A DICTIONARY OF CHEMISTRY

A DICTIONARY OF CHEMISTRY

J.L. SHARMA

CBS Publishers & Distributors Pvt. Ltd.

New Delhi • Bengaluru • Chennai • Kochi • Kolkata • Mumbai
Hyderabad • Nagpur • Patna • Pune • Vijayawada

ISBN: 81-239-0929-2

First Edition: 1988
Reprint: 1991, 1997, 2002, 2003, 2004, 2006,
2007, 2009, 2010, 2011, 2017

Published by **Satish Kumar Jain** and produced by **Varun Jain** for
CBS Publishers & Distributors Pvt. Ltd.,
4819/XI Prahlad Street, 24 Ansari Road, Daryaganj, New Delhi - 110002
delhi@cbspd.com, cbspubs@airtelmail.in • www.cbspd.com
Ph.: 23289259, 23266861, 23266867 • Fax: 011-23243014

Corporate Office: 204 FIE, Industrial Area, Patparganj, Delhi - 110 092
Ph: 49344934 • Fax: 011-49344935
E-mail: publishing@cbspd.com • publicity@cbspd.com

Branches:
- ***Bengaluru:*** 2975, 17th Cross, K.R. Road, Bansankari 2nd Stage, Bengaluru - 70 • Ph: +91-80-26771678/79 • Fax: +91-80-26771680 E-mail: cbsbng@gmail.com, bangalore@cbspd.com
- ***Chennai:*** No. 7, Subbaraya Street, Shenoy Nagar, Chennai - 600030 Ph: +91-44-26681266, 26680620 • Fax: +91-44-42032115 E-mail: chennai@cbspd.com
- ***Kochi:*** Ashana House, 39/1904, A.M. Thomas Road, Valanjambalam, Ernakulum, Kochi • Ph: +91-484-4059061-65 Fax: +91-484-4059065 • E-mail: cochin@cbspd.com
- ***Kolkata:*** 6-B, Ground Floor, Rameshwar Shaw Road, Kolkata - 700014 Ph: +91-33-22891126/7/8 • E-mail: kolkata@cbspd.com
- ***Mumbai:*** 83-C, Dr. E. Moses Road, Worli, Mumbai - 400018 Ph: +91-9833017933, 022-24902340/41 • E-mail: mumbai@cbspd.com

Representatives:
- Hyderabad: 0-9885175004
- Patna: 0-9334159340
- Vijayawada: 0-9000660880
- Nagpur: 0-9021734563
- Pune: 0-9623451994

Printed at:
J.S. Offset Printers, Delhi (India)

A

a-axis. One of the crystallographic axes used as reference in crystal description, usually oriented horizontally, front to back.

Abegg rule. 1. An empirical rule, holding for a large number of elements, that the sum of the maximum positive and negative valencies of an element equals eight. Also known as octet rule.

2. Most stable electronic configuration in atoms is that with completely filled *s* and *p* subshells of valence shell (noble gas configuration).

abrasion. The removal of surface material from any solid through the frictional act of another solid, liquid, or a gas or combination thereof; or by chemical degradation.

abrasive. A finely divided, hard material that can be used for grinding, honing, lapping, superfinishing, polishing, pressure blasting, or barrel tumbling. Its hardness on Mohs scale ranges from 6 to 10. It may be used in the form of a solid, a slurry or paste, or air suspension. Some of the natural abrasive substances are : corundum, diamond dust, feldspar, garnet, pumice, rouge (iron oxide), and silica. The important synthetic abrasives are : boron carbide, cerium oxide, fused alumina, and silicon carbide.

absinthe. A green liqueur having a bitter licorice flavor and high alcohol content.

absolute activity measurement. *See* absolute counting.

absolute activity of component. λ_B. A dimensionless quantity

$$\lambda_B = \exp\left(\frac{\mu_B}{RT}\right) \text{ or } \mu_B = RT \ln \lambda_B$$

where μ_B = chemical potential of B component, R = molar gas constant, and T = thermodynamic temperature.

absolute alcohol. Ethyl alcohol containing less than 1 per cent water, *i.e.*, atleast 99 per cent pure ethyl alcohol. Also known as anhydrous alcohol.

absolute configuration. Determination of real arrangement of atoms (or groups of atoms) around chiral centre. Absolute configuration is described according to *R-S* nomenclature. It has been established that absolute configuration of enantiomers of glyceraldehyde is in accordance with their arbitrarily adopted configuration.

absolute constants. *See* universal constants.

absolute counting. Direct measurement of total rate of radioactive decay, *i.e.*, measurement of number of disintegrations per unit time in the whole mass of the preparation examined. Also known as absolute activity measurement.

absolute electrode potential. Difference of inner potentials of electrode and electrolyte ; a nonmeasurable quantity (*cf.* relative electrode potential).

absolute error. Difference the between result of measurement (analytical determination) and value assumed as true.

absolute ionic mobility. *See* ionic mobility.

absolute oil. The pure essential oil obtained by double solvent extraction of flowers in the manufacture of perfumes.

absolute reaction rate. Reaction-rate constant of elementary reaction previously calculated on basis of properties of reacting molecules and activated complex, nowadays also determined experimentally.

absolute reaction rate theory. Reaction rate theory based on model of elementary reaction proceeding over activated complex. Also known as activated-complex theory ; transition-state theory.

absolute refractive index. Ratio of velocities of light in vacuum and in a given medium.

absolute scale. *See* absolute temperature scale.

absolute temperature. Temperature that is measured as a function of energy possessed by matter. Temperature measurement is based upon many properties of substances, for example the expansion of a gas, the change in resistance, the brightness of hot bodies etc. Kelvin was first to propose a thermodynamic scale of temperature in which changes of temperature are independent of the working substance used. Absolute temperatures are expressed either in degrees Kelvin or in degrees Rankine ; corresponding respectively to the Centigrade and Fahrenheit scales. Degrees Kelvin are obtained by adding 273 to the Centigrade temperature (if above 0°C) or subtracting the temperature from 273 (if below 0°C). Degrees Rankine are obtained by subtracting 460 from the Fahrenheit temperature. Also known as thermodynamic temperature.

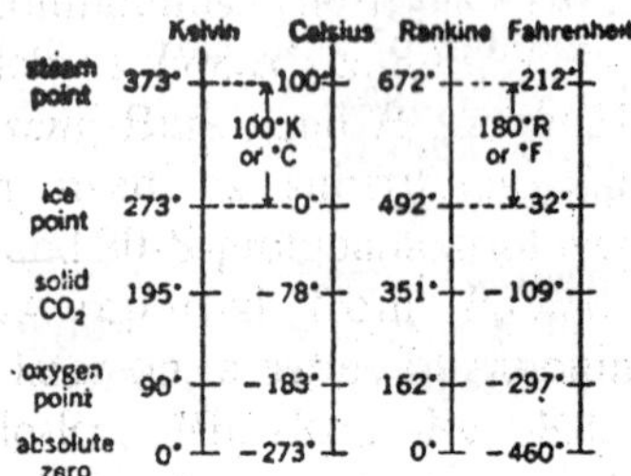

Fig. 1. **Comparisons of Kelvin, Celsius, Rankine, and Fahrenheit temperature scales. Temperatures are rounded off to nearest degree.**

absolute temperature scale. A scale with which temperatures are measured relative to absolute zero. Also known as absolute scale.

absolute unit. 1. A unit defined in terms of units of fundamental quantities such as length, mass, or time.

2. If a quantity y is uniquely defined in terms of quantities $x_1, x_2, x_3, \ldots$ by :

$$y = f(x_1, x_2, x_3, \ldots),$$

the unit U_y of y can be obtained from the units U_{x_1}, U_{x_2}, U_{x_3} of x_1, x_2, x_3 from the equation

$$U_y \propto f(U_{x_1}, U_{x_2}, U_{x_3}, \ldots).$$

In any given system an absolute unit is one for which the constant of proportionality is unity. All units of the SI system are absolute.

absolute value. The magnitude of a quantity without regard to its sign.

absolute zero. The lowest temperature theoretically possible ; the temperature at which molecular motion vanishes and a body would have no heat energy, *i.e.*, the thermal energy of random motion of the particles of a system in thermal equilibrium is zero. It is therefore, the zero of thermodynamic temperature :

$$0K = -273.15°C = -459.69°F$$

absorbance. Logarithm to base 10 of ratio of intensity of radiation passing through reference, I_0, and through investigated sample, I,

$$A = \lg I_0/I$$

Absorbance corresponds to loss of energy absorbed in a given medium in comparison with loss in reference. It is assumed that losses for reflection, solvent absorption, and refraction are compensated and that there is no interference due to scattered radiation. Also known as absorbancy ; optical density.

absorbancy. *See* absorbance.

absorbancy index. *See* absorptivity.

absorbed dose. D. Amount of energy imparted to matter by ionizing particles per unit mass of irradiated material at place of interest. In SI system it is expressed in Grays.

absorbing centres. *See* colour centres.

absorption. 1. Penetration of substance (absorbate) into body of another (absorbent).

2. Reduction in the flux of electromagnetic radiation on passage through matter. The radiation absorptive capacity of matter is utilized in analytical chemistry in various types of absorption spectroscopy.

3. The ability of some elements to pick up or capture thermal neutrons produced in nuclear reactors as a result of fission.

absorption bands. Dark bands or lines present in spectrum as a result of absorption by some intervening medium. Atoms absorb only a single wavelength, producing lines, such as the sodium D line. *See also* absorption line.

absorption cell. In studies of radiation absorption small vessel containing investigated sample (liquid or gaseous). Distance between the two parallel propagation windows, perpendicular to direction of radiation determines thickness of investigated sample. Also known as cuvette ; sample cell.

absorption coefficient. 1. *See* absorptivity.

2. Coefficient describing volume of gas (reduced to normal conditions) which dissolves in unit volume of liquid at the given temperature and under normal pressure.

absorption cross-section. Cross-section of nucleus of atom for absorption of bombarding particles.

absorption curve. 1. Dependence of absorption or of any of its functions on wavelength, wave number or frequency of electromagnetic radiation.

2. In magnetic resonance, curve representing dependence of energy absorbed by a given substance from alternating high-frequency magnetic field on strength of static magnetic field (at fixed frequency) or on frequency of field (at constant strength of static magnetic field). It represents changes of imaginary part x'' of magnetic susceptibility.

absorption edge. An abrupt discontinuity in the graph relating the coefficient of absorption of x-rays in a given substance with the wavelength of radiation. At certain critical absorption wavelengths the absorption shows a sudden decrease in value. This occurs when the energy quantum of the radiation becomes smaller than the work required to eject an electron from one or the other of the energy levels in the absorbing atom, and the radiation thus ceases to be absorbed in that level. Thus, the radiation of wavelength greater than the K absorption edge cannot eject electrons from the K level of the absorbing substance. Also known as absorption limit.

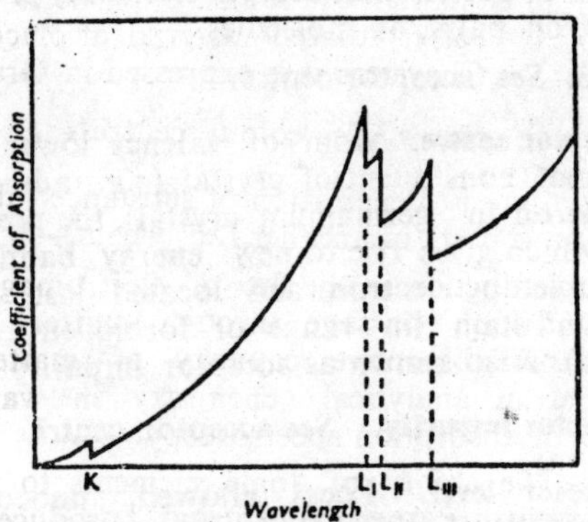

Fig. 2. Absorption edge

absorption filter. Optical filter absorbing radiation in some region of frequencies. Also known as colour filter.

absorption line. A minute range of wavelength or frequency in electromagnetic spectrum within which radiant energy is absorbed by the medium through which it is passing. *See also* absorption bands.

absorption of ionizing radiation. Whole of processes occurring when ionizing radiation passes through matter ; in result intensity of radiation is reduced and its composition changed.

absorption of light. Transformation of light energy passing through matter into energy of different type.

absorption oil. A coal tar or petroleum oil that is contacted with a vapour or gas mixture to remove heavy components, as in the recovery of neutral gasoline from wet natural gas. Also known as absorber oil ; scrubbing oil ; wash oil.

absorption peak. A wavelength of maximum electromagnetic absorption by a chemical sample ; used to identify specific elements, compounds, or radicals.

absorption spectroanalysis. Spectroanalysis based on investigation of absorption spectra.

absorption spectroscopy. Branch of spectroscopy comprising methods of determination of composition and structure of chemicals by study of absorption spectra.

absorption spectrum. Spectrum arising as a result of propagation of electromagnetic radiation through absorbing medium. When the light from a high temperature source producing a continuous emission spectrum is passed through a medium through a spectroscope, the spectrum reveals dark regions where absorption has taken place (continuous, line, and band types). In general medium absorbs those wavelengths which it would omit if its temperature were raised high enough. Solids and liquids show broad continuous absorption spectra, while gases give more discontinuous types.

absorption tube. A tube filled with a solid absorbent ; used to absorb gases and vapours.

absorptivity. Proportionality constant in Lambert-Beer law equation, equal numerically to absorbance of solution of unit concentration and unit path length. Also known as absorption coefficient ; specific absorbance ; absorbancy index.

ABS resin. Any of a group of tough and rigid thermoplastics made by blending acrylonitrile-styrene copolymer with a butadiene-acrylonitrile rubber or by interpolymerizing polybutadiene with acrylonitrile and styrene. Most contemporary ABS resins are true graft polymers consisting of an elastomeric polybutadiene or rubber phase, grafted with styrene and acrylonitrile monomers for compatibility, dispersed in a rigid styrene-acrylonitrile (SAN) matrix.

abundance. 1. The relative amount (% by weight) of a substance in the earth's crust, including the oceans and atmosphere. The abundance of some of the elements in the earth's crust is :

Element	Abundance % by weight
Oxygen	49.2
Silicon	25.7
Aluminium	7.5
Iron	4.7
Calcium	3.4
Sodium	2.6
Potassium	2.4
Magnesium	1.9
Hydrogen	0.9
Titanium	0.6
Chlorine	0.2
All others	0.9

It may be noted that on universal scale, most abundant element is hydrogen.

2. Content of particular isotope in given sample of the natural element, expressed as percentage, *e.g.*, 99.76% of oxygen-16 in natural oxygen. Also known as abundance ratio.

abundance ratio. *See* abundance.

Ac. Symbol for the element actinium.

acaricide. A pesticide used to destroy mites on domestic animals, crops, and man. Also known as miticide.

accelerated electrons. Electrons whose kinetic energy is increased in an electric potential.

accelerator. 1. A compound added to a photographic developer to increase its chemical activity, *e.g.*, quaternary ammonium compounds and alkaline substances.

2. A substance that greatly reduces the setting time when added to plaster, mortar, concrete, or cement.

3. A compound that greatly reduces the time required for vulcanization of natural and synthetic rubbers at the same time improving the ageing and other physical properties. The major organic accelerators include amines, guanidines, thiazoles, and dithiocarbamates.

4. *See* charged particle accelerator.

accelerator catalyst. A catalyst that increases the rate of chemical reaction.

accelofilter. A filtration device that uses a vaccum or pressure to draw or force the liquid through the filter to increase the rate of filtration.

acceptor. 1. In induced reactions, a substance which reacts with donor in system of coupled reactions.

2. A species that accepts electrons, protons, electron pairs, or molecules.

3. *See* acceptor centre.

acceptor centre. Atom of valency lower than normal constituent of crystal (*e.g.*, admixture of boron in germanium crystal), the presence of which gives rise to new energy band not occupied by electron and located just above ground state (in range of forbidden energy band). Also known as acceptor impurity.

acceptor impurity. *See* acceptor centre.

acceptor level. Local, allowed, unoccupied energy level situated in area of forbidden band, connected with presence of acceptor centre in crystal.

acceptor state. *See* acceptor level.

accretion. The process whereby stones or other inorganic substances add to their bulk by adding particles to their surface.

accumulator. Cell in which processes occurring during its work (discharge of accumulator), can be carried out in reverse direction by electrolysis (charging of accumulator). The unique property of the accumulator is that the chemical conditions necessary to produce the e.m.f. may be restored without structural alterations to the cell. Also known as secondary cell ; storage cell.

accuracy. Measure of agreement between result of measurement (determination) or mean in series of measurements and value of measured quantity assumed as true.

accuracy of method. Quantitative (absolute or relative) measure of agreement of mean value of measurement results obtained by a given method and value of measured property assumed as true.

acetal resin. A linear, synthetic polyoxymethylene thermoplastic polymer produced by ionically initiated polymerization of formaldehyde (HCHO) to obtain a linear molecule of the type :

$$-O-CH_2-O-CH_2-O-CH_2-$$

Also known as polyacetal.

acetamido-. A prefix indicating CH_3CONH- group. Also known as acetamino- ; acetylamino.

acetamino. *See* acetamido.

acetate. 1. A salt of acetic acid (CH_3COOH) in which the H atom of carboxyl group is replaced by a metal as in sodium acetate CH_3COONa.

2. An ester of acetic acid in which substitution by a radical takes place as in ethyl acetate, $CH_3COOC_2H_5$.

acetate film. A cellulose acetate resin sheet that is airproof, transparent and resistant to dust, grease and oil ; used for magnetic tapes, packaging, and photographic films.

acetate dye. 1. Any of a group of water-insoluble azo- or anthraquinone dyes that have been highly dispersed to make them capable of penetrating and dyeing acetate fibres.

2. Any of a class of water-insoluble amino-azo dyes that are made water-soluble by treatment with formaldehyde and bisulphite. After absorption by the fibre, the resulting sulphonic acids hydrolyze and regenerate the insoluble dyes.

acetate fibre. Generic name for a synthetic fibre in which the fibre-forming substance is cellulose acetate. in which not less than 92 per cent of the hydroxyl groups are acetylated. This fibre was formerly called acetate rayon or acetate silk. The use of the term 'rayon' is not permitted for this type.

acetate fibre, saponified. Regenerated cellulose fibres obtained by complete saponification of highly oriented cellulose acetate fibres ; possess high degree of crystallinity and great strength.

acetate process. Acetylation of cellulose (cotton linters or wood pulp) with acetic acid or acetic anhydride and sulphuric acid (catalyst) to obtain cellulose acetate resin or fibre.

acetic fermentation. Oxidation of alcohol to produce acetic acid by the action of bacteria of the genus *Acetobacter*.

acetic thiokinese. An enzyme that catalyzes the formation of acetyl coenzyme. A from acetate and adenosinetriphospate.

acetoacetate. A salt containing CH_3COCH_2COO- radical.

acetolysis. Metathesis between organic compound and acetic acid, the latter acting additionally as solvent, *e.g.*,

$$RCOOR'+CH_3COOH \rightarrow CH_3COOR'+RCOOH$$

acetone benzol process. A dewaxing process in petroleum refining, with acetone and benzol used as solvents.

acetone fermentation. Formation of acetone by the metabolic action of certain anaerobic bacteria on carbohydrates.

acetone number. A ratio used to estimate the degree of polymerization of substances such as drying oils ; it is expressed as weight in grams of acetone added to 100 grams of a drying oil to cause an insoluble phase to form.

acetone pyrolysis. Thermal decomposition of acetone into ketene.

acetone sugar. Any reducing sugar that contains keto group, *e.g.*, 1, 2-monoacetone-D-glucofuranose.

acetyl. The univalent group $CH_3CO—$, which occurs in acetic acid, acetic anhydride, and such compounds as acetyl chloride and acetylsalicylic acid. It contains one less oxygen atom than does the accetate group (CH_3COO). The process involving its introduction into other molecules is called acetylation.

acetylation. A reaction or process whereby an acetyl group $CH_3CO—$ is introduced into a compound, *i.e.*, substitution of hydrogen atom by acetyl group. Reagents often used for acetylation are acetic anhydride, acetyl chloride, acetic acid, etc. One typical example of acetylation reaction is :

$$C_6H_5OH + CH_3COCl \rightarrow CH_3COOC_6H_5 + HCl$$

acetylene black. The carbon black resulting from incomplete combustion or thermal decomposition of acetylene.

acetylene series. A series of unsaturated hydrocarbons having the general formula C_nH_{2n-2} and containing a triple bond between two adjacent carbon atoms, as $-C \equiv C-$. The name of the series is that of the simplest member acetylene ($HC \equiv CH$). The members of this series are also designated by changing the "*yl*" termination of the alcohol radicals, of like carbon content to "*yne*" ; *e.g.*, acetylene, C_2H_2, is thus named ethyne ; propylene ; C_3H_4, is named propyne, etc.

acetylenic bond. Triple bond between two adjacent carbon atoms as in the case of ethyne, $HC \equiv CH$.

acetylide. The anion $[C{\equiv}C]^{2-}$ or $[H{-}C{\equiv}C]^-$, or a compound containing one of these ions.

acetyl value. The acetyl value of a fat is the number of milligrams of potassium hydroxide required to neutralize the acetic acid liberated when 1 gram of acetylated fat is saponified. It is a measure of the number of free hydroxyl group in the fat.

acheson graphite. Collodial graphite of special purity, prepared so as to be miscible with water or with oil.

achirality. Lack of chirality, identity of configuration of molecule with its mirror image, caused by the presence of plane of symmetry, or centre of symmetry, or four-fold inversion (symmetry) axis in molecule.

achromatic. Transmitting white light without resolution, or correcting such resolution as has already been caused by lenses and other optical elements or systems.

achromic. Free from colour.

achromic period. The time required for complete fermentation of starch, as shown by its failure to produce a blue colour with iodine. This period is used as a measure of enzymatic activity, with a standard starch solution (commonly 1%) in water.

aci-. A prefix used to indicate the acid form, as aci-acetoacetic ester.

acicular. Shaped like needles.

acid 1. A compound of hydrogen in which some or all of the hydrogen atoms may be replaced by an atom or atoms of a metal, and which is capable of forming hydrogen ions when dissolved in water. Most of the acids are soluble in water and, have sharp taste, and turn litmus paper red. Most of them liberate carbon dioxide from a metallic carbonate. Most of the inorganic oxyacids may be regarded as a compound of an oxide with water. Acids are classified as monobasic, dibasic, tribasic polybasic, etc., according to the numbr (one, two, three, or more) of hydrogen atoms, replaceable by bases, contained in a molecule.

The acids are classified as organic if they contain the —COOH, carboxyl group(s), *e.g.*, acetic acid CH_3COOH ; propionic acid CH_3CH_2COOH ; benzoic acid, C_6H_5COOH ; oxalic acid COOH.COOH tartaric acid, COOH.CHOH.CHOH.COOH. The aromatic organic acids are further classified as ortho, meta, or para, according to the location of the carboxyl group, —COOH, in relation to another substituent in a cyclic compound.

All acids contain hydrogen. Inorganic acids (sometimes called mineral acids) are examplified by sulfuric, nitric, hydrochloric, and phosphoric acids. Organic or carboxylic acids contain one or more carboxyl groups (COOH) ; simple types are formic and oxalic acids. Carboxylic acids include the broad Subgroups of fatty acids and amino acids. some acids, such as carbonic and acetic, are weak, forming few ions in solution, while others are very strong (hydrochloric, sulfuric, nitric) and ionize completely. Concentrated strong acids are extremely corrosive to tissue and should be handled with care.

The organic sulphonic acids form an important class. These acids do not contain a —COOH group, but are characterized by the presence of $-SO_3H$ group, and behave as true acids. On the other hand compounds like carbolic acid (phenol), C_6H_5OH ; and picric acid, $C_6H_2(NO_2)_3OH$ (2,4,6,-trinitrophenol) behave as acids although they contain no —COOH, or $-SO_3H$ group.

2. According to Bronsted and Lowry, an acid is a proton donor, and a base is a proton acceptor. An acid always becomes a base after proton transfer. This base is called conjugate base of the acid. By the same logic, when a base accepts a proton in a protan transfer reaction, it becomes an acid. This acid is the conjugate acid of the base. Because new acids and bases are created, the proton transfer reaction can reverse itself in order to continue proton transfer, although it may go largely to completion in one direction or the other. For example,

$$\underset{\substack{\text{Acid}_1 \\ \text{(Very Strong)}}}{HCl} + \underset{\substack{\text{Base}_2 \\ \text{(Weak)}}}{H_2O} \rightleftharpoons \underset{\substack{\text{Acid}_2 \\ \text{(Strong)}}}{H_3O^+} + \underset{\substack{\text{Base}_1 \\ \text{(Very weak)}}}{Cl^-}$$

Here one conjugate acid-base pair is designated by subscript 1 ; the other, by the subscript 2.

According to this concept, following generalizations are made :

(*i*) Strong acids generate weak conjugate bases.

(*ii*) Strong base generate weak conjugate acids.

Bronsted's definition is valid for non-aqueous solution also, thus :

$$NH_3 \rightleftharpoons NH_2^- + H^+$$
$$NH_3 + H^+ \rightleftharpoons NH_4^+$$
$$\overline{2NH_3 \rightleftharpoons NH_4^+ + NH_2^-}$$

Thus compounds like NH_4I when dissolved in liquour ammonia, exhibit acidic properties. The Bronsted-Lowry definition of acids and bases is restricted in scope, since it limits discusion of acid-base phenomena to proton transfer reactions. There are many reactions that have all the characteristics of acid-base reactions but do not fit well in the Bronsted Lowry model.

3. G.N. Lewis has further extended the acid-base concept. According to this concept, an acid is a substance that can accept a pair of electrons, while a base is a substance that can donate a pair of electrons. For example :

$$\underset{\text{Acid}}{BF_3} + \underset{\text{Base}}{:NH_3} \rightarrow F_3B \leftarrow NH_3$$

Since Lewis acids seek substances having electron pairs to which they can become bound, Lewis acids are said to be electrophilic (electron loving) in character and an acid displacement reaction is said to be electrophilic displacement.

4. A useful modification of the Lewis concept introduced in 1963 is the classification of acids (and bases)as either "hard" or "soft", depending on such properties as electronegativity, tendency to polarize, and oxidation state, these in turn relating to the availability of vacant orbitals. Hard acids are in a high oxidation state, and their outer electrons are relatively stable ; they tend to associate with hard bases. Soft acids have the opposite properties.

See also amino acid ; carboxylic acid ; fatty acid ; hard and soft acids ; Lewis electron theory ; strength of acids ; strong and weak acids ; nucleophile.

acid amide. Any organic compound containing the group $-CONH_2$. The general formula is $RCONH_2$, in which R is an alkyl, aryl, or any other organic substituent.

acid anhydride. A compound derived from an acid by the elimination of one or more water molecules of the acid. The corresponding acids may commonly be regenerated from them by the addition of water, the process being often accompanied by the evolution of heat. For example, sulphur trioxide, SO_3, is regarded as the anhydride of sulphuric acid.

acid-base catalysis. Catalysis due to substances of acid or base type. In this type of catalysis, reaction of catalyst with substrate consists in proton transfer.

acid-base indicator. Weak acid or organic base which on reacting with water gives conjugated acid-base system. Acid-base indicators are used for approximate measurement of *p*H of solution and determination of end-point of acid-base titration by visual method.

acid-base titration. *See* acidimetry.

acid chloride. A compound containing —COCl group.

acid dye. An azo, triarylmethane, or anthraquinone dye with acid substituents such as nitro, carboxy, or sulphonic acid. They are most frequently applied in acid solutions to polyamides, silk and wool, and combine with the basic groups of proteins of those fibres. They do not form lakes with tannin and have little affinity for cotton. Application is usually made under acidic conditions which cause protonation of the basic groups. The dyeing process may be described as :

$$\text{Dye}^- + H_3O^+ + \text{Fibre} \rightleftharpoons \text{Dye}^-H^+ - \text{Fibre} + H_2O$$

It should be noted that this process is reversible. Generally, acid dyes can be removed from fibres. The rate of removal depends on the rate at which the dye can diffuse through the fibre under the conditions of washing. For a given fibre, the diffusion rate is determined by temperature, size, and shape of the dye molecules, and the number and kind of linkages formed with the fibre.

acid electrolyte. A compound such as sulphuric acid, that dissociates into ions when dissolved, forming an acidic solution that conducts the electric current.

acid gases. The gases such as sulphur dioxide, SO_2 ; sulphur trioxide, SO_3 ; hydrogen sulphide, H_2S ; carbon dioxide, CO_2 ; which, when combined with moisture, generally form corrosive acids. Also known as acidic gases.

acid halide. A compound of the type RCOX, where R is an alkyl or aryl radical and X is a halogen.

acid, hard. *See* hard acid.

acid heat test. The determination of degree of unsaturation of organic compounds by reacting with sulphuric acid and measuring the heat of reaction.

acid hydrazide. A compound containing the radical $—CONHNH_2$.

acid hydrogen. 1. The hydrogen atom in the acid group —COOH.

2. The hydrogen atom attached to a molecule that dissociates to give hydronium ion, H_3O^+.

acid hydrolysis. Decomposition of β-ketoacid ester by concentrated base leading to formation of corresponding acid salts and an alcohol, *e.g.*,

$$CH_3\overset{O}{\overset{\|}{C}}CH_2R\overset{O}{\overset{\|}{C}}OC_2H_5 \xrightarrow[H_2O]{NaOH} CH_3\overset{O}{\overset{\|}{C}}ONa + RCH_2\overset{O}{\overset{\|}{C}}ONa + C_2H_5OH$$

acidic. 1. Pertaining to an acid or its properties.

2. Forming an acid during a chemical process.

acidic gases. *See* acid gases.

acidic group. The part of a chemical (chelating agent) containing hydrogen ion which can be replaced by metal ion, *e.g.*, carboxyl group —COOH, hydroxyl group —OH, oxime group =NOH, thiol group —SH, and arsonium group $—AsO(OH)_2$ etc.

acidic oxide. The oxides of monmetals, such as CO_2, SO_2, SO_3, P_4O_{10}, N_2O_5, N_2O_4, Cl_2O_7, which from oxyacids when dissolved in water. *See also* acid anhydride.

acidic solvent. A solvent which is strongly

protogenic, *i.e.*, which has a strong tendency to donate protons and little tendency to accept them. Liquid hydrogen chloride and hydrogen fluoride are acidic solvent, and in them even such normally strong acids as nitric acid do not exhibit acidic properties, since there are no molecules which can accept protons, but on the contrary, behave to some extent as bases by accepting protons yielded by disociation of HCl or H_2F_2. Also known as protogenic solvent.

acidic titrant. An acid solution of known concentration used to determine the basicity of another solution by acid-base titration.

acidification. Addition of an acid to a solution or other system to increase the acidity, unit *p*H reaches a value less than 7.

acidimetry. The determination of the concentration of acid solutions or of the quantity of acid in a sample or of mixture. This is usually done by titration with a solution of base of known strength (standard solution) and an indicator is used to establish the end point.

acidity. 1. The amount of acid present, expressed for a solution either as the molecular concentration of acid, in terms of normality, molarity, etc., or the ionic concentration in terms of *p*H. The acidity of a base is the number of monobasic acid which one molecule of the base can neutralize.

2. Characteristic feature of electrolyte solutions in which concentration of so called 'hydronium ions' H_3O^+, is greater than that of hydroxyl ions, OH^-.

acidity function. H_0. Conventional, numerical approximate scale of acidity of solutions

$$H_0 = -\lg a_{H^+} - \lg \frac{f_B}{f_{BH^+}}$$

where a_{H^+} = hydrogen ion activity,

f_B and f_{BH^+} = activity coefficients of basic, electrically neutral and acidic forms of substance respectively.

Also known as Hammett acidity function.

acidity of base. Number of hydroxyl groups in molecule of base which may be exchanged by various acid radicals during neutralization process, *e.g.*, acidity of KOH and $Mg(OH)_2$ is 1 and 2 respectively.

acid number. *See* acid value.

acid of sugar. The trivial name of oxalic acid.

acidolysis. 1. A chemical reaction involving the decomposition of a molecule, with the addition of the elements of an acid to the molecule ; the reaction is comparable to hydrolysis or alcoholysis, in which water or alcohol respectively, is used in place of acid. Also known as acyl exchange.

2. Metasynthesis between organic compound and acid, the latter serving additionally as solvent, *e.g.*,

$$\text{CO—O—COR} + \text{R}'\text{COOH} \rightarrow \text{RCO—O—COR}' + \text{RCOOH}$$

acid phosphatase. Any nonspecific phosphatase requiring an acidic medium for optical activity ; less active than alkaline phosphatase.

acid phosphate. A mono- or dihydric phosphate such as M_2HPO_4 or MH_2PO_4 where M represents a monovalent metal atom. Also used to refer specifically to calcium phosphate monobasic $Ca(H_2PO_4)_2$, or superphosphate of lime.

acid pickle. Industrial waste water that is spent liquor from a chemical process used to clean metal surfaces.

acid process. A melting process carried out in a furnace lined with acidic materials which combine readily with the oxides present in the ore.

acid radical. Atom or group of atoms (uni-, di-, tri-, or polyvalent) that remain after splitting off one or more hydrogen atoms from molecule of acid, for example, chloride, Cl^-; sulphate, SO_4^{2-}.

acid salt. A compound derived from an acid and base in which only a part of the acidic hydrogen is replaced by a basic radical, for example, the acid sulphate, $NaHSO_4$; acid phosphate, Na_2HPO_4.

acid slag. Furnace slag in which there is more silica and silicates than lime and magnesia.

acid sludge. The residue left after treating petroleum oil with sulphuric acid for the removal of impurities.

acid solution. An aqueous solution containing more hydronium ions, H_3O^+ than hydroxyl ions, OH^-

acid soot. Carbon particles that have absorbed acid fumes as a by-product of combustion ; hydrochloric acid absorbed on carbon particles is frequently the cause of metal corrosion in incineration.

acid steel. Steel produced in a melting furnace employing siliceous-type refractories.

acidulant. An organic acid used as a multipurpose food additive ; among the more important functions of acidulants are prevention of rancidity, texture modification of doughs and baked goods, preservation of meats, enchancement and potentiation of flavors, and *p*H control. Citric, acetic, tartaric, and propionic acids are commonly used for these purpose. Succinic anhydride is used as an excellent leavening and dehydrating agent.

acid value. 1. The number of millgrams of potassium hydroxide required to neutralize the free acids present in one gram of oil, fat, or wax. The determination is made by titrating the sample in hot 95% ethyl alcohol using phenolphthalein as indicator. It is therefore, a measure of the degree of hydrolysis of the fat. Also known as acid number.

2. The acidity of a solution expressed in terms of normality.

acid wash. A solution of phosphoric acid applied to steel parts that neutralizes and removes the alkaline solutions used for grease removal after machining ; it also forms a metallic phosphate coating that accepts paint and, of itself, provides a high degree of protection against corrosion.

acid water pollution. Industrial waste waters that have *p*H below 7 (*i.e.*, acidic) ; usually appear in effluent from the manufacture of chemicals, artificial and natural fibres, batteries, mining, and fermentation processes.

acieration. Electrolytic coating of a thin metal plate with iron ; the iron hardens to steellike strength.

aci form. Tautomeric form of formula :

$$\begin{array}{c} \quad\ \ O{-}H \\ \quad\ \ | \\ | \qquad \\ C{=}{=}N{\rightarrow}O \end{array}$$

existing in equilibrium with primary or secondary nitro compound. Aci form is less stable than nitro compound. *See also* aci-nitro compound.

aci-nitro compound. One of a class of isomers of true nitro compounds, in which one of the two oxygen atoms that are joined to the nitro nitrogen by a double bond has become joined by one valence bond to another atom or radical, as by a tautomeric shift within the molecule. The nitrogen atom is then joined to the molecule by a double bond, instead of a single bond.

NO_2 | $R{-}OC_2H_5$	$NO.OC_2H_5$ ‖ $R{=}O$
True nitro compound	**Aci-nitro compound**

Acker process. A method of manufacturing sodium hydroxide from molten sodium chloride by electrolysis, with the addition of steam, using a cathode of molten lead.

Ackermann test for guanidine. On heating guanidine with aqueous sodium hydroxide solution and benzenesulphonylchloride, white needles (m.p. 210°C) are obtained.

Ackermann test for thio-*p*-tolyl-β-naphthylamine. With concentrated sulphuric acid thio-*p*-tolyl-β-naphthylamine forms violet-blue colour that changes to red-violet by addition of nitric acid.

Acree's reaction. A test for protein in which a violet-blue ring appears when concentrated sulphuric acid is introduced below a mixture of the unknown solution and a formaldehyde solution containing traces of ferric chloride.

acridine orange. A dye with affinity for nucleic acids ; the complexes of nucleic acid and dye fluoresce orange with RNA and green with DNA when observed in the fluorescence microscope.

acrinyl. The radical *p*-hydroxybenzyl,

$$HO{-}C_6H_4{-}CH_2{-}$$

acrolein dimer. $C_6H_8O_2$. A water soluble liquid used as intermediate for resins, dyestuffs, and pharmaceuticals. Also known as 2-formyl-3,4-dihydro-2H-pyran.

acrolein test. A test performed to detect the presence of glycerol or fats ; a sample is heated with potassium bisulphate ; if the test is positive, acrolein is released

acryl. The radical $-CH{=}CHCHO$, or

$$CH_2{=}\overset{|}{C}{-}CHO.$$

acrylate resin. Acrylic acid or ester polymer with a $-CH_2-CH(COOR)-$ structure ; used in paints, sizing and finishing for paper and textiles, adhesive, and plastics.

acrylic fibre. Any of numerous synthetic textile fibres made by polymerization of acrylonitrile.

acrylic resin. A thermoplastic organic polymer obtained by polymerization of acrylic derivatives such as acrylic acid, methacrylic acid, ethyl acrylate, and methyl acrylate ; used for adhesives and protective coatings.

acrylic rubber. Synthetic rubber containing acrylonitrile ; *e.g.*, nitrile rubber.

acrylyl. The radical $CH_2{=}CHCO-$.

actinic rays. Radiations effective in producing chemical changes and biological reaction. This term is usually applied to the violet and ultraviolet portion of the electromagnetic spectrum which consists of radiations relatively effective in causing these changes, as contrasted with radiation in the long wavelength portion of the spectrum.

actinide elements. *See* actinoids.

actinides. *See* actinoids.

actinide series. *See* actinoids.

actinism. The production of chemical changes in a substance upon which electromagnetic radiation is incident.

actinium. An element.	Symbol Ac	
Group IIIB	Atomic No.	89
State solid	Atomic Wt.	227
	Valence	3
	m.p.	1050°C

Actinium is a radioactive decay product of uranium-235 ; the 227 isotope occurs in nature with a half-life of about 22 years. Actinium does not have any stable isotope. Actinium is the first element of the actinide series. It is obtained as a whitish metal, and easily forms compounds with the halogens and with oxygen. It has bone-seeking properties, and finds limited use in trace studies. Isotopes of actinium include mesothorium-2 which has a mass number of 228 and a half-period of 6.14 hours. It is a member of the thorium series being formed from mesothorium-1 by particle β-particle emission, and forms in turn, radiothorium, also by β-particle emission. Other known actinium isotopes are with mass numbers 222, 223, 224, 225, 226, 229 and 230.

actinium D. AcD. Isotope of lead. Atomic number 82 ; mass number 207.

actinium series. Naturally occurring series with first and last members as uranium, uranium-235, and lead, lead-207, respectively. The mass number of each number of this series is

$$A=4n+3, \text{ where } n=\text{natural number}.$$

(*See also* Table on page 12).

actinoids. The sequence of radioactive elements immediately following radium in the Periodic Table ; all are members of Group IIIB, starting with actinium (atomic number 89) and including all the remaining elements. Those beyond uranium do not exist in nature and are produced synthetically ; these are called transuranic elements. The officially approved name for this series is actinoid, but it is seldom used. All the members have properties similar to actinium and are as follows :

Actinium	Berkelium
Thorium	Californium
Protactinium	Ensteinium
Uranium	Fermium
Neptunium	Mendelevium
Plutonium	Nobelium
Americium	Lawrencium
Curium	Elements 104, 105 and 106.

These elements are transition elements and form second series of inner transition elements starting with thorium (Seaborg) or neptunium (Dawson) filling of subshell 5 *f*.

The justification for this grouping is found in the existence in the higher elements of (III) oxidation states similar to actinium, and (IV) oxidation state similar to thorium. Certain similarities also exist between the atomic spectra and magnetic properties in the two

THE ACTINIUM SERIES

Radioelement	Corresponding element	Symbol	Radiation	Half life
Actinouranium ↓	Uranium	U^{235}	α	**7.07×10^{8} yr.**
Uranium Y ↓	Thorium	Th^{231}	β	**25.6 hr.**
Protactinium ↓	Protactinium	Pa^{231}	α	**3.4×10^{4} yr.**
Actinium (98.8% ↓ Radioactinium; 1.2% ↓ Actinium K)	Actinium	Ac^{227}	β and α	**21.7 yr.**
Radioactinium	Thorium	Th^{227}	α	**18.6 days**
Actinium K	Francium	Fr^{223}	β	**21 min.**
↓ Actinium X ↓	Radium	Ra^{223}	α	**11.2 days**
Ac Emanation ↓	Radon	Rn^{219}	α	**3.92 sec.**
Actinium A (∽100% ↓ Actinium B; ∽5×10^{-4}% ↓ Astatine-215)	Polonium	Po^{215}	α and β	**1.83×10^{-3} sec.**
Actinium B	Lead	Pb^{211}	β	**36.1 min**
Astatine-215	Astatine	At^{215}	α	**∽10^{-4} sec.**
↓ Actinium C (99.68% ↓ Actinium C′; 0.32% ↓ Actinium C″)	Bismuth	Bi^{211}	β and α	**2.16 min.**
Actinium C′	Polonium	Po^{211}	α	**5×10^{-3} sec.**
Actinium C″	Thallium	Tl^{207}	β	**4.76 min.**
↓ Actinium D (End Product)	Lead	Pb^{207}	Stable	

series. Also known as actinides; actinide elements; actinide series.

actinology. The study of electromagnetic radiation and its chemical effects.

actinometer. An instrument which measures the intensity of photochemically active radiation, by determining the fluorescence of a screen or the extent of a chemical decomposition reaction initated by the incident radiation.

actinometry. The determination of the photo chemical intensity of light.

actinon. An isotope of radon. Atomic number 86; mass number 219; half-period 3.92 seconds; produced as an emanation of actinium.

actinouranium. Isotope of uranium. Atomic number 92; mass number 235.

activated adsorption. Chemisorption characterized by fairly high energy of activation.

activated alumina. A highly porous and granular form of aluminium oxide having prefrential adsorptive capacity for moisture from gases, vapours, and some liquids. When saturated, it can be revived or reactivated by heating. It is also effective for the removal of oil vapour from commercial gases, such as oxygen, hydrogen, carbon dioxide, etc. It is also used as catalyst or as catalyst carrier. Activated alumina is also used to remove flouride from drinking water ; and in chromatography.

activated carbon. A highly porous form of carbon obtained by destructive distillation of carbon-rich materials to eliminate the volatile portions, followed by high-temperature treatment of the carbon with steam or carbon dioxide. The product obtained may have an internal surface area ranging from 420 to almost 1700 square metres per gram. This enables it to strongly absorb molecules of gases and vapours or colloidally suspended particles from liquids. Nut shells are used as a source of carbon for material of the smallest pore size, which is used for gas adsorption ; coal, wood, and similar materials are the basis of carbons used for adsorption from liquids. Activated carbon (sometimes called activated charcoal) is used to deodorize gases ; to reclaim solvents from the vapour phase, and to decolorize liquids. Also known as activated charcoal.

activated charcoal. *See* activated carbon.

activated clay. Clay whose absorbent character or bleaching action has been enhanced by acid-treatment. Bentonite clay is most frequently treated in this way.

activated complex. Unstable configuration of reactant atoms to which corresponds maximum of potential energy in reaction path. Also known as transition state ; transition complex ; critical complex.

activated molecule. Molecule which is able to react as a result of activation.

activated sludge. A biologically active sediment resulting from the repeated exposure of organic waste materials to atmospheric oxygen, permitting the growth of aerobic bacteria and other unicellular organisms that feed upon and destroy the pollutants in the waste. The activated sludge process is one of the major methods of treating municipal sewage and can also be applied to such industrial wastes as occur in canneries and other food processing plants. It involves mechanically mixing air with the waste material for several hours to promote growth of bacteria, followed by a shorter settling period ; this cycle is repeated until the purification is completed. About one kilogram of sludge is formed for every kilogram of organic waste digested. Phenolic wastes can be purified in this way by the development of special types of bacteria which can utilize them as food. *See also* aerobic.

activating agent. A substance added to another substance so that a physical or chemical change will take place more rapidly and/or completely.

activation. 1. Supplying of air and oxygen continuously to sewage sludge to promote growth of aerobic bacteria which digest (decompose) the organic waste material.

2. Increasing the activity of one substance by the addition of a second substance, usually in low concentration. Examples are the activating effect of fatty acids on thiazole accelerators, and of trace amounts of certain metals on phosphors. *See also* initiator.

3. Increasing the adsorptive capacity of a material, such as charcoal or alumina by exposing it in a finely divided state to steam or carbon dioxide at high temperature ; this treatment creates a high degree of porosity and thus increases the interior surface area.

activation analysis. A method of analysis by means of isotopes in which a small quantity of an element that is difficult to determine is exposed to activating particles (*e.g.*, deuterons in a cyclotron or neutrons in a nuclear reactor). One or more of the stable isotopes of the element are thus converted to radioisotopes which can be detected by their characteristic radiations and half-lives. By treating similarly a comparsion sample containing a known proportion of the given element the analysis can be made quantitative. *See also* nondestructive activation analysis.

activation energy. The excess energy over the ground state which must be acquired by molecules in order to take part in a particular reaction. The most common source of this additional energy is believed to be energy interchanged taking place during collisions.

activation induced by electrons. Activation by electrons with energy of at least 15 MeV.

activation of molecule. Uptake of activation energy by molecule.

activation polarization. Sum of transition and reaction polarizations. Active polarization is expressed by activation overvoltage.

activator. 1. A substance which renders a material or a system active ; commonly a catalyst. A special use of this term occurs in the flotation process, where an activator assists the action of the collector.

2. A substance which increases the effectiveness of rubber vulcanization accelerator, *e.g.*, zinc oxide, zinc laurate, litharge.

3. A substance which is required in trace quantities to impart luminescence to certain crystals. Silver and copper are used as activators for zinc sulphide and cadmium sulphide pigments.

active. Potent, effective, especially with the connotation of in motion, or producing motion or change.

active alkali. A general term in various processes for the total content of various alkali metal salts, often expressed as the equivalent NaOH that is available for a particular reaction.

active centre. Atoms which by their position on a surface, such as at the apex of a peak or on the edge or corner of a crystal, share with neighbouring atoms an abnormally small portion of their electrostatic field and, therefore have a large residual field available for catalytic activity or for adsorption.

active deposit. Solid radioactive material, deposited by radioactive emanations on surfaces in contact with them.

active earth. An absorbent prepared from a naturally occuring mineral, especially one that is found in a disintegrated solid state, *i.e.*, as an earth.

active immunization. Any process by which means of protection against bacteria or their products is elaborated by an organism.

active mass. Mass per unit volume, usually expressed in moles per litre (a concentration factor).

active principle. The chemical compound, or group of compounds, to which the physiological action of a drug is attributed.

active site. The region of an enzyme surface that binds the substrate molecule and transforms it.

active surface of adsorbent. Surface area at which various unbalanced forces act, resulting in adsorption of adsorbate by adsorbent.

active transport. Energy-requiring transport of a solute across a membrance in the direction of increasing concentration.

activity. This term has a number of specialized meanings in chemistry among which are the following :

1. The tendency of a metal high in the electromotive series to replace another metal lower in the series, from its compounds : for example, iron will replace copper in copper sulphate to form ferrous sulphate, releasing tree metallic copper. The electromotive series is also called the activity series or the displacement series.

2. The tendency of a metal, metallic oxide, or (rarely) an organic substance to accelerate the chemical combination of other substances ; this is known as catalytic activity. Some metal are active catalysts for given reactions and others are not. A fine state of subdivision usually increases the activity of a substance by exposing a maximum area of solid surface to the reacting gases.

3. Number of disintegrations of radioactive nuclei of a given quantity of a substance per unit time.

4. In the physical chemistry of chemical systems, particularly solutions, the term activity relates to the apparent concentration of a substance in a reactive system. Activity involves the thermodynamics of equilibrium systems and the concentrations of their compounds. It indicates the deviation of a system from the ideal state. Best defined in mathematical terms, when the ratio of the activity, a, to the actual concenrtation, $[A]$, is designated as f, in the expression, $a=f[A]$; f=a factor denoting the exent to which the activity of a substance differs from the actual concentration. In this case, f is the activity coefficient.

5. The term activity is also applied to an expression of the magnitude of interionic forces.

6. Activity is also the rate or speed at which an agent operates.

activity coefficient. f_M. Measure of deviation of thermodynamic properties of constituent in a given solution from its properties in ideal solution, defined by ratio $f_M = \frac{a_M}{x_M}$

where a_M=activity of solution constituent M. x_M=mole fraction of this constituent activity coefficient depends on pressure, temperature and other components of solution. In the case of gases, the effective pressure of a gas is represented by the *fugacity*, f, and the actual pressure of the gas by P. The activity coefficient, γ, of the gas is then given by $\gamma = f/P$. In solutions the activity coefficient is equal to unity at infinite dilution of the solute and then deviates from unity as the concentration increases.

activity coefficient of single ion, f_+ or f_-. Quantity defined by formula

$$f_+ = \frac{a_+}{c_+} \quad \text{or} \quad f_- = \frac{a_-}{c_-}$$

where a_+ and a_-=ion activities and c_+ and c_-=their concentrations ; this quantity is not measurable.

activity constant. In a reversible reaction which has reached equilibrium, the product of the activities of the substances produced by the direct reaction, divided by the product of the activities of the substances produced by the reverse reaction. Thus in the reaction

$$mA+nB\ldots\ldots \rightleftharpoons pC+qD\ldots\ldots$$

$$K=\frac{a_C^p\, a_D^q \ldots\ldots}{a_A^m\, a_B^n \ldots\ldots}$$

where K is the activitity constant.

activity, optical. *See* optical activity.

actor. In coupled or sympathetic reactions, the substance which takes part in both primary and secondary reactions as distinguished from the "inductor" and the "acceptor," both of which take part in but one of the reactions.

acyclic. Not possessing cycle or ring structure.

acyl. A carbonyl group (C=O) attached to an alkyl or aryl group. It may also be described as the group which remain after the removal of an OH group from an organic acid. Acyl groups occur in several series of organic compounds. Acetyl and benzoyl groups are specific types of acyl groups.

acylation. A reaction or process in which an acyl radical such as acetyl, benzoyl, etc., is introduced into an organic compound. Reagents often used for acylation are the acid anhydride, acid chloride, or the acid of the particular acyl radical to be introduced into the compound, *e.g.*

$$(RCO)_2O+C_2H_5OH \rightarrow RCOOC_2H_5+RCOOH$$

$$RCOCl+C_6H_6 \xrightarrow{AlCl_3} C_6H_5{-}COR+HCl$$

acyl carrier protein. A protein in fatty acid synthesis that picks up acetyl and malonyl groups from acetyl coenzyme A and malonyl coenzyme A and links them by condensation to form β-ketoacid acyl carrier protein, releasing carbon dioxide and the sulphydral form of acyl carrier protein. Abbreviated as ACP.

acyloin condensation. Linking together of two molecules of carboxylic ester under action of sodium ; also intramolecular reaction of dicarboxylic acid ester, resulting in formation of acyloin, *e.g.*

$$(CH_2)_n\begin{cases}COOCH_3\\COOCH_3\end{cases} \xrightarrow[2)\ 4H_2O]{1)\ 4Na} (CH_2)_n\begin{cases}C{=}O\\CHOH\end{cases} + 2CH_3OH + 4NaOH$$

adamantine compound. A compound having in its crystal structure an arrangement of atoms essentially that of diamond ; in which every atom is linked to its four neighbours by covalent bonds. An example of this type is zinc sulphide, but it is to be noted that the eight electrons involved in forming the four bonds are not provided equally by the zinc and sulphur atoms, the sulphur yielding its six valency electrons, and the zinc contributing two.

adaptor. A piece of apparatus in the shape of a gradually narrowing tube, commonly bend in an obtuse angle used to connect distillation and other apparatus, as a condenser and receiver. Also known as adopter.

adatom. A mobile, adsorbed atom.

addition. *See* addition reaction.

addition agent. A substance added to a process which without entering into the main reaction improves the quality or uniformity of the product.

addition compound. Compounds formed by linking of molecules of substance capable of independent existence. Also known as molecular compound.

addition polymer. A macromolecule resulting from the catalytic combination of many identical monomer units; the combination is initiated by free radicals formed by decomposition of the catalyst in the presence of heat or light. For example, the ethylene monomer ($CH_2=CH_2$) unites with others like it to give polyethylene, one of the most versatile synthetic resins ; the same is true of such monomers as butadiene, styrene, and acrylonitrile, which are the basis of many synthetic elastomers. *See also* free radical ; polymerization.

addition polymerization. Polymerization by repeated addition process.

addition reaction. 1. When two or more molecules react to produce but one product, the reaction is termed "addition" or, less commonly a synthetical reaction. The direct union of carbon and hydrogen to produce acetylene or sulfur and oxygen to produce sulphur dioxide are addition reactions.

2. Reaction of chemical compounds involving decrease of unsaturation of molecule. The following types of addition are known (depending on reaction mechanism) : electrophilic, nucleophilic and free-radical, *e.g.* electrophilic addition to double bond.

$$RCH=CH_2+HBr \rightarrow RCHBr-CH_3$$

additive. A nonspecific term referring to any substance added to a food, a petroleum product or a rubber or plastic mixture to impart a particular purpose or property. In most cases the proportion necessary to accomplish the desired results is one per cent or less. Food additives include antioxidants, leavening agents, emulsifiers, flavours, and colorants ; gasoline and lubricating-oil additives include gum inhibitiors, knock suppressants, ignition improvers, and pourpoint depressants ; while plastic additives include antioxidants, organic dyes, blowing agents, and accelerators.

additive properties. Properties which, for a given system, are some of corresponding properties of constituents.

additivity. Law according to which some definite property of a given set of elements is sum of corresponding properties of constituent elements, *e.g.*, molecular mass is sum of all masses of constituent atoms. Also known as additivity law.

additivity law. *See* additivity.

adduct. *See* clathrate compounds.

adelomorphic. Said of definite structure.

adenase. An enzyme that catalyzes the hydrolysis of adenine to hypoxanthine and ammonia.

adenosinediphosphatase. An enzyme that catalyzes the hydrolysis of adenosinediphosphate. Abbreviated as ADP_{ase}.

adenosinetriphosphatase. An enzyme that catalyzes the hydrolysis of adenosinetriphosphate. Abbreviated as ATP_{ase}.

adenylic acid. 1. A generic term for a group of isomeric nuclotides.

2. The phosphoric acid ester adenosine.

adhesion. In general, a condition in which two discrete entities or particles remain in close contact, or the force as a result of which such a condition is maintained. Specifically, the term adhesion is often used in chemistry to denote the attraction between the unlike particles, as distinguished from cohesion, which is the internal force of attraction, molecular or otherwise within a single substance or phase.

adhesion tension. The work required to enlarge the surface between a solid and a liquid is called the adhesion energy, and it may be expressed as the adhesion tension in units of force per unit of surface.

adhesive. A substance that has the property of attaching itself to the surfaces of other substances in such a way as to form a strong and relatively permanent bond between them. The adhesives may be natural substances of a proteinaceous of hydrocarbon nature, such as glues made from animal hides, blood and tendons, fish skins, casein, soyabeans, rubber, resin, asphalt, etc. Others are semisynthetics (water glass, inorganic cements of various types). More important than these are synthetic polymers, which may be thermoplastic or thermosetting and have a stronger bonding ability and are more resistant to deterioration than natural adhesive. Chief among them are epoxy and phenol-formaldehyde resins, widely used in plywood, reinforced plastics, and other composities; bot-melt adhesive (polyethylene, polyvinyl acetate, isobutylene); and various types of organic cements which are dispersions of an elastomer in a solvent. A very important group of synthetics is silicone resin cements. Adhesivies have been introduced which give a heat-resistant bond; for example, an organic material (polybenzinidazole) is effective up to 260°C, and mixtures of silica and boric acid are effective as adhesives up to 1100°C.

adiabatic. 1. A term used to characterize a process in which no heat is gained or lost as the conditions of operation are changed, *i.e.*, occurring without change in heat content. For example, certain fixed-bed reactors used in petroleum refining operate adiabatically.

2. Set of thermodynamic equilibrium states of the same system with identical entropy.

adiabatic calorimeter. A type of calorimeter in which heat exchange between calorimeter vessel and its outer jacket is practically negligible.

adiabatic cooling. A process in which temperature of a system is reduced without any heat being exchanged between the system and the surroundings.

adiabatic demagnetization. A method of attaining temperatures in the region of absolute zero by magnetizing a paramagnetic substance, such as potassium chrome alum or gadolinium sulphate, and allowing it to demagnetize adiabatically. During magnetization, between the poles of an electromagnet, the heat produced is carried away by helium; while during the adiabatic demagnetization process, cooling to very low temperatures takes place.

adiabatic elasticity. A term used to express the change of elasticity of the medium which is propagating an explosion wave assuming that the medium is discontinuous in the vicinity of the wave.

adiabatic expansion. Increase in volume without gain or loss of heat from outside the substance or system.

adiabatic invarient. A physical quantity which may be quantized and which, to a certain degree of approximation, remains unchanged under the slow variation of any parameter.

adiabatic law. The relationship which states that, for adiabatic expansion of gases,

$$P_{\sigma^{-\gamma}} = \text{constant};$$

where P=pressure; σ=density, and γ=ratio of specific heats=C_p/C_v.

adiabatic partition. Partition which does not allow mass or energy transfer in form of heat.

adiabatic process. Thermodynamic process, without any exchange of matter and heat with surroundings. Also known as adiabatic transition.

adiabatic transition. *See* adiabatic process.

adiactinic. Not transmitting photochemically active rays.

adion. An ion adsorbed on a surface that is held in such a way that it is free to move on the surface but not away from it.

adipyl. The radical —$OC(CH_2)_4CO$—.

adjacent position. In an organic compound having a ring structure, the position occupied by two or more atoms or radicals which are joined by valence forces to consecutive atoms in the ring.

adjective dye. Any dye that needs a mordent.

adjoint wave functions. Functions in Dirac electron theory which are formed by applying the Dirac matrix B to the Hermitian conjugates of the original wave functions.

adjuvant. A drug which assists the action of another drug.

Adler test for pentoses. On heating a mixture of equal quantities of aniline (or toluidine) and glacial acetic acid with pentoses, an intense red colour is produced.

Adler tests for blood. 1. On acidulating with acetic acid, an aqueous solution containing blood, and adding solutions of benzidine and hydrogen peroxide, a blue colour is produced.

2. Blood stains or spots on saturation with a solution of malachite green (leuco base form), and moistening with hydrogen peroxide, develop green colour.

Many modifications of these tests have been described.

Adrian test for aldehydes. To test for aldehydes present in ether, saturate it with gaseous ammonia. A precipitate of aldehyde ammonia is formed. The ether must be neutral before testing.

Adrian test for nitrite. Nitrites in acid solution give an orange-yellow colour with guaiacol.

adsorbate. A substance which is absorbed at the surface in the process of adsorption. Also known as adsorptive.

In some cases term adsorbate refers a substance which has already been adsorbed, whereas term adsorptive is restricted to substance (present in gaseous or liquid bulk phases) which can be adsorbed under given conditions.

adsorbent. Crystalline amorphous or liquid substance or gel with greatly increased outer or inner surface area at which adsorption takes place.

adsorption. Attachment of the molecules of a gas or liquid to the surface of another substance (usually a solid) ; these molecules form a closely adherent film or layer held in place by electrostatic forces that are considerably weaker than chemical bonds. The finer the particle size of the solid or the greater its porosity, the more efficient an adsorbent it will be because of the large surface area thus provided. Adsorption occurs on activated carbon, silica gel, and similar materials especially prepared for this purpose. Adsorption takes place only at the surface, which includes all capillaries, cracks, depressions, openings, and other types of irregularities. Adsorption is of primary importance in catalytic mechanisms, but should be distinguished from chemisorption, which involves much stronger attractive forces. *See also* chemisorption ; catalyst ; activated carbon.

adsorption, activated. Chemisorption (adsorption involving forces of chemical nature) in which the activation energy is relatively high.

adsorption, apolar. Adsorption of nonpolar substances on nonpolar media.

adsorption catalysis. Catalysis of a chemical reaction affected by adsorption of reactants on surfaces.

adsorption centre. The site on surface of adsorbent to which adsorbate molecule is bound. Also known as adsorption site.

adsorption chromatography. The type of chromatography in which solid that can adsorb components being separated is stationary phase.

adsorption coefficient. *K.* Constant in Langmuir equation equal to ratio of adsorption rate constant to corresponding desorption rate constant and which depends on kind of system and on temperature.

adsorption current. In polarography and related methods, current which is observed when substrate or product of electrode reaction is adsorbed on electrode surface.

adsorption, displacement. Displacement from a surface of one adsorbed substance by another.

adsorption equilibrium. Equilibrium between a substance that is adsorbed upon a surface, and the same substance in a solution or other medium that is in contact with the surface.

adsorption exponent. The exponential term *n* in the classical adsorption isotherm.

adsorption forces. Forces responsible for adsorption. They may be of different nature, depending on kinds of adsorption interactions, *e.g.*, physical adsorption or chemisorption.

adsorption hysteresis. Non-coincidence of adsorption and desorption isotherms.

adsorption indicator. Dyestuffs or other chemicals which are used to detect the end point of a precipitation titration. These substances are dissolved in the solution to be titrated and impart colour to it. The end point of the titration is signaled by disappearance of the colour from the solution, or a change of colour in the solution, attributable to adsorption of the indicator by the precipitate.

adsorption isobar. A graph showing how adsorption varies with some parameter, such as temperature at constant pressure.

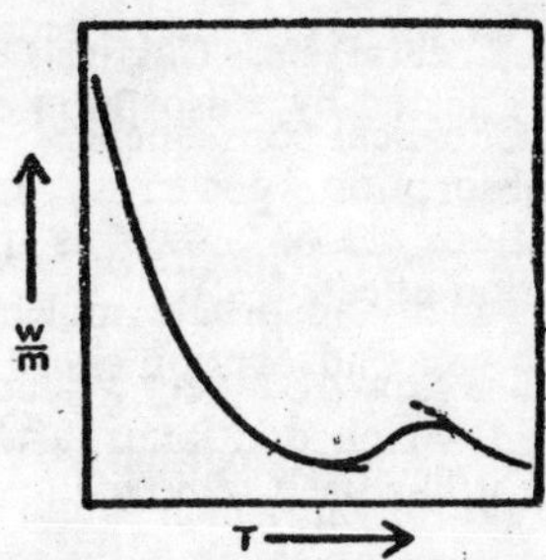

Fig. 3. Adsorption isobar

adsorption isostere. Curve which shows dependence of gas equilibrium pressure on its temperature determined for constant amount of gas adsorbed at surface of unit mass of adsorbent.

adsorption isotherm. A relationship between the mass of substance adsorbed at a given temperature and the mass of adsorbent. The Freundlich adsorption isotherm is of the form

$$\frac{x}{m}=kp^{1/n}$$

in which x = gas absorbed, m = mass of adsorbent, p = the gas pressure, and k and n are constants for the temperature and system. Numerous isotherm equations have been proposed in the chemical literature.

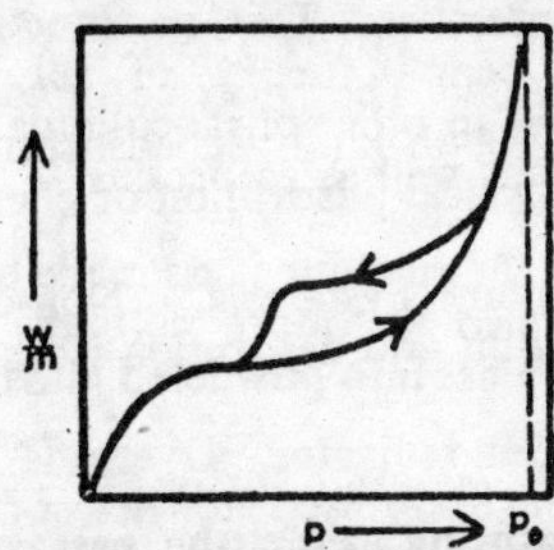

Fig. 4. Adsorption isotherm

adsorption, polar. *See* polar adsorption.

adsorption potential. The energy change experienced by a molecule (or ion) in passing from the gas (or solution) phase to the surface of the adsorbent.

adsorption, preferential. *See* adsorption, specific.

adsorption site. *See* absorption centre.

adsorption space. The thickness of an adsorbed layer.

adsorption, specific. 1. Preferential adsorption of one substance over another.

2. Quantity of absorbate held per unit area of adsorbent.

adsorptive. *See* adsorbate.

adsorptive capacity of surface. Quantity which describes tendency of surface (most commonly referred to defined unit of its area) of a given absorbent to adsorb various substances.

adulterant. A substance of inferior quality or lower cost that is used in a mixture or other preparation. Its presence may be due to improper handling as well as to intentional addition. Thus, a dirty material may also be considered as adulterated.

adulterate. To substitute one substance for another partly or entirely. The term connotes a deterioration of the quality of the product caused by the substitution. The substitution may be due to dirt, *i.e.*, to impurities present in the material because of careless handling or processing.

advection. Transfer of heat convection.

aeolotropism. The property possessed by certain solids (as crystals) and some liquids, of exhibiting differences in the physical properties of a spherical portion of the body when it is tested in different directions.

aerate. To impregnate or saturate a material (usually liquid) with air, carbon dioxide, or some similar gas.

aerating agent. A gas such as carbon dioxide, nitrous oxide, or food grade Freon used to flovour beverages or to dispense liquids from charged containers.

aeration cell. An electrolytic cell whose electromotive force is due to electrodes of the material located in different concentrations of dissolved air. Also known as oxygen cell.

aerobe. An organism whose metabolism demands free *i.e.*, uncombined oxygen.

aerboic. Requiring the presence of air or oxygen to live, grow, and reproduce ; the term is applied exclusively to microorganisms of various types, especially those used in the activated sludge process for industrial and municipal waste treatment. Its opposite, anaerobic, refers to an organism that can live without air or oxygen, or to a digestion process from which air is excluded. *See also* activated sludge.

aerogel. A colloidal solution of a gaseous phase in a solid phase, obtained usually by replacement of the liquid in the dispersed phase by air or gas.

aerosol Colloidal system in which dispersion medium is gaseous and solid or liquid is dispersed phase. If is particles are too small to settle out by gravity, the aerosol is permanent, at least until some forces are introduced to bring about coalescenace or precipitation. Colloidal suspensions of coal dust or other particles (smoke) and of fine water droplets (fog) are instances of aerosols that are undesirable. Aerosols may serve several useful purposes, as in the case of finely divided sprays of perfumes, sanitizing agents, and pesticides. These are released by a propellant gas such as carbon dioxide, which expels the liquid through the orifices in special nozzles. A common method of eliminating aerosols in industrial effluent gases is precipitation by electrical means.

Afanasiev test. The test for cyclopentadiene, performed by adding 1 drop of the liquid to 1 ml. chloroform and 1 ml. glacial acetic acid, then add 2 or 3 drops of sulfuric acid. A violet colour shows the presence of cyclopentadiene.

affination. A process in the sugar industry, in which the sucrose crystals obtained from the crude molasses are removed from residual molasses by treatment with a solvent followed by centrifugation.

affinity, chemical. *See* chemical affinity.

affinity curve. A graph obtained by plotting the heats of formation of various binary compounds of an element against the atomic number of the various elements with which it combines (or any regular arrangement of those elements).

after-chromed dyes. The dyes whose colour or fastness is improved by treatment with sodium dichromate, copper sulphate, or similar materials, after the fabrics have been dyed.

after-effect. Chemical consequences of ionizing radiation absorption, occurring much later after irradiation. Also known as post-effect ; post-irradiation effect.

after-flow. The flow of a very viscous liquid or a plastic solid, which continues after the pressure causing it has been removed.

after-glow. The emission of light or other radiation by a gas or other system persisting after the discharge, reaction, or other process causing it has terminated.

after-heat. Heat derived from residual radioactivity after a reactor has been shut down.

Ag. Symbol for the element silver.

agar. A starch-like natural polymer derived from red algae, a form of seaweed. It absorbs as much as 20 times its weight of water, forming a strong gel at about 40°C which melts at about 90°C. It is typical of the class of materials known as phycocolloids. The gelling property results from the trapping of water within the framework formed by the long-chain polysaccharide (carbohydrate) macromolecules. As little as 1% of agar dissolved in hot water will set on cooling as the slowly diminishing rotary motion of the molecules causes them to become entangled, and thus enclose water within the interstics. This is sometimes called the "brush-heap" theory of gel formation, which applies to other phycocolloids (carrageenan, algin) as well as to pectins.

agate glass. Multicolour glass made by blending glasses of two or more colours by rolling transparent glass into powdered glass of various colour.

ageing. Maturing with the passage of time. Natural ageing takes place without addition of other substances, directed change of envoirnment, or other intervention. Artificial ageing involves such intervention to hasten ripening or to obtain the effects of ageing in a shortened time, as in the case of alcoholic beverages.

ageing of catalyst. In heterogenous catalysis, gradual loss of activity by catalyst increasing during exploitation. Ageing of catalyst is most often caused by its recrystallization.

ageing of neutrons. The slowing down of neutrons.

ageing of precipitate. Change of properties of precipitate with time.

ageing of sols. Change of physical and chemical properties of colloidal solution with time.

agglomeration. Combination or aggregation of small particles suspended in a liquid into clusters of approximately spherical shape. The food industry uses this term in the sense of increasing the particle size of powdered food products. Because such powders tend to be hydrophobic due to the high surface tension of water, agglomeration causes them to be more readily dispersible in water. The operation is known as "instantizing". The agglomerates have varying degrees of voids (open spaces), and have loosely bound, foamlike structures. They are formed by mechanical means in chamber spray dryers, tubes, or fluidized beds, usually in the presence of moisture.

agglutination. A term used by biochemists and immunologists to refer to a form of aggregation occuring in antigen-antibody reactions in which proteinaceous particles, such as bacteria, blood cells, etc., form clumps or clusters. The action is quite specific to the proteins involved. *See also* aggregation.

agglutinin. One of a class of substances found in blood to which certain foreign substances or organisms have been added or admixed. As the name indicates, agglutinins have the characteristic property of causing agglutination, especially of the foreign substances or organisms responsible for their formation.

aggregate. A miscellaneous assortment of gravel, pebbles, cinder, etc., used as a filler for concrete, paving asphalt, and in greenhouse benches for nutrient plant culture.

aggregation. A general term describing the combination or coalescence of particles dispersed in a suspension into clusters or clots, which either precipitate or are removed by filtration. Such particles may be macromolecules of proteins, soaps, or other colloids (aggregates of which called micelles,) or larger particles, such as red cells in blood, rubber hydrocarbon in latex, and fat particles in milk. There are several types of aggregation :

(*i*) agglutination, which is chiefly the cohesion of bacterial cells, as in antigen-antibody reactions ;

(*ii*) coagulation, the irreversible clotting of proteins, etc., brought about by electrolytes, enzymes, or heat ;

(*iii*) flocculation, the formation of clumps of dispersed colloidal solids such as carbon black in rubber mixes ; and

(*iv*) agglomeration. *See also* agglomeration ; coagulation ; flocculation.

aggressin. A product of bacterial metabolism which impairs the defensive mechanisms of the blood of the host.

agitation. The act of exerting force on a solid or liquid mixture in order to bring about intimate mixing and uniform dispersion of the components. This is usually effected by stirring, grinding, shaking, kneadling, or plowing with any of a number of mechnanical devices ; it can also be done (in the case of an aerosol) by means of an air stream, as in the floatation of clays.

aglycone. The monocarbohydrate portion of a glucosidic molecule. *See* glucoside.

agon. The active portion of an enzymes molecule.

Agraz test reaction. A dilute solution of pyrrole, when mixed with a normal solution of iodine in potassium iodide and shaken with potassium hydroxide and ether, gives an intense blue colour (violet colour with chloroform). Upon shaking the blue test-mixture with zinc dust, a green colour is obtained.

Agrestini test. A solution of alloxan or alloxantin in sulphuric acid, upon addition of a solution of pyrocatechol, gives a blue-green colour which changes to green upon addition of water. Using resorsinol instead of pyrocatechol, a wine-red colour is obtained, changing to indigo blue upon addition of water.

Agulhon solution. A solution of 0.5 g. potassium dichromate in 100 ml. concentrated nitric acid ; used as a test reagent for certain reducing substances, such as alcohols, aldehydes, or carbohydrates. A blue colour, changing to green on heating, is given by the various reducing substances.

air. The mixture of gases that envelops the earth's crust ; the atmosphere. Its composition varies with the altitude at which a sample is taken. At sea level the composition is (in percent by volume) : nitrogen 78, oxygen 20.9, argon 0.94 and carbon dioxide 0.033. There are also trace amounts of other gases as well as varying proportions of water vapour. A low percentage of dissolved air is present in ocean water. The density of dry air is 1.29 grams per litre at STP. Air can be liquefied by compression and cooling. Nitrogen, oxygen, and argon for industrial use are separated from air by distillation. Most of the oxygen present in atmosphere is produced by photosynthesis, and the carbon dioxide by combustion and degradation of organic matter.

air drying. Drying by the evaporative action of atmospheric air currents.

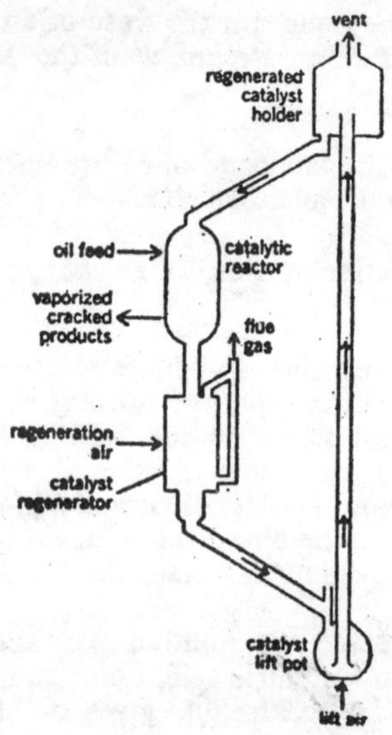

Fig. 5. Airlift thermofor catalytic cracking

airlift thermofor catalytic cracking. A continuous catalytic process for the conversion of heavy gas oils into lighter products ; utilizes a moving bed of small pellets or beads of catalyst travelling continuously through the oil cracking vessel and then through a regeneration klin.

air elutriation. The same as air separation.

air pollution. Introduction into the atmosphere of substances that are not normally present therein and that have a harmful effect on man, animals, or plant life. Important among these are sulfur dioxide, which forms sulfuric acid on contact with water vapour; automotive exhaust emission products (carbon monoxide, lead compounds, polynuclear hydrocarbons, nitrogen oxides), toxic metal dusts from smelters ; coal smoke, and other particulates, formaldehyde and aerolein ; and radioactive emanations. Control of these is exercised by the Environmental Protection Agency. As conventionally used, the term does not apply to interior air spaces such as industrial workrooms. Tolerances for the latter are established by the American Conference of Governmental and Industrial Hygienists (ACGIH) and enforced by the Occupational Safety and Health Administration (OSHA). Also known as atmospheric pollution.

air separation. A process for the classification of particles by the action of air currents.

air-standard cycle. A thermodynamic cycle in which working fluid is considered to be a perfect gas with such properties of air as a volume of 12.4 ft^3/lb at 14.7 psi and 492°R and a ratio of specific heats of 1.4.

alabamine. The name that was assigend to the element of atomic number 82 when its discovery was claimed by the magneto-optic method. *See also* astatine.

albedo. 1. Whiteness or a white tissue of substance.

2. In photometry the ratio of the amount of radiation reflected by a surface to the amount incident upon it.

3. The ratio of the neutron current density out of a (nonsource) medium to the neutron current density into it.

Alberger process. A method of producing high-quality sodium chloride from crude brine by fractional crystallization of calcium sulphate that is present, and flash evaporation of the purified brine.

Alberti test. To test for solanine and solanidine, dissolve the material in 1 drop glacial acetic acid, and 1 or 2 drops concentrated sulphuric acid and then add 1 drop of 0.5% hydrogen peroxide or 1% formaldehyde. A purple-red colour indicates the presence of solanine or solanidine.

albumin. A mixture of water-soluble globular proteins occurring in the tissues and fluids of the body. It crystallizes on drying but can be reconstituted with water. It is heat-sensitive and coagulates irreversibly at about 80°C. Albumin is the chief component of egg white in the form of ovalbumin and conalbumin, it also occurs in lower percentages in egg yolk, milk, and blood serum. It is produced for commercial use in food products and for photographic emulsions. Its molecular weight is about 50,000. The term is derived from the Latin word for white. *See also* protein.

albuminoid. One of a class of proteins that are insoluble in neutral solvents.

albuminoid ammonia. Ammonia obtained by decomposition of albuminous material. The quantity present is utilized in water analysis to determine the percentage of organic nitrogen in the sample.

albumose. A product obtained by the digestion of proteins with pepsin or dilute acids.

alchemy. 1. Medieval chemistry.

2. A term applied to the ancient attempts to transmute the base metals into gold and silver and to prepare the panacea for all diseases or the elixir of life. The most famous alchemists were Geber, Albertus Magnus, Roger Bacons, Raymond Lully, Basil Valentine. Paracelsus, Libavius, and Glauber.

Alchlor process. A process for the purification and treatment of lubricating oil, using aluminum chloride.

Alcock test for chromium. On treatment with an excess of sodium hydroxide solution, and then with sodium peroxide, chromium salts form yellow chromates. Addition of acetic acid to the solution containing hydrogen peroxide produces a violet or blue colour.

Alcock-Wilkin test. On heating 0.01 g. acetophenetidin with 5 ml. concentrated sulphuric acid a brown colour is obtained, which changes to red upon addition of water and ammonia.

alcogel. A gel formed by alcosol.

alcohol. 1. The common name for ethyl alcohol (ethanol).

2. Any one of a class of organic substances derived from the aliphatic hydrocarbons by the substitution of one or more hydroxyl groups for an equal number of hydrogen atoms, except that in rare cases and only where modifying constitutional influences are present, two hydroxyl groups or more are never united to the same carbon atom. The alkyl residue of the alcohol may be further substituted by aromatic nuclei, as in benzyl alcohol $C_6H_5CH_2OH$, thus forming the alcoholic derivatives of the carbocyclic series, but the alcoholic hydroxyl may not be directly alcoholic united to a carbon atom which is a member of the aromatic ring, because in that case, the compound is considered to be a phenol, which has certain distinctive properties. The alochols are named according to the Geneva plan by the substitution of "*ol*" for the final "*e*" of the parent hydrocarbon name, *i.e.*, ethane—ethanol ; propane—propanol.

Alcohol may be mono-, di-, tri-, or polyhydric, depending upon the number of hydroxyl groups per molecule, each attached to a different carbon atom. Examples are, respectively, ethyl alcohol, C_2H_5OH ; glycol $OHCH_2CH_2OH$; glycerol, $C_3H_5(OH)_3$; and pentaerythritol $C(CH_2OH)_4$ Their physical properties vary with molecular weight ; those having from one to four carbons are low-boiling, mobile liquids ; from five to eleven carbons, the viscosity and boiling points increase ; above eleven carbons, alcohols are waxy solids. Alcohols exhibit both acidic and basic behaviour. Several are toxic notably methyl and allyl, and most of them are combustible.

Primary alcohols are characterized by the grouping $—CH_2OH$; secondary alcohols by $=CHOH$; and tertiary alcohols by $\equiv COH$. It is evident that some compounds may contain all of these groups at once and so do not fall under any single one of the above classifications.

alcohol dehydrogenase. The enzyme tha

catalyzes the oxidation of ethanol to acetaldehyde.

alcohol, denatured. *See* denatured alcohol.

alcoholate. A compound derived from an alcohol by replacement of the hydrogen in the hydroxyl group by a metal, commonly one that forms a strong base. Also known as alkoxide.

alcoholic fermentation. Anaerobic process of hexose decomposition, *e.g.*, of glucose to ethanol and carbon dioxide, caused by zymase produced by yeast, *e.g.*,

$$C_6H_{12}O_6 \rightarrow 2C_2H_5OH + 2CO_2$$

alcoholometry. The determination of the proportion of ethanol in spirits and other solutions ; usually performed by measuring the relative density of the liquid at a standard temperature by a specially graduated hydrometer.

alcoholysis. Metathesis between organic compound and alcohol, the latter serving additionally as solvent, *e.g.*,

$$RCOCl + R'OH \rightarrow RCOOR' + HCl$$

alcosol. Mixture of an alcohol and a colloid.

aldehyde. Any of a series of unsaturated organic compounds, both aliphatic and aromatic, containing a carbonyl group, in which one of the bonds of the carbon atom is attached to hydrogen, $-\overset{\displaystyle O}{\overset{\|}{C}}-H$; *e.g.*, formaldehyde is HCHO. Aldehydes are closely related to ketones, but are, in general more chemically reactive. They are formed from alcohols by dehydrogenation, and the term aldehyde is derived from this reaction, *i.e.*, alcohols dehydrogenation. For example, formaldehyde (HCHO) is formed by removing two hydrogen atoms from a molecule of methyl alcohol (CH_3OH).

They are named (*i*) from the corresponding acids by combining the root of the acid with the word aldehyde, *e.g.*, formaldehyde, butyraldehyde ; and (*ii*) according to the Geneva system by substituting "*al*" for the final "*e*" in the name of the parent hydrocarbon, *e.g.*, ethanal, propanal, butanal, etc.

Aldehydes are important synthesizing agents ; they enter into condensation reactions, and are readily oxidized to organic acids. They also prevent deterioration of protein-rich substances, and thus are used as preservatives in the food and leather industries and for biological specimens. Among the more important aldehydes are : formaldehyde, acetaldehyde, and benzaldehyde. *See also* ketone ; aldol condensation ; condensation.

aldehyde lyase. Any enzymes that catalyzes the nonhydrolytic cleavage of an aldehyde.

aldehyde-ketone rearrangement. Acid-catalyzed conversion of aldehydes with no hydrogen atoms at α-position into isomeric ketones, involving rearrangement-1,2 of alkyl or aryl groups, *e.g.*,

$$(CH_3)_3CCHO \xrightarrow{H^+} (CH_3)_2CHCOCH_3$$

aldime. A compound containing the $-\overset{\displaystyle H}{\overset{|}{C}}=NH$ group which may be derived from an aldehyde by replacement of the carbonyl oxygen by an imido group.

aldohexose. One of a class of sugars that contain six carbon atoms and an aldehyde group, *e.g.*, glucose, mannose.

aldoketene. A compound containing the $-\overset{\displaystyle H}{\overset{|}{C}}=C=O$ group.

aldol condensation.. A reaction between two aldehyde molecules or between one aldehyde and one ketone molecule in which the position of one of the hydrogen atoms is changed so as to form single molecule having one hydroxyl and one carbonly group. Such a molecule formed is partly an alcohol (OH group) and partly a carbonyl (CO group) and represent a union of two smaller molecules.

Linking together of aldehydes and ketones (usually base catalyzed, containing hydrogen atom linked with α-carbon atom, resulting in formation of aldols, *e.g.*,

$$2\,RCH_2\overset{\displaystyle O}{\overset{\|}{C}}-H \xrightarrow{\text{Base}} RCH_2\underset{\displaystyle OH}{\underset{|}{C}H}\overset{\displaystyle R}{\overset{|}{C}H}\overset{\displaystyle O}{\overset{\|}{C}}-H$$

It can be repeated to form molecules of increasing molecular weight. The condensation of formaldehyde to sugar in plants, which on repetition builds up the more complex carbohydrate structures such as starch and cellulose, is thought to be a reaction of this type. Also known as aldolization.

aldolization. *See* aldol condensation.

aldopentose. One of a class of sugars that contain five carbon atoms and an aldehyde group ; *e.g.*, arabinose, ribose.

aldose. Any of a group of sugars whose molecule contains an aldehyde group and one or more alcohol groups. An example is glyceraldehyde ($HOCH_2.CHOH.CHO$), specifically called an aldotriose because it contains three carbon atoms.

aldoside. A compound resulting from the union of an aldose and an alcohol, a phenol or other hydroxylated substance by the elimination of water. The true glucosides belong to this class, as do also the mannosides, galactosides, rhamnosides, arabinosides, etc.

aldoxane. A condensation compound of an aldol and a carboxyl compound.

aldoxime. One of a series of compounds containing the group $-\overset{|}{C}{=}NOH$, or its tautomeric form.

Alekseevkii test. Chloropicrin in aqueous solution, when reduced with metallic calcium, gives a red precipitate with β-naphthylamine and sulphuric acid.

alembic. A form of retort, with a removable cap and neck used by early chemists and alchemists.

Aliamet test. In this test for copper, a solution of the metallic salt is added to a concentrated solution of sodium sulphite containing pyrogallol. A reddish-yellow to dark red colour indicates the presence of copper.

alicyclic. A major series of cyclic organic compounds whose molecules have a closed ring structure, but whose properties are much more like those of aliphatics than those of aromatics. The term is a combination of aliphatic and cyclic. They may be either saturated (cycloparaffins) or unsaturated (cycloolefins). They include a large number of alcohols, *e.g.*, cyclohexanol, menthol, terpineol, cholesterol. The rings vary greatly in size and may consist of from three to twelve or more constituents. Their chemical properties are strongly affected by the size of the ring, those with fewest constituents being the most reactive. Cycloparaffins were formerly called naphthenes, a name that is misleading and no longer in general use. *See also* cyclic compound.

alicyclic nucleus. An hydroaromatic ring.

Alimarin-Fried reagent. A strongly-acid solution of phenylarsonic acid, containing tartaric acid; used in the determination of columbium and tantalum. White precipitates are produced.

aliphatic. Derived from the Greek word for "fat," this term refers to a major series of organic compounds whose carbon atoms are arranged in straight or branched chains (sometimes called open chains). They may be saturated (single bonds only) or unsaturated (one or more double or triple bonds). Those having only single bonds are known as alkanes or paraffins ; those with one double bond are called alkenes or olefins ; and those with triple bonds are called alkynes or acetylenes. The aliphatic series includes hydrocarbons, aldehydes, ketones, alcohols, organic acids, and carbohydrates which have no ring structure. Some of the examples are as follows :

		typical	Formula	
common name	IUPAC mame	compound	molecular	generic
paraffin	alkane	methane	CH_4	C_nH_{2n+2}
olefin	alkene	ethylene	$H_2C{=}CH_2$	C_nH_{2n}
diolefin	alkadiene	isoprene	$H_2C{=}\overset{\overset{CH_3}{|}}{C}{-}CH{=}CH_2$	C_nH_{2n-2}
acetylene	alkyne	acetylene	$HC{\equiv}CH$	C_nH_{2n-2}

See also aromatic ; alicyclic.

aliquot. A fractional portion of a sample or solution taken for the purpose of analysis. For test purposes master lots are often prepared, which are divided into equal portions, to which various test substances are added ; each portion may be any desired fraction of the master lot, *e.g.*, one-half, one-quarter, one-tenth, etc. These are called aliquot parts. *See also* moiety.

alkali. This term is generally used to refer to hydroxides and carbonates of the elements of Group IA of the periodic table, as well as to ammonium hydroxide, all of which are bases, and their aqueous solutions range in *p*H above 7 to 14. Strong alkalies are also called caustics, their solutions being corrosive to the skin and other tissues Most alkali hydroxides are made by electrolysis of alkali chloride solutions, *e.g.*, sodium hydroxide (NaOH) from sodium chloride (NaCi), and potassium hydroxide (KOH) from potassium chloride (KCl). *See also* base ; alkali metal.

alkali alcoholate. A compound formed from an alcohol and an alkali metal base ; the alkali metal replaces the hydrogen of the hydroxyl group, *e.g.*, C_2H_5ONa.

alkali blue. The sodium salt of triphenylrosaniline sulphonic acid ; mainly used as an indicator.

alkali builder. An alkali added to soap which increases the alkalinity of materials to be washed. Among the alkali builders used for this purpose are the following : caustic soda, soda ash, various soluble basic salts such as trisodium phosphate, sodium orthosilicate and various mixtures of some of the above substances.

alkali metals. Elements of the first main group, *i.e.*, IA of periodic system with configuration of outer electronic subshells of atoms ns^1 : lithium, sodium, potassium, rubidium, caesium, and francium.

alkalimetric titration. *See* alkalimetry.

alkalimetry. The process of determining the amount of an alkali present in a sample by titration against a standard acid solution, or, more broadly, the system of analysis by titration whose end point is recognized by a change in hydrogen-ion concentration. Also known as alkalimetric titration.

alkaline. Exhibiting some or all of the properties of an alkali ; or an aqueous solution having an excess of hydroxyl ions over hydrogen ions (*p*H greater than 7.0).

alkaline earths. Three divalent metalic elements of Group IIA of the periodic table, namely barium, calcium, and strontium. They were originally called earths because of their noncombustibility and insolubility in water. All these elements form strong bases.

alkaline reaction. Any reaction characteristic of alkalies as the changes in a substance or system which are brought about by increase of its *p*H to values above 7.0.

alkalinity. 1. Possessing properties of alkalies.

2. In aqueous solution having a *p*H of more than 7.0.

alkali, vegetable. *See* vegetable alkali.

alkali, volatile. *See* volatile alkali.

alkalization. The act of communicating alkalinity to a compound or system.

alkalize. To render a solution or substance alkaline.

alkaloids. Any member of a class of organic compounds characterized by content of nitrogen and the property of combining with acids to form salts. The term is now restricted to basic substances derived from plants and excludes the simpler amino derivatives, as aniline, quinoline, propylamine, etc., which were formerly included in this classification. Certain other substances, *i.e.*, the purine bases, such as caffeine, theobromine, etc., although products of vegetable organisms, are not now included among the alkaloids. The following classification of alkaloids is widely accepted :

Derivatives of aryl-substituted amines.

Examples : adrenaline, benzedrine, ephedrine, neocynephrine, tyramine.

Derivatives of imidazole.

Example : pilocarpine.

Derivatives of pyridine and piperidine.

Examples : anabasine, coniine, ricinine.

Derivatives of pyrrole.

Examples : carpaine, hygrine, nicotine.

Complex alkaloids (containing condensed or fused ring system).

Aporphine alkaloids.

Examples : apomorphine, isothebaine, corydine.

Alkaloids containing pyrrole rings fused with other rings.

Examples : gelsemine, physostigmine, vasicine, yohimbine.

Tropine alkaloids.

Examples : atropine, cocaine, ecgonine, scopolamine, tropine.

Alkaloids containing a fusion of two piperidine rings.

Examples : pseudopelletierine, isopelletierine.

Berberine alkaloids.

Examples : berberine, emetine.

Cinchona alkaloids.

Examples : cinchonine, quinine, quinidine.

Lupine alkaloids.

Examples : lupanine, sparteine.

Cryptopine alkaloids

Examples : cryptopine, protopine.

Quinoline alkaloids.

Examples : dictamine, galipoline, lycorine.

Isoquinoline alkaloids.

Examples : peliotine, sarsoline, anhalidine.

Papaverine alkaloids.

Examples : codamine, homolaudanosine, papaverine.

Bis-benzylisoquinoline alkaloids.

Examples : bebeverine, trilobine.

Morphine and related alkaloids.

Examples : morphine, codeine, thebaine.

Phthalide isoquinoline alkaloids—narcotine alkaloids.

Examples : hydrastine, narcotine, narceine.

Other alkaloids.

Examples : brucine, colaoidine, strychuine.

alkaloidal reagent. A substance or mixture of substances used to separate or detect alkaloids, either by precipitating them, or by giving characteristic colour reactions with them, etc. Representative alkaloidal reagents are solutions of phosphomolybdic acid, potassium mercuric iodide. tannic acid, and chloroplatinic acid.

alkalosis. A metabolic condition in which the capacity of a body to buffer OH^- is diminished; usually accompanied by an increase in blood *p*H.

alkamine. A compound containing both the alcoholic hydroxyl group and the amine group.

alkane. One of the group of hydrocarbons of the paraffin series having the general formula C_nH_{2n+2}, *e.g.*, methane, ethane, propane, butane, etc.

alkanization. A term used in the petroleum industry to a particular reaction. It consists of the condensation, usually catalytic, of isobutane and various butenes, to form trimethyl butene and *iso*octane.

Alkar process. Catalylic alkylation of aromatic hydrocarbons with olefins to produce alkylaromatics, for example, production of ethylbenzene from benzene and ethylene.

alkene. One of a group of hydrocarbons having one double bond and the typical formula C_nH_{2n}, *e.g.*, ethylene, propylene, etc.

alkine. *See* alkyne.

alkone. One of a group of hydrocarbons which have the typical formula C_nH_{2n-1}, as by the possession of one triple bond and one double bond, as in butone, pentone, hexone, etc.

alkoxide. One of a group of compounds in which a hydrogen atom of an alcoholic hydroxide group is replaced by a metal.

alkoxy. A radical of the type RO—, in which R is an alkyl group.

alkyl. A univalent group derived from paraffinic hydrocarbons (alkanes), but containing one less hydrogen atom than the corresponding hydrocarbon ; for example, the methyl group (CH_3) has one less hydrogen, than methane (CH_4); similarly, the ethyl group (C_2H_5) ; and so on through the homologous series. Such groups are often represented in formulas by the letter R and have the generic formula C_nH_{2n+1}.

alkylarene. An arene (such as benzene) with one or more hydrogen atoms in the molecule replaced by alkyl groups ; *e.g.*, methylbenzene, $CH_3C_6H_5$.

alkylate. A reaction product containing an

alkyl group or radical characteristic of aliphatic hydrocarbons. (Here the suffix *-ate* means "product of, as in condensate.) The term alkylate has two distinct and somewhat different applications in chemistry.

(1) In detergent chemistry it refers to a group of compounds known as alkylbenzene sulphonates, made by reacting a long-chain alkane or alkene with benzene. Detergent alkylates made from straight-chain compounds are more biodegradable than those derived from branched-chain compounds and are called linear alkylates. These are now the more generally used because they are more readily decomposed by bacteria and thus do not seriously contribute to water pollution. Since the term "alkyl" applies to both straight- and branched-chain structures the word "linear" is used to indicate that the alkylate is a straight, unbranched chain containing at least ten carbon atoms.

(2) In the petroleum field, it designates a product obtained by catalytic reaction of an alkane (paraffin) with an alkene (olefin) to give a branched-chain paraffinic molecule used in high-octane gasoline, *e.g.*, neohexane.

alkylation. Addition of an alkyl group to an organic compound by means of catalytic or thermal processes ; it involves the synthesis of higher molecular weight compounds rather than the breaking down or cracking of large molecules. The catalysts most widely used are aluminum chloride, hydrogen fluoride, and sulphuric acid, at low temperatures and pressures, *e.g.*,

$$C_6H_6 + RBr \xrightarrow{AlCl_3} C_6H_5{-}R + HBr$$

$$CH_3I + NH_3 \rightarrow [CH_3NH_3]^+I^-$$

$$C_6H_5ONa + (CH_3)_2SO_4 \xrightarrow[\Delta]{H_2O} C_6H_5OCH_3 + CH_3SO_4^-Na^+$$

alkylene. Any radical related to an alkene by a difference of one hydrogen atom, *e.g.*, the ethylene radical C_2H_3—, the propylene radical C_3H_5—, etc.

alkylide. A compound of one or more alkyl radical and a metal.

alkylidene. A radical related to an alkane, or saturated aliphatic compound, by a difference of two hydrogen atoms, both from the same carbon atom, as ethylidene, CH_3CH—, propylidene, CH_3CH_2CH—, etc.

alkylogen. An alkyl ester of a halogen acid, as ethyl chloride ; these compounds may also be regarded as the monohalogen substitiution products of the aliphatic hydrocarbons, as monochloroethane.

alkylolamine. An aliphatic compound containing both hydroxy (—OH) and amino (—NH_2) groups.

alkyne. The series of unsaturated aliphatic hydrocarbons characterized by the presence of a triple bond ; their generic formula is C_nH_{2n-2}. The most important is ethyne, HC≡CH, the first member of the series.

alleiomorph. 1. One of two or more isomorphic substances which consist of the same atoms having the same valences, but possessing different linkages.

2. The first of two or more isomers to be recovered or separated from a system.

allelotropism. 1. When the two isomers of a tautomeric substance can exist in equilibrium and the proportions of either present can be changed by change of conditions such as temperature or concentration, the state is said to be one allelotropism. The acetoacetic ester is an example of this type.

2. The property by virtue of which, under certain conditions, a tautomeric substance (*see* tautomerism) is partly converted into its isomeric form and an equilibrium is established, the proportion of each isomer present depending upon the temperature, the solvent, and the degree of dilution.

Allen-Moore cell. An electrolytic cell used for the industrial production of chlorine and caustic soda from sodium chloride solution.

Allen test for phenol. A few drops of the liquid to be tested are mixed with hydrochloric acid and 1 drop of concentrated nitric acid is added to it. Appearance of red colour indicates the presence of phenol.

Allen test for vinegar. An extract of logwood in boiling water is spotted on a porecelain plate, and 1 drop of vinegar is added to it. A colour change from yellow to red, on drying shows the presence of free mineral acids in the vinegar.

allergen. Any substance that induces the formation of an antibody in the bloodstream of a susceptible individual; the allergen and antibody combine to form a histamine-like substance, which in turn weakens the blood vessels sufficiently to release fluids. This causes the commonly experienced edema, sneezing, and swelling well-known to hay fever sufferers. Only those who are predisposed to certain allergens are capable of forming such antibodies. Severe allergens can cause extremely serious conditions (anaphylaxis), which have been known to be quite fatal. Protein-containing substances are the most common allergens (wool, hair, pollen, etc.), but allergic reactions may be experienced by a few individuals from exposure to almost any substance.

Allinger's rule. Alicyclic conformer of small steric bulk (equatorial-axial conformer) has higher enthalpy, higher boiling point, higher density and higher refractive index than conformer having large steric bulk (equatorial-equatorial conformer).

allo-. A combining form generally meaning "other" as in all allotropic and polyallomer. More specifically, it refers to the more stable of two geometrical isomers.

allobar. A form of an element differing in its atomic weight from naturally occuring form and hence being of different isotopic composition.

allochromy. Any fluorescence, or re-radition of light in which the wavelength (and hence colour) of the emitted light differs from that of the absorbed light.

alloisomerism. *See* geometrical isomerism.

allomerism. A property shown by substances that differ in chemical composition but have the same crystalline form.

allomones. Allomones are chemicals produced by an organism which induce in a member of another species a behavioural or physiological reaction favourable to the emitter. These chemicals are involved in a variety of mutualistic and antagonistic relationships. The scents of flowers are mutualistic allomones; insects pollinate plants from which they obtain nectar in return. Ventoms and repellents, which organisms use in defense against predator, are antagonistic allomones.

allomorphism. A property of substances that differ in crystalline form but have the same chemical composition.

allosteric enzyme. Any of several regulatory enzymes whose catalytic activity is modulated by the noncovalent binding of a specific metabolite at a site other than the catalytic site.

allotriomorphic. Characterized by absence of typical crystal faces.

allotrope. One of a number of forms in which an element can exist. Both the chemical and physical properties of allotropes display marked differences for a given element. While most allotropes are those of crystalline metals, there may also be gaseous and liquid allotropes. For example, molecular oxygen has two allotropic forms, diatomic oxygen (O_2) and ozone (O_3); liquid helium also has two allotropic forms (helium I and helium II). Probably best-known are the allotropes of carbon (diamond, graphite, carbon black); phosphorus (white and red), sulphur (triclinic, orthorhombic) and tin (grey and white).

allotrpic, monotropic. *See* monotropic allotroph.

allotropic transformation. The change from one allotropic form to another. This change in form commonly associated with a change in energy, accompanied by absorption of heat, and occurring at a definite temperature (known as transition temperature).

allotropy. Occurrence of simple substance (chemical element) in two or more forms (at the same state of aggregation).

allotropy, dynamic. *See* dynamic allotropy.

allotropy, enantiomorphic. *See* enantiomorphic allotropy.

allowed energy band. Quasi-continuous range of energy states in crystal; which may be occupied by electrons according to Pauli exclusion principle. Also known as energy band in band theory of solids.

allowed transition. Transition between two energy levels whose probability, according to selection rules, is different from zero.

Alloxan reagent. A mixture of 2 g. of uric acid and 2 ml. of nitric acid is heated with 2 ml. water until it becomes clear, and is diluted with water to a volume of 100 ml. It gives characteristic colour reactions with certain cations, such as zinc, and also with glycine.

Alloxantin reagent. A solution of 1 g. alloxan in 100 ml. 1N sodium hydroxide solution. It gives characteristic blue colour with ferric ions.

alloy. A mixture of solution of metals, either solid or liquid, which may or may not include a nonmetal. In certain types of alloys the components are not completely miscible as liquids or tend to separate on solidification ; others, in which the components are miscible, can be considered as solid solutions. The most common nonmetal alloying agent is carbon, which is present in steel from 0.02% to 1.5% ; other elements (chromium molybdenum, etc.) are added to steel in amounts from 10 to 20% to impart specific properties such as corrosion resistance, hardness, etc. The properties of an alloy are usually quite different from those of its components. The two major classes of alloys are ferrous and non-ferrus, depending upon whether or not they contain iron.

Anfalgams are alloys of mercury with another metal and may be prepared in liquid form. An alloying element is used for a constructive and beneficial purpose rather than as an adulterant ; thus, is required in sterling silver and in yellow gold to effect a necessary increase in strength and hardness.

Fusible alloys, designed to melt at low temperatures, are represented by solders lead/tin and by Wood's metal (bismuth/cadmium) ; refractory alloys, which melt only above 1650°C are solutions of such metal as cobalt, nickel, tungsten, and molybdenum. *See also* amalgam; refractory.

alloy nuclear fuel. A material used in nuclear reactors that is an alloy of a fissonable substance and a nonfissionable metal or metals.

alloy steel. A steel whose distinctive properties are due to the presence of one or more element other than carbon.

allylic rearrangement. Rearrangement of compound containing allyl group, involving migration of an atom (or groups of atoms) from position 3 to 1, with simultaneous migration of double bond, *e.g.*,

$$\underset{R'}{\overset{R}{>}}\overset{3}{C}-\underset{X}{\overset{2}{C}}-\underset{R'''}{\overset{1}{C}}-R'' \rightarrow \underset{R'}{\overset{R}{>}}\overset{3}{C}=\overset{2}{C}-\overset{1}{C}\underset{X\ \ R'''}{\overset{R''}{<}}$$

Allylthiourea reagent. A solution of 50 g. allylthiourea in one litre water, used to test for cadmium. One drop of the reagent and 1 drop of 30% sodium hydroxide solution gives a yellow precipitate with 1 drop of the unkown solution, if cadmium is present in it.

Almen reagent for glucose. A solution of 40 g. Rochelle salt and 20 g. bismuth subnitrate in one litre 35% potassium hydroxide solution. This reagent gives a characteristic black precipitate on boiling with urine containing glucose.

Almen test for cyanide. The solution to be tested is mixed with yellow ammonium sulphide and evaporated to dryness, then water and hydrochloric acid are added, followed by the addition of ferric chloride solution. An orange-red colour is abtained if cyanide is present.

Aloy-Laprade solution. A solution of 100 g. uranium nitrate in 600 ml. water, that is neutralized with ammonium hydroxide, and diluted with water to one litre. It gives a red colour with phenol in neutral solution.

Alloy-Rabaut test. In this modification of the Lamal test, few drops of methanol and a crystal of uranyl nitrate give a red colour with morphine (if the morphine is present as its hydrochloride, uranyl acetate is used instead). Phenols give the same reaction.

Aloy test for alkaloids. A neutral solution of uranium nitrate or accetate, precipitates most alkaloids from solution.

Aloy test for uranium and hydrogen peroxide. With hydrogen peroxide and solid potassium carbonate, uranium compounds give a red solution, and a red precipitate on addition of alcohol. This reaction is also used in testing for hydrogen peroxide.

alpha decay. Radioactive decay in which an alpha particle is emitted by nucleus. Also known as alpha disintegration.

alpha-elimination mechanism. This mechanism in olves proton removal caused by base, deprotonation takes place at the same carbon from which leaving group X subsequently moves away. The latter stage is rate determining. α-elimination product is labile and undergoes further transformation, *e.g.*

$$CHCl_3+OH^- \rightarrow \bar{C}Cl_3+H_2O$$

$$\bar{C}Cl_3 \rightarrow Cl_2C:+Cl^-$$

$$Cl_2C:+H_2O \rightarrow Cl_2\bar{C}-\overset{+}{O}H_2 \rightarrow CO+2HCl$$

alpha emission. Ejection of alpha particles by the nucleus of an atom.

alpha iron. Iron with a body-centered cubic structure which is stable below 910°C.

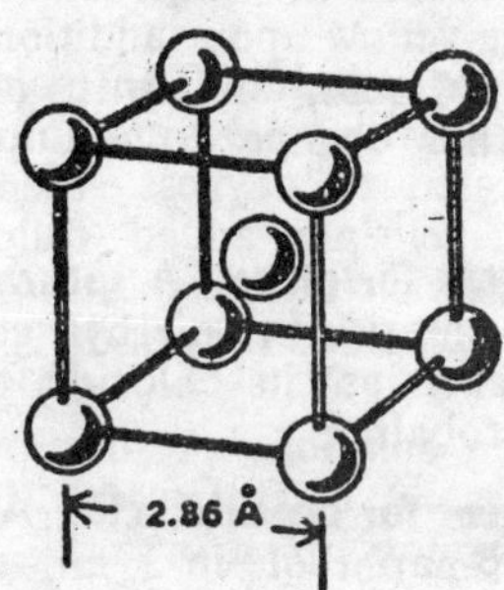

Fig. 6. Lattice of alpha iron

alpha irradiation. Subjection of a substance to a flux of alpha particles.

alpha olefin. An olefin in which the double bond is at alpha position, *i.e.*, between the two end carbons of carbon atom chain.

alpha particle. Helium nucleus, ^4_2He emitted in alpha radioactive decay.

alpha position. In chemical nomenclature, the position of substituent group of atoms in the main group of molecules; for example in a straight chain compound such as α-chloropropionic acid ($CH_3CHClCOOH$), the chloro group is in the alpha position.

alpha rays. A stream or α-particles (helium atomic nuclei), moving at similar speeds and in almost the same direction.

alphatopic. Pertaining to a relationship wherein the masses or composition of two nuclei differ by an α-particle.

alphyl. An abbreviation for alkylphenyl or a radical which contains both an alkyl and a phenyl group, as $CH_3.C_6H_4-$ (methylphenyl or toluyl.)

alternating copolymer. Copolymer formed of two kinds of monomeric units alternatively arranged.

alternating-current polarography. Method based on recording and analysis of alternating current which flows in polarographic circuit when voltage linearly increasing with time applied to electrodes is modulated with sinusoidal alternating voltage of frequency 50−60 Hz and amplitude 5−50 mV.

Altman solution. A mixture of equal parts of a 5% aqueous solution of potassium dichromate, and a 2% aqueous solution of osmic acid. It is mainly used as a fixative.

aludel. A pear-shaped vessel open at both ends and arranged so that several such vessels may be fitted into one another in succession to form a series. It is used in the sublimation of iodine, the distillation of nitric acid, etc.

alum. One of a class of double salts of the general formula $(M(III))_2(SO_4)_3(R(I))_2SO_4.24H_2O$. In which M may be any one of the three elements aluminum, iron or chromium, and R may be either potassium, sodium, caesium lithium, rubidium, thallium, silver, or ammonium. Alums crystallize as octahedral or as cubes and have many other properties in common. Ordinary alum in the crystalline double salt—potassium aluminium sulphate

$$(K_2SO_4.Al_2(SO_4)_3.24H_2O).$$

alumetize. To coat with aluminum, as by spraying the molten metal on a cleaned metal surface. Also known as aluminize.

aluminium. An element. Symbol Al

	Atomic No.	13
State Solid	Atomic Wt.	26.9815
Group IIIA	Valence	3
	m.p.	658°C

A strongly electropositive metal obtained in relatively pure state from bauxite by refining with alkalies to remove silica (Bayer process), followed by electrolytic reduction in which cryolite (a fluoride) is the electrolyte (Hall process).

Aluminium is amphoteric in nature and is notable for its ability to readily form a surface coating of aluminum oxide (alumina) which adheres strongly and permanently. This prevents further oxidation and makes possible a high degree of corrosion resistance, one of this metal's most valuable properties. This, along with its light weight, makes it an ideal construction material for the building as well as the automotive industries. The protection property of aluminium can be increased by anodizing.

Aluminium readily forms compounds with halogens and with both inorganic as well as organic groups. Its electrical conductivity is about two-thirds that of copper, making it economical for power transmission. It is almost completely nontoxic ; in powder form it is flammable, with strong evolution of heat. Its major uses other than construction are quite numerous ; as an alloying element with copper, manganese, magnesium, silicon, and zinc ; in special paints; as tubes and containers for ointments and toilet goods ; as packing foil, etc. Some of its compounds are important catalysts, *e.g.*, anhydrous aluminium chloride and triethylaluminium.

aluminium brass. Brass to which small amounts of aluminium has been added as a flux to improve the casting qualities, and with the addition of lead, the machining qualities.

aluminium bronze. An alloy of copper and aluminium which may also contain manganese, iron nickel, or zinc.

aluminium soap. Any of various salts of higher carboxylic acids and aluminium that are insoluble in water and soluble in oils ; used as lubricating greases, paints, and waterproofing substances.

aluminium solder. A solder containing upto 15% aluminium, having a melting point above that of the tin-lead solders.

aluminize. 1. To apply a film of aluminium to a material such as glass.

2. To form a protective surface alloy on a metal by treatment at elevated temperature aluminium or an aluminium compound. Also Also known as alumetize.

aluminon solution. A aqueous solution of 1 g. of the ammonium salt of aurintricarboxylic acid in 1 litre of water ; used in the colorimetric determination of aluminum.

aluminosilicate. A large class of compounds, both natural and synthetic, containing aluminium and silicon combined with oxygen in their structure. It includes clays, zeolites, micas, and many other important mineral materials.

Alvarez cholic acid reagent. A solution of 1 g. β-naphthol and 1 g. diphenylamine, in 1000 ml. of concentrated sulphuric acid ; used as a test reagent for cholic acid.

Alvarez nitrate, nitrite reagent. A solution of 1 g. resorcinol acid 1 g. diphenylamine, in 100 ml. concentrated sulphuric acid ; used as a test reagent for nitrates and nitrites. On contact with crystals of the salts, the reagent gives a greenish yellow colour with a blue border turning to orange-yellow upon addition of alcohol if nitrate is present, and with nitrite a dark blue colour that changes to red upon solution in alcohol.

Alvarez reagent for nickel. A saturated solution of hydrogen chloride in diethyl ether. It precipitates nickel as its chloride, even in the presence of cobalt.

Alvarez reagent for organic acid. A solution of of 0.02 g. β-naphthol in 1 ml. concentrated sulphuric acid. It yields melts of characteristic colours when heated with certain organic acids, such as malic acid, tartaric acid, and citric acid.

Amadori N-glycoside transformation. *See* Amadori reaction.

Amadori reaction. Transformation of aldose N-glycosides obtained from primary aromatic amines, into 1-amino-1-desoxyketoses under action of acid catalysis, *e.g.*,

```
CH3C6H4NH—CH——        CH3C6H4NH—CH2
          |    |                 |
       H—C—OH  |    H+       HO—C———
          |    O    —>          |   |
       H—C—OH  |             HO—C—H O
          |    |                |   |
```

Also known as Amadori rearrangement ; Amadori N-glycoside transformation.

Amadori rearrangement. *See* Amadori reaction.

Amagat's law. Total volume of mixture of different ideal gases V is equal to sum V_i of volumes of constitutents before mixing at the same temperatures and under the same pressure, equal to pressure of mixture.

$$V=\sum_{i=1}^{n} V_i$$

This law is empirical.

Amagat units.. A system of units in which the unit of pressure is taken as one atmosphere, and the unit of volume is taken as the gram-molecular volume (22.4 litres under standard conditions).

amalgam. A liquid or solid alloy or a mixture of mercury with another component which is usually a metal but may be a nonmetal in some cases. The component element must be soluble in mercury, for example, lithium, sodium, potassium and caesium. There is a strong tendency for these components to combine to form compounds under certain conditions. A well-known use of amalgams is for the repair of dental caries, in case, the amalgam contains silver and tin, forming a paste which quickly sets to a hard mass. Industrial applications of amalgams containing other components are numerous, such as in silvering mirrors, in special techniques in metallurgical analysis, and as catalysts. One method of recovering gold from ores is to form a gold amalgam from which the gold is separated by distilling off the mercury. Silver is similarly recovered from ores by the amalgamation process. *See also* alloy.

amalgamation. The process of forming an amalgam ; applied in electrochemistry to the coating of electrodes with mercury, and in metallurgy to a process for separating silver and gold from other metals or rocky material.

amalgam polarography. Variation of polarography where instead of dropping mercury electrode, dropping amalgam electrode containing metal to be investigated is used.

AAC1 mechanism. Mechanism of acid-catalyzed monomolecular esterification or hydrolysis of esters in which cleavage of acyl-oxygen bond occurs. The following reaction steps take place: protonation of acid or ester ; cleavage of acyl-oxygen bond with formation of acylium ion ; reaction of the latter with alcohol or water, *e.g.* AAC1 mechanism in hydrolysis

$$C_6H_5C(=O)\text{—}OR + H^+ \overset{\text{fast}}{\rightleftharpoons}$$

$$\left| C_6H_5\overset{+}{C}(OH)\text{—}OR \rightleftharpoons C_6H_5C(=O)\text{—}\overset{+}{O}(R)\text{—}H \right| \overset{\text{slow}}{\rightleftharpoons}$$

$$C_6H_5\overset{+}{C}{=}O + ROH$$

$$C_6H_5\overset{+}{C}{=}O + H_2O \overset{\text{fast}}{\rightleftharpoons} C_6H_5COOH + H^+$$

AAC2. mechanism. Mechanism of acid-catalyzed bimolecular esterification or hydrolysis of esters in which cleavage of acyl-oxygen bond takes place. The following reaction steps take place : protonation of acid or ester ; addition of alcohol (or water) molecule to carbonium ion ; cleavage of acyl-oxygen bond along with elimination of water (or alcohol) molecule, *e.g.* AAC2 mechanisms in hydrolysis

$$RC(=O)\text{—}OR' + H^+ \rightleftharpoons R\overset{+}{C}(OH)\text{—}OR' \underset{-H_2O}{\overset{+H_2O}{\rightleftharpoons}}$$

$$\left| R\text{—}C(OH)(\overset{+}{O}H_2)\text{—}OR' \rightleftharpoons R\text{—}C(OH)_2\text{—}\overset{+}{O}(R')\text{—}H \right| \underset{+R'OH}{\overset{\text{slow}}{\underset{-R'OH}{\rightleftharpoons}}}$$

$$R\overset{+}{C}(OH)_2 \rightleftharpoons RCOOH + H^+$$

AAL1 mechanism. Mechanism of acid-catalyzed monomolecular esterification or hydrolysis of esters in which cleavage of alkyl-oxygen bond takes place. The following reaction steps are postulated for case for hydrolysis : protonation of ester ; cleavage of alkyl-oxygen bond with formation of carbonium ion ; reaction of the latter with water, *e.g.*,

$$CH_3\text{—}C(=O)\text{—}O\text{—}C(CH_3)_2\text{—}CH_3 + H^+ \rightleftharpoons$$

$$CH_3\overset{+}{C}(OH)\text{—}O\text{—}C(CH_3)_2\text{—}CH_3 \overset{\text{slow}}{\rightleftharpoons}$$

$$CH_3COOH + CH_3\text{—}\overset{+}{C}(CH_3)_2$$

$$CH_3\text{—}\overset{+}{C}(CH_3)_2 + H_2O \rightleftharpoons CH_3\text{—}C(CH_3)_2\text{—}OH + H^+$$

americium. An element.

		Symbol	Am
		Atomic No.	95
State	Solid	Atomic Wt.	243 (?)
Group	Actinide	Valences	3, 4, 5, 6
IIIB	Series	m.p.	1000°C

Americium is an artificial transuranic element, it was discovered in 1944, and was found to exist only as radioisotopes. It is a whitish crystalline metal of the bone-seeking type, emitting gamma radiation. The isotope with longest half-life is Am-243 (7700 years); next longest is Am-241 (430 years). Americium of mass number 241 has been produced by bombardment of plutonium with neutrons in the chain-reacting uranium-graphite structure. Plutonium-241 is first formed, and it yields americium-241 by beta decay. The nuclear reaction is :

$$Pu^{239}\ (n, \gamma)\ Pu^{240}\ (n, \gamma)\ Pu^{241} \xrightarrow{\beta} Am^{241}$$

It is an α-emitter, yielding neptunium-237 ; in fact these two atomic species are members of the new fourth series of radioactive elements (the Neptunium series). There are other isotopes of americium of mass number 237, 238, 239, 240, 242, 243, and 244. It forms a large number of compounds with fluorine, oxygen, potassium, etc. It is used in radiography because of its gamma emission and as a source of curium isotopes.

Amicron. A name applied by Zsigmondy to individual disperse particles invisible under the ultramicroscope whose size is about 10^{-7} cm. They act as nuclei for the formation of sub-microns which are about five times as large.

amidase. A enzymes that catalyzes the hydrolysis of nonpeptide C=N linkage.

amidation. The formation of an amide, or any reaction by which it is effected.

amide. A generic term for various organic compounds derived from ammonia by replacement of one or all of its three hydrogen atoms by radicals. The term is properly restricted to compounds that contain acyl residues ; other substances should be referred to the class of amines but this strict classification is not always followed.

The acid amides are derived from ammonia by replacing hydrogen by acyl groups and are classified as primary, secondary, or tertiary, as one, two, or three hydrogen atoms are replaced, yielding compounds having the typical formulas H_2NOCR, $HN(OCR)_2$ or $N(OCR)_3$. Mixed amides may be formed by substituting in primary or secondary amides, other acyl group for the remaining ammoniacal hydrogen.

amide-imidol tautomerism. Type of prototropic tautomerism connected with reversible rearrangement of amide into imine

$$\underset{\underset{O}{\|}}{-C}-NH- \rightleftharpoons \underset{\underset{OH}{|}}{-C}=N-$$

amidines. Derivatives of the amides in which the carboxyl oxygen is replaced by the imide group and contain the radical $CNHNH_2$.

amido. The radical $-NH_2$, properly in acid groups only. However, some writers use the terms amide- and amino- synony-.

α-amidoalkylation. Introduction of amidoalkyl group RCONHCHR′ into a molecule in place of hydrogen atom, with the formation of new C—C bond ; this results from reaction of N-substituted amide with nucleophile, *e.g.*,

$$C_6H_5CONHCH_2Cl + :\underset{\underset{CH_3}{|}}{\bar{C}}(COOC_2H_5)_2 \xrightarrow{PCl_3}$$

$$C_6H_5CONHCH_2\underset{\underset{CH_3}{|}}{C}(COOC_2H_5)_2 + Cl^-$$

amidogen. An obsolete term for NH_2^-, especially in inorganic compounds.

amidoxime. One of a group of compounds derived from the amidines by substitution of hydroxyl for an hydrogen atom of the amido or imido group, *i.e.* ethenylamidoxime,

$$CH_3-\overset{\overset{N-OH}{\|}}{C}-NH_2$$

aminases. Enzymes that catalyze the hydrolysis of amines.

amination. Substitution of hydrogen atom in molecule by amino group $-NH_2$, $-NHR$ or

NRR′, *e.g.*

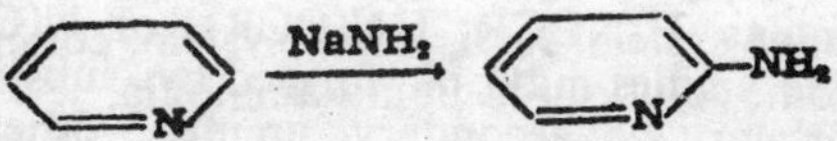

amine. Any of the various organic compounds of nitrogen in which one or more alkyl or aryl groups are attached to the nitrogen atom. Amines are ammonia derivatives and may be primary, secondary, or tertiary depending upon the number of the hydrogen atoms of ammonia (NH_3) replaced by the organic group. If one hydrogen is replaced, the amine is primary ; if two, it is secondary; and if three, it is tertiary, *i.e.* it contains no hydrogen attached to the nitrogen. Thus methylamine (CH_3NH_2) is primary, dimethylamine $(CH_3)_2HN$, is secondary, and trimethylamine, $(CH_3)_3N$, is tertiary amine. Industrially important amines are: aniline, the basis for an entire system of organic dyes ; triethanolamine, a useful solvent, detergent and plasticizer ; and hexamethylenetetramine, a catalyst used in the manufacture of formaldehyde resins. Many other types of amines are used as rubber accelerator and as chemical intermediates.

amino acid. An organic acid whose molecule contains both a carboxyl group (—COOH) as well as an amino group (—NH_2) coupled with an alkyl, aryl, or heterocyclic structure. Since amino group is basic and carboxyl group is acidic, amino acids are amphoteric ; in water solutions they form zwetterions, *i.e.* ions having a positive electric charge at one end and a negative charge at the other. All amino acids except glycine are optically active, *i.e.*, they contain one or more asymmetric carbon atoms ; most have the left-handed (L) configuration.

Amino acids can be obtained by the hydrolysis of proteins (which occurs in the digestive process), though many are now prepared synthetically. Amino acids have been prepared in the laboratary by passing an electric discharge through a mixture of ammonia, methane, and water vapour. It is believed that a similar reaction may have accounted for the origin of amino acids, and hence of life on earth. Eight amino acids are regarded as essential in the diet, since they cannot be synthesized within the body ; twelve others are considered nonessential (*see* given list).Over 80 amino acids have been identified in the free or uncombined state; of these, 22 are known to be constituents of proteins. Amino acids combine in chains of great complexity and form proteins. Molecular biologists have established the critical importance of their arrangement and sequence in these chains.

Nonessential		Essential
alanine .	glycine	isoleucine
arginine	histidine	leucine
aspartic acid	hydroxyproline	lysine
cysteine	serine	methionine
cystine	tyrosine	phenylalanine
glutamic acid		threonine
		tryptophan
		valine

amino-acid activation. ATP-dependent enzymatic esterification of the carboxyl group of an amino acid with the 3′-hydroxyl group of its corresponding transfer-RNA.

aminolysis. 1. Metathesis between organic compound and amine, *e.g.*,

$$RCOOR' + NH_2R'' \rightarrow RCONHR'' + R'OH$$

2. The conversion of diazoamido compounds into aminoazo compounds in the presence of a small amount of the hydrochloride of an aromatic base. Diazoaminobenzene (1,3-diphenyltriazene), $C_6H_5N_2NH{-}C_6H_5$ thus rearranges to *p*-aminoazobenzene, $C_6H_5N_2{-}C_6H_4NH_2$. In this rearrangement the azo nitrogen preferably enters in the para position with respect to the amino group, but when this is occupied—as with the derivatives of *p*-toluidine—the azo nitrogen will sometimes combine in the ortho position to the amino group. The velocity of the aminolysis is a function of the strength of the acid present.

aminomethylation. *See* Mannich reaction.

amino nitrogen. Nitrogen combined with hydrogen in the amino group.

aminopeptidase. An enzyme which catalyzes the liberation of an amino acid from the end of a peptide having a free amino group.

amino resin. A type of thermosetting high polymer (also called aminoplast) ; it results from a catalyzed condensation reaction between formaldehyde and either urea (having amide group) or melamine (having amine group) to form monomers containing either a triazine ring or an amide unit. They are then polymerized in carefully prescribed and closely controlled procedures. The properties of the resulting resins vary with the extent and degree of polymerization. On curing with heat and pressure their internal structure becomes cross-linked. Amino resins were among the earliest types of plastics and were notable because they were the first to permit the manufacture of white and coloured plastics.

amino sugar. A monosaccharide in which a nonglycosidic hydroxyl group is replaced by an amino or substituted amino group, *e.g.*, D-glucosamine.

ammine. A type of coordination compound in which the ligand, or electron-donating group, is ammonia ; it usually contains the metal ion, as the central atom which is attached directly to the nitrogen by a coordinate linkage, *e.g.*, $[Cu(NH_3)_4]^{2+}$, $[Co(NH_3)_6]^{3+}$. This term should not be confused with the more common "amine" in which nitrogen is bonded to carbon.

ammino. A combining term indicating content of the $—NH_2$ group in inorganic combination.

ammonate. A compound containing ammonia of crystallization. It is analogous to a hydrate.

ammonia oxidation process. A process for the production of oxides of nitrogen, or nitric acid itself, by the catalytic atmospheric oxidation of ammonia. Commonly a mixture of about 10% NH_3 by volume with air is passed over the catalyst at temperatures from 700 to 900°C. The first stage in the oxidation yields nitric oxide NO, which is subsequently oxidized to NO_2 which reacts with water to yield nitric acid.

ammonia-soda process. *See* Solvay process.

ammoniate. Certain compounds of ammonia, as the ammines or compounds which are used as fertilizers.

ammoniation. The process of treating or combining with ammonia.

ammonification. Addition of ammonia or its compounds, especially to the soil.

ammonium. The ion NH_4^+, which forms salts analogous to those of the alkali metals.

ammono-system. A dispersed system, commonly an ionic solution, in liquid ammonia.

ammonolysis. A process analogous to hydrolysis in which ammonia reacts with a compound to form an amide or amine and other products, commonly by the breaking of a valence bond in a compound, usually with the addition of an $—NH_2$ group to one fragment, and a hydrogen atom to the other. It is commonly regarded as a double decomposition reaction involving ammonia as reactant, *e.g.*,

$$RCOCl + NH_3 \rightarrow RCONH_2 + HCl$$

Amodel reagent. A solution of 2.5 g. guinine sulfate in 100 ml. glycerol, to which is added a solution of 4 g. potassium iodide in 100 ml. water. The reagent forms an orange precipitate with an acidified solution prepared from the ignited residue from urine, if bismuth is present in it.

amorphous. Lacking a crystal structure (literally, without shape) ; having random atomic arrangement without a three-dimensional structure.

amperometric titration. Method of analysis based on measurement of limiting current flowing in polargraphic circuit during titration of analysed substance with reagent at chosen contsant potential. Also known as amperometry.

amperometry. *See* amperometric titration.

amphi-. Meaning literally, on both sides, or present in both forms, and used commonly to designate certain isomers, as amphi-naphthoquinone, in which the oxygen atoms occupy amphi-positions.

amphichroic. A term applied to substances that exhibit two colours, or to indicators having two colours that are complementary.

amphi-position. The position of two substituent groups on atoms diagonally-opposite in β-position on symmetrical fused rings, as the 2, 6 or the 3, 7 positions which are identical) of a naphthalene ring.

amphiprotic solvent. Solvent whose molecules

may be both donors and aceptors of protons, *i.e.*, solvent which undergoes autoprotolysis reaction, *e.g.*, water, ammonia, acetic acid. Also known as amphoteric solvent.

ampholyte. A substances capable of acting either as a base or an acid ; in other words, it acts either as a proton acceptor or a proton donor, and forms salts with acids as well as with bases. In such substances intramolecular exchange of proton may occur, *e.g.*,

$$H_2N—R—COOH \rightleftharpoons {}^{+}H_3N—R—COO^-$$

i.e. in acidic solution $^{+}H_3N—R—COOH$ positive ions and in basic solution $H_2N—R—COO^-$ negative ions are formed. Also known as amphoteric electrolyte.

ampholytoid. A colloid that is amphoteric, adsorbing either hydrogen or hydroxyl ions.

amphoteric. Capable of acting either as an acid or as a base, *i.e.*, as a proton donor or acceptor, according to the nature of the environment. Thus, aluminic hydroxide dissolves in acids to form salts of aluminium, and it also dissolves in strong bases to form aluminates.

amphoteric ion. Ion with both positive and negative charge ; it may be formed as a result of intramolecular exchange of protons in amphoteric electrolytes, *e.g.*,

$$H_2NRCOOH \rightleftharpoons {}^{+}H_3NRCOO^-$$

Also known as zwitterion.

amphoteric ion exchanger. Ion exchanger simultaneously containing both cation and anion exchange groups.

amphoteric solvent. *See* amphiprotic solvent.

amphoterism. Ability of some complex and simple substances to exhibit both acidic as well as basic functions. Also known as amphoteric character.

amplification procedure. Analytical methods with amplification of measured physical quantities with respect to concentration of investigated component by using convenient and suitable stoichiometric reactions. Amplification procedure is frequently used in colorimetric analysis.

ampoule. A sealed glass container used for substances that must be kept out of contact with the atmosphere, such as very volatile liquids, small quantities of gases, and sterile solutions.

Amthor test. Caramel in alcoholic solution gives a brown precipitate with the sample if paraldehyde is present in it.

amyl. The hydrocarbon group containing five carbon and eleven hydrogen atoms ($—C_5H_{11}$) used in naming members of the fifth order of the homologous series of hydrocarbons. This is also, more logically, called pentyl, but amyl continues to be used for certain isomers of amyl alcohol and for amyl acetate, amylamine etc.

amylase. An enzyme that hydrolyzes reserve carbohydrates, starch in plants and glycogen in animals.

amylidene. The radical $CH_3(CH_2)_3CH=$.

amylolysis. Conversion of starch into sugar. It is essentially a hydrolysis and splitting reaction, or series of reactions, and is usually effected by heating with dilute acids, or by enzymatic action.

amylolytic. Any agent capable of hydrolyzing starches, particularly the amylase enzymes.

amylopsin. An enzyme in pancreatic juice that acts to hydrolyze starch into maltose.

amylose. A linear starch polymer.

anabolism. The assimilation of nutrient material by the living organism to build or restore its tissues and other living matter. It is a phase of intermediary metabolism concerned with the energy requiring biosynthesis of cell components from smaller precursor molecules.

Anaconda packed-cell process. A modification of the chamber process for the production of sulphuric acid in which the chambers are replaced by packed towers, each divided into compartments by partitions. Cooling is effected by circulation of large amounts of dilute acid.

anaerobic condition. The absence of oxygen, preventing normal life for organisms that depend on oxygen.

anaerobic glycolysis. A metabolic pathway in plants by which, in the absence of oxygen, hexose, is broken down to lactic acid and ethanol with some adenosintriphosphate synthesis.

anakinesis. A process in living organisms by which energy-rich molecules, such as adenosinetriphosphate are formed.

analgesic. A drug that relieves pain either by its effect upon the sensory nerve fibres or by direct action on the nerve centres.

analogue. One of a group of chemical compounds that are similar in structure, but different in elementary composition.

analysis. 1. Characterization and determination of the properties of elements, the structure and constitution of compounds, and the composition of mixtures comprises the field of analytical chemistry. Early methods were limited to determination either by weighing (gravimetric) or by titration (volumetric). These so-called "wet" methods served well for industrial qualitative and quantitative analysis for many decades and are still in general use. But more precise and sophisticated techniques were required by advances in theoretical science.

Now numerous instrumental methods have been developed for rapid and accurate chemical analysis ; these have largely replaced the older techniques for all but routine work. Among them are Raman spectroscopy, mass spectrometry, infra-red and x-ray diffraction, nuclear magnetic resonance, chromatography of various types, colorimetry, polarography, and use of radioactive tracers. *See also* infrared spectroscopy ; chromatography ; mass spectrometry ; colorimetry.

2. Study of the three-dimensional arrangements possible within a molecule, that is, its conformations, by movement of its constituent atoms or groups into various positions. Cyclohexane is a compound that has been studied extensively in this way. Such study is called conformational analysis *See also* conformation.

analysis, colorimetric. *See* Colorimetric analysis.

analysis error. *See* analytical error.

analysis, gas. *See* gas analysis.

analysis, gravimetric. *See* quantitative analysis.

analysis, isotopic dilution. *See* isotopic dilution analysis.

analysis, micro. *See* micro analysis.

analysis of variance. Method of statistical investigation (verification of hypothesis) by analysis of possible components of variance of a given feature. Analysis of variance allows determination of source and magnitude of errors of measurement and evaluation of significance of differences between investigated materials, procedures or methods.

analysis, proximate. *See* proximate analysis.

analysis, qualitative. *See* qualitative analysis.

analysis, quantitative *See* quantitative analysis.

analysis, ultimate. *See* ultimate analysis.

analytical absorption spectroscopy. Analytical methods based on the measurement of radiation absorption by a given medium.

analytical chemistry. A branch of chemistry that deals with qualitative and quantitative analysis of natural and artificial (man-made) products.

analytical curve. Plot of depending of measured quantity on concentration of analysed component.

analytical distillation. Precise resolution of a volatile liquid mixture into its components ; the mixture is vapourized by heat or vacuum and the vapourized components are recondensed into liquids at their respective boiling points.

analytical error. Difference between real and determined value of a given component in sample. Also known as analysis error.

analytical factor. Ratio of relative atomic mass of determined atoms or atom groups to relative molecular mass of weighed compound. Also known as stoichiometric factor ; chemical factor.

analytical gap. In emission spectral analysis, the region between two electrodes in which sample is excited either by arc or by electric spark. Also known as electrode gap.

analytical grade reagent. *See* analytical reagent.

analytical group. Group of cations or anions which exhibit identical reactions, *e.g.*, precipitation with group reagent under specified conditions.

analytical line. Spectral line used for analytical purposes.

analytically pure reagent. *See* analytical reagent.

analytical radiochemistry. *See* radiochemical analysis.

analytical reaction. Chemical reaction which may be used for analytical purposes.

analytical reagent. Reagent with producer's certificate guaranteeing content of specified impurities below given limits. Also known as analytical grade reagent ; analytically pure reagent.

anamorphosis. An optical process which produces a distorted image.

anaphoresis. Process of electrophoresis in which particles of dispersed phase migrate to anode.

ANA-position. The position of two substituent groups on atoms diagonally opposite, in α-positions on symmetrical fused rings, as the 1,5 or the 4,8 positions (which are identical) of the naphthalene ring.

anchimeric assistance. Rise of reaction rate caused by intervention of adjacent groups, *e.g.*,

$$RO^{\ominus} + -\overset{|}{\underset{|}{C}}-Cl \rightarrow RO-\overset{|}{\underset{|}{C}}- + Cl^{\ominus}$$

$$>C(O^{\ominus})-C(Cl)< \xrightarrow{10^3 \text{ times faster}} >C\overset{O}{—}C< + Cl^{\ominus}$$

anchimeric assistance effect. In S_{N2} reactions, effect exerted by nucleophile on reaction centre located in the same molecule not farther than 5 to 6 atoms away. Such an effect may lead to an increase in reaction rate.

anchoring. One of a number of processes resulting in the physical, or possible chemical association of organic molecules, or as those in biochemical processes, in drugs or dyes etc.

Anderson test for pyridine bases. Pyridine chloroplatinate, when boiled with water forms a precipitate of golden leaflets.

Andreasch test. When ferr chloride, and ammonia are added, a solution of cysteine hydrochloride, it becomes red-violet in colour. This reaction is also used in testing for iron.

Andre reagent for alkaloids. An aqueous solution of potassium dichromate, which precipitates many alkaloids.

Andre reagent for quinine, Upon treatment with chlorine and ammonia, a solution of quinine forms green colouration changing to blue and then to red upon addition of acid.

androgen. A class of steroid hormone produced in the testies and adrenal cortex which act to regulate masculine secondary sexual characteristics.

-ane. A suffix indicating a saturated aliphatic alicyclic compound, as in the names methane, octane, cyclopropane, etc.

anesthetic. A chemical compound used in surgery to eliminate pain. Anesthetics may be broadly classified as general (affecting the entire body), local (affecting a small area at the site of the operation), and basal (spinal), used for operations on the lower portion of the body group, *e.g.* lidocaine, (administered by injection).

ang-. The prefix used to denote an angular displacement of the rings in the structure of a substance.

Angeli-Rimini reaction. A reaction given by most of the aldehydes ; upon reacting with the sodium salt of nitrohydroxylamine, aldehydes give hydroxamic acids which, in turn, give purple colour with ferric chloride. This is the Angeli reaction. In the Rimini reaction, the aldehyde is heated with *N*-benezene sulphonylhydroxylamine to produce the hydroxamic acid.

$$RCH(=O)+HON=NO_2Na \rightarrow RC(OH)=NOH+NaNO_2$$

$$RC(=O)H+HONH-SO_2C_6H_5 \rightarrow RC(OH)=NOH+C_6H_5SO_2H$$

Angeli test for hydroxylamine. On heating with sodium nitroprusside and sodium hydroxide solution, a solution of hydroxylamine gives a fuchsin-red colouration.

angrstrom. Å. A linear dimensional unit, equal to one-ten thousandth micron or one-100 millionth centimetre (one-250 millionth inch). It is used to measure the spacing of atoms in crystals, the size of atoms and molecules, and the length of electromagnetic waves.

angular momentum. Vector product of particle momentum and its position vector relative to assumed origin of angular momentum. Also known as orbital angular momentum.

angular momentum conservation law. In an isolated mechanical system or in a system in external spherically symmetric potential field, if no frictional forces are present, angular momentum of centre of mass is constant.

anharmonicity 1. The term mechanical anharmonicity refers to a mechanical vibration in which the restoring force acting on the system does not vary linearly with the displacement of the system from its equilibrium position.

2. A phenomenon to which the term electrical anharmonicity is applied occurs in the calculation of the intensities of infrared bands. This phenomenon is a departure of the variation of dipole moment with internuclear distance from a strictly linear relationship.

anharmonic oscillator. Oscillator in which acting force directed towards equilibrium position is not proportional to displacement from equilibrium position.

anhydrase. Any enzyme that catalyzes the removal of water from a substrate.

anhydride. A compound formed by removing two atoms of hydrogen and one atom of oxygen from another compound (*i.e.* water molecule) *e.g.* sulphur trioxide (SO_3) is the anhydride of sulphuric acid (H_2SO_4), and carbon dioxide is the anhydride of carbonic acid. In organic chemistry, phthalic anhydride $C_6H_4(CO)_2O$, is formed from phthalic acid. $C_6H_4(COOH)_2$ by the elimination of one water molecule on heating.

anhydro-. A prefix denoting abstraction of water, as in anhydroglucose.

anhydrous. A term literally meaning "without water", it is used to describe a substance in which no water is present in the form of a hydrate or water of crystallization. For example, anhydrous copper sulphate is the pure compound $CuSO_4$ whereas the hydrated form contains 5 molecules of water $CuSO_4.5H_2O$.

"Anhydrous" is not synonymous with "anhydride" and should not be confused with it.

anilide. A compound formed from an aromatic amine by substitution of one or more acyl groups, or occasionally other groups, for hydrogen in the amino group. Referred especially to those compounds formed from aniline, as acetanilide, but the term may be extended to include all of such substances.

aniline ink. A fast drying printing ink which is a solution of a coal-tar dye in an organic solvent or a solution of a pigment in an organic solvent or water.

aniline point. The minimum temperature required for complete mixing of aniline and materials such as gasoline ; used in some specifications to indicate the aromatic content of oils and to calculate the approximate heat of combustion.

aniline thiocyanate reagent. A mixture of 10 ml. of a 10% aqueous solution of ammonium thiocyanate, and 18.6 g. aniline to which 5N hydrochloric acid is added until the emulsion becomes clear, then water is added to make the volume 100 ml., and ethyl alcohol is added until the solution is free from turbidity. This reagent forms a yellowish-brown colour with copper.

anilino. The radical C_6H_5NH-.

animal black. Finely divided carbon made by calcination of animal bones or ivory ; used in making pigments ; decolourizers, and purifying agents. Its varieties include bone black and ivoray black.

animal charcoal. Charcoal obtained by destructive distillation of animal matter at high temperatures ; it is mainly used to absorb organic colouring matter.

anion. A negatively charged ion. When a compound ionizes in water or any other suitable solvent, the molecule divides into ions of opposite electrical charges, those carrying a negative charge being anions and those with a positive charge cations. When electrodes are placed in the solution, one of them becomes the positive terminal, or anode, and the other the negative terminal, or cathode. When current is passed through the solution, the negatively charged anions migrate to the anode, and the positively charged ions (cations) move toward the cathode. This phenomenon is the basis of electrowinning and electrorefining of metals, electroplating, electrophoresis and many other similar processes.

anionotropy. Reversible migration of anion from one position to another, within the same molecule, *e.g.*,

$$CH_3-CH=CH-CH_2-Cl \rightleftharpoons CH_3-CH(Cl)-CH=CH_2$$

ansomeric. Not isomeric.

anisometric. Not isometric ; applied to crystals that have axes of different lengths.

anisotonic. Not isotonic.

anisotropic. A term used in crystallography to indicate a major group of crystalline structures in which the optical properties (such as refractive index) vary with the direction of the axes, that is, with the direction of the vibrations of the crystal. In isotropic crystals there is no such variation, as light passes through them at the same rate in all directions. The word literally means "not turning the same way".

Properties such as refractive index, elasticity coefficient, thermal conductivity, and dielectric constant may be regarded as anisotropic.

anisotropic liquid. A liquid in the mesomorphic state, which is also called a liquid crystal. It possesses the properties of true liquids, such as the ability to flow, but it is doubly refracting and gives interference patterns in polarized light, as do an isotropic crystal. However, an isotropic liquid does not possess any of the usual crystalline properties, and hence the term liquid crystal is misleading.

anisotropic substance. A substance in which the measured values for optical or physical properties depend on the direction with respect to the crystal axes.

anisotropy factor. A factor that appears in an expression of the magnitude of the effect called circular dichroism, or differential absorption of right- and left-circularly polarized light by an optically-active medium. The relationship is :

$$g=(K_l - K_r)/K$$

in which g = anisotropy factor (also called the dissymmetry factor), K_l and K_r = the absorption indices for left- and right-circularly polarized light, and K = the absorption index for ordinary light.

anisoyl. The radical p-$CH_3OC_6H_4CO-$.

anisyl. The radical $CH_3OC_6H_4-$, which is more commonly called methoxyphenyl. The term anisyl is sometimes used for methoxybenzyl.

anisylidene. The radical $pCH_3OC_6H_4-CH=$.

annealing. 1. An operation by which the properties such as strength, hardness, and durability of glass are greatly enhanced due to elimination of the internal stresses caused by rapid cooling. It is carried out by careful stepwise lowering of the temperature from a predetermined high point maintained for as long as three days (for plate glass) to successively lower temperatures maintained for shorter periods. This treatment, which is carried out in a specially designed oven called a lehr, brings the components into a more stable equilibrium state and prevents the distortions and weaknesses caused by permature crystallization.

2. The term is also applied to metals, especially steels, for a process which involves heating and cooling, and is usually applied to induce softening. The term also refers to treatments, intended to alter mechanical or physical properties, that produce a definite microstructure, or remove gases.

annealing point. The temperature at which the viscosity of a glass is 10^{13} poises. Also known as annealing temperature.

annealing temperature. *See* annealing point.

annihilation. Process in which particle-antiparticle pair meet and converts spontaneously into one or more photons and/or mesons. Both particles disappear during this process.

annihilation photon. Photon with energy 0.511 MeV formed during collision of a positron and an electron.

annihilation radiation. Radiation resulting from annihilation of a particle and its antiparticle, *e.g.*, electron and positron.

anode. The positive electrode in an electrolytic cell to which negatively charged ion, molecules, or colloidal particles migrate under the influence of an electric current. The anode may be in the form of a plate made of graphite, as in the manufacture of chlorine by the electrolysis of sodium chloride solution, or it may be made of aluminium (anodizing process) or of some other conducting surface. Electrochemical change occur at the point of contact between the anode and the electrolyte which involve electron transfer between them ; the nature of the electrolyte determines whether the anode gives up electrons or receives them. All anodic reactions are of oxidizing in nature.

In a primary cell (battery) the anode is negative terminal. In electrochemical corrosion, the material corroded, attacked, or dissolved is generally the anode in the galvanic circuit. *See also* electrode ; cathode.

anode copper. Refined blister copper used as anode in the electro-refining of copper.

anode corrosion. The disintegration of a metal acting as an anode.

anode effect. A condition produced by polarization of the anode in the electrolysis of fused salts and characterized by a sudden increase in voltage and a corresponding decrease in amperage.

anode film. The portion of solution in immediate contact with the anode.

anode mud. An insoluble substance or mixture of substances that collects at the anode in an electrolytic refining or plating process. Also known as anode slime.

anode slime. *See* anode mud.

anodic coating. A film of oxide produced on a metal by electrolysis with the metal as the anode.

anodic current density. Current density which flows across the metallic conductor-electrolyte phase boundary; it is equal to rate of oxidation at anode.

anodic oxidation. *See* electrolytic oxidation.

anodic reaction. The reaction in the mechanism of electrochemical corrosion in which the metal forming the anode dissolves in the electrolyte in the form of positively charged ions.

anodizing. An electrolytic method of applying a strongly adherent film or coating of oxygen on the surface of a metal, especially aluminium, in addition to the oxide film already formed by natural processes. This is accomplished by passing an electric current through a bath containing, for example, sulphuric or chromic acid as an electrolyte ; the negatively charged oxygen ions formed are deposited on the positively charged aluminium anode, building up a film of controllable thickness which increases the corrosion resistance of the metal. Anodizing is thus a type of electrodeposition. Such films can absorb particles of added colorant, so that the metal is in effect dyed by this method. *See also* anode ; electro-deposition.

anodyne. A drug that reduces or overcomes the sensation of pain.

anolyte. That part of electrolyte in the vicinity of an anode in which changes of physico-chemical properties occur during electrolysis or discharge of galvanic cell ; if solutions in vicinity of both electrodes of cell are separated, *e.g.* by membranes, it is that part of electrolyte surrounding anode.

anomalous dispersion. A discontinuity or number of discontinuities in the relationship between the refractive index of a medium and the wavelength of radiation passing through it, this relationship being normally an inverse proportionality. These discontinuities correspond to waves or bands in the absorption spectrum of the medium.

anomaly of strong electrolytes. The Arrhenius

theory of ionization is quite satisfactory for predicting the properties of dilute solutions of strong electrolytes, but it fails for their concentrated solutions. The Debye Huckel theory resolves this difficulty by recognizing that strong electrolytes are nearly completely ionized in water solution, and that there are practically no unionized molecules present. Instead, it is considered that the free ions become bound by acquiring an ionic atmosphere which reduces their mobility.

anomaly, optical. *See* optical anomaly.

anomers. Diastereoisomers of cyclic forms of sugars and their derivatives (*e.g.* glycosides), differing in configuration at chiral carbon atom, C_1 (in aldoses) or C_2 (in ketoses). Anomers are represented by symbol α or β, *e.g.*,

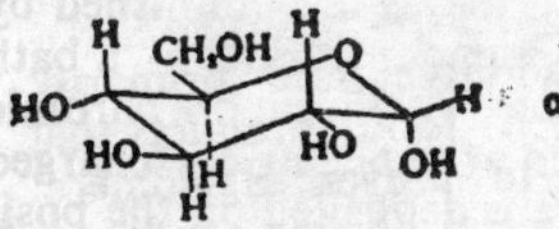

α-D-(+)-glucopyranose

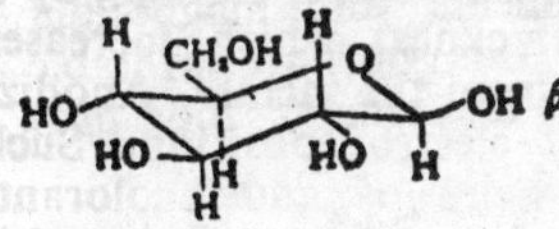

β-D-(+)-glucopyranose

ansa compounds. Macro-ring compounds composed of aromatic system and polymethylene bridge, linking directly (or by heteroatoms) meta- or para-positions of ring ; most often they are hydroquinone or resorcinol derivatives *e.g.*,

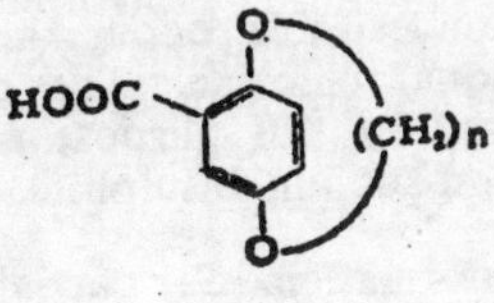

HOOC $(CH_2)_n$

antacid. A mildly alkaline substance suitable for internal use to neutralize excess stomach acidity ; commonly used antacids are aqueous solutions of sodium bicarbonate, magnesium hydroxide, and potassium sodium tartrate (Rochelle salt). Strongly effervescent types should be avoided. Some have a laxative effect if taken in large doses.

antagonism. A term used in biochemistry and chemotherapy to describe the inhibiting or retarding effect of one biologically active substance on another of closely similar molecular structure. An example is the antagonism that was found to exist between sulphanilamide and *p*-aminobenzoic acid, a growth-promoting substance. The molecules of the latter have almost the same structure as those of sulphanilamide, the the only difference being in the chemical nature of one substiuent group on the benzene ring ; yet this difference enables the sulpha drug to replace the *p*-aminobenzoic acid in an enzyme complex and to thus deactivate the enzyme. Structurally similar agents, therefore, compete with or "antagonize" each other, resulting in the impairment of enzyme growth functions. Substances that act as antagonsists are also called antimetabolites or growth inhibitors.

antagonism of ions. Effect of increasing coagulation value of one electrolyte due to addition of another electrolyte, it occurs during coagulation of negative sols with mixture of electrolytes ; *e.g.* $NaCl+CaCl_2$, $KCl+FeCl_3$.

anthocyan. One of a class of flower pigments, commonly those of blue or red flowers.

anthocyanidin. Any of the coloured aglycone plant pigments obtained by the hydrolysis of anthocyanins.

anthocyanin. One of a class of glucosides of various plant pigments responsible for most scarlet, purple, mauve, and blue colouration in higher plants.

anthoxanthin. One of a group of glucosides of various yellow plant pigments.

anthr-, anthra-. 1. Relating to coal, *e.g.* anthracite.

2. Relating to anthracene, *e.g.*, anthraquinone.

anti-. A prefix denoting opposite or opposed to as anti oxidant ; specifically, it denotes one of two geometrical isomers in which certain atoms or groups are on opposite sides of a plane, as anti-benzaldoxime.

anti-auxochrome. Electron-accepting group which shifts absorption spectrum towards longer wavelengths in dye molecule with system of conjugated π-bonds *e.g.*,

$$SO_2NH_2 < -C{\equiv}N <$$

$$< -\underset{OH}{\overset{O}{C}} \quad < -\underset{CH_3}{\overset{O}{C}} \quad < -\underset{H}{\overset{O}{C}} \quad < -\underset{O^{\delta-}}{\overset{O}{N^{\delta+}}}-O$$

(where groups are arranged according to their increasing power of spectrum shift). Also known as anti-auxochromic group.

anti-auxochromic group. *See* anti-auxochrome.

antibacterial. A drug or other substance that opposes or retards the growth of bacteria.

antibaryon. One of a class of antiparticles, including the antinucleons and antihyperons, with strong interactions, baryon number−1, and hypercharge and charge opposite to those of the particles.

antibiotic. A chemical substance produced by microorganisms that has the capacity, in dilute solutions, to inhibit the growth of, and even to destroy bacteria and other microorganisms, examples are : penicillin, streptomycin ; used largely in the treatment of infectious diseases caused by bacteria in man, animals and plants.

antibiotic like substances. Chemical substances with antimicrobial properties but produced by higher plants (quinine, emetine tomatin) and animals (lysozyme).

antiblock agent. In plastics terminology, an abherent material such as a silicate, wax, or finely divided mineral substance that is added to a mixture to prevent cohesion of films or layers of the plastic after processing. Waxes tend to "bloom" to the surface, forming a thin, dry coating which keeps the layers from sticking together, the mineral materials fulfill the same function by introducing small air pockets between the layers The term "block" means the undesired cohesion of plastic surfaces.

antibody. A protein (globulin) formed or synthesized in the blood as a protective agency when a proteinaceous infective organism enters the body; the antibody is capable of destroying such an organism. An antigen is usually a protein, of lower molecular weight than the antibody, which is intentionally introduced into the blood for the purpose of causing antibody formation, thus immunizing the recipient to a particular infective organisms for considerable period of time. The ability of an antibody to act upon bacteria and viruses in this way has been found to be due to its ability to combine or couple with specific chemical groups present in the antigenic protein molecules ; for example, $-COOH$ and $-SO_3H$. The forces holding the antibody antigen combination together are of the relatively weak hydrogen bond or van der Waals type.

antibonding electrons. Electrons occupying antibonding molecular orbitals.

antibonding orbital. Molecular orbital expressed as linear combination of atomic orbitals with energy higher than that of any valence atomic orbital contributing to it. Electrons occupying antibonding orbitals lead to decrease of chemical bond strength.

anticaking agent. An additive used primarily in certain finely divided food products that tend to be hygroscopic, to prevent agglomera. tion and thus maintain a free-flowing condition- Starch, calcium metasilicate and magnesium carbonate, are used for this purpose in table salt, flours, sugar, coffee and similar food products.

anticatalyst. A substance that slows down the action of a catalyst ; for example, lead inhibits the catalytic action of platinum.

antichlor. A term used chiefly in the textile and paper industries to refer to any substance that will neutralize chlorine-containing bleaching agents (such as sodium hypochlorite) in order to improve the colour of the products and to remove the undesirable odour and irritant effects of residual chlorine. The compounds most widely used for this purpose are sodium thiosulphate and sodium bisulphite.

anti-clinal conformation. *See* partially eclipsed conformation.

anticoagulant. Any substance having the ability to extend the normal clotting time of blood. Many anticoagulants are polysaccharides or complex carbohydrate polymers, an example is heparin, one of the most widely used types, which inhibits or prevents formation of thrombin from its precursor prothrombin. The uses of such compounds are almost entirely medicinal, though there has been some application in the field of rodenticides in which dosage leads to a lethal amount of internal bleeding.

anticodon. A specific sequence of three nucleotides in a transfer RNA, complementry to a codon for an amino acid in a messenger RNA.

anti-conformation. *See* fully staggered conformation.

antidote. A substance administered in cases of poisoning by any means (ingestion, inhalation, skin absorption, or injection) which has the property of counteracting the effects of poison or of eliminating it from the body. Emptying the stomach by means of an emetic or by administering a substance that acts as a neutralizing or adsorptive agent is usually effective if the patient remains conscious. Prompt action is essential, and a physician should be consulted immediately.

antiemetic. A drug that prevents vomiting.

antienzyme. One of a group of substances analogous to the antitoxins which are produced by the organism following the injection of various enzymes into the blood. These antienzymes are able to inhibit the normal action of the enzymes from which they are formed to a remarkable extent and, like the antitoxins, are selective in their action. Antibodies for many enzymes have been prepared including the enzymes trypsin, pepsin, lipase, emulsin, urease, lactase, tyrosinase, thrombase, and rennin.

antiferromagnetic Curie point. *See* Neel temperature.

antiferromagnetie substances. *See* antiferromagnets.

antiferromagnetism. A property possessed by some alloys, metals, and compounds of transition elements by which the atomic magnetic moments form an ordered array which alternates or spirals so as to give no net total moment in zero applied magnetic field. The susceptibility increases with increasing temperature upto a certain point, called the Neel temperature, and then falls with increasing temperature according to Curie-Weiss law. The material thus becomes paramagnetic above Neel temperature, which is analogous to the Curie point in the transition from ferromagnetism to paramagnetism.

Antiferromagnetism results from interactions between neighbouring atoms leading to antiparalled arrangement of adjacent magnetic dipole moments. The following diagram shows a crystal lattice, with the net spins of atoms represented by arrows. The unit cell of the normal lattice, *i.e.*, the determined by the position of atoms, is half the size of unit cell in the magnetic lattice.

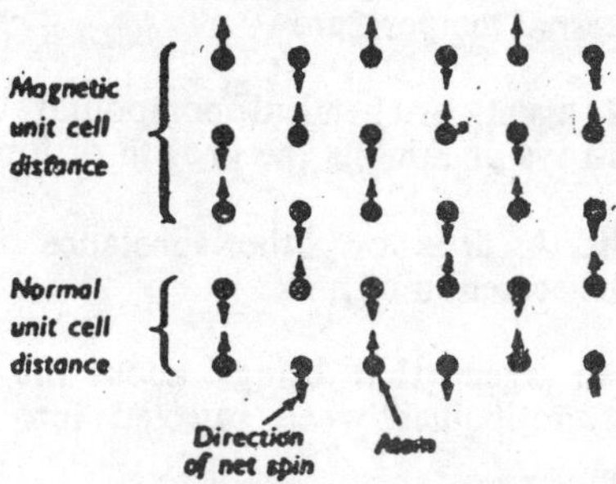

Fig. 7. Crystal lattice of an antiferromagnetism substance

antiferromagnets. Crystals built of two ferromagnetic sublattices compensating each other. Magnetic ordering in antiferromagnets arises below some characteristic temperature, called Neel temperature. Also known as antiferromagnetic substances.

antifertility agents. A natural or synthetic biologically active compound which is able to retard or prevent normal formation of ova in the female reproductive cycle. The steroid hormones progesterone and estrogen, which occurs naturally in the female, were found to possess this property but were not effective when taken orally. Many semisynthetic analogs of these hormones (including some non-steroid types) which inhibit conception when ingested as pills have been develoved ; some of these are found to have adverse side effects, which have tended to reduce their use.

antifouling paint. An organic protective coating especially designed for marine environments. Such paints are applied to ship bottoms, pilings buoys, and other structures immersed in salt water for long periods to reduce attack by barnacles, teredos, and other sea-dwelling organisms. The active chemical compounds often present are naphthenates of copper and lead, organic tin compounds, mercuric oleate and other mercury compounds having fungicidal properties.

antifreeze. 1. A substance added to a material or to a system to prevent freezing.

2. Specifically, a water soluble substance, such as ethylene glycol, glycerol, or ethyl alcohol, added to the water in the radiator of an internal-combustion engine to prevent freezing at low external temperatures.

antifungal agent. A chemical compound that either destroys or inhibits the growth of fungi.

antigalactic. A drug or other substance that reduces the secretion of milk.

antigen. An agent that brings about the formation of antibodies when injected into an organism.

antihemolytic. An agent that prevents the destruction, or loss from the organism, of red blood corpuscles.

antihistamine. One of about 25 synthetic organic compounds developed in recent years to inhibit the irritant and sometimes toxic effects of bistamine. The latter substance is a degradation product of the amino acid histidine ; it is a pharmacologically active compound formed in body tissues as a result of an external stimulus (allergen) in a manner similar to that of an antibody. The allergic effect is usually in the nasal tissues, and it is for this that antihistamines are generally used, though they are also effective in more severe disorders involving an allergic response to penicillin and other drugs. Chemically, they are complex aromatic amines. Since some have undesirable side effects, antihistamines must be used after proper investigations.

antiknocking agent. A substance commonly added to the fuel of an internal combustion engine to prevent premature excessively-rapid and irregular combustion of the fuel-air mixture. The "knocking" properties of various fuels vary widely with their chemical structures and are expressed by their "octane rating."

antilysin. A substance elaborated by the animal organism to counteract the lysins produced by bacterial metabolism.

antimatter. Matter composed of antiparticles, *e.g.* antinuclei (composed of antiprotons and antineutrons), antiatoms (composed of antinuclei and positrons), antimolecules (composed of antiatoms).

antimer. One of a pair of substances having the same plane structural formula, but showing a difference in spatial configuration such that the space formula of one substance of the pair is the mirror image of the other. The chief difference in properties is optical, *i.e.*, in the direction of rotation of the plane of polarized light.

antimonide. A binary compound of antimony with an electropositive element. Also known as stibide.

antimonite. The anion $(SbO_2)_n^{n-}$ (meta), or a compound containing it.

antimono. The group —Sb=Sb—.

antimony. An element.

		Symbol	Sb
		Atomic No.	51
State	Solid	Atomic Wt.	121.75
Group	VA	Valence	3, 5
		Isotopes	2 stable
		m.p.	630.5°C

Antimony is metallic element, in the form of a crystalline solid, though one of its two allotropic forms is amorphous. It is not a good conductor of heat or electricity. The major source of antimony is stibnite ore (Sb_2S_3). Its chief uses are as an additive to harden lead and in metal bearings ; it also has some application as a solder and in type metal. It is too soft for independent metallurigical uses. The highly purified metal has semiconducting properties. Antimony forms many compounds which are quite toxic, as are fumes of the metal itself ; the toxicity depends largely upon the chemical state of the metal or compound. One of the most poisonous compounds of this element is antimony hydride.

antimony electrode. An electrode of metallic antimony that has sufficient antimony oxide (Sb_2O_3) on its surface to function as an oxide electrode for the measurement of *p*H.

antimonyl. The radical SbO—.

antineuralgic. A drug used to treat neuralgia.

antineutrino. $\bar{\nu}$. An energy-carrying particle whose formation is postulated in the processes supposed to occur when a positron is emitted by an atomic nucleus. In this pocess a proton is transformed into a neutron, a positron and a third particle of zero mass and charge which accounts for the energy distribution among the positrons and is called an antineutrino. The use of this term does not assert a difference between this particle and the neutrino which is postulated to accompany the conversion of a neutron into a proton.

antineutron. $\bar{n}$. Antiparticle corresponding to neutron, of baryon number $B=-1$ and third component of isospin $I_3=1/2$; electrically neutral and unstable.

antioxidant. An organic compound which has the power to greatly reduce the normal tendency of oxygen to combine chemically with hydrocarbons in petroleum products, animal fats, vegetable oils, rubber, and similar substances, with consequent degrading effects on the material. The protective effect is considered to be due to free radical mechanisms and is obtained with extremely low percentages. The maximum content of antioxidants in foodstuffs is 0.02% and some will function at a concentration of only 0.0025%. Antioxidants are added to gasoline to prevent oxidative gum formation ; to natural and synthetic rubbers, in which they increase service life by a factor of from 5 to 10 ; and to food stuffs to inhibit rancidity or spoilage.

antiozonant. An inhibitor effective in preventing ozonation by atmospheric oxygen.

antiparticle. Elementary particle defined by corresponding particle but having opposite sign : electrical charge $Q \rightarrow -Q$, baryon number $B \rightarrow -B$, lepton number $L \rightarrow -L$, strangeness $S \rightarrow -S$, third component of isospin $I_3 \rightarrow -I_3$, and magnetic moment $\mu \rightarrow -\mu$. Mass m, spin quantum number J, isospin I mean lifetime and in case of bosons parity P of antiparticle are identical as for corrosponding particle. Annihilation may occur in the event of interaction of antiparticle with particle.

anti-periplanar conformation. *See* fully staggered conformation.

antiphlogistic. 1. A drug which retards the spread of inflammation.

2. Designating a theory proposed by Lavoisier directly contradicting the older phlogiston theory.

antiproton, $\bar{p}$. Antiparticle corresponding to proton, of negative elementary electric charge, baryon number $B = -1$ and third component of isospin $I_3 = -1/2$, stable. It is produced by the collision with a copper target of protons previously accelerated to an energy of 6200 Mev in the bevatron.

antipruritic. An agent, such as comphor that relieves itching.

antipyretic. A drug used to reduce body temperature in fever.

antipyrotic. An agent used to treat burns.

antirachitic. A drug or substance used to prevent rickets.

antiresonance. The condition in which as vibrating system responds with minimum amplitude is an alternating driving force, by virtue of the inertia and elastic constants of the system.

antiscorbutic. A substance effective in the treatment of scurvy. Such substances have been shown to owe their action to their content of vitamin C.

antiscorch. A substance used to retard the catalytic activity of rubber accelerators during processing.

antiseptic. 1. A drug or other substance used to oppose sepsis by its action upon microorganisms.

2. Any substance which will destroy or inhibit the growth of bacteria or other infective organisms when in contact with the tissue of humans or animals.

Antiseptics should be distinguished from disinfectants, which are applied to non-living objects rather than to peopele because of their high toxicity (*e.g.* inorganic mercury compounds, cresol), and also form sterilants, which include agencies such as heat and ultraviolet radiation as well as chemical substances.

The most commonly used antiseptics are organic mercury compounds (thiomersal), essential oils (thymol, menthol), silver compounds (argyrol), and oxidizing materials (hydrogen peroxide, potassium permanganate). Alcohol also exhibit antiseptic properties ; iodine solutions (3%) have been widely used but are considered too drastic for most applications.

antiserum. Any immume serum that contains antibodies active chiefly in destroying a specific infecting virus or bacterium.

antishock agent. A substance, such as a caesium salt, that relieves a state of shock.

antisideric. A drug that counteracts the physiological effects of iron.

antiskinning agent. A substance used to prevent the skinning of various varnishes. Antiskinning agents are usually phenolic compounds such as guaiacol and catechol.

antispasmodic agent. A drug used to decrease or prevent spasmodic or violent contractions of voluntary muscles.

antistatic agent. A compound added to a thermoplastic polymer which will migrate to the surface to form a conductive film, thus reducing the tendency of the plastic to accumulate static electric charges. The materials used for this purpose include amines, phosphate esters, and quatennary ammonium compounds. Such agents are especially desirable in objects made of nylon and other thermoplastic fibres, which attract unsightly dust particles because of their static surface charge.

anti-stokes lines. Lines, in fluorescence or Raman spectra of molecules attributable to the emission of radiation of a shorter wavelength, and hence higher energy, than the exciting radiation.

antisudorific. A drug that reduces perspiration.

antitoxin. A substance produced by the organisms following the injection of, or eleboration of, toxin, derived from pathogenic bacteria into the blood. These substances appear to combine with and neutralize the corresponding toxin and so immunize the organism against it, but they are inactive toward other toxins. Eletich considered this as due to an asymmetric configuration so that only those antitoxins which are constituted similarly to a certain toxin can unite with it.

antitussive. An agent, such as benylin expectorants, that relieves coughing.

antivenin. An immune serum that neutralizes the venoms of certain poisonous snakes.

antiviral agent. A substance such as interferon that decreases virus multiplication in the body.

antivitamin. Any substance that prevents a vitamin from normal metabolic functioning.

antizymotic. A substance that prevents, inhibits, or retards fermentation, and is frequently used for that purpose in medicine, in food products, etc.

Antonoff rule. The tension at the interface between two saturated liquid layers which are in equilibrium is equal to the difference between the individual surface tensions against air or vapour of the two saturated solutions.

antozonide. An oxide produced by "antozone", *i.e.* the peroxides of hydrogen, potassium, sodium, and others.

aperient. A drug or other substance tnat has mild purgative action upon the intestinal tract.

aphrodisiac. A drug or other substance that stimulates sexual interest.

apo-. A prefix denoting formation from or relationship to, another compound, *e.g.*, 5-apomorphine.

apparent equilibrium. When the velocity of a reaction is so small that is appears to remain unchanged with time, it is in a state of apparent, but not real, equilibrium. It differs from true equilibrium in that is not re-established automatically after the system has been disturbed.

apparent activation energy. Activation energy of reaction taking place in multiphase system determined from Arrhenius equation. Apparent activation energy is smaller than activation energy of the same reaction in one-phase system by value of heat of adsorption of activated complex on catalyst.

apparent half width. Experimentally observed line width which is larger than true width because of instrument's imperfection (optical, electric and mechanical errors) ; it is usually given as apparent half-width $\Delta \overset{A}{\nu}_{1/2}$. Also known as apparent width.

apparent molar heat capacity. ϕ_s. Intensive quantity which expresses excess of heat capacity of solution above that of pure solvent alone, calculated for one mole of particular solute, *viz.*,

$$\phi_s = \frac{C_p - n_{solv}\ C^0_{p,\,solv}}{n_s}$$

where C_p=heat capacity of solution, $C^0_{p,\,solv}$= molal heat capacity of pure solvent n_{solv} = number of moles of solvent n_s= number of moles of solute.

apparent order of reaction. Order of reaction in cases where it is not equal to molecularity of reaction. Also known as pseudo-order of reaction.

apparent width. *See* apparent half width.

appearance potential. The minimal potential which the electron been in the ion source of a mass spectrometer must traverse in order to acquire enough energy to produce ions of a specified nuclide or molecular fragment.

applied chemistry. Branch of chemistry dealing with studies about manufacture of chemical products on industrial scale as well as with applications of chemical research in other branches of science and technique.

approximate equilibrium constant. *See* equilibrium constant.

aprotic solvent. Solvent whose molecules are neither donors nor acceptors of protons, *e.g.*, liquid hydrocarbons. Also known as indifferent solvent.

apyrase. Any enzyme that hydrolyzes adenosinetriphosphate, with liberation of phosphate and energy, and that is believed to be associated with actomyosin activity.

aqua. Latin word for water.

Aquadag. A trade name for colloidal graphite, made by the Acheson process ; dispersed in water (sold as a dark grey paste).

aqua destillata. Latin name for distilled water.

aqua dissolutiva. An alchemical name for concentrated nitric acid. It was also called "aqua fortis".

aqua fortis. Another name for concentrated nitric acid.

aqua regia. The mixture of acids that dissolves gold—about 3 parts concentrated hydrochloric with 1 part concentrated nitric acid. The mixture contains nitrosyl chloride (NOCl), and also free chlorine which is the active agent in dissolving noble metals such as gold and platinum.

aqua vieja. The mother liquor from caliche (crude sodium nitrate) after the nitrate has been crystallized. It contains sodium iodate that is the main source of iodine.

aqua vitae. Alcoholic spirit such as brandy or whisky.

aquametry. Determination of water in substances by means of Karl Fischer reagent and similar other reagents.

aquation. Formation of a complex that contains water by replacement of other coordinated groups in the complex.

aqueous. A solution or suspension in which the solvent is water. The term is often used to describe a gaseous compound dissolved in water, for example, aqueous formaldehyde, a form in which the gas is commercially handled. Aqueous solutions of hydrogen chloride, hydrogen fluoride, and hydrogen iodide are known as hydrochloric acid, hydrofluoric acid, and hydriodic acid, respectively. The standard abbreviation is "*aq*".

aquilina solution. A solution of platinic chloride used in testing for alkali iodides. It is added to the solution to be tested, and a wine-red colour indicatates the presence of alkali iodides.

aquobasic salt. A basic salt formed by hydrolysis.

aquo-complex. A complex in which water molecules are ligands.

aquo-ion. A complex ion containing one or more H_2O molecules.

arabic gum. A water-soluble polymer composed of complex carbohydrate units (polysaccharide) ; the major constituents are galactose, glucuronic acid, arabinose, and similar sugars, the units being linked together to give a polymer structure having a molecular weight of about 250,000.

aralkyl. A radical in which an aryl group is substituted for an alkyl hydrogen atom; derived from arylated alkyl.

aramid. Generic name for a distinctive class of highly aromatic polyamide fibres characterized by their flame-retardant properties. Some types are also suitable for protective clothing, dust-tilter bags, and bullet-resistant structures. Their chemical nature and physical properties are different from those of nylon.

arbor dianae. The branching growth of silver amalgam obtained when a little mercury is added to silver nitrate solution.

Arbusov rearrangement. In general sense, rearrangement of trialkylphosphites into dialkyl phosphonate taking place on heating the former with alkyl halides, *e.g.*,

$$P(OR)_3 + R'X \xrightarrow{\Delta} [R'\overset{+}{P}(OR)_3]^+X^- \rightarrow R'-P(O)(OR)_2 + RX$$

Ar_{cm}. The temperature at which austenite is converted to cementite upon cooling a hypereutectoid steel.

arc spectrum. Emission spectrum of an element obtained by its excitation in electric arc; it contains chiefly emission lines of neutral atoms but, in the case of atoms with low ionization potentials, also spectral lines of singly ionized species.

arene. Class name for unsaturated cyclic (aromatic) compounds, of which benzene is typical; several rings may be present, either chemically bonded, as in diphenyl, or fused, as in anthracene. *See also* aromatic.

argentic. Containing silver.

argentiferous. Containing silver.

argentometry. A volumetric analysis that employs precipitation of insoluble silver salts, such as chromate or chloride.

argentous. Containing monovalent silver (as of a compound).

arginase. An enzyme that produces ornithine and urea by splitting arginine; found in liver.

arginyl. The radical $H_2NC(:NH)NHCH_2CH_2CH_2CH(NH_2)CO-$.

argol. Crude wine lees from which potassium hydrogen tartrate (cream of tartar) can be extracted.

argon. An element.

		Symbol	Ar (or A)
		Atomic Wt.	39.948
State	Gas	Valence	0
Atomic No.	18	Isotopes	3 stable
		b.p.	−186°C

One of the few truly inert or "noble" elements, argon, is a component of air to the extent of 0.94% by volume; obtained as a by-product of liquid air distillation operations which produce oxygen and nitrogen. It does not form compounds with other elements in the usual sence, though ionic combinations with hydrogen have been observed in electric discharge tubes; quite stable hydrates and clathrates are also possible, but none of these involves actual chemical bonding. The most important industrial use of argon is in arc welding, where it serves as a shielding medium; it is also used as a filler gas in incandescent and fluorescent lamps and in electron tubes. Argon has a particularly stable electronic arrangement.

Armani-Barboni test for caffeine. Heat the material with potasium hydroxide solution; cool and add phosphomolybdic acid until a white precipitate forms, then add 50% potassium hydroxide solution until the precipitate dissolves. An intense blue colour indicates the presence of caffeine.

Armani-Barboni test for gold and silver. A solution of 2 parts formaldehyde and 1 part 20% potassium hydroxide solution precipitates gold or silver in deeply-coloured colloidal form.

Arndt-Eistert synthesis. A series of reactions for converting an organic acid or its derivative to its next higher homologue or its derivative. The synthesis consists of three essential steps, as follows:

(*i*) Formation of the acid chloride, followed by (*ii*) its reaction with diazomethane to form a diazoketone;

$$RCOCl + 2CH_2N_2 \rightarrow RCOCHN_2 + CH_2Cl + N_2$$

and finally, (*iii*) rearrangement of the diazoketone, by reaction with water, an alcohol, or an amine, in the presence of a catalyst (commonly certain colloidal metals). Step (*iii*) with an alcohol, gives an ester

$$RCOCHN_2+R'OH \rightarrow RCH_2CO_2R'+N_2$$

Arnaud-Pade reagent. The substance cinchonamine used as a reagent for nitrate. An insoluble precipitate is formed.

Arnold-Mentzel reagents for milk. 1. A 2-3% alcoholic solution of *p*-diethyl-*p*-phenylenediamine.

2. A 2-3% alcoholic solution of *p*-diaminodiphenylamine hydrochloride. These reagents give red, and blue-green colours, respectively, with unboiled or unpasteurized milk, probably by reaction with peroxidase.

Arnold-Mentzel test for hydrogen peroxide. A solution of 1 g vanadic acid in 100 ml. dilute sulphuric acid; used in testing for hydrogen peroxide. A red colour indicates the presence of hydrogen peroxide.

Arnold-Mentzel test for ozone in water. A saturated solution of tetramethyl-*p*-diaminodiphenylmethane in methyl alcohol. One or two drops of this reagent are added to 1·2 ml. of a 2% silver nitrate or 10% manganese sulphate solution, and 25 ml. of the water to be tested is added. A blue colour indicates the presence of ozone.

Arnold solution. A mixture of one volume of a 1% aqueous solution of sodium nitrite, with two volumes of a 1% aqueous solution of *p*-aminoacetophenone hydrochloride. This is a reagent for testing acetoacetic acid in urine. A brownish-red colour, in ammonical solution, indicates the presence of acetoacetic acid.

Arnold tests for alkaloids. 1. On heating with syrupy phosphoric acid for about 10 minutes on the water bath, coniine produces a green to bluish-green colour, while nicotine gives yellow to orange-red colour.

2. These alkaloids also give colour reactions on warming with concentrated sulphuric acid, then adding an excess, by drops of 30-40% potassium hydroxide solution.

3. On heating with a few drops of concentrated sulphuric acid and phenol, narceine or veratrine forms a cherry-red colour changing to dirty-yellow on the addition of water. Codeine gives a dirty red-violet to brown colour.

Arnold test for proteins. Upon the addition to 1-2 ml. of the protein solution, of 2-4 drops of a 5% solution of sodium nitroprusside, and a few drops of ammonia, a purple-red colour is formed.

Arny-Dimler test. To detect lactic acid in pharmaceuticals, the preparation is shaken with 20 ml. ethyl acetate, and the acetate extract is washed with water and dilute sulphuric acid. After filteration and evaporation, the residue is dissolved in 5 ml. of 1% resorcinol solution and layered upon 5 ml. concentrated sulphuric acid. A red colour indicates the presence of lactic acid.

aromatic. A term used to denote major series of unsaturated cyclic hydrocarbons (also called arenes) whose carbon atom are arranged in close rings typified by the benzene nucleus (C_6H_6); the rings may be either single or fused, that is attached to each other in groups (naphthalene, anthracene, phenanthrene). Aromatics are characterized by their chemical reactivity and versatility as intermediates; the hydrogen atoms on the ring are readily replaced with other elements chlorobenzene, C_6H_5Cl), with groups (phenol, C_6H_5OH), or with side chains of various types (dodecylbenzene, ($C_6H_5C_{12}H_{25}$).

aromatic bond. System of σ-bonds and delocalized π-bonds present in molecules of aromatic compounds, *e.g.*, in benzene molecule.

aromatic character. Characteristic features of aromatic molecules: ring like, sterically plane molecule containing $(4n+2)\pi$-electrons in conjugated system; relatively high resonance energy ensuring stability of system; tendency to undergo electrophilic substitution (rather than addition). Also known as aromaticity.

aromaticity. *See* aromatic character.

aromatic nucleus. *See* aromatic ring.

aromatic ring. Polyenic plane ring containing (according to Huckel rule) $(4n+2)$ π-electrons in conjugated system (n=0, 1, 2, 3...). Generally, it is a six- or five membered ring with a sextet of π-electrons, *e.g.*, benzene, thiophene or pyrrol ring

Also known as aromatic nucleus.

aromatic sextet. Set of six π-electrons in aromatic molecules or ions.

aromatization. Formation of aromatic rings from non-aromatic compounds as a result of dehydration or elimination, *e.g.*,

$$CH_3(CH_2)_5CH_3 \rightarrow C_6H_5CH_3 + 4H_2$$

$$3\,C_6H_{10} \xrightarrow{Pt} 2\,C_6H_{12} + C_6H_6$$

Arreguine test for citric acid. The dilute slou-tion to be tested in acidified with sulphuric acid and oxidized with a 4% acid potassium permanganate solution, then 0.1 g. resorcinol is added, and sulphuric acid until a red colour develops. The solution is then extracted with ether, and water and a few drops of ammonia are added to the extract. An intense blue fluorescence indicates the presence of citric acid.

Arreguine test for glycerol. The material is oxidized with bromine, an equal volume of concentrated sulphuric acid is then added, and 1% alcoholic solution of veratrole in superimposed. An intense blue colour in the zone of separation indicates the presence of glycerol.

arrest point. A temperature at which a system of more than one component that is undergoing heating or cooling absorbs or yields heat without change in temperature, thus interrupting the heating or cooling process.

Arrhenius complex. In homogenous catalysis, substrate-catalyst complex has rate constant of decay into starting compounds substantially higher than rate of decay into reaction products.

Arrhenius equation. Equation describing dependence of reaction-rate constant on temperature.

$$\ln k = \ln A - \frac{E}{RT}$$

where k=rate constant, A=Arrhenius coefficient (specific for given reaction), T=thermodynamic temperature, E=activation energy R=universal gas constant.

Arrhenius-Guzman equation. The relation between the viscosity η of a liquid and the Kelvin temperature T at constant pressure :

$$\eta = A \exp (B/RT)$$

where A and B = constants and R = gas constant.

Arrhenius theory of acids and bases. Theory according to which acidic properties of substance are connected with presence of hydrogen which may dissociate as H^+ ion ; basic properties are connected with presence of hydroxyl groups which may dissociate to form OH^- ions.

Arrhenius theory of activation. The theory which states that an equilibrium is reached between "normal" and "active" molecules in every system, and that only active molecules take part in reactions. "Active" molecules are considered to be those molecules which have acquired the requisite activation energy to enter chemical reactions.

Arrhenius theory of electrolytic dissociation. The theory proposed by Arrhenius, which states that when an electrolyte (acid, base, or salt) is dissolved in water, a substantial portion of its molecules dissociate spontaneously into positive and negative ions, which, upon the application of an electrical potential difference to the solution, are attracted to the electrode of opposite sign and discharge, thus conducting current through the solution. The dissociation increases the number of particles in the solution, and thus changes the osmotic pressure, elevation of the boiling point, and depression of the freezing point to an extent determined by the degree of dissociation and concentration of the electrolyte. The degree of dissociation increases with dilution, becoming complete at "infinite dilution." Modern discoveries and interpretations have modified considerably this view of electrolytic dissociation.

arsenic. An element		Symbol	As
State	Solid	Atomic No.	33
Group	VA	Atomic Wt.	74.9216
		Valence	2, 3, 5

Arsenic is a soft, solid substance classified as a metalloid. It sublimes at 613°C at 760 mm pressure, and at its melting point of 817°C it has a vapour pressure of 28 atmospheres. The pure material has semiconducting properties and is used commercially in transistors and other semiconducting devices in both elemental and compound form (gallium arsenide. It has few other uses, though it is a metallurgical additive in some lead and copper alloys). It has several allotropic forms, one of which is amorphous. It readily forms compounds, some of which are used as pesticides ; arsine (AsH_3) is an intensely toxic gas resulting from electrochemical reactions involving arsenic compounds.

arseno. The radical —As=As— in organic compounds.

arsenoso. The radical O=As— in organic compounds.

arsinico. The radical (HO)OAs=(pentavlent arsenic).

arsino. The radical H_2As—.

arso. The radical O_2As—.

arsonation. Substitution of hydrogen atoms of aromatic nucleus, *e.g.*, in phenols or aromatic amines by arsonic group —AsO_3H_2.

arsonium. The radical —AsH_4 ; it may be considered analogous to the ammonium radical in that a compound such as AsH_4OH may form.

arsono. The radical $(HO)_2OAs$—.

arsylene. The radical >AsH.

Arthaud-Butte reagent. A solution of 20 g. of sodium thiosulphate, 40 g. of Rochelle salt, and 1.484 g. of cupric sulphate in 1 litre of water. This reagent is used as a precipitant for uric acid.

artificial aging. The heat treatment of an alloy at moderately elevated temperature to accelerate precipitation of a component from the supersaturated solid solution.

artificial radioactivity. Radioactivity induced in stable elements by bombardment with alpha particles, protons, deuterons, neutrons, gamma rays, etc. Thus aluminium on alpha ray bombardment emits a neutron, forming radiophosphorus of mass 30.

$$_{13}Al^{27}+{}_{2}He^{4} \rightarrow {}_{15}P^{30}+{}_{0}n^{1}$$

Radiophosphorus emits a positron to form silicon of mass 30, a stable isotope

$$_{15}P^{30} \rightarrow {}_{14}Si^{30}+{}_{+1}e^{0}$$

The second process being an example of induced radioactivity. Other alpha ray bombardments, as well as bombardment with deuterons, neutrons, etc., may yield electron-emitting radio-elements, as the process,

$$_{37}Rb^{85}+{}_{0}n^{1} \rightarrow {}_{37}Rb^{84}+2\,{}_{0}n^{1}$$

the radio-element rubidium of mass 84 is an electron-emitter.

$$_{37}Rb^{84} \rightarrow {}_{38}Sr^{84}+{}_{-1}e^{0}$$

There are also radio-elements which decay by emission of alpha particles, by capturing one of their own K-electrons, etc.

aryl. A univalent group derived from aromatic hydrocarbons and having a ring structure of benzene, naphthylene, etc. Examples are phenyl (C_6H_5) and naphthyl ($C_{10}H_7$). Such groups are often represented in general formulas by the letter *R*. Compounds made up of both aryl and alkyl groups are sometimes called aralkyl (a shortened form of arylalkyl), depending on where the available bond is located. For example, the benzyl group ($C_6H_5CH_2$) is an arylalkyl group, since the open bond is on the alkyl portion of the molecule, and the tolyl group ($C_6H_4CH_3$, or methylphenyl) is an alkylaryl group, since the open bond is on the aryl portion of the molecule. *See also* alkyl.

arylation. Subtstitution of hydrogen atom by aryl group in molecule, *e.g.*,

$$Br\text{—}C_6H_4\text{—}\overset{+}{N}{=}N\overset{-}{Cl}+C_6H_6+NaOH \rightarrow$$

$$Br\text{—}C_6H_4\text{—}C_6H_5+N_2+NaCl+H_2O$$

arylene. A bivalent radical derived from an aromatic hydrocarbon by removal of a hydrogen atom from each of the two carbon atoms of the nucleus ; for example, phenylene, naphthylene, biphenylene.

arylide. A compound formed from a metal and an aryl radical, *e.g.*, PbR_4, where R is an aryl radical.

aryloxy compound. One of a group of compounds useful as weed killers, such as 2-4, dichlorophenoxyacetic acid.

Arzberger test. One drop of peppermint oil is warmed with 5 ml. formaldehyde ; it develops a pink colour, which changes to red, red-violet, and dirty brown upon the addition of glacial acetic acid.

asbestos. Fibrous magnesiu.n silicate occurring in two forms :

(*i*) chrysotile or serpentine asbestos, which

is relatively pure and can be handled on textile machinery and

(*ii*) amphibole asbestos, which contains other silicates as impurities and has fibres that are too hard to weave or spin. Being non-combustible, its primary use is as a fireproofing additive to heavy textile products, brake linings. etc., as well as in rubber, plastic, and paint compositions, where heat resistance is a factor. Asbestos dust is strongly carcinogenic, and inhalation should be avoided.

ascending chromatography. A technique for the analysis of mixtures of two or more compounds in which the mobile phase rises through the fixed phase.

ase-. A sufix characterizing the names of many enzymes, *e.g.*, diastase cholinesterase, etc. However, the names of some enzymes have the sufix -in (pepsin rennin).

ash. The residue left after a substance has undergone complete combustion, and when further heating in the presence of oxygen produces no further change in wight.

Asmacher test. To test for a histamine salt, treat the solution with sodium hydroxide, then extract with hot chloroform, and add 0.2 g. anhydrous cupric sulphate. A dirty blue colour indicates the presence of histamine.

asparagyl. The radical

$$H_2NCOCH_2CH(NH_2)CO—.$$

aspartase. A bacterical enzyme that catalyzes the deamination of aspartic acid to fumaric acid and ammonia.

asphalt. A black semisolid sticky substance composed of bitumen with mineral matter. It consists mainly of complex hydrocarbons ; occurs naturally in asphalt lakes or in deposits mixed with sandstone and limestone ; made artificially by adding mineral matter to bitumen ; used in road-making and building and in paints and varnishes.

A product khown as blown asphalt or "mineral rubber" is made by permeating asphalt with air, giving a hard, brittle material used as a diluent in cheap rubber goods and as a roofing sealant.

asphalt cement. Fluxed on unfluxed asphalt especially prepared for direct use in making bitumenous pavements.

asphaltene. Any of the dark, solid constituents of crude oils and other bitumens which are soluble in carbon disulphide but insoluble in paraffin naphthas.

asphalt flux. An oil used to reduce the consistency or viscosity of hard asphalt to the desired level.

asphalt mastic. A mixture of asphalt with sand asbestos, crushed rock, or similar material, used like cement.

aspiration condenser. An ion-counter collecting element consisting of cylindrical condenser which when charged produces a radical field that collects ions from the aspirated air.

assay. A form of analysis in which certain constituents of a substance or components only are determined, the others being usually neglected ; applied particularly to minerals and drugs.

associated molecules. Set of two or more identical molecules, kept together by hydrogen bonds or by dipole interactions as $(H_2O)_2$ and $(H_2O)_3$ are formed from H_2O and N_2O_4 is formed from NO_2.

associated production. Simultaneous production of two strange particles in strong interactions (in accordance with strangeness conservation law valid in these interactions),

association. A loose chemical union between molecules of the same or different types, characterized by relatively weak bonding forces (hydrogen bonding of water molecules to each other or of acetic acid to water). In some cases such as complex ion formation, coordinate covalent bonds are involved. Associated groups of molecules dissociate readily ; thus, association is a revesible phenomenon, quite different from polymerization, which is irreversible. An example is the protein hemoglobin, made up of four chains of polypeptides which are associated, but which dissociate when the *p*H changes markedly in either direction ; this dissociation is reversible. Another instance is that of aqueous solutions of soaps or synthetic detergents, which are sometimes referred to as association colloids.

association colloid. Colloid composed of micelles formed by association of particles of dispersed substance under influence of van der Waals forces. Also known as semicolloid.

association degree of ions. In Bjerrum's theory of ionic association, fraction of number of ions in solution which associate into stable ion pairs or higher ionic associates.

A-stage resin. A resin formed by condensation of a phenolic compound and an aldehyde in the presence of a catalyst and a base.

astatine. An element.

		Symbol	At
State	Solid	Atomic No.	85
Group	VIIA	Atomic Wt.	211
		Valence	1, 3, 5
		m.p.	302°C

Astatine the heaviest of the halogen elements, is classified as a nonmetal. It occurs in nature in trace quantities, the total in the earth crust not exceeding 50 grams ; thus, its physical properties are not definitely known. All its isotopes are strongly radioactive, the longest-lived having a half-life of 8·5 hours. It has no stable isotope. It is capable of compound formation with other halogens, with oxygen, and with some organic groups. It is a thyroid-seeking element similar to iodine. Astatine was one of the first elements to be made synthetically by alpha particle bombardment of of bismuth but the largest quantity made at one time is less than 0.1 microgram.

astringent. A chemical used to produce contraction of tissues especially to lessen secretions from mucous membrane and surfaces of wounds.

astron. A proposed thermonuclear device in which a deuterium plasma is confined by an axial magnetic field produced by a shell of relativistic electrons.

asymmetric carbon atom. Carbon atom bound to four different atoms (or groups of atoms). Molecule containing one asymmetric carbon atom is said to be asymmetric and exits in two enantiomeric forms, *e.g.*,

```
     CHO                    CHO
      :                      :
  H—C—OH                HO—C—H
      :                      :
    CH₂OH                  CH₂OH
D-(+)-glyceric aldehyde   L-(–)-glyceric aldehyde
```

asymmetric synthesis. Synthesis of optically active compound, resulting in formation of new chiral centre in molecule with one configuration (of the two possible) predominating *e.g.*,

$$C_6H_5CHO + HCN \xrightarrow{\text{quinine}^*} C_6H_5\overset{*}{C}H(OH)CN$$

asymmetric top. A molecule which nas no three-fold or high-fold axis of symmetry, so that during rotation all three principal moments of inertia are in general different. Examples are water molecule, ethylene molecule, and CH_2BrCl.

asymmetry. A molecular arrangement in which each bond of the central element (usually carbon) is attached to a different element or group.) This results in three-dimensional optical isomers having mirror-image configurations called enantiomorphs or enantiomers. Carbon is the most common asymmetric element, but the phenomenon also exists with sulphur, nitrogen, cobalt, and others. A compound may contain several asymmetric atoms ; the number of possible isomers for any compound having 2 or more asymmetric carbons is 2 to the *n*th power, where *n* equals the number of asymmetric carbons. Each isomer displays optical rotation to the left or right under polarized light, a property of many sugars, amino acids, aldehydes, and terpenes. An asymmertic atom is conventionally denoted by an asterisk, for example, C*. It is possible for a molecule to be asymmetric even in the absence of an asymmetric atom, *i.e.*, by having two different organic groups attached to one end of a carbon chain, as in allenes. *See also* enantiomorph ; optical rotation ; racemic ; stereoisomer.

Atack reagent for nickel. An alcoholic solution of α-benzildioxime, which gives a voluminous red precipitate with nickel compounds in solution.

Atack test for almuinum. To 5 ml. of the solution to be tested, which has been made acidic or neutral, add 1 ml. of a 0.1% filtered alizarin-*S* solution, and then add ammonia until a purple colour appears. Boil, cool and acidify with acetic acid. A red colour or precipitate indicates the presence of aluminum.

atactic polymer. Regular polymer in whose macromolecules there is essential randomness with regard to configurations at all main-chain sites of steric isomerism.

Fig. 8. Atactic polymer

-ate. A suffix that indicates a salt whose metal or radical is in the higest oxidation state, *e.g.*, cobaltic sulphate, mercuric nitrate.

Athermal solution. Solution characterized by enthalpy of mixing H_M (*See* functions of mixing equal to zero, *i.e.*, it has the same value as in ideal solution and entropy of mixing S_M is not equal to entropy of mixing of ideal solution :

$$S_M \neq -R \sum_i x_i \ln x_i$$

where R=universal gas constant, x_i=molar fraction of solution constituent, $\sum_i$=summation of all constituents of solution.

atmolysis. The separation of a mixture of gases by means of their relative diffusibility through a porous portion, as burned clay. The rates of diffusion are inversely proportional to the square roots of the densities of the gases. Hydrogen, thus, is the most diffusible gas.

atmosphere. 1. The gaseous enovelope surrounding the earth (or other heavenly body). The composition of the earth's atmosphere varies very slightly in different localities and according to altitude. Volume composition of dry air sea-level (average values) is ; nitrogen, 78.03% ; oxygen, 20.98% ; argon, 0.94% ; carbon dioxide, 0.04% ; neon, 0.0018% ; helium, 0.0005%; krypton, 0.0001%; xenon, 0.00001%. Air generally contains, in addition to the above, water vapour, hydrocarbons, hydrogen peroxide, sulphur compounds and dust particles in small and variable amounts.

2. A unit of pressure. The pressure that will support a column of mercury 760 mm high (29.92 inches) at 0°C, sea-level and latitude 45°. 1 normal atmosphere = 101325 newtons per square metre. Atmospharic pressure fluctuates about this value from day to day.

atmospheric corrosion. The gradual destruction or alteration of a metal or an alloy by contact with substances present in the atmosphere, such as oxygen, carbon dioxide, moisture, and compounds of nitrogen, chlorine, and sulphur.

atmospheric distillation. Distillation operation conducted at atmospheric pressure, in contrast to vacuum distillation or pressure distillation.

atmospheric layer. The gaseous layers into which the earth's atmosphere can be divided according to change in the physical properties, especially temperature. The altitude figures given in the diagram are approximate, as they vary over the earth's surface, and also show seasonal and diurnal changes. There are main five layers : troposphere, stratosphere, mesosphere, thermosphere, and exosphere. The

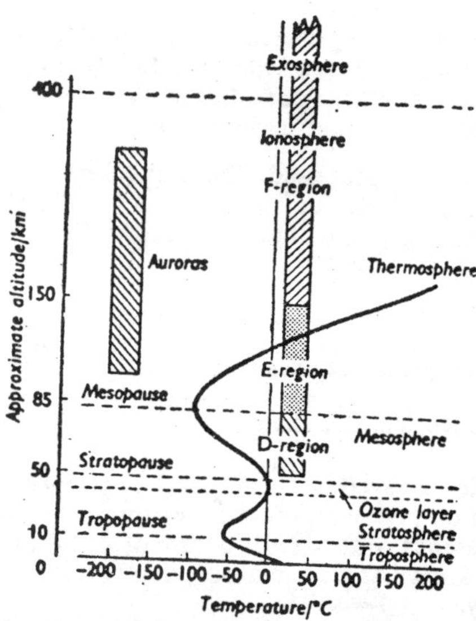

Fig. 9. Atmospheric layer

ionosphere extends from the stratosphere into the exosphere.

atom. Derived (though erroneously) from the Greek, meaning "indivisible" an atom is the smallest unit of an element that can exist. Atoms have long been known to be made up of subatomic particles of matter called protons, neutrons, and electrons. The nucleus of an atom contains one or more proton, which are positively charged and two or more neutrons (except in hydrogen), which have no electric charge. Each proton and neutron has a mass number of 1, they are bound together in the nucleus by exceedingly strong forces in a few special cases they can be separated by bombardment with high-energy particles from an external source. When this occurs, some of the binding energy is released during the fission process for nuclear energy. A few types of atoms are radioactive, and spontaneously, releasing their energy, in some cases over a period of centuries.

The electrons move around the nucleus in shells (groups of orbitals) which are determined by their energy levels or wave functions. An electron is a negatively charged unit which behaves as both a particle and a wave, *i.e.*, it is partly mass and partly energy. Every atom has the same number of electrons as protons and is thus electrically neutral It might be asked why the electrons, being negatively charged, do not combine with the positively charged nucleus in accordance with the law of attraction of oppositely charged bodies. The explanation lies in the dual properties of the electron ; its wave function rather than its particulate nature is the controlling factor in the stability of the atom. Atoms which have gained or lost one or more electrons are called ions. *See also* element ; electron ; periodic table ; orbital.

atom annihilation. The reverse of atom creation. In the most familiar case, a pair of positive and negative electrons disappear, and their equivalent energy appears as two γ-rays quanta.

atom, asymmetric. *See* assymetric.

atom, labeled. *See* labeled atom.

atomic absorption analaysis. Spectroanalysis based on investigation of absorption spectrum of gaseous (atomized) phase of the sample. Also known as atomic absorption spectrophotometry.

atomic absorption spectrophotometry. *See* atomic absorption analysis.

atomic bomb. Explosion system based on chain reaction of uranium ^{235}U or plutonium ^{239}Pu nuclides with slow neutrons. Also known as fission bomb.

atomic cloud. The cloud of hot gases, smoke, dust, and other matter that is carried after explosion of a nuclear weapon in the air or near the earth's surface; generally it has a mushroom shape.

atomic constants. The physical constants including the electronic charge, electronic mass, speed of light, Avogadro number, and Planck's constant.

atomic core. Atom with valence electrons removed.

atomic cross-section. Products of isotopic cross-section and relative abundance of a given isotope in a natural element.

atomic crystals. Crystals with covalent bonds between atoms predominant, they are characterized by high hardness, low ionic conductance and low electron conductivity. Also known as covalent crystals.

atomic energy level. A definite value of energy possible for an atom, either in ground state or in excited state.

atomic fluorescence analysis. Emission spectral analysis based on investigation of fluorescence spectrum of gaseous (atomized) sample. Also known as atomic fluorescence spectrometry.

atomic fluorescence spectrometry. *See* atomic fluorescence analysis.

atomic ground state. The state of lowest energy in which an atom can exist.

atomic heat. *See* atomic heat capacity.

atomic heat capacity. Product of atomic mass and heat capacity measured either at constant pressure or at constant volume. Also known as atomic heat ; atomic specific heat.

atomic line. *See* atom line.

atomic magnetic moment. *See* magnetic moment of atom.

atomic mass. The mass of an atom of an element usually expressed in atomic mass units.

atomic mass scale. Scale of relative atomic and nuclear masses. *See also* : chemical scale of atomic weights ; physical scale of atomic weights ; carbon-12 atomic mass scale. Also known as scale of atomic masses ; scale of atomic wegights).

atomic mass unit. An arbitrarily defined unit in terms of which the masses of individual atoms are expressed ; the standard is the unit of mass equal to 1/12 of the mass of the carbon atom, having as nucleus the isotope with mass number 12.

atomic nucleus. System of nucleus (protons and neutrons) bound by nuclear forces ; central part of atom with which almost its entire mass (about 99.9%) is associated. Atomic nucleus is defined usually by two numbers ; atomic number Z (number of protons in nucleus), and mass number *A* (total number of nucleons).

atomic number. The number of protons, or positively charged mass units, in the nucleus of an atom, upon which its structure and properties depend. This number represents the location of an element in the periodic table ; it is always the same as the number of negatively charged electrons in the shells. Thus an atom is electrically neutral, except in an ionized state that is, when one or more electrons have been gained or lost. Atomic number range from 1, for hydrogen to 106, for the most recently discovered element. *See also* periodic table ; atomic weights ; mass number.

atomic orbital. An allowed wave function of an electron is an atom obtained by a solution of Schrodinger's wave equation. A precise orbit cannot be considered as in Bohr's theory of the atom but the behaviour of the electron is described by its wave function Ψ, which is a mathematical function of its position with respect to the nucleus. The significance of the wave function is that its modulus squared $|\Psi|^2$ is proportional to the probability of finding the electron at a particular point. Schrodinger's equation for hydrogen atom is :

$$\frac{d^2\Psi}{dx^2}+\frac{d^2\Psi}{dy^2}+\frac{d^2\Psi}{dz^2}+\frac{8\pi^2m}{h^2}\left(E+\frac{e^2}{r}\right)=0$$

where m = mass of the electron, and E = its total energy. When equation is solved and boundary conditions applied to make the solution meaningful in physical terms, it is found that the electron can only have certain allowed wave functions (eigenfunctions). Each of these corresponds to a probobility distribution in space given by the manner in which $|\Psi|^2$ varies with position. They also have an associated value of the energy E. These allowed wave functions, or orbitals, are characterized by three quantum numbers similar to those characterizing the allowed orbits in the earlier quantum theory of the atom.

atomic parachor. Contributions of atomic parachors of determined experimentally in parachor of chemical compound, *e.g.*, parachor of chloroform is equal to sum of atomic parachors

$$P_{CHCl_3} = P_C + P_H + 3P_{Cl}$$

Also known as parachor equivalent.

atomic plane. A plane passed throughout the atoms of a crystal space lattice, in accordance with certain rules relating its position to the crystallographic axes.

atomic polarizability. Dielectric polarization (per molecule) arising in unit local field due to shift of atomic nuclei.

atomic polarization. Dielectric due to translation or rotation of atoms or ions arsing from the change in dipole moment accompanying the streching of chemical bonds between unlike atom in molecules. The measure of atomic polarization is defined by

$$P_A = \frac{1}{3\varepsilon_0} N_A \alpha_A \text{ (in SI units)}$$

where N_A = Avogadro constant, α_A = atomic polarizability, ε_0=permittivity of free space.

atomic radius. In quantum mechanical concepts the atom has no definite radius. The atomic radius would be the effective radius of an atom as calculated from physical data such as viscosity or cross-sections.

atomic refraction. Part of experimental value of molar refraction computed for atom in molecule by using additive scheme ; atomic refraction computed in this way is different from atomic refraction of elementary substances.

atomic scattering factor. The mean amplitude of

a wave of x-rays scattered by atoms in a plane of a crystal lattice structure.

atomic specific heat. *See* atomic heat capacity.

atomic spectroanalysis. Spectroanalysis based on investigation of atomic spectra.

atomic spectroscopy. Branch of spectrosocopy dealing with investigation of atomic emission and absorption spectra.

atomic spectrum. The spectrum of radiations due to transitions between energy levels in an atom, either absorption or emission.

atomic standard. Any supposedly immutable property of an atom, such as wavelength or frequency of a characteristic spectral line, in terms of which a unit of a physical quantity is defined.

atomic stopping power. For an ionizing particle passing through an element, the particle's energy loss per atom within a unit area normal to particle's path ; equal to the linear energy transfer (energy loss per unit path length) divided by the number of atoms per unit volume.

atomic susceptibility. The change in magnetic moment of one gram-atom of a substance produced by the application of a magnetic field of unit strength.

atomic term. Set of quantum mechanical states of atomic electrons with defined total orbital and spin angular momentum.

atomic transmutation. The changing of an atom into an atom of different atomic number or, in other words, into an atom of a different element. The process of transmutation occurs in nature in the course of the disintegration of the various radioactive elements and may also be effected by artificial means, such as by bombardment with neutrons, α-particles, γ-radiations, etc.

atomic units. System of units with $h/2\pi$ (h= Planck constant), electron mass, and absolute value of the electron charge all set equal to unit value.

atomic vibration. Periodic, nearly harmonic changes in position of the atoms in a molecule giving rise to many properties of matter such as molecular spectra, heat capacity, and heat conduction.

atomic volume, V_a. Volume of one gram-atom of given element, *i.e.*, ratio of relative atomic mass (in grams) and element density.

atomic weight. The average weight (or mass) of all the isotopes of an element, as determined from the proportions in which they are present in a given element, compared with the mass of the 12 isotope of carbon (taken as precisely (12.000), which is now the official international standard. The true atomic weight of carbon, when the masses of its isotopes are averaged, is 12.01115. The total mass of any atom is the sum of the masses of all its constituents (protons, neutrons, and electrons). The atomic weight of an element expressed in grams is called the gram atomic weight. *See also* atomic number ; mole.

atomization. The process of breaking up a liquid into small droplets.

atom line. Spectral line in emission spectrum of excited atoms. Also known as atomic line ; arc line, in emission spectral analysis.

atropisomerism. Type of stereoisomerism caused by restricted rotation about single bond. High value of rotational barrier (ca. 25 30 kcal/mole) enables isolation of enantiomeric atropisomers, *e.g.*, 6,6'-dinitrodiphenyl acid

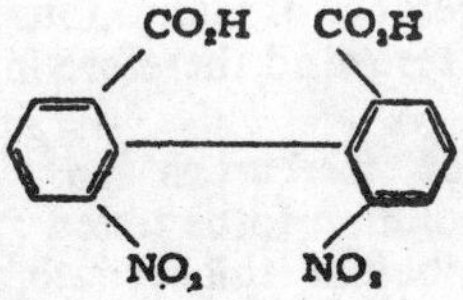

CO_2H CO_2H

NO_2 NO_2

attenuated total reflectance. A method of spectrophotometric analysis based on the reflection of energy at the interface of two media which have different refractive indices and are in optical contact with each other. Also known as internal reflectance spectroscopy.

Aubry test. A mixture of (*i*) a solution of 1 g. of quinine sulphate in 20 ml. of water containing 4 drops of sulphuric acid, and

(*ii*) a solution of 2 g. of potassium iodide in 10 ml. of water ; the mixture being then made up to 100 ml. It gives an orange colour if bismuth is present in urine. The urine sample is evaporated and the residue is dissolved in dilute nitric acid, before testing with this reagent.

Audiffren test. This test is used for chrysanthemum-monocarboxylic acid. To 1 ml. of a dilute solution of the acid, add 1 ml. acid mercuric sulphate solution, and underlay with 0.5 ml. concentrated sulphuric acid. On shaking, a red colour, changing to violet, then green and, after standing for 24 hours, giving a yellow precipitate, indicates the presence of chrysanthemum-monocarboxylic acid.

Aufrecht test. Methanol is detected by oxidation with chromic acid. The distillate gives a blue colour with dimethylaniline and sulphuric acid, followed by lead peroxide.

Auger effect. Transition of atom from excited electronic energy state to lower state with emission of electron instead of photon; it is analogous to internal conversion in nuclear transitions.

Auger electrons. Electrons ejected in Auger effect, differing from β^--radiation in spectrum and generally having lower energy.

Augusti test for manganese. To 1 drop of the solution to be tested, add 1 drop of sodium hydroxide solution on a watch glass, let it stand for 1 minute, evaporate to dryness and add 1-2 drops of a 1% solution of strychnine in sulphuric acid. A blue-violet colour, changing to red, indicates the presence of manganous ion. Cobalt gives a similar test, and therefore interferes.

Augusti test for mercurous ion. Evaporate 1 drop of the solution to be tested ; add 1 drop of dilute ammonium thiocyanate solution, 1 drop of cobalt nitrate solution; let it crystallize under cover ; and examine microscopically (300 diameters). Blue crystals indicate the presence of mercurous ion.

Auld-Hantzsch test for aldehydes. In this test for aldehydes, a little sodium hydroxide solution is added to a few drops of 0.1N mercuric chloride solution, followed by 2-3 ml. of the solution to be tested. A white precipitate is formed by aldehydes.

auriferous. Containing gold.

auro. A combining term for monovalent gold.

auroauric. The combining term for aurous and auric gold in the same compound.

aurum fulminans. The "earth" obtained by precipitating gold from its solutions by adding ammonia. When dry, it detonates when struck. Its properties were known to Mayow and Scheele but its composition is complex.

austenitic steel. A steel in which the iron component is present in the gamma modification, namely, a face-centered lattice structure, which occurs at temperatures between 730 and 1100°C in contrast to the alpha modification called ferrite, which has a body-centered lattice. These two modifications of iron are allotropic forms, the gamma (austenite) being nonmagnetic and the alpha, magnetic. In austenitic steels the carbon atoms are able to diffuse through the iron atoms, which is an important factor in making a steel susceptible to heat treatment. Some stainless steels are austenitic.

autocatalysis. A name to the condition which obtains when one of the products of a reaction, or one of the factors, acts as a catalyst and accelerates or retards the velocity of the reaction, *e.g.*, in the hydrolysis of esters the acid products formed exert an influence to increase the velocity of the hydrolysis. Autocatalysis may be positive or negative according as the result of the catalytic action is acceleration or retardation.

autocatalyst. product or reactant acting catalytically.

autoclaving. Heating of liquids or sterilizing of equipment at high steam pressure.

autocomplex. Complex compound formed in salt solution through association of simple primary molecules, *e.g.*, in solutions of cadmium chloride following autocomplexation reaction occurs :

$$2CdI_2 \rightarrow Cd[CdI_4] \text{ ; or } 3CdI_2 \rightarrow Cd[CdI_3]_2$$

autoignition. Ignition of substance due to exothermal process taking place in it, with no apparent energy impulse from outside.

autoignition point. The lowest temperature at which a material will catch fire without the aid of a flame or spark ; it is also called the ignition point. Some substances, such as white phosphorus, have such a low autoignition point that they will ignite spontaneously on exposure to air ; materials like paper, thin wood shavings, and cotton fibers will burn when exposed to temperatures of from 200 to 260°C. Nitrocellulose will ignite at about 135°C. The lowest ignition point for any solvent is 100°C for carbon disulphide. This property should not be confused with flash point. *See also* flash point ; combustible material.

autoinduction. Chemical induction in cases when concentration of inductor increases as function of time.

autoionization. Electron detachment from excited atom or molecule with simultaneous transition of another excited electron to ground state. Autoionization involves at least doubly excited states.

autolytic enzyme. A bacterial enzyme, located in the cell wall that causes disintegration of the cell following injury or death.

autoprotolysis. Electrolytic dissociation of solvent only, as a result of proton exchange between its molecules, *e.g.*,

$$2H_2O \rightleftharpoons H_3O^+ + OH^-$$
$$2CH_3COOH \rightleftharpoons CH_3COOH_2^+ + CH_3COO^-$$

Autoprotolysis occurs between amphiprotic solvents, *e.g.*,

$$NH_3, H_2O, CH_3COOH, H_2SO_4$$

autoradiography. Determination of distribution and content of radioactive substances in object examined by means of a photographic emulsion placed in close contact with subtances emitting radiation. Also known as radioautography.

autoradiolysis. Radiolysis caused by ionizing radiation from an internal source.

autoxidation. An oxidation that takes place spontaneously in a substance exposed to air or oxygen at temperatures below 150°C. It is activated by a free radical chain mechanism (autocatalysis) and is characteristic of many hydrocarbons ; thus it is applied to a number of industrial operations in the chemical industry, such as the production of acetone and phenol from cumene. Autoxidation also is responsible, at least in part, for development of rancidity in food products, the drying of certain types of vegetable oils, the formation of "gum" in petroleum products, and the deterioration of vulcanized rubber.

Autenrieth-Hinsberg test. A test for acetophenetidin based on the formation of its mononitro derivative on boiling with 10-12% nitric acid. The nitro derivative crystallizes from water in needles having a melting point of 103°C.

Autenrieth test for methanol. This test is based on the formation of the methyl ester of *p*-bromobenzoyl chloride by reaction of the latter substance with methanol in alkaline solution. The ester has an anise-like odour, and melts at about 77-78°C.

auxiliary. A term used almost exclusively in the textile-processing industry to include a large number of functional materials which have no chemical relationship ; among these are fats and oils used to lubricate fibers, natural and synthetic surface-active agents, film-forming materials (starches, gums, etc.) for coating and sizing, delustering agents, and waterproofing materials. The term "assistant" is used in almost the same sense in the industry, but it also applies to the fixing of dyes on fabrics, for example, a mordanting assistant. Dyestuffs are not usually regarded as auxiliaries as their function is essential.

auxin. One of a group of hormones which regulate or control the growth of plants and vegetation ; they affect a number of processes, including the cell wall structure of stems; enabling the plant to lean one way or another in response to sunlight, as well as the length and direction of roots, and the development of buds and fruit. The auxins include indoleacetic acid and 2,4-D, the latter is effective in very small amounts, as it occurs in the plant but can be lethal to some plants if applied in high concentrations. *See also* plant growth regulator ; 2,4-D.

auxochrome. Electron-donating group which shifts absorption spectrum towards longer wavelengths in dye molecule with system of conjugated π-bonds, *e.g.*,

$$-CH_3 < -OH < -OCH_3 < -NH_2 < -NHCH_3 < -N(CH_3)_2$$

(where groups are arranged according to their approximate increasing power of spectrum shifts). Also known as auxochromic group.

auxochromic group. *See* auxochrome.

Auwers-Skita rule. A method of predicting which of the two possible stereoisomers will result in the catalytic hydrogenation of an unsaturated cyclic material from which stereoisomeric polymethylene products are possible and where labile configurations do not result. The rule states that reduction in acid solution yields the *cis*-configuration, and reduction in neutral or alkaline solution, the *trans*-configuration.

Auwers synthesis. A ring rearrangement of halogen (usually bromine) substituted coumaranones, brought abought about by the action of alkali, with the formation of flavonols.

CBrCHBrR + H_2O →

+ 2 HBr.

available energy. *See* Helmholtz free energy.

available net work. *See* net maximum work.

available work at constant temperature. *See* Helmholtz free energy.

aviation gasoline. Stable fuel with high volatility and high octane, especially suited for use in aircraft reciprocating engines.

aviation mix. Antiknock fluid containing tetraethyllead, ethylene dibromide, and dye ; used in aviation gasoline.

Avogadro's constant. N_A. Number of molecules in one mole of substance : $N_A = 6.02252 \times 10^{23}$ mol^{-1}. Also known as Avogadro's number.

Avogadro's hypothesis. *See* Avogadro's law.

Avogadro's law. Equal volumes of different ideal gases at the same pressure and temperature contain the same number of molecules. Molar volumes of ideal gases are the same at identical pressures and temperatures. Also known as Avogadro's hypothesis.

Avogadro's number. *See* Avogadro's constant.

Axenfeld test for Albumin. A 0.1% solution of gold chloride used in testing for albumin in solution. The solution is acidulated with formic acid and the reagent added to it. A pink to purple-red colour on heating indicates the presence of albumin.

axial bond. One of the six bonds parallel to three-fold axis in symmetry in chair form of cyclohexane. Axial bond direction are alternately upwards and downwards, parallel to each other and perpendicular with respect to "mean" plane of ring, *i.e.*, plane bisecting all C—C ring-forming bonds.

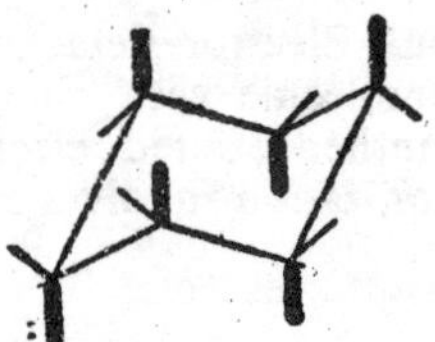

Fig. 10. Axial bond

axial element. The lengths, length ratios, and angles which define a crystal's unit cell.

axial haloketone rule. Particular case of octant rule ; according to this introduction of chlorine, bromine of iodine atoms into axial position adjacent to carbonyl group in cyclohexene derivatives influences in defined way the sign of Cotton effect in initial ketone. Introduction of halogen atom into equatorial position in ketone does not change sign of Cotton effect.

axial plane. 1. A plane that includes two of the crystallographic axes.

2. The plane of the optic axes of an optically biaxial crystal.

axial ratio. The ratio obtained by comparing the length of a crystallographic axis with one of the lateral axes taken as unity.

axial symmetry. Property of a geometric configuration which is unchanged when rotated about a given line.

Aymonier solution. A solution of 1 g. potassium dichromate and 1 ml. of nitric acid in 100 ml of water. It is used as a test reagent for α-naphthol. A dark precipitate with this reagent indicates the presence of α-naphthol.

azeotrope. A term used to denote a mixture of two components in such proportions as to result in either the lowest or the higest constant boiling point attainable with any mixture of the same components. Thus, a blend of ethyl alcohol (b.p. 78.5°C) and water (b.p. 100°C) when mixed in the mole fraction of 89.4% alcohol and 10.6% water, has the lowest boiling point, 78.15°C of any possible mixture of these substances. Similarly, HCl and water mixtures have a constant maximum boiling point. Numerous of combinations of substances exhibit this behaviour. The vapours of azeotropic mixtures have the same percentage composition as the original liquid mixture. In azeotropic distillation, complete separation of the components of the mixture being distilled is aided by adding another substance, *e.g.*, benzene, which is known to form an azeotrope with one of these components ; as the azeotropic mixture has a different boiling point, it readily distills off. *See also* eutectic.

azeotropic agent. Invariable component in series of two-component azeotropic systems in which second component is compound belonging to defined homologous series.

azeotropic point. Point in phase diagram which defines composition and boiling temperature, or composition and vapour pressure of azeotrope.

azeotropic range. Range of temperature covering boiling points of homologues which form azeotropic system with azeotropic agent.

azeotropic system. System of constituents forming azeotrope.

azeotropy. Boiling (distillation) of mixture of liquids without change of composition.

azide. Any of a group of detonating explosive compound whose molecule are comprised of a chain structure of double-bonded nitrogen atoms to which is attached a metal or metal complex, a halogen, hydrogen, an ammonium radical, or an organic radical. Hydrogen azide and all the heavy-metal azides are highly sensitive and can be detonated by slight shock, heat or friction ; less sensitive are the azides of barium, sodium, and calcium ; organic azides lie midway between, in respect to sensitivity. Shipment and storage of azides are legally specified, as is the case with all high explosives.

azido-. In inorganic compounds, a prefix denoting the group N_3—. In organic compounds azido- means triazo-.

azimethylene group. The group $N_2C=$, found in diazomethane, diazoacetic ester, etc.

Azimuthal quantum number. An integer obtained in quantizing the angular momentrum of a particle, such as an electron, moving in an elliptical path. The total momentum is resolved into components, one directed radially and the other tangentially to the orbit. The latter has values given by the expression $hl/2\pi$ in which h is Planck's constant, and l is the azimuthal quantum number.

azine. A heterocyclic compound of six atoms in the ring. one or more of which is nitrogen and a ring structure resembling benzene. Thus pyridine, C_6H_5N, is an azine.

azine dyes. Benzene-type dye derived from phenazine ; members of the group, such as nigrosines and safranines, are quite varied in application.

azino. The group =N—N= in organic compounds.

azo. 1. Compounds which contain nitrogen.

2. Compounds which contain the azo group —N=N— united on either side to a benzene nucleus ; as, in azobenzene ;

$$C_6H_5N=N-C_6H_5$$

or to an aliphatic and an aromatic group, as in benzene azomethane,

$$C_6H_5-N=N-CH_3$$

When the two nuclei are the same the compound is called "symmetrical" ; and, if one is aromatic and the other aliphatic, the compound is termed "mixed." Compounds which contain two or three azo gtoups are termed "disazo" and "trisazo".

azo dyes. The most versatile and widely used group of dyestuffs ; the term azo refers to the nitrogen content of the molecule. Two reactions are involved in their formation. The azo component is derived by reacting a primary aromatic amine with nitrous acid, plus a mineral acid. This reaction is called diazotization. It yields a compound containing an

—N=N—, or diazo, group which performs the colour-imparting function and this is called a chromophore. The diazo compound then undergoes a second reaction, known as coupling, with other organic compounds, such as phenols or amines.

azoimino. The group —N=N—NH—. It is found, for example, in compounds such as benzotriazole, $C_6H_4N_3H$, where the azoimino group forms a five-membered ring with two adjacent carbon atoms of the benzene nucleus.

azole. One of a group of heterocyclic, five-membered ring compounds, such as pyrrol, oxazole, the diazoles, etc.

azote. The french word for nitrogen, derived from the prefix *a*=(not) and the base *zoo*, meaning "alive" (*zoon*=animal). This entry is included to facilitate recognition of nitrogen-containing compounds indicated by such chemical terms as azo, azide, thiazole, azobenzene, carbazole, etc. The derivation is due to the comparative chemical inactivity of nitrogen.

azotize. To combine with nitrogen.

B

B. Symbol for the element boron. Also, symbol for brightness, or luminance.

b. Symbol for constant in vander Waal equation. Symbol for Wien displacement constant. Symbol for Richardson equation factor.

babbitt. A group of bearing alloys used as coatings on steel ; there are several modifications, including those in which lead, tin or cadmium comprise the basis metal. They absorb heat developed by friction, retain lubricants, and thus protect the steel bearing from deterioraion and seizing.

Babkin test for manganese. A test for manganese in which 1-2 ml. of the solution is boiled with excess sodium hydroxide and 2-3 drops hydrogen peroxide, the solution is filtered, and the precipitate is washed. The precipitate is boiled with lead dioxide and 2-3 ml. nitric acid. A violet colour indicates the presence of manganese.

Babo's law. A law stating that relative lowering of a solvent's vapour pressure by a solute is the same at all temperatures.

Bach reagent for copper and nickel. A mixture of equal quantities of 20% formaldehyde and hydroxylamine hydrochloride. Add 0.5 ml. of this reagent and 0.5 ml. 15% potassium hydroxide solution to 15 ml. of the solution to be tested. A violet colour is given by copper while an orange-yellow colour is given by nickel.

Bach reagent for hydrogen peroxide. A solution of 0.03 g. of potassium dichromate and 5 drops of aniline in 1 litre of water. Five ml. of this solution, to which 2 drops of 5% oxalic acid solution have been added, give a violet colour with 5 ml. of a solution in which hydrogen peroxide is present.

Bachmeyer test. With a tannin solution, caustic alkalies and ammonia produce a red to reddish-colour which, after, a while, turns to a dirty green.

Bachstez-Cavallini test. A reaction for differentiating ascorbic and isoascorbic acids. Add 2 drops of 10% uranium acetate solution and a few drops of concentrated sodium hydroxide solution to a 1% solution of the material to be tested, made fanitly alkaline. Ascorbic acid produces a brownish colour discharged by the alkali and then an amorphous precipitate of sodium urnate is formed. Isoascorbic acid produces a dark brownish-red colour and the solution remains clear.

back donation. A form of chemical bond in which a ligand forms a sigma bond to an atom or ion by donating a pair of electrons, and the central atom donates electrons back by overlap of its filled orbitals with vacent orbitals on the ligand.

background. 1. Ionizing radiation coming from sources other than the radiation to be detected or measured, *e.g.*, from naturally occurring radioactive nuclides, cosmic radiation or radioactivity contamination in laboratory.

2. Absorption due to all components except for the one to be determined.

3. Counting rate recorded by a counter in absence of a radioactivity sample.

back mutation. A mutation that causes a mutant gene to regain its wild-type base sequence.

backscattering. Scattering of radiation at angle greater than 90°.

back-scatter peak. Peak in gamma radiation spectrum formed by photoelectric absorption of radiation scattered at angle of 180°.

back strain effect. Effect displayed by B-strain —one of the series strains which are attribute to difference in molecular compactness between initial and final stages of reaction, *e.g.*, formation of ammonium compound from amine R—N—R causes compression of R—N—R bond angle due to change from planar to pyramidal arrangement of nitrogen substituents. Also known as B-strain effect.

Bacovesco reagent. A solution of 15 g. molybodic acid in 85 g. concentrated sulphuric acid. It forms a blue-violet ring with solutions containing alcohols or phenols.

bacteria. Microorganisms composed chiefly of proteins and nucleic acids. It is neither plant nor animal. In shape, some are spherical, some rod-like, and some spiral. They have many important beneficial chemical functions, some of which are utilized in the manufacture of ethyl alcohol, beer, and antibiotics by fermentation; baking industry (yeast), soil fixation of nitrogen; sewage treatment by the activated sludge process; formation of proteins from hydrocarbon; manufacture of sulphur from gypsum; organic oxidation processes; and reaction with cellulose for production of high protein foods. Bacteria are 0.5-2.0 μm in length or breadth and reproduce by binary fission. Bacteria also have undesirable properties, as they are the cause of many types of food spoilage, toxic effects, and infectious diseases.

bactericide. An agent having the power of destroying bacteria.

bacteriology. The science and study of bacteria, including their anatomy, growth, characteristics, culture, and identification.

bacteriolysis. The destruction and dissolution of bacteria cells commonly one due to a bacterial or biochemical agent.

bacteriophage. A substance of biological origin which has a lytic (dissolving) action on bacteria and thus destroys them. Little is known of the nature of bacteriophages; they are ultramicroscopic and pass through filters readily.

bacteriostat. A compound having the ability to inhibit or stop the proliferation and growth of infectious microorganism without actually killing them. It thus acts in the manner of an antiseptic.

Badische process. One method of working the contact process for the manufacture of sulphuric acid. Sulphur dioxide and air (in calculated excess) mixture—purified and preheated—is passed through an iron converter containing vertical iron tubes packed with platinized asbestos. The name 'Badische process' was also used at one time for a modification of the Birkeland-Eyde process.

Baekeland process. The polymerization of phenols and formaldehyde to yield resins. The reaction starts with the addition to the carbonyl group of formaldehyde. The hydrogen atoms in the ortho and para positions are reactive. One of these adds to the oxygen atom and the rest of the phenol molecule adds to the carbon atom:

$$C_6H_5OH + HCHO \rightarrow o\text{-}HOC_6H_4CH_2OH$$

These molecules can condense with more phenol and more formaldehyde forming molecules with several reactive groups which continue to react until the final molecules are too complex to crystallize and so form resins.

Baert test. A test for reducing sugars in raw sugars made by dissolving approximately 10 g. of the sugar in 50 ml. of Fehling solution and 2 ml. of 1% methylene blue solution. A funnel is placed at the mouth of the flask and the mixture is brought to a boil in 2-3 minutes. The blue colour is discharged if the sample contains more than 0.05% of invert-sugar.

Baeyer-Drewson synthesis. Synthesis of indigo from *o*-nitrobenzaldehyde and acetone, acetaldehyde or similar compounds.

$$2\ C_6H_4(CHO)(NO_2) + 2\ CH_3COCH_3 \xrightarrow[NaOH]{dil} 2\left[C_6H_4(NO_2)\text{–}CHOH\cdot CH_2 \vdots COCH_3\right]$$

$$\downarrow$$

$$\text{indigo} + 2\ CH_3COOH + 2\ H_2O$$

Two molecules of the intermediate compound undergo hydrolysis as indicated above, lose water, and condense to form indigo.

Baeyer-Drewson test for acetone. Add some *o*-nitrobenzaldehyde to the solution containing acetone and heat the mixture to boiling, then add a few drops of sodium hydroxide or potassium hydroxide solution. If acetone is present, a blue colour is produced. A number of modifications of this test have been developed.

Baeyer reaction. A method of preparation of dihydroxyl-diaryl alkenes by condensation of two molecules of a phenol with one molecule of an aldehyde ; *e.g.*,

$$2\ C_6H_5OH + RCHO \rightarrow HO\text{–}C_6H_4\text{–}CH(R)\text{–}C_6H_4\text{–}OH + 2\ H_2O$$

baeyer's reagent. An important test reagent for unsaturation in organic compounds. A solution of potassium permanganate, made alkaline with sodium carbonate, is decolourized with the precipitation of brown manganese dioxide when shaken with an unsaturated compound. An acid solution of permanganate would oxidise, too strongly.

Baeyer strain theory. Former theoretical explanation of differences in chemical and physical properties of cyclic compounds. Baeyer theory assumes that alicyclic compounds are planar and that their stability depends on angles of valency bonds. Cyclic compound should be the more stabe, the more nearly the angles of valency bonds in the cycle approximate to 109°28′. Later it was shown that six-membered and more rings are not planar and the Baeyer theory partly lost its importance, reserved only for cyclic compounds containing less than 6 carbon atoms.

Baeyer test for glucose. 1. When a solution containing glucose is boiled with a solution of *o*-nitrophenylpropiolic acid in aqueous solution carbonate, indigo precipitates.

2. Alkaline potassium permanganate is reduced by glucose to produce a green colour.

Several modifiacations of these reactions have been developed.

Baeyer test for phenol. When boiled with a mixture of concentrated sulphuric acid and a few drops of aldehyde, phenol produces a white, cement-like mass, soluble in sodium hydroxide solution to give a violet colour. A number of modifications of this reaction have been developed.

Baeyer test for resorcinol. 1. Concentrated sulphuric acid gradually added to a mixture of resorcinol and benzaldehyde forms a red resinous substance which is soluble in alkalies to give a violet colour.

2. If resorcinol is heated with phthalic anhydride almost to the boiling point of the latter and the melt is dissolved in sodium hydroxide solution, a green fluorescence is produced.

Baeyer-Villiger oxidation. Oxidation of aldehydes and ketones to esters, effected with hydrogen peroxide or peracids, *e.g.*,

$$R-\overset{O}{\overset{\|}{C}}-R' \xrightarrow[\text{peracids}]{H_2O_2\text{ or}} R-\overset{O}{\overset{\|}{C}}-OR'$$

CH_3, CH_3 — peracids → CH_3, CH_3

Also known as Baeyer-Villiger peracid rearrangement

Baeyer-Villiger peracid rearrangement. *See* Baeyer-Villiger oxidation.

Bailey test for sulphur. When sulphur is fused with sodium carbonate, and dissolved in water, it gives a blood-red colour upon the addition of sodium nitroprusside solution

Baine reagent. A solution obtainted by mixing 30 ml. of 10% sodium hydroxide solution, 20 ml. glacial acetic acid, 1 ml. 0.25% sodium fluoresceinate solution and 50 ml. water. It is a test reagent for bromides, giving a characteristic pink colour upon addition of 0.0001N chlorine water, the colour disappearing upon addition of an excess of the chlorine water.

bainite. Steel formed by austempering, having an acicular structure of ferrite and carbides, exhibiting considerable toughness, and combining high strength with high ductility.

Baker-Venkataraman transformation. The change of *o*-aroyloxyacetophenones into *o*-hydroxydiaroylmethanes.

$OCOC_6H_5$, $COCH_3$ — KOH →

OH, $COCH_2COC_6H_5$

bagasse. The cellulosic residue of sugar-cane after it has been disintegrated to extract the sugar. It is converted by high-temperature compression into a heavy board of high thermal insulating value which is useful for heat- and soundproofing in building construction. Paper can be made from bagasse on a commericial basis ; also applicable in the manufacture of furfural ; and used as an extender in animal feeds.

baking powder. A synthetic leavening agent used in the baking industry. There are several types, all of which contain a carbonate, a weak acid, and a filler. A typical composition is sodium bicarbonate, tartaric acid or monobasic calcium phosphate, and cornstarch. On exposure to water and heat, the acid reacts, with the bicarbonate to evolve carbon dioxide, which produces a stable foam. The baked product is thus a dispersion of a gas in a solid.

Balandin multiplet. Active centre composed of several atoms or ions of catalyst, distributed in regular manner and remaining in geometrical consistence with distribution of ions or atoms in molecules of reactants which participate in catalytic reactions. Also known as multiplet.

Balandin theory of multiplets. Theory of heterogeneous catalysis which assumes progress of catalytic reaction on active centres of multiplet nature. Also known as theory of multiplets.

Balavione test. To distinguish grape wine from cider, extract 25 ml. of the liquid with 10 ml. ether. Wash the ether extract, and to it add 2 ml. of 0.5% ammonia and several crystals of *p*-phenylendiamine hydrochloride. A cider extract is coloured cherry red and a white grape wine extract becomes yellow.

Balbach process. An electrolytic process for the separation of gold and silver, in which the metal to be separated forms the anode and is electrolyzed in a bath of silver nitrate, and the silver deposits on the cathode.

Ball and Wingham process. A metallurigical process for the desulphurization of molten metals, especially iron, by the action of an alkaline cyanide flux.

ball clay. A type of clay used in ceramics that is characterized by strong binding properties, a tendency to ball, and excellent plasticity.

Ball test for hydroxylamine. If the hydroxylamine solution is boiled with 1-2 drops of yellow ammonium sulphide to incipient sulphur separation, and 2 ml. ammonia is added, followed by the addition of an equal volume of alcohol, a purple-red colour is obtained.

Ball reagents. Reagents used for testing the alkali metal ions.

1. The reagent for rubidium and cesium is a solution of 50 g. sodium nitrite and 10 g. bismuth nitrate in dilute nitric acid.

2. The reagent for sodium is a solution of 50 g. potassium nitrite and 10 g. bismuth nitrate in dilute nitric acid, to which 25 ml. of 10% caesium nitrate solution is added.

The first reagent yields a yellow precipitate with solutions containing caesium or rubidium, and the second reagent gives a yellow precipitate with solutions containing sodium ions.

Balmer series. A group of lines in the visible spectrum of atomic hydrogen represented by the formula :

$$\bar{\nu}=R_H\left(\frac{1}{n_1^2}-\frac{1}{n_2^2}\right)$$

in which $\bar{\nu}$ is the wave number, R_H is the Rydberg number and n_1 is 2, while n_2 has various integral values.

balsam. A sticky, resinous, fragrant substance obtained from several varieties of trees and shrubs throughout the world. It has a strong, pleasant aroma and is used as a base for perfumes, cough syrups, and pharmaceutical preparations. The chemical composition varies with source ; in general, it includes essential oils, terpenes, benzoic acid and cinnamic acid,.

Bamberger reagent for aldehydes and ketones. Para-nitrophenylhydrazine is used as a reagent for aldehydes and ketones. Precipitates of characteristic crystalline form are obtained.

Bamberger test for ortho-diketones. Addition of potassium hydroxide solution, in the absence of air, to a heated alcoholic solution of the *o*-diketone gives a dark red to black colour, which disappears on shaking in presence of air.

banana bond. Informal name for the type of electron deficient bond holding the B—H—B bridges in boranes and similar compounds. *See also* bent-bond.

band. A restricted range in which the energy of electrons in solids lie, or from which they are excluded, as understood in quantum-mechanical terms. *See also* band spectrum.

band gap. *See* forbidden band.

band head. In rotation-ocillation-electronic spectrum, direction of convergence limit of group of rotation lines. Also known as band edge.

band scheme. The identification of energy bonds in solids with levels of independent atoms from which they arise as the atoms are brought together to form the solid, together with the width and spacing of bands.

band spectrum. Type of spectrum characteristic for molecules. Band spectrum consists of several closely spaced groups of lines corresponding to rotation-vibration-electronic transitions.

band theory of solids. Quantum machanical theory connecting physical and chemical properties of solid state with electronic structure of atoms in substance, and particularly successfully describing electrical properties of metals and semiconductors. According to this theory, particular energetic states of electrons belonging to isolated atoms (ions) have corresponding energy band in solid, which result from splitting of these states due to atomic interactions, and are extended throughout the whole crystal.

bar. A c.g.s. unit of pressure equal to 10^5 pascals or 10^6 dynes per square centimetre.

Barbache reagent for glycerol. A solution of 0.25 ml. phenol in 1 litre water, to which a few drops of a saturated solution of ferric chloride are added. It is used in testing for glycerin, which decolourizes this reagent.

barberite. A nonferrous alloy with good resistance to sulphuric acid, mine waters, and sea water ; consists of 88.5% copper, 5% nickel, 5% tin, and 1.5% silicon.

Barbier test. To detect alcohol in volatile oils, distill off 10% of the volume of the oil, and add potassium acetate to the residue. The alcohol can be reclaimed and estimated by distillation from the separated layer.

Barbier-Wieland degradation. A method of elimination of one carbon atom at a time from an aliphatic acid type of side chain. The method consists essentially of the reaction of the ester of the acid with an aryl-magnesium halide and its removal by hydrolysis and oxidation of the compound at the resulting double bond.

iodine solution (an iodine-potassium iodide solution acidified with acetic acid) and 3 ml. ammonia. Yellow needles are formed by proteins.

Bardhan-Sengupta synthesis. Phosphorus pentoxide and other powerful dehydrating agents act upon 2-β phenethyl-1-cyclohexanol to form octahydrophenanthrene compounds.

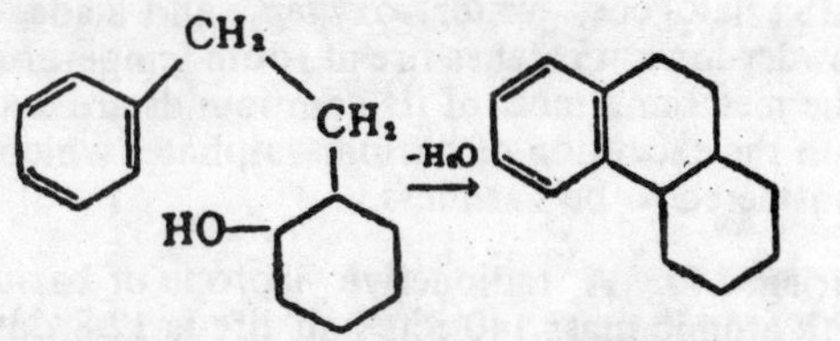

CH_2 CH_2 HO— $\xrightarrow{-H_2O}$

Barff's process. A process for oxidizing the surface of metals, by the action of superheated steam to increase their resistance to corrosion by forming a protective film of Fe_3O_4.

Barfoed's reagent. A test reagent for all monosaccharoses. It is made by dissolving cupric ace-

$$RCH_2COOH + C_2H_5OH \xrightarrow{-H_2O} RCH_2COOC_2H_5$$

$$RCH_2COOC_2H_5 + 2C_6H_5MgX + 2HX \xrightarrow[-C_2H_5OH]{-2MgX_2} RCH_2C(OH)(C_6H_5)-C_6H_5$$

$$RCH_2C(OH)(C_6H_5)-C_6H_5 \xrightarrow{-H_2O} RCH{=}C(C_6H_5)_2 \xrightarrow{[O]} RCOOH + C_6H_5COC_6H_5$$

barbiturate. A class of hypnotic, habit-forming drugs of which barbituric acid NHCONHCOCH$_2$CO, and barbital NHCONHCOC$(C_2H_5)_2$CO, are the best-known examples ; they act by depressing the central nervous system. Chemically, they are pyrimidine derivatives, containing nitrogen in the molecule. About 25 types of barbiturates are now in approved medical use. They are highly toxic, and their administration is limited to prescriptions.

Bardach test for proteins. To 5 ml. of a fairly dilute solution of the sample, add 3 drops of 5% acetone solution, 0.1—0.2 ml. Lugol's

tate in water (about 6% solution) and adding dilute acetic acid. Cuprous oxide is precipitated on warming with a monosaccharose.

Bari-Sol process. A process for removal of waxes from liquid hydrocarbons by extraction of the wax with a mixed ethylene dichloride-benzene solvent, followed by separation from the hydrocarbon is a centrifuge.

barium. An element.

		Symbol	Ba
		Atomic No.	56
State	Solid	Atomic Wt.	137.34
Group	IIA	Valence	2
		Isotopes	7 stable
		m.p.	729°C

Barium is a heavy alkaline-earth metal derived from barytes (barium sulphate) and witherite (barium carbonate) ; found in Missoori, Georgia, Mexico, and Canada. It can be extruded and machined and is used in special alloys, as a "getter" in vacum tubes, and as a thin-film lubricant in electronic instruments. It exhibits a green colour when exposed to flame. Barium is chemically active, reacting with halogens, water, oxygen, and acids. In powder form it catches fire at room temperature. The metal and most of its compounds are toxic, with the exception of barium sulphate, which is considered to be harmless.

barium-140. A radioactive isotope of barium with atomic mass 140 ; its half life is 12.8 days, and decays by negative beta-particle emission.

barium number. Absorption of barium hydroxide solution (commonly (0.25N) by a textile sample, or the ratio of the amount absorbed by a given textile to that absorbed by a standard textile, such as untreated cotton.

Barkhausen effect. The effect observed when a ferromagnetic substance is magnetized by a slowly increasing magnetic field ; the magnetization does not take place continuously, but in a series of small steps. The effect is due to orientation present of magnetic domains in the substance.

Barlow's rule. The volumes of space occupied by the various atoms in a given molecule are approximately proportional to the valencies of the atoms ; whenever an element exhibits more than one kind of valency the lowest value is generally selected.

barn, *b*. Obsolete unit of surface area used in nuclear physics to define values of cross sections. In SI system $1b = 100\ fm^2$.

Barnard reagent. A solution of 0.42 g. hydrazine in 1 litre water, to which has been added 7.5 ml. of a 2% acid fuchsin solution. This reagent gives a characteristic pink colour with aldehydes.

Barnebey test. To detect cyanides in the presence of ferrocyanides, ferricyanides and thiocyanides, add ammonia to a dilute aqueous solution of cupric sulphide until the precipitate redissolves, then pass a small quantity of hydrogen sulphide, precipitating a little cupric sulphide and follow with the solution being tested. If the precipitate of cupric sulphide dissolves, cyanide is present.

barometric formula. In colloid chemistry, relation between height of rise and concentration of sol at sedimentation equilibrium (analogous) to relation between altitude and air pressure). In case of monodisperse sol with spherical particles, barometric formula can be expressed as

$$\frac{RT}{N_A} \ln \frac{n_0}{n} = \frac{4}{3}\pi r^3(\gamma - \gamma_0)gh$$

where R = gas constant, N_A = Avogadro constant, n_0=number of particles at zero level, n = number of particles at height h, r=radius of particle, γ and γ_0= densities of dispersion medium and dispersed phases respectively.

Barreswil test for chromate. A solution containing chromic acid gives an intense blue colour with a slightly acidic 3% solution of hydrogen peroxide containing ether, the blue colour passing into the ether layer on shaking.

Barreswil test for vanadium. Hydrogen peroxide, in limited amount, gives a reddish-brown to red colour in acidic vanadium solution.

Bartlett force. A force between two nucleons in which spin is exchanged.

Bart reaction. Transformation of aromatic diazonium salt into corresponding arylarsonic acid, effected by sodium arsenite in presence of catalyst (copper or its salts), *e.g.*,

$$C_6H_5N_2Cl + Na_3AsO_3 \xrightarrow{Cu} C_6H_5AsO(ONa)_2 + NaCl + N_2$$

Also known as Bart arylarsonic acid synthesis.

baryon. Any elementary particle which can be transformed into a nucleon with some number of mesons and lighter particles. Also known as heavy particle.

baryon number, *B*. Additive quantum number attributed to every particle and antiparticle and their systems. For proton and particles decaying to proton, B=1, for corresponding antiparticles $B = -1$. Other particles and antiparticles have B=0. Baryon number is conserved in all interactions.

baryon number conservation law. Sums of baryon numbers of initial and final particles in given process are equal. Baryon number conservation law is observed in all interactions.

baryon octet. The group of one lambda, three sigma, and two xi hyperons and two nucleons, all having spin ½ and positive parity, and forming a symmetrical pattern as suggested by SU_3 symmetry.

baryon resonances. Resonances with baryon number $B=1$.

basal metabolic rate. The rate of oxygen consumption of a body at complete rest, long after a meal.

basal orientation. A crystal orientation in which the surface is paralled to the base of the lattice or to the lattice plane which is normal to one of the lattice axes.

basal plane. The plane perpendicular to the long or C, axis in all crystals except those of isometric system.

base. A base is a substance that :

(*i*) liberates hydroxyl ions when dissolved in water (Arhenius).

(*ii*) that liberates negative ions of various kinds in any solvent (Franklin) ;

(*iii*) that receives a hydrogen ion (proton) from a strong acid to form a weaker acid (Bronsted-Lowry) ;

(*iv*) that gives up two electrons to an acid, forming a covalent bond with the acid (Lewis) ; Reactions (*iii*) and (*iv*) occur whether or not the substances are in solution. Lewis bases are considered "hard" if they have high electronegativity and are difficult to oxidize and "soft" if they have low electronegativity and are easily oxidized. These properties relate to the presence or absence of vacant orbitals. Bases react with acids to form salts and water; when the proper proportions are used, neutralization occurs. All bases give solutions having a *p*H of more than 7.0, the neutral point.

The term alkali is closely related in meaning ; it refers to hydroxides and carbonates of the alkali metals (lithium, potassium, sodium, and others), which are strongly electropositive; typical alkalies are sodium hydroxide, and potassium carbonate, all widely used in industry. *See also* acid ; *p*H ; alkali.

base exchange. This process takes place when a solution is passed through a medium and the latter removes certain cations from the solution, replacing them with different ,but equivalent, ions furnished from the medium itself. Thus in one process for softening water, the water is passed through "permutit" (an artificial zeolite) which removes calcium and magnesium ions, replacing them with inocuous sodium ones. Many artificial resins are now manufactured for selective replacement in particular ions—either anions or cations.

base line method. Technique in quantitative spectrophotometric analysis. In order to set up reference point for absorption evaluation of the determined component and to eliminate base influence, supplementary line is drawn on absorption curve.

base metals. 1. In contradistinction to the noble metals, metals that corrode, tranish, or oxidize on exposure to air, moisture, or heat.

2. The principal metal of an alloy.

base pair. Two nucleotides that are in different nucleic acid chains and whose bases pair by hydrogen bonding.

basic dye. One of a group of dyes that form soluble salts with mineral acids and certain organic acids, and that form insoluble compounds with acidic fibres.

basicity. Characteristic feature of electrolytic solutions in which concentration of hydroxyl ions OH^- is greater than that of hydronium ions H_3O^+. Also known as alkalinity.

basicity of an acid. The number of replaceable hydrogen atoms contained in one molecule of the acid. Thus nitric acid (HNO_3) and acetic acid (CH_3COOH) are monobasic, each forming one sodium salt ; sulphuric acid (H_2SO_4) and oxalic acid $(COOH)_2$ are dibasic, each forming two different sodium salts. Orthophosphoric acid (H_3PO_4), is tribasic since it forms three different sodium orthophosphates.

basic salt. A salt whose molecule contains, beside the normal acid radical, one or more hydroxyl groups. Substance is often formed when a solution of the pure salt is evaporated to dryness. Thus pure cupric carbonate is said not to exist—commonly it has the formula $2CuCO_3.Cu(OH)_2$. The salt of weak acids are often hydrolyzed in this way.

basic solvent. *See* protophilic solvent.

Basileios test for iodate. To 10 ml. of the 5% solution to be tested, add 2 ml. chloroform, 1 ml. 0.001 N sodium thiosulphate, and 1 ml. N sulphuric acid. After standing for 1 minute, the solution is shaken. A blue colour in the chloroform layer indicates the presence of iodate.

Basileios test for iodide. Shake 10 ml. of the neutral solution to be tested about 20 times with 2 ml. 0.5% iodine solution in chloroform. Add 3 drops of 1% starch solution and turn the container 4-5 times. If iodide is present the aqueous layer turns blue. Bromate gives a violet colour. This test works well even in presence of bromate, chlorate, and iodate.

Bassett-Snyder reagent. A reagent prepared by mixing 3 parts glacial acetic acid, 4 parts nitric acid, and 16 parts water. It is used in metallography to etch lead and lead alloys.

batch process. Any industrial procedure in which raw materials are mixed in individual lots or batches. Many basic materials are made in this way, *e.g.*, soap, rubber, paper pulp, (fermented liquors, and confectionery and food products). Batching is particularly necessary when special aging and enzymatic reactions are involved which require long holding periods for maturation purposes. Continuous processing is chiefly used in making finished products from the original batch-prepared material, as in the manufacture of sheet metals, paper, glass etc.

batch rectification. Batch distillation in which the boiled off vapour is re-condensed into liquid form and refluxed back into the still to make contact with the rising vapours.

Bate equation. A relationship of the form :

$$\log_{10}\left(\frac{\Lambda\eta}{\Lambda_0\eta_0}\right)^2 \frac{C}{1-\dfrac{\Lambda\eta}{\Lambda_0\eta_0}} = k + k'\left(\frac{C\Lambda\eta}{\Lambda_0\eta_0}\right)$$

$\frac{\eta}{\eta_0}$ = ratio of viscosity of a solution to that of of water at the same temperature ; $\frac{\Lambda\eta}{\eta_0}$ = corrected equivalent conductance ; k, k' h, and Λ_0 are empirical constants; C is the concentration of the solution.

bathochrome. Atom or group of atoms which, when substituted into molecule or organic compound, shifts its absorption spectrum towards longer wavelengths.

bathochromic group. *See* bathochrome.

bathochromic shift. Shift of light absorption towards lower frequencies.

bathoflore. An atom or radical which by its substitution in a molecule tends to shift its fluorescent radiation band in the direction of longer wavelength.

bating. A unit process in leather manufacture in which the dehaired skins or hides are treated with enzyme-containing materials to provide desirable softness and flexibility (plumpness) prior to tanning. The most effective enzymes for this purpose are pancreatin and trypsin.

Battelli-Stern solution. A solution perpared by mixing a 1% potassium iodide solution with twice its volume of a 3% starch solution, and acidifying with acetic acid. It is oxidized, giving the characteristic blue colour of iodine-starch by peroxidases in animal tissue.

Baubigny test. A filter paper that has been treated with a solution of fluorescein in 40-50% acetic acid and then dried, becomes rose coloured when exposed to traces of bromine.

Baudisch reagent. A solution of cupferron, the ammonium salt of nitrosophenylhydroxylamine, used in testing for copper and iron.

Bauer test for milk. One drop of a 0.25% aqueous solution of Nile blue sulphate is added to 3 ml. of the milk. Cows' milk becomes green-blue, while human milk becomes violet. On shaking with ether, cows' milk changes to blue, and human milk becomes colourless.

Baumann benzoyl chloride reaction. When carbohydrates, diamines, and polyhydric alcohols in dilute aqueous solution are shaken with benzoyl chloride and sodium hydroxide, a precipitate of the benzoic acid esters forms.

Baumann test for iodide. Solutions of alkali iodides give a black precipitate with palladous chloride solution.

Baumann test for corn starch in wheat flour. One-tenth g. of the flour is shaken for 2 minutes with 10 ml. potassium hydroxide solution (1.8%); then 4-5 drops of 25% hydrochloric acid are added, and a microscopic examination is made. Corn starch is unchanged, but the wheat grains are completely swollen.

b-axis. A crystallographic axis that is oriented horizontally, right to left.

Bayer process. For the extraction of aluminium by electrolysis, pure aluminium oxide has to be obtained from natural bauxite. In the Bayer process, which is commonly used, the ground ore is heated with about 10% caustic soda solution for an hour or more. The ferric oxide impurity ("red mud") precipitates and is removed. The sodium aluminate formed is hydrolyzed by stirring with more water for two or three days and the solution is then "seeded" with fine crystals of aluminium hydroxide to encourage precipitation of the hydroxide from solution. The precipitate is removed and calcined to pure oxide (Al_2O_3).

Bayer test reaction for adrenaline. If 2 ml. adrenaline solution is mixed with 1 ml. sulphanilic acid solution, 2 ml. solution bi-iodate solution, and 1 ml. 10% phosphoric acid, various colours are obtained ranging from reddish yellow to yellow as concentration decreases.

Bayer test reaction for gold. A drop of rubidium chloride solution and a drop of 0·1% silver nitrate solution, upon addition to a drop of gold chloride solution, give blood-red microscopic crystals.

B band. In electronic spectrum of benzene derivatives and its homologues, band corresponding to π-π^* electronic transition and analogous to 254 mm band of benzene, *i.e.*, band of rather low intensity with well-developed vibrational structure.

B-B fraction. A mixture of butanes and butenes distilled from a solution of light liquid hydrocarbons.

B complex. A closely related but independently active group of growth-promoting substances (vitamins) produced by living cells ; each member of the complex is essential, and no member can be substituted for any other member. Their physiological effect is additive, throughout each is a distinct compound which has specific functions in metabolism. The complex may be thought of as a rope, each strand of which is represented by an individual and unique substance. The complex occurs in all the cells of all organisms, both plant and animal, and among its components are thiamine ; riboflavin, niacin, biotin, pyridoxine, folic acid, and cobalamin. *See also* vitamin.

beam hole. Space accessible from outside, which is close to, or inside core of nuclear reactor, and enables utilization of produced radiation for experimental purposes. Also known as reactor channel for experiments.

beam of radiation. Ionizing radiation (corpuscular or electromagnetic) propagating through space at a specified solid angle.

Beattie-Bridgeman equation of state. Thermal equation of state of real gas.

$$pV_m^2=RT\left[Vm+B_0\left(1-\frac{b}{Vm}\right)\right]\left(1-\frac{c}{VmT^3}\right)+A_0\left(1-\frac{a}{Vm}\right)$$

where p = pressure, V_m = molar gas volume, T= thermodynamic temperature, R=universal gas constant, A_0, B_0, a, b, c=constant characteristic for the given gas.

Bechamp reaction. A reaction for the preparation of aromatic arsonic acids by the interaction of arsenic acid with phenols, aromatic amines, or their derivatives, *e.g.*,

$$C_6H_5OH+H_3AsO_4 \rightarrow HO-C_6H_4-AsO(OH)_2(p)+H_2O$$

Bechamp reduction. Reduction of nitro compounds to amines with iron (or ferrious salt) and dilute acid, *e.g.*,

$$R-NO_2+2Fe+6HCl \rightarrow R-NH_2+2H_2O+2FeCl_3$$

Bechamp test for alkali sulphides. Alkali sulphides give a purple-red colour with a 0.4% aqueous solution of sodium nitroprusside. For greater sensitivity, add sodium hydroxide to the solution to be tested.

Bechamp test for nitrobenzene. The oil is distilled with ferric acetate and chlorinated lime solution is added to the distillate. A blue colour indicates the presence of nitrobenzene. The test is applicable for nitrobenzene even in presence of oil of bitter almond.

Bechi-Hehner solution. A solution of 1 g. silver nitrate in 250 ml. ethyl alcohol, with the addition of 50 ml. of diethyl ether and 0.1 ml. concentrated nitric acid. The reagent gives a dark red colour with oily mixtures if cottonseed oil is present.

Bechi solution. A solution of 1 g. silver nitrate in 100 ml. 98% ethyl alcohol ; used as a test reagent for cottonseed oil in olive oil. A dark colour, obtained on heating the sample with the reagent and additional alcohol, indicates the presence of cottonseed oil.

Beckmann mixture. An oxidizing reagent consisting of 60 parts potassium dichromate, 80 parts concentrated sulphuric acid, and 270 parts water.

Beckmann rearrangement. A rearrangement whereby ketoximes are converted into isomeric amides, usually effected by treatment with phosphorus pentachloride, but strong mineral acids may also be employed. The change occurs through entire rearrangement of the molecule : the hydroxyl group exchanges positions with the alkyl group in the *anti* position ; then the hydroxyl hydrogen shifts to the nitrogen atom so that the double bond formerly between the nitrogen and carbonyl carbon is now found between the latter and the hydroxyl oxygen. It is represented by the following steps :

$$\underset{\text{Ketoxime}}{\begin{matrix} R'-C-R \\ \| \\ HO-N \end{matrix}} \rightarrow \begin{matrix} R'-C-OH \\ \| \\ R-N \end{matrix} \rightarrow \begin{matrix} R'-C=O \\ | \\ NHR \end{matrix}$$

The reaction has proved to be useful in determining the constitution for *syn-anti* isomers, for, from the acid formed hydrolyzing the amide, one can determine the group *cis* to the oxime hydroxyl group.

Becquerel. *Bq.* Unit or nuclear activity giving one disintegration per second.

Becquerel rays. Radiations emitted by radioactive substances ; later renamed as alpha, beta and gamma rays.

Behrens reagent for aldehydes and ketones. An aqueous solution of *p*-nitrophenylhydrazine hydrochloride, clarified by the addition of a few drops of acetic acid, and used in the microscopic detection of aldehydes and ketones.

Beijerinck reagent. The substance isatin hydrochloride, used in testing for indican in plant cells.

Beilstein test. A simple procedure to detect the presence of halogen in an organic compound. The substance is heated in a Bunsen flame at the end of a piece of thick, clean copper wire. If halogen is present the formation of volatile copper halide colours the flame green. Pure copper oxide in the loop of a platinum wire may also be used instead of the copper wire. The test is not too good as some nitrogenous compounds may, under these conditions, produce cuprous cyanide, which also gives a green flame. If nitrogen first be proved absent, the test is useful.

Beissenhirtz test. Aniline, when dissolved in concentrated sulphuric acid, gives a transitory blue colour with 1-2 drops of 5% potassium dichromate solution.

Belgian process. When zinc is obtained from its sulphide ore (blende), after concentration by a flotation process the ore is roasted to form the oxide. The oxide is then reduced with carbon by heating in special retorts either of the Belgain or Silesian type (*see also* Silesian process). Belgain retorts are fireclay arranged horizontally and sloping downwards to their open end. Another smaller fireclay vessel is attached to the open end of each retort in which the zinc vapour condenses. Modern furnaces have something of both types and are known as Belgo-Silesian furnaces, though vertical retorts are steadily replacing the horizontal ones.

bell metal. An alloy of copper and tin containing 15-25% tin and 60-85% copper.

Bellier reagent for wheat. I. A solution of 5 g. pottasium hydroxide in 15 ml. glycerin and 85 ml. water.

II. A mixture of 100 ml. of (I) and 5 ml. glycerin.

III. A mixture of 1 part of (I) and 3 parts water. These reagents are used to differintiate starches from various sources by their swelling properties.

Benda solution. A mixture of 4 parts of 2% aqueous solution of osmic acid, 15 parts of 1% aqueous solution of chromic acid, and a small amount of glacial acetic acid; used as a fixative.

Bender process. Treatment of petroleum liquids

with lead sulphide catalyst to sweeten (to convert mercaptans io disulphides) by oxidation.

Bender's salt. Potassium ethyl thiocarbonate—prepared by passing carbonyl sulphide (COS) into alcoholic potash. Its formula is $C_2H_5O.CS.OK$ and on treatment with dilute hydrochloric acid, it evolves pure carbonyl sulphide.

bending vibration. Vibrations which lead to changes of valence angles.

Benedict acetate reagent. A solution prepared by saturating 20 ml. of a normal cobalt nitrate solution with hydrogen sulphide, and then adding about 25 drops of normal acetic acid. It is used to test for acetate.

Benedict-Hopkins-Cole reagent. Add 250 ml. saturated oxalic acid solution, slowly and with cooling, to 10 g. magnesium powder. Filter and acidify with acetic acid, and dilute to 1 litre. This reagent is used to test for tryptophane or proteins yielding it. The substance to be tested is mixed with the reagent, and a ring-test is performed with concentrated sulphuric acid. A red-violet ring indicates the presence of tryptophane.

Benedict's solution. This is used for the qualitative and quantitative estimation of glucose. It is preferred to Fehling's Solution by many chemist and doctors because the solution keeps better and needs only one solution. It contains the following in the correct weighed proportions; sodium citrate, sodium carbonate, potassium thiocyanate and copper sulphate, dissolved in distilled water. Its method of employment is similar to that used for Fehling's Solution. For quantitative work, the solution is prepared thus : 200 gm. sodium carbonate (cryst.), 200 gm. sonium citrate, and 125 gm. of potassium thiocyanate dissolved in about 800 ml. of hot water. To this is added a solution of cupric sulphate (18 gm. in 100 ml. of water) with constant shaking. Finally 5 ml. of a 5% solution of potassium ferrocyanide is added and the total volume made up to exactly one litre .25 ml. of Benedict's solution is equivalent to 0.05 gm. of glucose.

Benedict uric acid reagent. A solution of 1 g. of sodium tungstate and 3 g. arsenic pentoxide in 70 ml. water, which is then boiled with 5 ml. concentrated hydrochloric acid and made up to 100 ml. This reagent gives a blue colour with solutions containing uric acid, upon the addition of sodium carbonate solution.

benefication. A term used in extractive metallurgy to refer to methods of concentrating metallic ores preparatory to the reduction process ; they include mechanical classification fragmentatation, magnetic separation, flotation, etc.

Benfield process. A method of removing carbon dioxide and hydrogen sulphide from fuel-gases by absorbing them in potassium carbonate solution at about 120°C.

Benoist test for ozone. A test for ozone in air, in which a 0.0001% solution of fluorescein is shaken with the sample of air. If the dye losses its colour, ozone is present. More concentrated solution lose their fluorescence, but not their colour.

bent-bond. Chemical bond occuring in strained ring systems, when axes of bonding orbitals do not correlate with bond directions, *e.g.*, in cyclopropane. Also known as banana bond.

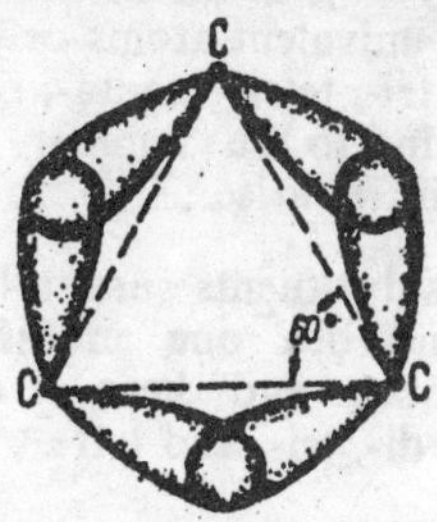

Fig. 11. Bent-bond

Bentzen test. A test for formaldehyde in paper in which the paper is boiled with fresh aniline-water is an apparatus designed to avoid direct contact with air. A turbidity indicates the presence for formaldehyde.

benz-, benzo-. Relating to benzene ; as benzoic; specifically, denoting presence of the benzene ring, as benzoquinoline.

benzene ring. Also called the benzene nucleus, the carbocyclic structure is one of the most important in organic chemistry. The full representation, with the symbols included is shown in (*a*) below, and the once widely used outline in (*b*) though the double bounds are often omitted. The six carbon atom may be numbered from the upper apex, as shown in (*c*) these numbers being used to designate the position of the carbon atoms or of the elements or groups attached to them. Thus, 2 is the ortho- (or *o*-) position, 3 is the meta (or *m*-) position, and 4 the para (or *p*-) position.

(*a*) (*b*) (*c*)

Benzene exhibits the phenomenon ef resonance, which is a mathematical way of stating that the position of the double bonds cannot be precisely pictured by any one diagram but rather is intermediate among a number of representations.

benzene, nomenclature of substitution products. All of the hydrogen atoms in benzene may be replaced by univalent atoms or groups forming mono-, di-, tri-, tetra-, penta-, or hexa-, derivatives according to the number of substituents. Two possibilities arise :

1. The substituents are all of one kind. Here we find but one modification of the mono-, penta-, and hexa-, derivatives and three of the di-, tri-, and tetra-, derivatives.

(*a*) The di-derivatives are named according to the relative positions which the substituents assume around the ring as ortho-, meta-, or para- ; ortho- where adjacent carbon atoms are involved, meta- when an unsubstituted carbon rests between the two substituted carbons, and para- if two unsubstituted carbon atoms occur between the substituted carbons. Diagrammatically :

o-dibromobenzene *m*-dibromobenzene

p-dibromobenzene

(*b*) The tri- derivatives are named adjacent (vicinal), unsymmetrical (asymmetrical), and symmetrical according as the groups take the positions (1.2,3) (1,2,4) or (1,3,5).

v-tribromolenzene *unsym*-tribromobenzene.

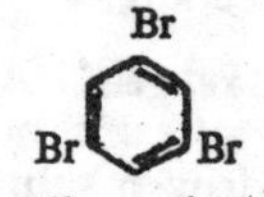

sym-tribromobenzene

(*c*) The tetra- derivatives are named adjacent, symmetrical, or unsymmetrical according as the positions assumed by the substituents are (1,2,3,4), (1,2,4,5) or (1,2,3,5).

adjacent-tetrabromobenzene *sym*-tetrabromobenzene

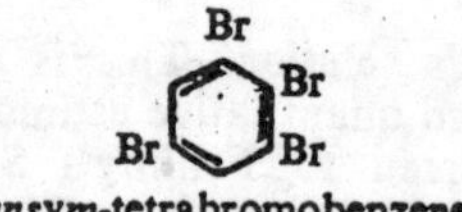

unsym-tetrabromobenzene

2. The substituents are of two or more kinds. Here the number of isomers is greatly multiplied ;

(*a*) The di-derivatives which contain two unlike substituents may be distinguished by the prefixes ortho-, meta-, and para-, as *o*-chloronitrobenzene, or the positions of the groups may be designated by number as 1,2-chloronitrobenzene.

(*b*) The system of numbering is usually followed in naming polysubstitution products of benzene, the compound being referred back to benzene or to another substance derived from benzene whose characteristic group is present. In this latter class the nunamed group is always regarded as assuming the 1 position, *i.e.*, 3,6-chloronitrobenzoic acid is represented,

3,6-chloronitrobenzoic

benzenoid. Having the structure of benzene, particularly the Kekule constitution, as distinguished from the "quinoid" from.

benzhydryl. The radical

$$\begin{array}{c} C_6H_5 \\ | \\ CH- \\ | \\ C_6H_5 \end{array}$$

Also known as benzohydryl.

Benzidine reaction. A test for blood (hemoglobin) made by acidifying the same with glacial acetic acid, extracting with ether, and treating the ethereal extract with a solution of benzidine in glacial acetic acid, to which hydrogen peroxide has been added. In the absence of certain metals, a blue or green colour, changing to deep blue or purple, indicates the presence of blood.

Benzidine rearrangement. Acid-catalyzed conversion of hydrazobenzene and its derivatives into benzidine (and its derivatives), *e.g.*,

$$C_6H_5-NH-NH-C_6H_5 \xrightarrow{H^{\oplus}} NH_2-C_6H_4-C_6H_4-NH_2$$

benzidino. The radical $p\text{-}H_2NC_6H_4C_6H_4NH-$ (from benzidine).

benzilic acid rearrangement. Base-catalyzed conversion of aromatic α-diketones into corresponding α-hydroxy acids, involving formation of carboxylic group and migration of one of aryl groups (with rearrangement-1,2), *e.g.*,

$$Ar-\underset{\underset{O}{\|}}{C}-\underset{\underset{O}{\|}}{C}-Ar' \overset{\overset{\ominus}{O}H}{\rightleftharpoons} HO-\underset{\underset{O^{\ominus}}{|}}{\overset{Ar}{C}}-\underset{\underset{O}{\|}}{C}-Ar' \xrightarrow{\text{slow}}$$

$$HO-\underset{\underset{O}{\|}}{C}-\underset{\underset{O^{\ominus}}{|}}{\overset{Ar}{C}}-Ar' \xrightarrow{H^{\oplus}} HO-\underset{\underset{O}{\|}}{C}-\underset{\underset{OH}{|}}{C}\begin{smallmatrix} Ar \\ Ar' \end{smallmatrix}$$

benzilidene. The radical $C_6H_4-CH=$; preferably benzylidene.

bedziloyl. The radical

$$(C_6H_5)_2C(OH)CO-.$$

benzimidazolyl. The radical $C_7H_5N_2-$ (from benzimidazole).

benzimido. The radical $C_6H_5C(=NH)-$.

benzo-. A combining term for the radical $C_6H_4=$; especially denoting the presence of the benzene ring.

benzofuryl. The radical C_8H_5O-.

benzohydryl. The radical $(C_6H_5)_2CH-$.

benzohydrylidene. The radical $(C_6H_5)_2C=$.

benzoin condensation. Specific reaction of aromatic or heterocyclic aldehydes, catalyzed by cyanide ions, resulting in formation of benzoins, *e.g.*,

$$2C_6H_5-\underset{\underset{H}{|}}{\overset{\overset{O}{\|}}{C}} \xrightarrow{CN^-} C_6H_5-\overset{\overset{O}{\|}}{C}-\overset{\overset{OH}{|}}{CH}-C_6H_5$$

benzopyranyl. The radical C_9H_7O-(2-*a*, etc.) (from benzopyran).

benzoxy. The radical C_6H_5COO-.

benzoyl. The radical C_6H_5CO-.

benzoylation. Substitution of hydrogen atom in molecule by benzoyl group C_6H_5CO-, *e.g.*,

$$C_6H_5COCl+(CH_3)_2NH \rightarrow C_6H_5CON(CH_3)_2+HCl$$

benzoylene. The radical $-C_6H_4CO-$.

benzyl. The radical $C_6H_5CH_2-$.

benzylation. Substitution of hydrogen atom in molecule by benzyl group $C_6H_5CH_2-$.

benzylidene. The radical $C_6H_5C\equiv$.

Berg reaction for aldehyde sugars. This reaction is based on the conversion of the aldose into a hydroxy acid by bromine water and then adding Berg reagent to produce an intense yellow colour.

Berg reagent. A solution of 4 drops of 60%

ferric chloride solution and 2 drops of concentrated hydrochloric acid in 100 ml. water.

Berg-Teitelbaum test for selenite. To 2 ml. of the solution. add 1 ml. 5% ferric chloride solution and dilute to 10 ml. with phosphoric acid ; then add a few drops of 1% solution of pyrrole in alcohol. A deep blue colour indicates the presence of selenite.

Bergius process. A method for making synthetic hydrocarbon oil by a hydrogenation process. Powdered coal, or creosote, is heated with hydrogen to a temperature between 400° and 500°C., in the presence of catalyst and under a pressure of 250 to 300 atmospheres. The product is fractionally distilled to give petrol and lubricating oils.

Bergmann azlactone peptide synthesis. A method of synthesizing peptones from amino acids and azlactones of acetylated amino acids :

$$C_6H_5CHO + \underset{|}{\overset{HNOCR}{}}CH_2{-}COOH \xrightarrow[\text{Anhydride}]{\text{Acetic}} C_6H_5CH{=}\underset{N}{C}{-}{-}\underset{O}{C}{=}O \quad (\text{ring: } N{-}C(R){-}O)$$

$$+\ NH_2CHR'{-}COOH \downarrow$$

$$C_6H_5CH_2\overset{NHOCR}{\overset{|}{CH}}{-}CONH{-}CHR'{-}COOH \xleftarrow{\text{Red.}} C_6H_5CH{=}\overset{NHOCR}{\overset{|}{C}}{-}CONH{-}CHR'{-}COOH$$

Bergmann degradation. A series of reactions for the mild degradation of polypeptides sidewise, so that the end amino acids can be determined The reactions include condensation with phenyl isocyanate, followed by treatment with diazomethane, hydrazine, nitrous acid, and benzyl alcohol, with a final combined reduction and hydrolysis.

Bergmann-Zervas carbobenzoxy method. A method of protection of the amino groups, during a peptide synthesis, by blocking them by carbobenzoxy groups, which are later to be removed by reduction ;

$$H_2N.CHR.COOCH_3+C_6H_5.CH_2.O.COCl \xrightarrow{HCl} C_6H_5CH_2.O.CO.NH.CHR.COOCH_3$$

berkelium. An element. Symbol Bk

State	Solid	Atomic No.	97
Group	Actinide Series	Atomic Wt.	243 (?)
		Valence	3,4
		m.p.	986°C

This element was discovered in 1949, at Berkeley, California, in the form of Bk^{243} as a product of the cyclotron bombardment of americium isotope 241 with helium ions ; it is eighth member of the actinide transition series, and is a radioactive transuranium element ; has been prepared and several compounds, chiefly oxides and halides of oxidation states 3 and 4, have been identified. Larger amount of Bk-249 isotopes have been made so that its properties can be investigated. The isotope is made by intense neutron bombardment of curium-244. There are as yet no known uses of berkelium.

Berthelot equation of state. Empirical (thermal) equation of state of real gas

$$\left(p+\frac{a}{V_m^2 T}\right)(V_m-b)=RT$$

where p = pressure, V_m = molar gas volume, T=thermodynamic temperature, R=universal gas constant ; a, b = constants characteristic for the given gas.

Berthelot-Michel test for α-and β-naphthol. A violet colour is produced when a 1% α-naphthol solution is added to the chloramine-*T* reagent (15 g. chloramine-*T* in 85 ml. water). A brownish-red colour is produced by the addition of β-naphthol on warming.

Berthelot-Nernst distribution law. Distribution of a micro- and macrocomponent between crystals and solution, for two substances forming mixed crystals at real thermodynamic equilibrium, is expressed by the equation :

$$\frac{x}{y} : \frac{a-x}{b-y} = D$$

where x, y = quantities of micro- and macrocomponent, respectively, which passed to crystalline phase, a, b=initial quantities of micro- and macrocomponent in system, D = crystallization coefficient. Also known as homogeneous distribution law.

Berthelot reagent for peroxide in ether. The substance lead ammonium iodide which is coloured yellow on contact with ether containing peroxide.

Berthelot test for carbon monoxide. Add ammonia drop by drop to an aqueous solution of silver nitrate. Continue until the precipitate formed just dissolves. A brown colour is formed with this reagent in the cold and a black precipitate on heating, if carbon monoxide is present.

Berthelot test for ethyl alcohol in methanol. If methanol is treated with twice its volume of concentrated sulphuric acid, methyl ether is formed. Ethyl alcohol forms ethylene under the same conditions ; this can be combined with bromine and determined.

Berthelot rule. A means for predicting whether a reaction will take place. The rule states that if one of the reaction products would leave the system under the given conditions, as by precipitation, evolution (gaseous), or other means then the reaction will take place.

Bertsch test. A test for vinyl alcohol in ether in which the ether is shaken with mercuric oxychloride. If a white precipitate forms, vinyl alcohol is present. Sodium hydroxide converts the precipitate into a black, explosive powder.

beryllate. The anion BeO_2^-, or a compound containing it.

beryllate (hydroxo-) The anion $Be(OH)_4^-$, or a compound containing it.

beryllium. An element.

State	Solid	Symbol	Be
Group	IIA	Atomic No.	4
		Atomic Wt.	9.0122
		Valence	+2
		m.p.	1280°C

Beryllium is a unique metal in many respects; it is lighter (sp. gr. 1.85) than aluminium, with a high ratio of strength to weight, and is extremely penetrable by *x*-rays. It is an excellent neutron reflector (better than graphite for slow neutrons), and it is a good source of neutrons, especially when mixed with radium. Hotpressed blocks of beryllium are used for aerospace instruments and inertial guidance equipment, as well as in nuclear reactors. The metal is obtained from the ore called beryl, $Be_3Al_2(SiO_3)_6$, by oxidation and chemical processing. In metallurgical applications, it is used as an alloying agent (with copper) in the manufacture as well as of springs and diaphragms. The metal and its compounds are quite toxic, especially in the form of powder, dust or fume.

beryllium bronze. A nickel-copper alloy containing small amount of beryllium.

beryllium copper. An alloy of copper and beryllium having less than 3% beryllium. Also known as beryllium bronze.

Bessemer process. A method of steel production using a special "converter". Molten iron from the blast furnace is poured into the converter when in a horizontal position (the converter being lined with a basic lining only if phosphorus is known to be present). A blast of air under a pressure of 20—25 lb. per square inch. is blown through the molten metal and the converter immediately swung into an upright position. The "blow" lasts for only about twenty minutes, the impurities being removed by rapid oxidation. Much heat is evolved simply from the oxidation of the carbon, sulphur, etc. This type of converter is used for other metals nowadays. Copper, for example, is often purified by a similar "bessemerization" process.

beta. (or β) (pronounced bay-ta). A term or symbol having several meanings analogous to those of alpha. Its most common chemical designation are :

(*i*) the position of a substituent atom or radical in a compound.

(*ii*) the second position in a naphthalene ring, or

(*iii*) the fact that a chemical unit is attached to the side-chain of an aromatic compound. Another meaning used by metallurgists, refers to an allotropic modification of a metallic or crystalline structure. The term is also used to denote a type of radioactive decay.

beta brass. A variety of brass containing almost equal proportions of copper and zinc.

beta decay. Radioactive decay in which an electron (β^--decay) or position (β^+-decay) is emitted and, respectively, an antineutrino $\bar{\nu}$ or a neutrino ν. Also known as beta disintegration.

beta factor. In plasma physics, the ratio of plasma kinetic pressure to the magnetic pressure.

beta globulin. A heterogenous fraction of serum globulins containing transferrin and various complement components.

beta iron. An allotropic (*see* allotropy) form of pure iron, stable between 768°C and 910°C, similar to alpha-iron except that it is non-magnetic.

beta particle. An electrically charged particle emitted by an atomic nucleus (for example, radium) during radioactive decay. If the particles are negatively charged, they are identical with electrons ; they may, however also be positively charged (positrons). They have moderate energy (upto 4 million electron volts) and can be damaging to human tissue ; effective shielding can be obtained with thin metal sheets. Collectively, such particles are often called beta rays or beta radiation.

beta particle absorption technique. Method of analysis based on measurement of attenuation of a beta particle stream in layer of material to be tested. It is used for determining composition of mixtures mainly for hydrogen content.

beta particle back scattering technique. Method of quantitative analysis in which use is made of the relation between intensity and energy of reflected β radiation, and atomic number of elements occuring in material to be examined.

betaines. Inner anhydrides of amino-acid derivatives containing a hydroxyl attached to the nitrogen atom which split out water with the carboxyl group, thus joining the nitrogen to the carboxyl carbon atom. They have the general constitution :

$$\begin{array}{l} H_2C—C{=}O \\ \quad | \qquad\ | \\ R_3N—O \end{array}$$

betatron. An electromagnetic device for accelerating electrons (beta particles). Its action is similar in principle to that of an electric transformer, in which the secondary windings are replaced with focusing magnets. The electrons travel around the core in a vacuum tube placed between the magnets. At each revolution around the core the electrons pick up the same energy as the voltage that would have been induced in one turn of wire at that point. The betatron can generate electrons beams upto 320 MeV.

Bet equation. Equation of the isotherm for multilayer adsorption of vapour :

$$\frac{p}{x(p_0-p)}=\frac{1}{x_mC}+\frac{C-1}{x_mC}\cdot\frac{p}{p_0}$$

where x=amount of gas adsorbed by unit mass of adsorbent, x_m=amount of gas necessary for formation of monomolecular layer at surface of unit mass of adsorbent, p=equilibrium pressure, p_0=saturated vapour pressure for pure adsorbate at temperature of isotherm, C=constant characteristic for given system and temperature. Also known as Brunauer, Emmett and Teller equation.

Bethe cycle. *See* carbon-nitrogen cycle.

Bethe-Salpeter equation. The relativistic analog of the integral form of the two-body Schrodinger equation, the two particle interaction kernel being the analog of the potential.

Bet isotherm. Adsorption isotherm corresponding to Bet (Brunauer, Emmett and Teller) equation the mlutilayer adsorption of vapours. Also known as Bet adsorption isotherm.

Bett test for manganese. A test for manganese in which the sample is heated with sodium carbonate paste and potassium chlorate. A green colour indicates the presence of manganese.

Bettel test for molybdenum. A test for molybdenum in which a slighty ammonical solution of molybdic acid is coloured red-brown by the addition of hydrogen peroxide.

Bettendorff-Winkler reagent. A solution of 1 g. stannous chloride in concentrated hydrochloric acid, adjusted with the water to a volume of 1 ml. and clarified by the addition of 1 g. of powdered glass. The reagent is used in testing for arsenic. A brown colouration on heating with a hydrochloric acid solution of the sample indicates the presence of arsenic.

Bettendorff's test. For arsenic in the pressence of antimony and bismuth compounds. If arsenious oxide is dissolved in hydrochloric acid and warmed with freshly made stannous chloride solution, a brown colour and precipitate of arsenic is formed.

Bett's process. A method of purifying lead by electrolysis. Impure lead is the anode, pure sheet lead the cathode, and the complicated electrolyte consists of an aqueous solution containing lead fluosilicate ($PbSiF_6$), hydrofluosilicic acid (H_2SiF_6), and gelatine. When the electric current is passed, lead passes from anode to cathode and silver and gold may be recovered from the anode slime.

Bey reagent A 5% etheral solution of resorcinol, which gives a blue ring with cadmium chloride solutions, and a blue colour with stannic tin solutions, under test conditions.

Bezssonov reagent. A solution of 30 g. sodium tungstate and 1 g. phosphomolybdic acid in 400 ml. water, 50 ml. 5 N sulphuric acid, and 2 ml. 85% phosphoric acid. It gives characteristic colour reactions with many polyphenols and with antiscorbutic extracts.

Bhabba scattering. The scattering of positrons by electrons.

bi-. A prefix either meaning "two," as in the words binary, bidentate, etc., or indicating the presence of hydrogen in the names of certain inorganic compounds such as sodium bicarbonate ($NaHCO_3$), sodium bisulphate ($NaHSO_4$), etc. In a few compounds name, it is interchangeable with di-, but the latter is preferred, *e.g.*, carbon disulphide, diphenyl, etc.

bi-amperometric titration. "Dead stop" or "dead stop end point" titration in which the two strictly identical electrodes, usually platinum, immersed in the titration cell a constant voltage (·0-500 mV) is applied and current passing through cell is measured as a titrant is added. Also known as amperometry with two polarized electrodes.

Bianchi-Nola test for nickel. A test for small amounts of nickel, an adaptation of the Tschugaev test, in which 1-2 drops of concentrated hydrochloric acid or nitric acid are added to the substance to be tested. This solution is transferred to a spot plate. It is made alkaline with ammonia, exposed to ammonia fumes, acidified with 1 drop of acetic acid, and a few drops of a saturated alcoholic solution of dimethylglyoxime added. A red colour is produced if nickel, is present.

biaxial crystal. A crystal of low symmetry in which the index ellipsoid has three unequal axes.

Bickel-French test reaction. A test reaction for alcohols in which they produce, with α-naphthylisocyanate, crystalline urethanes that can be identified by their melting points.

bicyclic. Having two rings, as of a compound, specifically designating certain bridged compounds, as bicycloheptane.

bidentate. The literal meaning of this term is "having two teeth"; it refers to a ligand, in a coordinatation compound, which is bound to metal atoms by two bonds. *See also* ligand; coordination compound.

bilayer. A double layer of oriented amphipathic lipid molecules; the hydrocarbon tail faces inward to form a continuous nonpolar phase.

bile. A complex organic liquid secreted by the liver of vertebrate animals and comprised chiefly of cholic acid and its derivates. It functions in the body as an emulsifying agent of ingested fats and is stored in the gall bladder. The bile acids are steroids having 24 or more atoms and one or more hydroxyl groups. Organic chemists have extracts important steroid complexes for research purposes from the bile of sharks, oxen, and reptiles.

bile salts. Amphipathic steroid derivatives with

detergent properties, participating in digestion and absorption of lipids.

Billiter process. For the production of caustic soda, this is one of several cells designed for the electrolysis of brine. Other process are the Castner-Solvay, Nelson, and Townsend. In the Billiter cell (German) the carbon anode is separated from the iron cathode by an asbestos diaphragm supported on ion gauze. The cathode and diaphragm lie horizontally.

Biltz-Mecklenburg test for zirconium. Add a few drops of sodium phosphate solution to a zirconium solution which has been strongly acidified with hydrochloric or nitric acid and warm. A white hydrogel, containing zirconium and phosphoric acid is formed.

Biltz reagent for carbonate. A 5% aqueous solution of mercuric chloride, used in judging the amount of carbonate present in sodium bicarbonate. A reddish-brown turbidity indicates more than 4% carbonate.

Biltz test for water. A test paper prepared by saturating filter paper with an acetone solution of potassium lead iodide, and then drying it. With water it gives a deep yellow colour.

Bimolecular reaction. Elementary unit reaction of molecularity equal to two.

binary. In reference to chemical compounds, term indicates a compound composed of two elements, of an element and a group (hydroxyl), methyl, etc.), or of two groups, *e.g.*, oxalic acid (two carboxyl groups). In reference to solutions, it refers to the presence of two phases or components, as in alloys, glass, etc.

binary alloy. An alloy composed of two principal metallic components.

binary compound. *See* compound, binary.

binary eutectic. Eutectic composed of two constituents.

binary separation. Separation by distllation or solvent extraction of a fully miscible liquid mixture of two chemical compounds.

binary system. System composed of two independent constituents. Also known as two-component system.

binder. In genernal, any soft, sticky substance used to hold together such dry solids as for example, propellants, nonwoven fabrics, and other composites. Specifically, in paint technology, the resin or drying oil that acts as the film-forming component of the paint ; acrylic latexes and linseed oil are examples of commonly used paint binders.

binder test. A test for nitrate in water, in which a pinch of zinc dust is shaken with water, a few drops of dilute sulphuric acid added to it and shaken again followed by the addition of potassium iodido-starch. A blue colour indicates the presence of nitrate or nitrite.

Binder-Weinland reagent for oxygen. An aqueous solution of ferrous ammonium sulphate (free from ferric salts) and pyrocatechol, alkalinized with sodium hydroxide. It gives a red colour with free oxygen.

binding energy. The energy that holds the protons together in an atomic nucleus. Since protons are positively charged, they exert strong mutually repellet forces, and tremendous energy is required to keep them from moving apart. This energy is so great that it results in a slightly low value for the mass of nucleus taken as a whole then for the sum of its constituents taken individually. The phenomenon is of vast significance, for it means that a small fraction of mass has been converted into energy within the nucleus, as shown by Einstein's equivalence equation $E=mc^2$. Thus, when a uranium nucleous (92 protons) is split in the fission process, a proton of its binding energy (equivalent to the mass difference) is released ; it amounts to about 200 million electron volts per nucleus. *See also* mass defect ; fission ; energy.

bio-. A prefix indicating life or the presence and activity of living organisms, as in biochemistry, biodegradable, bioluminescence, etc. It is also appears in words in other sciences as well as in literature (biology, biography).

bioassay. Determination of the potency af activity of drugs of derivatively, the amount of active ingredient they contain, by observing their effect upon animals. Also known as biological assay.

biocatalyst. Organic substance, usually of complicated structure which acts catalytically on chemical reactions proceeding in living organisms, *e.g.*, enzymes, hormone, vitamin.

biochemical fuel cell. A fuel cell in which small amounts of electric power can be produced continuously for a long time by some form of biological system.

biochemical oxygen demand. BOD. It is the amount, in milligrams per litre, of dissolved oxygen required by aerobic bacteria to decompose organic matter in water solution. The BOD is determined by adding oxygen-saturated water to sample of the contaminated water and and then measuring the dissolved oxygen in the mixture at once and again after several days. The BOD value is thus an index of the contamination of the water. It is an important consideration in sewage treatment, in which proper aeration of the organic material is essential.

biochemistry. The science devoted to the chemistry of living organisms, including plants, bacteria, animals, and man. Within its scope are all the elements and compounds necessary for nutrition and metabolic functions in the organisms ; activating substances, such as enzymes, vitamins, hormones, etc. ; infectious bacteria and viruses and the medicines used to combat them ; the chemistry of immunity ; the nature of the cell and its nucleus, including genes and chromosomes ; and the complex reaction cycles which maintain the chemical balance of the organism. It includes certain aspects of both inorganic and organic chemistry, as well as of colloid and physical chemistry.

biochemorphology. The science dealing with the chemical structure of foods and drugs and their reactions and living organisms.

biochrome. Any naturally occurring plant or animal pigment.

biocide. General name for any substance that kills or inhibits the growth of microorganisms, such as bacteria, molds, slimes, fungi, etc. Many of them are also toxic to humans. Biocidal chemicals included chlorinated hydrocarbons, organometallics, halogen-releasing compounds, metallic salts, organic sulphur compounds, quaternary ammonium compounds, and phenolics. *See also* antiseptic, disinfectant, fungicide.

biocolloid. A general term including all biochemically active aggregates in the colloidal size range, such as protein macromolecules, nucleic acid complexes, and various coenzymes, bacteria, and viruses.

biodegradability. The susceptibility of an organic material to decomposition as a result of attack by microogranisms. The term is applied especially to detergents and insecticides, which vary widely in this respect. For ecological reasons, a high degree of biodegradation is desirable to minimize the advese environmental effect of such materials. Sewage is highly biodegradable, and present methods of treatment are based on this property. Phosphate compounds and chlorinated hydrocarbons such as DDT are not biodegradable, and its largely for this reason that their use is restricted. Biodegradable plastic containers have been developed to get rid of the solid waste problem.

biogas. Methane derived from animal manures. Large-scale production is under way in several countries including India and China. *See also* biomass.

biological assay. *See* bioassay.

biological oxidation. Oxidation of chemical compounds caused by enzymes, which act as electron or hydrogen atom carriers.

biological shield. Layer of material of suitable absorption characteristics and thickness, placed between source of ionizing radiation and operator, securing attenuation of radiation to admissible level.

biological value. A measurement of the efficiency of the protein content in a food for the maintenance and growth of the body tissues of an individual.

bioluminescence. Chemiluminescence accompanying certain chemical reactions of living organisms.

biological oxygen demand. *See* biochemical oxygen demand.

biomass. Plant growth in all its forms, from algae and terrestrial vegetation to agricultural products and their residues, garbage, and metabolic wastes (manures). Biomass is becoming a renewable energy source of increasing importance. Its most important component is wood, body by direct combustion and by chemical or bacterial conversion to alcohols and other liquid fuels.

biomaterial. Any of the various materials, used either within the body or as a prosthetic device in contact with external tissue under the supervision of a surgeon of dentist. Such materials must meet standards of tissue compatibility, resistance to degradation, toxicity, and functional dependability. Among the materials used are titanium, tantalum, cellulose, graphite, and reprocessed animal bone ; alloys (amalgams, stainless steel) ; many kinds of plastics, including nylon ; ceramics, composites, and elastomers of various kinds.

biosynthesis. Synthesis of organic compounds, *e.g.*, alkaloids, proteins, antibiotics, terpenes, steroids, effected by living organisms.

biphenylene. The radical $-C_6H_4-C_6H_4-$.

biphenylenedisazo. The radical

$$-N{:}NC_6H_4-C_6H_4N{:}N-.$$

biphenylyl. The radical (2-, 3-, or 4-) $C_6H_5-C_6H_4-$ (from biphenyl).

biphenylylcarbonyl. The radical

$$C_6H_5-C_6H_4CO-.$$

biphenylyloxy. The radical $C_6H_5-C_6H_4O-$.

biradicals. Free radicals possessing unpaired electrons at each of two different atoms, *e.g.*, propene biradical CH_3CH-CH_2, oxygen biradical $\cdot\ddot{O}-\ddot{O}\cdot$ Also known as diradicals.

Birch reduction. Hydrogenation of arenes with metallic sodium and alcohol in liquid ammonia, *e.g.*,

birefringent. A term used in crystal optics to describe a type of crystal which has the property of resolving the divergent components of a light ray into two beams that are at right angles to each other. These perpendicular beams separate as they emerge from the crystal, so two images appear, each of which is the result of a light ray that vibrates in only one direction. This is called plane-polarized light ; crystals having the property, such as Iceland spar (a form of calcite), are used in Nicol prisms.

Birkelland-Eyde process. A process for the "fixation" of atmospheric nitrogen that has now been superseded by the Haber process. Air, often enriched with oxygen, is passed over electric arcs spread out by magnets. A little nitric oxide is formed at such high temperatures by combination of nitrogen with oxygen. On passing away from the arcs and cooling, the nitric oxide combines with more oxygen to give nitrogen dioxide from which nitric acid nitrates can be readily obtained.

bis-. A prefix used in the names of certain organic compounds to indicate that a particular group occurs twice. For example, in bisphenol, $(CH_3)_2C(C_6H_4OH)_2$ the "bis" refers to the phenolic group $-C_6H_4OH$, as the name indicates, though two methyl groups are also present. The prefixes di- and bi- have a similar meaning, as in dibutylamine $(C_4H_9)_2NH$ and biphenyl $(C_6H_5)_2$ but the these are not interchangeable. It may be noted that in the element bismuth, the first syllable is not a prefix, but an integral part of word.

Bischler-Napieralski reaction. Preparation of 3,4-dihydroisoquinoline from acyl derivatives of β-phenylethylamine under action of dehydrating agents, *e.g.*,

bismuth. An element. Symbol Bi

State Solid		Atomic Wt.	208.9806
Group VA		Atomic No.	83
		Valence	+3, 5
		m.p.	271°C

Bismuth, is a hard, brittle metal whose crystals have a pronounced rhombohedral structure ; it has only one stable form and has unusual properties. It expands 3.3% when it solidfies, and it is strongly repelled by magnetic fields, assuming a position at right angles to the lines of magnetic force. It readily forms compounas with halogens, oxygen, nitrogen, and sulphur.

The most important uses of bismuth are :

(*i*) as a component of a number of low melting (fusible) alloys used in fire protection equipment, metal joining, heat-transfer media, etc. ; (*ii*) in pharmaceutical and medicinal products for stomach trouble and treatment of syphilis ; (*iii*) in electrical equipment (thermoelectric alloys and permanent magnets) ; and (*iv*) as a catalyst, especially in the manufacture of acrylonitrile.

An unusual aspect of bismuth is the existence of five naturally radioactive isotopes, at least one of which is involved in the actinium decay series. Though it is not normally considered a radioactive element, it is next above lead in the periodic table and thus is not completely stable.

bittern. The mother-liquor remaining after the crystallization of common salt, NaCl, from seawater ; source of compounds of magnesium, bromine, and iodine.

bitter pattern. A pattern produced when a drop of a colloidal suspension of ferromagnetic particles is placed on the surface of the ferromagnetic crystal, the particles collect along domain boundaries at the surface.

biuret test. When urea is heated to a temperature just above in melting-point, two molecules of urea condense, with the loss of a molecule of ammonia, to form a compound called "biuret". If this residue is dissolved in dilute caustic soda solution, the addition of a dilute copper sulphate solution produces a violet colouration. This colour reaction does not give a specific test for biuret, as many protein substances behave in the same way.

bivariant phase system. System with two thermodynamic degrees of freedom. Also known as bivariant system.

Bjerrum association theory of ions. Theory which predicts formation of pair from ions of opposite charges if distance separating them l is :

$$a \lessgtr l \leqslant \frac{|z_i z_j|\, e^2}{2\varepsilon kT}$$

Life-time of this pair as a result of coulombic interactions is sufficiently long to consider it as unit resistant against thermic motions in solution ; a=effective ionic diameter, while other symbols have their usual meanings.

Bjerrum theory of acids and bases. Attempt at combination of Bronsted and Lewis theories of acids and bases ; Bjerrum defined acid as a substance having tendency to lose protons, antibase—with tendency to attach electron pairs, and base as a species having tendency to add on protons or to lose electron pairs to form bond.

black acids. Sulphonates in the sludge formed during treatment of peteroleum products with sulphuric acid ; soluble in water but insoluble in naphtha, benzene, and carbon tetrachloride.

black ash. A carbon product made by furnace heating of black liquor from paper making processes.

black body. Body which absorbs completely all incident radiation falling upon it, no matter what the wavelength of radiation and temperature is.

black copper. The impure copper (70—99%) produced in the blast furnaces when running on oxide ores or roasted sulphide material.

black lead. Plumbago, graphite. Natural crystalline form of carbon. A soft grey-black solid ; used for making vessels to resist high temperatures, in pencils, and as a lubricant.

black light. Invisible light, such as ultraviolet rays which fall on fluorescent materials, and cause them to emit visible light.

Blaise ketone synthesis. A method of forming ketones from organic zinc derivatives and acid halides, *e.g.*,

$$R'ZnCl + R''COCl \rightarrow R'COR'' + ZnCl_2$$

See also Blasie-Maire reaction.

Blaise-Maire reaction. A method of forming β-hydroxy ketones, or α, β unsaturated ketones, from organic zinc derivatives and α-acetoxy and halides, *e.g.*,

$$R'ZnCl + R'\overset{OCH_3}{\overset{|}{C}}HCH_2-COCl \xrightarrow{-ZnCl_2} R'\overset{OCH_3}{\overset{|}{C}}HCH_2COR' \xrightarrow{NaOH} R'CHOH-CH_2COR' + CH_3ONa$$

$$\downarrow -H_2O$$

$$R'CH=CHCOR'$$

See also Blaise ketone synthesis.

Blaise reaction. A method of formation of β-ketoesters from α-bromoesters and nitriles :

$$R'R''CBrCOOR''' + R'''CN + Zn \rightarrow R'R''\overset{R'''C=NZnBr}{\overset{|}{C}}-COOR'''$$

$$H_2O \downarrow$$

$$R'R''\overset{R'''C=O}{\overset{|}{C}}-COOR'' + NH_3 + ZnBrOH$$

blackstrap. A term used in sugar technology to refer to the molasses which remains after all the economically recoverable sugar has been removed from cane or beet syrup. It can be used as a source of alcohol and other fermentation products and as an animal feed base. *See also* molasses.

Blagden's law. When a solute is dissolved in a solvent, the lowering of the freezing-point of the solvent is proportional to the concentration of the solution. The interesting observation was largely overlooked for about a hundred years until the time of Raoult.

Blanc chloromethylation reaction. A method of formation of chloromethyl compounds by the action upon aromatic hydrocarbons of formaldehyde and hydrochloric acid, in the presence of zinc chloride.

$$C_6H_6 + HCHO + HCl \xrightarrow[-H_2O]{ZnCl_2} C_6H_5CH_2Cl$$

blanching. A term used in the food industry to describe the mild heating of fruits and vegetable at 93-100°C primarily to inactivate enzymes that would cause deterioration or loss of flavour. This process usually precedes canning, dehydration, freezing, and other preservation methods. Notwithstanding the name, it has little effect on colour.

Blanc reaction. The method of formation of cyclic ketones by heating anydrides of dicarboxylic acids. The reacton yields ketones when adipic acid (6 carbon atoms) and pinelic acid (7 carbon atoms) are heated with acetic anhydride, as expressed in Blane's rule. On the other hand, succinic acid (4 carbon atoms) and glutaric acid (5 carbon acids) yield cyclic anhydrides ; *e.g.*,

$$C_4H_8(COOH)_2 \xrightarrow{(CH_3CO)_2O} C_4H_8C{=}O + CO_2 + H_2O$$

Blanc rule. Conversion of dicarboxylic acid into cyclic ketone (upon heating with acetic anhydride) proceeds with good yield when resulting ketone is 5- or 6-membered.

The acids containing six or more carbon atoms are stated to yield chiefly ketones, and those with less than six carbon atoms yield the corresponding anhydrides.

Blanchetiere reagent for sodium. Two solutions:

(*i*) a solution of 100 g. uranium acetate acid in water enough to make 1 litre ; and

(*ii*) a solution of 333 g. magnesium acetate and 60 ml. glacial and in water enough to make 1 litre. Equal volumes of the two solutions are mixed to form the reagent, which is used as a precipitate for sodium.

blank. Test carried out under specified conditions with all reagents with exception of determined substance to account for content of this substance in reagents used. Also known as blank test; blank determination.

blank determination. *See* blank.

Blank test. *See* blank.

blast furnace. An apparatus for the reduction of iron ore. It consists of a tall cylindrical chamber with a charging device at the top through which quantities of coal and coke, lime and iron oxide are admitted; near the bottom is a ring of tubes, called tuyeres, through which hot air is blown into the furnace; below is the hearth with lateral openings for drawing off the slag and the molten iron separately. The ore is brought to a white heat, the top of the furnace and as it descends is reduced to molten metal when much of the phosphorus, sulphur, and silicon originally in the ore combines with the lime to form the slag. Blast furnaces are now fitted with checker-work chambers of brick which are heated by the waste gases from the furnaces and serve to preheat to air for the tuyeres. The product of the blast furnace is known as pig iron.

Blau test for ferrous ion. The formation of deep-red compounds with *o*-phenanthroline relatively stable to acids and ammonium sulphide, indicates the presence of the ferrous ion.

bleach. To remove or decolourize impurities occurring in numerous materials, including textiles, paper pulp, vegetable and mineral oils, as well as such earth products as barytes and clays in order to achieve whiteness. Bleaching usually involves a chemical reaction such as oxidation or reduction.

(*i*) Oxidation, by far the more important and more generally employed, consists in decolourizing the colouring matter with moist chlorine, hydrogen peroxide, chlorine dioxide, or other oxidizer.

(*ii*) Reduction consists of converting the colour into a colourless compound, as by the use of moist sulphur dioxide of other reducing agent. Oils may be treated with special clays of high adsorptive power to achieve the same purpose. Similar exposure to air and sunlight has a similar effect over a long time period.

bleaching agent *See* bleach.

bleaching assistant. A material added to textile bleach baths to cause better penetration by bleach; includes pine oils, borax, and sulphonated oils.

bleaching clay. Absorbed clay contacted with petroleum, vegetable, and other oils to obtain decolourized products.

blending. In general, the elimination of discontinuities in form and structure, or differences in appearance. Blending materials means mixing them to form a homogenous mass. Blending colours means modifying their hues or shades so that their over-all pattern shows no sharp changes in hue or intensity.

blending agent. A term applied in the petereoleum industry or hydrocarbons, commonly those produced by polymerization, alkylation, and other processes, which have a high antiknock rating and which are mixed with gasoline to improve this property.

block. Portion of polymer macromolecule comprising many constitutional or configurational feature not present in adjacent multiple-unit portions.

block brazing. The process of joining metals by applying heated blocks to the joint and using a nonferrous filler metal with a melting point above 427°C.

blocking group. 1. *See* protecting group.

2. *See* steric hindrance.

block polymer. A combination long-chain macromolecule comprised of any given polymer and either another polymer of different chemical nature, or a so-called coupling group of relatively low molecular weight.

AAAAA—BBBBB—AAAAA—

A stereoblock polymer is a chain comprised of only one chemical entity (*e.g.*, polypropylene) in which orderly and random molecular configurations occur in alternate sequence. The properties of block and stereoblock polymers are notably modified by their structure and composition; indeed, the segments may have very different properties, resulting in a material which can have more than one form (that is, hard and soft) depending on the solubility properties of its components.

block polymerization. Process in which one or more monomers and a polymer are cenverted together into block polymer.

Term block copolymerization has been reserved for case of block polymerization with two or more participant monomers.

blood (human). Considered to be liquid tissue. blood is a heterogenous suspension containing the followings :

(*i*) Red cells, or erythrocytes, which contain hemoglobin, an iron-protein complex ; they are not actually living cells, but rather are aggregates of hemoglobin, liquids, and water.

(*ii*) White cells, or leucocytes, which are true biological cells ; they contain nucleoproteins and liquids and function as a protective mechanism against infections.

(*iii*) Platelets, made up of cephalin and other proteins, which play a part in blood clotting. Besides these major components, blood contains many proteins, sugars, cholesterol, fatty acids, and in organic substances in ionized form. Blood acts in the body as a transport agent for nutrients and for oxygen and carbon dioxide. It is strongly buffered system and maintains a *p*H of from 7.3 to 7.5. The coagulation mechanism involves the protein fibrinogen ; serum is the fraction remaing after coagulation.

blood groups. Four different types of blood possess different clotting agents. These clotting agents can be labelled *a* and *b* and the blood can contain one agent or both or neither. Blood group *A* contains agent *a* and this type of blood is immediately clotted by agent *b*. Blood group *B* contain agent *b*, and is immediately clotted by agent *a*. Blood group *AB* contains agent *a* as well as *b* and is not clotted by adding either agent. Blood group *O* contains neither clotting agent *a* nor *b* and is clotted by both *a* and *b*. Hence blood group *AB* is the universal acceptor and blood group *O* is the universal donor.

Blomstrand test. The cyanate ion is detected by a blue colour or crystals produced by reaction of (potassium) cyanate solution with cobaltous acetate solution.

bloom. 1. A fluorscence which characterizes certain organic compounds. Many petroleum distillates, especially of paraffin base petroleum have a pronounced bloom. This term is also applied to a bluish cast which occasionally forms on the surfaces of dried lacquer or paint films.

2. Migration of one or more ingredients to the surface of a finished products. The term is used partieularly in the rubber industry to refer to uncombined sulphur which appears on the surface of a vulcanized article after long standing, or to waxes added to protect the product from degradation due to sunlight.

3. Name of a scale used to determine the viscosity of gelatin.

4. Any sudden increase in the population of marine piant such as algae.

blowing agent. A compound, suitable for incorporation in plastics, rubber, or food products, which will evolve an inert gas (carbon dioxide or nitrogen), usually at high temperature ; those used in foamed-in-place plastics react at room temperature. Sodium bicarbonate is a typical blowing agent, as it may be used to make sponge rubber, cellular plastics, and bread and other baked products, all of which are dispersions of a gas in a solid. Sodium bicarbonate and similar compound give off carbon dioxide at a temperature just below that at which the blown material "sets up," and and the globules of gas are thus permanently entrapped within the solid, forming a stable foam. *See also* foam ; baking powder.

blown oil. A vegetable of mineral oil through which air is passed at moderately high temperature. Such vegetable oils as linseed, soyabean and castor are thickened by this treatment, as a result of oxidation and partial polymerization, to become suitable for the modification of lubricants, paints, plasticizers, and the like. The most widely used blown mineral oil is an air-treated bituminous residue, the product being known as blown asphalt, or mineral rubber, it is a hard, brittle solid used as a dilutant in low quality rubber goods, as an impregnant for burlap and other coarse fabrics, and in hot-melt coatings. *See also* castor oil ; linseed oil.

blue gas. A gas consisting chiefly of carbon monoxide and hydrogen, formed by the action of steam upon hot coke ; used mainly as a source of hydrogen and in synthesis of other chemical compounds. Also known as blue water gas.

Blum reagent. A mixture of :

(*a*) a solution of 0.05 g. manganous chloride in dilute hydrochloric acid ; and

(*b*) a solution of 3 g. lead peroxide in 10 g.

metaphosphoric acid and 95 ml. water. It is used in testing for albumin.

Blum test for ferrous ion. Add a crystal of potassium nitrate and a excess of concentrated sulphuric acid to the soultion to be tested. The appearance of red streaks about the crystal indicates the presence of ferrous ion, even if ferric ions are present.

blunt test. Silver is detected in lead by dissolving the material in nitric acid, and adding a little saturated aqueous solution of lead chloride. A turbidity is given by silver.

blush. Condensation of atmospheric moisture on a freshly painted surface as a result of too rapid evaporation of solvent from the paint; the rapid evaporation causes a lowering of the temperature of the air near the surface, which precipitates water vapour and gives an unsightly appearance. It can be avoided by using a less volatile solvent and by applying the paint under condition of minimum humidity.

B_{A1}1 mechanism. Mechanism of monomolecular hydrolysis of esters in basic medium involving cleavage of alkyl-oxygen bond. Two reaction steps are postulated; cleavage of alkyl-oxygen bond with formation of carbonium ion and acid anion, and reaction of the former with OH^- ion, *e.g.*,

$$R{-}\overset{\overset{O}{\|}}{C}{-}O{-}R' \rightarrow R\overset{\overset{O}{\|}}{C}{-}O^- + R'^+$$

$$R^+ + OH^- \rightarrow ROH$$

B_{AC}2 mechanism. Mechanism of bimolecular hydrolysis reaction of esters in basic medium, involving cleavage of acyl-oxygen bond. The following reaction steps are postulated: addition of OH^- ion to carbonyl carbon atom of ester, cleavage of acyl-oxygen bond with formation of acid and alcoholate ion, proton exchange between acid and alcoholate ion, *e.g.*,

$$HO^- + \underset{\underset{R}{|}}{\overset{\overset{O}{\|}}{C}}{-}OR' \xrightarrow{\text{slow}} \left| HO{-}\underset{\underset{R}{|}}{\overset{\overset{O^-}{|}}{C}}{-}OR' \right| \xrightarrow{\text{fast}}$$

$$HO{-}\underset{\underset{R}{|}}{\overset{\overset{O}{\|}}{C^+}} + R'O^- \rightarrow RCOO^- + R'OH$$

B-meson. An elementary particle with strong nuclear interactions; baryon number B=0, and mass=1237 MeV.

boat form. Labile (flexibie) conformation in saturated six-membered carbocyclic and heterocyclic compounds, *e.g.*, cyclohexane. In this conformation carbon bond angles maintain value of 109.5°; however, C—C bond system at two pairs of adjacent carbon atoms is ecliptic and repulsion between substituents is observed at 1,4-flag-pole position.

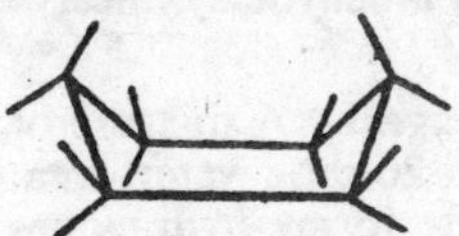

Fig. 12. Boat form

Bobierre test. A test for lead in tin in which a drop of glacial acetic acid is placed on the metal, which is then heated, and a drop of potassium iodide solution is added to it. A yellow colour indicates the presence of lead.

Bochichio test. A test for salicyclic acid in milk in which 5 drops of 10% sodium nitrite solution and 5 drops of 10% cupric sulphate solution are added to a mixture of 5 ml each of milk and distilled water, followed by heating on the water bath until the casein separates. A red colour in the supernatant liquid shows the presence of salicyclic acid.

BOD. *See* biochemical oxygen demand.

Bodde test. To distinguish resorcinol in solution from certain other phenolic compounds add solution of hypochlorite solution. A violet colour, changing to yellow, and becoming brown on warming is given by rosorcinol.

Bodeker test. A mixture of zinc sulphate solution with a little sodium nitroprusside solution gives a red to dark-red colour in a neutral solution of a sulphite which has been neutralized with acetic acid or sodium bicarbonate. The sensitivity is increased by addition of potassium ferrocyanide solution.

bodied oil. A vegetable oil, such as linseed, whose viscosity has been increased considerably by heating.

Bodroux-Chichibabin aldehyde synthesis. Preparation of aldehydes by treating ethyl orthoformate with Grignard reagent, *e.g.*,

$$RMgX + HC(OC_2H_5)_3 \rightarrow RHC(OC_2H_5)_2 + XMgC_2H_5$$

$$RHC(OC_2H_5)_2 \xrightarrow[H_2O]{H^+} RCHO + 2C_2H_5OH$$

Also known as Bodroux-Chichibabin synthesis.

Bodroux-Chichibabin synthesis. *See* Bodroux-Chichibabin aldehyde synthesis.

Boeseken reagent. A mixture of 2 mg. phenylhydrazine in 20 ml. water, treated is complete. This reagent forms hydrazones with carbonyl compounds.

Bogert-Cook synthesis. By the action of sulphuric acid, derivatives of 1-β-phenethyl-cyclohexanol yield octahydrophenanthrene derivatives, *e.g.*,

$CH_2—CH_2$ OH →

$+ H_2O.$

In the course of this reaction, initial dehydration sometimes occurs; the cyclization of the resulting unsaturated compounds or similar substances is called Bogert synthesis.

Bogert synthesis. *See* Bogert-Cook synthesis.

Bohn-Schmidt reaction. A method of introducing hydroxyl groups, or addition hydroxyl groups, into anthraquinones by the action of sulphuric acid (or fuming sulphuric acid) and boric acid. Mercury is generally used as catalyst.

O OH

$\xrightarrow[H_2SO_4]{H_3BO_4}$

O

HO O HO

HO HO O HO

Bohr magneton. μ_B (β). Unit of atomic electronic) magnetic moment; $1\ \mu_B = 9.273.10^{-24}\ Am^2$.

Bohr orbit. Circular or elliptic orbit around nucleus. In old quantum theory this was considered as electron path in atoms.

Bohr postulates. Postulates of old quantum theory. They refer to existence of stationary states of electrons in atoms and to transitions between these states.

Bohr radius. a_0. Radius of lowest energy. Bohr orbit of hydrogen atom (1*s*). For hydrogen atom in 1*s* states distance of maximum electron density is

$$a_0 = \frac{h^2}{4\pi me^2} = 0.529167 \times 10^{-10} m$$

where m=electron mass, e=elementary charge, h=Planck constant.

Bohr-Sommerfeld theory. A modification of the Bohr's theory in which elliptical as well as circular orbits are allowed.

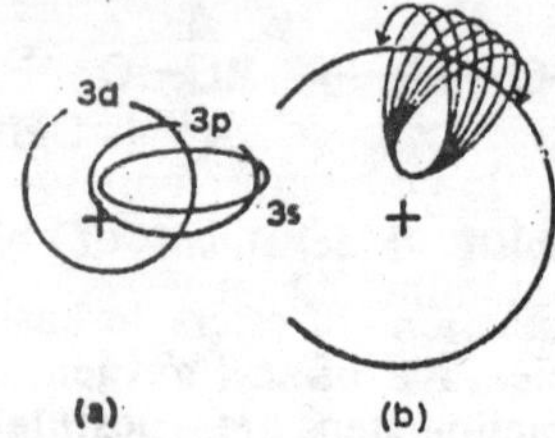

Fig. 13. Bohr-Sommerfeld theory

Bohr theory. The electrons surrounding the nucleus of an atom move in closed orbits about the nucleus; more than one such stable orbit, or energy level, is possible tor a given elcctron; in fact, the number of such orbit is determined by the condition that the angular monentum of the electron be an integral multiple of $h/2\pi$ (where h is Planck's constant); emission of radiation result when an electron moves suddenly ftom one orbit to another in which it has less energy; and, conversely, adsorption of radiation is attended by a jump of an electron from a lower energy level to a higher.

Since there are numerous energy levels in each atom, there can be various transitions, and hence numerous spectral lines are possible.

Bohr-Wheeler theory of fission. An analytical theory of the nature of nuclear fission and the conditions under which it might occur, based upon a liquid-drop analogy. One conclusion was that if the ratio Z^2/A exceeded 45, no additional energy would be necessary to cause fission to take place. (Z=atomic number; A=mass number.) An element having a Z^2/A ratio of 45 would have an atomic number of 120, thus according to this theory the elements of higher atomic number are not stable.

boiled oil. A vegetable oil such as linseed that has been heated with catalysts until it has become partly oxidized. It is used in paint manufacture because it dries more rapidly and uniformly than linseed oil which has not been treated in this way.

boiler scale. An extremely hard incrustation of calcium and/or magnesium compounds formed on the inner surfaces of boilers and hot-water lines after so-called "hard" water has been in contact with them for a long period of time. The deposition of these insoluble carbonates and sulphates results in heat loss and increasingly impairs the efficiency of the boiler; it also clogs feed lines and ultimately may block them almost completely. The best prevention is to test the water for hardness and to treat it prior to use ; it can be demineralized or "softened' by ion-exchange methods. Scale may be prevented in small, low-pressure boilers by using soda ash, tannins. or phosphates which precipitate the contaminating materials as a sludg. *See also* ion-exchange.

boiling point. For an unenclosed liquid or mixture of liquids, the temperature at which the upward pressure of molecules escaping from the surface (vapour pressure) equals the downward pressure of the atmosphere. When the liquid is in a closed container, the boiling point may be defined as the temperature at which the liquid and its vapour are in equilibrium, that is, when evaporation and condensation are occurring at the same rate at constant atmospheric pressure. The temperature is the same in both cases. The boiling point is increased somewhat by the presence of molecules of dissolved substances and substantially by the presence of ions. It decreases with decreasing atmospheric pressure. *See also* equilibrium; vapour pressure.

Bollenback reagent. An ammoniacal solution of ammonium persulphate used; to precipitate lead and bismuth as their higher oxides, and thus to separate them from the other metals of the hydrogen sulphite group.

Boltzmann constant. k. Quotient of universal gas constant R and Avogadro number N_A

$$k=\frac{R}{N_A}=1.38054\times10^{-23}\ \mathrm{J\ K^{-1}}$$

$$=1.38054\times10^{-16}\ \text{erg per }^\circ\text{C}.$$

Boltzmann distribution function. *See* Maxwell-Boltzmann distribution.

Boltzmann equation. Conservation equation for unimolecular partition function

$$\frac{\partial\rho_1}{\partial t}+v\frac{\partial\rho_1}{\partial x}+\frac{F}{m}\frac{\partial\rho_1}{\partial v}=\left(\frac{\partial\rho_1}{\partial t}\right)_{\text{coll}}$$

where $\rho_1\,(t, v, x)$=unimolecular partition function, t = time, x = molecule position vector and v= molecule velocity, F= external forces and m= molecular mass,

$$\left(\frac{\partial\rho_1}{\partial t}\right)_{\text{coll}}=\text{collision integrals.}$$

Boltzmann equation describes processes in rarified gases. Also known as Boltzmann transport equation.

Boltzmann factor. Exp $(-E/kT)$ where E= energy of molecule, k= Boltzmann constant, T= thermodynamic temperature. Boltzmann factor occurs in formula for Maxwell-Boltzmann distribution, etc.

Boltzmann transport equation. *See* Boltzmann equation.

bond. An electrostatic attraction acting between atoms of the same or different elements enable ing them to unite to form molecules or mettallie crystals. The number of bonds that characterize each element, this is, the number of combining forces it can exert, is called its valence and is determined by its electronic configuration. The energetic value of a carbon bond is about 5 electron volts. The several types of bonds (covalent, ionic, metallic, and hydrogen) are described in separate entries. In conventional structural formulas a single bond is indicated bp a (dash (—), a double bond by two dashes (=), and a triple bond by three (≡) ; dots are used in electronic formulas. *See also* valence ; orbital.

bond atomic. A valence linkage between atoms consisting of a air of electrons, one of which has been contributed by each of the atoms bonded.

bond, coordinate. *See* coordinate linkage.

bond, colvant. *See* convalent bond.

bond, dative. *See* coordinate linkage.

bond dipole moment. Dipole moment previously ascribed to given chemical bond according to additivity concepts. Bond dipole moment was assumed to be parallel to axis ; however, because of asymmetry to charge distribution in atoms with long electron pairs, its direction need not have been parallel to that of total molecule dipole moment. Also known as bond moment.

Term group dipole moment is recommended instead of this term.

bond, electrostatic. *See* ionic bond.

bond energy. *See* chemical bond energy.

bonderizing. A process by which a phosphate film is formed on the surface of iron, thus protecting it from corrosion, parkerizing and granodizing are similar processes.

bond force constant. *k* (Fr.) Constant characterizing harmonic forces due to changes of bond length during vibrations of atom in molecules. It is equal to second derivate of total molecular energy with respect to a given bond length and computed at position of nuclear equilibrium. Also known as stretching force constant.

bond, heteropolar. A valence linkage between two atoms consisting of a pair of electrons. This bond is characterized by an unequal distribution of charge due to a displacement of the electronic-pair so that the effect of the bond is to make one atom differ in polarity from the other.

bond, homopolar. A valence linkage between two atoms consisting of a pair of electrons that are held equally by both atoms, so that no difference in polarity exists between the atoms.

bond, hydrogen. A valence linkage joining two electronegative atoms through a hydrogen atom. Since a stable hydrogen atom cannot be associated with more than two electrons, the hydrogen bond may be regarded as representing a resonance phenomenon, by which it is alternatively attached to one or the other of the two atoms. The ion HF_2^- may consist of two fluoride ions joined by a proton, through a hydrogen bond, whereas many associated molecules, such as those in water itself, may well owe their existence to the formation of hydrogen bonds. Intermolecular hydrogen bonds serve to explain the properties of certain keto-esters and other organic compounds.

bonding electrons. Electrons assumed to occupy bonding molecular orbitals. They play important rôle in formation of chemical bonds.

boding orbital. Molecular orbital represented as linear combination of atomic orbitals ; its energy is lower than that of any atomic orbital co tributing to it. Electrons occupying bonding orbitals lead either to formation of chemical bond or to strengthening of already existing bond.

bond length. Distance between nuclei of two atoms forming chemical bond, measured in molecular ground state. Also known as internuclear distance.

bond, metallic. A special type of bond existing in metals, in which the valence electrons of the constituent atoms are free to move in the periodic lattice. This type of bonding accounts for the observed metallic properties.

bond, molecular. A valence linkage between two atoms consisting of a pair of electrons, both of which have been furnished by one of the atoms.

bond moment. *See* bond dipole moment.

bond order. Number denoting bond multiplicity ; for conjugated double bond rational number between 1 and 2.

bond pair. Electron pair taking part in formation of both chemical bond and system of hybridized orbitals.

bond polarity. Effect or non-uniform distribution of electronic charge along bond. Electron density is shifted towards one atom and leads to bond dipole moment ; characteristic for bonds between atoms of different electronegativities.

bond strength. Measure of stability of chemical bond. In molecular orbital method bond strength is determined by overlap of atomic orbitals used to construct molecular orbitals and indirectly by degree of hybridization of atomic orbitals.

bone. Industrial source of several products (bone char, bone oil, bone meal). Bone char, or bone black, results from calcination of animal bones and is used as an adsorbent in sugar refining to remove colour and as a pigment in shoe polishes, etc. Bone oil is obtained by destructive distillation of bones; it has been used as a denaturant for alcohol because of its repellent odor. Bone meal is made by steaming and pulverizing animal bones. Its chief use is as a fertilizer and soil conditioner for its high phosphorus content, as well as an ingredient of fine china clay.

bone ash. A white ash consisting primarily of tribasic calcium phosphate obtained by burning bones in air; used in cleaning jewelry and in pottery.

bone black. *See* bone; black.

bone char. *See* bone.

bone meal. *See* bone.

bone oil. *See* bone.

bone seeker. Any element that tends to concentrate in the bones and teeth of animals and man. Most important are calcium, an essential components of bony structure, and fluoride, which in very low concentration (1 ppm) can inhibit tooth decay. Strontium also belongs to this class; the radioactive isotope strontium-90 is extermely dangerous, as it replaces calcium and cause radiation damage in blood-and marrow-forming structure. It occurs in the fallout from atomic bombs, is picked up by vegetation, and finds its way into the body via milk. *See also* fluoridation.

Bongiovanni test for thiocynate. Thiocyanate ion is detected by the red colour, becoming green on dilution, produced when its solution is treated with vanadium trichloride.

Bonnes test. To detect formic and acetic acids, distill the sample with sulphuric acid. Neutralize with calcium carbonate, evaporate and distill the residue over a flame, into a little water. Then treat this solution with :

1. fuchsin-bisulphate which gives a rose colour if formic acid is present.

2. alkaline sodium nitroprusside solution, which gives a yellow colour becoming red with acetic acid, if acetic acid is present.

Bonnet test for formaldehyde. 1. Formaldehyde gives a pink to blue colour to a solution of 0.35 g. morphine sulphate in 100 ml. concentrated sulphuric acid when the reagent is floated in a wateh glass on the surface of a sample containing the formaldehyde.

2. The above reagent may be mixed directly with the sample, if the colour of the latter does not interfere.

Bonz test for tellurium in presence of bismuth. A solution of l g. of a bismuth salt in 2.5 ml. hydrochloric acid gives a black colour with 2.5 ml. Bettendorf-Winkler solution if tellurium is present; with twice as much reagent, the colour is light green.

Boord synthesis. A system of synthesis of pure olefins, applied with notable success to the production of all twentyseven possible structural isomers of heptene, C_7H_{14}. The synthesis depends on the following successive reactions :

1. The treatment of an aldehyde with an alcohol and hydrochloric acid to form an α-chloroether.

2. The reaction of the chloroether with bromine.

3. The reaction of a Grignard reagent with the resultant α,β-dibromoether to replace the α-bromine with an alkyl group.

4. The removal of the bromine and alkoxyl group by the interaction of the β-bromoether and zinc. The product is an olefin.

boracic. *See* boric.

borate. The anions $(BO_2)_n{}^{n-}$ or $H_2B_5O_{10}{}^{3-}$ (meta); $BO_3{}^{3-}$ (ortho); or $B_4O_7{}^{=}$ (tetra or pyro); or a compound containing one of them.

borate, meta-. The anion $(BO_2)_n{}^{n-}$ or $H_2B_5O_{10}{}^{3-}$ or a compound containing any of these anions.

borate, ortho-. The anion BO_3^{3-}, or a compound containing it.

borate, pyro-. *See* borate (tetra-).

borate, tetra-. The anion B_4O_7 , or a compound containing it.

Borcher process. A process for the electrorefining of a silver, in which the impure silver is the anode and the pure silver is deposited on the cathode of an electrolytic cell having an electrolyte consisting of an aqueous solution of silver nitrate and nitric acid.

Borde reagents. Three standard reagents used for the determination of iodine number, they are :

1. a solution of 18.8 g. antipyrine in 1 litre alcohol ;

2. a solution of 5 g. iodine in 100 ml. alcohol ; and

3. a solution of 6 g. mercuric chloride in 100 ml. alcohol. The alcohol used should be somewhat weaker than the usual 95%.

Bordeaux mixture. An insecticide composed of copper sulphate and lime, used primarily on potato bugs and other common garden pests. It is applied as a suspension in water and should be kept out of reach of pets and livestock.

boride. A binary compound of boron and a metal formed by heating a mixture of two elements.

Born equation. Equation which describes Gibbs free energy of solvation ΔG of one mole of ions derived from assumption that it is equivalent to difference of electrical field energy of ions in solvent

$$\Delta G = -\frac{N_A z_B^2 e^2}{2a}\left(1 - \frac{1}{\epsilon_r}\right)$$

where a = ionic radius and ϵ_r =relative permittivity.

Born-Haber cycle. Imaginary thermodynamic cyclic process used for calculating energy of ionic crystal lattice.

A cycle of changes, chemical and physical, applied to a chemical substance, commonly a crystalline metallic halide, to calculate the electron affinities of certain atoms. The stages include the dissociation of the molecules of the crystal into gaseous ions, the neutralization of these ions by transfer of electrons from the negative ions to the positive ones, the condensation of the gaseous atoms to form solid molecules of the two oppositely charged ions (*e.g.*, metal and halogen), and the recombination of the solid molecules to reform the original crystalline compound. From this cycle, it is possible to derive the equation :

$$E = Q + S + \frac{D}{2} + I - U_{MX}$$

in which E is the electron affinity of the halogen atoms, Q is the heat of formation of the compounds, S is the heat of sublimation of the metal, D is the heat of dissociation of the molecular halogen, I is the ionization potential of the metal, and U_{MX} is the lattice energy of the crystal.

Born-Oppenheimer approximation. In molecular electronic state lying far enough energetically from other electronic states nuclei move in effective potential field resulting from electron density distribution in this state.

Born theory of solvation. Theory which considers solvation process as ordering action of electrical field of ion on polar molecules of solvent.

Bornemann reaction. A modification of Etard reaction for the oxidation (to carbonyl groups) of heterocyclic bound methyl groups. Bornemann used proportions of slightly less than 2 moles of chromylchloride to one of the substance, both dissolved in carbon disulphide.

Bornet reagent. A freshly-prepared, neutral, saturated solution of cryogenine used to give colour reactions with heavy metals.

Borntrager test for amyl alcohol. Amyl alcohol is detected in ethyl alcohol by the production of a raspberry-red colour with 3 drops concentrated hydrochloric acid and 10 dropsc of olourless aniline.

boron. An element	Symbol B
State Solid	Atomic No. 5
Group III A	Atomic Wt. 10.811
	Valence 3
	m.p. 2300°C

A hard, nonmetallic solid, may be either a

crystalline solid or an amorphous powder, depending on the method of production. It can be produced in several ways :

(*a*) by reduction of boron oxide with magnesium or aluminium ;

(*b*) by electrolysis of fused potassium halide salts in which boron-containing compounds are dissolved ;

(*c*) by passing gasoeus boron compounds and hydrogen over heated metal wires, upon which pure boron deposits. This method is unique, but is slow and expensive.

Boron has a number of unusual properties. The boron-10 isotope has the higest neutron-absorbing capacity of any known substance. In addition to forming conventional chemical compounds with hydrogen, nitrogen, oxygen, and the halogens, boron combines with carbon and silicon to form carbides, carbonate, and various borosilicates. In combination with metals, it also forms a large array of refractory borides, which have crystalline structures in which the boron atoms are uniquely bonded to produce extremely hard, stable materials of high thermal conductivity and very high melting point.

The elemental uses of boron include high strength filaments used in composites, neutron-absorbing devices for nuclear reactor control, alloying agent with iron, manganese and other metals, and deoxidizing additive in steels and copper. It is an essential plant micronutrient and is nontoxic in low concentration.

borosilicate glass. A heat-resistant glass in which the principal ingredient in addition to silica, soda, and lime, is boric oxide (or boric acid), at a concentration of about 5%. The inclusion of boron greatly reduces the heat expansion property and raises the softening point of such glasses to approximately 650°C. It also increases the transmission of ultraviolet radiation compared with that of regular glass. Borosilicate glasses have become quite common for cooking utensils, laboratory ware, and other high-termperature uses, as well as in sun lamps. Their use for high-level nuclear waste disposal is under considersation.

Borsche-Drechsel synthesis. Ring closure of aryl hydrazones of alicyclic ketones, yielding hydrogenated carbazoles.

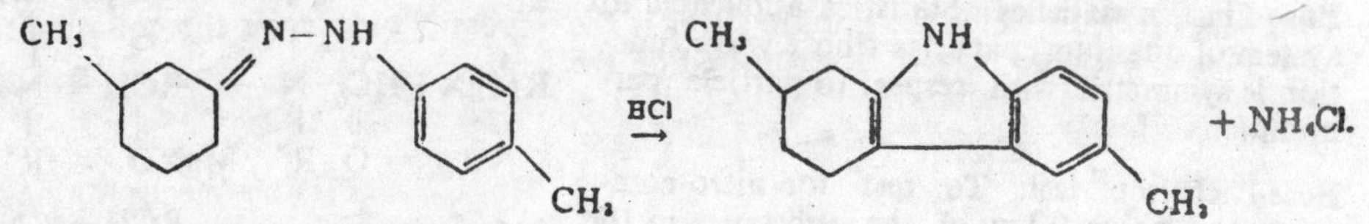

CH_3 N–NH CH_3 $\xrightarrow{HCl}$ CH_3 NH CH_3 $+ NH_4Cl.$

Bosch-Meiser urea process. An industrial method of producing urea from carbon dioxide and ammonia. High temperature and pressures favour the reaction.

$$2NH_3+CO_2 \rightarrow H_2N-CO-NH_2+H_2O$$

Bosch process. To obtain hydrogen from water-gas by means of the catalysed reaction between steam and carbon monoxide. Water-gas is made at a temperature of about 700°C., and a mixture of this with steam is passed over the catalyst (ferric oxide with promoters such as chromic oxide) at a lower temperature (about 450°C.) The carbon monoxide reacts with the steam to produce more hydrogen and carbon dioxide. The latter is removed by dissolving in water under a pressure of some 50 atmospheres. Any remaining carbon monoxide gas can be absorbed in ammoniacal cuprous chloride or formate solution. The Bosch process is often used to provide the hydrogen necessary for the synthesis of ammonia by the Haber process :

$$CO+H_2O \rightarrow CO_2+H_2$$

Bose distribution function. *See* Bose-Einstein distribution.

Bose-Einstein condensation. State of system of identical noninteracting bosons at low temperatures. It corresponds to occupation number of the lowest single-particle energy level comparable with total number of particles in system.

Bose-Einstein distribution. Equilibrium distribution of particles among single-particle energy levels

$$\langle N_\varepsilon \rangle = \frac{g_\varepsilon}{\frac{1}{\lambda}\exp\frac{\varepsilon}{kT}-1}$$

where k=Boltzmann constant, T=thermodynamic temperature, λ=absolute activity and g_ε=degeneracy of energy level ε, $<N\varepsilon>$= average occupation number of this level Bose-Einstein distribution can be used for weakly interacting systems of identical bosons. Also known as Bose distribution function.

Bose-Einstein statistics. Statistics applicable to system of quantum particles whose wave function is symmetric with respect to particle permutations

Bose-Nicholson test. To test for nitro-compounds, dissolve 0.1 g. of the substance in 10 ml. acetate, and add 3 ml. 5% sodium hydroxide. A purple-blue colour shows dinitrocompounds, and a blood-red colour, trinitrocompounds. Mononitrocompounds give no colouration.

Bose test for nitro-group in organic compounds. Heat 0.01—0.05 g. of the substance for 1—2 minutes with 1. ml. of a solution of 10 g. potassium hydroxide in 6 ml. water. Cool rapidly, add 1 ml. water, acidify with 50% accetic acid. A rose-red colour with Griess-Ilosvay reagent indicates the presence of the nitro-group.

bosons. Elementary particles or complex system with integral spin quantum number, *e.g.*, mesons, photons, nuclei of even number of nucleons. Bosons are described by Bose-Einstein statistics.

bottled gas. Butane, propane, or butane-propane mixtures liquified and bottled under pressure for use as domestic cooking fuel.

Bouguer-Beer law. *See* Lambert-Beer law.

Bouguer's law. *See* Lambert's law.

bound electron. An electron whose wave function is negligible except in the vicinity of an atom.

bound energy. Extensive thermodynamic function TS, where T = thermodynamic temperature and S=entropy.

bond level. An energy level in a nucleus so close to the ground state that it can only decay by gamma emission.

bound oxygen. In autooxidation, the part of the oxygen that unites with the substance undergoing oxidation.

bound water. A thin film of water absorbed on a molecule or other particle, as a result of electrical affinity. It is often found on protein molecules and is extremely difficult to remove.

Bouveault aldehyde synthesis. Preparation of aldehydes by treating Grignard reagents with disubstituted formamide derivatives, *e.g.*,

$$RMgX + HC(=O)-N(R')(R'') \rightarrow RCH(OMgX)-N(R')(R'') \xrightarrow{HX} RCH{=}O + R'NHR'' + MgX_2$$

Bouveault-Blanc reduction. Reduction of esters to alcohols with sodium and ethanol, *e.g.*,

$$RCOOC_2H_5 \xrightarrow[Na]{C_2H_5OH} RCH_2OH + C_2H_5OH$$

Bouwer-Barff process A process for producing a corrosion-resistant film on the surface of a metal, chiefly iron, by oxidation with superheated steam, followed by treatment with hot linseed oil.

Boyd, Schubert and Adamson equation. An ion-exchange equation of the form :

$$X_A = \frac{kb_1a_A}{1+b_1a_A\ b_2a_B}$$

where X_A=amount of A absorbed per gram, a_A and a_B = the cation activities in equilibrium solution, k=total exchange capacity, and b_1 and b_2 = constants.

Boyle's law. Product of pressure p and volume V of the given mass of gas is constant at constant temparature ; pV=constant Boyle's law is empirical.

This rulé strictly applies only to an ideal gas, since all actual gases deviate from it slightly, especially carbon dioxide. The principle may be visualized by a piston-in-cylinder arrangement; when the pressure on the piston doubles, the piston moves into the cylinder to a point where the volume of the gas is halved. Also known as Mariotte's law. *See also* gas.

Boyle's point. *See* Boyle's temperature.

Boyle's temparature. T_B. Temparature at which range of low pressure, perfect gas satisfies Boyle-Mariotte's law, *i.e.*,

$$\left(\frac{\partial(pV)}{\partial p}\right)_{T_B,\ p\to 0}=0$$

where p=pressure, V=gas volume ; for gas satisfying van der Waals equation $T_B=a/Rb$, where a and b = constants entering this equation, R=molar gas canstant. Also known as Boyle's point.

Brabender farinograph. A twinbladed, water-jacketed mixer directly coupled to an electric motor which is supported so it is free to turn in a vertical plane and to the housing of which is connected a pen that can write on a clock-work-driven band of ruled paper. This instrument is used to test flour, by recording the varying resistance of the dough to a given mixing operation.

brachy axis. The shorter lateral axis, usually the a axis, of an orthorhombic or triclinic crystal. Also known as brachydiagonal.

Brackett series. A group of lines in the infrared spectrum of atomic hydrogen represented by the formula :

$$\bar{\nu}=R_H\left(\frac{1}{n_1^2}-\frac{1}{n_2^2}\right)$$

in which $\bar{\nu}$ = the wave number, R_H = the Rydberg number, n_1 = 4, and n_2 has various integral values.

Bragg angle. One of the characteristic angles at which x-ray reflect specularly from planes of atom in a crystal.

Bragg curve. Graph for average mumber of ions per unit distance along beam of initially monoenergetic α-particles passing through gas.

This original definition is sometimes extended to other ionizing particles and other media.

Bragg-Gray cavity chamber. Hollow chamber filled with gas inside solid medium, used for absorbed dose measurements, mainly by ionization methods.

Bragg ionization spectrometer. Device for direct measurement of reflection angle for x-ray radiation reflected by set of parallel crystallographic planes ; for appropriately chosen position of crystal (*see* Bragg equation) reflected ray appears, which is recorded either by Geiger-Muller or by scintillation counter. Also known as Bragg spectrometer.

Bragg method of crystal analysis. A beam of x-rays is directed against a crystal, and its atoms, because of their lattice arrangement, reflect the rays as would a series of plane surfaces. The measurements of the diffraction patterns formed by the reflected radiations furnish a means of calculating the spacings between the atomic planes, if the wavelength of the x-rays is known.

Bragg-Pierce law. A relationship for determining an element's atomic absorption coefficient for x-rays when the atomic number of the element and the wavelength of the x-rays are known.

Bragg rule. An empirical rule according to which the mass stopping power of an element for alpha particles is inversely proportional to the square root of the atomic mass.

Bragg's equation. Condition under which monochromatic X-ray beam of wavelenght λ is reflected from set of parallel planes in crystal of indices h, k, l : $2d_{hkl}\sin\theta=n\lambda$, where d_{hkl}= distance between neighbouring lattice planes, θ=angle between hkl plane and reflected beam, n=order of interference (n=1, 2, ...). Also known as Bragg's law.

Bragg's law. *See* Bragg's equation.

Bragg spectrometer. *See* Bragg ionization spectrometer.

branched chain. A molecular structure induced in C_4 to C_8 paraffinic hydrocarbons and the corresponding alcohols by a catalytic refining process called isomerization. Such molecules are chracterized by a subordinate chain of one or more carbon atoms attached to the principal chain, as indicated below :

```
 H   H   H   H
 |   |   |   |
HC — C — C — CH   or   CH3CH2CH2CH3
 |   |   |   |
 H   H   H   H
```

normal butane
(straight-chain)

```
  H   H   H
  |   |   |
 HC — C — CH
  |   |   |
  H   |   H        or   CH3CH(CH3)CH3
     HCH
      |
      H
```

$CH_3CH(CH_3)CH_3$

isobutane
(branched-chain)

Branched-chain compounds are isomers of the normal or straight-chain compounds from which they are derived, and are designated by the prefix iso-. They are much more reactive than the normal compounds and are particularly effective in motor fuels, for which they were originally developed ; for example, isooctane has a much higher antiknock rating than its straight-chain isomer octance. *See also* isomerization ; octane number.

branch head. In rotation-oscillation spectrum of molecules, convergence limit for rotational lines of a given branch.

branching. In radiochemistry, existence of at least two competitive modes of decay of radioactive nuclide.

branching chain reaction. Chain reaction which proceeds with chain branching.

branching ratio. In cases where a radioactive element may undergo more than one radioactive disintegration, the ratio of the quantities of the element entering into the various types of disintegrations is called the branching ratio.

brass. An alloy of copper and zinc, often containing some tin. There are many special types of brass, each designed for a specific use, for example, red brass (85% copper, 15% zinc), admiralty brass (73% copper, 26% zinc, 1% tin), and cartridge brass (70% copper, 30% zinc). Brass is corrosion resistant and is widely used for marine equipment, fire-hose nozzles, couplinge, etc. *See also* bronze.

Braun test for cyanide. An aqueous solution of picric acid gives a red colour on heating with a solution of alkali cyanide.

Braun test for manganese. On fusion of a substance with sodium pyrophosphate in the oxidizing flame (a bead test) and moistening with nitric acid, a violet colour indicates manganese.

Braun test for molybdic acid. An aqueous solution of molybdic acid gives :

(*i*) a carmine-red colour with a little zinc and potassium thiocyanate solution on the addition of hydrochloric acid ;

(*ii*) a blood-red colour and brown-black crystalline precipitate when boiled for some time with ammonia and ammonium sulphide.

Braun test for nickel. A rose-red colour with an aqueous solution of potassium sulphocarbonate indicates the presence of nickel.

Braun test for picric acid. When alkaline solution of picric acid is heated wiih glucose, red colouration appears.

Braun test for pyrophosphate. Dilute solutions of alkali pyrophosphates give a pale red-yellow precipitate with a concentrated aqueous solution of cobaltic hexammine chloride.

Braun test for tartaric acid. On boiling an aqueous solution of tartaric acid with a solution of 1 g. cobaltic chloride hexammine in 12 ml. water, and adding sodium hydroxide solution, a green colour changing to blue-violet, is obtained.

Bravais lattice. 14 basic types of crystal lattice, of different symmetry, built by simple repetition of 14 types of Bravais cells in direction of their three edges on distances equal to length of edges.

brazing. A type of welding involving the use of nonferrous alloys as filler materials between the pieces of metal to be joined at temperatures above 540°C. The "joins" formed by brazing are stronger than those made by soldering, as the filler alloy cannot be remelted once the union is complete. Numerous ternary and quaternary alloys are used for this purpose.

breadth of spectral line. *See* line width.

breakthrough. *See* column breakthrough.

breakthrough capacity of column. Q_B. In ion exchange chromatography number of miliequivalents of given ion retained by column up to moment of breakthrough.

breakthrough curve. In frontal analysis, diagram showing dependence of substance concentraton in effluent, *C*, (or concentration ratio in effluent and original solution respectively, C/C_0) upon effluent volume or time. Also known as effluent concentration history, exchange isoplane.

Bredig's method. A useful means of obtaining colloidal suspensions of the noble metals. For colloidal platinum, as an example, an electric arc is struck under distilled water platinum wires. Metal is torn from the positive wire and, after filtering the larger particles, the filtrate contains colloidal patinum.

Bredt's rule. In polycyclic compounds (excluding very large cycles), C=C and C=N double bond systems cannot exist at nodal carbon atoms.

Breeder reactor. A type of nuclear reactor for power generation, which is far more efficient than conventional reactors. It permits conversion of about 70% of the energy in uranium-238 compared to the less than 2% in current practice. In fast breeder reactors the heavy uranium isotope-238 is irradiated by neutrons from fission of uranium, 235 and is thus converted to plutonium ; any unconverted uranium-238 can be reprocessed and returned to the breeder until its energy content has been fully exploited. Thus, the reactor yields more nuclear fuel than it consumes. Liquid sodium is used as a coolant, enabling the breeder to operate at a higher temperture, with a corresponding gain in efficiency.

Breit-Wigner formula. An expression for the nuclear cross section of a reaction $X(a, b) Y$:

$$\sigma=\frac{\lambda^2}{4\pi}\cdot\frac{\Gamma a\Gamma b}{(E-Er)^2+\frac{1}{4}\Gamma^2}$$

in which σ=the nuclear cross section, λ=the equivalent wavelenght of the incident particle as derived from its mass and velocity by the de Broglie equation, Γa and Γb = the level widths representing the probability of emission of particles a and b, by the compound nucleus in a specific quantum state, Γ=the total level width, E=total energy of the incident particle, Er=the energy value which would give exact resonance with the specified quantum level of the compound nucleus.

bremsstrahlung. A German word, meaning literally "braking radiation", applied to radiations, usually radiation bands, produced during deceleration of charged particles.

brewing. The production of beer and ale by enzymatic conversion of the starches contained in barlay malt to wort, or malt extract This is then hydrolyzed to sugars and proteins by a process known as mushing, followed by boiling with hops and fermentation with yeast. These processes (all of which are of the batch type) involve complex reactions induced by enzymes and require extremely close control and careful selection of ingredients. Barley is the grain chiefly used as a source of malt; its enzymes are activated by controlled cycles of water absorption and aeratian, which induce partial germination of the barley. Beer and ale also contain colloidally suspended proteins which cause foaming ; they are clarified by filtration through adsorptive clays or diatomite.

brewster angle. The angle of incidence, for a given material, at which a beam of plane-polarized light is shifted in phase by 90°.

Brewster process. A process for the concentration of dilute acetic acid by extraction with solvents, such as isopropylether, which are subsequently recovered by distillation.

bridged complex. *See* polynuclear complex.

bridging atom. Atom of bridging group linked with two central atoms of polynuclear complex.

bridging group. Group attached to two central atoms of polynuclear complex.

brightener. 1. In the electroplating field, this term refers to an additive used in certain nickel-plating formulations which imparts increased brightness and reflectively to deposits on smooth surfaces ; they may be sulphonic acid derivatives, metallic ions of zinc or cadmium, or such compounds as thiourea.

2. An organic fluorescent compound (an ultraviolet absorber), which emits enough blue radiation to conceal off-colours of paper, textiles, and the like. These products are often called optical brighteners and have much the same effect as bleaching agents.

brillouin zones. Zones in space of wave vector limited by such values of vector for which waves coupled with electron (or phonon) movement in crystal are standing waves (Bragg condition is fulfilled. *See* Bragg's equation.

brine. A water solution of sodium chloride of a higher concentration than that of sea water

(2.6%). The brines of many lakes are virtually saturated salt solutions. Brines are used in the chemical industry as a source of chlorine and caustic, sodium bicarbonate, soda ash, and sodium chloride; they are also used for curing and picking hides and as supercooling media.

Brin's process. Before liquefaction processes became particable, Brin's process was used to obtain oxygen from the air. Air was passed under pressure over heated barium oxide (BaO) and barium peroxide (BaO_2) being formed. On reducing the pressure, oxygen was released from the peroxide and was collected:

$$2BaO+O_2 \rightleftharpoons 2BaO_2$$

Bringhetti test. To detect nitrate in solution, add to the evaporated residue of the solution à little salicin and concentrated sulphuric acid. A blood-red colour, changing to violet on dilution with water, indicates the presence of nitrate.

britannia metal. A silver-white tin alloy, similar to pewtar, containing about 7% antimony, 2% copper, and often small quantities of zinc and bismuth.

Brodie's ozoniser. This produces ozonised oxygen by the passage of a silent electric discharge through oxygen gas which slowly travels between vessels containing copper sulphate solution, or dilute sulphuric acid, in which wires from an induction coil are immersed. Also called Berthelot's ozoniser.

bromination. Substitution of hydrogen atom in molecule by bromine atom, *e.g.*,

$$C_6H_6+Br_2 \xrightarrow{Fe} C_6H_5Br+HBr$$

bromine. An element.

		Symbol	Br
State	Liquid	Atomic Wt.	79.904
Group	VIIA	Valence	1,3,5,7
		Atomic No.	35

A highly reactive element, bromine exists as a liquid at room temperature, though it is highly volatile, it does not occur naturally in elemental form but always in combined state. Itis obtained commercially from brines, and was the first element to be recovered from sea water. The isotopic composition of bromine is unusual, the percentage of its stable isotopes (79 to 81) being almost equal. Both liquid and vapour are diatomic (Br_2). The vapour is over five times as dense as air, and the liquid form boils at 58.8°C. Bromine reacts violently with aluminum and potassium but does not attack most other metals unless moisture is present. An extremely strong oxidizing agent, it is widely used in bleaches for textiles and paper, and in water purification. Its major industrial use has been in antiknock gasoline (as ethylene bromide), where it acts to keep cylinders free from lead oxide deposits; this use may be excepted to decline in the future. Bromine is also important in organic synthesis, as a laboratory reagent, and general sanitizer; it forms a large number of inorganic and organic compounds, *e.g.*, hydrobromic acid, bromates, and bromides. It is toxic by inhalation and strongly irritant to eyes and skin and should be handled with proper protective measures.

bromine absorption number. Fatty oils add bromine directly and the amount of the bromine so absorbed is used as an analytical test for the purity of the oil. This bromine number may be converted into the "iodine number" by multiplying it by 1.5875.

bromo-. A prefix designating the presence of the bromine atom —Br.

Bronsted-Bjerrum equation Epuation describing dependence of reaction-rate constant on activity coefficient and activated complex:

$$k'=k_0 \frac{f_A f_B}{f^*}$$

where k'=reaction-rate constant in real solution, k_0=reaction-rate constant in ideal solution, f_A, f_B=activity coefficients of substrates *A* and *B*, f^*=activity coefficient of activated complex.

Bronsted catalysis law. *See* Bronsted relationship.

Bronsted-Lowry theory. A broad generalized conception of the nature of acids and bases, by which an acid is defined as any substance, molecular or ionic, that can yield a proton (hydrogen ion) to anothar substance; whereas a base is any substance which can combine with a proton. Substances such as the H_2O molecule which can yield a proton to form OH^- ions, or combine with a proton to form H_3O^+ complexes, are both acids and bases. Every acid has a base which differs from it by a proton, and vice versa, and such acids and bases are said to be conjugate to one another. An acid may react with a base not conjugate to it, however, producing their respective conjugate base and conjugate acid. Since free protons do not exist to any extent in solution, the acidic or basic properties of a substance cannot be evident unless the solvent itself has basic or acidic properties, that is, unless its molecules can accept or give protons.

Bronsted relationship. Empirical law according to which catalytic reaction-rate constant k of acid- or base-catalyzed reaction is linearly proportional to acidity (alkalinity) coefficient of catalyst K to αth power

$$k=GK^{\alpha}$$

where G and α are constants for given reaction. Also known as Bronsted catalyst law.

Bronsted test. To test for tartaric acid, add calcium acetate solution to a 0.1% aqueous solution of the acid. A precipitate of calcium tartrate forms after standing for hours; however a precipitate of calcium racemate appears immediately if 1 drop of an *l*-tartrate solution is added.

Bronsted theory of acids and basis. Theory according to which acid is substance which is able to lose proton, base is substance which binds proton (*see* protolysis), irrespective of whether these substances exist as neutral molecules or ions, *e.g.*,

$$\begin{array}{ccc} H_2SO_4 & \rightleftharpoons & HSO_4^- + H^+ \\ HSO_4^- & \rightleftharpoons & SO_4^{2-} + H^+ \\ \textbf{acid} & & \textbf{base} \end{array}$$

bronze. 1. A mixture of alloy, normally comprised of 94 to 95% copper and 5 to 10% tin, which gives a dark reddish-brown appearance which does not take a high polish. Special types of bronze also contain small percentages of aluminium, silicon, or phosphorus, the last being called phosphor bronze. These alloys are used for special electrical applications, cuttings tools, springs in precision equipment and for the special wire used in papermaking on the fourdrinier machine. In powder form, uspensions of bronze particles in a solvent are used as a pigment for metal coating and decoration.

2. Descriptive of various inorganic pigments, *e.g.*, iron blue and Red Lake C, as well as of suspensions of bronze powder in organic solvents (bronzing liquids). *See also* brass.

Brown alcohol test. To test ethyl alcohol for the presence of other alcohols, dissolve 0.1 g. vanillin in 10 ml. of the alcohol, and pour 1 ml. concentrated sulphuric acid down the side of the tube. Characteristic colours are obtained in the interface and the liquid layers.

Brownian motion. The discontinuous movement of colloidal particles in a gaseous or liquid suspension, giving the appearance in a micro scope of a "dance" or zigzag effect. It was later shown by Einstein that the motion is caused by the impact of the molecules of the suspending medium, and it thus provides visible evidence of molecular kinetics. The phenomenon can be observed in rubber latex using an optical microscope.

Browning-Palmer test. To test for the ferrocyanide, ferricyanide, and thiocyanate ions in solution, acidulate the solution and add thorium nitrate solution, which precipitates the ferrocyanide. Ferricyanide is precipitated from the filtrate with cadmium nitrate. Filter again, and add ferric chloride solution to the filtrate, obtaining a deep red colour if thiocyanate is present.

browning reaction. A condensation reaction occuring in many food products between amino acids and sugars, without the aid of enzymes. The hydroxyl groups of the sugar, *e.g.*, glucose, react with the amide groups of protein to form undersirable brownish end products, which impair appearance, quality, and storage life. In the case of egg white, the glucose can be removed by bacterial fermentation or enzyme action. It is also called the Maillard reaction.

Brown rule. A means of predicting positions upon the benzene ring taken by substituent atoms or groups, proposed by Crum Brown. It states that meta substitution occurs wherever the replaced hydrogen atom can be oxidized directly to a hydroxyl group. Otherwise, the ortho or para position is substituted.

b-strain effect. *See* back strain effect.

Bucher process. A method of "fixing atmospheric nitrogen by converting it to sodium cyanide. Bricks consisting of sodium carbonate, carbon, and iron (to act as a catalyst) are heated in atmosphere of nitrogen. The sodium cyanide formed is extracted with liquid ammonia:

$$Na_2CO_3+4C+N_2 \rightarrow 2NaCN+3CO$$

Bucherer-Bergs hydantoin synthesis. Preparation of hydantoin derivative from carbonyl compounds, hydrogen cyanide and ammonium carbonate, *e.g.*,

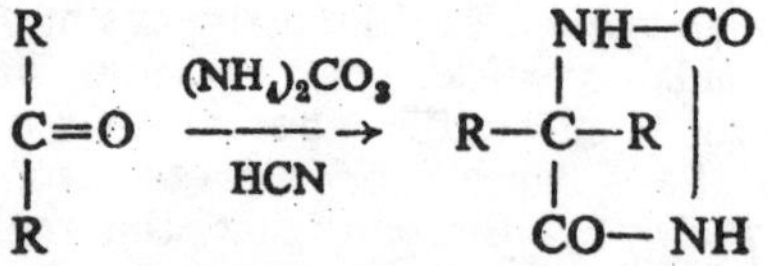

$$R_2C{=}O \xrightarrow[HCN]{(NH_4)_2CO_3} R_2C(NH{-}CO)(CO{-}NH)$$

Also known as Bucherer hydantoin synthesis.

Bucherer carbazole synthesis. A synthesis of carbazoles from naphthols (or naphthylamines) and aryl hydrazines, in the presence of sodium bisulphite.

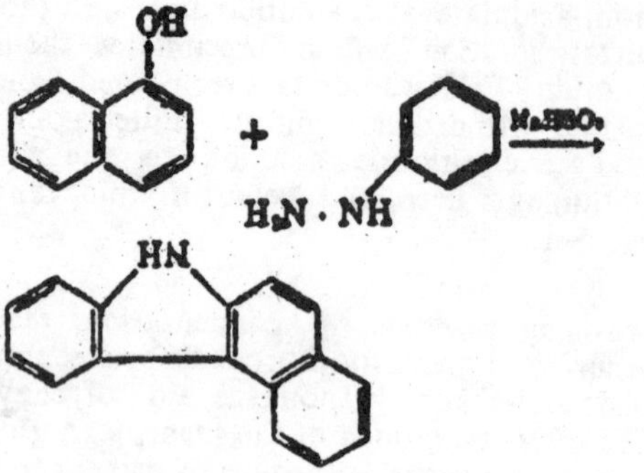

OH + $H_2N \cdot NH$ $\xrightarrow{NaHSO_3}$ HN

Bucherer reaction. Substitution of amino group in primary aromatic amines (mainly naphthlamines) by hydroxyl group, effected by sodium hydrogen sulphite and sodium hydroxide ; also reverse process ; substitution of hydroxyl group in naphthols by amino group effected by ammonium sulphite and ammonia.

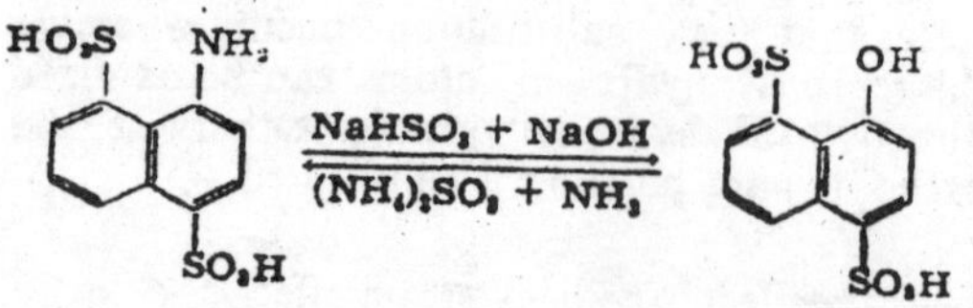

HO_3S NH_2 SO_3H $\underset{(NH_4)_2SO_3\ +\ NH_3}{\overset{NaHSO_3\ +\ NaOH}{\rightleftharpoons}}$ HO_3S OH SO_3H

Buchner-Curtius-Schlotter-Beck reaction. The direct addition, with loss of nitrogen, of diazo compounds and aldehydes to form ketones.

$$R'CHN_2+R''CHO \rightarrow R'CH_2COR''+N_2$$

(R' should be aliphatic).

Buell test for uranium. Dissolve the sample in nitric acid and add zinc shavings ; a yellow deposit on the zinc indicates the presence of uranium.

buffer. An acid-base balancing or control reaction by which the *p*H of a solution is protected from major change when acids or bases are added to it. The protection is afforded by the presence in the solution of a weak acid and related salt (for example, acetic acid and sodium acetate), which maintain the equilibrium by means of ion transfer and neutralization. The same effect can be obtained by use of a blend of two acid salts ; phosphates, carbonates, and ammonium salts are common buffering agents. An example of biochemical buffering in nature is the extremely close maintenance of the acid-base balance of the blood which contains a weak acid (carbonic) and its salt (bicarbonate). Many commercial products are approximately buffered to retain their original strength. *See also* acid base ; *p*H.

buffer solution. *See* buffer.

builder. A detergent additive which promotes the effectiveness of a natural or synthetic surface-active agent. Phosphates have been used for many years for this purpose but have been considered undersirable because they along with other nutrients, promote the growth of algae ; as a result, detergent wastes are ecologically destructive, especially when discharged into lakes and rivers. Nitrilotriacetic acid is also an effective builder, but its use has been restricted due to possible toxicity. Other compounds that have shown promise in this field are carboxymethylcellulose and ethylenediaminetetraacetic acid (EDTA) *See also* detergent.

building-block molecule. A biomolecule serving as a structural unit of a biological macromolecule, *e.g.*, an amino acid, a fatty acid, or a sugar.

build-up factor. Ratio of intensity of observed effect of absorption of ionizing radiation to effect of absorption of particles or photons of the primary radiation.

bulk polymerization. A term applied to polymerization reactions that take place without a solvent or other medium, directly between the reacting molecules.

bumping. The formation of large bubbles during boiling, due to local superheating, and the consequent violent effect of their passage through the liquid.

Bunsen cell. A primary cell in which the anode consists of zinc and is immersed in dilute sulphuric acid, and the cathode consists of carbon immersed in concentrated nitric acid.

Bunsen coefficient. The volume of gas under standard conditions of temperature and pressure (S.T.P.) which is absorbed by a unit volume of gas solution. Also known as absorption coefficient.

Bunsen reaction for acetate. On heating an alkali acetate with arsenic trioxide, the characteristic odor of poisonous cacodyl appears.

Burgess reagent for aromatic compounds. A solution of 10 g. mercuric sulphate in enough 25% sulphuric acid to make a volume of 100 ml. This is a general reagent for aromatic compounds, many of which give characteristic colour reactions.

Burgess-Kamm test. A modified cobaltinitrite test in which 10 ml. of a solution are tested for potassium by adding 1 drop of 25% sodium cobalti nitrate solution and a little 0.01N silver nitrate solution. A yellow to orange precipitate indicates the presence of potassium.

Burian test for xanthine basis. Adenine, guanine and other xanthine bases, in alkaline solution, give a red colour with diazobenzenesulphonic acid.

burn. To oxidze so rapidly that the products of the oxidation are rendered incandescent.

burn-up. In radiochemistry, destruction or transformation of specified nuclei as a result of neutron capture reaction. In reactor technique, degree of consumption of initial load of reactor fuel as a result of reactor operation.

burn-up fraction. In radiochemistry fraction, usually expressed as percentage, of initial quantity of nuclei of a given type which has undergoing fission.

burnt-up fuel elements. Nuclear fuel elements which have reached final degree of burn-up, as defined for the particular type or batch. Also known as spent fuel element.

Bury theory. A modification of the Langmuir theory of electronic arrangement around the nucleus. Bury suggested that the maximum number of electrons in the outermost shell of any atom is limited to 8, and that a new layer must commence to form in the case of the next element. The formation of the forth shell would commence, for example, when the third shell contains 8 electrons, even though the ultimate capacity of the third shell is 18 electrons, and this number is undoubtedly present in higher elements. The Bury modification is supported by much evidence, including the properties of the rare earths.

Busch reagent. A solution of 10 g. nitron in 90 g. 5% acetic acid. This solution is used as a test reagent for nitrate. The solution to be tested is acidified with dilute sulphuric acid and a few drops of reagent added. A white precipitate indicates the presence of nitrate.

Burton process. The first commercially-successful petroleum cracking process in the United States. It was a batch process, in which the petroleum was heated to a temperature of about 400°C, under a pressure of 75–100 pound per square inch.

Butamer process. A method of isomerizing normal butane into isobutane in the presence of hydrogen and a solid, noble-metal catalyst.

butter. 1. The glycerides of the fatty acids present in milk, of which about half is butyric acid, from which the product is named. The fat particles coalesce to a semisolid as a result of mechanical agitation, which ruptures the protective protein coating and allows them to cohere. The product is colourless, but permissible colorants are added for acceptability.

2. Obsolete term for various metallic chlorides whose hygroscopic nature give them a viscosity suggestive of butter, *e.g.*, butter of tin.

buttressing effect. Effect typical of atropoisomer derivatives of biphenyl and similar systems. Substitutional of 3,3′-and 5,5′-hydrogen atoms increases stability of atropoisomers (by decreasing racemization rate); *e.g.*, in 2′-

methoxy-3′ methyl-2′-nitrodiphenyl-6-carboxylic acid, buttressing effect is exhibited by methyl group :

CO_2H OCH_3 CH_3

NO_2

butyl. The univalent group $—C_4H_9$, the fourth member of the homolgous series of paraffin hydrocarbons ; it is derived from butane by removing one hydrogen atom. There are four isomeric forms. When a second hydrogen atom is dropped from butane, the divalent butylene group results, $—C_4H_8—$ which represents the corresponding olefin. The abbreviation Bu is often used in formulae.

butyl, iso. *See* isobutyl.

butyl, normal. *See* butyl.

***sec*-butyl.** The radical

$$(C_2H_5)CH_3)CH—.$$

***tert*-butyl.** The radical $(CH_3)_3C—$.

butyl rubber. A synthetic elastomer produced by catalytic copolymerization of isobutene (isobutylene) with no more than 3% of isoprene ; the latter is necessary to permit valcanization with sulphur-accelerator systems. An early form of synthetic rubber, butyl can be used as a component of tire carcases, though it is not especially suitable for trends. It is superior to natural rubber in resistance to attack by oxygen and ozone, in dielectric strength, and particularly in ability to retain gases, a property which makes it valuable as an inner lining for tubeless tires. In latex form it is an excellent insulating material.

butyric fermentation. Type of oxidative fermentation of hexoses, *e.g.*, of glucose, caused by *Bacillus butylicus*, leading to decomposition of carbohydrate with formation, of *n*-butanol, butyric acid, ethanol, formic acid, acetic acid, lactic acid and carbon dioxide.

Buznea-Cernatesco test. Nitric acid is detected by a red colour produced with a freshly-prepared solution of diaminophenol hydrochloride in concentrated sulphuric acid.

byerite. Bituminous coal that does not crack in fire and melts and enlarge upon strong heating.

by-product. A secondary product of a reaction or of manufacture obtained in addition to the primary product.

Byers process. A process for the production of wrought iron with a minimum of hand labour, as distinguished from the old manual-working process. The molten metal passes through several stages in desulphurization and other operations in purificatien, including a "cold-slag" treatment.

C

C. Symbol for the element carbon.

°C. Symbol for centigrade temperature.

***c*.** Symbol for the velocity of light.

Cabanne's factor. An equational factor to correct for the depolarization effect of the horizontal components of scattered light during the determination of molecular weight by optical methods.

cacodyl. An organic monovalent radical containing arsenic. It is derived from arsine (AsH_3) and has the formula $As(Me)_2—$.

Cadet test. Arsenic trioxide is detected by the odour of cacodyl (poisonous) on heating with sodium acetate.

Cadiot-Chodkiewicz reaction. Formation of conjugated acetylenic system by coupling of two asymmetric acetylene derivatives (ethylenic and 1-bromoacetylanic derivatives) in presence of Cu^+ ions.

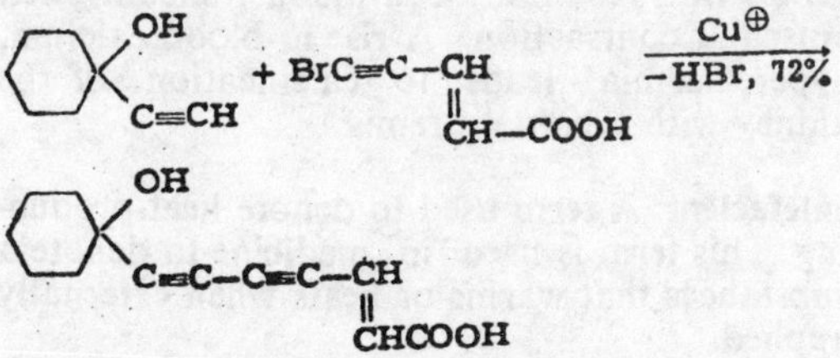

(cyclohexane ring with OH and C≡CH) + BrC≡C–CH(=CH–COOH) $\xrightarrow[-HBr,\ 72\%]{Cu^{\oplus}}$

(cyclohexane ring with OH and C≡C–C≡C–CH=CHCOOH)

cadmium. An element.

	Symbol	Cd
Group IIB	Atomic No.	43
	Atomic Wt.	112.4
	Valence	+2
	Isotopes	8 stable
	m.p.	320.9°C

Cadmium is a soft metal, and is tarnished in air. Two of its notable properties are its extremely high capture cross-section for neutrons (2500 barns), which makes it unique in its ability to control the rate of nuclear reactions in a reactor, and its toxicity, which is sufficient enough to cause poisoning by inhalation of fume or dust and also to prevent its use in any material in contact with foodstuff. It should be handled with adequate respiratory protection. Ingestion of 15 ppm of cadmium in food, or about 15 times the normal amount, on produce mild symptoms of poisoning. It is caimarily a respiratory poison. It is used in prazing alloys, electrical contacts, and in elecbroplated coatings; nickel-cadmium storage tratteries and cadmium-based alloys find use bn heavyduty bearings. Control rods in nuclear ireactors are made of cadmium.

cadmium cell. A standard or "normal" cell usually constructed in the "H" form. The cathode is an amalgam of 12.5 parts of cadmium and 875 parts of mercury by weight. The anode may be made of highly purified mercury or of amalgamated platinum. A saturated solution of cadmium sulphate in water is used as electrolyte. The cathode is surrounded by undissolved cadmium sulphate crystals, and the anode is covered with a paste made of mercurous sulphate and cadmium sulphate solution. The cell is sealed to prevent evaporation. At 20°C, the cadmium cell furnishes an electromotive force of 1.0186 volts, and this varies only 0.00007 volts per degree charge of temperature.

cadmium-silver oxide cell. An alkaline electrolytic cell which may be used without recharging in primary batteries or which may be recharged for secondary battery use.

cadmium sulphide cell. A photoconductive cell in which a small wafer of cadmium sulphide provides an extremely high dark-light resistance ratio.

caesium. An element.

	Symbol	Cs
State Liquid	Atomic No.	55
Group IA	Atomic Wt.	132.9055
	Valence	+1
	m.p.	28.5°C

Caesium has a notably low melting point, and is one of the three metals that are liquid at room temperature. It is the most reactive of the alkali metals and indeed is the most electropositive and the most reactive of all the elements. It reacts vigrously with oxygen and members of the halogen groups, causing ignition, and with sulphur and phosphorus it reacts explosively. In the earth's crust, caesium is present upto 7 parts per million. Early uses of caesium were in photoelectric cells and as a greater in vacuum tubes; more recently its powder-generating ability has been studied for possible thermoelectric applications, especially for spacecraft. Caesium compounds are used in glass and ceramic production, as absorbents in carbon dioxide purification plants, and in medicine as antishock agents after administration of arsenic drugs.

cage effect. Increased (higher than anticipated from diffusion) recombination of free radicals, originating from the same molecule.

Cailletet and Mathias law. Average density of liquid and its saturated vapour is linear function of temperature: intersection of this straight line with curve describing dependence of density of liquid and saturated vapour on temperature determines density of this substance in critical state. Also known as law of the rectilinear diameter.

calcarious. Containing, composed of, or resembling calcium carbonate.

calcic. Derived from or containing calcium.

calcination. Heating an inorganic material such as limestone, gypsum, magnesium carbonate, or a metallic ore to a temperature below its melting point but high enough to effect evolution of carbon dioxide, and removal of bound water and of other impurities by oxidation, reduction, etc. Calcination also induces phase changes in some metal ores and in glass. In metallurgy it is called roasting when oxidation is involved and smelting when a reduction eaction occurs. *See also* pyrolysis ; smelt ; rroast.

calcined clay. Clay that has been heated to drive out volatile materials.

calcined coke. Coke that has been heated to expel volatile substances.

calcium. An element.

Group IIA	Symbol	Ca
	Atomic Wt.	40.08
	Atomic No.	20
	Valence	+2
	Isotopes	40, 42, 43 44, 46, 48
	m.p.	845°C

Calcium a soft metal of the alkaline earth series that can be derived in the pure state ; does not occurs naturally calcium is fifth elements and third among metals in abundance in the earth's crust. Its compounds make 3.64% of the earth's crust. It oxidizes in air and decomposes water and evolve hydrogen. It is a metabolically essential mineral which is deposited in bones and teeth, a process which is catalyzed by vitamin D ; the best nutrient source is milk. The metal is employed as an alloying agent for aluminium bearing metal, as an oil in removing bismuth from lead and is a controller from graphite carbon in cast iron. It is also used as deoxidiser in the manufacture of many steels, as a reducing agent in the preparation of such metals as chromium, thorium, zirconium, and uranium, and as a separating material for gaseous mixtures of argon and nitrogen.

calcium metabolism. Calcium an essential element needed by all animals and animal cells, substances four function in mammels :

(*i*) as an integral part of bone mineral ;

(*ii*) as an integral part of biomembranes ;

(*iii*) as the link between excitation and contraction in all forms of muscle, and similarly as the link between excitation and secrelion in both endcorine and exocrine glands ; and

(*iv*) as a activator, regulator, or inhibitor of key enzymes.

A fall in blood calcium, hypocalcemia, leads to tetany, the spontaneous firing of nerves with resultant continuous, uncontrolled muscular contraction. A rise in blood calcium, hypercalcemia, leads to calcification of the kidney with eventual uremia.

calefacient. A term used to denote heat-producing. This term is used in medicine to denote a substances that warms or heats when externally applied.

Caley test for calcium. To detect calcium in the presence of strontium and barium, ignite the malerial at 900°C, the alkaline earth group precipitated as carbonates, leach with 25 ml. water concentrate the solution acidify with hydrochloric acid, and boil, add 1 g. potassium iodide and then 0.1 g. yellow mercuric oxide. A white turbidity indicates the presence of calcium.

Caley test for lithium. Treat the precipitate of alkali chlorides by digestion with amyl alcohol, and add a solution of 1.5-2.0% stearic acid in ether which has been treated with ammonia gas to form the ammonium stearate, if turbidity appears, lithium chloride is present.

Caley test in oxalic acid. Dissolve 0.1 g. of the material in 20 ml. water and shake for 1-2 minutes with 1 ml. 5 N sodium hydroxide solution. A white crystalline precipitate show the presence of oxalate.

californium. An element.

	Symbol	Cf
State Solid	Atomic No.	98
Group IIIB	Valence	+2,3,4

Californium is an artificial radioactive element of the transuranic portion of the actinide series having all of its isotopes radioactive it was made by helium bombardment of curium. The 249 isotope has a half-life of 360 years. The 252 and 249 isotopes have been made in minute quantities. The chemical properties of californium are similar to those observed for other +3 actinide elements. It can be separated and identified in the presence of other actinides by ion-exchange chromatography. Californium is quite volatile and can be distilled at temperatures of the order 1100-1200°C. It forms compounds with halogens and oxygen. Californium is a bone seeking element for which the body has a very low tolerance ; it has a few medical applications. It also had an important influence on the development of counters and electronic systems.

calking compound. A mixture of substances used to fill cracks and keep them liquid-tight and in some cases, gas-tight. Ideally, calking compounds should bond with various surfaces and retain their elasticity.

calomel electrode. A half-cell consisting of a mercury electrode covered with calomel (mercury (I) chloride) and a solution of mercury in potassium chloride. It is used as a standard electrode, its potential being 0.2415 volt at 298 K, with respect to a hydrogen electrode. Electrode Hg, $Hg_2Cl \mid Cl^-$ is used as reference electrode : electrode reaction is

$$\tfrac{1}{2}Hg_2Cl_2 + e^- \rightleftharpoons Hg + Cl^-$$

and potential of electrode,

$$\varepsilon = \varepsilon^\circ - \frac{RT}{F} \ln a_{Cl^-}$$

where ε°=standard electrode potential. Also known as calomel half-cell ; calomel reference electrode.

calomel half cell. *See* calomel electrode.

calomel reference electrode. *See* calomel electrode.

Caloric equation of state. Equation which gives phase internal energy U dependence on its temperature T, volume V and number of moles of its constituents $n_1, n_2 \cdots, n_c$

$$U=(T, V, n_1\ n_2 \cdots, n_c)$$

calorie. A unit of heat defined as the heat required to raise the temperature of one gram of water from 14.5°C to 15.5°C (the 15° calorie). If the word is spelt with a capital letter it denotes the larger unit—the kilogram calorie—which, however, is now usually represented by the abbreviation *kcal.* Another artificial calorie, used in engineering steam tables is the International Table calorie ; 1 I.T. calorie =1/860 international watt-hour = 0.00116298 absolute watt-hour. Conversion to other energy units gives :,

1 cal. = 0.003:6573 B.T.U.
1 cal. = 0.0412917 litre-atmosphere
1 cal. = 0.999346 I. T. cal.

15° calorie, cal_{15}. Obsolete energy unit ; in SI system 1 cal_{15}=4.1855 J.

calorifacient. A drug or other substance that produces heat within the organism.

calorific intensity. The maximum temperature attainable by combustion of a given fuel with atmospheric oxygen under atmospheric pressure.

calorific value. The number of units of heat obtained by complete combustion of unit mass of a substance. Determination of calorific value are very commonly made in the evaluation of fuels, the study of foods, etc.

calorific value, gross. The quantity of heat produced by the combustion of a unit mass of a substance with oxygen under pressure, as in a bomb calorimeter. If this value is corrected for the latent heat of evaporation of the water present, then the net calorific value is obtained.

calorigenic. Heat-generating.

calorimetry. Measurement of the quantity of heat involved in various processes, such as chemical reactions, changes of state, and formation of solutions, or in determination of the heat capacities of substances. Under these circumstances the gain in the internal energy is equal to the difference between the heat absorbed and the work done by the system. Calorimetric measurements are useful in determining important thermodynamic properties of substances, for example, heat capacity, entropy, and free energy.

calorizing. A process for impregnating or containing a surface of iron, steel, etc., with aluminum by heating it with aluminum, alumina, and ammonium chloride in an atmosphere of hydrogen. Articles so treated are in many cases highly resistant to corrosive materials, and at high temperature are resistant to oxidation.

calutron. An electromagnetic apparatus for separating isotopes of uranium and othre elements according to their masses, using the principle of mass spectrograph.

Campbell-Strake test reaction. To detect hydrogen peroxide, float an equal amount of ether on the sample liquid, add a few drops of 10% chromic acid, and shake. Formation of blue colour confirms the presence of hydrogen peroxide.

Campo-Cerdan test reaction. Zinc is detected in weakly-ammoniacal solution by the formation of a blue colour (characteristic absorption spectrum) with alcoholic resorcinol solution.

Camps quinoline synthesis. A method of formation of substituted hydroxyquinolines by ring closure of *o*-acylaminoacetophenones and related compounds.

COR′ CH₂R″ C=O NH $\xrightarrow{-H_2O}$ R′ R″ N OH

Canfield reagent. A solution of 4 g. ferric chloride, 3.3 g. nickel nitrate, and 30 g. cupric chloride, dissolved in 15 ml. of hot water, to which is then added 100 ml. of methyl alcohol and 0.5 ml. of nitric acid. The reagent is used to detect phosphorus segregation in steel.

Cannizzaro reaction. The formation of acids of alcohols by the simultaneous oxidation and reduction (a process called dismutation) of a pair of aldehyde molecules, most commonly one that has no alpha carbon atom, or no hydrogen atoms on an alpha carbon atom. Thus, benzaldehyde yields benzyl alcohol and benzoic acid, while formaldehyde gives methyl alcohol and formic acid. Mixed aldehydes may be used.

$$2C_6H_5CH \xrightarrow{OH^-} C_6H_5CH_2OH + C_6H_5COO^-$$

$$2HCHO \xrightarrow{OH^-} CH_3OH + HCOO^-$$

canonical assembly. *See* canonical ensemble.

canonical distribution. *See* canonical ensemble.

canonical ensemble. Statistical ensemble given by following probability distribution function

$$P(Q) = \exp\left[\frac{F - E(Q)}{kT}\right]$$

where $E(Q)$ = energy of system in stage Q, k = Boltzmann constant, T = thermodynamic temperature, and F=free energy. Canonical ensemble is utilized for statistical description of thermodynamic equilibrium in conservative systems. Also known as canonical assembly, canonical distribution.

canonical structures. *See* resonance structures.

Canton's phosphorus. Impure calcium sulphide, CaS, having the property of phosphorescence after exposure to light; used in luminous paints.

capillarity. Rise to fall of meniscus of liquid in capillary tubes. Also known as capillary action.

capillary action. *See* capillarity.

capillary column. In gas chromatography, column with small diameter, without packing in which layer of liquid held at inner walls of column serves as stationary phase. Also known as golay column.

cappillary condensation. Condensation of vapours in small pores of adsorbent (preferentially in its capillaries) due to fact that saturated vapour pressure of liquid adsorbate in capillary tube is lower than that above its plane surface.

caprolactam. The monomer used in the manufacture of nylon-6, it is derived by several methods from cyclohexane or from phenol, catalytic synthesis being involved, together with complex molecular rearrangements. In addition to its use in synthetic fibers, it is an ingredient or paints and plasticizers and also serves as a cross-linking agent. Its formula is $CH_2(CH_2)_4$—NHCO. It can also be used to synthesize the amino acid lysine.

capture cross-section. Cross-section for radiative capture of nucleon by nucleus.

caramel. A brown substance of complex composition, formed by the action of heat on sugar or other carbohydrate materials. Its chemical nature is not fully known, and its reactions vary with its method of preparation. It is used as a colouring agent for foodstuffs and drinks.

Caratheodory's principle. For every state there are other states which cannot be reached from this state *via* adiabatic process. Also known as principle of inaccessibility.

carbamate. The anion H_2NCOO^-, or a compounds containing it.

carbamic. The radical $-NH-\overset{\overset{\displaystyle O}{\|}}{C}-O-$.

carbamido. The radical $H_2NCONH-$.

carbamino. A compound formed by the combination of carbon dioxide with a free amino acid in an amino acid or protein.

carbamyl. The radical H_2NCO-. Also spelled as carbamoyl.

carbanion. Anion with negatively charged carbon atom *e.g.*, $R'-\overset{-}{\underset{\underset{\displaystyle R'''}{|}}{C}}-R''$.

It is produced by cleavage of certain C—H; C-halogen, C-metal, and C—C bonds.

carbazide. A compound of the type-formula

RHN—NH—CO—NH—NHR′

carbazone. A compound of the type-formula

R—N=N—CO—NH—NHR′

carbene. A short-lived and strongly reactive group containing a carbon atom having only six instead of eight valence electrons. It rapidly adds to alkenes to give cyclopropane products. The composition of this group, which is derived by the action of ultraviolet radiation on ketone, is $:CH_2$. The carbon atom has only two valences, which accounts for the exceptional activity of carbene and its value as an initator of organic reactions.

Chemical properties of a carbene depend on its electronic structure. When spins of nonbonding electrons are anti-parallel, electronic structure of carbene corresponds to less stable but more reactive singlet stat $\uparrow\downarrow\underset{|}{\overset{|}{C}}$. When spins parallel, electronic structure corresponds to more stable but less reactive triple state $\uparrow\uparrow\underset{|}{\overset{|}{C}}$.

carbenium ion. *See* carbonium ion.

carbenoid. Transient intermediate reacting under certain conditions in a way typical for a carbene.

carbethoxy. The radical C_2H_5OOC-.

carbide. A compound composed of carbon and a metal or nonmetal. Carbides are usually made by heating the substances in an electric furnace. Some are characterized by extreme hardness and resistance to high temperature; these are used as abrasives and refractory furnace linings (silicon carbide) and for metal-cutting drills and similar tools (tungsten carbide). Carbides may be pulverized, mixed with a similarly powdered metal such as cobalt or iron, and compressed at high temperature to form so-called cemented carbides.

carbinol. Either a primary alcohol, of type-formula RCH_2OH; or the first of the primary alcohols, methanol, CH_3OH; or acetyl methyl carbinol.

carbo-cation. Cation with positively charged carbon atom $R'-\overset{+}{\underset{\underset{\displaystyle R'''}{|}}{C}}-R''$.

carbocyclic. Any cyclic compound in which carbon atoms appears in the ring, *e.g.*, cyclohexane (alicyclic) and benzene (aromatic). *See also* heterocyclic.

carbodiazone. A compound of the type-formula

R—N=N—CO—N=N—R′

carbodithioic. The radical —C(:S)SH.

carbohydrase. Any enzmye that catalyze the hydrolysis of disaccharides and more complex carbohydrates.

carbohydrate. A class of compound which are basic components of plants of all types; they collectively consitute the most abundant group of natural organic substances. They include both simple compounds (sugars) and polymers of these (starches and cellulose), the latter being called polysaccharides. Carbohydrate molecules are composed of carbon, hydrogen, and oxygen, the ratio of the two being the same as exists in water. The atoms are so arranged that each molecule contains a hydroxyl group and a carbonyl group—a structure known as a saccharose unit.

```
      |
   H—C—C—
      |  ||
     HO  O
```

The simple sugars include fructose (levulose), glucose (dextrose), and sucrose ; the polymers comprise all varieties of starches, seaweeds, natural gums, and cellulose.

carbohydrate metabolism. The breakdown and synthesis of simple sugars, oligosaccharides, and polysaccharides, and the transport of sugars across cell membranes and tissues is dealt with in biochemistry and physiology. The breakdown of simple sugars, particularly glucose, is one of the principal sources of energy for living organisms. The dissimilation may be anaerobic, as in fermentations or aerobic, that is respiratory. In both types of metabolism, the breakdown is accompanied by formation of energy rich bonds, chiefly the pyrophosphate bond of the coenzyme adenosinetriphosphate (ATP) ; which serves as a coupling agent between different metabolic processes. In higher animals, glucose is the carbohydrate constituent of blood, which carries it to the tissue of the body. In higher plants, the disaccharide sucrose is often stored and transported by the tissues. Certain polysaccharides, especially starch and glycogen, are stored as endogenous food reserves in the cells of the plants, animals, and microorganisms. Others, such as cellulose, chitin, and bacterial polysaccharides, serve as structural components of cell walls. As constituents of animal and plant tissues, various carbohydrates become available to those organisms for their source of nutrients. Hence, all naturally occurring carbohydrates can be dissimilated by some animals or microorganisms.

carbohydrate nomenclature. The following rules for carbohydrate nomenclature were proposed by the ACS Committee in 1953 with the recommendation that they be adopted by the American Chemical Society after being tentative for one year.

Rule 1. Carbohydrate nomenclature should follow the general principles of established organic nomenclature.

Rule 2. As few changes as possible will be made in terminology universally adopted.

Rule 3. The names "aldose" or "ketose" will be used in a generic sense to denote the respective character of the reducing, or potentially reducing, group of the monosaccharide or derivative thereof. In an aldose, the carbon atom of the aldehyde function is atom number one ; and, in a ketose, the carbonyl carbon atom has the lowest possible number.

For indicating the number of carbon atoms in the chain, the appropriate one of the following names will be used : triose, tetrose, pentose, hexose, heptose, octose, nonose, etc.

Rule 4. Configurational relationships shall be denoted by the capital letters D and L which in print should preferable be small capital Roman letters and which are pronounced "dee" and "ell" (not "dextro" and "levo"). Such symbols will be placed immediately before the sugar stem name, and be employed only with compounds which have been definitively related to the reference-standard glyceraldehyde (*see* Rule 5). In a definitive name, the configurational symbol should not be omitted.

If the optical rotational sign under specified conditions is to be indicated, this may be done by adding (*dextro*) or (*levo*), which are italicized in print, or by adding (+) or (—). Racemic modifications may be indicated by the prefixes DL, or (±), or *inactive*, the last being italicized in print.

Examples :

D-glucose or D(*dextro*)-glucose or D (+) glucose

DL-glucose, or (±)-glucose, or *inactive*-glucose

Rule 5. Carbohydrates having the same configuration of the highest numbered asymmetric carbon atom as that of D(*dextro*)-glyceraldehyde will belong to the D-configurational series ; those having the opposite configuration will belong to the L-series.

D(*dextro*) Glyceraldehyde, the configurational reference standard, is written as follows :

```
     CHO
  H-<|>-OH
    CH2OH
```

Rule. 6. The configuration of a group of consecutive and adjacent asymmetric carbons, such as CHOH, CHOCH$_3$, CHOAc, or CHNH$_2$, containing one to four asymmetric carbons is designated by the appropriate one of these prefixes :

Number of Asymmetric Carbons	
One	*glycero*
Two	*threo, erythro*
Three	*arabino (arabo), ribo, xylo, lyro*
Four	*gluco, manno, gulo, ido, galacto, (gala), talo, allo, altro*

Each is D or L, as D-*talo* or L-*manno*. The prefix, which is derived by omitting the last two letters from the name of the aldose having the same configuration as the group to which it refers, is to be uncapitalized, italicized (in print), and attached by hyphens to the names to which it refers.

Rule 7. Ketoses having the carbonyl group at carbon atom number two will be named by means of suffix "*-ulose*" ; before this will be a prefix denoting the number of carbon atoms in the chain, which, in turn, will be preceded by the prefix denoting the configuration of the group of asymmetric centers present (*see* Rule 6).

Ketoses having the carbonyl group at a carbon atom other than number two will be named by inserting the appropriate numeral immediately before the prefix denoting the number of carbon atoms in the chain.

Rule 8. When an alcoholic hydroxyl group of a monosaccharide is replaced by the hadrogen atom, the compound will be named by attaching by a hyphen, before the sugar name, the appropriate number (indicating position), a hyphen, and the prefix "*deoxy*". The configuration of the sugar will be designated, when necessary, as given in Rule 6. This deoxy moiety can be further substituted.

Rule 9. When the hydrogen atom of an alcoholic hydroxyl group of a carbohydrate is substituted, an italic capital letter *O* (for oxygen) will be attached by a hyphen directly before the substituting prefix. The *O* prefix need not be repeated for multiple substitutions by one group. Similar principles apply where necessary to substitution or nitrogen (prefix, *N*). The prefix *C* may be used to indicate substitution or carbon to avoid possible ambiguity.

Example :

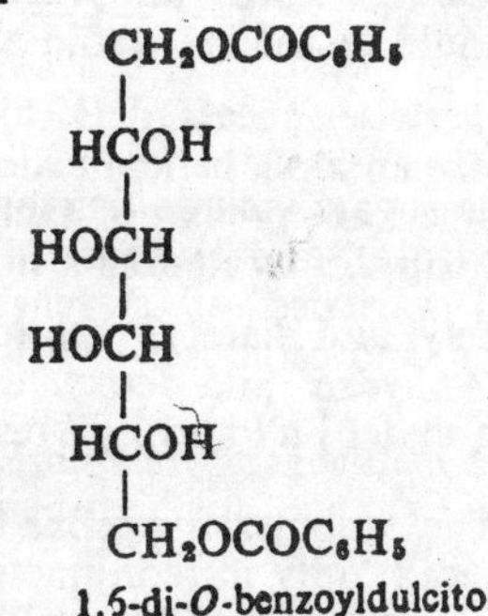

1,6-di-*O*-benzoyldulcitol

Rule 10. When a hydrogen atom of an alcoholic hydroxyl group of a carbohydrate (*see* Rule 9) is substituted by another atom or group, the name of the parent compound may be retained as the root for the substituted compound. In such names, the prefix (denoting the substituent) is to be attached directly to the root and not spaced from it.

Examples :

2,3,4,6-tetramethyl-α-D-glucose
hexa-*O*-acetyldulcitol
2-*O*-methyl-β-D-glucose
penta-*O*-propionyl-β-D-galactopyranose.

Rule 11. An ester formed from a sugar or sugar derivative by reaction with one or more of its alcoholic hydroxyl groups will be named by placing, after the sugar name and separated therefrom by a space, the appropriate numeral (indicating position) and a hyphen as prefix to the name of the group derived from an acid.

Rule 12. Class terms (excepting amine) such as acetal, alcohol, anhydride, ether, glycoside, ketone, sulphide, xyloside, and the like, which when used singly, represent no definite unsubstituted compound, are used as separate words.

Rule 13. When ethers of polyols (glycols, glycerol, polyhydric phenols, carbohydrates, and the like) are named as ethers, the name of polyol (a one-word name) shell be the first word, "ether" the last word, and the name of the appropriate radical (or radicals) shall be the middle word (or words).

Rule 14. When a prefix is attached to one of the words in a two-or three-word is attached and does not modify the remaining words in the name. But if a preceding word in this name is the name of a compound, numerals to indicate position of substitution in it may be placed before the following word, and, if necessary, parentheses should be used to avoid ambiguity.

Unless otherwise specified (Rules 15 and 17), prefixes take an alphabetical order, regardless of the numerical prefix of each; a compound radical name is treated as a unit.

Thus, triacetyl and diacetyl are to be listed under acetyl. Anhydro and deoxy are subject to alphabeting under "*a*" and "*d*" respectively.

Rule 15. The anomeric prefix (α- or β-), which can be used only in conjunction with a configurational prefix (D or L), will immediately precede the latter. The configurational prefix with directly precede the stem name (*see* Rule 6).

Rule 16. In conformity with established practice, hyphens shall be used in names to connect letters or numerals to syllables, or to separate different kinds of characters such as Roman letters from Greek letters or letters from numerals.

The preferred style is to connect syllables directly (no hyphens). Hyphens may be inserted, however, for the sake of clarity.

Examples :

α-D-glucose
3-*O*-methyl-β-L-mannose
penta-*O*-acetyl-α-D-glucopyranose
methyl tri-*O*-acetyl-α-D-glucopyranoside.

Rule 17. The acyclic nature of a sugar of derivative containing an unmodified CHO or CO groups as the primary function will be indicated by inserting the italicized prefix *aldehydo*, or *keto*, respectively, immediately before the configurational prefix and stem name.

Examples :

aldehydo-D-glucose pentaacetate
3,6-anhydro-*aldehydo*-D-galactose
keto-D-fructose pentabenzoate

Rule 18. The size of the ring in the heterocyclic forms of monosaccharides (aldoses and ketoses) may be indicated by replacing, in the sugar name, the letters "se" by "pyranose" for the 6-atom ring; "furanose" for the 5-atom ring; and "septanose" for the 7-atom ring. Likewise, for the glycosides (aldosides and ketosides), the size of the ring may be revealed by replacing the syllable "-side" by "pyranoside", "furanoside," or "septanoside."

Examples :

α-L-iodofuranose
methyl β-D-*altro*-heptulopyranoside

Rule 19. The root "glyc" in glycose or glycoside shall be used in a generic sense to denote any simple sugar or derivative thereof, rather than some specified sugar.

Examples :

glycose, methyl glycoside } generic

β-L-glucose, methyl *a*-D-glucopyranoside, ethyl b-D-altropyranoside, methyl β-L-fructofuranoside } specific

Rule 20. A glycoside is a mixed acetal resulting from the exchange of an organic radical for the hydrogen of the hemiacetal hydroxyl group of a cyclic form of an aldose or ketose. It is named by substituting "*ide*" as a suffix in place of the terminal "*e*" of the corresponding sugar name and placing before this word, seprated by a space, the name of the organic substituent.

Examples :

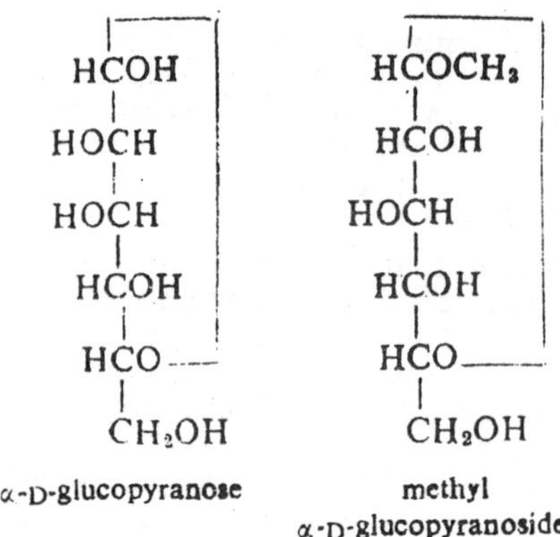

α-D-glucopyranose   methyl α-D-glucopyranoside

methyl-2-amino-2-deoxy-α-D-glucopyranoside (common name : methyl α-D-glucosaminide).

Rule 21. If the hemiacetal hydroxyl is detached from a cyclic modification of an aldose or ketose, the residue is a glycosyl glycopyranosyl, glycofuranosyl, glycoseptanosyl radical. It is named by substituting "*yl*" as a suffix in place of the terminal "*e*" of the corresponding sugar name.

Example :

```
        |‾‾‾‾‾‾‾‾‾‾‾‾‾‾|
       HCBr            |
        |              |
   CH3OCOCH            |
        |              O
   CH3OCOCH            |
        |              |
       HCOCOH3C        |
        |              |
       HC——————————————|
        |
       CH2OCOCH3
```

tetra-*O*-acetyl-α-D-mannopyranosyl bromide

Rule 22. A monosaccharide containing more than four configurational asymmetric carbon atoms will be named by adding two or more prefixes indicating the configurations of those asymmetric carbon atoms to a root indicating the number of carbon atoms in the chain and ending with the suffix "-ose" for aldoses and "-ulose" for ketoses.

Rule 23. Names for the polyhydric alcohols may be derived from the names of the corresponding aldose sugars by changing the suffix "ose" to "itol," using for nonmeso compounds the same family-determining asymmetric carbon as that characterizing the name of the sugar.

Rule 24. Aldonic acids, formed from aldoses by oxidation of only the hemiacetal or aldehydic carbon atom to $—CO_2H$, may be named by substituting "onic acid" as a suffix in place of "ose', of the corresponding aldose. Esters, salts, acid chlorides, lactones amides, and the like, are named in the conventional manner.

Rule 25. Uronic acids, formed from aldoses having a terminal $—CH_2OH$ group by oxidation only of this group to —COOH, may be named by substituting "uronic acid" as a suffix in place of "ose" of the corresponding aldose name. The hemiacetal or aldehydic carbon atom is carbon atom number one, and the syllable "*ur*" has the significance of "ω".

Esters, salts, acid chlorides, lactones amides, nitriles, and the like, are named in the c onventional manner.

Examples :

α-D-mannopyranuronic acid.

tetra-*O*-acetyl-β-D-talopyranuronic acid (or β-D-talopyranuronic acid tetraacetate).

methyl β-L-galactopyranuronate.

3-*O*-methyl-α-D-ribofuranurono-5,2-lactone.

α-D-mannopyranurono-6,2-lactone.

Rule 26. If the glycoside radical (*see* Rule 20) of an aldose glycoside possesses a terminal $—CH_2OH$ group, and if this group of the glycoside is oxidized to a carboxyl group, the product may be named by substituting "uronic acid" as a suffix in place of the terminal "*e*" of the parent glycoside name. The glycoside hemiacetal carbon atom is carbon number one.

Esters, salts, acid chlorides, lactones, amides, nitriles, and the like, may then be named in the conventional manner.

Examples :

methyl α-D-mannopyranosiduronic acid.

methyl α-D-glucopyranosidurono-γ-lactone (or 6,3-lactone).

ethyl (methyl β-L-galactopyranosid) uronate

butyl (propyl tri-*O*-acetyl-β-D-talopyranosid) uronate

Rule 27. α, ω-Dicarboxylic, sugar acids (aldaric or glycaric acids), formed by the oxidation of aldoses at both terminal carbon atoms, may be named by substituting "aric acid" as a suffix in place of "ose" of the corresponding aldose name.

Examples :

(*a*) Permissible name established by usage of some of the compounds are :

tartronic acid	for	glyceraric acid
dextro-tartaric acid	for	L-threaric acid
meso-tartaric acid	for	erythraric acid
saccharic acid	for	D-glucaric acid
idosaccharic acid	for	idaric acid
mannosaccharic acid	for	mannaric acid
mucic acid	for	galactaric acid
allomucic acid	for	allaric acid
talomucic acid	for	talaric acid

(*b*) Names requiring D or L :

threaric acid

arabinaric (arabaric) acid

glucaric acid

talaric acid

idaric acid

mannaric acid

(*c*) Names used without D or L :

glyceraric acid
erythraric acid
ribaric acid
xylaric acid
allaric acid
galactaric acid

The names of meso forms can be used advantageously with D or L in naming derivatives which have become optically active by substitution.

(*d*) Equivalent names :

lyxaric acid and arabinaric acid
talaric acid and ultraric acid
L-gularic acid and D-glucaric acid.

Rule 28. The "glycosides of other ester structure" may be named as the ortho esters with the carbohydrate group given as the first term in the name.

Example :

```
 ┌────────┐
 │        │
 │        HCO    *   OCH3
 │        │    \ C /
 │        HCO  /   \ CH3
 O        │
 │        HCOOCH3
 │        │
 │        HCOOCCH3
 │        │
 └────────CH2
```

D-ribose 1,2-(methyl orthoacetate) 3,4-diacetate

It may be noted that this compound can also be named according to Rule 29 as 3,4-di-*O*-acetyl-1,2-*O*-(1-methoxyethylidene)-D-ribose.

Rule 29. Cyclic acetals which are formed by the reaction of carbohydrates with aldehydes or ketones may be named with bivalent radicals as prefixes in accordance with Rule 7, such radicals to follow the momenclature set forth in I.U.P.A.C. Rule 56.1. In representing more than one cyclic acetal grouping, the numeral pairs are separated typographically when the exact position of the acetal groups is known.

Examples :

```
  CH2OH
   │
  HCO──────┐
   │       │
 HOCH     CH2
   │       │
  HCO──────┘
   │
  CH2OH
```

2,4-*O*-methylenexylitol

```
 ┌──────────OCH2
 │           │
 CH2        HOCH
 │           │
 └──────────OCH
             │
            HCO──────┐
             │       │
            HCOH    CH2
             │       │
            CH2O─────┘
```

1,3;4,6-di-*O*-methylene-D-mannitol

Rule 33. An intramolecular anhydride, formed by the elimination of the elements of water from two hydroxyl groups of a monosaccharide molecule (aldose or ketose), is named by attaching by a hyphen before the sugar name the prefix "anhydro" ; this, in turn, is preceded by a pair of numerals identifying the two hydroxyl groups involved. Anhydride, of sugar acids, lactones, alcohols, and the like are named similarly.

Rule 34. An intermolecular anhydride, formed by condensation of two monosaccharide molecules with the elimination of the elements of two molecules of water, will be named by the word "dianhydride" placed after the names of the two parent sugars. The position of each anhydride link is indicated by a pair of numerals showing the positions of the two hydroxyl groups involved ; the numerals relating to one sugar (in a mixed dianhydride, the second sugar named) will be primed. Both pairs of numerals will immediately precede the word "dianhydride".

Examples :

di-D-fructopyranose 2,1′:2′,1-dianhydride.
di-β-D-fructofuranose 2,3′:2′,1-dianhydride.
β-D-fructofuranose β-D-*threo*-pentulofuranose.
2,1′:2′,1-dianhydride

Rule 32. An oligosaccharide is a compound which, on complete hydrolysis, gives monosaccharide units only, in relatively small number per molecule (in contrast to the high-polymeric polysaccharides).

carbon. An element.

		Symbol C
	Atomic No.	6
Group IVA	Atomic Wt.	12.01115
	Valence	(2), 4
	m.p.	3550°C
	b.p.	4830°C

A nonmetal, present in all organic compounds and is essential to the photosynthetic reaction on which all living organisms depend. Carbon and its compounds are found widely distributed in nature. It is estimated that carbon makes up about 0.032% of the earth's crust. In the atmosphere carbon is present in amounts of up to 0.03% by volume as carbon dioxide. Though inactive at room temperature, it is highly reactive above 550°C. Carbon occurs in compounds that number in the hundreds of thousands, such as hydrocarbons (petroleum) and carbohydrates (plants). The free element finds many uses, ranging from ornamental applications of diamond in jewelry to the black-coloured pigment of carbon-black which is used in automobile tires and printing inks. Carbon forms binary compouns called carbides with many metals and some nonmetals. Its electronegative nature makes it a good reducing agent for metallic oxides ; and its high electrical conductivity accounts for its use as electrodes, brushes, contacts, and other electrical equipment. Chemically pure carbon is prepared by thermal decomposition of sucrose in absence of air. Its physical and chemical properties are dependent on its crystal structure. Carbon exists in several allotropic forms, two of which (diamond and graphite) are crystalline, the others being amorphous (coal, carbon black, activated carbon, and charcoal). The latter (except coal) (are generally known as industrial carbon. A unique feature of carbon is its ability to notably affect the properties of metals in which it is present in very low concentrations ; this is especially true of steel, in which carbon content varies from 0.02 to 1.5%. Since the C-12 isotope comprises over 99% of carbon, its mass is taken as the international standard for determination of atomic masses.

carbon-14. A naturally occurring radioisotope of carbon having a mass number of 14 and half life of 5780 years. It is used in radiocarbon dating and in the elucidation of the metabolic path of carbon in photosynthesis.

carbonation. 1. In beet sugar refining, the process of precipitating, with a stream of carbon dioxide, the lime which has been added to the juice to neutralize the free acids and precipitate the albuminoids.

2. The reduction of carbon containing compounds to elemental carbon.

3. Saturation with carbon dioxide.

4. The introduction of a carboxyl group (—COOH) into an organic compound (in other words, the preparation of an organic carboxylic acid) by the action of carbon dioxide on certain organic compounds, especially alkylmagnesium halides. For example :

$$(CH_3)_3CMgCl + CO_2 \rightarrow (CH_3)_3CC(O)OMgCl$$

$$\xrightarrow[H_2O]{\Delta} (CH_3)_3CCOOH + MgClOH$$

carbon black. A type of amorphous carbon notable for its extremely small particle size, It is produced commercially by thermal or oxidative decomposition of hydrocarbons.

There are four grades of carbon black :—

1. channel black, made by high-temperature decomposition of natural gas, the particles being deposited on a metal bar or channel immediately the flame (sometimes called impingement above black for this reason).

2. Fumace black, made by partial combustion of a mixture of hydrocarbon oils, gases, or vapours in an enclosed chamber.

3. Thermal decomposition black, made by heating the gas in the chamber without air being present.

4. Acetylene black, made by decomposition of acetylene in a special refractory unit. It is used principally in rubber goods, pigments, and printer's ink. It is not an inert filler but enhances and signiforces various properties of rubbers.

carbon chain. System of mutually linked carbon atoms forming skeleton of the compound, *e.g.*,

$$-\overset{|}{\underset{|}{C}}-\overset{|}{\underset{|}{C}}-\overset{|}{\underset{|}{C}}-\overset{|}{\underset{|}{C}}-\overset{|}{\underset{|}{C}}-\overset{|}{\underset{|}{C}}-$$

carbon cycle. This term refers to two quite different phenomena ; one occurring in the sun and other stars, while the other in the earth's biosphere.

1. As to the first, carbon acts as a catalyst of the thermonuclear reactions responsible for the sun's energy, namely, the formation of helium from four hydrogen nuclei (protons). The carbon is not transformed in the process. *See also* carbon-nitrogen cycle.

2. The second meaning involves the complex reaction known as photosynthesis, in which carbon is absorbed from the air by plants as carbon dioxide, then moves through photochemical reactions catalyzed by chlorophyll, and finally through decay or combustion sequences wherein it reappears as carbon dioxide.

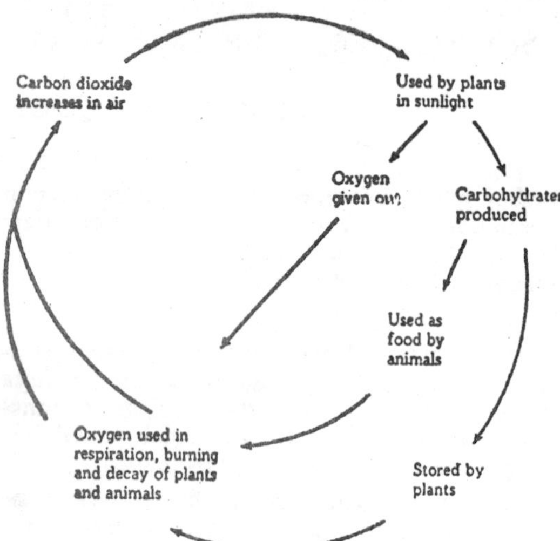

Fig. 14. Carbon cycle occurring in the earth's biosphere

carbonic anhydrase. An enzyme which aids carbon dioxide transport and release by catalyzing the synthesis, and the dehydration, of carbonic acid from, and to, carbon dioxide and water.

carbonium ion. An unstable form of carbon in which the carbon atom has only six valence electrons instead of the normal eight. This results in a positively charged carbonium ion which is an extremely active reaction intermediate in, for example, catalytic cracking of petroleum and many aromatic reactions. The carbonium ion is one of the most important of such unstable initiators, others being free radicals and carbenes.

carbonium-ion-induced rearrangements. In many reactions carbonium-ion intermediates in which the positively-charged, centre is adjacent to a highly branched (substituted) carbon atom may rearrange by a shift of one of the neighbouring substituents :

$$R-\overset{R}{\underset{R'}{C}}-\overset{+}{\underset{R'}{C}}-R' \xrightarrow{\text{R shift}} R-\overset{+}{\underset{R}{C}}-\overset{R}{\underset{R'}{C}}-R'$$

Such carbonium-ion rearrangements are most often observed when they result in an improvewent in ion stability or in a relief of ring strain or nonbonded repulsions. Such rearrangements do not usually involve more than one functional group. *Also see* carbocation.

carbonize. 1. To convert into carbon.

2. To cause combination with, or addition of carbon, as in the cementation process for making steel.

3. To cleanse wood of vegetable matter by soaking it in a bath of aluminium chloride (or dilute sulphuric acid) ridding it of excess moisture, and placing it in preheated chambers where the aluminium chloride is decomposed. The hydrochloric acid thus formed attacks the foreign matter and renders it so friable that it is easily removed in a beating machine.

carbon-nitrogen cycle. Series of thermonuclear reactions leading to synthesis of helium from hydrogen.

In the cycle, nuclei of carbon and nitrogen are involved.

$$^{12}C(p,\gamma)\ ^{14}N(\beta^+ \nu)\ ^{13}C(p,\gamma)\ ^{14}N(p,\gamma) \rightarrow\ ^{15}O(\beta^+ \nu)\ ^{15}N(p,\alpha)\ ^{12}C$$

Carbon-nitrogen chain is the source of energy of stars. Also known as carbon cycle ; Bethe cycle.

carbonyl. 1. The group $-\overset{|}{C}=O$.

2. A compound formed by the union of carbon monoxide with a metal, *e.g.*, nickel tertra

carbonyl $Ni(CO)_4$, iron pentacarbonyl $Fe(CO)_5$, cobalt pentacarbonyl, $Co(CO)_5$ are important compounds of this type.

carbonylation. Addition of carbon monoxide molecule to the molecule of an organic or inorganic compound ; *e.g.*,

$$>C{=}C< + CO + H_2 \xrightarrow[\text{30 atm, catalyst}]{200°C} \overset{|}{\underset{|}{C}}H{-}\overset{|}{\underset{|}{C}}{-}\overset{O}{\overset{\|}{C}}{-}H$$

carborane. The parent substance of a group of unique organic compounds containing boron, carbon, and hydrogen ($B_{10}C_2H_{12}$) some members also contain unsaturated organic groups (isopropenylcarborane). Carborane can be prepared by reaction of acetylene with decaborane ($B_{10}H_{14}$) and diethyl sulphide. Not all compounds of carbon, boron, and hydrogen can be considered as carboranes. To be called as carborane, a compound must have at least one carbon atom in the three-dimensional skeleton of the structure. For example, $C_2H_5B_{12}H_{11}^{2-}$ is a derivative of $B_{12}H_{12}^{2-}$ in which one hydrogen atom is replaced by an ethyl group ; it is thus not a carborane even though it is composed of carbon, boron and hydrogen. The unusual crystal structure is that of a 20-sided polyhedron. The nucleus common to these compounds ($B_{10}C_2$) often has a closed, cage-like form. Carborane is a solid, melting at about 260°C ; it burns with intense heat and is highly toxic.

carboxylase. An enzyme that catalyzes the carboxylation or decarboxylation reaction.

carboxylation. Introduction of carboxylic group —COOH into the molecule of an organic compound usually effected by the action of carbon dioxide on metal-organic molecule with subsequent decomposition of formed salt, *e.g.*,

$$RMgX \xrightarrow{CO_2} RCOOMgX \xrightarrow{H_2O_2/H^+} RCOOH$$

$$RLi \xrightarrow{CO_2} RCOOLi \xrightarrow{H_2O_2/H^+} RCOOH$$

carboxylic. Pertaining to the carboxyl group, —COOH, characteristic of organic acids.

carboxylic acids. Any of the several compounds incorporating the carboxyl (—COOH) functional group, one of the highest commonly encountered **oxidation** state of carbon. Carboxylic acids are identified by IUPAC nomenclature with ending *-ioc* acid. Carboxylic acids have substantially higher boiling points than other organic compounds of equivalent molecular weight as a result of hydrogen-bonded association of acid molecules. The preparation methods include :

(*i*) Oxidation of primary alcohols.
(*ii*) Oxidation of aldehydes.
(*iii*) Oxidation of aryl side chains.
(*iv*) Oxidative cleavage of distribution alkenes and alkynes.
(*v*) Reaction of Grignard reagents or alkyl lithium reagents with carbon dioxide.
(*vi*) Hydrolysis of nitriles.

carboxymethylation. Substitution of hydrogen atom (bound with carbon, nitrogen or oxygen atom) of organic compound molecule by carboxymethyl group $—CH_2COOH$, *e.g.*,

$$\underset{\underset{O}{\|}}{RC}CH_3 + ClCH_2COOR' \xrightarrow{NaNH_2} \underset{\underset{O}{\|}}{RC}CH_2CH_2COOR'$$

$$\begin{matrix}CH_2NH_2\\ |\\ CH_2NH_2\end{matrix} \xrightarrow[H_2O/NaOH]{HCHO+NaCN} \begin{matrix}CH_2N(CH_2COOH)_2\\ |\\ CH_2N(CH_2COOH)_2\end{matrix}$$

carboxypeptidase. Any enzyme that catalyzes the hydrolysis of peptide at the end of a molecule containing the free carboxyl group.

carburetion. The process of enriching a gas by adding volatile carbon compounds, such as hydrocarbons ; to it, as in the manufacture of carbureted water gas.

carburize. To surface-harden steel by converting the outer layer of low-carbon steel to high-carbon steel by heating the steel above the transformation range in contact with a carbonaceous material.

carburizer. A substance used in the surface-heat-treatment of certain metals to increase the carbon content, and hence the hardness, of the portion of the metal at or near the surface. This process is known as case hardening.

carbylamine reaction. Reaction of primary amines with chloroform and sodium (or potassium) hydroxide, involving isonitrile formation (manifested by very unpleasant smell); carried out for detecting the amino group, *e.g.*,

$$RNH_2+CHCl_3+3NaOH \rightarrow R-N^+\equiv C^- + 3NaCl + 3H_2O$$

Also known as isocyanide reaction.

carcinogen. Any agent which has been found to induce the formation of cancerous tissue in experimental animals. A number of benzenoid compounds are found to be carcinogenic, *e.g.*, benzopyrene (in cigarette tars), benzidine, and phenanthrene, as well as other types such as the nitrogen mustards. The most dangerous is benzopyrene, since it involves chronic inhalation affecting the large surface area of the lungs. The number of suspected carcinogens is constantly increasing; some (such as asbestos fibres) are well documented, but others are not.

Carius's method. For the quantitative determination of halogen in an organic compound, the substance is oxidised by heating with fuming nitric acid and silver nitrate in a sealed "Carius tube". The tube is wrapped in asbestos and heated in a special furnace to about 260°C and kept at that temperature for about four to six hours. Precautions are observed against the possibility of explosion. The silver halide formed is eventually washed out, filtered, dried and weighed. Sulphur, or phosphorous can also be determined by a similar process.

carminative. Any drug that promotes the expulsion of gas from the gastrointestinal tract.

Carmody's indicator. For acid-carbonate titrations; a screened indicator of about 0.5 gram. of dimethyl yellow with one-twentieth of that amount to methylene blue dissolved in 500 ml. of ethanol.

Carney test. A solution of 5.0 g. tetramethyldiaminodiphenylmethane and 10 g. citric acid in 1 litre water, when added to gold in solution, the reagent forms a purple to blue colour.

Carnot cycle. A hypothetical thermodynamic cycle used as a standard for comparison for actual cycles. The Carnot cycle shows that, even under ideal conditions, a heat engine cannot convert all the heat energy supplied to it into mechanical energy some of the heat energy must be rejected.

In a Carnot cycle, an engine accepts heat energy from a high-temperature source, or hot body, converts part of the received energy into mechanical (or electrical) works, and rejects the remainder to to low-temperature sink, or cold body. The greater the temperature difference between the source and sink, the greater is the efficiency of the heat engine.

The Carnot cycle (*see* illustration) consists first of an isentropics compression. then an isothermal heat addition, followed by an isentropic expansion, and concludes with an isothermal heat rejection process. In short, the processes are compression, addition of heat, expansion, and rejection of heat, all in a qualified and definite manner. The net effect of the cycle is that heat is added at at constant high temperature, somewhat less heat is rejected at a constant low temperature, and the algebraic

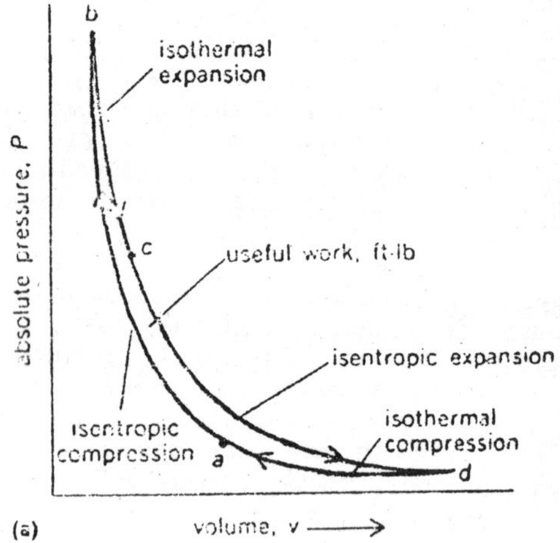

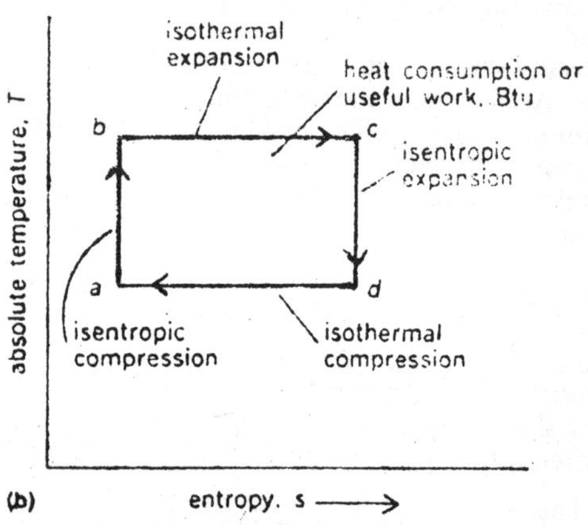

Fig. 15. Carnot cycle for air. (a) Absolute pressure versus volume. (b) Absolue temperature versus entropy.

sum of these heat quantities is equal to the work done by the cycle.

A Carnot cycle consists entirely of reversible processes ; thus it can theoretically operate to withdraw heat from a cold body and to discharge that heat to a hot body. To do so, the cycle requires work input from its suroundings. The heat equivalent of this work input is also discharged to the hot body. Just at the Carnot cycle provides the highest efficiency for a power, cycle operating between two fixed temperatures, so does the reversed Carnot cycle provide the best coefficint of performance for device pumping heat from a low temperature to a higher temperature.

There are various difficulties that arise when one tries to make and actual Carnot engine. The necessarily high peak pressures and temperatures limit the practical thermal efficiency that an actual engine can achieve. Although the Carnot cycle is independent of the working substance, and hence is applicable to a vapour cycle, the difficulty of efficiently compressing a vapour liquid mixture renders the cycle impractical.

Carnot's principle. Yield of Carnot cycle is the same for all substances. Carnot's principle follows from second law of thermodynamics.

carotenase. Any enzymes that effects the hydrolysis of carotenoid compounds ; used in bleachhing of flour.

carotenoid. Any of a class of yellow, orange, red, and purple pigments that are widely distributed in nature. Carotenoids are generally fat-soluble unless they are complexed with proteins. In plants, carotenoids are usually located in quantity in the grana of chloroplasts in the form of carotenoprotein complex. Carotenoprotein complexes give blue, green, purple, red, or other colours to crustaceans, echinocerms, nudibranch mollusks, and other invertbrate animals. Some coral coelenterates exhibit purple, pink, orange, or variuos other colours due to carotenoids in the calcareous skeletal material. Cooked or denatured lobster, crab and shrimp show the modified colours due to presence of carotenoproteins.

The general structure of carotenoid is that of aliphatic and aliphatic-alicyclic polyenes, with a few aromatic-type polyenes. Most carotenoid pigments are tetraterpenes with a 40-carbon (C_{40}) skeleton. More than 350 carotenoids of known structure are recognized, and the number is still on the rise.

There are several biochemical functions in which the role of carotenoids is well understood. These include carotenoid in the photosynthetic apparatus of green plants, algae, and photosynthetic bacteria, where carotenoids function as a blue light harvesting pigment (antenna or accessory pigment) for photosynthesis. Thus carotenoids make it possible for photosynthetic organisms more fully to utilize the solar energy in the visible spectral region.

Another important function of carotenoids is to protect biological systems as the photosynthetic apparatus from photodynamic damage.

Carr-Price tests for vitamin A. 1. On adding 1 ml. of the Carr-Price reagent to 0.1 ml. of the oil to be tested, a blue colour indicates the pressence of vitamin A.

2. Stannic chloride, dissolved in chloroform, gives a deep blue colour changing to purple with Vitamin A.

3. Anhydrous ferric chloride, on addition to an oil containing Vitamin A, dissolved in chloroform, gives a fluorescent red-violet colour.

4. Powdered anhydrous aluminum chloride gives red-violet colour fading to brown with an oil containing Vitamin A.

Carrel-Dakin solution. An isotonic solution of sodium hypochlorite, used as an antiseptic in surgical treatments. It is prepared by dissolving 30.8 g. chlorinated lime (U.S.P.), 12.8 g. sodium bicarbonate, and 15.4 g. sodium carbonate in 2 litres of water.

carrier. Substance introduced into system in macro-amounts in order to separate or retain quantitatively a microcomponent (*e.g.*, impurities, radioactive substances) which undergoes the same transformations in the system as the macrocomponent.

carrier distillation. In spectroanalysis, fractional distillation in presence of spectroscopic carrier.

carreir free radioactive preparation. Radioactive isotope which does not contain non-radioactive isotopes. It usually has a high specific activity.

carrier gas. Gas used to elute sample from column in gas chromatography.

carrier metal. A metal serving as the base for supporting a second metal, especially as applied in photoelectric cells, where extremely thin films of the active metal are used.

carrier, spectroscopic. A material added to a sample to facilitate its vapourization into an excitation source. The carrier may serve to sweep the entire sample rapidly into the source or it may be limited in its action to assisting in the fractional distillation of the sample.

Carter process. An improved modern version of the old Dutch process for the manufacture of white lead. Metallic lead which has been blown to a fine powder with steam or air reacts with acetic acid, air, water, and carbon dioxide in large revolving wooden cylinders. The white lead (basic lead carbonate) is produced in about two weeks as against three months or so by the original Dutch process.

Cascade process. A term used ;

1. for an early method devised for gases that liquefy with difficulty—it depends on the successive cooling of the gas by other gases already liquefied, and

2. for a method used to concentrate sulphuric and manufactured by the "chamber" process—water being caused to evaporate by a stream of hot air.

case hardening. Turning wrought iron into steel on the surface only by heating it in contact with carbon. The term may also be used for other substances where the surface is made harder than the interior.

casting alloy. An alloy which cannot be forged or rolled by can be shaped only as casting.

cast iron. Any carbon iron alloy cast to shape and containing 1.8-4.5% carbon, that is in excess of the solubility in austenite at the eutectic temperature. Usually silicon is present upto 3% but special compositions are made containing upto 6% (Silal) and upto 12% (Durison).

Castner process. Two processes are named after Castner :

1. The production of metallic sodium by the electrolysis of sodium hydroxide fused in a specially designed cell. This method has now given way to that in which fused sodium chloride is electrolysed,

2. The production of sodium cyanide by first passing ammonia gas over fused sodium to make sodamide, and then pouring the fused sodamide on to red-hot charcoal to give sodium cyanide.

Castner-Kellner process. In a specially designed rocking cell, sodium hydroxide was produced by the electrolysis of brine. It is obsolete, as a modification of the process in the Kellner Solvay cell is now used.

catalysis. Phenomenon of acceleration or retardation of chemical reaction due to presence of catalyst.

catalyst. Element or compound that changes rate of chemical reaction but remains unchanged in chemical composition after reaction. If the reaction $A+B \rightarrow C$ occurs very slowly but is catalyzed by some catalyst Z, the addition of Z must open new channels for the reaction;

$$A+Z \rightarrow AZ$$
$$AZ+B \rightarrow C+Z$$
$$\overline{A+B \rightarrow C}$$

The catalysts most used in industrial processing are inorganic substances, chiefly metals or metallic oxides, usually in the form of powders or porous masses. They function by either physical or chemical adsorption. Only a few parts per million of catalyst are required to activate a large-scale reaction, the same catalyst charge can be used for 1000 hours or more since it is not consumed during the course of reaction. To be effective, catalysts must be in a finely divided state to furnish maximum surface area for adsorption as the reacting substances pass over or through them ; their effect is due to submicroscopic projections on the surface of their particles (active points), where a bond is formed with the reactants. If the adsorption is physical, these bond are relatively weak ; if it is chemical, they are about as strong as chemical bonds.

Catalysis is conventionally divided into three categories ; homogeneous, heterogenous, and enzyme. Heterogenous catalysis plays a dominant role in chemical processes in chemical industries. Homogeneous catalysis is also important in the petrochemical and chemical industries. Organic catalysts called enzymes are essential in the functioning of animal metabolism ; the part played by chlorophyll in photosynthesis is an example of catalysis in plants, promoting formation of sugars from carbon dioxide and water.

Following is a list of some of the catalysts and the types of reaction they catalyze ; (the asterisk indicates a destructive effect).

aluminium chloride	condensation (Friedel-Crafts reaction)
aluminium alkyl + titanium chloride	Ziegler catalyst for stereospecific polymers
aluminium oxide	hydration ; dehydration
chromic oxide	methanol synthesis aromatization ; polymerization
cobalt	hydrocarbon synthesis ; Oxo process
copper salts	oxidation (of rubber)*
iron	ammonia synthesis ; hydrocarbon synthesis
iron oxide	dehydrogenation (oxidation)
manganese dioxide	oxidation
molybdenum oxide	dehydrogenation; polymerization ; aromatization ; partial oxidation
nickel	**hydrogenation (oils to fats)**
platinum metals	**hydrogenation ; aromatization ; oxidation**
silica-alumina	**cracking hydrocarbons**
silver	**hydration ; oxidation**
vanadium pentoxide	oxidation (manufacture of surphuric acid)

catalyst activity. Quantitative expression of ability of a catalyst to change rate of reaction. Also known as catalytic activity.

catalyst carrier. *See* catalyst support.

catalyst poison. In heterogenous catalysis, substance adsobed at surface of catalyst, blocking access of substrates and therefore diminishing, or even destroying activity of catalyst. Also known as catalytic poison.

catalyst poisoning. In heterogenous catalysis, loss of catalyst activity, due to action of catalytic poison.

catalyst promoter. In heterogeneous catalysis, a substance which is not a catalyst or possesses weak catalytic properties, but which when mixed with a catalyst causes growth of its catalytic activity (sometimes also its selectivity of persistence).

catalyst stripping. Introduction of steam to remove hydrocarbons retained on the catalyst ; the steam is introduced where the spent catalyst leaves the reactor.

catalyst support. Substance which is not active catalytically, usually of large specific surface acting as support for catalyst. Also known as catalytic carrier.

catalytic activity. *See* catalyst activity.

catalytic coefficient. Quotient of rate constant and concentration of catalyst. Also known as catalytic constant.

catalytic constant. *See* catalytic coefficient.

catalytic cracking. Conversion of high-boiling hydrocarbons into lower-boiling hydrocarbons using a suitable catalyst.

catalytic current. In polarography and related methods, current which results from catalytic chemical reaction which transforms product of electrode reaction into substrate.

catalytic hydrogenation. Hydrogenation taking place in the presence of a catalyst such as nickel or palladium.

catalytic poison. *See* catalyst poison.

catalytic polymerization. A process for the polymerization of hydrocarbon gases, usually consisting chiefly of paraffins and olefins, by catalytic action, to yield gasoline and other liquid products.

catalytic reaction. Reaction proceeding with participation of catalyst. Also known as catalyzed reaction.

catalytic reforming. A process used for upgrading gasoline by improving its antiknock characteristics (increasing the octane number). It is widely used for the production of aromatic hydrocarbons for the petrochemical industry. The process utilizes a supported platinum catalyst and involves a number of different reactions.

Under suitable conditions it is possible to convert 40% of the naphtha to LPG, the by-product being high octane gasoline.

catalyzed reaction. *See* catalytic reaction.

cataphoresis. The drift of a disperse phase through its medium towards anode or cathode. As this term would seem to imply a drift to the cathode only (true of a positive colloid but not of a negative one) the term electophoresis is usually perferred.

cat craker. A term used in the petrochemical industry for the plant in which hydrocarbons of high molecular weight are broken down into simpler ones (*i.e.*, "craked") in the presence of a catalyst.

catecholamines. Harmones such as adrenaline, that are amino derivatives of catechol.

catenanes. Compounds whose molecules are constructed of two or more large rings (usually saturated) having no common carbon atoms (or atoms of any other element) ; such rings form chain-link structures, *e.g.*,

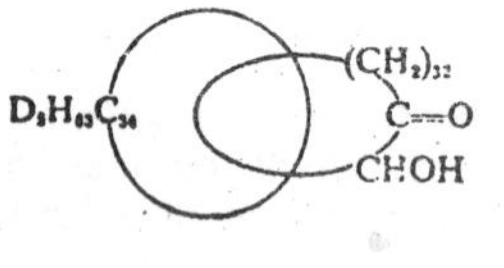

$D_5H_{63}C_{34}$ $(CH_2)_{32}$
$C=O$
$CHOH$

catenate. A term used in chemistry to indicate the tendency or ability of an element to unite with itself to form chains ; carbon is notable in this regard, and several other elements, such as sulphur, phosphorus and silicon, exhibit this property to a limited extent. It is noteworty that the elements whose atoms behave in this manner are all fairly close to carbon in the periodic table, and they all possess atoms that are electronically unsaturated.

cathartics. Agents used to produce evacuation of the bowl. They are too frequently used and should probably be administered only after possible organic causes of constipation have been considered.

cathode. The negative electrode of an electrolytic cell through which current is being passed. It is the electrode at which reduction takes place and at which electrons enter (current leaves) an electrolyte. Among the reducing reactions occurring at the cathode are discharge of positive ions, formation of negative ions, and reduction of chemical elements from higher to lower oxidation state. It may be noted that in a battery the cathode is the positive terminal. In electroplating, cations (positively charged ions) migrate to the cathode, upon which they are deposited to form a coating. In an electron or vacuum tube, the negative electrode is the cathode.

cathode current density. Current density which flows across metallic conductor-electrolyte phase boundary, equal to the rate of reduction as cathode. Also known as cathode partical current density.

cathodoluminescence. The luminescence resulting from the bombardment of a substance with an electron beam. Its major application is in cathode-ray oscilloscopes and in television picture tubes.

cathode ray polarography. *See* oscillopolarography.

cathodic partial current density. *See* cathodic current density.

cathodic polarization. Portion of electric cell polarization occuring at the cathode.

cathodic protection. Protecting a metal from electrochemical corrosion by making it as the cathode of a cell with a sacrificial anode. Also known as electrolytic protection.

catholyte. Part of an electrolyte in vicinity of cathode in which changes of physico-chemical properties occur during electrolysis or discharge of galvanic cell ; if solutions in vicinity of both electrodes of a cell are separated, *e.g.*, by membranes it is that part of electrolyte surrounding cathode.

cation. An ion, having one or more positive charges, which migrates to the cathode in a solution when an electric current is passed. *See also* anion.

cation exchanger. Ion exchanger containing cations that can be exchanged for other cations present in solution.

cationic current. That fraction of the total current which is carried by the cations.

cationic detergent. A member of a group of detergents that have molecules containing a quaternary ammonium salt cation with a group of 12 to 14 carbon atoms attached to the nitrogen atom in the cation, *e.g.*, alkyltrimethyl ammonium bromide.

cationic polymerization. A polymerization reaction catalyzed by cationic species.

cationotropy. Reversible migration of cation from one position to another in molecule.

Ionization of certain tautomeric organic compounds, whereby one of their equilbrium forms dissociates into a simple cation (such as H^+ and a complex anion.

caustic. A term which has the general meaning of corrosive and is applied to the water-soluble hydroxides of the light metals to distinguish them from their carbonates. It is also used in medicine to designate substances that destroy body tissues ; thus lunar caustic is silver nitrate.

caustic embrittlement. The development of britleness in metals such as steel or ferrous alloys upon prolonged exposure to alkaline substances, like caustic soda, in solution. Failures and explosions in boilers and evaporators have been caused by this action.

cavitation. A method of making a vapour-liquid emulsion by reduction of the hydrodynamic pressure within the liquid to a value below the vopour pressure.

cavity field. Part of local electric field in cavity in dielectric (obtained by removing a molecule) due to influence of external electric field.

c-axis. A vertically oriented crystal axis, usually the principal axis ; the unique symmetry axis in tetragonal and hexagonal crystals.

cell. 1. In electrochemistry, the term cell refers to a device for producing an electric current by chemical means (battery) or for performing electrolysis, the essential difference being that the former generates electricity whereas the latter consumes it.

2. In bichemistry, a cell is the basic unit of tissues structure, composed of an outer wall or membrane, an interior fluid called cytoplasm, and a nucleus which contains chromosomes and genes (nucleic acids).

3. One of a set of elementery regions in a heterogenous reactor, all of which have the same geometricals form and the same neutron characteristics.

4. The word cell may also mean a hollow structural unit of a plastic foam. *See* cellular

cell, cadmium. *See* cadmium cell.

cell, Clarke. *See* Clarke cell.

cell, combination. *See* combination cell.

cell, concentration. *See* concentration cell.

celll constant of conductomertic vessel, *k*. Characteristic parameter for vessels used in comparative measurements, of specific conductivity of electrolyte solutions :

$$k=Rx$$

where R and x=resistance and specific conductivity of standard solution of KCl respectively. Also known as vessel constant.

cell, diffusion. *See* diffusion cell.

cell, displacement. *See* displacement cell.

cell, oxidation-reduction. *See* oxidation-reduction cell.

cell, primary. *See* primary cell.

cell, secondary. *See* secondary cell.

cell, standard. *See* standard cell.

cell, transition. *See* transition cell.

cellophane. A transperent cellulose, similar to rayon, produced by the viscose process and extruded in the form of thin sheets. It has adequate strength and a high degree of transparency ; used as an excellent packing material for general purpose. It is not as good as moisture-vapour barrier as more recently developed plastics films.

cellular. A term used in the plastics and rubber industries to describe a foam-like structure, either flexible or rigid, comprised of closed pores formed by the action of a blowing agent; this gives a soft, spongy feel to flexible products, such as "sponge" rubber. The word "cellular" is not synonymous with "porous" since the latter includes both closed and open pores.

cellulose. The most abundant organic compound in nature, cellulose is a carbohydrate polymer belonging to the general class of polysccharides. Its formula can be represented as $(C_6H_{10}O_5)n$, in which the n stand for an undertermined number of carbohydrate units. It is a straignt-chain molecule comprised of glucose units connected by oxygen atoms and can be converted to simpler forms (starches, etc.) by hydrolysis. Its molecular weight ranges from 150,000 to over 500,000. The molecule has been shown to possess both crystalline and amorphous segments. Cellulose does not disslove in any solvent, but it swells in dilute NaOH solution to from alkali cellulose, which is used as an intermediate in the manufacture of visocose.

α-cellulose. A fraction of cellulose polymer mixture consisting of those cellulose molecules which remain unaffected by alkaline solution.

cement. 1. A type of ceramic, a hydraulic cement is a blend of varying percentages of calcium oxide (CaO), silica (SiO_2) alumina (Al_2O_3), and sometimes also iron oxide (Fe_2O_3) which is converted from a powder to a soft, plastic mass and then to a rigid solid by addition of water. Hydrates of these compounds are formed by chemical reaction with the water. There are two basic types ; those containing about one-third alumina (aluminous cement) and those containing little or no alumina (Portland cement). The mixture is often diluted with sand before addition of water ; plastics can also be added in liquid or latex form to impart a high degree of flexibility. Hydraulic cements are manufactured as dry powders, the water and modifying ingredients being admixed shortly before pouring.

2. A mixture of sticky, adhesive substance such as glue, casein, rubber hydrocarbon, etc. with a solvent, used to form a temporary bond between wood veneers, paper, fabrics, and the similar substances.

3. A mixture of a high-polymer resin such as epoxy, silicone, or highly accelerated rubber with a solvent, strong ; permanent bonds can be obtained when these mixtures cross-link on exposure to air room temperature. They are used chiefly in the furniture and woodworking processes.

cementation. A term used in metallurgy to refer to a coating (usually on steel) formed by heating the steel in contact with another metal or nonmetal which then diffuses into the base metal to give an alloy or intermetallic compounds. The coating agent may be a powdered metal, a gas, or a liquid; high temperatures are required. The process of cementation is carried out to protect the base metal from corrosion and to impart surface hardness, as in case-hardening (nitriding). Other cementatian methods are known as carburizing (carbon), sherardizing (zinc alloy), chromizing (chromium), and calorizing (aluminum).

cementite. Fe_3C. A hard, brittle, crystalline compound occurring as lamellae or plates in steel. Its unit cell contains 12 iron and 4 carbon atoms at interstitial positions.

centigrade. The temperature scale universally used by scientists in which the freezing point of water is represented by 0 and its boiling point by 100 ; it is also called Celsius. When no indication of a scale is given in a scientific notation, it may be assumed that centigrade is meant ; 20 to 25 degrees centigrade is considered to be "room temperature". To convert centigrade to Fahrenheit, multiply °C by 9/5 and add 32 to the product ; for example,

$$30°C=(30\times 9/5)+32=54+32=86°F$$

centigram method. Method of analysis where mass of investigated sample is $x.10^{-2}$g and in the case of gases volume is $x.10^{0}$ cm^3. Also known as semi-micro method.

central atom. In coordination chemistry, atom or ion in the complex around which ligands are coordinated.

centre of inversion. A point in a crystal lattice such that the lattice is left invarient by an inversion in the point.

centre of symmetry. A point in an object through which any straight line encounters exactly similar points on opposite sides. Also known as symmetry centre. The centre of symmetry in chair conformation of cyclohexane can be seen below :

Fig. 16. Centre of symmetry

centrifugal barrier. Part of kinetic energy in system of two particles, related to their relative circulation (non-zero angular momentum). Centrifugal barrier is a potential barrier preventing mutual approach of particles.

cephalin. Any of several acidic phosphatides whose composition is similar to that of lecithin but having ethanolamine, serine, and inositol instead of choline; found in many living tissues.

ceramal. *See* cermet.

ceramic. Any product made from earth-derived materials such as clays, silicates, sand and the like, usually requiring the applications of high temperature in a kiln or oven at some stage in the process. They include the following: all types of household china, pottery, etc.; brick, tile, and similar structural products; porcelain and porcelain enamels; glass in all its various forms; refractories; hydraulic cements; silicon carbide and fused alumina, used as abrasives. Hydraulic cements set by the action of water and do not require high-temperature treatment.

Cerenkov counter. Particle counter in which Cerenkov light is observed.

Cerenkov effect. *See* Cerenkov radiation.

Cerenkov radiation. Polarized electromagnetic (visible) radiation produced when charged particle traverse a transparent medium with velocity exceeding velocity of light in the medium. This type of radiation is analogous to the emission of a shock wave by a projectile moving faster than sound, since in both cases the velocity of object passing through the medium exceeds the velocity of the resulting wave disturbance in the medium. Also known as Cerenkov effect.

cerium. An element. Symbol Ce

	Atomic No.	58
	Atomic Wt.	140.12
State Solid	Valence	+3,4
Group IIIB	isotopes	136, 138, 140, 142
	m.p.	798°C
	b.p.	3257°C

A reactive metal, and a member of the rare earth family. It occurs naturally in monazite sands and as the ore bastnasite. A radioactive α-emitter, cerium-142 has a half life of 5×10^{16} years. Cerium oxidizes so strongly that it is a dangerous fire hazard at temperatures above about 275°C, it ignites at temperates in the range of 150-175°C. It is used as an oxidizing agent when in the +4 valence state, while the metal is used as a reducing agent.

cermet. A divided composite of such metals as aluminum, chromium, tungsten, or titanium and a ceramic component, *i.e.*, metallic, oxides, borides carbides and nitrides. Of these, only the oxide and carbide-based types are in actual commercial use. Cermets display physical properties superior to those of either component alone. They are manufactured by powder metallurgy methods; after the powders are blended they are compressed and subjected to high temperature in a process called sintering, as a result of which the particles interlock and bond together, forming a ceramic-in-metal matrix. Cermets are used for refractory purposes, in aerospace equipment in high-speed tools, and in nuclear engineering devices. Also known as ceramal.

cesium. *See* caesium.

cetane number. The percentage by volume of cetane (cetane number 100) in a blend with α-methylnaphthalene (cetane number 0); indicates the ability of a fuel to ignite quickly after being injected into cylinder of an engine.

cetane number improver. A chemical which has the effect of increasing a diesel fuel's cetane number; *e.g.*, nitrates, nitroalkanes, and peroxides.

chain branching. Formation of two or more chain carriers in reaction of chain initiation or in elementary reaction of chain propagation.

chain breaking reaction. *See* chain termination.

chain carrier. Active variety of molecule (*e.g.*, free radical) which is recreated many times in subsequent links of chain and secures progression of chain reaction. Also known as chain propagator.

chain explosion. Explosion caused by chain-like process.

chain inductor. *See* chain initiator.

chain initiation. Elementary reaction resulting in formation of first carrier of reaction chain.

chain initiator. Substance which enters into elementary reaction with substrate, thus initiating chain. Chain also known as chain inductor.

chain isomerism. Type of structural isomerism caused by different structure of carbon chain in isomeric compounds. It is illustrated by the difference between normal pentane,

$$CH_3{-}CH_2{-}CH_2{-}CH_2{-}CH_3,$$

and, for example, tetramethylmethane

$$CH_3{-}\overset{\overset{CH_3}{|}}{\underset{\underset{CH_3}{|}}{C}}{-}CH_3$$

which is isomeric with it.

chain length. Number of unit steps in reaction initiated by one carrier of chain of reactions, formed during initation stage.

chain length of polymer. Total chain length of linear macromolecule, measured from one atom to another along chain.

chain, molecular. The sequence of carbon atoms in an organic molecule. A straight or open chain is one in which the carbons extend in a linear sequence, such chains may have one or more branches. A closed chain is a cyclic compound in which the carbon atoms form a ring (benzene) or other geometric figure (cyclohexane), a ring in which one or more of the atoms is not carbon is called heterocyclic. A side chain is a straight chain attached to one of the atoms of a closed chain.

chainomatic. Pertaining to a method of weighing by means of a chain, one end of which is attached to one arm of a balance and the other end attached to a vertical slider. The amount of weight applied by the chain is adjusted by varying the position of the slider, which moves over a vertical scale. The use of small-size weights or of riders is eliminated in this method of weighing.

chain propagation. Multiple reproduction of chain carrier.

chain propagator. *See* chain carrier.

chain reaction. 1. A chemical reaction in which many molecules undergo chemical reaction after one molecule becomes activated. It is initiated by a free atom, ion, or radical of transitory existence as a result of rupture of a chemical bond. Under certain conditions these set up a limited sequence of reactions ending in the formation of a stable compound. For example, free chlorine atoms formed in a mixture of hydrogen and bromine can induce the sequence.

$$Br_2 \rightarrow 2\,Br^{\cdot}$$
$$Br^{\cdot} + H_2 \rightarrow HBr + H^{\cdot}$$
$$H^{\cdot} + Br_2 \rightarrow HBr + Br^{\cdot}$$
$$H^{\cdot} + HBr \rightarrow H_2 + Br^{\cdot}$$
$$2\,Br^{\cdot} \rightarrow Br_2$$

Such reaction chains often occur in photochemistry and also in reactions involving polymerization, combustion, and oxidation of fats, oils, rubber etc.

2. A nuclear reaction in which each of the two or three neutrons released by the fission of one atomic nucleus splits another atomic nucleus, thus creating a continuous and self-sustaining energy release.

chain terminat'on. Reaction resulting in chemical change of propagat on carrier of chain into non-reactive product.

chair conformation. *See* chair form.

chair form. Privileged conformination in saturated six-membered carbocyclic and heterocyclic compounds, *e.g.*, cyclohexane. In chair conformation carbon bond angles maintain value of 109.5°, C—C bond system at adjacent carbon atoms is staggered. In this conformation each carbon atom has one axial and one equatorial bond. Chair conformations in stereoismers of 1,4-dimethyl cyclohexane are shown below :

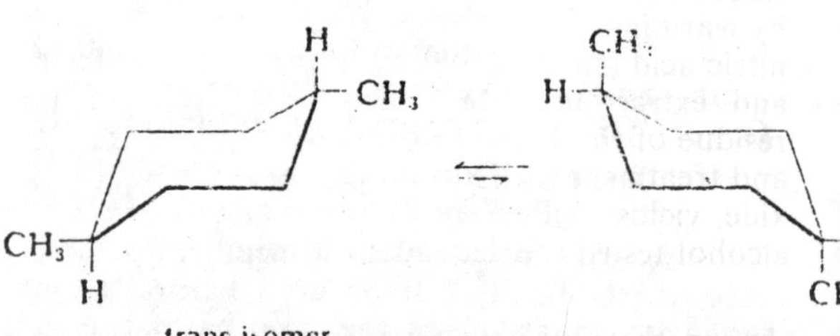

Fig. 17. Chair conformations in stereoisomers of 1,4-dimethylcyclohexane

chalcogens. Elements of sixth main group of periodic table with configuration of outer electronic shells of atoms ns^2np^4 : oxygen, sulphur, selenium, tellurium, and polonium.

chalones. Substances considered to be molecules of protein-peptide class that are produced as a part of the growth-control systems of the tissues ; known to inhibit cell division by acting on several places in the mitotic cycle.

chamber process. One of the two chief methods of making sulphuric acid. Essentially sulphur dioxide gas, oxygen, and water are combined in a chamber (usually lined with lead) with the help of oxides of nitrogen acting catalytically. Since the first use of the method during the late eighteenth century, the process has been made more efficient by the addition of the Gay-Lussac and Glover towers ; and it can now produce acid, fairly pure, of about 70% concentration. Also known as lead chamber process.

chamie aggregates. Aggregates of radioactive substance indicated by unequally distributed darkenings of the radiograms of gases or liquids probably formed due to adsorption of radioactive substance on surface of a photographic emulsion.

Chance-Claus process. A method devised to recover sulphur from alkali waste such as that produced by the Le Blanc process. Carbon dioxide gas is blown through a suspension of the sulphide waste to produce carbonate and hydrogen sulphide gas, and the latter is then burned in a Claus kiln to give sulphur. The method is obsolete, but Claus kilns are still employed, *e.g.*, in the petrochemical industry.

Chancel test. Secondary alcohols are detected by warming 1 ml. of the alcohol with 1 ml. nitric acid (sp. gr. 1.35), diluting with water, and extracting with ether. The evaporated residue of this extract on dissolving in alcohol, and treatment with alcoholic potassium hydroxide, yields yellow prismatic crystals if the alcohol tested is a secondary alcohol.

change, chemical. An alteration in the atomic constitution or molecular structure of a substance; this phenomenon always results in the formation of one or more new and different substances. Such changes usually occur by chemical reactions of various types (combination, decomposition, replacement, etc.), involving the formation and rupture of chemical bonds. A chemical change may also occur by rearrangement of atoms within a molecule, as in the formation of urea from ammonium cyanate :

$$NH_4OCN \rightarrow (NH_2)_2CO$$

Chemical changes should be distinguished from (*i*) physical changes, in which only the form of a substance is changed, *e.g.*, the melting freezing, and evaporation of liquids : and (*ii*) nuclear changes, which involve alteration of an atomic nucleus rather than one of the bonds between atoms.

channeled spectrum. A spectrum in which there are interference bands, usually produced by the interaction of light rays approximately one-half wavelength apart in phase, as those resulting from reflection from parallel surfaces.

channeling in solids. The steering of energetic charged particles by the atomic rows or atomic planes of a crystalline solid. It occurs when swift particles such as α-particles, electrons, protons, or heavy ions from an accelerator move in a crystal along one of the channel directions, when this occurs, the particle tends to be gently deflected away from atoms by a series of very small angle, scatterings ; in this way the particle tends to stay in the open spaces of the crystal as it passes through.

Chapman-Enskog method. Method for solution of Boltzmann equation based on assumption that unimolecular partition function depends on time only through time dependence of temperature, density and local velocity.

Chapman rearrangement. Intramolecular rearrangement of iminoesters, into *N*-disubstituted amides, it is effected by heating the former to about 200°C, *e.g.*,

$$\underset{\substack{|\\ O-R}}{C_6H_5-C}=N-Ar' \xrightarrow{\Delta} \underset{\substack{\|\\ O}}{C_6H_5-C}-\underset{\substack{|\\ R}}{N}-Ar'$$

characteristic coordination number. Coordination number characteristic for given central atom, generally equal to maximum coordination number with some exceptions, *e.g.*, for Cu^{2+} ion it is 4, while maximum coordination number is 6.

characteristic frequency. 1. Maximum frequency of elastic wave in crystal at any defined temperature. Also known as Debye frequency.

2. Oscillation frequency for a part of molecule relatively independent of vibrations of other fragments of molecule. It can be easily identified and measured in a given spectrum.

characteristic functions. *See* thermodynamic functions.

characteristic photographic curve. *See* emulsion calibration curve.

characteristic temperature, θ. Temperature at which energy $(k\,\theta)$ is equal to energy of elastic wave in crystal with frequency maximum ω_D at a given temperature, $k\theta = h\,\omega_D$, where k=Boltzmann constant, and h=Planck constant.

characteristic x-radiation. Discrete electromagnetic radiation of spectrum characteristic for the element that emits it. It is connected with rearrangement of electrons in inner shell of atoms.

characteristic x-ray spectrum. Emission spectrum with lines corresponding to transitions between inner shell atomic energy levels.

charcoal. A highly porous form of carbon obtained from wood by destructive distillation or from animal bones by calcination ; it is also called char. It is used to remove odors and other impurities from gases by adsorption as a component of low, explosives, and for recovery of solvents from their vapours. Its efficiency can be increased by steam activation.

Chardonnet process. An earlier process to produce synthetic fibres. Cellulose is nitrated with the usual nitric/sulphuric acid mixture and the product is dissolved in an ether/alcohol solvent. The solution is then squirted through fine nozzles into a stream of warm air. The process did not long survive, as the product was too inflammable, though efforts were made to denitrate the threads by immersing them in a bath of alkaline sulphide. The whole process was, however, expensive.

charge cloud. Spatial distribution of electric charge of a particle.

charge conjugation operation. The operation of changing every particle into its antiparticle.

charge density. The charge per unit area on a surface or per unit volume in space. It is equal to the product of particle charge and corresponding probability density.

charge density wave. The ground state of a metal in which the conduction-electron charge density is sinusoidally modulated in space. The periodicity of this extra modulation is unrelated to the lattice periodicity. Instead, it is determined by the dimensions of the conduction-electron Fermi surface in momentum space.

charged particle accelerator. Device for acceleration of electrons or other charged particles in electric or electromagnetic fields. Also known as accelerator.

charged-particle activation analysis. Activation method of analysis in which a stream of charged particles, *e.g.*, protons, deuterons, α-particles is used for activation.

charge multiplets. Families of elementary particles having close values of mass, identical baryon number B, strangeness S, lepton number L, quantum spin number J, but differing in electrical charge. Value of isospin I of particles belonging to given charge multiplet is defined by formula $n=2I+1$, where n=number of particles belonging to given charge multiplet (*e.g.*, nucleons have $I=1/2$; there exists an isospin proton-neutron doublet). Also known as isomultiplets.

charge parity. The eigenvalue of the charge conjugation operation ; it exists only for a system which goes into itself under the operation.

charge quantization. The principle that electric charge of an object must equal an integral multiple of a universal basic charge.

charge-transfer band. In electronic spectra of molecules and intermolecular complexes band corresponding to electronic transition with substantial transfer of charge between molecular fragments or complex components ; *e.g.*, in spectra of transition metal complexes transfer of charge from ligands to central ion or vice-versa.

charge-transfer complex. *See* donor-acceptor complex.

charging current. current arising from charging of electrical double layer to a given potential.

Charle's law. The statement that the volume of a given mass of gas kept under constant pressure is directly proportional to the absolute temperature. It may also be expressed as : the volume of a fixed mass of gas at constant pressure increases by 1/273 of its volume at 0°C for each 1°C rise in temperature. It would hold exactly only for an ideal gas. Gay-Lussac also clearly stated the law but generously attributed the prior, though unpublished, discovery to Charles. At constant pressure, volume V_t of a given mass of gas depends on temperature according to formula :

$$V_t = V_0(1+\alpha t) \quad \text{or} \quad V_t = \frac{V_0}{273.15\ \text{K}} T$$

where V_0=volume of gas at the given pressure at temperature 273.15 K(=0°C),
t=(empirical) temperature in °C,
T=thermodynamic temperature, and
α=expansion coefficient of gas.

Chauvenet process. A method of making anhydrous aluminium chloride on a commercial scale. A mixture of chlorine and carbonyl chloride is passed over heated aluminium oxide.

chelate. An organic coordination (complex) compound in which the metal ion is bound to atoms of nonmetals, *e.g.*, nitrogen, carbon, or oxygen, to form a heterocyclic ring having coordinate covalent bonds, *e.g.*,

$$Cu^{2+} + \begin{array}{l} CH_2-NH_2 \\ | \\ CH_2-NH_2 \end{array} \longrightarrow$$

$$\left[\begin{array}{ccccc} CH_2-H_2N & & & & NH_2-CH_2 \\ | & \searrow & & \swarrow & | \\ & & Cu & & \\ | & \nearrow & & \nwarrow & | \\ CH_2-H_2N & & & & NH_2-CH_2 \end{array}\right]^{2+}$$

The nonmetal atoms are called ligands ; these may be attached to the metal ions by from one to six linkages. They are called uni- bi-, tridentate, etc., meaning one-, two-, or three-toothed. The chelate compounds are frequently found in an interdisciplinary field of science called bioinorganic chemistry. The biological significance of chelates is demonstrated by the large number of biologically important compounds that are either metal chelates or chelating agents.

chelate effect. Increase in stability of chelate complex, compared with corresponding non-chelate complex, as a result of chelate ring formation.

chelate ring. Heterocyclic ring formed by linking central atom with multidenate ligand.

chelating agent. Organic compound forming chelate complexes with cations, *e.g.*, EDTA.

chelatometric titrations. *See* chelatometry.

chelatometry. Branch of compleximetry dealing with the study of compounds (usually aminopolycarboxylic acids or salts) forming water-soluble chelates with titrated ion. Also known as chelotometric titration.

chemical adsorption. *See* chemisorption.

chemical affinity. 1. The attractive force between elements by means of which compounds may be formed. The conception was extended by Thomsen and Bertholet, who thought that the heat evolved in a chemical reaction was a measure of the "affinity" of the substances involved in the reaction. A more recent view (Gibbs and Helmholtz) is that affinity is the intensity factor of chemical energy, the capacity factor being the equivalent weight of the element. The affinity determines the course of reaction in a mixture where many reactions are possible.

2. Intensive quantity being a force of chemical reaction

$$A = -\sum_{B} \nu_B \mu_B$$

where ν_B=stoichiometric coefficient of reagent B (positive for products, negative for substrates), μ_B=chemical potential of reagent B, and $\sum_B$ denote summation over all components.

chemical analysis. Identification and determination of components, (elements, ions, radicals, molecules) in analysed sample.

chemical bond energy. For diatomic molecule

bond energy is equal to dissociation energy into atoms in their ground states. In polyatomic molecule bond energy cannot be defined in unique way and is defined as part of total binding energy corresponding to given bond. Chemical bond energy is obtained experimentally by using indirect procedures. Also known as bond energy.

chemical change. *See* change, chemical.

chemical compounds. Substance composed of two or more elements which do not vary in composition from sample to sample, and which have fixed and definite physical properties, such as density and refractive index. The elements in compounds cannot be separated by simple physical or mechanical mean, but only by chemical treatment. When compounds are formed from their elements, heat is generated or absorbed. These properties distinguish them from mixtures.

Most chemical compounds are formed in fixed and definite proportions by weight from their elements, and they obey the laws of chemical combination. However, there are a number of solid compounds, known as nonstoichiometric compounds, that exhibit departures from the law of definite proportions.

chemical conversion. The term for the chemical change from reactants to products of a chemical industrial process. Preferred for decades in the petroleum industry, the term is being used to an increasing extent for the entire chemical process industries in place of unit processes, since it is a more exact definition of industrial chemical reactions. The following are important chemical conversions :

Alkylation	Halogenation
Amination	Hydroformylation (oxo)
Ammonolysis	Hydrogenation, Hydrogenolysis
Aromatization	Hydrolysis, hydration
Calcination	Ion exchange
Combustion	Isomerization
Condensation	Neutralization
Dehydration	Nitration
Diazotization and coupling	Oxidation
Esterification (sulphation)	Polymerization
Fermentation	Pyrolysis, cracking
	Reduction
	Sulphation
	Sulphonation

All these terms refer to the classes of chemical changes, each embracing many individual reactions or chemical conversions into which chemical industrial processes can be divided.

chemical dating. Determination of the relative or absolute age of minerals and of ancient objects and materials by measurement of their chemical composition. By inference this method of age determination may be extended to the dating of geological formations and to the dating of geological and human events.

Almost all chemical dating methods are based on measurements of : (*i*) the proportion of some stable element known to vary in a systematic way ; (*ii*) the degree of epimerization or racemization of an amino acid in residual organic matter ; (*iii*) the ratio of the weight of a decomposition product of radioactivity to the weight of original radioactive element or elements still present ; or (*iv*) the residual activity of a radioactive isotope.

The oldest and least reliable method is based on the increase in the fluorine content of bones with increase in time elapsed since they were buried in the soil. This increase is due to contact of the bones with groundwater containing fluoride ions and the consequent partial replacement of the phosphate of the bones with fluoride. This method must be used with great caution, and is usually applicable only where all conditions appear to have been fairly constant over long periods, as in caves.

A much superior method for dating ancient bones is based on the measurement of the degree of epimerization or racemization of one of the amino acids they often contain. The amino acids in living bone are, with the exception of glycine, mostly in the form of the L-isomers of these acids. On death of the organism, these isomers change slowly and progressively, at a rate governed by temperature, to the D-isomers of the acids, except for L-isoleucine which changes by epimerization to the nonprotein amino acid D-alloisoleucine.

chemical dosimetry. Branch of radiation technique dealing with determination of absorbed doses of ionizing radiation on basis of chemical changes in system.

chemical dynamics. That branch of physical chemistry which seeks to explain time-dependent phenomena, such as energy transfer and chemical reaction, in terms of the detailed motion of the nuclei and electrons which constitute the system.

chemical ecology. Chemical ecology is concerned with the interaction of organisms mediated by the chemicals they produce. *See also* allomones ; kairomones ; pheromones.

chemical energy. In most chemical reactions, heat is either taken in or given out. By the law of conservation of energy, the increase or decrease in heat energy must be accompanied by a corresponding decrease or increase in some other form of energy. This other form is the chemical energy of the compounds involved in the reaction. The rearrangement of the atoms in the reacting compounds to produce new compounds causes a change in chemical energy. This change in chemical energy is equal numerically and of opposite sign to the heat change accompanying the reaction.

It is possible to measure an absolute value for the chemical energy of a compound ; only changes in chemical energy can be measured. It is therefore necessary to make some arbitrary assumption as a starting point. One such assumption would be to take the chemical energies of the free atoms as zero and measure the chemical energies of all elements and compounds relative to this standard. If this were done, all chemical energies would then be negative quantities. Heat is given out when all elements and compounds are formed from their atoms. Since chemical energy can be regarded as a form of potential energy, it is interesting that the formation of chemical bonds is always accompanied by a decrease of potential energy. The reason, in quantitative terms at least, lies in the quantum theory. When chemical bonds are formed between atoms, electrons are shared between the two atoms, and this electron sharing produces a lowering of the potential energies of the shared electrons, and thus a lowering of the potential energy of the molecule relative to the free atoms.

Although it would be more fundamental to take the chemical energies of the separated atoms as zero, in practice it is more convenient to take a more arbitrary starting point and to assume that the chemical energies of the elements are zero. For precision, the standard states of the elements at 25°C and 1 atmosphere pressure are chosen.

chemical engineering. The branch of engineering serving those industries that chemically convert basic raw materials into a variety of products. Starting with ores, salt, sulphur, limestone, coal, natural gas, petroleum, air, water, and so forth, these industries, by chemical processing techniques, produce widely diversified products, such as aluminium, copper, iron, platinum and titanium metals and alloys; refined petroleum fractions, such as fuels and solvents; synthetic fertilizers; synthetic fibres, resins, and plastics; antibiotics ; wood pulp and paper and petrochemicals.

chemical equation. An expression, in symbols, of the substances that enter into a chemical reaction, and those that result from it, with numerical coefficients to indicate the proportionate number of moles of each substance that enters into the reaction, or the proportionate number of gram-atomic weights of each atom or ion.

chemical equilibrium. 1. In a dynamic or kinetic sense, chemical equilibrium is a condition in which a chemical reaction is occuring at equal rates in its forward and reverse directions, so that the concentrations of the reacting substances do not change with time.

2. In a thermodynamic sense, it is the condition in which there is no tendency for the composition of the system to change ; no change can occur in the system without the expenditure of some form of work upon it.

3. From the view point of statistical mechanics the equilibrium state places the system in a condition of maximum freedom (or minimum restraint) compatible with the energy, volume, and composition of the system. The statistical approach has been merged with thermodynamics into a field called statistical thermodynamics ; this merger has been of immense value for its intellectual stimulus, as well as for its practical contributions to the study of stimulus, as well as for its practical contributions to the study of equilibria.

chemical equivalent. Ratio of relative atomic mass to valence of a given element.

chemical formula. Abbreviated notation which shows quantitatively and qualitatively composition of chemical compound and sometimes also its electronic structure and spatial arrangement.

The formula of simple diatomic molecules of a single element are designated by the symbol for the element with subscript 2, indicating that it contains 2 atoms. Thus the hydrogen molecule is represented as H_2; the nitrogen molecule, N_2; and the oxygen molecule, O_2. Polyatomic molecules of a single element are designated by the symbol for the element with a numerical subscript corresphnding to the number of atoms in the molecule.

Diatomic covalent molecules containing unlike elements are given a similar designation. The formula for lithium chloride is LiCl. The more electropositive element is always designated first in the formula.

For polyatomic covalent molecules containing unlike elements numerical subscripts are used to designate the number of atoms of each element present in the molecule. An example is aluminium (III) chloride, $AlCl_3$. Again, as in diatomic molecules, the more electropositive element is placed first in the formula.

Ionic inorganic compounds are designated by a similar notation.The positive ion is written first in the formula, followed by the negative ion ; subscripts are again used to denote the number of ions of each element present in the compound. The formulas for several common compounds are sodium chloride, NaCl; ammonium nitrate, NH_4NO_3 ; and ferric sulphate, $Fe_2(SO_4)_3$.

More complex inorganic compounds are designated in a similar manner. The positive ion is written first, but may contain attached or coordinated groups, and this is followed by the negative ion. Examples are hexammine cobalt (III) nitrate, $[Co(NH_3)_6](NO_3)_3$. Hydrates of inorganic compounds, such as coper (II) sulfate pentahydate, are designated by the formula of the compound followed by the formula for water, the number of water molecules being designated by a numerical prefix. Thus the symbol for the above compound is $CuSO_4 \cdot 5H_2O$.

Because there are many more organic than inorganic compounds, the designation or notation for the first group becomes exceedingly complex. Many different types of organic compounds are known. The system of notation used must distinguish between the various hydrocarbons as well as setting this group of compounds apart from others such as alcohols, ethers, amines, esters, and phenols.

chemical induction. Incitement or acceleration of induced (secondary) reaction by primary reaction in system of coupled reactions.

chemical inhibitor. A substance capable of stopping or retarding a chemical reaction.

chemical kinetics. Branch of physical chemistry dealing with investigation of chemical reaction rates. *See also* reaction kinetics.

chemical potential. μ_B. In a thermodynamic system or several constituents, the rate of change of the Gibbs function of the system with respect to the change in the number of moles of a particular constituent. It is an intensive quantity.

$$\mu_B=\left(\frac{\partial U}{\partial n_B}\right)_{S,\,V,\,n_C}=\left(\frac{\partial H}{\partial n_B}\right)_{S,\,p,\,n_C}=$$
$$=\left(\frac{\partial F}{\partial n_B}\right)_{T,\,V,\,n_C}=\left(\frac{\partial G}{\partial n_B}\right)_{T,\,p,\,n_C}$$

where n_B=number of moles of B component in phase, n_C=number of moles of other components in this phase, U, H, F, and G=internal energy, enhalpy, Helmholtz free energy and Gibbs free energy, respectively, S= entropy, V=volume of phase, T=its thermodynamic temperature and p=pressure. The importance of the chemical potential lies in its relation to the affinity or driving force of a chemical reaction.

chemical relaxation. Establishment of chemical equilibrium previously perturbed *e.g.*, by change of temperature, pressure, electric field etc.

chemical shift. Shift of resonance frequency ν_0 or of resonance strength of static magnetic field H_0 in nuclear magnetic resonance ; caused by magnetic shielding of nucleus by surrounding electrons; in practice chemical shift denotes relative chemical shift

$$\frac{\nu_0-\nu_0'}{\nu_0}=\frac{H_0-H_0'}{H_0'}$$

where ν_0 and H_0 refer to investigated resonance signal, and ν_0' and H_0' correspond to resonance signal of suitably chosen standard (reference substance).

chemical shim. A chemical, usually boric acid, that is placed in the coolant system of a nuclear reactor to serve as a neutron obsorber and that compensates for fuel burnup during normal operation.

chemical species. Atom, molecule, ion, free, radical, ion radical, cluster, solvated ion etc. which may be identified as exhibiting specific properties notwithstanding short time period of existence.

chemical stage of radiolysis. Final phase of changes due to absorption of ionizing radiation conventionally taken to be longer than 10^{-8} s from moment of passage of ionizing particle or quantum.

chemical sterilization. The use of bactericidal chemicals to sterilize solutions, solid surfaces and air.

chemical symbol. A system of symbols and notation for 106 chemical elements. The system consists of letters to denote the chemical element which generally has only first or first and one of following letters taken from their Latin names. These symbols give concise and instantly recognizable description of the element and greatly simplify the language of chemistry.

chemical thermodynamics. The application of thermodynamic principles to systems involving physical and chemical transformation in order to (*i*) develop quantitative relationships among the identifiable forms of energy and their conjugate variable, (*ii*) establish the criteria for spontaneous change, for equilibrium, and for thermodynamic stability, and (*iii*) provide the macroscopic base for the statistical-mechanical bridge to atomic and molecular properties. The thermodynamic principles applied are the conservation of energy as embodied in the first law of thermodynamics, the principle of internal entropy production as embodied in the second law of thermodynamics, and the principle of absolute entropy and its statistical thermodynamic formulation as embodied in the third law of thermodynamics.

chemiluminescence. The type of luminescence wherein a chemical reaction supplies the energy responsible for the emission of light (ultraviolet, visible, or infrared) in excess of that of a blackbody (thermal radiation) at the same temperature and within the same spectral range. Below (500°C), the emission of any light during a chemical reaction is a chemiluminescence. The blue inner cone of a bunsen burner or the Coleman gas lamp are examples. of this phenomenon.

Many chemical reactions generate energy. Usually this exothermicity appear as heat ; whereas, for a visible chemiluminescence to occur, one of the reaction products must be generated in an excited electronic state from which it can undergo deactivation by emission of a photon. Hence a chemiluminescent reaction can be regarded as the reverse of a photochemical reaction.

Only very exothermic, or "exergonic," chemical processes can be expected to be chemiluminescent. Partly for this reason, most familiar examples of chemiluminescence involve oxygen and oxidation processes ; the most efficient examples of these are the enzyme-mediated bioluminescences.

chemiosmotic coupling. Coupling of ATP synthesis to electron transport *via* an electrochemical H^+ gradient across a membrane.

chemisorption. A phenomenon related to adsorption in which atoms or molecules of reacting substances are held to the surface atoms of a catalyst by electrostatic forces having about the same strength as chemical bonds. The surface at which chemisorption takes place is usually a metal or metallic oxide; the chemisorbed molecules are always changed in the process, and often the molecules of the surface are changed as well. Chemisorption is an essential feature of catalytic reactions and accounts for large measure of the specialized activity of catalysts.

chemistry. Science dealing with studies regarding formation, properties, constitution and structure of substances as well as their transformations and conditions which determine directions and rates of these transformations.

chemistry, analytical. That branch of chemistry dealing with the determination of qualitative or quantitative composition of substances and materials.

chemistry, clinical. *See* clinical chemistry.

chemistry, colloid. *See* colloid chemistry.

chemistry, cosmic. *See* cosmochemistry.

chemistry, cyto. *See* cytochemistry.

chemistry, electro. *See* electrochemistry.

chemistry, forensic. *See* forensic chemistry.

chemistry, geo. *See* geochemistry.

chemistry, industrial. *See* industrial chemistry.

chemistry, inorganic. *See* inorganic chemistry.

chemistry, magneto. *See* magnetochemistry.

chemistry, medicinal. *See* medicinal chemistry.

chemistry, micro. *See* microchemistry.

chemistry, nuclear. *See* nuclear chemistry.

chemistry, organic. *See* organic chemistry.

chemistry, pharmaceutical. *See* pharmaceutical chemistry.

chemistry, photo. *See* photochemistry.

chemistry, phyto. *See* phytochemistry.

chemistry, stereo. *See* stereochemistry.

chemistry, stoichiometric. *See* stoichiometry.

chemistry, structural. *See* structural chemistry.

chemistry, synthetic. *See* synthetic chemistry.

chemistry, theoretical. *See* theoretical chemistry.

Chemistry, thermo. *See* thermochemisrry.

chemokinesis. The process by which a chemical substance increases the activity of an organism.

chemonuclear reactor. Nuclear reactor in which moderator and/or coolant is medium of useful chemical reactions initiated by ionizing radiation.

chemosmosis. The phenomenon of chemical action taking place through an intervening membrane.

chemosterilant. A chemical compound which adversely affects the reproductive ability of an insect exposed to it. Such compounds have been successfully used on both male and female insects of several species, including the screw-worm fly. This method of control may eventually considerably reduce the need for insecticides. The chemicals used so far, are antimetabolites, organotin, and boron compounds.

chemosynthesis. The synthesis of organic compounds from carbon dioxide by microorganisms using energy derived from chemical reactions.

chemotaxis. Sensing of and movement toward (or away from) a specific chemical agents by cells.

chemotherapy. The treatment of disease by administering synthetic drugs with the object of destroying harmful invading bacteria with negligible inconvenience to the human beings. It is the modern iatrochemistry.

chemurgy. The employment of the methods of chemistry, and the resources of chemical knowledge, to increase the number of uses of agricultural products and thereby to build a broader farm-factory economy.

Chichibabin amination reaction. Process of amination of heterocyclic systems, *e.g.*, pyridine, quinoline and their derivatives, with metal amides, *e.g.*,

$$\text{(pyridine)} + NaNH_2 \longrightarrow \text{(2-pyridyl)}NHNa \xrightarrow{H_2O} \text{(2-pyridyl)}NH_2$$

Chichibabin pyridine synthesis. A condensation of carbonyl compounds with ammonia (or amines) to form pyridine derivatives.

$$4CH_3CHO + NH_3 \xrightarrow{\Delta}$$

$$\text{(pyridine ring with } C_2H_5 \text{ and } CH_3 \text{ substituents)} + 4H_2O.$$

Chien-Shih solution. A 0.2% solution of resorcylaldoxime in 5% alcohol, used in testing for ferric iron, which forms a purple colour in slightly acidic solution.

chimeric DNA. Recombinant DNA containing genes from two different species.

chimeric protein. Covalently joined proteins from different species ; made in response to chemeric DNA.

chiral centre. The smallest grouping of atoms (usually fragment of molecule) responsible for existence of chirality in molecule ; such a molecule is non-superimposable on its mirror image and is said to be optically active (with the exception of the *meso* form). Asymmetric atom is the simplest chiral centre. More complex chiral centres are present in specially substituted allene derivatives, alkylidenecycloalkanes, spiranes, biphenyl and deformed aromatic systems. Also known as chirality centre.

chirality. 1. Non-identity in steric structure (configuration) of molecule with its mirror image, caused by total lack of symmetry elements or presence only of simple symmetry axes. The term is applied to molecules that display the type of optical activity characteristic of enantiomorphs, *i.e.*, having structures which are mirror images of each other, analogous to the left and right hands. *See also* enantiomorph ; asymmetry.

2. The characteristic of particles of spin 1/2 *h* that are allowed to have only one spin state with respect to an axis of quantization parallel to the particle's momentum ; if the particle's spin is always parallel to its momentum, it has positive chirality.

chirality centre. *See* chiral centre.

chitin. A white or colourless polysaccharide having a basic structure similar to that of cellulose but also containing amine (nitrogen) groups ; it forms hard layers or accretions and is found in the integuments of shelfish and some insects. It is insoluble in water and most solvents but reacts with concentrated acids.

chitinase. An externally secreted digestive enzyme produced by certain microganisms and invertebrates that hydrolyzes chitin.

chlorate. A salt of chloric acid, $HClO_3$ in which the oxidation state of chlorine is +5.

chloride. The salt of hydrochloric acid (HCl), in which the oxidation state of chlorine is −1.

chloride-shift. The reversible exchange of chloride and bicarbonate ions between erythrocytes and plasma to effect transport of carbon dioxide and maintain ionic equilibrium during respiration.

chloridization. Treatment of mineral ores with hydrochloric acid or chlorine to form the chloride of the main metal present in the ore.

chlorinate. The combine with chlorine. Specifically, the process of adding chlorine to or substituting chlorine, especially for hydrogen, in a compound.

chlorinated hydrocarbon. Any of a large group of synthetic organic chemicals made by replacing one or more of the hydrogen atoms of a hydrocarbon with chlorine. Well-known and widely used examples are carbon tetrachloride, chloroform, trichloroethylene, hexachloroethane, *p*-dichlorobenzene, and chloronaphthalene. The hydrocarbons may be either aliphatic or aromatic and the materials either solid or liquid ; they are used as cleansing agents, fumigants, and insecticides.

chlorination. The process of chlorinating, *e.g.*,

$$CH_4 + Cl_2 \xrightarrow{h\nu} CH_3Cl + HCl$$

$$C_6H_6 + Cl_2 \xrightarrow{Fe} C_6H_5Cl + HCl$$

chlorine. An element **Symbol Cl**

Atomic No. 17	Atomic Wt.	35,453
Group VII A	Valence	1,3,4,5,7
	Isotopes	2 stable
	m.p.	−100.98°C
	b. p.	−34.05°C

Chlorine is highly reactive element and is the second member of the halogen family, it is a strong electron acceptor (electronegative) and thus is a powerful oxidizing agent. In addition to its elemental form, chlorine exists in the valence states of −1, +1, +3, +4, +5 and +7, indicative of its great reactivity. It is estimated that 0.045% of the earth's crust is chlorine. The diatomic gas (Cl_2) has a molecular weight of 70.906. It critical temperature is 144°C, the critical pressure is 76.1 atmosphere, and the critical volume is 1.745 ml/g ; and the density at critical point is 0.573 g/ml. It is obtained industrially by subjecting sodium chloride solution to electrolysis (electrolytic cell). The isotopic composition of chlorine is unique, its one of the two isotopes comprises about 25% of the element. Chlorine is unusually capable of forming ionic bonds and free radicals. It is toxic when inhaled as a gas and is a strong skin irritant in liquid form.

chlorinolysis. Decomposition of molecule of chemical compounds by chlorine, *e.g.*,

$$ClCH_2CH_2SSCH_2CH_2Cl + Cl_2 \rightarrow 2ClCH_2CH_2SCl$$

chlorite. A salt of chlorous acid. $HClO_2$, in which the oxidation state of chlorine is +3. The most common chlorite it sodium chlorite.

chloritization. The introduction of, production of, replacement by, or conversion into chlorite.

chlorohydrin. Any of a number of aliphatic compounds containing one or more hydroxyl groups and at least one chlorine atom, thus, they are both alcohols and organic chlorides and comprise quite a reactive series of compounds. A general method of preparation is the addition of hypochlorous acid to alkenes, *e.g.*,

$$RCH{=}CH_2 + HOCl \rightarrow RCHOHCH_2Cl$$

Chlorohydrin itself is made by reacting glycerol with hydrogen chloride, giving a liquid that is a good solvent for cellulose derivatives. Its formula is $CH_2OHCHOHCH_2Cl$. b.p. 213°C (decomposes).

chloromethylation. Substitution of hydrogen atom of aromatic ring by chloromethyl group $-CH_2Cl$, effected by formaldehyde and hydrogen chloride in presence of anhydrous $ZnCl_2$, *e.g.*,

$$C_6H_6 + HCHO + HCl \xrightarrow{ZnCl_2} C_6H_5CH_2Cl + H_2O$$

Also known as Blanc reaction.

chlorosulphonation. Substitution of hydrogen atom in molecule of an organic compound by chlorosulphonic group $-SO_2Cl$, usually affected by chlorosulphonic acid $HOSO_2Cl$ or sulphur dioxide and chlorine, *e.g.*,

$$C_6H_6 + 2HOSO_2Cl \rightarrow C_6H_5SO_2Cl + H_2SO_4 + HCl$$

$$RH + SO_2 + Cl_2 \xrightarrow{h\nu} RSO_2Cl + HCl$$

Also known as sulphochlorination.

Christensen reagent for quinine. A solution of 1 g. iodine in a mixture of 1 g. 50% hydriodic acid 0.8 g. sulphuric acid, and 50 g. 70% ethyl alcohol. This solution is used as a test reagent for quinine. Characteristic coloured crystals are obtained.

cholesterol. An unsaturated polycyclic alcohol (sterol) having one hydroxyl group and one double bond. It is closely related to phenanthrene in structure and falls into the general classification of lipids. Cholesterol is synthesized by all higher animals; its oxidation product in the body are bile acids and steroid hormones. In esterified form it is a component of the saturated fatty acids occurring in animal fats such as butter; it is thought by some workers to have an adverse effect on the circulatory system, but according to recent researches, this has not been proved.

cholinesterase. An enzyme in the body of animals and man which reacts with the actylcholine formed by nerve functioning; as a result of this, the extremely toxic acetylcholine splits into acetic acid and choline and is thus detoxified.

chromadizing. Treating the surface of aluminium, or aluminium alloys with chromic acid to improve paint adhesion.

chromatin. A filamentous complex of DNA, histones and other proteins constituting eukaryotic chromosomes.

chromatofuge. An apparatus in which chromatographic adsorption takes place on the radial flow of a solution through a disc or cylinder from the axis to the perimeter, in which the process may be assisted by centrifugal forces to give greater speed and clearer zone definition. The process is adapted to the recovery of products on a laboratory or even a small plant scale.

chromatogram. Fixed image of results of chromatographic separation in form of : (*a*) sheet or disc of filter paper or plate with adsorbent, showing after development spots due to substances being separated ; (*b*) column with sorbent after development and detection of separated substances ; (*c*) registration obtained from detector that recorded concentrations of substances coming out of chromatographic column or separated on filter paper or chromatographic plate.

chromatographic band. Distribution of adsorbate on surface or within volume of stationary phase (on filter paper, in column etc.).

chromatographic column. Tube (most often cylindrical) filled with stationary phase and equipped with inlet and outlet for mobile phase.

chromatography. Set of separation methods that make use of different rates of migration of components being separated in porous media, in which one phase is immobile layer of developed surface and the other is stream of gas or liquid flowing through it.

The best-known types of chromatography are gas, liquid, paper, ion-exchange, and thin-layer, the name depending on the characteristic aspect of the method. Basically chromatography involves passing a gaseous or liquid mixture such as refinery gases or gasoline, called the mobile phase, through a column of porous material sometimes coated with a nonvolatile liquid, called the stationary phase. The components of the mixture are adsorbed selectively and pass through the porous material at different rates, emerging as distinct separation zones at the bottom the column. A carier gas or liquid is necessary to provide movement of the material through the adsorbent. When the components have been thus separated, the identity of each can be determined by an appropriate analytical method. In thin-layer chromatography, the adsorbent is placed on a glass plate in a layer less than 0.5 millimetre thick, and a solution of the mixture to be separated is placed near one edge of the of the thin layer, separation occurs by adsorption as the components move through the layer at different rates. The commonly used adsorbents are silica gel, cellulose (paper), alumina, and diatomaceous earth.

chromatophore. Any pigmentary cell or colour producing plastid, such as those of the deep layers of the epidermis ; a chlorophyll-containing granule in certain bacteria.

chromatopolarography. Electroanalytical method which combines chromatographic separation of mixture of ions or molecules with their polarographic detemination in effluent.

chrome dye. A mordant dye, most frequently one in which sodium dichromate is used as the mordant.

chrome pigment. Any inorganic pigment containing chromium compounds. These are quite stable and resistant to sunlight, weathering, and chemical action than the brighter organic dyes.

chromic. Containing or pertaining to trivalent chromium.

chromite. The anion CrO_2^- or CrO_3^{3-}, or a compound containing one of these anions ; a combination of chromic oxide with another metallic oxide, especially ferrous oxide.

chromium. An element. Symbol Cr

Atomic No. 24	Atomic Wt.	51.996
	Valence	2,3,6
Group VIB	Isotopes	50.51.52.53,54
	m.p.	1875°C
	b.p.	2672°C

Chromium is a grayish metal, though many of its compounds display various colours. It is obtained by reduction of chromite ore. It is an excellent coordination metal and owes much of its commercial use to its corrosion-resistant properties. The metal itself is not toxic except in the form of fume, but some of its compounds are irritant and damaging to the skin, especially those involving hexavalent chromium. Chromium has relatively poor forging, rolling, and drawing properties. However, when absolutely free from oxygen, nitrogen, carbon and hydrogen, it is relatively ductile and can be forged and drawn, but it is difficult to keep it free from these elements. Its major uses are as an alloying agent in stainless steel and other alloys and for electroplated coatings on exposed metal parts. It can also be plated on plastics. Its isotope, chromium-51, is radioactive and is, obtained by neutron bombardment of chromium; it radiates gamma rays.

chromizing. Surface alloying of metals in which an alloy is formed by diffusion of chromium into the base metal.

chromogen. A substance that, although having no colour itself, gives a coloured substance when it is oxidised. It may be regarded as the parent of a dye-stuff. For example, hydrazobenzene ($C_6H_5NH.NHC_6H_5$). Alternatively the word "chromogen" is used in a somewhat wider sense to mean any coloured substance that contains a chromophore but is unsuitable to be used as a dye.

chromoisomerism. Isomerism in which the isomers exhibit different colours.

chromophore. An atom or group of atoms which, when introduced into a molecule causes the substance to exhibit colour, for example; the nitro group $—NO_2$, the azo group —N=N—, the carbonyl group —C=O, and the quinonoid group.

Such groups do not confer dyeing properties upon the compounds which contain them; dyes are formed when the substance is further substituted by a salt-forming or auxochrome group.

chromophoric electrons. Electrons in the double bonds of the chromophoric groups. Such electrons are not bound as tightly as those of single bonds and can thus be easily excited to higher energy levels with less expenditure of energy. Their electronic spectra appear at frequencies in the visible or near ultraviolet region of the spectrum.

chromoproteins. A class of protein substances characterized by being coloured. The prosthetic group is a coloured compound in such cases. Hemoglobin and hemocyanin are the best known examples of this class of proteins.

chromosome. Any of the protein-nucleic acid complex formed from chromatin in the nucleus of the biological cell; it is made up of DNA, the genetic code carrier, and various other nucleo-proteins. Chromosomes are unit structures formed during cell division from standards of the parent complex, chromatin, the number of chromosomes in a given cell being characteristic of a particular plant or animal species. They contain the genes, which are the specific agents of hereditary transmission.

chromotrypsins. An important group of enzymes which are secreted into the intestine from pancreas; act specifically on peptide linkages next to phenylalanine or tyrosine.

chromous. Containing or pertaining to divalent chromium.

chronoamperometry. Electroanalytical method dealing with the of analysis of dependence of current on time constant potential of indicator electrode placed in non-stirred solution or in molten salt.

chronocoulometry. Method of investigation of of kinetics of electrode reactions and adsorption of electroactive substances consisting in analysis of dependence of charge flowing in electrolytic cell during time of electrolysis carried out at constant potential of indicator electrode.

chronopotentiometric analysis. Analytical method that measures time of transition in a programmed-current (usually constant) electrolysis.

chronopotentiometry. Electrochemical method which consists in recording and analysis of changes of potentials of indicator electrode during time of electrolysis carried out at programmed current intensity (usually at contant current intensity).

Chugaev reaction. Transformation of alcohol to alkene involving formation of xanthogenate (first stage) and then thermal decomposition of the latter, *e.g.*,

$$RCH_2CH_2OH \xrightarrow[-H_2O]{NaOH,\ CS_2} S{=}\underset{\displaystyle SNa}{\overset{\displaystyle OCH_2CH_2R}{C}} \xrightarrow{\Delta} RCH{=}CH_2 + HS{-}\overset{\displaystyle O}{\overset{\|}{C}}{-}SNa$$

Also known as Tschugaeff dehydration.

Cimmino reagent. A modified Kopp reagent consisting of diphenylamine and sulphuric acid. It is used in testing for nitrate, which forms a blue colour with the reagent and sulphuric acid.

cinder. 1. Slag from a metal furnace. 2. Scale cast off in forging metal.

cinder pig. Pig iron produced from a mixture of slag in the furnace and crude metal or ore.

cinders. Incombustible residual form a burning process; in particular, small pieces of clinker from the burning of soft coal.

cinnamic. The radical $C_6H_5CH{=}CH—$.

cinnamoyl. The radical $C_6H_5CH{=}CHCO—$.

cinnamyl. The radcal $C_6H_5CH{=}CHCH_2—$.

circular dichroism. Dichroism caused by different absorption of left and right circularly polarized light by optically active samples. Circular dichroism is caused a result of elliptical polarization of transmitted light.

circular polarization of light. Fixing of direction of light wave electric vector *E*.

circulating reactor. A nuclear reactor in which

the fissionable material circulates through the core in fluid form or as small particles suspended in the fluid.

cis-form. *See* cis-isomer.

cis-isomer. 1. Diastereoisomer in which identical or similar groups are situated on the same side of plane passing through double bond or through ring surface, *e.g.*,

$$\begin{array}{cc} H_3C & CH_3 \\ | & | \\ C & = C \\ | & | \\ H & H \end{array} \quad (\textit{cis}\text{-2-butene})$$

2. In coordination chemistry, isomer in which two similar ligands are near each other, *i.e.*, in square complexes $[MA_2B_2]$ the ligands occupy adjacent vertices of square, and in octahedral complexes $[MA_4B_2]$ adjacent corners of octahedron. Also known as *cis*-form.

cis-trans isomerism. A type of diastereoisomerism resulting due to restricted rotation about double bonds or considerable restriction in rotation about single bonds in ring systems. *Cis-trans* isomerism is observed in ethylene-1,2-dicarboxylic acids.

$$\begin{array}{c} H-C-COOH \\ \| \\ H-C-COOH \end{array} \qquad \begin{array}{c} H-C-COOH \\ \| \\ HOOC-C-H \end{array}$$

Maleic acid (*cis*) Fumaric acid (*trans*)

In coordination chemistry, type of isomerism based on different arrangements around central ion by two similar ligands. This isomerism occurs in square planar and octahedral complexes, but does not occur in tetrahedral complexes and in complexes of coordination number 2 or 3. Also known as geometric isomerism.

cis-trans isomerization. Establishment of thermodynamic equilibrium between *cis* and *trans* isomers, caused by conversion of one isomer into another.

citric acid cycle. A cyclic system of enzymatic reactions for the oxidation of acetyl residues to carbon dioxide, in which formation of citrate is the first step.

citric acid fermentation. Type of oxidative fermentation of hexoses, *e.g.*, of glucose, caused by Citromicetes, Aspergilla and Penicilla resulting in decomposition of carbohydrates to citric acid.

cladding. A term used to designate a type of protective coating consisting of a relatively thick layer of a metal (such as nickel) mechanically applied to a substrate metal (steel or copper). The coating is not less than 5% of the total thickness and usually is much more (up to 25%). Cladding supplies a combination of desired properties not found in any one metal. A base metal can be selected for cost or structural properties, and another metal added for surface protection as some special property such as electrical conductivity. A permanent intermetallic bond is formed between the coating and substrate. Clad metals are used widely in the electrical field, for semiconductors, corrosion-resistant equipment, and nuclear fuel elements.

Claisen ester condensation. Condensation of easter with compound containing active methylene group (*e.g.*, ester, ketone or nitrile), effected by basic catalyst (sodium alcoholate, sodium amide, triphenylmethylsodium etc.) resulting in formation of β-ketoester, β-diketone or β-ketonitrile, respectively, *e.g.*

$$RCH_2-\overset{O}{\overset{\|}{C}}-OC_2H_5 + \underset{R}{\underset{|}{HC}}=\overset{O^{\ominus}}{\overset{|}{C}}-OC_2H_5 \rightleftharpoons \left[RCH_2-\overset{O^{\ominus}}{\overset{|}{C}}(OC_2H_5)-\underset{R}{\underset{|}{CH}}-\overset{O}{\overset{\|}{C}}-OC_2H_5 \right]$$

acceptor donor a hemiketal

$$\Updownarrow$$

$$RCH_2-\overset{O}{\overset{\|}{C}}\overset{\ominus}{\cdots}\underset{R}{\underset{|}{C}}\cdots\overset{O}{\overset{\|}{C}}-OC_2H_5 + C_2H_5OH \rightleftharpoons RCH_2\overset{O}{\overset{\|}{C}}-\underset{R}{\underset{|}{CH}}-\overset{O}{\overset{\|}{C}}-OC_2H_5 + C_2H_5O^{\ominus}$$

a β-keto ester enolate base

Other related reactions involving condensation of active methylene groups with carbonyl groups include the aldol condensation, the acetoacetic ester synthesis, the Claisen-Schmidt condensation, and the Perkin reaction.

Claisen rearrangement. A rearrangement of alyl ethers of certain type-compounds, such as phenols or enols, whereby an allyl group attached to the oxygen atom of the ether shifts to an adjacent carbon atom, leaving a hydroxy or carbonyl group instead of the ether linkage, *e.g.*,

$$C_6H_5-O-CH_2-CH=CH-C_2H_5 \xrightarrow{\Delta} o\text{-}(OH)C_6H_4-CH(C_2H_5)-CH=CH_2$$

$$CH_3-C(O-CH_2-CH=CH_2)=CH-COOC_2H_5 \rightarrow CH_3-C(=O)-CH(CH_2-CH=CH_2)-COOC_2H_5$$

Claisen-Schmidt condensation. A form of the Claisen condensation used for the preparation of α, β, unsaturated aldehydes or ketones by the condensation of aromatic aldehydes with aliphatic aldehydes or ketones, *e.g.*,

$$C_6H_5CHO+CH_3COC_6H_5 \xrightarrow{NaOH} C_6H_5CH=CH-COC_6H_5+H_2O$$

$$C_6H_5CHO+CH_3CHO \xrightarrow{NaOH} C_6H_5CH=CHCHO+H_2O$$

Clapeyron's equation. *See* Clausius-Clapeyron equation.

Clapeyron's relation. *See* Clausius-Clapeyron equation.

clarification. Removal of colloidally dispersed solids from a liquid either by coalescence and sedimentation or by adsorption on active material surfaces. For example, aluminium sulphate causes flocculation and settling of solid particle in purification of potable water; finely divided clays, carbon and certain proteins effect clarification of vegetable oils, sugar solutions, beverages, etc. by adsorbing colloidal impurities. The operation is sometimes called decolourization.

Clark and Lubs indicator. A mixed indicator of methyl-red and thymol-blue that shows colour changes between *p*H 4 and *p*H 10.

Clarke cell. A standard cell having anode, consisting of a zinc rod, is immersed in a saturated zinc sulphate solution. The mercury cathode is covered with a paste of mercurous sulphate. The cell must be kept below the transition temperature (at 39°C) of $ZnSO_4.7H_2O$ into $ZnSO_4.6H_2O$ to prevent serious changes in the electromotive force. A 20°C the Clarke cell furnishes an emf of 1.4267 volts ; the emf values are very sensitive to even small variation in temperature.

Clark process. The removal of temporary hardness from water by adding the calculated amount of slaked lime to precipitate the soluble calcium compounds as carbonate and the magnesium compounds as hydroxide.

classical gas. *See* ideal gas.

classical thermodynamics Theory of equilibrium states in macroscopic systems based in a few phenomenological laws called laws of thermodynamics.

classification. 1. Separation of grading of fragmented solids (ores, coal, crushed stone) or products of varying unit size (peas, beans, cherries, etc.) into groups having the same or nearly the same dimensions, by passing them through screens, sifters, or a similar selective device, or by air floatation.

2. A grouping of substances having closely similar chemical and physical properties, for example, hydrocarbons, aromatic compounds, alkaloids, terpenes, solvents etc.

clathrate. A unique type of solid mixture in which an atom or molecule of one substance (for example, argon) is entirely entrapped within the crystal lattice of another (*e.g.*, hydroquinone). The two substances do not form a chemical compound, the only attractive forces between them being relatively weak, such as hydrogen bonds or van der Waals forces. These compounds are formed during recrystallization (from solution or in gaseous atmosphere). Certain ("host") compounds are capable of enclosing other foreign ("guest") molecules or atoms in free spaces of their crystal lattice. Clathrate structures known as gas hydrates can be formed with water and several gases, *e.g.*, bromine, propane, and hydrogen sulphide. Urea can form clathrates with aliphatic compounds. Cathrate structures are often called "cage" complexes, adducts, or inclusion complexes. They are useful in chemical separation processes such as desalination of seawater, petroleum refining.

Claude process. Synthesis of ammonia from nitrogen and hydrogen at about 900 atmospheres pressure and 600°C. The term Claude process is also applied to a method of liquefaction of air by a series of operations, including cooling by expansion through an orifice, and cooling by expansion against external pressure in a piston engine.

Clausius-Clapeyron equation. Equation which determines relation between thermodynamic temperature T and pressure p in one-component two-phase system in thermodynamic equilibrium :

$$\frac{\partial p}{\partial T}=\frac{H_m^a-H_m^b}{T(V_m^a-V_m^b)}$$

where H_m=molar enthalpy, V_m=molar volume and a and b denote phases.

Also known as Clapeyron's equation, Clapeyron's relation.

Clausius equation of state. Empirical (thermal) equation of state of real gas :

$$\left[p+\frac{a}{T(V_m+c)^2}\right](V_m-b)=RT$$

where p=pressure, V_m=molar gas volume, T= thermodynamic temperature, R=universal gas constant, and a, b, c=constants characteristic for the given gas.

Clausius law. The law that the specific heat of an ideal gas (at constant volume) does not depend on temperature.

Clausius-Mossotti equation. Equation relating permittivity ϵ to polarizability α of molecule

$$\frac{\epsilon-1}{\epsilon+2}\frac{M}{\rho}=\frac{4}{3}\pi N_A\alpha$$

where M=molar mass, ρ=density, N_A=Avogadro number.

clay. A group of crystalline, finely divided earthy materials having similar physical and chemical properties ; some types have a particle size within or slightly above the colloidal range. The shape of the particles varies widely from one type to another. With some exceptions, clays can be considered as hydrates of alumina and silica with iron oxide and magnesia as common minor components ; a generalised chemical formula might be $Al_2O_3SiO_2{\cdot}nH_2O$. The best known types are kaolin (china clay), attapulgite, montmorillonite, and bentonite. Clays readily adsorb water to from a plastic matrix that can be shaped at room temperature and permanently hardened by baking or firing in a kiln ; in the terminology of plasties, they are thermosetting.

clay wash. A light oil such as nephtha or kerosine used to clear fuller's earth after it has been used in a filter.

cleaning. Removal of soil or other foreign matter from a material by the use of : (*i*) detergents in aqueous solution, for light-weight textiles, plastics, linaleum, etc., (*ii*) solvents for dry-cleaning (Stoddard solvent), for suitings and other heavy fabrics, (*iii*) pressurized steam, for cement and concrete, (*iv*) abrasives (sandblast), for building stone, granite, etc., (*v*) solvents for metal degreasing, chiefly such chlorinated hydrocarbons as carbon tetrachloride, trichlorothylene. etc.

clear gasoline. Gasoline free from antiknock additives.

cleavage. 1. The splitting of organic compounds by reactions with various reagents, *e.g.*, proteins by hydrolysis.

2. A property of crystals by virtue of which they split more readily in certain directions than in others, leaving nearly smooth faces. It is due to the fact that there is a minimum of cohesion between the atoms in the direction of cleavage.

cleavage crystal. A crystal fragment bounded by cleavage faces giving it a regular geometry.

cleavage plane. Plane along which a crystalline substance may split.

Clemmensen reduction. Reduction of carbonyl group by nascent hydrogen obtained from by zinc (or its) amalgam and hydrochloric acid, *e.g.*,

$$RCOR'+4[H]\xrightarrow[HCl]{Zn(Hg)}RCH_2R'+H_2O$$

clinical chemistry. A branch of chemistry which deals with behaviour and oomposition of all types of body fluids ; also deals with analysis and testing of these fluids.

clinoaxis. The inclined lateral axis that makes an oblique angle with the vertical axis in the monoclinic system.

clinohedral class. A rare class of crystals in the monoclinic system having a plane of symmetry but no axis of symmetry. Also known as domatic class.

clinopinacoid. A form of monoclinic crystal whose faces are parallel to the inclined and vertical axes.

closed cycle. A thermodynamic cycle in which the thermodynamic fluid does not enter or leave the system, but it is used over and over again.

closed system. A system which is isolated so that it cannot exchange matter or energy with its surroundings and therefore attain a state of thermodynamic equilibrium.

cloud point. The temperature at which a solution becomes cloudy as it is cooled at a specified rate. The cloud point is an important property in the specification of lacquers, oils, and other important liquids and solutions.

cluster. 1. A group of closely-related or interacting molecules which has an independent existence within a larger molecular domain ; the postulation of such clusters leads to quite satisfoctory treatments of certain properties of liquids, such as condensation and the critical state.

2. Group of nucleons inside atomic nucleus forming structure of the whole nucleus.

cluster model. Model of atomic nucleus which describes nucleus as system of comparatively weakly bound lighter atomic nuclei, *e.g.*, helium nuclei in alpha model. Cluster model describes properties of excited nucleus in terms of nucleus-cluster properties.

coacervation. The process of producing, by coagulation of a hydrophilic sol, of a liquid phase, which often appears as viscous drops, instead of forming a continuous liquid phase, *e.g.*, during salting out with electrolytes. One constituent of separated phase is a concentrated sol, and the other, a dilute sol.

coagel. A gel formed by precipitation or coagulation, as distinguished from gel formed by swelling of solid colloid.

coagulation. 1. Process of decreasing number of particles of dispersed phase in unit volume of collodial system by gathering of single particles into larger species (aggregates).

2. The result of an alteration of a disperse phase or of a dissolved solid which causes the separation of the system into a liquid phase and an insoluble mass. Agents which induce coagulation are usually strong electrolytes (acids or alkalies) which form strongly charged ions in the suspension, thus neutralizing the oppositely charged particles. As a result, the particles coalesce and precipitate. Enzymes also have effective coagulant properties. Familiar examples of coagulation are : (*i*) blood, initiated by the enzyme thrombin ; (*ii*) the proteins of egg white, coagulation being caused by heat ; (*iii*) coalescence of fat particles of whole milk or cream by agitation or beating, which mechanically ruptures the protein coating of the particles, allowing them to cohere ; (*iv*) rubber latex, where coagulation is brought about by addition of acetic or formic acid.

coagulation concentration. Smallest concentration of electrolyte, expressed most often as mmoles/dm^3, causing quick visible coagulation of sol. Also known as flocculation value.

coalescence. Separation of disperse system, usually emulsion, into two continuous phases, caused by gathering of particles of dispersed phase.

coal gas. Flammable gas derived from coal either naturally or by destructive distillation of coal in iron retorts ; average composition by volume is : hydrogen 50%, methane 30%, carbon monoxide 8%, carbon dioxide and oxygen 8% and other hydrocarbons 4%.

coal gasification. The conversion of coal, coke or char into a gaseous product by reaction with air, oxygen, steam, carbon dioxide, or mixture of these.

coalification. Conversion of plant remains in coal by the processes of diagenesis and metamorphism Also known as carbonification ; incarbonization ; incoalation.

cobalamin. A compound, called vitamin B_{12} is a member of the B complex. has several forms, one of which (nitrocoblamin) has the formula $C_{62}H_{90}N_{14}O_{16}PCo$. It is an essential metabolic factor, affecting the formation of nucleic acids and the interconversion of fats and carbohydrates by its complexing activity. It is effective in counteracting anemia and certain forms of acute neuritis. It occurs in extremely low concentrations in milk, meat and eggs and is stored in the liver; it is recovered from sugar beet and skim milk residues.

cobalt. An element.

Group VIII

Symbol	Co
Atomic No.	27
Atomic Wt.	58.9332
Valence	+2,+3
m.p.	1493°C
b.p.	2870°C

Cobalt is similar to iron and nickel in both its free and combined states. It is distributed in nature, making up about 0.01% of the igneous rocks of the earth's crust, compared with 0.02% for nickel.

The metal is obtained by calcining and subsequent reduction. Cobalt has exceptional properties as a coordinating element. It is also unusual for its magnetic properties which make it useful in alloys used for magnets. About 80% of the cobalt consumed is used in the manufacture of several important nonferrous alloys. Cobalt is one of the trace elements required for plant nutrition. Cobalt itself is essentially nontoxic; however, the highly radioactive artificial isotope cobalt-60 is dangerous unless used under medical supervision, as for cancer therapy. The natural element has only one stable isotope. Some of its compounds are used as blue pigments in glass and cosmetics and as catalysts.

cobalt bomb. Common name for cobalt-60 source of ionizing radiation; used for therapeutical purposes and for irradiation of materials and reacting systems.

codimer. A copolymer formed from the polyerization of two dissimilar olefin molecules, *e.g.*, the product of polymerization of isobutylene with one of the two normal butylenes.

codon. A sequence of three adjacent nucleotides in a nucleic acid that codes for a specific amino acid.

coefficient of compressibility x. Relative change of gas volume V caused by unit change of preseure p at constant thermodynamic temperature T considered with opposite sign

$$x = -\frac{1}{V}\left(\frac{\partial V}{\partial p}\right)_T [\text{atm}^{-1}]$$

or $[\text{Pa}^{-1}]$ in SI system.

Coefficient of compressibility is used sometimes also in meaning of adiabatic coefficient of compressibility, which describes relative change of volume due to pressure, but in adiabatic conditions. Also known as compressibility; isothermal compressibility.

coefficient of purity. An approximate factor used in the sugar industry obtained by multiplying the polarization of the juice by 100 and dividing the product by the reading it gives with the Brix hydrometer. It furnishes an approximation of the amount of pure sucrose present. Also known as **quotient of purity.**

coefficient of thermal expansion (of gas), α. Relative change of volume V of gas, caused by change of its thermodynamic temperature T by 1 K at constant pressure p

$$\alpha = \frac{1}{V}\left(\frac{\partial V}{\partial T}\right)_p [\text{K}^{-1}]$$

Coefficient of expansion of ideal gas is

$$\alpha = \frac{1}{273.15}\ \text{K}^{-1}$$

coenzyme. An organic cofactor or prosthetic group (nonprotein portion of the enzyme) whose presence is required for the activity of many enzymes. In addition, many enzymes need metal ions (such as Cu^{2+}, Mn^{2+}, Mg^{2+}) for activation. A number of the coenzymes are nucleotides; all play an important role in vitamin activity and related functions. For example, Coenzyme I catalyzes oxidations, Coenzyme A activates acetylation (acetylcholine formation), and Coenzyme Q is involved in the citric acid cycle. The members of the B complex are components of coenzymes; their mechanism of action is that of a prosthetic group.

coenzyme A. A pantothenic acid—containing coenzyme serving as an acyl group carrier in certain enzymatic reactions.

coercive force. 1. Magnetic field strength corresponding to zero value of magnetic induction and magnetization in ferro- or ferrimagnets during their overmagnetization.

2. The magnetic force necessary to demagnetize a body previovsly magnetized.

cofactor. A small-molecular weight, heat-stable, inorganic or organic substance required for the action of an enzyme.

coferment. Any substance that increases or makes possible the action of an enzyme. Thus phosphates and a complex organic phosphates have been shown to increase the activity of the yeast ferment and blood does not clot in the absence of calcium salts, apparently because calcium salts are necessary for the conversion of the blood zymogen into thrombase, the clotting ferment. *See also* coenzyme.

cofermentation. A condition of fermentation in which the principal enzyme is unable to carry on its specific reactions in the absence of a coferment.

conere. Of a material or substance, to stick tightly together (as opposed to adhere, meaning to stick to another substance, as an adhesive). Cohesion is a property of most resins, gums, mucilages, and other materials that are sticky in the raw state; many of them also display good adhesive properties.

coherent. The term "coherent," as applied to light rays emananting from lasers, refers to a high-energy beam of light having only one wavelength and one frequency, which can be used as a penetrating or cutting device of tremendous efficiency and accuracy.

coherent precipitate. A precipitate that is a continuation of the lattice structures of the solvent and has no phase or grain boundary.

coherent scattering. Scattering due to simultaneous interaction with more than one scattering centre, resulting in interference of waves scattered on particular centres.

cohesion. Molecular attraction between the particles of any given mass by virtue of which the mass tends to resist physical disintegration. It differs from adhesion which refers to surface attractions.

cohesion pressure. The addition term a/V^2 used in the van der Waals equation to correct the pressure by adding the attractive force of the molecules where, V=the volume of the gas, and a=constant for a given gas.

cohobation. A process of distilling in which the distillate or a portion of the distillate is repeatedly returned to the still.

co-ions. Mobile ions (able to diffuse freely) on the same charge as that of ion exchanger's skeleton.

coke. The end-product of the destructive distillation of bituminous coal or of the cracking of petroleum hydrocarbons. Coal-derived coke is used chiefly for blast-furnace fuel. Petroleum-derived coke (also called metallurgical coke) is used to make electrolyic and electrothermic electrodes and also as refractory electrothermal furnance linings. It is somewhat purer, having about 95% carbon. Coke is generally regarded as a form of industrial carbon. An important chemical use of coke is in the manufacture of synthesis gas and water gas.

coke oven gas. A gas formed during carbonization of coal to coke; it contains hydrogen, methane, carbon monoxide, ammonia, and traces of benzene, etc.

coping. A process for thermal conversion of the heavy residual bottoms of crude oil entirely to lower boiling products and by-product petroleum coke.

Colasanti test for thiocyacate. Solutions of thiocyanates give (*i*) a persistent green colour with cupric sulphate solutions; (*ii*) an intense violet colour with a 0.1% gold chloride solution made alkaline with sodium carbonate.

cold anodizing. Dipping light alloys in 50% nitric acid (aqueous) for 1-2 minutes to produce a slight thickening of the neutral oxide film.

cold cathode. A cathode whose operation does not depend on its temperature being above the ambient temperature.

cold galvanizing. Painting iron-surface with a zinc-rich paint.

cold neutron. A very low-energy neutron in a reactor; has wavelength of the order of crystal lattice spacings.

cold plasma. Plasma having temperature of order of tens of thousands kelvins.

cold process. 1. A method of low temperature saponification once used widely in the soap industry. The fat is melted, emulsified with sodium hydroxide solution or other alkali, and allowed to stand until saponification is complete or, rather, until saponification has progressed to the desired extent.

2. A low temperature polymerization method used in the synthetic rubber industry.

cold settling process. A simple process for the dewaxing of petroleum, consisting chiefly of mixing it with gasoline or naphtha, cooling, and standing, where upon the wax settles. After sometime the gasoline or naphtha is separated by distillation.

collagen. A protein occurring in the connective tissue of the body, having a fibrous polypeptide chain comprised of many amino acids ; possesses the unique property of shrinking in hot water within a specific temperature range from 62-65°C. This behaviour is a critical factor in leather tannage, for leather, the shrinkage temperature increase within the extent of tannage. In addition to leather, it is used to some extent in the manufacture of animal glues and in many medical applications such as dialysis membranes, sutures, etc. Collagen is converted into gelatin by hydrolysis, after purification it is used as a protective colloid and gel-former in food products, for sausage casings, and for coating photographic film.

colligative properties. Properties which depend primerily on the number of particles in a system, being independent of the size or nature of the particles. Considering dilute solutions, for example, vapour pressure and osmotic pressure of these are colligative properties. Such properties are chiefly encountered in the study of solutions.

collision diameter of molecules. The distance of closest approach between the centres of any two molecules during a collision.

collision, elastic. A colloision between particles in which only kinetic energy, and not internal energy, is exchanged.

collision integral. Internal term in Boltzmann equation

$$\left[\frac{\partial \rho_1}{\partial t}\right]_{\text{coll.}} = n \int d^3 v \int d\phi\, \sigma(\phi) \mid v - v_1 \mid \times$$
$$\times [\rho_1(v')\rho_1(v_1') - \rho_1(v)\rho_1(v_1)]$$

where t=time, n=particle density, ρ_1=unimolecular partition function, ϕ=angle between vectors $v-v_1$ and $v'-v_1'$, $\sigma(\phi)$=differential cross-section for two molecule collision with initial velocities v, v_1 and final velocities v', v_1'. Collision integral takes into account influence of intermolecular collisions on partition function and their effect on gas phase processes.

coilision number, $\bar{z}$. A term used in reaction rate theory to denote the number of collisions between molecules occurring per second per unit of concentration.

Average number of two-molecular collisions in unit time interval which take place in unit volume of rarified gas in equilibrium conditions

$$\bar{z} = d^2 \frac{\pi}{4}\left(\frac{m}{\pi k T}\right)^{3/2} \int_0^\infty \sigma v^3 \exp\left[-\frac{mv^2}{4kT}\right] dv$$

where k=Boltzmann constant, T=thermodynamic temperature, d=molecule density, v= relative velocity of pair of molecules, and σ= cross-section for two-molecular collision. In hard sphere core model σ is constant and then

$$\bar{z} = 2d^2x^2\left(\frac{\pi k T}{m}\right)^{\frac{1}{2}}$$

where x=molecule diameter.

collision theory of reaction rates. Reaction rate theory based on model of elementary chemical reaction as due to collisions of molecules possessing defined surplus of energy (called activation energy).

This theory fails in many instances and offers at best in incomplete explanation of the factors involved.

colloid. Disperse system of high degree of dispersion and developed surface of separation of phases in which dispersed phase consists of colloidal particles (colloid) or system physically homogeneous containing macromolecules as one of components (molecular colloid).

The colloidal state is neither solution nor suspension but is obtained when small particles of size within definite limits) of solid, liquid or gas as a phase are distributed in a gas, liquid or solid as a medium. All gases being miscible with one another, a colloidal system of gas distributed over gas is not possible. Colloidal dispersions have quite different properties from those of true solutions or suspensions. They are divided into two main classes, lyophil and lyophobe and are of great importance in nature (*e.g.*, fog, milk) and for synthetic materials such as plastics. All colloidal particles are electrically charged. Ostwald distinguished between two classes of colloidal liquids, one in which the suspended colloid does not sensibly affect the properties of the dispersive medium such as suspensions of metals, metallic sulphides or clay ; and the class in which the reverse is true as in the case of gelatin solutions which "set" to gels below a certain temperature.

colloidal electrolyte. A compound having a long hydrocarbon chain terminating in a group that can ionize. Colloidal electrolytes resmble non-electrolytes in some of their properties and electrolytes in others. Thus, the alkaline salts of the fatty acids, for example, have the osmotic properties of a nonelectrolyte, but they show a marked electrical conductance and other properties of weak electrolytes.

colloidal equivalent. A term applied to the dispersed phase of a colloidal system, denoting the number of molecules per unit electric charge.

colloidal metals. Colloidal solutions or suspensions of metals, the metal being distributed in the form of very small electrically charged particles. They are prepared by striking an electric arc between electrodes made of the metal, under water or by the chemical reduction of a solution of a salt of the metal ; used in medicine and paints.

colloidal particles. Particles of dispersed phase of dimensions from 1 nm to 500 nm which can be observed under ultramicroscope, including particles of two or only one dimension of this order (laminar and thread colloidal particles).

colloidal state. State of matter characterized by appropriate degree of colloidal dispersion (*see* colloid, colloidal particles).

colloid chemistry. The study of phenomena occurring when any form of matter has at least one dimension that is less than 1 micron (the limit of resolution of the optical microscope), and more than 1 millimicron (10 angstrom), which is the approximate size of an average molecule. Thus, it is concerned with the size range that lies between molecular dimensions and particles that are just visible in a compound microscope. It is important to note that in colloid chemistry it is the dimension that is significant, rather than the nature of the materials ; thus it involves not only particulate matter but films, foams, fibres, interfaces, and surface irregularities such as occur, for example, in catalysts.

colloid, heteropolar. *See* heteropolar colloid.

colloid, homopolar. *See* homopolar colloid.

colloid mill. Device in which direct mechanical disintegration of substance suspended in dispersion medium takes place until particles of colloidal size are obtained.

colloid, protective. *See* protective colloid.

colloid, reversible *See* reversible colloid.

colorant. A general term for any substance that imparts a distinctive and relatively permanent colour. There are both natural and synthetic colorants which are classified as dyes and pigments. Most dyes are synthetic organic compounds ; pigments may be either natural or synthetic and either organic or inorganic. Some metals in the from of compounds have colorant properties, *e.g.*, iron, cobalt, and chromium. Some of the natural organic colorants are chlorophyll, xanthophyll, carotene, and other plant pigments.

colorimeter. An instrument used to perform colorimetric analysis either by absorption measurements or by comparison of absorption of solution. Measurements are carried out with white light or simple monochromatic light is used. This term is also used to describe photo-colorimeter.

colorimetric analysis. Analytical method utilizing measurement of colour intensity of solution for determination of amount of substance which is coloured or which forms a coloured compound in chemical reaction. Amount of a compound in solution can be determined by measuring the intensity of its colour by either visual or photometric methods. Such determinations depend on the light absorption and transmission properties of the substance measured. Colorimetric techniques can be used to measure extremely low concentrations, for example, of chromium in steel. They are also used in medical analysis and in food and pharmacological studies. Also known as colorimetry.

colorimetric titration. Method of colorimetric analysis : a coloured reaction in investigated solution is carried out in one of the absorption cells ; in other cell all the reagents are mixed in the same quantities and then solution of component to be determined is added from micro-burette until solutions in both cells become identically coloured.

colorimetry. 1. *See* colorimetric analysis.

2. Branch of optics dealing with quantitative determination of colours based on interpretation of absorption or re-emission spectrum for using specially devised and normalized measurement system which enables all colours to be synthesized from the three primary colours.

colour centres. Atomic and electronic defects of various types which produce optical absorption bands in otherwise transparent crystals such as alkali halides. These are produced by gamma-radiation, x-radiation, and by addition of impurities. A well known example is that of F-centre in NaCl. Colour centres find application in radiation dosimeters.

colour temperature. Temperature at which black body radiation spectrum is indentical with radiation spectrum of grey body at a given temperature.

columbium. Former name of the element niobium.

column breakthrough. In chromatography, appearance of given component in effluent from column (in practice, moment when concentration of this component exceeds certain conventional value).

column chromatography. A chromatographic procedure in which a sample dissolved in a small amount of solvent is placed on the top of a chromatographic column. In the course of the elution process, the different materials in the sample separate out on the column as discrete bands. The chemical nature of both the sorbent and the eluting solvent exert primary control over the degree in which individual mixture components are retained on the column.

column efficiency. *See* column performance.

column performance. Measure of chromatographic band spreading expressed in terms of number of theoretical plates. Also known as column efficiency.

Combes quinoline synthesis. A method of formation of quinolines from β-diketones and aromatic amines, followed by dehydration of the intermediate compound formed ; *e.g.*,

$$C_6H_5NH_2 + R'COCH_2COR \xrightarrow[-H_2O]{\Delta} C_6H_5N{=}C(R){-}CH{=}C(OH)R' \xrightarrow[-H_2O]{H_2SO_4} \text{(quinoline with } R' \text{ at 4 and } R \text{ at 2)}$$

combination. A type of chemical reaction in which one compound is formed, either from two elements: $C_2+O_2 \rightarrow CO_2$, from an element and a compound: $C_2H_2+2Br_2 \rightarrow C_2H_2Br_4$, or from two simpler compounds : $NH_3 + HNO_3 \rightarrow NH_4NO_3$. This term is also loosely used in the sense of any union of molecules, either weakly bonded or cross-linked. *See also* association ; polymerization.

combination band. In vibration spectrum band with frequency equal to sum or difference of two or more fundamental vibrations ; it appears due to anharmonicity of vibrations. Also known as summation band or difference band.

combination cell. An electrolytic cell in which one electrode is composed of an active metal (such as zinc) and the other electrode of an active nonmetal (such as chlorine) and current is produced in an external circuit by the formation of ions at the electrodes (zinc ions at the zinc electrode and chloride ions at the chlorine electrode). It is called a combination cell because the cell reaction is the same as the combination reaction between the metal and the nonmetal.

combining weight. *See* equivalent weight.

combustible material. Technically defined as any material that will burn when exposed to a sufficient degree of heat in an atmosphere of air or oxygen, the term is usually applied to materials which ignite above 64°-65°C and burn relatively slowly. In this sense, "combustible" is distinguished from "flammable." Combustible materials are typified by paper, wood and other cellullosics in their gross or bulk state as distinct from a finely divided state. Combustible materials are nonflammable, that is, they do not ignite instantaneously, as do flammable materials. "Nonflammable" should be distinguished from "noncombustible," which means literally "incapable of combustion" (carbon dioxide, water, oxygen, etc.). *See also* flammable material ; combustion ; autoignition point.

combustion. Rapid exothermal reaction accompanied usually by phenomenon of light emisson; most often reaction with oxygen.

Most commonly, the chemical combination of oxygen with another element or compound, usually induced by high temperature, resulting in the formation of one or more new compounds (generally oxides). It is often called burning. In the case of organic materials, where decomposition of the original compound occurs, combustion is the reverse of photosynthesis; the reaction is usually rapid and is accompanied by release of energy in the form of heat, and usually light as well. Combustion of hydrogen results in the formation of water, the oxide of hydrogen. In the case of sodium and phosphorus, combustion occurs at room temperature. Combustion will take place in air when an organic material is heated to its autoignition point, either by an external flame, or spark, or by exposure to a sufficiently high ambient temparature.

combustion analysis. Most organic compounds are composed largely of carbon and hydrogen. If necessary, the presence of these elements can be conformed by detecting carbon dioxide and water among the products of combustion. Other elements such as nitrogen, phosphorus, sulphur or halogens, may also be present and qualitative tests for these involve destructive reduction with molten sodium, followed by the analysis of resulting inorganic ions.

To determine the amount of carbon and hydrogen in an organic substance, it is simply burnt (a weighed sample) and the amount of CO_2 and H_2O produced is measured :

$$C_xH_yO_z \xrightarrow{\text{Combustion}} xCO_2 + \frac{y}{2}H_2O$$

comminution. Reduction in size. The term is commonly used in reference to process such as grinding, crushing, shredding, etc., of materials.

common intermediate. A chemical compound common to two chemical reactions, as a product of one and as reactant of the other.

common ion effect. The depression of the solubility of an ionized substance by adding more of one of the ions already present. Thus if hydrogen chloride gas is bubbled through a saturated solution of common salt, crystalline salt begins to precipate. In this case chloride is the "common ion", thus NaCl may be purified by this method.

compact doule layer. Part of electrical double layer at metal-electrolyte solution interphase, it directly adheres to metal surface and is built from adsorbed or electrostatically bound ions ; identical with Helmholtz medel. *See also* theories of double layer.

comparator. In colorimetric analysis, instrument for determination of concentration of coloured substances by visual comparison with standard scale.

comparison solution. Solution with colour identical with that which titrated solution, should have just before or after end-point of titration.

compatibilily. The ability of two (or more) materials to exist together in the form of mixtures, laminates, or composites without exerting a damaging or harmfull effect on one another over long periods of time. The term is usually applied to solvents which can be blended in all proportions and do not tend to separate, for example, water and alcohol. It is also applied to mixtures of polymers of different molecular structure. The term compatibility is also used when two or more ligands simultaneously form the complex with the same metal ion.

competitive inhibition. A type of enzyme inhibition reversed by increasing the substrate concentration.

complementry DNA (cDNA). A DNA that is usually made by reverse transcriptase and is complementary to a given messenger RNA ; used in DNA cloning.

complementarity. According to the principle of complementarity, nature has "complementary" aspects ; an experiment which illustrates one of these aspects necessarily simultaneously obscures the complementary aspect. To put it differently, each experiment or sequence of experiments yields only a limited amount of information about the system under investigation ; as this information is gained, other equally interesting information (which could have been obtained from another sequence of experiments) is lost. Of course, the person performing experiment does not forget the results of previous experiments, but at any instant, only a limited amount of information is usable for predicting the further course of the system. Wave-particle duality and the uncertainty principle are thought to be examples of the more profound principle of complementarity.

complement-fixation test. A sensitive reaction used in serology for the detection of either antigen or antibody, as in the diagonosis of many bacterial, viral and other diseases. It involves two stages : stage I is the binding or fixation of compliment if certain antigen-antibody reactions occur, and stage II is the detection of residual unbound compliment, if any, by its hemolytic action on the sensitized erytherocytes subsequently added.

complete internal equilibrium. *See* thermodynamic equilibrium.

completely polarizable electrode. Electrode (half-cell) with no flow of charged particles between bordering phases of metallic conductor and electrolyte, *e.g.*, mercury in solutions of alkali metal chloride in a certain potential range.

complete miscibility. Ability of mixture to undergo uniform mixing in any proportion. Also known as unlimited compatibility.

complex. *See* coordination compound.

complex compound. *See* coordination compound.

complex dielectric polarization (molar). P_m^*. Quantity defined by :

$$P_m^* = \frac{\epsilon^*-1}{\epsilon^*+2} \frac{Mr}{\rho}$$

where ϵ^*=complex permitivity, Mr=relative molecular mass, ρ=density.

complex formation. *See* coordination.

compleximetric titration. *See* compleximetry.

compleximetry. Titration based on reactions of formation of soluble complexes of determined ion with titrant. Also known as complexometry ; compleximetric titration ; complexometric titration.

complex ion. The species formed when an ion links with a natural molecule or radical, or with another ion of opposite charge. When the complex has formed, the simple ion ceases to give its usual ionic reactions in solution. Two fairly simple examples are (*i*) the complex ion formed when plumbous chloride dissolves in concentrated hydrochloric acid (here therefore the common ion effect does not appear), and (*ii*) complex formed when iodine dissolves in an excess of potassium iodide solution.

complexometric titration. *See* compleximetry.

complexometry. *See* compleximetry.

complexones. Reagents introduced by Schwarzenbach in 1945 which remove certain ions from solution by forming complexes. The Chelate compounds remove ions in this way by a "sequestration" effect.

complex permitivity, ω^*. Quantity defined by $\omega^*=\omega-i\omega'$, where ω=permitivity, $i=\sqrt{-1}$, ω'=dielectric losses.

complex reaction. System of two or more mutually connected elementary reactions.

complex salt. A compound formed by the combination of two or more salts and which is regarded as the normal salt of a complex acid. Complex salts do not split into a mixture of the constituent salts in solution but furnish a complex ion which contains one of the bases, *e.g.*, potasium ferrocyanide, and potassium platino-chloride.

component. 1. Out of the elements or compounds present in a system such as a phase, a mixture, a solution, or a suspension, in which it may or may not be uniformly dispersed. For example, chromium as a component of stainless steel, and water is a component of milk. *See* also constituent ; mixture.

2. In physical chemistry, one among the smallest number of chemical substances which need to be specified in order to reproduce a given chemical system.

composite material. Any combination or blend of solid materials whose particles are large enough to be visible to the unaided eye and which are chemically different from each other. Attempts are often made to differentiate composite materials from conventional materials on the basis of the heterogenous or multiphase nature of the former, but many materials which are considered conventional by generally accepted usage are also multiphase. There are a number of different kinds of composites. Notable among them are combinations of extremely high-strength fibres (graphite, silicon carbide) with thermosetting plastics. Another important type includes reinforced plastics, which usually involve glass fibres. Even blends of natural and synthetic fibres in both woven and nonwoven fabrics can be considered as composites.

compound. A homogeneous, pure substance composed of two or more essentially different chemical elements, which are present in definite proportions ; compounds usually possess properties differing from those of the constituent elements.

Compounds are represented by formulas which specifically indicate their atomic or ionic content and the proportion by weight of their elements ; some types of formulas also show the spatial arrangement of elements in the compound. Chemical bonds or valences hold the compound together. Its properties are almost invariably different from those of the individual constituents. A significant feature of compounds is their homogeneity, that is, the fact, that any given quantity of a compound has the same properties throughout. The constituents can be separated only by a chemical change induced by a reagent, by heat, or by electrical energy.

compound, addition. A compound that is formed by the junction or union of two simpler compounds.

compound, associated. A compound formed by the union of two or more molecules, usually of the same or similar chemical composition, to form a single complex molecule.

compound, asymmetric. A compound containing an asymmetric carbon atom.

compound, binary. A compound made up of only two elements, in one definite molecular ratio.

compound chromophores. Two or more chromophores within one molecule with common conjugated bond system ; they exhibit fairly strong light absorption usually shifted strongly bathochromically and hyperchromically as compared with those of separate component chromophores. Also known as conjugated chromophores.

compound, coordinate. *See* coordinate compound.

compound, covalent. *See* covalent compound.

compound, cyclic. *See* cyclic compound.

compound, heterocyclic. *See* heterocyclic compound.

compound, inorganic. *See* inorganic compound.

compound, intermetallic. *See* intermetallic compound.

compound, interstitial. *See* interstitial compound.

compound, ionic, *See* ionic compound.

compound, isocyclic. *See* homocyclic compound.

compound, molecular. *See* molecular compound.

compound nucleus. An intermediate state in a nuclear reaction in which the incident particle combines with the target nucleus and its energy is shared among all the nucleons of the system. Final state of such reactions is reached independently of initial state, as result of decay of compound nucleus.

compound, organic. *See* organic compound.

compound, organo-metallic. *See* organo-metallic compound.

compound, polar. *See* polar compound.

compound, quaternary. *See* quaternary compound.

compound saturated. *See* saturated compound.

compound, spiro. *See* spiro compound.

compound, unsaturated. *See* unsaturated compound.

compressed gas. Any gaseous material that is subjected to specific pressure and introduced into metal cylinders or special tanks for shipment in either liquid or non-liquid form. Common inorganic gases handled in this way are nitrogen, oxygen, ammonia, chlorine, carbon dioxide, helium, fluorine, hydrogen and nitrous oxide. Liquefied petroleum gases (LPG) comprise a subgroup of compressed organic gases ; they include butene, butane, propane, and propylene and are chiefly used as household and industrial fuels. Other organic gases in compressed forms are vinyl chloride, acetylene, and butadiene, the reasons for compression are economy and convenience in shipping, storge, and handling, and in the case of flammable gases, the safety factor.

compressibility. Dependence of volume of substance on pressure.

compressibility factor, *z*. Empirical coefficient depending on nature of substance, pressure *p* and thermodynamic temperature *T*, applied in description of properties of real gas by equation of state in the form

$$z = \frac{pV_m}{RT}$$

where V_m=molar volume of real gas, and R= universal gas constant.

compression distillation. A distillation process in which the vapours from the still are subjected to compression. The vapours heated in this manner are then used to furnish heat to other units of equipment.

Compton continuum. Energy spectrum of electrons liberated in Compton effect.

Compton edge. Maximum energy which can be gained by electron in Compton effect.

Compton effect. Scattering of gamma radiation, the wavelength of which is increased as a result of energy transfer to orbital electrons. This increase in wavelength is caused by the interaction of the radiation with the weakly bound electrons in the matter in which the scattering takes place. This effect illustrates one of the most fundamental interactions between radiation and matter and displays in a very graphic way the true quantum nature of electromagnetic radiation.

concentration. The quantity of any substance, present in a specified weight or volume of a mixture. The units used for mixtures of solids are usually percent by weight or by volume. These may also be used for liquids, *e.g.*, seawater is a 2.6% sodium chloride solution containing 2.6 grams of NaCl per 100 grams of solution. For solutions, concentrations are more accurately expressed in terms of molality, molarity, and normality. Square brackets are often used in formulas to indicate concentration, *i.e.*, [M].

concentration, absolute. The quantity of a substance, or form of energy or other entity that exists in a unit volume, expressed in mass per unit volume (joules per cubic metre) or number or particles (as of atoms, alpha particles hydrogen ions, etc.) per unit volume.

concentration cell. An electric cell in which the E.M.F. is obtained by using two electrodes of the same material each separately immersed in a different concentration of the same electrolyte the two electrode compartments being connected by a suitable bridge. In concentration cell electrical work results from equalization of concentrations of electrolyte, or composition of metallic phase of electrodes, or pressures of gases which comprise given electrode systems.

concentration cell without transference. Concentration cell in which electrolytes of different concentrations m' and m'' are not in direct contact, *e.g.*,

$$\text{Ag, AgCl} \mid \text{NaCl}(m') \mid \text{Na}_x\ \text{Hg} - \text{NaHg}_x \mid \mid \text{NaCl}(m'') \mid \text{AgCl, Ag}$$

or concentration cell with one electrolyte and different partial pressures p' and p'' of gases in electrode systems, *e.g.*,

$$\text{Pt, H}_2(p') \mid \text{HCl} \mid \text{Pt, H}_2(p'')$$

concentration cell with transference. Concentration cell with two different concentrations m' and m'' of electrolyte which are in contact (for example through diaphragm), *e.g.*,

$$\text{Pt, H}_2 \mid \text{HCl}(m') \mid \text{HCl}(m'') \mid \text{Pt, H}_2$$

concentration, critical. *See* critical concentrations.

concentration, ionic. *See* ionic concentration.

concentration, molal. *See* molal concentration.

concentration, molar. *See* molar concentration.

concentration, normal. *See* normal concentration.

concentration polarization. Type of electrolytic polarization consisting in changes of electrolyte concentration at electrode as a result of flow of polarizing current. Concentration polarization is expressed by concentration overvoltage.

conchoidal. A term generally used in mineralogy

to describe a type of surface formed by fracturing a hard solid by impact. Certain materials present involutely curved fracture surfaces suggestive of the shape of the shells of bivalves (conch), from which the term is derived. Examples of this type of substances are glass, blown asphalt, and numerous minerals.

condensation. 1. Linking together of two or more molecules, resulting in the formation of larger molecule, usually proceeds with elimination of some simple substance, *e.g.*, water, ammonia or hydrogen halide, *e.g.*,

$$2C_6H_5Cl + Cl_3CCHO \xrightarrow{H_2SO_4} \begin{array}{c} ClC_6H_4 \\ | \\ CHCCl_3 + 2H_2O \\ | \\ ClC_6H_4 \end{array}$$

$$2H_3PO_4 \rightarrow H_4P_2O_7 + H_2O$$

There are a number of special types designated by such names as aldol, Claisen, and Friedel-Crafts.

2. The change of water or other substances from vapour to liquid phase on contact with a cool surface, as in distillation.

condensation method. In colloid chemistry, methods of obtaining colloids from systems of molecular disintegration by aggregation, polymerization or polycondensation of ions, atoms or molecules.

condensation point. *See* condensation temperature.

condensation polymer. Polymer formed by condensation polymerization. Condensation polymer is a linear or three-dimentional macromolecule resulting from a catalyzed reaction between two organic molecules, often of the aldehyde or ketone type, usually with the formation of water or an alcohol as the by-product. Several kinds of condensation polymers are made by such repetitive or multistage reactions (called polycondensation) ; *e.g.*, phenolformaldehyde, polyamides, polyesters, and polyurethanes.

condensation polymerizatoin. Polymerization by repeated condensation, *i.e.*, with simultaneous elimination of some simple substance as by-product. Also known as polycondensation.

condensation temperature. Temperature at which vapourized substance is converted into liquid or solid state. Also known as condensation point.

condensed nuclei. *See* condensed ring system.

condensed phases. Liquids and solid phases.

condensed polycyclic compound. *See* condensed ring system.

condensed polyhedral structures. Compounds in which two or more coordination polyhedrons are united to form a more complex total structure.

The classic homologous series of compounds in organic chemistry provide useful examples involving the condensation of polyhedrons containing the same central element in the individual units. The series of saturated or aliphatic hydrocarbons, having the general formula C_nH_{2n+2}, contains a large number of compounds extending from the lowest member, methane, CH_4, to polyethylene, a plastic of economic importance in which n is a very large number. There are two ways for the linking together of these tetrahedrons. This gives rise to two molecular forms, both of which are stable, well-known compounds. It is an essential part of these structures that each C—C link is linear (because it is merely a σ-bond) ; however, when two carbon atoms are linked to a third, the C—C—C angle is essentially determined by the bond angle of the central carbon atom (that is, the other carbons may be treated as ligands to the first) The other familiar homologous series of organic chemistry differ from the saturated hydrocarbons in having at least one unique coordination polyhedron of a different type. The olefins contain two doubly bonded, or unsaturated, carbon atoms, whose polyherdal structures are trigonal planar, and the remainder of the carbons are tetrahederal. As in the case of the aliphatic hydrocarbons, the olefins exhibit an isomerism which is associated with the branching of the chain structure. In addition, the presence of two linked trigonal planar carbon atoms and the fact that the polyhedrons cannot rotate about the double bond give rise to a different kind of isomerism, called cis-trans isomerism.

condensed ring system. System of two or more rings fused together, having common pairs of atoms, *e.g.*, naphthalene. Also known as condensed rings ; condensed nuclei ; condensed polycyclic compound.

condensed system. System composed of condensed phases only.

condition of isothermal mechanical stability. Condition $x>0$, where x = isothermal compressibility coefficient of phase. It ensures that phase cannot decompose irreversibly into parts with different pressure.

condition of material stability. Condition according to which phase cannot decompose irreversibly into parts with different values of chemical potential of the same constituent if matrix $[\mu_{ij}]$ is positive definite, where

$$\mu_{ij} = \frac{\partial \mu_i}{\partial x_j}$$

∂_i=chemical potential of i-th constituent in a given phase, x=mole fraction and i, j refer to given phase constituents.

condition of thermal stability. Condition $Cv>0$, where Cv=phase molar heat capacity at constant volume ; it ensures that phase cannot decompose irreversibly into parts with different temperature.

conductance. The capacity to conduct, as applied particularly to heat or electricity ; or the quantity of electricity which flows through a unit volume (unit cube) under unit difference of electrical potential per unit time. It is the reciprocal of resistance.

conductance, equivalent. *See* equivalent conductance.

conductance, ionic. *See* ionic conductance.

conductance, molar. *See* molar conductance.

conductance, specific. *See* specific conductance.

conduction band (in band theory of solids). Energy band derived from overlap of lowest unoccupied energy levels of all atoms or ions forming crystal lattice.

conductivity. 1. The property of a substance or mixture of transmitting heat uniformly throughout its mass, the energy being passed from one atom to another with little if any loss. Crystalline solids (especially metals and alloys) are good thermal conductors because of their high density ; liquids (water, glass) and high polymers (rubber, cellulose) usually are bad conductors.

2. The property of a substance of transmitting an electric current by the flow of electrons through a dense solid (metal) or by movement of the ions of a dissolved electrolyte to the electrodes when a potential difference exists between them. In the case of solids, no chemical change occurs when the current is passed, but in electrolytic solutions, decomposition of the electrolyte takes place. The term "conductance" is often used in preference to "conductivity" when referring to electrolytic solutions.

conductivity cell. A cell for determining the conductivity of a solution (or fused solid), consisting of a chamber containing two electrodes.

conductivity coefficient. The amount of energy, *i.e.*, heat or electricity, passing through a unit length of a medium in a unit time, under a unit difference of temperature or potential.

conductivity water. For the measurement of the conductance of solutions the water used for making the solutions must itself have negligible conductahce, *i.e.*, its specific conductance must not exceed $4\times10^{-6}ohm^{-1}cm^{-1}$. This so-called "condutivity water" was formerly obtained by a tedious distillation process from dilute potassium permanganate solution in a specially prepared glass apparatus. Now it is readily obtained by passing ordinary water through carefully prepared ion-exchange resins.

conductometric analysis. *See* conductometric titration.

conductometric titration. Method of quantitative analysis consisting in measurements of changes of conductivity of solution during titration of analysed substance with suitable reagent, for example, the end-point of an acid/alkali titration can be accurately determined by measuring the conductance of the solution continuously during the titration process. Hydronium and hydroxyl ions carry a larger proportion of the current than any others. If acid is being run into alkali, the conductance is at first largely due to the hydroxyl ions and, as these are neutralised, the conductance becomes less. When the end-point is reached, excess hydronium ions at once cause the conductance to increase. The point of minimum conductance therefore indicates the end-point.

conductometry. Method of determination of material present in mixture based on measurement of its influence on electrolytic conductivity of mixture.

conductor of electricity. Material of low specific resistance (conventionally lower than $10^{-4}\Omega$ cm) ; often used as general term for metallic conductors characterized by negative temperature coefficient of conductance. According to band model of solid state, crystal is conductor with continuous zone of incompletely occupied quantum states, accessible to electrons.

Cone-Cady reagent. Two solutions : a 1% aqueous solution of potassium ferricyanide, and a 1% glacial acetic acid solution of diphenylamine ; used in testing for zinc. A brown, green, or purple precipitate indicates the presence of zinc.

configuration. Steric arrangement of atoms (or groups of atoms) within the chiral or rigid (double bond or ring) part of molecule ; disregarding changes caused by rotation about simple bonds. Configuration of molecule possessing a few chiral centres is fully determined when configuration of each centre is known.

configurational base unit (of polymer or oligomer). Constitutional base unit of which configuration is defined as least at one site of steric isomerism in main chain. In regular polymer, configurational base units must correspond to constitutional repeating unit.

configurational block. Block containing only one species of configurational base unit.

configurational formula. A graphic device used to emphasize or portray the fact that a given molecule has a steric configuration. that is, it exists in three dimensions. This is especially true of high-polymer substances, and configurational formulas are essential to a proper understanding of their structures. Though, all molecules have three dimensions, configurational formula are seldom used for the simpler structures. Representation of the molecular structure of cellulose, sugars, proteins, and high polymers often include heavy lines or shaded areas to represent their three-dimensional shape.

configuration, atomic. The arrangement in space of the atoms of a molecule.

configuration, axially symmetric. The spatial arrangement of the atoms in the trans or fumaroid form of a stereoisomer. Also known as centrally symmetric configuration.

configurational thermodynamic functions. Those parts of thermodynamic quantities which can be expressed in terms of configurational integral ; other parts do not depend on intermolecular interactions. Also known as configurational properties.

configuration interaction. Interaction between ground and excited states of atom, ion or molecule assumed for interpretation of hyperfine structure of spectra of electron spin resonance. Also known as configurational interaction.

conformation. A term used by organic chemists to refer to any possible three-dimensional or steric pattern of substituent atoms in a molecule as they rotate around single-carbon bonds. Since the substituent atoms or groups (for example, hydrogen) tend to restrict rotation by repelling each other, the preferred conformation of a given organic molecule is one in which these atoms are most widely separated. From an infinite number of possible conformations, the most stable is the one in which all interactions between mutually non-bound substituents are the weakest.

conformational analysis. Analysis of physical and chemical properties with respect to conformation of a molecule in ground, transition or excited states.

conformational isomers. *See* conformers.

conformers. The different spatial orientations that may be assumed by the atoms of a molecule, as a result of rotation about single bonds. The conformations of ethane are shown below :

H H H H H
H C—C H ≡ H H ≡ H H
H H H H H H H H

H H H H H
C—C ≡ H H ≡ H
H H H H H H H H
H H

Conformations of molecules in equilibrium are impossible to be isolated (rotational barrier is approximately 2—10 kcal/mole). Also known as conformational isomers.

congo red solution. An aqueous solution of sodium tetrazodiphenylnaphthionate, used as an indicator of hydrogen-ion concentration. The colour changes from blue to red in the *p*H range of 3.5 to 5.0.

congurent melting point. Point on phase diagram in which solid phase melts and changes into liquid phase of the same composition.

conjugate acid-base pair. An acid and a base which are so related that the acid molecule is formed by the addition to the base of a hydrogen ion (proton) and the base molecule is formed by dissociation of a hydrogen ion (proton) from the acid. Thus, in the equilibrium

$$A \rightleftharpoons H^+ + B^-,$$

A and B^- are conjugate acid and base respectively.

conjugated double bonds. Where four or more atoms in a molecule are linked by alternate single and double bonds the arrangement is known as a conjugated system, and the double bonds in the system as "conjugated double bonds". Examples are furnished by 1,3-butadiene, ($H_2C{=}CH{-}CH{=}CH_2$), and 1,3,5-hexatriene, ($H_2C{=}CH{-}CH{=}CH{-}CH{=}CH_2$).

conjugate particles. A particle and its antiparticle.

conjugated proteins. The proteins which are characterized by nonprotein components or prosthetic groups. Conjugated proteins include the following :

Nucleoproteins ; the prosthetic group of these onjugated proteins is a nuclic acid.

Lipoproteins ; the lipid prosthetic group in these proteins is variable, but usually contains glyceride, phosphatide, and cholesterol.

Mucoproteins ; those substances having a carbohydrate prosthetic group, which almost always contain some hexosamine.

Chromoproteins ; the prosthetic groups of this class are not easily classified except for their colour, *e.g.*, haemoglobin.

conjugate solutions. A system in equilibrium consisting of two liquid phases and two components ; if the components of such a two component system are designated as A and B, then one phase is a solution of component A in component B, and the other phase is a solution of component B in component A. Such liquids are generally considered as partially miscible.

conjugation. A relationship of neighbouring π-electrons functions in which the *p* orbitals on all the atoms of such systems overlap when oriented parallel to each other. The LCAO treatment of *n* overlapping *p* orbitals generates $n\pi$-molecular orbitals, half of which are bonding and half antibonding. This phenomenon is of much importance in the formation of certain so-called conjugated molecules, as are found among the complex proteins ; or formation of conjugate double bonds or compounds containing them.

conjugative effect. A type of electron displacement where an electron pair migrates from a bond linking two atoms to an adjoining position. Thus C=C—C might in this way become C—C=C. This effect is commonly signified thus : C=C—C (with curved arrows), and it has been used to explain, for example, the mechanism of the conversion of trimethylethylene into tertiary amyl alcohol, when the amylene is treated with 46% sulphuric acid and then hydrolysed.

Conrad-Limpach synthesis of quinolines. A method of formation of 4-hydroxyquinolines, by condensing β-keto-esters and aromatic amines followed by ring closure of the intermediate compounds, *e.g.*,

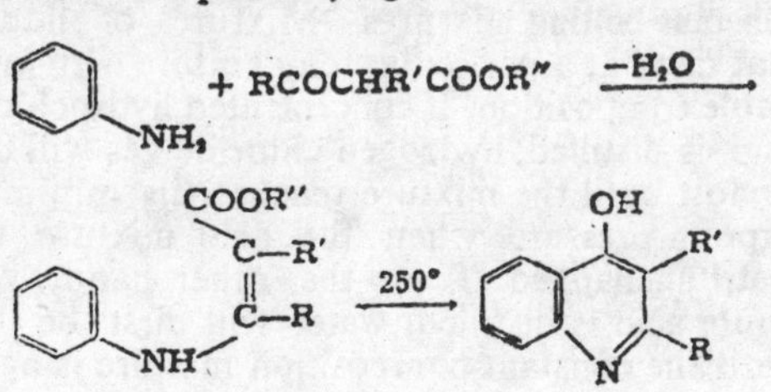

$$C_6H_5NH_2 + RCOCHR'COOR'' \xrightarrow{-H_2O}$$

$$C_6H_5NH{-}C(R){=}C(R'){-}COOR'' \xrightarrow{250^\circ} \text{4-hydroxy-2-R-3-R'-quinoline (OH, R', R)}$$

consecutive instability constant. Reciprocal of consecutive stability constant. Also known as stepwise dissociation constant.

consecutive reactions. A continuous chain of reactions in which one or more of the products of one reaction become one or more reactants for the next.

$$A \rightarrow B \rightarrow C \text{ etc.}$$

Examples may be found in the reaction between bromine and acetone in aqueous solution, and in the hydrolysis of an ester of a dibasic acid by an alkali. In such reactions some of the stages may be instantaneous and the overall rate of reaction will be determined by the rate of the slowest stage.

consecutive stability constant, *Kn*. Equilibrium constant of consecutive formation reaction of complex $ML_{n-1} + L \rightleftharpoons ML_n$; under conditions guaranteeing constancy of activation coefficients;

$$K_n = \frac{[ML_n]}{[ML_{n-1}]\,[L]}$$

where $[ML_n]$ and $[ML_{n-1}]$=equilibrium concentrations of complexes, and L=equilibrium concentration of ligand. Also known as stepwise formation constant.

Consolute. Completely miscible. This term is generally applied to liquids when they are miscible in all proportions, *i.e.*, mutally completely soluble, under certain given condition. It is not usually applied to gases which are all miscible.

consolute temperature. *See* critical solution temperature.

constant. A magnitude which suffers no change during a specific operation.

constant, Avogadro. *See* Avogadro constant.

constant boiling mixtures. Mixtures of liquids that distil at a particular temperature with invariable composition. If concentrated hydrochloric acid is distilled, hydrogen chloride gas will first be lost until the mixture reaches its minimum vapour pressure when the acid mixture will distil unchanged. If on the other hand, very dilute acid is distilled, water will first be lost until the constant composition mixture is again reached. Some important cases of azeotropic mixtures are :

Mixture	*B. Pt.*	*Composition*
Hydrochloric acid/water	110°C	20.22% acid by weight
Nitric acid/water	121°C	68.2% acid by weight
Sulphuric acid/water	338°C	98.3% acid by weight
Ethanol/water	78.13°C	95.59% alcohol

Also called "azeotropic mixtures".

constant-current coulometry. Electroanalytical method of determination of substance from the charge which flows in time taken to reduce or oxidize the substance completely at constant current.

constant, dissociation. *See* ionization constant.

constant, equilibrium. *See* equilibrium constant.

constant freezing mixtures. A name sometimes used for eutectic mixtures of constant freezing-point. For example at —11°C, solid potassium chloride, ice, solution, and water vapour can exist as separate phases in equilibrium, and adding more ice or solid potassium chloride will not alter the composition of any other phase.

constant, gas. *See* gas constant.

constant, Planck. *See* Planck's constant.

constant, Rydberg. *See* Rydberg constant.

constant, Stefan-Boltzmann. *See* Stefan-Boltzmann constant.

constituent. One of the elements or groups present in a chemical compound, or one of the molecules in a macromolecule or high-polymer substance. For example, oxygen is a constituent of water; amino acids are constituents of proteins. *See also* component; compound.

constitutional base unit. Smallest possible regularly repeated constitutional unit of regular polymer.

constitutional block. Block containing only one species of constitutional base unit.

constitution formula. A formula that shows the molecular structure (or constitution) of a substance in two dimensions, *e.g.*,

```
        H
        C
      /   \\
    HC     CH
    |      ||
    HC     CH
      \\   /
        C
        H
```

is a constitutional formula for benzene, and CH_3-COOH is the constitutional formula for acetic ecid. It is to be noted that the constitutional formula shows the atomic linkages when they are most significant to the chemist, and does not show, as in the case of the structural formula, the valence linkages of every atom.

constitutional isomers. Isomers differing in the manner in which atoms are connected or bonded together are called constitutional isomers. They will always have different IUPAC names, whereas stereoisomers must be identified by an additional nomenclature term, such as *cis-* or *trans-* prefixes. It may be noted that interconversions of conformational isomers is often rapid at room temperature, while stereoisomers are configurationally stable under normal conditions.

constitutive enzyme. Enzymes of central metabolic pathways ; always present in normal cells.

constitutive property. Any property of a system or of a substance that depends mainly on the way in which atoms are arranged and not, to any extent, on their number or nature, *e.g.*, optical activity. The term may also be used to mean a property that depends on the quality of matter present, such as atomic weight, or melting-point.

contact angle. θ. In system of coexisting liquid-solid-gas phases, angle between the flat surface of solid body and tangent to liquid surface at common point of three interfaces ; in equilibrium state :

$$\cos\theta = \frac{\sigma_{sg} - \sigma_{sl}}{\sigma_{lg}}$$

where σ_{sg} = solid-gas surface tension, σ_{sl} = solid-liquid surface tension, and σ_{lg} = liquid-gas surface tension. Also known as wetting angle.

contact catalysis. Process of change in structure of gas molecules absorbed on to solid surface ; the basis of many industrial processes.

contact filtration. A process in which finely divided adsorbent clay is mixed with oil to remove coloured substances and to improve oil's stability.

contact potential. A difference of electrical potential existing between two substances in direct contact. All metals, electrolytic solutions, and other substances containing "free" ions or electrons, exhibit slight difference of potential on direct contact.

contact process. The most important method for the production of pure sulphuric acid. Sulphur dioxide (obtained by burning sulphur or roasting metallic sulphides) is mixed with air and passed over a catalyst heated to about 450°C. Vanadium pentoxide has now largely replaced platinised preparations as the catalyst because it is not easily poisoned by the impurities such as arsenic. Sulphur trioxide is obtained:

$$2SO_2 + O_2 \text{ (from air)} \rightarrow 2SO_3$$

As at the working temperature all three substances are in the gaseous phase, it follows from Le Chatelier's principle that increased pressure should increase the yield of trioxide. In practice, however, the yield is over 90% of the maximum—so increased pressure is seldom used. The sulphur trioxide fumes are absorbed in 93% sulphuric acid. The concentration is thus increased to 100% and, if no further water be added, oleum ($H_2S_2O_7$) is obtained :

$$H_2SO_4 + SO_3 \rightarrow H_2S_2O_7$$

contaminant. Any foreign and often deleterious matter present in an otherwise relatively pure substance or mixture. Though generally similar in meaning to "pollutant," it applies to any extreneous agent that has found its way into a normal material or organism. For example, surfur dioxide is an air contaminant (or pollutant) ; insecticidal residues are water and food contaminants, though they are often called "unintentional additives."

contamination (radioactive). Pollution of environment of any objects, plants, animals, or human environment by substances controlled and removed by methods of radiological protection.

continuity of state. Transition between the gaseous and liquid states, in either direction, without discontinuity, or abrupt change in physical properties. Although this transition is not realizable in practice by mere pressure-volume change, it can be accomplished by some processes, as by a sequence of temperature changes in one direction at constant volume, followed by temperature changes in the other direction at constant pressure, or vice versa.

continuous phase. *See* dispersion medium.

continuous solid solution. Solid solution of unlimited miscibility of constituents.

continuous spectrum. A spectrum without dark lines or bands caused by the absence of radiations of certain frequencies. A well-known example is the spectrum of white light that contains all the colours from red to violet and shows no discontinuities at any point. The spectra from incandescent bodies, molten metals, and incandescent lamps are often continuous.

continuous system. Macroscopic system with properties such as temperature, pressure, concentration of constituents, etc.. changing continuously in space.

control chart. Graphical method of time variation control of parameter ; usually represented by diagram with central line and two parallel lines which determine tolerance limits. Numbers of subsequent measurements are given on abscissa and values of parameter or deveriations from its nominal value are presented on ordinate axis. Control chart is used for production, quality control, investigation of conditions of process, and for accuracy and precision control in analytical methods.

controlled potential electrolysis. Electrolysis carried out in conditions with potential of working electrode having constant value or changing only within small limits as a result of changes of total potential applied to electrodes.

control line pair. In emission spectral analysis, pair of lines of approximately equal intensity. Ratio of their intensities depends crucially on excitation conditions ; it is used to control stability of excitation source. Also known as fixation pair.

conventional analysis. Determination of component or properties of investigated sample under conventional but strictly defined conditions. As a result one obtains not absolute value but one dependent on method of analysis.

converse piezoelectric effect. Mechanical deformation of crystal due to polarizing influence of external electric field.

conversion. 1. A change in numerical value of a quantity resulting from the use of a different unit in the same or a different system of measurement.

2. An intramolecular rearrangement of organic substances in which the relative positions of the radicals are modified. The Beckmann rearrangement is a case of this type. Radicals may be transferred from carbon, oxygen, or nitrogen to carbon ; from carbon or oxygen to nitrogen ; from side chains to nucleus, etc. The specific examples are discussed under the names of individual investigators.

conversion electrons. Electrons emitted by atoms in internal conversion. As opposed to beta rays, they possess a linear energy spectrum.

conversion factor. A number used to multiply a quantity in order to obtain its equivalent value in other units, which may be either in the same system of weights and measures, or in another system.

conversion of chair forms. *See* interconversion of chair forms.

Cook formula. A relationship for calculating the acetyl number of an organic substance from the saponification titers before and after acetylation. It is equal to their difference, divided by a correction factor that approaches unity as the initial saponification value decreases.

cooking. 1. Changing a foodstuff from the raw state to a softer and more palatable condition by heat treatment of various types from 90° to 260°C. A number of chemical and physical changes occur, for example, hydrolysis of the collagen in the connective tissue of meats, causing tenderness ; softening and partial hydrolysis of cellulose and starches to sugars ; denaturation and cleavage of proteins in meat, resulting in a less tightly ordered structure ; coagulation of egg albumin and wheat gluten (cooked eggs and bakery products) ; modification or "shortening" of wheat flour by added fats, which coat the particles to form a laminate ; evolution of carbon dioxide by the carbonates in baking powder, which causes bread and cake to "rise" ; browning of bakery products due for reaction between sugars and amino acids (nonenzymatic) ; deactivation of enzymes. One adverse effect of cooking is the large loss or deactivation of water-soluble vitamins.

2. A term used in the paper industry to refer to digestion of wood pulp with such chemicals as sodium bisulphite, sodium hydroxide, and sodium sulphide, to separate the cellulosic content from the lignin.

cooling time (of reactor). Time allowed to elapse between removal of radioactive product from reactor and its chemical treatment, to reduce its activity by decay.

Cooper reagent. A solution of 100 g. 2,4-dihydroxyacetophenone in 1 litre alcohol, which gives a red colour with ferric ion.

cooperative phenomenon. Any process for whose occurrence the simultaneous interaction between several molecules or systems is required.

coordinate induction. Induction of a set of related enzymes by a single inducer.

coordinate linkage. A bond between two atoms where the two electrons necessary for the bonding are both furnished by one of the atoms, and not one from each as in an ordinary covalent bond. Molecules that have a "lone pair" of electrons, *e.g.* those of ammonia readily from coordinate linkages. Also known as dative bond ; dative covalency ; semipolar bond ; co-ionic bond.

coordinate valence. *See* coordinate linkage.

coordinate of thermodynamic system. *See* state variable.

coordinating atom. Atom of ligand linked directly with central atom or ion. Also known as ligating atom ; donor atom.

coordinating group. Part of chelating agent containing donor atom, *e.g.*, amine group $-NH_2$, $-NHR$ or NR_2, azo group $-N{=}-$, carbonyl group $=CO$, ether group $-O-$.

coordination. Process leading to formation of complex. Also known as complex formation reaction.

coordination chemistry. Chemistry of complex compounds, *i.e.*, the chemistry of metal ions in interaction with coordinating species.

coordination compound. Compound containing complex ion or compound which is neutral complex. Coordination compounds are usually derived by addition from simpler inorganic substances. Coordination compounds are essentially compounds to which atoms or groups have been added beyond the number possible on the basis of electrovalent linkages or the usual covalent linkages, to which each of the two atoms linked donates one electron to form the dublet. The coordinated groups are linked to the atoms of the compound usually by semipolar convalences, in which both the electrons in the bond are furnished by the linked atom of the coordinated group. The ammines and complex cyanides are representative coordination compounds.

coordination isomerism. Type of isomerism of complex compounds containing complex cation and complex anion, depending on different distribution of particular ligands in these complex ions, *e.g.*, $[Co(NH_3)_6][Cr(CN)_6]$ and $[Cr(NH_3)_6][Co(CN)_6]$.

coordination number. 1. The maximum number of coordinate linkages that an atom can form after its normal valency bonds have been formed.

2. Number of closet neighbours of atoms or ions in crystal lattice, characteristic for particular type of lattice.

coordination position isomerism. Isomerism generally occurring in polynuclear complexes consisting of different distribution of ligands around central atoms :

$$\left[(H_3N)_3ClCo \overset{\overset{H}{O}}{\underset{\underset{H}{O}}{\rightleftarrows}} Co(NH_3)_3Cl \right] SO_4$$

and

$$\left[(H_3N)_2Cl_2Co \overset{\overset{H}{O}}{\underset{\underset{H}{O}}{\rightleftarrows}} Co(NH_3)_4 \right] SO_4$$

coordination sphere. The space around central atom occupied by coordinates ligands.

coordinatively saturated complex. Complex in which number of coordinate bonds is equal to maximum coordination number of central atom, *e.g.*, $[Fe(CN)_6]^{3-}$

Cope rearrangement. Intramolecular thermal rearrangement of 1,5-dienes involving migration of subtituents from allylic to vinylic position, *e.g.*,

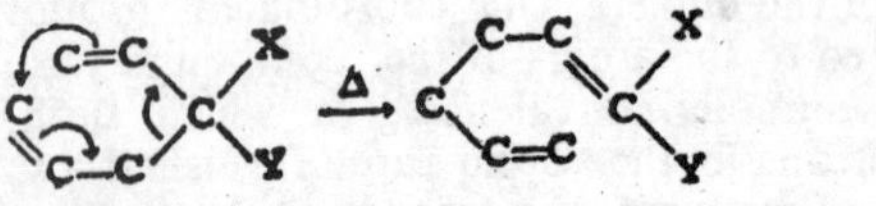

$$C=C-C(X)(Y)-C=C \xrightarrow{\Delta} C-C=C(X)(Y) \ldots C=C$$

X I Y = —COOR, —COOH, —CN, —C_6H_5.

coplanarity. Arrangement of two or more planar groups such as : —OH, $>C=O$, —NO_2, —$CH=CH_2$, aromatic rings, etc. in one plane common from them.

copolymer. A high-polymer substance, usually an elastomer, made up of two or more different kinds of monomer, for example, styrene and butadine. Copolymers are made by simultaneous polymerization of the monomers in the same operation, usually in emulsion form ; as a result, the constituent monomers are combined into a common macromolecule, in contrast to the blending of two separately polymerized monomers (called homopolymers). When the latter method is used, the product is called a polyblend, which is a mixture of homopolymers, the components of polyblends are likely to be incompatible.

co-polymerization. An addition polymerization which involves two or more distinct molecular species, each of which is capable of polymerizing alone. The molecule formed contains each molecular constituent, or an essential unit therefrom, as a distinct entity in its structure.

copper. An element. Symbol Cu

	Atomic No.	29
Group IB	Atomic Wt.	63.546
	Valence	1,2
	m.p.	1083°C
	b.p.	2582°C

A reddish metal, occuring in the form of sulphide and oxide ores. It is one of the transition elements and an important nonferrous metal. Its usefulness is accounted for by its combination of physical, chemical, mechanical and electrical properties and its fairly abundant supply. It is distinctive in its high electrical conductivity and in its resistance to corossion ; these properties contribute to its main use in communication wiring and in many other electrical application. It is also widely used as an alloying metal (brass and bronze). Copper forms a large number of complexes and is a trace element required for the proper nutrition of plants and animals. It is essentially non-toxic. Its compounds are used as oxidation catalysts for many organic materials ; and a number of them are used as fungicides and insecticides.

copper family. *See* copper group.

copper group. Elements in first sub group of periodic system with structure of outer electronic shells of atoms $(n-1)d^{10}ns^1$; copper, silver, gold. Also known as copper family.

copper intoxication. Copper and its salts are remarkably nontoxic to mammalian tissues. It is necessary to ingest a large quantity of a soluble copper salt such as copper sulphate to produce intoxication. Ingestion of smaller amounts of copper salts dissolved from the walls of vessels produces symptoms and does not present a threat to life. The symptoms that occur are mild (nausea and vomiting). Inhalation of fumes of copper compounds can cause congestion and irritation of the upper airway.

copper number. An expression of the quantity of a reducing carbohydrate, in terms of the number of milligrams of metallic copper required for reduction of that quantity of Fehling's solution, which is reduced by on gram of the sample.

co-precipitation. Precipitation of required substance together with precipetate of other substances present in solution, *e.g.*, impurities or very small amount of radioactive substance with precipate of carrier.

core. 1. The central part of a structure.

2. The active portion of a nuclear reactor, containing the fissionable material.

corona. 1. A crownlike part or structure.

2. A luminous circle around one of the heavenly bodies, specically the irregular, radial streams of light seen around the sun during a total eclipse.

3. The pattern of light and other radiation produced at electrodes during an electrical discharge at high voltage. It causes ionization of oxygen and the formation of ozone. It is particularly evident in the air close to high-tension wires and spark-ignited automotive engines. The ozone formed has a drastic oxidizing effect on wire insulation, cable covers, and hose connections.

corpuscular radiation. Radiation composed of particles of rest mass greater than zero, *e.g.*, α-, β-, neutron, proton, fission fragment radiation etc.

corrected selectivity coefficient, $k_{A,B}$. Selectivity coefficient of ion exchange reaction calculated by taking into account activity coefficients of ions in solution.

correction factor. A quantity used to multiply an experimental result in order to correct for a source of error of known magnitude.

correlation of configurations. Specification of mutual correlation between configuration of an examined compound and that of a reference compound having relative configuration, or a compound having established absolute configuration.

correlation of electrons. *See* electron correlation.

correspondence principle. Since classical mechanics and Maxwell's electromagnetic theory accurately describe macroscopic phenomena, quantum mechanics must have a classical limit in which it is equivalent to the older classical theories. Although there is no rigorous proof of this principle for arbitrarily complicated quantum-mechanical systems, its validity is well established in numerous illustrations.

corresponding states. If any two or more substances are at the same reduced pressure or the same fraction or multiple of their respective critical pressures, and are at equal reduced temperatures or the same fraction or multiple of their respective critical temperatures, their reduced volumes should be equal. These substances are said to be in corresponding states, and the above statement is the law of corresponding states.

corrigent. A corrective drug, *i.e.*, a drug that modifies the action of another drug in a desired manner.

corrosion. An electrochemical reaction occurring on a metal surface caused by reaction of the metal with one or more substances with which it is in contact for long periods ; the effect is usually deleterious. As air is usually the environment to which metals are exposed, oxidation is one of the commonest forms of corrosion, as in the rusting of iron. This reaction is catalyzed by moisture and leads to formation ferric oxide. Oxidation may be beneficial to metals, *e.g.*, aluminium drives its immunity to corrosion from the tenacius film of aluminium oxide, formed on its surface, which inhibits degradation.

Another form of resistance is called which is passivity due to formation of very thin oxide films on chromium and nickel. This is not true of copper, which resists corrosion because of its lower position in the electromotive series. Corrosion is accelerated by impurities present in the environment such as ionizing acids and alkalies, which act as electrolytes, *e.g.*, sulphur compounds, salt, etc.

Corrosion is basically an electrochemical reaction in which the metal is ionized and assumes positive charges and is accompanied by evolution of hydrogen at the cathode and generation of a detectable amount of electric current ; thus, it requires the presence of an anode, a cathode, and an eletrolyte.

cosmic chemistry. *See* cosmochemistry.

cosmochemistry. Branch of chemistry dealing with studies on composition, abundance, formation and exchange of substances present in celestial bodies, cosmic dust and interstellar matter. Also known as cosmic chemistry; astrochemistry; space chemistry.

cosmotron. A particle accelerator capable of accelerating particles to energies of billions of electron volts. *See also* bevatron.

Cotton effect. The characteristic wavelength dependence of the optical rotatory dispersion curve or the circular dichroism curve or both in the vicinity of an absorption band.

When an initially plane-polarized light wave traverses an optically active medium, two principal effects are manifested : a change from planar to elliptic polarization. and a rotation of the major axis of the ellipse through an angle relative to the initial direction of polarization. Both effects are wavelength dependent. The first effect is known as circular dichroism, and a plot of its wavelength (or frequency) dependence is referred to as a circular dichroism (CD) curve. The second effect is called optical rotation and, when plotted as a function of wavelength, is known as an optical rotatory dispersion (ORD) curve In the vicinity of absorption bands, both curves take on characteristic shapes, and this behaviour is known as the

Cotton effect, which may be either positive or negative (*see* illustration). There is a Cotton effect associated with each absorption process, and hence a partial CD curve or partial ORD curve is associated with each particular absorption band or process.

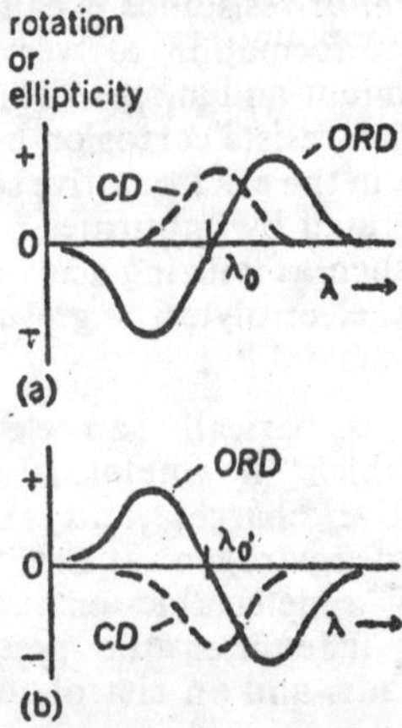

Fig. 18. Behaviour of the ORD and CD curves in the vicinity of an absorption band at wavelength λ_0 (idealized). (a) Positive Cotton effect (b) Negative Cotton effect.

The rotational strengths actually observed vary over quite a few orders of magnitude ; this variation in magnitude is useful in stereochemical interpretation of molecular structure.

Cotton-Mouton effect. A magneto-optic effect concerned with the double refraction of light in a liquid when the liquid is placed in a transverse magnetic field. It is analogous to the electro-optical Kerr effect, and is observed in liquids with complicated molecular structure. If the molecule has a magnetic moment, the field tries to orient the molecule, but the thermal motion tends to oppose this action. There is thus a degree of orientation which is dependent on the temperature. If the molecule itself is optically anisotropic, the liquid also will be anisotropic and will exhibit double refraction.

The Cotton-Mouton effect is observed chiefly in nitrobenzene and many other aromatic organic liquids. Aliphatic compounds have a considerably smaller effect.

Coulomb potential barrier. Potential barrier of coulomb (electrostatic) repulsive forces. In nuclear physics, barrier surrounding atomic nucleus and preventing penetration of positively charged particles, *e.g.*, protons or alpha particles, into nucleus or escaping from nucleus.

coulometric analysis. A number of methods based on Faraday's laws of electrolysis used mainly in measurements of quantity of electricity and analytical determinations.

A condition of 100% current efficiency must exist for a coulometric analysis ; that is all the current must be used either directly or indirectly to deplete the desired substance.

coulometric titration. Determination of substance by its reaction with reagent generated electrolytically with constant current. Final result is calculated from product of current intensity and time of generation of reagent.

coulometry at controlled potential. Electroanalytical method of determination of substance from charge which flows in time taken to reduce or oxidize this substance completely at constant potential of electrode.

coulostatic analysis. Method of investigation of kinetics of electrode reactions from changes of potential of indicator electrode after injection of known electric charge to electrolytic system.

counter (electron and nuclear). An instrument used to detect and measure emanations, especially those of a radioactive nature. These electron and nuclear counters, also called Geiger-Mueller counters, are used not only in the enumeration of charged particles and radiations —x-rays, gamma rays, and cosmic rays, but also in the counting of neutrons, even the extent of distinguishing between fast and slow neutrons. A common form of this apparatus consists of an ionization chamber in which the charge on the wall is of an opposite sign to the charge upon the central wall.

2π-counter. Windowless radiation counter with semigeometrical counting efficiency.

4π-counter. Radiation counter with active volume completely surrounding source of radioactivity, and geometrical counting efficiency unity.

counter characteristic curve. The curve of the counting rate against voltage, all pulses counted being greater than a certain minimum size, determined by the sensitivity of the receiving circuit.

countercurrent flow. A term frequently used in chemical engineering denoting the movement relative to one another of two or more streams of materials (gas, liquid, or solid) to effect chemical, physical, or thermal changes between the respective streams. This type of flow is most frequently applied to multi-stage unit operations such as drying, evaporation distillation, leaching, washing of solids, solvent extraction. etc., to achieve maximum efficienty and economy. Heat exchangers utilize countercurrent flow to obtain maximum heat transfer between a material being cooled and a material being heated. In the laboratory, a good example is the common water-cooled condenser, wherein the coldest water entering at the bottom is across the condenser wall from the cooled condensate exit, while the warmer water leaving at the top is near the hot distillate vapour inlet.

counter dead time. The time interval, after recording a count, that the counter is completely insensitive and does not detect other ionizing events occurring inside it.

counter efficiency. The efficiency of a counter is defined as the probability that a count will take place when the entity to be detected enters the counter.

counter electrode. Electrode placed in front of the electrode containing sample.

counter gas amplification. The number of additional ions produced by each electron produced in the primary ionizing event as it travels to the central wire.

counter-ions. Mobile (*i.e.*, able to diffuse freely) ions of opposite charge to that of ion exchanger skeleton.

coupled reactions. System of two parallel reactions in which path of secondary reaction (induced reaction) is determined by result of primary reaction ;

$A+B \rightarrow X$ primary reaction

$A+C \rightarrow Y$ induced (secondary) reaction

where A = actor in coupled reactions, B = inductor in coupled (primary) reaction, C = acceptor in coupled (secondary) reaction. Also known as induced reactions.

coupling. 1. A chemical reaction which takes place in the union of amino acids to form proteins ; the reaction is essentially a condensation polymerization, which can be achieved synthetically only by suppressing the active sites on the amino-acid molecules ; when this is done, a peptide linkage can be formed, *i.e.*, coupling can occur.

2. Reaction of diazonium salt with phenol or aromatic amine, resulting in formation of coloured azo compound, *e.g.*,

$$(C_6H_5{-}N{\equiv}N)^{\oplus}X^{\ominus} + C_6H_5{-}N(CH_3)_2 \longrightarrow$$
$$C_6H_5{-}N{=}N{-}C_6H_4{-}N(CH_3)_2 + HX$$

3. Polymerization of certain phenols (especially those containing two substituted methyl groups) by means of oxygen and a nitrogenous catalyst to form a thermoplastic polymer ; the process is called oxidative coupling.

coupling constant. Value characterizing force of interaction between elementary particles ; occurs as coefficient in interaction hamiltonian.

covalence. Number of covalent bonds formed by the atom of a given element.

covalent bond. Chemical bond formed by sharing valence electrons in pairs, each electron originating from a different atom, *e.g.*, in molecules of H_2, H_2O, CH_4, PCl_5, SF_6 and H_2O_2.

covalent compound. A compound formed by the sharing of electrons, between atoms ; as distinguished from electrovalent compounds, in which there occurs a transfer of electrons.

covalent radius. One half of bond length in homonuclear diatomic molecule. Sum of covalent radii of two different atoms determines to good approximation covalent bond length in corresponding molecule.

cracking. A process used to reduce molecular weights of hydrocarbons by breaking molecular bonds by thermal, catalytic, or hydrocracking methods. This process involves decomposition and molecular recombination of organic compounds, especially hydrocarbons obtained by distillation of petroleum, by means of heat, to form simpler molecules suitable for fuels, monomers, and other industrial purposes. A series of condensation reactions take place accompanied by transfer of hydrogen atoms between molecules which brings about fundamental changes in their structure. Cracking is carried out by thermal, catalytic, or hydrocracking methods. Increasing demand for gasoline and other middle distillates relative to demand for heavier fractions makes cracking processes important in balancing the supply of petroleum products. Among the chemical changes induced are conversion of alicyclic compounds (cyclohexane) to aromatic compounds (benzenoid) and of straight-chain to branched-chain structures. Cracking reactions are exothermic. Free radicals, carbonium ions, and other chain-initiating agents are involved in these rearrangement. The fluidized bed technique is often used now-a-days. Modified aluminosilicate compounds (zeolites or molecular sieves) are largely replacing many cracking catalysts formerly used. Hydrocracking is based on catalytic formation of hydrogen radicals to break carbon-carbon bonds and saturate olefinic bonds.

Cram's rule. Rule describing steric addition in asymmetric synthesis of organometallic compound to acyclic carbonyl compounds with chirality centre in α-position. If substituents are denoted by : L>M>S (depending on their steric bulks), nucleophilic attack on carbonyl group in compound with energetically privileged conformation (*see* example below) will take place from the most uncovered side, *e.g.*,

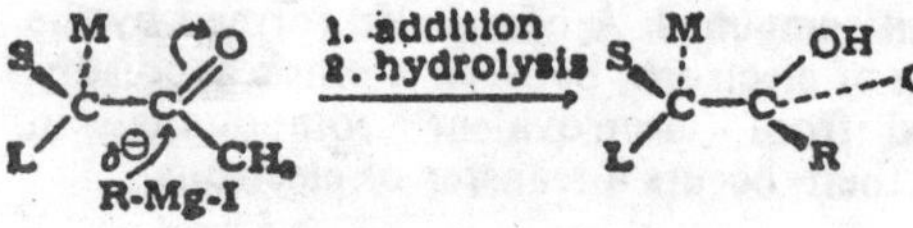

S, M, L–C–C(=O)–CH_3 + R-Mg-I —(1. addition, 2. hydrolysis)→ S, M, L–C–C(OH)(R)–CH_3

Criegee reaction. The splitting of a glycol compound between the carbon atoms attached to the hydroxyl groups of the glycol using lead tetraacetate, *e.g.*,

$$\begin{matrix} R'R''C\text{—}OH \\ | \\ R'''R''''C\text{—}OH \end{matrix} + Pb(OOCCH_3)_4 \rightarrow$$

$$\begin{matrix} R' \\ | \\ C{=}O \\ | \\ R'' \end{matrix} + \begin{matrix} R''' \\ | \\ C{=}O \\ | \\ R'''' \end{matrix} + Pb(OOCCH_3)_2 + 2CH_3COOH$$

Criswell reagent. A solution of 35g. cupric sulphate in 100ml. of water and 200g. of glycerol, to which 450 ml. 20% sodium hydroxide solution is then added, followed by boiling for 15 minutes, and dilution to 1 litre. This reagent is used in testing for glucose, which causes reduction of the solution and appearance of red precipitate of cuprous oxide.

critical. *See* criticality.

critical coefficient. *k*. An additive property of substances which is also a measure of the space actually occupied by the molecules and is proportional to the critical volume. It is expressed as the ratio between the critical temperature T_c and the critical pressure P_c, or

$$k = \frac{T_c}{P_c}$$

(Some writers define the critical coefficient as the product ; $RT\ T_c/P_c$.

critical composition. Systems, consisting of two liquid layers that are formed by the equilibrium between two partially-miscible liquids, frequently have a consolute temperature or a critical solution temperature, beyond which the two liquids are miscible in all proportions. At this temperature, the phase boundary disappears, and the two liquid layers merge into one: The composition of the mixture at that point is called the critical composition.

critical constants. *See* critical properties

critical indices. χ. Numbers characterizing speed of approaching zero by a given thermodynamic quantity X when reaching critical state

$$\chi^{\pm} = \lim_{T \to T_c^{\pm}} \frac{\ln \chi(V, T)}{\ln[\pm(T - T_c)]}$$

where V=system's volume, T=thermodynamic temperature, T_c=critical temperature ; way of approaching critical state is separately defined for each quantity ; most frequently $V{=}V_c$.

critical isotherm. *p-V* isotherm of real gas at critical temperature. Inflection point of critical isotherm has coordinates p_c, V_c.

criticality. A term used in nuclear chemistry to denote the condition of a reactor wnen the flow of fission-generated neutrons is just sufficient to produce electric power. Below this stage the reactor is said to be subcritical.

critical mass. The minimum amount of fissionable material required to achieve an uncontrolled chain reaction, as in an atomic bomb. It is increased by the presence of neutron absorptive materials and is reduced by a moderator, such as graphite or heavy water.

critical point. The point at which a significant and notable change occurs in the properties of a substance or in a state of matter; for example the glass transition temperature. The point may be that of temperature, pressure, concentration electrical charging, rate of nuclear fission etc.

critical point, ternary. The point where, upon adding a mutual solvent to two partially miscible liquids (as adding alcohol to ether and water), the two solutions become consolute and results in the formation of one phase.

critical potential. The potential required to raise one of the electrons surrounding an atomic nucleus from a lower to a higher energy level, the highest level being that in which the electron is totally removed, and the atom becomes an ion. Since the charge on the electron is constant, the magnitude on the critical potential is a direct measure of the energy expended in the change.

Two specific types of critical potential are : (*a*) the resonance potential, which is the amount of energy necessary to raise an electron from its lowest energy level to any other level ; and (*b*) the ionization potential, the amount of energy necessary to remove entirely an electron in the lowest energy level fron the atom (to "infinite distance").

critical pressure. 1. The pressure of a vapour at its critical point, the temperature above which the vapour can exist only in the form of a gas.

2. In fiuid dynamics, the term critical pressure is used to denote a value of the final pressure of a fluid flowing through an orifice or nozzle, above which the volume of flow depends on final pressure.

critical properties. Values of intensive quantities in critial state of system. Also known as critical constants.

critical solution temperature. In a system that consists of two partially miscible liquids, as the temperature rises the mutual solubility will increase until a temperature is reached (called the "consolute temperature") when the two are completely miscible and the two phases become one homogeneous phase At this temperature interface vanishes in system of two liquids of limited mutual solubility. System has one phase in whole range of concentations above upper or below lower critical solution temperature. Also known as consolute temperature.

critical temperature. The maximum temperature at which a gas or vapour can be liquefied (by application of the critical pressure). Above this temperature the substance exists only as a gas.

critical volume. The volume occupied by unit mass, commonly one mole, of a substance at its critical temperature and critical pressure.

cross bombardment. A method of determination of the atomic number of a radio-element, by producing it by a number of different nuclear reaction. As an illustration, in order to determine the atomic number of a 47-day, β-activity isotope of iron produced by deuteron bombardment, cobalt oxide was treated with neutrons of medium energy. It was observed that a 47-day, β-activity developed, and that the isotope having this activity could be extracted by chemical methods for iron. It was evident, therefore, that deuteron bombardment to a stable isotope of iron, and neutron bombardment of a stable isotope of cobalt, produced the same radio-isotope of iron.

crosslinking. Process of numerous intermolecular covalent bonds between polymer chains either by heating in the presence of a substance capable of forming a chemical bond between the two chains, or by exposing the polymer to ionizing radiation. Both can be illustrated by the vulcanization of rubber in which sulphur or an organic peroxide forms a bond with hydrocarbon chains, a schematic example of which would be :

```
C—C—C—C—C—C
   |       |
   S       S
   |       |
C—C—C—C—C—C
```

or, radiation effects the union by removing two or more hydrogen atoms, thus permitting direct carbon-to-carbon linkage. Free radical mechanisms play an important role in both methods. Conversion of a thermoplastic to a thermoset ting material, with accompanying increase in strength and durability, is an important outcome of cross-linking in rubber.

crossover point. In a multienzyme system, a point at which inhibition causes accumulation of the preceding intermediates and decreased concentration of the subsequent products.

crown conformation. Fairly stable conformation of cyclooctane and its derivatives.

Also known as crown form.

crown ethers. The macrocyclic polyethers which are large enough to encircle metal cations. Such compounds possess cavities which can encapsulate metal cations and have ability of forming stable and selective complexes with monoatomic or molecular ions, as such, are potential receptor, carrier, or catalyst molecules.

crown form. *See* crown conformation.

crown glass. A type of optical glass that has low index of refraction and low light dispersion; both these interrelated properties are critical factors not only in prescription lenses but in scientific instruments as well. Crown glass is of the soda-lime type.

Crum-Brown (and Gibson) rule. When a second substituent is introduced into the molecule of a monosubstituted benzene compound, if the group already present forms a compound with hydrogen that can be oxidised directly into the corresponding hydroxyl compound, the new substituent will enter the meta-position. Thus the $—NO_2$ group is metadirecting, as HNO_2 can be oxidised directly to HNO_3. The —OH group, on the other hand is ortho and para-directing, because H_2O cannot be oxidised directly to H_2O_2.

Crum's test for manganese. A managanous compound when boiled with 1 : 1 nitric acid and a little lead dioxide, gives a purple colour due to the formation of permanganate ions.

cryogenics. The study dealing with the properties of matter at extremely low temperatures. Such temperatures, which approach absolute zero, can be attained only by use of liquefied gases such as oxygen, ntirogen, helium, hydrogen.

cryohydrate. The crystalline substance of invariable composition that separates as the eutectic mixture from a salt and water system.

cryohydric point. The temperature at which a cryohydrate eutectic mixture separates from solution.

cryometry. *See* cryoscopy.

cryoscopic constant, *K*. Quantity given by equation

$$K = \frac{RT^2}{\Delta H} M$$

where R=molar gas constant, T=thermodynamic temperature of freezing of solvent at pressure $0.980\ 665.10^5$ Pa, ΔH=molar enthalpy (heat) of fusion of solvent at this temperature, and M=molar mass of solvent.

cryoscopy. Methods for measurement of freezing temperature of uni- or multi-component systems. Cryoscopic methods are used for determination of molar masses, determination of purity of substances, for investigation of liquid-solid phase equilibrium, etc. Also known as cryometry.

cryosol. Colloid stable only at relatively low temperatures, *e.g.*, ice in chloroform, is stable at about —20°C.

cryptoclastic. Composed of very fine, almost submicroscopic, broken or fragmental particles.

crystal. A homogeneous solid body or definite geometrical form bounded by plane surfaces, formed when certain liquid or gaseous substances pass into the solid state (or crystallize). Most compounds possess a definite crystal form in the solid condition and are said to be crystalline. Substances which crystallize in two three, or more forms are termed di-, tri-, or polymorphous. The shape of a crystal is an indication of its orderly internal structure called a lattice; the atoms comprising the lattice act as a diffraction grating which permits determination of the structure by means of *x*-rays. Solids are made up of crystals of various forms, or "habits," united in aggregates which can be split apart along their cleavage planes (adjacent crystal surfaces). The shapes of crystals always involve flat surfaces and straight lines and may be cubes, rhomboids, lozenges, needles, plates, etc. (but never spheres). The magnetic and optical properties of crystals make them useful in lasers, computers, and many other electronic devices.

crystal axes. System of three (sometimes four) axes intersecting at one point and connected with crystal in such a way that symmetry operations mutually transform axes. Edges to unit cell are parallel to axes, according to accepted convention. Also known as crystallographic axes.

crystal, biaxial. A doubly refracting crystal which has two optic axes. There are two direction parallel to which light travels with one definite velocity. Crystals of the rhombic, monoclinic, and triclinic systems are biaxial.

crystal classes. Thirty two classes among infinite number of symmetry classes, occurring in ideal crystals.

crystal defects. *See* lattice defects.

crystal elements. The angles, plus the axial ratios or intercept ratios, in terms of which the position of any crystal face may be described.

crystal field. Electric field at a given point inside crystal produced by surrounding ions or dipoles.

crystal field splitting energy, $\triangle$(10 Dq). Difference in energies of orbitals in crystal field theory, *e.g.*, between e_g and t_{2g} orbitals of central atom or ion in the case of octahedral complex.

crystal field stabilization energy. Difference between average and true orbital energy of *d* electrons of cental atom or ion in complex. Also known as ligand field stabilization energy.

crystal field theory. Theory assuming bond between central ion of transition metal and ligand to be of ionic character, and considering influence of field of negative ligands surrounding the cation on energy of its *d* orbitals. This theory is essentially a very specialized form of the more complete molecular orbital theory, and some aspects of the transition metal behaviour can only be interpreted in terms of covalent bonding.

crystal habit. The external shape of a crystal, which depends on the relative development of the different faces, as well as upon the interfacial angles characteristic of the crystal.

crystal, hemihedral. *See* hemihedral crystal.

crystal, holohedral. *See* holohedral crystal.

crystal, isomorphous. *See* isomorphism.

crystal lattice. A lattice from which the structure of a crystal may be obtained by associating with every lattice point an assembly of atoms identical in composition, orientation, and arrangement. Also known as space lattice ; lattice.

crystalline polymer. Polymer containing considerable regions of crystalline species.

crystal, liquid. *See* liquid crystals.

crystallinity. The extent to which the atomic structure has controlled the outward form of a substance. Taking silica (SiO_2) as an example, it may develop in four ways : (*i*) as perfect crystal of quartz, *i.e.*, showing crystallized ; (*ii*) as irregular grains of quartz with a fully developed atomic arrangement but not displaying crystal faces, *i.e.*, crystalline ; (*iii*) as a very finely crystalline aggregate, chalcedony, in which individual units are so small as to be indistinguishable except under powerful magnification *i.e.*, cryptocrystalline ; (*iv*) as the material opal, in which there is no regular arrangement of atoms, *i.e.*, amorphous.

crystallite. A microscopic, often skeletal, crystal unit which is the initial form of crystalline material developing in a volcanic glass.

crystallization. To assume the crystal state by transformation from another state, which is commonly, that of a solute in solution, although it may also be the state of a liquid, a non-crystalline solid, or (less commonly) a gas.

crystallization, fractional. *See* fractional crystallization.

crystallization polarization. Type of electrolytic polarization consisting in slow removal or accumulation of ion in lattice of electrode metal in comparison to other steps of electrode process. Crystallization polarization is expressed in crystallization overvoltage.

crystalloblastic. The term used to describe the texture produced by the simultaneous recrystallization of several minerals as a result of metamorphic processs. A characteristic feature of the texture thus produced is that any of the minerals involved may be found as inclusions in any of the other minerals.

crystallographic point groups. 32 groups among infinite number of point groups, constructed from common axes or one-, two-, three-, four-. and six-fold axes which may occur in crystal lattices.

Systems	Number of classes	Characteristic symmetry elements
Cubic or Isometric	5	4 iii-fold axes
Tetragonal	7	unique iv-fold axis or a iv-fold inversion axis
Hexagonal	7	unique vi-fold axis or a vi-fold inversion axis
Trigonal	5	unique iii-fold axis or a iii-fold inversion axis
Orthorhombic	3	one or three ii-fold axes of symmetry, and if planes of symmetry are present, there are at least two
Triclinic	2	no axes or planes of symmetry
Monoclinic	3	unique ii-fold axes or a ii-fold inversion axis with a maximum of one plane of symmetry

crystal structure. The arrangement of atoms or ions in a crystalline body.

crystal symmetry. The existence of nontrival operations, consisting inversions, rotations around an axis, reflections and combination of these, which bring a crystal into a position indistinguishable from its original position.

crystal systems. General mode of repartition of crystal substances in respect to geometrical relations between lengths of elementary cell a, b, c and angles between them α, β, γ. There are seven crystal systems :
triclinic
($a \neq b \neq c, \alpha \neq \beta \neq \gamma \neq 90°$),
monoclinic
($a \neq b \neq c, \beta \neq \alpha = \gamma = 90°$),
orthorhombic
($a \neq b \neq c, a = \beta = \gamma = 90°$),
trigonal (rhombahedral)
($a = b = c, \alpha = \beta = \gamma < 120°$),
hexagonal
($a = b \neq c, \alpha = \beta = 90° \ \gamma = 120°$),
tetragonal
($a = b \neq c, \alpha = \beta = \gamma = 90°$),
cubic
($a = b = c, \alpha = \beta = \gamma = 90°$).

crystal, twin. *See* twin crystal.

crystal, uniaxial. *See* uniaxial crystal.

crystal whiskers. Single crystals that have grown in a filamentary form. Whiskers have been grown by spontaneous extrusion or out of a supersaturated medium, the medium being supersaturated by physical methods or by chemical reaction. In all instances whiskers apparently form singularities in the medium.

crystal zone. Set of planes (not necessary crystal faces) which have one common direction in space (axis of zone). Also known as crystalographic zone.

cumene process. An industrial process for making phenol from benzene. A mixture of benzene and propene is passed over phosphoric acid catalyst at 250°C. The product is oxidised by air and hydrolysed with dilute acid to give phenol and propanone.

cumulated double bonds. Double bonds located in molecule next to each other, *e.g.*,

$$R_2C{=}C{=}CR_2.$$

cumulative formation constant. *See* stability constant.

cumulative instability constant. *See* overall instability constant.

cupellation. The removal of base metal from a more noble metal by heating the mixture strongly in a special crucible ("cupel") in a muffle furnace. Thus the base metal is oxidised, being either absorbed by the cupel or blown off the surface by a blast of air. Silver may be freed from lead in this way during one stage of the desilverization of lead.

curie. C_i. The accepted unit of radioactive decay, which has been found to be 3.7×10^{10} disintegrations per second. The term is abbreviated C_i.

Curie constant, C. Constant appearing in Curie law and Curie-Weiss law ; $C = N_A \mu^2/3k$, where N_A=Avogadro constant, μ=atomic or molecular magnetic moment and k=Boltzmann constant.

Curie law. Physical law which determines temperature dependence of paramagnet's magnetic susceptibility χ, $\chi = C/T$, where C denotes Curie constant.

Curie point. *See* Curie temperature.

Curie temperature. The critical or ordening temperature for a ferromagnetic or a ferrimagnetic material. The Curie temperature T is the temperature below which there is a spontaneous manetization M in the absence of an externally applied magnetic field, and above which the material is paramagnetic. In the disordered state above the Curie temperature, thermal energy overrides any interaction between the local magnetic moments of ions. Below the Curie temperature, these interaction are predominant and cause the local moments to order or align so that there is a net spontaneous magnetization.

In the ferromagnetic case, as temperature T increases from absolute zero, the spontaneous magnetization decreases from M_0, its value at T=0. At first this occurs gradually, then with increasing rapidity until the maganetization disappears at the Curie temperature. In ferrimagnetic materials the course of magnetization with temperature may be more complicated, but the spontaneous magnetization disppears at the Curie temperature.

In antiferromagnetic materials the corresponding ordering temperature is termed as Neel temperature. Below the Neel temperature the magnetic sublattices have a spontaneous magnetization, though the net magnetization of the material is zero. Above the Neel temperature the material is paramagnetic.

The ordering temperature for magnetic materials vary widely. The ordering temperature for ferroelectrics is also termed the Curie temperature, below which the material shows a spontaneous electric moment. Also known as Curie point.

Curie-Weiss law. A relation between magnetic or electric susceptibilities and the absolute temperature which is followed by ferromagnets, antiferromagnets, nonpolar ferroelectrics and antiferroelectrics, and some paramagnets. The Curie-Weiss law is usually written in the form of following equation, where χ=the susceptibility

$$\chi = C/(T-\theta)$$

C=a constant for each material, T=absolute temperature, and θ=Curie temperature. Antiferromagnets and antiferroelectrics have a negative Curie temperature. The Curie-Weiss law refers to magnetic and electric behaviour above the transition temperature of the material in question. It is not always precisely followed, and it breaks down in the region very close to the transition temperature. Often the susceptibility will behave according to a Curie-Weiss law in different temperature ranges with different values of C and θ.

curing. A process, applied to many types of organic materials, which often involves application of heat and/or chemical reagents to bring about physicochemical changes that make the product suitable for use, for example, tobacco is cured by exposure to a temperature ranging from 27 to 83°C for several days; this reduces moisture content, converts starches to sugars, and eliminates the green colouration. Curing of meat is done by addition of common salt, sodium nitrite, sugar, etc ; some types are smoked after curing. The curing or vulcanization of rubber involves addition of sulphur and accelerator and short exposure to heat; the change here is from an unstable thermoplastic to a thermosetting material as a result of cross-linking.

curium. An element

	Symbol	Cm
	Atomic No.	96
	Atomic Wt.	242(?)
Group IIIB	Valence	+3, +4
	m.p.	1340±40°C

A radioactive and electropositive metal ; member of actinide series ; which is classified as a bone-seeker. Curium does not exist in the terrestrial environment, but may be produced artificially. The chemical properties of curium are similar to those of the typical rare earths that, if it were not for its radioactivity, it might easily be mistaken for one of these elements. There are nine known isotopes of curium which include mass numbers 238-250. The 242 and 244 isotopes produced in small quantities are useful for power generation in spacecraft.

curium series. Radioactive series with first member of reasonably long half-life curium, ^{245}Cm; and last member bismuth, ^{209}Bi, respectively. The mass number of each member of this series is $A = 4n+1$, where n = a natural number. Previously this series was called the neptunium series.

curoids. Inner transition elements belonging to actinide series of atomic number $Z=96$ to 103 : curium, berkelium, californium, einsteinium, fermium, mendelevium, nobelium, and lawrencium.

Curtin-Hammet principle. Composition of *cis-* and *trans-*alkenes in elimination product depends on activation energy of process (not on presence of conformers satisfying requirements for *trans-*elimination).

Curtius degradation. *See* Curtius reaction.

Curtius reaction. A chemical change resulting in the formation of a primary amine (RNH_2) or a urethane ($RCOONH_2$) from an acid azide. The process may be carried out by heating an acid chroride with sodium azide (NaN_3) in toluene, or by treating an ester successively with hydrazine and nitrous acid, and hydrolyzing the acide azide by heating in presence of HCl. The isocyanate is an intermediate product.

$$RCOCl+NaN_3 \rightarrow RCON_3+NaCl$$
$$RCON_3 \rightarrow RNCO+N_2$$
$$RNCO+H_2O \rightarrow RNH_2+CO_2$$

$$R-\overset{O}{\overset{\|}{C}}-Cl+NaN_3 \xrightarrow{NaCl} \left| R-\overset{O}{\overset{\|}{C}}-\underset{\cdot\cdot}{N}=\overset{+}{N}=\overset{-}{N}: \right|$$

$$\longleftrightarrow \left| R-\overset{O}{\overset{\|}{C}}-\overset{-}{\underset{\cdot\cdot}{N}}-\overset{+}{N}\equiv N \right| \xrightarrow{-N_2} R-\overset{O}{\overset{\|}{C}}-N: \rightarrow$$

$$R-N=C=O \xrightarrow{H_2O} \left| R-\underset{H}{\underset{|}{\ddot{N}}}-COOH \right| \longrightarrow$$

$$R-\ddot{N}H_2+CO_2$$

cyanine dye. One of a group of dyes derived from the compound cyanine, in which the $-CH=$ group linking two nitrogen—containing heterocyclic rings is present. An important special use of the cyanine dyes is as sensitizers in photographic emulsions.

cyanoethylation. Substitution of acidic hydrogen atom in molecule of chemical compound by cyanoethyl group $-CH_2CH_2CN$, effected by vinyl cyanide in presence of a basic catalyst, *e.g.*,

$$H_2S+CH_2=CHCN \xrightarrow{base}$$

$$HSCH_2CH_2CN \xrightarrow{CH_2=CHCN} \begin{matrix} CH_2CH_2CN \\ | \\ S \\ | \\ CH_2CH_2CN \end{matrix}$$

$$C_6H_5COCH_3+3CH_2=CHCN \xrightarrow{base} C_6H_5COC(CH_2CH_2CN)_3$$

cyanomethylation. Substitution of nitrogen-bound hydrogen in molecule of chemical compound such as amine by cyanomethyl group $-CH_2CN$, effected by sodium hydrogen sulphite :

$$R_2NH+HCHO+NaCN \xrightarrow[-Na_2SO_3]{NaHSO_3} R_2NCH_2CN+H_2O$$

cyanohydrins. Organic compounds formed by the addition of hydrogen cyanide to aldehydes or ketones (in the presence of a base).

cybotaxis. The three-dimentional arrangement of molecules of a substance ; in general, the term is applied to liquid, noncrystalline substance. Two of the most common arrangements are the end-to-end (AB. . .BA) and the side-by-side $\left(\begin{matrix} AB \\ \vdots \\ AB \end{matrix}\right)$ forms, with coordinate bonds existing between certain continuous atoms or radicals as indicated by the dotted lines.

cyclamates. Salts of the acid, $C_6H_{11}.NH.SO_3H$, where $C_6H_{11}-$ is a cyclohexyl group. Sodium and calcium cyclamates were formerly used as sweetening agents in soft drinks, until their use was banned when they were suspected of causing cancer.

cycle. 1. A period of time, at the end of which a sequence of events repeats.

2. A series of events which repeats.

3. Thermodynamic process with identical final and initial state.

cyclic AMP (cyclic adenylate). The second messanger within cells, its formation by adenylate cyclase is stimulated by certain hormones. It is involved in controlling gene expression and cell division, in immune responses, and in nervous transmission.

cyclic compound. An organic compound containing one or more closed rings. If the ring contains only carbon atoms, it is called carbocyclic, represented by alicyclic compounds (cyclohexane) and aromatics (benzene). Alicyclic rings are saturated and have various geometrical shapes ; aromatic rings are unsaturated. *See* also carbocyclic, heterocyclic.

cyclic electron flow. In chloroplasts, the light induced flow of electrons originating from and returning to photosystem I.

cyclic form. Tautometric form of cyclic structure, existing in equilibrium with its open-chain form. Tautometric equilibrium often exists in several cyclic forms, differing in size, *e.g.*, open-chain D-ribose exists in tautometric equilibrium with α- and β-D-ribofuranose and with α- and β-D-ribopyranose.

cycle nucleotides. Mononucleotides in which phosphate moiety is attached to both the third and the fifth carbon atoms of the ribose component of the molecule, thus forming a cyclic diester. They are more correctly referred to as 3′,5′-mononucleotides, but the usage of the adjective cyclic is very common.

cyclic triangular wave method. *See* cyclic voltammetry.

cyclic voltammetry. Method of study of mechanism of electrode processes based on electrolysis carried out under conditions of linearly changing potential in cyclic manner between two previously prescribed potential. Product of reduction formed during cathodic half-cycle may be oxidized in anodic one. Also known as cyclic triangular wave method.

cyclization. The process of establishing a ring structure within a molecule by intramolecular bond linkage, *e.g.*,

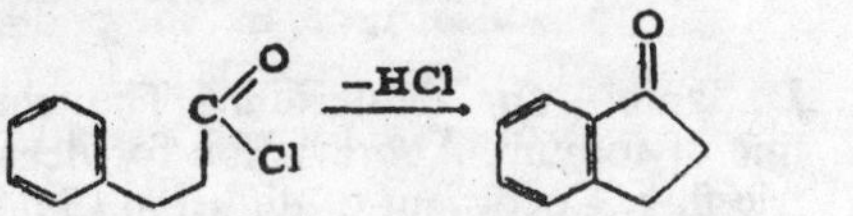

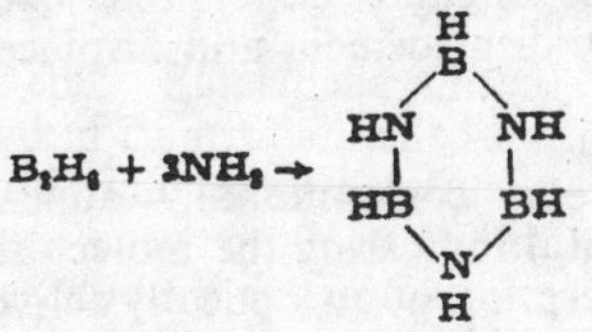

$$C_6H_5CH_2CH_2COCl \xrightarrow{-HCl} \text{(indanone)}$$

$$B_2H_6 + 2NH_3 \rightarrow \text{(ring: HB, HN, NH, HB, BH, NH)}$$

1,1-cycloaddition (of carbenes and nitrenes). Addition of carbene or nitrene in singlet state to unsaturated system with formation of three-membered ring ; reaction is stereospecific, *e.g.*,

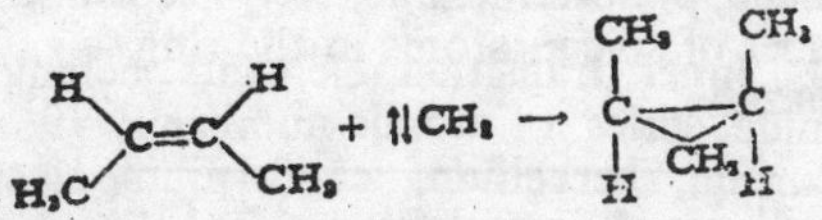

$$\text{cis-}CH_3CH{=}CHCH_3 + {:}CH_2 \rightarrow \text{cis-1,2-dimethylcyclopropane}$$

1,2-cycloaddition. Dimerization of unsaturated compounds containing electron-withdrawing substituents, leading generally to formation of four-membered ring, *e.g.*,

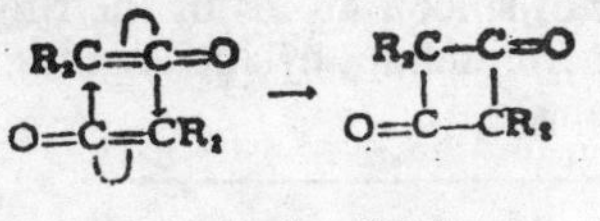

$$2\,R_2C{=}C{=}O \rightarrow \text{(four-membered ring } R_2C{-}C{=}O \,/\, O{=}C{-}CR_2)$$

Also known as 2+2 cycloaddition.

2+2 cyloaddition. *See* 1,2-cycloaddition.

cycloalkane. *See* cycloparaffin.

cycloalkene. *See* cycloolefin.

cycloalkyne. A cyclic compound, containing one or more triple bonds between carbon atoms.

cyclodiolefin. An unsaturated hydrocarbon with cyclic structure having two double bonds, *e.g.* cyclopentadiene,

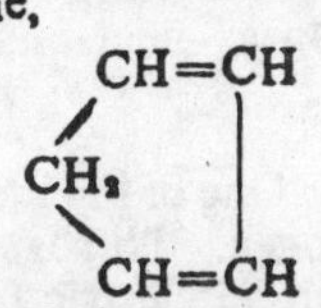

$$\text{(ring: } CH{=}CH,\ CH_2,\ CH{=}CH)$$

cycloolefin. An unsaturated hydrocarbon with cyclic structure having the formula C_nH_{2n-2} which contains one double bond, *e.g.*, cyclopentene,

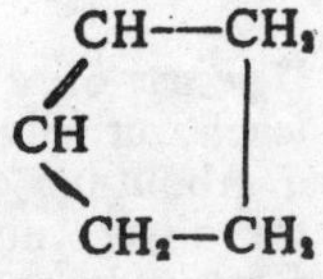

$$\text{(ring: } CH{-}CH_2,\ CH,\ CH_2{-}CH_2)$$

cycloparaffin. Saturated hydrocarbons with a cyclic or ring structure. They have the general formula C_nH_{2n}, for example, cyclohexane (C_6H_{12}). Also known as cycloalkanes.

cyclosilanes. Cyclic silicon compounds of general formula $(SiH_2)_n$, which are called cyclotrisilane, cyclotetrasilane, etc, according to the number of members in the ring ; they have the generic name cyclosilanes.

cyclosilazanes. Cyclic compounds of general, formula $(SiH_2NH)n$, which are called cyclotrisilane, cyclotetrasilane, etc., according to the number of silicon atoms in the ring, *e.g.*, cyclotrisilazane,

$$\overline{HN-SiH_2-NH-SiH_2-NH-SiH_2}.$$

cyclosiloxanes. Cyclic compounds of general formula $(SiH_2O)n$, which are called cyclodisiloxane, cyclotrisiloxane, etc., according to the number of silicon atoms in the ring; they have the generic name cyclosiloxanes, *e.g.*, cyclotriciloxane,

$$\overline{O-SiH_2-O-SiH_2-O-SiH_2}.$$

cyclotron. A circular electromagnetic device for accelerating positively charged particles (protons, deuterons, alpha particles). The acceleration is achieved by successive application of small accelerations at low-voltage synchronized with the rotational period of the particles in a magnetic field. Energies of over 700 MeV for protons and over 900 MeV for alpha particles have been attained. The energized particles emerging from the cyclotron impinge upon a target nucleus, resulting in formation of radioactive isotopes, neutrons, and ionizing radiation.

cyanamide process. One of the methods of "fixing" atmospheric nitrogen. Nitrogen is heated with calcium carbide in an electric furnace. Calcium cyanamide ("nitrolim") (CaNCN) and graphite are formed, the former being a useful nitrogenous fertiliser;

$$CaC_2+N_2 \rightarrow CaNCN+C$$

cyanide process. The use of a very dilute cyanide solution to leach out silver or gold from worthless mineral. About 0.5% sodium cyanide solution is used for silver, and an even more dilute potassium cyanide solution is used for gold extraction. In either case the double cyanide is formed (sodium argento- or potassium auro-) in solution, and from this the metal is easily recovered.

cytase. Any of several enzymes in the seeds of cereals and other plants, which hydrolyze the call-wall material.

cytochemistry. A branch of biochemistry which deals with the chemical nature of the living cell and the behaviour of its components, such as membranes, nucleus, protoplasm, etc., including nutrient and metabolic factors. Both plant and animal cells are studied in this science.

cytochromes. Haem proteins serving as electron carriers in respiration and photosynthesis.

cytokinins. Plant harmones (phytohormones) that act together with other phytohormones, such as auxins, in regulating virtually every aspect of plant growth and development.

cytosol. The continuous aqueous phase of cytoplasm, with its dissolved solutes.

Czyhlarz-Furth test. Peroxidases liberate iodine from a solution of potassium iodide which is slightly acidified with acetic acid, in the presence of hydrogen peroxide.

D

D. Symbol for deuterium. The charactertstic line of sodium. Abbreviation for density of electric flux. Coefficient of diffusion (fluid). Abbreviation for angular dispersion. Abbreviation for electric displacement and displacement flux density.

D-. A prefix conventionally appearing as a small capital indicating the molecular structure or configuration of an optically active substance it stands for "dextro," the "right-handed" enantiomorph of an optical isomer. It does not indicate that the substance is dextrorotatory.

d-. 1. A perfix indicating that a compound is dextrorotatory, that is, it turns the plane of polarized light to the right. A plus sign (+) is preferably used instead of the letter. Do not confuse with D-, which refers to molecular configuration only.

2. Symbol for grating space between corresponding points.

Dakin reaction. A method for the replacement by hydroxyl of an aldehyde group, or an aceto group in phenolic aldehydes or ketones by the action of warm hydrogen peroxide and sodium hydroxide.

$$C_6H_4(OH)(CHO) \xrightarrow{H_2O_2,\ NaOH} C_6H_4(OH)_2 + HCOOH$$

Also known as Dakin hydroxylation reaction.

Dakin solution. An aqueous solution containing 0.5% sodium hypochlorite, in which the *p*H has been carefully adjusted ; used to sterilize cuts and wounds.

Dakin-West acylamino-ketone synthesis. *See* Dakin-West reaction.

Dakin-West reaction. A method of formation of α-acylamino ketones from α-amino acids and acid anhydrides or acyl fluorides, in the presence of a base (usually pyridine) *e.g.*,

$$C_6H_5CH_2-\underset{\displaystyle NH_2}{\underset{|}{CH}}-COOH+(CH_3CO)_2O \rightarrow$$

$$C_6H_5CH_2-\underset{\displaystyle NHCOCH_3}{\underset{|}{CH}}-COCH_3+CO_2+H_2O$$

Also known as Dakin-West acylamino-ketone synthesis.

dalton. The weight of single hydrogen atom (1.66×10^{-21} kg).

daltonides. *See* stoichiometric compounds.

Dalton's atomic theory. Theory forming the basis of the accepted modern atomic theory, according to which, reactions must take place between atoms or group of atoms, and the atoms of the same elements are all alike but differ from the atoms of other elements.

Daltion's law of partial pressures. Total pressure p of mixture of gases is equal to sum of partial pressures p_i of constituents of mixture

$$p=\sum_{i=1}^{n} p_i$$

It may be noted that this law is empirical.

dammar. A natural resin of the group known as "recent" in the geological sense ; it is obtained from various types of East Indian trees. It is soluble in nonpolar solvents but insoluble in water. It is used to some extent in baked enamels, lacquers, and varnishes, as well as being a component of coatings for fabrics, paper, leather, etc.

Dane test for formaldehyde. α-Naphthol dissolved in a little sodium hydroxide solution, on the addition of a little formaldehyde solution gives a green colour, changing to dark blue on warming. The reaction is used conversely to test for α-naphthol.

Danheiser reagent. A solution prepared by mixing 0.1g. dimethyglyoxime, dissolved in 10 ml. ethyl alcohol, with 5 g. citric acid, dissolved in 90 ml. ammonium hydroxide solution (sp. gr. 0.90). This reagent is used as a test agent for solutions of nickel, which give with it a red colour or precipitate.

Daniel cell. Cell of :

$$Cu \mid CuSO_4(aq) \mid ZnSO_4(aq) \mid Zn \text{ type}$$

A primary cell with constant electromotive force of 1.1 volts having a negative pole of amalgamated zinc, standing in a porous pot containing dilute sulphuric acid. This pot stands in cupric sulphate solution which also contains the positive pole, a copper plate. On completion of the external circuit, a current flows and the following reactions take place :

$$Zn \rightarrow Zn^{2+} + 2e^-$$

$$Cu^{2+} + 2e^- \rightarrow Cu$$

at the negative pole, zinc sulphate being formed ; at the positive pole, copper is deposited.

Dantec test for antipyrine. To test for antipyrine add to 0.1 g. of sample 1 ml. of a 10% solution of xanthydrol in acetic acid, and then 2 ml. glacial acetic acid ; heat to boiling. A red colour indicates the presence of antipyrine.

Danziger test for cobalt. Cobalt is detected by acidifying 5 ml. of a very dilute solution with hydrochloric acid, adding solid ammonium thiocyanate and a few drops of stannous chloride solution, followed by shaking with amyl alcohol ; the non-aqueous layer becomes blue in the presence of cobalt.

dark reactions. In photosynthetic cells, the light-independent enzymatic reactions concerned in the synthesis of glucose from carbon dioxide, ATP, and NADPH.

Darzens-Claisen condensation. Reaction of aldehyde or ketone with α-haloester in presence of basic condensation agent (*e.g.* sodium alcoholate, sodium amide), resulting in formation of glycidic ester, The glecidic ester yield on saponification the corresponding carboxylic acid of the ethylene oxide series, which on loss of carbon dioxide yield aldehydes or ketones, *e.g.*,

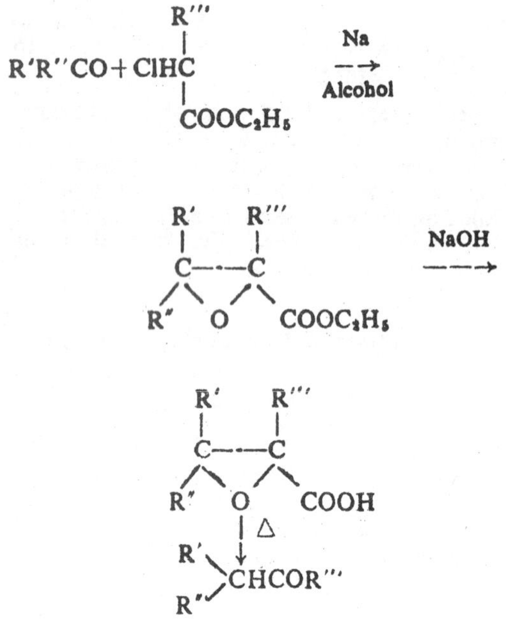

$$R'R''CO + ClHC(R''')COOC_2H_5 \xrightarrow[\text{Alcohol}]{\text{Na}}$$

$$R'R''C\!-\!O\!-\!C(R''')COOC_2H_5 \xrightarrow{\text{NaOH}}$$

$$R'R''C\!-\!O\!-\!C(R''')COOH \xrightarrow{\Delta} R'R''CHCOR'''$$

Also known as Darzens condensation.

Darzens condensation. *See* Darzens-Clasien condensation.

Darzens synthesis of tetralin derivatives. A method of formation of tetralin derivatives by ring closure of benzylallylacetic acid and ıelated compounds :

$$C_6H_5CH_2CH(COOH)CH_2CH{=}CH_2 \xrightarrow{H_2SO_4}$$

(tetralin ring bearing COOH and CH_3)

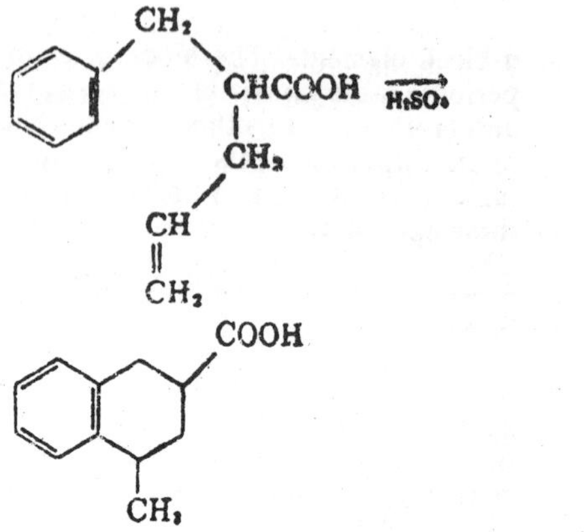

Darzens synthesis of unsaturated ketones. A method of formation of unsaturated ketones by reaction of the corresponding unsaturated hydrocarbon with an acid chloride, followed by removal of hydrochloric acid, *e.g.*,

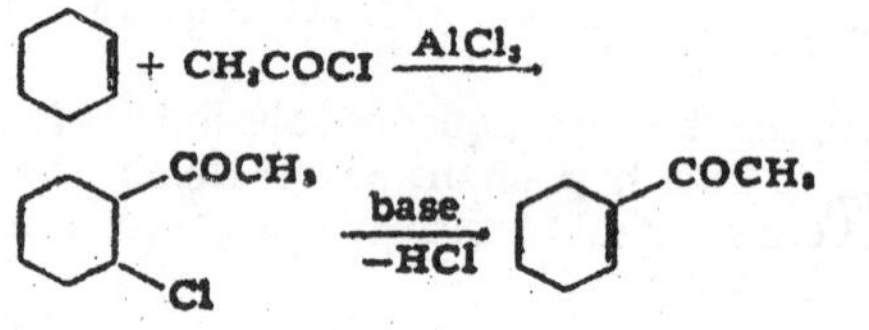

$$\text{(cyclohexene)} + CH_3COCl \xrightarrow{AlCl_3}$$

$$\text{(2-chlorocyclohexyl)}COCH_3 \xrightarrow[-HCl]{\text{base}} \text{(cyclohexenyl)}COCH_3$$

dative bond. *See* coordinate bond.

dating, radiocarbon. *See* radiocarbon dating.

daughter element. Any member of a series of nuclides formed by radioactive disintegration of an unstable elements, *e.g.*, uranium, which is called the parent. The daughter nuclides in tern emit energy in the form of alpha or beta particles so that a sequence results, terminating in a stable nucleus. For example, radium and radon arc daughter elements of uranium. *See also* decay ; radioactivity.

David test for alcohol (in essential oils). Extract the oil with a little water, and superimpose the water, on a solution of molybdic acid in concentrated sulphuric acid. A blue ring indicates the presence of alcohol. If the sample contains an aldehyde, it must be removed from the sample of oil with petroleum ether before performing the test.

Davy reagent A solution of 50 g. molybdic acid in 1 kilogram concentrated sulphuric acid used as a test reagent for varous phenols, especially phenol itself. The latter gives a yellow colour, changing to purple-red, except in dilute solution, where a green colour, changing to blue, is obtained.

d-block elements. The block of elements in the periodic table consisting of scandium, yttrium, and lanthanum together with the three periods of transition elements: titanium to zinc, zirconium to cadmium, and hafnium to mercury. All these elements have two outer *s*-electrons and *d*-electrons in their penultimate shell, *i.e.*, an outer electronic configuration of the type $(n-1)d^x ns^2$, where x is 1 to 10. *See also* transition elements.

de-, des-. Indicating removal of something from the molcule ; as desoxybenzoin, $C_6H_5CH_2CO$-C_6H_5 (benzoin with oxygen atom removed).

deacetylation. The removal of an acetyl grouping from a molecule.

deacidification. Removing or neutralizing an acid in a system.

Deacon process. A method of making chlorine by oxidising hydrogen chloride with air, using a catalyst. A mixture of hydrogen chloride and air is passed over clay balls soaked in cupric chloride solution and heated to a temperature of about 440°C.

$$2HCl+O_2 \rightarrow Cl_2+H_2O$$

The resulting gas seldom contains more than 10% chlorine. A more efficient version mixes hydrogen chloride with oxygen and passes the gases over a mixture of ferric and potassium chlorides molten at 450°C. This process is now practically obsolete.

deactivation. A substance used to modify selectively the action of an activator, reducing its effect upon an undesired substance.

deactivation of catalyst. Loss of ability to catalyze by catalyst, *e.g.*, occurring because of ageing, sintering or poisoning.

deactivation of excited state. Loss of excitation energy of atom or molecule due either to nonradiative or radiative transitions or to chemical reaction.

deactivation of molecule. Loss of energy by molecule which previously was able to react.

dead space. 1. The volume of a vessel not occupied by a porous solid (as in adsorption) or to that portion of the volume of a vessel through which no discharge takes place (in discharge tubes), etc.

2. When the surface tension of a system increases as chemical action proceeds, capillarity will tend to stop the action. If any part of the system is then subjected to capillary action, as in a capillary tube, no reaction takes place. This is called "dead space" of the reaction.

dead time. Time immediately after receiving a stimulus during which counter is insensitive to another impulse or stimulus. Also known as insensitive time.

dead volume In chromatography, volume of mobile phase contained between lower end of bed of stationary phase and outlet of column.

deagglomeration. Size-reduction process in which loosely adhered clumps (agglomerates) of powders or crystals are broken apart without further disintegration of the powder or crystal particles themselves.

dealkylation. Elimination of alkyl group from molecule of organic compound.

deamidase. An enzyme that catalyzes the removal of an amido group from a compound.

deamidate. The removal of amido group from the molecule.

deaminization. Any process for removing the amino group from an amide, *e.g.*,

$$CH_3CONH_2 + HCl + H_2O \rightarrow CH_3COOH + NH_4Cl$$

Also known as desamidization ; disamidinization.

deamination. Any process involving the removal of an amino group from a compound, *e.g.*, by diazotization and subsequent boiling with alcohol, *e.g.*,

$$2CH_3(CH_2)_2NH_2 \xrightarrow[-N_2]{HNO_2} CH_3(CH_2)_2OH + CH_3CH{-}CH_2$$

Also known as desamination.

deaminase. An enzyme that catalyzes the hydrolysis of amino group.

de Boer test for zirconium and hafnium. Both zirconium and hafnium give a violet colour with alizarinsulphonic acid which is not discharged by hydrochloric acid, but which is changed to yellow by even traces of fluoride.

Debray reagent. An aqueous solution of phosphomolybdic acid, which is used to test for salts of cesium, potassium, rubidium, and thallium, giving yellow precipitates with these ions.

de Broglie theory. The theory that particles of matter have wavelike properties which can give rise to interference effects, and electrons in an atom are associated with standing waves on a Bohr orbit.

de Broglie waves. A concept arising from the dual nature of smail quantities of matter, which may be regarded as possessing both particle as well as wave characteristics.

Matter wave ascribed to moving paiticle. De Broglie wavelength $\lambda=h/p$, where frequency $\nu=E/h$, where h= Planck constant, E=particle energy and p=particle momentum.

Debye-Falkenhagens effect. Increase of equivalent conductance of electrolyte as a result of disappearance of relaxation effect in case of very large frequencies (above 10^6 Hz) of alternating electric field.

Debye frequency. The maximum allowable frequency in the computation of the Debye specific heat.

Debye-Huckel's equation. Semiempirical relation which describes mean activity coefficient $f\pm$ of strong electrolyte ;

$$\lg f_{\pm}=-\frac{A \mid z_+z_- \mid \sqrt{J}}{1+Ba\sqrt{J}}$$

$$B\equiv\left(\frac{8\pi N_A e^2}{1000k}\right)^{\frac{1}{2}} \frac{10^{-8}}{(\varepsilon_r T)^{1/2}}=\frac{50.29}{(\varepsilon_r T)^{1/2}}$$

where a=effectiee diameter of ion ; for other symbols *see* Debye-Huckel's limiting law.

Debye-Huckel limiting law. The mean activity coefficient of the ions in a dilute solution is proportional to the product of valences of the ions and the square root of the ionic strength of the solution. Therefore, the departure from ideal behaviour is independent of the chemical nature of the electrolyte, being determined solely by ionic valences and ionic strength.

Formula which describes mean activity coefficiennt $f\pm$ of strong electrolyte in diluted solution is :

$$\lg f_{\pm}=-A \mid z_1z_2 \mid \sqrt{J}$$

$$A\equiv\sqrt{\frac{2\pi N_A}{1000}}\,\frac{e^3}{2.303(k\varepsilon_r T)^{3/2}}=\frac{1.8246\,.\,10^6}{(\varepsilon_r T)^{3/2}}$$

where e=elementary charge, ε_r=relative permittivity, k=Boltzmann constant, J=ionic strength ; it gives results which agree with experiment if J does not exceed 0.02—0.03 (in aqueous solution).

Debye-Huckel-Onsager's limiting law for conductivity. Formula for equivalent conductivity Λe of diluted solution of strong electrolyte :

$$\Lambda c=\Lambda_0-\left[\frac{2.801\times10^6 \mid z_+z_- \mid q}{(\epsilon_r T)^{3/2}(1+\sqrt{q})}\Lambda_0+\frac{41.25(\mid z_+ \mid + \mid z_- \mid)}{\eta(e_r T)^{1/2}}\right]\sqrt{J}$$

where :

$$q\equiv\frac{\mid z_+z_- \mid}{\mid z_+ \mid + \mid z_- \mid}\,\frac{\lambda_{0+}+\lambda_{0-}}{\mid z_+ \mid \lambda_0 + \mid z_- \mid \lambda_{0+}}$$

and η=viscosity of strong, Λ_0=limiting equivalent ionic conductivity, ε_r=relative permitivity of solution, J=ionic strength ; in aqueous diluted solutions of 1,1-electrolytes ($c\leq10^{-3}$ mole/dm^3), this law gives results which agree with experimental results.

Debye-Huckel screening radius. *See* Debye shielding length.

Debye-Huckel's theory of strong electrolytes. Theory which describes simplified model of strong electrolyte : (*a*) interionic interactions are exclusively coulombic in nature and are small in comparison to energy of thermal agitation, (*b*) ions are non-polarized spherical charges, and dielectric constant of solution is equal to that of pure solvent, (*c*) electrolyte is completely dissociated ; theory introduces concept of ionic atmosphere and describes model mathematically.

Debye Janncey scattering. In coherent background scattering of x-rays from a crystal in directions between those of the Bragg reflections.

Debye length. *See* Debye shielding length.

Debye-Scherrer method. X-ray diffraction technique for investigation of crystal structure.

X-ray beam is scattered by powdered microcrystalline sample and diffracted rays are recorded.

Debye shielding length. A characteristic distance in a plasma beyond which the electric field of a charged particle is shielded by particles having charges of the opposite sign. Also known as Debye length; Debye-Huckel screening radius.

Debye theory. Theory of dielectric polarization which was the first to take into account orientation polarization. Assuming that local field is given by Lorenz field, Debye theory expresses relative permittivity ε_r, and density of medium ρ in terms of induction polarizability α_1 and permanent dipole moment μ

$$P_m=\frac{\varepsilon_r-1}{\varepsilon_r+2}\frac{M_r}{\rho}=\frac{N_A}{3\varepsilon_0}\left(\alpha_1+\frac{\mu^2}{3kT}\right)$$

where, P_m=(molar) polarization, M_r=relative molecular mass, N_A=Avogadro constant, ε_0=permittivity of free space, k=Boltzmann constant, and T=thermodynamic temperature.

Debye T³ law. At very low temperature, *i.e*, those below $\theta/10$, atomic heat capacities of crystalline simple substances are approximately proportional to cube of thermodynamic eemperature, where θ = characteristic Debye ttmperature.

Debye unit, D. Unit of dipole moment; $1D=1.10^{-18}$ e.s.u. of electric diplole moment; in SI units $1\ D=3.33.10^{-30}$ Cm.

decalescence. Absorption of heat, usually by an alloy, without rise in temperature, due to an allotropic transformation.

decantation. Pouring, or siphoning, off the clear supernatant liquid after a substance held in suspension has settled to the bottom of the containing vessel.

decarbonization. Removal of carbon from any system which contains it. The substitution of oxygen for carbon dioxide in the blood in the lungs is termed decarbonization, as is also the burning out of a portion of the carbon in cast iron to make steel.

decarbonylation. Elimination of carbon monoxide molecule from molecule of organic compound, *e.g.*,

$$RCOCH_2COCOOR \rightarrow RCOCH_2COOR+CO$$

decarboxylase. An enzyme that hydrolyzes the carboxyl radical.

decarboxylation. The removal of one or more carboxyl groups from the molecule of a compound by loss of carbon dioxide. The term is also applied to the loss of carbon dioxide from proteins or amino-acids by bacterial action. Carboxylic acids having a β-carbonyl function or a β, γ double bond often suffer loss of carbon dioxide on heating. A cyclic transition state involving a concerted hydrogen transfer and double bond shift is proposed for these reactions:

Deckert reagent for zinc. One ml. of a solution of dithizone in 0.01*N* sodium hydroxide is diluted with 90 ml. zinc-free water. The mixture is then added to the test solution which has previously been adjusted to the same *p*H. The formation of a red colour confirms the presence of zinc.

Deckert test for ethylene oxide in air. Pass 50 ml. of the air through 1–2 ml. of a 40% solution of potassium thiocyanate contaning 1 drop of 0.1% alcoholic phenolphthalein. The test is negative for ethylene oxide if no red colour appears in 2 minutes.

decoction. A solution that is made by boiling a solid material to dissolve one or more of its component substances.

decolourize. To remove the colour from ; to bleach. Decolourization may be carried out in a variety of ways ; (*i*) by adsorption, in which the colouring matter is removed from solution by placing it in contact wiih charcoal, activated carbon, alumina. etc. ; (*ii*) by precipitation ; many colouring matters form insoluble compounds with aluminium, lead, and other heavy metals ; (*iii*) by destruction, *e.g.*, oxidation or reduction. The agent in the process is termed a decolourizer.

decomposition. A type of chemical reaction in which one compound divides or splits into two or more simpler substances. which may be either elements or compounds. The decomposition of an inorganic compound into two elements is examplified by the reactions shown below :

$$2H_2O \rightarrow 2H_2+O_2$$
$$2Hg \rightarrow 2Hg+O_2$$
$$CaCO_3 \rightarrow CaO+CO_2$$

Energy is always supplied for such reactions.

decomposition, double. *See* double decomposition.

decomposition, sensitized. *See* sensitized decomposition.

decomposition voltage, U_d. The minimum electromotive force which must be applied to a given solution and given electrodes to produce steady electrolysis. Value of overvoltage extrapolated to I_0 corresponding to charcteristic bend of curve for current of electrolysis I and electrolysis voltage U; especially well observed in case of gaseous products of electrolysis.

This term is used mainly in technical electro chemistry and has no strict physical interpretation.

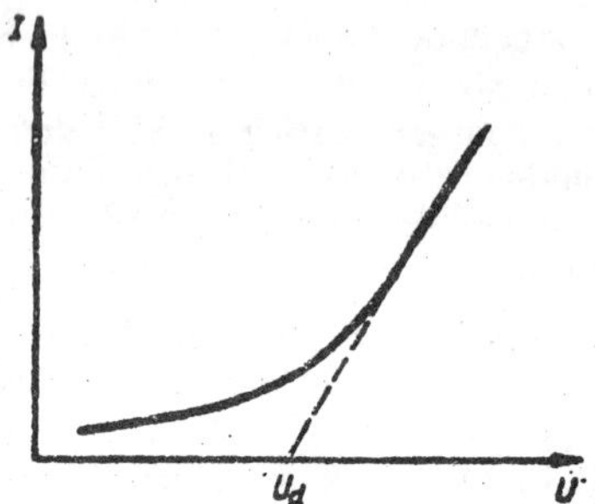

Fig. 19. Decomposition voltage

decontamination. In general, the removal of chemical, biological, or rediological contamination., from an area or a material ; specifically this term refers to treatment of clothing, equipment, buildings, and the like to remove radioactive substances to which they have been exposed. Standard methods of decontamination include thorough washing with a soap/water solution or with potassium permanganate solution with subsequent application of 5% sodium bisulphite solution. Sequestering agents such as ethylenediaminetetraacetic acid are also effective. Steam blast can be used on buildings and metals. The effectiveness of the decontamination can be checked with a radiation counter.

decontamination factor. Ratio of amount of rodioactive impurities present in substance before purification to that present after purification.

decrepitation. A crackling noise produced when certain crystals are heated, caused by changes in structure resulting generally from loss of water of crystallization.

defecation. A term used chiefly in food technology to refer of the clarification or removal of impurities from sugarcane or beet juice by heating in the presence of lime to precipitate undesirable substances. The resulting mother liquor is then drained off and concentrated by evaporation and boiling. *See also* clarification.

defervescence. Cessation or discontinuance of boiling or of effervescence.

deflagration. A chemical reaction accompanied by vigrous evolution of heat, flame, sparks, or sputtering of burning particles. usually containing potassium or sodium nitrate (black powder) or nitrocellulose (smokeless powder). It is induced by heat, friction, or impact. Deflagration occurs at the particle surfaces of materials classified as low explosives, in which the combustion products flow away from the unreacted material. It differs from detonation, characteristic of high explosives, where the decomposition products flow toward the unreacted mass under high pressure. When a low explosive deflagrates in a confined area, the combustion rate increases rapidly to the point of detonation (nitrocellulose). *See also* detonation ; explosive.

deflocculation. The reverse process of flocculation, or the process of preventing flocculation, *i..e*, the process of breaking up dispersing agglomerates to form a stable compound.

De Florez process. A process for the distillation and cracking of crude oil (or a fraction distilled therefrom) by the application of heat and pressure. The preheated oil passes into a huge pipe still, externally heated, from which the vapour is conducted to a tower. By varying the pressures at which the tower and still are operated it is possible to vary yields of oil and gasoline as well as to change the antiknock value of the gasoline.

defoliant. A chemical, sprayed on plants, that causes leaves to fall of prematurely ; used for military purposes. Most compounds used for this purpose are ecologically damaging, as they tend to deposit residues of varying degrees of toxicity in the soil, which may contaminate water supplies. Chemically, defoliants comprise a number of groups, including organic nitrogen compounds (thiocyanates, trichloropicolinic acid), phenoxyacetic derivatives, arsenates, etc. *See also* herbicide ; silvicide.

deformation of atomic nuclei. Deviation of surface of atomic nuclei from sphericity. Deformed atomic nuclei are those with total number of protons and/or neutrons differing widey from a magic number.

deformation of ion. The electronic field of one ion may be considerably distorted by the fields of neighbouring ions of opposite charge. This effect was investigated by Fajans who, in 1928, pointed out that the tendency to form ionic or covalent links is related to the deformability of the electron shells. The action of negative ions on positive ones is slight as the positive ions are usually smaller and less easily deformed.

deformation polarization. *See* induced polarization.

defrother. An agent which prevents frothing.

degasification. Removal of gas, as applied particularly to the removal of the last traces of gas from wires used in vacuum tubes, from metals to be plated, and from substances to be used in other specialized applications.

degeneracy. *See* degeneration of energy level.

degeneracy temperature. *See* Fermi temperature.

degenerate. 1. This expression was used in the kinetic theory of gases to describe a gas which did not obey the ideal gas laws, in other words, any real gas. The greater the deviation of the real gas from ideality, the greater its degeneracy.

2. In quantum mechanies the term applies to any system for which two or more states correspond to the same eigenvalue.

degenerate electron gas. Group of electrons in metal or semiconductor which may be treated as group of particles obeying laws of quantum mechanics, travelling freely in field of constant potential or in periodic field (in range of whole crystal). Distribution of energy in degenerate electron gas is described by Fermi-Dirac law.

degenerate matter. Matter that has been stripped of its orbital electrons, so that the nuclei are pack closed together.

degenerate state. Energetic state of quantum mechanical system described simultaneously by more than one linearly independent wave function.

degeneration of energy level. For given energy level there are two or more linearly independent quantum states ; in this case the energy value is not sufficient for unique description of quantum state of system on given energy level.

degradation. 1. The breakdown of complex organic structures to simpler compounds by the influence of bacteria, usually accelerated by oxygen and sunlight. High-polymer substances are specially subject to this type of decomposition, which is used industrially in the treatment of municipal wastes. Infectious organisms can bring about degradation of proteins in the nervous system of the body.

2. Decomposition of organic compounds by various methods resulting in formation of compounds of simpler structure, *e.g.*,

$$(CH_3)_3\overset{+}{N}CH_2CH_2\overset{-}{O}H \xrightarrow{\Delta} H_2O+N(CH_3)_3+CH_2{=}CH_2$$

degradation of acids. A method of reducing the number of carbon atoms in the molecule of an acid ; especially a fatty acid by the decomposition of its calcium or barium salt in the presence of a salt of acetic acid, followed by oxidation of the resulting methyl ketone, *e.g.*,

$$(R{-}CH_2{-}COO)_2Ca+(CH_3{-}COO)_2Ca \longrightarrow 2R{-}CH_2{-}CO{-}CH_3+2CaCO_3$$

$$\downarrow CrO_3$$

$$2RCOOH+2CH_3COOH$$

Also known as Kraft method.

degradation of polymer. Degradation of macromolecules caused by physical, chemical or biological factors, involving structural change of polymer and lowering of polymerization degree. Degradation generally decreases the quality of polymer.

degreasing agent. A solvent used to remove grease, either a fat or oil or a mixture of both, as from a metal in a plating operation.

degree of association. Ratio of the number of associated monomer molecules to the total number of monomer molecules.

degree of degeneracy. The number of linearly independent wave functions corresponding to stationary states of system with the same energy.

degree of depolarization of light. Ratio of scattered light intensity in direction parallel to incident light beam and scattered light intensity perpendicular to incident beam.

degree of dispersion. A relationship that is characteristic of a colloid. The degree of dispersion of a precipitate can be varied by the correct choice of the concentration of the solutions involved.

$$\delta = \frac{C}{S}\,\eta$$

where δ = the fineness of the particles, S = slight solubility of the disperse phase, C the state of supersaturation that would exist if the disperse phase had remained in solution, and η=viscocity of the solution. Thus any suspension may be changed into a colloidal dispersion by suitable manipulation.

degree of dissociation, α.

$$\alpha = \frac{i-1}{\nu-1} = \frac{\Lambda_c}{\Lambda_0}.$$

where i=van't Hoff isotonic coefficient, ν= number of ions arising from one molecule of electrolyte, Λ_0 and Λ_c=limiting equivalent donductivity and equivalent conductivity at a given concentration c respectively ; this value is not identical with true degree of dissociation.

degree of formation, α_n. Ratio of equilibrium concentration of complex [MLn] to overall metal concentration c_M

$$\alpha_n = \frac{[ML_n]}{c_M}$$

degree of freedom. 1. In the statement of the phase rule a degree of freedom is one of that number of variable factors such as pressure, temperature, or concentration, which must be fixed to define completely the state of a system.

2. In terms of the energy of a system the number of degrees of freedom is the number of independent squared terms of the type $\frac{1}{2}mv_x^2$ or $\frac{1}{2}Ir^2$ or $\frac{1}{2}kx^2$, which must be specified in order to determine uniquely the energy of the system. In a diatomic gas the two atoms require six coordinates between them, giving six degrees of freedom. Commonly these are interpreted as six independent ways of storing energy : on this basis the molecule has three degrees of freedom for different directions of translational motion, and in addition there are two degrees of freedom for rotation of the molecular axis and one vibrational degree of freedom along the bond between the atoms.

degree of freedom of thermodynamic system. Independent variable which may be changed without disturbance of thermodynamic equilibrium.

degree of ionization. Ratio (chiefly expressed as percentage) of the number (or concentration) of ionized molecules to their total number (or concentration) in solution investigated.

degree of polymerization. A number indicating the extent to which the molecules of a monomer have combined to form a polymer ; it is determined by calculating the number of such molecules present in an average molecule of polymer in a sample. The degree of polymerization of viscose rayon, for example, is 700 while for pure natural cellulose it is 3000 ; for synthetic polymers it is usually much higher. In plastics manufacture, the properties of the product can be modified and controlled to a considerable extent by keeping the degree of polymerization within specified limits. *See also* polymerization.

De Hass test for β-naphthol. One ml. of an aqueous solution of the substance is added to 5 ml. acetic acid, and the solution is floated on 5 ml. concentrated sulphuric acid. A coloured ring at the interface, and fluorescence on shaking, indicates the presence of β-naphthol.

De Hass-Van Alphen effect. Oscillatory changes of magnetic susceptibility of certain metals with increasing magnetic field strength at low temperature.

dehalogenation. Elimination of one or more halogen atoms (F, Cl, Br or I) from the molecule of chemical compound, *e.g.*,

$$BrCH_2CH_2Br + Zn \rightarrow CH_2{=}CH_2 + ZnBr_2$$

Dehan-Scott test for aromatic amines. A 0.1% alcoholic solution of the substance is treated with 1-2 drops of ammonia and 2-3 drops sodium hypobromite solution. Characteristic colours are obtained with many aromatic amines.

Dehan-Scott test for phenolic compounds. A 0.1% alcoholic solution of the substance is treated with 2-3 drops of sodium hypobromite solution. Characteristic colours are obtained for many phenolic compounds. If a drop of ammonia is added before the hypobromite, other colours are obtained in several instances.

dehydrase. An enzyme which catalyzes the removal of water form a substrate.

dehydration. 1. Removal of 95% or more of the water from a food product by intensive oven drying, spraying, or other means for the purpose of saving space, weight, and transportation cost. A number of common foods are available in dehydrated form (potatoes, bouillon cubes, fruit juices), requiring only addition of water to restore them to edible condition (reconstitution). A process called dehydrofreezing removes only about half the water content, after which the vegetable is frozen.

2. Elimination of water molecule from the molecule of a chemical compound, *e.g.*,

$$CH_3CH_2OH \xrightarrow[\Delta]{H_2SO_4} CH_2{=}CH_2 + H_2O$$

$$CuSO_4.5H_2O \xrightarrow[-5H_2O]{\Delta} CuSO_4$$

3. Removal of chemically combined water from castor oil by heating it in the presence of a catalyst, thus converting it from a nondrying to a drying oil suitable for use in protective coatings.

4. Excessive or abnormal loss of water from the body as a result of dysentery, diarrhea, or vomiting, which results in severe chemical imbalance.

dehydro-. Denoting (*a*) removal of hydrogen ; as, dehydrocholic acid ; (*b*) sometimes, removal of water ; as dehdromucic acid.

dehydrochlorination. A process whereby a molecule of hydrogen chloride is removed from an organic chloride leaving a double or triple bond in the organic compound. It is the principal process for manufacturing vinyl chloride from ethylene dichloride (1,2-dichloroethane), by the reaction :

$$CH_2ClCH_2Cl \rightarrow CH_2{=}CHCl + HCl$$

It can be conducted thermally at an elevated temperature or at lower temperatures in the presence of an alkali which reacts with the liberated HCl.

dehydrocyclization. Elimination of hydrogen molecule from hydrocarbon molecule (open-chain, aromatic or hydroaromatic) with formation of compounds containing one or more cyclic structures in molecule, *e.g.*,

$$CH_3(CH_2)_5CH_3 \rightarrow \text{[benzene ring]}{-}CH_3 + 4H_2$$

$$\text{[benzene ring]}(CH{=}CH_2)(CH{=}CH_2) \rightarrow \text{[naphthalene]} + H_2$$

dehydrogenases. Engymes catalyging the removal of pairs of hydrogen atoms from their substrates.

dehydrogenation. A chemical reaction, normally requiring a catalyst, in which hydrogen atoms are removed from a saturated compound (an alcohol, paraffin, or alicyclic compound) to unsaturated aldehydes, olefins, or aromatic compounds. This is a form of oxidation (electron transfer), for example, acetaldehyde is formed by removing two hydrogen atoms from ethyl alcohol : $CH_3CH_2OH \rightarrow CH_3CH{=}O + H_2$. The saturated cyclic hydrocarbon cyclohexane is dehydrogenated to benzene in the catalytic reforming process.

dehydrohalogenation. Elimination of molecule of hydrogen halide from molecule of organic compound with formation of unsaturated compound, *e.g.*,

$$CH_3CH_2X \xrightarrow{HO^-} CH_2{=}CH_2 + HX$$

deionization. Process of removing ions from solution. Also known as demineralization.

delayed critical. The condition in which a nuclear reactor is critical because of delayed neutrons alone, without requiring the contribution of prompt neutrons.

delayed fluorescence. Fluorescence with relatively long life-time ; starting upper singlet state from which emission of light originates is achieved either through triplet-triplet annihilation process (P-type delayed fluorescence) or optical electrons are thermally excited from lower triplet electronic state (E-type delayed fluorescence).

delayed neutron. Fission neutrons, emitted with delay, by primary and secondary fission fragments of atomic nucleus (half-life of order of seconds). Delayed neutrons constitute about 1% of all neutrons emitted in fission reactions.

delayed proton. Protons emitted spontaneously from a nucleus as a consequence of excitation left from a previous radioactive decay event.

Delepine primary amine synthesis. A method of obtaining amines from organic halides by forming the hexamethylenetetramine addition product, and treating it with hydrochloric acid and alcohol.

$$RCH_2X + (CH_2)_6N_4 \rightarrow [RCH_2(CH_2)_6N_4]^+X^- \xrightarrow[C_2H_5OH]{HCl,\ H_2O} RCH_2NH_2$$

deletion mutation. Mutation resulting from deletion of one or more nucleotides from a gene.

deliquescence. The literal meaning of this term (from the Latin) is "becoming liquid". Substances are said to be deliquescent if they will absorb enough water from the air to dissolve themselves, and hence become liquid. Many substances are hygroscopic (*which see*), but only a smaller number—such as caustic soda, some salts of calcium and magnesium, etc.—are deliquescent.

delocalization energy. Difference between energy of real molecule with conjugated double bonds and energy of hypothetical molecule with localized double bonds.

delocalized electrons. Electrons assumed to occupy delocalized molecular orbitals.

delocalized molecular orbital. Molecular orbital spread over whole molecule or substantial part of it, *e.g.*, orbitals in conjugated double bond molecules ; also known as delocalized orbital.

delocalized orbital. *See* delcoalized molecular orbital.

delta electrons. *See* delta rays.

delta-iron. An allotropic (*see* allotropy) form of pure iron which is nonmagnetic and exists between 1400°C and its melting point.

delta metal. An alloy of copper (55%) and zinc (43%) with small amounts of iron and other transition metals.

delta rays Non-nuclear electron radiation generated when ionizing particles or photons pass through matter and having energy sufficient to cause further ionization of atoms of medium. Also known as delta electrons.

Demarcay test for rhodium. A neutral or weakly-acid solution of rhodium ammomium chloride when treated with a slight excess of sodium hypochlorite solution, gives a yellow precipitate. The precipitate dissolves in 20% acetic acid solution to give an orange-yellow colour, which fades to give a grey precipitate, and then a sky-blue colour.

demethylation. Elimination of methyl group—CH_3 from the molecule of an organic compound, *e.g.*,

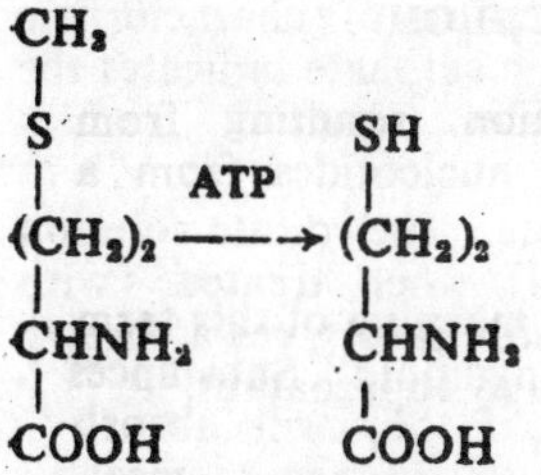

$$\begin{array}{c} CH_3 \\ | \\ S \\ | \\ (CH_2)_2 \\ | \\ CHNH_2 \\ | \\ COOH \end{array} \xrightarrow{ATP} \begin{array}{c} SH \\ | \\ (CH_2)_2 \\ | \\ CHNH_2 \\ | \\ COOH \end{array}$$

Demianov rearrangement. Rearrangement of structure that accompanies the treatment of certain primary aliphatic amines with nitrous acid ; change in size of the ring frequently occurs ; *e.g.*

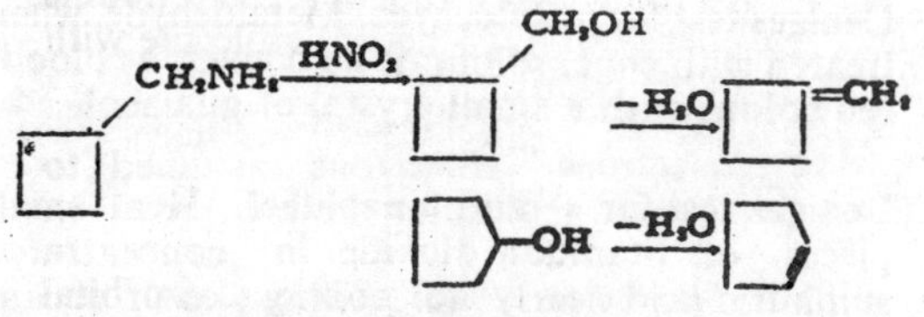

$$CH_2NH_2 \xrightarrow{HNO_2} CH_2OH \xrightarrow{-H_2O} =CH_2$$

$$-OH \xrightarrow{-H_2O}$$

demineralization. *See* deionization.

demulsification. The intentional destruction of the undesirable emulsions such as that occur in petroleum extraction, where subterranean pressure has created a highly stable emulsion of saline water in the petroleum. A wide variety of materials and methods have been used to "break" these emulsions, including altermating current, neutralization by multivalent ions, centrifugation.

denaturant. A substance added to ethyl alcohol to prevent it being used for internal consumption. This applies chiefly to ethyl alcohol intended for industrial use. The contaminating material being added to insure that it is not diverted to beverge use (for taxation purposes). Methyl alcohol is used in completely denatured alcohol because of its toxicity; specially denatured alohol may contain a number of specified materials, among which are tert-butyl alcohol, brucine, quassin, and sucrose octaacetate. Many other additives have been used unofficially in the past with the idea of making the alcohol obnoxious as to odour, taste or internal effect.

denaturation. A reordering of the molecular structure of some proteins (globulins) induced by a number of environmental factors, such as heating to just below the boiling point, change of *p*H, or exposure to various detergents. These factors cause rupture of the hydrogen bonds in the molecule, but not of the stronger peptide bonds. As a result the structure of the protein becomes somewhat more random, and its enzymatic actitivity is greatly reduced. The process is reversible, *e.g.*, the protein can be restoredto its original state. Denatured proteins are less soluble than normal proteins and lose their ability to crystallize.

denatured alcohol. Ethyl alcohol containing, sufficient methyl alcohol, acetone, methyl isobutyl ketone, hydroxybutyraldehyde, or other organic compounds to render it unsuitable for beverage use.

Deniges reagent for benzoyl group. A solution of 1 ml. 37% formaldehyde in 50 ml. concentrated sulphuric acid; used in testing for the presence of the benzoyl group. A brown-red colour, obtained on heating, indicates the presence of the benzoyl group.

Deniges reagent for halogens. A solution of 0.01 g. fuchsin in 10 ml. of water, decolourized by the addition of 100 ml. of a 5% aqueous solution to sulphur dioxide followed by acidification with glacial acetic acid and, concentrated sulphuric acid. This reagent gives a violet-red colour with free bromine, and a yellow colour with free chlorine.

Deniges reagent for (phosphate-arsenate). A volume of 50 ml. 10% aqueous ammonium molybdate solution of which 50 ml. concentrated sulphuric acid is added. This reagent is used, with stannous chloride solution, in testing for phosphate and arsentae. A blue colour indicates the presence phosphate or arsenate.

Deniges test for anilides. Many anilides, on boiling with alcoholic sodium hydrobromite solution, give a yellow-red precipitate and pungent smell of methyl cyanide.

Deniges test for benzoic acid. An aqueous solution of benzoic acid, when heated with acetic acid, ferric chloride solution, and hydrogen peroxide, gives a violet colour.

Deniges test for cadmium. Add enough ammonia to 5 ml. of the solution to form the ammine complex ion, and boil with 0.5-1.0 ml. of 5% thiourea solution. A yellow precipitate indicates the presence of cadmium.

Deniges test for chlorate. A solution of resorcinol in an aqueous solution of sulphuric acid gives a green colour when treated with chlorate.

Deniges test for cobalt, copper, nickel, and manganese. A solution of 3 g. trioxymethylene, 7 g. hydroxylamine chloride, and 15 ml. water is boiled until clear. One drop of this reagent and 2 drops of 1.0 N solution of sodium hydroxide give characteristic colours with 10 ml. of aqueous solution containing various metallic ions.

Deniges test for cyanide. To a mixture of 2 ml. 10% ammonia, 1 drop of 5% potassium iodide solution, add 20 ml. water, and 1 drop of 2% silver nitrate solution. The sulphides in the sample are precipitated with mercurie chloride, and the filtrate is treated with zinc and sulphuric acid, the gas evolved being absorbed in sodium hydroxide solution, which is then added to the opalescent reagent. The presence of cyanide causes the opalescence to disappear.

Deniges test for cyclic aldehydes. The addition of 0.02 g. α- or β-naphthol, dissolved in 1 ml. ethanol to a 1% alcoholic solution of many cyclic aldehydes, followed by the addition of 2 ml. concentrated sulphuric acid, yields intense colours or fluorescence.

Deniges test for ethanol in methanol. Add 5 ml. of 0.6% (by volume) bromine water to 0.2 ml. of the methanol. Heat in boiling water bath until it is decolourized (not more then 5-6 minutes). Cool and add fuchsin-sulphurous acid. A red to violet colour, appearing in 5-8 minutes, shows the presence of ethanol.

Deniges test for glycol. On oxidation with potassim permanganate and treatment with resorcinol dissolved in sulphuric acid, a wine red colour indicates the presence of glycol.

Deniges test for hydrogen peroxide. Mix 2 ml. 5% tartaric acid solution with 2 drops 5% ferrous ammonium sulphate solution. Add 1–2 drops of the hydrode solution to be tested, than 5–6 drop sodium hydroxide solution and shake. A violet color shows the presence of hydrogsn peroxide.

Deniges test for isothiocyanates. A solution of 5g. mercuric oxide in 20 ml. sulphuric acid and 75 ml. water, on shaking this reagent with one-half its volume of the liquid to be tested, filtering and boiling, precipitation of characteristic crystals of dithiomercuric sulphate indicates the presence of isotheocyanates.

Deniges test for maganese. The dilute solution of manganese ions (II) when treated with sodium hypobromite solution, gives a brown blak precipitate, and a red supernatant.

Deniges test for mercaptans, If an alcoholic solution of a mercaptan is added to a few ml. of a solution of 1 g. isatin in 10 ml. concentrated sulphuric acid to which several volumes of concentrated sulphuric acid have been added, a green colour is formed.

Deniges test for metaldehyde. Metaldehyde, when treated with conc. sulphuric acid gives a blood-red colour with a small crystal of guaiacol.

Deniges test for α- and β-naphthol. Heat small pieces of titanium dioxide in concentrated sulphuric acid nearly to boiling; cool, decant the clear liquid, which gives a green colour with α-naphthol and a blood-red colour with β-naphthol; the addition of glacial acetic acid changes the α-naphthol colour, only, to violet-red.

Deniges test for nickel. With 1–2 ml. concentrated hydriodic acid solution, a drop of 4% nickel solution gives a blood-red colour which disappears on dilution with water.

Deniges test for nitrite. A few ml. of the solution to be tested is boiled with a solution of 2 ml. aniline in 40 ml. glacial acetic acid and 60 ml. water. In the presence of nitrite a yellow colour is obtained.

Deniges test for seleniun. The dry material is treated in a porcelain dish with a drop of 5% thiourea solution, followed by the addition of drop 1 N hydrochloric acid, selenite ion gives a red precipitate at once; selenate only after several minutes.

Deniges test for sulphanildes. Several mg. of the substance are heated in a test tube for 20-30 seconds with 0.02-0.03 g. potassium ferrocyanide (powdered). The peculiar smell of mercaptan confirms the presence of sulphanilides.

Deniges test for tartrate. The testing material is boiled with 1 ml. of a solution of 2 g. resorcinol in 100 ml, water and 0.5 ml. concentrated sulphuric acid. A red colour indicates the presence of tartarate. Any oxidizing substance if present, must first be reduced with zinc and hydrocholoric acid.

denitrification. 1. Any process for removing or altering the nitro group in an organic compound. The nitro group may be altered by reduction, being converted into the amino group and then the nitrogen may be wholly removed from the compound by diazotizing the reduction product and boiling with water or alcohol.

2. Bacterial decomposition of nitrates with production of gaseous nitrogen. The bacteria which effect the change are termed as denitrifiers. Also known as denitration.

density of probability. In quantum mechanics density of probability is defined as limit of ratio of probability of finding system in some volume element to its volume. Density of probability is given by modulus square of corresponding wave function.

density of states. Ratio of number of quantum mehanical states of system with continuous or quasi-continuous energy sprectrum in a very small energy interval ΔE to value of this interval. Derivative of number of qantum mechnical states of system with respect to its energy.

dental gold. An alloy of gold containing 5 to 12% silver and 4 to 10% copper.

deodorant. A substance, either with or without an independent odour, which has the effect of reducing, removing, or replacing the undesireable odours of other substances. It acts in several ways. For example, activated carbon adsorbs molecules of malodorous materials ; aluminium chlorohydrate neutralizes acidic components of perspiration ; materials having a pungent but pleasant smell replace or mask the unwanted odour, *e.g.*, peppermint, pine oil, menthol, camphor, etc.

deoxidiser. Any substance which reduces the amount of oxygen in a substance, especially a metal, or reduces oxide compounds. Also known as deoxidant.

deoxygenation. Removal of oxygen from a substance, such as blood or polluted water.

deoxyribonucleic acid. *See* DNA.

deoxyribonucleotides. Nucleotides containing 2-deoxy-D-ribose as the pentose component.

deoxy sugar. A substance that has the chracteristics of a sugar, but shows a deviation from the required hydrogen to oxygen ratio.

dephlegmation. A process for increasing the efficiency of fractional distillation by forcing the vapours from the still to bubble through shallow, layers of condensate in a column or "dephlegmator," whereby the amount of low-boiling component in the vapour is increased and a substantial portion of the higher-boiling components is retained in the condensate.

depleted materials. The material in which the amount of one or more isotopes of a constituent has been reduced by an isotrope separation process or by a nuclear reaction.

depolarization in metal deposition. The deposition of a metal by electrolytic process at the cathode at higher potentials than normal, by virtue of the ability of the metal to form, a solid solution or a compound with the cathode.

depolarizer. Agent preventing polarization of electrode, *e.g.*, manganese dioxide MnO_2 in Leclanche cell.

depolymerization. Reversion of polymerization ; decomposition of polymer with formation of simpler components ; monomers, dimers etc.

deposition potential, ϵ_W. Electrical potential which should be exceeded to observe effective course of a given electrode process, $\epsilon_W = \epsilon + \eta$, where ϵ=reversible electrode potential and η= overvoltage of tested electrode process.

depressant. 1. A term occurring in the flotation process, where a depressant is used to reduce the concentration of undesired substances in the air-solution interface ; and consequently, to redues the amount of these undesired substances appearing in the product.

2. A narcotic or sedative agent that acts upon the cerebrospinal nervous system.

depth dose. Dose of ionizing radiation at defined depth (mostly at 0.1 metre) ; usually depth dose is defined relatively to surface dose as percentage.

depurant. A drug used to effect purification of the system by stimulating excretion.

derivative. A term used in organic chemistry to express the relation between certain known or hypothetical substances and the compound formed from them by simple chemical processes in which the nucleus or skeleton of the parent substance exists. Thus phenol, aniline, and toluene are derivatives of benzene, and many of the terpenes are derivatives of cymene.

derivatography. Branch of thermal analysis that examines substances by simultaneous thermogravimetry and differential thermal analysis.

derosination. Removal of excess of resins from wood by saponification with alkaline aqueous solutions or organic solvents.

desalination. Removal of the mineral salts from seawater or saline waters (brines) to produce potable fresh water conforming to standard purity requirements. This can be done in a number of ways. The three methods that have proved most satisfactory on a large scale are flash distillation, reverse osmosis and electrodialysis. Ordinary solar evaporation has been utilized on a small scale in several localities. An alternative term with virtually the same meaning is demineralization.

desamination. *See* deamination.

desaturation. The revese process of saturation, as applied to an organic compound, whereby a saturated compound becomes unsaturated, as a hydrocarbon by catalytic dehydrogenation.

desensitization. 1. The action of rendering less subject to reactian brought about by light, as *e.g.*, in the case of a photographic emulsion.

2. The action of destroying or inactivating immune bodies.

desiccants. 1. Chemicals that kill leaves of plants, the leaves may either drop of or remain attached. These are used on many seed crops to hasten harvest ; the leaves are cleaned from seed in hervesting. Such chemical have also been used during war to destroy vegetation.

2. Substance used to withdraw moisture from other materials. *See also* desiccation.

desiccation. Removal of water vapour from a material by a hygroscopic substance, such as anhydrous calcium chloride, phosphorus pentaoxide, or silica gel, placed in an air-tight container with the material to be dried (often under vacuum). The term is conventionally restricted to laboratory control or chemical reagents, test samples, and the like and is not used for large-scale drying or dehydrating operation.

desmolase. Any of a group of enzymes which catalyze rupture of atomic linkages that are not cleaved through hydrolysis, such as the bonds in the carbon chain of D-glucose.

desmotropism. Obsolete term denoting tautomerism in which equilibrium rate is relatively low, thus enabling isolation of tautomers, *e.g.*, ketonic and enolic forms of ethyl acetoacetate, were called desmotropes. Also known as desmotropic isomerism.

desorption. The reverse of absoption or adsorption, as in the release of one substance which has been "taken into" another by a physical process, or the release of a substance which has been held in concentrated form upon a surface.

desoxy compound. A compound which has lost oxygen, by replacement of a hydroxyl group by a hydrogen atom.

destearinate. A process of removing from a fatty oil the lower melting point compounds.

destructive activation analysis. Activation method of analysis in which activity of the element to be determined is measured after its separation from an irradiated sample by chemical methods.

destructive distillation. Heating complex substance to produce chemical changes in it, and distilling off the volatile substances so formed, *e.g.*, the destructive distillation of coal produces coal-gas and many other valuable products.

destructive hydrogenation. *See* hydrogenolysis.

desulphurization. Elimination of sulphur atom from molecule of chemical compound; usually effected with Raney nickel, *e.g.*,

$$R_2S+Ni+C_2H_5OH \rightarrow 2RH+NiS+CH_3CHO$$

detection. 1. The identification of an element or compound in a substance or a material.

2. Process leading to making visible or detection of chromatographic bands or spots of

normally colourless substances in column, on filter paper etc.

3. Detection and characteristics of nature, energy and number of particles or photons emitted by the sample examined.

detergent. A substance used to enhance the cleansing action. It is a surface-active compound, either natural or synthetic. Oil soluble detergents are used in gasoline and lubricating oils to hold particulate impurities in suspension. Among the water soluble detergents, alcohols and common soaps are effective. Still more so are the synthetic types (syndets) such as sulphonated dodecylbenzene and similar alkylates. The linear alkyl sulphonates (LAS) are more biodegradable than are the branched-chain type ; they are made from petrochemicals by various cracking and polymerization techniques. Detergent action is promoted by phosphatic compouuds called builders. Detergents may be nonionic, cationic. or anionic, depending on the nature and behaviour of the molecules involved in emulsification.

determination. Quantitive estimation of content of a given component in studied sample. Also known as estimation

detonation. The almost instantaneous decomposition of a high explosive substance as a result of ignition, shock, or impact, resulting in the propagation of an intense high-pressure wave traveling from 1 to 10 km a second at the point of initiation. Well-known detonating explosives are trinitrotoluene (TNT), nitroglycerin, dynamite, tetryl, cyclonite, pentaerythritol tetranitrate (PETN), mercury fulminate, lead azide, and ammonium nitrate-fuel oil mixture. Detonation is also possible with some low explosives (nitrocellulose) when confined and exposed to friction or impact.

detonation wave. The specific value for the rate at which an explosive combustion spreads throughout a body of gas when it is once started at any point. It is much faster than the velocity of sound in the same gas *e.g.*, for $2H_2+O_2$; it is 2.810×10^3 meters per second, and for $C_2H_2+2O_2$ 2195×10^3 meters per second. Also known as explosion wave.

deuteration. Replacement of hydrogen atom in molecule of chemical compound by deuterium atom. Also known as deuterium exchange.

deuterium. The rare natural isotope of hydrogen having atomic mass of 2.014 instead of the normal 1.008 ; the extra mass is due to the presence of a neutron in the nucleus in addition to the proton. Deuterium is often called heavy hydrogen, and water containing it, heavy water (deuterium oxide). The natural occurrence of this isotope is one in every 6500 parts of normal hydrogen. All the chemical properties of deuterium, including high flammability, are identical with those of hydrogen.

deuteron. The nucleus of a deuterium atom ; it contains one proton and one neutron and thus has a mass of 2 and a positive charge of 1 ; used to bombard other nuclei to produce radioactive isotopes, as in a cyclotron. *See also* deuterium.

Devarda's alloy. An alloying containing copper (50%), aluminium (45%), zinc (5%). When a substance containing a nitro-group is warmed with this alloy and caustic soda solution, its nitrogen is released in the form of ammonia gas. If used as a test for a nitrate, the ammonium ion must first be proved absent.

De vathaire process. A metallurgical process for the desulphurization of impure molten iron by treatment with alkaline earth cyanides and carbon.

developer. 1. A reducing agent used in the development of films and other materials containing photosensitive substances which have been exposed to the action of light.

2. In dying technology, an organic compound which will unite or combine with another compound in or on the fibre to form or "develop" a new colour, often having improved properties.

development. 1. In general, development is the growth and differentiation in the structure of an entity, such as a crystal or an organism, and the acquisition of new characteristics.

2. In photography, development is a process whereby the exposed light-sensitive film or other material is treated with a chemical agent to reduce or otherwise change enough of the photosensitives substance (such as silver bromide to free silver) in order to produce a vesible (reverse) image of the object photographed. This step is necessary because the initial exposure merely transforms enough of the photosensitive substance to serve as a

starting point (probably as a system of nuclei) for the development.

3. In charomatography, passing of appropriate mobile phase through column or layer of stationary phase to get separation as result of differences in migration rates of components being separated.

devitrification. The crystallization of glass, detected by the appearance of opaque areas.

dextran. Any of several polysaccharides, $(C_6H_{10}O_5)n$ that yield glucose units on hydrolysis.

dextrin. A polymer of D-glucose which is intermediate in complicity between starch and maltose.

dexitrinization. The process of converting a starch into dextrins.

dextro-levo modifieation. *See* racemic modification.

dextrorotatory. An organic compound containing an asymmetric carbon atom, which has the property of turning the plane of polarized light to the right; such compounds usually exist in the form of so-called optical isomers, one of which is dextrorotatory and the other levorotatory, the latter turning the plane of polarized light to the left. Dextrorotatory is indicated either by the italic letter *d* prefixed to the name, or by a plus sing (+); levoratory isomers are indicated by italic *l*, or by a minus sign (—). The use of + and — signs is now perferred.

dextrose. A dextrorotatory sugar, also called glucose, which occurs naturally in corn and grapes and is also found in blood. A member of the general class of carbohydrates, it is formed in plants by photosynthesis; it is a monosaccharide having the formula $C_6H_{12}O_6$. Dextrose is an optical isomer of levulose (fructose), which is levorotatory. Dextrose polymers form amylose, a basic constituent of starch.

di-. A prefix meaning "two; " in the names of compound, it indicates the presence of two atoms of the same element (sulphur dioxide, SO_2). It also appears in more general terms such as dipole (two electric poles), diolefin (two double bonds), dimer (two molecules united), and diatomic (two atoms); the last of these has no connection with diatom or diatomaceous earth, which are named from a biological genus. *See also* dia- ; bi-.

dia-. A prefix having several meanings: 1. "passing through," as in dialysis, diaphragm, diameter; 2. "opposite to," an in diamagnetic; 3. "complete" or "throughout," as in diagnosis It is not a prefix in the word diamond.

diabatic. Involving a thermodynamic change of state of a system in which there is a transfer of heat across the boundaries of the system.

diacidic base. A base which, for its complete neutralization, requires two molecules of a monobasic acid.

diactinic. Having the property of transmitting actinic (chemically active) radiation.

diactinism. The property of transmitting chemically active radiation.

dialysed iron. Ferric hydroxide colloidally dispersed in aqueous solution. It is a positive sol, and is used in various medical preparations.

dialysis. The separation of a colloid from ions and molecules in solution by means of a parchment membrane. Ions and molecules pass through the membrane but the colloid is retained. If the mixture is placed in a parchment bag, and water is constantly flown round the bag, eventually a complete "washing" of the colloid will be effected.

diamagnetic. A diamagnetic substance is repelled by a magnet and will tend to take up a position at right-angles to the field of an electromagnet. Such substances have magnetic permeabilities that are less than unity. Most stable molecules are diamagnetic because their electrons are paired. Molecules that have unpaired electrons are paramagnetic.

diamagnetic anisotropy. Anisotropy of magnetic susceptibility of diamagnetic crystal given by three fundamental susceptibilities X_1, X_2 and X_3 measured along three mutually prependicular fundamental magnetic axes.

diamagnetic bodies. *See* diamagnetics.

diamagnetics. Substances with negative magnetic susceptibility and magnetic permeability less than one. Also known as diamagnetic substances ; diamagnetic bodies.

diamagnetic screening of nucleus. *See* diamagnetic shielding of nucleus.

diamagnetic shielding of nucleus. Participation of electrons in magnetic shielding of nucleus, leading to nuclear magnetic resonance shifts in direction of higher static field or lower frequencies of alternating magnetic field. Also known as diamagnetic screening of nucleus.

diamagnetic substance. *See* diamagnetics.

diamagnetic susceptibility. Negative magnetic susceptibility induced by external magnetic field in all bodies and related to Larmor precession.

diamagnetism. The property of a substance that has a small negative magnetic susceptibility and is repelled by magnets. This type of magnetism is due to a change in the orbital motion of the electrons in the atoms of the substance consequent on the application of an external magnetic field. The phenomenon occurs in all substances, although the resulting diamagnetism is often masked by the much greater effects due to paramagnetism or ferromagnetism.

diamine oxidase. A flavoprotein which catalyzes the aerobic oxidation of amines to the corresponding aldehyde and ammonia.

diaphorase. Mitochondrial flavoprotein enzymes which catalyze the reduction of dyes, such as methylene blue, by reduced pyridine nucleotide such as reduced diphosphopyridine nucleotide.

diastase. An enzyme that catalyzes the hydrolysis of starch to maltose.

diastereoisomerism. Type of stereoisomerism caused by different spatial arrangement of atoms or groupings of atoms (*i.e.*, by different configuration) in compound that are not enantiomers. This different spatial arrangement does not result from restricted rotation about single bond. Stereoisomers having two or more chiral centres are said to be diastereoisomeric when they have identical configuration at some chiral centres.

diastereoisomers. Stereoisomers which are not enantiomers. The following combination are possible : both diastereoisomers are chiral (I) ; one is chiral, the other achiral (II) ; both are achiral (III and IV)

```
     COOH          COOH
  H—|—OH        H—|—OH
  H—|—OH       OH—|—H
     CH₃           CH₃
            I

     COOH          COOH
  H—|—OH        H—|—OH
 HO—|—H         H—|—OH
     COOH          COOH
            II

     COOH          COOH
  H—|—OH        H—|—OH
  H—|—OH       HO—|—H
  H—|—OH        H—|—OH
     COOH          COOH
           III

H—C—COOH        H—C—COOH
  ‖               ‖
H—C—COOH     HOOC—C—H
           IV
```

diathermal wall. *See* diathermic partition.

diathermic partition. Partition which allows energy transfer in the form of heat but does not allow for mass or energy transfer in the form of work. Also known as diathermal wall ; thermally conducting wall.

diatomaceous earth. A light, bulky, high-silica material considered to be the petrified remains of microscopic sea life of an earlier geologic period. It has considerable ability to absorb liquids and thus being used as a decolourizing and purifying agent. Its most important application are as a filter medium, as a diluent in many types of industrial mixture, in paper coating, and as a carrier for catalysts. Its low conductivity of heat and sound account for its use in both thermal and acoustic insulation. The material is also called diatomite and sometimes kieselguhr.

diatomic gas. 1. A molecule composed of two atoms of the same element, which is a gas at room temperature ; the elements which normally occur as diatomic gases are nitrogen (N_2), oxygen (O_2), hydrogen (H_2), and the halogens.

The molecular form of these elements should be distinguished from their atomic form, which occurs in compounds.

2. A molecule composed of two atoms of different elements which is a gas at room temperature, *e.g.*, carbon monoxide, hydrogen chloride. Unless otherwise stated, meaning (1) is generally assumed.

diatomite. *See* diatomaceous earth.

diazine. A cyclic compound having two nitrogen atoms in the ring. In many cases, the six-membered ring-diazine compounds have individual names, thus

```
        N
      /   \
    HC     CH
    ||     |
    HC     CH
      \   /
        N
```

is pyrazine (*p*-diazine). Similarly, *m*-diazine is called pyrimidine, and *o*-diazine is called pyridazine.

diazo. The radical —N=N— or N≡N=.

diazoamine. The grouping —N=NNH—. Also known as azimino.

diazole. A cyclic hydrocarbon with five atoms in the ring two of which are nitrogen atoms and three are carbon atoms.

diazoate. A substance of the general formula R—N=N—OM, in which R is an organic (usually aryl) radical and M is a metal ion, or ammonium radical, etc.

diazonium compound. A derivative of the diazonium hydrates

```
     R
     |
   N≡N
     |
     OH
```

in which the hydroxyl group is replaced by an acid radical.

diazo reaction (Griess). The method of diazotization by the action of nitrogen trioxide on primary aromatic amines in acid solution, as represented by the equation :

$$2C_6H_5NH_2+N_2O_3+H_2O+2HNO_3 \rightarrow 2C_6H_5N{=}NNO_3+4H_2O$$

The name of Griess is also mentioned to denote the diazotization reaction itself, not being limited to the specific reaction above in which nitrogen trioxide is used.

diazo reaction (Knoevenagel). Diazotization reaction, in which the aromatic amines are treated with an alkyl nitrite or nitrosyl chloride, *e.g.*,

$$C_6H_5NH_2+RONO+HCl \rightarrow C_6H_5N{=}NCl+ROH+H_2O$$

diazo reaction (Witt). Diazotization reaction in which the aromatic amines are dissolved in nitric acid, to which is added a reducing agent to form the nitrous acid for the diazotization, *e.g.*,

$$2C_6H_5NH_2+4HNO_3+Na_2S_2O_5 \rightarrow 2C_6H_5N{=}NNO_3+Na_2S_2O_7+4H_2O$$

diazotization. The introduction the diazo group into a compound, usually effected by treating an amine with any compound of nitrogen capable of releasing nitrogen oxides, as from nitrites or nitrous acid. The amino group is converted into the diazo group, *e.g.*,

$$C_6H_5NH_2+NaNO_2+HCl \xrightarrow{0^\circ\text{–}5^\circ} C_6H_5{-}N{=}N{-}Cl$$

dibasic. 1. A term used to describe an acid either inorganic or organic, whose molecule contains two hydrogen atoms that can be replaced by basic elements to form salts. Examples are sulphuric acid (H_2SO_4) and oxalic acid (HOOCCOOH). Dibasic inorganic acids liberate two hydrogen ions when dissolved in water.

2. An inorganic compound whose molecule contains two atom of a basic univalent element, for example, dibasic sodium phosphate (Na_2HPO_4).

dichroism. Feature of plate cut of optically anisotropic material that, viewed in the directions of principal optical axes, has different colours. Dichroism is caused by differences of light absorption coefficients in directions of principal optical axes.

didymium. 1. A mixture of the metals or oxides of several rare-earths extracted from monazite sand. Its salts are used to some extent in manufacture of special glasses and in electronic equipment.

2. A name given to a mixture of praseodymium and neodymium which was originally thought to be an element in the rare-earth series.

Dieckmann intramolecular cyclization. *See* Dieckmann reaction.

Dieckmann reaction. A method of effecting ring closure between an ester group and a δ- or ε-methylene group, by heating with sodium and alcohol, as, for example,

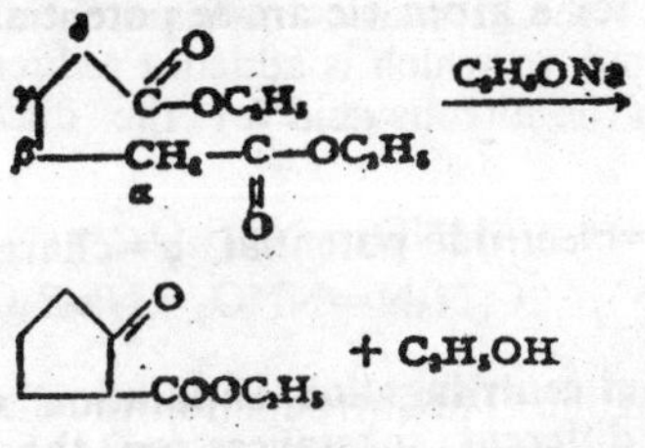

$$\text{(δ, γ, β, α)}\ \ \text{C(=O)–OC}_2\text{H}_5 \ \ \text{CH}_2\text{–C(=O)–OC}_2\text{H}_5 \xrightarrow{\text{C}_2\text{H}_5\text{ONa}} \text{(cyclopentanone)–COOC}_2\text{H}_5 + \text{C}_2\text{H}_5\text{OH}$$

This reaction is a special case of Claisen condensation.

dielectric. Substance undergoing electric polarization and of very low electric coductivity (insulator).

Liquid dielectrics often called transformer oils, include silicone oils, minerals oils, and chlorinated hydrocarbons (askarels).

dielectric constant. A value that serves as an index of the ability of a substance to resist the transmission of an electrostatic force from one charged body to another, as in a condenser. The lower the value, the greater the resistance.

dielectric dispersion. Decrease of dielectric permittivity with increasing frequency of electric field.

dielectric polarization. 1. Veotor quantity equal to electric dipole moment per unit volume of dielectric.

2. Formation of macroscopic dipole moment in dielectric due to external electric field.

Value of induced dipole moment is usually refered to unit volume or to 1 mole.

dielectric relaxation. Delay of dielectric polarization with respect to electric field changes.

dielectric relaxation time. Time interval after electric field is switched off in which dielectric polarization decreases to $1/e$ its original value.

dielectric saturation. Limit of the change of permittivity induced by external electric field.

dielectric spectroscopy. Branch of spectroscopy dealing with investigation of dielectric properties of matter as function of frequency of applied electromagnetic fields ; it covers measurements of absorption and dispersion dielectric spectra.

Diels-Alder reaction. A synthesis which takes place by addition to the 1,4 position of a compound containing two conjugated double bonds of another unsaturated compound, commonly an anhydride of an unsaturated acid, although other unsaturated compounds may be used. *e.g.*,

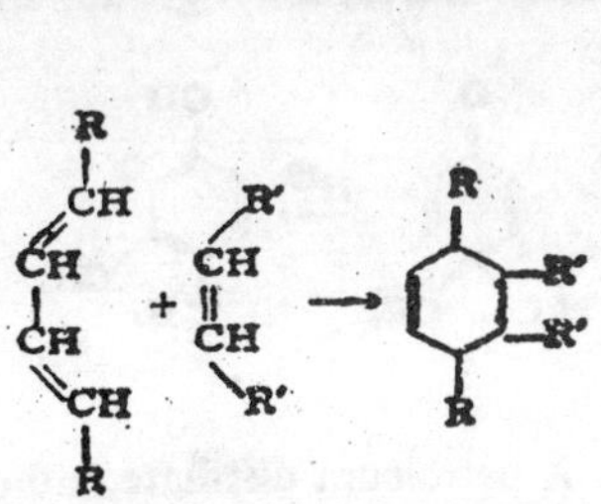

$$\text{R–CH=CH–CH=CH–R} + \text{R'–CH=CH–R'} \longrightarrow \text{(cyclohexene ring with R, R', R', R)}$$

Since two π-bonds are converted to sigma bonds in the course of such tronsfarmations, the resulting increase in thermodynamic stability causes most Diels-Alder reactions to be exothermic. At high temperatures Diels-Alder reactions are reversible. Also known as Diene synthesis.

Diene analogues. Dienes containing conjugated bonds between heteroatoms or between carbon atom and a heteroatom, *e.g.*, α, β-unsaturated aldehydes or ketones,

$$\text{H–CH=CH–}\overset{\text{H}}{\overset{|}{\text{C}}}\text{=O} \qquad \text{R–CH=CH–}\overset{\text{R'}}{\overset{|}{\text{C}}}\text{=O}$$

Also known as Diene anologs.

dienes. Alkenes that contain two carbon-carbon double bonds. Dines are divided into three classes according to the arrangement of the double bonds. Double bonds that alternates with single bonds are conjugated. Double bonds that are seperated by more than one single bonds are isolated. Double bonds that share a carbon are cumulated, and the compounds are called allenes. For example,

$CH_2=CH-CH=CH_2$ 1,3-Butadiene (conjugated diene)

$CH_2=CH-CH_2-CH=CH_2$ 1,4-Pentadiene (Isolated diene)

$CH_2-CH=C=CH_2$ 1,2-Butadiene (cumulated diene)

The chemical properties of a diene depend upon the arragement of its double bonds.

diene synthesis. *See* Diels-Alder reaction.

dienone-phenol rearrangement. Acid-catalyzed rearrangement of alicyclic dienones to correspoding phenols, involving migration of two hydrogen atoms, or in certain cases, of one hydrogen atom and an alkyl gronp, *e.g.*,

O H⊕ OH

H_3C CH_3 CH_3 CH_3

diesel fuel. A petroleum distillate, either stright-run or partially cracked, used as a power source for diesel engines ; it is equivalent to the No. 2 grade of domestic fuel oil. It contains a high percentage of aliphatic hydrocarbons. It is suitable for use in heavy automotive equipment and is being increasingly used in automobiles. Its performance is rated by the cetane scale. *See also* cetane number.

diesel fuel additives. Compound added to diesel fuels to imporve performance such as cetane number improvers, metal deactivators, corrosion inhibitors, antioxdants, rust inhibitors, and dispersants.

diesterase. An enzyme such as nuclease which splits the linkages binding individual nucleotide of a nucleic acid.

Dieterici equation. A form of the equation of state, relating pressure, volume, and temperature of gas, and the gas constant. The Dieterici equation applies a correction to the van der Waals equation to allow for variation in density throughout a gas, due to the higher potential energies of molecule on or near the boundaries. One form of this equation is

$$p(Vm-b)=RT\exp\left(\frac{-a}{RTVm}\right)$$

where p = pressure, Vm = molar gas volume, T=thermodynamic temperature, R=universal gas constant, a, b=constants characteristic for the given gas.

differential absorptiometry. *See* differential spectrophotometry.

differential capacity of double layer, *C*. Capacity of electrical double layer at electrode-solution interface for a given electrode potential

$$C=\frac{dq}{d\varepsilon}$$

where ε=electrode potential, q=charge of the electrode.

differential centrifugation. Saparation of molecules of different substances on the basis of their different rates of sedimentation in a centrifugal field.

differential colorimetry. *See* differential spectrophotometry.

differential cross-section. Cross-section for nuclear process whereby an angle is specified (relative to direction of incidence) for emission of particles or phtons per unit solid angle.

differential flotation. Separation of a complex ore mixture into two or more mineral components and gangue by flotation.

differential heat of dilution. *See* partial heat of solution.

differential method (of determining the order of reaction). Method of determination of reaction order n, consisting in determination of reaction rate with respect to defined concentrations of reaction substance. Logarithm of rate v is linear function of logarithm of concentration c and slope of line is equal to order of reaction n

$$n=\frac{\lg v_2-\lg v_1}{\lg c_2-\lg c_1}$$

differential polarography. Polarography based on recording and analysis of dependence of derivative of current with respect to potential on potential of dropping mercury electrode.

differential process. A process in which a system is caused to move through a bubble point and as a result to form two phases, the minor phase being removed from further contact with the major phase ; thus the system continuously changes in quantity as well as composition.

differential spectrophotometry. Spectrophotometric method of determination of concentration of investigated solution by measurement of its absorption with respect to standard solution of substance to be determined and of known and similar concentration. Also known as differential colorimetry ; differential absorptiometry.

differential thermal analysis, DTA. Thermal analysis carried out under comparison of increases in temperatures of specimen and reference substance on heating at a constant rate.

differential thermogravimetric analysis. Thermal analysis in which the rate of material weight change upon heating versus temperature is plotted ; used to simplify reading of weight-versus-temperature thermogram peaks that occur close together.

differential thermometric titration. Thermometric titration in which titrant is added simultaneously to the reaction mixture and to a blank in identically equipped cells.

differentiating solvent. Solvent in which equivalent conductivity of electrolytes is strongly dependent on nature of electrolyte ; for salt—solvent which does not form stable crystalline solvent, for acids—protogenic solvent—and for bases, protophilic solvent.

diffuse series. A series of lines in the spectra exhibited by many atoms which, either in their normal state or as the result of an ionization, possess one, two or three electrons in the outer shell. The diffuse series differs from the other series for such elements in having a somewhat distinctive physical appearance, and in having a charateristic formula,

$$\nu_D = L - \frac{R}{(m+c)^2}$$

where ν_D = the wave number of a line in the diffuse series, L and c = constants for the diffuse series, m = variable integer, whose values give the various lines in the diffuse series and R = Rydberg constant. Atoms possessing but a single electron, such as hydrogen, singly ionized helium, doubly ionized lithium, etc., do not give rise to such a series.

diffusion. The mutual permeation of two or more substances due to the kinetic activity of their molecules. so that a uniform mixture or solution results. Diffusion occurs with all forms of matter ; it is most rapid for gases somewhat, slower for liquids and for solids in solution. Gases of different densities will mix uniformly counter to gravity.

For gases, the rate of diffusion is inversely proportional to the square roots of their densities. Miscible liquids of different molecular weight diffuse into each other, *e.g* , alcohol and water. Solids in solution (suger, salt) move through the solvent unit a uniform concentration results, as, for example, salts in ocean water. Two metals in close contact also show a slight tendency to diffuse. Diffusion also takes place when a barrier or film of a microporous solid (metal or cellulosic) is placed between two gases or between two liquid solutions of different concentrations ; in the latter case, the rate depends on the relative strength of the concentrations.

diffusion analysis. The determination of the relative size or molecular mass of particles by comparing their diffusion rates or by comparing them by differential diffusion methods.

diffusion bonding. A solid state process for joining metals by applying only heat and pressure to achieve atomic bonding.

diffusion cell. A chamber used for the extraction of soluble materials from mixtures with insoluble solids. The process is slow, because of the time required for diffusion from the interior of the mass, and, therefore, counter-current flow is usually employed and sufficient capacity provided to give sufficient time for the process to be completed.

diffusion coefficient. Magnitude D defined by Fick's first law, equal to quantity of diffusing component through unit area in unit time, when change of one unit of concentration occurs at unit length.

diffusion current. In polarography with a dropping-mercury electrode, the flow that is controlled by the rate of diffusion of the active solution species across the concentration gradient produced by the removal of ions or molecules at the electrode surface.

diffusion kernel. The neutron flux resulting from a point source emitting one neutron per second; it is a function of the distance between the source and the point where the flux is measured.

diffusion layer. Layer of electrolyte with different concentration of potential-determining ions in comparison to bulk of solution; it forms near electrode as result of diffusion polarization.

deffusion model of radiolysis. Model explaining chemical effects of ionizing radiation absorption by diffusion of intermediate products of radiolysis in bulk of solution from spurs where they are formed in high concentration.

diffusion number. A dimensionless number used in the study of mass transfer, equal to diffusivity of a solute through a stationary solution contained in the solid, times a characteristic time divided by the square of the distance from the mid point of the solid to the surface.

diffusion plant. A plant which separates isotopes by isotopic diffusion or thermal diffusion.

diffusion polarization. Type of concentration polarization; it is due to transport of reactants to or from electrode surface, slow in comparison to electrode reaction rate. Diffusion polarization is expressed by diffusion overvoltage.

diffusion potential. When liquid junctions exist where two electrolytic solutions are in contact, as in the case of two solutions of different concentrations of the same electrolyte, diffusion of ions occurs between the solutions, and the differences in rates of diffusion of different ions set up an electrical double layer, having a difference of potential, known as the diffusion potential or liquid junction potential.

diffusivity analysis. Analysis of (difficult to separate) materials in solution by diffusion effects, using, for example, dialysis, electrodialysis, interferometry, amperometric titration, polarography, or voltammetry.

digestion. 1. The breakdown of cellulosic fibres by the action of heat and chemicals (both acids and alkalies), as occurs in the pulping of wood and in the reclaiming of automobile tires. As a result of digestion with sodium hydroxide solution, for example, the cellulose is separated from the lignin in wood pulp, and the fabric content of tires is separated from the rubber.

2. Preferential dissolving of mineral constituent during concentration of ores.

3. Decomposition of solid or semisolid organic wastes such as garbage, cellulosics, sewage, etc., by the action of bacteria, either with or without the presence of air. Air is used in the activated sludge method of treating sewage wastes and in the compositing of garbage and agricultural wastes.

4. The metabolic sequence of events by which food is decomposed in the body. *See also* metabolism.

dihexagonal. Said of crystals, having a symmetrical form with 12 sides.

dihexagonal-dipyramidal. Characterized by the class of crystals in the hexagonal system in which any section perpendicular to the six-fold axis is dihexagonal.

dihexahedron. A type of crystal that has 12 faces, such as a double six-sided pyramid.

dihydrate. A compound with two molecules of water of hydration.

dihydric. An alcohol characterized by the presence of two hydroxyl (OH) groups; this classification is represented by the glycols. The term diol is sometimes used synonymously. *See also* glycol.

diketones. Organic compounds containing two keto (—C=O) groups. They are classified according to number of carbon atoms separating the two keto groups. α- 1,2 diketones are formed from their monoximes. β- 1,3-diketones ($R.CO.CH_2.CO.R$) are obtained by the reaction between an ester and a ketone in the presence of metallic sodium or sodamide. γ or 1,4-diketones ($R.CO.CH_2.CH_2.CO.R$) are formed by treating sodium acetoacetic ester with α-bromoketones and hydrolysing the product.

dilatancy. The property of certain colloidal solutions of becoming solid, or setting under pressure. Dilatancy is one of the gel-sol transformations known under the general term of thixotropy.

dilatation. The increase in volume per unit volume of any continuous substance, caused by deformation.

dilation number. Ratio of the volume of a liquid to the volume of a solid of the same composition at the same temperature.

diluent. An inert substance used to increase the volume of some other substance or solution.

dilute. Not concentrated. A solution in which the solvent is in great excess. A relative term of inexact nature unless qualified by a statement of the actual concentration.

dilute solution method. Method of dipole moment measurement of polar compound in non-polar solvent based on assumption of additivity of molar polarizations of components.

dilution method. Method of colorimetric analysis for determination of concentration of coloured solution by equalizing its absorption with that of standard after dilution of one of these solutions. Then,

$$c_1 l_1 = c_2 l_2$$

where l_1, l_2 correspond to absorbing layer thickness and c_1, c_2 = concentration of investigated and comparative solution respectively.

dilution ratio. The ratio of the maximum volume of a liquid which can be added to a solution without causing precipitation, to the total volume of solution.

dimer. A compound consisting of a combination of two molecules of the same compound.

dimerization. Combination of two identical simple molecules of chemical compound (monomers) resulting in formation of more complex molecule (dimer), *e.g.*,

$$2(CH_3)_2C{=}CH_2 \xrightarrow{H_2SO_4} (CH_3)_3CCH_2\overset{\overset{\displaystyle CH_3}{|}}{C}{=}CH_2$$

$$\text{butadiene} + \text{butadiene} \xrightarrow{\Delta} \text{4-vinylcyclohexene}$$

diminoflore. An atom or group which, by its substitution in a molecule, tends to reduce the intensity of the fluorescent radiation bands of that molecule.

diol. *See* dihydric.

diolefin. Any of a series of unsaturated hydrocarbons containing two double bonds; they are also called dienes or alkadienes. Diolefins fall into two groups ; those in which the double bonds are conjugated and those in which they are not conjugated. Conjugated diolefins are either straight-chain (1,3-butadiene) or cyclic structures (cyclopentadiene), which readily undergo polymerization.

diolefin hydrogenation. A fixed bed catalytic process used to hydrogenate diolefins in C_4 and C_5 fractions to mono-olefin in alkylation feedstocks.

-dione. Suffix indicating the presence of two keto groups in a molecule.

diose. A member of a class of monosaccharides that have two carbon atoms ; the only compound that belongs to this class is glycoaldehyde.

dip brazing. Soldering by dipping the job into a hot, molten salt or metal bath and by using a nonferrous metal with a melting point above 427°C.

dipeptidase. An enzyme that hydrolyzes the dipeptide linkage.

1,3-dipolar addition. Reaction of $\overset{+}{a} - \ddot{b} - \overset{-}{c}$ dipole molecule with alkene molecule, resulting in formation of cyclic system, *e.g.*,

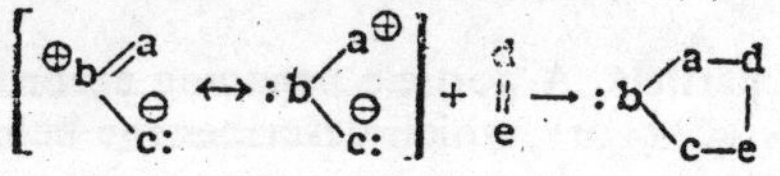

$$\left[{}^{\oplus}b{\lower{0.3em}{}}\begin{smallmatrix} // a \\ \backslash \overset{\ominus}{c}: \end{smallmatrix} \leftrightarrow :b\begin{smallmatrix} / a^{\oplus} \\ \backslash \overset{\ominus}{c}: \end{smallmatrix} \right] + \begin{smallmatrix} d \\ \| \\ e \end{smallmatrix} \longrightarrow :b\begin{smallmatrix} / a - d \\ \quad\;\; | \\ \backslash c - e \end{smallmatrix}$$

dipole-dipole interaction. Electrostatic intermolecular interaction between two polar molecules ; two permanent parallel dipole moments μ_1 and μ_2 separated by distance r in medium of electric permittivity ε interact with energy :

$$\text{(a)}\ U_{(r)} = \pm \frac{2\mu_1\mu_2}{\varepsilon r^3} \qquad \text{(b)}\ U_{(r)} = \pm \frac{\mu_1\mu_2}{\varepsilon r^3}$$

(formulae in e.s.u. CGS system) where + sign corresponds to repulsive energy for the same direction of both dipoles and — sign represents attractive energy for antiparallel dipoles.

dipole interaction. *See* dipole-dipole interaction.

dipole moment A force vector exhibited in molecules having closely juxtaposed positive and negative charges, which constitute an electric dipole, absolute (scalar) value equal to

$$|\mu| = |q| \cdot d$$

where $|q|$ = absolute value of one of pole charges ; d = mutual distance between poles.

Sometimes opposite definition of dipole moment direction is utilized which is in disagreement with definition of polarization vector direction. In this case dipole moment should be represented by →.

The value of a given dipole moment is generally expressed in electrostatic units (e.s.u). It is due to variations in the location of nuclear (positive) charges and electronic (negative) charges in the molecule. It occurs in such polar compounds as nitrobenzene, acetonitrile, benzaldehyde, water, alcohols, and amino acids ; hydrocarbon liquids have a very low value, and carbon dioxide and carbon tetrachloride have zero. In SI units it is expressed in coulomb . metre. *See also* dielectric constant ; polar compound.

diprotic acid. An acid capable of dissociating two protons.

Dirac equation A relativistic wave equation for an electron in an electromagnetic field, in which the wave function has four components corresponding to four internal states specified by a two-valued spin coordinate and an energy coördinate which can have a negative or positive value.

Dirac particle. A porticle behaving according to the Dirac theory, which describes the behaviour of electrons and neutrons except for radiative corrections, and is envisaged as describing a central core of a hadron of spin 1/2 h which remains when the effects of nuclear forces are removed.

Dirac theory. Theory of electron based on Dirac equation, which accounts for its spin angular momentum and gives its magnetic moment and its behaviour in an electromagnetic field (except for higher-order corrections).

diradical. A molecule possessing two separate free electrons, *e.g.*,

$$(C_6H_5)_2\dot{C}.C_6H_4.[CH_2]_4 C_6H_4.\dot{C}(C_6H_5)_2$$

direct dye. A water-soluble organic dye, usually a sodium or potassium salt of an azo dye, which is adsorbed directly by the fibres of cotton, rayon, and other cellulosic materials. Alkaline assistants are often added to promote efficient concentration, and detergents are commonly used as well. Such dyes may be introduced in colloidal form, but they will not be effective until a molecular dispersion is achieved (by increasing the temperature of the bath). The alkaline addition retards ionization of the dye molecules, which would prevent satisfactory dyeing action ; only the undissociated molecule of the dye can be absorbed by the fibres. *See also* dye.

directing effect. The effect of substituent groups already present in benzene and other aromatic derivatives which forces new substituent groups, about to enter the molecule, into definite positions relative to the original groups.

direct isotope dilution. Isotope dilution in which substance of natural isotopic composition is determined by addition of the substance labelled with isotopic tracer.

disaccharides. Carbohydrates consisting of two covalently joined monosaccharide units.

discharge. 1. The effluent from a plant, process, apparatus, etc.

2. The action by which it is expelled. The latter meaning has a common connotation of suddenness, from its use for electric spark discharges

3. In dyeing technology, to cause a colour to disappear from a fabric by means of a chemical reaction ; substances used for this purpose are called discharging or stripping agents, *e.g.*, titanous sulphate.

4. Neutralization of electrical charge of ion by exchange of electron ; usually this description is limited to exchange of electrons between ion and electrode.

5. In electrochemistry, to withdraw or subtract electrical energy from a system, such as a battery or an electrically stabilized colloidal suspension.

discharge potential. A charateristic value of the electrode potential, observed in the electrode potential-current relationship determined for an electrode in contact with an ionic solution The distinguishing feature of this value is that it marks a point of inflection, at which the current increases very rapidly with small increase in electrode potential. The high current value is marked by discharge of ions upon the electrode.

discomposition. The process in which an atom is knocked out of its position in a crystal lattice by direct nuclear impact, as by fast neutrons or by fast ions that have been previously knocked out of their lattice positions.

discontinuous spectrum. *See* discrete spectrum.

discontinuous system. System composed of parts with discontinuities of thermodynamic properties at interfaces.

discrete spectrum. A spectrum in which the component wavelengths constitute a discrete sequence of values rather than a continuum of values. In spectroscopic terminology, the term is used for line and band spectra. Also known as discontinuous spectrum.

disinfectant. A substance having the ability to kill or inactivate bacteria, but usually of too great strength or toxicity for use on living tissue. Among these are certain-mercury compounds, phenols, formaldehyde, quaternary ammonium salts, and some synthetic detergents. High temperature and ultraviolet radiations are also employed for similar purpose. *See also* antiseptic.

disinfestant. A substance that acts to destroy insects, worms, ants, mice, and other animal pests. *See* rodenticide, insecticide etc.

disintegration. 1. Loss of form or powdering.

2. The passage of a metal into colloidal solution when it is used as an electrode under certain conditions.

3. Transformations of radioactive elements are sometimes termed disintegrations, when they result from radioactivity.

dismutation. A mutation, or change, which yields two products from one, as observed in the Cannizzaro reaction.

dispergation. Pulverization of relatively large particles of a given substance in order to obtain disperse system.

disperse dyes. Dyes of all chemical types that are applied in the form of fine suspensions in water to man-made fibres, such as cellulose nylon, and polyester fibres. They are insoluble in water, but are usually soluble in organic solvents, such as esters.

disperse medium. The medium in which a colloid is dispersed, in a manner analogous to that of the solvent in a true solution. Also known as dispersive or dispersion medium; continuous phase.

disperse phase. The distributed phase in a colloidal system, *i.e.*, the phase which is composed of the distributed particles.

disperse system. Colloidal system physically inhomogeneous consisting of two phase.

dispersing agent. *See* surface-active agent.

dispersion. 1. A system comprised of two phases, one of which is in the form of finely divided particles, often in the colloidal size range, distributed throughout a bulk substance; the particles are usually called the internal or disperse phase and the medium in which they are distributed, the external or continuous phase. Under natural conditions is seldom uniform, but under controlled conditions it can be made so by use of wetting or surface-active agents, such as a fatty acids. There are a number of possible systems: gas/liquid (foam); solid/gas (aerosols); gas/solid (cellular rubber); liquid/gas (fog); liquid/liquid (emulsion); solid/liquid (paint); and solid/solid (carbon black in rubber). Dispersions of solids in liquids are called suspensions. If the solid or liquid particles are larger than colloidal, they will eventually agglomerate, coalesce, and settle out by gravity. Some dispersions (fat particles in milk) can be stabilized with protective colloids; on the other hand, they can be precipitated by addition of electrolytes, as in water clarification process.

2. In optical terminology dispersion refers to the retardation of a light ray as it passes through or into a transparent medium; a change of direction is ustally involved. The extent of the phenomenon depends on the frequency of the radiation and the refractive index of the medium. Dispersion is a critically important property of optical glass. *See also* refractive index.

dispersion effect. One of the consequent of intermolecular forces. Dispersion effects leads to attractive forces between molecules of electrically neutral non-polar character and can be explained in terms of electron density fluctuations in interacting sub systems.

dispersion medium. Component or components of disperse system forming continuous phase. Also known as continuous phase.

dispersoid. A colloidal system in which the dispersity is relatively great, as in emulsoids and suspensoids.

disphenoid. 1. A crystal form with eight scalene triangles combined in pairs.

2. A crystal form with four similar triangular faces combined in a wedge shape ; can be tetragonal or orthorhombic.

displacement. 1. A chemical reaction in which one molecule, atom, or radical is replaced by another, as, for example, in the reaction $Zn+CuCl_2 \rightarrow Cu+ZnCl_2$, in which molecular zinc replaces copper atoms (ions) in the compound cupric chloride. forming zinc atoms (ions) and metallic copper.

2. Chromatographic method that consists in washing out of mixture of components from column with the help of agent whose affinity to stationary phase is greater than that of any of components being separated.

displacement cell. An electrolytic cell in which the essential chemical reaction is the ionization and entry into solution of atoms of one element; and the discharge and deposition from solution of the ions of another. A well-known displacement cell is the Daniell cell, in which metallic zinc dissolves in a zinc sulphate solution, yielding zinc ions, while copper ions are discharged and deposited from the copper sulphate solution, with accompanying flow of electricity in an external circuit.

disproportionation. A type of decomposition reaction in which one ion or compound is simultaneously oxidized and reduced. The reaction usually require heat and a catalyst). For example,

$$2Cu^+ \rightarrow Cu + Cu^{2+}$$

$$2C_6H_5CHO \xrightarrow{\overline{OH}} C_6H_5COOH+C_6H_5CH_2OH$$

$$2C_2H_4 \rightarrow C_2H_6+H_2C{=}CH_2$$

Alternatively, a redistribution of groups around a central atom, *e.g.*,

$$2PF_4Cl \rightarrow PF_3Cl_2 + PF_5$$

Also known as dismutation.

disproportionation of radicals. Stabilization of free radicals, involving hydrogen atom transfer from one radical to another ; two stable molecules are thus formed, *e.g.*, ethylene and ethane from two ethyl radicals

$$2C_2H_5\cdot \rightarrow H_2C{=}CH_2+H_3C{-}CH_3$$

dissipation. The interaction between matter and energy incident on it, such that the portion of energy used up in the interaction is no longer available for conversion into useful work.

dissociation. A specific kind of decomposition occurring (*a*) when a molecule of a diatomic gas (Cl_2) is separated by heat into its constituent atoms, and (*b*) when an inorganic compound in aqueous solution separates into charged particles (ions), *e.g.*, hydrochloric acid in water dissociates to form positively charged hydrogen ions (H^+) and negatively charged chloride ions (Cl^-) (electrolytic dissociation). In sense dissociation is synonymous with ionization. *See also* decomposition ; ionization ; electrolysis.

dissociation constant. *See* instability constant.

dissociation field effect. Increase of equivalent conductance of an electrolyte as a result of increase of number of ions in solution in case of high electric field (10^4—10^5 V/cm).

dissymetry factor. *g*. A quantity used to express conveniently the magnitude of circular dichroism (refer to the Cotton effect). It is defined by the following formula :

$$g = \frac{(K_l - K_r)}{K}$$

where g = dissymmetry factor, K_l and K_r = absorption indices for the left- and right-circularly polarized light, and K = absorption index for ordinary light of the same wavelength. Also known as anisotropy factor.

distillate fuel. A broad term for any one of the wide variety of fuels obtained from fractions boiling above gasoline in the distillation of petroleum. The most important distillate fuels are kerosine, furnace oils, and diesel fuels.

distillation. Separation of the components of a mixture (usually of liquids or solutions) by heating to the boiling point and condensing the resulting vapour. In mult-component mixtures such as petroleum, the various fractions have different boiling points ; thus it is possible to effect separation by condensing the vapour of each component in turn, the lower-boiling fractions distilling-off first (fractional distillation). Distillation of petroleum thus yields fuel oils, gasoline, kerosine, naphthas, and ultimately a tarry or waxy residue, depending on the geographical origin of the petroleum. Distillation is also employed to purify many other organic liquid products.

distillation, compression. *See* compression distillation.

distillation, destructive. *See* destructive distillation.

distillation, fractional. *See* fractional distillation.

distillation, steam. *See* steam distillation.

distillation, vacuum. *See* vacuum distillation.

distribution. In its most general sense, the arrangement, occurrence, or presence of a substance in a defined space or area. Specifically, the types of distribution important in chemistry include (*i*) the amount or concentration of a substance in two or more phases of a multiphase system, (*ii*) the occurrence of a substance in the earth's crust, (*iii*) the scattering and local concentration of a food or drug throughout the animal organism, (*iv*) the relative amount of an acid which reacts with two bases present in a reaction system, or of a base with two acids, etc.

distribution coefficient, D_g. Ratio of equilibrium concentrations of substance in stationary and mobile phase respectively.

distribution isotherm. In chromatography, isotherm characterizing dependence between equilibrium concentrations of given substance in stationary and mobile phase respectively.

distribution law. If two partially or nearly immiscible liquids are in contact and a substance which is soluble in both liquids be added to the system, the added will be distributed between them in such a way that the ratio of the concentration of the two solutions formed is a constant regardless of the quantity of solute. (Measurable deviations from this law take place especially in concentrated solutions, because of association, ionization, chemical action, etc.) The constant is termed the distribution ratio, constant, or coefficient, and the partition coefficient. Also known as the partition law; distribution law of Nernst.

disulphide. One of a group of organosulphur compounds, R S-S-R′, that may be symmetrical (R=R′) or unsymmetrical (R≠R′). They are of great biochemical interest, since S-S link occurs in natural products ; the S-S cleavage in proteins has biological and industrial interests in dehairing of hides and in the preparation of cysteine from wool.

disulphide bridge. A covalent cross-link formed between two polypeptide chains by a cystine residue.

diuretic. A drug that increases the secretion of urine. It may act by stimulating the functional activity of the kidneys, by raising the osmotic pressure of the blood, or by increasing blood pressure. Among the most common diuretics are the acetate and citrate of potassium, digitalis, buchu, uva ursi, and caffeine.

divergence. In a nuclear reactor, the condition wherein the number of neutrons produced increases in each succeeding generation.

divers liquid. A concentrated solution of ammonium nitrate in liquid ammonia. This solution is known for its solvent action, especially upon metals, metallic oxides, and metallic hydroxides.

***dl*-.** A prefix indicating a mixture of equal parts of dextro- and levorotatory crystals, which results in optical inactivity. The symbol ± is also used. *See also* meso-(1) ; racemic.

DL-. A prefix indicating that a compound contains equal parts of D and L stereoisomers. *See also* racemic ; meso-(1).

D line. The yellow line that is the first line of the major series of the sodium spectrum ; the doublet in the Fraunhofer lines whose almost equal components have wavelengths of 5895.93 and 5889.96 Å respectively.

DNA (deoxyribonucleic acid). A polynucleotide having a specific sequence of deoxyribonucleotide units and serving as the carrier of genetic information.

DNA chimera. A DNA containing genes from two different species.

DNA ligase. An enzyme that creates a phosphodiester bond between the 3′ end of one DNA segment and 5′ end of another, while they are base-paired to a template strand.

DNA polymerase. An enzyme catalyzing template-dependent synthesis of DNA from its deoxyribonucleoside 5′-triplephosphate precursors.

DNA replicase system. The entire complex of enzyme and specialized proteins required in biological DNA replication.

Dobell solution. An aqueous solution of 1.5%

sodium borate, 1.5% sodium bicarbonate, phenol, and glycerol. It is used as an antiseptic commonly for the throat.

Dobner reagent. A solution of 5.0g. guaiaconic acid in 1 litre alcohol and 1 litre water. It is used to detect cyanides, hydrogen peroxide, or blood, each of which gives a blue colour with this solution. With blood in feces, the colour with this reagent may be green instead of blue.

doctor test. A method used in petroleum technology to determine the content of obnoxious-smelling thiols in gasoline and other distillates. These odors can be diminished (a process called "sweetening" the product) by treating the gasoline with a solution of lead oxide in sodium hydroxide, usually with addition of sulphur (doctor solution). By this means the offensive thiols are changed to disulphides, which have a less noticeable smell.

Doebner-Miller synthsis. A method of formation of quinoline derivatives from aromatic amines and two molecules of an aldehyde (or one molecule of an aldehyde and one molecule of a ketone) in the presence of HCl or certain other mineral acids.

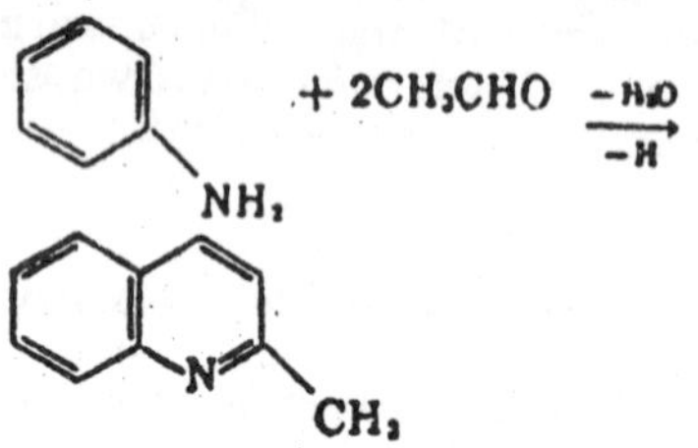

NH_2 + $2CH_3CHO$ $\xrightarrow[-H]{-H_2O}$

CH_3

Doebner reaction. *See* Doebner synthesis.

Doebner synthesis. Preparation of 2-substituted derivatives of cinchonic acid by condensation of arylamine, aliphatic (or aromatic) aldehyde and pyruvic acid, *e.g.*,

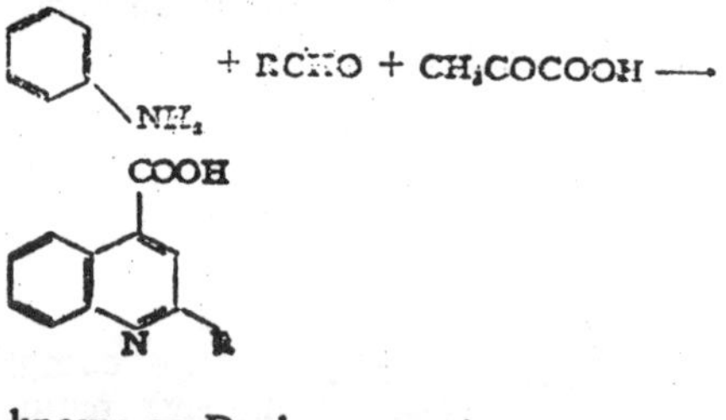

NH_2 + RCHO + $CH_3COCOOH$ ⟶

COOH

N R

Also known as Doebner reaction.

Dohmee reagent. An aqueous solution of trichloracetic acid and picric acid plus acetic acid or citric acid; used as a precipitant for albumin.

domains. Regions of spontaneous magnetization in magnetic materials (*e.g.*, in ferromagnets or spontaneous polarization in ferroelectrics.

domain structure. Structure exhibited by ferromagnets and ferroelectrics due to presence of large number of zones (domains) of different mutual orientation in absence of external magnetic field (for ferromagnets) or electric field (for ferroelectrics).

Donnan equilibrium. The particular equilibrium set up when two coexisting phases are subject to the restriction that one or more of the ionic components cannot pass from one phase into the other. Commonly the restriction is caused by a membrane which is permeable to the solvent and small ions but impermeable to colloidal ions or charged particles of colloidal size. The presence of membrane is not essential, since the restriction of movement on the charged colloid can be provided by a centrifugal or gravitational field or by gel coherence.

Donnan potential. *See* membrane potential.

donor. A nucleophilic atom or ion which donates an electron pair to another atom, thus creating a covalent bond. The electron-deficient atom, called the acceptor, is said to be electrophilic. Donor and acceptor atoms are involed in acid-base reactions, carbon linkage formation, and coordination compound formation. The term is derived from the Latin word for "give." *See also* nucleophile.

donor-acceptor complex. Combination of molecules which are electron donors with molecules which are acceptors of electrons. Linked molecules are capable of independent existence. Also known as charge-transfer complex ; molecular complex.

donor centre. Atom of valency higher than normal constituent of crystal (*e.g.*, admixture of arsenic in germanium crystal), the presence of which causes formation and occupation by electron of new allowed energy band, located just below conductivity band (in range of forbidden band). Also known as donor impurity.

donor impurity. *See* donor centre.

donor level (donor state in band model of solid state). Local, filled energy level situated in area of forbidden band and connected with presence of donor centre in crystal.

dope. 1. A substance (usually a metal or metallice oxide) added in trace amounts to laser crystals and semiconducting elements to provide essential properties for these applications. For example, neodymium and chromic oxide are used as activators for yttrium-garnet and ruby lasers, while arsenic is added to germanium to enhance its semiconducting properties.

2. A carbon-containing additive to dynamite.

Dorn effect. The development of a difference in potential by the motion of particles through water. The potential difference is established between the particles and the water. Also known as electrophoretic potential; sedimentation potential.

dose. 1. Industrially, the term is often used in reference to the percentage of an active ingredient added to a mixture. as, for example, the accelerator dosage in rubber mixture.

2. In medicine, it refers to the amount of any medicine prescribed by a physician.

3. In radiation therapy it means the amount of radiation of any type administered to a patient; the so-called permissible dosage of X-radiation is 0.3 roentgen a week.

double bond. A linkage between two multivalent atoms, usually carbon, in which one valence of each atom is unsatisfied; the two "free" valence are thus available to unite with univalent atom of other elements such as hydrogen, chlorine or any other element under appropriate conditions. Double bonds are weaker than single bonds, but compounds containing them are much more reactive than saturated compounds.

double bond, cumulated. Two double bonds linked to same carbon atom as in

$$R_2C=C=CR_2$$

double bond shift. The shift of a double bond within a chemical compound as in

$$RCH=CH-CH_3 \rightarrow RCH_2-CH=CH_2$$

double comparator. A device used to project and to compare standard and sample spectrum. Also known as twin comparator; comparator.

double decomposition. A term used to express the interaction of molecules which exchange one or more of their constituent atoms or radicals to form new substances, *e.g.*,

$$NaCl+AgNO_3 \rightarrow AgCl+NaNO_3$$

double escape peak. Peak in gamma radiation spectrum generated as a result of formation of electron-positron pair, annihilation of positron formed and escape of both annihilation photons from detector.

double helix. The natural coiled conformation of two complementary, antiparallel DNA chains.

double resonance. Magnetic resonance with two alternating fields, one H_1 of frequency equal to resonance frequency of spin system I (nuclear or electronic) and another H_2 corresponding to resonance frequency of spin system II (nuclear or electronic). If two systems interact this may lead to substantial changes in resonance signal of spin system I and in turn to its simplification.

double salt. A salt that upon hydrolysis forms two different anions or cations.

2. A compound of two salts formed by crystallization from a solution containing both of them. When redissolved, the double salt ionizes as two salts. For example, potassium sulphate and aluminium sulphate in solution together will crystallize as the double salt

$$K_2SO_4.Al_2(SO_4)_3.24H_2O$$

doublet. In atomic spectroscopy, set of spectral lines arising from energetic transitions between two atomic doublet terms.

doubly magic nucleus. Atomic nucleus in which both number of protons and number of neutrons are equal to magic numbers, viz. nucleus with occupied proton and neutron shells. Doubly magic nucleus has particularly high binding energy:

$$^4He,\ ^{16}O,\ ^{40}Ca,\ ^{48}Ca,\ ^{208}Pb$$

Also known as proton-and-neutron magic nucleus.

Downs process. A process for extracting sodium by the electrolysis of molten sodium chloride. A small amount of potassium fluoride is added to sodium chloride to lower its melting point. The Downs cell has a central carbon (graphite) anode surrounded by cylindrical steel cathode, chlorine released is led away through a hood over the anode. Molten sodium is formed at the cathode and is liquid at operating temperature, is trapped above the cathode. Since it is lighter than the molten sodium chloride, sodium is forced up into the rise and overflows into storage.

Dow process. The process for the extraction of magnesium from sea-water by precipitation of $Mg(OH)_2$ by adding $Ca(OH)_2$ followed by dissolution of the hydroxide in hydrochloric acid.

dowtherm. Mixture of high-boiling organic substances used for purposes of heat exchange.

drag effect. The effect of interionic attraction in reducing the freedom of an ion to move in an electrical field, because of the interference of the ions of opposite charge by which a given ion is surrounded. The drag effect is an essential feature of the explanation of the Debye-Huckel theory of the anomalous properties on concentrated solutions of strong electrolytes.

Draper effect. An increase in volume at constant temperature which sets in at the start of a gaseous combination; the phenomenon was discovered in the reaction between hydrogen and chlorine.

Draper law. The only radiation which is effective in causing a chemical change is that which is absorbed.

Drew number, N_A^D. A dimensionless group used in the study of diffusion of a solid material *A* into the stream of vapour initially composed of substance *B*, equal to ;

$$\frac{Z_A (M_A - M_B) + M_B}{(Z_A - Y_{AW}) M_B - M_A} \cdot \ln \frac{M_V}{M_W}$$

where M_A and M_B=molecular weights of components *A* and *B*, M_V and M_W=molecular weights of the mixture in the vapour and at the wall, Y_{AW} and Z_A=mole fractions of *A* at the wall and in the diffusing stream, respectively.

drier. A substance having the ability to catalyze the combination of oxygen with the unsaturated linkages of fatty acids in drying oils and to accelerate polymerization of synthetic resins in paints and printing inks. Such substances are metals heavier than sodium or compounds of these with unsaturated acids such as naphthenic, linoleic, etc. The most effective and widely used metals are cobalt and manganese, either as such or in the form of heavy-metal soaps (cobalt naphenate, manganese linoleate). *See also* drying

dropping mercury electrode. Electrode constructed from glass capillary with internal diameter of order of 5.0×10^{-5} m from which mercury flows in small drops.

dropping point. The temperature at which grease changes from a semisolid to a liquid state under standardized conditions.

drop time. In polarography, time between detaching of two successive drops of mercury from polarographic capillary, usually in interval 1 to 8 seconds.

dross. Oxidized metallic residues, or other metallic waste-products, such as the scum-material which forms on the surface of molten metals during refining or casting.

Drude equation. A relationship between the specified rotation of an optically-active substance and the wavelength of the light; of the form :

$$[\alpha] = \frac{k}{\lambda^2 - \lambda_0^2}$$

where $[\alpha]$=specific rotation. λ = wavelength, and k and λ_0^2 are constants, known as the rotation constants and the dispersion constant.

drug. A natural or synthetic chemical substance or mixture (also called a pharmaceutical) which has one or more of the following effects: (*a*) killing or inhibiting the growth of infectious organisms : (*b*) affecting the activity of a specific organ of the body ; (*c*) stimulating or depressing the central nervous system (narcotics, tranquilizers, and other psychotropic agents). Study of the chemical nature and behaviour of drugs is called medicinal or pharmaceutical chemistry ; the science of drug preparation is called pharmacy ; pharmacology includes study of both, with emphasis on the effects on the organisms.

dry cell. A primary battery (usually net rechargeable) ; these are two types, one of which is a self-contained assembly of the component chemicals, including the electrolyte (Leclanche cell), the other reserving the chemicals in dry form and adding electrolyte later. Dry cells have a relatively short life and tend to deteriorate on long standing, especially in a moist atmosphere. They are used chiefly in flashlights and small electrical systems requiring low energy output. *See also* battery.

dry chemical. A preparation designed chiefly for fire fighting, especially for fires involving flammable liquids, pyrophoric materials, and electrical equipment. Common types contain sodium or potassium bicarbonate, sodium chloride, and free flowing additives. *See also* extinguishing agent.

dry gas. A gas that does not contain fractions which may easily condense under normal atmospheric condition, for example, natural gas with methane and ethane.

dry ice. Solid carbon dioxide having temperature of 194K used to refrigerate foodstuffs in transit, for carbonation of liquids and for cold traps in laboratories. It sublimes from solid state to gaseous state with liquefying.

drying. 1. Evaporative loss of water or other solvent from a substance, usually a solid, with the aid of heat. Many food products and industrial materials are dried as an integral step in processing. The spray drying of such products as milk and soap to a powdered form can be considered as a type of dehydration. Organic coatings (both solvent- and water-based) also dry to evaporation, through polymerization is also involved in the case of paints containing organic solvents. Evaporative drying is not as intensive as dehydration, which removes over 95% of the water.

Removal of water by a mechanical device such as a screen or filter is called dewatering.

2. Polymerization of a vegetable oil or high polymer base in paints and varnishes, resulting in the formation of a protective film ; it is catalyzed by oxygen and is quite distinct from evaporative drying, which occurs simultaneously (but much more rapidly) in paints.

drying agents. Substances used to absorb moisture, especially in a desiccator and in towers through which moist gases are passed. The principal laboratory drying agents are sulphuric acid, fused calcium chloride, solid sodium hydroxide, calcium oxide, and phosphorus pentaoxide.

drying oil. Relatively highly unsaturated oil, such as cottonseed, soyabean, and linseed oil, that has the property of forming a hard, continuous film when exposed to air ; the atmospheric oxygen induces polymerization of the unsaturated fatty acids (glycerides) in the oil. The largest volume use of drying oils is in exterior paints, printing inks, and putty. They have been largely replaced in paints by synthetic latexes, such as acrylic, which polymerize in a similar manner.

dry point. In a laboratory distillation the thermometer reading observed when the last drop of liquid evaporates from the lowest point in the flask.

Duane-Hunt law. The increment in energy of an electron passing through an X-ray tube determines the maximum frequency of X-rays obtainable.

Dubbs process. A process for the simultaneous cracking and distilling of crude oil (or a fraction distilled therefrom) by the application of heat and pressure. The oil is preheated to about 670K and is circulated through steel tubes heated to about 720K, under a pressure of more than 10 pascal. The charge passes continuously into a chamber in which the vapour separates from the remaining liquid and carbon.

Dubsky-Wagner tests for magnesium. 1. To 50 ml. of the solution to be tested add 5 drops 0.05% solution of alizarin in alcohol, or 0.03% naphthazarin solution, then add a slight excess of 2.5 N sodium hydroxide. A blue precipitate (on warming if necessary) indicates the presence of magnesium.

2. With 0.03% naphthazarin and 10% ethylenediamine solution in 5 : 1 proportions, magnesium ions give a blue colour.

Duckert test reaction for antimony. A saturated alcoholic solution of 2,3,7-trihydroxy-9-methyl-6-fluorone give a bright red precipitate with antimony at *p*H 4.

Dudley solution for glucose. A solution of bismuth subnitrate in nitric acid to which an equal volume of acetic acid and 10 volumes of water are added. It is a test reagent for glucose. A black or grey colour, obtained on heating in alkaline solution, indicates the presence of glucose.

Duff-Bills phenolic aldehyde synthesis. Perparation of *o*-hydroxybenzoic aldehyde derivatives from phenols and hexamethyltetramine in acidic medium, *e.g.*,

$$C_6H_5OH \xrightarrow[H_2SO_4]{(CH_2)_6N_4} o\text{-}HOC_6H_4CHO$$

Dufour effect. Abnormal Zeeman effect. Individual lines show Zeeman effect in band spectra, if observed in a direction parallel to field and if circular vibrations are converted into plane ones with a quarter-wave plate, through Nicol prism.

Dufour number, Du_2. A dimensionless number used in studying thermodiffusion, equal to increase in enthalpy of a unit mass during isothermal mass transfer divided by the enthalpy of a unit mass of mixture.

Duhem-Margules relation. Equation which determines relation between volatilities a_{pi} of components of gas mixture at constant temperature T and pressure p :

$$\sum_i x_i (d \ln a_{pi})_{T,p} = 0$$

where x_i = mole fraction of i-th component and $\sum_i$ denotes summation over all components. Also known as Duhem-Margules equation).

Duhring rule. The rule that a plot of the temperature at which a liquid exerts a particular vapour pressure against the temperature at which a similar reference liquid exerts the same vapour pressure produces a straight or nearly straight line.

Dulong and Petit law. The product of the atomic weights and the specific heats of the solid element (*i.e.*, their atomic heats or thermal capacities) have nearly always the same numerical value, about 6.4. Many substances obey this law. Exceptions include silicon, boron beryllium, and carbon ; at high temperatures even these substances give values approaching 6.

Dumas' Method. A method for the quantitative estimation of nitrogen in an organic substance. A weighed amount of the compound is heated with a large excess of pure copper oxide in a combustion tube, and the nitrogen gas evolved is collected in a nitrometer over a 40% solution of caustic potash. Between the copper oxide mixture and the nitrometer the nitrogen passes over a hot copper gauze to reduce any oxides of nitrogen formed. A stream of carbon dioxide gas is passed through the apparatus before and after the heating.

duplex iron. Cast iron heated in an electric furnace after it has been melted in a cupola.

duplex process. A two step process in which steel is refined by one process (usually the Bessemer process) and finished by another process (usually open hearth or electric furnace).

duralumin. A light and hard aluminium alloy containing about 4% copper, and small amounts of magnesium, manganese, and silicon.

duriron. Iron containing small amount of carbon and more than 15.5% silicon.

Durour effect. Cross effect opposite to thermodiffusion, *i.e.*, heat flux accompanying isothermic diffusion.

Durrant test reaction. Cobalt is detected by adding to its dilute solution an excess of sodium bicarbonate and then some hydrogen peroxide or chlorine or bromine, with the development of an apple-green colour.

dust. An air suspension of solid particles ranging from 10 to 50 microns in diameter. The chemical nature of such particles may vary widely, as represented by coal and oil particulates (smoke), metal and metallic oxide fume, calcium carbonate, and organic materials such as flour, pesticides, etc. Most such dusts, when sufficiently concentrated in air, constitute a serious fire hazard and are capable of causing a severe explosion, if exposed to static sparks or flame under certain conditions. They are also a health hazard, particularly if they contain toxic components. Electrostatic precipitators have been used with considerable success in industry, and there are a number of dust-collecting devices available for manufacturing areas where dust may be unavoidable. Silica dust and mine dust are damaging to the lungs and require special precaution.

dusting agent. A powdery solid used as an abherent and mold-release agent in the plastics and rubber industries. Typical materials in general use are talc (soapstone), mica, fine sand, slate flour, and the like. Graphite and mica have a flat crystal structure which causes them to act as lubricants, and thus are especially effective in preventing sheets or slabs of hot solid mixtures from sticking together when stacked.

Dutch metal. An alloy of 80% copper and 20% zinc that is ductile, is easily drawn, and takes a high polish used for low-priced jewelry.

Dutch process. A process for making white lead; metallic lead is placed in vessels containing dilute acetic acid, and the vessels are stacked in bark or manure.

dye. Any substance capable of being absorbed from solutiou by fibres or of combining with them when mordanted to impart a colour to textiles and similar materials. Dyes are classified as direct, mordant, substantive, adjective, monogenetic, polygenetic, natural, synthetic, mineral, etc., according to their origin and mode of application.

dye, acid. A dyestuff that dyes animal fibres directly from an acid bath. Acid dyes are of little use for applcation to vegetable fibers, *e.g.*, nitro and azo dyes.

dye, acid mordant. An acid dye which requires a mordant for achieving best results on animal fibres.

dye, acridine. A dyestuff derived from acridine,

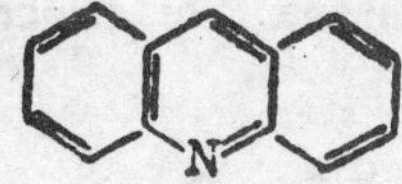

dye, adjective. A dyestuff that requires a mordant, as alizarin.

dye, artificial. A synthetic dyestuff, as distinguished from natural products. The most important synthetic dyestuffs are the coal-tar colours including azo dyes and phthaleins.

dye, azine. A dyestuff having the chromophore

group, R (N, N) R.

dye, azo. A dyestuff which has the azo group, —N=N— as its chromopore.

dye, basic. *See* basic dye.

dye, cyanine. *See* cyanine dye.

dye, direct. *See* direct dye.

dyeing assistant. Material such as sodium sulphate added to a dye to control or promote the action of a textile dye.

dye, ingrain. *See* ingrain dye.

dye, mineral. *See* mineral dye.

dye, monogenetic. *See* monogenetic dye.

dye, mordant. *See* mordant.

dye, natural. *See* natural dye.

dye, nitro. *See* nitro dye.

dye, nitroso. *See* nitroso dye.

dye, oxyazine. *See* oxyazine dye.

dye, polygenetic. *See* polygenetic dye.

dye, pyranine. *See* pyranone dye.

dye, substantive. *See* substantive dye.

dye, thiazine. *See* thiazine dye.

dye, triphenylmethane. *See* triphenylmethane dye.

dye, vat. *See* vat dye.

dynamic allotropy. A class of allotropic phenomena in which the transition from one form to another is reversible but with no definite transition temperature. The proportions of the allotropes depend upon the temperature.

dynamic isomerism. Isomerism due to intramolecular rearrangements by virtue of which one substance may react in accordance with two structural formulas, viz., cyanamide may react as $N{\equiv}C{-}NH_2$ or $HN{=}C{=}NH$. The terms dynamic isomerism and desmotropism have also been applied to the cases where the two forms have been found to exist, usually they are interconvertible; in fact, the compound exists as a mixture of the two forms in equilibrium. Also known as energy isomerism; dynamical isomerism.

dynamic reactivity indices. Reactivity indices following from consideration of electronic structure of molecule in transition state of given reaction. Dynamic reactivity indices provide measure of activation energy, *e.g.*, localization energy.

dynamite. A mixture of either nitroglycerin or ammonium nitrate with a carbon-containing material such as wood pulp or charcoal.

dysprosium. An element.

Group IIIB
(Lanthanide Series)

Symbol	Dy
Atomic No.	66
Atomic Wt	162.50
Valence	+3
Isotopes	6 stable
m.p.	1409°C
b.p.	2335°C

Dysprosium is a member of the rare earth family and occurs in gadolinite and several other ores. Dysprosium is paramagnetic, but as the temperature is lowered, it becomes antiferromagnetic at the Neel point (178 K) and ferromagnetic at the Curie point (85 K). At very low temperatures it shows strong anisotropic magnetic properties. It is uniquely noncorrosive in air. Dysprosium is relatively stable at room temperature. It reacts rapidly at high temperatures with a number of elements including halogens, oxygen, boron, hydrogen, and carbon. Its neutron cross-section is quite high (1100 barns), which has led to its use in measuring neutron concentrations and in reactor control.

dystectic mixture. A mixture of two or more substances in such proportions as to yield the maximum melting point, so that upon altering the proportions the melting point is lowered.

E

E. Symbol for ebullioscopic constant electromotive force, electrode potential, the einstein, a unit of energy, entrainment ratio for total energy, electric field strength, illuminance, and Young's modulus of elasticity.

E alloy. An alloy containing 76.5% aluminium, 20% zinc, 2.5% copper, 0.5% manganese, and 0.5% magnesium.

Eau de Cologne. Certain perfumed oils dissolved in alcohol and the mixture distilled. The oils used may include lemon, orange, bergamot neroli, and rosemary.

Eau de Javel(le). The solution obtained when chlorine is passed into cold alkali solution. It contains chloride and hypochlorite and may be used for bleaching. "Milton" and "Dakin's solution" are similar.

Eau de Labarraque. A solution similar to the above containing sodium hypochlorite and used for bleaching.

Eau de Vie. The name given to a variety of Brandy.

Eboli test reaction. Many alkaloids give characteristic colours when 1-2 mg of them are treated on a watch glass with 5-6 drops of a 1 : 1 sulphuric acid solution, followed by addition of a small piece of potassium dichromate.

ebulliometry. Accurate measurement or determination of the boiling point of a liquid under varying conditions of temperature and pressure. Ebulliometric method are used for determination of molar mass, degree of purity of substance, for investigation of liquid-vapour phase equilibrium, etc. Also known as ebullioscopy.

ebullating-bed reactor. A type of fluidized bed in which catalyst particles are held in suspension by the upward movement of the liquid reactant and gas flow. As known as slurry bed reactor.

ebullioscopic constant, *E*. Quantity given by equation

$$E = \frac{RT^2}{\Delta H} M$$

where R = molar gas constant, T = normal boiling temperature of solvent (in kelvins), ΔH = molar evaporation heat of solvent at boiling point, and M = molar mass of solvent.

ebullition. The phenomenon of bubble formation such as that accompanying boiling.

-ecane. A suffix indicating a 10-membered ring.

echelon grating. A diffraction grating designed for use in high orders and at angles of illumination and resolving power by the use of high orders of interference.

eclipsed conformation, $\pm sp$. Conformation in which the most bulky substituents at two adjacent carbon (for any other element, *e.g.*, silicon or nitrogen) atoms are sterically as near one another as possible. In Newman's projection formula, bond angles of less remote and more remote substituents equal 0°. This type of conformation is the least stable :

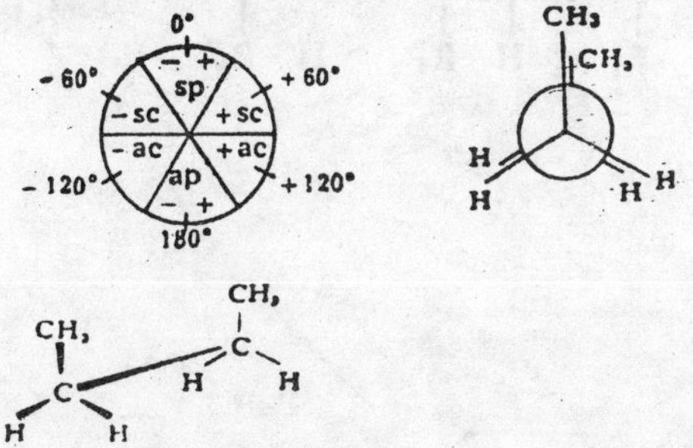

0°
−60° +60°
sp
−sc +sc
−ac +ac
−120° +120°
ap
180°

CH_3 CH_3
H H H H

CH_3 CH_3
C C
H H H H

Edeleanu process. An extraction process utilizing liquid sulphur dioxide for the removal of aromatic hydrocarbons and polar moleculas from petroleum fractions.

edge-bridging ligand. A ligand that forms a bridge over one edge of the polyhedron of a metal cluster structure.

edge dislocations. Rows of atoms forming edges of lattice planes running through parts of crystal only.

edible oil. Any of the fatty oils obtained from vegetables, nuts, and seeds, commonly used in food products, either as a liquid or in hydrogenated form. They include corn, soyabean, olive, safflower, cottonseed, coconut, peanut, and citrus seed oils. These oils are comprised largely of oleic, palmitic, linoleic, and other fatty acids. Fish- and shark-liver oils, used as dietary supplements for their vitamin content, and castor oil are also classed as edible oils. It may be noted that flavouring oils derived from flowers, such as wintergreen, coriander, clove, and citrus peels, are of different chemical composition and are called essential oils, even though they are edible. *See also* vegetable oil.

Edison cell. A secondary cell in which the plates are impregnated steel grids. The positive plate is a nickel/nickel hydrate mixture and the negative one is iron oxide. Potassium hydroxide is used as electrolyte. The cell is lighter and more durable than lead cells and is capable of delivering heavy currents having e.m.f. ≅ 13 volts.

This reaction is specific for *d*-amino functions. Repetition of it discloses the order of amino acid units at each of the peptide chain, and in the case of small to moderate-size peptides the complete sequeuce can be determined. An illustration of this reaction is :

$$H_2N{-}CH(R_1){-}C({=}O){-}NH{-}CH(R_2){-}C({=}O){-}NH{-}CH(R_3){-}C\ldots + \underset{\text{phenyl isothiocyanate}}{C_6H_5N{=}C{=}S} \xrightarrow{pH=9} C_6H_5NH{-}C({=}S){-}NH{-}CH(R_1){-}C({=}O){-}NH{-}CH(R_2){-}C\ldots$$

$$\xrightarrow{H^+} H_2N{-}CH(R_2){-}C({=}O){-}NH{-}CH(R_3){-}C\ldots + \underset{\text{a thiazolinone}}{C_6H_5NH{-}C{=}N{-}CH(R_1){-}C({=}O){-}S\ (\text{ring})}$$

$$\xrightarrow{H^+} \underset{\text{a phenylthiohydantoin}}{C_6H_5{-}N{-}C({=}S){-}NH{-}C(R_1){-}C({=}O)\ (\text{ring})}$$

Edlbacher test for proteins. Many proteins, after shaking with sodium hydroxide solution and dimethyl sulphate, give a blue-red ring test with concentrated sulphuric acid.

Edlefsen test for resorcinol. Resorcinol solution, when treated with an aqueous solution of β-naphthoquinone after the addition of ammonia, is coloured blue-green, changing to red with nitric acid. This test may also be used for β-naphthoquinone.

Edman degradation. In protein analysis, an approach to amino-end-group determination involving the use of a reagent, phenylisothiocyanate, that can be applied to the liberation of a derivative of the aminoterminal residue witout hydrolysis of the remainder of the peptide chain.

Eegriwe micro-test for phenol. A drop of the solution to be tested is added to a little *m*-nitrobenzaldehyde in a test tube ; after addition of 2 ml. 63% sulphuric acid, the mixture is heated to 340K. Appearance of pink colour indicates the presence of phenol.

Eegriwe reagent for tin. A solution of 0.01 g. diazine green S in 100 ml. water to which hydrochloric acid is added until the solution is blue. The solution to be tested is reduced with iron and hydrochloric acid, then the test reagent is superimposed on it. A violet ring, becoming red, indicates the presence of tin.

Eegriwe reagents for zinc. 1. A solution of 5-10 mg. metanil yellow or orange IV in 100 ml. water. One drop of it, mixed with 3 drops of 2% aqueous potassium ferricyanide solution, and acidified to a red colour with hydrochloric acid, becomes colourless in 5 minutes on addition of 1 drop of a weakly-acidic zinc solution.

2. A mixture of 0.25 ml. 2% aqueous potassium ferrocyanide solution and 0.3 ml. of an 0.25% diethylaniline (which must be free from monoethylaniline) solution in 50% phosphoric acid (The diethylaniline solution is added to potassium ferrocyanide.) One drop of a weakly-acidic zinc solution gives a brown-yellow to brown-red colour with this reagent.

Egriwe tests for cobalt. Add to 1 drop of the neutral solution to be tested, 5-10 drops of 0.02% solution of Eriochrome blue-balck B and 1 drop of a 3.5% sodium nitrite solution and acidify with 0.5 N acetic acid. A violet colour indicates the presence of cobalt (brown-violet if nickel is also present).

Egriwe test for lactic acid. One drop of the solution to be tested is heated with 1 ml. sulphuric acid for 2 minutes at 85°C, cooled to 25°C, and mixed with a little solid *p*-hydroxydiphenyl. A violet colour on standing confirms the presence of lactic acid.

Egriwe test for magnesium. The neutralized solution to be tested is treated with a 0.1% solution of benzoazurine-G, followed by the addition of 1 ml. concentrated ammonia. A blue precipitate indicates the presence of magnesium.

Egriwe test for nitrite and nitrate. Treat 1 ml. of the solution to be tested with 1 drop of a solution of 0 03 g. Safranine-T in 100 ml. water, and acidify with dilute sulphuric acid. A blue colour indicates the persence of nitrite.

Concentrate the solution to be tested, and add 3 drop of the Safranine-T solution, add some magnesinm powder and a few drops 2 N sulphuric acid, followed by a few more drops of the sulphuric acid after evolution of gas is over. A violet to blue colour indicates the presence of nitrate.

Egriwe tests for tartrate. 1. On heating with sulphuric acid containing β,β′-binaphthol, a green fluorescence shows the presence of tartrate.

2. On heating with sulphuric acid containing tannic acid, a blue, blue-green or green-yellow colour shows the presence of tartrate.

effect. 1. As a verb, to cause or bring about, as to effect a change of colour, state, condition or porperty.

2. As a noun a chamber in a series of evaporation and condensation units which is heated by the latent heat evolved by the condensing vapour from the preceding unit ; it is a type of heat exchanger. The number of effects in such a series is usually designated, *e.g.*, double-effect, triple-effect, etc., evaporator.

effective atomic number. Total number of electrons surrounding central atom of metal in complex. This number often is equal to atomic number of nearest noble gas.

effective collision. Collision of substrate molecules bearing activation energy. Collision results in change of substrates into products if it takes place with appropriate geometrical orientation.

effective cross-section for reactions of radicals. Quantitative expression for probability of inelastic collisions between free radical and second reactant which is stable compound or (sometimes) another free radical.

effective height of theoretical plate. It is the plate height in chromatography. It is defined as the thickness of column segment in which mean concentration of substance is in equilibrium with its own effluent.

effective mobility of ions. The average velocity of an ion due to electric force taken over a long time and including the periods of rest, *i.e.*, when the ion is neutralized ; or the average velocity of all the ions including those neutralized at the time.

effective number of Bohr magnetons, μ_{ef}. Magnetic moment of atom, ion or molecule determined from experimentally measured magnetic susceptibility according to assumption of its temperature dependence given either by Curie law or by Curie-Weiss law :

$$\mu_{ef} = 2.83\sqrt{C_M}\,\mu_B = 2.83\sqrt{\chi_M(T-\theta)}\,\mu_B$$

where μ_B=Bohr magneton, χ_M=molar magnetic susceptibility at temperature T, C_M=molar Curie constant, θ=paramagnetic Curie temperature.

effective quantum number. Number characteristic for given spectroscopic term of many-electron atom, defined as

$$n_{ef} = \sqrt{R/Tn}$$

where R = Rydberg constant and Tn=term energy. Effective quantum number differs from principal quantum number of given type of electron shells by approximately the same value ; it takes into account screening of nucleus by electrons.

effect of the state of aggregation. Differences in yield of products of radiolysis in the same system, but in different states of aggregation during irradiation.

effervescence. The formation of gas bubbles in a liquid as a result of chemical reaction. It occurs during fermentation, during the action of acids upon carbonates, etc. Boiling is not regarded as effervescence, nor is the frothing produced in such actions as that of concentrated sulphuric acid upon sugar.

efflorescence. The process in which a crystalline hydrate loses water, forming a powdary deposit. It depends on the partial pressure of water vapour in the air. When it is less than the dissociation pressure of the hydrated compound the latter gives up all or part of its water of crystallization and becomes powdery. Substances that are ordinarily efflorescent are sodium sulphate decahydrate, sodium carbonate decahydrate, magnesium sulphate heptahydrate, and ferrous sulphate heptaydrate. When the saturated solution of a substance in water has water vapour pressure greater than that of the surrounding atomosphere, evaporation of the water from solution takes place.

effluent. Any liquid, slurry, or gas emerging from a pipe or similar outlet. It is usually used in connection with waste disposal of chemical or manufacturing plants, such as stack gases and residual liquid or semi-liquid mixtures discharged into rivers or lagoons.

effluent volume. Volume of solution collected from chromatographic column up to given moment during run.

effusion. A process taking place when a gas under pressure escapes through a small orifice. Graham's Law applies to effusion as well as to diffusion of gases, and it is often more convenient to measure rates of effusion rather than rates of diffusion.

Ehrlich diazo reagent. A reagent prepared by mixing 1 ml. of a 0.5% aqueous solution of sodium nitrite and 50 ml of hydrochloric acid in water. This reagent is used for testing urine, determining urea, phenols etc.

Ehrlich reaction for indole. Dissolve the substance to be tested in 10 ml. benzene, add 2 ml. alcoholic solution of *p*-dimethylaminobenzaldehyde, and shake with 0.5 ml. hydorchloric acid. Indole imparts a violet-red colour to the aqueous layer.

Ehrlich-Sachs reaction. The condensation of aromatic nitroso compounds with compounds containing active methylene groups ;

$$RCH_2X + C_6H_5NO \rightarrow \overset{\displaystyle X}{\overset{|}{R C}}{=}NC_6H_5 + H_2O$$

Nitrones (compounds containing the group :C:NO—) may also be formed.

Ehrlich theory. A theory by which the mechanism of immunity from disease is explained in chemical terms. The process is explained in terms of two major classes of substances (each in turn composed of many sub-classes), present in the organism—the antigens and the antibodies.

Antibodies are present in the body as a result of action to counteract antigens which are really extraneous to the body, such as foreign protein produced by bacteria or injected, etc. They may or may not be toxic. Thus diphtheria or tetanus toxoid are nontoxic foreign proteins which cause the body to develop diphtheria or tetanus antitoxin (antibody).

To affect the cells, the antigens must enter into a chemical combination with the protoplasm, probably by means of side chains which couple together. The side chains may, according to Ehrlich, break away from the protoplasm, and circulating in the blood where they can combine with the antigens of the disease before the latter can reach the protoplasm. Thus, these broken-off side chains are the antibodies which render the organism immune to the disease.

Eichler amine reaction. A solution of 2 g. resorufin and 2 g. sodium carbonate in 1 litre of water, used as a test reagent for diazonium salts. The formation of a brown dye indicates the presence of diazo group. This solution is called an amine reagent because it can be used in testing for ordinary amines, after first diazotizing them.

Eichler nitrate reagent. A solution of 0.1 g.

magadala red in 100 ml. of formic or acetic acid, used as a reagent for nitrite in the presence of nitrate. Nitrites cause the disappearance of the fluorescence of this reagent and the appearance of a blue colour.

Eichler resorcinol solution. A solution of 0.5 g. resorcinol in 100 g. sulphuric acid; used in testing for nitrate, nitrite, and related inorganic anions. A violet colour, resulting from alkalinizng the residue obtained by evaporating the sample with the reagent,—indicates the presence of the nitrate, nitrite, or other inorganic anions.

Eichler test for nitrobenzene. Heat the material with sulphuric acid and resorcinol until a violet colour appears or sulphur trioxide is evolved. Cool, dilute, and neutralize with sodium carbonate. A violet colour indicates the presence of nitrobenzene. The test can be used conversely to detect resorcinol (or phenol).

eigenfunction. Solution of time-independent Schrodinger wave equation. It describes quantum-mechanical stationary states with definite energy values of system.

eigenvalue. If an equation containing a variable parameter possesses nontrival solution only for certain special values of the parameter these solution are called eigenfunctions and the special values are called eigenvalues, *i.e.*,

$$O\phi = c\phi$$

where O=operator, c=eigenvalue, ϕ=eigenfunction corresponding to this eigenvalue c.

The eigenfunction-eigenvalue relation is of particular importance in quantum mechanics because of its prominence in the equation which relate the mathematical formalism of the theory with physical results.

Eiloart test reaction for quinine. An aqueous solution of quinine gives a red colour on addition of the mixture of bromine water, mercuric cyanide solution, and calcium carbonate.

einstein. A unit of light energy used in photochemistry, equal to Avogadro's number times the energy of one photon of light of the frequency in question.

Einstein diffusion equation. An equation for the displacement, due to Brownian movement, of spherical colloidal particles, which may be expressd in the form :

$$\frac{x^2}{2\tau} = \frac{RT}{6\pi r\eta N}$$

in which x=mean displacement, along a given axis, of a particle in time τ, R=gas constant, T= absolute temperature, r = radius of the particle, η=viscosity of the gas, and N=Avogadro's constant.

Einstein equation for heat capacity. A quantum relationship for the heat capacity at constant volume of an element, of the form :

$$Cv = 3R\left(\frac{h\nu}{kT}\right)^2\left(\frac{e^{h\nu/kT}}{(e^{h\nu/kT}-1)^2}\right)$$

in which Cv=the heat capacity at constant volume for one gram atom of an element, R= the gas constant, h=Planck's constant, k= Boltzmann constant, ν= the chiracteristic frequency of oscillation of the atoms of the element, T=the absolute temperature in kelvin, and e=the natural logarithmic base.

einsteinium. An element

	Symbol	Es
	Atomic No.	99
State Solid	Atomic Wt.	254
Group IIIB	Valence	3
	m.p.	860°C

The first pure isotope found was ^{253}Es, produced by prolonged treatment of plutonium-239 with neutrons in the Arco, Idaho, Testing Reactor. The most stable is ^{254}Es, half-life 270 days and therefore the mass number 254 is carried in the atomic weight table. Others include ^{245}Es—^{246}Es, ^{248}Es—^{251}Es, and ^{253}Es, ^{255}Es.

The ion Es^{3+} is stable. The istopes of mass number 245, 252, 253 and 254 decay by alpha-particle emission ; that of mass number 250 by electron capture, those of mass number 246, 248, 249 and 251 by both of these processes, while those of mass number 255 and 256 emit electrons to form the corresponding fermium isotopes.

Einstein number. A dimensionless number used in magnetofluid dynamics; equal to the ratio of the velocity of a fluid to the speed of light.

Einstein's equation, $E=mc^2$, where E is the energy equivalent of a mass m, and c is the velocity of light. A direct consequence of Einstein's special theory of relativity, this equation is the basis of all nuclear energy.

Einstein shift. A slight displacement towards the red of the lines of the solar spectrum due to the sun's gravitation field; predicted by Einstein's general theory of relativity and subsequently verified experimentally.

Einstein-Smoluchowski equation. Formula for mean path projection Δ_x covered by particle in rectilinear Brownian movement, on abscissa:

$$\overline{\Delta}_x = \sqrt{\frac{RT}{N_A} \cdot \frac{1}{3\pi\eta r} \cdot t}$$

where R=gas constant, T=thermodynamic temperature, N_A= Avogadro constant, η= viscosity coefficient of dispersion medium, r= radius of colloidal particle, and t=time. Also known as Einstein-Smoluchowski formula.

Einstein-Smoluchowski formula. *See* Einstein-Smoluchowski equation.

Einstein's principle of relativity. The principle that all the laws of physics must assume the same mathematical form in any inertial frame of reference, thus it is impossible to determine the absolute motion of a system by any means.

Ekkert test for alcohol. Two ml. of alcohol containing 0.01 g. resorcinol gives a pale pink to red ring-test with 1 ml. sulphuric acid. With more acid and less alcohol, a deepening red colour is obtained on heating.

Ekkert test for alkaloids. Three to four drops of a reagent, consisting of 1 g. of a 1% aqueous solution of furfural and 10 g. concentrated sulphuric acid, on adding to 0.02 g. of various alkaloids, produce characteristic colours.

Ekkert test for barbiturates. 1. On addition to ten times its weight of fused potassium hydroxide, barbital gives a rancid odor; phenobarbital a honey-like odor becoming pungent; and propanal an aromatic odor becoming pungent.

2. With solution of 0.01-0.02 g. the substance in 1-2 ml. alcohol containing 1 drop salicyldehyde, all three of the above barbiturates give a deep red ring-test with concentrated sulphuric acid.

3. With 0.5-1 ml. 3-12% formaldehyde and 4 ml. concentrated sulphuric acid, and heating, 0.01-0.02 g. barbital or propanal give a yellowish colour; phenobarbital gives a rose-pink colour, changing to wine-red.

Ekkert test for glycerin. A mixture of glycerin, sulphuric acid, and codeine becomes deep blue on heating. If codeine is replaced by resorcinol, the colour formed is deep-red.

Ekkert test for lactic acid. When a lactic acid solution is floated on a 1% solution of pyrocatechol in sulphuric acid, a blood-red ring test is obtained.

Ekkert test for levulose (fructose). Add to 10-30 mg. levulose. 3-5 drops 3 N sodium hydroxide and 0.5-1.0 g. solid sodium hydroxide. A red zone appears around the sodium hydroxide; the mixture becomes blood-red in colour.

Ekkert test for nitrate and nitrite. Add 0.1 g. sodium nitrite to 5 ml. 33% hydrochloric acid containing 0.02-0.03 g. resorcinol. A saffron-yellow colour appears, changing to brown-red and then to dark mulberry-red. After 20-25 minutes, add enough 0.2 N sodium hydroxide to produce a dark green liquid. This liquid colours methyl acetate violet-red, ethyl acetate rose to eosin-red; and it turns violet red and then green with red fluorescence on dilution.

To 0.01 g. potassium nitrate add 5 ml. 33% hydrochloric acid containing 0.02-0 03 g. resorcinol. A pale-yellow colour forms after 5 minutes, turning yellow, peach-red, and mulberry-red on heating in a boiling water bath. The addition of 0 2 N sodium hydroxide produces a green liquid, which colours methyl acetate violet-red or lilac with a red fluorescence on dilution.

Ekkert test for saccharin. On shaking 1-2 ml. water with 0.2 g. saccharin and adding 3-6 drops 30% hydrogen peroxide and 0.02-0.04 g. sodium nitrite, a yellow colour is produced which changes to brown-red with ammonia.

Ekkert test for salicylate. A solution of 0.01-0.02 g. salicylate and 0 002 g. sodium nitrite in 0.5 ml. water gives with 1 ml. sulphuric acid a red ring, a red mixture on shaking, changing to green with excess sodium hydroxide solution. With salol a green colour is obtained on mixing, becoming red on dilution, and blue-green with excess sodium hydroxide solution.

Ekkert test for tartaric acid. On mixing 0.01 g. tartaric acid with 0.02 g. pyrogallol adding 5 ml. sulphuric acid, and heating on the water bath, a violet colour is obtained. With β-naphthol instead of pyrogallol, a blue-green colour is produced. Citric acid produces no colour or a light yellow colour ; lactic acid, a red or brown colour.

elaborate. A term used in biochemistry to describe chemical transformations within the organism resulting in the formation of specific types of substances; for example, plants elaborate vitamins and fats, and some poisonous snakes elaborate their own venom. It also refers to formation of metabolic end-products such as purines and uric acid.

Elaidin reaction. A test that differentiates non-drying oils such as olein from semi-drying and drying oils ; nitrous acid converts olein into its solid isomer, while semi-drying oils in contact with nitrous acid thicken slowly, and drying oils such as tung oil become hard and resinous.

elastase. A proteinase from mammalian pancreas which hydrolyses elastin. It acts on peptide bonds between amino-acids which possess non-polar (alkyl) side chains.

elastic collision. *See* collision, elastic.

elasticity. 1. A property of matter by virtue of which solids resist deformation and resume their original form or volume when the stress cease to act.

2. The ratio of the stress to the strain which it produces. For gases the formula $E=pV/v$ is used, in which E = elasticity ; p = increase in pressure ; V = original volume ; and v=diminution in volume.

A material which recovers 100% of its shape after distortion is said to be perfectly elastic (*e.g.*, glass) ; rubber and many elastomers, on the other hand, tend to be permanently deformed, that is, they may be only 90 to 95% elastic after being stressed to the breaking point, while exhibiting elongation of up to 1000%. *See also* elastomer.

3. In physical chemistry, this term refers to the fact that atoms and molecules maintain their energy in spite of continual mutual collision ; thus, an elastic collision is one in which the particles, for example, of a gas in a closed container, collide with each other or the walls of the container indefinitely with no net energy loss.

elastomer. Of natural or synthetic origin, an elastomer is a polymer possessing elastic (rubbery) properties. A polymer is a substance consisting of molecules which are, in the most part, multiples of low-molecular-weight units or monomers. As an example, isoprene (2-methyl-butadiene-1,3) is C_5H_8, whereas polyisoprene is $(C_5H_8)x$, where $x \geqslant 2$ and normally varies from 1,000 to 10,000 for rubbers. Although they differ in composition from natural rubber, many of these high-molecular-weight materials are termed synthetic rubbers.

Among the early synthetic elastomers were polychloroprene, styrene-butadiene copolymer, butyl rubber and sodium polysulphide polymer. More recent development produced silicone rubbers, polyurethanes, polyisoprene (an exact duplication of natural rubber), and a number of others.

Elbs anthracene synthesis. *See* Elbs reaction.

Elbs persulphate oxidation. Oxidation of monohydroxyphenols to dihydroxyphenols by the action of potassium persulphate in akaline medium, followed by the hydrolysis of persulphate compound formed, *e.g.*,

$$C_6H_5OH \xrightarrow[K_2S_2O_8]{OH^{\ominus}} HO\text{-}C_6H_4\text{-}OSO_3K \xrightarrow{HOH} HO\text{-}C_6H_4\text{-}OH + KHSO_4$$

Elbs reaction. The formation of anthracene derivatives by dehydration and cyclization of diaryl ketone compounds which have a methyl group or methylene group.

$$\text{(2-methylbenzophenone)} \xrightarrow{400-450^\circ} \text{(anthracene)} + H_2O$$

The reaction is commonly accomplished by heating, usually to fairly elevated temperatures. Also known as Elbs anthracene synthesis.

electret. Substance preserving macroscopic field induced dipole moment when electric field is switched off. Electrets are made by cooling suitable dielectrics from elevated temperatures in strong electric fields.

electrical double layer. A region of characteristic properties which exists at the surface of separation between two phases. Present-day opinion tends to the view that at a solid-liquid boundary, for example, the double-layer consists of a monomolecular or monoionic layer of liquid that is closely held to the solid surface, and then a diffuse layer which extends into the liquid for some distance. Also known as electrochemical double layer.

electric current carrier. Collective term for particles able to transport electric charges. In general, the term is applied only to mobile charge carriers, *i.e.*, free electrons and electron holes. *See also* electron conductivity; hole conductivity.

electric dipole. System of charges with non-coinciding. centres of gravity of negative and positive charge. In the simplest case, system of two equal but opposite and displaced point charges. Also known as carrier.

electric dipole moment. *See* dipole moment.

electric steel. A high-alloy steel made by heating the components in an electric furnace; it usually contains substantial percentages of nickel, chromium, and molybdenum.

electride. A member of a class of ionic compounds in which the anion is believed to be an electron.

electro-analysis. Methods of chemical analysis based on phenomena occurring during electrode reactions and/or flow of current through electrolyte solutions.

Many metals may be rapidly and accurately determined by depositing them on a weighed cathode and subsequently determining the difference in weight. Concentration may be determined by measuring potentials and conductivities, the end point of a galvanometer in place of an indicator, and the concentration of hydrogen ions in acid and bases may be determined electrolytically. Also known as electro-analysis.

electrocapillarity curve. Curve which represents dependence of surface tension of metal (*e.g.*, mercury) at metal-electrolyte interface on potential of metal.

electrocapillary phenomenon. Changes produced in the surface tension of a liquid by an electric field.

electrochemical analysis. *See* electro-analysis.

electrochemical double leyer. *See* electrical double layer.

electrochemical equivalent (E.C.E.). The mass of any element or group liberated in an electrolytic cell divided by one coulomb. As, by Faraday's law, the gram equivalent of any element is liberated by 96,594 coulombs, the electrochemical equivalent is given by the chemical equivalent divided by the Faraday (96,494 coulomb). Thus for silver the E.C.E. is 108 divided by 96,594, *i.e.*, 0.001118 g./coulomb.

electrochemical generation of titrant. Production of titrant by electrolytic oxidation or reduction. Quantity of produced titrant is calculated on the basis of charge which passes through circuit during time of generation.

electrochemical potential (of a given sort of ions) $\tilde{\mu}_B$. Intensive thermodynamic quantity:

$$\tilde{\mu}_B = \mu_B + z_B F\varphi$$

where μ_B=chemical potential of ions B, z_B= valency of ion and φ=inner potential of phase.

electrochemical series. *See* electromotive series.

electrochemistry. The study dealing with the chemical changes accompanying the passage of an electric current, or the reverse process in which a chemical reaction is used as the source of energy to produce an electric current.

Electrochemistry is directly involved in chemical bonding, ionization, electrolysis, metallurgy battery technology, and corrosion—in short, in any situation in which a chemical change is caused by, or associated with, electrical phenomena. (It does not include electronics, in which electrons are not bound within the atom and in which no chemical changes occur).

electrochromatography. Type of chromatography that utilizes application of an electric potential to produce an electric differential. Also known as electropherography.

electrocratic. A term used in colloid chemistry to denote a dispersion of solid particles of colloidal size in a liquid, whose stability is maintained by either positive or negative electric charges on the particles. Since the charges are alike, they repel each other and thus offset the attraction of gravity. Such dispersions, made with colloidal gold, silver, and other metals, have certain medical applications.

electrocyclic reactions. Under the influence of heat or light, a conjugated polyene can undergo isomerization to form a cyclic compound with a single bond between the terminal carbons of the original conjugated system ; one double bond disappears, and the remaining double bond shift their positions. The thermal cyclization of conjugated trienes and the cleavage of cyclobutenes are examples of electrocyclic reactions :

CH_3 CH_3 ⇌ (Δ) CH_3 H H CH_3

trans, cis, trans 2,4,6-octatriene **cis-5,6-dimethyl-1,3-cyclohexadiene**

CH_3 CH_3 → (Δ) CH_3 CH_3

electrode. 1. The means whereby the electric current gains entrance to or leaves a cell.

2. The ends of a metallic circuit between which the current travels in a medium different from the rest of the circuit are termed electrodes The negative electrode, or cathode, is that through which the current leaves the cell ; the positive electrode, or anode, is that through which the current enters the cell. This discussion follows the convention of positive current; actually, electrons leave the cell at the anode and enter at the cathode.

3. In emission spectroscopy, either of two terminals between which an electrical discharge occurs, and act as source of excitation.

4. In electrochemistry system of two or more conducting phases, at least one of which is electrolytic conductor. These phases border in such a way as to enable flows of electric charges or ions across interfacial surfaces.

electrode, calomel. *See* calomel electrode.

electro-decantation. Modified electrodialysis in which concentration of dispersed phase occurs simultaneously with dialysis due to electrophoresis and gravitational sedimentation ; clear solution lying above concentrated dispersed phase is removed by decantation.

electrode, gas. *See* gas electrode.

electrode, glass. *See* glass electrode.

electrode, hydrogen. *See* hydrogen electrode.

electrode of first order. Electrode (half-cell) of metallic conductor/electrolyte solution type, *e.g.*, silver, copper, hydrogen electrodes.

electrode of second order. Electrode (half-cell) composed of metal M covered with thin layer of its poorly soluble salt MA and dipped into solution of fairly soluble salt of some metal M′A with anion common with salt MA. Solution of M′A is saturated with salt MA, *e.g.*, calomel electrode, silver chloride, electrode, oxide electrodes.

electrode of third order. Electrode (half-cell) composed of metal M covered with thin layer of its poorly soluble salt MA, and layer of poorly soluble salt of other metal M′A dipped into solution of well soluble salt of metal M′ ; solution is saturated with respect to salts MA and M′A ; *e.g.*, Zn, ZnC_2O_4, CaC_2O_4 | Ca^{2+}.

electrodeposition. A general term for the coating of an electrode with a metal or other substance as a result of the migration of charged particles, in aqueous solution or suspension, caused by passage of an electric current. The particles may be ions, as in electroplating, large molecules (proteins), colloidal micelles, or still larger units (rubber particles in latex), as in electrophoresis. Thus, the term includes such processes as electroplating, electrocoating electroforming, electrophoresis, and anodizing. *See also* electrolysis ; electroplating ; electrophoresis ; anodizing.

electrode potential. The potential difference produced between the electrode and the solution in a half-cell. Its magnitude depends upon both the element and the concentration of the solution. Under conditions when no net current flows between the electrode and solution, the system is said to behave reversibly and the potential is termed the reversible electrode potential. It is not possible to measure it directly, since any measurement involves completing the circuit with the electrolyte, thereby introducing another half-cell. Standard electrode potentials (E°) are thus defined by measuring the potential relative to a standard hydrogen eleectrode half-cell using 1.0 mole solution at 298 K.

electrode, quinhydrone. *See* quinhydrone electrode.

electrode reaction. Oxidation or reduction of substance occurring at electrode surface ; reaction which takes place at electrode—electrolyte interface whose course determines potential of electrode.

electrode, reversible. *See* reversible electrode.

electrodialysis. The separation of ionizing substances from other materials in a solution, and also from the solvent, by use of one or more semipermeable membranes, and an electric current (electrolysis). This methods is being used in some installations for desalination of sea water and for other forms of demineralization. *See also* dialysis.

electroendosmosis. Cataphoresis in which the solid is stationary and the water phase is displaced and migrates toward the electrode.

electroforming. A method of making intricate metal objects, especially those having specifically contoured surfaces, by means of electrolytic deposition. The ions of the coating metal attach themselves to a previously prepared negative mold of the object to be manufactured, to which graphite has been applied to act as a conductor. This method is used in making printing plates, phonograph records, and similar products in which the surface configuration is of primary importance. *See also* electroplating.

electrographic analysis. Method of analysis based on electrolytic transfer of ions from analysed sample onto surface of another material (for instance on papers saturated with electrolyte), where these ions are identified.

electrogravimetry. Weight determination of metallic elements quantitatively deposited from solution on cathode as metal or on anode as oxide.

electrokinetic phenomena. Phenomena associated with the movement of charged particles through a continuous medium or with the movement of a continuous medium over a charged surface. The four principal electrokinetic phenomena are electrophoresis, electro-osmosis, streaming potential, and sedimentation potential, or Dorn effect.

eletrokinetic potential. *See* zeta potential.

electroless plating. A chemical reduction process which once initiated, is autocatalytic. The process is similar, to electroplating except that no outside current is needed. The metal ions are reduced by chemical agents in the plating solutions, and deposit on the substrate. It is used for plating nonmetallic substrates.

electroluminescence. A luminescence resulting from the application of an electric field to a material, usually solid. The phenomenon is utilized in the luminescent lamp.

electrolysis. Decomposition of a chemical compound by means of an electric current, the extant being proportional to the quantity of electricity passing through the solution. The ions present move to the oppositely charged electrode, where they are deposited ; metallic ions discharged on an electrode form a coating, *i.e.*, an electrodeposit. Water can be separated in this way into its component gases, hydrogen and oxygen. Many industrial operations, utilize electrolysis, *e g.*, metallurgical separations, electroplating, electroforming, anodizing, etc., as well as the manufacture of important inorganic chemicals.

electrolyte. A term used for any liquid, fused solid, or solution that will conduct electricity by furnishing the necessary ions. Whereas ordinary metallic conductors conduct without chemical change and are merely heated, electrolytes are decomposed by the current that passes through them.

electrolytic bridge. *See* salt bridge.

electrolytic cell. An electrochemical device in which electrolysis is performed, such as for the manufacture of chlorine and sodium hydroxide from sodium chloride solution (brine). Its essential features are a graphite anode and a steel or mercury cathode. The types employing steel cathodes (Hooker, Vorce) also utilize a porous asbestos diaphragm cells ; the mercury cathode type is represented by the Castner and DeNora cells. The Downs cell is used for extraction of sodium from a molten mixture of sodium chloride and calcium chloride. When current is passed through an electriclytic cell, the sodium chloride is ionized to Na^+ and Cl^-; it thus acts as an electrolyte, and the ions move to the respective electrodes. Chlorine is evolved then at the anode and sodium hydroxide at cathode, with evolution of hydrogen. Modified electrolytic cells also used for electroplating.

electrolytic conductivity. *See* specific conductance.

electrolytic conductor. *See* ionic conductor.

electrolytic dissociation. Decomposition of substance into thermodynamically stable, free ions as result of interactions between dissolved substance and solvent.

electrolytic dissociation classical constant, K_c. Equilibrium constant of electrolytic dissociation reaction expressed by concentrations *c*, *e.g.*, for 1.1-electrolyte,

$$MA \rightleftharpoons M^+ + A^-$$

$$Kc = \frac{c_{M^+} + c_{A^-}}{c_{MA}}$$

equation applies approximately to diluted solutions of weak electrolytes. *See also* electrolytic dissociation constant.

electrolytic dissociation constant, *Ka*. Thermodynamic equilibrium constant of electrolytic dissociation reaction ; for instance for 1.1-electrolyte

$$MA \rightleftharpoons M^+ + A^-$$

$$Ka = \frac{a_{M^+}a_{A^-}}{a_{MA}} = \frac{c_{M^+}c_{A^-}}{c_{MA}}\ \frac{f_{M^+}f_{A^-}}{f_{MA}} = Kc\frac{f_{M^+}f_{A^-}}{f_{MA}}$$

where Kc=electrolytic dissociation classical constant ; equation applies to all electrolytic solutions.

electrolytic gas. The highly explosive mixture of two volumes of hydrogen and one volume of oxygen obtained when, for exmple, a dilute aqueous solution of sulphuric acid, is electrolysed and the gases from the electrodes collected together.

electrolytic oxidation. Oxidation taking place at anode in course of electrolysis, *e.g.*,

$$2Cl^- \xrightarrow{-2e^-} Cl_2$$

$$\begin{array}{ccc} & & CO_2 + R^{\cdot} \rightarrow \text{other products} \\ & & \uparrow \\ R{-}COO^- & \xrightarrow{-e^-} & R{-}COO^{\cdot} \\ & & \downarrow -e^- \\ & & CO_2 + R^+ \rightarrow \text{other products} \end{array}$$

Also known as anodic oxidation.

electrolytic polarization. Processes which occur during flow of anodic or cathodic current exceeding exchange current through electrode—solution interphase ; they result in deviation of half-cell from equilibrium due to one or several steps of electrode processes.

electrolytic rectifier. An electrolytic system which converts alternating current to direct current. It consists essentially of a combination of two electrodes and an electrolyte which produces a polarizing film on one of the electrodes that practically bars the flow of current into it from the solution, while freely permitting flow in the opposite direction. Groups of these cells may be arranged to utilize both halves of the alternating-current cycle.

electrolytic reduction. Reduction taking place at cathode in electrolysis, *e.g.*,

$$Na^+ \xrightarrow{e^-} Na$$

$$C_6H_5N(\rightarrow O)(=O) \xrightarrow[+2H^+]{2e^-} C_6H_5N(\rightarrow O){-}OH \rightleftharpoons C_6H_5\ddot{N}(OH)_2$$

$$\overset{+}{H} \rightleftharpoons C_6H_5\overset{\overset{+}{O}H_2}{\overset{|}{N}}\!\!\!\!\underset{OH}{} \quad \overset{+}{H} + 2e^- \underset{-H_2O}{\rightleftharpoons} C_6H_5\overset{H}{\overset{|}{N}}\!\!\!\!\underset{OH}{}$$

electrolytic refining. Purification of metals by electrolysis. A large block of impure metal is used as the anode and a thin strip of pure metal is made the cathode. Insoluble impurities settle out as a sludge, or anode mud. Soluble impurities—other metal ions-remain in solution because the operating voltage is selected so it will be insufficient for their deposition. If this is impossible on a practical basis, other ions may be added which selectively complex or precipitate the impurity ions, thus preventing their electrodeposition.

electrolytic tautomerism. A type of tautomerism in which a substance exhibits different electronic configuration, often resulting in differences in chemical behaviour, corresponding to changes in the electric character of the environment. This type of tautomerism is shown by amphiprotic substances which are capable of acting as proton donors or proton acceptors.

electrolytic thermocell. Galvanic cell constructed from two identical electrodes, which however remain at different temperatures.

electrolyze. To submit to the process of electrolysis ; to decompose by means of an electric current.

electromagnetic interaction. Interaction of particles which gives rise to processes taking place within time range of $10^{-18}-19^{-15}$ second. Real or virtual photons participate in electromagnetic interaction.

electromagnetic radiation. Periodical changes of electromagnetic field propagated through space with finite velocity.

electromagnetic units. A system of electrical units derived from dynamic data usually written e.m.u. or emu. The starting point in this system is the unit magnetic pole, which is defined by the expression $m=r\sqrt{F\mu}$, where m =the magnitude of the pole r = its distance from a like pole, F = force of repulsion between them, and μ = magnetic permeability (unity for air). Then the unit of magnetic field intensity H is defined by the expression

$$H = \frac{F}{m}, \text{ etc.}$$

electromeric effect. Shift of electron density in molecules with multiple, and especially conjugated bonds, induced by external electric field.

electromotive force, emf. Difference of potentials between electrodes of thermodynamically reversible cell.

electromotive series. An arrangement of elements in order of decreasing potentials of their electrodes in equilibrium with solutions of their ions. Since the electrode potential of a metal in equilibrium with a solution of its ions cannot be measured directly, the values in the electromotive force series are, in each case, the difference between the electrode potential of the given metal in equilibrium with a solution of its ions, and that of hydrogen in equilibrium with a solution of its ions. In experimental procedure, the hydrogen electrode is used as the standard with which the electrode potentials of other substances are compared. Some of the metals in the decreasing order of reactivity are sodium, magnesium, aluminium, manganese, zinc, cadmium, iron, cobalt, nickel, tin, lead, hydrogen, copper, mercury, silver, and gold. Also known electrochemical series.

electron, e (e^-). Stable elementary particle, a lepton, of : mass m, $= 9.109558\times10^{-28}$g $= 0.5110041$ MeV, with negative elementary charge Q=4.803250×10^{-10} ES units=1.6021917×10^{-19} C, baryon number B=0, electronic lepton number Le=1 and spin quantum number J=1/2.

The sign of the electron's charge is negative by convention, and that is of equally charged proton is positive. This is somewhat unfortunate convention, because the flow of electrons in a conductor is thus opposite to the conventional direction of the current.

Electrons may occupy from one to seven energy levels (depending on the element involved) which are at varying distance from the nucleus. These are called shells, or groups of orbitals ; each shell contains a specific number of electrons ranging from 1 to 32, though in many cases the shells are not filled. Those in the outer shell are known as valence electrons, as they play a predominant role in chemical bonding : for example, fluorine has two shells, the inner one being occupied by two electrons and the outer one by seven electrons, which represents its valence. Thus, there is a definite relationship between the number of outermost electrons and the chemical activity of an element. No orbital can contain more than two electrons ; two electrons in the same orbital are known as paired electrons.

The negative charge on, or represented by, an electron is regarded as being diffuse rather than concentrated, and thus has the appearance of a charge-cloud around the nucleus which becomes gradually less dense as it extends outwards, the density being indicated by the square of the wave junction. Electrons may be detached from the nucleus of an atom by application of energy ; in this free state they can flow along a conductor or through a vacuum tube or semiconductor in the form of an electric current. Electrons are emitted as beta particles from radioactive nuclei such as radium and uranium. The electron obeys the Fermi-Dirac statistics, and for this reasons is often called a fermion.

electron acceptor. Atom capable of accepting pair of electrons from donor.

electron affinity. Energy ensuing from electron capture by atom or molecule resulting in formation of negative ion. For an atom or molecule X, it is the energy released for the electron-gain reaction

$$X(g) + e^- \rightarrow X^-(g)$$

often this is measured in joules per mole or electron volts. Alternatively, the molar enthalpy change, ΔH can be used.

electron beam. Fast electrons moving along straight, almost parallel tracks. Electron beam is produced in accelerating devices. Its power is defined by intensity (in amperes) and energy of electrons (in mega-electronvolts).

electron capture. Radioactive transition whereby nucleus captures one of its orbital electrons (most often from K shell, more seldom from L or M shells) with emission of neutrino. Excited nucleus returns to ground state emitting characteristic x-rays and Auger electrons.

electron cloud. Distribution of electrons around atomic nucleus ; it is usually accepted that they occupy atomic orbitals.

electron conductivity. Transfer of electric charge through crystal under external field. Electrons occupying quantum states in range of conduction band move to neighbouring unoccupied quantum states in range of this band in opposite direction to vector of electric field. Also known as n-conduction.

electron configuration. *See* electron distribution.

electron correlation. Difference between real electron motion and the one following from self-consistent field method description.

electron-deficient structures. A significant number of chemical compounds are known in which the bonding cannot be accurately described by the utilization of a pair of electrons for each bond and between contiguous atoms. Rather, examples exist where the total number of valence-electron pairs is less than the number of bonds. Such molecules are said to have electron-deficient structures which are characterized by the formation of an electron-pair bond between more than two atomic centres. An example is diborane, B_2H_6. A total of only 12 valence electrons (3 from each boron atom and 1 from each hydrogen atom) is available to form what, under normal circumstances, would be 8 covalent bonds. The bonding in this electron-deficient case can be understood by postulating the existence of a three-centre two-electron bond for each B—H—B bridge. That is, the three atoms are joined together by a single electron pair. The formation of such multi-centre bonds in response to electron deficiency frequently leads to molecular structures which are cyclic or cage-like. An example involing metal-to-carbon bonds is trimethylaluminium. Electron deficiency leads to a dimeric structure with bridging methyl groups. The bridges are joined by three-centre two-electron bonds.

electron density. In atom or molecule, density of electron cloud ; defined by modulus square of atomic or molecular orbital respectively. Also known as electronic density.

electron diffraction. Beams of high-speed electrons exhibit diffraction phenomena analogous to those exhibited by light, thus showing the wave-like character of electron beams. Such patterns are useful in the interpretation of the structure of gases or solids.

electron distribution. An arrangement of electrons, especially the arrangement of electrons in orbits or shells around the nucleus of an atom or an ion, it is given by symbols of all occupied shells with superscript number equal to number of electrons in shell, *e.g.*, electron configuration of ground electronic state of sulphur atom is $1s^2 2s^2 2p^6 3s^2 3p^4$.

electron donor. When the valence bond between two atoms is that type of covalent linkage in which both the electrons of the duplet are supplied by one atom, then that atom, or portion of the molecule of which it forms a part, is called the electron donor, and the other atom in the linkage is called the electron acceptor.

electron dublet. A pair of electrons which is shared by two atoms, and is equivalent to a single, nonpolar chemical bond.

Two electrons with opposite orientation of their spins ; according to Lewis theory they form single covalent bond, *e.g.*, in H_2 molecule.

electron duplet. *See* electron dublet.

electronegative element. An element which has a relatively great tendency to attract electrons, whereby the bond energy of its linkage with another and different atom is found to exceed the mean of that found in linkages between the two pairs of identical atoms (*i.e.*, the $A-B$ bond energy exceeds the mean of the values for $A—A$ and $B—B$). Electronegative elements generally form acidic oxides ; their outer shell contains four or more electrons, and they tend to gain electrons to complete it. They are commonly non-metals.

electronegativity. The extent to which an atom can attract shared pair of electrons in a molecule and thus become negatively charged; this tendency is due to the attractive force exerted by the nuclei of atoms having valancies in their outer shells. This attraction makes possible the formation of polar chemical compounds.

electron-excess semiconductor. Semiconductor in which electrons transferred to conductance band are main carriers of electric ourrent. Also known as *n*-type semiconductor.

electron exchangers. Solids able to participate in reversible oxidation-reduction reactions.

electron, free. *See* free electron.

electron gas. The concept that the free electrons in a solid, liquid, or gas may be treated as a gas and compared with a real gas dissolved in the appropriate material. Such an electron gas obeys a totally different energy distribution than a real gas, obeying Fermi-Dirac statistics rather than the Maxwell-Boltzmann statistics obeyed by an ordinary gas. It also has a vanishingly small specific heat.

electronic antineutrino, $\bar{\nu}_e$. Antiparticle corresponding to electronic neutrino of lepton electronic number $Le = -1$ and positive (right-handed) helicity ; stable.

electronic band. In molecular electronic spectra, band corresponding to transition between rotation-vibration-electronic states.

electronic conductor. *See* metallic conductor.

electronic defects. Imperfections of crystal lattice consisting in occupation of certain interstitial positions by ions of abnormal charge (*e.g.*, Fe^{3+} in FeO crystal), neutral atoms, electrons or localized holes respectively in anionic or cationic vacancies. The number of defects of one sign must be compensated by stoichiometric number of defects of opposite sign. Also known as ionic defects.

electronic density. *See* electron density.

electronic formula. Structural formula with distribution of valency electrons marked by bars and lone pairs of electrons represented by dots, *e.g.*, acetylene H:C:::C:H, ammonia H:N:H. (with lone pair dots above N and H below: $\overset{..}{\text{H:N:H}}$ over $\vdots$ H)

electronic internal partition function. *See* electronic partition function.

electronic isomerism. Existence of different electronic configurations (states of different multiplicity) in molecules of a given chemical compound ; *e.g.*, Chichibabin's hydrocarbon exists in singlet or triplet forms :

$$(C_6H_5)_2C{=}\langle\rangle{=}\langle\rangle{=}C(C_6H_5)_2 \rightleftharpoons$$

$$\rightleftharpoons (C_6H_5)_2\dot{C}{-}\langle\rangle{-}\langle\rangle{-}\dot{C}(C_6H_5)_2$$

electronic lepton number, L_e. Number attributed to elementary particles; for electronic neutrino, $L_e = 1$, for their antiparticles, $L_e = -1$. Other particles and antiparticles have $L_e = 0$. Electronic lepton number is conserved in all interactions.

electronic neutrino, ν_e. Elementary particle, a lepton, with rest mass probably zero, electrically neutral, stable, of baryon number $B = 0$, quantum spin number $J = 1/2$, negative helicity and electronic lepton number $L_e = 1$.

electronic orbital. An electron remaining with a high degree of probability in the immediate neighbourhood of a nucleus, where it occupies a quantized orbital.

electronic partition function. $e(T)$. Function

$$e(T) = \sum_{\varepsilon_e} g(\varepsilon_e) \exp\left(-\frac{\varepsilon_e - \varepsilon_{e_0}}{kT}\right)$$

where $g(\varepsilon_e)$ = degeneracy of electronic level equal to its statistical weight,

ε_{e_0} = energy of electronic ground state,

k = Boltzmann constant,

T = thermodynamic temperature, and summation take place overall electronic state of molecule. Electronic partition function determines influence of molecular electronic structure of gas molecules on its thermodynamic properties. For $T << \frac{\varepsilon_{e_1} - \varepsilon_{e_0}}{k}$, electronic partition function simplifies to $e(T) \approx g(\varepsilon_0)$. Also known as electronic internal partition function.

electronic polarizability, α_E. Dielectric polarization (per molecule) arising in unit local fieled due to deformation of electron density.

electronic polarization. *See* electron polarization.

electronic polarization. Measure of electronic polarization defined by :

$$P_E = \frac{1}{3\varepsilon_0} N_A \alpha_E \text{ (in SI units)}$$

where N_A = Avogadro constant, α_E = electronic polarizability, and ε_0=permittivity of free space.

electronic shell. Set of atomic orbitals with the same principal quantum number. The arrangement of extranuclear electrons in different groups of orbitals which are characterized by different principal quantum numbers. In the classical Bohr model of the atom, all electrons in a given shell moved in orbits of approximately the same distance from the nucleus. Different shells are then characterized by different dimensions of the electronic orbits. Also known as electron shell.

electronic specific heat. Contribution of free or semi-free electrons to total specific heat of metal. It is experimentally determined from low-temperature behaviour of specific heat.

electronic spectroscopy. Branch of spectroscopy dealing with study of electronic spectra of atoms and molecules.

electronic spectrum. Spectrum in visible and ultraviolet region arising due to transitions between different electronic energy levels of a given system.

electronic subshell. Set of atomic orbitals with the same principal and orbital quantum numbers.

electronic theory of catalysis. Theory of heterogeneous catalysis which ascribes principal role in catalytic process to chemisorption of molecules of substrates on surface of catalyst.

π-π^* electronic transition. According to one-electron excitation model, transition involving electron jump from bonding to antibonding π^*-orbital.

σ-π^* electronic transition. According to one-electron excitation model, transition involving electron jump from bonding σ-orbital to antibonding π^*-orbital.

n-π^* electronic transition. According to one-electron excitation model, transition corresponding to electron jump from non-bonding lone pair orbital, n, to antibonding π^*-orbital.

n-σ^* electronic transition. According to one-electron excitation model, transition involving electron jump from non-bonding lone pair orbital, n, to antibonding σ^*-orbital.

electronic-vibration-rotation spectrum. Molecular spectrum corresponding to transitions between electronic energy levels with simultaneous change of vibrational and rotational energy of molecule. Also known as rotation-vibration-electronic spectrum.

electron lens. An electric field used to focus a stream of electrons on a target. This may be achieved, for example, by use of a circular hole in a charged conductor.

electron microprobe x-ray analyzer. Device which enables qualitative and quantitative analysis of chemical composition of micro-regions (of diameter of a few μm) to be performed on sample surface from x-ray spectrum excited by precisely focused electron beam. Also known as electron probe micro-analyzer.

electron multiplier. An arrangement of electron emission surfaces such that, for each jumping electron, a large number of additional electrons are expelled toward the next surface. In such a manner a cascading electron stream may be obtained.

electron, nuclear. An electron which is emitted from the nucleus of an atom. Its formation within the nucleus is believed to be due to the transformation of a proton into a neutron. It is now not believed that electrons exist as such inside the nucleus.

electron octet. Eight electrons filling s- and p-subshells of valence shell of an atom.

electron optics. The control of the movement of free electrons by means of electric fields, and their utilization in research investigation of electronic diffraction phenomena, in direct analogy to the effect of lenses on light. Electron beams are used to determine the microstructure of crystals and many other materials. (*See* electron microscope and electron diffraction.)

electron, orbital. *See* electronic orbital.

electron pair. *See* electron dublet.

electron paramagnetic resonance, (EPR). A method of spectroscopic analysis similar to nuclear magnetic resonance except that micro-wave radiation is employed instead of radio frequencies. It is used for studying free radicals, crystal centres, transition elements and structures involving unpaired electrons. Also known as electron spin resonance.

electron-position pair production. A process in which a negative electron and a positive electron (position) are simultaneously created in the vicinity of a nucleus or an elementary particle. In external pair production, a photon is absorbed and creates an electron pair. The absorption of high energy gamma-rays is mainly due to this effect. Internal pair production is not associated with observable electromagnetic radiation and may occur when an exited nucleus releases some of its internal energy.

electron polarization. Polarization due to deformation of electron density distribution. The part of the total induced polarization of a molecule that is due to the distortion or deformation of the electron shells or orbitals under the influence of external electric fields.

electron probe microanalysis (EPM). A method of analysing a very small quantity of a substance by directing a finely focused electron beam on to it so than an x-ray emission is produced characteristic of the elements present in the simple. The diameter of the beam is usually about 1 μm and quantities as small as 10^{-14} gm can be detected by this method. The method may be used quantitatively for elements whose atomic numbers exceed 11.

electron shell. *See* electronic shell.

electron spin. Rotation of the electron about its own axis. This rotation contributes to the total angular momentum of the electron and is quantized It gives rise to multiplicity in line spectra, which may be characterized by introduction of the spin quantum number.

electron spin resonance. *See* electron paramagnetic resonance.

electron theory of metals. Theory based on following assumptions : (*a*) crystal of metal consists of positive metal ions which are in equilibrium with electrons moving freely in lattice space (electron gas); (*b*) electrons obey laws of classical mechanics and kinetic theory of gases as concerns their movements in lattice space of crystal. Also known as free electron theory of metals Drude-Lorentz theory.

electron transfer. The process of shifting of an electron from one electrical field to another, as in the formation of an electrovalent bond, in which an electron moving in an orbit about one atom shifts to move in an orbit about the two bonded atom.

electron transport chain A sequence of biochemical oxidation-reduction reactions that forms the final stage of aerobic respiration. It results in the transfer of electrons or hydrogen atoms derived from Krebs cycle to molecular oxygen, with the formation of water. At the same time it conserves energy in the form of ATP. The chain comprises a series of electron carriers that undergo reversible oxidation—reduction reactions, accepting electrons and then donating them to the next carrier in the chain. In the mitochondria, NADH and $FADH_2$, generated by the Krebs cycle, transfer their electrons to a chain comprising flavin mononucleotide (FMN), coengyme *Q*, and a series of cytochromes. This process is coupled to the formation of ATP at three sites along the chain. The ATP is then carried across the mitochondrial membrane in exchange for ADP. An electron transport chain also occurs in the light reaction of photosynthesis.

electronvolt, *eV*. Unit of energy. 1 eV is equal to the change of energy of an electron which passes through an electrical potential difference of one volt. In SI system $1\ eV = 1.60206.10^{-19} J$.

The repture of a chemical bond yields from 5 to 10 electronvolts. Whereas the splitting of an atomic nucleus releases about 200 million elctron volts. Approved. abbreviation for electron volt is eV and MeV for million electron volts.

electro-osmosis. The movement of an electrolyte through a fine tube or membrane under the influence of an electric field. Under conditions of pressure equality on each side of the partition, the volume of liquid transferred depends upon the nature of the electrolyte. It is independent of the area and thickness of the partition, being approximately proportional to the resistivity of the solution. A contact potentiai difference (*see* contact) between the membrane and electrolyte has been postulated to explain the effect. Also known as electroendosmosis.

electrophile. Reagent which acts as acceptor of electron pair belonging to carbon atom (or to atom of another element). Positive ions of molecules, containing electron deficient atoms (Lewis acids) and molecules with highly polarized bonds are electrophiles, *e.g.*,

$$H_3O^+,\ R_3C^+,\qquad \underset{\displaystyle R}{\overset{\displaystyle R}{\overset{|}{\underset{|}{C^{\delta+}}}}}=O^{\delta-},\quad BF_3$$

Also known as electrophilic reagent.

electrophilic addition. An addition reaction in which the first step is the attack by an electrophile on the electron rich site of the molecule.

electrophilic reagent. *See* electrophile.

electrophilic substitution. A substitution reaction in which the first step is the attack by an electrophile. Electrophile substitution is a feature of reactions of benzene in which a positively charged species approaches the delocalized pi electrons on the benzene ring.

electrophoresis. If a colloidal dispersion is placed under the influence of an electric field, the particles of the colloidal phase will drift either to the cathode if it is a positive colloid or to the anode if a negative one. This induced movement of the colloidal phase is known as "electrophoresis". It was formerly called "cataphoresis" but this rather gives a wrong impression—as if such movement is always towards the cathode. Rubber-plating may be carried out by electrophoresis. Protein molecules, which may have either a positive or negative charge depending on the *p*H of their environment, also respond to electrophoresis : research on this behaviour has been an important phase of investigation of immunology, especially as applied to allergens. *See also* electrodeposition.

electrophoretic effect. Hindering of ionic motion in electric field as a result of movement in opposite direction of counter ions (ionic cloud) with their solvation sheaths.

electrophoretic potential. *See* Dorn effect.

electroplating. A type of electrodeposition in which a substrate (metal or plastic) is coated with a fine film of metal for corrosion protection or for decorative purposes. An electrolytic cell is used in which the metal being coated is the cathode and the metal being deposited is either the anode, or is present as ions in the solutions. The solution, or bath, contains ionized salts of the metal being deposited. When the curent is passed through the solution, the positively charged metal ions are impelled to the cathode, on which they deposit a uniform layer of controllable thickness. The metallic anode may be ultimately consumed in the process.

electropositive. Elements and radicals which readily give up valence electrons and accumulate a positive charge. During electrolysis they are deposited on the cathode. Electropositive elements are generally metallic and base-forming ; they tend to lose electrons, and thus to acquire a positive character, and enter into combination with nonmetals.

electrorefining. Any of the method for the purification of elements, chiefly metals, by electrodeposition.

electroselectivity. Preference for ions of higher charge shown by ion exchanger in dilute solutions.

electrosol. A colloidal solution produced by electrical means, as by passing a spark between metal electrodes in a liquid.

electrostatic bond. Ionic bond, hydrogen bond and electrostatic interaction of multipoles.

electrostatic precipitation. A widely used method of controlling the pollution of air or other gases). The gas, containing solid or liquid particles suspended in it, is subjected to a uni-directional electrostatic field, so that the particles are attracted to, and deposited upon, the positive electrode.

electrostriction. The phenomenon of the contraction of a solvent attributable to the electrostatic field in a dissolved electroyte.

electrosynthesis. The production of synthetic reactions by means of the electric current. The electrolysis of a mixture of potassium acetate and potassium ethyl succinate yield ethyl butyrate, viz.,

$$C_2H_5OOCCH_2CH_2COOK + CH_3COOK + 2H_2O \rightarrow C_2H_5OOCCH_2C_2H_5 + 2CO_2 + 2KOH + H_2$$

This type of reaction might well be termed electrocondensation.

electrovalence. Number of electrons given or accepted by an atom during formation of ionic bond.

electrovalent bond. *See* ionic bond.

electroviscous effect. Relation between viscosity of sol and charge of particles of dispersed phase.

electrotwinning. An electrometallurgical process involving the recovery of a metal, usually from its ore by dissolving a metallic compound in a suitable electrolyte and reducing it electrochemically through passage of a direct electric current.

electrum 1. A natural alloy of gold (55%-85%) and silver.

2. A German-silver alloy containing 52% copper, 26% nickel, and 22% zinc.

element. An element is a substance made up of atoms with the same atomic number. A unique arrangement of fundamental units of matter having characteristic properties ; 106

elements are presently known, of which 92 occur in nature, the others being synthetic. Many more synthetic elements are theoretically possible. The number of protons in the atomic nucleus (atomic number) and the arrangement of electrons around them determine the properties of an element, especially in relation to chemical bonding and reactivity. When arranged in order of increasing atomic number, the elements are shown to have recurring similarity of certain properties. The origin of chemical elements is believed to be the result of the synthesis by fusion processes at very high temperatures (100,000,000 K) of the simple nuclear particles first to heavier atomic nuclei such as those of helium and then on to the heavier and more complex nuclei of the light elements. The helium atoms bombard the atoms of light elements and produce neutrons. The neutrons are captured by the nuclei of elements and produce heavier elements. These two processes—fusion of protons and neutron capture—are the main processes forming the chemical elements. About 75% of the elements are metals, and all those beyond lead are radioactive. All atoms of a given element are identical in every respect except mass, the presence of one or more extra neutron in the nucleus accounts for the existence of isotopes. Besides the major groups of elements of the Periodic Table, there are several classifications or series based on type or properties ; some of these lie within a major group, while others straddle several groups. These are the alkali metals (group IA, except hydrogen) : the alkaline earth metals (group IIA, except beryllium) ; the transition metals (several groups, including the platinum metals of group VIII) ; the halogen elements of group VIIA; the lanthanide series (rare earth metals) : and the actinide series, which includes the transuranic (synthetic) elements. The last two series occupy group IIIB of periodic table.

element-104. The first element beyond actinide series, and the twelfth transuranium element. The scientists have claimed the preparation of element-104, mass number-260, by irradiating plutonium-242 with neon-22 ions. Two alpha-emitting isotopes of element-104 with mass numbers 257 and 259 are also obtained by bombarding californium-249 with carbon-13. The International Union of Pure and applied chemistry has not yet adopted an official name for element-104.

element-105. A chemical element which is second beyond actinide series. It has a half life of 1.6 seconds and decays by emitting alpha particles with energies 9.06, 9.10, 9.14 MeV. It was shown to be of mass number 260, by identifying lawrencium-256 as its daughter by two different methods.

element-106. The element with atomic number 106 is the fourteenth of the synthetic transuranium elements, on the basis of the projected position in the periodic table, element-106 is expected to have chemical properties similar to those of tungsten.

elemental. Consisting of an element only as distinguished from a compound of an element, *e.g.*, elemental iron is Fe (not Fe_2O_3 or other iron compound). The term elementary is often used in this sense but should be avoided because of its more common nontechnical meaning of "simple" or "easy."

elementary analysis. The quantitative determination of the elements in a compound, the term being applied to the analysis of an organic compound by combustion, followed by determination of the products obtained. Also known as element analysis.

elementary entity. Elementary unit of matter ; atom, molecule, ion free radical, elementary particle. Also known as elementary unit.

elementary particle. Any of the particles of matter that cannot be subdivided into smaller particles. Elementary particles are described by a set of quantum numbers describing their intrinsic properties, such as charge and spin. The stable particles are the electron, proton, photon, and neutrino. The neutron is also stable when bound in an atomic nucleus. The electron is the natural unit of electric charge.

Elementary particles can be classified in groups according to the type of nuclear interaction to which they are subject. These groups are the hadrons (including the neutron and proton), the leptons (including the electron and neutron), and the photon, which is in a group by itself.

elementary process of radiolysis. Electronic excitations, especially ionization occurring as a result of interaction of ionizing quanta or particles with secondary electrons.

elementary quantum. *See* Planck's constant.

elementary reaction. Reaction proceeding without intermediary stages and in one direction only, from substrates to products.

elementary work, $\delta W(W_{el})$. Infinitely small amount of work exchanged between system and its surroundings in an elementary thermodynamic process. Also known as elementary quantity of work.

elimination reaction. Reaction involving removal of atoms, groups of atoms or ions from molecules (or ions) with formation of unsaturated or cycle compounds, *e.g.*,

```
 |  |          |  |
—C—C—    →    C=C + XY
 |  |          |  |
 X  Y
```

Elinvar. Trade name for a nickel-chromium steel containing about 36% nickel, 12% chromium, and smaller proportions of manganese and tungsten. Its elasticity does not vary with temperature.

elixirs. Pharmaceutical solutions, frequently containing alcohol, used as sweetening or flavouring agents for drugs.

Ellms-Hauser test. To detect the presence of free chlorine in water, add to 100 ml. of water, 1 ml. of a 0.1% solution of *o*-tolidine in 10% hydrochloric acid. In the presence of free chlorine a yellow to green colour develops; useful in colorimetric determination.

eluate. In paper- and column chromatography, solution containing substances washed out of filter paper or column after separation.

eluent. Gas or liquid used for selective washing out of substances retained on chromatographic column.

elution. In general, a process for extracting a solid substance from a mixture of solids by means of a liquid; as in the recovery of a vitamin adsorbed on an adsorbent by means of a solution. Specifically, a process for the recovery of sucrose from molasses. Quicklime in the proportion of 25% of the weight of the molasses is added, the resulting mass is freed from much impurity by percolating (in "eluators") with 35% alcohol and is then decomposed by carbon dioxide which liberates the sucrose.

elution curve. Diagram showing dependence of substance concentration in eluate upon effluent volume or elution time.

elutriation. The process of suspending finely divided particles in an upward flowing stream of air or water to wash and separate them into sized fractions. It is basically a sedimentation operation, in which the mixed particles are subjected to a flow of water in an appropriately designed container; as the water moves upward through the mixture, the heavier particles fall to the bottom of the container, while the water carries the lighter ones over edge into a collection device.

emanating power. Ratio of magnitude of emission of radioactive emanation released by solid material to total emission produced in material in given time interval.

emanation method. Method used for studying structure, surface, etc. solid materials, and changes occurring in these solids. It consists of the introduction into the material studied of radionuclide (*e.g.*, ^{226}Ra) which decays to give gaseous emanation, the rate of evolution of which is measured.

emanations. In general, a gaseous substance given off from radioactive material. Specifically, collective name for three radioactive gases (isotopes of the element radon) occurring in natural radioactive series of:

radon — $^{22}_{86}Rn$, actinon — $^{219}_{86}An$, and

thoron — $^{220}_{86}Th$.

embossing. Forming a pattern on the surface of metal articles by forcing portions of its surface upwards into a depressions in die.

embrittlement. A term used in metallurgy to describe the tendency of a metal or an alloy such as steel to become brittle on exposure to a specific environment, with consequent failure known as brittle fracture. The main agent causing this problem is hydrogen, which is liberated in many electroplating and pickling processes or by corrosive acids. It diffuses into the metal surface, where it become trapped and eventually ruptures the metal. The extent of embrittlement depends somewhat on the nature and composition of the alloy; titanium and high-strength steels are especially subject to this effect.

Emde degradation reaction. A method of breaking carbon-nitrogen bonds, often opening ring-structures in the process by treating a quaternary ammonium halide, in alcoholic or aqueous solution, with sodium amalgam, *e.g.*,

$$\left[\text{(tetrahydroquinolinium, } \overset{\oplus}{N}(CH_3)_2)\right] Cl^{\ominus} \xrightarrow{Na(Hg)} C_6H_5-CH_2-CH_2-CH_2-N(CH_3)_2$$

This reaction is a modification of the Hofmann degradation.

Emde test. Methylaniline is differentiated from dimethylaniline by recrystallization of the platinic chloride double salts from hot water. The latter decomposes, while the former does not.

E_1 mechanism. Mechanism involving formation of carbonium ion as first reaction step ; in second step elimination of proton attached to β-carbon atom takes place with formation of unsaturated compound, *e.g.*,

$$H-\overset{|}{\underset{|}{C}}-\overset{|}{\underset{|}{C}}-X \xrightarrow[-X^{\ominus}]{slow} H-\overset{|}{\underset{|}{C}}-\overset{|}{C}^{\oplus}$$

$$H-\overset{|}{\underset{|}{C}}-\overset{|}{C}^{\oplus} + OH^{\ominus} \xrightarrow{fast} >C=C< + H_2O$$

Also known as mechanism of unimolecular elimination.

E_2 mechanism. Mechanism involving attack of base on β-hydrogen atoms with simultaneous elimination of group X as anion and formation of double bond. Rate of formation of active complex determines overall reaction rate, *e.g.*,

$$H\ddot{O}:^{\ominus} + H-\overset{|\beta}{\underset{|}{C}}-\overset{|\alpha}{\underset{|}{C}}-X \rightarrow$$

$$\rightarrow \left[H\ddot{O}\cdots H\cdots \overset{|}{\underset{|}{C}}=\overset{|}{\underset{|}{C}}\cdots X\right] \rightarrow H_2O + >C=C< + X^{\ominus}$$

activated complex

Also known as mechanism of bimolecular elimination.

emetic. A drug that induces vomiting.

emission lines. Spectral lines resulting from emission of electromagnetic waves by atoms, ions, or molecules during transition from excited states to the lower energy states.

emission spectral analysis. Spectroanalysis based on investigation of emission spectra. Also known as emission spectroanalysis.

emission spectroanalysis. *See* emission spectral analysis.

emission spectroscopy. Branch of spectroscopy dealing with study of spectra emitted by excited systems.

emission spectrum. Spectrum of radiation emitted by a given source. A spectrum of the type produced by an incandescent gas, which shows definite lines or bands at various frequencies. If these frequencies lie within the visible range, then their corresponding lines or bands are of characteristic colours.

emissive power. The intensity of radiation of given wavelength emitted at a given temperature.

emissivity. The total emissive power of a surface divided by that of a black body at the same temperature.

emmenagogue. A drug that initiates or increases the menstrual flow.

emollient. A pharmaceutical preparation or drug, which soothes irritated skin when applied externally.

empirical. Denoting a result that is obtained by experiment or observation rather than from theory.

empirical formula. The simplest formula for a compound that shows the elements and the relative numbers of their atoms present in it. It does not necessarily give the actual number of atoms in the molecule or their arrangement. The molecular formula may be the same as the empirical or a simple multiple of it, but the molecular formula cannot usually be established until the molecular mass has been determined. The empirical formula of benzene, for example, is shown by quantitative analysis to be CH. As its molecular mass is found to be 78, its molecular formula must be C_6H_6.

emulsification. The process of preparing an emulsion of one liquid in another.

emulsifying agent. A substance which aids the

formation of an emulsion, or which extends the range of temperature, concentration, etc., over which the emulsion remains dispersed, and, in general, increases the stability of the emulsion.

emulsion. A permanent suspension or dispersion, usually of oil or fat particles in water; the reverse also may occur, in which water is dispersed in an oil or fat. These are often designated as o/w (oil in water) and w/o (water-in-oil) emulsions, the latter occurring frequently in crude petroleum. The intimate and uniform mixture of naturally immiscible liquids is made possible by the action of an emulsifying agent, commonly fatty acids or long chain alcohols, at the oil-water interface. A fatty acid is comprised of a hydrocarbon chain which is insoluble in water and a negatively charged (polar) carboxyl radical (—COOH) which is attracted by water (also polar). As a result, the fatty acid molecule orients itself with the water-soluble carboxyl radical in the water and the insoluble hydrocarbon chain in the oil. The monomolecular film thus formed reduces the repulsion between the two liquids and creates a stable emulsion.

In such natural emulsions as milk and rubber latex, the particles of fat and rubber hydrocarbon are coated with a thin layer of protein, which keeps them from cohering; emulsifying agents of this type are called protective colloids, *e.g.*, alginates, agar, etc., and find many applications such as in ice cream, frozen desserts, etc. Polymerization is often carried out with monomers in emulsion form. *See also* interface; surface tension; emulsion polymerization.

emulsion calibration curve. Curve representing the following dependence: $S=f(\lg H)$, where S=blackening of photographic emulsion, H=radiation energy per unit surface. Also known as characteristic photographic curve; characteristic curve.

emulsion polymerization. An important technique for the manufacture of liquid dispersions of synthetic rubber latexes and paint resins such as acrylic and vinyl coatings. The oil-soluble monomers are emulsified with water at temperatures from about 265—333 K, the polymerization being accelerated with catalysts. This method is also applicable to systems involving two or more types of monomers (copolymerization), for example, of styrene and butadiene. *See also* **polymerization**; coplymer; emulsion.

emulsoid. Historical term used to define lyophilic sol. A colloidal dispersion formed when a liquid phase is dispersed over a liquid medium. These will not separate on standing. The term "emulsoid" parallels that of "suspensoid" for a solid phase dispersed over a liquid medium. In practice, however, the term emulsion is used loosely to cover both ordinary emulsions and colloidal ones.

enamel. 1. A hard ceramic coating, consisting principally of silicates, which is bonded to a metal surface in the molten state, the ceramic mixture is first applied to the metal in powder form, and the composite is then fired to the temperature where the coating melts to form a uniform, strongly bonded protective surface when cooled. This is called a porcelain enamel.

2. An organic protective coating similar to a paint, comprised of varnish or of oil-modified alkyl resin and urea or melamine resins, plus necessary pigments; after application, the coated product is exposed to heat or infrared radiation. Such coatings are called baked enamels.

enamines. Vinylamines; those having a hydrogen atom on nitrogen are usually unstable and rearrange to the corresponding imine:

```
        H
|   |   |              |
C═C—N    ⇌    —C—C═N—R
|   |   |              |  |
        R              H
```

But those with no hydrogen on nitrogen are stable. These are easily prepared from ketones with an α hydrogen and a secondary amine in presence of an acid catalyst.

enantiomeric configurational unit. Both of two substituted configurational units, whose configuration of chiral and prochiral atoms can be obtained as mirror reflection of one from the other in plane of main chain

```
       H                    CH₃
       |                    |
—CH₂—C—       and     —CH₂—C—
       |                    |
      CH₃                   H
```

enantiomer. *See* enantiomorph.

enantiomorph. One of two or more isomers containing an asymmetric element (usually carbon), which has the effect of causing the plane of polarized light to rotate to either right or left when the substance is placed under crossed nicol prisms. Each enantiomorph (or enantiomer) is a mirror image of its twin, that is, its tetrahedral (pyramidal) structure compares with its reversed image in the same way as right and left hands. These are sometimes called chiral arrangements. Enantiomorph is taken from the Greek, meaning "having an opposite form."

The illustration I, II is a schematic drawing of a mirror-image molecule, in which C is an asymmetric carbon and 1, 2, 3, and 4 are different univalents or groups. The illustration III, IV is an actual compound (lactic acid) which displays this arrangement ; glyceraldehyde is another such compound. In both cases, structures I and II are enantiomorphs :

```
     I                 II
L=left-hand       D=right-hand

     1                  1
     |                  |
  2—C—4             4—C—2
     |                  |
     3                  3

    III                IV
    CH3                CH3
     |                  |
HO—C—H             H—C—OH
     |                  |
    CO2H               CO2H
```

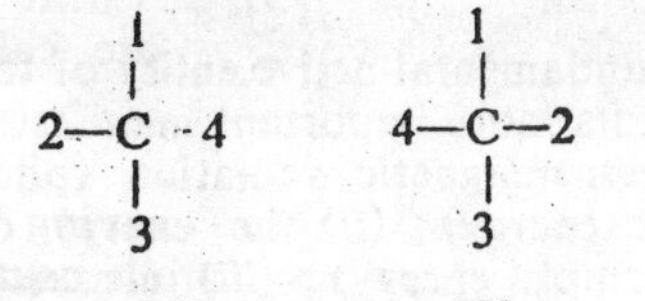

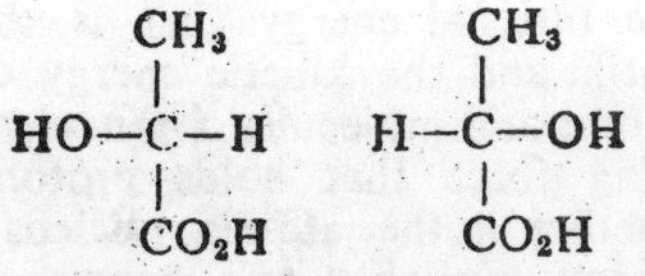

D and L are conventionally used to denote these configurations, the D standing for dextro (right-hand) and the L for levo(left-hand). These designations refer only to the configuration of the molecule and do not indicate the actual rotation the latter is represented by the symbols + and — (sometimes by *d* and *l*). Some D isomers are levorotatory and vice versa. Also known as enantiomer ; optical antipode.

enantiomorphic allotropy. A class of allotropic phenomena in which the transition from one form to another is reversible and takes place at a definite temperature, above or below which only one form is stable, *e.g.*, the alpha and beta forms of sulphur.

enantiotropic phases. Solid phases characterized by temperature of transition of one into another lower than melting temperatures of both phases.

enantiotropy. The reversible transformation of one form or one allotrope into another at a definite translation temperature.

encapsulation. 1. The coating or covering of an integrated group of small parts such as in an electrical or electronic assembly with a plastic or similar material, often in the form of a foam. The encapsulating material holds the components in position and thus aids the manufacture of complex circuitry for computers. aerospace equipment, etc. The materials used for this purpose are also called potting compounds : among them are polyurethane, epoxy, and polyester resins.

2. Microencapsulation refers to the formation of very small capsules of the order of 20 to 150 microns in diameter, containing a variety of materials. The capsule is a semipermeable membrane made of gelatin or any other similar polymer, which hinders or prevents release of the contained material until desired. Enzymes are immobilized in such microcapsules until they reach the desired stage or site of an enzymatic process. Medicines are also microencapsulated for controlled release in the body. The process is also used for adhesives for carbon or dyes for copy paper, and for perfumes, so that these materials remain stable until the capsules are broken by pressure, heat, or dissolution when the contents are to be released.

endo-. Combining term used in chemical nomenclature to indicate an inner position, specifically (*i*) in the ring and not in a side chain ; or (*ii*) attached to a bridge within the ring.

endocrine. Pertaining to ductless glands, or to their products or secretions.

endocyclic compounds. Unsaturated cyclic derivatives in which the double bond or bonds occur in the nucleus.

endo-exo isomerism. Isomerism of norborane (bicyclo[2.2.1]heptane) derivatives and their analogues ; derivatives with substituent in six-membered ring (at positions 2, 3, 5 or 6), located on side of bridge, are commonly designated as *exo-*; derivatives with substituents on opposite side—as *endo-*, *e.g.*,

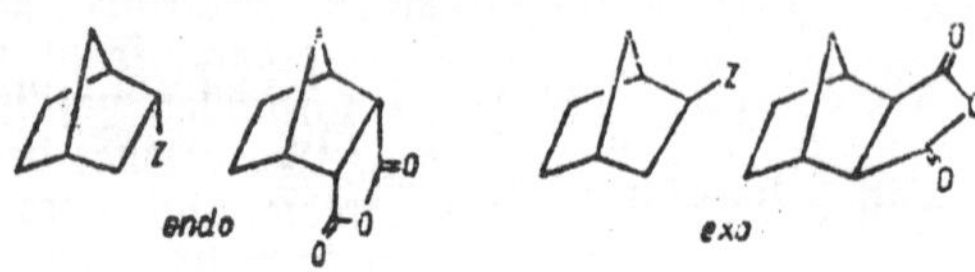

endopeptidases. A class of peptide cleaving enzymes which act at points in the interior of polypeptide chains rather than at terminal groups.

endothermal reaction. *See* endothermic reaction.

endosmosis. A type of osmosis in which the solvent dialyzes into the system. Exosmosis is the reverse process. The two processes may be illustrated by the conditions in the living cell; when the plasma is hypertonic, solvent passes from the cell into the plasma (exosmosis); when the plasma is hypotonic the solvent passes from the plasma into the cell (endosmosis).

endothermic reaction. A chemical reaction which requires absorption of heat from an external source, as, for example, the formation of carbon monoxide and hydrogen from coke and water (steam);

$$C + H_2O \xrightarrow{\text{heat}} CO + H_2;$$

also the formation of magnetite (mixed oxide of iron) from iron and water:

$$3Fe + 4H_2O \xrightarrow{\text{heat}} Fe_3O_4 + 4H_2$$

Also known as endothermal reaction.

end point. That point in a titration at which no further addition of titrating agent is necessary; it is usually denoted by a change in colour of an added substance called an indicator. The end point is often almost identical with the equivalence point, *i.e.*, the natural point between the titrant and the subject compound. End points are also indicated by instrumental methods. *See also* neutral; indicator.

end-product. 1. As generally used, this term refers to a substance or mixture that is primarily used "as is," without further chemical processing, for example carbon black, gasoline, fuel oils, waxes, etc. Many substances, though, are used not only for terminal purposes but as sources or intermediates for other products. For instance, sodium chloride is used both as such and as a source of chlorine; and chlorine also is used as a direct agent (as in bleaching and water treatment) as well as in the manufacture of hundreds of chemicals. The same is true of ethyl alcohol, ethylene dichloride, and many other organic chemicals. Thus, many substances are simultaneously end-products and intermediates, depending on their intended use.

2. The stable element at the conclusion of a radioactive decay series, for example, lead-206.

-ene. A suffix indicating the presence of one or more double bonds in a compound; thus it appears in the names of alkenes, cycloolefins and aromatics. For this reason, the spellings gasolene and kerosene are less desirable than gasoline and kerosine.

energy. Energy is an intangible quality by which a body is enabled to perform work (against an external resistance or force) to the surroundings.

Energy is the fundamental active entity of the universe. Among its more important manifestations are (*i*) electromagnetic radiation (photons, or radiant energy); (*ii*) the energy of combustion (thermal energy); (*iii*) electrical energy; (*iv*) kinetic energy (the energy of motion); (*v*) the internal energy that is the sum of the potential and the kinetic energy of its component atoms and molecules, (*vi*) nuclear energy, the binding force that holds protons and neutrons together in the atomic nucleus; and (*vii*) free energy available to a substance for reaction with other substances. The three laws of thermodynamics state the energy condition which determine the nature and extent of chemical reaction. The first and best-known of these (conservation of energy) is that the total of energy in the universe is constant and cannot be increased or diminished. Einstein formulated the concept of the equivalence of energy and mass, expressed by the equation $E=mc^2$.

energy balance. In nuclear reactions, the amount of energy released per individual reaction. It is positive when the energy is released, and negative when it is absorbed.

energy bands. In a single atom, according to

quantum theory, the orbiting electrons can only have certain discrete energies. The atom has a number of associated energy levels and the electrons occupy the levels with increasing order of energy and obey the Pauli's exclusion principle, *i.e.*, not more than two electrons can occupy each level. In a solid the situation is more complicated. As atoms come close together, the narrow energy levels become bands of allowed energies (Fig. 20), each band consisting of a large number of

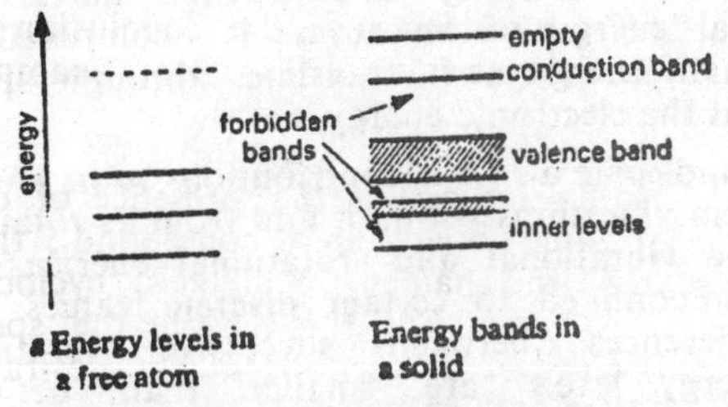

Fig. 20. Energy bands

closely spaced energy levels capable of containing two electrons. In general, within a band the number of levels is approximately equal to the number of atoms in the crystal The bands of permissible energy are called the allowed bands. Within any allowed energy band the number of constituent discrete energy levels varies with the energy.

The energy bands may either be filled or vacant depending on whether they correspond to filled or vacant levels in the free atoms. The energy regions between the bands are called forbidden band. The band of energies of the valence electrons in a solid is called the valence band.

If an electric field is applied to a solid the electrons can be accelerated by the field and they thus gain energy. This can only occur if they can move from their own energy level within the band to an unoccupied level at a higher energy. If the valence band is completely filled and there is a wide forbidden band between it and the next highest empty band than the substance behaves as an insulator. If the valence band is not completely filled or it overlaps with a higher empty energy band, then there are vacant levels where the electrons can go. The substance then behaves as a good conductor of electricity.

In the case of semiconductors there is a small forbidden gap between the valence band and higher vacant band. At absolute zero, all the electrons occupy the valence band and the substance acts as an insulator. As the temperature is raised some electrons gain sufficient thermal energy to escape from the valence band and cross the forbidden gap into the conduction band, leaving the valence band unfilled. As a result of it, conduction is possible i n both bands and the conductivity increases with the temperature.

At absolute zero all the electrons in a solid occupy the lower energy levels and the valence band is filled to a certain energy, while no higher levels are occupied. This level of maximum energy is called the Fermi level, E_F. At temperatures above absolute zero some electrons gain thermal energy and the distribution of electrons in the given energy levels

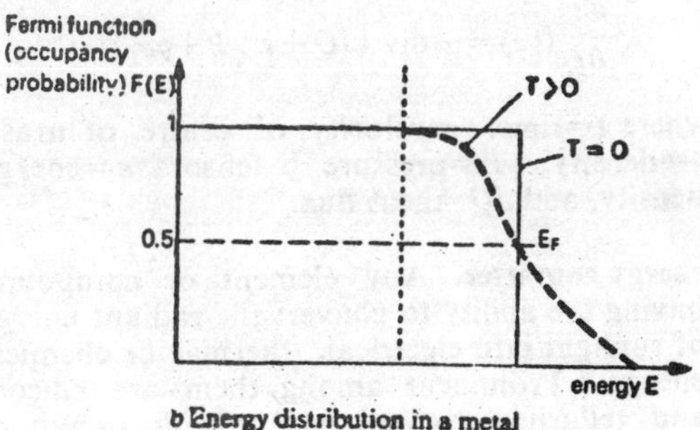

b Energy distribution in a metal

Fig. 21

can be derived by Fermi-Dirac statistics. The probability of finding an electrons at a particular energy is its Fermi function, F(E). Fig. 21 shows the function for a metal at absolute zero and a temperature above absolute zero. The Fermi level is then defined as the energy at which the probability of finding an electron is ½. The Fermi level is approximately constant

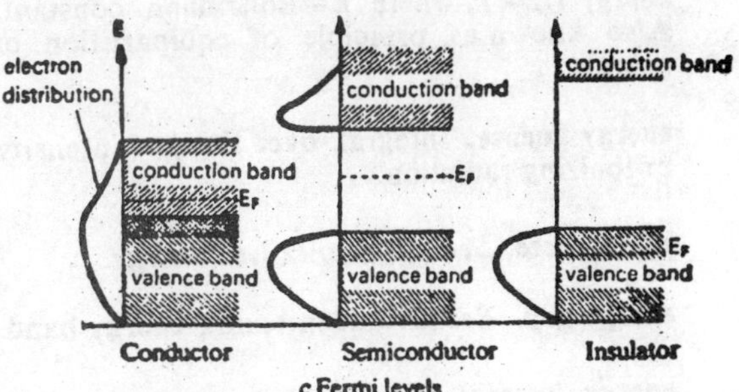

c Fermi levels

Fig. 22

with temperature. In semiconductors electrons are distributed between the valence band and the conduction band and the Fermi level lies in the forbidden gap between the two (Fig. 22). In an insulator the Fermi level lies in the valence band. The electronic distribution curves on Fig. 22 show how the number of electrons in each band varies with energy.

energy, binding. *See* binding energy.

energy conservation law. In isolated system. sum of all energies is constant, provided no nuclear reactions take place.

energy conservation law in continuous system. Equation :

$$\frac{\partial}{\partial t}(\rho e) = -\text{div}\,(JQ + v \,.\, P + \rho e v)$$

where t=time. v=velocity of centre of mass, ρ=density, P=pressure tensor e=energy density, and JQ=heat flux.

energy converter. Any element or compound having the ability to convert the radiant energy of sunlight into electrical, thermal or chemical energy. Prominent among them are silicon, and tellurium, as well as the chlorophyll of plants in photosynthesis.

energy degradation. Changes in form of energy take place in the direction of inereasing entropy, hence lesser availability

energy equipartition principle. At sufficiently high thermodynamic temperature T each additive energy term, which is quadratic either in generalized coordinate or in generalized momentum of particle corresponds to average energy $1/2\,kT$, where k=Boltzmann constant. Also known as principle of equipartition of energy.

energy fluence. Integral, over time, of intensity of ionizing radiation.

energy, free. *See* Helmholtz free energy.

energy gap. *See* forbidden band ; energy band.

energy, internal. *See* internal energy.

energy, lattice. *See* lattice energy.

energy levels. The possible values of energy of an atom or molecule.

Quantum theory states that only certain fixed values are possible and these may only change by an integral multiple of some fixed value. An electron orbiting the nucleus of the hydrogen atom may only occupy certain orbits of different energy. These allowed states of energy of the atom are called electronic energy levels. The ground state is the lowest possible energy level, higher states being called excited states. The total energy of an atom is composed of kinetic energy, as it translates through space, and the electronic energy.

A molecule also has contributions to its energy from vibrations within it and from its rotation. The vibrational and rotational energies are also confined to certain discrete values. The differences between successive vibrational energy levels are smaller than between electronic energy levels, rotational energy levels having even smaller differences. Each electronic energy level has several associated vibrational levels, which in turn have numbers of rotational levels. Change in the energy level result from the emission or absorption of photons of radiation. *See also* nuclear energy.

energy metabolism. Living cells carry on sequences of chemical reaction, the overall energetics of which are such as to lebel processes as spontaneous, *i.e.*, exergonic, in terms of the change in free chemical energy. A few of the chemical intermediates in such sequences are sufficiently reactive as they are so formed that inorganic phosphate may in turn be 'activated' chemically and thus be able to form substituted phosphoric acid anhydrides, adenosinetriphosphate (ATP) or its energetic equivalents. The ATP becomes a reactant in numerous energy-requiring reactions, both relatively simple (fatty acid activation) and relatively complete (muscle contraction).

energy of nuclear reaction. Difference between sum of the kinetic energies of nuclides (particles) after reaction, and corresponding sum of energies before reaction. This difference, considering the equivalence of mass and energy, is equal to the mass defect in the reaction.

energy of radioactivity. Difference between energies of mother nuclide and transformation products calculated from mass defect in a nuclear reaction.

energy, radiant. *See* radiant energy.

energy of rotation. The specific heat ratio for gases has a different value for monatomic, diatomic, triatomic, gases. The reason for this is that if a molecule consists of more than one atom, some of the heat supplied at constant volume goes to increasing the kinetic energy of rotation of the molecule and also, in some cases, to increasing the energy of vibration of the atoms within the molecule.

energy surface. In statistical mechanics a 2f-1 dimensional subspace of phase space, containing all phase points which satisfy equation :

$$H(q_1, \ldots, q_f, p_1, \ldots, p_f) = E,$$

where H=Hamilton function, E=energy, q=coordinates, p=momenta and f=number of degrees of freedom of system. For a free electron gas according to Fermi-Dirac distribution function, the surface is a sphere with

$$k = \tfrac{1}{8}(\pi/2)^{1/2}\,(3n)^{3/2}$$

where n=the density of electrons. When the variation in potential are taken into account, the energy surface becomes more complicated, but it always retains the symmetry of the reciprocal lattice.

energy sources. The sources of energy described here include both natural materials and man-made devices. Mechanical sources (wind, water, geothermal, oceans, etc.) are not considered, as they involve little or no chemistry.

Non-renewable sources are those of geologic origin. *i.e.*, petroleum, natural gas, coal, shale oil, oil sands, and uranium, which cannot be replaced once their supply is exhausted. Renewable material sources can be replenished on a predictable basis; include such cellulosic products as wood, bagasse, agricultural wastes, and residue from forest products industries (shavings, sawdust, bark, etc.), as well as methane from animal manures (biogas) and seaweed products (algae). The entries listed below give detailed information :

		fission
algae	biomass	fusion
bagasse	breeder	fuel cell
battery	cellulose	fuel oil
biogas	coal	gasoline
natural gas	gasohol	petroleum
nuclear energy	geothermal	shale oil
oil sands	energy	solar cell
peat	hydrogen	wood
ethyl alcohol	methane	

energy value. measure of the heat energy available by the complete combustion of a stated weight of the food ; often expressed in joules per kilogram or large calories per lb. It takes no account of the value of the food from any other point of view, or sometimes even of the suitability of the food for use by the human organism.

enfleurage. A process for the extraction of volatile oils and odoriferous substances from plants. The plants or flowers are spread on glass plates which have been coated with grease, fat, vaseline, or glycerol, that absorbs the oils. The essential oils are subsequently extracted from the absorbent by alcohol, or other solvents.

Engel-Precht process. Potassium bicarbonate cannot be made by a parallel process to the Solvay (as used for sodium bicarbonate) as, under similar conditions, it is too soluble and does not separate. The Engel-Precht procsss utilises hydrated magnesium carbonate to convert potassium chloride to potassium carbonate, also with the help of carbon dioxide. The magnesium carbonate is recovered and used again. The double salt first formed of potassium bicarbonate and magnesium carbonate ($KHCO_3.MgCO_3.4H_2O$) is known as "Engel's salt". Potassium carbonate is obtained from this either by treatment with water under pressure at 410K, or with an aqueous suspension of magnesium oxide, keeping the temperature below 293K.

Engel test. 1. Glycocoll is detected by its deep red colour (destroyed by acid) with ferric chloride.

2. With one drop phenol, and then some sodium hypochlorite solution, glycocoll gives a blue colour instantaneously.

engineering plastic. A type of plastic that is hard and stable enough to be treated as a metal, such materials are capable of sustaining high loads and stresses and are machinable and dimensionally stable. They are used in construction, as machine parts, automobile components, telephone handsets, and numerous other items. Among the more important are nylon, acetal resins, polycarbonate resins, and ABS resins.

enhanced oil recovery. Extraction of oil trapped in rock strata so firmly that it cannot be recovered by conventional pumping. The techniques in present use are as follows (*i*) chemical flooding. in which mixtures of strong detergents and salt water are introduced into the formation under high pressure to reduce the surface tension of the oil so that it will flow (a modification of this method, called micellar flooding, involves a second-step addition of a water-soluble high polymer), and (*ii*) hydraulic fracturing, in which a water solution of guar gum (in which bauxite is dispersed) is pumped into the strata, this pressure creates small fissures in the rock formation that are held open by the suspended bauxite particles (called "proppants"), permitting the trapped oil to flow through the apertures.

enhancer. A food additive that brings out the taste of a food without having any taste of its own. Monosodium glutamate is widely used for this purpose. The effective concentration of enhancers is much greater than that of potentiators, being measured in parts per thousand, as compared with parts per billion for potentiators.

enimization. A reversible intramolecular rearrangement of amines to yield imines :

$$\underset{\text{enamic form}}{RC{=}CH{-}NHR'} \rightleftharpoons \underset{\text{enimic form}}{RCH{-}CH{=}NR'}$$

enkephalins. Two pentapeptides, *met*-enkephalin (H-tyr-gly-gly-phe-met-OH) and *leu*-enkephalin (H-tyr-gly-gly-phe-leu-OH) which occur naturally in the brain and have similar analgesic and other properties to the opiates, morphine, cadeine, pethidine etc.

enolate anion. Mesomeric anion formed as a result of proton removal from the electronic-deficient atom bond with carbonyl group. One of the resonance structures has enol form, *e.g.*,

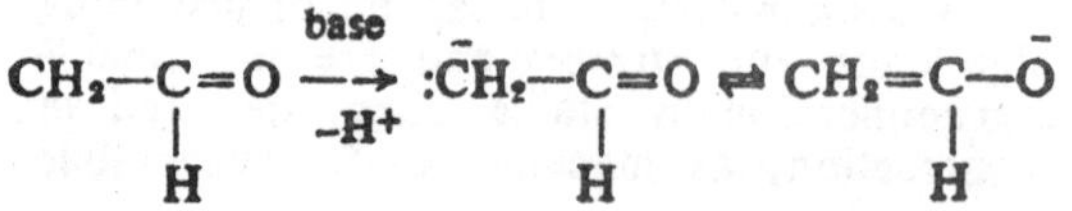

$$\underset{\substack{|\\H}}{CH_2{-}C}{=}O \xrightarrow[-H^+]{\text{base}} :\bar{C}H_2{-}\underset{\substack{|\\H}}{C}{=}O \rightleftharpoons CH_2{=}\underset{\substack{|\\H}}{C}{-}\bar{O}$$

enol form. Tautomer of constitution of α, β unsaturated alcohol, existing in equilibrium with keto form.

The enol form is formed from the keto form by migration of hydrogen atom from the adjacent carbon atom to the carbonyl group, producing the type :

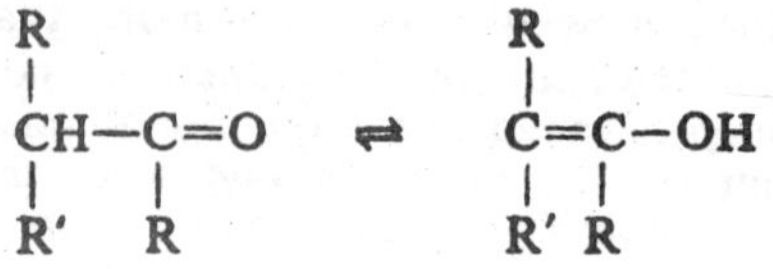

$$\overset{\substack{R\\|}}{\underset{\substack{|\\R'}}{CH}}{-}\underset{\substack{|\\R}}{C}{=}O \rightleftharpoons \overset{\substack{R\\|}}{\underset{\substack{|\\R'}}{C}}{=}\underset{\substack{|\\R}}{C}{-}OH$$

In this type of rearrangement the hydrogen is especially reactive and is easily replacably by other elements. The reaction is called enolization and occurs in many racemic compounds.

In most cases equilibrium is shifted toward keto form, so that enols cannot be isolated. Enolic esters and ethers form stable derivatives, *e.g.*,

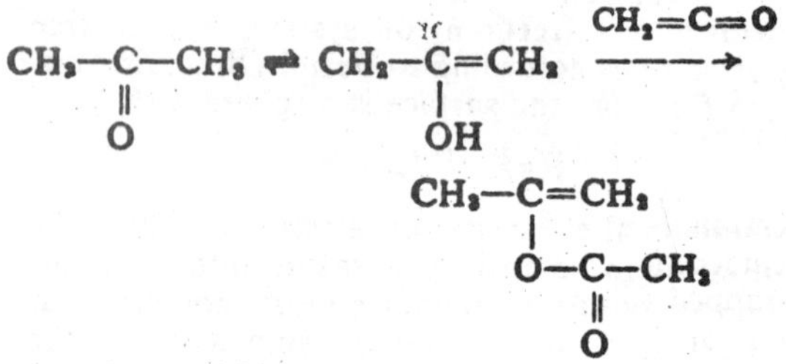

$$CH_3{-}\underset{\substack{\|\\O}}{C}{-}CH_3 \rightleftharpoons CH_2{-}\underset{\substack{|\\OH}}{C}{=}CH_2 \xrightarrow{CH_2=C=O} CH_3{-}\underset{\substack{|\\O-\underset{\substack{\|\\O}}{C}-CH_3}}{C}{=}CH_2$$

See also enol form.

enolization. Transformation of carbonyl compound into unsaturated alcohol (enol) ; *e.g.*,

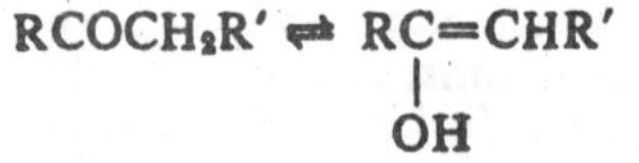

$$RCOCH_2R' \rightleftharpoons R\underset{\substack{|\\OH}}{C}{=}CHR'$$

enriched material. In radiochemistry, material in which content of one of the isotopes is increased over its natural abundance.

enrichment. 1. Any process which changes the isotopic ratio.

2. A process which increases the ore content of the lower levels of a deposit at the expense of the upper.

enrichment factor. In radiochemistry, quotient of abundance ratios of particular isotopes after and before enrichment.

enthalpy, H. Extensive thermodynamic function defined by the equation; $H=U+pV$, where U= internal energy, p=pressure, and V=volume.

At constant pressure the change in enthalpy measures the quantity of heat exchanged by the system with surroundings. Previously, enthalpy was referred to as total heat or heat content, but these terms are misleading. Enthalpy is, from the viewpoint of mathematics, a point function, as contrasted with heat and work, which are path functions. Point functions depend only on initial and final stages of the system undergoing a change they are independent of the paths or character of the change. Also known as enthalpy function.

enthalpy function. *See* enthalpy.

enthalpy of activation, ΔH^*. Intensive quantity equal to difference of molar standard of activated complex and enthalpies of substrates. For reaction in liquids enthalpy of activation is connected with activation energy *Ea* of collision theory :

$$\Delta H^* = Ea - RT$$

where R=molar gas constant and T=thermodynamic temperature.

entrainment. The state of being shut in or occluded, as of small units of gases of liquids trapped within a different phase, for example, air bubbles in a solid or liquid or water droplets in a solid. It also has the sense of "being carried along" when used in reference to liquid droplets present in a stream of vapours, as may occur in evaporation or distillation.

entropy. Extensive thermodynamic function. The internal and unavailable energy of a system, a quantity which rarely enters directly into calculations, but rather in the form of its increments or changes. It is arrived at in thermodynamics in the form of the conception of a change in the entropy of a system, which change in entropy is equal to the heat taken up during each infinitesimal stage of a reversible and isothermal process, divided by the temperature at which it is absorbed. For the entire change in the system, the change in entropy is equal to the summation of the infinitesimal terms as denoted by the expression,

$$\Delta S = \Sigma \frac{q}{T}$$

where ΔS = the change in entropy and $\Sigma q/T$=the summation of the terms obtained by dividing the infinitesimal amounts of heat by the temperatures at which they are gained or lost. At absolute zero the entropy of a system become zero ; it is a maximum usually when the available energy is a minimum. Most thermodynamic processes are accompanied by an increase in entropy. It is measured in joules per kelvin per mole (J/K. mol).

entropy density, S_V. Entropy per unit volume $S_V = S/V$, where S=entropy and V=volume of macroscopic element of system, respectively.

entropy factor. In absolute reaction-rate theory the value exp $(\Delta S^*/R)$, where S^* = entropy of activation, R=universal gas constant. Entropy factor is counterpart to the steric factor P in the collision theory.

entropy flow. J_s. Thermodynamic vector quantity, whose component J_{s_n} perpendicular to any surface at a given point is equal to entropy transferred through unit element of surface in units time.

entropy flux. *See* entropy flow.

entropy of activation. ΔS^*. Intensive quantity equal to difference of molar standard entropies of activated complex and substrates, defined by

$$\Delta S^* = \frac{\Delta H^* - \Delta G^*}{T}$$

where ΔH^* = molar standard activation enthalpy, ΔG^*= molar standard thermodynamic potential of activation, T=thermodynamic temperature. Activation entropy can be correlated with steric factor P of collision theory, *i.e.* for bi-molecular reaction :

$$\exp\left(\frac{\Delta S^*}{R}\right) \equiv P$$

where R=molar gas constant

entropy of fusion. The unavailable energy during a fusion, which is the quantity obtained when the heat absorbed in the conversion of a given substance from the solid to the liquid state is divided by the temperature at which the process takes place.

entropy of mixing. $S^M_{T,p}$. Intensive quantity equal to entropy increase S during isothermal isobaric formation of one mole of mixture from its components.

entropy source strength. *See* local entropy production.

entropy, standard. *See* standard entropy.

envelope conformation. Conformation in ring in which at least four cyclic-structure forming atoms are coplanar. Such conformation is observed in carbocyclic five-membered compounds (I) and in heterocyclic six-membered boron compound having plane sterical structure (II):

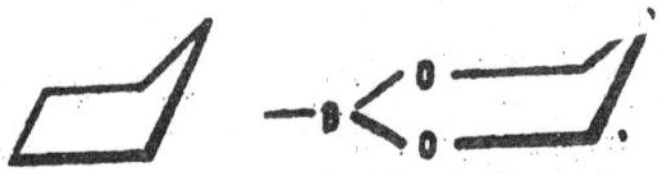

I II

environment. The collective total of external influences to which plants, animals, and man are exposed. This includes many chemical factors such as nutrients, *p*H, toxic substances, temperature, air, water, waste disposal, pesticides, etc. The study of these and their various maladjustments is called environmental chemistry.

enyl complexes. Complexes formed by organic ligands in which an odd number of electrons must be considered to be donated to the metal, *e.g.*,

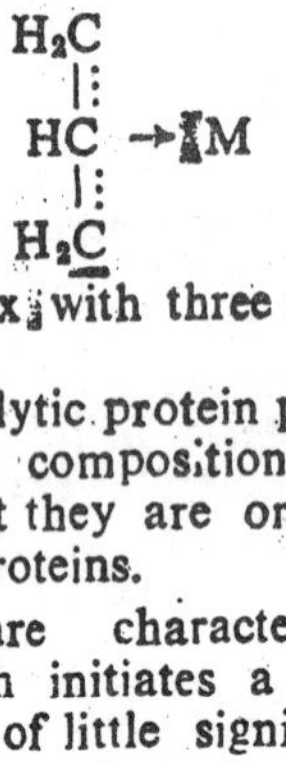

H_2C
⁝
HC → M
⁝
H_2C

a π-allyl complex with three electrons donated.

enzyme. A catalytic protein produced by living cells. The exact composition of most enzymes is unknown, but they are organic compounds related to the proteins.

Enyzmes are characterized by their specificity ; each initiates a certain chemical reaction, but is of little significance for other reaction. There are four types : (*i*) those which effect removal of water. (*ii*) those which aid transfer of electrons, (*iii*) those which transfer radicals, and (*iv*) those which act on a single carbon-carbon bond without removal or transfer of radicals.

All enzymes are proteins of high molecular weight ranging from about 10,000 to more than 1,000,000. An enzyme molecule may contain one or more polypeptide chains. The sequence of amino-acids within the polypeptide chain is characteristic for each enzyme and is believed to determine the unique three-dimensional conformation in which the chains are folded. This conformation, which is necessary for the activity of the enzyme, is stabilized by interactions of amino-acids in different parts of the peptide chains with each other and with the surrounding medium. These interactions are relatively weak and may be disrupted readily by temperature or *p*H variations, or changes in the polarity unfolding of the peptide chains and a concomitant loss of enzymatic activity, solubility and other properties characteristic of the native enzyme.

Enzymes have a vast number of specific function, among which are synthesis of proteins, conversion of starches to sugars, catalysis of fermentation processes, promotion of digestive reactions, etc.

They act by lowering the overall activation energy of a reaction sequence by involving a series of intermediates, or mechanism different from the spontaneous uncatalyzed reaction. Most enzymes show their activity within a narrow *p*H range and at around 300-310 K and are destroyed at higher temperatures.

The names of most enzymes terminate in either *-ase* or *-in*, for example, rennin, diastase, amylase, phosphatase, cholinesterase, and epimerase. Enzymes are similar to proteins in their chemical nature and often are closely associated with them (coenzymes). An example is ribonuclease, composed of 124 amino acids arranged in a specific sequence and having four disulphide cross-links.

enzyme inhibition. The prevention of an enzymic process as a result of the interaction of some substance with an enzyme so as to decrease the rate of the enzymic reaction. Enzyme inhibition are important as chemotherapeutic agents, as regulator in normal control of enzymic processes in living organisms, and as useful agents in the study of of biochemistry.

enzymolysis. A term applied to any reaction catalyzed by an enzyme.

Eotvos rule. Temperature coefficient *K* of molar surface energy has approximately constant value, which for liquids not undergoing association is $K=2.12$.

$$K = -\frac{d\,(V_m^{2/3}\,\sigma)}{dT}$$

where V_m =molar volume of liquid, σ=surface tension, T=thermodynamic temperature.

-epane. A suffix indicating a seven-membered ring.

Ephraim reagent for copper. A solution of 10 g. salicylaldoxime in 50 ml. of alcohol, which is then diluted to 1 litre with hot water; used as a test reagent for copper. A green precipitate indicates the presence of copper.

Ephraim test for thallous ions. The test reagent is prepared by making a solution of antimony trichloride in a slight excess of hydrochloric acid, adding water until no further turbidity occurs, then treating with solid potassium iodide. This solution gives a bright red to orange precipitate with an acidified or neutral solution of a thallous ions.

Ephraim test for vanadium. Evaporate mixture of 1 ml. of the solution to be tested and 1 ml. concentrated hydrochloric acid down to 0.4 ml. volume. Cool, add one drop of freshly prepared 0.1% ferric chloride solution and 2 drops of 1% dimethylglyoxime solution, and alkalinize with ammonia. A red colour indicates the presence of vanadium.

epi-. (Greek upon, on, to) Denoting certain relations, as follows: (*a*) the 1,5-position in naphthalene; as epidichloronaphthalene: (*b*) in aldoses and related compounds, identity of structure except arrangement about the α-carbon atom; as, epirhodeose (epimer of rhodeose); (*c*) a bridge connection: as 9,10-epidioxyanthracene (anthracene 9,10-peroxide).

epimer. One of a pair of isomeric substances which differ in structure only in the positions of one hydrogen atom and one hydroxyl radical, both of which are on the same asymmetric carbon atoms, usually the carbon atom is at the end of a carbon. Epimers are fairly common among the sugars. Also known as epimeride.

epimeride. *See* epimer.

epimerization. Process of changing configuration of atoms or groups of atoms at one of the chiral centres (at last two chiral centres should be persent in molecule); *e.g.*, epimerization at chiral carbon atom adjacent to aldehydic or ketonic group of a monose:

D-glucose (CHO; HO–; –OH; –OH; –OH; CH_2OH) ⇌ ($OH^{\ominus}$) eudiol (CH–OH; ‖ C–OH; HO–; –OH; –OH; CH_2OH) ⇌ D-mannose (CHO; HO–; HO–; –OH; –OH; CH_2OH) and D-fructose (CH_2OH; =O; HO–; –OH; –OH; CH_2OH)

-epin, -epine. A suffix indicating a seven-membered ring.

epitaxy. A method of growing a thin layer of material upon a single-crystal substrate, such as silicon, so that the lattice structure of the layer is identical to that of the substrate. The material, which may be the same as the substrate or a different one, is usually deposited from a gaseous mixture.

epithermal atoms. Atoms having kinetic energy slightly above their thermal agitation energy.

epithermal neutrons. Neturons of kinetic energy between 0.1 eV and 100 eV.

epoxidation. Oxidation of compound containing carbon-carbon double bond, resulting in formation of appropriate 1,2-epoxy (oxirane) derivative, *e.g.*,

$$\text{RHC}=\text{CHR} + \text{HO–OCOR}' \rightarrow \text{RHC}\overset{\text{O}}{—}\text{CHR} + \text{R}'\text{COOH}$$

epoxide. An organic compound containing a heterocyclic skeleton made up of two carbon atoms, both of which are attached to an oxygen atom by a single bond, as shown below:

$$-\text{C}\overset{\text{O}}{—}\text{C}-$$

Epoxides are quite reactive towards oxidizing and reducing agents and towards acids, and they also polymerize easily in presence of heat or catalyst, to yield epoxy resins. Epichlorohydrin and ethylene oxide are examples of this type.

epoxy resin. A type of synthetic resin made by reacting an epoxide compound (usually epichlorohydrin) with a hydroxyl-containing substance such as bisphenol-A or a polyhydric alcohol (glycerol). Such resins are thermosetting and have high strength and low shrinkage. Epoxy coatings have high resistance to attack by chemicals corrosion and weathering, and to electricity.

Eppinger test. Glyoxylic acid is detected in solution by adding a 0.1% indole solution, and floating the mixture on concentrated sulphuric acid. A red ring indicates the presence of glyoxylic acid.

equalizing solvent. *See* levelling solvent.

equation, Beattie and Bridgeman. *See* Beattie and Bridgeman equation.

equation, Berthelot. *See* Berthelot equation.

equation, chemical. *See* chemical equation.

equation, Clapeyron-Clausius. *See* Clapeyron-Clausius equation.

equation, Dieterici. *See* Dieterici equation.

equation, electronic. An equation, or partial equation, showing the transfer or liberation or gain of electrons. For example,

$$Na \rightarrow Na^+ + e^-$$
$$2S_2O_3^{2-} \rightleftharpoons S_4O_6^{2-} + 2e^-$$
$$2I^- \rightarrow I_2 + 2e^-$$

equation, Eötvös. *See* Eötvös, equation.

equation, Fanning. *See* Fanning equation.

equation, Geiger-Nuttall. *See* Geiger-Nuttal rule.

equation, Gibbs-Helmholtz. *See* Gibbs-Helmholtz equation.

equation, ionic. *See* ionic equation.

equation, Keyes. *See* Keyes equation.

equation, Kirchhoff. *See* Kirchhoff equation.

equation Langmuir. *See* Langmuir equation.

equation, molecular. *See* molecular equation.

equation, Morse. *See* Morse equation.

equation of continuity. An expression of the conservation of mass for a fluid, wherein the excess of flow of fluid mass into a region, over the flow from the region, is equated to the time rate of increase of density. The equation is commonly written in the form :

$$\frac{\partial \rho}{\partial t} = -\nabla \cdot V$$

where $\partial\rho/\partial t$ is the rate of increase of density, ∇ is the vector differential operator, V is the mass of fluid flowing through unit cross-section in unit time, and $-\nabla . V$ is the excess of inward over outward flow, or the convergence of the fluid.

equation of reference kinetic curves. Kinetic equation in which concentrations of substrates are expressed by fraction of initial concentrations.

equation of state. A relationship which defines, or partly defines, the physical condition of a homogeneous system by relating its pressure, temperature, volume or concentration, and the gas constant. Furthermore, all equations of state, except the simple $pV=RT$, contain additional constants or variable. (*Also see* equation of state, general ; equation of state, thermodynamic ; Keyes equation ; Berthelot equation ; Beattie and Bridgeman equation ; van der Waals equation ; Dieterici equation ; and Clausius equation.)

equation of state, general. *See* general equation of state.

equation of state, reduced. *See* reduced equation of state.

equation of state, thermodynamic. *See* thermodynamic equation of state.

equation of state, virial. *See* general equation of state.

equation, oxidation-reduction. *See* oxdation-reduction equation.

equation, Stark-Einstein. *See* Stark-Einstein equation.

equation, Stefan-Boltzmann. *See* Stefan-Boltzmann equation.

equation, Svedberg. *See* Svedberg equation.

equation transmutation. *See* transmutation equation.

equation, van der Waals. *See* van der Waals equation.

equatorial bond. One of the six bonds which extend outward and away from three-fold axis of symmetry in chair form of cyclohexane. Equatorial bonds are declined 19.5° alternately upwards with respect to mean plane of ring, *i.e.*, plane bisecting all C—C ring-forming bonds :

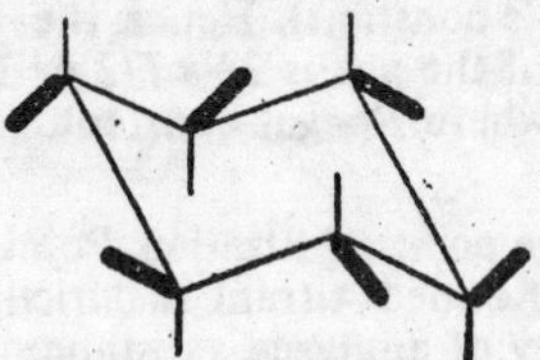

Fig. 23. Equatorial bond

equilibrium. A state of balance in terms of the molecular concentration of compounds undergoing a reversible reaction. The equilibrium constant, *K*, is the ratio of the molecular concentration of the reaction products to that of the starting materials. It is strongly affected by temperature, which increases the rate of the reaction. Equilibrium exists when the rates of the two reactions are equal at a given temperature.

Physical equilibrium is said to exist when, in a liquid partially filling a closed container, the number of molecules expelled from the surface by internal molecular impact is equal to the number of molecules attracted back into the liquid at the interface when the air-space has become saturated, that is, when it can retain no more molecules of vapour. Thus, there is a reversible physical reaction which reaches equilibrium condition between two molecular concentration (of the liquid and the vapour, though no chemical change occurs. *See also* vapour pressure.

equilibrium, apparent. A condition of apparent equilibrium in a system which is brought about by the interference of some factor (usually accidental) that prevents the system from proceeding to a true equilibrium. Often the interfering factor is a great diminution in the velocity of one of the reactions. Also known as false equilibrium.

equilibrium asymmetric transformation. Change of configuration at one chiral carbon atom in compound containing two or more chiral carbon atoms, proceeding till new thermodynamic equilibrium is established.

equilibrium, chemical. *See* chemical equilibrium.

equilibrium, chemical law of. *See* law of chemical equilibrium.

equilibrium constant. Consider the general reaction :

$$aA + bB \rightarrow cC + dD$$

occurring at constant temperature *T* and pressure *P* when all of the substance involved are in their standard states of unit activity. The quantity ΔG° is known as the

$$\Delta G^0 = [c\mu^\circ_C + d\mu^\circ_D] - [a\mu^\circ_A + b\mu^\circ_B] \qquad (1)$$

standard free energy change of the reaction at that temperature and pressure are the chosen standard states (Standard state properties are commonly designated by superscript, ΔG°, μ°,) Since each of the standard chemical potentials (μ°) is a unique property determined by the temperature, pressure, standard state, and chemical identity of the substance concerned, the standrad free energy change ΔG° is a constant (parameter) characteristic of the particular reaction for the chosen temperature, pressure, and standard states.

When the system has come to chemical equilibrium at constant temperature and pressure, $\Delta G = 0$, and ΔG° is given by Eq. (2), where the value of K° is shown as Eq.

(3), and the activities are the quilibrium values. The ratio of the activities

$$\Delta G^\circ = -RT \ln K^\circ \quad (2)$$

$$K^\circ = \left| \frac{a_C^c \, a_D^d}{a_A^a \, a_B^b} \right| \quad (3)$$

at equilibrium, K°, is called the equilibrium constant or more precisely, the themodynamic equilibrium constant. (The terms K° and Q° are written with superscripts to emphasize that they represent ratios of activities.) The equilibrium constant is a characteristic property of the reaction system, since it is determined uniquely in terms of the standard free energy change. The term $-\Delta G^\circ$ represents the maximum net work which the reaction could make available when carried out at constant temperature and pressure with the substances in their standard states.

The equilibrium constant K is also defined as ratio of product of equilibrium partial pressures of products and product of equilibrium partial pressures of substrates partial pressure) of each reactant is raised to power equal to corresponding stoichiometric coefficient. Equilibrium constant can be expressed in terms of: mole fractions (K_x), molar concentration (K_c), molalities (K_m) or partial pressures (K_p); it depend on temperature, pressure and composition of system. Also known as approximate equilibrium constant.

equilibrium diagram. A graphical representation, commonly plotted from temperature and pressure data, which shows the condition of equilibrium between various phases of a substance, or system of substance.

equilibrium fluctuations. Fluctuations in system in thermodynamic equilibrium. Also known as thermodynamic fluctuation.

equilibrium, heterogeneous. *See* heterogeneous equilibrium.

equilibrium, homogeneous. *See* homogeneous equilibrium.

equilibrium, isothermal. *See* isothermal equilibrium.

equilibrium, metastable. *See* metastable equilibrium.

equilibrium, photochemical. *See* photochemical equilibrium.

equilibrium, polyphase. *See* equilibrium, heterogeneous.

equilibrium, radioactive. *See* radioactive equilibrium.

equipartition of energy. In any physical system in thermal equilibrium the average energy per degree of freedom is the same, and equals $kT/2$, where k=Boltzmann's constant and T= thermodynamic temperature of the system. This provides a means of calculating the total thermal energy of a system. Thus, in one mole of a monoatomic gas each atom possesses three degrees of freedom (due to its translatory motion), and the total number of atoms is N Avogadro's constant). Hence the total energy per mole of the gas is $3NkT/2$ or $3RT/2$, since $k=R/N$, where R=gas constant.

equivalence point of titration. Point at which the amount of added titrant is strictly equivalent to quantity of analysed substance in solution. Also known as theoretical end-point of titration.

It is the theoretical end point of the titration, which differs from that found on analysis, because of the limitations of the indicator or indicating system, and of the observational error.

equivalent. A terms used generally in chemistry to connote equal combining power. Thus the equivalent weight of an elements is its atomic weight divided by its valence in the particular reaction in the question.

equivalent conductivity, Λc. Conductivity of 1 gram equivalent of electrolyte in solution with a given concentration :

$$\Lambda c = \frac{1000x}{c}$$

where x =specific conductance of solution with concentration c gram equivalents/dm^3.

equivalent conductivity at infinite dilution. *See* limiting equivalent conductivity.

equivalent electrons. For an atom, electrons in the same orbital (whereby they have the same principal quantum number and the same azimuthual quantum number). For a molecule, electrons having the same quantum numbers, apart from spin, and the same symmetry *g* or *u*.

equivalent of acid. The number of parts by weight of the acid that contain 1.008 parts by weight of hydrogen replaceable by a metal.

equivalent of base. The number of parts by weight of the base that will exactly neutralise the equivalent weight of an acid (defined as above) ; or (more directly) the number of parts by weight of the base that will react with 1.008 parts by weight of hydrogen replaceable by a metal to form a salt and water.

equivalent of oxidising agent. The number of parts by weight of the compound that will furnish 8 parts by weight of oxygen for the oxidising reaction.

equivalent weight. The weight of an element that will combine with 7.9997 grams (one-half the atomic weight of oxygen. This weight of oxygen will combine with exactly 1.0079 grams of hydrogen (*i.e.*, the atomic weight of hydrogen). Thus, 1.0079 grams of hydrogen can be taken as equivalent to 7.9997 of oxygen and hydrogen, is said to have an equivalent weight of 1. As hydrogen is the lightest element, the combining power of all other elements is greater than 1. The equivalent weight principle was formerly used in determination of atomic weights, but this method has been replaced by the mass spectrograph. Equivalent weight, is now called the combining weight.

erbium. An element.

	Symbol	Er
	Atomic No.	68
State Solid	Atomic Wt.	167.26
Group IIIB	Valence	+3
	Isotopes	6 stable
	m.p.	1522°C
	b.p.	2510°C

Erbium closely related to yttrium and teribium, is a member of lanthanide series, and is strongly electropositive element.

It is readily flammable and has a quite high electrical resistivity, 87 microhm-cm as compared with copper, 1.67 microhm-cm, at room temperature. At low temperatures the metal is anti-ferromagnetic and at still lower temperatures becomes strongly ferromagneic. It is used in lasers, magnetic alloys, and similar specialized devices. It forms compounds with the halogens and also forms nitrate, oxalate, phosphate, carbonate, and acetate.

Erdmann reagent for potassium. Dissolve 30 g. cabalt nitrate in 60 ml. water and add 100 ml. 50% sodium nitrite solution and 10 ml. glacial acetic acid. This reagent gives a yellow precipitate with potassium and rubidium salts. Many modifications of this reagent have been developed.

Erdmann test for nitrite. 100 ml. of the solution to be tested is mixed with 10 ml. of an acidified solution of 2 g. per liter sodium sulphanilate, and then is added 1.0 g. 1-amino-8-hydroxynaphthalene-4,6-disulphonic acid. A bright Bordeaux-red colour indicates the presence of nitrite.

eremacausis. Slow combustion or oxidation such as the rusting of iron, decay of wood, or oxidation of phosphorus in air.

erg. A unit of work or energy in cgs system of units, being the work done when a steady force of one dyne produces a displacement of 1 cm in the direction of the force.

ergodic systems. System with time average of any integral of motion which is symmetric function of dynamic variables of all particles, depending solely on energy of system.

ergodic theorem. In isolated system time average are equal to average values in microcanonical ensemble.

Several conditions for validity of ergodic theorem have been given. However, they cannot be checked in the case of real microscopic system.

ergon. 1. A quantum of energy which is calculated for any given oscillator by multiplying the frequency of the oscillator by Planck's constant.

2. This term is used also by some writers to denote an enzyme which has a vitamin as part of the prosthetic group.

Erlenmeyer-Plochl azlactone and amino acid synthesis. A reaction of carbonyl compounds and acylglycines which yields unsaturated alzactones which undergo reduction and hydrolysis to yield amino acids *e.g.*,

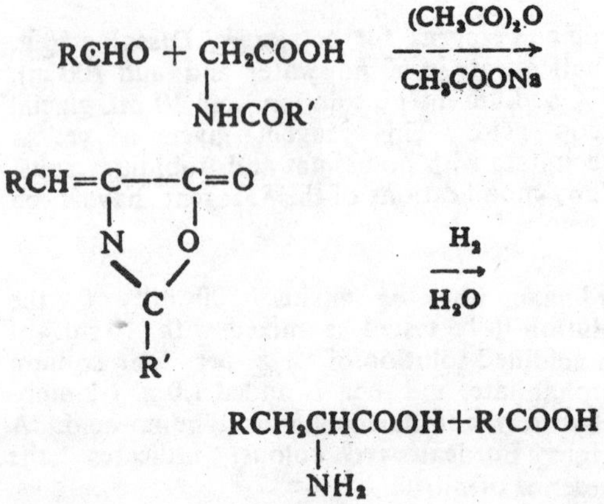

$$RCHO + \underset{\displaystyle NHCOR'}{\underset{|}{CH_2COOH}} \xrightarrow[CH_3COONa]{(CH_3CO)_2O}$$

$$\begin{array}{l} RCH{=}C{-}{-}C{=}O \\ \quad\;\; | \qquad | \\ \quad\;\, N \qquad O \\ \qquad \diagdown \;\; \diagup \\ \qquad\;\; C \\ \qquad\;\; | \\ \qquad\;\; R' \end{array} \quad \xrightarrow[H_2O]{H_2}$$

$$\underset{\displaystyle NH_2}{\underset{|}{RCH_2CHCOOH}} + R'COOH$$

Erlenmeyer rule. This originally postulated as that all unsaturated alcohals of the types

$$C{-}CHOH \text{ and } \overset{|}{\underset{|}{C}}{-}COH{-}\overset{|}{\underset{|}{C}}{-}$$

were unstable and that any reaction leading to this would give instead the aldehyde or keto forms

$$\overset{|}{\underset{|}{CH}}{-}CHO \text{ or } \overset{|}{\underset{|}{CH}}{-}CO{-}\overset{|}{\underset{|}{C}}{-}$$

Later findings have modified this rule, especially when the carbon atoms concerned are connected with carbonyl, or carbonyl-group, but it still holds good for monohydric unsaturated alcohols.

erosion. Physical removal of material from a surface by mechanical means such as flowing water, stream, or gas. It is often accelerated by abration from entrained particles or by corrosion.

erythrocyte. The most important component of mammalian blood, chiefly composed of the protein-iron complex called haemoglobin and commonly known as the red cell of the blood. Erythrocytes can be removed from blood by centrifugation, to give plasma.

erythro form. Diastereoismer having two adjacent non-equivalent chiral centres of configuration shown below :

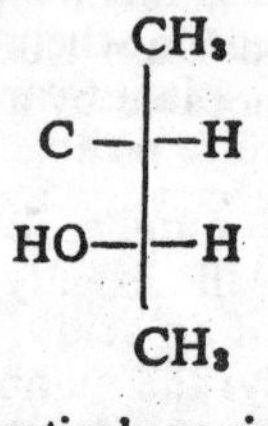

$$\begin{array}{c} CH_3 \\ | \\ C{-}|{-}H \\ | \\ HO{-}|{-}H \\ | \\ CH_3 \end{array}$$

i.e., two identical or similar atoms (or groups of atoms) situated on the same side of Fischer's projectional formula.

Esbauch reagents. Aminopyrine and ammonium thiocyanate, used as reagents for copper. In Martini's microtest, a drop of dilute copper solution is treated with a drop of saturated ammonium thiocyanate solution, and then with a drop of aminopyrine. A grey-brown precipitate is obtained.

escape peak. Peak in gamma radiation spectrum caused by escape of one or two annihilation photons or X-rays from detector after photoelectron emission.

Eschaich test for cyanide. 1 ml. of a 10% aminopyrine solutions is mixed with 1 ml. of 25% cupric sulphate solution and 10-12 drops glacial acetic acid ; then the solution to be tested is added dropwise. A blue colour, formed by a turbidity, indicates the presence of cyanide.

Eschaich test for phenol. Add to the solution to be tested, 10 drops of ammonia, 0.05 g. sodium or ammonium persulphate and 4-5 drops of 0.1N sodium nitrite. A green colour, changing to bule, indicates the presence of phenol.

Eschweiler-Clarke reaction. Methylation of primary and secondary amines with formaldehyde and formic acid (in excess) at 373 K, *e.g.*,

$$RNH_2 + 2HCHO + 2HCOOH \rightarrow RN(CH_3)_2 + 2CO_2 + 2H_2O$$

eso-. (Greek) Within ; a prefix denoting immediate attachment to a ring atom.

essential aminoacid. An amino acid, that is not synthesized by the animal organism but must be obtained externaliy, that is, by ingestion of plant products of one type or another.

essential element. Any of a number of elements required by living organims to ensure normal growth, development, and maintenance. Apart from the elements present in the organic compounds (C, H, N, O), plants, animals, and microorganisms all require a range of elements in inroganic forms in varying amounts. The major elements, present in tissues in relatively large amounts (greater then 0.005%) are Ca, P, K, Na, Cl, S, and Mg. The trace elements occur at much lower concentrations, the most important of which are, Fe, Mn, Zn, Cu, I, Co, Se, Mo, Cr, and Si.

essential fatty acids. Fatty acids that must normally be present in the diet of certain animals, including man. Essential fatty acids, which include linoleic acid and linolenic acid, all possess double bonds at the same two position along their hydrocarbon chain and so can act as precursors of prostaglandins.

essential oil. Odoriferous, oily products of plant origin which are distillable. These are nonfatty oil with a strong, usually pleasant, odour and taste. Terpenes are the chief components of many essential oils; others are mixtures of aldehydes, acids, alcohols, like, *e.g.*, benzaldehyde and hydrocyanic acid occur in oil of bitter almond. Essential oils are subject to evaporation. in contrast to fixed vegetable oils, which are not. They are obtained from a wide variety of plant life, some having such exotic names as oil bois de rose, neroli oil, ylang-ylang oil, geraniol, rose otto, patchouli oil, and citrous peel oils. They are used in perfumes, odorants, and food flavourings. An exception is turpentine oil, used chiefly as a solvent and paint thinner. The term "essential" refers to the distilled "essence" of a material, not to its importance. Though they are products of vegetation, essential oils are not classified as vegetable oils.

ester. A compound formed from an alcohol and an organic or inorganic acid by the elimination of water. The alcohol residue takes the position assumed by cations in the inorganic salts. The general formula for an ester is RCOOR. While the reaction

$$ROH + RCOOH \rightarrow RCOOR + H_2O$$

appears analogous to the salt-forming acid-base neutralization of inorganic chemistry, its mechanism is different. *See also* esterification.

esterase. Any enzyme or ferment which brings about the hydrolysis of esters.

ester gum. A synthetic gum resin prepared by the reaction of a natural gum resin with a polyhydric alcohol, such as glycerol, at moderate temperatures.

esterification. Process of obtaining esters from carboxylic acids (or their derivatives such as chlorides) and alcohol (or phenols), *e.g.*,

$$CH_3COOH + HOC_2H_5 \overset{H^+}{\rightleftharpoons} CH_3COOC_2H_5 + H_2O$$

$$R{-}C(=\ddot{O})(\ddot{O}{-}H) \underset{-H^{\oplus}}{\overset{H^{\oplus}}{\rightleftharpoons}} R{-}C^{\oplus}(\ddot{O}{-}H)(\ddot{O}{-}H) \underset{-R'\text{-}^{18}OH}{\overset{R'\text{-}^{18}OH}{\rightleftharpoons}} R{-}C(\ddot{O}{-}H)(\ddot{O}{-}H){-}^{18}\ddot{O}^{\oplus}(H)R'$$

$$\Updownarrow$$

$$R{-}C(=\ddot{O})({}^{18}\ddot{O}{-}R') \underset{H^{\oplus}}{\overset{-H^{\oplus}}{\rightleftharpoons}} R{-}C^{\oplus}(\ddot{O}{-}H)({}^{18}\ddot{O}{-}R') \underset{H_2O}{\overset{-H_2O}{\rightleftharpoons}} R{-}C(\ddot{O}{-}H)({}^{\oplus}OH_2){-}^{18}\ddot{O}R'$$

Although esterification superficially resembles the neutralization of a base by an acid (assuming that the alcohols are sources of hydroxyl group, which of course, they are not), nothing could be further from the actual state of affairs. The mechanism of esterification is probed by using an isotopically labeled alcohol as a reactant, it is seen that ^{18}O label is retained in ester, rather than being lost to water. The mechanism, which not only accounts for the labeled oxygen, but also explains the steric hindrance and the acid catalysis, is shown on the last page.

esterification constant. A constant that depends upon the velocity of the esterification of an acid dissolved in an alcohol in the presence of N/20 alcoholic hydrochloric acid. As the reaction velocity varies with the temperature and the alcohol employed the constant is qualified thus :

$$E^{20^\circ}_{EtOH} \quad \text{or} \quad E^{15^\circ}_{MeOH}$$

esterification law. *See* law of esterification.

ester number. A ' constant" of a fat or wax. It is calculated from the amount of alkali needed to saponify the netural esters in a given fat and is equal to the saponification number minus the acid number. Specifically the number of milligrams of potassium hydroxide required to saponify 1 gram of oil, fat, or wax.

Ester test reaction. Vanillin is detected by a violet colour formed on boiling the solution to be tested with a solution of mercury in nitric acid and water.

Esteve test. To detect barium in the presence of strontium and calcium, add to 5 ml. of the solution to be tested, 1 ml. of 1 : 100 sulphuric acid and 1 ml. of 1 : 1000 potassium chromate solution (without mixing the liquids). A white ring changing to yellow, at the interface indicates the presence of barium.

Estill-Nugent test. Aluminium is detected by dissolving the sample to be tested in hot 6 N sulphuric acid, adding 5-10 ml. water and enough alkanet tincture to colour the solution ruby-red. Add 6 N ammonium hydroxide until the colour changes to blue, and add 3.5 ml. in excess. A purple precipitate which appears in about 5 minutes (rising to the surface as a compact mass) indicates the presence of aluminium.

estrogen. Collective term for naturally occurring steroid compounds formed in the ovary; they are also prepared synthetically. Estrogens have hormonal activity and are essential for normal female sexual development. Among the more important are estrone and estradiol. They can be obtained from the urine of pregnant animals and have appilication in the oral contraceptive field and for specialized medical purposes. *See also* antifertility agent.

-etane. A suffix indicating a four-membered ring.

Etard reaction. The direct oxidation of an aromatic or heterocyclic bound methyl group to an aldehyde group by chromyl chloride or certain metallic oxides ;

$$RCH_3 \xrightarrow{CrO_2Cl_2} RCHO$$

When benzene homologues with longer side chains are treated with CrO_2Cl_2 a ketone is the usual product, but with ethylbenzene a mixture of phenylacetaldehyde and acetophenone is formed.

etching. Suitable selective attack, of the surface of polished metal for metallographic examination. It may be conducted by chemical attack, electrolytic dissolution, heating in air or vacuum.

-ete. A suffix indicating a four-membered ring.

-etene. A suffix indicating a four-membered ring.

ethanolysis. Alcoholysis in which the alcohol formed is ethyl alcohol.

ethenoid. Containing an ethene or ethylene linkage.

ethers. A class of compounds derived from two alcohol molecules by the elimination of water.

$$\begin{matrix} CH_3CH_2OH & & CH_2CH_3 & \\ & & | & \\ + & \rightarrow & O & + H_2O \\ & & | & \\ CH_3CH_2OH & & CH_2CH_3 & \end{matrix}$$

Ethers in which the alcohol radicals are identical are termed simple ethers ; those in which they are different are mixed or complete ethers.

Most common ethers are liquids, and some are extremely flammable. The ethers of ethylene glycol form a well-known group of useful solvents and plasticizers. There are a few solid ethers of cellulose. The term "petroleum ether" for petroleum derived naphtha is a misnomer.

etherification. Process of obtaining ethers R—O—R′, usually by substituting hydrogen atom or aryl group, *e.g.*,

$$R{-}OH + CH_3OSO_2OCH_3 \xrightarrow{\text{base}} R{-}O{-}CH_3 + CH_3OSO_3H$$

ethical drug. A drug obtainable on prescription not offered for open sale.

ethide. A compound of a metal and the ethyl radical. as zinc ethide, $Zn(C_2H_5)_2$. The ethides may be regarded as ethane in which one hydrogen atom has been substituted by a univalent metal.

ethinyl. *See* ethynyl.

ethinylation. The reaction between ethyne and organic substrates to produce substances having an intact ethynic bond, *e.g.*,

$$HCHO + HC \equiv CH \rightarrow HO{-}CH_2{-}C \equiv C{-}CH_2{-}OH$$

ethoxalyl. The radical C_2H_5OOCCO—.

ethoxy. The radical C_2H_5O—.

ethyl. The univalent group, CH_3CH_2—, the second member of the homologous series of paraffinic hydrocarbon (alkyl) radicals ; it is derived by removing one hydrogen atom from ethane. CH_3CH_3. and often appears in formulas as C_2H_5—. When a second hydrogen atom is removed from ethane, the divalent ethylene group is formed, $-CH_2CH_2-$. The corresponding olefin, $H_2C{=}CH_2$, is also called ethylene, and the two meanings of ethylene are sometimes confused in naming compounds. Like the methyl group, the ethyl group is present in a large number of organic compounds.

ethylation. The formation of a compound by introduction of the ethyl radical.

Ethyl-Dow process. A method for the recovery of bormine from sea water. Treatment with chlorine displaces the bromine from bromides present, then air is passed through the acidulated sea water to remove the bromine, and this air is passed through bromine-absorption columns where the bromine is absorbed in a solution of sodium carbonate, which is then acidfied, and steam-distilled to obtain the bromine.

ethylene. The radical $-CH_2CH_2-$.

ethyldnedioxy. The radical

$$-O{-}CH_2{-}CH_2{-}O{-}.$$

ethylene linkage. $\overset{|}{\underset{|}{C}}{=}\overset{|}{\underset{|}{C}}$. Carbon-carbon double bond. Also known as olefinic link.

ethylidene. The radical $CH_3CH{=}$.

ethylidyne. The radical $CH_3C{\equiv}$.

ethynyl. The radical $CH{\equiv}C$—.

ethynylation. Introduction of ethynyl group $-C{\equiv}CH$ (or $-C{\equiv}CR$) into molecule of organic compound, *e.g.*,

$$-C \equiv CH + -\overset{|}{C}{=}O \xrightarrow{\text{KOH}} -C \equiv C{-}\overset{|}{\underset{|\atop OH}{C}}{-}$$

ethynylene. The radical—$C \equiv C$—.

-etidine. A suffix indicating a four-membered ring.

-etine. A suffix indicating a four-membered ring.

etio-. (Greek aitia) cause ; a prefix used tc denote certain degradation products.

Etti test reaction. Resorcinol is detected by a violet colour formed on triturating a solution containing it with vanillin and hydrochloric acid. This test is also used to detect vanillin.

euchlorine. A name given by Davy to the gas that is evolved when potassium chlorate is warmed with concentrated hydrochloric acid. Pebal proved that it is actually a mixture of chlorine and chlorine dioxide.

eucolloid. A colloid composed of relatively large particles, *i.e.*, exceeding 0.25 micron in length.

europium.

	Symbol	Eu
	Atomic No.	63
State Solid	Atomic Wt.	151.96
Grop IIIB	Valence	+2,3
	Isotopes	5 stable
	m.p.	822°C
	b.p.	1597°C

Europium, the second most volatile of the rare-earths, is relatively soft metal. It has a body-centered cubic crystal structure at 298K Europium dissolves readily in dilute mineral acids and reacts with water at room temperature. The metal is not known to be toxic,but because of its high reactivity in air, great care in handling it is required.

Europium is very soft as compared with the other rare-earth metals. Two stable isotopes of the element occur naturally: ^{151}Eu and ^{153}Eu. Upon absorption of thermal neutrons, ^{151}Eu forms ^{152}Eu with a half-life of 13 years. The isotope ^{153}Eu forms ^{154}Eu with a half-life of 16 years. The latter further decays to ^{155}Eu with a half-life of 1.7 years. In terms of abundance, europium is present on the average of 1.2 ppm in the earth's crust, making its potential availability greater than those of antimony, bismuth, or cadmium.

Because of the desirable nuclear properties of the element, europium has received serious consideration for the construction of nuclear reactor hardware. In some optically-read memory systems, ferromagnetic europium chalcogenides (sulphides, selenides, and tellurides) have been used. Other electronic and semiconductor uses of europium are under serious investigation.

Eury test. Formaldehyde in milk is detected by heating to boiling 5 ml. of the milk, with 5 ml. sulphuric acid, and 5 drops of 0.01 N ferric chloride solution. A violet colour indicates the presence of formaldehyde.

Euston process. A procedure for the manufacture of white lead. Refined metallic lead is treated to obtain a solution of basic lead acetate, which then reacts with carbon dioxide to form white lead, which settles down as precipitate.

eutectic. 1. A term used in metallurgy and glass technology to indicate the lowest melting point attainable with a solution of two or more components by varying the percentage of the components. For example, an alloy or solid solution which melts at a lower temperature than any other alloy of the same metals is called an eutectic alloy. In a given alloy system, at a fixed pressure, all phases will have fixed composition during the isothermal transformation. The temperature at which freezing occurs is known as the eutectic temperature, while the composition of the liquid phase is called the eutectic composition. On a temperature-composition binary phase diagram, the eutectic point is determined by the eutectic composition and the eutectic temperature. In general, an alloy of the eutectic composition freezes at a minimum temperature.

2. A term used is petrology to indicate a discrete mixture of two or more minerals, in definite proportions, which have simultaneously crystallized from the mutual solution of their constitents.

3. A term used in the physical chemistry of solutions, *e.g.*, of electrolytes in water, to designate the point at which two or more components precipitate together in a constant ratio as the temperature of a saturated solution is charged (usually lowered) or as the concentration is changed by removal of solvent (*e.g.*, evaporation of water).

eutectic bond. A thermometallurgical bond, generally used to provide contacts between semiconductor chips. It is formed by having a eutectic mixture and then allowing it to cool.

eutectic halt. An arrest point in the equilibrium diagram of two or more components, due to the appearance of eutectic mixture.

eutectic point. Point on phase diagram which describes composition of solution coexisting with at least two solid phases.

eutectic temperature. Temperature of equilibrium coexistence of liquid phase with two or more solid phases.

eutectoid. Solid eutectic formed as result of decay of solution during cooling.

The best known eutectoid reaction is that which occurs in steel where the austenite phase, stable at high temperatures, transforms into the eutectoid structure known as pearlite. In this transformation, the austenite phase, containing 0.8% carbon in solid solution, transforms to a mixture of ferrite (nearly pure body-centred cubic iron) and iron-carbide (Fe_3C). At atmospheric pressure, the equilibrium temperature for this reaction is 996 K. This temperature is the eutectoid temperature.

eutrophication. A term which has come into prominence in recent years as a result of concern over water pollution. It refers specifically to the "fertilization" of lakes, rivers, and coastal bays resulting from disposal of phosphate-bearing detergents in waste water. The phosphate stimulates the growth of algae to the point where most of them die due to lack of light and thus pollute the water with their decomposition products, removing oxygen in the process with the resulting death of marine organisms.

eutropy. The effect of the atomic number of an element upon the isomorphous series of salts which it forms.

Evans-Carpenter process. For the removal of carbon disulphide from coal-gas ; the gas is passed over a catalyst generally nickel at a temperature of about 673K. The carbon disulphide reacts with the hydrogen of the coal-gas to give methane and hydrogen sulphide, the latter being then removed with the usual ferric oxide purifier.

even-even nucleus. Atomic nucleus containing even number of protons and even number of neutrons.

even-odd nucleus. Atomic nucleus containing even number of protons and odd number of neutrons.

evolution. The act of giving off or emitting a gas or vapour as the result of a chemical reaction, for example, acid evolve hydrogen when treated with a metal or metal-containing compounds ; carbon dioxide is evolved by combustion. In biology and mathematics the term has quite different meanings.

Ewald reagent. A solution of ferric chloride and potassium thiocyanate used in determining hydrochloric acid in gastric juice.

EXAFS. Abbreviation for Extended X-ray Absorption Fine Structure Spectroscopy. A spectroscopic technique which can determine interatomic distances very precisely.

exaltation. The positive difference between the observed and the calculated values of the molar refractivity of a substance.

excess function. $Z^E_{T,p}$. Mixing function for a mixture decreased by some of mixing functions for the same mixture calculated under assumption that this mixture is ideal. Also known as excess thermodynamic quantities.

excess thermodynamic quantities. *See* excess functions.

exchange adsorption. Exchange of one substance adsorbed on adsorbent surface by another.

exchange current density, j_0. Density of current which flows across electrode-electrolyte phase boundary when electrode reaction is at equilibrium :

$$j_0 = j_+ = j_-$$

where j_+ and j_- = densities of anodic and cathodic current respectively corresponding to rates of electrode reaction at equilibrium.

exchange energy. Part of electrostatic electron interaction energy due to indistinguishability of electrons.

exchange fraction. In radiochemistry, ratio of concentration of molecules or atoms labelled at a given time to their concentration corresponding to their distribution at equilibrium.

exchange interaction. Quantum mechanical interaction of electrostatic nature which follows from theory of covalent bond and leads to several type of magnetic ordering in crystals.

exchange rate. Quantity given by reciprocal of the mean life time of atom in a given molecule ($1/\tau$) in chemical exchange process.

exchange reaction. 1. Process of transformation of two or more substrate molecules, involving mutual exchange of their atoms or ions, *e.g.*,

$$NaOH + HCl \rightarrow NaCl + H_2O$$

Also known as replacement reaction.

2. Nuclear reaction consisting in exchange of one or several nucleons between interacting atomic nuclei.

exchange scattering. Scattering in which particle colliding with system (atomic nucleus, atom) knocks out identical particle, but is absorbed itself by system. This effect cannot be distinguished from simple scattering and both processes are always observed together.

excimers. Molecular associates, of two or several molecules, existing only in electronic, excited states. Excimers play a role in fluorescence and different kinds of radiation-induced luminescence.

excitation. The process of absorption of energy by atomic nuclei, atoms or molecules which is accompanied by their transition from ground state to states of higher energy (which are called excited states).

excitation energy. Energy necessary to transfer molecule, atom or atomic nucleus from ground to excited state. In molecule, energy is in general sum of electronic excitation oscillation and rotation excitations.

excitation function. Relation between cross-section of a given nuclear reaction and energy of bombarding particles.

excitation source. Energy source used to evaporate and excite investigated sample thus leading to emission of electromagnetic radiation. Also known as energy source.

excited molecule. Molecule in which energy levels are higher than in ground state.

excited nucleus. Atomic nucleus in energetic state higher than energy of ground state, unstable. Excited nucleus decays with emission of γ-quanta or other particles.

excited state. A higher than normal energy level (vibrational frequency) of the electrons of an atom, group, or molecule, resulting from absorption of photons (quanta) from a radiation source (arc, flame, spark, etc.) in any wavelength of the electromagnetic spectrum, X-ray ultraviolet, visible, infrared, microwave, and radio frequencies are used for excitation in various types of spectroscopy. When the energizing source is removed or discontinued, the atom or molecule returns to its normal or stable state either by emitting the absorbed photons or by transferring the energy to other atoms or molecules. The increased vibrational activity of the atom or molecule yields line or band spectra characteristic of its structure, thus permitting identification. Photochemical reaction are induced by excited chemical entities, which are also responsible for the phenomenon of luminescence (phosphorescence and fluorescence).

exciton. Electronic state of excitation in crystal. Exciton is formed as electron-hole pair, *e.g.*, in effect of absorption of ionizing energy radiation, it may move through crystal, thus transporting energy but not charge.

exclusion principle. *See* Pauli exclusion principle.

exhausting agent. A substance which is added to a dye bath to effect a greater absorption of dye by the fibre, and to cause a high exhaustion of dye from the dye bath.

exhaustive methylation. The introduction of methyl groups into a compound until all the replaceable hydrogen atoms have been replaced, *e.g.*,

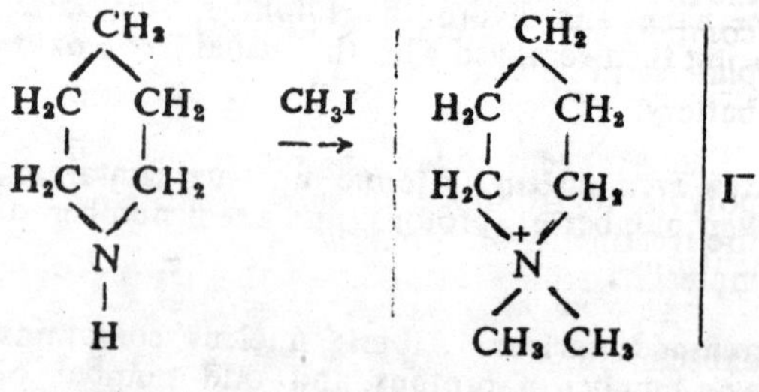

$$CH_2(CH_2)_2(CH_2)_2NH \;(\text{ring: } CH_2,\ H_2C\text{—}CH_2,\ H_2C\text{—}CH_2,\ N\text{—}H) \xrightarrow{CH_3I} \left[CH_2(CH_2)_2(CH_2)_2\overset{+}{N}(CH_3)_2\right] I^-$$

exo-. (Greek) Outside, out of ; as, exotoxin (an excreted toxin) : specifically, denoting attachment in a side chain. *See* endo-, eso-.

exocyclic compound. An unsaturated cyclic compound in which the double bond occurs in the side chain.

exocellular enzyme. An enzyme that may readily be isolated from association with living cells, *e.g.*, pepsin, maltase, zymase. Also known as extracellular enzyme.

exosmosis. An osmotic process by which a diffusible substance passes from the inner or closed, to the outer parts of a system, as in the loss of substances, from a portion of a plant root to water in the surrounding soil.

exothermal reaction. *See* exothermic reaction.

exothermic reaction. Process (chemical reaction or physical process) accompanied by decrease of internal energy or enthalpy of system due to heat emission for example, the formation of sulphur dioxide from sulphur and oxygen :

$$S + O_2 \rightarrow SO_2 + \text{heat}$$

also the reaction between metallic sodium and water to form sodium hydroxide :

$$2Na + 2H_2O \rightarrow 2NaOH + H_2 + \text{heat.}$$

exotic. A term occasionally used to describe or indicate materials of particularly high efficiency, derived from an unusual source for a given application ; for example, when boron-derived fuels for rocket engines were developed they were known collectively as exotic fuels. A number of new and unusually powerful solvents have also been so described. There are also so-called exotic metals, *e.g.*, titanium, hafnium, zirconium, etc.

expander. 1. In storage batteries, a composition made up of carbon black, barium sulphate, and wood lignin ; when added in the amount of about 1 percent to the lead oxide used to coat the negative plates of the battery, this expander composition maintain the capacity of the plates and helps to extend the active life of the battery.

2. An agent added to blood plasma, *e.g.*, polyvinylpyrrolidone, or substituted for it in the treatment of wounds, burns, etc. Such materials are called plasma volume expanders.

expectorant. A drug which promotes the secretion of mucus from tissues of the respiratory system.

explosion. A chemical change that produces large quantities of energy or an increase in the volume of the system, or both at a rate sufficiently rapid to have considerable effects, often destructive, upon the surroundings.

explosive. An unstable chemical compound of which nitrogen usually is the active constituent which decomposes more or less violently when shocked or ignited, particularly when confined. Low explosives, typified by black powder and smokeless powder, burn or deflagrate rapidly, with evolution of gases. High explosives detonate, with production of a rapidly traveling shock wave of destructive violence. Initiating explosives are those used in blasting caps to detonate dynamite, TNT, etc., which are less shock-sensitive than many types. Silver acetylide and copper acetylide are instances of explosives that do not contain nitrogen. While explosions can occur by ignition of dusts and vapours of organic liquids, these are not classified as explosive materials.

explosive limits. Range of one of parameters of chemical reaction (pressure, composition or temperature) above which (lower explosion limit) or below which (upper explosion limit) reaction proceeds explosively at defined value of remaining parameters.

A concentration below the lower limit is not sufficient to support combustion, and above the upper limit the mixture is too "rich" to burn (as when a carburetor is flooded). Flammable or explosive limits for some common substances in air are as follows :

	Lower (%)	Upper (%)
acetylene	2.5	80
benzene	1 5	8
carbon disulphide	1	50
butadiene	2	11.5
methane	5	5
butane	1.9	8.5
natural gas	3.8	17
hydrogen	4.1	75.5
ether	1.73	23.3
ethanol	4.16	19
hydrogen sulphide	4.3	46
propane	2.4	9.5

exposure *X*. Amount of ionizing radiation (gamma or X-rays) energy defined by ability to ionize air

$X = \Delta Q/\Delta m$, where ΔQ = sum of electric charges of all ions of the same sign, formed in unit of air mass Δm, in conditions where all electrons (negatons and positrons) released by photons are totally stopped in that volume of air. Also known as exposure dose.

exposure dose. *See* exposure.

extensive parameters. *See* extensive quantities.

extensive properties. *See* extensive quantities.

extensive quantities. The properties of a system that are equal to the sum of the values of those properties for the constituents of the system ; used for quantities such as the internal energy and the various thermodynamic potentials, which are proportional to the mass of a system in equilibrium, other things remaining equal. Also known as extensive properties ; extensive variables ; extensive parameters.

extensive variables. *See* extensive quantities.

extent of reaction, ξ. Parameter characterizing advance of chemical reaction :

$$\xi = \frac{\Delta n_B}{\nu_B}$$

where Δn_B=number of moles of reactant B used or produced in chemical reaction, ν_B= stoichiometric coefficient of this reactant (positive for products, negative for substrates) : value of extent of reaction is the same for all reactants and is proportional to number of gram-equivalents used in reaction. Also known as degree of advancement of reaction; reaction variable.

external indicator. Indicator which is not added to titrated solution ; reaction between external indicator and titrated solution is carrid out externally by taking a drop of analyzed solution and treated on a spot-plate with the indicator. The titration is continued until this test shows that the end point of the reaction has been reached.

external reference. *See* external standard.

external return Restitution of substrate by internally associated ionic pair, by recombination of X^- ions originating from different molecules of dissociated compounds. Intramolecular processes, such as inversion, racemization or rearrangements, often accompany external return

$$A—X \rightleftharpoons A^+X^- \rightleftharpoons A^+\ X^- \overset{X'^-}{\rightleftharpoons}$$
$$\rightleftharpoons A^+ \parallel X'^- \rightleftharpoons A^+X'^- \rightleftharpoons (A—X')\ (X{=}X')$$

external standard. 1. A standard sample used for direct comparison with the unknown sample.

2. In spectroanalysis, component absent in investigated sample but present on counter electrode. Its spectral line(s) is (are) used as reference for measurement of spectral line intensities of determined elements.

3. In NMR spectroscopy, reference substance external to investigated sample, used to determine chemical shifts.

extinction coefficient (molar). A constant quantity that appears in one of the forms of statement of Beer's law expressing the amount of light absorption of a solution at various wave lengths, as in the relationship :

$$I=I_0.10^{-\epsilon cd}$$

in which I = intensity of light transmitted and I_0 = intensity of incident light (both for a given wave length), ϵ = molar extinction coefficient for that wavelength, c = concentration of the solution in moles per litre, and d = thickness of the transmitting layer of solution.

extinguishing agent. Any compound used to put out fires. Water is, of course, the best-known : it not only has a powerful cooling effect but also serves to keep oxygen away from the flame. It is especially effective in the form of spray or mist, and as such it can be used to extinguish fires in heavy oils. A direct stream of water should never be used to fight fires involving gasoline, hydrocarbon liquids, or any other material of specific gravity less than 1.00. Carbon dioxide is often used on these and other fires. Dry chemical (a mixture of sodium chloride and sodium bicarbonate) is useful for extinguishing fires in metals and electrical equipment. Fires in hydrocarbon liquids are best handled by use of chemical foam (carbon dioxide in water). Such toxic halogenated hydrocarbon as carbon tetrachloride and methyl bromide should be avoided. *See also* flame retardant.

extraction. 1. Separation method that makes use of differences in partition of various substances beween two immiscible liquids. Numerous solvents are used in anayltical chemistry, pharmacy, etc., for example, a sample of vulcanized rubber can be analyzed for specific components by extracting it with acetone or chloroform. Solvent extraction is an industrial method of removing impurities from liquids and also of obtaining essential oils from plant sources Steam distillation is also an extraction method.

2. In metallurgy, the term is applied to the mining of metals and separation of pure metals from their ores (sometimes also called winning).

extraction chromatogrphy. Chromatography in which organic extractant adsorbed on solid support serves as stationary phase Also known as reversed phase partition chromatography.

extrinsic semiconductor. Semiconductor whose electrical properties are dependent on impurities added to the semiconductor crystal, in contrast to intrinsic semiconductor, whose properties are characteristic of ideal pure crystal.

extrusion. A fundamental mechanical operation

of the process industries, applied in one variation or another in the manufacture of a wide range of plastics and rubber articles, synthetic fibres and filaments, plastic film and sheet, wire and cable coating, some metals, and such food items as spaghetti, etc. The base material may be a low-viscosity liquid such as molten glass or a polymer dispersion passed through a spinneret ; a viscous liquid polymer as used in injection molding ; or a semisolid mass such as a rubber or plastic composition. In the case of high-viscosity materials, the process involves passing the mass over a revolving screw of varying pitch in an enclosed chamber ; this forces it through a metal form or die to impose the required shape. Film is made by extrusion through a slit of predetermined width and thinkness. Polymer fibres are usually hardened by passing them through a bath of formaldehyde or similar agent. Extrusion involves application of rheological principles of some complexity ; viscosity, temperature, and rate are critical factors.

Eykman formula. An empirical relationship for the molal refraction of a liquid, of the form :

$$r = \frac{M(n^2-1)}{\rho(n+0.4)} = \frac{V(n^2-1)}{n+0.4}$$

in which r = the molal refraction for a given optical frequency, n=the index of refraction for that frequency, M = the molecular weight, V=the molecular volume, and ρ=the density.

E-Z system. Conventional system for specification of *cis-trans* configuration of stereoisomers of ethylene or other unsaturated derivatives. This convention (similarly to R-S nomenclature) is based on sequence rule. When atoms or groups of atoms of high atomic numbers are attached to double-bond carbon atoms from the same side, Z-configuration is ascribed to system. In the reverse case, configuration is said to be (E)-, *e.g.*,

```
        Cl  Cl
        |   |
(Cl > H)  C=C   (Br > Cl)
        |   |
        H   Br
```

E-1-bromo-1,2-dichloroethen

```
CH3—C—C2H5
    ||          (C2H5 > CH3)
    N
    |           (OH > zero)
    OH
```

Z-butanone axime

F

F. Symbol for the element fluorine. Symbol for Fahrenheit temperature Abbreviation for the faraday; unit of electrical quantity. Symbol for hyperfine quantum number ($=I+J$). Abbreviation for magnetomotive force.

f. Abbreviation for degree of freedom. Symbol for Fanning friction factor. Symbol for activity coefficient, molal basis. Symbol for friction coefficient. Abbreviation for fugacity. Symbol for distribution function. Abbreviation for frequency (electrical, mechanical, acoustical). Abbreviation for resonant frequency.

faber flow. A deformation in the superconducting material which acts as a nucleation centre for the growth of a superconducting region.

Fabinyi test. To 0.25 ml. acetone, add 1 g. salicylaldehyde and 4 ml. 1N sodium hydroxide. A red colour on shaking, after standing for 15 minutes, is obtained. To test for benzaldehyde, add a crystal of potassium hydroxide and a little acetone to the alcoholic solution of the material under examination. A red colour indicates the presence of benzaldehyde.

Fabry-Perot interferometer. Instrument used for multi-beam interference of radiation. Main parts are two glass or quartz plates exactly parallel and neatly polished ; each one slightly wedged (the angle between wedge planes is about 30′).

face-centred lattice. A lattice whose unit cells are cubes, with lattice points at the centre of each face of the cube, as well as at the vertices, *e.g.*, structures of austinite, copper, aluminium etc.

facet. The flat, usually highly reflective surface of a crystal, a cut stone, or other fractured surface.

factice. A synthetic softener made by reacting a vegetable oil (usually corn oil) with sulphur chloride ; it is a brown to light-tan semisolid material used in special types of rubber and plastic products to impart a soft, smooth feeling, as well as to make art gum erasers. It is also called rubber substitute and vulcanized oil.

factor. A term used chiefly by biochemists to indicate any member of a biologically active complex, especially if its exact chemical nature is unknown or if its function in cellular metabolism has not been elucidated. Several of the B complex vitamins were originally referred to as "factors" until their identity had been established by research.

factor, conversion. *See* conversion factor.

factor, correction. *See* correction factor.

factor, gravimetric. *See* gravimetric factor.

factor, titrimetric. *See* titrimetric factor.

FAD (flavin adenine dinucleotide). A coenzyme important in various biochemical reactions. It comprises a phosphorylated vitamin (B_2) molecule linked to the nucleotide adenine monophosphate (AMP) It is usually tightly bound to the enzyme forming a flavoprotein. It functions as hydrogen acceptor in hydrogenation reactions and is reduced to $FADH_2$, which in turn is oxidised to FAD by the electron transport chain, thereby generating ATP.

Fages test reaction. To detect stannous ions in alkaline solution, add a few drops of sodium nitroprusside solution. Stannons ions give a grey red colour, changing to blue with hydrochloric acid, but decolourized by an excess of the acid.

Fairhall test. Lead is detected by the formation of a black hexanitrite of potassium, copper, and lead, showing rectangular plates or cubes under the microscope.

Fajans method. The use of a dye which is adsorbed near the end of a titration, thus producing a clearly visible colour change. An example is the use of dichlorofluorescein in titration of chloride with siliver nitrate solution.

Fajans' rules. The rule enable to predict whether a bond is likely to be covalent or ionic. An electrovalent link is likely to be replaced by a covalent one if (*i*) the charge on either ion is large, (*ii*) the radius of the cation is small, (*iii*) the radius of the anion is large. Opposite condition favour the reverse change.

Fajans-Soddy law. *See* law of radioactive displacement.

fallout. Radioactive fission products resulting from nuclear and thermonuclear explosions; these may drift for hundreds of kilometres from the explosion site, contaminating the earth's surface as they go. Much potentially dangerous radioactivity has already been added to the environment by nuclear testing, especially in the form of strontium-90. No adequate proection from fallout occurs from controlled fission reactions in atomic power plants, whose deleterious products are neutralized within the plant area or shipped elsewhere for treatment or disposal.

false chemical equilibrium. Thermodynamic state of reacting system with reaction rates equal to zero due to kinetic hindrances but with non-zero affinity. Also known as unstable chemical equilibrium.

family of elements. Set of elements with similar properties, such as valence, behaviour toward reagents, etc. • For example, the alkali metal family includes lithium, sodium, potassium, rubidium, cesium, and francium. The halogen family consists of fluorine, chlorine, bromine, iodine, and astatine.

Fanning equation. An equation expressing the drop in pressure, because of friction in a fluid flowing in the pipe. It is of the form :

$$\Delta p_f = 2f\left(\frac{v^2}{g}\right)\left(\frac{l}{d}\right)$$

where Δp_f = frictional drop in pressure,

f = function of the Reynolds number, v = the rate of flow, g=the acceleration of gravity, l = length of the pipe element, and d = its diameter.

farad, F. The SI unit of capacitance. A capacitor has a capacitance of one farad when a charge of one coulomb increases the potential difference between its plates by one volt. The farad is too large for most practical purposes, the submultiples microfarad, nanofarad and picofarad being more convenient.

Faradaic rectification method. Method of studying kinetics of electrode processes based on non-linear and asymmetric characteristics of electrodes. When sinusoidal voltage of significant frequency is applied to electrode system, constant current component called Faradaic rectification current is observed.

Faraday constant, ***F.*** Fundamental constant having the value 9.648670×10^4 coulombs per mole. It is the quantity of electricity that is equivalent to one mole of electrons and that can deposit or liberate one mole of a univalent ion. It is equal the product of electron charge and Avogadro constant.

Faraday effect. The rotation of the plane of polarization of light by transparent substances when they are placed in a magnetic field. It is a function of the nature of the substance, the frequency of the light, the intensity of the magnetic field, and the temperature.

Faraday's gold. Colloidal gold made by the action of reducing agents on a solution of gold chloride.

Faraday's laws I. Amount of a given substance undergoing reaction at electrodes are proportional to quantity of electricity passing through electric circuit

II. Amounts of different substances undergoing reactions at electrodes, in case of equal quantities of electricity passing through circuit are proportional to their chemical equivalents.

faradization. Therapeutic use of induced currents.

farinaceous. Containing starch.

far infrared. Electromagnetic radiation in the range of wavelength between ca. 25 μm to ca. 800 μm.

Farrant solution. A solution of 2 g. arsenious oxide and 50 g. gum acacia in 50 ml. glycerol and 50 ml. water; used as a preservative.

Farrar process. A method of producing high-quality case-hardened iron from pig iron by treatment with manganese dioxide, ammonium chloride, and potassium ferrocyanide.

far ultraviolet, FUV. Electromagnetic radiation in the range of wavelength between ca. 170 nm to ca. 200 nm.

fast breeder reactor. A type of fast nuclear reactor that uses highly enriched fuel in the core, fertile meterial in the blanket, and a liquid metal coolant, having breeding ratio equal to one or more than one.

fast burst reactor. A nuclear reactor that produces microsecond pulses of fast neutrons which are used in biomedical research.

fast dye. A term used to describe a dye or pigment whose colour is not impaired by prolonged exposure to light, steam, high temperature, or other environmental conditions. Inorganic pigments are normally superior in this respect to organic dyes.

fast effect. Increase in neutrons due to fissions caused by fast neutrons in a thermal reactor.

fast neutrons. Neutrons moving with the speed at which they emerge from a ruptured nucleus and possess kinetic energies greater than 1 MeV as opposed to "slow" or thermal neutrons whose speed has been reduced by impinging on a moderating substance such as graphite.

fast reactor. A nuclear reactor in which fission is produced by fast neutrons, with little or no moderator to slow down the neutrons.

fat. A solid to semisolid glyceride of a fatty acid of high nutritional value. Fats are chemically classified as lipids. Natural fats are produced by both plants and animals; the former are represented by coconut and cocoa "butters," and the latter by lard, tallow, and milk-derived butter. Chemically, such fats have the same composition as oils of the same origin. Generally, fats are glycerides of stearic, palmitic, oleic, and similar fatty acids, varying only in the extent of their saturation, the animal fats being the more highly saturated. Thus, the only difference between a vegetable or animal fat and a similarly derived oil is that fats are solid and oils are liquid at room temperature. Some fats show traces of crystal formation on cooling. Synthetic fats are made by catalytic hydrogenation of vegetable oils to a solid consistency, chiefly for cooking purposes. Some fish oils are also hydrogenated for use as dispersing agents. Fats can be hydrolyzed or "split" by reacting the glyceride with water at about 533K to form glycerol and free fatty acids.

fatigue. Failure of a material by repeated applications of stresses, each of which is individually to cause failure. Many materials such as non-ferrous alloys, have a finite life for any given number of reversals of stress.

fatliquor. A mixture of neatsfoot oil and water, emulsified with a fatty acid or sulphonated oil ; the neatsfoot oil is derived from water extraction of animal tendons. Fatliquors are used primarily in the leather industry to lubricate skins and hides, which tend to become hard and dry as a result of tanning. This treatment enables the finished leather to bend easily without cracking and to withstand the stresses it receives during fabrication into shoes and other products.

fatty acid. 1. A general term for a group of monobasic organic acids derived from hydrocarbons by the equivalent of oxidation of a methyl group. They include both saturated and unsaturated acids ; for example,
formic acid, $HCOOH$;
propionic acid, CH_3CH_2COOH ;
sorbic acid, $CH_3CH{=}CHCH{=}CHCOOH$.

2. Three members of the fatty acid series (those whose glyceryl esters compose the largest part of the most fats), namely, palmitic acid, $C_{15}H_{31}COOH$; stearic acid, $C_{17}H_{35}COOH$; and oleic acid, $C_{17}H_{33}COOH$. Fatty acids are in the general classification of lipids. Natural fats contain many unsaturated fatty acids having up to six double bonds along the chain (polyunsaturates), and many isomeric structures are possible. Saturated types occur in animal fats and some nut fats (coconut) ; unsaturated acids occur chiefly in such vegetable oils as castor, linseed, and safflower. Most fatty acids are mixtures of several types of glycerides. They are produced commercially by catalytic hydrolysis ("splitting") of the fat or oil to separate the acid from it (Twitchell process), with glycerol as a by-product. The best known saturated fatty acids are stearic, palmitic, butyric, and lauric ; among the unsaturates are oleic, linolenic linoleic, and ricinoleic. Some fatty acids are synthesized within the animal and are thus called non-essential ; others that are nutritionally necessary but are not formed within the organism and thus must be obtained from external sources and are hence called essential. These are arachidonic, linoleic ; and linolenic acids. Fatty acids are used primarily as raw materials for soap manufacture, as dispersing and activating agents in the rubber industry, in synthetic detergents, and in candle making. *See also* glyceride ; lipid.

fatty alcohol. An aliphatic alcohol containing from 8 to 20 carbon atoms in the chain ; they are derived from natural sources by reduction, hydrolysis, or hydrogenation and may be saturated (octyl and stearyl) or unsaturated (oleyl and linoleyl). Those having more than 12 carbons in the molecule are solids. Fatty alcohols are used as solvents, detergents, and in pharmaceutical products.

fatty oil. A nonvolatile oil of vegetable or animal origin, and consisting of glyceryl (and other) esters of fatty acids (sometimes other organic acids), often with some of the free acid present.

Favorskii-Babayan acetylenic alcohol synthesis. Preparation of acetylenic alcohol by condensation of ketones with acetylenic hydrocarbons in presence of anhydrous potassium hydroxide, *e.g.*,

$$RR'C{=}O + HC{\equiv}CR' \xrightarrow{KOH} RR'C(OH){-}C{\equiv}C{-}R'$$

Favorskii rearrangement. One of a number of rearrangements of α-haloketones to acid or esters, catalyzed by bases, *e.g.*,

$$ClCH_2\overset{O}{\overset{\|}{C}}R + NaOH \rightarrow RCH_2COOH + NaCl$$

$$\text{2-chlorocyclohexanone} \xrightarrow[-NaCl]{+NaOH} C_5H_9{-}COOH$$

Favrel test reaction. Citirc acid is detected by heating for 5-10 minutes with sulphuric acid, cooling, diluting with water, and extracting with ether. On evaporation of the ether, the extract gives a red colour with ferric choride solution.

f-block elements. The block of elements in the periodic table consisting of the lanthanide series (from cerium to lutetium) and the actinide series (from thorium to lawreneium). They are characterized by having two *s*-electrons in their outermost shell and *f*-electrons in their inner shell.

f-centres. Colour centres formed as result of trapping of electrons by anionic vacancies in ionic crystal.

Fearon test reaction for cyanate. To a slightly acid or neutral cyanate solution, add 2-5 drops of 6% alcoholic benzidine solution and a few drops of cupric acetate solution. A red colour, becoming brown confirms the presence of cyanate.

Feder test for hydrogen peroxide. To detect hydrogen peroxide in milk, warm 5 ml. milk with 5 ml. concentrated hydrochloric acid, add a few drops of formaldehyde and keep at 3₃0K for a few minutes. A blue-violet colour indicates the presence of hydrogen peroxide.

feedstock A term used in the petroleum and synthetic organic chemical industries to refer to petroleum or petroleum-derived hydrocarbon (liquids or gaseous) from which gasoline and petrochemicals are produced by cracking, reforming, and similar operation. It also sometimes called the charging stock It should not be confused with animal feedstuffs.

Fehling solution. A freshly mixed solution of cupric sulphate, sodium tartrate, and sodium hydroxide, used for determining reducing compounds, especially reducing sugars, by reduction of the cupric ions to insoluble cuprous oxide. Fehling solution is commonly prepared by mixing two solution—(*i*) a solution of 69.30 g. cupric sulphate in 1 litre water; and (*ii*) a solution of 346 g. of Rochelle salt and 250 g. potassium hydroxide in 1 litre distilled water.

Feigl-Demant test. Selenium is detected in solution by mixing 4 drops of a 1% solution of *as*-diphenylhydrazine in glacial acetic acid on a spot plate with 1 drop of 2 N hydrochloric acid and 1 drop of the solution to be tested. A red colour indicates the presence of selenium.

Feigl-Krumholz test for palladium. When a rapid stream of carbon monoxide is passed through a boiling pre-acidified solution containing palladium and phosphomolybdic acid, a blue to green colour appears in a few minutes.

Feigl test reaction for cerium. When cerium oxide is moistened with a solution of benzidine in acetic acid, a bright blue colour is obtained. Other cerium salts act similarly, but not the fluoride, bisulphate, or carbonate.

Feigl-Zappert-Vasquez test for methyl ketones. The material to be tested is dissolved in a solvent other than alcohol, heated and treated with 1 drop of alkaline solution of *o*-nitrobenzaldehyde, and evaporated. On treatment with chloroform, a blue colour indicates the persence of methyl ketones.

Fenton reagent. Aqueous solution containing hydrogen peroxide and ferrous ions. System genrates free hydroxyl radicals (.OH) without radiation of high energy.

Fenton test for malonic acid. The substance to be tested is allowed to stand with anhydrous alcohol containing hydrochloric acid. After a few minutes, it is neutralized, bromomethylfurfurol is added, and the mixture barely alkalinized with potassium hydroxide solution. A blue fluorescence indicates the presence of malonic acid.

Fermat principle. Light beam in medium moves between points A and B in such way that its optical path, *i.e.*, $\int_A^B 1/\nu \, . \, ds$ is minimum,

where ν = phase frequency of light wave, and ds = path element.

ferment. A material which catalyzes certain orgnic reactions and which consists of an enzyme (a catalyst which is the product of a living organism or organisms, and which has an organic chemical composition) in association with other substances produced by the living organism, or with the organism or cell itself.

ferment, inorganic. *See* inorganic ferment.

fermentation. An anaerobic, energy-yielding reaction brought about or catalyzed by enzymes or bacteria and involving the decomposition of carbohydrates (sugars and starches) to alcohol and carbon dioxide. The ethyl alcohol in spiritous liquors is derived in this way from cereals and fruits. The fundamental reaction is :

$$C_6H_{12}O_6 \rightarrow 2C_2H_5OH + 2CO_2$$

Yeast contains enzymes which activate this reaction, and the bacteria of some induce the fermentation responsible for growth of antibiotics. Bacterial action also accounts, for the souring of milk, spoilage of vegetables, and similar types of organic decomposition. Proteins can be obtained from petroleum by means of bacteria-induced fermentation. Several vitamins, including riboflavin and vitamin B_{12}, are also products of fermentation.

fermentaion, acetic. A fermentation which produces acetic acid, commonly in the dilute form (vinegar) from alcohol-containing solutions or substances.

fermentation, alcoholic. A fermentation which produces ethyl alcohol, commonly by the action of a yeast, such as *Saccharomyces cerevisiae*, on a sugar, or a sugar-containing solution.

fermentation, amylolytic. In general, this term means a fermentation of starch ; specifically, it is an incomplete fermentation of starch that does not yield simple sugars.

fermentation, butyric. A fermentation reaction which produces butyric acid.

fermentation, lactic. *See* lactic fermentation.

ferment oil. A volatile oil produced by the fermentation of plant material in which the oils are not pre-existent.

Fermi-Dirac distribution. Equilibrium distribution of particles among single-particle levels given by :

$$<N_\epsilon> = \frac{g_\epsilon}{\frac{1}{\lambda}\exp\frac{\epsilon}{kT} + 1}$$

where k = Boltzmann constant, T=thermodynamic temperature, λ= absolute activity and g_ϵ=degeneracy of energy level ϵ, $<N_\epsilon>$= average occupation number for this level. Fermi-Dirac distribution can be used for systems of weakly interacting fermions.

Fermi-Dirac statistics. A system of quantum statistics that is used to describe the behaviour of solids in terms of a free electron model. In this model the most weakly bound electrons of the constituent atoms are considered to behave as a gas subject to certain conditions ; the electrons are free to move in any direction throught the solid, they do not interact with each other, and are subject to the Pauli exclusion principle.

The probability of an energy level of energy E being occupied by an electron is given by the Fermi-Dirac distribution function, $f(E)$:

$$f(E) = 1/[e^{(E-\mu)^{kT}} + 1]$$

where μ = constant and a function of temperature, k = Boltzmann constant, and T = themodynamic temperature.

The free electron model is used to explain a number of important physical properties of metals.

Fermi energy. *See* **fermi level.**

Fermi-gas model. Model of atomic nucleus which describes nucleus as consisting of mutually non-interacting nucleons being in constant movement (similar assumptions are made in consideration of gas). Fermi-gas model is applied in a simplified analysis of heavier atomic nuclei.

fermi level. At 0 K, highest occupied energy level in metals ; at higher temperatures inflection point on energy dependence of density of states. Also known as Fermi energy.

fermions. Elementary particles or complex systems of spin quantum number equal to one half unit, *e.g.*, leptons, baryons, nuclei with odd number of nucleons each of which has a spin angular momentum of $\sqrt{3}h/4\pi$, where h = Planck's constant ; this is equivalent to stating that each fermion has a spin quantum number of magnitude $\frac{1}{2}$.

Fermions are described by Fermi-Dirac statistics.

fermi resonance. In vibrational molecular spectra abnormal increase of intensity of two absorption bands of the same symmetry of vibration and sufficiently close frequencies.

Fermi surface. Of a metal, semimetal, or semiconductor, that surface in momentum space which separates the energy states which are filled with free or quasi-free electrons from those which are unfilled. Constant energy surface corresponding to Fermic level in system of fermions in k-space, where k is wave vector.

Fermi temperature. T_F. Parameter expressed in units of tempertaure :

$$T_F = \frac{\epsilon_F}{k}$$

where ϵ_F=Fermi level, k=Boltzmann constant. At temperatures low in comparison with Fermi tempereature. Fermi gas is degenerate. Also known as degeneracy temperature.

fermium. An element	Symbol	Fm
	Atomic No.	100
State Solid	Atomic Wt.	253
Group IIIB	Valence	+3

Fermium isotopes are made (*i*) by heavy iron bombardment of uranium and plutonium isotopes, (*ii*) by the action of alpha particles on californium isotopes, and (*iii*) from several of the other transuranium elements by multiple neutron capture—or in the case of the heaviest istopoes, from einsteinium by single neutron capture.

All known isotopes of fermium are radioactive. They include isotopes of mass numbers 248($t_{1/2}$=0.6m), 249($t_{1/2}$=150s), 250($t_{1/2}$=0.5h.), 251($t_{1/2}$=7h), 252($t_{1/2}$=23h), 253($t_{1/2}$=4.5d), 254($t_{1/2}$=3.24h), 255($t_{1/2}$=22h), 256 ($t_{1/2}$=160m), and an isotope of mass number 257 which has a half-life of about 10 days.

Ferrario reaction. A reaction of diphenyl ethers and sulphur to yield phenoxathin and its derivatives.

Ferrate (II). The anion FeO_2^-, $Fe(OH)_4^-$, or $Fe(OH)_6^{4-}$ or a compound containing one of these ions ; the last two of these ions and their compounds, are called hydroxoferrates (II).

ferredoxins. Non-haem iron-containing proteins isolated from a number of bacteria and plants. They possess low redox potentials. Ferredoxins are involved in nitrogen fixation and photosynthesis.

Ferreira da Silva solution. A solution of 0.5 g. ammonium selenite in 10 g. concentrated sulphuric acid ; used as a test reagent for alkaloids. Characteristic colour reactions are obtained.

ferri-. A prefix indicating content of ferric iron, as in ferricyanide.

ferric. Indicating, the oxidation states of +3 for the metal in a given compound, *e.g.*, ferric chloride ($FeCl_3$). An alternative nomenclature recommended for fuch compounds is iron (III) chloride. Undoubtedly because of possible confusion with nonscientific meanings, the word "ironic" is not used in chemistry.

ferriferrous. Containing both trivalent and divalent iron.

ferrimagnetics. *See* ferrimagnets.

ferrimagnetic substances. *See* ferrimagnets.

ferrimagnets. Highly magnetic solids with properties similar to ferromagnets but of more complicated temperature dependence of sturation magnetization below Curie temperature and of magnetic susceptiblliy above Curie point (*e.g.*, magnetite, pyrrhotite). Such materials are important because they are usually insulators and hence have low eddy-current losses in radiofrequency applications, while exhibiting substantial magnetic moments at room temperature, although less than those of ferromagnetics. Alse known as ferrimagnetic substances ; ferrimagnetics.

ferrite. A solid compound consisting of the iron oxide Fe_2O_3 and FeO, the latter being replaceable by oxides of several other transition metals such as copper, nickel, or cobalt. Their characteristic property is their magnetic moment, for which they are used in computers, tape recorders, and many related communication devices where magnetic properties are essential. A simple example of a ferrite is the mineral magnetite, whose composition is FeO. Fe_2O_3

ferrites. A group of ceramic materials that exhibit the property of ferrimagnetism. They consist of iron oxide to which small quantities of transition metal oxides (*e.g.*, cobalt and nickel oxides) have been added. The spinel ferrites have the formula $MO.Fe_2O_3$ where M is a divalent transition metal ion. By suitable combination of metallic oxides, ferrites can be made which exhibit ferromagnetism, but as they are electrical insulators and therefore do not suffer from the effects of eddy currents, they can be used as cores in coils and transformers in electronic equipment at frequencies that would be impossible with ordinary ferromagenetic materials.

Ferrites are manufactured by ceramic methods involving grinding, pressing, and sintering. Some types substitute a nonmagnetic oxide component, *e.g.*, sodium, zinc, or aluminium.

ferroalloy. An alloy containing varying proportions of iron and some other metal, such as molybdenum, manganese, titanium, etc., commonly added to steel for purposes of strength, heat resistance and the like. Such alloys are used as a means of introducing the specific element into the "melt" and have no independent applications. The are also called ferrous alloys.

ferroaluminium. An alloy of aluminium (up to 80%) and iron.

ferroborn. An alloy of iron and boron that is added to steel to make it hard.

ferrochrome. An alloy of chromium with 30% —40% iron, obtained by the reduction of chromite with carbon in an electric furnace.

ferroelectric crystals. Crystalline substances exhibiting spontaneous electric polarization, characterized by high permittivity and occurrence of polarization hysteresis ; electric analogue of ferromagnets. Such substances are particularly useful as detectors of vibrations.

ferromagnetic. *See* ferromagnets.

ferromagnetic substances. *See* ferromagnets.

ferromagnets. Crystalline substances with magnetization in absence of external magnetic field which appears due to long-range ordering of elementary magnetic mements. Also known ferromagnetic substances ; ferromagnetics.

ferromagnetism. A phenomenon observed in certain solids in which the magnetic properties change abruptly at a certain characteristic temperature known as the Curie point. Below the Curie point the soild exhibits ferromanetic properties. Above this temperature the thermal energy of the atoms is sufficient to produce magnetic properties typical of paramagnetism : the susceptibility obeys the Curie-Weiss law approximately, the value of the Weiss constant being close to that of the Curie point and a few degrees higher.

The chief ferromagnetic elements are iron, cobalt, and nickel ; there are also many ferromagnetic alloys based on these materials. Ferromagnetic materials are characterized by a large positive susceptibility ; very large values of magnetization are produced by relatively

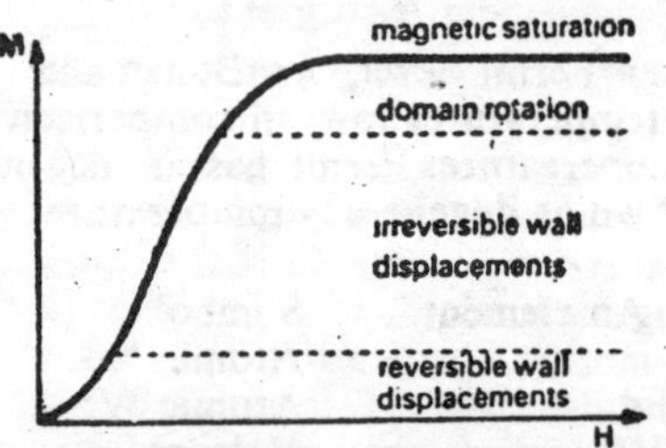

Fig 24. Typical magnetization curve of a ferromagnetic substances

small magnetic fields, the magnetization varying nonlinearly with field strength (Fig. 24). Maximum intensity of magnetization (magnetic saturation) is achieved at fairly low field strengths and a certain amount of magnetization is retained when the magnetizing field is removed, *i.e.*, the materials exhibit magnetic hysteresis.

The magnetic moments of the atoms arise from the spin of electrons in an unfilled inner shell. In any stable material in the absence of an applied magnetic field, the detailed arrangements of the magnetic moments result from the interaction between the various forces operating within the sample. It is always such as to produce the minimum energy possible. In ferromagnetic materials this minimum energy state occurs when the electron spins of the atoms within a domain are arranged in parallel.

Ferromagnetic materials are classified as either hard or soft. Hard materials have a low relative permeability , very high coercive force, and are difficult to magnetize and demagnetize; soft materials have a high relative permeability low coercive force, and are easily magnetized and demagnetized.

Hard ferromagnetics, such as cobalt steel and various ferromagnetic alloys of nickel, aluminium, and cobalt, retain a high percentage of their magnetization and have a relatively high hysteresis loss. They are most suitable for use as permanent magnets, as used in sound amplification devices. A high degree of dislocation is introduced into their stucture during manufacture. Hard materials are frequently heated to high temperatures and then quenched in a suitable liquid to introduce strains. Alternatively they may be produced as compressed powders in which each particle in sufficiently small so as to be a single domain ; magnetization can then only proceed by domain since the energy required for wall movement is so great.

Soft ferromagnetics, such as silicon steel and soft iron, retain very little magnetization and have extremely small hysteresis loss. The ease of magnetization and demagnetization makes them very suitable for uses involving changing magnetic flux, as in electro-magnets, electric motors, generators, and transformers. They are also useful for magnetic screening. Their properties are enhanced by careful manufacture, as by heating and slow annealing in order to achieve a high degree of crystal purity.

ferromanganese. An allow of manganese (70% to 80%) and iron.

Ferron solution. A solution of 2 g. 7-iodo-8-hydroxyquinoline-5-sulphonic acid in 100 ml. water ; used in the colourimetric determination of iron. A green colour in a solution acid to water methyl orange is positive for ferric iron.

ferrosilicon. An alloy of silicon (15%) and iron ; used in special steels.

ferrosilicon process for hydrogen. A method of preparing hydrogen of high purity by reaction of powdered ferrosilicon with a 20% aqueous solution of caustic soda at about 360K.

ferrous. Containing or pertaining to divalent iron.

ferruginous. Containing iron.

ferrous metals. Three chemical elements grouped horizontally in eighth, additional, group of periodic system in period IV : iron, cobalt, nickel.

fertile material. Isotopes that can be transformed into fissile material by the absorption of neutrons, *e.g.*, thorium-232 ; uranium-238.

fertilizer. An agricultural chemical (which may be an element, compound, or mixture) containing one or more soil nutrients. Fertilizers are usually made artificially and applied either as soilds or solutions. The elements essential for soil fertility are chiefly nitrogen, phosphorus, and potassium ; several others are of less importance (sulphur, calcium, and trace elements). Fertilizers used in largest amount are ammonium nitrate, superphosphate (20% phosphoric acid), and potassium chloride. Controlled-release fertilizers are made by impregnating the fertilizer pellets with sulphur to permit gradual release of the fertilizer elements under varying moisture conditions. Some fertilizer are obtained from organic sources, such as processed municipal wastes, various types of manures, and tankage. The chemical characteristics of a soil are important in the selection of an optimum fertilizer.

Feynman diagrams. Diagrammatic representation of elements of matrix describing interaction processes, *e.g.*, of elementary particles.

fibre. An elongated crystalline stucture ranging in length from a few millmetres to several metres (for some woody fibres) and in diameter from 1 to 1,270 micron. Their strength varies greatly, from upwards of one million psi for single- crystal metal fibres (often called whiskers) to about 40,000 psi (theoretically) for cotton. Many common natural fibres are of vegetable origin (cotton, flax, ramie, jute, etc.) ; there are also animal fibres (wool, mohair, silk) and natural inorganic fibres cuch as occur in asbestos. Semisynthetic fibres are rayon (cellulose-derived), glass, boron nitride, graphite, and a number of other materials. Syntheic fibres are essentially plastics passed through fine nozzles in liquid form into a hardening bath ; these can be cut to any length or manufactured in continuous lengths called filament. Polymides (nylon), polyesters, and polyethylene are among the more familiar types.

fibre-reactive dye. An organic dye, often of the azo type, which can form chemical bonds with cellulose and thus become an integral part of the fibre. They can also be used to dye a large number of man made fibres.

fibrin. An insoluble blood protein precipitated in the blood of vertebrates in the form of a meshwork of fibres during the process of clotting. It is formed when thrombin acts upon fibrinogen.

fibrinogen. A major protein component of blood plasma ; when activated by the enzyme thrombin at the onset of beelding, the fibrinogen under-goes chemical modification to fibrin; this in turn triggers the protective agglutination or clotting of blood. Fibrinogen is water-soluble and has a fibrous structure ; it is synthesized in the liver. Blood clotting is an involved series of reactions in which fibrinogen plays the vital role.

Fick's first law. Tranport by diffusion J_D, defined as number of moles, particles or units of mass of defined constiuent flowing across unit area in unit time, is proportional to concentration gradient, grad c.

$$J_D = -D \text{ grad } c$$

where D = diffusion coefficient ; in one-dimensional problems when ; concentration gradient does not depend on time, Fick's first law is reduced to the form :

$$m = -D \frac{dc}{dx} At$$

where m = amount of constituent flowing across area A perpendicular to direction of diffusion in time t (x coordinate).

Fick's second law. Relationship resulting from Fick's first law and defining partial derivative of concentration c with respect to time t at defined unit volume as

$$\left(\frac{\partial c}{\partial t}\right)_{xyz} = -\text{ div } (D \text{ grad } c)$$

where D = diffusion coefficient, grad c = concentration gradient. In one-dimensional problems, when diffusion coefficient does not depend on concentration, Fick's second law is reduced to the form :

$$\left[\frac{\partial c}{\partial t}\right]_x = -D\left[\frac{\partial^2 c}{\partial x^2}\right]_t$$

Fiehe test for glucose. To detect commerical glucose in food products, dilute or dissolve 10 g. of the sample with 10 ml. of water, warm it if neccessary to make solution. Add 10 ml. of a saturated solution of ammonium oxalate and boil. Add animal charcoal and boil again. Filter and place 2 ml of the clear filtrate in a test tube, add 2 drops of hydroehloric acid and 20 ml. of 95% alcohol and mix. In the presence of commercial glucose or dextrins, a marked white turbidity will be formed.

Fiehe reagent for invert sugar. A solution of 1 g. resorcinol, in 100 g. hydrochloric acid ; used in testing honey for invert sugar, a substance used in making artificial honey. A violet red colour indicates the presence of invert sugar. This test can also be applied to detect the presence of artificial honey.

field effect. Effect exerted by dipole of bond linking substituent with rest of molecule on distribution of electron density of molecule. Unlike inductive effect, this effect is not transferbale by bond system but acts sterically in direct way. Also known as direct field effect.

field emission. The emission of electrons from a metal or semiconductor into vacuum (or dielectric) under the influence of a strong electric field. In field emission, electrons tunnel through a potential barrier, rather than escaping over it as in thermionic or photoemission. It occurs because the wave function of an electron does not vanish at the classical turning point, but decays exponentially into the barrier. Thus there is a finite probability that the electron will be found on the outside of the barrier.

field strength effect. Increase of equivalent electrolytic conductance in high electric field (10^4—10^5 V/cm) as a result of progressive disappearance of ionic atmosphere. Also known as Wien's effect.

Filhol test. Alkali hydroxides are detected by a blue colour given with an aqueous solution of sodium nitroprusside saturated with hydrogen sulphide.

filler. A very fine-ground soild, usually inorganic in nature, used in considerable tonnages in the plastics and rubber industries, partly to save costs and partly for the heavy, deadening effect they produce in such items as floor coverings, gaskets, heels, etc. The materials, used include whiting (calcium carbontae), barytes (barium sulphate), certain types of clays, wood flock, etc. They have neither reinforcing nor colouring effect.

filter. In the most general sense of the term, a filter is a device for removing one or more components of a mixture on passage through it. The nature of the mixture is widely variable. It may be any kind of matter, or material particles, or not matter at all, as in the case of an optical filter, which absorbs certain frequencies of radiant energy and transmits other.

filter aid. Any material used in a finely divided state to effect filtration of a liquid. Sand can serve as a filter in water purification ; in the laboratory, such materials as clays, diatomite, coarse cellulosic structures, and glass fibres are used. These are sufficiently porous to allow passage of water and other liquids of similar viscosity, the foreign particles adhering to the surfaces of the filter aid.

filter plate. A porous, circular disc used in funnels or other supports for purposes of filtration ; it may be packed around the edges with asbestos or secured permanently with cement.

filter press. A type of apparatus consisting of alternate plates and frames with filter paper or cloth between each frame and the adjacent plate. The materials to be filtered are forced through by a pumping device, the residue is left in the hollow space inside the frames, and the effluent is discharged through a manifold.

filter pump. Any vacuum pump used to assist filtration by evacuating the receiver. The term is used specifically to designate a short tube containing a tepered constriction, which is attached to the water faucet and develops a vacuum in accordance with the Bernoulli principle. Filter pumps are also available in positive pressure types.

filtrate. Solution separated from precipitate by filtration.

filtration. In most common sense, an operation involving liquid-soild separation, used in chemistry and chemical engineering ; it consists essentially of either gravity or forced flow of a liquid containing dispersed solid particles through a structure having a pore size small enough to retain the particulates. Special papers, cloth, fine-mesh wire screens, and membranes of collodion or other plastic are all used. In water purification, a bed of fine sand is effective ; in the paper industry, the formation of the sheet on the fourdrinier wire is a practical example. Filter paper, glass fibre mats, and similar materials are used for laboratory filteration. *See also* filter aid.

fine chemical. A chemical produced in comparatively small quantities and in a relatively pure state. Pharmaceutical and biological products, perfumes, photographic chemicals, and reagent chemicals are examples of fine chemicals.

fineness. 1. The extent of subdivision of a substance.

2. The number of particles in a unit volume of a material.

3. The gold content of an alloy, expressed in parts per thousand.

fine spectrum The resolution of lines in atomic emission spectra, by high-power spectroscopes, into two or more fine lines situated close together. The fine lines in atomic spectra arise from so-called term multiplicities, *i.e.*, from transition between groups of higher, to groups of lower, levels, the levels comprising each group lying close together. Groups of lying-close-levels are obtained by coupling the orbital angular momentum vector with the spin angular momentum vector of the atom in a variety of possible combinations.

fine structure. Structure of spectra lines or atomic terms arising due to interaction between spin and angular momentum of electrons.

fingerprint region. Spectral range in infrared from 650 to 1480 cm^{-1} with a number of bands characteristic for a molecule as a whole and non-characteristic for separate functional groups.

fining agent. A substance added to a liquid to clarify it. Examples are the addition of certain colloids or other materials to fermented beverages to remove suspended matter, and the use of certain oxides, such as arsenious oxide, in molten glass to aid in the removal of air bubbles.

finishing agent (material, or substance). A substance used to confer certain desired properties upon another substance, such as resistance to shrinking, oxidation, combustion, etc., and which is commonly applied or incorporated in the latter stages of the manufacturing process.

first heat of solution. Enthalpy change in

process of dissolving one mole of a given substance in infinitely large bulk of solvent.

first law of thermodynamics. In any process increase of internal energy ΔU of closed system is equal to energy supplied in this process in form of work W and heat Q, *i.e.*,

$$\Delta U = W + Q$$

first-order asymmetric transformation. Spontaneous epimerization taking place in solution of optically unstable diastereoisomers. Consequently, new equilibrium between epimers is established, *e.g.*, if compounds A and B are able to form salt A.B, than first-order asymmetric tranformation can be expressed by equation :

$$2(\pm)A + 2(-)B \rightarrow \underset{50\%}{(+)A.(-)B} + \underset{50\%}{(-)A.(-)B}$$

$$\rightleftharpoons \underset{(50+x)\%}{(+)A.(-)B} + \underset{(50-x)\%}{(-)A.(-)B}$$

first-order phase transition. Change of physical state of matter accompanied by sudden change of first-order derivative of Gibbs free energy with respect to pressure and temperature, *i e.*, volume and entropy.

first-order reaction. Reaction with kinetic equation characterized by sum of powers in which concentrations of reactants occur being equal to one.

Fischer-Hepp rearrangement. The rerrangement of a N-nitroso-N-alkyl or N-aryl derivatives of anilines to a *p*-nitrosoarylamine, which is brought about by an alcoholic solution of hydrogen chloride, and similar reagents, *e.g.*,

$C_6H_5N(CH_3)NO \xrightarrow{H^{\oplus}} p\text{-}ON{-}C_6H_4{-}NHCH_3$

Fischer indole synthesis. A method of formation of indole derivatives by ring closure of aromatic hydraozones, *e.g.*,

$C_6H_5NH{-}N{=}C(R'){-}CH_2R \xrightarrow{180-200^\circ}$ 2-R'-3-R-indole $+ NH_3$

Fischer oxazole synthesis. A method of formation of oxazoles from aldehyde cyanhydrins and aldehydes, *e.g.*,

$$R'CHOHCN + R''CHO \xrightarrow[\text{ether}]{HCl} \text{(oxazole, R', R'')} + H_2O$$

Fischer peptide synthesis. A method of synthesis of peptides in which α-amino acids (or peptides containing a free amino group) react with acid halides of α-haloacids, followed by amination with ammonia :

$$\underset{(1)}{ClCHR'COCl} + \underset{(2)}{H_2NCHR''COOH} \xrightarrow{-HCl}$$

$$\underset{(3)}{ClCHR'CONHCHR''COOH} \xrightarrow{NH_3}$$

$$\underset{(4)}{NH_2CHR'CONHCHR''COOH}$$

The above reaction can be used repeatedly by forming the acid chloride of the intermediate product (3), and condensing it with another molecule of an α-amino acid, (2), to form another intermediate molecule of type (3), before the final amination of the terminal carbon atom.

Fischer phenylhydrazine synthesis. The method of production of aromatic hydrazines by reducing diazo compounds to hydrazine-sulphonic acids, followed by hydrolysis, *e.g.*,

$$RN_2Cl + 2Na_2SO_3 + H_2O \rightarrow$$

$$RNHNHSO_3Na + NaCl + Na_2SO_4$$

$$\downarrow H_2O,\ HCl$$

$$RNHNH_2HCl + NaHSO_4$$

Fischer phenylhydrazone and osazone reaction. The reaction of pheyhydrazine with sugars with the formation of phenylyydrazones and di-phenylhydrazones (osazones).

Fischer projection formula. Projection formula of chiral molecule in which chiral atom is placed in plane of projection, so that its bonds with adjacent atoms and carbon chain are beyond projection plane, but at equal angles to it, The more oxidized part of chain is at the top of formula; remaining two atoms (or groups) linked with chiral carbon atom project towards viewer (at equal angles to plane).

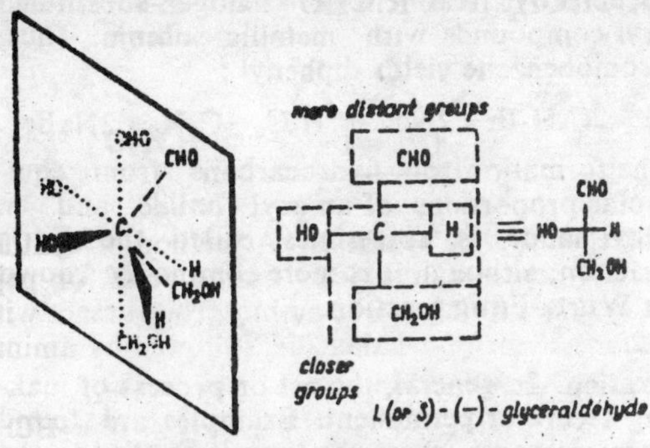

Fig. 25. Fischer projection formula

Fischer reagent for aldehydes and ketones. A solution of 1 part phenylhydrazine hydrochloride and 1 part sodium acetate in 10 parts water. It forms hydrazones with aldehydes and ketones.

Fischer reagent for beryllium. An alkaline, violet solution of quinalizarin, which changes to blue with alkaline solution of beryllium ion.

Fischer reagents for cobalt. 1. Glyoxaline, which gives violet-blue precipitates; 2. An ammoniacal solution of diphenylthiocarbazone, it gives a violet colour.

Fischer's salt. The yellow hydrated potassium cobaltinitrite ($K_3Co(NO_2)_6)xH_2O$. It insoluble in water, and is used as a pigment.

Fischer-Speir method. A method for the conversion of fatty acid to ester. To make ethyl acetate a mixture of alcohol and glacial acetic acid is boiled and dry hydrogen chloride gas is passed through. The method avoids the use of concentrated sulphuric acid in the cases where the alcohol is too readily dehydrated.

Fischer test reaction for benzaldehyde. When benzaldehyde is heated with twice its volume of dimethylaniline and sulphuric acid, leucomalachite green is formed. On dilution with water and addition of potassium dichromate and sodium acetate, the green colour of malachite green appears.

Fischer test for cobalt. An aqueous solution of potassium nitrite and acetic acid produces a yellow precipitate with a cobalt salt solution.

Fischer test for tertiary amines. An aqueous solution of potassium ferrocyanide; when added in amount equivalent to that of the hydrochloride of the tertiary amine in aqueous solution, gives a precipitate which recrystallizes from alcohol to yield colourless leaflets, becoming blue in air.

Fischer-Tropsch process. A process for the manufacture of liquid hydrocarbon fuels. It is basically a catalyzed reaction of carbon monoxide and hydrogen, yielding aliphatic hydrocarbons and oxygen-containing organic chemicals. The gaseous mixture of hydrogen and carbon monoxide can be obtained from petroleum or coal (water gas or synthesis gas). A number of metallic catalysts have been successfully used. Variations of this process are being applied to coal gasification.

Fishel test for ketose. A method for determining levulose by treatment with a freshly-prepared aqueous solution of Rochelle salt, disodium phosphate, sodium carbonate, and cupric salphate.

fish salt. Sodium chloride in the form of large coarse-grained crystals obtained by the slow evaporation of brine at about 305K.

fissile material. Material containing nuclides with nuclei undergoing fission with emission of neutrons in reaction with neutrons. Sometimes the term is restricted to isotopes that are capable of undergoing fission upon impact with a slow neutron (*e.g.*, U 233, U-235, Pu-239). Also known as fissionable material.

fission. A nuclear reaction brought about by direct impact of a neutron upon the uranium isotope 235 or upon the artificial element plutonium-239. This causes the nucleus to split or divide into two fragments (fission products); for example, U-235 yields radioactive isotopes of barium and krypton, the lost mass appears as energy in amount $\triangle E = c^2 \triangle m$, where $\triangle m$ is the change in mass, and c^2 the square of the velocity of light. The process of fission is initiated by the bombardment with certain particles and radiations, especially neutrons of resonance energy, of certain fissionable atomic species, such as the uranium isotopes U-235 and U-238, the transuranic element plutonium Pu-239 (which may also have other fissionable isotopes), a certain isotopes of the transuranic element neptunium

More important is the tremendous energy release, amounting to about 200 million electron volts for each nucleus split, which represents a portion of the binding energy of the nucleus. In addition, fission produces two or three fast neutrons per nucleus, each of which is then able to impinge upon and divide another nucleus. In this way, a progressive and self-sustaining chain reaction occurs. For effective fission, the fast neutrons must be retarded by contact with a moderating substance such as graphite ; in this condition, they are called slow or thermal neutrons. Fission reaction can be closely controlled; their most important use is for electric power generation.

fission chain reaction. Chain of nuclear reactions; in neutron fission chain reaction, neutron hitting fissionable atom causes fission resulting in number of neutrons which in turn cause other fissions with emission of further neutrons ; number of fission may deminish with time, remain constant or increase rapidly.

fission fragments. Nuclei formed in nuclear fission process with kinetic energy obtained during this process.

fission neutrons. Neutrons emitted in atomic nuclear fission reactions, immediately or with delay. Spectrum of fission neutrons is continuous with maximum at 1 MeV.

fission parameter. *x*. Ratio of square of atomic number *Z* divided by mass number *A* of nucleus to critical value of this quotient

$$x = \frac{Z^2}{A} \Big/ \left(\frac{Z^2}{A}\right)_{cr}$$

where $\left(\frac{Z^2}{A}\right)_{cr} \approx 50$. In liquid-drop model, fission parameter gives expression for the stability of a nucleus of spherical shape, thus describing the ability of a nucleus to undergo fission. Also known as fissility parameter.

fission products. Fission fragments from atomic nucleus and products of their radioactive decay.

fission yield. Fraction of fissions leading to formation of product of specified mass number.

Fittig reaction. The synthesis of aryl hydrocarbons by treatment of halogen-substituted aryl compounds with metallic sodium. Thus, bromobenzene yields diphenyl ;

$$2C_6H_5Br + 2Na \rightarrow H_5C_6-C_6H_5 + 2NaBr$$

The formation of hydrocarbons from equimolar proportions of an aryl halide and an alkyl halide is sometimes called the Fittig reaction, although it is more commonly known as Wurtz-Fittig reaction.

fixation. In general, the act or process of making secure or permanent. Examples are found in microscopy, where the term is applied to the preparation of slides from specimens or sections cut from them ; in photography, the term is applied to the removal from photographic film or other media, after exposure, of the unchanged light-sensitive substances, to prevent further change and hence marring the picture ; in immunology, the term is applied to the method of preventing hemolysis by the complement ; in perfume and flavour formulation, to the use of high boiling components to make the evaporation of the mixture uniform ; and in chemistry, it refers to reactions and processes by which free nitrogen enters into chemical combination. (*See* nitrogen fixation.)

fixative. 1. A reagent, or mixture of reagents, used to preserve organs and organisms intended for microscopic examination.

2. In dyeing technology, either an adhesive substance which holds a dye in contact with a fibre, or a metallic complex (mordant) which chemically combines with the dye and thus binds it so the fibre.

3. A quick-drying cellulosic solution applied as a spray to pencil and ink drawings to maintain distinctness of the lines.

4. In the perfume industry, a substance that retards the evaporation rate of the volatile components and thus stabilizes the odour ; a number of natural materials have been used as perfume fixatives (ambergris, musk), but these have now largely been replaced by synthetics.

fixed. As applied to nitrogen, the term refers to atmospheric nitrogen that has been made available to plants by soil bacteria or has been combined by synthetic processes into useful chemical compounds, especially ammonia.

fixed air. Former name for carbon dioxide, CO_2.

fixed alkali. Former name for potassium or sodium corbonate, to distinguish them from volatile alkali, ammonium carbonate.

fixed oil. A nonvolatile oil of animal or vegetable origin, consisting usually largely of fatty acids and certain of their esters. Fixed oils may be solid, semi-solid or liquid at atmospheric temperature.

flame. A reaction or reaction-product, partly or entirely gaseous, which yields heat and more or less light, as the result of a chemical reaction, commonly oxidation.

flame colour. A characteristic colour imparted to a nonluminous flame by certain atoms or substances containing them, due to the excitation of their flame spectra.

flame photometer. Instrument used to measure intensities of radiation in flame-excited spectra of samples.

flame photometry. Branch cf emmission spectral analysis using flame as excitation source.

flame retardant. A substance applied to or incorporated in a combustible material to reduce or eliminate its tendency to ignite when exposed to a low-energy flame such as a match or cigarette. There are three methods of application ; (*i*) as a coating or surface finish (non-durable, readly removed) : (*ii*) in solution form to penetrate the fibres (semi-durable, reasonably, stable) ; and (*iii*) as an integral part of the polymer stucture of a synthetic fibre (durable, not removable). The latter method provides permanent protection, as it not only makes the material self-extinguiushing, but cannot be leached out by laundering or drycleaning. Substances commonly used in methods (*i*) and (*ii*) include such inorganic salts as ammonium sulphamate, zinc borate, and antimony oxychloride ; chorinated organic compounds such as chlorendic anhydride ; alumina trihdyrate and certain organic phosphates and phosphonates. Major uses of flame-retardant chemicals are in carpets, rugs, upholstery, plastics used in consruction, and miscellaneous wearing apparel.

flame spectrophotometer. Flame photometer which measures intensity of radiation of a given wavelength after its separation by monochromator.

flame test. A simple test for metals, in which a small amount of the sample (usually moistened with hydrochloric acid) is placed on the tip of a platinum wire and held in Bunsen flame. Certain metals can be detected by noticing the colour of the flame : barium (green) lithium (crimson), potassium (lilac), sodium (yellow).

flash. A term used to describe several quite different physicochemical operations in the general sence of "extremely rapid" or almost instantaneous." In flash photolysis, for example, an actual flash of light is used to initiate a reaction ; flash distillation and flash evaporation involve very fast conversions of liquid to vapour, taking place in thousandths of a secound. Flash pasteurization involves heating the product, *e.g.*, milk for only 15 seconds at 343K. Flash pyrolysis converts waste solids to usable materials, including fuel oil, by applying a temperature of 753K for 30 minutes.

flash drying. *See* flash evaporation.

flash evaporation. Very rapid evaporation, especially as applied in industrial processes, in which liquids are heated under pressure is subsequently suddenly reduced causing the liquid, which is then superheated, to evaporate rapidly. Also known as flash drying.

flash pasteurization. A pasteurization technique in which a heat-labile liquid such as milk, is briefly subjected to temperature around 383K.

flash photolysis. Photolysis generated by very short but high-intensity flash of light. Flash photolysis is a method of investigating the mechanism of extremely rapid photochemical reactions involving the formation of free radicals (both inorganic and organic). This is done by irradiating a given reactions mixture with a flash of high-intensity light ; this excites the molecules and produces the short-lived radicals which activate photochemical reactions. These products are instantaneously analyzed spectroscopically, which permits identification of the radical species from the spectra obtained. The time lapses involved in this technique are about

10^{-6} second. It has also been applied to study of the exceedingly fast reactions occurring in flames and explosions.

flash point. The temperature at which an organic liquid forms a high enough pressure of vapour at or near its surface to form an ignitable mixture with air. Flash points range from far below 273K for volatile liquids like diethyl ether to several hundred kelvins for heavy, nonvolatile liquids such as vegetable oils, petroleum, etc. A flash point from 300 to 311K is considered by most authorities to be the dividing line between flammable and combustible liquids.

flash spectroscopy. Branch of molecular spectroscopy which use technique of light pulses to obtain high population of molecular excited states for observation of absorption spectrum.

flat. A term used in industrial chemistry to describe a paint or simlar coating meterial which contain enough coarse solid particles to give a slightly roughened surface when applied ; the effect of this is to decrease direct reflectivity by scattering light rays at angles, rather than reflecting them in a direction normal to the surface. The most effective flatting agents are diatomite, silica, and low percentages of heavy-metal soaps.

flat-bed chromatography. A common form of liquid chromatography that takes place in flat chromatography beds. Two methods which belong to this technique are paper chromatography and thin-layer chromatography.

flavonoid 1. Any of a series of widely distributed plant constituents related in one way or another to the aromatic heterocyclic skeleton 2-phenylbenzopyran, or flavan. The three most important classes are anthocynins, the flavons, and the flavon-3-ols, or flavonols. Other classes are chalcones, isoflavons, and leucoanthocynidins. The various flavonoid classes are biogenetically related, all being derived from a common precursor. In contrast to alkaloids, flavonoids are rather inactive pharmacologically. An economically significant property of flavonoids is their contribution to taste and flavour in foods.

flavoproteins. Yellow conjugated proteins in which the prosthetic group is either flavin mononucleotide of flavin adenine dinucleotide. Flavoproteins are enzyme of the dehydrogenase type.

flavour. 1. Approximately synonymous with taste. Though much research has been expended on analyzing this sense, no correlation between flavour and chemical type or structure has been determined, The basic tastes are bitter, sweet, salty, and sour ; beyond this, the problem is physiological and psychological, rather than chemical. Taste, like odor is a property widely used by chemist for identification purposes.

2. A substance having a strong characteristic taste, often obtained by extraction from the leaves, twigs, or flowers of plants ; many are now made artificially. Among the more common natural flavouring materials are vanillin and chocolate (from beans), oils of wintergreen, peppermint, clove, and cinnamon (from plant leaves or blossome), oil of bitter almond (from nuts), and citrus flavours (from seeds or rinds of oranges, lemons, etc.). Over 1,500 flavouring materials are known. *See also* potentiator ; enhancer.

Fleck test for zinc. A solution of picric acid in 10% hydrochloric acid gives a blue colour on addition of zinc ions. Dinitrocresol gives a blood-red colour.

Fleig blood reagent. A test reagent for testing the presence of blood in urine, made by adding 10 g. powdered zinc to a solution of 0.25 g. fluorescein and 20 g. potasssum hydroxide in 100 ml water. A fluorescence, in the presence of hydrogen peroxide, indicates the presence of blood.

Fleig test for carbohydrates. 1. On heating 0.5 ml. of a dilute solution of many of the carbohydrates with 4 ml. hydrochloric acid, a yellow to orange-red colour forms on addition of 4 drops of 0.1% alcoholic indole solution.

2. On addition of 2 drops of a saturated solution of carbazole in alcohol, and 1 ml. sulphuric acid to 0.5 ml. of the carbohydrate solution, a violet-red colour is produced.

Fleischmann test. Alcohol is detected in volatile oils by shaking the oil with water and, adding potassium dichromate and sulphuric acid to the water-extract. A green colour indicates the presence of alcohol.

flexibility of macromolecules. Capacity of changing conformation characteristic of macromolecules due to intramolecular thermal movements of certain fragments or action of external forces.

Flick solution. A solution of 15 ml. hydrochloric acid and 10 ml. hydrofluoric acid in 90 ml. water ; used for etching aluminium.

flint. 1. A term used in glass technology to denote a type of optical glass characterized by a high refractive index and high light dispersion properties ; it generally contains lead oxide, which increases the refractivity. Lead-containing glass has the brilliance characteristic of genuine cut glass.

2. A naturally occurring hard crystalline silica similar to quartz ; used as an abrasive material for spark ignition, in pulverizing devices, and in powder form as an extender in various materials.

floatation. Method for separation of crushed solid substances making use of difference in wettability of the particular substaneces in (soild—liquid—gas) three-phase system.

flocculating agent. A substance added to dispersion medium to bring about flocculation of fine particles.

flocculation. A type of aggregation of finely divided solid particles dispersed in a liquid or semiliquid matrix ; under certain conditions they tend to clump together to form small clusters or "flocks" similar in appearance to tufts of fibre. This often occurs with colloidal dispersions of carbon black, clays, etc., in rubber and plastic mixes, drilling muds, and paints. The effect can often be reversed by agitation where as coagulation cannot. The word is derived from the Latin word for tuft of wool. *See also* aggregation ; coagulation.

flock. 1. A finely divided, low-gravity pulverized material made from vegetable fibres ; it is flammble when suspended in air as a dust. Its uses are as a diluent in rubber, plastics, and paint mixtures. Cotton linters can be considered as a type of flocculation.

2. *See* flocculation.

Flood reaction. A method for the preparation of trialkylhalosilanes from (*i*) trialkylsilylsulphates and hydrogen chloride, or from

(*ii*) hexaalkalyldisiloxanes on treatment with sulphuric acid and ammonium halide. On treatment with sulphuric acid, the hexaalkyldisiloxanes yield the trialkylsilylsulphates that are the initial reactants in (*i*) :

$$(R_3Si)_2SO_4 + 2HCl \xrightarrow{(NH_4)_2SO_4} 2R_3SiCl + H_2SO_4$$

$$R_3SiOSiR_3 + H_2SO_4 + 2NH_4Cl \rightarrow 2R_3SiCl + (NH_4)_2SO_4 + H_2O$$

flow diagram. A graphic or pictorial representation used by physical chemists to indicate the various successive steps in the production of a chemical. It is sometimes also called a flow sheet, the term flow in this instance referring to the progress of the various reactants through the system. Such diagrams also indicate quantities, energy input and output, by-products, waste, etc., as well as efficiencies and other relevant production data. Flow diagrams are essential in setting up a pilot, as well as for full-scale operations.

flue dust. Fine particles of alloys or metals emitted along with the gases of metallurgical furnaces.

flue gas. The gaseous products of combustion from a boiler furnace consisting predominantly of carbon dioxide, carbon monoxide oxygen, nitrogen and steam. Analysis of the flue gases is used to check the efficiency of furnace.

fluid. Substance which at given conditions in macroscopic dimension has no defined shape and fills vessel in which it is contained or melts away in space. Fluids include ; gases, liquids and also solid substances in delicate disintegration and suspension in gas or liquid.

fluidity. The property of a substance that expresses its ability to flow, as contrasted with viscosity, which is the resistance to flow. Fluidity is a measure of the rate, at which a fluid is deformed by a shearing stress, and is mathematically of the viscosity.

fluidization. *See* fluidized bed.

fluidized bed. A device originally developed for catalytic cracking of petroleum gases ; it consists of a container partially filled with finely divided solids through which a uniform stream of hydrocarbon vapours is passed upward through the bottom of the container. The catalyst is incorporated in the bed of solids, and as the gases move uniformly through the solids, they attain a random motion; and the bed tends to expand. Thus, the surface of the bed assumes the appearance of a boiling liquid, which gave rise to the name "fluidization" for this method. The cracking reaction occurs at the surface of the solid particles. This is an example of heterogeneous catalysis. Other applications of fluidization include the oxidation of naphathalene to form phthalic anhydride, the decomposition of limestone to produce lime and carbon dioxide, coal gasification, and the roasting of sulphide ores to produce metallic oxides and sulphur dioxide.

fludized-bed combustion. A method of burning fuel in which the fuel is continually fed into a bed of reactive or inert material while a flow of air passes up through the bed, causing it to act like a turbulent fluid.

fluo- (or fluor- or fluoro-). A prefix indicating content of fluorine, as fluobenzene, fluorochloroform. The prefix fluo- also indicates the presence of fluorescence.

fluorescence. Type of the photoluminescence depending on emission of light during transition of atoms or molecules from electronically excited state other energetically lower electronic state of like multiplicity.

Among inorganic substances having the property of fluorescence are sodium vapour, numerous compounds of zinc, cadmium, magnesium, and calcium with sulphur, tungsten, silicon, boron, and others. Such materials (called phosphors) are utilized in fluorescent lights, televisian tubes, and similar devices. Organic substances which fluoresce are anthracene, fluorescein, and other fused ring sturctures, used in fluorescent dyes and as tracer materials.

fluorescence analysis. Methods of analysis based upon irradiation with ultraviolet light, and observation of the colour and intensity of of the fluorescent radiation emitted by the sample. Also known as fluorometric analysis; fluorimetry; fluorescimetry; fluorophotometry.

fluorescence excitation spectrum. Dependence of fluorescence intensity at some wavelength recorded as function of exciting radiation wavelenth.

fluorescence spectrum. Spectrum of electromagnetic radiation resulting from re-emisson of previously absorbed excitation by a given sample.

fluorescent indicator. An indicator which shows a change in a chemical system, such as the end point of a reaction, by an increase or decrease in fluorescence.

fluorescimetry. *See* fluorescence analysis.

fluorimetry. *See* fluorescence analysis.

fluoridation. In a broad sence, this term signifies the addition of fluorine to a substance much as chlorination means the addition of chlorine. In a more specific, but commonly used sense fluoridation means the addition of very small amounts of a fluoride-containing compounds to water supplies for the purpose preventing dental caries. It has been shown over a number of years that the introduction of about 1 part per million (ppm) of fluoride to drinking water will reduce the incidence of tooth decay in children by as much as 60 per cent as compared with similar groups of children who consume nonfluoridated water.

fluorination. Introduction of fluorine atom into an organic molecule usually by substituting hydrogen atom. Usually, this reaction is effected indirectly in presence of catalysts, *e.g.*,

$$RH + 2CoF_3 \rightarrow RF + HF + 2CoF_2$$

or by hydrogen atom exchange (Swart reaction), *e.g.*,

$$C_6H_5CCl_3 + SbF_3 \xrightarrow{SbCl_5} C_6H_5CF_3 + SbCl_3$$

fluorine. An element.

		Symbol	F
		Atomic No.	9
State	Gas	Atomic Wt.	18.9984
Group	VIIA	Valence	—1
		b.p.	—188.13°C

At an estimated 0.065% of the earth's crust, fluorine is roughly as plentiful as carbon, nitrogen or chlorine, and much more plentiful than copper or lead, though much less abundant than aluminium or iron. Fluorine is the most reacitive member of the halogen family. Its outer shell contains seven electrons, which accounts for its tendency to acquire an eighth electron to complete the shell ; for this reason, it is extremely electronegative. Its oxidation state is —1. Thus, it combines easily with other elements (except helium. neon, and argon) to form fluorides, fluorocarbons, etc. It is a strong oxidizing agent and therefore is a fire hazard in the presence of combustible materials. Although only the isotope with atomic mass 19 is stable, the other, radioactive isotopes between atomic mass 17 and 22 have been artificilly prepared. Fluoride substances show toxicity in both animals and plants when encountered in fumes and dusts from industrial facilities as well as natural emissions from the eruption of volcanoes. Abnormally high levels of fluoride in water also have caused fluorine toxicity in animals and mottled teeth in humans.

It has the highest bactericidal activity of all the halogens ; and is classed as a boneseeking element.

fluorocarbon. Any of the compounds of fluorine and carbon. Large numbers of such compounds are known ; in many of their properties they resemble the hydrocarbons. The series C_nF_{2n+2} shows a sequence of increasing boiling points in successive members that is closely analogous to that of the paraffin hydrocarbons. The chemical inertness of the fluorocarbons makes them useful solvents, lubricants, and insulators.

The unsaturated aliphatic fluorocarbons such as vinyl fluoride ($H_2C{=}CHF$) and tetrafluoroethylene ($F_2C{=}CF_2$) are the basis of an importaut series of heat-resistant thermoplastic polymers. The aromatic fluorocarbons, *e.g.*, hexafluorcbenzene (C_6F_6) are valuable intermediates from which many useful compounds can be obtained.

Use of chlorofluorocarbons as aerosol propellants has been discontinued because of the possibility that they may deplete to atmospheric ozone layer.

fluorocarbon resin. Any of a group of organic polymers containing fluorine and having a number of exceptional properties, among which are relativly high heat resistance, permitting them to be used at temperatures of 530K or more ; resistance to electricity and to attack by chemicals, oxidation, and severe environmental conditions ; they are also nonflammable and non-toxic. Examples are polyvinylidene fluoride, polytetrafluoroethylene, and polychlorotrifluoroethylene. All are thermoplastic and are available in several forms. Their uses include numerous types of high-temperature application (insulation and nonstick coatings for cooking utensils, steam packing, etc,). *See also* fluorocarbon.

fluorochrome. A substance that causes another material, upon contact, to become fluorescent.

fluorogen. A radical which, by its presence in a compound, causes fluorescence.

fluorimetric analysis. A method of chemical analysis in which a sample exposed to radiation of one wavelength, absorbs this radiation and re-emits radiation of the same or longer wavelength. If this re-emission occurs in about 10^{-6} second or more, it is called plosphorescence, and if it occurs in about 10^{-9} second, it is called fluorescence. This type of analysis utilizes the re-emitted light to determine the material, which is the source of fluorescence.

flushed colour. A pigment dispersed in oil, varnish, etc., the transfer from the water phase to the oil phase having been effected without drying and subsequent grinding of the dry pigment. Flushed colours are as such ready for use.

flux. 1. Substance added to other compound in order to lower its melting point or to transform it into soluble compound.

Many substances may act as a flux on one material when added to it in small proportions and yet may have their own melting point decreased when the situation is reversed. Fluxing agents are chiefly used in ceramic glazes and in ore smelting. It is also known as fusing agent.

2. The quantity of a force which passes through unit area in a given time.

3. Flow, often with the connotation of periodic reversal in direction.

flux converter. Small quantity of fissionable substance introduced into thermal column of reactor to produce local fast neutron flux. Also known as neutron converter.

fluxional compounds. Molecules that undergo rapid intramolecular rearrangements among equivalent structures in which the component atoms are interchanged, *e.g.*, PF_5 involves inter conversion of the tringonal bipyramidal molecule to square planer configuration and back.

flux of radiation. Radiation power or energy (or number of particles or photons) per unit time passing through a surface.

fly ash. Fine particles introduced into the air by burning pulverized coal ; they can be recovered within the stack by electrostatic precipitation, as an aid to air purification. The collected ash finds application as a cement additive, especially for use in oil-well casings. Fly ash has been tried as a means of combating oil spills on sea water.

foam. Dispersed system in which disersion medium is liquid or solid (solid foam) and dispersed phase is gas. The gases present are usually air or carbon dioxide. Examples of liquid foams are the froth on beer and ale (proteins and fats being excellent foam-formers), soapsuds, fire-extinguishing foam, shaving creams, etc. Soild foams, are exemplified by flexible and rigid plastic foams, cellular rubber, and in the food field, by bread and other baked products. Special blowing agents (nitrogen) are used in plastics; baking powders and yeast provide the carbon dioxide for edible solid foams.

foam glass. A light, opaque, cellular glass formed by adding powdered carbon to crushed glass and firing the mixture.

foam metal. Cast metal with tiny gas bubbles evenly distributed throughout the body of the metal.

Foges test. Chlorates and bromates are detected by treating a solution containing a few drops of either of them with 1 ml. of a solution of 0.8 g. strychinine in 24 ml. nitric acid (sp. gr. 1. 334). A red colour is obtained if any of these is present.

Folin-Denis reagent for phenols. A solution of 100 g. sodium tungstate, 20 g. phosphomolybdic acid, and 50 ml. 85% phosphoric acid in water, adjusted to a volume of 1 litre ; used as a test reagent for phenols. A blue colour indicates the presence of phenols.

Folin-McEllroy reagent. A solution of 50 g. sodium carbonete, 100 g. sodium pyrophosphate, and 30 g. disodium phosphate dissolved in 1 littre of water, the resulting solution being then mixed with a solution of 13 g. cupric sulphate dissolved in 1 litre water. This reagent is used for testing the presence of glucose in urine. A greenish-yellow or red precipitate indicates the presence of glucose.

Folin mixture. An aqueous solution of 500 g. ammonium sulphate, 5 g. uranium acetate, and 6 g. acetic in a volume of 1 litre ; used in testing for acids.

food. A substance used to maintain certain essential biological proccsses in living organisms, notably to furnish cell and tissue-building materials, and to provide heat and energy, as well as to supply auxiliary substances needed for the functioning of these processes. The basic food requirements of animals and man are fats, carbohydrates, proteins vitamins, and minerals, all of which are obtained by the ingestion of plants or their assimilated forms (meat, milk). The energy stored in the food is made available by oxidation, hydrolysis and similar chemical reactions.

food additive. Any substance intentionally added to a foodstuff or mixture of foodstuffs with the purpose of providing a specific purpose or property. All substances that effect flavour (salt-sweeteners, spices, synthetic or natural flavouring agents colour and texture modify the properties of taste, apperance, and feeling, respectively, substances that aid in processing and preservation are functional in nature, *i.e.*, they have a specific physicochemical action in the food product. Among this group are nutrients, preservatives, antioxidants, antimicrobials, emulsifiers thickners, colouring agents, anticaking agents, artificial sweetners, foam regulators, aerating agents, buffering agents, enzymes and the like. Additives are not used for nutritional purpose ; even though some have nutrient value, *e.g.*, sugar, starches, and fats used in low percentage as sweeteners, thickeners, and shortening, respectively. Vitamins and amino acid added as fortifiers should more properly be considered as dietary supplements rather than food additives.

food preservation. The prevention of chemical decomposition and the development of harmful bacteria in foods. It is generally affected by the sterlization of the food (*i.e.*, by the destruction of bacteria in it) by heating in sealed vessels, *i.e.*, canning ; or by making the conditions unfavourable for the development of bacteria, by pickling, drying, freezing, smoking, etc.

foots. Sediment that accumulates at the bottom of a tank or other vessel containing crude liquids, such as vegetable oils.

forbidden band. Range of energy states which cannot be occupied by electrons in ideally periodic crystal lattice. Also known as forbidden energy band ; band gap ; energy gap in band theory of solids.

forbidden energy band. *See* forbidden band.

forbidden transition. Transition between two energy levels of system whose probability, according to selection rules, is equal to zero.

forensic chemistry. The application of chemical knowledge to the solution of legal problems. Important subdivisions of forensic chemistry are crime detection and the entire body of patent law as it applies to chemical products and processes.

forked chain. System of mutually linked atoms with branching chain in a definite place, *e.g.*,

```
  |  |  |  |              |
—C—C—C—C—            —C—
  |  |  |  |              |
     —C—           —C—C—C—
      |              |  |  |
                       —C—
                        |
```

Also known as branched chain.

formation curve In coordination chemistry, curve relating ligand number n and equilibrium concentration of free ligand [L], usually expressed in logarithmic form : $\overline{n}=f(p[L]$, where $p[L]$ is negative logarithm of ligand concentration.

formazyl. The radical

```
C6H5N=N
       |
       C—
       ‖
C6H5NHN
```

form oil. An oil utilized on the contact surface of wooden or metal concrete forms to prevent concrete from sticking.

formolite. The solid product obtained by treating with sulphuric acid and formaldehyde those mineral oils which contain unsaturated cyclic hydrocarbons.

formoilte number. The weight of air-dry formolite obtained from 100 g. of oil is known as the formolite number of the oil.

formol tiration. A method of estimating carboxyl groups in amino-acid and free carboxyl groups in proteins, devised by Sorensen. Methanal reacts with the amino-groups to most amino-acid to form neutral methylene derivatives. Thus the presence to methanal the carboxyl groups can be estimated by titration with alkali.

formula. 1. A statement in chemical symbols of the composition of a substance.

2. A recipe for the preparation of some mixture or compound.

3. A mathematical statement of a law.

formula, chemical. *See* chemical formula.

formula, constitutional. *See* constitutional formula.

formula, electronic. *See* electronic formula.

formula, empirical. *See* empirical formula.

formula, general. *See* general formula.

formula, Lewis-Langmuir. *See* Lewis-Langmuir formula.

formula, molecular. *See* molecular formula.

formula, product. *See* product formula.

formula, stereoisomeric. *See* stereoisomeric formula.

formula, structural. *See* structural formula.

formula, weight. The sum of the atomic

weights from the formula written for the molecule, although it may be known that the substance does not exist as separate molecules, *e.g.*, some proteins. For many subsances it is molecular weight, but in the case of common salt, for example, 58·5 respresents its formula weight rather than is molecular weight—as any such crystal is a "giant molecule" of ions.

formylation. Substitution of hydrogen atom in organic compound molecule by formyl group —CHO, *e.g.*, Gattermann-Koch reaction.

Forster-Decker amine method. A method of formation of secondary amines by reaction of an alkyl halide with one of the Schiff bases, with subsequent hydrolysis, *e.g.*,

$$RX + R'N{=}CH{-}C_6H_5 \rightarrow C_6H_5{-}CH{=}NRR'X$$

$$\downarrow H_2O$$

$$C_6H_5CHO + HNRR' + HX$$

fortification. A term used in the food industry to describe the addition of essential nutritional factors (vitamins, minerals, proteins, etc.) to certain food products to replace losses incurred in the processing of raw materials, and to meet standard nutritional requirements. It is practiced especially with milled wheat flours, prepared mixes, meat and fish by-products, margarine, and infant foods. In cases where the food is baked after fortification, a large percentage of the vitamins so added may be inactivated by heat. *See also* food additive.

Forward process. The name given to a new hydrometallurgical method of treating mineral concentrates for the recovery of metals. In this process, solvent extraction methods working at high temperatures and pressures are used for the successive extraction of certain base metals. The "pressure leaching" process was first devised by Professor Forward at Vancouver for recovering nickel from a nickel copper sulphide ore. It has also been successfully applied to uranium ores. In the case of the nickel and copper ore, ammonia is used for the leaching process, and from the solution obtained copper may be precipitated as sulphide. Nickel is present as nickel ammine sulphate (the metal being obtained by reduction with hydrogen), cobalt is separated as sulphide, and finally ammonium sulphate is recovered from solution.

fossil. A term used in chemistry to indicate that a material is composed of geologically ancient animal or vegetable matter which has lain underground from a depth of a few metres to a kilometre or more. Thus fossil fuels include coal (vegetable) and petroleum (animal) : there are also fossil waxes (ozocerite), fossil resins (amber), and silicated (petrified) woods. Peat is a semifossilized carbonaceous material in the process of becoming lignite, brown coal. Their value as fuel depends on the exothermic oxidation of carbon to form carbon dioxide and the oxidation of hydrogen to form water.

fossil fuel. *See* fossil.

Foucry test reaction. To test for amines, add to 5 ml. of aqueous solution to be tested, which has been neutralized with acetic acid. 5 ml. of a solution of 1 part quinone and 5 parts glacial acetic acid in 100 parts alcohol. A bright-red to violet colour is given, on boiling, by many amines.

Foulger reagents. To solutions (*i*) a solution of 40 g. urea in 80 ml. (40% by volume) sulfuric acid, to which 2 g. stannous chloride is added, and the solution diluted to 100 ml. with 40% sulphuric acid ; and (*ii*) a solution of 25 g. quinidine in 100 ml. 40% sulphuric acid which is then saturated with stannous chloride. These solutions give characteristc colours with sugars. Solution (*i*) is useful in differentiating between aldose and ketose sugars.

foundry sand. 1. A mixture of silica and a binding material, used in metal-forming molds in the dry-sand casting operation; the binder may be sodium silicate, casein, or a thermosetting resin. The mixture is heated to form a hard shell for the molding of units having thin or intricate shapes.

2. Sand used in a metal casting operation without a binder, often called greensand. It is used for molding objects of simple design, without thin projections.

Fourier law. The rate of head flow at a given point in a body is proportional to the area of the cross-section and the temperature gradient, at the given point. The form of this relationship is :

$$\frac{dQ}{dt} = -kA\frac{dT}{dl}$$

where Q = quantity of heat, t=time, k = the proportionality constant (thermal conductivity) A=the cross-sectional area, T=temperature, and l = distance in the direction of heat flow.

fourth dimension. Time in the theory of relativity in which space and time are conceived as particular aspects of four-dimensional world.

Fox test. Hydrocyanic acid in air decolourizes the bluish cloudiness present in a solution of 1 drop 5% potassium iodide solution of 1 drop 0.001 N silver nitrate solution in 1 ml. 5% potassium hydroxide solution.

fraction. Any homogeneous component of a mixture which can be separated in relatively pure form by a number of operations, *e.g.*, chromatography and distillation (for liquids) and centrifugation, electrophoresis, filtration, and crystallization for solids. One of the most widely used types of separation into fraction is distillation, especially of petroleum ; the many components of petroleum differ widely in boiling point, which makes it possible to boil off and condense each in turn, thus obtaining vasaline and naphthas, straight-run gasoline, kerosine, and fuel oils of different grades.

fractional crystallization. The separation of a crystalline substance from a mixture, or its purification, by a series of crystallizations. The mother liquor is rejected, the crystals redissolved and crystallized a second time. The process may be repeated several times.

fractional distillation. A method for the separation of several volatile components of different boiling points, conducted by distilling the mixture at the lowest possible boiling point and collecting the distillate as one fraction until the temperature of the vapour rises showing that a higher boiling component or mixture is beginning to distill. The receiver with fraction No. 1 is disconnected at this stage from the condenser and a new receiver substituted for it which collects fraction No. 2, the next higher boiling fraction desired. When the temperature again rises a third receiver is substituted to collect fraction No. 3, and this method is continued untill the highest boiling fraction has been distilled. For solutions whose boiling point changes continuously with changes in composition, fractional distillation is also achieved in stages. The original solution is distilled until a certain fraction of the liquid has been vapourized ; the distillate is then separately redistilled untill a certain fraction of it is volatilized, and this process is kept up through several stages. If the process is repeated long enough or if the "cuts" have been made appropriately, then the different fraction will each be rich in one particular component of the original solution. In many industrial operations especially designed fractionation columns are used which permit fractional distillation to be carried out continuously in one stage.

fractional free volume. Ratio of free volume to total volume of chromatographic column. Also known as fractional void volume.

fractional void volume. *See* fractional free volume.

fractional collector. Device for automatic collection of fractions of effluent from column.

fragmentation reaction. Elimination reaction resulting in formation of organic moieties, originating from fission of carbon chain, *e.g.*,

$$>\ddot{N}-\underset{\alpha}{C}-\underset{\beta}{C}-\underset{\gamma}{C}-X \longrightarrow >\overset{\oplus}{N}=C< + >C=C< + X^{\ominus}$$

where X = halogen atom or tosyl group.

fragrance. Any substance having a pleasant smell it is virtually synonymous with "perfume," but may be considered to include odoriferous materials that are not used specifically for perfumery but for making unpleasent odors or for imparting a "natural" smell to such items as leather substitutes and other imitative products ; for example pine oil and balsam.

Franchimont reaction. A method whereby α,β-dicarboxylic acids may be obtained. The reaction is that of KCN on α-bromo acids or esters. The resulting α-cyano-α,β-dicarboxylic acid derivatives yield the α,β-dicarboxylic acids on hydrolysis and decarboxylation :

$$2C_6H_5CHBr{\cdot}COOR + KCN \rightarrow \begin{array}{c} CN \\ | \\ C_6H_5-C-COOR \\ | \\ C_6H_5-C-COOR \\ | \\ H \end{array} + HBr + KBr$$

$$\downarrow H_2O$$

$$\begin{array}{c} C_6H_5-CH-COOH \\ | \\ C_6H_5-CH-COOH \end{array} + 2ROH + NH_3 + CO_2$$

francium. An element.

		Atomic No.	87
Symbol	Fr	Atomic Wt.	223 (?)
Group	IA	Valence	+1

Francium is a radioactive metal having no stable isotope. Its longest-lived isotope (223) is the only one that occurs naturally, with a half-life of 21 minutes. From the properties of the known isotopes, it is certain that no long-lived form of franicium will ever be found in nature or synthesized artifically.

The isotopes of francium that occur in nature are found in thorium and uranium ores, in which they are continually formed by disintegration chains. These start with ^{232}Th ($4n$ family), ^{237}Np ($4n+1$ family), aud ^{235}U ($4n+3$ family). It is estimated that 1 ton of natural uranium contains about 3.8×10^{-8} g of ^{223}Fr and 10^{-17} g of ^{221}Fr. The tracer studies show that the element has all the properties expected of the heaviest alkali metal.

Studies have shown that francium fixes itself in induced sarcomas in rats. Because of the short half-lives of ^{223}Fr and ^{212}Fr, which would cause no radiation risk to organisms, the property could become useful for the early diagnosis of certain kinds of cancers.

Franck-Condon principle. Time required for electronic transition in molecule is so short (about 10^{-15}s)—compared to period of vibration of molecule (about 10^{-13}s)—that during act of absorption and excitation to excited electronic state, nuclei do not appreciably alter their relative positions (*i e.*, internuclear distance remain^ԑ practically constant) or their kinetic energies.

Frank test. To test for magnesium in water, add to to 2-3 drops of a solution of 0.02 g. *p*-nitrobenzeneazoresorcinol in 100 ml. sodium hydroxide solution, and then add concentrated sodium hydroxide solution until the solution becomes red or violet in colour. Magnesium is present if a blue precipitate forms after agitation.

Frankland-Duppa reaction. A reaction of dialkyl oxalates and alkyl halides, with zinc and HCl, yieding α-hydroxyesters.

$$2RI + R'OOC{\cdot}COOR' + 2Zn + 2HCl \rightarrow R_2C(OH)COOR' + R'OH + ZnCl_2 + ZnI_2$$

Frankland reaction. A condensation similar in principle to the Wurtz reaction but using zinc alkyls or zinc alkyl halides to react with the halogenated hydrocarbons, instead of metallic sodium as a condensing agent. The zinc alkyls or zinc alkyl halides are prepared by action of metallic zinc on alkyl halides. Many of these metal alkyl compounds are spontaneously flammable and, therefore, this reaction is limited to specific syntheses which cannot well be accomplished by other methods such as the production of cartain hydrocarbons :

$$2(CH_3)_3CCl + (C_3H_7)_2Zn \rightarrow 2(CH_3)_3CC_3H_7 + ZnCl_2$$

Frasch process. The sulphur deposits in Louisiana and Texas lying well over 30 metres below ground were discovered accidentally by oil prospectors. Owing to the clay and quicksand above, it was found impossible to mine the deposit by the ordinary methods. Commonly, three concentric tubes, the outermost one being only about 25 cm in diameter, are sunk into the bed. Superheated water under high pressure at a temperature of about 435K, is sent down the outside pipe and a mixture of molten sulphur and hot water collects round the bottom of the pipes. Air is then forced down the innermost pipe impelling a foam of air, sulphur, and hot water up the space between the other two pipes. The sulphur, obtained by this process is at least 99.5% pure.

Frases test reaction. A solution of 0.1 g. vanadium pentoxide in 10 ml. sulphuric acid gives an emerald-green colour with quinine hydrochloride; a blood red colour becoming violet, with quinine sulphate; and with rotenone, a dark red colour with violet streaks.

Fraude solution. A solution of 25 g. perchloric acid in 100 ml. water; used in testing for alkaloids. Various colour reactions are obtained with different alkaloids.

Fraunhofer lines. A series of dark lines which cross the solar spectrum and whose location is fixed. They are designated by letters and occur in great numbers. The are produced by atoms in the cooler outer atmosphere of the sun, which absorb principally radiations of those wavelengths they wou'd emit if heated to a high temperature. Therefore the missing wavelengths correspond to the spectra of various elements, which are thus identfied as present in the solar atmosphere. (In applying this method, attention must be paid to selective absorption by atoms and molecules as it passes through the earth's atmosphere.)

free electron. 1. An electron which is not restrained to remain in the immediate neighbourhood of a nucleus or an atom.

2. The term free electron is also applied to any electron in the outer electronic shell of an atom, when that electron is not shared by another atom, and especially when that electron is free to be so shared (to form a covalent bond).

free electron density. Number of electrons in unit volume (*e.g.*, in 1 cm^3 which may participate in charge transfer. Also known as electron density.

free energy. *See* Helmholtz free energy.

free enthalpy. *See* Gibbs free energy.

free internal rotation. *See* free rotation.

free radical. The reactive portion of a stable molecule occurring as a result of rupture of one or more single bonds as by thermal decomposition or ionizing radiation. For example, serveral free radicals can formed by breaking the carbon-to-hydrogen linkages in methane (CH_4) namely $CH_3^{\cdot}$, $CH_2^{\cdot}$ and $CH^{\cdot}$ All such radical have one or more free electrons, which may be either paired or unpaired. Because of their extreme reactivity, the life of a free radical is very short, of the order of 0.1 second. The original evidence for the existence of free radical and the elucidation of the chain mechanisms by which they initiate such reactions as oxidation, polymerization, etc. was obtained by photochemists about 75 years ago. *See also* chain reaction.

free-radical polymerization. Polymerization in which free radicals or macroradicals take part in all stages of process.

free radical reaction. Process in which substrates or end-products are free radicals. Also known as radical reaction.

free rotation. Rotation of two parts of molecule about single bond, due to small difference in potential energy (at defined temperature) of conformers. Rotational barrier does not surpass 2.5 kJ/mole. Also known as free internal rotation.

free space. The region used as an absolute standard and characterized by an absence of gravitational an electromagnetic fields. Free space was formerly referred to as a vacuum. The electric constant and the magnetic constant are the formally defined values of the permittivity of free space and the permeability of free space, respectively. The velocity of light in free space is constant and is the maximum possible value.

free surface. Surface of liquid separating liquid and gaseous phase.

free surface energy. Work needed to increase liquid surface by unit area.

free volume. Volume occupied by mobile phase in chromatographic column (total column volume minus volume of stationary phase). Also known as interstitial volume; void volume.

freeze-drying. A unique method of dehydrating solid or solid/liquid suspensions of organic meterials or mixtures. It is especially valuable in the pharmaceutical and medical fields for preservation of vacciness, blood plasma, and similar materials which are readily degraded even at normal room temperature. The method has also been applied to some food products, notably coffee. The material is frozen under vacuum and kept at between 253 K and 233 K; at this temperature the ice sublimes, removing about 99% of the water. *See also* drying; dehydration.

freezing mixture. Two or more substances which initiate, upon being brought together, an endothermic process. They are used in chemical work to absorb heat, as in conducting freezing point determinations, reactions at lower temperatures, ete.

freezing point. The temperature at which a liquid becomes a solid. This is not always identical with the melting point of the solid for many mixtures, particularly of fats and waxes which do not solidify unit they have been cooled several degrees below their melting points. If a liquid be cooled under pressure the freezing point rises if the solid is of higher specific gravity, than the liquid; if it is of lower specific gravity, as in the case of water, the freezing point is lowered. Since the freezing point varies slightly with pressure, the pressure should be stated in reporting a freezing point. However, atmospheric pressure is commonly understood unless otherwise specified.

Frehden-Goldschmidt test for amines. Amines are detected by treating them in a crucible with 2 drops of a solution of 10 drops furfural in 10 ml. glacial acetic acid. On gentle evaporation, and moistening with a few drops of acetic acid, characteristic colours are obtained. *p*-dimethylaminobenzaldehyde solution may be used instead of furfural.

French process. A process for the manufacture of zinc oxide in which the metal or spelter is volatilized, and its vapours are oxidized by air to form the oxide. Because the metal or spelter must first be produced from the ore, this process is also called the indirect process.

Frenkel defects. Imperfections of crystal lattice consisting in localization of certain number of atoms or ions in interstitial positions. A part of nodes may remain unoccupied.

frequency. In periodic (oscillation movement, number of returns of system to initial position or state in unit time. Frequency is equal to reciprocal of oscillation period. When applied to electromagnetic radiation, the frequency is defined by the expression :

$$\nu = \frac{c}{\lambda}$$

in which ν = the frequency of the radiation, λ = its wavelength, and c = the velocity of light.

fresnel A unit of frequency equal to 10^{12} cycles per second.

Freudenberg's rule of shift. Chiral molecules of similar structure, undergoing the same chemical conversions, may display considerable changes in optical rotation in the same directions.

Freundlich adsorption isotherm. *See* Freundlich isotherm.

Freundlich equation. Empirical equation of the adsorption isotherm :

$$x = kp^{n} \quad \text{or} \quad x = kc^{n}$$

where x=amount of gas adsorbed by unit mass of adsorbent, p=equilibrium pressure, c=equilibrium concentration of adsorbate, k, n=constant characteristic of a given system and temperature.

Freundlich isotherm. Adsorption isotherm corresponding to Freundlich equation. Also known as Freundlich adsorption isotherm.

Freund reaction. A method of preparation of alicyclic hydrocarbons by the action of sodium on open-chain dihalo compounds. *e.g.*;

$$BrCH_2{-}CH_2{-}CH_2{-}CH_2Br + 2Na \rightarrow \begin{matrix} H_2C{-}CH_2 \\ | \quad\quad | \\ H_2C{-}CH_2 \end{matrix} + 2NaBr$$

friable. Easily crumbled, rubbed or pulverized into powder.

Friedel-Crafts reaction. Alkylation or acylation of aromatic and aliphatic compounds with alkyl and acyl halides or anhydrides in presence of Lewis acids as catalysts (usually anhydrous $AlCl_3$, $FeCl_3$, $ZnCl_2$, BF_3, etc), *e.g.*,

$$ArH+RX \xrightarrow{AlCl_3} ArR+HX$$

$$ArH+(RCO)_2O \xrightarrow{AlCl_3} ArCOR+RCOOH$$

$$CH_3\underset{\underset{O}{\|}}{C}CH_2CH_2\underset{\underset{O}{\|}}{C}Cl+H_2C{=}CH_2 \xrightarrow[-HCl]{AlCl_3}$$

$$CH_2{=}CH\underset{\underset{O}{\|}}{C}CH_2CH_2\underset{\underset{O}{\|}}{C}CH_3$$

Friedlander synthesis. A method of formation of quinoline derivatives by condensation of *o*-aminobenzaldehydes with compounds containing $-CH_2-CO-$ group, *e.g.*,

$$o\text{-}C_6H_4(CHO)(NH_2) + \underset{CO-R'}{\overset{CH_2-R}{|}} \xrightarrow{-2H_2O} \text{quinoline (R', R)}$$

Fries rearrangement. Rearrangement of phenolic esters into *o*- and *p*-hydroxyketones in presence of anhydrous aluminium chloride, *e.g.*,

$$2\,C_6H_5OCOR \xrightarrow{AlCl_3} o\text{-}HOC_6H_4COR + p\text{-}HOC_6H_4COR$$

Fries rule. During the course of a reaction, or whenever change is posible, any aromatic ring in a polynuclear compound tends to assume the bond structure most nearly approaching that of the benzene ring.

frit. Fragmented or finely ground glass particles used as components of ceramic glazes, porcelain enamels. etc. It is sometimes mixed with fluxes and colourants. Frits used as components of glazes are usually made by special methods to make possible the use of water-soluble substances (alkalies and borates) in the glaze.

Fritzmann test. Nitrate in milk is detected by a blue to violet ring which appears when milk containing formaldehyde and nitrate is floated over concentrated sulphuric acid. Various modifications of this test have been developed.

frontal analysis. Chromatographic method in which mixture to be separated is continuously fed to column. This enables isolation of only one component (that most weakly retained by column) in pure form. Also known as frontal chromatography.

frontal chromatography. *See* frontal analysis.

frontier-orbital symmetry. The theory according to which rate of reaction depend on geometries and relative energies of highest occupied molecular orbital (HOMO) of one reactant and the lowest unoccupied molecular orbital (LUMO) of the other.

front pinacoid. The {100} pinacoid in an orthorhombic, monoclinic or triclinic crystals.

frother. Substances that make longer lasting air bubbles by reducing surface tension, *e.g.*, used in froth flotation process.

froth flotation. A very valueable method for separating different particles from a crushed ore, and its importance is steadily increasing. Its effectiveness depends on the fact that different particles have different "wettabilities". If a particle is easily wetted by a solution, it will sink ; but if not it can be carried to the surface in a froth. The mixture used usually contains an oil, such as pine or eucalyputs, and the air is forced through the emulsion to create violent agitation and frothing. The mixture is made to flow through a series of cells and the oiled and unwetted particles are carried to the surface in the froth, continuously overflowing the rims of the cells. The method is particularly useful because, by altering the composition of the mixture, particles of different types can be removed in succession. Thus, for example, the sulphides of lead and zinc, which are commonly found in the same crude ore, are easily separated in this manner. The galena (PbS) particles are taken off first and then, after altering the composition of the mixture, the zinc blende (ZnS). Again, in the modern plant for the extraction of nickel, copper and iron sulphides are successfully and successively separated. In the flotation mixture for this process potassium ethyl xanthate is an important ingredient.

Fry reagent A solution of 90 g. cupric chloride in 120 ml. hydrochloric acid and 100 ml. water used in etching steel.

Fryer-Weston reagent for fats. A mixture of methyl and amyl alcohols, with which fats and fatty oils produce clear solutions at various temperatures.

f-sum rule. The rule that the sum of the *f*-values of adsorption transitions of an atom in a given state, minus the sum of the *f*-values of the emission transition in that state, equals the number of electrons that take part in these transitions. Also known as Thomas-Reiche-Kuhn sum rule.

fuel. Any substance that evolves heat as a result of combustion can be used as a fuel. The most common materials used for heating and electric power production are the so-called fossil fuels (coal, petroleum, and the gases or liquids derived from them). Economic feasibility is usually the critical factor in selection of a fuel for a given purpose. Many organic waste products are used as fuels in locations where they are a disposal problem. *e.g.*, sugarcane waste, com shucks, and other farm wastes. Rocket fuels are a special group, requiring nearly instantaneous combustion and high temperature ; among them are hydrogen peroxide, hydrazine, and boron hydride. Quite distinct, from combustible fuels are the nuclear fuels whose energy is derived from controlled disintegration of atomic nuclei ; they are used exclusively in electric power reactors. *See also* fuel oil ; combustible material ; fission.

fuel cell. An electric cell that converts the chemical energy of a fuel directly into electric energy in a continuous process. Such cell has total reaction consisting in oxidation of easily available fuels (*e.g.*, coal, hydrocabons, water gas). An electrochemical reaction takes place at the electrodes and will continue as long as fuel is supplied. An electrolyte is necessary toact as a conducting medium. The electrodes are of generally porous carbon to permit diffusion of the gases, *e.g.*, hydrogen and oxygen, into the cell.

The electrode reactions are comprised of the oxidation of hydrogen on the anode (the negative electrode) to hydrated protons with the release of electrons ; and on the cathode the reaction of oxygen with protons to form water vapour with the consumption of electrons. Electrons flow from the anode through the external load to the cathode and the circuit is closed by ionic current transport through the electrolyte. In an acid cell, the current is carried by proton.

The cell voltage and the free energy of the underlying reaction are defined by

$$U = \frac{\Delta G}{nF}$$

where U=theoretical cell voltage ; n=number of electrons transferred in the reaction ; and F=Faraday constant.

Since $\Delta G = \Delta H - T\Delta S$, it follows that depending upon the value of ΔS, the electrical energy to be derived from the cell can be larger or smaller than the energy ΔH obtained by direct combustion of the fuel.

The thermodynamically possible conversion efficiency, however, is only partly realized in a practical fuel cell. Two basic losses are encountered : (*i*) the ohmic loss and (*ii*) the electrode polarization, that is, the deviation of the actual from the thermodynamic electrode potential. The polarization is the result of the irreversibility of the electrode process, that is, the activation polarization and the voltage loss which develops from concentration gradients of the reactants.

fuel cell catalyst. A substance such as nickel, platinum or silver, from which the electrodes of a fuel cell are made, and which accelerate the reaction of the cell.

fuel cell electrolyte. The substance which conducts electric current between the electrodes of a fuel cell.

fuel cell fuel. A substance such as alcohol, carbon monoxide, hydrocarbon, or hydrogen, which reacts with oxygen to generate energy in a fuel cell.

fuel element. A fabricateed rod, or other shape which consists of or contains the fissionable fuel for use in a nuclear reactor.

fuel oil. Liquid petroleum fractions or residual refinery products used for heating and power generation. There are several grades designated by numbers.

fuel pellet. A form of nuclear fuel element consisting of flat sheet of fuel which is generally a sandwitch of uranium fuel protected by metallic cladding.

fugacity. a_p. A function that facilitate the application of thermodynamics to real systems, effective gas pressure in uni- or muliti-component system defined by

$$\mu = \mu^- + RT \ln a_p$$

where μ =molar thermodynamic potential (in uni-component systems) or chemical potential of component (in multi-component systems), μ^{-}=molar thermodynamic potential or chemical potential of component in standard state, respectively, R=molar gas constant and T= thermodynamic temperature.

fugitive. A term used in chemistry and chemical technology to denote an ingredient which tends to be partially deactivated during or immediately after processing. This occurs with certain organic dyes, rubber accelerators, softeners, etc., and may be due to adsorption, neutralization, heat, or other physicochemical action.

Fujiwara test reaction. When a solution containing chloroform or other trihalogenated compound is treated with pyridine and sodium hydroxide solution, a pink colour is produced.

fully staggered conformation, ±ap. Conformation in which the most bulky substituents at two adjacent carbon (or any other element *e.g.*, silicium or nitrogen atoms are sterically as far away one another as possible. In Newman's projection formula, bond angle of the most bulky substituents equal 180°. Fully staggered conformation is the most stable when no hydrogen bond is present between substituents :

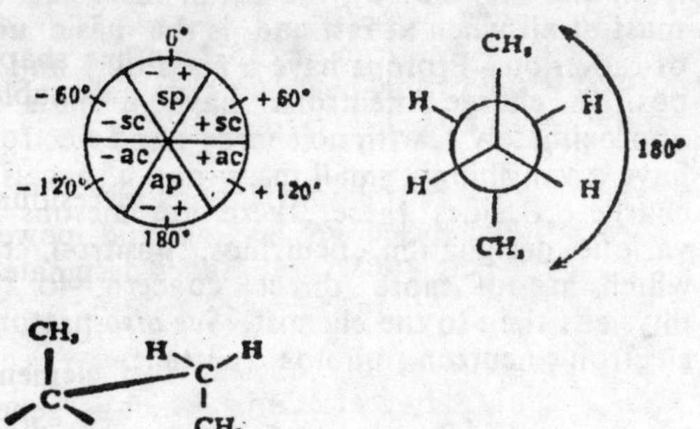

fulminate. A compound containing the —ONC group. Fulminates are isomeric with cyanates, and are commercially important.

fulminating. Literally to cause a flash like lightning. A term used for explosive substances of a particular type.

fulminating gold. A green powder formed when auric hydroxide is heated with ammonia solution. Its composition is doubtfull, but when dry it detonates violently when struck.

fulminating silver. A black substance, explosive when dry, that deposits when a solution of silver oxide in ammonia is exposed to the air. It may be a nitride of silver (Ag_3N).

Fulton reactions for phenols. 1. To 0.5 ml. alcoholic solution of the substance to be tested, add on the spot plate 3 of drops hydrogen peroxide and 2 drops of 50% ammonium hydroxide solution. On stirring with copper wire, phenols give a pink colour changing to yellow or brown.

2. To 5 ml. alcoholic or aqueous solution of the substance to be tested, add, 0.5-1.0 ml. hydrogen peroxide, 0.5 ml. ammonium hydroxide, and a 0.1% cupric sulphate solution drop by drop. Phenols give a red or pink colour.

fulvenes. Hydrocarbons of the general formula $H_4C_5{=}CRR'$. They are dark coloured compounds and are prepared by base-catalyzed condensation of cyclopentadiene and the appropriate keto-compound, they behave as conjugated dienes and peroxidse easily. The parent hydrocarbon fulvene (R=R'=H) is known and is isomeric with benzene.

fumarase. The enzyme catalyzing the reaction between fumaric acid and water to form (—) malic acid in the citric acid cycle.

fume. Derived from the Latin word for smoke, this term has several distinct, though related meanings : (*a*) vapours given off by strong inorganic liquids or by evaporation of organic solvents ; (*b*) the combination of smoke and gases resulting from incomplete combustion, as from a gasoline (exhaust fumes) ; (*c*) the submicroscopic particles emitted by heated metals or metallic oxides (usually in the singular, as metal fume).

fume closet. An enclosed space that is ventilated for the safe removal of gases, vapours, smokes, etc. It is essential for performing experiments that produce unpleasant or toxic gases or vapours.

fumigant. A pesticide or bactericide applied either indoors or in a closely restricted locality in the form of a vapour or gas. Common fumigants are para-dichlorobenzene (fabrics), sulphur dioxide (grains), and hydrogen cyanide (tree crops). Phenol and naphthalene, as well as sulphur compounds are used for disinfection of sickrooms.

fuming. A term used in inorganic chemistry to describe the property characteristic of highly active liquids which evolve visible smoke-like emanation on contact with air. Most familiar are the examples of nitric acid and sulphuric acid designated as "fuming." These are not pure concentrated acids : low percentages of nitrogen dioxide and water are persent in fuming nitric acid, and fuming sulphuric acid contains dissolved sulphur trioxide. Hydrofluoric acid (a mixture of hydrogen fluoride and water) also fumes.

functional group. The properties of organic compounds are largely governed by the particular groups present in the molecules. Thus an organic acid contains one or more carboxyl groups (—COOH), nitro compounds have one or more nitro groups ($—NO_2$) and so on. These are the groups known as "functional." The term is not often used in inorganic chemistry, but it might well be.

functional group analysis. Methods of analysis of organic compounds consisting in identification and determination of compounds according to their functional groups.

functional group isomerism. Type of structural isomerism caused by persence of different functional groups in isomeric compounds, *e.g.*, in ethanol CH_3CH_2OH and dimethyl ether CH_3OCH_3.

functional tautomerism. A type of tautomerism in which the isomers possess different chemical functions, as keto-enol, amide-imido, etc., tautomerism.

function of mixing $Z^{M}_{T,\,p}$. Molar values of state quantity Z of mixture decreased by sum of pure components' Z function for one mole of mixture.

functions of state. *See* state quantities.

fundamental band. In IR spectroscopy band corresponding to transition from state with vibrational quantum number 0 to state with vibrational quantum number 1.

fundamental constants. *See* universal constants.

fundamental equation. *See* Gibbs relation.

fundamental interactions. Fundamental forces that act between the elementary particles of which all matter is composed of. So far, four types of fundamental interactions are distinguished :

(*i*) gravitational interaction manifests itself as a long-range force of attraction between all elementary particles.

(*ii*) The electromagnetic interaction is responsible for the long-range force of repulsion of like and attraction of like charged particles. At considerable distances, the ratio of gravitational to electromagnetic interactions is approximately 4×10^{-37}.

(*iii*) The weak nuclear interaction, whose characteristic strength for low-energy phenomena is a thousand times weaker than electromagnetic ; the range of such force being much smaller than 10^{-17} m.

(*iv*) The strong nuclear interaction between protons and neutrons is also short-range, though the range is approximately 10^{-15} m rather than $<<10^{-17}$ m.

fundamental particle. Ultimate units occurring in the atom or formed by impact of high-energy particles from an outside source. For the chemist, the most important fundamental particles are the proton, the neutron, the electron, and the photon ; the last of these has no mass at all when at rest and is the basic unit of radiation. Protons have a mass of 1 and a positive charge ; neutrons have a mass of approximately 1, with no charge ; and electrons have a vanishingly small mass and a negative charge. Besides these, there are mesons of various designation, neutrinos, positron, etc., which are of more direct concern to the physicist than to the chemist. *See also* proton ; electron ; neutron ; photon ; particle.

fundamental series. A series of lines in the spectra (*see* spectrum) of many atoms which have one, two, or three electrons in their outer shells, either in their neutral state or as a result of ionization. (Excluded are the atoms which have only one electron in all, such as hydrogen, singly-ionized helium, doubly-ionized lithium, etc.). The fundamental series differs from the other series for such elements in having a somewhat distinctive physical appearance, and in having a characteristic formula,

$$\bar{\nu}_F = L - \frac{R}{(m+c)^2}$$

where ν=the wave number of a line in the fundamental series, L and c = constants for, the fundamental series, m=a variable integer whose values give the various lines in the fundamental series, and R = the Rydberg constant.

fungicide. Synthetic or biosynthetic compounds used to control fungal diseases. Chemical compounds are used to control plant diseased caused by fungi. Fungicides now used include both inorganic and organic compounds. Older fungicidal agents for agricultural purposes included sulphur, lime, and their combinations ; inorganic copper compounds such as Bordeaux mixture and copper oxychloride. Mercury compounds have not been used since 1971 because of their toxicity to humans. Various metallic naphthenates have been used to impregnate tent fabrics and clothing for the military. Fungus infections in humans are a complicated and serious medical problem as many types are extremely persistent and require sophisticated medical treatment.

fungicidin. An antibiotic substance capable of destroying fungi.

fungistasis. Inhibition of growth of fungi.

fungistat. A substance that checks the growth of fungi.

fungitoxic. A substance that exerts a toxic effect upon fungi.

fungus. A broad group of plantlike organisms which reproduce both sexually and asexually and which do not form chlorophyll. Authorities are not agreed as to whether fungi should be considered plants or unicellular bacteria ; they include molds, yeasts, smuts, rusts, mushrooms, etc., and often act as parasites on living organisms.

funicular distribution. The distribution of a two-phase, immiscible liquid mixture in a porous system when the wetting phase is continuous over the surface of the solids.

furfuryl. The radical

O—CH=CH—CH=CCH₂— (ring closed between O and C)

furfurylidene. The radical

O—CH=CH—CH=CCH= (ring closed between O and C)

2-furoyl. The radical

O—CH=CH—CH=CCO— (ring closed between O and C)

3-furoyl. The radical

CH=CH—O—CH=CCO— (ring closed between first CH and C)

fury l. The radical

O—CH=CH—CH=C— (ring closed between O and C)

furylidene. The radical

CH=CH —O—CH_2—C= (ring closed between first CH and C)

fuse. The primary meaning of this term as used in chemistry is to melt or soften from a solid to a liquid or semiliquid state ; closely associated with this meaning is the idea of joining or uniting. The word has number of derived forms in chemical literature, each with a rather specific meaning, as follows : (*i*) two metals may be fused together, *i.e.*, joined by melting, as in welding ; (*ii*) fusible alloys are low-melting alloys which fuse (melt) on slight heating ; (*iii*) fused salts are melted or molten salts ; (*iv*) nuclear fusion is the union of light atomic nuclei to form heavier nuclei at high temperature ; (*v*) fused rings occur in many cyclic structures, where two or more rings have a side in common. (In the last two the joining concept has displaced the melting concept.)

Nonchemical meanings are : (*i*) a strip of conductive metal that melts when subjected to too high a voltage, and (*ii*) a cord or strip of flammable material used to detonate explosives.

fused salt. A molten (liquefied) halide or nitrate salt of a metal such as sodium,potassium, barium, or calcium ; these are useful for electrolytic processes because of their high conductivity. They are also used for the heat treatment of metals at high temperatures and as coolants for nuclear reactors. Their heat-transfer capacity is similar to that of water. They are also called molten salts.

fusel oil. A mixture of alcohols, fatty acids and esters existing as impurities in ethyl alcohol derived by fermentation (yeast enzymes) of molasses and other materials rich in sugar ; after separation from ethyl alcohol, its major components are various amyl alcohols (expect normal primary), propyl alcohol, and low percentages of other alcohols and esters. So-called refined amyl alcohol is produced from fusel oil by distillation. Its composition depends upon both the material fermented and the yeast used.

fusible alloy. Any of a number of mixture of metals such as bismuth, tin, lead, cadmium, etc., which melt at a relatively low temperature (550K or less). The best known is Wood's metal, used as heads on automatic fire-extinguishing water lines, for vent control on tanks for compressed gases, and for similar uses.

fusion fuel. A substance that can generate energy in a fusion reaction, such as deuterium, tritium, helium-3.

fusion mixture. A mixture of sodium and potassium carbonates. It is commonly used in qualitative analysis to break down insoluble salts by double decomposition. Thus barium sulphate fused with this mixture would yield barium carbonate and the alkali sulphates.

fyrel. A flexible multifilament fibre made of nickel-chromium alloy that withstands heat upto 2500K ; used in space applications.

G

g. Symbol for degeneracy (statistical weight) Lande factor.

G. Symbol for modulus of shear elasticity. Abbreviation for Gibbs function, and symbol for the gravitational constant.

Ga. Symbol for gallium.

Gabriel ethylenimine synthesis. A method for preparing ethylenimines from aliphatic compounds having terminal halogen and amino groups, by eliminting HX by the action of an alkali, *e.g.*,

$$BrCH_2{-}CH_2{-}CH_2{-}NH_2 \xrightarrow{KOH} \begin{matrix} H_2C{-}CH_2 \\ | \quad\; | \\ H_2C{-}NH \end{matrix} + H_2O + KBr$$

Gabriel primary amine synthesis. Prepartion of primary aliphatic amines by hydrolysis of N-alkyl phthalimide derivatives, formed from alkyl halides and phthalimide potassium salts, *e.g.*,

$$C_6H_4(CO)_2NK + RX \xrightarrow{-KX} C_6H_4(CO)_2NR \xrightarrow{KOHaq} C_6H_4(COOK)_2 + RNH_2$$

Gabutti test for formaldehyde. When formaldehyde is treated with a solution of carbazole in sulphuric acid, it becomes violet-red at room temperature and turns blue or gives a bluish-green precipitate on heating.

gadolinium.	An element	Smybol Gd
	Atomic No.	64
State solid	Atomic Wt.	157.25
Group IIIB	Valence	3
	Isotopes	8 stable
	m.p,	1585K
	b.p.	3446K

Gadolinium is a member of the lanthanide series, and occurs in low percentages in monazite and bastnasite ores. It is a heavy crystalline metal, not unlike steel in appearance. Gadolinium is paramegnetic and becomes strongly ferromagnetic below room temperatures. The Curie point, where the transition occurs, is about 16K. The natural mixture of gadolinium has the greatest thermal-neutron-absorption cross section of all elements, 40,000 barns. This is approximately 10 time greater than the next two elements, samarium (5800 barns) and europium (4300 barns). However, gadolinium is limited to nuclear applications mainly as a start-up and shutdown material because only two of the natural isotopes. ^{155}Gd and ^{157}Gd behave in this manner. These are separated by isotopes which do not so react—hence, no chain relationship exists. The isotopes ^{155}Gd and ^{157}Gd make up 31% of the total weight of elemental gadolinium. The metal has a low acute-toxicity rating. It is also used in laser garnets as a substitute for yttrium. The selenide is used for thermoelectric power generation, The metal is flammable in dust or powder form. Gadolinium metal and several of its salts are under consideration for use in a magnetic heat pump device.

galactan. Any of a number polysaccharides composed of galactose unit. Also known as galactesan.

glactoglucomannan. Any of a group of polysaccharides which are prominent components of coniferous woods ; consist of D-glucopyranose and D-mannopyranose units.

galactomannan. Any of a group of polysaccharides which are composed of D-galactose and D-mannose units.

galactoside. A glycoside formed by the reaction of galactose with an alcohol ; yields galactose on hydrolysis.

Gallagher-Hollander degradation. A series of reactions for the degradation of amino acids by which two carbon atoms are eliminated. This method has been applied effectively to side chains of bile acids and other polynuclear compounds :

$$R(CH_2)_2COOH \xrightarrow{SOCl_2} R(CH_2)_2COCl \xrightarrow{CH_2N_2} R(CH_2)_2COCHN_2$$

$$\downarrow HCl$$

$$RCH_2CHBrCOCH_3 \xleftarrow{Br_2} R(CH_2)_2COCH_3 \xleftarrow[CH_3COOH]{Zn} R(CH_2)_2COCH_2Cl$$

$$\downarrow (Collidine)$$

$$RCH{=}CHCOCH_3 \xrightarrow{CrO_3} RCOOH + [CH_3COCOOH]$$

gallium. An element

	Symbol	Ga
	Atomic No.	31
	Atomic Wt.	69.72
State Liquid	Valence	1,3
	Isotopes	2 stable
Group IIIA	m.p.	302.78K

Galium is chemically similar to aluminium. It is amphoteric but slightly more acidic than aluminium. Gallium has low melting point and the liquid form looks much like mercury. Thus gallium is one of only three metals that are liquid at this temperature. Gallium metal has no industrial uses, but several of its compounds (arsenide, antimonide, and phosphide) have semiconducting properties and are used in electric and solid state equipment (lasers, microwave generators, and electroluminescent devices). It forms low, melling eutectic alloys with several metals intermetallic compounds with many others. The two stable isotopes of gallium are ^{69}Ga and ^{71}Ga. The eight radioactive isotopes include ^{64}Ga through ^{68}Ga, ^{70}Ga, ^{72}Ga, ^{73}Ga. All have a relatively short half-life, the longest, ^{67}Ga, with a half-life of 78 hours.

galvanic. Pertaining to electricity produced by chemical action in cells.

galvanic cell. System consisting of two half-cells of such construction that after their connection with metallic conductor, flow of electrons across this circuit is observed; then electro-reduction occurs on one electrode and electro-oxidation on the second one; for practical reasons one classifies galvanic cells as chemical or concentration cells, or as primary non-regenerated or secondary cells (*see* accumulator).

galvanic corrosion. Electrochemical corrosion associated with the current in a galvanic ceil, caused by dissimilar metals an electrolyte because of difference in potential of two metals.

galvani electric potential difference. Difference of inner potentials of two phases. Also known as galvani potential.

galvanizing. Application of a protective layer of zinc to a metal, chiefly steel, to prevent or inhibit corrosion. The length and extent of the protection are dependent upon the weight or thickness of the zinc coating. It is applied by (*a*) the hot-dipping process by passing the metal through molten zinc, or by (*b*) electro-deposition of zinc by a plating process, usually onto strip or wire. The former method gives a unique mottling or "spangle" pattern on the surface, formed as the zinc crystallizes, while the latter results in either a white matte surface or one which is bright and reflective. Galvanized metal is used chiefly on inexpensive products for utilitarian service (pipe, nails, wire, containers, etc.) and represents one of the largest uses of zinc.

galvanostatic methods. Methods of study of kinetics af electrode reactions consisting in recording and analysis of potential changes of indicator electrode during electrolysis carried out with current of constant intensity.

gamma (γ or Γ). Used as a prefix to denote the third carbon atom in a straight chain compound, or a derivative in which a substituted group is attached to that carbon atom (γ-).

The position in a polycycyclic compound following the β-position (*see* beta), and away from the α-position (*see* alpha), or a derivative in which a substitu ed group occupies that position (γ-). Symbol for microgram. Symbol for activity coefficient, molal basis. Symbol for weight rate of flow per unit width. Ratio of specific heats of a gas Cp/Cv (γ). Symbol for surface tension and specific weight.

gamma constant, Γ. Ratio of exposure dose rate of electromagnetic radiation of high energy emitted by a point source at distance of 1 m from source to its activity.

gamma emission. A transition between two energy levels of a nucleus in which a gamma ray is emitted. Also known as gamma decay.

gamma heating. Heating of a substance due to absorption of gamma rays.

gamma-iron. An allotropic form (*see* allotropy) of iron, which is nonmagnetic and exists between 1173K and 1673K.

gamma photon activation. Activation by gamma quanta. Also known as γ-ray activation.

gamma quantum. High energy photon.

gamma radiation. A form of highly energetic radiation emanating from unstable atomic nuclei and characterized by ultrashort wavelengths (about 1 angstrom unit). It is emitted slowly by decaying radioactive nuclei (radium) and very rapidly in the fission process.

The gamma ray is an electromagnetic radiation pulse—a photon—of very short wavelength. The electric (E) and magnetic (H) fields associated with individual radiations oscillate in planes matually perpendicular to each other and also to the direction of propagation with a frequency (*v*) which characterizes the energy of radiation. The **E** and **H** fields exhibits various specified phase-and-amplitude relations, which define the character of the radiation as either electric or magnetic. They range in energy from a few keV to 100 MeV, although most radiations are in the range 50-6000 keV.

Gamma radiation is highly dangerous to body tissues and may cause genetic damage or even death on prolonged exposure. Cobalt-60 has been used in industry as a source of gamma rays for initiating the synthesis of ethyl bromide and the cross-linking of polyethylene and other high polymers. Gamma radiation is used for spectroscopic analysis and in medicine (cancer treatment).

gamma-ray absorption analysis. Method of analysis based on measurement of attenuation of a beam of γ-rays in layer of material tested. It is used for measuring thickness, density and for analysing composition of mixtures (particularly binary mixtures).

gamma-ray activation. *See* gamma-photon activation.

gamma-ray activation analysis. *See* photoactivation analysis.

gamma-ray cascade. Process by which two (or more) γ-rays are emitted successively from one radioactive nucleus.

gamma rays. *See* gamma radiation.

gamma-ray spectrometer. Instrument designed for measuring energy spectrum of gamma radiation.

gamma space (γ-space). A hyper-space of $2nr$ dimensions, where n=the number of (identical) molecules, and $2r$=the number of coordinates required to specify the exact mechanical condition of a molecule, both its instantaneous position and its momentum.

Ganassini test for acrolein. Add to 10 drops of the aqueous solution to be tested, 2 drops of a solution of 2 ml. phenylhydrazine in 3 ml. glacial acetic acid and 5 ml. water; after shaking, add 5 ml. concentrated hydrochloric acid and 1 drop of 0.5% aqueous potassium chloride solution. A violet-red colour indicates the presence of acrolein.

Ganassini test for mercury. Shake the solution to be tested with metalic copper. Wash with water, and alcohol, and dry the amalgam. Place in a test tube, introduce a piece of paper that is wet with cuprous iodide solution, and heat. If mercury is present, the paper is coloured rose.

gangue. A term used in extractive metallurgy to refer to the waste rocky or siliceous content of metal ores which is separated by flotation or elutriation. It is also a component of slag, which separates from the ore on smelting. Ore residues are sometimes called tailings; the latter term is also used in other industries for any residual processing waste.

Gapchenko-Sheintzis test for bismuth. A solution of 1 g. quinoline in 100 ml. alcohol mixed with 20 ml. 25% potassium iodide solution gives a red-orange colour with bismuth

Gapchenko-Sheintzis test for titanium. Saturate a filter paper with a 10% tannin solution. Apply to it a drop of 20% antipyrine solution, and to the latter a drop of the solution to be tested. Titanium gives a red colour which is not removed by 25% sulphuric acid solution.

Garmask test for strontium. To the solution to be tested, add one-fifth its volume of a saturated solution of sodium acetate, acidify with acetic acid, and add an excess saturated potassium dichromate solution. Filter, add an equal volume of saturated ammonium sulphate solution, and heat to boiling. If strontium is present, a precipitate is formed.

gas. A state of matter, in which the molecules move freely, and consequently the entire mass tends to expand indefinitely, occupying the total volume of any vessel into which it is introduced. Gases follow, within considerable degree of fidelity, certain laws relating their conditions of pressure, volume, and temperature ; they mix freely with each other.

Gases behave like fluids ; any gas can be liquefied when subjected to sufficient pressure and low temperature. The molecules of a gas are in continuous motion, exerting pressure equally in all directions as a result of their kinetic energy. The volume of a confined gas is inversely proportional to the pressure applied to it if the temperature remains constant (Boyle's Law). A perfect or ideal gas is one that conforms exactly to this and other gas laws (although no gas behaves in the ideal manner), it is a characteristic of gases to diffuse into each other to form uniform mixtures, regardless of their weight. Equal volumes of the same or different gases contain the same number of molecules (Avagadro's Law).

gas analysis. Qualitative and quantitative determination of composition of mixture of gases.

gas battery. A concentration cell (*see* cell, concentration) in which the electrodes are virtually gaseous. Also known as gas cell.

gas black. Fine carbon particles formed by partial combustion of natural gas. Also known as carbon black ; channel black.

gas carbon. A hard deposit consisting of fairly pure carbon, found on the walls of the retorts used for the destructive distillation of coal in the manufacture of coal-gas. It is a good conductor of electricity, and it is used for making carbon electrodes. Also knwn as retort carbon.

gas chromatography. A very sensitive method

of analysing the components of a complex mixture of volatile substances. The apparatus consist of a long narrow tube, packed with an inert support material of uniform particle size (*e.g.*, diatomaceous earth) that has been coated with a non-volatile liquid, called the stationary phase, the whole tube and its content being maintnined in a thermostatically controlled oven. The sample to be analysed is carried through the tube by a noble gas (*e.g.*, agron) so that the progress through the tube of various components of the mixture is selectively interfered with the satationary phase, some components passing through the tube more rapidly than others. A detector measures the electrical or thermal conductivity, or some other chracteristic property, of the gas leaving the column, differences being recorded on a strip chart, which indicates peaks corresponding to the various components. The instrument is calibrated by analysing samples of known compositions.

gas constant, *R*. Constant value in ideal gas equation :

$$R=\frac{pV_m}{T}=8.31433\ JK^{-1}mol^{-1}$$

where p = pressure, Vm=molar volume of ideal gas, T=thermodynamic temperature. Gas constant describes work done by 1 mole of ideal gas when it increases its volume due to temperature increase of 1 K at constant pressure. Also known as molar gas constant, **universal gas constant.**

gas conversion process. A method of petroleum cracking in which thermal cracking and naphtha reforming take place in the same reaction zone, specifically by subjecting the C_3 and C_4 hydrocarbons to partial conversion before the naphtha is added to the stream.

gas degeneracy. Violation of ideal gas equation $pV_m=RT$ due to inadequacy of Maxwell-Boltzmann distribution for description of equilibrium partition of gas particles among enregy levels when thermal de Broglie wavelength is greater than or comparable with cubic root of average volume per gas particle.

gas electrode. Electrode (half cell) constructed usually from noble metal dipped into solution saturated with appropriate gas and containing ions resulting from oxidation or reduction of this gas, *e.g.*, hydrogen, oxygen, or halogen electrodes.

gas hydrate. A type of hydrate in which a molecule of a gas is enclosed (without chemical bonding) in a multisided "cage" of water molecules ; this results in an insoluble crystalline clathrate or inclusion compound in which the combining ratio of gas to water molecules varies from about 1 to 18 for propane a low as 1 to 6 for some other gases. Gas hydrates form in pipelines, causing considerable operating difficulty. The structure has been found useful in separating fresh water from brine; a salt-free cage compound is obtained by use of propane-seawater mixture. Many gases can form hydrates of this kind, including the noble gases fluorocarbons, acetylene, carbon dioxide, cyclopropane, ethyl chloride, and ethane. *See also* hydration; clathrate.

gas ideal. *See* ideal gas.

gasification. Production of gaseous or liquid hydrocarbon fuels from coal (*a*) by direct addition of hydrogen to form methane (hydrogasifications, (*b*) by reacting steam with hot coal (1070K) in the presence of air or oxygen to form carbon monoxide and hydrogen (synthesis gas), followed by a methanation reaction ; (*c*) by underground combustion. In method (*a*) and (*b*), the coal enters the reaction sequence in finely divided form hydrocarbon gases, naphta and fuel oils of various grades can be produced by several modifications, *e.g.*, the Fischer-Tropsch process. In method (*c*), air is pumped down to previously ignited coal seams and the combustion products evolved are collected.

Many variation of methods (*a*) and (*b*) have been researched in the U.S. since 1945, but none was economically competitive with the then lowpriced crude oil. Several have advanced to the pilot stage, and projections of cost, investment. and installation for large-scale operation have been made. Environmental and geographic considerations have also been investigated. The controlling factor for future development is the price of crude oil.

gas, inert. *See* noble gases.

gas laws. *See* Boyle's Law ; Gay-Lussac's Law ; Charles' Law.

gas multiplication. Multiplication of charge value collected at electrodes of gas-filled counter tube, as a result of secondary ionization of gas.

gasohol. A fuel, chiefly for internal combustion engines, composed of a 9/1 ratio by volume of unleaded gasoline and water-free ethyl alcohol. It octane number is essentially equivalent to that of gasoline.

gas oil. A liquid petroleum distillate with viscosity and boiling range between kerosine lubricating oil, usually includes diesel fuel, heating oils and light-fuel oils.

gasoline. A refined mixture of hydrocarbons having an octane number ranging from about 60 to 100 or more, used primarily as a fuel for automobiles and airplanes. The mixture consists of more than 100 different hydrocarbons. Its vapours are flammable, and its partial combustion products toxic in high concentrations. Generally high octane gasoline is made by catalytic cracking, platinum being one of the most effective catalyst. Branched-chain paraffins (iso-octane), cycloparaffins, and aromatic compounds predominate. Straight-run gasoline is obtained by direct distillation of petroleum, and casinghead (natural) gasoline from various hydrocarbon gases present in natural gas ; these two types are not cracked and have low-power fuels for motor boats, etc. They can be upgraded by catalytic reforming. Antiknock gasoline of adequate octane number is now in general use without addition of tetraethyllead, which is being gradually replaced dy methyl tert-butyl ether.

gasometric analysis. Determination of components of sample based on measurement of volume of gas evolved in a given reaction.

gas tar. Coal tar, the tarry matter produced in the distillation of bituminous coal, and obtained from coal gas by separation.

gas, water. *See* water gas.

Gastaldi synthesis. A method of forming dicyanopyrazines from isonitrosoketones by reaction with sodium bisulphite and potassium cyanide, followed by the condensation of two molecules by action of HCl :

$$RCOCH = NOH + 2NaHSO_3 + KCN \rightarrow RCOCH(CN)NHSO_3K + Na_2SO_3 + H_2O$$

NC, $NHSO_3K$ — CH — C(R)=O + O=C(R) — CH — KSO_3NH, CN $\xrightarrow[\text{[O]}]{2HCl}$

(pyrazine ring with NC, R, R, CN substituents) $+ H_2O + 2H_2SO_4 + 2KCl$

Gattermann aldehyde or ketone synthesis. A reaction between phenols, hydrogen chloride, and hydrogen cyanide in the presence of anhydrous aluminium or zinc chloride to yield, on hydrolysis, hydroxy aldehydes. Ketones are produced by using organic cyanides instead of hydrogen cyanide, *e.g.*,

OCH_3-benzene $+ HCN + HCl \xrightarrow{ZnCl_2}$

CH_3O-C_6H_4-$HC{=}NH{\cdot}HCl$ $\xrightarrow{H_2O}$ CH_3O-C_6H_4-CHO $+ NH_4Cl$

Gattermann diazo-reaction. Substitution of diazo group by halide, in presence of metallic copper as catalyst, *e.g.*,

$$ArN_2^+Cl^+ \xrightarrow{Cu} ArCl + N_2$$

$$ArN_2^+ + CN^- \xrightarrow{Cu} ArCN + N_2$$

Gattermann-Koch aldehyde synthesis. Perparation of aromatic aldehydes by action of carbon monoxide—hydrogen chloride mixture on aromatic hydrocarbons, in presence of Lewis acids as catalysts (usually anhydrous aluminium chloride, *e.g.*,

CH_3-C_6H_4-CH_3 $+ (CO + HCl) \xrightarrow{AlCl_3}$ CHO-$C_6H_3(CH_3)_2$ $+ HCl$

Gattermann-Skita synthesis. A method of formation of pyridine derivatives by condensation of esters of the type of diethyl sodiomalonate with amines such as dichloromethylamine :

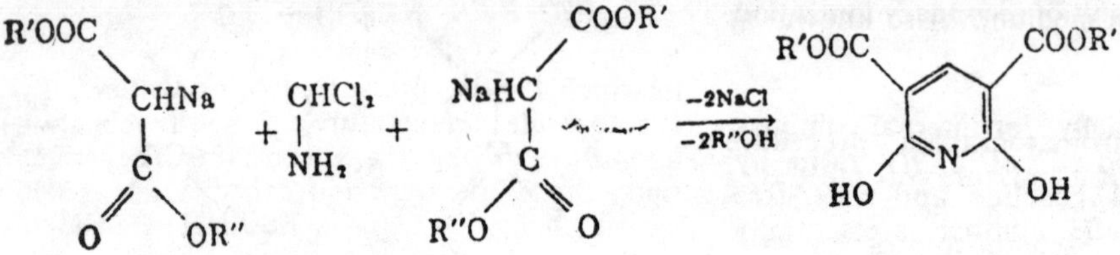

R'OOC–CHNa–C(=O)OR'' + $CHCl_2NH_2$ + NaHC(COOR')–C(=O)OR'' $\xrightarrow[-2R''OH]{-2NaCl}$ pyridine with R'OOC, COOR', HO, OH substituents

Gauche conformation. ±sc. Conformation characteristic for staggered position of the most bulky substituents located at two adjacent carbon (or any other elements, *e.g.*, silicium or nitrogen) atoms. In Newman's projection formula, bond angles between less remote and more remote substituents equal 60° :

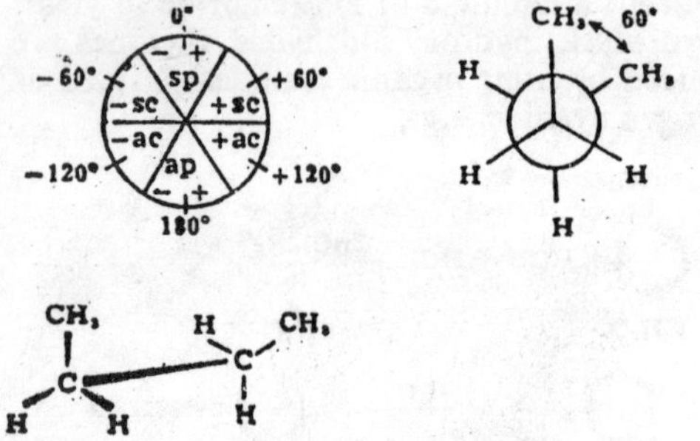

0°, −60°, +60°, −120°, +120°, 180°; sp, −sc, +sc, −ac, +ac, ap

CH_3, 60°, H, CH_3, H, H, H

Also known as skew conformation.

Gay-Lussac's law. *See* law of combining volumes.

Geiger-counter. *See* Giger-Muller counter.

Geiger formula. A relationship between the initial velocity of α-particles and their range. This relationship, which was derived from measurements on radium-C and was later found to apply to α-particles from various sources which have ranges from 3 to 7 cm, is of the form :

$$V_0^3 = aR$$

where V_0 = the initial velocity of the α-particles at the source ; a = a constant having the same value for α-particles from various sources, namely 1.03×10^{27}, provided V_0 is given in centimeters per second ; and R, the usual range of the α-particles, is given in the number of centimetres of air at 288K and a pressure of one atmosphere, which the α-particles traverse their source to a point at which they no longer produce appreciable ionization.

Geiger-Muller counter. Gas filled counter operating at a gas amplification such that charge collected at electrodes during each pulse is constant and independent of charge liberated by initial ionizing event. Also known as Geiger-counter ; G-K counter.

Geiger-Nuttall rule. The equation relating the radioactive constant (decay constant) of a radio element, and the range of the α-particles which it emits. This relationship takes the form

$$\log \lambda = B + A \log R$$

where λ = the radioactive constant, B = a constant for each series, A = a constant, and R = range of the α-particles.

Geiger region. The part of the characteristic curve of pulse size versus voltage in which pulse size is independent of the number of ions produced in the initial ionizing event.

gel. A term used in colloid chemistry to denote a structure formed by substances of high molecular weight, in which the macromolecules consist of long chains or fibres. Substances which produce gels readily are, common soap, certain proteins (collagen), and carbohydrates such as starches, complex sugars, and related compounds (pectin). They absorb many times their own weight of water, with consequent swelling and set to a viscous or semisolid jelly (gel) when cool. The macromolecules become entangled with one another as their motion slows with decreasing temperature, water being occluded in the interlocked network so formed ; when warmed, such gels resume their liquid form and thus called reversible. Some heavy-metal soaps have a similar tendency. Gels such as dextran can be used as sieves to separate molecules of other substances, an operation called gel filtration.

gelation. Stiffening of colloidal system into uniform mass without separating dispersed phase and dispersion medium. Also known as gelling.

gel filtration. A chromatographic procedure for the separation of a mixture of molecules on the basis of size, through the capacity of porous polymers to exclude solutes above a certain size.

gelignite. An explosive consisting of a mixture of nitroglycerin, cellulose nitrate, potassium nitrate and wood pulp.

gel permeation chromatography. (GPC). A separation technique involving passage of a liquid moving phase through a column containing the stationary phase which consists of a porous meterial (gel). Gel permeation chromatography (GPC) affords a rapid method of separating high molecular weight material, with separation based on differences in molecular size.

gem-. Abbreviation of geminate (said of two groups attached to the same atom), as the *gem*-dimethyl grouping in camphor.

gene. A chromosomal segment that codes for a single polypeptide chain or RNA molecule. It is a basic unit of inheritance, comprising part of a chromosome, which controls an individual inherited characteristic of an organism and which is capable of mutation as a unit. The gene is regarded as being a particular molecular configuration of the nucleic acids at a particular point on the length of a chromosome. There is considerable evidence to support the belief that genes function by controlling the manufacture of specific proteins in cells.

general acid-base catalysis. Acid-base catalysis due to all acid or bases present in solution.

general chemistry. Branch of chemistry dealing with the most general and fundamental chemical laws and principles.

general equation of state. The most general form of the equation of state relating the pressure, volume, and temperature of a gas, and the gas constant. It is of the form

$$PV=RT\left(1+\frac{B}{V}+\frac{C}{V^2}+\frac{D}{V^3}\cdots\right)$$

in which P=the pressure, V=the volume, T= the absolute temperature, R = gas constant, and B, C, D, etc., are constants, dependent upon the temperature and called virial coefficients. The equation is sometimes referred to as the virial equation of state.

general formula. A formula that represents the composition of more than one substance by the use of symbols which represent more than one kind of atom or more than one number, as HX represents hydrochloric, hydrobromic or hydriodic acid and as $CoCl_n$ might represent cobaltous chloride and cobaltic chloride.

generalized spectrophotometry. Method of analysis of two component system with such a choice of conditions of analysis (wavelength, *p*H, temperature equilibrium, etc.) that calculation of unknown concentrations from appropriate equation is possible for results of two to four spectrophotometric measurements.

generic *n*-th order phase distribution, ρ_n. (1, 2, ..., n). Partition function for n particles, where $0 \leqslant n \leqslant N$ and N is maximum number of particles in given system ; determines probability that one particle is in state 1, one in state 2, ..., and one in state n, independently of way of ascribing particles to states and also independently of number of particles in other states. Particle state is defined by particle dynamic variables ; if $n=N$, generic phase distribution contains maximum possible information about system.

genetic code. A natural computer code provided in the genes by deoxyribonucleic acid and activated by ribonucleic acid two extremely complex substances that are present in the nuclei of all living cells. The code programs not only the specific amino acids required in a protein, but also their sequence in the molecular chain of which the protein is composed, some of which contain several hundred amino acid units.

The code is expressed by the molecular configuration of the chromosome of cells. Chromosomes consist of deoxyribonucleic acid (DNA) and protein, the code-bearing material being the DNA. Four different nitrogenous bases (adenine, cytosine, guanine and thymine) occur in the nucleotides of DNA, and it appears that the sequence of three of these bases constitues a unit of the genetic code, in that each sequence of three bases codes for one of the twenty different amino ac ds that go to make up the enzymes that control the characteristics of a cell. Chromosomes, which almost always exits in the nuclei of cells, transfer their coded information to the cytoplasm of these cells (where the enzyme proteins are assembled in units called ribosomes) by way of a 'messenger' nucleic acid (ribonucleic acid).

geochemistry. A branch of chemistry dealing with the chemical composition and distribution of elements in earth's crust, including oceans and atmosphere. It is based largely on the detailed analysis of minerals and on the application of the chemistry of crystals to mineral formation.

geometrical ınversion. The conversion of a geometrical isomer into its opposite form by physical or chemical means. Fumaric acid, on heating, is converted into the anhydride of maleic acid ; nitrous acid converts oleic into elaidic acid.

geometrical isomerism. *See* cis-trans ismerism.

geothermal energy. Superheated water and steam trapped in rock strata in areas characterized by volcanic activity or by intrusions of molten magma. Its temperature ranges from 420 to 570K. It escapes either from natural surface vents (geysers, fumaroles, hot springs) or from boreholes drilled through the strata. A contributing source of heat is the natural radioactivity of rocks in the earth's upper mantle.

germanium. An element.

		Symbol	Ge
		Atomic No.	32
State	Solid	Atomic Wt.	72.59
Group	IVA	Valence	+2,4
		Isotopes	5 stable
		m.p.	1210.4K

Germanium, is a rare element present in low percentages in a few widely scattered ores and in coal in trace amounts. There are five natural isotopes, ^{70}Ge, ^{72}Ge through ^{74}Ge. and ^{76}Ge. Seven radioactive isotopes include ^{67}Ge through ^{69}Ge, ^{71}Ge, ^{75}Ge, ^{77}Ge, and ^{78}Ge. All have a relatively short half-life the longest, ^{68}Ge, with a half-life of 275 days. In terms of abundance, germanium ranks 32nd among the elements in the earth's crust and thus is about as abundant as galium, selenium, arsenic, and bromine. It is usually classed as a nonmetal ; its structure is similar to that of carb›n. Its distinguishing feature is its ability to act as a semiconductor. It forms perfect crystals and can be made in extremely pure form. Germanium can be readily "doped" with impurities on a controlled basis, an essential feature of semiconduction. For these reasons it has been ideal for the study of solid state physics. Mercury-doped and copper-doped germanium are used as infrared detectors. It is also used in special alloy and in brazing.

The addition of as little as 0.35% germanium to tin doubles the hardness of tin. Similarly, germanium improves the strength and hardness of aluminum and magnesium alloys. These applications are limited, however, because of the current high costs of germanium. Germanium silicon alloys are under intensive study for use in thermoelectric generators. Advantages claimed for these metals include better thermoelectric qualities abave 870K, an improved efficiency per unit weight factor, and virtually no corrosion or decomposition.

German silver. An alloy of copper, zinc, and nickel ın varing proportion approximating to 50% copper, 25% nickel, and 25% zinc.

germicide. A substance or chemical which kills disease germs and other microorganisms.

Germuth reagent for nitrite. Two solution : (*i*) a solution of 1g. sulphanilic acid in 100 ml. water ; and (*ii*) 5.25 g. dimethyl-α-naphthylamine in 1 liter of a 4 N methanol solution of acetic acid. These solutions are used in the determination of nitrite which gives a purple-red colour.

Germuth test reaction for lactate. To a solution of 0.5-5.0% lactic acıd, or a weakly-acid (hydrochloric acid) lactate solution, add 0.5 ml. 15% potassium thiocyanate solution for each 1% lactic acid present. An orange to red colour develops, which remains unchanged by heating.

getter. A metal used in vacuum tubes and similar evacuated devices to adsorb (scavenge) residual molecules of oxygen, nitrogen, and other gases. Rare earth metals and misch metal are commonly used.

Geuther test. A modified Welman test for detecting vegetable oils in animal oils or fats, in which the reagent is a solution of 5 g. sodium phosphomolybdate in 25 ml. water and 25 ml. nitric acid (sp. gr. 1.4). On treatment with this reagent and chloroform, vegetable oils give a dark green colour in about 2 minutes.

gibberellins. A group of plant hormones, that promote the growth of plant stems and fruit, and have other beneficial effects.

Gibbs adsorption equation. *See* Gibbs adsorption theorem.

Gibbs adsorption theorem. Quantitative relation describing isothermal adsorption at surface of liquid phase; for liquid two-component systems this relation is :

$$\Gamma = -\frac{c}{RT}\left(\frac{\partial \sigma}{\partial c}\right)_{q,\,T}$$

where Γ=surface concentration of absorbate absorbed at surface of liquid phase, in moles per unit area of surface, c=concentration of adsorbate in bulk liquid phase, R=gas constant, σ = surface tension, q = surface area of liquid phase, T=thermodynamic temperature.

Gibbs concentration triangle. Equilateral triangle with each side equal to unit length which makes possible presentation of three-component mixture composition :

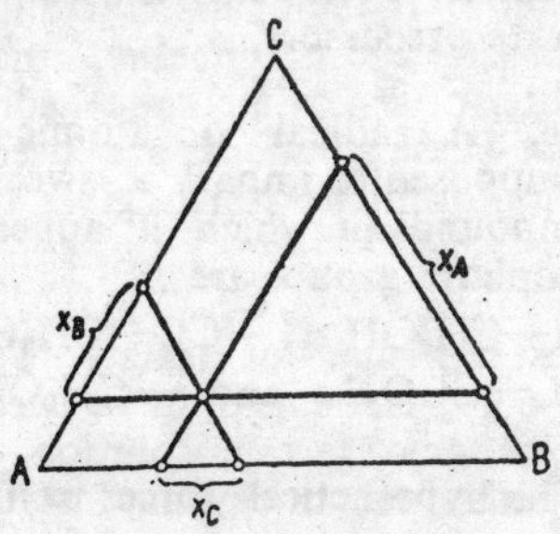

where x_A, x_B, x_C=molar fraction of particular components of solution.

Gibbs-Duhem equation. Equation expressing relation between intensive state parameters of a given phase α :

$$S^{\alpha}dT^{\alpha} - V^{\alpha}dp^{\alpha} + \sum_i n_i^{\alpha}d\mu_i^{\alpha} = 0$$

where S=entropy, V=volume, n_i=number of moles of i-th component, μ_i=its chemical potential, T=thermodynamic temperature, p=pressure, and n=indicator of a given phase.

Gibbs free energy, *G*. Extensive thermodynamic function, $G=H-TS$, where H=enthalpy, T=thermodynamic temperature, and S= entropy. Also known as free enthalpy ; Gibbs free energy function, thermodynamic potential.

Gibbs-Helmholtz equations. Thermodynamic identities expressing relations between Helmholtz free energy F and internal energy U and between Gibbs free energy G and enthalpy H

$$\left|\frac{\partial \frac{F}{T}}{\partial \frac{1}{T}}\right|_v = U \qquad \left|\frac{\partial \frac{G}{T}}{\partial \frac{1}{T}}\right|_p = H$$

where T=thermodynomic temperature and V and p=volume and pressure respectively.

Gibbs phase rule. Number of thermodynamic degrees of freedom s of system containing α independent components and β phases is given by :

$$s = 2-\alpha-\beta$$

Gibbs phthalic anhydride process. An industrial method of producing phthalic anhydride by atmospheric oxidation of naphthalene at 470-720K. Vanadium pentoxide is an effective catalyst in this process.

Gibbs relation. Equation :

$$T^{\alpha}dS^{\alpha} = dU^{\alpha} + p^{\alpha}dV^{\alpha} - \sum_i \mu_i^{\alpha}dn_i^{\alpha}$$

where S=entropy, V=volume, n_i=number of moles of i-th component of mixture, μ_i=its chemical potential, and α numbers phases. Also known as fundamental equation.

Giblin-Chapman test. A modified Griess test in which nitrite is detected by a red colour formed on addition to 10 ml. of the solution tested of 2 drops of a solution of 1 g. dimethylaniline and 1.5 g sulphanilic acid in 100 ml. 0.5 N hydrochloric acid.

Gies Biuret solution. An aqueous solution of potassium hydroxide to which has been added a solution of cupric sulphate. It is used as a test reagent for proteins.

Girard reagent. Various quaternary ammonium compounds which form soluble compounds with substances containing carbonyl groups, the latter being readily regenerated by treatment of the compound formed. The Girard reagents are used in certain separations of carbonyl-containing substances, especially in separation of the sex hormones from urine. A representative reagent of the group is Girard's reagent *T*, which is trimethylacethydrazine ammonium chloride.

glacial. A term applied to a number of acids (acetic, phosphoric) which in a highly pure state, have a freezing point slightly below room temperature. For example, glacial acetic acid is 99.8% pure and crystallizes at 20°C.

glance. A mineralogical term meaning brilliant or lustrous, used to describe hard, earth-derived materials that have a bright, reflecting surface or fracture. It is applied to hard asphalts, which are often called glance pitch, as well as to galena (PbS) as lead glance, an ore of lead.

glass-ceramic. A mixture based on the silica-soda-lime composition of regular glass (an amorphous or noncrystalline material) but also containing an ingredient which causes crystal formation by a nucleating process ; the glass is thus devitrified, that is, it becomes a crystalline solid rather than a liquid. Such products are resistant to extreme heat and can be used for laboratory hoods, restaurant ranges, etc.

glass electrode. A thin-walledglass membrane, separating a solution of known *p*H from another solution whose *p*H is to be determined. A standard electrode dips into each of these two solutions. From the total electromotive force of the cell and the *p*H of the standard solution, the *p*H of the unknown may be calculated.

glass fibre. An extruded filament of glass, often only a few microns in diameter, which can be twisted into yarns and woven into fabrics. It is used as such in insulation bats, filter aids, tire cord, drapes, etc., and also in composites with phenol-formaldehyde and other resins.

glassine. A type of paper in which are cellulose fibres have beeen subjected to extensive breakdown by mechanical action during manufacture and to which a small amount of paraffin is usually added to achieve a high degree of proofness to water vapour. It is translucent, flexible, and of very low friction coefficient.

Glide reflection plane. Symmetry element of space group. combined from two symmetry operations reflection in mirror plane and translation in the given direction in space. Also known as glide plane.

globular protein. Any protein that is soluble in aqueous medium and in which polypetide chain is lightly folded in three dimensions to yield a globular shape.

globulins. Group of proteins soluble in dilute solutions of mineral salts, such as sodium chloride. They generally contain glycine and coagulate when heated. They occur in many animal and vegetable tissues and fluids ; *e.g.*, lactoglobulin in milk, serum globulin in blood, vegetable globulins in seeds. Globulins are the main proteins of antibodies.

gluc-, gluco-. Relating to glucose ; as glucopyranose, glucuronic.

glucinium. Trivial name for the element beryllium.

glucogenic amino acids. Amino acids whose carbon chain can be metabolically converted into glucose or glycogen.

gluconeogenesis. The biosynthesis of new carbohydrate precursors.

glucophore. A radical or atomic grouping which is supposed to impart a sweet taste to many compounds in which it appears. Common glucophore groups are :

$-CHOH-CH_2OH$; $-CO-CH_2OH$; $-CHNH_2-COOH$; and $-CH_2ONO_2$.

gluons. The hypothetical force particles which

are believed to bind quarks into elementary particles. Although theoretical models in which the strong interactions of quarks are mediated by gluons have been successful in predicting, interpreting, and understanding many phenomena ; free gluons remain undetected in experiments.

glutelin. A general name for a class of proteins which are insoluble in water, alcohol or neutral salt solutions, but readily dissolve in dilute acids and alkali. Glutelins are mixture of various similar proteins.

glyc-, glyco-. (Greek) Sweet, or relating to sugars or glycine, as glycogen, glycoside, glycocholic.

glyceride. An organic ester in which the alcohol radical is glyceryl derived from glycerol; *e.g.*,

Triacetin	Tristearin
$CH_2O—OC—CH_3$	$CH_2O—OC—C_{17}H_{35}$
$CHO—OC—CH_3$	$CHO—OC—C_{17}H_{35}$
$CH_2O—OC—CH_3$	$CH_2O—OC—C_{17}H_{35}$

If more than one type of fatty acid is present, as is usually the case in natural fats, the product is a mixed triglyceride. Glycerides are the major components of animal and vegetable fats and oils and may be saturated or unsaturated. They are readily hydrolyzed to fatty acids and glycerol. Monoglycerides are excellent emulsifying agents. Unsaturated glycerides are often hardened to make margarines and shortenings by catalytic addition of hydrogen.

glycogen. A starch polymer which is classed as a polysaccharide and is found chiefly in the liver of animal organisms where it acts as a reserve of energy. It can be broken down to simpler forms by the action of enzymes, a reaction called glycolysis.

glycogenesis. The metabolic formation of glycogen from glucose.

glycogenolysis. The metabolic breakdown of glycogen.

glycolipids. Complex lipids that consist of compounds of fatty acid with carbohydrates and contain nitrogen but no phosphoric acid ; found in brain tissues.

glycol. Any of a class of compounds characterized by having two hydroxyl groups on two different carbon atoms of an organic structure, *e.g.*,

$$
\begin{array}{cc} HO & OH \\ | & | \\ —C— & C— \\ | & | \end{array}
$$

glycolysis. Enzymatic decomposition of sugars, starches, a type of reaction occurring in yeast fermentation and in certain metabolic processes. Lactic acid is one of the products formed. The root word is glyco- ("sugar"), not glycol ("alcohol").

glycoside. Any of a member of a large class of carbohydrate derivatives characterized by the replacement of the hydrogen atom of the hemiacetal hydroxyl group by an alkyl or aryl moiety, the aglycon. The glycosides are stable compounds and, do not undergo many of the reactions of sugars, *e.g.*, they show no reducing properties, they do not mutarotate etc. The non-sugar part of a glycoside is known as the aglycon, Natural glycoside constitute a large and biologically important class of sugar derivatives. Many natural pigments and dyestuffs, poisons and drugs, are glycosides.

Glycosides are classified according to the sugar formed during their hydrolysis as glucosides, fructosides, rhymnosides, galactosides, mannosides, arabinosides, xylosides, sorbosides, glucoheptosides, etc., or as aldosides, or ketosides if formed from aldoses or ketoses. Other classifications are based upon the nature of the nonsugar or "aglycone" group formed when glycosides are hydrolyzed.

Gogte synthesis. A method of formation of α-pyrone derivatives by treatment of β-substituted glutaconic anhydrides with acyl chlorides, followed by decarboxylation.

R′, OH, O + R″COCl $\xrightarrow{-HCl}$

R″CO, R′, OH, O $\xrightarrow[-CO_2]{\Delta}$ R′, R″, O

gold. An element

State	Solid	Symbol	Au
Group	IB	Atomic No.	79
		Atomic Wt.	196.9665
		Valence	+1, 3
		m.p.	1337.43K

Gold is a deep-yellow, soft, and very dense metal. It is classed as a heavy metal and as a noble metal

The density of gold is 19.3 times that of water. It does not tarnish or burn in air. It is inert to strong alkaline solutions and to all pure acids except selenic acid. Gold has 19 isotopes, ^{185}Au through ^{203}Au. Though not particularly reactive, it readily forms compounds with the halogen elements. Its softness (ductility) enables it to be extended into sheets (leaf) as thin as 50 angstrom units which have become extremely useful in surgical techniques. Even in thin layers, gold is highly reflective to radiation and is used in space applications, such as the face masks of astronauts suits. It can also be prepared in colloidal suspension and mixed with molten glass to give the red colour of ruby glass.

The use of gold in the electrical, electronic, and other industrial fields has grown considerably in recent years. The electrical and thermal conductivity, resistance to oxidation, and ease of being electroplated make gold an excellent coating for electrical contacts. This has been particularly true in metallized ceramics for use in microelectronics and other electronic components.

gold number. An index of the protective action of a colloid. It is found by determining the value of the colloid in preventing coagulation of a metal sol by an ionic solution. It is defined as the smallest concentration of protective colloid, expressed in mg. per 10 cm^3 of solution, which prevents colour change of standard gold sol from poppy red to violet after addition of 1 cm^3 of 10% solution of NaCl or 3.7% solution of KCl.

Goldschmidt detinning process. A process for the recovery of tin, based on the action of dry chlorine on scrap tin-plate. The tin reacts readily to form stannic chloride, and the iron reacts only slightly. By fractional distillation the stannic chloride is separated from the small amount of ferric chloride that is formed.

Goldschmidt process. A method of direct synthesis of formates by heating sodium hydroxide with carbon monoxide under pressure. Further heating yields oxalates :

$$NaOH + CO \xrightarrow{473K} HCOONa$$

$$2HCOONa \xrightarrow{650K} \begin{array}{l} COONa \\ | \\ COONa \end{array} + H_2$$

Goldschmidt reduction process. A process based on the reaction of various metallic oxides with metallic aluminium, resulting in the oxidation of the aluminium to its oxide, and the reduction of the metallic oxide to the free metal. This process used in the production from their oxides of many metals, such as chromium, zirconium, cobalt, etc. Furthermore the reaction is strongly exothermic and is applied in welding by igniting a mixture of aluminium and ferric oxide, which is known as thermite.

Golodetz reagent. A solution of a few granules of benzoyl peroxide in concentrated sulphuric acid ; it gives a blood red colour with formaldehyde.

Gomberg-Bachmann-Hey reaction. Preparation of diaryl compounds by action of benzene (or its homologues) on dizonium salt solutions in presence of sodium hydroxide. *e.g.*,

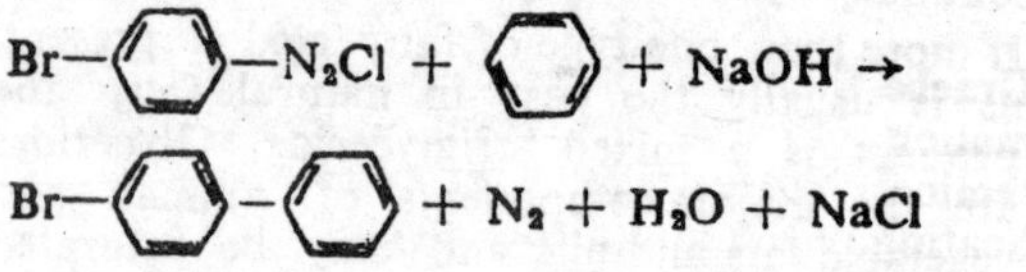

$$Br{-}C_6H_4{-}N_2Cl + C_6H_6 + NaOH \rightarrow$$

$$Br{-}C_6H_4{-}C_6H_5 + N_2 + H_2O + NaCl$$

Goodman-Suzanne reagent. A solution of 1.5 g phosphoric acid and 5 g. hydrochloric acid in 93.5 g. ethyl alcohol used in testing for albumin in urine.

Goppelsroder reagent. A 0.1% alcoholic solution of morin which gives a strong green flourescence with aluminum salts.

Gould-Jacobs reaction. A method of formation of 4-hydroxyquinoline by ring closure of α-carbalkoxy-β-aniloacrylic esters ; *e.g.*,

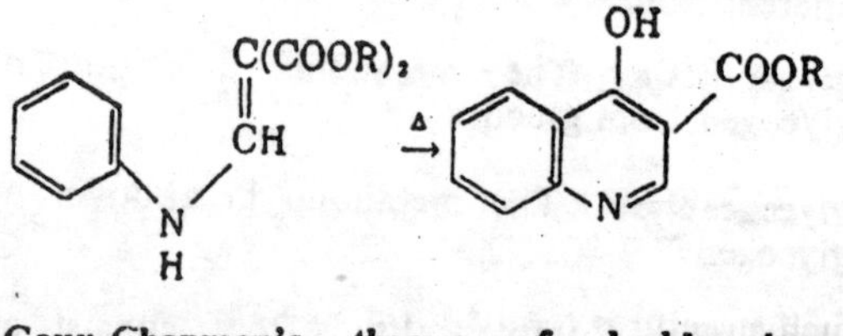

$$C_6H_5{-}NH{-}CH{=}C(COOR)_2 \xrightarrow{\Delta} \text{4-hydroxy-3-(COOR)quinoline}$$

Gouy-Chapman's theory of double layer. Theory referring to Helmholtz model (*see* Helmholtz's theory of double layer), in which it is assumed that neutralising charge on electrolyte side is not located strictly in interface, but it distributed statistically in solution, analogously to that in Debye-Huckel's ionic cloud.

Gouy magnetic susceptibility balance. Instrument for the measurement of magnetic susceptibility of cylindrical samples of length of about 10—20 cm; main parts are magnet and balance used to measure forces acting on sample in inhomogeneous magnetic field.

Gover process. A process for the dewaxing of petroleum oils by the use of a solvent consisting of a mixture of benzene and acetone which may be partly replaced by various other ketones or mixtures of them. Since ethyl methyl ketone (2-butanone) is one of these solvents the process is also known as the ethyl methyl ketone process, as it was once known as the benzol-acetone process. The final separation of the wax is done by filtration.

gradient elution. Elution in which composition (concentration, *p*H, etc.) of eluent is changed continuously.

Graebe-Ullmann synthesis. A method of formation of carbazoles from 2-aminodiphenylamines, by treatment with nitrous acid, and heating of the intermediate compound.

Graft polymer. Polymer in whose macromolecules one or more species or block is attached as side chains, these side chains being different from the main chain, *e.g.*,

```
.....AAAAAAAA.....
      |   |
      X   X
      X   X
      X   X
```

Such structures results form free radical initiation at active points on the main chain; their composition and structure are subject to close control so that copolymers of many types and properties can be constructed by chemical "grafting" of subchains to the backbone of the major component. Styrene, vinyl acetate, and acrylonitrile have been attached in this way to polyethylene and other polymers.

Graham's dialyzer. Device for separation of colloids from dissolved substances of low molecular weight by means of dialysis.

Graham law of diffusion. At constant conditions of temperature and pressure, the rate of diffusion of a gas is inversely proportional to square root of the density of the gas.

gram-atom. Mass in grams of element equal to its relative atomic mass. In view of introduction of mole as unit of amount of substance, molar mass should be used in preference of gram-atom. Also known as gram atomic weight.

gram-atomic weight. *See* gram-atom.

gram equivalent. Mass in grams of element equal to its relative atomic mass divided by its valency number.

gram method. Method of analysis where mass of investigated sample is $x . 10^{-1} — x . 10^{0}$ g and in the case of gases volume is $x . 10^{1} — x . 10^{3}$ cm^3. Also known as macro method, classical method.

gram-molecular volume. The volume occupied by 1 mole of an element at 273K. and 760 mm. pressure. For an ideal gaseous element it is 22.242 litres.

gram-molecular weight. *See* mole.

gram-molecule. *See* mole.

grand canonical ensemble. Statistical ensemble with following probability distribution function

$$P(Q_N, N) = \exp\left[\frac{\Omega - E(Q_N, N) - \mu N}{kT}\right]$$

where $E(Q_N, N)$ = energy of system of N identical particles in state Q_N, k=Boltzmann constant T= thermodynamic temperature, μ=chemical potential of particle, and Ω= grand thermodynamic potential. In this form formula refers to systems composed of differ- ent particles this formula must be suitably generalized. Grand canonical ensemble is utilized for description of thermodynamic equilibrium in open systems and in systems undergoing phase transition of chemical reactions. Also known as grand canonical statistical function.

grand partition function, Ξ Function defined by

$$\Xi(T, V, \mu)=\sum_{N}\sum_{Q_N} \exp\left[-\frac{E(N, Q_N)-\mu N}{kT}\right]$$

where T=thermodynamic temperature, V=volume of system, μ=molecular chemical potential, k=Boltzmann constant and $E(N,Q_N)$ =energy system of N identical particles in state Q_N. Grand partition function determines all equilibrium thermodynamic properties of system.

grand potential. *See* grand thermodynamical potential.

grand thermodynamical potential Ω. Ω function $=-kT \ln \Xi$, where k=Boltzmann constant, T=thermodynamic temperature and Ξ=grand partition function. Grand thermodynamical potential determines all equilibrium properties of system. In thermodynamic limit $\Omega=-pV$, where p=pressure and V=volume of system.

gravimetric analysis. A branch of quantitative chemical analysis. The amount of a substance present is determined by converting it, by a suitable chemical reaction, into some other substance of known chemical composition, which can be readily isolated, purified and weighed.

gravimetric factor. A number used to multiply the weight result of a given quantiative analysis in order to obtain the amount of a substance to be determined.

gray, *Gy*. Unit of absorbed dose of ionizing radiation correseponding to 1 J of absorbed energy per 1 kg of medium.

gray body. An energy radiator which has a blackbody energy distribution, reduced by a constant factor, throughout the radiation spectrum or within a certain wavelength interval. The designation "gray" has no relation to the visual appearance of a body but only to its similarity in energy distribution to a blackbody, Most metals, for example, have a constant emissivity within the visible region of the sepectrum and thus are gray bodies in that region.

grease. 1. A cholesterol fatty-acid ester with an unpleasant odour produced by the hair follicles of some animals, especially sheep and goats. This material must be separated from the wool before the latter can be used.

2. A mixture comprised of a petroleum derived oil thickened until becomes a semisolid, by means of soaps of heavy metals such as calcium, aluminium, lead, etc. ; copper pthalocyanine, rosin, and colloidal silica are also used. The high viscosity of these greases enables them to withstand the severe mechanical action of machine parts, gears, and bearings even at temperature up to 535K. Corrosion inhibition and other special-purpose additive may also be included.

greenhouse effect. Absorption of infrared radiation by the carbon dioxide and water vapour in the atmosphere, which retards dissipation of heat from the earth's surface. This phenomenon significantly affects global temperature. The carbon dioxide content of the air is not constant; at present, it averages 0.033%. Authoritative estimates indicate that the combustion of fossil fuels increased it by 10 to 12% between 1900 and 1950, causing a rise of about 1°C in average global temperature. Presumably, an equivalent rise will have occurred by 2000, for a total of 2°C for the century. Coal and coal-derived fuels produce substantially more carbon dioxide; on combustion than either oil or natural gas. Environmentalists warn that, since the temperature increase is considerably greater at the poles than near the equator, sufficient melting of polar ice may eventually occur to raise the level of the oceans enough to threaten coastal cities.

grex. A term used in the textile industry to designate the weight per unit length of a filament. *i.e.*, its diameter or "fineness ;" a filament is called 1 grex if 10,000 meters of it weigh 1 gram.

Griess phenylenediamine test for nitrite. A solution of 5 g. *m*-phenylenediamine dissolved in 1 litre water acidified with sulphuric acid gives a brownish-yellow colour with even traces of nitrite in solution.

Griess test for nitrite. The solution to be tested is

acidified with sulphuric acid, and a solution of sulphanilic acid is added, followed after a few minutes by colourless solution of α-naphthylamine sulphate. A red colour is given even with traces of nitrite. Many modifications of this test have been developed.

Grignard degradation. A method of removing the halogen atoms from a polyhalo compound step-by-step by formation of the magnesium addition compound (Grignard reagent) and decomposition with water.

$$\text{2,5-dibromothiophene} \xrightarrow{Mg} \text{5-bromo-2-thienyl-MgBr} \xrightarrow[-MgBrOH]{H_2O}$$

$$\text{2-bromothiophene} \xrightarrow{Mg} \text{2-thienyl-MgBr} \xrightarrow[-MgBrOH]{H_2O} \text{thiophene}$$

Grignard synthesis. Any one of a vast number of reactions, commonly condensations, involving the various Grignard reagents, which is usually preparation of organomagnesium compound from alkyl (or aryl) halide and magnesium in anhydrous diethyl ether (Grignard reagent); the latter is treated with compound containing multiple bond between atoms differing in electronegativity (C=O, C=S, C≡N, N=O), *e.g.*,

$$RX + Mg \xrightarrow{\text{ether}} RMgX$$

$$R'(R'')C{=}O + RMgX \rightarrow R'{-}C(R')(R){-}OMgX \xrightarrow{H_2O} R'{-}C(R')(R){-}OH + Mg(OH)X$$

Grimm's law. Law defining conditions of isomorphism of two chemical substances. Two substances are isomorphous if; (*a*) types of chemical formula are identical; (*b*) types of unit cell of space lattices are the same; (*c*) dimensions of unit cells are approximately equal in both compounds.

Grote reagent. A solution in 10 ml. water of 0.5 g. sodium nitroferricyanide, 0.5 g. hydroxylamine hydrochloride, and 1 g. sodium bicarbonate, to which 2 drops of bromine are added, and the volume made up to 25 ml. It is used to test for sulphur in organic compounds and for thiourea in orange juice. A purple colour indicates the presence of organic sulphur, and a blue or blue-green colour is given by thiourea in orange juice.

Grotthus-Draper law. Only that part of incident radiation may be photochemically active which is absorbed by reacting system.

ground colour. A foundation coat of a colour which will intensify the chromatic value of more transparent colours that are to be applied later.

ground state. In quantum mechanics the stationary state of lowest energy of a particle or a system of particles. The ground state may be bound or unbound; when bound, its energy generally is a finite amount less than the energy of the next higher or first excited state. In the typical circumstance that the potential energy is zero at infinite separation, the magnitude of the negative ground-state energy in the binding energy, that is, the energy required to separate all the particle infinitely.

group. 1. Any set of elements which is equipped with an operation (called multiplication) that is associative, has an identity element, and has an inverse element for each element of the set, is called a group.

2. A number of elements having similar electronic structure and chemical properties as classified according to the Periodic Law and appearing in vertical columns in the Periodic Table. There are nine major groups, seven of which are divided into two subgroups, designated A for the major group elements and B for transition elements. The two groups that are not so divided are VIII (transition elements only) and the noble gas group (sometimes called Group zero. Thus, the numbered groups in a widely used type of Periodic Table are as follows; IA, IIA, IIIB, IVB, VB, VIB, VIIB, VIII, IB, IIB, IIIA, IVA, VA, VIA, VIIA, and noble gas.

3. Two or more associated elements which tend to remain together during a reaction. The term group properly refers to these only when no dissociation is involved. Thus, there are inorganic groups such as OH^- (hydroxyl), CO_3^{2-} (carbonate), SO_4^{2-} (sulphate), as well as organic group such as COOH (carboxyl), CO (carbonyl), $CH_3^{\cdot}$ (methyl) and homologous

univalent alkyls, and C_6H_5 (aryl) groups. Alkyl groups may acquire an unpaired electron when the break away from their molecules in which case they are called free radicals. Besides the above, there are a number of combinations of elements that are characteristic of large classes of compounds these are also called groups, *e.g.*, COH (alcohol or methanol), CHO (aldehyde). $CONH_2$ (amide), CH_3CO (acetyl) NH_4 (ammonium), and SH (sulphhydryl).

group reagent. In systematic qualitative analysis, reagent which precipitates from solution a given group of cations or anions.

Gryszkiewicz-Trochimowski and McCombie method. A method of formation of fluorine compounds from chlorine compounds and potassium fluoride at high temperatures and pressure (autoclave). The reaction applies particularly to chloroesters and chloroalcohols.

$$ClCH_2.COOR + KF \xrightarrow{460K} FCH_2.COOR + KCl$$

Guerbet reaction. The direct condensation of alcohols, in the presence of alkali and metallic catalysts and at elevated pressure and temperature. Straight chain alcohols add to form a single molecule containing one hydroxyl group and twice the number of carbon atoms, some of which are in a side chain. Close control of conditions is necessary to minimize the extent of the side reactions.

Guerin solution for selenium. A solution of 10g. mercuric nitrate and 10 ml. nitric acid in 100 ml. water, used as a reagent for selenium. Characteristic precipitates are obtained with selenic acid and selenites.

Guldberg and Waage law. A theory which embodied the principle that the rate of a chemical reaction is proportional to the active masses of the reacting substances. Guldberg and Waage were interested in the "affinity" coefficient, later "velocity" coefficients for reactions, which they found were especially useful for reversible reactions because they furnished a means for "determining the result of the reaction from any original condition of the four substances."

Guldberg's rule. Normal (thermodynamic) boiling temperature *Tw* of liquids not undergoing association amounts to about 2/3 of their critical temperature *Tc*.

gulfining. Hydrodesulphurization of heavy distillate gas oils. The charge is gas oils including vacuum distillate. Products are low sulphur fuel oil or catalytic cracking unit, charge stock.

gun-metal, A class of copper alloys containing about 90% copper, 8%-10% tin and up to 4% zinc.

Gunning reagent. A solution of zinc acetate; used for precipitating blood pigments.

Gustavson reaction. A method of formation of alicyclic hydrocarbons by the action of zinc on open chain dihalocompounds :

$$XCH_2.CH_2.CH_2X + Zn \rightarrow H_2C\overset{CH_2}{\diagup\diagdown}CH_2 + ZnX_2$$

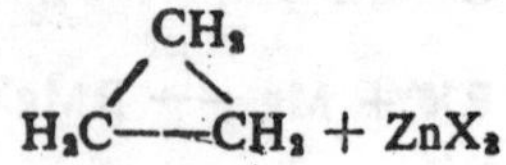

Gutknecht pyrazine synthesis. A method of formation of dihydropyrazines by reduction of α-oximinoketones and condensation ; *e.g.*,

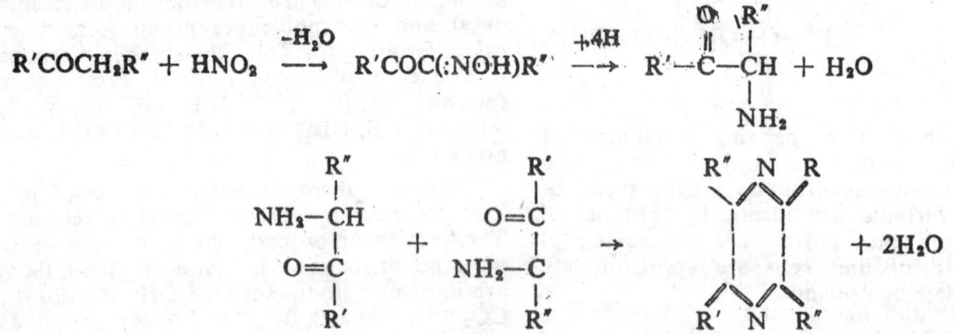

$$R'COCH_2R'' + HNO_2 \xrightarrow{-H_2O} R'COC(:NOH)R'' \xrightarrow{+4H} R'-\overset{O}{\overset{\|}{C}}-\underset{NH_2}{\underset{|}{CH}}-R'' + H_2O$$

$$\begin{array}{c} R'' \\ | \\ NH_2-CH \\ | \\ O=C \\ | \\ R' \end{array} + \begin{array}{c} R' \\ | \\ O=C \\ | \\ NH_2-C \\ | \\ R'' \end{array} \rightarrow \begin{array}{c} R'' \quad N \quad R \\ \text{(dihydropyrazine ring)} \\ R' \quad N \quad R'' \end{array} + 2H_2O$$

Guyot reagent for ammonia. Potassium bromide solution is added to an acid solution of mercuric nitrate until the precipitate formed redissolves. Then potassium hydroxide solution is added until a permanent precipitate is formed. The clarified liquid gives a white precipitate or turbidity with ammonia.

gyromagnetic effects. Phenomena of magneto-mechanical character with enable gyromagnetic rations to be determined and depend on : (*i*) magnetization during rotation of ferromagnet (Barnett effect) ; (*ii*) rotation following magnetization of ferromagnet change (Einstein-de Haas effect). Also known as magneto-mechanical effects.

Gyromagnetic ratio. Ratio of system's magnatic moment and its mechanical momentum ; for angular momenta gyromagnetic ratio is $\gamma_1 = e/2m_0c$, for spin momenta $\gamma_s = e/m_0.c$ where e=electronic, charge, m=electron mass, c=speed of light in vacuum.

Gyro process. A petroleum-craking process that operates on crude oil which is preheated and flashed. The reduced crude oil is introduced into the fractionator and the "bottoms" from the tower are sent to a viscosity-breaking coil.

H

H. Symbol for hydrogen. The symbol for the gauss, unit of magnetic field strength. The symbol for the henry, unit of inductance. Symbol for Boltzmann function; and Henry law constant.

h. Symbol for Planck's constant. Abbreviation for hetero-.

Haber-Bosch process. A process for the synthesis of ammonia from nitrogen and hydrogen under a pressure of about 200 atmosphere, and at a temprature of about 773K, in the presence of a special iron catalyst, plus oxides of potassium, aluminum, and other metals to promote the catalytic activity.

habit. A term used in crystallography to denote the type of geometric structure a given crystalline material invariably forms, *e.g.*, thin plates or sheets, fibres, cubes, rhomboids, etc. The detailed morphology of crystals is a science in itself, with a multitude of classes and subclasses, but the crystal habit of a given substance under comparable condition of formation is quite constant and predictable. *See also* crystal.

hadrons. The generic name of a class of particles which interact strongly with one another. Examples of hadrons are neutrons, protons, the π-, K-, and D-mesons, and their antiparticles.

haemoglobin. *See* hemoglobin.

haemolysin. *See* hemolysin.

haemolysis. *See* hemolysis.

hafnium. An element	Symbol	Hf
State Solid	Atomic No.	72
Group IVB	Atomic Wt.	178.49
	Valence	2,3,4
	Isotopes	5 stable
	m.p.	2495K
	b.p.	4876K

Hafnium is one of the less abundant elements in the earth's crust. It is a lustrous, silvery-white, ductile corrosion-resistant metal. The chemistry of hafnium is almost identical with that of zirconium, which is a consequence of the lanthanide contraction. It is separated from zirconium by chlorination and solvent extraction, followed by reduction of hafnium chloride with magnesium (Kroll process).

The alpha form of elemental hafnium has a close-packed hexagonal crystal structure ; the beta form, a body-centered cubic structure. Metallic hafnium, like zirconium, exhibits passivity in air due to formation of adherent coatings of oxide or nitride.

While harmless from the toxicity stand-point,

it is a fire hazrad in powdered form. It is classed as a rare metal.

Several uses have been found for hafnium : (*i*) as a control material in water-cooled nuclear reactors. Also hafnium is an effective flux-depressor in a reactor for absorbing neutrons to decrease the peaks in neutron flux ; (*ii*) as a filament in gas filled incandescent light blubs ; (*iii*) as an alloying ingredient to add strength to tungsten and molybdenum filments and electrodes used in high-pressure discharge (*iv*) as a cathode in x-ray tubes ; (*v*) as a getter material in vacuum tubes and system ; (*vi*) as a minor alloying ingredient in nichrome heating elements where hafnium appears to singnificantly increase the lifespan of the elements ; and (*vii*) usually with zirconium, as an ingredient of several alloys.

Hager reagent for glucose. A solution of 48 ml. glacial acetic acid, 60 g. sodium acetate, 100 g. sodium chloride, and 60 g. mercuric oxide in one litre water ; used as a reagent for glucose. A precipitate of mercurous chloride is given by glucose on heating.

Hager test for nitrate and nitrite. Solution of nitrates or nitrites in concentrated sulphuric acid give with a 1% solution of naphthol in alcohol a yellow to dark cherry-red colour.

Hager test for glycerol. An aqueous solution of borax coloured blue by litmus becomes red when added to glycerol or to neutral solutions containing it.

Hahn reagent. The compound 8-hydroxyquinoline ; used in 5% alcoholic solution it the determination of zinc, aluminium, and magnesium, in certain analytical separations, etc.

Hahn reagent for nitrite. The compound. 2,4-diamino-6-hydroxy-pyrimidine, which gives a strawberry-coloured precipitate with sodium nitrite.

Hahn's precipitation rule. A microcomponent (*e.g.*, radioactive substances) contained in solution may be incorporated in crystalline precipitate to be separated when it is found in structure of crystal lattice of a macrocomponent, *i.e.*, when it is isomorphic or isodimorphic with macrocomponent.

Haine reagent. A solution of 8.314 g. cupric sulphate and 40 ml. glycerol in 400 ml. water, to which is added 500 ml. 5% aqueous potassium hydroxide solution. It is a test reagent for glucose, yielding a precipitate of cuprous oxide.

hair-salt. A native form of aluminium sulphate ($Al_2(SO_4)_3.18H_2O$). Also called "feather alum".

Halden solutions. Two solution—(*i*) a solution 0.1 g. pyrogallol in 100 g. absolute alcohol ; and (*ii*) 10 g. anhydrous aluminum chloride in 110 ml. absolute alcohol. They are used in testing for vitamin D. A deep violet colour is given by vitamin D dissolved in benzene chloroform or ether.

half-cell. *See* electrode.

half-intensity width. $\Delta\nu_{1/2}$. Width of spectral range where intensity of spectral line is equal to one half of maximum intensity. Also known as half-width.

half-life. 1. The time required for an unstable element or nuclide to lose one-half of its radioactive intensity in the from of alpha, beta, and gamma radiation. Half-lives of radionuclides range from microseconds to millions of years ; that of radium is 1620 years. *See also* decay ; radiocarbon dating.

2. The time required for a reaction to be half-completed or for one-half of a reactant to be consumed. The relation between specific rate constant (*k*) and half-life ($t_{1/2}$) for a first order reaction is given by :

$$t_{1/2}=\frac{2.303}{k}\log\frac{1}{1/2}=\frac{0.693}{k}$$

half-thickness. The thickness of an absorbing medium necessary to reduce the intensity of the transmitted radiation to one-half its incident value. Also known as half-value layer.

half-value layer. *See* half-thickness.

half-value width. Width of energy peak at half of its height.

half-wave potential. Potential corresponding to one-half of amplitude of limiting current of polarographic wave.

half-width. *See* half-intensity width.

halide. A binary compound of a halogen

(fluorine, chlorine, bromine, or iodine) and another element most commonly a metal.

Hall effect. Effect occurring in strip of conducting material carrying electric current *I* when constant magnetic field *H* is applied at right angles to face of strip. Potential difference (Hall potential *V*) is created across conductor in direction orthogonal to directions of both magnetic field and current flow. Sign of Hall potential depends on the kind of mobile charge carriers, *i.e.*, free electrons or electron holes.

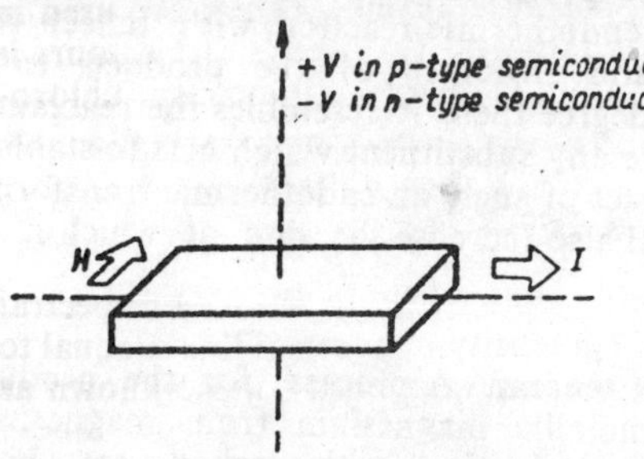

Fig. 26. Hall effect

Hall-Heroult cell. A cell for the production of aluminium by electrolysis of alumina dissolved in a bath of molten salts. This cell uses six or more performed carbon electrodes which are suspended in the cell by means of copper bars.

Hall process. The basic method for the separation of aluminum from alumina (Al_2O_3), whose most important source is bauxite, an earthy material rich in aluminum oxide (alumina). The process involves electrolysis in which the alumina is mixed with used cryolite (Na_3AlF_6).

Hall reheating process. A process for the removel of organic sulphur compounds from petroleum oils before they are used in gas manufacture.

Haller-Bauer reaction. A reaction for the preparation of trisubstituted acetic acids. The usual starting substance is a phenyl alkyl ketone in which the (*i*) the α-methylene group is fully alkylated by the action of an alkyl halide and sodamide, then (*ii*) the resulting compound is split between the phenyl and carbonyl groups by action of sodamide and hydrolysis and (*iii*) the trisubstituted amide is oxidized to the acid :

$$C_6H_5.CO.CH_2R' + 2R''X + 2NaNH_2 \rightarrow C_6H_5.CO.CR'R''_2 + 2NH_3 + 2NaX$$

$$C_6H_5.CO.CR'R''_2 + NaNH_2 + H_2O \rightarrow H_2N.CO.CR'R''_2 + C_6H_6 + NaOH$$

$$CR'R''_2.CO.NH_2 + HNO_2 \rightarrow CR'R''_2.COOH + H_2O + N_2$$

hallucinogen. Any of a group of cyclic organic compounds which cause various aberrations of perception and feeling, as will as a undesirable physical reactions. Many of these compounds are from natural sources and encompass six distinct types. The best-known of these are derivatives of lysergic acid, chiefly the diethylamide (LSD-25), which is one of the most powerful ; mescaline, a phenylethylamine ; and the tetrahydrocannabinol group occurring in marijuana and its concentrated form, hashish. *See also* psychotropic agent.

halochromism. The phenomenon of colour-development from colourless carbonyl compounds when they are dissolved in mineral acids. It is thought to be due to the formation of an oxonium salt, *e.g.*,

$$R_1R_2C{=}O + H_2SO_4 \rightarrow [R_1R_2C{=}O{-}H]\,HSO_4$$

haloform reaction. Reaction of organic compounds containing $—COCH_3$ group, or corresponding alcohols with hypochlorites, hypobromites or hypoiodites of alkali metals involving formation of $CHCl_3$ $CHBr_3$, or CHI_3 respectively ; *e.g.*,

$$RCOCH_3 \xrightarrow{NaOCl} RCOONa + CHCl_3$$

halogen. The term whose literal meaning is "saltmaker," refers to the five elements of Group VIIA of the Periodic Table. In the order of their activity these are fluorine chlorine, bromine, iodine, and astatine ; they are all electronegative and thus are strong oxidizing agents. They are classified as nonmetals.

halogenation. A chemical reaction or process which results in the formation of chemical bond between a halogen atom and another atom of some other element. Reactions resulting in the formation of halogen-carbon bonds are especially important, *e.g.*,

$$R - H + X_2 \rightarrow RX + HX$$

Halphen reagent for cottonseed oil. A solution of 1 g. sulphur in 100 ml. carbon disulphide, used in detecting cottonseed oil. Three ml. of this reagent is heated with 3 ml. of the oil to be tested and 3 ml. amyl alcohol for 15 minutes, in a concentrated aqueous solution of sodium chloride. A red colour is given by cottonseed oil.

Halphen reagent for linseed oil. A solution of sufficient bromine in 10 ml. carbon tetrachloride to bring the volume to 15 ml., used in detecting linseed oil. One ml. of the reagent is added to 0.5 ml. of the oil tested and 30 ml. ether at 300K. A turbidity which appears in 2 minutes is given by linseed oil.

hamiltonian. Quantum mechnical operator of total energy of system given as sum of kinetic and potential energy operators. Eigenfunctions of hamiltonian describe stationary states of system and its eigenvalues correspond to all possible total system energies.

Hammersten solution. A mixture of 5 ml. 25% nitric and 95 ml. 25% hydrochloric acids, used in testing for bile pigments in urine. A green colour is given by bilurubin.

Hammett equation. Equation describing influence exerted by substituent on rate or equilibrium constants of reaction :

$$\lg k - \lg k_0 = \rho \sigma$$

where k, k_0=reaction rate or equilibrim constants of substituted and non-substituted compounds respectively, σ = constant characteristic for substituent X, independent of type of reaction but dependent on type and location of substituent X with respect to reaction centre Y, ρ=reaction constant, dependent on reaction centre Y and reaction conditions (ρ expresses reaction sensitivity to substituent X). In case of benzene derivatives, Hammet equation is applicable to meta- and para-compounds :

Y

X

Hammick reaction. A method of formation of heterocyclic carbinols by decarboxylation of picolinic or related acids by reaction with carbonyl compounds :

N COOH + RCHO → N CHOH—R + CO_2.

Hammond postulate. The transition state of a strongly endothermic reaction with reflect the energy and structure of the products to a greater degree then it resembles the reactants. Therefore any substituent which acts to stablize the product of such an endothermic transformation will also increase the rate at which it is formed.

Hansgrig process. A process for the production of metallic magnesium from magnesium oxide by reduction with carbon at high temperatures, followed by quenching in a blast of hydrogen or natural gas.

Hantzsch pyridine synthesis. Preparation of pyridine derivatives by condensation of two moles of β-ketoester with aldehyde and ammonia, followed by nitric acid oxidation of resulting condensation product, *e.g.*,

ROOC R' COOR
CH_2 CHO CH_2 →
CO + CO
NH_3
H_3C CH_3

ROOC R' H COOR $\xrightarrow{HNO_3}$ ROOC R' COOR
H_3C N CH_3 H_3C N CH_3

In other variants of this reaction, cyanoacetic acid derivatives may be used instead of acetoacetic ester or a mole of malonic ester may be used instead of a mole of acetoacetic ester.

Hantzsch pyrrole synthesis. A method of formation of pyrrole derivatives, using as starting materials an α-chlorocarbonyl compound, a β-ketoester, and ammonia (or an amine) :

$$\underset{CH_3\quad O}{\overset{CH_2Cl}{C}} + \underset{O\quad CH_3}{\overset{CH_2-COOR}{C}} \xrightarrow[-2H_2O]{-HCl} \text{(pyrrole: } CH_3, COOR, N\text{-}H, CH_3)$$
$$+\ NH_3$$

Haptophore. The chemical group which joins with the amboceptor which is a heat resistant substance found in blood that unites the cell body with the complement.

hard acid. A Lewis acid of low polarizability, small size, and high positive oxidation state ; it does not have easily excitable outer electrons, *e.g.*, H^+, Li^+, Mg^{2+}, Al^{3+}

hard base. A Lewis base having high polarizability and low electronegativity, it is easily oxidised, or possess lowlying empty orbitals, *e.g.*, OH^-, H_2O, F^-, CN^-, OCH_3^-.

hardened steel. Steel hardened by quenching from high temperatures.

hard glass. A variety of glass containing potassium and high silica content ; used for making glassware. Also known as Bohemian glass.

hard iron. Iron or steel which is not easily magnetized by induction.

hardness. 1. The most familiar property of solid materials, which is difficult to define accurately. It is measured by determining the extent to which a material resists the force applied by a needle-like instrument under a specific load. Various hardness testers of this type are used for metals, glass, plastics, rubber, etc. Among the more important are Brinell and Rockwell testers (for steel and iron) and the Shore Durometer (for rubber and plastics). The hardness of minerals is indicated by the Mohs scale.

2. The amount of inorganic matter contained in a sample of water ; the contaminant is usually a calcium or magnesium compound picked up by the water from the rocks and soil over which it has flowed. The mineral content is usually expressed in parts per million.

3. In reference to radiation, hardness refers to wavelengths beginning about the middle of the x ray spectrum and moving downward through the gamma and cosmic ranges. These have extremely high energy and called "hard" radiation. *See* x-ray.

4. The term also applied to Lewis acid and bases having certain properties.

hardness permanent. *See* permanent hardness.

hardness scale, Moh. *See* Moh's scale.

hardness temporary. *See* temporary hardness.

hard radiation. Ionizing radiation of high energy and penetrating power, *e.g.*, β- and γ-radiation of energy exceeding 1 MeV.

hard sphere potential. Model intermolecular interaction potential :

$$u(r) = \begin{cases} \infty & \text{for } r < a \\ 0 & \text{for } r > a \end{cases}$$

where u=potential energy of pair of molecules (particles), r=intermolecular (interparticle) distance and a=the closest approach distance. Also known as hard core potential, hard sphere core model.

hardwater. Water that does not form an immediate lather with soap, owing to the presence of calcium, magnesium, and iron compounds dissolved in the water. The addition of soap produces an insoluble scum consisting of salts of these metals with the fatty acids of the soap, until no more is left in solution. Hardness is divided into two types : (*a*) temporary hardness, due to hydrogen carbonates (bicarbonates) of the metals. These enter the water by the passage of the water, containing dissolved carbon dioxide, over solid carbonates (chalk or limestone deposits, etc.).

Such hardness is removed by boiling, the soluble bicarbonats being decomposed into the insoluble carbonates, carbon dioxide and water. (*b*) Permanent hardness, due to sulphates of the metals. This is destroyed by the addition of washing soda, sodium carbonate, which precipitates the insoluble carbonates. All hardness may be destroyed by passing the water through zeolites.

harmonic oscillator. Oscillator in which acting force directed towards equilibrium position is proportional to displacement from equilibrium position.

Harris process. A process for the "softening" (partial purification) of lead, in which the oxidized impurities are treated by certain sodium salts (sodium nitrate, sodium hydroxide etc.) in a specially-designed cylindrical chamber provided with means for agitating. mixing, removal of molten impurities (salts of arsenic, antimony, tin, etc.) and removal of the "softened" lead.

Hartley test reaction. Ceric salt in acid or neutral solution give a brown precipitate, which later darkens, on addition of sodium acetate and hydrogen peroxide.

hartree. Atomic unit of energy equal to e^2/l_0, where e = charge of an electron and l_0 = the atomic unit of length. It is equal to 4.360×10^{-18} joule or 27.21 eV.

hartree-fock method. Approximate quantum chemistry method based on one-electron approximation. Coulomb electron-electron interaction is replaced by effective, self-consistent interaction potential following from variational minimization of total average energy of many-electron system. Also known as self-consistent field method ; SCF method.

Hass cyclopropane reaction. A method of preparation of cyclopropane by chlorination of propane, and treatment of the resulting 1,3-dichloropropane with zinc dust in aqueous alcohol :

$$ClCH_2{-}CH_2{-}CH_2Cl + Zn \rightarrow \underset{H_2C{-}{-}CH_2}{\overset{CH_2}{\triangle}} + ZnCl_2$$

Haworth methylation reaction. The use of dimethyl sulphate and sodium hydroxide to prepare methyl ethers of carbohydrates :

$$\begin{array}{c}|\\CHOH\\|\\CHOH\\|\end{array} + (CH_3)_2SO_4 + 2NaOH \rightarrow \begin{array}{c}|\\CH_2OCH_3\\|\\CH_2OCH_3\\|\end{array} + 2H_2O + Na_2SO_4$$

Haworth synthesis. A method for the preparation of multi-ring hydrocarbons by preparing the substituted butyric acids with aromatic radicals in the γ-position, followed by reduction of the carbonyl group, cyclization, reduction, and aromatization.

Naphthalene + $\begin{array}{l}CH_2{-}COOH\\|\\CH_2{-}COOH\end{array}$ $\xrightarrow[-H_2O]{AlCl_3}$ $COCH_2CH_2COOH$ (naphthyl)

Reduction (Zn, HCl) ↓

$CH_2CH_2CH_2COOH$ (naphthyl) $\xrightarrow{H_2SO_4}$ ketone (O)

Reduction (Zn, HCl) ↓

tetrahydrophenanthrene $\xrightarrow{Se}$ phenanthrene

hazardous material. Any material which, if improperly handled, can be damaging to health and well-being of human being. These may be poisons or toxic agents, corrosive chemicals, flammable materials, explosives, and radioactive substances.

heat. A mode of energy associated directly with and proportional to the random molecular activity (motion) of a material system. It maintains or raises the temperature of the system and can be transferred to another body (gas, liquid, or solid) by radiation, convection, or conduction. It can also be converted to other forms of energy, *e.g.*, electricity and motion. Heat is also defined as energy which is transferred under a temperature gradient or difference from one body to another. Heat is variously generated *e.g.*, by chemical reaction, flow of electricity, friction, nuclear fission and fusion, etc. Exchange of internal energy or enthalpy defined by appropriate equations which balance these quantities. In open systems concept of heat is not explicit.

Heat is sometimes, traditionally, identified with internal energy or enthalpy (*i.e.*, kinetic energy of random movement of particles and potential energy of their mutual interactions).

heat balance. Comparison of total amount of energy supplied in form of heat to system in a given process with total sum of energy consumed in all particular conversions.

heat content. A thermodynamic property which may be regarded as the total heat of a substance or system, and is defined as the sum of its internal energy plus the product of its pressure and volume, as in the relationship :

$$H = E + PV$$

where H = the heat content, E = the internal energy (*see* energy, internal) P = the pressure, and V = the volume. Heat content is also called the heat function, and the enthalpy. The form in which this concept enters most commonly into chemical calculations is that of changes in heat content when a system changes for one state to another.

heat capacity at constant pressure, Cp. Extensive thermodynamic function

$$Cp = \left(\frac{\partial H}{\partial T}\right)_p$$

where H=enthalpy, T=thermodynamic temperature, and p=pressure.

heat capacity at constant volume, Cv. Extensive thermodynamic function

$$Cv = \left(\frac{\partial U}{\partial T}\right)_v$$

where U=internal energy, T=thermodynamic temperature, and V=volume.

heat engine. System in which process takes place such that in each cycle some fraction of energy is transferred to surroundings by way of work and some fraction is accepted in the form of heat.

heat index. The quantity is essentially the same as the Maumene number. It is determined by mixing a given amount, such as 20 ml. of an oil with a given amount, such as 4 or 5 ml. of sulphuric acid and noting the temperature rise. Its magnitude indicates the degree of unsaturation of the oil, and hence its effectiveness as a drying oil. Also known as heat number.

heat number. *See* heat index.

heat of activation. The increase in heat content accompanying the transformation of a substance from a less active to a more reactive form. This process applies commonly to enzymes, and to many instances of the excitation of atoms or molecules, as well as to the irradiation of molecules.

heat of adsorption. The change in heat content when one mole of a given substance is adsorbed upon another specified substance. It is also necessary to state whether the adsorption is of the van der Waals type or of the activated type, since higher values are obtained from latter process.

heat of combustion. The heat evolved when a definite quantity of a substance is completely oxidized (burnt) ; usually stated for a standard state of 25°C and one atmosphere pressure for reactants and products in kilocalories per gram-formula weight of the substance. It is applied most commonly to the combustion of fuels and organic compounds but may also be applied to many inorganic substances, *e.g.*, the burning of sulphur to form sulphur dioxide It is a special type of heat of formation and is closely related to the heating value commonly expressed as BTU per pound of fuel.

heat of condensation. Change of enthalpy associated with isothermal and isobaric transition of a given amount of substance from gaseous state either to liquid state (heat of liquefaction) or to solid state (heat of condensation of solid phase).

heat of crystallization. The heat evolved or absorbed when a crystal forms from a saturated solution of a substance; usually expressed in kilocalories per gram-formula weight of the crystalline substance. In water solutions, the crystal formed often contains water of the crystallization, *e.g.*, $Na_2SO_4 . 10H_2O$. For engineering calculations, the value is often taken as the negative of the heat of solution of the crystalline form, thereby neglecting the much smaller heat of dilution, which is the actual difference between the heat of solution and the heat of crystallization.

heat of dilution. Enthalpy change of system associated with change in concentrations of one mole of a given solute within defined interval of concentrations c_1 and c_2, caused by diluting solution under consideration with appropriate amount of solvent. Also known as integral heat of dilution.

heat of dissociation. Change of enthalpy in process of breaking bonds in molecules, *e.g.*, heat of atomization, heat of electrolytic dissociation D_{ch} is obtained by subtracting vibrational zero-point energy E_0 of molecules from energy corresponding to dissociative vibrational level D, *viz.* :

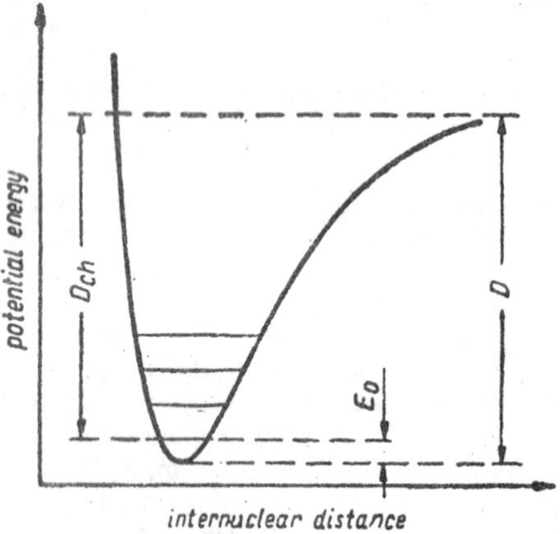

Fig. 27. Heat of dissociation

heat of formation. The increase of heat content of the system when one mole of a substance is formed from its elements. If the physical state of the various elements are not specified they are assumed to be in the state at which they would normally exist at atmospheric pressure and ordinary temperature.

heat of fusion. Enthalpy increase of system during isothermal and isobaric transition of defined amount of substance from solid phase to liquid under conditions of phase equilibrium.

heat of hydration. 1. The heat associated with the hydration or solvation of ions in solution, usually expressed in kilocalories per gram-formula weight or per mole of the ion involved.

2. The heat evolved or absorbed when a hydrate of a compound is formed *i.e.*, the difference between the heats of solution of the anhydrous and hydrated forms of the compound, *e.g.*, Na_2SO_4 and $Na_2SO_4 . 10H_2O$; usually expressed as kilocalories per mole of the compound. *See also* hydration.

heat of mixing (molar) Q^M. Change of enthalpy of system associated with formation of one mole of mixture from its liquid or gaseous components.

heat of neutralization. Enthalpy change of system in reaction of neutralization of one gram equivalent of acid by base, in dilute solution.

heat of racemization. The increase in heat content when one mole of an optically active substance changes to its racemic form.

heat of radioactivity. Heat released continuously and spontaneously by any radioactive substance; it depends on half-life of a nuclide, kind of radiation and conditions of absorption. For radium, in equilibrium with its first four daughters, heat of radioactivity is about 175 J/kg s.

heat of reaction. The heat evolved or absorbed when a chemical reaction occurs, in which the final state of the system is brought to the same temperature and pressure as that of the initial state of the reacting system. The value usually is accompanied by a chemical equation expressing the reaction and the number of gram-moles involved in it. The heat change is usually expressed in kilocalories per gram-formula weight of the products.

heat of solution. Enthalpy change of system in process of dissolving n_2 moles of a given substance in n_1 moles of solvent, per mole of solute under consideration. Also known as integral heat of solution.

heat of solvation. Enthalpy change of system for one mole of a given solute due to mutual solute-solvent intermolecular interactions in investigated solution.

heat of sublimation The heat required to convert a unit mass of a substance from the solid to the vapour state (sublimation at a specified temperature and pressure, without the appearance of the liquid state. It is equal to the sum of the heats of fusion and vaporization for the substance; usually expressed in kilocalories per gram-formula weight of the substance.

heat transfer salt. A mixture of salt, commonly 50% sodium nitrite and 50% potassium nitrate used in molten form (melting point of this mixture) as a heat transfer medium in high temperature processes.

heat of transition. The heat evolved or absorbed when a unit mass of given substance is converted from one crystalline form to another crystalline form. It can be calculated from the respective heats of formation of each crystalline form and is usually expressed in kilocalories per gram-formula weight of the substance.

heat of vaporization. The heat required to convert a substance from the liquid to the gaseous state with no temperature change; also called the latent heat of vaporization. It is usually measured at the normal boiling point of the substance, *i.e.*, the temperature at which the liquid boils at one atmosphere pressure. It is usually expressed as the heat required to convert a definite weight of the substance into a gas, *e.g.*, kilocalories per gram-formula weight.

heavy. As used in chemistry, that word has several meanings; (*i*) in the phrase "heavy-metal" soaps, it refers to metals of atomic weight greater than sodium (22.99) which form soaps, on reaction with fatty acids, *e.g.*, aluminium, lead, cobalt, and others; (*ii*) the term heavy isotope refers to deuterium, the isotope of hydrogen having an atomic weight of 2.016, which occurs in heavy water; (*iii*) the term heavy chemical is applied to chemicals produced on a very large scale, without reference to their actual weight, *e.g.*, soda ash, borax, sulphuric acid, etc.

heavy chemical. *See* heavy.

heavy hydrogen. *See* heavy.

heavy metals. Metals having a specific gravity greater than four. Sulphides of such metals are usually insoluble in water.

heavy oxygen. Isotope of oxygen. Atomic number 8. Mass number 18.

heavy platinum metals. Three chemical elements grouped horizontally in eight sub-group of periodic system (in period VI): osmium, iridium, platium. Also known as third triad.

heavy water. A form of water also known as deuterium oxide (D_2O), in which the symbol D_2 stands for two atoms of heavy hydrogen (H^2), an isotope of hydrogen containing one proton and one neutron. The specific gravity of heavy water is 1.1 and its boiling point at normal atmospheric pressure is 101.4°C. Its occurrence in H_2O is in the ratio of approximately 1 to 6000 parts. It was used as moderator in early types of nuclear reactors but has no other important application. *See also* deuterium.

Hedvall effect. Increase of catalytic activity of solids in vicinity of their phase transition temperature; also for ferromagnets in vicinity of their Curie temperatures.

Heermann reagent. A solution of stannous chloride in absolute alcohol saturated with hydrogen chloride gas. It gives a turbidity or precipitate with sodium.

Heintz test for potassium. Aqueous solutions of potassium salts acidified with hydrochloric acid, and on mixing with double their volume of a mixture of equal parts of ether and alcohol, give an octahedral crystalline precipitate on addition of platinic chloride solution on standing.

Heintz test for sulphite. Heating with stannous chloride and hydrochloric acid gives a precipitate if sulphites are present. If only a colour develops add cupric sulphate, which gives a black precipitate of copper sulphide.

Heisenberg relation. *See* uncertainty principle.

Heitler-London method. A quantum mechanical theory describing the nature of homopolar bonds. According to this theory the orbital wave functions for the complete molecule are determined by summing over products of the atomic wave functions.

Helferich method. The replacement of an acetoxy group on the first carbon atom of an acetylated aldose, by a phenoxy group, by heating with phenol. Acid catalysts are used, and influence the configuration of the resulting compound :

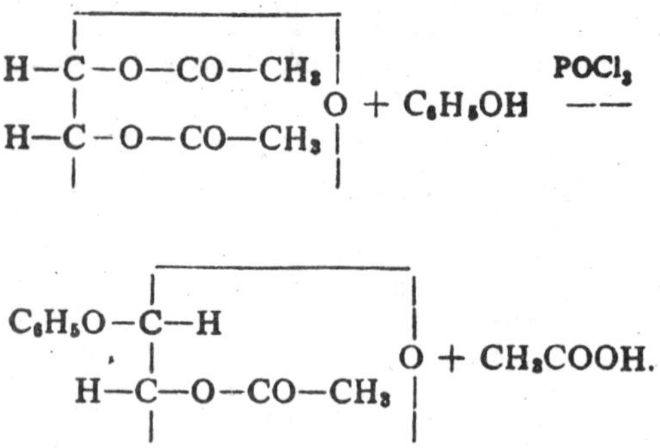

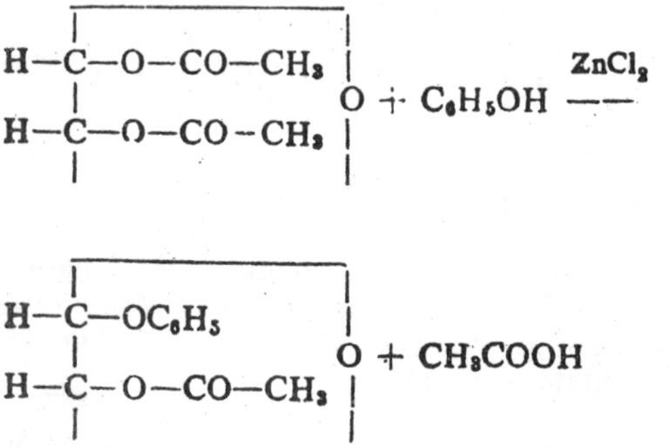

$$\begin{matrix} H-C-O-CO-CH_3 \\ H-C-O-CO-CH_3 \end{matrix} \Big] O + C_6H_5OH \xrightarrow{POCl_3}$$

$$\begin{matrix} C_6H_5O-C-H \\ H-C-O-CO-CH_3 \end{matrix} \Big] O + CH_3COOH.$$

$$\begin{matrix} H-C-O-CO-CH_3 \\ H-C-O-CO-CH_3 \end{matrix} \Big] O + C_6H_5OH \xrightarrow{ZnCl_2}$$

$$\begin{matrix} H-C-OC_6H_5 \\ H-C-O-CO-CH_3 \end{matrix} \Big] O + CH_3COOH$$

helicity. A fundamental quantized variable used in quantum mechanics to specify the relative orientations of spin and linear momentum of massless particles. It is the requirement of fundamental Dirac quantum mechanics that such particles have their spins aligned either parallel or antiparallel to their linear momentum. Particles have parallel alignment are arbitrarily assigned helicity +1; those have antiparallel alignment, −1.

helimagnetism. A property possessed by some metals, alloys, and salts of transition metals in which the atomic magnetic moments, at sufficiently low temperatures, are arranged in a spiral or helix. Simple antiferromagnets and ferromagnets can be considered as nonconical helimagnets with helical angles of 180° and 0°, respectively.

helium. An element

		Symbol	He
		Atomic No.	2
State	Gas	Atomic Wt.	4.00260
Group	Noble Gas	Valence	0
		Isotopes	2 stable

It is component of natural gas, from which it is separated by compressing the gas at low temperatures until all the other components have been liquefied. Helium does not become liquid until a temperature of 4.2 Kelvin (about −269°C) is reached and is thus a cryogenic liquid, which remains fiuid at temperatures near absolute zero. At standard conditions, helium is a colourless, tasteless, odourless, gas. There are two natural isotopes, ^3He and ^4He, with ^4He being slightly less than 100% abundant. The boiling point is 3.2 K for ^3He. Radioactive ^5He and ^6He have extremely short half-lives

Industrially helium is used to provide an inert gaseous shield for arc welding, for growing transistor crystals, in the production of titanium and zirconium, to fill the space between optical lenses in instruments, as the carrier gas in some chromatographic apparatus, as a liquid bath for masers and cryotrons, as a refrigerant for furnishing the low temperature required for superconducting electrical equipment, in lasers as a diluent gas in deep-sea diving applications, as a heat-transfer medium in gas-cooled nuclear reactors, and as a leak-detecting medium for testing pressure and vacuum equipment, Now, to a rather limited extent, helium is used as a lifting gas for airships and for balloons used in metereological investigations.

helium II. Upon cooling, ^4He liquefies at atmospheric pressure at 4.216 K to form an essentially normal liquid, liquid helium I. On further cooling to the lambda-point, 2.178 K at one atmosphere, a change occurs to liquid helium II. The latter has a very low viscosity (hence the name "superfluid") and a very high thermal conductivity, which produce such phenomena as the creeping of a film over the edge of the container, and the fountain effect, in which the liquid sprays out of a capillary.

The most abundant helium atoms, ^4He, are bosons, but the ^3He, atoms are fermions. This has a consequence that liquid ^3He does not show superfluidity—a property very probably connected with a Bose-Einstein statistics obeyed by the ^4He atoms.

Hell-Volhard-Zelinsky reaction. The direct

halogenation of an anhydrous aliphatic acid, with the production of the α-halogenated acid halide. The presence of a small amount of phosphorus causes halogenation (by an ionic mechanism) to take place exclusively at the alpha position. This reaction is used extensively in the production of pure α-halogenated acids, which are obtained by hydrolysis of the acid halides :

$$RCH_2COOH \xrightarrow[Br_2]{P} RCH_2COBr \xrightarrow{Br_2}$$

$$RCHBrCOBr \xrightarrow{H_2O} RCHBrCOOH$$

Helmholtz free energy, *F.* It is a property of a system defined as the difference between the heat content and the product of the entropy and temperature. In the older literature, the term "free energy" was used for the quantity now called the work function. Extensive thermodynamic function $F=U-TS$, where U=internal energy, T=thermodynamic temperature, and S=entropy. Also known as free energy, Helmholtz function, available energy, Helmholtz potential, available work at constant temperature, work function,

Helmholtz function. *See* Helmholtz free energy.

Helmholtz potential. *See* Helmholtz free energy.

Helmholtz theory of double layer. Theory which describes model of electrical double layer at electrode—electrolyte interface ; on electrode surface there exists excess of ions or electrons which is accompanied by excess of ions of opposite charge on solution side ; this system is analogous to plate condenser.

hem-, hemo-. Relating to blood or its colour ; as, hemoglobin, hemin.

hemat , hemato-. Relating to blood or its colour ; as hematoporphyrin, hematein.

hemiacetal. A hemiacetal is formed by the addition of the nucleophilic alcohol molecule to the carbonyl group. A hemiacetal molecule is both an ether and an alcohol. With a few exceptions hemiacetal are too unstable to be isolated :

$$R'-\overset{\displaystyle H}{\overset{|}{C}}=O + ROH \overset{H^+}{\rightleftharpoons} R'-\underset{\underset{\displaystyle OH}{|}}{\overset{\overset{\displaystyle H}{|}}{C}}-OR$$

Hemiacetal

In acidic medium, hemiacetals react with more of the alcohol to form the acetal :

$$R'-\underset{\underset{\displaystyle OH}{|}}{\overset{\overset{\displaystyle H}{|}}{C}}-OR + ROH \overset{H^+}{\rightleftharpoons} R'-\underset{\underset{\displaystyle OR}{|}}{\overset{\overset{\displaystyle H}{|}}{C}}-OR + H_2O$$

hemicellulose. A fraction of cellulose containing relatively few monomer units, compared with normal cellulose ; as the name suggests, it is a sort of "half-cellulose". It is soluble in mild solution of sodium hydroxide and is a minor component of wood ; it is sometimes also called beta- or gamma-cellulose. High percentages occur in corn cobs and in other agricultural wastes.

hemihedral crystal. A crystal having half of its faces developed.

hemihydrate. A compound that has one molecule of water of crystallization for every two molecules of the compound. Plaster of Paris, $2CaSO_4.H_2O$ or $CaSO_4.\frac{1}{2}H_2O$, is sometimes called hemihydrate plaster.

hemiterpene. One of a class of substances related to the terpenes of the formula C_5H_8, *e.g.*, isoprene.

hemitrope. A twin crystal.

hemocynin. A blue copper-containing blood pigment, and the second most abundant blood pigment after haemoglobin and function similarly in acting as oxygen-carrier in the blood. Also spelled haemocynin.

hemocyte. A blood cell especially in invertebrates.

hemoglobin. The iron-protein complex which is the characteristic component of red blood cells (erythrocytes). Its chief function is the transport of oxygen in the body. It exists in the form of molecule of high molecular weight, each containing one atom of iron ; the symbol Hb is often used. Hemoglobin is able to pick up oxygen from the air inhaled into the lungs it also picks up carbon monoxide very much more readily, resulting in dangerous and sometimes fatal poisoning from exposure to atmospheres containing more than 20 ppm of carbon monoxide.

hemolysin. One of a group of metabolic products of bacteria, some plants, snakes, toads, bees, spiders, etc., which have the power of producing hemolysin. Certain of these exist normally in blood serum or are produced during immunization.

hemolysis. 1. The separation of hemoglobin from the stroma of the blood and its appearance in the serum. This is effected by hypotonic solutions, a number of chemical compounds (ether, chloroform, alkalies, and especially saponins) and by hemolysins.

2. The actual destruction of red blood corpuscles.

hemostatic. A drug or other agent which, upon external application, arrests or retards the flow of blood form the body, as from wounds or lesions.

Henderson's equation. Formula which describes diffusion potential, ϵd derived from assumption that in boundary layer, concentrations of all ions change linearly in direction of diffusion :

$$\epsilon d = -\frac{RT}{F}\,\frac{\sum\frac{\lambda_i}{z_i}(m_i^{II}-m_i^{I})}{\sum\lambda_i(m_i^{II}-m_i^{I})}\ln\frac{\sum\lambda_i\, m_i^{II}}{\sum\lambda_i\, m_i^{I}}$$

where m_i^{I} and m_i^{II} = concentrations of ion i in neighbouring solutions I and II respectively, and λ_i=ionic conductivity.

Henderson's method for calculation of diffusion potential. Method based on assumption of linear change in direction of diffusion of concentration of each type of ions in boundary layer between two electrolytic solutions.

Henry alcohol reactions. 1. Acetyl chloride forms acetates with primary and secondary alcohols, but gives chlorides with tertiary alcohols.

2. On solution in fuming hydrochloric acid, tertiary alcohols yield an oil (the chloride) which rises to the surface. Primary and secondary alcohols may give an upper layer, but it contains unchanged alcohol.

3. Bromine is used to distinguish between secondary and tertiary alcohols.

Henry reaction. A method of formation of nitroalcohols by the condensation of nitroparaffins (primary or secondary) with aldehydes in the presence of a base.

$$CH_3.CH_2.NO_2 + RCHO \rightarrow RCHOH.CH_2.CH_2.NO_2$$

Henry's law. Mass m of gas dissolved at constant temperature in defined volume of liquid is proportional to partial pressure p of that gas over solution ; $m=kp$, where $k=$ proportionality factor, which depends on gas and temperature.

hepatic gas. An eighteenth-century name for hydrogen sulphide.

hepatic water. A natural spring water that contains hydrogen sulphide or an alkali sulphide.

Herbert-Heim test. Arsine (AsH_3) in air is detected by passing the air through a solution of cuprous chloride in hydrochloric acid, and then over mercuric chloride paper. A yellow colour is formed.

herbicide. Any chemical used to destroy or inhibit plant growth, especially of weeds or other undesirable vegetation. They may include weeds-killers, silvicides and defoliants. There are both organic and inorganic herbicides ; the latter is typified by common salt, sodium borate, and various arsenical compounds and the former by 2,4-D and similar chlorinated compounds and by the defoliant picloram. Some herbicides will kill only the weeds while leaving the desirable plants unharmed (selective) ; others (called silvicides) are especially effective on heavy growths such as trees and shubbery (ammonium sulphamate). *See also* pesticide ; defoliant ; silvicide.

Herman-Mauguin symbols. International symbol for representation of point and spatial symmetry of crystal lattice.

Hermans test for nitrate. Two ml. of the liquid tested are mixed with a few drops acetic acid, 2 ml. 5% potassium oxalate solution, 1 ml 5% manganous sulphate solution, and a few drops hydrogen peroxide. A red colour indicates nitrite. The test may be rearranged to detect manganese.

Hermite process. An electrolytic process for producing sodium hypochlorite solution from sodium chloride.

Herz reaction. A method of formation of the so-called "Herz-Compounds, which are arylthiazathionium chlorides, from aromatic amines (primary) and sulphur chloride :

$$CH_3NH\text{-}C_6H_3\text{-}NH_2 + S_2Cl_2 \rightarrow CH_3NH\text{-}C_6H_3(S\text{-}S(Cl)=N)$$

Hess's law. Total heat effect in chemical reaction and other processess carried out at constant volume or at constant pressure, if no useful work is done, is independent of path of process but depends only on starting and final states of system under consideration. Also known as law of constant heat summation.

hetero-. A prefix having the meaning "different" or "unlike", as in heterogeneous (different kinds") and heterocyclic ("different atoms in the ring").

heteroatom. A term applied to the members of a ring structure other than carbon atoms ; as in pyridine, the nitrogen atom, and in thiophene, the sulphur atom, are heteroatoms.

heteroazeotrope. Mixture composed of two or more liquid phases, distilling without change of mean composition. Also known as heteroazeotropic mixture.

heteroazeotropic mixture. *See* heteroazeotrope.

heteroazeotropic point. Point on phase diagram describing composition and boiling temperature, or composition and vapour pressure of heteroazeotrope.

heteroazeotropic system. Azeotropic system of constituents forming heteroazeotrope.

heterocyclic compound. An unsaturated cyclic compound containing one or more atoms other than carbon as part of the ring structure. The rings may be hexagonal or pentagonal, the latter appearing in the furan, purine, and pyrrole families of heterocyclics.

Substances of cyclic structure, as acid anhydrides, lactides, lactams, lactones, cyclic ethers, and cyclic derivatives of dicarboxylic acids which are formed by the elimination of water from aliphatic compounds, are not considered among the heterocyclic substances. Derivatives of pyridine, quinoline, thiophene, thiazole, pyrone, etc., which contain heterocyclic ring that persist in the compound through chemical reactions, are considered the true members of this class.

heterogeneous. Consisting of more than one phase. *See* equilibrium, reaction, catalysis.

heterogeneous catalysis. Catalysis in systems in which catalyst forms separate phase, most often solid.

heterogeneous equilibrium. Equilibrium between two or more phases, as between a solid and a gas, or a liquid and its saturated vapour. The system calcium oxide-calcium carbonate-carbon dioxide is an example of an heterogeneous equilibrium state.

Such systems are usually studied at constant pressure, since at last one of the phases will be a solid or liquid. The imposed pressure may be that of an equilibrium gaseous phase, or it may be an externally controlled pressure.

In describing such systems, the nature of each phase must be specified. In the following example, the terms *s*, *l*, and *g* identify solid, liquid, and gaseous phases, respectively. For solutions or mixture, the composition is needed in addition to the temperature and pressure, to complete the specification of the system. If not obvious, the identity of the solvent must be given.

For the following equilibrium reaction,

$$H_2O(l) \rightleftharpoons H_2O(g)$$

This relationship holds,

$$\Delta G^0 = \mu_g^0 - \mu_l^0 = -RT \ln \frac{p}{N}$$

Here $K^0 = p/N$, the ratio of the vapour pressure p to the liquid mole fraciton N. For pure water, the equilibrium constant is simply the standard vapour pressure p^0, and the Clausius-Clapeyron equation is just a special case of the Gibbs-Hemholtz equation. Now when a small amount of solute is added, decreasing the mole fraction of solvent, the vapour pressure p must be lowered to maintain equilibrium (Raoult's law). The effect of the total applied pressure P

upon the vopour pressure p of the liquid is given by the Gibbs-Poynting equation,

$$\left[\frac{dp}{dP}\right]_T = \frac{V_l}{V_g}$$

where V_l and V_g are the molar volumes of liquid and vapour. The vapour pressure will increase as external pressure is applied (activity increases with pressure). If the external pressure is applied to a solution by a semipermeable membrane, an applied pressure can be found which will restore the vapour pressure (or activity) of the solvent to its standard state value.

Other heterogeneous equilibria are solubility equilibria, reactions involving two immiscible phases, and reactions involving condensed and immiscible phases. Also known as polyphase equilibrium.

heterogeneous isotopic exchange. Isotopic exchange occurring in a polyphase system.

heterogeneous radiation. Radiation having a number of different frequencies, different particles, or different particle energies.

heterogeneous system. Thermodynamic system composed of finite (but greater than one) number of homogeneous phases. Also known as multiphase system.

heterolysis. *See* heterolytic dissociation.

heterolytic dissociation. Fission of covalent bond in molecule, resulting in formation of two ions bearing, different charges. Also known as heterolysis, heterolytic fission.

heterolytic fission. *See* heterolytic dissociation.

heterometric titration. Titration method with end point determined from point of inflection on curve representing dependence of opacity changes on volume of added reagent. Also known as turbidimetric titration.

heteronuclear. A condition in which two (or more) substituents occur in different rings or nuclei of compounds which cantain two or more rings, as, *e.g.*, 1,8-dichloronaphthalene. When substituents are both located in the same ring conditon is termed isonuclear.

heteropolar bond. *See* ionic bond.

heteropolar colloid. A colloidal system in which the dispersed particles are polar compounds.

heteropolyacids. Acids derived from two or more other acids, under such conditions that the negative radicals of the individual acids retain their structural indentity within the complex radical or molecule formed. The term heteropolyacids is usually restricted to complex acids in which both radicals are derived from oxides, such as phosphomolybdic acid.

heteropolymerization. Copolymerization of monomers of various structures, when one monomer is not able to polymerize with difficulty.

heterozeotropic system. Zeotropic system of limited mutual miscibility of liquid constituents.

hetp. An abbreviation used in chemical engineering ; it stands for "height equivalent to a theoretical plate" in a fractionating (distillation) column. The value in a given case is obtained by dividing the height of the column or tower by the number of theoretical plates present. *See also* theoretical plate.

Heumann indigo synthesis. A method of synthesis of indigo by fusion of phenylglycine with sodamide to form indoxyl, which is then oxidized to indigo.

The *o*-carboxy derivative of phenylglycine may be used, yielding on fusion with caustic soda. indoxylic acid, which gives indigo on decarboxylation and oxidation.

hexagonal system. A crystal system that has three equal axes intersecting at 120° and lying in one plane, a fourth unequal axis is perpendicular to the other three.

hexon bases. The amino acids lysine, arginine, and histidine which contain six carbon atoms.

hiding power. The extent to which a pigment is able to conceal or "cover" another colour when imposed over it ; it is also sometimes called covering power. It depends on various factors, chiefly refractive index and fineness of subdivision. Carbon black and titanium dioxide are black and white pigments of maximum hiding power. The term is used chiefly in the paint industry, mostly in reference to white pigments. *See also* pigment ; opacity.

high-elastic state. State in which elastic deformations involve dislocation of particular segments only of macromolecule chain. High-elastic state is achieved by heating polymer in vitreous state to temperatures higher than so called vitrification temperature, T_v. Relaxation of strains in this state is appreciably faster than in vitreous state. Also known as rubber-like state of polymers.

high explosive. An explosive whose shattering power, or brisance, is due to detonation brought about by hear or mechanical shock. Some are much more readily detonated than others, among the more sensitive are mercury fulminate and nitroglycerin ; TNT and ammonium nitrate are much more stable. *See also* explosive.

higher order phase transition. Transition taking place in some range of temperature and characterized by anomalous process of change of some physico-chemical properties, *e.g.*, molal heat capacity, magnetic susceptibility.

higher order reactions. Reaction with kinetic equation characterized by sum of exponents in which concentrations of reactants occur being higher than three.

high frequency titration. Titration for which end point is determined from changes of frequency and intensity of current in special oscillometric circuit. Also known as oscillometric titration.

high-pressure chemistry. Chemistry at very high pressures arbitrarily chosen to be above 10,000 bars, and mainly concerned with solid and liquid states. At 25°C, and 10 kilobars, nearly all ordinary gases are liquid or solid, and only a few liquids are not frozen ; thus most high-pressure chemistry involves either high temperatures, at which chemical reactions can occur at appreciable rates, or studies of internal arrangements in solids.

high polymer. A natural or synthetic polymer of high molecular weight (*i.e.*, 5000 or more). Such polymers may contain as many as several thousand monomer units, the molecular weights sometimes running into the millions. Units of such large size are called macro-molecules and are in the colloidal size range ; they include such bio-chemically active agencies as enzymes and viruses. High-polymer molecules are chain-like structures that may be linear, coiled, helical, or cross-linked. Among the natural high polymers are carbohydrates (starch, cellulose, polysaccharides), proteins, and certain unsaturated hydrocarbons ; the exact number of units present is not definitely known. These are the basis for many types of plastics and fibres : (*i*) cellulose and its derivatives (rayon, cellophane. nitrocellulose. carboxymethylcellulose) ; (*ii*) proteins (casein, soyabean) ; (*iii*) and hydrocarbons (rubber and related materials.)

high-speed steel. A very hard steel containing 12%-22% tungsten, with chromium, vanadium, molybdenum and small amounts of other elements which remains hard and tough at red heat ; used for tools which remain hard even at red heat.

high-spin complex. Complex in which number of unpaired electrons is maximal (from viewpoint of their possible distribution on t_{2g} and e_g orbitals). Also known as spin-free complex.

high-temperature chemistry. The study of chemical phenomena occurring above 500 K. High temperatures represent one of the important variables available to chemists for increasing the variety of possible chemical reactions over that expected for classical ground-state atoms and molecules. The relative population of excited rotational, vibrational, and electronic states can be enhanced by increasing the temperature and thus effectively create new mechanisms for the reaction.

Traditional high-temperature chemistry deals with the chemical phenomena in the range of 500-3000K, although exotic flames can produce temperature upto $\sim$ 25,000 K, electric archs can be operated in constricted modes to produce temperatures of $\sim$50,000K, and nuclear processes begin to occur at temperatures in the millions of degrees range. Laser-excitation of selected energy states can produce species with effective temperature in the range of 10^8 K.

Hilger test for malic acid. On heating to boiling with palladous chloride in neutral or weakly alkaline solution, malic acid gives a dark-coloured precipitate of palladium.

Hillebrand test for vanadium. Several drops of hydrogen peroxide added to an appropriately prepared extract of the sample give a brownish yellow colour if vanadium is present. If chromium is present, hydrogen peroxide and ether are added to an acidified portion of the extract. The ether is coloured blue by the chromium ; and the aqueous solution, yellow by vanadium.

Hill reaction. The oxygen evolution and photo reduction of an artificial electron acceptor by a chloroplast preparation in the absence of carbon dioxide.

hindrance. Partial or complete blocking of a reaction resulting from the three-dimensional structure of a molecule, often referred to as steric hindrance. For example, differences in the geometric arrangement of alkyl groups in saturated acids may cause substantial retardation of their rates of esterification ; trimethylacetic acid esterifies at only a small fraction of the rate of acetic acid because the reaction is hindered by three methyl groups attached to the first carbon atom. *See also* stereochemistry.

Hinsberg indole synthesis. A method of synthesis of oxindoles by formation of the third (indole) ring by the action of the sodium bisulphite addition product of glyoxal on such aromatic amines as β-naphthylamine.

in potassium hydroxide solution, while secondary amines give sulphonamides insoluble in alkali, and tertiary amines do not react.

histochemistry. A branch of biochemistry dealing with the study of detailed structure and chemical composition of the tissues of plants and animals. Since this involves the study of the cells of which the tissues are composed, there is some overlap between histochemistry and cytochemistry. Most histochemical procedures involve microscopic examination of tissues section of smear of cells that have been treated with reagents that convert specific cell constituents into visible derivatives or, in the case of enzymes, treatment with substrate solutions which yield a visible reaction product at their sites of activity.

histones. Basic proteins which occur in the nuclei of both plant and animal cells. They are less basic than the protamines, having isoelectric point at about pH 11. Some investigator restrict the term histone to only those basic proteins anatomically and chemically associated with DNA (deoxyribonucleic acids).

Histones by blocking some areas of the DNA molecule, may permit only part of the

NH_2 + CHOH—SO_3Na | CHOH—SO_3Na → N H SO_3Na + $NaHSO_3$ + $2H_2O$

$-H_2O$

N H O + $NaHSO_3$.

Hinsberg test for *o*-diamines. Prepare a solution of phenanthrenequinone in glacial acetic acid by heating, and add one drop of it to an alcoholic solution to be tested, then heat to boiling. A yellow precipitate, turned deep red by adding hydrochloric acid, is formed by *o*-diamines.

Hinsberg test for primary and secondary amines. On reaction with benzene sulphonylchloride ($C_6H_5SO_2Cl$) and dilute aqueous alkali, primary amines give sulphonamides soluble

DNA base sequences to act as templates for the formation of messenger RNA. Thus histones, by controlling messenger RNA formation may ultimately control protein biosynthesis within the cell. Or, the primary role of histone may be structural, histone being essential for stabilizing the DNA helix, for the integration of DNA strands into complex chromosomal structures, and for fixing and maintaining during cell division chromosomal changes occurring during differentiation and development.

Hittorf's method for determination of transport numbers. Method based on determination of changes of anolite and catholite resulting from different mobilities and hence different transport numbers of anion and cation.

Hock-Campbell ethylenimine synthesis. A Grignard method for the preparation of ethylenimines from ketoximes :

$$R'-\overset{\overset{NOH}{\|}}{C}-CH_2-CH_3 + 2R''MgX \xrightarrow{2HCl}$$

$$R'-\underset{R'}{C}(-NH-)CH-CH_3 + R''H + 2MgXCl + H_2O$$

Hoesch synthesis. *See* Houben-Hoesch synthesis.

Hofer-Moest reaction. A method of obtaining methyl alcohol by the electrolysis of an acetate in the presence of strong electrolytes :

$$CH_3COONa + NaOH + \tfrac{1}{2}O_2 \rightarrow CH_3OH + Na_2CO_3$$

Hofmann degradation. *See* Hafmann elimination.

Hofmann elimination. Exhausting methylation of amine and thermal degradation of quaternary ammonium hydroxide of tertiary amine and alkene, *e.g.*,

$$RCH_2CH_2NH_2 \xrightarrow{CH_3I} RCH_2CH_2\overset{+}{N}(CH_3)_3I^- \xrightarrow[H_2O]{Ag_2O}$$

$$RCH_2CH_2\overset{+}{N}(CH_3)_3\overset{-}{O}H \xrightarrow{100\text{-}200°C} RCH = CH_2 + N(CH_3)_3 + H_2O$$

An illustration of the preparation of the quaternary hydroxide precursor via exhaustive methylation followed by anion exchange is shown below :

H_2N–(bicyclic diamine)–NH_2 $\xrightarrow{6CH_3I,\ NaOH}$ $(CH_3)_3N^{\oplus}$–(bicyclic)–$N^{\oplus}(CH_3)_3$ $2I^{\ominus}$ $\xrightarrow{2AgOH}$ $(CH_3)_3N^{\oplus}$–(bicyclic)–$N^{\oplus}(CH_3)_3$ $2OH^{\ominus}$ + 2AgI $\xrightarrow{\Delta}$ $2H_2O + 2(CH_3)_3N +$ barrelene

The sequential Hofmann's eliminations of a cyclic amines is shown below :

2-methylpiperidine $\xrightarrow{2CH_3I,\ NaOH}$ N,N-dimethyl-2-methylpiperidinium $I^{\ominus}$ $\xrightarrow{AgOH}$ N,N-dimethyl-2-methylpiperidinium $OH^{\ominus}$ $\xrightarrow{\Delta}$ $CH_2=CH(CH_2)_3N(CH_3)_2$ (with =CH₂) $\xrightarrow{CH_3I}\xrightarrow{AgOH}$ $CH_2=CH(CH_2)_3\overset{+}{N}(CH_3)_3\ {}^{\ominus}OH$ $\xrightarrow{\Delta}$ $CH_2=CH(CH_2)_2CH=CH_2 + (CH_3)_3N$

Also known as Hofmann degradation.

Hofmann-Sand reaction. A general reaction of alkenes with mercuric salts in alkaline solution, to form compounds containing mercury :

$$RCH{=}CH_2 + Hg(NO_3)_2 + NaOH \rightarrow HOCHRCH_2HgNO_3 + NaNO_3$$

Hofmeister reactions for aliphatic amino acids. Amino acids give a red colour with ferric chloride, and blue with cupric sulphate. They reduce mercuric nitrate to mercury, which they precipitate in the presence of sodium carbonate, and they bring about the solution of cupric hydroxide in alkalies.

Hofmeister series. *See* lyotropic series.

Hohnel reagent for silk. A saturated solution of chromic acid which has been diluted with an equal volume of water, used in testing for silk, which dissolves rapidly in this reagent.

Hold-Back carrier. Carrier added to solution in order to retain a microcomponent in solution, *e.g.*, to prevent coprecipitation or sorption of radioactive substances on to precipitates to be separated.

hole. A term used in semiconductor technology to refer to an energy deficit in a crystal lattice due to (*i*) electrons ejected from unsatisfied covalent bonds at sites where an atom is missing (vacancy) or (*ii*) to electrons supplied by atoms of impurities present in the crystal, *e.g.*, arsenic or boron. The free electrons from these two sources move through the crystal leaving energy deficits which are positively charged ; these deficits sites, or holes, are also considered to move as they become alternately filled and vacated by electrons ; thus, a flow of positive electricity results.

Holmes-Manley process. A process for the simultaneous cracking and distillation of crude oil (or a fraction distilled therefrom) by the application of heat and pressure. The oil is heated with stirring in large stills, to a high pressure.

holmium. An element

		Symbol	Ho
		Atomic No.	67
State	Solid	Atomic Wt.	164.930
Group	IIIB	Valence	3
		m.p.	1743K
		b.p.	2973K

Holmium, is a rare earth metal prepared by reducing holmium fluoride with calcium. In terms of abundance, holmium is present in the earth's crust on the average of 1.2 ppm, ranking ahead of bismuth, antimony, cadmium, and mercury in potential availability. Elemental holmium has a close-packed hexagonal crystal structure at room temperature. It is strongly electropositive ; It has a high magnetic moment and electrical resistivity. It also has scavenging properties. The metal is paramagnetic but as the temperature is lowered, it changes to antiferromagnetic and then to ferromagnetic system. There are no important industrial uses of holmium, though it is of considerable theoretical interest. Tnere is one natural isotope ^{165}Ho, and 18 artificial isotopes have been produced. The natural isotope is not radioactive.

holocellulose. The carbohydrate component of wood ; depending on the species and botanical nature of the wood, its holocellulose content varies between 67 and 80% the remainder being lignin.

holohedral crystal. A crystal that has all of its faces developed.

Holton test. Iodine is detected in the presence of bromine by boiling 0.5 ml. of the solution tested with 15 ml. saturated sodium carbonate solution, filtering, adding excess nitric acid to 1 ml. of the filtrate, then 3 drops of 8% potassium chromate solution and 1 ml. of carbon disulphide, which becomes violet if iodine is present.

Holzer-Reif test reaction. α-Naphthylamine gives a blue or red-violet precipitate with gold chloride, palladium chloride, or ferric chloride.

homo-. A prefix having the meaning of "the same," as in the terms homogeneous ("the same kind"), homologous ("the same proportion)", homopolymer, etc.

Homoazeotrope. Homogeneous mixture of liquids, which distils without change of composition.

homoazeotropic system. Azeotropic system of constituents forming homoazeotrope.

homochromoisomerism. The phenomenon in which different structural modifications of organic compounds exhibit the same colour and identical absorption bands in solution.

homocyclic. A ring or nucleus composed of atoms of the same element which is usually carbon. This is true of cycloparaffins, cycloolefins, benzene and its derivatives, and cyclic terpenes. The term carbocyclic is also used for rings composed only of carbon.

homocyclic compound. An organic compounds containing a homocyclic ring, *i.e.*, a ring containing carbon atoms only. Also known as isocyclic compound.

homodesmic. Pertaining to a crystal, having atoms bonded in a single manner.

homogeneous catalysis. Catalysis in systems where catalyst and reactants constitute one phase.

homogeneous distribution coefficient. Magnitude D in Berthelot-Nernst distribution law indicating how many times ratio of content of a microcomponent to a macrocomponent in a crystalline precipitate is greater ($D > 1$) or smaller ($D < 1$) than analogous ratio in solution containing precipitate.

homogeneous equilibrium. Equilibrium conditions in a system that constitutes a single phase, *i.e.*, reactions in solution or among gases the products of which remain in the same phase as the reactants. In most cases, solid solutions are so far from ideal that equilibrium constants cannot be evaluated, and such systems are treated in terms of the phase rule. A typical gas-phase equilibrium is the ammonia synthesis,

$$N_2 + 3H_2 \rightleftharpoons 2NH_3$$

A typical liquid-phase equilibrium is the dissociation of acetic acid in water,

$$CH_3COOH + H_2O \rightleftharpoons H_3O^+ + CH_3COO^-$$

homogeneous isotopic exchange. Isotopic exchange occurring in a monophase system.

homogeneous precipitation. Slow precipitation of solid by action of suitable reagent which result from chemical homogeneous reaction in whole solution. Also known as precipitation from homogeneous solution.

homogeneous radiation. Radiation having an extremely narrow band of frequencies, or a beam of particles each having same energy.

homogeneous system. Thermodynamic system composed solely of one homogeneous phase.

homogenization. Reduction of the sizes of solid or semisolid particles in aqueous suspension to colloidal dimensions by mechanical action, the purpose being to stabilize the suspension so that the particles will neither rise to the surface nor precipitate. This is performed, for example, on pigments use in latex dispersions. A protective film of a hydrophilic nature (gelatin, casein) is first formed on the particles by wetting them in a water solution of these materials. The coated particles are then passed through a homogenizer, or "colloid mill," which exerts a strong shearing force that reduces the particles to uniform diameter. So-called homogenized milk is made in this way, except that its fat particles have their own protein coating. The operation may also be applied to paints and similar solid-liquid dispersions. The products are not homogeneous in the strict sense of the word. *See also* homogeneous ; heterogeneous.

homogeneous pair. In spectrographic analysis an homologous pair consists of the particular spectral line utilized in the determination of the concentration of an element and an internal standard line, such that the ratio of the intencities of the radiation producing the lines remain unchanged with variations in the conditions of excitation.

homologous series. A series of carbon compounds of the same type which conform to a general formula and in which each member differs from the preceding member by a constant increment of the atomic group CH_2. For example, in the paraffin series we have the general formula C_nH_{2n+2}, and the compounds :

CH_4	methane
C_2H_6	ethane
C_3H_8	propane
C_4H_{10}	butane
C_5H_{12}	pentane
etc.	

The phenomenon is known as homology, the compounds are homologous and any one of them is the homologue of any other in the series.

homologue. A member of an homologous series.

homology. Systematic change of physical properties and similarity of chemical properties displayed by members of homologous series.

homolysis *See* homolytic dissociation.

homolytic dissociation. Fission of covalent bond in molecule, resulting in formation of two atoms or free radicals. Also known as homolysis, homolytic fission.

homolytic fission. *See* homolytic dissociation.

homopolar bond. *See* covalent bond.

homopolar colloid. A colloidal system in which the dispersed particles are nonpolar compounds.

homopolymer. A high polymer made by polymerizing only one monomer substance, as compared with a copolymer, which is made from two or more different monomers. Examples of homopolymers are natural rubber whose monomer is isoprene, and polyethylene, whose monomer is ethylene. *See also* monomer.

homotope. One of the elements in a vertical group of the periodic system, as sodium is a homotope of lithium, potassium, rubidium, cesium, and francium.

honing. The process of removing a relatively small amount of material from a surface by means of obrasive stones to obtain a desired finish or extremely close dimensional tolerance.

Hooker reaction. A shifting of substituent groups in certain naphthoquinones which accompanies side-chain oxidation with alkaline permanganate ; *e.g.*,

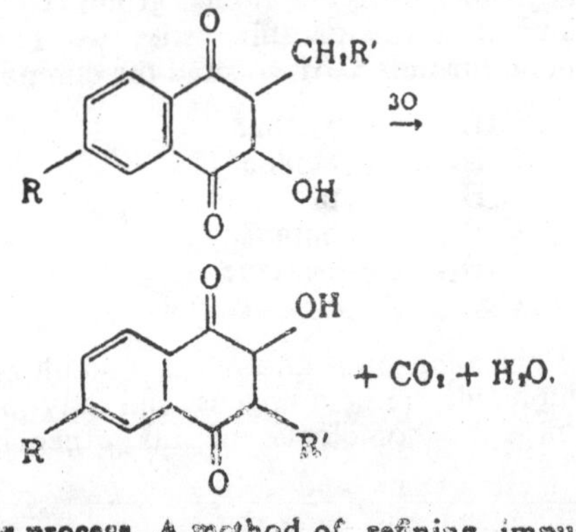

O, CH_2R', R, OH, O $\xrightarrow{3O}$

O, OH, R, R', O $+ CO_2 + H_2O.$

Hoopes process. A method of refining impure metallic aluminium by its electrolysis in a cell in which the anode of the crude aluminium rests on the bottom, the electrolyte is molten cryolite containing some barium fluoride, and the cathode is a layer of pure aluminium floating on the surface.

hormone. One of a number of complex organic substances which control or regulate various metabolic processes in plants and animals. In man they are formed in the so-called ductless glands (adrenal cortex, pituitary, pancreas, thyroid) and are secreted directly into the blood stream. Examples are adrenaline. ACTH, thyroxine, insulin, cortisone esterogen, and testosterone. Some are steroids, others, amino acids, proteins, and polypeptides ; most have been synthesized, but some are made from the specific organs of animals. They regulate such metabolic functions as blood-sugar level (insulin), reproductive functions (esterogen), metabolic rate (adrenaline), and other body processes. They have often been described as chemical messengers. Plant hormones are preferably called plant growth regulators.

Horoszkiewicz-Marx test. To detect carbon monoxide in blood, add 2 ml. blood to 4 ml. hot aqueous 8% quinine hydrochloride solution. Heat to boiling. Cool, add 2 drops fresh ammonium sulphide solution. A bright red colour indicates the presence of carbon monoxide in the blood. Normal blood gives a dirty blue green colour.

hot-atom chemistry. Branch of chemistry concerned with study or reactions occurring in system containing hot atoms.

hot atoms. Atoms formed in nuclear reactions, and of energy corresponding to a temperature of the order of 10^5 K, and taking part in numerous specific chemical reactions. Also known as recoil atoms.

hot cell. Space or set of rooms, shielded biologically, used for handling by remote control of highly radioactive materials for purpose of chemical and mechanical processing, investigation, reloading etc.

hot-melt. In the adhesives and sealants fields, hot-melt refers to a material which is easily liquefied by a relatively low temperature so that it can be poured or spread and which sets quickly on cooling to form a strong and permanent bond. Many hot-melt adhesives contain such synthetics as polyethylene ; hot-melt sealants for highway construction are usually composed of combinations of asphalt, rubber, coal-tar pitch, etc. Low-melting waxes are used in packaging.

hot plasma. Plasma of temperature of order of several millions kelvins.

hot radical. Free radical of substantial kinetic energy, higher than its share of thermal movement for the particular medium and temperature.

hot reactions. Chemical reactions in which hot atoms of energy considerably in excess of 0.025 eV, characterized by their independence of surrounding temperature, state of aggregation and presence of radical scavengers take part.

Houben-Fischer synthesis. Preparation of aromatic nitriles by hydrolysis of trichloromethyl-aryl ketimines ; the hydrolysis must be carried out in an alkaline medium, since acid hydrolysis yields ketones instead of nitriles. The trichloromethylaryl ketimines are prepared from aromatic hydrocarbons and trichloroacetonitrile as in the Hoesch synthesis :

$$C_6H_6 + Cl_3C{-}CN \xrightarrow[AlCl_3]{HCl} C_6H_5{-}C(=NH{\cdot}HCl){-}CCl_3 \longrightarrow$$

$$\xrightarrow{KOHaq} C_6H_5{-}CN + CHCl_3 + KCl + H_2O$$

Houben-Hoesch synthesis. Preparation of aromatic hydroxy ketones by condensation of phenols (or their ethers) with nitriles in presence of hydrogen chloride and zinc chloride (or aluminium chloride), *e.g.*,

$$C_6H_4(OH)_2 + CH_3CN \xrightarrow[ZnCl_2]{HCl} (HO)_2C_6H_3{-}C(=NH{\cdot}HCl)CH_3 \xrightarrow{H_2O} (HO)_2C_6H_3{-}COCH_3$$

Houdry process. A process for the catalytic cracking of the crude oil by the action of activated aluminium hydrosilicate. The charge is heated in a still to about 750K, whence it passes to a vaporizer, from which the vaporized fractions pass to catalyst chambers, after which they are fractionated. The process varies considerably with the nature of the oil changed and the products desired.

Hubl number. The iodine number of a fat or an oil.

Huckel's equation. Semiempirical formula which describes mean activity coefficient $f\pm$ of strong electrolyte :

$$\lg f\pm = -\frac{A\,|\,z_+z_-\,|\,\sqrt{J}}{1+Ba\sqrt{J}} + CJ$$

where a and C=empirical constants.

Huckel's rule. Aromatic character is displayed only by organic compounds containing $(4n+2)$ π-electrons (where n is an integer). Also known as $4n+2$ rule.

Hudson Isorotation rule. The rotational contribution of the terminal carbon atom of an aldose sugar is affected only slightly by changes in any other part of molecule than a contiguous atom ; and changes in the atoms or radicals attached to the terminal carbon atom affect only slightly the rotation of the remainder of the molecule.

Hudson lactone rule. When γ-lactones of aldonic acids are represented by the usual planar projection formula, the lactones having the γ-hydroxyl on the right will be dextrorotatory, and those having it on the left, levorotatory.

Hugoniot equation. Equation

$$\Delta U_m = -\left(p + \frac{1}{2}\,\Delta p\right)\Delta V_m$$

which determines dependence of molar internal energy change ΔU_m on pressure Δp and molar volume ΔV_m changes in shock wave.

humectant. A hygroscopic liquid used to maintain constant moisture content in materials with which it is mixed or associated. Common types are glycerol, some glycols, sorbitol, etc. Humectants are used chiefly in tobacco, as a top dressing on leather and plastic products, in textile products, and in cosmetic preparations (skin creams and lotions). When not actually mixed with the materials, they are able to keep the humidity reasonably constant in small containers for tobacco, etc.

Hume-Rothery phases. Phases which occur in metallic alloys where besides phases of structures characteristic of pure constituents, also phase of regular space-centred structure, phase of complex regular lattice containing 52 atoms, and phase of hexagonal lattice and closest packing are to be seen.

Hume-Rothery rules. When alloy system form distinct phases, it is found that the ratio of the number of valence electrons to the number of atoms is characteristic of the phase (*e.g.*, β, γ, ϵ) whatever the actual elements making up the alloy. Thus both $Na_{31}Pb_8$ and Ni_5Zn_{21} are γ structures, with the electron-atom ratio 21 : 13 The rules are explained by the tendency to form a structure in which all the Brillouin zones are nearly full, or else entirely empty.

humus. That portion of a soil comprised of semidecomposed organic matter (dead vagetation), the modification resulting primarily from the action of bacteria. The lignin, cellulose, and proteins interact to from a diverse range of substances, including aromatic compounds amino acids, polysaccharides, and organic phosphorus compounds. The part played by microorganisms in humus formation is critical, as they not only effect the decomposition of the vegetation but structurally modify its chief components (lignin and carbohydrates); they also are able to synthesize the numerous aromatic substances found in humus.

Hund's rule. Rules which enable the lowest energy term of atom or ion to be determined Russell-Saunders coupling, provided electronic configuration is known.

In atomic spectra, the ground term is associated with the largest multiplicity possible for the available electrons. In general, the lowest energy state of any atom or ion is considered to be the one in which the maximum number of the electrons, compatible with the Pauli's principle have unpaired spins.

Hunsdiecker-Borodin reaction. Decomposition of silver salts of carboxylic acids on treatment with halogens in anhydrous medium, resulting in formation of alkyl halides and carbon dioxide, *e.g.*,

$$RCOOAg + X_2 \rightarrow RX + CO_2 + AgX$$

hybridization. Mixing of atomic valence orbitals with different orbital quantum number *l*. Orbitals constructed in this way have more pronounced directional properties than the original ones. Angles between them are also different from original ones.

hybridized orbital. Atomic orbital constructed by hybridization of atomic orbitals with different orbitals quantum numbers. It has more pronounced directional properties than component orbitals; *e.g.* sp^3 hybridized orbitals constructed of $2s$, $2p_x$, $2p_y$ and $2p_z$ atomic orbitals of carbon atom are used to explain geometry of methane.

hydramine. One of a series of amines derived from the glycols in which one hydroxyl is replaced by an amino group, *e.g.*, oxyethylamine, $CH_2OH.CH_2NH_2$.

hydramine fission. A reaction characteristic of alkaloids having a hydroxyl group in the α-position to the aromatic nucleus and an amino group in the β-position. The nitrogen from the β-position is removed as an ammonia derivative, and the alcoholic group is converted into a carbonyl group.

hydrate. *See* hydration.

hydration. 1. As used by inorganic chemists, this term refers to combination of one or more molecules of water with a crystalline inorganic compound, usually a salt, without rupture of the H—OH bond. Such compounds are called hydrates, the structure being indicated by a centered dot. *e.g.*, $Na_2SO_4 \cdot 10H_2O$. When the water (often called water of crystallization) is removed by heating or other means, the compound is called anhydrous. The same substance may be capable of forming several hydrates, which are designated mono-. tetra-, decahydrates, etc., according to the number of water molecules present. A common group of hydrates are the alums (named from aluminium); the best known of these is $KAl(SO_4)_2 \cdot 12H_2O$. Hydration occurs readily in solution, where the negative portion of the water molecule is attracted to positively charged metal ions.

2. Hydration also refers to the strong affinity of water molecules for ions of dissolved substances, an interaction which is the fundamental cause of electrolytic dissociation. Ions and other charged particles thus acquire a tightly held film of water. Such particles are said to be solvated. This phenomenon may lead to hydrate formation, as defined in (1); it also as important effects in stabilization of colloidal solutions.

hydration isomerism. Type of isomerism based on different arrangement of water molecules in first coordination sphere and beyond it, *e.g.*, $[Cr(H_2O)_6]Cl_3$, $[Cr(H_2O)_5Cl]Cl_2.H_2O$, $[Cr(H_2O)_4Cl_2]Cl.2H_2O$. Also known as hydrate isomerism.

hydrazide. A compound of the general type, $R-\overset{\overset{\displaystyle O}{\|}}{C}-NH-NH_2$, in which R is commonly an alkyl group.

hydrazino. The radical $H_2N=NH-$.

hydrazo. The radical $-HN=NH-$ (the two bonds are not attached to the same atom).

hydrazone. A compound of the general type $RNH-N=CR'R''$ formed by reaction between a hydrazine and compound containing a carbonyl group.

hydrazono. The radical $H_2NN=$.

hydride. A compound formed by combination of hydrogen either with a single metal (lithium hidride, LiH), with two metals (sodium aluminium hybride, $NaAlH_4$), or with a metal and a nonmetal plus an organic group. The latter are called organometallic hydrides. Hydrides are hazardous materials which may catch fire when rubbed or agitated. They are powerful reducing agents used in chemical conversion reactions; they are also employed as sources of hydrogen and as catalysts. The boron hydride, or boranes, have been researched extensively because of their high energy capability; they evolve hydrogen in the presence of water and are spontaneously flammable. The gas arsine (AsH_3) is extremely poisonous. The organometallic hydrides are assuming prominence and are competitive with the inorganic type.

hydrido complexes. Complex hydrides containing a hydride ligand bonded to a central metal atom. The prefix hydro- instead of hyddrido is sometimes used. All are soluble in aromatic hydrocarbons.

hydro-. A prefix derived from the Greek word for water; in many chemical terms such as hydrocarbon and hydrogenation, it merely indicates the presence of hydrogen. Closely related is the prefix hygro, meaning "dampness" or "moisture," as in hygroscopic (absorbing moisture").

hydroboration. Addition of diborane $(BH_3)_2$ to unsaturated organic compound with formation of trialkylborane, *e.g.*,

$$6RCH=CH_2+(BH_3)_2 \rightarrow 2(RCH_2CH_2)_3B$$

hydrocarbon. Any compound composed of carbon and hydrogen; hydrocarbons may be gases (methane), liquids (benzene) or solids (waxes).

These are regarded as the parent substances in organic chemistry from which all other organic compounds may be considered derived. They are classed as saturated, unsaturated, aliphatic, aromatic, etc.

Their chemical structure may be straight- or branched-chain, alicyclic. The chief sources are coal, natural gas, petroleum and plant life. They have multitudinous uses as heating fuels, solvents, gasoline, and as starting materials for synthetic chemicals.

hydrocolloid. A hydrophilic colloidal material used largely in food products as emulsifying, thinkening and gelling agents. They readily absorb water, thus increasing viscosity and imparting smoothness and body texture to the product, even in concentrations of less than 1%. Natural types are plant exudates (gum arabic), seaweed extracts (agar), plant seed gums or mucilages (guar gum), cereal gums (starches), fermentation gums (dextran), and animal products (gelatin). Semisynthetic types are modified celluloses and modified starches. Completely synthetic types are also available, *e.g.*, polyvinylpyrrolidone. Most are carbohydrate polymers, but a few, such as gelatin and casein, are proteins.

hydrocooling. Removing heat from freshly harvested fruits and vegetables by immersion in ice water, then while still wet, subjected to vacuum. The evaporation of water chills the fruits and vegetables.

hydrocracking. Cracking of petroleum or its products in the presence of hydrogen and a suitable catalyst.

hydrodelkylation. A term used in petroleum technology to describe a method of removing methyl groups (or other alkyl groups) from a hydrocarbon compound and replacing them with hydrogen. This effected by treating the compound with hydrogen at high temperatures and pressures. For example, toluene ($CH_3C_6H_5$)

can be converted to benzene (C_6H_6) in this way The process is also useful in improving the quality of more complex petroleum distillation product.

hydrodistillation. Removal of essential oils from plant components by using high temperature system.

hydrodynamic stage. In statistical mechanics, last stage of time evolution of microscopic system in which dissipative processes occur leading from local equilibrium to thermodynamic equilibrium of the whole system.

hydrofining. A high-pressure catalytic process for the hydrogenation of low-grade petroleum fractions, to produce gasolines and lubricating oils that are exceptionally high in quality. Pressures are used as high as 3500 pounds per square inch, temperatures of 410-430°C, and a widely used catalyst is molybdenum oxide.

hydroforming. The operation of converting hydrocarbons of low octane number and other undesirable properties into a stable fuel of higher octane rating. The operation may be conducted by subjecting the material to temperatures ranging from 480°C-540°C, at a pressure of 150-300 pounds per square inch, including a high partial pressure of hydrogen to minimize carbon formation, and a suitable catalyst. During the process various reactions occur, including considerable cracking and aromatization.

hydroformylation. Aaddition of carbon monoxide and hydrogen to unsaturated compound with formation of aldehyde, *e.g.*,

$$\geq C{=}C\leq + CO + H_2 \xrightarrow[\text{3MPa, Catalyst}]{200^\circ C} -\overset{|}{\underset{|}{C}}H-\overset{|}{\underset{|}{C}}-\overset{O}{\overset{\|}{C}}-H$$

Also known as oxo process.

hydrogasification. Production of gaseous of liquid fuels by direct addition of hodrogen to coal.

hydrogel. A colloidal gel in which water is the dispersion medium for example, coagulated silicic acid.

hydrogen. An element :

		Symbol	H
		Atomic No.	1
		Atomic Wt.	1.00797
State	Gas	Valence	1
Group	IA	Isotopes	
		(stable)	^1H ; ^2H
		(radioactive)	^3H
		m.p.	13.8K
		b.p.	20.13K
		critical temperature	30.0K
		critical pressure	13.0 atm.
		critical density	0.0301g/cm^3

Hydrogen is by far the most abundant element in the universe. Solid hydrogen has a hexagonal crystal structure. Hydrogen at standard conditions is a colourless, odourless, tasteless gas, suffocating, but not toxic. Atomic hydrogen, made up of one proton and one electron, is represented by H ; molecular hydrogen is a diatomic molecule represented by H_2 ; the isotope deuterium (one proton and one neutron in the nucleus) is represented by ^2H ; or D; the isotope tritium (one proton and two neutrons is indicated by ^3H or T. Normal hydrogen (protium) and deuterium are stable, whereas tritium is radioactive, with a half-life of 12.26 years. Tritium emits a negative electron to form ^3He. It is estimated that the isotopic abundance of ^1H (protium) in natural occurring hydrogen is 99.9851% and on the basis of carbon=12 (atomic weight scale), protium has a mass of 1.007825 amu. The isotopic abundance of ^2H deuterium) is estimated at 0.0149% with a mass 2.014101 amu. The artificially-prepared ^3H (tritium), $^9Be + ^2H \rightarrow 2\,^4He + ^3H$, has a mass of 3.01605 amu. Hydrogen is the lightest of all elements and is extremely flammable over a concentration range of 4 to 75% by volume. As hydrogen is a major potential energy source, there is containing active research on its use as a fuel.

Hydrogen is the characteristic element of acids and is a constituent of water, hydrocarbons and is widely distributed not only on the earth but throughout the universe. Among its many chemical uses are production of ammonia and methyl alcohol, numerous hydrogenation reactions (especially of fatty acids) and oxidation-reduction reactions. It is essential in many catalytic reaction in petroleum refining (hydrocracking, hydrodealkylation, etc.). It is also used in welding and in meteorological balloons.

hydrogenation. Process of catalytic addition of

hydrogen molecule to organic compound molecule containing multiple bond, *e.g.*

$$C_6H_6 + 3H_2 \xrightarrow[200^\circ C,\ 20\ MPa]{Ni} C_6H_{12}$$

Destructive hydrogenation, in which organic molecules split into smaller ones capable of reacting with hydrogen, occurs in catalytic hydrocracking of gasoline (hydrogenolysis). Reactions of hydrogen with inorganic materials are not considered as hydrogenation.

hydrogenation of coal. The manufacture of artificial mineral oil from coal by the action of hydrogen. This depends on causing the carbon in coal to combine with hydrogen to form hydrocarbons.

hydrogenation of oils. Artificial hardening of liquid animal and vegetable oils by the action of hydrogen. Liquid fats and oils contain a high percentage of liquid triolein, $C_{57}H_{104}O_6$, which may be converted into a solid tristearin, $C_{57}H_{110}O_6$, by the action of hydrogen in the presence of finely divided nickel as catalyst ; the result being a hard fat of higher melting point.

hydrogen bomb. Explosion system based on synthesis reaction of light nuclei of deuterium and tritium, occurring at temperature of the order of 10^6 K.

hydrogen bond. Weak chemical bond formed between hydrogen and strongly electronegative atoms, such as nitrogen, oxygen or fluorine.

This attractive force effects an association between the molecules of liquids such as water and alcohols, holding them together almost as if they were one huge molecule. Hydrogen bonding at least partially accounts for the fact that alcohols and water do not evaporate rapidly. Bonding of this type is relatively weak ; it may be represented by :

```
 H   H   H
:Ö:H:Ö:H:Ö:H
 ..  ..  ..
```

hydrogen-bonded crystals. Crystals built of molecules kept together by hydrogen bonds. They are characterized by tendency to polymerize and by increased energy of crystal lattice.

hydrogen electrode. Electrode (half-cell) constructed from platinum or palladium covered by platinum black, dipped into solution containing hydrogen ions and saturated with hydrogen, $Pt, H_2/H_3O^+$; electrode reaction is

$$1/2H_2 + H_2O \rightleftharpoons H_3O^+ + e^-$$

and electrode potential

$$\epsilon = \epsilon^\circ + \frac{RT}{F} \ln \frac{a_{H_3O^+}}{a_{p_{H_2}}}$$

where ϵ° = standard electrode potentiol and ap_{H_2} = volatility of hydrogen.

The hydrogen electrode reversible to hydrogen ion and its electrical potential is a logarithmic function to hydrogen-ion activity. Because of this reaction, this electrode is used to measure hydrogen-ion activity. It cannot be used in reducing or oxidising solutions or in solutions that poison the surface of the noble metal.

hydrogen equivalent. The effective acidity of an acid, or basicity of a base, as measured by the number of hydrogen equivalents per mole of acid (or, in other words, the number of replaceable or reactable hydrogen atoms per molecule), or the number of hydroxyl equivalents per mole of the base.

hydrogenolysis. Catalytic hydrogen reduction with partial destruction of substrate and formation of molecules of lower molecular weight (than original ones) or with ring opening, *e.g.*,

$$\text{cyclo-}(CH_2)_5 \xrightarrow{[H]} CH_3(CH_2)_3CH_3$$

Also known as destructive hydrogenation.

hydrogen, ortho and para. *See* ortho and para hydrogen.

hydrolases. A class of enzymes that control hydrolysis ; *e.g.*, esterases; proteases.

hydrolysis. A chemical reaction in which water reacts with another compound so that both it and the compound are cleaved or split ; the water decomposes to its ion, hydrogen and hydroxyl, each of which reacts with a portion of the cleaved compound. In inorganic chemistry, it refers to hydrolysis of salts of a weak acid and strong base to give a basic solution, *e.g.*, $CH_3COONa + H_2O \rightarrow NaOH + CH_3COOH$, or of salts of a strong acid and a weak base to give an acidic solution, *e.g.*, $SiCl_4 + 4H_2O \rightarrow SiO_2.xH_2O + 4HCl$. Hydrolysis also refers to the interaction of water with certain molecules, such as phosphorus tribromide ; $PBr_3 + 3H_2O \rightarrow P(OH)_3 + 3HBr$. The rate of reaction with water is generally increased with the addition of an acid or base to increase the concentration of hydrogen or hydroxyl ions. In organic chemistry, many types of hydrolysis are important, among them are :

(1) formation of a fatty acid and an alcohol by hydrolysis of an ester $CH_3COOC_2H_5 + H_2O \rightarrow CH_3COOH + C_2H_5OH$) ;

(2) conversion of starch to sugar by enzyme-catalyzed hydrolysis ;

(3) hydroytic separation (cleavage) of proteins to amino acids ;

(4) fat-splitting and saponification reactions. Catalysts are normally required to accelerate hydrolysis; enzymes and bacteria are frequently involved in such catalysis. *See also* solvolysis, saponification.

hydrolysis constant, K_h. Equilibrium constant of hydrolysis reaction (*see* hydrolysis) ; for salt of weak acid (HA) and strong base :

$$K_h = \frac{a_{HA}\, a_{OH^-}}{a_{A^+}} = \frac{L_{H_2O}}{K_{HA}}$$

for salt of strong acid and weak base (B) :

$$K_h = \frac{a_B a_{H_3O^+}}{a_{BH^+}} = \frac{L_{H_2O}}{K_B}$$

and for salt of weak acid (HA) and weak base (B) :

$$K_h = \frac{a_{HA} a_B}{a_{A^+} a_{BH^+}} = \frac{L_{H_2O}}{K_{HA}\, K_B}$$

where K_{HA} and K_B=dissociation constants of weak acid and base respectively, L_{H_2O}=ionic product of water.

hydrolytic adsroption. Exchange adsorption with participation of hydrogen or hydroxylic ions.

hydrolytic dissociation. 1. The hydrolysis of a salt upon solution in water, *e.g.*, sodium phenolate hydrolyzes as follows :

$$C_6H_5ONa + H_2O \rightarrow NaOH + C_6H_5OH$$

2. Ionization upon solution in water.

hydrolytic enzyme. An enxyme that catalyzes, such as pepsin, maltase, emulsin, invertase.

hydrolytic processes. The reactions of both organic and inorganic chemistry where in water affects a double decomposition with another compound, hydrogen going to one component, and hydroxyl to another ; *e.g.*,

$$AB + H_2O \rightarrow H{-}B + A{-}OH$$

$$KCN + H_2O \rightarrow H{-}CN + K{-}OH$$

$$C_5H_{11}Cl + H_2O \rightarrow H{-}Cl + C_5H_{11}{-}OH$$

hydrolytic reactions can be classified as :

(*i*) hydrolysis with water alone ;

(*ii*) hydrolysis with dilute or concentrated acids ;

(*iii*) hydrolysis with dilute or concentrated alkali ; and

(*iv*) hydrolysis with fused alkali with little or no water at high temperature.

hydrometallurgy. The extráction and recovery of metals from their ores by processes in which aqueous solutions play a predominant role. Hydrometallurgy occupies an important role in the production of aluminium, copper, cobalt, gold, nickel, platinum metals, selenium, silver, tellurium, tungsten, zinc and other metals.

hydrone process. A method of preparing hydrogen of high purity by reaction of a lead-sodium alloy with water.

hydronium ion. An ion (H_3O^+) formed by the transfer of a proton (hydrogen nucleus) from one molecule of H_2O to another ; a companion ion (OH^-) is also formed ; the reaction is $2H_2O \rightarrow H_3O^+ + OH^-$. Formation of such ions is very infrequent, resulting from the interaction of water molecules in a ratio of about 1 to 550 million.

hydroperoxide. An organic peroxide having the generalized formula ROOH. In which R represents an organic group (either alkyl or aryl). An example is ethyl hydroperoxide (C_2H_5OOH).

hydrophilic. 1. With the literal meaning of "water-loving," this term refers to substances that tend to absorb and retain water; this results in swelling, often accompanied by formation of gels. This property is characteristic of some proteins (collagen, gelatin), water-soluble gums (arabic, tragacanth), pectins, and starches, as well as of some types of clay such as bentonite. Hydrophilic agents are widely used as stabilizers and thickeners in food products, pharmaceuticals, and coatings for textiles, paper, etc. The term should not be confused with hydroscopic. *See also* gel; bentonite; hydroscopic; hygrocolloid.

2. The term is also applied to the surfaces of solids which are readily wetted by water or on which water is adsorbed easily. Thus, wetting is important, *e.g.*, in detergency and in the secondary recovery of oil which involves the displacement of oil from sand by water.

hydrophobic. Literally meaning "water-hating," this term describes substances which repel water and thus are difficult to "wet" or emulsify. Most notable of these are fats, waxes, and oils, but this property is also found in many solids in finely divided form, *e.g.*, carbon black, magnesium carbonate, and metal powders. Rubber notably hydrophobic, as are many synthetic polymers. In liquids, this property is often due to differences in surface tension.

hydrosol. A colloidal system in which the dispersion medium is water.

hydrosulphate. A salt formed when an organic base, (*e.g.*, an alkaloid) combines with sulphuric acid. The salt so formed is usually more soluble than the base.

hydrosulphide. A compound containing the univalent —HS group.

hydrosynthesis. The correlative of hydrolysis or condensation reaction in which water is eliminated.

hydrous. Containing either admixed or combined water.

-hydroxamamide. A suffix indicating the group —C(=NOH)NH_2, commonly introduced by replacement of the carboxy radical.

-hydroxamic. A suffix indicating the radical —C(=NOH)(OH) or its tautomer —C(=O)-(NHOH), commonly introduced by replacement of the carboxy radical.

hydroxamino. The radical HONH—.

hydroxylation. Reaction of alkenes with oxidizing agents ($KMnO_4$, H_2O_2 etc.) resulting in formation of 1,2-diols, *e.g.*,

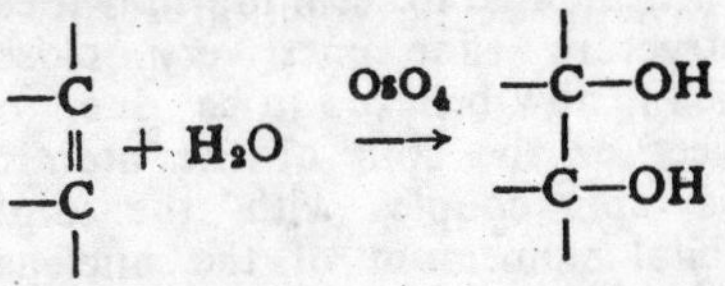

$$\begin{array}{c} | \\ -C \\ \| \\ -C \\ | \end{array} + H_2O \xrightarrow{OsO_4} \begin{array}{c} | \\ -C-OH \\ | \\ -C-OH \\ | \end{array}$$

hydroxymethylation. Introduction of hydroxymethyl group $—CH_2OH$ into molecule of organic compound, *e.g.*,

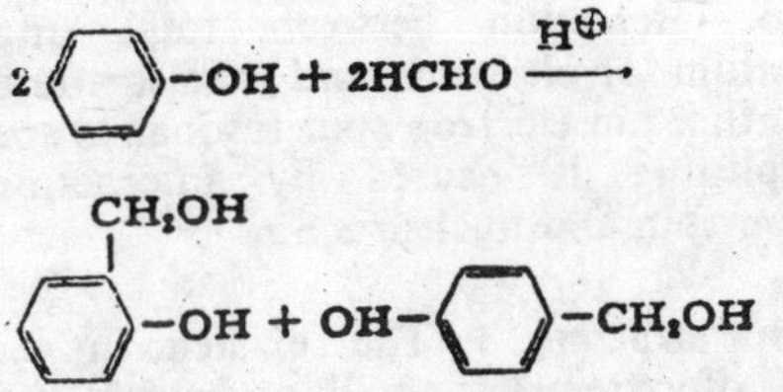

$$2\ C_6H_5\text{—}OH + 2HCHO \xrightarrow{H^{\oplus}}$$

$$\text{(o-}CH_2OH\text{)}C_6H_4\text{—}OH + OH\text{—}C_6H_4\text{—}CH_2OH$$

hygroscopic. A term used to describe solid or liquid materials which pick up and retain water vapour from the air. Some solids having a high internal surface area are made especially for this purpose; by adsorbing vapour molecules they can maintain a small volume of air virtually free from moisture.

hypercharge, Y. Additive dimensionless quantum number defined of hadrons and photons as sum of baryon number and strangeness $Y=B+S$. Hypercharge always has internal values. Hypercharge was introduced to formalize the observation that certain decay modes of baryons expected to proceed by means of the strong nuclear force simply were not observed.

hyperconjugation. Conjugation of σ-electron of C—H bonds in alkyl groups with adjacent π-electrons of double bonds, *e.g.*, in toluene:

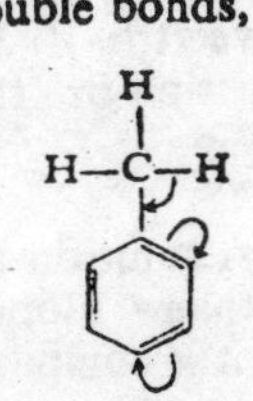

$$\begin{array}{c} H \\ | \\ H\text{—}C\text{—}H \\ | \\ C_6H_5 \end{array}$$

hyperfine interaction. Interaction between electron magnetic moments and nuclear magnetic moments in atom, ion or molecule which leads to hyperfine structure of spectral lines in atomic spectra and electron spin resonance spectra.

hyperfine spectrum. In the case of atomic emission spectra, there is, in addition to the fine strucure (*see* spectrum, fine) of the spectral lines attributable to term multiplicities a hyperfine structure (fine lines very close together), which is now believed to be due to an isotope effect or the spin of the atomic nucleus. This spin couples with the total angular or orbital momentum of the nucleus and yields a series of resulting vectors representative of closely spaced energy levels.

hyperfine splitting. Splitting of energy levels due to interaction between total angular momentum of electrons and nuclear angular momentum ; in electron spin resonance spectra this splitting is caused by interaction of electron spin and nuclear spin.

hyperfine structure. 1. The existenc in certain spectra of extremely fine lines, which become evident only at very high resolution, or very high sensitivity, and were overlooked in early investigations, of the fine structure. The hyperfine structures are explained in some cases as due to the spin momentum of the atomic nucleus, which produces, by interaction with the resultant quantum number of the electronic system, a series of values for the total angular momentum of the whole atom.

2. Splitting of resonance lines due to interaction between electron spin and nuclear spin.

hyperons. Elementary particles, hadrons, having mass greater than that of the neutron and less than that of deuteron. Hyperon is a collective name for any baryon with nonzero strangeness number *s*. The name hyperon has generally been limited to particles which are semistable, *i.e.*, which have long lifetimes relative to 10^{-22}s and which decay by photon emission or through weaker decay interactions.

hypertonic solution. A solution having a higher osmotic pressure than blood or another solution with which it is compared.

hypo-. 1. A prefix used in inorganic chemistry to denote acids and salt whose central multivalent positive element is in its lowest oxidation state ; it is also the acid or salt containing the least oxygen. Examples are hypochlorous acid, HOCl, in which Cl has a valence of +1, and hypophosphorous acid, H_3PO_2, in which phosphorus P has a valence of +1. Salts of these acids also carry the prefix hypo.

2. Other meanings of hypo vary some what but have the general sense of "below," "less than," and "underneath," which appear in such terms as hypodermic ("underneath the skin"). It is the opposite of hyper.

3. Hypo is often used as a slang term in the photographic industry to refer to sodium thiosulphate, a solution of which is a developing assistant. This compound is erroneously called sodium hyposulphite.

hypochromic effect. Decrease of absorption coefficient due to structural changes of absorbing substance.

hypotonic solution. A solution having a lower osmotic pressure than blood or another solution with which it is compared.

hypsochrome. Atom or group of atoms which, when substituted into molecule of organic compound, shift its absorption spectrum towards shorter wavelengths. Also known as hypsochromic group.

hypsochromic group. *See* hypsochrome.

hypsochromic shift. Shift of light absorption towards higher frequencies.

hysteresis. The dissipation of energy in one form or another in a material, when the forces acting on it are reversed. This applies, for example, to the magnetic induction of iron and iron alloys which does not respond reversibly to change in the magnetizing force, as well as to the resilient energy of rubber and other elastomers, some of which is "lost" when the deforming force is reversed, the energy decrement appearing as heat. The term actually means "lagging behind."

I

I. The symbol for iodine. Symbol for moment of inertia. Symbol for light intensity. Symbol for electric current. Symbol for instantaneous electric current. Symbol for ionic strength. Symbol for candle power, or luminous intensity. Symbol for integration constant of Gibbs function equation (I). Symbol for nuclear spin. Symbol for strength of magnetic shell (I).

i. Abbreviation for *iso* or inactive. The van't Hoff factor, mole factor or van't Hoff coefficient.

-ic. A suffix used in naming inorganic compounds to indicate that the multivalent positive element in the compound is in its highest valence state.

ice point. The temperature at which liquid and solid water are in equilibrium under atmospheric pressure.

-ide. A suffix used in naming compounds comprised of two elements ; in such names, the first element, being electropositive, retains its name without change, but the second, being elecronegative, utilizes the suffix *-ide* as a modification of the elemental name ; for example, calcium hydroxide, sodium chloride, lithium nitride, calcium carbide etc.

ideal. Description of a substance or system which exists only in theory, that is, which is in exact accord with the principles governing its behaviour. The term perfect is also used in the same sense.

ideal gas. Gas which satisfies equation of state $pVm=RT$, where p = pressure, Vm = molar volume, T=thermodynamic temperature, and R=molar gas constant. In statistical mechanics this means that there is no interaction between particles of such a gas. Also known as classical gas, perfect gas.

ideal gas equation of state. Thermal equation of state resulting from empirical laws of ideal gases :

$$pVm = RT$$

where p=pressure, Vm=molar gas volume, T=thermodynamic temperature, R=universal gas constant.

ideal solution. A solution which behaves exactly in accordance with Raoult's law and various relationships derived from it, all temperatures and concentrations, *i.e.*, the solution whose mixing thermodynamic potential G^M satisfies equation :

$$G^M = RT\sum_B x_B \ln x_B$$

where R=molar gas constant, T=thermodynamic temperature, x_B=mole fraction of component B ; mixing enthalpy and volume of ideal mixture are equal to zero. Many real solutions approach ideal behaviour more or less closely when highly dilute, deviations from ideality becoming more marked the higher the concentration.

-idene. This suffix or word-part, added to any radical, usually means a double bond at the point of attachment.

identification. In qualitative analysis determination of identity of investigated substance. Chemical reaction which enables detection of a given chemical substance is known as identification reaction.

identification reaction. *See* identification.

identity period. In any polymeric substance, the characteristic repeating unit, or monomer, which may occur an indefinite number of times in the natural or synthetic molecule ; its length is usually measured in angstrom unit. The structure within the brackets in the following example indicate identity period of anhydro-glucose units in cellulose.

idiomorphous. Appearing in distinct crystals.

ignition. 1. The process of complete oxidation.

2. The initiation of such a process.

3. The process of heating a substance until it ceases to lose-weight, indicating that all thermal decomposition, including losses of moisture and volatile matter which may occur up to the temperature of heating; has been completed.

ignition point. Lowest temperature necessary to start combustion of substance in precisely defined and usually normalized conditions. It is also called ignition temperature.

ignition temperature. *See* ignition point.

Ilinski-Knorre reagent for cobalt and nickel. A solution of α-nitroso-β-naphthol in 50% acetic acid; it forms a red precipitate with cobalt solutions, and a brown precipitate with nickel solutions.

Ilkovic equation. Equation:

$$i_t = 607\, n\, m^{2/3} t^{1/6}\, D^{1/2} C^{\circ}$$

which relates polarographic limiting current i_t to concentration of reactant C°, its diffusion coefficient D; n = number of electrons transferred in electrode reaction, m = efficiency of capillary and t = drop time.

imazine. The radical =C=N—CH=N—.

-imide. A suffix indicating the radical —NH or —CONHCO—, introduced in the case of the former, by replacement of two acid hydroxide groups, or in the case of the latter, by replacement of two methyl groups.

imidic. A suffix indicating the radical

—C(:NH)OH

introduced by replacement of a carboxy group.

imido. The radical NH= (properly in acid groups only; sometimes used synonymously with imino).

-imine. A suffix indicating the —NH radical, introduced by replacement of two hydrogen atoms attached to the same atom. Such compounds are highly reactive more so than the carbon-nitrogen triple bond characteristic of nitriles.

imino. The radical NH=.

iminoquinole. One of a series of compounds of the general type formula:

HO R

NH

in which R is an alkyl radical.

immiscible. A term used to describe substances of the same phase that cannot be uniformly mixed or blended. It usually applies to liquids, such as oil and water, but may also refer to solids in powder form which differ widely in some physical property, such as magnesium carbonate and barium sulphate. In the case of liquids, immiscibility is due to differences in their chemical nature, which can often be overcome by addition of a third substance called an emulsifier or detergent.

immunochemistry. The chemistry of antibodies and antigens and their disease-protective mechanism in animals and man. It primarily involves the study of specialized proteins, structural antagonism, allergies, and related responses.

immunoelectrophoresis. A combination of techniques of electrophoresis and immunodiffusion used to separate the components of a mixture of antigens and make them visible by reaction with specific antibodies.

immunofluorescence. A technique that used a fluorochrome to indicate the occurrence of a specific antibodies.

immunoglobulin. Any of a set of serum glycoproteins which have the ability to bind other molecules with a high degree of specificity.

impalpable. A term used to refer to a powder composed of particles that are too small to be sensed as such by manipulation with the fingers. Such powders usually have a slippery feeling, such as talc and mica, and thus have definite lubricating properties.

impermeable. Relatively resistant to the passage of a gas, vapour, or liquid. For example, many synthetic rubbers are said to be impermeable to air by which is meant that air will pass through them much less slowly than through natural rubber. There are few materials that are absolutely impermeable to gases ; glass most nearly approaches this, but helium will migrate through it at cryogenic temperatures.

impingement. A term used in the chemical industry to refer to a carbon black made by combustion of natural gas in an open burner the carbon given off, being collected on a metal surface (called a channel) immediately above the burner.

impregnation. The incorporation of one substance into another, usually in a finely-divided or finely-separated form.

improver. A bleaching or whitening agent, as nitrosyl chloride, or chlorine, which is added to flour to remove or mask the colour ; or a mixture of starch and salts added to flour to stimulate the yeast and improve the rising properties of the bread.

impurity. An extremely low percentage of an extraneous substance either naturally present in a material or added to it accidentally or intentionally. Often it is impossible to completely eliminate naturally occurring impurities by any separation method, but there are many processes that are effective in reducing them to an acceptable minimum. So small are the amounts involved that impurities are usually indicated in parts per million (ppm).

In solid state chemistry, imperfections in crystal lattice consisting in occupation of some nodes or interstitial positions by atoms or ions of other elements.

incineration. The process of complete oxidation.

inclusion compounds. Molecular compounds in which molecules of first ("guest") component are enclosed in intermolecular free spaces present in crystalline structure or crystal lattice of second ("host") component.

incoherent scattering. Scattering on more than one scattering centre in which incident wave (particle) interacts with each centre separately. During incoherent scattering interference effects do not occur because intensity (but not amplitude) of scattered wave is sum of intensities of waves scattered on particular centres.

incompatibility. In pharmacy a condition which arises when two substances possess properties which cannot be harmonized. Incompatibility is termed chemical, pharmaceutical, or physiological according to whether the compounds react upon each other in an undesirable manner, are immiscible like oil and water or liquefy like mixtures of camphor and methol, or are physiological antagonists like atropine and pilocarpine or strychnine and chloral hydrate.

incompressible volume. That portion of the total volume of a gas which consists of the actual bulk of the gas molecules, rather than the spaces between molecules. It is because of the large amount of empty space between molecules that gases are easily compressible ; the ideal gas law describes the behaviour of a (hypothetical) gas which has no incompressible volume. It is denoted by the quantity *b* in the van der Waals equation.

incongruent melting point. Point on phase diagram in which solid phase disintegrates partially into liquid phase and in part into another solid phase ; new phases differ in chemical composition.

increment. Portion of investigated material taken once from one part of material.

indamines. Dyestuffs derived from one of the indoanilines by substitution of —NH for the quinone oxygen. Phenylene blue,

$$C_6H_4{-}N{-}C_6H_4NH_2$$
$$\diagdown\diagup$$
$$NH$$

is a representative indamine.

independent component of phase system. Component which has to be defined qualitatively and quantitatively. Such definition is necessary and sufficient for description of chemical composition of every phase in system.

indeterminancy principle. *See* uncertainty principle.

indicator. A substance which shows by a colour change, or other visible manifestation, some change in or particular condition of, the chemical nature of a system. Thus acid-base indicators may be used to indicate the end point of a particular neutralization reaction, or they may also be used to indicate the *p*H value of a system.

Many indicators are organic dyes (Congo red, methyl orange, methylene blue, litmus) which change colour within a specific range of *p*H, as from red to yellow or blue to red. Others are derivatives of phthalic anhydride (phenolphthalein), which are colourless under acid conditions and red under basic conditions.

indicator, adsorption. An indicator which shows the end point of a titration by a change in its colloidal condition, commonly by being released from adsorption, or by being adsorbed upon the precipitate, so that the precipitate, which had been coloured by the adsorbed dye, becomes colourless, or much less strongly coloured ; or vice-versa.

indicator electrode. Electrode (half-cell) with potential dependent on the kind and concentration of electroactive substance.

indicator error of acid-base indicator. Error due to change of concentration of protons or hydroxyl ions by their reaction with indicator.

indicator, external. *See* external indicator.

indicator, fluorescent. *See* fluorescent indicator.

indicator, internal. *See* internal indicator.

indicator, neutralization. *See* neutralization indicator.

indicator, oxidation-reduction. *See* redox indicator,

indicator, radioactive. *See* radioactive indicator.

indicator, universal. *See* universal indicator.

indium. An element

State Solid		Symbol	In
Group IIIA		Atomic No.	49
		Atomic Wt.	114.82
		Valence	1,3
		Isotopes	2 stable
		m.p.	429.6K

Indium occurs in the earth's crust to the extent of about 0.000001% and is normally found in concentrations of 0.1% or less. It is a very soft, silvery metal, always occurring as a component of ores of other metals ; it is corrosion-resistant at room temperature and thus used as a coating for bearings. It alloys readily with many other metals, the products being used for brazing and soldering. It is also useful in semiconductor and electronic technology. In reaction, indium is able to form covalent rather than ionic bonds. It has no toxic properties.

indophenine reaction. Coloured (blue) reaction of isatine with thiophene in presence of sulphuric acid, applied for identification of thiophene.

induced activity. Radioactivity induced in irradiated material by activation.

induced dipole. Dipole formed by charge separation due to external electric field and vanishing when field is absent.

induced dipole moment. Dipole mement induced by electric field and determined by sum of electronic and atomic polarizations.

induced enzyme. An enzyme that is not made by the cell (*i.e.*, is repressed) unless it is induced by its substrate or a closely related compound.

induced fission. Fission taking place only as a result of bombardment of nucleus with neutrons, gamma rays or other carriers of energy.

induced fit. A change in the shape of an enzyme to confirm to the structure of its substrate.

induced polarization. Sum of molar atomic and electronic polarizations, approximately equal to molar refraction. Also known as deformation polarization, distortion polarization.

induced radioactivity. The production of radioactive elements by bombardment of other elements, commonly the stable ones, with alpha particles, neutrons, protons, and other particles or radiations. The artificial radioactive elements (commonly called radioelements) usually, but not always, have short life periods ; they emit electrons, positrons, and other particles, as well as gamma rays, in their decomposition.

induced reaction. A reaction that is accelerated when one or more, but not all, of its reactants enter into another reaction with one or more other substance.

In system of coupled reactions, path of secondary reaction which depends on simultaneous run of primary, initiating reaction. *See also* coupled reactions.

induction. 1. The initiation or occurrence of an induced reaction.

2. The production of an electric charge or magnetic field in a substance by the approach or proximity of an electrified body, a magnet or any other source of an electric or magnetic field, the term induction implying that there is a relatively poor conduction of electricity, or a relatively non-magnetized medium, between the body in which the electric or magnetic effect is induced and the electrified body, or other source of the electric or magnetic field.

induction effect. One of the components of intermolecular forces. Induction effect leads to attractive intermolecular forces between pair of molecules one of which is charged or has permanent higher multipole moment in other molecule.

induction factor. In coupled reactions, ratio of acceptor concentration loss to loss of inductor concentration.

If the substances entering into a simple induced reaction are designated as follows :

For the induced reaction,

$$A + B \rightarrow X \ldots$$

and for the reaction which accelerates the induced reaction,

$$A + C \rightarrow Y \ldots$$

then the induction factor is :

$$\frac{\text{Rate at which } B \text{ is transformed}}{\text{Rate at which } C \text{ is transformed}}$$

induction period. Time elapsing between point at which system is ready to react and actual start of reaction.

inductive effect in organic chemistry. Polarization of bonds in organic molecule by dipole existing in bond linking electronegative substituent of electronegativity other than that of hydrogen with rest of molecule (it is assumed that inductive effect of C—H bond is zero). Inductive effect is more pronounced in molecule containing more polarizable double bonds :

$$CH_3 \rightarrow CH_2 \rightarrow Cl$$

$$CH_2 \rightarrow CH \rightarrow CH_2 \rightarrow Cl$$

Arrows indicate direction of electron shift.

inductor. In induced reactions, the substance which takes part in the accelerating reaction as distinguished from the actor which takes part in both, and from the receptor which takes only in the induced reaction. Thus if the induced reaction is

$$A + B \rightarrow X \ldots$$

and the reaction which accelerates it is

$$A + C \rightarrow Y \ldots$$

then *C* is the inductor, *A*, the actor, and *B*, the receptor.

induline. One of a group of black or blue dyes containing the ring structure

$$HN{=}C_6H_3 \overset{N}{\underset{NR}{\langle\rangle}} C_6H_4$$

industrial alcohol. This term includes four items (*i*) pure ethyl alcohol used by chemical manufacturers for nonbeverage use, with or without payment of tax, depending on the circumstances of its use (scientific research, government agencies, etc.) ; (*ii*) completely denatured alcohol ; (*iii*) specially denatured alcohol ; and (*iv*) proprietary solvents made from these. *See also* denaturant.

industrial carbon. A general term considered to include all forms of carbon used for industrial purposes with the exception of fuels ; it does not include graphite and diamond but does encompass carbon black, charcoal, activated carbon, and similar products. Most of the uses on these amorphous carbons are based on their strong adsorptive capacity, electrical conductivity, reinforcing ability, and pigmenting property. *See also* carbon black ; activated carbon.

industrial chemistry. That branch of chemistry which is concerned with the application of chemical facts and principles in the production in industry of chemical, or nonchemical materials. For many years this term was used to describe a practical mixture of general chemistry and chemical engineering, applying to large-scale manufacturing in which chemical reactions are involved ; it embraced the so-called process industries, including paint, plastics, textiles, inorganic and synthetic organic chemicals, leather, paper, rubber, etc. In recent years it has fallen into disuse in educational circles ; though it is no longer generally regarded as an independent discipline.

-ine. A suffix meaning a base or a potential base.

-ine is generally characteristic of nitrogenous substances, *e.g.*, amine, benzidine purine, thiamine, serine, lysine, etc. The spelling benzine for benzene is thus inadmissable. In names of halogen elements, the terminal -ine is not a suffix but is an integral part of the word.

inelastic scattering. Scattering of particles in which the kinetic energies of scattered particles are changed in system's centre of mass.

intert. Having little or no chemical affinity or activity. The six elements comprising the noble-gas group of the Periodic Table are either wholly or relatively inert. The first three (helium, neon, argon) have a valence of 0 and do not enter into any chemical combination. The last three (krypton, xenon, radon) have several valences but are capable of only limited compound formation. Thus, these gases are collectively called "noble." Less specifically, nitrogen and carbon dioxide are often referred to as "inert atmospheres," as they are unreactive under normal conditions ; they are used to protect certain highly reactive substances from contact with atmospheric oxygen. In the same sense, inert solids are generally considered to be clays, asbestos, talc, sand, etc. The phrase inert ingredients on labels usually refers to water, the most common example of an inactive solvent.

inert complex. Complex characterized by small exchange rate of ligands.

intert gases. *See* inert ; noble gases.

infection. 1. The invasion and successful growth in an organism of one or more species of bacteria or parasites.

2. Transmission of disease by contact.

infiltration. In general, the passage of a liquid or gas through interstices, or into restricted spaces. Specifically, the passage of injected liquid from the point of introduction into the tissues; or the penentration of a liquid or solution into the interstices of a rock, usually with subsequent solidification and modification of the composition of the original rock.

infinitely thick layer. Target of such thickness that there is complete, or nearly complete, absorption of incident particles or photons.

infinitely thin layer. Target in which practically no reduction of intensity of radiation due to absorption of self-absorption is observed.

infinitesimal process. Thermodynamic process with final state only infinitesimally different from initial one.

inflammable. This term is not acceptable to safety authorities ; proper word is flammable.

informational molecules. Molecules containing information in the form of specific sequences of different building blocks ; include proteins and nucleic acids.

infrared radiation. Electromagnetic radiation possessing wavelengths between those of visible light and those of radio waves, *i.e.*, from approximately 0.75 micrometre to 1000 micrometres. Infrared radiation has the power of penetrating fog or haze, which would scatter ordinary visible light. Infrared radiation is produced by vibrational or rotational motion of molecules.

infrared spectroscopy. An instrumental technique of analytical chemistry in which substances of any type (gases, liquids, or solids) are identified by their tendency to absorb light (energy) of infrared wavelength (2 to 40 microns). The resulting absorption spectrum makes it possible to analyze complex mixtures quantitatively, to identify impurities and other unknown components, and to determine the various kinds of atomic groups in a molecule ; in short, the infrared spectrum offers an infallible molecular "fingerprint."

infusible. Solid substances which cannot be transformed into the liquid state under specified or implied conditions.

infusion. An aqueous solution of the soluble components of a plant made by immersing a quantity of the plant in water, allowing the mixture to steep until cold, and straining off the liquid portion.

ingrain dye. A dyestuff produced in the fibre by successive treatment with the components of the dye or with dye in its leuco (reduced and soluble) form, followed by oxidation.

inhibitor. Any substance that retards or reduces the rate of a chemical reaction ; the opposite of a catalyst. Antioxidants are well-known inhibitors of oxidation reactions in foods, rubber, and other organic materials. Protective coatings of various kinds inhibit the corrosion of metals. Spontaneous polymerization reactions are prevented in reactive monomers, *e.g.*, acrylic acid, by incorporation of suitable inhibitors during storage and shipment.

initiating explosive. An explosive of high shock sensitivity used to cause detonation of a less sensitive explosive such as dynamite or TNT, usually in the form of blasting caps or similar devices. Initiating explosives regularly used are mercury fulminate, lead azide, and diazonitrophenol.

initiator. A substance exhibiting unusual chemical activity, which enables it to set in motion, or induce, a chemical reaction such as polymerization, oxidation, or detonation. Well-known initiators are peroxides, which evolve atomic (nascent) oxygen, organic ions (carbanions and carbonium ions), and free radicals. Benzoyl peroxide is an instance of an organic initiator.

inner complex salt. A member of a special class of internal salts in which an acid group and a neutral group coordinate with metals to form a cyclic complex. These salts occur widely in analytical chemistry, where they are formed between metallic ionic reagents, in dyestuffs, in life processes (chlorophyll and hematin belong to this class of compounds), and in many other fields.

inner-electric potential, ϕ. Electrical potential between point in phase and point at infinity $\phi = \psi + x$, where ψ = outer potential and x = surface potential of phase.

inner electrons. Electrons of atomic shells with principal quantum number n less than that for for valence shell. Also known as inner-shell electrons.

inner-orbital complex. Complex in which d orbitals of smaller principal quantum number than for s and p orbitals take part in hybridization of central ion orbitals ; in octahedral comlex $(n-1)\ d^2nsp^3$.

inner quantum number. A term sometimes applied to the sum of the azimuthal quantum number and the spin quantum number, representing the resultant of the two corresponding contributions to the angular momentum of the electron.

inner transition elements. Transition elements the atoms of which have partially-filled d subshell and also a farther partially unfilled f subshell. Two series of these elements are distinguished : lanthanoids and and actinoids.

inorganic analysis. The operating principles of all systematic inorganic qualitative analysis schemes for the elements are similar : separation into group by reagents producing a phase change ; isolation of individual elements within a group by selective reaction ; and confirmation of the presence of individual elements by specific test.

Many instrumental methods of quantitative analysis can be adapted to qualitative analysis.

Emission spectroscopy is important in establishing the presence or absence of a suspected element also The simple qualitative flame test developed into flame photometry and subsequently into atomic absorption spectrometry.

Bombardment of surfaces by *x*-rays, elec trons, and positive ions has given rise to a number of methods useful in analytical chemistry. *x*-ray diffraction is used to determine crystal structure and to identify crystalline substances by means of their diffraction patterns. *x*-ray fluorescence analysis employs *x*-

rays to excite emission of characteristic x-ray by elements. The electron microprobe uses electron bombardment in a similar manner to excite x-ray emission.

Neutron activation analysis, where neutron bombardment induces radioactivity in isotopes of elements not naturally radioactive, involves measurement of the characteristic gamma radiation and modes of decay produced in the target atoms.

inorganic chemistry. Branch of chemistry dealing with studies on properties and transformations of all chemical elements and their compounds, excluding only majority of carbon compounds. Primarily, the field of inorganic chemistry centres around the elements and their compounds, including much of physical chemistry, atomic structure, chemical bonding, electro-chemistry, and coordination chemistry.

Sometimes, however, it is convenient to extend this branch of chemistry to cover certain simple carbon compounds, such as the oxides of carbon, the metallic carbides, etc.

There is no sharp dividing line between inorganic and organic chemistry in view of the many borderline cases such as organometallic compounds, electroorganic reactions, etc.

inorganic compound. In general, a compound that does not contain carbon atoms. Some very simple carbon compounds, such as carbon monoxide and dioxide, binary metallic carbon compounds (carbides) and carbonates, are usually also included in the group of inorganic compounds.

inorganic ferment. A term sometimes used, improperly, for a colloidal solution of a metal which acts catalytically in a similar manner to organic ferments, showing analogous changes of activity by time and temperature, and whose activity is destroyed by substances which render the enzymes inert.

inorganic ion exchanger. Ion exchanger which consists of inorganic skeleton bearing excess electric charge and mobile counter ions.

insecticide. A chemical compound that is lethally toxic to insects either by ingestion or by body contact; it is applied to vegetation, crops, and insect-breeding areas either as liquid spray or as dry powder. There are five major types; (*i*) inorganic metallic compounds, for example, Bordeaux mixture (copper sulphate-lime); (*ii*) natural organic compounds, such as rotenone; (*iii*) chlorinated hydrocarbons, typified by DDT; (*iv*) organic phosphorus esters (parathion and its derivatives) (*v*) methylcarbamates, such as carbaryl (1-naphthyl N-methylcarbamates). Of these the fourth is by far the most toxic to man. Insecticides are also classified according to the type of action as: stomach poisons, systemic poisons, furrigants, repellents, attractants, insect growth regulators, etc. They may act in one or more than one way.

insertion reaction. Reaction characteristic for carbenes and intrenes, involving insertion of appropriate group between the carbon and hydrogen atoms linked together, *e.g.*,

$$-\overset{|}{\underset{|}{C}}-H + {}^{1}CH_2 \underset{\text{singlet state}}{} \rightarrow -\overset{|}{\underset{|}{C}}-CH_2-H$$

instability constant. The dissociation constant for complex ion, which may be expressed in terms of activities, by dividing the product of the activities at equilibrium of each of its simpler ions (raised to the proper power) by the activity of the complex ion; or in terms of concentrations, where permissible, by dividing the product of the concentrations at equilibrium of each of its simpler ions (raised to the proper power) by the concentration of the complex ion. Also known as dissociation constant.

instrumental analysis. As ordinarily used, this term refers to methods of analytical chemistry in which rather sophisticated instruments are required. Most important are those involving light or radiant energy (optical methods), which are used in the many types of spectroscopy (infrared, x-ray, NMR, etc.), and those utilizing electrical measurements, including potentiometry, coulometry, magnetic susceptibility, and mass spectrometry.

instrumental error. Measurement (determination) error due to improper construction or working of instrument.

instrumentation. Application of specialized devices, often electronic, to measure continuously, and in some cases control, such phenomena as temperature, chemical composition, light, electrical activity, and radioactivity.

insulator. Non-conducting material (gas, liquid or solid) of high specific resistance, generally accepted as $>10^{10}\ \Omega$ cm (dielectric). According to band theory of solids, crystal with broad forbidden band.

integral. 1. A whole, or composed of constituent parts making a whole.

2. An essential part, either a constituent or a component.

3. A mathematical symbol denoting summation, or a mathematical expression carrying such a symbol.

integral capacity of double layer, *K*. Capacity of electrical double layer at electrode — solution interphase, defined by equation :

$$K=\frac{q}{\epsilon-\epsilon_0},$$

where ϵ =electrode potential, ϵ_0=zero charge potential of electrode, q = charge of electrode given by

$$q=\int_{\epsilon_0}^{\epsilon} C d\epsilon$$

and C = differential capacity of double layer.

integral detector. Device that measures continuously total amount of substance in gas or liquid coming out of chromatographic column.

integral dose. Amount of energy of any kind of ionizing radiation imparted to sample or organism and absorbed by it.

integral heat of adsorption. Total amount of heat which is liberated (or absorbed) in adsorption which involves defined masses of adsorbate and pure adsorbent engaged in process.

integral heat of dilution. *See* heat of dilution.

integral heat of solution. *See* heat of solution.

intensive parameters. *See* intensive quantities.

intensive properties. *See* intensive quantities.

intensive quantities. Thermodynamic quantities independent of system's mass. Also known as intensive properties, intensive variables, intensive parameters, intensities.

intensive variables. *See* intensive quantities.

interaction. 1. Identical with reaction.

2. Mutual effect due to proximity of charges, ions, dipoles, or molecules on each other's properties.

intercombination transition. Radiative electronic transition between states of different multiplicity, *e.g.*, between triplet state and singlet state.

interconversion of chair forms. Conversion of one chair conformation of a six-membered ring into another chair form with intermediate formation of skew boat form. In the majority of cyclohexane derivatives, conversion of chair forms is responsible for establishing equilibrium between conformers, differing in axial or equatorial location of substituent, *e.g.*,

[chemical structures: chair form (R) ⇌ [skew boat form (R)] ⇌ chair form (R)]

Also known as conversion of chair forms.

interface. The area of contact or boundary layer between two forms of matter or two phases of a dispersion, such as : (*i*) solid particles in contact with a gas or vapour; (*ii*) solid particles in contact with a liquid ; (*iii*) liquid droplets dispersed in another liquid ; (*iv*) solid surfaces in contact with each other, as in protective coatings. Interfaces are physicochemically active areas at which a considerable force exists because of the adsorptive power of finely divided solids and the surface tension of liquids. Together these comprise what is known as interfacial tension.

interfacial surface energy. The work necessary to enlarge the surface of separation between two immiscible or partially-miscible liquids.

interfacial tension. The contractile force of an interface between two liquids, resulting from their surface tensions, and the attraction between the molecules of the two liquids. It is commonly determined by measuring the interfacial surface energy.

interference. An opposing action, commonly between two forces or force systems, which results in partial or complete nullification of their individual effects. The term arises most commonly in chemistry in regard to wave systems, especially of radiant energy, where the process results in partial or even complete loss of energy in certain areas (destructive interference) and exaltation of energy in other areas (constructive interference).

interference filter. Optical filter whose action is based on principle of light interference in thin plates or membranes.

interfering nuclear order reaction. In activation analysis, nuclear reaction of constituent of a sample, other than that to be determined, gives the same product as that from the element to be detemined (result is too high), or reaction which leads to decrease the product to be determined (result is too low).

interfering second order reaction. In activation analysis, nuclear reaction in which from the matrix atoms the same radioisotope is formed in two successive activations as that formed from constituent to be determined.

interferometric analysis. *See* interferometry.

interferometry. Method of analysis based on measurement of difference of refractive indices for investigated sample and standard sample by using interferometer. Used mostly in gas analysis, sometimes also for liquids. Also known as interferometric analysis.

interhalogen compound. A binary compound composed of two elements of the halogen family.

intermediate. A substance used in the manufacture of dyes, drugs, and other organic products, which has been obtained usually br chemical treatment of crudes or other chemical raw materials.

For example : (1) benzene may be reduced to aniline, the parent substance of a large family of dyes ; (2) oxidation of naphthalene gives phthalic anhydride, from which are produced plasticizers, dyes, resins and pharmaceuticals. In these examples, aniline and phthalic anhydride are intermediates.

The term intermediate is much less specific now than formerly and is often loosely used for any organic compound from which many others can be made.

intermediate frequency. In superheterodyne radio receivers, the carrier wave frequency of the incoming radio wave is changed to a fixed intermediate frequency by heterodyne action, for ease of amplification before detection.

intermediate neutrons. Neutrons with kinetic energies between those of epithermal and fast neutrons, *i.e.*, between 100 to 100, 000 electron-volts.

intermediate phases. Intermetallic compounds, which are somtimes called intermediate phases because they are commonly found in the matrix of another phase at intermediate compositions in an alloy.

intermediate reactor. A nuclear reactor in which chain reaction is sustained mainly by intermediate neutrons.

intermetallic compound. A term used in metallurgy to describe an alloy formed by the heat-induced diffusion of two metals at the interface between them : for example, when one metal is coated with another for protective purposes, an intermetallic layer often is formed. This occurs in the process known as cementation. The alloys are not true compounds in the chemical sense but are actually mixtures or solid solutions of two or more metals.

intermetallic phases. Solid phases in alloys of metals with space lattices different from those of each constituent.

intermittency effect. The departure from the reciprocity low when the exposure of a photographic emulsion is made in a series of discrete installments rather than in a continuous exposure to the same total energy.

intermolecular energy transfer. Transfer of different kinds of energy (*i.e.*, electronic vibrational, and translational energy) from one molecule to another in different media.

intermolecular forces. Interaction forces between molecules (or order of 10^{-7} cm); attractive (van der Waals) or repulsive forces.

intermolecular hydrogen bond. Hydrogen bond in which hydrogen atom is linked with two atoms of two different molecules, *e.g.*, in formic acid dimer

```
        O......H—O
       /          \
  H—C              C—H
       \          /
        O—H......O
```

intermolecular potential, $u(r)$. Potential energy of pair of molecule as function of their relative positions.

intermolecular reaction. A reaction between individual molecules, which is the usual kind of reaction. The term used to distinguish these reactions from intremolecular reactions, where the action takes place between portions of the same molecule.

internal. A term used frequently in chemistry to express the idea that a phenomenon is confined within a molecule, as internal compensation, internal oxidation.

internal adsorption. Adsorption from solution of microamounts of foreign ions on surface of a precipitate, connected with incorporation of ions into interior of crystals due to growth of crystals.

internal compensation. A condition of optical inactivity in a molecule containing two, or a multiple of two, asymmetric carbon atoms, due to the fact that two carbon atoms, one of which is dextrorotatory, the other of which is levorotatory, neutralize the optical effect of each other.

internal conversion. 1. Transition of excited atomic nucleus to lower energy state ; the energy difference between initial and final states being given to orbital electron (not to γ-photon).

2. Isoenergetic radiationless transition between two electronic states of like multiplicity.

internal conversion coefficient, α. Ratio of number af internal conversion electrons N_e to number of gamma quanta $N\gamma$ emitted in given transition, *i.e.*, ratio of probability of electron emission λ_e to probability of photon emission $\lambda\gamma$:

$$\alpha = \frac{N_e}{N\gamma} = \frac{\lambda_e}{\lambda\gamma}$$

internal electrolysis. Electrolysis occurring spontaneously in cell constructed of two electrodes with appropriate potentials without applying external voltage to electrodes.

internal energy U. Extensive thermodynamic function equal to difference between total energy E of system and its macroscopic kinetic energy E_k and potential energy E_p :

$$U = E - E_k - E_p$$

Only a change in internal energy can be measured, not its value for any single stage. For a given process, the change in internal energy is fixed by initial and final states and is independent of the path by which the change in state is accomplished.

internal indicator. An indicator used in the usual way, by adding it to the system under analysis or control. Contrast indicator, outside.

internal partition function $j(T)$. Partition function for intramolecular degrees of freedom

$$j(T) = \sum_{\varepsilon} g_\varepsilon \exp\left[-\frac{\varepsilon}{kT}\right]$$

where g_ϵ = degeneracy of the energy level ε, k=Boltzmann constant, and T = thermodynamic temperature. Sum is taken over all internal (*i.e.*, non-translational) degrees of freedom. Internal partition function determines internal partition function determines influence of intramolecular degrees of freedom on thermodynamic proporties of corresponding gas.

internal pressure. Quantity defined by $\left(\frac{\partial U}{\partial V}\right)_T$

where U = internal energy of phase, V = its volume and T=phase temperature. Also known as cohesion pressure.

internal reference. *See* **internal standard.**

internal resistance of galvanic cell. Electrical resistance in internal circuit of galvanic cell; it depends on dimensions and separation of electrodes, electrical conductivity of electrolyte; resistance at electrode—electrolyte interphase and, if present, on nature of diaphragm.

internal return. Recombination of internally associated ionic pair, leading to restitution of substrate. No ions coming from other molecules present in system take part in internal return. Intramolecular processes, such as inversion, racemization or rearrangements, often accompany internal return :

$$A{-}X \rightleftharpoons A^{+}X^{-} \rightleftharpoons A^{+}\ X^{-}$$

internal salt. A compound in which the acidic or basic groups which react to produce the salt linkage (which may or may not entail the formation of water), are in the same molecule. This particular salt linkage may consist of a polar or a nonpolar bond.

internal standard. 1. Components added or already present in the same concentration in standard and investigated samples whose spectral line(s) is (are) used as reference lines for measurement of spectral line intensities of determinee elements.

2. In NMR spectroscopy, reference substance dissolved in investigated solution ; used for determination of chemical shifts.

internal standard line. A spectral line of an internal standard, with reference to which the radiant power of an analytical line is measured.

internal-standard method. Analytical method based on addition to analysed sample of known quantity of some substance (internal standard), for which analytical curve in the given conditions of determination is identical with that for determined component. Using linear relationship between quantity measured for standard and analysed substance and knowing concentration of standard one may calculate amount of analysed substance.

internal strain. Changes in steric interactions (angular, conformational and transannular strains) taking place in reactions of alicyclic compounds, mainly due to change in valence state of carbon atom forming reaction centre. These strains may stimulate of hinder reaction. Also known as I-strain.

International Union of Pure and Applied Chemistry. *See* IUPAC.

interphase. The boundary surface between two phases.

interstitial. 1. In a crystal lattice, an atom of another element (impurity). which causes a defect or dislocation, for example, the presence of an atom of carbon or nitrogen in an iron crystal, or of arsenic in a semiconductor.

2. In biochemical terminology, a substance (usually water) occurring between the cell of other structural units in a tissue.

interstitial compound. A compound of a metal or metals and certain metalloid elements, in which the metalloid atoms occupy the interstices between the atoms of the metal lattice. Compounds of this type are, for example, TaC, TiC, ZrC, NbC, and similar compounds of carbon, nitrogen, boron and hydrogen with metals. Such compounds are frequently nonstoichiometric in that they do not have definite formulas.

interstitial position. *See* interstitial site.

interstitial site. Position in between periodic nodes in crystal lattice, occupied by iron or atom. Also known as interstitial position.

interstitial solid solution. Solid solution in which atoms or ions of dissolved substance occupy interstitial positions in lattice in-between atoms or ions of matrix substance.

intersystem crossing (in photochemistry). Isoenergetic radiationless transition between the two electronic states of different multiplicity.

intertraction. Increase in density of a colloidal solution caused by loss of solute by diffusion into a salt solution which is in contact with the colloidal solution.

intramolecular hydrogen bond. Hydrogen bond in which hydrogen atom is bound with two different atoms of the same molecule, *e.g.*, in 2-nitrophenol :

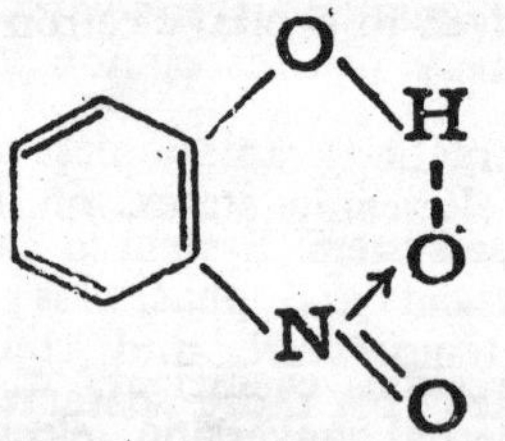

intramolecular oxidation. The oxidation of a compound in which the oxygen required by the reaction is furnished by the compound it self, *e.g.* nitrolactive acid oxidizes itself to oxalic acid, hydrocyanic acid and water, *viz.*,

$$\begin{array}{l} CH_3 \\ | \\ HCNO_2 \\ | \\ COOH \end{array} \rightarrow \begin{array}{l} COOH \\ | \\ | \\ | \\ COOH \end{array} + HCN + H_2O$$

intramolecular reaction. Process in which formation of product results from reaction of functional groups present in the same molecule.

intrinsic efficiency of detector. Ratio of number of particles or photons which give rise to counts, to number of particles or photons reaching sensitive part of detector.

intrinsic semiconductor. Semiconductor in which electrons transferred to conduction band as well as positive holes left in the same number in ground band are carriers of electric current. Intrinsic conductivity occurs in very pure crystals, free from defects. It may also occur in crystals with defects at temperatures high enough to neglect the number of carriers formed by ionization of impurities and in crystals containing equivalent numbers of donor and acceptor centres.

intrinsic viscosity $[\eta]$. Limiting value of reduced viscosity obtained by extrapolation to zero concentration :

$$[\eta] = \lim_{c \to 0} \eta_{red} = \lim_{c \to 0} \frac{\eta_{sp}}{c}$$

where η_{red}=reduced viscosity, η_{sp} = specific viscosity, c = concentration. Also known as limiting Staudinger function.

introfaction. The effect of an introfier upon a liquid, whereby its rate and extent of penetration or impregnation is increased. The effect is due primarily to dissociation of complex molecules.

invariant phase system. System in which number of constituents and phases is determined explicitly by temperature and concentration ; change of each of those parameters causes change of number of constituents or phase. Also known as invariant system.

invariant system. *See* invariant phase system.

invasion. The solution of a gas in a liquid. *See* absorption of gases.

invasion coefficient. A factor used to denote the number of milliliters of a gas under standard conditions absorbed by one square centimeter of surface in one minute.

inversion. Reversal in the direction of optical rotation of a carbohydrate molecule as a result of acid hydrolysis ; it may be either from right (dextro) to left (levo), or the opposite. Sucrose the common form of sugar, is dextrorotatory; it can be readily hydrolyzed to glucose and fructose. The resulting mixture is levorotatory and thus is called invert sugar. Inversion of sucrose can also occur by fermentation in the presence of the enzyme invertase.

2. The conversion of a stereo chemical isomer into its opposite form, as a levorotatory to a dextrorotatory substance or a cis to a trans form.

inversion axis. Coupling of n-fold rotation axis (revolution by $360/n°$ angle) with reflection in symmerty centre placed on axis. Also known as inversion symmetry axis.

inversion, geometrical. *See* geometrical inversion.

inversion line. In spectroscopy, band corresponding to transition between inversion levels of lowest vibrational state of molecule ; lies in microwave region.

inversion of configuration. Change in configuration of chiral centre of molecule caused by chemical reaction.

inversion, optical. *See* optical inversion.

inversion point. *See* inversion temperature.

inversion spectrum (of ammonia). Spectrum of ammonia in microwave region corresponding to transition between two energy levels arising from splitting of zeroth vibrational level by inversion motion of molecule ; inversion spectrum arises due to existence of two equivalent forms of molecule separated by energy barrier.

inversion symmetry axis. *See* inversion axis.

inversion temperature, *Ti*. Temperature at which Joule-Thomson coefficient changes sign.

Also known as Joule-Thomson inversion temperature ; inversion point.

inversion, Walden. *See* Walden inversion.

inverting enzyme. An enzyme that catalyzes the inversion of a sugar, *i.e.*, its hydrolysis to yield simpler sugar molecules, as invertase hydrolyzes sucrose to yield glucose and fructose.

in vitro. An experiment (usually of a biochemical nature) that is carried out in laboratory equipment rather than on living organisms. The opposite meaning is given by the expression in vivo.

in vivo. An event or brocess occurring naturally or spontaneouly within a living organism.

iodination. Substitution of hydrogen atom in molecule of organic compound by iodine atom.

iodine. An element.

State	Solid	Symbol	I
Group	VIIA	Atomic No.	53
		Atomic Wt.	126.9045
		Valence	1,3,5,7
		m.p.	113.6°C

Iodine is one of the less active members of the halogen family of elements and is classed as a nonmetal.

There is one stable isotope, ^{127}I, and fourteen radioactive isotopes, ^{122}I, through ^{126}I, and ^{128}I, through ^{136}I. The lengths of the half-lives of the isotopes vary widely, the shortest, ^{136}I, with a half-life of 86 seconds ; the longest, ^{129}I, with a half-life of 1.72×10^7 years. In terms of abundance in the crust of the earth, the element ranks 53rd and is about as plentiful as tin, antimony, cesium, and barium.

It is quite poisonous in the concentrated state, and even the 3% solution used as an antiseptic is dangerously toxic if swallowed, though it can be applied topically without risk. It is extracted from Chilean nitrate, which contains about 0.2%, from natural brines and to a limited extent from seaweed.

The dietary requirement for iodine was established many year ago as needed for the maintenance of cell growth in humans and animals. The largest concentration of iodine occurs in the thyriod gland where the hormone thyroxine $C_{15}H_{11}O_4I_4N$ is present.

It is used in iodized salt for protection against goiter, as a chemical reagent, as a catalyst, as an indicator of chemical uusaturation, and in organic synthesis.

First ionization potential 10.44 eV ; second, 19.4 eV. Oxidatioh potentials $I^- \rightarrow \frac{1}{2}I_2 + e^-$, -0.535 V ; $I^- + H_2O \rightarrow HIO + H^+ + 2e^-$, -0.99 V ; $I^- + 3H_2O \rightarrow IO_3^- + 6H^+ + 6e^-$, -1.085 V; $\frac{1}{2}I_2 + 3H_2O \rightarrow IO_3^- + 6H^+ + 5e^-$ -1.195 V ; $\frac{1}{2}I_2 + H_2O \rightarrow HIO + H^+ + e^-$, -1.45 V : $IO_3^- + 3H_2O \rightarrow H_5IO_6 + H^+ + 2e^-$, ca. -1.7 V; $I^- + 6OH^- \rightarrow IO_3^- + 3H_2O + 6e^-$, -0.26 V ; $I^- + 2OH^- \rightarrow IO^- + H_2O + 2e^-$, -0.49 V; $IO + 4OH^- \rightarrow IO_3^- + 2H_2O + 4e^-$, -0.56 V ; $IO_3^- + 3OH^- \rightarrow H_3IO_6^{2-} + 2e^-$, ca. -0.70 V.

Iodine is not required by plants, but if iodine is present in the soil, it is taken up by most plants and moves on into the diets in forms that are effective in preventing goiter.

Studies of the geochemistry of iodine indicate that this elements is volatilized from oceans, carried overland by winds, and deposited on the soil by rain.

iodine carriers. Substances added to organic reaction mixtures to cause combination of iodine with various compounds or to direct the course of the reaction in some specific way. Phosphorus, iron wire, ferrous iodide, ferric choride, mercuric oxide, etc., are examples.

iodine number. The amount of iodine, in percent by weight, that is chemically added to a given quantity of an unsaturated material, especially one in which the double bonds are not conjugated. This technique for determining the extent of chemicals unsaturation is used primarily for fatty acids (vegetable oils) rubber, and similar materials, The iodine number (or value) increases rapidly with the number of double bonds present.

iodo compound. An organic compound which may be regarded as derived from hydriodic acid. as iodobenzence, C_6H_5I, iodomethane, CH_3I.

iodometry. Analysis by means of iodine, commonly consisting of the titrimetric determination of substances which can, under certain conditions, oxidize an iodide, such as potassium iodide, to free iodine; or else of substances which combine with iodine or reduce it.

iodous. 1. Related to iodous acid, HIO_2.

2. Containing trivalent iodine.

ion. Atom or group of atoms with electrical charge equal to elementary charge or its multiple. The properties of ions are quite different from those of the neutral units from which they are derived, because of the presence of the electric charge. In a solution. they are closely associated with molecules of the solvent; they also may exist in solids and gases.

ion association complex. Species formed through association (mainly due to electrostatic interaction) of two oppositely charged ions, of which at least one is complex ion, *e.g.*,

$$[Co(NH_3)_6]^{2+}[SO_4]^{2-}$$

Also known as ion pair, outer sphere complex.

ion beam. A beam of charged particles which compare in velocity to those yielded by radioactive substances, or which exceed that velocity Ion beams are produced by the application of electrical forces to ordinary ions and other particles.

ion cluster. Hypothetical conglomerate of positive ion with attached neutral molecules in gases, recently experimentally confirmed to be solvation of ions in mass-spectrometry at higher than usual pressures (1.3 kPa and higher). Also known as ionic cluster.

ion exchange. Substitution of one ion, either positive (cation) or negative (anion), for another of the same charge when an ion-containing solution is passed into a molecular network having either acidic or basic substituent group which can be readily ionized. The ions in the solution attach themselves to the network, replacing the free or mobile ions contained therein.

ion exchange capacity of strongly acidic/basic groups. Number of equivalents of ionogenic groups, able to exchange ions from neutral salt solution per unit mass or volume of exchanger. Also known as exchange capacity of high dissociated cationic/anionic groups.

ion exchange chromatography. A chromatograghic method based on the ability of polymers to absorb ionized solutes reversibly. It can be carried out in columns as well as on sheets.

ion exchange column. Cylindrical tube filled with inlet and outlet for solution being separated, purified etc.

ion-exchange isotherm in chromatography. Isotherm characterizing dependence of equilibrium concentrations of counter-ion in ion exchanger and external solution respectively (in given conditions).

ion exchanger. Insoluble substance containing ions that can be exchanged for other ions from solution.

Many insoluble substances, both inorganic and organic which have an interlocking molecular structure (cage) can act as ion exchangers, *e.g.*, aluminosilicates (clays) cross-linked organic polymers (ion-exchange resins), sulphonated coal and cellulose, and, to some extent, proteins and nucleic acids. Ion exchange is a reversible phenomenon with many uses : water softening (zeolite), chromatographic analysis, elimination of ionic impurities (demineralization) of rare earth separations, acid removal, etc. Because of their predominantly siliceous nature, soils exhibit ion-exchange activity, which has a important bearing on fertilizer application *See also* mixed-bed de-ionization.

ion density. The number of ion pairs in unit volume of irradiated medium also the number of ion pairs per unit length track of the ionizing particle. Also known as ionization density.

ion-exchanger membrane. Ion exchange material of arbitrary geometrical form (usually sheet or foil) which can be used as boundary between two solution.

ion exclusion. Method for separation of strong electrolytes from weak electrolytes and nonelectrolytes on ion exchangers. Strong electrolytes are excluded from exchanger's phase (Donnan effect) and are eluted from column ahead of weak electrolytes and non-ionic compounds.

ion pair. As postulated in the Debye-Huckel theory, in concentrated solutions of strong electrolytes (two or more) ions may occasionally approch each other so closely that they may form pairs (or groups) without entering into permanent chemical combination.

ionic atmosphere. A term used to characterize a diffuse population of ions surrounding a charged particle in a solution, the particle may be an ion, a molecule, or a colloidal micelle. Most of the ions in the "atmosphere" have a charge opposite from that of the particle they surround, and the net strength of the charge diminishes with their distance from the central particle.

ionic bond. Chemical bond formed between atoms of distinctly different electronegativity. Valence electron of less negative atom passes to more negative one and ion thus formed are held together by electrostatic forces. Also known as electrovalent bond ; heteropolar bond ; polar bond ; electrostatic bond.

ionic compound. One of a class of compounds which ionize readily in a aqueous solution, and which are formed when atoms combine to produce molecules having stable configurations by the transfer of one or more electrons within the molecule.

ionic concentration. The number of gram-ions (calculated from the atomic weight of the substance or subtances composing the ion) contained in unit volume of solution.

ionic conductance (λ_+ or λ_-).

$$\lambda_+ = Fu_+ \quad \text{or} \quad \lambda_- = Fu_-$$

where u_+ and u_- = mobilities of cation and anion respectively; also conductance of 1 gram equivalent of a given sort of ion in solution of these ions with concentration c.

ionic conductor. Conductor conducting electrical current by ions. Also known as electrolytic conductor.

ionic crystals. Crystals composed of positive and negative simple or complex ions; they are characterized by low electric conductivity at low temperature and high ionic conductance at high temperatures.

ionic equation. An equation expressing an ionic reaction in terms of the symbols or formulas of the ions or molecules which react, and the ions or molecules which are formed by the reaction, with integral coefficients showing the proportional number of ions or molecules involved (which is the proportional number of equivalent weights of each ion or of gram-molecular weights of each molecule). For example :

$$Ba^{++} + SO_4^{2-} \rightleftharpoons BaSO_4 \text{ (precipitate)}$$
$$Pb^{++} + 2CH_3COO^- \rightleftharpoons Pb(CH_3COO)_2$$
$$Zn + Pb^{++} \rightleftharpoons Zn^{++} + Pb.$$

ionic equilibrium. In any ionization, at any particular temperature and pressure, the conditions at which the rate of dissociation of unionized molecules, or other particles to form ions, is equal to the rate of combination of the ions to form the unionized molecules, or other particles so that activities and concentration remain constant as long as the conditions are unchanged.

ionic isomerism. 1. The isomerism of the acid and non-acid forms of pseudo-acids and the basic and non-basic forms of pseudo-ammonium bases.

2. Isomerism between ions attributable to valence differences. as Fe^{2+} and Fe^{3+}, Cr^{2+} and Cr^{3+}. These ions are considered isomeric and are termed as ionic isomers.

ionic migration. The movement of charged particles of an electrolyte toward the electrodes under the influence of the electric current.

ionic mobility, u. Ratio of velocity of ion in cm/s to electrical field in V/cm in which ion is travelling. Also known as absolute ionic mobility.

ionic polymerization. Polymerization catalyzed by acids, bases or complexes in which ions or macroions take part in all stages of process.

ionic product. K (L). Product of activities of cation and anions resulting from dissociation of weak or weakly soluble electrolytes

$$K = a_+^{\nu+} \cdot a_-^{\nu-}$$

where a_+ and a_+=concentration activities of cation and anion, respectively, ν_+ and ν_-= quantities of cations and anions resulting from one molecule of electrolyte. Value of ionic product depends on temperature.

ionic product of solvent. Equilibrium constant for autoprotolysis reaction of solvent if activity of undissociated part is equal to one.

ionic product of water. Equilibrium constant for water autoprotolysis reaction, written as

$$L_{H_2O} = a_{H_3O^+} \cdot a_{OH^-}$$

since $a_{H_2O}=1$ due to negligible self-dissociation of water.

ionic radius. Sum of ionic radii of two neighbouring ions determines ionic bond length.

The distance usually measured in Angstrom units, from the center of a charged atom or group of atoms to the periphery of the effective sphere, generally calculated from crystal structure data.

ionic reaction. Reaction in which substrates, intermediates or products are ions.

ionic refractivity. Part of experimental value of molar refraction for ion in ionic compound computed according to additive scheme.

ionic sieves. Ion exchangers (most often inorganic) of such pore dimensions which enable exchange of smaller ions while mechanically excluding larger ones ; in case of big differences in counter ion dimension also organic ion exchangers can act sieves.

ionic strength J or J* . A mathematical quantity used to evaluate the effectiveness of the forces restricting the freedom of ions in an electrolyte and defined as :

$$J \equiv \frac{1}{2} \sum c_i z_i^2 \text{ or}$$

$$J^* \equiv \frac{1}{2} \sum m_i z_i^2$$

where c=molar concentration, m=molality of ions in solution, z=ion charge.

ionic valency. Number of positive or negative charges of given ion.

ionic yield, M/N. Ratio of number of molecules which number of the ion pairs formed by ionizing radiation in the same volume.

ion implantation. A process of introducing impurities into the near-surface region of solids by directing a beam of energetic ions at the solid. The advantages of this process are ; precise control of the type of impurity to be introduced, the amount of impurity introduced, and the impurity distribution in depth. The applications of ion implantation has been in the field of semiconductor device fabrication.

ionium. Isotope of thorium. Atomic number 90. Mass number 230. Ionium has a half-period of 8.3×10^4 years, emitting α-particles and γ-rays.

ionization. A chemical change by which ions are formed from a neutral molecule of a solid, liquid, or gas. The most common type of ionization occures when an ionically bonded inorganic compound, such as NaCl or H_2SO_4, is dissolved in water (or other solvent) ; the molecule separates, or dissociates, into two ions, the metallic ion being positively charged by loss of an electron and the nonmetallic ion being negatively charged by gaining an electron (electrolytic dissociation). The degree of dissociation varies with the type of compound, the solvent, and the temperatre. Gaseous molecules can be ionized by electric energy.

ionization chamber. Hollow chamber with electrodes, filled with suitable gas, enabling measurement of intensity of ionizing radiation from intensity of current due to ions formed.

ionization constant. The analog of dissociation constant, which is equal to the product of the activities of each of the ions produced as a result of the dissociation (if more than one ion of a given kind is produced, its activity is raised to the corresponding power) divided by the activity of the unionized molecules. Concentrations may be substituted for activities, if the result is multiplied by a similar term consisting of the corresponding activity coefficients of ions and unionized molecules, or if activity coefficients are assumed to have values of unity as in dilute solutions.

ionization, degree of. *See* degree of ionization.

ionization density. *See* ion density.

ionization energy. Smallest amount of energy necessary to remove an electron from one mole of kind of atom or molecule to an infinite distance.

ionization isomerism. Type of isomerism of complex compounds concerned with different distribution of anions in first coordination sphere and beyond it, *e.g.*, $[Co(SO_4)(NH_3)_5]Br$, and $[CoBr(NH_3)_5]SO_4$.

ionization potential. Energy in electronvolts necessary to detach the weakest bound electron from atom or molecule.

ionizing particle. A particle that produces ion pairs in its passage through a substance. Ionizing particles may be divided into two groups : (*i*) directly ionizing particles—charged particles (electrons, protons, alpha, particles, and so on) having sufficient kinetic energy to produce ionization by collision ; and (*ii*) indirectly ionizing particles—uncharged particles, such as neutrons and photons, which can liberate directly ionizing particles or can initiate a nuclear reaction.

ionizing radiation. Any radiation consisting of directly or indirectly ionizing particles, or a mixture of both. Ionizing radiation, unless controlled, poses a biological and environmental hazard.

ion line. Spectral line in emission spectrum of excited ions. Also known as spark line in emission spectral analysis.

ion-molecule reaction. Reaction of ion-radical with stable molecule.

ionomer. A type of cross-linked noncrystalline copolymer of unsaturated hydrocarbons, such as ethylene, and unsaturated acid salts ; these form aggregates on moderate heating and bring about cross-linking, but at higher temperatures, they are weakened to the point that the material becomes thermoplastic.

ionotropy. The ionization of a tautomeric form of a substance in which a charged atom or radical separates from an unsaturated molecule, having an oppositely charged fragment. If the atom or radical is negative, the process is called anionotropy ; if positive, cationotropy.

ion pair (in radiology). Parent positive ion and electron formed as result of ionization. *See also* **ion association complex.**

ion retardation. Method for separation of strong elrctrolytes from weak electrolytes and non-electrolytes on amphoteric ion exchangers, which makes use of differences in sorption strength of individual components ; strong electrolytes are more strongly retarded when passing column with amphoteric exchanger than weak electrolytes and non-ionic compounds.

ion-selective electrode. Electrode (half-cell) in which potential, dependent on activity of a certain ion of electrolyte, arises at the interphase of electrode material and electorolyte.

ion spectrum. Spectrum of singly or multiply ionized atom.

Ipatiev reaction. An organic reduction, most commonly of ketones to alcohols, brought about by heating under pressure with hydrogen in the presence of a metallic oxide catalyst, usually nickel oxide.

iridescence. The exhibition of the colours of the rainbow, commonly by diffraction of light of the various wave lengths reflected from superficial layers in the surface of a substance.

iridium. An element

	Symbol	Ir
	Atomic No.	77
	Atomic Wt.	192.22
State Solid	Valence	1,2,3,4,6
Group VIII	Isotopes	2 stable
	m.p.	2686K
	b.p	4403K

A member of the so-called platinum group of metals, iridium is the heaviest of all elements with a density, 22.65 g/cm³ twice that of lead.

Elemental iridium has a face-centered cubic crystal structure. The two stable isotopes of iridium are ^{191}Ir and ^{193}Ir. The ten unstable isotopes are ^{187}Ir through ^{190}Ir, ^{192}Ir, and ^{194}Ir. In terms of earthly abundance, iridium is one of the scarce elements.

It is extremely resistant to corrosion and other forms of chemical attack. It is the only metal which can be used unprotected in air upto 2600K, with any degree of life expectancy. It is not attacked by any acid, including aqua regia. It has a strong tendency to form coordination compounds. In finely divided form it is used as a catalyst, especially for petroleum products ; its major industrial application is as an alloying elements with platinum to produce electrical contacts, resistance theremal devices, and the like. Its electrical conductivity is about twice that of platinum. Iridium has considerably less oxidation resistance than platinum or rhodium, but more so than ruthenium or osmium. With its numerous valences, it is quite reactive, forming many oxides, halogen salts, and sulphides.

iron. An element

	Symbol	Fe
	Atomic No.	26
	Atomic Wt.	55.847
State Solid	Valence	2,3
Group VIII	Isotopes	4 stable
	m.p.	1813K
	b.p.	~3275K

Iron is the fourth most abundand element in the earth's crust (5%), iron occurs widely, usually in the form of oxides (hematite, taconite) ; it is present in most soils in a concentration of from 1 to 6% There are nine isotopes of iron, ^{52}Fe, through ^{60}Fe. Isotopes 54, 56, 57, and 58 are fully stable, whereas four others have fairly short half-lives, ranging from 8.9 minutes for ^{53}Fe to 2.94 years for ^{55}Fe. The half-life of ^{60}Fe is approximately 3×10^5 years. Iron ores are reduced by heating (smelting) with coke and calcium carbonate to yield pig iron, primarily used for steel manufacture. It is a tough, malleable, silver-gray, magnetic metal. The four stable, naturally occurring isotopes have masses of 45, 56, 57 and 58. Iron has important electrochemical and magnetic properties ; it will remove hydrogen from water and thus is easily oxidized to form rust (corrosion), a reaction in which water acts as catalyst. Finely divided and purified iron is used as a chemical reagent and catalyst, as well as in magnets.

There are several allotropic forms of iron, Ferrite or α-iron is stable upto 1033K. The change of β-iron involves primarily a loss of magnetic permeability because the lattice structure (b.c.c.) is changed.

The allotrope γ-iron has the cubic close-packed arrangements of atoms and is stable from 1183K to 1673K, δ-iron is stable above 1673K and has a lattice similar to that of α-iron.

Its physical properties can be heat treatment (tempering) and by the presence of law percentages of carbon. Biochemically, it is essential in life processes and is the primary constituent of red blood cells (hemoglobin).

First ionization potential is 7.896 eV; second 16.5 eV. Oxidation potentials : $Fe \rightarrow Fe^{2+} + 2e^-$, 0.441 V ; $Fe \rightarrow Fe^{3+} + 3e^-$, 0.036 V ; $Fe^{2+} \rightarrow Fe^{3+} + e^-$, —0.771 V ; $Fe + 2OH^- \rightarrow Fe(OH)_2 + 2e^-$, 0.877 V ; $Fe(OH)_2 + OH^- \rightarrow Fe(OH)_3 + e^-$, 0.56 V ; $Fe(OH)_4^- + 4OH^- \rightarrow FeO_4^{2-} + 4H_2O + 3e^-$, E=0.55 V (80°C; 40% NaOH).

Iron deficiency is a serious problem in crop production in certain regions of the world and some nutritionists consider iron deficiency anemia to be one of the most frequently observed mineral element deficiency conditions in humans. Yet iron fertilization of soils is not likely to be effective in decreasing the incidence of this deficiency. Iron-deficient plants are generally stunted and chlorotic, *i.e.*, normally green leaves are yellow or streaked with yellow. When the iron deficiency is treated by adding soluble iron to the soil, the plants turn green, grow larger and yield more, but sometimes the concentration of iron per unit weight of plant material may be no higher than in the stundted iron-deficint plants. Thus, in terms of forage plants, correction of iron deficiency in the plant does not necessarily improve the plant as a source of dietary iron. The iron-treated plants, however may contain a higher concentration of carotene or provitamin A than the yellow, stunted, deficients plants. Thus iron fertilization can be more useful in improving the vitamin A than the iron level in diets.

iron blue. A blue pigment whose molecule is made up of iron in combination with carbon, nitrogen, and hydrogen (ferriferrocyanide). It is also called Prussian blue, it is insoluble in water and organic solvents but is attacked by alkalies. It is used as a colourant in paints, baked enamels, printing inks, and laundering additives.

iron group. Three elements in eighth sub-group

of periodic system with structure of outer electronic shells of atoms : iron—$3d^6 4s^2$, ruthenium—$4d^7 5s^1$, osmium—$4d^6 6s^2$.

iron-steam process. A method used for the manufacture of hydrogen. Steam is passed over heated iron at high temperatures, producing iron oxide and hydrogen.

irradiation. Subjection of a substance to radiation of a specific type or wavelength in order to initiate a chemical change. There are several kinds of irradiation ; (*i*) ultraviolet irradiation of milk to increase its vitamin D content (no longer widely practiced) ; (*ii*) gamma-ray irradiation of ethylene and hydrogen bromide to synthesize ethyl bromide ; (*iii*) cross-linking of polyethylene and vulcanization of rubber by high-energy irradiation. *See also* radiation.

irradiation chamber. Space in irradiation divice in which objects are placed for purpose of ionizing radiation treatement.

irradiation loop. Closed-circuit system of pipes passing through or closed to core of nuclear reactor. Irradiation loop is used for : (*i*) direct irradiation of through-flowing liquids or gases, (*ii*) (n, γ) activation of circulating molten metal which release energy as pure gamma radiation (*i.e.*, without neutrons) in irradiation chamber through which loop passed.

irregular polymer. Polymer is irregular when its macromolecules cannot be split into constitutional unit of one species and in one sequential arrangement.

irreversible. A chemical or physicochemical change of state that is permanent and cannot be reversed.

irreversible coagulation. Coagulation in which product (precipitate or gel) cannot be reversibly transformed into sol state, *e.g*,, denaturation of proteins, coagulation of lyophobic colloids by action of electrolytes.

irreversible colloid. A colloidal system that cannot be restored to its original form after coagulation or precipitation, for example, the hardening of egg white or milk protein by heat the formation of butter from milk (mechanical action), and the coagulation of rubber latex by acid (chemical action).

irreversible process. Thermodynamic process accompanied by production of entropy either in system or at boundings between system and surroundings ; if irreversible process take place, then according to second law of thermodynamics, simultaneous return of both system and surroundings to initial state is impossible. Also known as irreversible change.

irreversible reaction. A chemical reaction that can proceed in only one direction, *i.e.*, to the right, giving a product that is stable and that cannot revert to the original constituents, most reactions are of this type.

Irving-Williams series. Divalent cations of metals of second haif of first transition series arranged by stability of their complexes :

$$Mn^{2+} < Fe^{2+} < Co^{2+} < Ni^{2+} < Cu^{2+} < Zn^{2+}$$

Also known as Irving-Williams stability series.

Irving-Williams stability series. *See* Irving-Williams series.

isentropic change. *See* isentropic process.

isentropic process. Thermodynamic process with constant entropy of system. Also knwon as isentropic change.

Ishibashi-Mori test. Tellurium in minerals is detected by adding copper to a dilute solution of the mineral in hot sulphuric acid. A red precipitate indicates the presence of tellurium.

isidioms. A term suggseted by Ladenberg to describe different compounds or different elements that behave in a similar chemical manner, as pseudotropine and scopoline, benzene and thiophene, cobalt and nickel, niobium and tantalum.

ising model. Abstract model of crystal composed of space-fixed atoms whose spin that is also magnetic moments have only two possible opposite directions with respect to some selected direction. It is assumed that only nearest-neighbours interact. Ising model is used in statistical mechanics to describe higher-order phase transitions, *e.g.*, in ferromagnetics and antiferromagnetics.

iso-. A prefix used in chemical and biological term meanig "the same," for example, isotope isomorphic, isomer. When used in combination with the name of an aliphatic compound, it means that the molecular structure of the compound is a branched chain, for example, isopentane, isooctane, isopropyl alcohol.

isoabsorptive point. Point on wavelength scale with equal absorption coefficients for two or more substances.

isoantigen. A type of antigen that induces antibody production in members of a species that have different genetic constitution.

isobar. 1. A line connecting points at equal pressure, such as that which appears on a meteorological chart.

2. One of two or more atomic species, or elements, which have the same mass number, but which differ in other respects, such as atomic numer, *i.e.*, having identical number of nucleons but different number of protons.

isobaric process. A thermodyamic process in which the heat transfer to or the gaseous system cause a volume change at constant pressure.

isochore. The variation of the pressure of a gas or liquid with varition in temperature, at constant volume ; or the graph of that function.

isochoric process. Thermodynamic process with constant volume of system.

isochromatic. Of the same colour, as of lines of the same tint in the interference figures of biaxial crystals.

isochrone. A line connecting points having the same time values, as points of the same gelation time or colloidal solutions.

isodimorphism. Ability to form substitutional solid solutions (in limited range of compositions) by two compounds which occur in different crystallographic systems (*e.g.*, $NaClO_3$ of regular lattice, with $AgClO_3$ of tetragonal lattice).

isodisperse system. Disease system in which particles of dispersed phase have the same sizes. Also known as monodisperse system.

isodose. Curve or surface connecting points of equal dose rate in irradiated system.

isoelectric point. The pH at which the positive and negative charges on the particles of a colloidal solution cancel each other so that the particles become electrically neutral. This condition is brought about by altering the original pH by addition of acids or alkalies to the solution. The pH at which the isoelectric point occurs varies with the chemical nature of the particles ; for example, it is about 6.0 (faintly acid) for glycine and near 10 (moderately alkaline) for lysine. At the isoelectric point, particles will not migrate in an electric field ; the system becomes unstable, and coagulation or precipitation occurs, unless the change of *p*H is great enough to cause reversal of the charge by "jumping" the isoelectric point.

isoelectronic molecules. Molecules with the same number of valence electrons, *e.g.*, N_2 and CO.

isoelectronic principle. Molecules with the same number of electrons have similar molecular orbitals, and consequently, also similar molecular orbitals, and consequently, also similar physico-chemical properties, *e.g.*, CO and N_2 molecules.

isoelectronic sequence. A term used in spectroscopy to designate the set of spectra produced by different chemical elements ionized in such a way that their atoms or ions contain the same number of electrons. Examples of isoelectronic sequence are shown in the following table :

Designation of spectrum	Emitting atom or ion	Atomic number
Ca I	Ca	20
Sc II	Sc (I)	21
Ti III	Ti (II)	22
V IV	V (III)	23
Cr V	Cr (IV)	24
Mn VI	Mn (V)	25

isohydric solution. Solutions that possess the same concentation of hydrogen ions. They may be mixed without alteration of the degree of ionization of either solute. By extension the term is applied to all solution which have a common ion in the same concentration.

isolated double bonds. Double bonds isolated one from another by two or more single bonds.

isolated system. System which cannot exchange either energy or mass with surroundings.

isolation. In chemistry, the identification and separation of a particular element or compound often the first step in la'ge-scale production of laboratory synthesis. Usually complex analytical techniques, extensive fractionation, and purfication procedures are required.

isolation method of ostwald. Method of determination of partial order of reaction *n* with respect to one substrate consisting in elimination of changes in consisting of remaining substrates by introducing them to system in high stoichiometric excess. During run of reaction, its rate, defined as decay of concentration of deficient reactant, should be proportional to its concentration to power *n*.

isologous series. Carbon compounds, similar chemically, but differing from one another in composition by a difference other than nCH_2 (characteristic of homology) are isologous and form an isologous series as :

ethane	C_2H_6	benzene	C_6H_6
ethylene	C_2H_4	naphthalene	$C_{10}H_8$
acetylene	C_2H_2	anthracene	$C_{14}H_{10}$

isomer. One of two or more compounds having the same molecular weight and formula but often having quite different properties and somewhat different structure stucture. A vast number of isomers are possible in organic chemistry, *e.g.*, in alcohols, benzene derivatives, and petroleum hydrocarbons. The following example indicates the nature of such closely related substance, the difference between them in this case being the position of the bromine atoms attached to the benzene ring. Dibromobenzene has the formula $C_6H_4Br_2$, but it has three distinct configurations all having identical molecular weights.

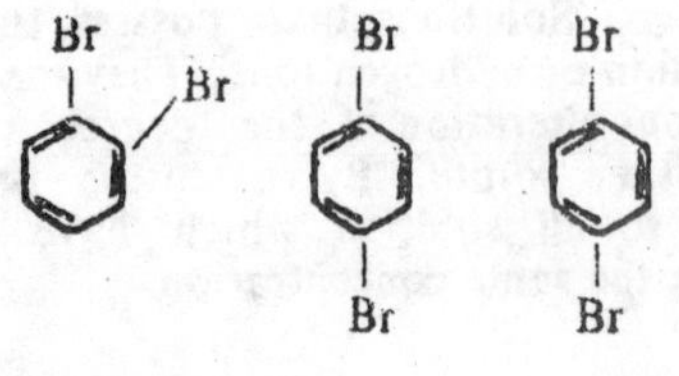

isomeric isotopes. Two (or more) atomic species with the same mass number and the same atomic number, but with different radioactive properties. They are believed to have isomeric nuclei, *i.e.*, nuclei which are composed ultimately of the same number of protons and the same number of neutrons, but which differ in their energy levels. Such isomeric nuclei are found among naturally radioactive elements as well as artificially radioactive ones. Two well-known examples of the latter are radiozinc of isotopic atomic weight 69, which emits a gamma radiation to yield another radioactive zinc of isotoic atomic weight 69 ; and a radioactive krypton which has an atomic weight of 83 and is, therefore, an isomeric isotopes of ordinary nonrarydioactive krypton.

isomeric nucleus. *See* atomic nucleus in excited nuclear state of long lifetime in comparison to normal excited state of this nucleus. Also known as metastable nucleus.

isomeric transition. Radioactive transition from one nuclear isomer to another of lower energy, with emission of gamma radiation or conversion electrons.

isomerism. A phenomenon attributable to the structure of chemicle compounds in which two or more compounds of different properties may possess identical ultimate compositions, *e.g.*, two substances of the formula C_4H_{10} are known, *viz.*, butane, $CH_3-CH_2-CH_2-CH_3$, and isobutane,

$$\begin{array}{c} CH_3 \\ | \\ HC-CH_3. \\ | \\ CH_3 \end{array}$$

There are many types of isomerism, as will be apparent from the listings that follow.

isomerism, chain. *See* chain isomerism.

isomerism, cis-trans. *See* cis-trans isomtrerism.

isomerism, desmotropic. *See* desmotropism.

isomerism, dynamic. *See* dynamic isomerism.

isomerism, geometrical. *See* cis-trans isomerism

isomerism, ionic. *See* ionic isomerism.

siomerism, linkage. *See* linkage isomerism.

isomerism, meta. *See* metamerism.

isomerism, nuclear. *See* nuclear isomerism.

isomerism, optical. *See* optical isomerism.

isomerism, position. *See* position isomerism.

isomerism, pseudomeric. *See* pseudomeric isomerism.

isomerism, stereochemical. *See* stereoisomerism.

isomerism, structural. *See* structural isomerism.

isomerism, syn-anti. *See* syn-anti isomerism.

isomerization. A method used in petroleum refining to convert straight-chain to branched-chain hydocarbons or alicyclic to aromatic hydrocarbons, to increase their suitability for high-octane motor fuels. Isomerization techniques were introduced on large scale during World War II.

isomorph. 1. One of two or more substance that crystallize in the same form.

2. One of a group of elements whose compounds with the same other atoms or radicals crystallize in the same form. The elements may be classified on this basis into eleven groups.

isomorphism. Similarity of crystalline forms of two chemical compounds which enables them to form substitutional solid solutions and alternate crystal growth of both compounds on each other's crystals. Necessary conditions of isomorphism are : identical type of unit cell of both compounds, similar dimensions of unit cells and the same type of chemical formula (*e.g.*, KNO_3 and $CaCO_3$).

isoplere. A curve or graph corresponding to the condition of constant volume, as *e.g.*, a plot of pressure versus temperature for a gas held at constant volume. Also termed isochore, isometric, and isopycnic.

isopolyacid. Polyacid containing only one acid-forming element, *e.g.*, 7-molybdic acid $H_6[Mo_7O_{24}]$.

isoprene rule. Nearly all the terpenes (found in essential oils of many plants) have carbon skeletons made up of isoprene units :

$$(CH_2=C(CH_3)-CH=CH_2)$$

joined together in a regular, head-to-tail manner. This rule has been of great help in working out structures of terpenes. Following structural formulas illustrate this rule :

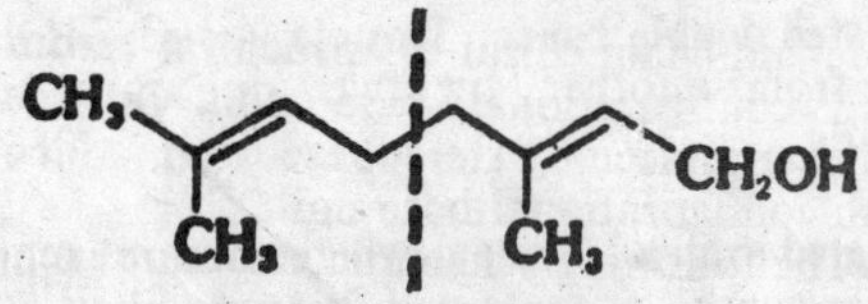

CH₃ CH₃ CH₂OH CH₃ CH₃

geraniol
($C_{10}H_{18}O$)

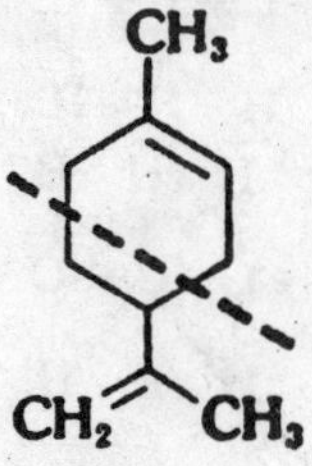

CH₃ CH₂ CH₃

limonene
($C_{10}H_{16}$)

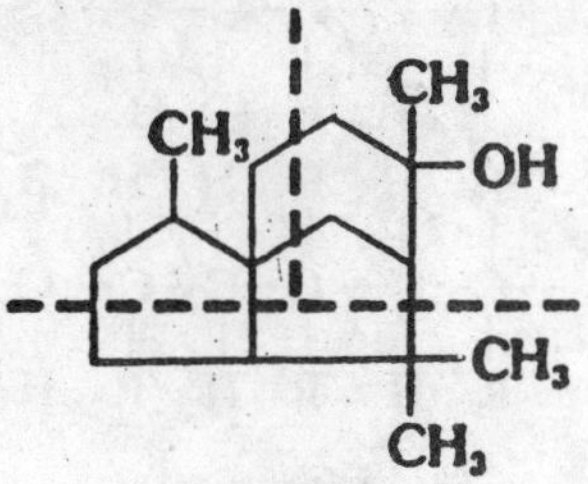

CH₃ CH₃ OH CH₃ CH₃

cedrol
($C_{15}H_{26}O$)

isorotation rules. *See* Hudson isorotation rules.

isosbestic point. Point on wavelength scale of equal absorption coefficients of two or more compounds existing in chemical equilibrium.

isosmotic. Having an identical osmotic pressure.

isospin. Quantum number attributed to elementary particles and atomic nuclei according to formula $n=2I+1$, where n denotes number of states in isospin multiplet. Also known as isotopic spin, isobaric spin.

isosteres. Pairs of compounds which show notable agreement in physical properties (as carbon dioxide and nitrous oxide ; carbon monoxide and nitrogen) and which (according to the octet theory) have the same number and arrangement of electrons in the molecule. The term applies also to radicals and groups of atoms which hold pairs of electrons in common. These are termed isosteric compounds, and the phenomenon is called isosterism.

isostructural compounds. Two or more chemical compounds crystallizing in the same type of structure in spite of difference in chemical composition.

isotactic polymer. Regular polymer composed of macromolecules having regular repetition of identical configurational base units at least at one main-chain chiral or prochiral atom in each configurational base unit. In isotactic polymer molecule,, stereobase unit is identical with configurational base unit.

The following schematic structure suggests the isotactic arrangement, though it is over-simplified since in the actual molecule the carbon atoms are not in the same plane :

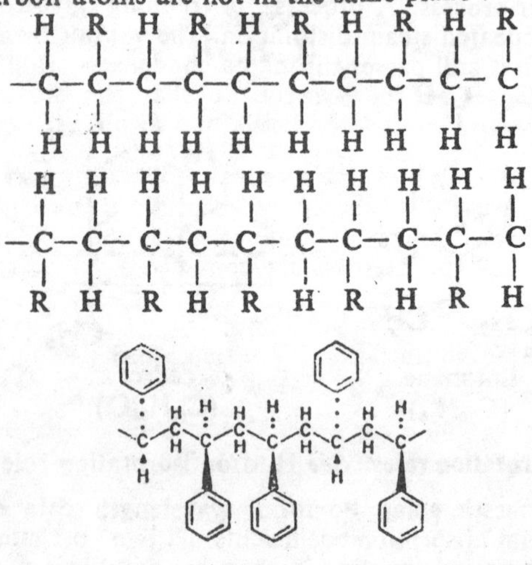

```
 H  R  H  R  H  R  H  R  H  R
 |  |  |  |  |  |  |  |  |  |
-C--C--C--C--C--C--C--C--C--C
 |  |  |  |  |  |  |  |  |  |
 H  H  H  H  H  H  H  H  H  H

 H  H  H  H  H  H  H  H  H  H
 |  |  |  |  |  |  |  |  |  |
-C--C--C--C--C--C--C--C--C--C
 |  |  |  |  |  |  |  |  |  |
 R  H  R  H  R  H  R  H  R  H
```

Such polymers are made with stereospecific catalysts developed by Ziegler and Natta and are distinguished from the older type by having a crystalline rather than an amorphous structure. They are made from propylene, styrene, and other olefinic monomers : isotactic polypropylene has been notably successful in the fiber field.

isotherm. A relationship, or its mathemetical or graphical expression, for which the temperature is constant.

isothermal change. *See* isothermal process.

isothermal equilibrium. An equilibrium reached by a system that remains at constant temperature during the entire process.

isothermal process. A thermodynamic process which occurs with a heat addition or removal rate just adequate to maintain constant temperature. The change in internal energy per mole U accompanying a change in volume in an isothermal process is

$$U_2-U_1=\int_{V_1}^{V_2}\left[T\left(\frac{\delta P}{\delta T}\right)_V-P\right]dV$$

where T=temperature, P=pressure, and V= volume per mole. Also known as isothermal change, isothermic transition.

isothermic transition. *See* isothermal process.

isotones. Nuclides having the same number of neutrons A-Z but different number of protons Z in their nuclei.

isotonic. Having equal osmotic pressure (of solutions) ; an isotonic salt solution is one containing the same concentration of sodium chloride as occurs naturally in body fluids (about 1%). For this reason, such a solution can be used effectively to restore osmotic balance in tissues when too much water has been lost from the body as a result of injury. It is also called physiological salt solution.

isotope. Any of two or more forms of an element whose weights differ by one more mass units as a result of variation in the number of neutrons in the nuclei. Isotopes of an element have the same atomic number Z but different mass number A, *i.e.*, of the same number of protons but different number of neutrons.

A few elements have only one stable atomic form, *e.g.*, manganese, sodium, beryllium, iodine : this form is commonly referred to as an isotope, though strictly it should not be, since there are no other forms that are like it, Such an element can correctly be said to have no isotopes, because at least two forms must exist to comply with the definition active isotope.

isotope effect. 1. Change of reaction rate caused by introduction into molecule of isotope of atom whose removal is kinetically the slowest process. Isotope is located at the same place original atom occupied. Deuterium and tritium are applied as substituents for hydrogen due to the largest difference in their isotopic mass.

2. Changes in properties of substance owing to replacement of an element by its isotope. Effects are most distinct when hydrogen is replaced by deuterium or tritium (the largest relative difference in mass between an element's isotopes).

isotope shift. A small difference between the different isotopes of an element in the transition energies corresponding to a given spectral line transition. For a spectral line transition between two energy levels 1 and 2 in an atom or ion with atomic number Z, the small difference $\Delta E_{12}=E_{12}(A')-E_{12}(A)$ in the transition energy between isotopes with mass numbers A' and A in the isotope shift.

isotopic analysis. Determination of particular isotopes in a given element or its compounds.

isotopic carrier. Carrier for radioactive substance chemically identical with substance, *e.g.*, inactive SO_4^{2-} ions for $^{35}SO_4^{2-}$ ions.

isotopic cross-section. Cross-section for specified isotone of a given element for a definite nuclear reaction.

isotopic dilution analysis. Method for determination of substance by tracing change in its isotopic composition caused by addition of known amount of the substance of different isotopic composition.

isotopic enrichment. Increase in content of specified isotope in mixture of isotopes.

isotopic exchange. Process whereby distribution of isotopes between different phases, different chemical compounds or inside molecules changes.

isotopic neutron source. Source emitting neutrons (usually besides radiation of other types) as a result of a nuclear reaction occurring in material of source.

isotopic spin. *See* isospin.

isotopic tracer. Isotope which is introduced into a system in order to examine it.

isotrimorphism. The condition in which two isomorphous substances are each trimorphous and each of the three pairs of forms is isomorphous. Also know as triple isomorphism.

isotropism. Independence of physical property of direction (most often crystallographic). All scalar physical properties are isotopic. Also in regular crystal all properties which may be described by vectors are isotropic. Also know as isotropy.

isozymes Different molecular forms of proteins with the same enzymatic activity. They differ from each other in their substrate affinity, in their maximum activity, or in regulatory properties. Also known as isoenzymes.

it calorie. cal (cal_{IT}). Obsolete energy unit ; in SI system 1 cal=4.1868 J. Also known as international steam table calorie.

-ite. A suffix indicating an intermediate oxidation state of the central element of a metallic salt, analogous to -ous for acids, *e.g.*, sodium sulphite (Na_2SO_3) which contains one less oxygen atom than the sulphate, and in which the sulphur has a valence of four, compared with a valence of six in the sulphate.

Ittner process. A process for refining glycerol by repeated steam distillation. The vapour from the first still passes through a condenser which condenses out the glycerol. So that the steam can be used in a second still, and so on.

-ity. A suffix meaning a property of a substance. For example, absorptivity, density, solubility, resistivity (which is simpler than the older term, specific resistance), coductivity, and so on.

IUPAC. Abbreviation for International Union of Pure and Applied Chemistry.

A voluntary, nonprofit association of national organizations representing chemists in 45 member countries. It was formed in 1919 with the object of facilitating international agreement and uniform practice in both academic and industrial aspects of chemistry. Examples are ; nomenclature, atomic weight s, symbols and terminology, physicochemical constants, and certain methods of analysis and assay. Reports on such subject are presented at the biennial conferences of the Union by the numerous Commissions dealing with them, discussed, and, after approval, are published. Its offices are in Basle, Switzerland.

Ivanov reaction. Reaction of organomagnesium compound (obtained from phenylacetic acid salt—Ivanov reagent) with carbonyl compounds, resulting in formation of β-substituted α-phenyl-β-hydroxypropionic acids, *e.g.*,

$$C_6H_5CH_2COONa \xrightarrow{(CH_3)_2CHMgX} C_6H_5CH(MgX)COOMgX$$

$$C_6H_5\underset{\underset{MgX}{|}}{C}HCOOMgX \xrightarrow{RCOR} R-\overset{\overset{OH}{|}}{\underset{\underset{R}{|}}{C}}-\underset{\underset{C_6H_5}{|}}{CH}-COOH$$

Iwanow test for rhodium. Rhodium solution on heating with stannous chloride solution turn brown and then raspberry-red.

izal. An emulsion of tar oils, widely used as a disinfectant and deodorant.

J

J. Abbreviation for joule. Symbol for mechanical equivalent of heat.

j. Symbol for inner quantum number.

Jablokoff test. To detect mineral oils in fatty oils, mix 1 part of the oil with 4 parts of aniline. The presence of mineral oils causes turbidity.

Jackson reaction for titanium. Hydrogen peroxide colours an aqueous solution of titanium compounds yellow to orange-yellow.

Jacobsen rearrangement. Migration of an alkyl group or a halogen atom in polyalkyl- or halogenopolyalkylbenzenesulfonic acides, effected by concentrated sulphuric acid, *e.g.*,

SO_3H, H_3C, CH_3, H_3C, CH_3 $\xrightarrow{H_2SO_4}$ SO_3H, CH_3, H_3C, CH_3, CH_3

Also known as Jacobsen reaction.

Jacquemart reagent. An aqueous solution of mercuric nitrate acidified with nitric acid ; used as a test reagent for ethyl alcohol. A black precipitate, produced upon addition of concentrated ammonium hydroxide, indicates the presence of ethyl alcohol.

Jaffe test reaction for molybdenum. Two to three ml. of the molybdate solution are acidified with hydrochloric acid. With triethanolamine, this solution gives a green ring test, becoming turbid and forming a blue precipitate, soluble in excess triethanolamine.

Jaffe test reaction for vanadium. A boiling solution of acidified vanadate forms green colour with triethanolamine ; on standing, the green colour changes to bright blue.

Jager test reaction for cholesterol. On heating with isobutyric anhydride cholesterol forms its isobutyrate.

Jahn-Teller effect. 1. Inseparability of nuclear and electronic motions in degenerate electronic states of non-linear polyatomic molecules.

2. Decrease in symmetry of complex (*e.g.*, from octahedral to tetragonal) caused by internal asymmetry due to incomplete filling with electrons of nonbonding *d* orbitals of central ion.

3. Jahn-Teller effect is most commonly observed in the optical and microwave spectra of point defects and localized impurity centres in solids. Such a centre has certain point symmetry, that is, there is a group of coordinate transformations which leave the centre and its surroundings unaltered. If this symmetry is high enough, some of the electronic states of the centre will be orbitally degenerate. *See also* Jahn-Teller theorem.

Jahn-Teller theorem. The most favourable energetic state of non-linear paramagnetic molecule is the one having lowest non-degenerate energy level of paramagnetic atom. This leads to spontaneous deformation of molecules (exception—*see* Kramers' theorem).

Jannasch reagent. A mixture of 15-20% hydrogen peroxide and 65% nitric acid, used in oxidizing organic matter, as a preliminary step in determination of inorganic substances present.

japan. A type to varnish orginally developed by japanese craftsmen for use on ceramics and other object of art. It contains a natural resin, a drying oil ; various pigments, and lead oxide ; after baking, it forms a hard, durable, and shiny coating.

japan wax. A mixture of glycerides obtained from a plant grown in the Far East ; it has a pronounced odour similar to tallow and a light yellowish colour. Its uses are similar to those of beeswax.

Japp-Klingemann reaction. A method of formation of hydrazones by the action of aryl diazo compounds on various activated methylene groups, *e.g.*,

$$CH_3COCH(CH_3)COOC_2H_5 \rightleftharpoons CH_3C(OH){=}C(CH_3)COOC_2H_5 +$$

$$Ar\overset{+}{N}{\equiv}NCl^- \xrightarrow{\overset{-}{OH}} CH_3COC(COOC_2H_5)(CH_3){-}N{=}NAr \xrightarrow{H_2O}$$

$$CH_3COOH + CH_3C(COOC_2H_5){=}N{-}NHAr$$

Jaworowski test for cobalt in presence of nickel. Neutralize the liquid tested with sodium carbonate, shake with sodium pyrophosphate until the precipitate has dissolved, dilute until almost colourless, shake 8 ml, of this solution with 1.5 g. sodium carbonate and 8 drops bromine water. A green colour indicates cobalt.

Jean test for soap in lubricating oils. An ethereal solution of the oil gives a precipitate of the soap on addition of an alcoholic solution of metaphosphoric acid.

Jean viscosity equation. An equation relating the viscosity of a gas to the temperature, having the from $\eta = kT^n$, where k is a constant, T is the absolute temperature, and n is an empirical constant differing for different gases.

jelly. 1. A modified (transliterated) from of gel. this term refers specifically to the colloidal dispersions fromed by warming and tern cooling mixture of pectins, sugar, and water. The socalled high-ester pectins have a recognized jelly grade when over 50% sugar is used ; low ester pectins form gels of the gelatin type.

2. This term is also used in nontechnical designations such as mineral jelly or petroleum jelly as alternative names for petrolatum.

jet fuel. Any of a number of combustible mixtures used in turbine-propelled aircraft ; some types are blends of gasoline and light petroleum fractions, others are specially prepared kerosines. Their composition and properties are closely controlled by specifications. *See also* kerosine.

j-j coupling. Interaction between spin and angular momentum of electron giving total angular momentum determined by quantum number *j*; each total angular momentum interacts with total angular momenta of other electrons in atom or ion and contributes to total angular momentum of whole system.

Johnstone test. To detect silver in lead, dissolve the lead in nitric acid, nearly neutralize with sodium carbonate and introduce strips of zinc and of copper. Lead is precipitated on the zinc and silver on the copper.

Jones process. A process for the manufacture of a fuel gas from oil, which consists essentially of thermal decomposition of the oil to yield gaseous hydrocarbons, and production of water gas by the intermittent admmision of steam. A relatively small amount of lampblack is formed.

Jonescu test. To detect benzoic acid in foods, acidify with sulphuric acid and distill with steam. Extract the distillate with ether and evaporate it. The residue is dissolved in water, and treated with ferric chloride, solution and hydrogen peroxide. A violet colour indicates benzoic acid.

Jorissen reagent for peroxide in ether. A solution of 0.4 g. vanadic acid in 4 ml. concentrated sulphuric acid and 100 ml. water. Shake 10 ml. of the ether with 2 ml. of reagent. A rose-red to blood-red colour is given if peroxide is present.

Josephson effect. The passage of paired electrons (cooper pairs) through a weak connection between superconductors, as in the tunnel passage of paired electrons through a thin dilectric layer separating two superconductors.

Joule's law. Internal energy of ideal gas depends only on its temperature.

Joule-Thomson coefficient, μ. Coefficient characterizing quantitatively Joule-Thomson effect, viz. :

$$\mu = \left(\frac{\partial T}{\partial p}\right)_{H_m}$$

where T=thermodynamic temperature, P= pressure, Hm=molal enthalpy of gas. Numerical value of μ is measure of departure of real gases from ideal gas behaviour.

Joule-Thomson effect. Temperature change in adiabatic process of free expansion of real gas without any external work being done.

In passing or gas at high pressure through a porous plug or small aperture, a difference of temperature between the compressed and released gas may be noticed. Hydrogen and helium become warmer and all other gases cooler at ordinary temperatures and pressures. This phenomenon is called the Joule-Thomson effect. It is due to the departure of real gases from the ideal gas laws. With a perfect gas no difference should be observed.

Joule-Thomson inversion temperature. *See* inversion temperature.

Jourdan-Ullmann-Goldberg synthesis. A method of sythesis of acridones by ring closure of diphenylamine *o*-carboxylic acids.

J particle. An elementary particle with an unusual long lifetime and large mass which does not fit into any of the schemes for classifying the large number of previously known particles. The dicovery of *J* particles in proton-proton (p, p) and electron-positron (e^-, e^+) collisions was of great importance for elementary particle physics. The energy spectrum of *J* particle family is very similar to the positronium spectrum. It is estimated that the *J* particle is a bound state of a new type of quark and antiquark.

juvenile hormone. A hormone secreted by endochrine glands associated with the brain in insects that prevents metamorphosis into the adult form and maintains the presence of larval characteristics.

juvenile water. Water in earth's crust that has come from magma.

K

K. Symbol for the element potassium. Symbol for Kelvin temperature.

k. Symbol for specific reaction rate or reaction velocity constant. Symbol for individual mass transfer coefficient. Symbol for thermal conductivity. Symbol for Boltzmann constant. Symbol for compressibility factor, or coefficient of compressibility. Symbol for force constant. Miller indices (h, k, l). Symbol for radius of gyration. Symbol for specific magnetic susceptibility. Symbol for overall mass transfer coefficient; expression for equilibrium constant.

kairomones. Kairomones are chemical substance that benefit the recipient living organism rather than the organism emitting it. These compounds elicit positive responses of predators to their prey, herbivores to their food plants, and parasites to their hosts.

Kamlet reaction. A method of formation of nitroalcohols by the condensation of the sodium salts of *aci*-nitroparaffins with the sodium bisulphite addition products of aldehydes in the presence of weak acid or alkali.

$$CH_2 : NO_2Na + RCHOH.SO_3Na \rightarrow RCHOH.CH_2.NO_2 + Na_2SO_3$$

kaolin. The most widely used industrial type of clay (aluminium silicate) : it is relatively free from impurities and has small and uniform particle size ; its neutral colour and high heat resistance have led to its use as the primary ingredient of fine ceramics.

Karaglanov sulphite test. To detect sulphite in the presence of thiosulphite, dilute the solution until addition of acetic acid causes no precipitation. Then add 2N acetic acid, and pass in hydrogen. The vapours will decolourize starch iodine solution if sulphite is present.

k band. Intensive absorption band characteristic of conjugated systems corresponding to allowed π-π^* electronic transition.

Kekule structures. Formulae of benzene and its derivatives, proposed by Kekule, describing benzene as a cyclohexatriene in which double bonds are in constant oscillation between adjacent position (which were to explain lack of expected isomers of the two and higher substituted derivatives), *e.g.*,

CH_3 CH_3 CH_3 CH_3

k-electron. An electron in the first shell surrounding the atomic nucleus; such electrons (two in number) are statistically nearest to the nucleus.

k-electron capture. Capture by a nucleus of an electron of the "K" shell, or the innermost shell of electrons surrounding the nucleus. This process accompanies the decay processes of artificially-radioactive atomic nuclei, notably those emitting positrons.

Kellogg equation. An equation of state, relating the pressure, absolute temperature, and density of a gas. It is of the form :

$$p = RT\rho + \left(B_oRT - A_o - \frac{C_o}{T^2}\right)\rho^2 + \left(bRT - a - \frac{c}{T^2}\right)\rho^3$$

in which p = pressure, T = absolute temperature, p = density, R = gas constant, and A_o, B_o, C_o, a, b, and c are constants.

Kelvin, *K.* Unit of thermodynamic temperature equal to 1/273.16 of thermodynamic temperature of triple phase point of water.

Term kelvin and symbol K are used both for denoting temperature value (previously marked °K), and for denoting temperature interval (previously marked degree). Also known as degree Kelvin ; degree absolute.

Kelvin equation. Equation describing dependence of saturated vapour pressure (at constant tempearture) on curvature of surface of a liquid; the equation enables maximum radius of capillary filled with liquid of given vapour pressure to be determined for capillary condensation, *viz.* :

$$\ln \frac{p}{p_0} = -\frac{2\sigma V}{rRT} \cos \theta$$

where V=molar volume of liquid, σ=surface tension of adsorbate, θ=wetting angle of adsorbent, r = radius of capillary, T = thermodynamic temperature, R = gas constant, p_0 = satrurated vapour pressure of adsorbate for flat liquid surface.

Kentmann reagent. A solution of 10 g. morphine hydrochloride, in 100 ml. concentrated sulphuric acid ; used as a test reagent for formaldehyde. If a liquid containing formaldehyde is floated on the reagent, a reddish-violet colour in the aqueous layer indicates the presence of formaldehyde.

keratin. A class of natural fibrous proteins occurring widely in animals and man; they are characterized by their high content of several amino acids, especially cystine, arginine, and serine. They are generally harder than the fibrous collagen group of proteins ; the softer keratins are components of the external layers of skin, wood, hair, and feathers, while the harder types predominate in such structures as largely due to the extent of cross-linking by the cystine molecules, which makes them difficult to dissolve. *See also* wool.

kerma. Energy supplied to defined medium by gamma or neutron radiation as kinetic energy of secondary charged particles.

Kern test reaction. Gold in solution gives an orange precipitate on warming with a potassium thiocyanate solution.

kerogen. The bituminous component of shale oil, which has the approximate compoition; carbon 75%, hydrogen 10%, nitrogen 2.5%, sulphur 1.5%, and oxygen 9%. On refining, it yields about 18% gas oil, 25% lube oils of various weights. It is formed by the conversion of plant and animal remains. It is the most common form of the organic carbon on earth; and it has been estimated that there is 1000 times as much kerogen as coal.

Kerr constant. A constant in the relationship between the different refractive indices of the same medium when exhibiting the properties of double refraction by electrical polarization (Kerr effect). The reduced form (independent of wave length of light) for the expression for K is :

$$K = \frac{n_p - n_s}{nE^2},$$

in which n is the refractive index of the medium for the incident light, and n_p and n_s are the refractive indices of the emergent polarized light vibrating in planes parallel and perpendicular to the direction of the field, and E is the field strength.

Kerr effect. Electric field induced anisotropy of refractive index of liquids.

ketazine. One of a class of nitrogenous derivatives of the ketones, of the type

$$RR'C{=}N{-}N{=}CR''R'''$$

in which R term represent univalent aryl or alkyl groups. For example, tetramethyl ketazine,

$$(CH_3)_2C{=}N{-}N{=}C(CH_3)_2$$

ketene. A class of organic compounds characterized by the presence of two double bonds. The term also applies to the compound which is the most important member of this class; its formula is $H_2C{=}C{=}O$. Others are derived by replacement of the CH_2 group with one or more methyl groups (CH_3) to form methylketene, dimethylketene, etc. These are all quite reactive compounds. Ketene itself is a severely toxic gas made by heat treatment (pyrolysis) of acetone or acetic acid. It has numerous applications in organic synthesis, especially as an acetylating medium.

ketimine. A class of organic compounds in which the oxygen atom of the keto-group has been replaced by the imino, =NH group. The type formula is :

```
  R
  |
  C=NH
  |
  R'
```

keto-. A prefix which indicates content of the carbonyl group, =CO, which confers ketonic properties.

ketoamine. A compound containing a carbonyl group (=CO), and an amino group ($-NH_2$).

keto-enol tautomerism. Type of prototropic tautomerism connected with reversible rearrangement of α, β–unsaturated alcohols (enols) into ketones and, in wider sense, of enols into carbonyls :

```
 |  |             |
 C=C     ⇌     —C—C—
 |  |             |  ‖
    OH            H  O
```

keto form. Tautomeric form having carbonyl group in molecule and at least one hydrogen atom at α-carbon $H{-}\overset{|}{C}{-}\overset{O}{\overset{\|}{C}}{-}$. Keto form exists in tautomeric equilibrium with enol form

```
CH3—C—H      ⇌     CH2=C—H
    ‖                  |
    O                  OH
```

keto-hexose. A six-carbon monosaccharose which contains a carbonyl group, *e.g.*, fructose.

ketol. A compound containing a carbonyl group (=CO), and an alcohol group (—OH).

ketone. A class of unsaturated and reactive compounds whose formula is characterized by a carbonyl group to which two organic groups are attached : these groups may be either paraffinic (alkyl) or aromatic (aryl). The best-known example of this class is acetone, or dimethylketone. $(CH_3)_2C{=}O$. Other important ketones are methyl ethyl ketone, acetophenone, and cyclohexanone The reactions of ketones are generally similar to those of aldehydes. Their major uses are in the solvent field, especially in the plastics, textile, paint, and lacquer industries. They are particularly good solvents for cellulose derivatives. The ketones are named in various ways : (*i*) By combining the names of the redicals (alkyl or aryl) with "ketone," as dimethyl ketone, ethyl methyl ketone, etc. (*ii*) The Geneva names are formed by adding the suffix "one" to the root of the parent hydrocarbon. Thus, acetone is propanone; ethyl methyl ketone is butanone. Simple ketones contain two alkyl or aryl groups of one kind; in mixed ketones the alkyl or aryl groups are different, *e.g.*, ethyl methyl ketone.

ketonic hydrolysis. Decomposition of β-ketoacid esters by water, leading to formation of corresponding ketones, alcohols and carbon dioxide; process involves hydrolysis of esters with subsequent decarboxylation of acid formed, *e.g.*,

$$CH_3\overset{O}{\overset{\|}{C}}CH_2COOC_2H_5 \xrightarrow[H_2O]{H^+} CH_3\overset{O}{\overset{\|}{C}}CH_3 + CO_2 + C_2H_5OH$$

ketose. Any sugar that contains a carbonyl group.

ketoside. Any glycoside which, on hydrolysis, yields a ketose, *e.g.*, methylfructoside.

ketosis. An excessive accumulation of ketone bodies in the tissues, blood, and urine. Ketone bodies are formed by the oxidation of fatty acids by the liver.

Keyes equation. An equation of state for a gas, deduced from the concept of the nuclear atom. This equation is designed to correct the van der Waals equation for the effect upon the term *b* of the surrounding molecules. The equation is written as

$$P=\frac{RT}{V-Be^{-\alpha/V}}-\frac{A}{(V+l)^2}$$

in which P=pressure. T=absolute temperature, V=volume, R=gas constant, e=2.718 . . . . and A, α, B, and l are constants for each gas.

Kick's law. An expression for the energy consumed in grinding in term of the fractional reduction in average size of the particles. It is of the form :

$$E = k \log \frac{l_1}{l_2}$$

where E=the energy consumed, k = a proportionality contant, and l_1 and l_2 are the linear dimensions of the initial and final particles, respectively.

Kikuchi lines. A series of spectral lines obtained by directing an electron stream against the surface of a crystal, due to the scattering of electrons by lasers of atoms in the crystal structure.

Kiliani-Fischer synthesis. Method for extending aldose chain by formation of epimeric cyanohydrins, followed by hydrolysis to -onic acids and consecutive reduction ; *e.g.*,

$$CHO\text{–}(CHOH)_n\text{–}CH_2OH \xrightarrow{HCN} H\text{–}{}^*C(CN)(OH)\text{–}(CHOH)_n\text{–}CH_2OH \xrightarrow{H_3O^+} CO_2H\text{–}C(H)(OH)\text{–}(CHOH)_n\text{–}CH_2OH \xrightarrow{\text{lactone formation}} \xrightarrow{[H],\ Na/Hg} CHO\text{–}C(H)(OH)\text{–}(CHOH)_n\text{–}CH_2OH$$

$$CHO\text{–}(CHOH)_n\text{–}CH_2OH \xrightarrow{HCN} HO\text{–}{}^*C(CN)(H)\text{–}(CHOH)_n\text{–}CH_2OH \xrightarrow{H_3O^+} CO_2H\text{–}C(HO)(H)\text{–}(CHOH\text{–}CH_2OH \xrightarrow{\text{lactone formation}} \xrightarrow{[H],\ Na/Hg} CHO\text{–}C(HO)(H)\text{–}(CHOH)_n\text{–}CH_2OH$$

HCN

Kindling temperature. The minimum temperature to which a substance, or mixture of substances in specified proportions, must be heated in order to cause them to burn continuously. In this definition, to burn means to undergo vigorous oxidation accompanied by the production of heat and light.

kinematic viscosity. A relationship defined as the ratio of the viscosity of a fluid in centipoises to its density : the value is expressed in centistokes. Determination is made by noting the time required for the test fluid to pass through an aperture of small diameter. *See also* viscosity; poise.

Kinetic current. Current resulting from electrode process of substance which forms at electrode surface from other electrodically inactive specia.

kinetics. As applied to chemistry, kinetics is the study of matter as conceived of discrete moving particles and the forces resulting from their behaviour at various temperatures. The term is derived fron the Greek word for moving. The basic principal of kinetics are emobdied in the gas laws of Boyle, Charles, Dalton, and Avogadro. This is one of the two fundamental approaches to the problems of rate changes in chemical phenomena, the other being thermodynamics.

Thermodynamics determines the driving potential for a system to change from one state to another, *i.e.*, whether a chemical reaction will proceed and how far it will proceed. Kinetics determines the rate at which a system changes and what resistance must be overcome to allow the change to occur. In chemical reaction, the latter is indicated by the activation energy needed to initiate the change.

kinetic spectrophotometry. Absorption or emission spectrophotometry of high time resolution, which enables investigation of short-living species (radicals and radical ions) to be carried out.

kinetic stage. In statistical mechanics, intermediate stage of time evolution of macroscopic system. During this stage bi- and polymolecular partition function depend only on unimolecular partition function but the whole system does not yet reach local equilibrium.

kinetic theory of gases. Branch of statistical mechanics which deals with properties of rarified gases by application of unimolecular partition function; *e.g.*, in order to describe macroscopic properties of ideal gas by, this theory one uses a molecular model, according to which gas is treated as ensemble of either dimensionless points or hard spheres moving randomly and mutually non-interacting except for elastic collisions. Form kinetic theory of gases one can deduce equation of state of ideal gas, Maxwell-Boltzmann distribution law, expression for mean free path, etc.

kinins. Chemical substance which stimulate differentiation of plant cells that otherwise may have lost permanently the power of differentiation. The kinins contain adenine, which seems to give these substance their biological activity.

Kirchhoff equation. The basic relationship between the variation of heat of reaction with temperature to the change in heat capacity accompanying the process. The generalized form of this equation is :

$$\left(\frac{\partial(\Delta H)}{\partial T}\right)_p = \Delta C_p$$

in which ΔH = the reaction at constant pressure, T=the absolute temperature, ΔC_p=the difference in heat capacities of the final and initial states. A similar equation can be deduced for reactions at constant volume.

Kirchhoff's radiation law (for thermal radiation). At a given thermodynamic temperature T and for a given wavelength λ ratio between emissive and absorptive power $E(\lambda, T)/A(\lambda, T)$ is the same for all thermally excited bodies and is equal to emissive power of perfectly black body $E_{bb}(\lambda, T)$.

Kishner cyclopropane synthesis. A method of formation of cyclopropane derivative from α,β-unsaturated ketones or aldehydes by reaction with hydrazine :

```
     R'
     |
  R—C
     ||              NH₂           -H₂O
    HC        +      |             ——>
     |               NH₂
     C=O
     |
     CH₃
```

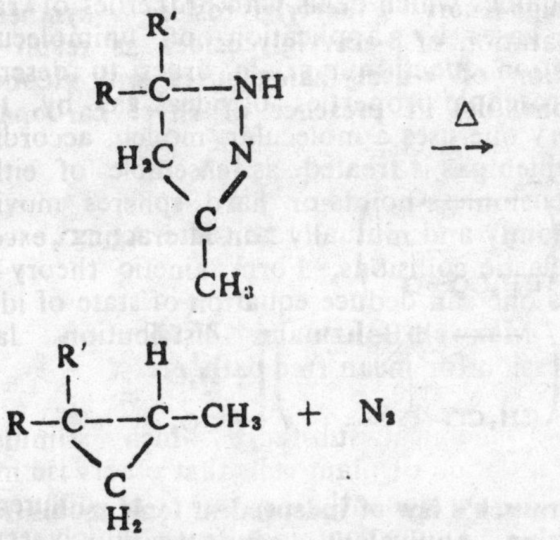

```
        R'
        |
   R—C——NH
        |     |          Δ
   H₂C    N         ——→
      \  //
        C
        |
       CH₃

    R'    H
    |     |
R—C——C—CH₃  +  N₂
   \    /
     C
     H₂
```

Kjeldahl method. Analytical method for determination of nitrogen in certain organic compounds. It involves addition of a small amount of an hydrous potassium sulphate to the test substance and heating the mixture with concentrated sulphuric acid and a catalyst; ammonium sulphate is formed. Ammonia is distilled off after alkalizing with sodium hydroxide the nitrogen present being determined by titration.

K-line. 1. One of the characteristic lines the X-ray spectrum of an atom produced by K-electron excitation.

2. The designation used for a strong line in the emission spectrum of calcium, useful in fixing spectrographic positions.

K-meson. Elementary particle, a hadron, of baryon number $B=0$, lepton number $L=0$, quantum spin number $J=0$, strangeness $S=1$, isospin $I=1/2$, party $P_j=-1$; unstable. K-meson occurs in two states of charge (isospin doublet): of positive elementary electric change (K^+-meson; mass $m=493.84$ MeV, third component of isospin $I_3=1/2$, mean lifetime 1.237×10^{-8} s); and electrically neutral (K^0-meson; $m=497.79$ MeV, $I_3=-1/2$). Neutral K^0-mesons are mixture of K^0_s particles with mean lifetime 0.862×10^{-10}s and of K^0_L particles with mean lifetime 5.172×10^{-8} s. K^+-meson and K^0-meson have corresponding antiparticles, K^- and $\overline{K}^0$.

Kniga test. To test for ferricyanide, treat one drop of the unknown solution on filter paper, with one drop of alkaline phenolphthalein. A brilliant red colour shows ferricyanide.

knight shift. Shift of resonance frequency or resonance magnetic field strength in nuclear magnetic resonance of metals, measured with respect to position of resonance signal for identical nuclei but in non-metallic substance. Knight shift arises due to interaction between nuclei and electrons of conduction band.

knock. Undesired ignition of a portion of a motor fuel in the cylinder head due to spontaneous oxidation reactions rather than to the spark. This is not only noisy but causes loss of power, particularly in high-compression systems. It is reduced by the presence of branched-chain hydrocarbons in the fuel and virtually eliminated by anti-knock agents such as tetraethyllead and manganese tricarbonyl. The use of these is declining because of their toxicity, their reputed contribution to air pollution, and their adverse effect on catalytic exhaust gas converters. In their place, increasing use is being made of non-metallic antiknock agents, such as methyl tertbutyl ether (MTBE) or a mixture of methanol and *tert*-butyl alcohol.

knock-out reaction. Nuclear reaction of direct interaction in which incident nucleon interacts with nucleon in target nucleus, knocking it out but itself becoming bound in nucleus.

Knoevenagel condensation. Condensation of aliphatic or aromatic aldehyde with compounds having active hydrogen (*e.g.*, malonic and cyanoacetic acids and their esters) in presence of catalyst such as piperidine:

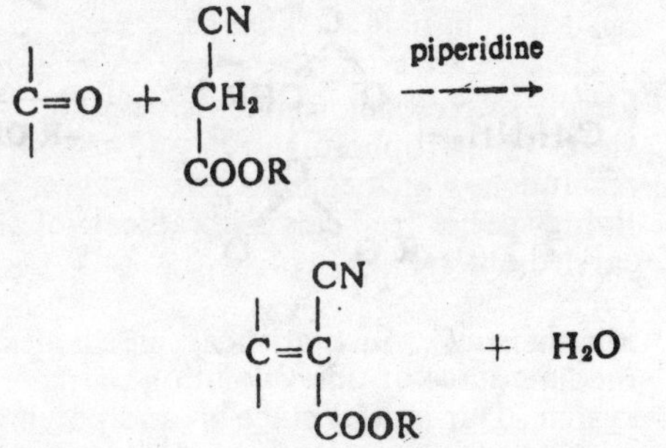

```
            CN
 |          |         piperidine
 C=O  +  CH₂       ——————→
 |          |
           COOR

                    CN
                |  |
                C=C         +  H₂O
                |  |
                   COOR
```

Knorr pyrazole synthesis. A method of formation of pyrazoles from β-dicarbonyl compounds and hydrazines:

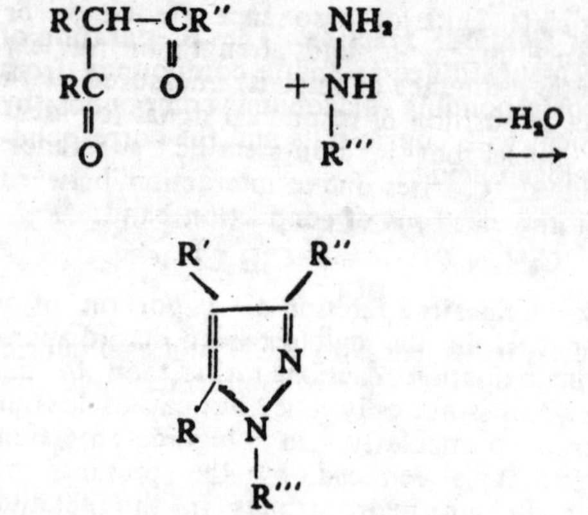

$$R'CH{-}CR''(=O)\text{, } RC{=}O \;+\; NH_2{-}NH{-}R''' \xrightarrow{-H_2O}$$

(pyrrole ring with substituents R′, R″, R and N–R‴)

Knorr pyrrole synthesis. Preparation of pyrrole and its derivatives by condensation of α-aminoketones with compounds containing $-CO-CH_2-$ group, *e.g.*,

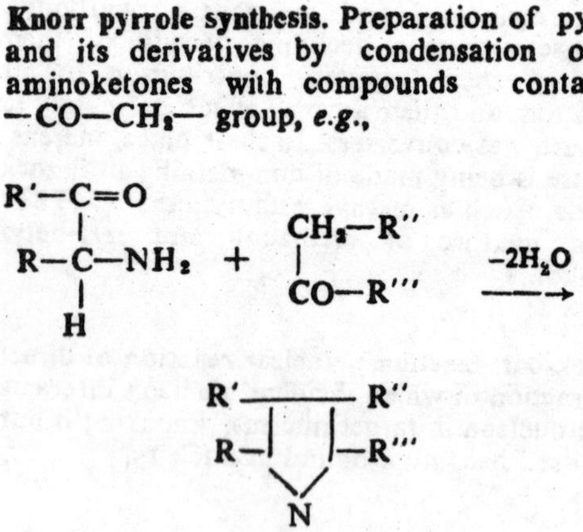

$$R'{-}C{=}O,\; R{-}C(H){-}NH_2 \;+\; CH_2{-}R'',\; CO{-}R''' \xrightarrow{-2H_2O}$$

(pyrrole ring with substituents R′, R″, R, R‴ and N)

Knorr quinoline synthesis. A method of formation of α-hydroxy quinolines by ring closure of aromatic amides of β-keto esters :

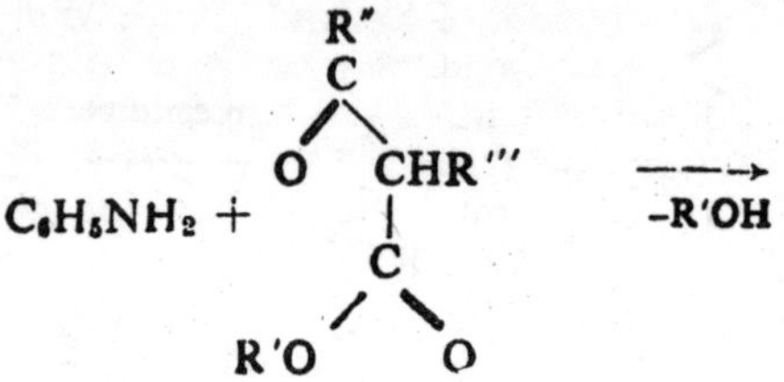

$$C_6H_5NH_2 + R''C(=O){-}CHR'''{-}C(=O)OR' \xrightarrow{-R'OH}$$

(anilide: $C_6H_5{-}NH{-}C(=O){-}CHR'''{-}C(=O){-}R''$)

$$\downarrow H_2SO_4,\ -H_2O$$

(quinoline with R″ at position 4, R‴ at position 3, OH at position 2)

Koenigs-Knorr acetylglycoside synthesis. Preparation of β-acetylglycosides as result of reaction of α-acetylhalogenoses with alcohols (or phenols), in presence of silver carbonate, *e.g.*,

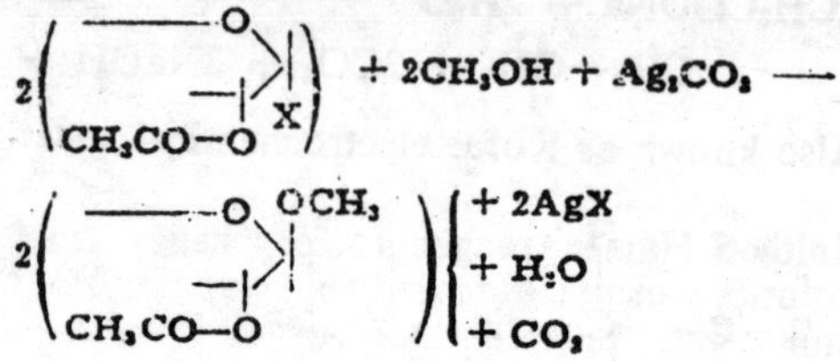

$$2\,(\text{acetylglycosyl-X, } CH_3CO{-}O) + 2CH_3OH + Ag_2CO_3 \longrightarrow 2\,(\text{acetylglycosyl-}OCH_3\text{, } CH_3CO{-}O) + 2AgX + H_2O + CO_2$$

Kohlrausch's law of independent ionic mobilities. Limiting equivalent conductivity Λ_0 of electrolyte is sum of limiting ionic equivalent conductivities λ_{0+}, λ_{0-} : $\Lambda_0 = \lambda_{0+} + \lambda_{0-}$. Also known as law of independent migration of ions, Kohlrausch's additive law.

Kohn test for glycerin. The glycerin is oxidized with potassium bisulphate to acrolein, which is detected by Schiff reagent.

Kolbe electrochemical reaction. *See* Kolbe synthesis.

Kolbe-Schmitt reaction. Preparation of phenoloacids (*e.g.*, salicylic acid) from sodium phenolate and carbon dioxide at 400K, under precsure of 0.4—0.7 MPa, *e.g.*,

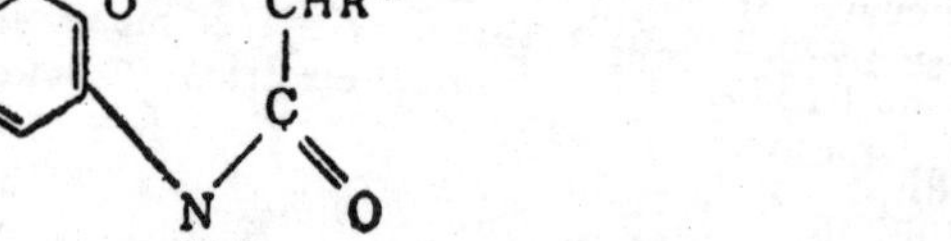

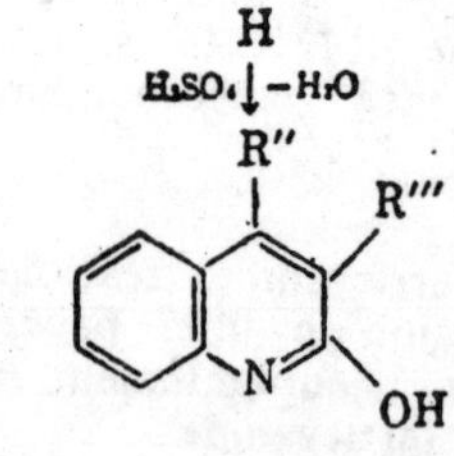

$$C_6H_5ONa + CO_2 \longrightarrow C_6H_4(OH)COONa$$

Kolbe synthesis. Method of hydrocarbons by electrolysis of aqueous solution of carboxylic acid salts, *e.g.*,

$$2CH_3COONa + 2H_2O \xrightarrow{\text{electrolysis}} CH_3{-}CH_3 + 2CO_2 + 2NaOH + H_2$$

Also known as Kolbe electrochemical reaction.

Kolthoff-Hamer reagents for heavy metals. Solutions of pyridine and thiocyanate, of pyridine and bromide, or of antipyrine and thiocyanate. They precipitate metals.

Kondakoff rule. Those alkenes which add mineral acids easily react with bromine or chlorine by replacement to yield unsaturated monohalides, while those alkenes which react sluggishly with mineral acids, add the bromine or chlorine to give dihalides.

$$(CH_3)_2C{=}CH_2 \xrightarrow{Br_2} (CH_3)_2C{=}CHBr \text{ or } CH_2{=}C(CH_3)CH_2Br + HBr$$

$$CH_2{=}CH_2 \xrightarrow{Br_2} CH_2Br{-}CH_2Br$$

Kondo effect. The large anamolous increase in the resistance of certain dilute alloys of magnetic materials in nonmagnetic hosts as the temperature is lowered.

Konowaloff's laws. Laws describing liquid-vapour equilibrium in systems of unlimited miscibility in liquid phase : (*i*) Gas phase is enriched in that component which, when added to liquid, causes increase of vapour pressure above it (*i.e.* in component which lowers boiling point of liduid); (*ii*) Maximum on curve of vapour pressure correponds to minimum on the curve of boiling points and vice versa ; these are azotropic points.

Kopp solution. A solution of 0.1 *g.* diphenylamine in 5 ml. concentrated sulphuric acid and 5 ml. water, which is then made up to a volume of 1 liter with concentrated sulphuric acid. It is used in testing for nitrates and nitrites, which give a blue colour with it. Many modifications of this test have been reported.

Kopp's rule. Molal heat capacity of solid compound is approximately equal sum of atomic heat capacities of its constituent elements.

Korner-Contardi reaction. The preparation of halogen-substituted aromatic compounds from the corresponding diazonium compounds by treatment with cupric salts and the corresponding halogen acid :

$$C_6H_5N_2Cl \xrightarrow[HCl]{CuCl_2} C_6H_5Cl + N_2$$

Similarly, treatment with KCN and the cupric salt yields nitrile. *See also* Gatterman reaction and Sandmeyer reaction.

Korner method. An absolute method for the establishment of the orientation of the substituents in derivatives of benzene based upon the number of isomers that can be produced by further substitution in the ring. For example, nitration of *o*-dibromobenzene leads to two isomeric (mono-nitro) derivatives ; *m*-dibromobenzene leads to three isomers ; *p*-dibromobenzene can lead to only one isomer.

Kostanecki synthesis of chromones and coumarins. Preparation of chromones and coumarins by treating *o*-acylphenols with fatty acid anhydrides and fatty acid sodium salts, in presence of triethylamine, *e.g.*,

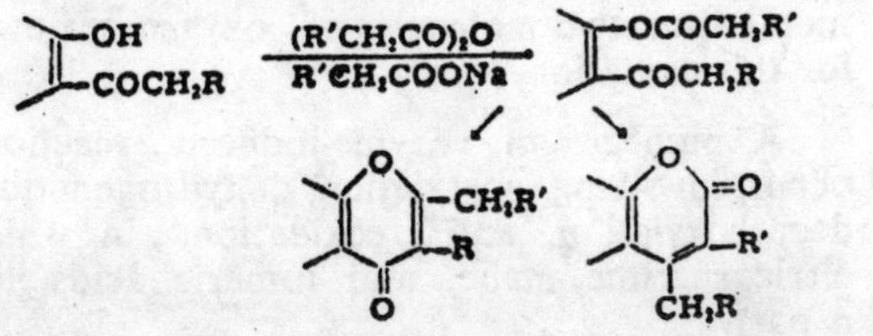

OH, $COCH_2R$ $\xrightarrow[R'CH_2COONa]{(R'CH_2CO)_2O}$ $OCOCH_2R'$, $COCH_2R$ → chromone (CH_2R', R, O) / coumarin (=O, R', CH_2R)

Kostanecki synthesis of flavones. Preparation of flavones or benzylideneeoumaranones by action of alkalis on dibromides of *o*-hydroxy-and *o*-acetoxychalcones. Flavones or coumaranones are formed depending on relative uf both bromine :

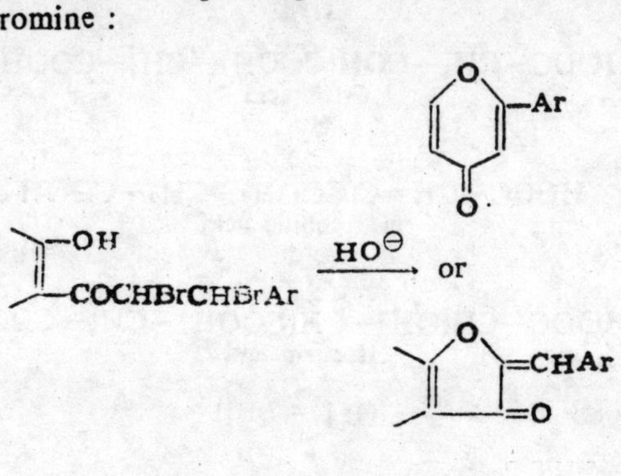

OH, COCHBrCHBrAr $\xrightarrow{HO^{\ominus}}$ flavone (O, Ar, O) or coumaranone (O, =CHAr, =O)

K-radiation. The radiation, or rather radiations, emitted when K-electrons are excited. These radiations are x-rays of relatively high frequency, and of similar spectral distribution for the various elements, except that they are displaced in the direction of decreasing wave length as the atomic number of the element increases. They are commonly obtained by bombardment with high-speed electrons of the particular element, usually in the form of the metal.

Kramers' theorem. In atom with odd number of electrons electric field of any symmetry leaves at least two-fold spin degeneracy which can be destroyed by magnetic field only.

Krase process. A process for the production of urea by the reaction of liquid carbon dioxide and liquid ammonia in an autoclave.

Krebs cycle. A sequence of enzymatic reactions that is involved in the oxidation metabolism of many organisms, especially those that carry out respiration. Tnough this sequence, or pathways, the two-carbon acetyl unit, an important metabolic intermediate derived from a variety of substrates, can be oxidised to two molecules of carbon dioxide. In aerobic metabilism, two molecules of oxygen are used for this oxidation.

A number of enzyme-induced reactions occur, involving acetylation, dehydrogenation, decarboxylation, and reoxidation, in which citric. succinic, malic, and fumaric acids play a part.

$$\underset{\text{Oxaloacetic acid}}{HOOC{-}CH_2{-}\overset{\overset{\displaystyle O}{\|}}{C}{-}COOH} + \underset{\text{Acetyl group of acetyl coenzyme A}}{CH_3{-}\overset{\overset{\displaystyle O}{\|}}{C}{-}}$$

(1) ↓

$$HOOC{-}CH_2{-}COH(COOH){-}CH_2{-}COOH$$
Citric acid

(2) ↓

$$HOOC{-}CH{=}C(COOH){-}CH_2{-}COOH$$
cis-Aconitic acid

(3) ↓

$$HOOC{-}CH(OH){-}CH(COOH){-}CH_2{-}COOH$$
Isocitric acid

(4) ↓ −2[H]

$$CO_2 + HOOC{-}\overset{\overset{\displaystyle O}{\|}}{C}{-}CH_2{-}CH_2{-}COOH$$
α-ketoglutaric acid

(5) ↓ −2[H]

$$CO_2 + HOOC{-}CH_2{-}CH_2{-}COOH$$
Succinic acid

(6) ↓ −2[H]

$$HOOC{-}CH{=}CH{-}COOH$$
Fumaric acid

(7) ↓

$$HOOC{-}CH_2{-}CHOH{-}COOH$$
Malic acid

(8) ↓ −2[H]

$$HOOC{-}CH_2{-}\overset{\overset{\displaystyle O}{\|}}{C}{-}COOH$$
Oxaloacetic acid

The Krebs cycle is a multi-faceted stepwise biological oxidation process, the energy of oxidation being retained as adenosine triphosphate. Also called the citric acid or incarboxylic acid cycle (TCA cycle).

Kroll process. A method of extraction of titanium from its ores, in which the essential step is the reaction of titanium tetrachloride with metalic magnesium to form magnesium chloride and metalic titanium. The exothermic reaction gives off enough heat to maintain the temperature at about 800°C for the reaction :

$$TiCl_4 + 2Mg \rightarrow Ti + 2MgCl_2$$

The operation is conducted under an inert atmosphere, and the magnesium chloride separates by leaching; or in the more recent modification, high temparature vacuum technique is used, wherein the magnesium chroride is distilled from the reaction mass. After separation the magnesium metal and chloride arc recovered by electrolysis of the magnesium chloride. The titanium metal is obtained in the form of a fused solid mass or a sponge.

The process is also used to produce pure hafnium and zirconium from their tetrachlorides.

Krumholz-Feigal-Rajmann reagent for palladium and platinum. p-Dimenthylaminebenzylidenerhodanine, which gives violet precipitates with palladium and platinum; used in spot tests.

Krumholz-Kruh test for cadmium. Decolourize the ammoniacal solution tested with potassium cyanide, add 5 drops of the solution of 1 g. sodium selenite and 0.5 g. potassium cyanide in 100 ml. water. On cooling, shake with 1 ml. ether. A red-brown colour in the interface indicates the presence of cadmium.

krypton. An element.

		Symbol	Kr
		Atomic No.	36
State	Gas	Atomic Wt.	83.80
Group	Noble Gas	Isotopes	6 stable
		mp.	116K
		b.p.	120.7K

Krypton is one of the noble gases placed in zero group of periodic table. It is estimated that about $2\times10^{-8}\%$ of the weight of the earth is krypton. Solid krypton has a face-centered cubic crystal structure. At standard conditions, krypton is a colourless, odourless gas. Natural krypton is a gas occuring in trace percentages in air, from which it is extracted by fractionation processes. It was formerly classed as an inert gas but later was found to form a few transient compounds with fluorine. Krypton forms a hydrate at 14.5 atm pressure and 273K. The element also forms addition compounds with a number of organic substances, such as $Kr.2C_6H_5OH$ with phenol, which has a dissociation pressure of 6-10 atm at 273K. Krypton also forms compounds, possibly clathrates, with certain substances in nonstoichiometric proportions. It is more than twice as dense as air and can be prepared in liquid and solid forms at very low temperatures. The principal use for krypton is in filling electric lamps and electronic devices. Krypton-argon mixtures are widely used to fill fluorescent lamps. The radioactive krypton-85 is used in analytical determinations.

K-shell. The innermost shell of electrons surrounding the atomic nucleus; this shell consisting of the K-electrons.

Kucherov synthesis. Direct addition of water to acetylenic hydrocarbons taking place in dilute sulphuric acid medium, in presence of mercuric salts as catalysts. Unstable adduct isomerizes to form carbonyl compound, *e.g.*,

$$HC\equiv CH + H_2O \xrightarrow[H_2SO_4]{Hg} [CHOH{=}CH_2] + CH_3CHO$$

Kuhn-Roth method. A method of determination of terminal methyl groups by oxidation of the compound with chromic acid-sulphuric acid. The terminal methyl groups are converted to acetic acid which is easily determined.

Kunz-Kraus reagent for cyanogen. A mixture of 1.0 ml. freshly-prepared 1 : 1000 aqueous cupric sulphate solution, with 1.5 ml. alcohol in which a granule of guaiaconic acid has been dissolved. Traces of cyanogen give a blue colour instantly.

kurie plot. A graphical relationship resulting from the Fermi equation for β-decay. The quantity (N/f) is plotted against $E + 1$, where N is the number of β-particles that have a momentum, or energy, lying within a certain narrow range, and f is a function of the corresponding calculated values of the β-particle energy E. In accordance with the Fermi neutrino theory, this plot should be a straight line. This plot is also called the Fermi plot.

kyanize. To protect against decay by saturating with aqueous mercuric chroride.

L

L. Symbol for Azimuthal or orbital quantum number.

L. A prefix conventionally appearing as a small capital, indicating the moleular structure or configuration of an optically active subsance, at stand for "levo", the left-handed enantiomorph of an optical isomer. It does dot mean that tne substance is levorotatory.

labelled compound. Chemical compound with some molecules containing isotopic tracer (radioactive or stable).

labile. A system or compound that is unstable, suffering conversion into a more stable form on slight disturbance. Thermolabile means modified by moderate heating, as certain isomers, enzymes, and bacteria.

labile complex. Complex in which ligands may easily be replaced by other ligands. Labile complex is characterized by high exchange rate of ligands. Also known as kinetically unstable complex.

Lachman process. A purification process for petroleum products obtained by craking, in which the hot hydrocarbon vapour is treated with concentrated zinc chloride solution.

lacquer. A type of organic coating in which rapid drying is effected by evaporation of solvents, as distinguished from a point, where drying is largely due to polymerization of a resin of oil. Nitrocellulose lacquers are the most important industrially: their largest use is for automobiles, furniture, and other products requiring a decorative and permanent finish. The rate of drying is rapid enough to permit economical large-scale operation. Other components of nitrocellulose lacquers (in addition to colourant) are plasticizers, alkyl or other resins, and solvents (both active and latent).

lactam. One of a group of cyclic amides containing the —NH—CO— grouping. For examples, two of the more common types of lactams are derived from the γ and δ aminocarboxylic by elimination of water—an intramoleccular condensation. They correspond to the γ and δ lactones and are of the general type:

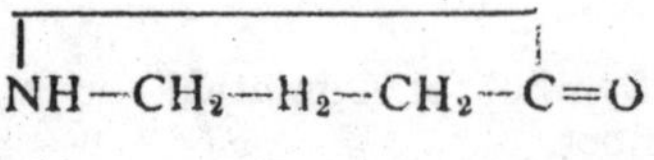

$$\overline{\text{NH}-\text{CH}_2-\text{H}_2-\text{CH}_2-\text{C}=\text{O}}$$

(γ lactam), and

$$\overline{\text{NH}-\text{CH}_2-\text{CH}_2-\text{CH}_2-\text{CH}_2-\text{C}=\text{O}}$$

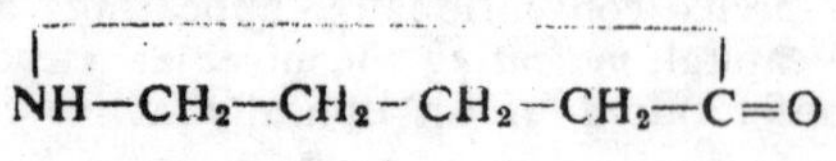

(δ lactam). They are named from the fatty acids of like carbon content.

lactase. An enzyme found in mammals, honeybee larvae, and some plants. It is a β-glactosidase which hydrolyzes lactose to galactose and glucose.

lactazam. A type of compound which may be regarded as a lactam (group —NH—CO—), in which the lactam-nitrogen is joined to a second nitrogen atom, *e.g.*, 3-methylpyrazolone:

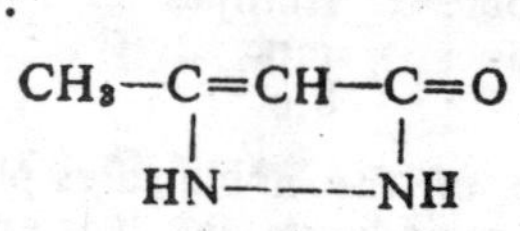

```
CH₃—C=CH—C=O
    |      |
    HN————NH
```

lactic fermentation. Type of oxidative fermentation of hexoses, *e.g.*, of glucose by Bacillus Delbruckii, resulting in decomposition of carbohydrate to lactic acid.

lactide. One of a group of cyclic double esters of the α-hydroxy acids. The lactides have the general type-formula:

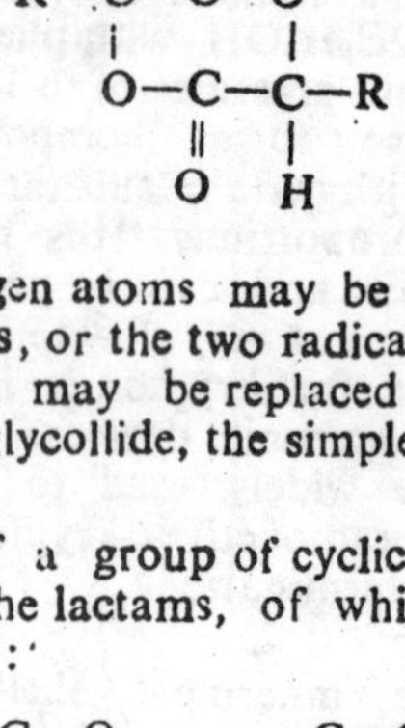

```
    H  O
    |  ||
 R—C—C—O
    |     |
    O—C—C—R
       ||  |
       O   H
```

The two hydrogen atoms may be replaced by organic radicals, or the two radicals (R) in the above formula may be replaced by hydrogen atoms to give glycollide, the simplest lactide.

lactim. One of a group of cyclic compounds, isomeric with the lactams, of which they are the enol forms:

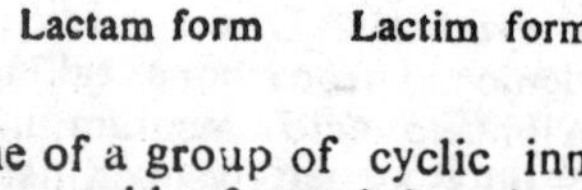

```
—C=O        —C—OH
 |            ||
—NH          —N
Lactam form   Lactim form
```

lactone. One of a group of cyclic inner esters of the hydroxy acids formed by the elemination of the elements of water from one molecule of the hydroxy acid. They are classified as α, β, γ, and δ according to the position relative to the carboxy carbon atom of the carbon atom connected to the hydroxy group.

Thus, the γ-hydroxy acid of type-formula,

$$RCHOH—CH_2—CH_2—COOH$$

yields a γ-lactone,

$$\overbrace{RCH—CH_2—CH_2—C}^{O}=O$$

and the δ-hydroxy acid of type formula

$$RCHOH—CH_2—CH_2—CH_2—COOH$$

yields a δ-lactone

$$\overbrace{RCH-CH_2—CH_2—CH_2—C}^{O}=O.$$

lactone rules. *See* Hudson lactone rules.

ladder polymer. A cross-linked high polymer comprised of double chains or strands of monomers or similar molecular groupings joined at regular intervals by hydrogen (or chemical) bonds, thus stimulating a ladder-like structure. Such polymers occur in nature in the proteins, where polypeptide chains are crosslinked with hydrogen bonds, in deoxyribonucleic acid, the inter-locked chains have a curved or helical conformation. The tanning of leather and the vulcanization of rubber approximate this mechanism. Some inorganic silicon compounds also exhibit a ladder structure, as do many synthetic organic polymers :

$$\left[\begin{array}{c} C_6H_5 \\ | \\ —Si—O— \\ | \\ O \\ | \\ —Si—O— \\ | \\ C_6H_5 \end{array}\right]$$

Ladenburg's law. The speed of a photoelectron is proportional to the square root of the excitation voltage.

laevo-, levo-. (Latin laevus, left) To the left, as in levorotation : rotating the plane of polarization to the left : as, levovaline. Abbreviation, *l* ; as, *l*-valine.

laevo-rotation. Specific effect in optically active substance ; when plane-polarized light passing through an optically active substance has its plane of polarization rotated in anti-clockwise direction (when viewed from opposite side to light source), such subsance is side (—), *i.e.*, laevo-rotatory (obsolete-notation : *l* —).

lake. A class of water-insoluble organic pigment made by precipitating base (aluminum hydrate). Soda ash, calcium salts, and other metallic salts can be used as precipitants. Lakes are limited in their service aspects because of their sensitivity to light ; their chief uses are in printing inks, interior paints, etc., where there is minimum exposure to sunlight, and in food colorants.

lambda. (Λ or λ). The eleventh letter of the Greek alphabet, used to denote : the eleventh carbon atom in a straightchain compound, or a derivative in which a substituent group is attached to that carbon. Symbol for latent heat of evaporation. Symbol for wavelength, Symbol for liner charge density. Decay or radioactive disintegration constant. Symbol for linear mass density.

lambda hyperon (Λ-hyperon). Elementary particle, a hadron, the lightest of hyperons, $m=1115.59$ MeV, electric charge $Q=0$, baryon number $B=1$, lepton number $L=0$, spin quantum number $J=1/2$, strangeness $S=-1$, isospin $I=0$, third component of isospin $I_3=0$, unstable, of mean lifetime 2.517×10^{-10} s (has antiparticle $\bar{\Lambda}$).

lambda point (λ-point). The temperature at which the transition of helium I to helium II take place. Under orthobaric conditions, liquid helium under-goes this change at 2.19 K. ; but the temperature at which this change occurs decreases with increasing external pressure.

Lambert-Beer law. For monochromatic light passing through solution of absorbing substance in non-absorbing solvent absorbance A is proportional to concentration c and path length b, $A=acb$, where a=absorptivity. Also known as Bouguer-Beer law.

Lambert's law. For monochromatic light passing through homogeneous medium absorbance A is proportional to path length b, $A=acb$, where a=absorptivity. Also known as Bouguer's law.

laminate. A composite structure made up of alternating strips or layers of the same or different materials, which are joined tightly with adhesives. Plywood is a familiar type of laminate in which the wood placed with the grain at right angles on successive layers to achieve maximum strength, the bonding agent usually being a phenolic resin. Similar structures are made with glass fibers (reinforced plastics). Adhesive-bonded paper and cloth are also used. Laminates of this type usually exhibit high strength and electrical resistance and are widely used in the construction industries. Rubber/fabric laminates, used in tire carcases, and textile fibers bonded with adhesive, as in nonwoven fabrics, are others, examples of laminates.

lande factor. Dimensionless quantity in formula for magnetic moment of paramagnetic atom ; depends on quantum numbers *J, L* and *S*. Also known as spectroscopic splitting factor.

landmark process. A process for the production of ammonia from nitrogen, steam and carbon using titanium nitride as an intermediate substance. Carbon monoxide is also a product of the process, and must be utilized for economic operation. The basic reaction is

$$2TiN_2+3H_2O+3C \rightarrow 2TiN+2NH_3+3CO$$

followed by the renitrification of the titanium nitride,

$$2TiN + N_2 \rightarrow 2TiN_2$$

Langheld test reaction. Benzaldehyde, on heating with dimethylaniline and ethyl metaphosphate forms malachite green.

Langmuir adsorption isotherm. *See* Langmuir isotherm.

Langmuir equation. Equation of adsorption isotherm derived on assumption that only monolayer adsorption occurs :

$$x = x_m \frac{Kp}{1 + Kp}$$

where x=amount of gas adsorbed by unit mass of adsorbent, x_m=amount of gas necessary for formation of monomolecular layer at surface of unit mass of adsorbent, p=equilibrium pressure, K=adsorption coefficient.

Langumuir isotherm. Adsorption isotherm corresponding to Langmuir equation. **Also known as Langmuir adsorption isotherm.**

lanolin. A mixture of cholesterol esters occurring in the sebaceous glands of sheep and similiar animals, which exudes into the wool. The crude product is known as degras ; the type resulting from tanning chamois leather with various fish oils is callon moellon degras. When removed by scouring and purified, the product becomes lanoline (from Latin word for wool).

lanthanide contraction. The name given to an unusual phenomenon encountred in the rare-earth series (lanthanides). The radii of the atoms of the members of this series decrease slightly as the atomic number increases. As the charge on the nucleus increases across the lanthanide series, all elctrons are pulled closer to the nucleus so that the radii of the lanthanide ions decrease slightly as the compounds go across the lanthanide series. Any given compound of the lanthanides is very likely to crystallize with the same structure as any other lanthanide. However, the lattice parameters become smaller and the crystal denser as the compounds proceed across the series. This contraction of the lattice parameters is known as lanthanide contraction. As a consequence of lanthanide contraction, the second and third rows of transition elements are much like.

lanthanides. *See* lanthanide series.

lanthanide series. Series of elements in groups IIIB of periodic system.

Their names, symbols and atomic numbers are :

Lanthanum	La	57
Cerium	Ce	58
Praseodymium	Pr	59
Neodymium	Nd	60
Promethium	Pm	61
Samarium	Sm	62
Europium	Eu	63
Gadolinium	Gd	64
Terbium	Tb	65
Dysprosium	Dy	66
Holmium	Ho	67
Erbium	Er	68
Thulium	Tm	69
Ytterbium	Yb	70
Lutetium	Lu	71

The elements with atomic numbers 57-62 are known as cerium subgroup. and 63-67 are the yttrium subgroup. Yttrium, atomic number 39, although not a rare-earth element, is found associated with the rare-earths and is separated with great difficulty.

Lanthanides are transition elements and, except for lanthanum and lutetium, form first series of inner transition elements (filling of 4*f* electronic sub-shell).

They are more commonly known as rare earth. They spelling recommended by IUPAC is lanthanoid, but this has not been generally followed by authors. Also known as lanthanides, lanthanide series, lanthanide elements lanthanons, lanthanoids.

lanthanoids. *See* lanthanide series.

lanthanons. *See* lanthanide series.

lanthanum. An element

	Symbol	La
	Atomic No.	57
State Solid	Atomic Wt.	138.9055
Group IIIB	Valence	3
	m.p.	1191K
	b.p.	3737K

The first the rare-earth metals comprising the lanthanide series of the Periodic Table. It is recovered from monazite sands and the ore bastnasite.

Elemental lanthanum has a double close-paked hexagonal crystal stucture at room temperature. Pure metallic lanthanum is silvery gray, in colour, but with a luster that remains only briefly upon exposure to air, rapidly oxidizing to a white powder. The oxide is hygroscopic and tends to spall, thus exposing fresh su.faces of the metal for oxidation, Thus the metal must be handled in an inert atmsophere. Chips and powdered lanthanum are pyrophoric,

Two solid forms known, the α-form, stable at ordinary tempratures, density 6.194 ; the β-form obtained by heating at 623K, density 6.17.

There are two natural isotopes, ^{139}La and ^{138}La. The latter is mildly radioactive with a half-life of $10^{10}—10^{15}$ years, The element becomes a superconductor below 6 K. There are 19 known artificial isotopes, all radioactive Of the light (or cerium group) rare-earth metals, lanthanum is the second most plentiful and ranks 57th in abundance of elements in the earth's crust, exceeding gold, tantalum, platinum, mercury, bismuth and several other commonly known elements.

It has some application in high-energy fuels and as a reducing agent, but its prineipal use is in alloys such as misch metal. Lanthanum compounds are used in glass and ceramics, as phosphors in fluorescent lamps, and as analytical reagents.

Larmor frequency. Frequency of nuclear or electronic moment precession about direction of external magnetic field *cf*, Larmor precession).

Larmor precession. Precession of vector of spin orbital or total angular momentum in external magnetic field arising when axis of momentum vector does not coincide with magnetic field direction.

Larson test reaction. Cholesterol and its esters are detected by a dark brown colour given by a 25% solution of antimony pentachloride in chloroform.

laser. This term is made up from the initial letters of "light amplification by stimulated emission". The emission referred to is that of a controlled beam of high-energy radiation of constant wave-length and frequency (called coherent light). It results from photon-initiated atomic vibrations in certain crystals, such as garnet and ruby when activated by trace addition of other metals (yttrium, chromium), in gases (argon, carbon dioxide), and in other materials (plastics, glasses). The exciting energy is due to photons from an external source (flash lamp) which initiates continuosly increasing emission of photons within the laser crystal ; in chemical lasers it is due to the bond rupture of a chemical reaction. Laser beams are exceedingly powerful and highly accurate cutting agents; adequate protection for the eyes is essential. They have been adapted to surgical techniques, diamond and metal cutting, missile guidance, and other high-precision work. One of the most successful applications of lasers to chemistry has been the enrichment of uranium isotopes for preparation of more effective reactor fuels.

laser chemistry. The branch of physical chemistry in which chemical reactions are altered, induced, or monitered by laser light.

latent heat. The quantity of energy, in calories per gram, absorbed or given off as a substance undergoes a change of state, that is, as it changes from liquid to solid (freezes), from solid to liquid (melts), from liquid to vapour (boils), or from vapour to liquid (condenses). No change in temperature occurs.

latent solvent. An inactive solvent (invariably an alcohol) used in conjunction with a true solvent for nitrocellulose, usually in the ratio of 1 volume alcohol to 2 volumes of active solvent. Alcohols alone are not good solvents for nitrocellulose but are less costly than active solvents such as ketones, and glycols and are effective when blended with them in nitrocellulose lacquers. For this reasion, their solvent power is said to be latent, *i,e.*, hidden. An example is isopropyl alcohol. The term cosolvent is often used synonymously.

latex. An aqueous suspension of proteins and resins occurring in some plants, trees, and shrubs, such as sapodilla, guayule, and especially the tree *Hevea braziliensis*, from which natural rubber latex obtained.

Latimer's equation. Empirical formula which describes standard partial molar entropy S_B of monoatomic ion in aqueous solution :

$$\bar{S}_B = \frac{3}{2} R \ln A_r + 37 - 270 \frac{|z_B|}{r_B^2}$$

where r_B = effective ionic radius solution : larger by 0.1 nm and 0.2 nm for anions and cations respectively than their crystallograghic radius, z_B = valency of ion.

lattice. The stable geometric arrangement of atoms in a crystal (metals, nonmetals, and their compounds).

A regular periodic arrangement of points in three-dimensional space ; it consists of all those points p for which the vector from a given fixed point to p has the form :

$$n_1a + n_2b + n_3c$$

where n_1, n_2, and n_3 are integers, and a, b, and c are fixed, linearly independent vectors.

The lattice structure constitutes a submicroscopic three-dimensional grating, or network of atoms, which refracts incident light of short wavelenth. Measurement of the angles of this refraction has made it possible to determine with x-rays the arrangement of atoms in a crystal with a high degree of accuracy. Vacancies or dislocations may occur in lattices due to lack of enough atoms to satisfy all the covalent bonds ; such imperfections have a marked effect on the electrical and optical properties of the crystal.

lattice constant. A parameter defining the unit cell of a crystal lattice, *i.e.*, the length of the edges of the cell or an angle between edges. Also known as lattice parameter.

lattice defects. All deviations from ideal periodicity of crystal lattice. Also known as crystal defects, lattice imperfections.

lattice energy. The energy required to separate the ions of a crystal to an infinite distance from each other ; usually expressed as kilocalories per mole.

lattice imperfections. *See* lattice defects.

lattice parameter. *See* lattice constant.

lattice plane. Plane incorporating at least three nodes which are not placed on the same straight line and which is parallel to one of possible faces of crystal. Also known as net plane of lattice.

lattice vibrations. Periodic oscillation of the atoms in a crystal lattice about their equilibrium positions. As the crystal is heated, the amplitude of vibration increases. If the heating is continued, a stage reaches when the vibrations are so violent that the atoms break away from their lattice sites. and the solid melts. On the other hand, if the crystal is cooled to absolute zero, the amplitude of vibrations does not subside entirely. A residual vibration or quantum-mechanical origin remains ; which is called zero point vibration.

Laue method. A basic method of diffraction of x-rays by crystals, or prepared section patterns, usually recorded photographically.

Laue pattern. Population of dark spots in photographic layer, of characteristic distribution, often symmetrical, obtained by irradiating fixed flat crystal with narrow beam of x rays of continuous spectrum.

Lauth test for aromatic amines. One drop, or a tiny particle, of the amine is treated on a watch glass with about ten drops of 30% acetic acid. A little lead peroxide is placed on the edge of the watch glass, and moistened by the solution. Characteristic colours are obtained with many aromatic amines.

laves phases. Solid phases formed from atoms of constant ratio of diameters, *e.g.*, Cu_2Mg, Au_2Bi, KBi_2.

law of combining volumes. In any chemical reaction, volumes of all gaseous substrates and products measured at the same constant pressure and temperature may be expressed in ratios of small integers. Also known as Gay-Lussac's law.

law of combining weights. In every chemical compound the proportion by weight of each element may be denoted by a fixed number (a different one for each element) or by some integral multiple of that number.

law of conservation of energy. The total quantity of energy in a closed system is constant. This law has been restated, in light of the relativistic relationship between matter and energy, in a form that applies to the total quantity of matter and energy in a system, taken together as a single entity.

law of conservation of mass. This law has been put in the form that matter can neither be created nor destroyed. More accurately, the total mass of any system remains constant under all transformations. In light of the relativistic relationship between mass and energy, this law has been restated in a form that applies to the total quantity of mass and energy in a system, taken together as a single entity. Also known as law of the conservation of matter.

law of constant angles. Angles between characteristic faces of particular kind of crystal at constant temperature remain independent of size of crystal, and of defects connected with process of growing.

law of constant composition. *See* law of definite proportions.

law of constant heat summation. *See* Hess's law.

law of constant properties. Properties of a pure substance are independent of its origin or previous treatment (strictly observed only for gases and liquids because in solids certain properties may vary depending on their treatment).

law of constant proportions. *See* law of definite proportions.

law of corresponding states. If any two or more substances have the same reduced pressure (the same fraction or multiple of their respective critical pressure) and are at equal reduced temperature (the same fraction or multiple of their respective critical temperature), their reduced volumes should be equal. These substances are said to be in corresponding states.

law of definite proportions. Proportion of masses of constituent elements or components in any definite chemical compound is fixed and constant. Also known as law of constant composition ; law of constant proportions ; Proust's law.

law of diffusion. *See* Grahm's law of diffusion.

law of distribution. *See* Nernst distribution law.

law of Dulong and Petit. *See* Dulong and Petit's law.

law of equivalent proportions *See* law of reciprocal proportions.

law of esterification. When the hydrogen atoms in the two positions ortho to the carboxyl group in a substituted benzoic acid are replaced by radicals such as chlorine, bromine, nitro, methyl, and carboxyl, an acid results which can be esterified by means of hydrochloric acid and alcohol only with difficulty or not at all.

law of impenetrability of matter. Two bodies cannot occupy the same region of space at the same time.

law of independent migration of ions. *See* Kohlrausch's law of independent ionic mobilities.

law of mass action. For a homogeneous system the rate of a chemical reaction is proportional to the active masses of the reacting substances. In state of chemical equilibrium reactant activities satisfy equation :

$$\prod_{C} (a_C)^{\nu_C} \Big/ \prod_{B} (a_B)^{\nu_B} = K_a$$

where a_B, a_C=activities, ν_B, ν_C=stoichiometric coefficients of substrates B and products C, respectively. Ka=thermodynamic chemical equilibrium constant.

law of multiple proportions. When two elements combine in more than one proportion the quantities of the first which are combined with a given amount of the second stand in the ratio of small whole numbers.

law of octaves. Newland's name for his hypothesis of the periodic system. His arrangement was a simple grouping of the elements in order of increasing atomic weight, beginning with lithium, in horizontal rows of eight elements each, beginning each new row directly beneath the previous one.

law of radioactive decay. Number of nuclei which undergo radioactive decay in unit time dN/dt is proportional to number N of unchanged nuclei present ; *i.e.*,

$$-\frac{dN}{dt} = \lambda N$$

where λ=disintegration constant. A statistical law. Also known as decay law.

law of radioactive displacement. The atomic number of an element produced by a radioactive disintegration is determined by the atomic number of the parent element and by the particle emitted. Specifically, emission of an α- or a β-particle by an element results in a new element with atomic number 2 units lower or 1 unit higher respectively, than that of the parent element. Also known as group displacement law.

law of rational indices. If face P of crystal, chosen as unitary, intercepts on three chosen crystallographic axes sections a, b, c respectively, then every other face R of this crystal intercepts on these axes sections a', b', c' respectively, related according to equation $a/a' : b/b' : c/c' = h : k : l$ at the same time ratio of face numbers $h : k : l$ (called indices of face R) is always rational, *i.e.*, may be expressed as integers.

law of reciprocal proportions. Elements combine with one another in definite amounts by weight corresponding to their equivalent weights. Also known as law of equivalent proportions.

law of the rectilinear diameter. *See* Cailletet and Mathias law.

law of successive reactions. In the formation of a consecutive series of intermediate compounds in a chemical process the compound which involves the smallest loss of free energy will be formed first, and the one which involves the next smallest loss of free energy second, and so on. This is also known as the law of intermediate reactions, or of intermediate stages.

lawrencium. An element.

		Symbol Lw
State	Solid	Atomic No. 103
Group	IIIB	Atomic Wt. 257
		Valence +3

Lawrencium is the eleventh transuranium element, and completes the actinide series of elements.

Lawrencium is an experimentally developed radioactive element. It was identified by irradiating californium with boron ions. The nuclear properties of all the isotopes of lawrencium from mass 255 to mass 260 have been established. Lawrencium-260 is an alpha-emitter with a half-life of 3 minutes and consequently is the longest-lived isotope known. An isotope, ^{256}Lw, half-life of about 45 second, was reported by the U.S.S.R. in 1965. It was said to have been produced by impact of oxygen atoms (^{18}O) on americium (^{243}Am). It decayed by alpha particle emission and electron capture to form ^{252}Fm.

leaching The removal of a soluble fraction, in the form of a solution, from an insoluble, permeable solid, with which it is associated. Leaching processes fall into two principal classes : those in which the leaching is accomplished by percolation, and those in which particulate solids are dispersed into the extracting liquid and subsequently separated from it. In either case, the operation may be a batch process or continuous.

lead. An element.

	Symbol	Pb
	Atomic No.	82
	Atomic Wt.	207.19
State Solid	Valence	2,4
Group IVA	Isotopes	4 stable
	m.p.	600.4K
	b.p.	2013K

Lead is a soft heavy metal obtained chiefly from the sulphide ore galena.

First ionization potential 7.415 eV; second 14.970 eV. Oxidation potentials $Pb \rightarrow Pb^{2+} + 2e^-$, 0.126 V ; $Pb^{2+} + 2H_2O \rightarrow PbO_2 + 4H^+ + 2e^-$, — 1.456 V; $Pb + 2OH^- \rightarrow PbO + H_2O + 2e^-$, 0.576 V; $Pb + 3OH^- \rightarrow HPbO_2^- + H_2O + 2e^-$, 0.540 V.

In terms of abundance, lead is scarcely represented in the earth's crust, the average composition of igneous rocks containing only 0.002% Pb by weight. Lead has four naturally occurring isotopes. In order of abundance, these are ^{208}Pb, ^{206}Pb, ^{207}Pb, and ^{204}Pb. There are ten unstable isotopes, 201-203, 205, and 209-214.

The atomic mass varies because of natural variations in the isotopic composition of the element caused by the various isotopes having different origins: ^{208}Pb is the end product of the thorium decay series, while ^{207}Pb and ^{206}Pb arise from uranium as endproducts of the actinium and radium series, respectively. Lead-204 has no existing natural radioactive precursors.

Elemental lead has a face-centered cubic structure with an edge of 4.950 Å.

A calcined mixture of lead zirconate and lead titanate (PZT) is used as a piezoelectric material. Other important applications of metallic lead are as grids in storage batteries, solders, vibration absorbers in heavy construction, type-metal alloys, piping, and cable sheathing exposure to lead results in a clinical picture of hypertensive encephalopathy, neuropathy, and hemolytic anemia characterized by coarse basophilic stippling in red blood cells. The mechanism of lead's action on human tissue is complex. For one thing, lead blocks heme synthesis. This leads to a buildup of red blood cell protoporphyrin. Lead interferes with cell metabolism by causing a deficiency of pyrimidine 5′-nucleotidase. Lead attacks erythrocyte membrane phospholipids with resultant loss of potassium and interference with the sodium-potassium balance. Diagnosing lead poisoning may involve a determination of the free erythrocyte protoporphyrin level as well as determination of blood and urine levels.

lead storage cell. A cell in which the original active materials can be regenerated by forming a current through, in the opposite direction to that in which it flows during discharge is called a storage cell. The lead storage cell is extremely useful, for its sturdy, capable of recharge, and relatively inexpensive. The electrodes are made of lead or an alloy of lead and antimony and the electrolyte consists of dilute sulphuric acid. One plate is created with brown lead oxide PbO_2, and acts as the positive pole. The other is coated with spongy lead, and acts as the negative pole. When the two terminals are connected. the electrons flow in the external circuit from lead plate. to the plate coated with PbO_2. The reactions during discharge are :

Reaction at the lead plate

$$Pb + SO_4^{2-} \rightarrow PbSO_4 + 2e^-$$

Reaction at the PbO_2 plate

$$2e^- + PbO_2 + 4H^+ + SO_4^{2-} \rightarrow PbSO_4 + 2H_2O$$

Overall reaction

$$Pb + PbO_2 + 2H_2SO_4 \rightarrow 2PbSO_4 + 2H_2O$$

The reactions are reversed during charging. Each cell gives an e.m.f. of about 2.2 volts, and in motor vehicles a 12 volt battery of six-cells is generally used.

The concentration of sulphuric acid in a charged battery is much higher than in a discharged battery; hence the statement that a charged battery never freezes in cold weather—the sulphuric acid lowers the freezing point of the solution. Usually the limits of specific gravity of sulphuric acid are 1.3 for a charged battery and 1.15 for a dead one.

leavening agents. The generation of carbon dioxide for use as dough leavening is produced by reacting sodium bicarbonate (baking soda) with one of several leavening acids.

Claims for use of acidic phosphate salts, in addition to formation of carbon dioxide, are the buffering effects for providing an optimal pH for the backed product, as well as interactions with protein constituents of flour, with resulting optimal elastic and viscosity properties of the dough batter.

Lebedev process. A method of producing butadiene by heating ethanol with a suitable catalyst.

$$2CH_3CH_2OH \xrightarrow{570-670K} CH_2 = CH-CH = CH_2 + 2H_2O + H_2$$

Le Bel-Vant Hoff theory. Theory constituting foundation of stereochemistry and explaining optical activity as consequence of steric structure of organic compounds. Theory assumes that four atoms (or groups of atoms) on carbon atom are distributed round it at positions corresponding to corners of tetrahedron, carbon atom being located in centre of that tetrahedron. When all, substituents *a, b, c, d* are different, molecule *Cabcd* is not superimposable on its mirror image, displays optical activity and forms two isomers.

Le Blanc process. A method for the production of sodium carbonate from salt, sulphuric acid, limestone, and coal. The salt is treated with the sulphuric acid, forming sodium sulphate, which is reduced to sodium sulphide by fusion with the coal (or coke), and finally the sodium sulphide is heated with the limestone to yield sodium carbonate.

Le Chatelier's principle. If a stress, such as change of temperature, pressure, or concentration, is applied to a system in equilibrium, the equilibrium is shifted in such a manner as to undo the effect of the stress. Also known as principle of mobile equilibrium.

lectins. A group of proteins, also referred to as phytohemagglutinins and phytolectins, which possess the unique ability to agglutinate erythrocytes and other types of cells. Lectins are widely distributed in plant kingdom. There is some evidence to indicate that lectins may serve to protect plants against certain pathogenic fungi and insect predators.

Leclanche cell. A primary cell, consisting of ammonium chloride solution, and electrodes of zinc and carbon, *i.e.*,

Cell of C | MnO_2, NH_4Cl (20%) | Zn type.

Lederer-Manasse reaction. A method of preparation of phenolic alcohols by the controlled addition of phenols to formaldehyde :

$$C_6H_5OH + HCHO \rightarrow C_6H_4(OH)CH_2OH$$

Legal solution. An alkaline solution of 10 g. sodium nitroprusside in 30 ml. water, used in testing for acetone in urine. A characteristic series of colour changes, beginning with red, is obtained.

Lemoult test reaction. On heating with phosphorus pentachloride at 80—100°C dimethylaniline produces a blue colour, which disappears at higher temperatures.

Lenard Ray. Fluorescence radiation of characteristic appearance obtained on passage of cathode rays (electrons) through metallic films or sheets.

Lennard-Jones potential. Semiempirical potential for intermolecular interactions :

$$u(r) = \frac{A}{r^n} - \frac{B}{r^m} \quad (m < n)$$

where r=intermolecular distance ; A, B, m, n are constants. If van der Waals forces are present it is usually assumed that $m=6$ and $n=12$.

Leone test. Cottonseed oil is detected by the formation of a brown ring on heating the oil tested with a 1% alcoholic solution of silver nitrate to which 0.5% nitric acid has been added.

lepton number, *L*. Number, attributed to elementary particles ; for neutrino, electron and μ^--lepton, $L=1$, for their antiparticles, $L=-1$; other particles and antiparticles have $L=0$. Lepton number is conserved in all interactions.

lepton number conservation law. Sums of lepton numbers of initial and final particles in a given process are equal. Lepton number conservation law is valid for all interaction.

leptons. Group of light elementary particles taking part in electromagnetic and weak interactions, of baryon number $B=0$, lepton number $L=1$, quantum spin number $J=1/2$. To group of leptons belong : electronic neutrino, ν_e ; muonic neutrino, ν_μ, electron, e^- ; and mu-lepton, μ^-. Antiparticles are respectively :

$$\bar{\nu}_e, \bar{\nu}_\mu, e^+, u^+$$

Leptons are very small, less than 10^{-18} m in size which is less than 1/1000 the size of a nucleus and less than 10^{-8} the size of an atom. Leptons are much simpler than hadrons in both their nature and behaviour, hence they are considered to be more elementary than hadrons.

Le Roy test for free chlorine in hydrochloric acid. The presence of chlorine is indicated by a blue colour on the addition of diphenylamine to the acid.

lethal dose. Dose of ionizing radiation which when absorbed by given population of living organisms, causes death of certain part of this population, after fixed period of time.

Letts synthesis. A method of formation of nitriles by heating acids with metallic thiocyanates :

$$RCOOH + NaSCN \xrightarrow{\Delta} RCN + NaHS + CO_2$$

leuc-, leuco-. (Greek) Colourless, white, as leucine ; specifically, denoting a colourless or weakly coloured compound closely related to a coloured compound, as leucomethylene blue.

leucine. One of a series of unsaturated glycines of the general formula :

$$C_nH_{2n-4}O_2N$$

Leuckart thiophenol reaction. A method of formation of thiophenols (or their alkyl ethers) from diazo compounds and xanthates. The reation takes place in two stages :

$$(i)\ ArN_2Cl + NaS.CS.OR \xrightarrow{\Delta} ArS.CS.OR + N_2 + NaCl$$

The intermediate compound yields the thiophenol on hydrolysis in alkaline solution, or the thioether by simple heating ;

$$(ii)\ ArS.CS.OR + H_2O \rightarrow ArSH + HSCOOR, \text{ or}$$

$$(ii)\ ArS.CS.OR \xrightarrow{\Delta} ArSR + COS.$$

Leuckart-Wallach reaction. Conversion of aldehydes and ketones into amines by heating them with formamide or ammonium formate, *e.g.*,

$$RR'CO + 2HCOONH_4 \rightarrow RR'CHNHCHO + NH_3 + CO_2 + 2H_2O$$

$$RR'CHNHCHO \xrightarrow{H_2O} RR'CHNH_2 + HCOOH$$

leuco base. One of the great number of colourless reduction products of certain dyestuffs, notably of the triphenylmethane derivatives, which on oxidation are converted back into dyestuffs.

leucomaine. One of a number of protein degradation products, formed in animal tissues, which are somewhat similar to the ptomaines.

level To promote maximum uniformity of a dissolved dye by means of an additive in the bath which acts as a wetting or dispersing agent. For sulphonic acid dyes, lignin is effective as it forms lignosulphonates in the dye solution.

levelling effect. The effect of a protophilic solvent, such as water, in equalizing the difference between acids in their tendency to ionize.

levelling solvent. Solvent in which different electrolytes have large equivalent conductivities of the same order ; for salts—solvent forming crystalline solvates, for acids—protophilic solvent, for bases—protogenic solvent. Also known as equalizing solvent.

Levenstein process. An industrial method of producing mustard gas from sulphur chloride and ethylene :

$$2CH_2 = CH_2 + S_2Cl_2 \rightarrow ClCH_2.CH_2S.CH_2CH_2Cl + S$$

levigate. To grind solid materials into powders of approximately uniform particle size, either in the dry form or mixed with liquid ; the term is also used in the broad sense of effecting a uniformly dispersed mixture of solids, pastes, or gels by mechanical agitation.

Lewis-Langmuir formula. A formula for a substance which shows each atom and the electrons that participate in the valence bonds uniting it to other atoms. For example, this type of formula for methane,

H
H:C:H,
H

shows the central carbon atom joined to four hydrogen atoms, in each case by a valence bond composed of a pair of shared electrons. To consider another type of compound, the formula for potassium chloride:

$\overset{+}{K}$:$\overset{-}{Cl}$:,

Lewis-Langmuir theory of atomic structure. A fundamental conception of the structure of the atom, in which the electrons surrounding the nucleus of an atom are considered to be arranged in shells. The number in the successive shells that appear in atoms of increasing atomic number, are inferred from the total number of electrons in the rare gases of the atmosphere whose chemical inactivity is attributed to their possession of complete shells. Since the atomic numbers of these elements are 2, 10, 18, 36, 54, and 86, the successive differences between these numbers are considered to be the number of electrons in the successive shells. Moreover, the theory is extended to explain the properties of other atoms which, by their gain or loss of electrons to achieve a complete shell structure, or by their sharing of electrons with other atoms, from the various types of chemical compounds.

Lewis-Randall's ionic strength law. In diluted solutions of strong electrolytes of the same ionic strength $J < 0.02$, mean activity coefficient of a given electrolyte has identical value independent of type of solution.

Lewis-Sargent's equation. Formula which describes liquid junction potential ϵd of bordering solutions of 1:1 electrolytes of equal concentration with common anion or cation:

$$\epsilon d = \frac{RT}{F} \ln \frac{\Lambda^{(1)}}{\Lambda^{(2)}}$$

where $\Lambda^{(1)}$ and $\Lambda^{(2)}$ are equivalent conductivities of solutions (1) and (2) respectively.

Lewis theory of acids and bases. Theory according to which acids are substances which may accept free electron pair from atom or group of atoms, forming coordinate bond; substances which have such an electron pair from group of bases. An acid is thus an electron acceptor. Hydrogen ion (proton) is the simplest substance that will do this, but many compounds, such as boron trifluoride, BF_3, and aluminium chloride, $AlCl_3$, exhibit the same behaviour and are therefore properly called acids. Such substances show acid effects on indicator colours when dissolved in the proper solvents.

Lieben iodoform reaction. A method of formation of haloforms by treatment with hypohalites, of acetaldehyde, methyl ketones, their halogenated derivatives, or compounds yielding them on reaction. The reaction is general for hypohalites, but derives its name from the "iodoform test" whereby the compounds listed above give the characteristic odour of iodoform with iodine in alkaline solution:

$$CH_3CHO + 3NaOX \rightarrow CX_3CHO + 3NaOH$$
$$CX_3CHO + NaOH \rightarrow CHX_3 + HCOONa$$

Liebig combustion. The oxidation of organic substances for analytical purposes so that their carbon and hydrogen are quantitatively converted to carbon dioxide and water, respectively, and absorbed in suitable materials.

liesegang rings. Concentric bands of precipitate formed in gel due to rhythmic precipitation of sparingly soluble sols. Thus, for example, if silver nitrate is dissolved in a warm gelatin sol which is then allowed to set, and a drop of sodium dichromate solution is deposited on its surface, the resulting silver chromate precipitate will appear in the gel as a series of rings, with clear areas between them.

ligand. Derived from the Latin word for bind, a ligand is a molecule, ion, or atom that is capable of furnishing or donating one or more pairs of electrons to a transition-metal ion, thus forming a coordination compound. Common substances that act as ligands are ammonia. water, and chlorine, When organic nitrogen compounds behave as ligands, a heterocyclic ring is formed and the product is called a chelate. The number of points of attachment of the ligand to the metal is called its coordination number and is normally 2, 4, or 6. Ligands which coordinate by donation of electrons from more than one atom are known as bidentate (*e.g.*, ethylenediamine), tridentate, and so on, the multidentate type being the most stable. Ligands may be neutral, positively charged, or negatively charged.

ligand field. Electric field defined by symmetry of complex formed by ligands in complex and causing splitting of energy levels (terms) of central ion.

Ligand field theory. Theory of electronic structure of complex compounds which is modification of crystal field theory and which takes into account covalence of coordinate bond (on basis of principal concepts of molecular orbital theory).

ligand number, $\overline{n}$. Average number of ligands of given type linked with central atom :

$$\overline{n} = \frac{c_L - [L]}{c_M}$$

where c_L = total ligand concentration. [L] = equilibrium ligand concentration. c_M = total concentration of metal in solution. Also known as average ligand number.

ligasoid. A colloidal system, in which the dispersed particles (or the dispersed phase) are liquid, and the dispersion medium (or the continuous phase) is gaseous.

light hydrocarbon. A gaseous or liquid aliphatic or aromatic hydrocarbon obtained from natural gas by fractionation or cracking and used in the manufacture of synthetic organic chemicals ; they include ethane, methane, propane, ethylene, acetylene, benzene, toluene, etc. Some are used as liquefied petroleum gases.

light metals. The term is generally used to refer to metals having a specific gravity of less than 3.5 that are capable of being used for construction purposes: these are aluminium, magnesium, and beryllium. Many others have low specific gravity, especially the alkali metals, but they are too reactive and much too soft for any but chemical use.

light oil. A coal-tar or petroleum fraction obtained by distillation, which boils between 110 and 214°C. It contains a number of important organic solvents, including phenol and cresol, which can be separated from it by further fractionation processes.

light platinum metals. Three chemical elements grouped horizontally in eighth sub-group of periodic system (in period V) : ruthenium, rhodium, palladium.

light water. Ordinary water, as distinct from heavy water (deuterium oxide). It is widely used as a moderator in nuclear reactors.

lignin. The noncellulosic portion of wood, of which it constitutes from 25 to 35%. It is an amorphous organic polymer whose function is to hold the cellulose fibers together.

It is used as an extender in plastics, as a binder in heavy emulsions and drilling muds, and as a leaving agent in dye baths. It is a source of vanillin ; phenol and benzene can made by fluidized bed cracking of lignin.

lignosulphonate. A waste product from pulp digesters in which the lignin of the wood is removed in the sulphide and sulphate pulping processes ; it is a component of the so-called black liquor.

ligroin (pronounced lig-ro-in). A low-boiling petroleum-derived solvent, sometimes also called petroleum-ether, the latter name is not recommended since the material is not an ether in the true chemical sense.

lime-soda process. A method of manufacture of sodium hydroxide by treatment of calcium hydroxide (slaked lime) with a solution of sodium carbonate. Calcium carbonate is precipitated, and the sodium hydroxide remains in solution.

liminal value. The minimum concentration, usually expressed in normality, of a solution of a drug which produces an observable physiological reaction.

limiting concentration. *See* limiting dilution.

limiting current. In electroanalysis, current which for given conditions is controlled by transport rate of reactant to electrode.

limiting curves. Any line on a phase diagram, or other graphical representation of the conditions of a system, at which two phases are coexistent. Usually these limiting curves are the plotted curves that separate phases.

limiting density. The value which the density of a gas approaches as its pressure-volume relationship approaches the constant value (at constant temperature) of an ideal gas.

limiting diffusion current. In electroanalysis, maximum value of current, independent over some range of electrolysis voltage ; it arises if in system there exists mainly diffusion polarization.

limiting dilution. Dilution of solution of analysed substance for which one half of performed tests still give positive result. Also known as limiting concentration.

limit of detection. Lowest concentration of analysed component of sample which can be determined by a given method.

limits of autoignition. Limiting values of combustible constituent concentration, or pressure above which (upper limit) or below which (lower limit) autoignition of gas mixture occurs, at the given temperature.

limits of inflammability. Boundary concentrations of inflammable constituent in gas mixture or (seldom) range of pressures of this mixture, at which inflammation may occur. Also known as ignition limits.

Lindar catalyst. A specially prepared variety of palladium used as a catalyst in the hydrogenation of alkynes to obtain almost entirely *cis*-alkenes :

$$R{-}C{\equiv}C{-}R + H_2 \xrightarrow[\text{catalyst}]{\text{Lindar}} \begin{matrix} R & & R \\ | & & | \\ C & = & C \\ | & & | \\ H & & H \end{matrix}$$

Linde test for glycerin. In the presence of glycerin, borax colours the flame green. A borax solution, to which litmus has been added, changes from blue to red with glycerin.

Lindo test for nitrate. To 0.5 ml. of the solution tested, add 1 drop of hydrochloric acid, 1 drop 10% of aqueous resorcinol solution, and 2 ml. concentrated sulphuric acid. A purple-red colour indicates the presence of nitrate.

linear adsorption isotherm. BET isotherm in the case of adsorption on ideal adsorbent (flat, non-porous surface).

linear attenuation coefficient, μ. Decrease in intensity of beam of ionizing radiation J (expressed as fraction of intensity of primary beam) after passing through absorber of unit thickness x

$$\frac{dJ}{J} = -\mu\, dx$$

linear dispersion (of spectrograph). Derivative $dx/d\lambda$, where dx=distance, along surface of detection, of two closely spaced spectral lines of wavelength difference $d\lambda$; usually expressed in millimetres per nanometre.

linear energy transfer, LET. Amount of energy transferred to defined medium by ionizing particle or quantum per unit length of track of particles or path of quantum propagation.

linear molecule. Molecule, whose atoms lie on straight line, *e.g.*, O=C=O.

linear polymer. Polymer composed of macromolecules forming long unbranched chains.

line defects. Irregularities in formation of crystal, occurring in structure along certain lines. Also known as linear defects, dislocations.

line interference (in emission spectral analysis). Partial or complete overlap of two or more spectral lines of close wavelength.

line pair. In spectroscopy, an analytical line and the internal standard line with which it is compared.

line spectrum. A discontinuous spectrum characteristic of excited atoms, ions, and certain molecules in the gaseous phase at low pressures. If an electric arc or spark between metallic electrodes or an electric discharge through a low pressure gas, is observed through a spectroscope, images of the spectroscope slit are seen in the characteristic colours emitted by the atoms or ions present.

line width. Quantity which defines degree of monochromacity of a given line in spectrum; usually given as half-width of spectral line.

lining. A ceramic inner wall, or surface, of a furnace or other high temperature apparatus, which is composed of either siliceous material, or material containing lime, magnesia, and substances giving basic reactions under the other operating conditions.

linkage isomerism. Type of isomerism of complex compounds which may occur when unidentate ligand contains two different atoms capable of coordinating, *e.g.*, SCN^- ion may be coordinated either through sulphur atom M—SCN (thiocyanates) or through the nitrogen atom M—NCS (isothiocyanates).

Linter reaction for salicylic acid. On addition of a little 10% acid mercuric nitrate to the solution tested, boiling for 2 minutes and cooling, the addition of a few drops dilute sulphuric acid and a few drops of a solution of sodium nitrate give a red colour if salicylic acid is present.

Liouville's equation. Conservation equation for generic *n*-th order phase distribution :

$$\frac{\partial \rho}{\partial t}+\sum_{k}\left(\frac{\partial H}{\partial p_k}\frac{\partial \rho}{\partial q_k}-\frac{\partial H}{\partial q_k}\frac{\partial \rho}{\partial p_k}\right)=0$$

where ρ = generic *n*-th order phase distribution in phase space of system. H = Hamilton function of system, t = time, p = momenta, and q = coordinates. Summation extends over all degrees of freedom of system. In classical statistical mechanics Liouville's equation determines time evolution of isolated system.

Liouville's theorem. The time of change of point density near a given point moving through gamma-space is zero. This implies that an assembly of points, which fills a certain part of phase space with a given density, will move through phase space in such a manner as to leave its density unaltered.

lipid. One of a broad class of organic compounds formed in the cells of plants and animals as metabolic products : they include fats, waxes, lecithins (phosphatides), sterols, carotenoids, and fat-soluble vitamins. Fatty acids and their glycerides occur in many lipids found in animal and vegetable oils.

Lipids are generally classified into the following groups.

Simple lipids :

1. Triglycerides or fats and oils and fatty acid esters of glycerol, *e.g.*, corn oil, cotton-seed oil, lard, butter.
2. Waxes are fatty acid esters of long-chain alcohols.
3. Steroids are lipids derived from partially or completely hydrogenated phenanthrene, *e.g.*, cholesterol and ergosterol.

Complex lipids :

1. Phosphatides or phospholipids are lipids which contain phosphorus and, in many instances nitrogen ; *e.g.*, lecithin, cephalin.
2. Glycolipids are lipids which contain carbohydrate residues ; *e.g.*, sterol glycosides, cerebrosides, and plant phytoglycolipids.
3. Sphingolipids are lipids containing the long-chain amino alcohol sphingosine and its derivatives, *e.g.*, ceramides, sphingomyelins.

Lipids are transported in the blood in the form of lipoproteins, which are synthesized in the liver.

lipolysis. The solution or decomposition of fats and fatty substances.

lipolytic enzyme. An enzyme that catalyzes the hydrolysis of fats and other esters to yield alcohols and acids. Also known as lipase, stearolytic enzyme.

Lippmann's equation. Formula which expresses dependence between tangent to electrocapillary curve and charge density on both sides of metal η^M-solution η^S interface :

$$\left(\frac{\partial \sigma}{\partial \epsilon}\right)_{p,T,\eta} = -\eta^M = \eta^S$$

where σ=surface tension and ϵ=potential of electrode.

liquation. Fractionation of an ore or alloy whose components have appreciably different melting points, by application of heat to the mixture ; the lower-melting components are thus removed, leaving the pure metal (in the case of an ore) or the base metal (in the case of an alloy or bimetallic structure).

liquefaction. Transformation to the liquid state ; term is applied more commonly to the change of gases to liquids than to the melting of solids.

liquefied natural gas. (LNG). A product of natural gas which consists primarily of methane. One property which differentiates liquefied natural gas from liquefied petroleum gas is the low critical temperature (200K). This means that natural gas cannot be liquefied at ordinary temperature simply by increasing the pressure, as in the case with liquefied petroleum gas, instead, natural gas must be cooled to cryogenic temperatures to be liquefied and must be well insulated to be held in the liquid state.

liquefied petroleum gas. (LPG). Any of a group of hydrocarbon fuels which constitute a portion of the broader group of compressed gases. Liquefied petroleum gases (usually abbreviated LPG) include butane, isobutane, propane, and propylene. All have ignition points above 703K but extremely low flash points, below 203K.

liquid. A state of matter intermediate between gaseous and solid ; liquids differ from gases because of their greater density and more complex molecules, and from solids because of their random (amorphous) molecular arrangement, which is the distinctive nature of the liquid state.

Liquids possess important transport properties, notably their capacity to transmit heat, to transfer momentum under shear stresses, and to attain a state of homogeneous composition when mixed with other miscible liquids.

Two classes of liquids are distinguished on the basis of their response to an applied force :

(*i*) Newtonian liquids, which flow immediately when stressed, the rate of flow being directly proportional to the stress, and assume any shape imposed upon them ;

(*ii*) non-Newtonian liquids, which do not flow until a force of critical magnitude is applied. Examples of this are thick colloidal aggregates such as putty and under certain conditions, asphalt and rubber. These exhibit what is called plastic flow. Many common materials resembling solids are either combinations of amorphous and crystalline phases or change from one to the other when under stress. Cellulose has been found to consist of crystalline structures in an amorphous matrix, unvulcanized rubber is amorphous when unstretched but develops crystallinity when stretched. Glass is technically a Newtonian liquid of such high viscosity that it is rigid. Thus, liquids are often difficult to differentiate from solids, as both conditions can exist in the same material.

liquid chromatography. Chromatography employing liquid as mobile phase. The mobile phase is percolated through the column by means of either gravity or under pressure pumps. The two principal forms of liquid chromatography are ion-exchange chromatography and gel chromatography.

liquid counter. Counter of the Geiger-Muller type used to measure ionizing radiation emitted by liquids.

liquid crystal. A state of matter intermediate between amorphous and crystalline, sometimes designated by the terms mesophase and mesomorphic. The most common examples are cholesterol derivatives. Materials of this nature combine the properties of liquids and crystals, that is, they have fluidity but at the same time have optical properties associated with crystal structures. They are known to occur in such biological forms as muscles and nerves. Liquid crystals have some applications in medicine, as well as in electronics, especially in colour television tubes.

liquid-drop model. Model of atomic nucleus in which nucleus is imagined as behaving like drop of liquid. Liquid-drop model takes into account strong coupling between nucleons. It explains approximate constancy of binding energy per nucleon, enables approximate calculation of mass of nuclei to be made in explaining fission ; it is valid for medium and heavy nuclei. Also known as hydrodynamical model.

liquid ion exchanger. Solution of compound containing ionogenic groups in water immiscible organic solvent, *e.g.*, solution of long chain aliphatic, sulphonic and phosphoric acids are used as cation exchangers, and solution of long chain aliphatic amine salts as anion exchangers, respectively.

liquid junction potential. *See* diffusion potential.

liquid curve. In a temperature-concentration diagram, the line connecting the temperatures at which fusion is just completed for the various compositions.

liquor. Any aqueous solution of one or more chemical compounds. In sugar manufacturing it refers to the sirups obtained from various refining steps (mother liquors). The paper industry uses this term extensively as follows : (*a*) black liquor is liquid digester waste (also called spent sulfate liquor) containing sulphonated lignin, rosin, acids, and other waste wood components, from which tall oil is made ; (*b*) green liquor is a solution made by dissolving chemicals recovered in the alkaline pulping process in water ; (*c*) white liquor is made by adding caustic soda to sodium sulfide solution. In dyeing technology, red liquor is a synonym for mordant rouge.

lisoloid. A colloidal system made up of a liquid phase surrounded by a solid phase.

lithium. An element.

	Symbol	Li
State Solid	Atomic No.	3
Group IA	Atomic Wt.	6.939
	Valence	1
	m.p.	452K
	b.p.	1613K

The first member of the alkali-metal series, lithium, has some unusual properties.

Lithium is lightest in weight of all the chemical elements that are solid at standard conditions. Elemental lithium in the solid phase has abody-centered cubic crystal structure. In comparison with other members of the alkali metal series, lithium has the smallest ionic radius, the highest ionization potential, least electropositivity, and the greatest heat capacity.

There are two naturally occurring isotopes, ^{6}Li and ^{7}Li. They are not radioactive. Two radioactive isotopes have been identified, ^{5}Li and ^{3}Li, both with very short half-lives, measured in fractions of a second. Among elements occurring naturally in the earth's crust, lithium ranks 28th, with an estimated average content of about 10-20 ppm. In terms of content in seawater, lithium ranks 17th. It has the lowest gravity (0.54) of any of the solid elements and is also one of the softest, rating 0.6 on the Mohs scales.

In metallurgy, lithium metal is used as a deoxidizer, desulfurizer, and degasifier in the production of a number of molten metals, notably copper and copper alloys.

Lithium is attractive for use in batteries for a number of reasons. Lithium is the most reducing of the alkali metals and also has the lowest equivalent weight.

The metal also has potential as a coolant and heat-trasfer medium for nuclear reactors. Very important potentially, lithium can be used as a tritium source for controlled-fusion reactors.

When bombarded with neutrons, it yields the hydrogen isotope tritium.

lithium-drifted germanium detector. Spectrometric semiconductor detector of γ radiation consisting of germanium (type *p*) in which an active layer is produced by drifting lithium atoms. Also known as Ge(Li) detector.

lithium primary cell. A primary cell whose anode is made up of lithium. It has a number of advantages over other primary cell systems. The cell is primarily designed for cardiac pacemakers and works with a typical current drain of 30 microamperes.

lixiviation. A process for separating soluble from insoluble matter by dissolving out the soluble substances and drawing off the solution from the residue.

local entropy production, σ. Rate of increase of locally produced entropy due to dissipative processes ; according to second law of thermodynamics local entropy production is always non-negative. Also known as entropy source strength.

local equilibrium. State of volume element in which its measured thermodynamic parameters correspond to values which could be obtained after isolation of this element from surroundings and when its thermodynamic equilibrium is reached.

localization energy. Dynamic reactivity index which gives some measure of reactivity of given position in molecule.

localized adsorption. Adsorption localized at definite sites of surface preventing motion of molecules along surface.

localized electrons. Electrons assumed to occupy localized molecular orbitals.

localized molecular orbital. Molecular orbital limited to some part of molecule, *e.g.*, σ orbital of C—H bond in methane. Also known as localized orbital.

local potential, $\Psi(t)$. Functional :

$$\Psi(t)=\int d^3xL(T, T_o; \mu_1, \mu_{1_o}, \ldots, \mu_n \mu_{n_o}; v, v_o)$$

where V=volume of system, $T(x, t)$=temperature as function of position and time, $\mu_i=\mu_i(x,t)$=chemical potential of i-th component as function of position and time, $v=v(x,t)$=local velocity of centre of mass function of position and time ; quantities supplied with subscript "*o*" refer to stationary state and quantities without this subscript change over all comparative states satisfying the same boundary conditions. Local potential reaches its minimum value at $T\equiv T_o$, $\mu_i \equiv \mu_{i_o}$, $v\equiv v_o$; in statistical mechanical interpretation local potential is measure of information gain which would have to accompany the system transition from a given state to comparative state.

london forces. Forces due to mutual perturbations of the electron clouds of two atoms or molecules which, when the molecules are in their ground electronic states, are attractive. The principal part of these forces is due to interactions between the instantaneous dipole moments and gives a potential energy varying inversely as the sixth power of the molecular separation.

long distance effect. Influence exerted by remote substituent in steroidal systems on reaction rate of reacting centre, *e.g.*,

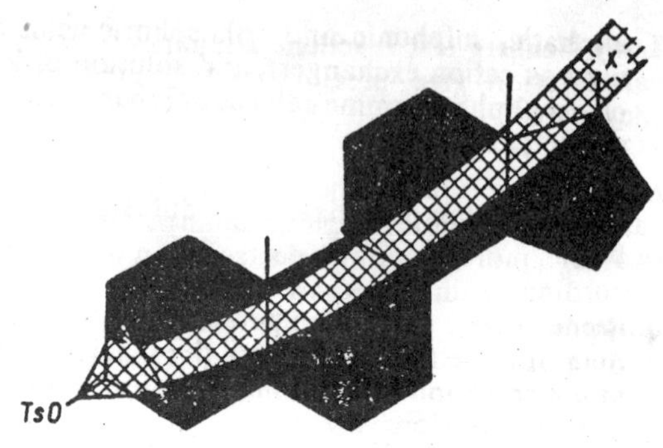

Ts=tosyl ($-SO_2C_6H_4CH_3$)

long oil. A term used in paint or varnish containing an unusually high proportion of drying oil, which makes it suitable for prolonged use in outdoor service for example, spar varnish.

Lorentz-Lorenz equation. Equation relating molar refration Rm of chemical compound to its electronic polarizability

$$R_m = \frac{[n^2-1]}{[n^2+2]}\frac{M}{\rho} = 4/3\,\pi N_A\alpha$$

where n = refractive index, M = relative molecular mass, ρ = density, N_A=Avogadro's constant.

Lorenz field. Local field of strength E_L acting on molecule in isotropic dielectric :

$$E_L=E + 4/3\pi P$$

where : E = external electric field vector, P= dielectric polarization.

Lossen rearrangement. The rearrangement of aromatic hydroxamic acids or their derivatives into isocyanates. The change is effected by heat or by certain reagents, such as an alkali, or thionyl chloride :

$$R-\overset{\overset{O}{\|}}{C}-\overset{\overset{H}{|}}{N}-O-\overset{\overset{O}{\|}}{C}-R' \xrightarrow{\text{Base}} RNCO \xrightarrow{H_2O} RNH_2$$

low-spin complex. Complex in which some or all of unpaired electrons of free metal ions are paired.

Lowy-Neuberg test reaction. Diamines in ethereal solution give precipitates with phenylisocyanate.

L-S coupling. One of the possible methods of calculating the total angular momentum of the two or more orbiting electrons in an atom. According to this method the orbital angular momentum and the spin angular momentum vectors of the elctrons are added separately to obtain a resultant orbital and a resultant spin angular momentum vector. The two resultants are then combined vectorially to obtain a series of allowed total angular momentum vectors. Interaction of total spin and total angular momenta of all electrons giving total angular momentum of atom :

$$p_J = h \sqrt{J(J+1)}$$

where J is total angular momentum quantum number. Also known as Russel-Saunders coupling.

lubricant. An inclusive term embracing a wide variety of substances (solid, semisolid, liquid, and even gaseous) whose molecules (or crystals) are able to pass over one another freely when slight shearing force is applied.

The majority of lubricants are oils of various types derived from petroleum and greases made by compounding mineral oils with soaps of heavy metals. There is also a wide variety of synthetic lubricants based on silicone compound, polyglycols, phosphate esters, and chlorofluorocarbons.

Lucas theory. A theory of the effect of substituent groups upon the electronic configuration of atoms, which has been applied to explain many structural phenomena, including the differences in properties of position-isomers or place-isomers, especially of benzenoid compounds. One of the salient points of this theory is that a substituting radical, especially in an organic compound, attracts or repels electrons of neighbouring and other atoms and thus modifies the chemical reactivity of those atoms.

Luggin capillary. Capillary extension of reference electrode or salt bridge in measurements of polarization (overvoltage) ; tip of capillary is placed very near and perpendicularly to investigated electrode in order to decrease pseudo-resistance (overvoltage) polarization.

luminescence. Radiation of any wavelength emitted by the atoms or molecules of a substance (solid, liquid, or gas) as a result of absorption of exciting energy (photons, electrons, chemical reactions) and subsequent release of some of that energy on return of the excited atoms to their normal state, without accompanying evolution of heat. The wavelength ranges include the entire visible spectrum (reds, greens, blues, etc,) and extend into the ultraviolet and infrared. There are several types of luminescence, designated by the nature of the energy source ; electroluminescence is induced by an electric impulse or current ; chemiluminescence results from chemical bond formation, electron capture, or oxygen elimination ; bioluminescence occurs in organisms (insects, marine fauna) by oxidation catalyzed by the enzyme luciferase; photoluminescence is due to shortwave radiation (photons). Two cases of luminescence are fluorescence and phosphorescence.

luminophores. Substances displaying luminescence after their excitation, *e.g.*, solid solutions of some fluorescent dyes or activated crystal phosphorus.

luster. The reflection of the light from the surface of an object or material, and the appearance of the surface by that reflected light. The luster of minerals is a property which is useful in their identification. The luster of a mineral may be metallic, vitreous, adamantine, resinous, pearly, greasy, silky, dull, or earthy.

lutetium. An element.

	Symbol	Lu
State Solid	Atomic No.	71
Group III B	Atomic Wt.	174.97
	Valence	3
	Isotopes	1 stable
	m.p.	1948K
	b.p.	3575K

Lutetium is least abundant of the lanthanide elements, estimated as present on the average of 0.5 ppm in the earth's crust. Potentially, however, it is more plentiful than mercury, cadmium, or any of the precious metals.

Lutetium is a very rare metal and the heaviest member of lanthanide series. Lutetium is recoverd from monazite sands in which it occurs in concentrations of as low as 0.003%. It is quite similar to erbium and holmium.

Elemental lutetium has a close-packed hexagonal crystal structure at 25°C. Pure metallic lutetium is a silvery-gray coloured and retains its lustre at room temperature indefinitely. There are two natural isotopes, ^{175}Lu and ^{176}Lu. The latter isotope is radioactive, with a half-life of 2.2×10^{10} years. Fourteen artificial isotopes are known. Because it is expensive to produce, it has no industrial application but is of considerable interests to scientists studying magnetism. Lutetium is classified with a low acute-toxicity rating.

luteo. Orange-yellow, brownish yellow ; specifically, designating certain series of coordination compounds, as $[M(NH_3)_6]Cl_3$ (the members of which are not necessarily all yellow).

lyate ion. Product of autoprotolysis ; base formed from molecule of solvent after proton removal, coupled with equivalent amount of simultaneously formed acid, *i.e.*, lyate ion; *e.g.* lyate ions of water and formic acid :

$$2H_2O \rightleftharpoons \boxed{OH^-} + H_3O^+$$

$$2HCOOH \rightleftharpoons \boxed{HCOO^-} + H-\overset{\displaystyle OH}{\underset{\displaystyle OH}{C^+}}$$

Lyman series. A series of lines in the ultraviolet region of the spectrum of atomic hydrogen. The wave number of the lines in this series are given by the relationship :

$$\bar{\nu} = R_H \left(\frac{1}{n_1^2} - \frac{1}{n_2^2} \right)$$

where ν is the wave number of a line in the Lyman series, R_H is the Rydberg constant, n_1 is 1, and n_2 has various intergral values.

lyogel. Gel rich in liquid produced in gelation process when bonds between molecules of sol, making structure rigid, are formed.

lyonium ion. Product of autoprotolysis ; acid formed from solvent molecule and proton, coupled with equivalent amount of simultaneously formed base, *i.e.*, lyonium ions of water and formic acid :

$$2H_2O \rightleftharpoons OH^- + \boxed{H_3O^+}$$

$$2HCOOH \rightleftharpoons HCOO^- + \boxed{H-\overset{\displaystyle OH}{\underset{\displaystyle OH}{C^+}}}$$

lyophilic. Having strong affinity for a liquid ; the term is usually used to describe a finely divided or colloidal substance in a solvent dispersion, *e.g.*, sol of gelatin in water, sol of caoutchouc in benzene.

lyophilization. Solvent removal from the frozen state by sublimation ; commonly referred to as freeze-drying. It is accomplished by freezing the material to be dried below its eutectic point and then providing the latent heat of sublimation.

lyophobic. A term used to describe a finely divided or colloidal substance that repels liquids *e.g.* sols of noble metals in water.

lyotropic liquid crystals. The liquid crystals that possess atleast two components, one of these is water and the other is amphiphile (a polar head group attached to one or more long hydrocarbon chains). In the lamellar form, water molecules are sandwiched between the polar heads of adjacent layers while the hydrocarbon tails lie in a nonpolar environment. Lyotropic liquid crystals have very complex structures, but occur abundantly in nature, particularly in living systems.

lyotropic series. A series of anions or cations arranged in the order of magnitude of their effect upon reactions in colloidal solutions. These ions indirectly influence a reaction by exerting a lyophilic or lyophobic effect upon the solvent. Definite order of arrangement of ions according to their capability of bonding dispersion medium as function of their ionic radius, *i.e.*, of their hydration is :

Univalent cation form Li^+, Na^+, K^+, Rb^+, Cs^+ series ;

Divalent cations form Mg^{2+}, Ca^{2+}, Sr^{2+}, Ba^{2+} series ;

Univalent anions form Cl^-, Br^-, NO_3^-, I^-, CNS^- series.

Lyotropic series may be observed in coagulation, adsorption, and other processes. Also known as Hofmeister series.

lysin. A term used to describe substances that will disrupt a living cell with the release of some of its constituents.

-lysis. A suffix commonly used in chemical terminology. When referring to substances, the meaning is more clearly expressed by the term decomposition of as in hydrolysis, glycolysis, solvolysis.

lytic reaction. A term used in serology to describe a reaction that leads to the disruption or lysis of a cell.

M

M. Abbreviation for molar solution and mass.

***m*-.** Abbreviation for the chemical prefix meta; abbreviation for molal solution.

m. Abbreviation for metre. Symbol for magnetic moment. Symbol for order of spectrum. Magnetic quantum number.

maceration. The steeping of a solid material in a liquid, in order to soften it or break down its structure.

mache unit. A unit of quantity of radioactive emanation, defined as the quantity of emanation which sets up a saturation current equal to one thousandth of the electrostatic unit of current. It is equal to 3.6×10^{-10} curie.

macro-analysis. Analysis of sample with mass exceeding 0 1 g or, in the case of gases, volume larger than 10 cm^3.

macro-component. Component of system which can be detected or determined by analytical methods.

macromolecular colloid. *See* molecular colloid.

macromolecular compound. Chemical compound composed of macromolecules. Also known as high molecular weight compound.

macromolecule. A large molecule whose size may be in the lower colloidal range (0.5 to 1 micron). Such giant molecules are in general of two types : (*i*) Individual entities (compounds) that cannot be subdivided without losing their chemical identity. Typical of these are proteins, many of which have molecular weights running into the millions. (*ii*) Combinations of repeating chemical units (monomers) linked together into chain or network structures called polymers. Each monomer has the same chemical constitution as the polymer, *e.g.*, isoprene (C_5H_8) and polyisoprene $(C_5H_8)x$. Synthetic elastomers (plastics) are typical of macromolecule.

macroporous ion exchanger. Ion exchanger having pores that are big in comparison with atomic dimensions.

macroscopic cross-section. Product of microscopic cross-section σ and number of particles N contained in 1 cm^3.

macroscopic state. State of macroscopic system characterized by such macroscopic properties as volume of system, its density, internal energy, electric current strength, etc. Also known as thermodynamic state.

macroscopic thermodynamics. Theory of macroscopic systems based on experimentally justified phenomenological laws such as laws of thermodynamics, phenomenological equations, etc. Also known as phenomenological thermodynamics.

Madelung constant. A constant appearing in the term for the Coulomb energy ϕ of an ionic crystal. It may be defined by α in the equation :

$$\phi = -\frac{\alpha e^2}{R}$$

where R=separation of nearest neighbours in the crystal, and is evaluated by adding the mutual electrostatic potential energies of all the ions in the particular lattice.

magic nucleus. Atomic nucleus containing a magic number of protons or neutrons, *viz.*, nucleus with completed proton or neutron shells. Magic nucleus has high binding energy.

magic numbers. Numbers of protons or neutrons in atomic nuclei of high binding energy, equal to 2, 8, 20, 28, 50, 82, 126. Nuclei with magic number of protons or neutrons have completed proton or neutron shells.

They have anomalously low capture probabilities for additional neutrons and protons respectively.

magnesia mixture. An aqueous solution of magnesium chloride, ammonium chloride, and ammonium hydroxide, used for the determination of arsenates and phosphates.

magnesium. An element.

	Symbol	Mg
State Solid	Atomic No.	12
Group IIA	Atomic Wt.	24.312
	Valence	2
	Isotopes	3 stable
	m.p.	922K
	b.p.	1380K

Magnesium is the third most abundant structural metal in the earth's crust exceeded only by aluminium and iron. Elemental magnesium has a close-packed hexagonal crystal structure, as do the common alloys of magnesium except those that contain lithium in excess of 11%.

Magnesium is a light, strongly electropositive metal obtained from sea-water by electrolysis of molten magnesium chloride (Dow process) ; in another widely used method, magnesium oxide, is reduced with ferrosilicon at high temperature.

There are three naturally occurring isotopes ^{24}Mg through ^{26}Mg, and three radioactive isotopes have been identified ^{23}Mg, ^{27}Mg and ^{28}Mg, all with comparatively short half-lives measured in seconds, minutes, or hours.

As a catalyst, magnesium is useful for promoting organic condensation, reduction, addition, and dehalogenation reactions.

Biochemically, it is of great importance, as it is the characteristic element in chlorophyll ; it also has metabolic functions in the body.

Magnesium finds principal uses as a primary metal to which other metals are added in varying amounts, as an alloying ingredient for other metals, as an important metallurgical chemical in the form a deoxidizer and desulphurizer, and as the constituent of numerous important inorganic and chemical compounds.

magnesium alloys. The most important alloying ingredients used in magnesium alloys are aluminium, manganese, rare-earths, silicon, zinc, and zirconium. The specific gravity of magnesium alloys range from 1.74 to 1.83. Magnesium alloys are most commonly used in the form of die castings, which account for 75% of their total usage in structural applications.

magnetic criterion. Criterion which enables division of complex into ionic, or outer-orbital and covalent or inner-orbital, basing on comparison of number of unpaired electrons in free and central metal ions.

magnetic dipole. System of magnetic mass with distinct negative and positive magnetic centres of gravity. In the simplest case system of two displaced point magnetic monopoles, positive and negative, with equal magnetic mass.

magnetic field. A region in which a magnetic force or the characteristic effects of a magnet are apparent or theoretically apparent. Or the actual force system of a magnet, expressed in terms of lines of force.

magnetic field strength H. Vector quantity together with magnetic induction B describing magnetic field and defining value and direction of force acting on magnetic pole at a given point in field. Also known as magnetic field intensity.

magnetic flux, ϕ. Flux of induction vector B through surface S :

$$\phi = \int_S B \cos \theta \, dS$$

where $B \cos \theta$ = perpendicular component of vector B with respect to surface S.

magnetic induction, B. Quantity characterizing effective magnetic field in any substance

$$B = H + 4\pi J$$

if B, H and J are parallel

$$B = \mu H$$

where μ=magnetic permeability, H=magnetic field strength, J=magnetization.

magnetic moment of atom. Vector quantity responsible for interaction between atoms and external magnetic field; for atoms with low atomic number magnetic moment of atom is given by $\sqrt{J(J+1)}g(L, S, J,)\mu_B$ (Russel-Saunders coupling), where J=total angular momentum quantum number of atom, $g(L, S, J,)$=Lande' factor and μ_B=Bohr magneton; for atoms with high atomic number magnetic moment of atom is equal to sum of magnetic moments of individual electrons (*j-j* moment. Also known as atomic magnetic coupling).

magnetic permeability, μ. Tensor quantity defined by $B=\mu H$, where B=magnetic induction, H=external magnetic field strength.

magnetic potential. Since the curl of a magnetostatic field in a current-free region vanishes, *i.e.*,

$$\nabla \times \mathbf{B}=0, \qquad \nabla \times \mathbf{H}=0;$$

the vectors **B** and **H** are derivable from scalar potentials,

$$\mathbf{H} = -\nabla \mathbf{U}$$

This scalar potential must be used with caution when electromagnetic fields are considered, because these fields are not conservative.

magnetic quantum number, m (m_l). Number which defines allowed values of projection of electron angular momentum onto some chosen direction, *e.g.*, direction of external magnetic field. For given value of orbital quantum number l allowed values of m are 0, ± 1, ± 2, ..., $\pm l$.

magnetic resonance. Absorption of alternating electromagnetic field energy of characteristic frequency ν which satisfies resonance condition $h\nu=\Delta E=g\mu_B H$, where ΔE=spacing of adjacent Zeeman levels, g=*g*-factor, μ_B=Bohr or nuclear magneton, H=magnetic field strength. Also known as paramagnetic resonance.

magnetic spin quantum number, m_s. Number which defines allowed values of projection of particle spin angular momentum onto given direction, *e.g.* direction of external magnetic field; for electrons m_s assumes only two numerical values $+1/2$ and $-1/2$.

magnetic susceptibility, x. Tensor quantity characterizing ability of a given substance to change magnetization J upon change of magnetic field strength H, $J = x$H, where x = magnetic susceptibility of 1 cm^3 of substance. Magnetic susceptibility is also defined sometimes for 1 g ($^x g$) or 1 mole ($^x M$) of substance.

magnetocaloric effect. Decrease or increase of para- or ferromagnet temperature resulting from adiabatic change of magnetic field strength.

magnetochemistry. The branch of chemistry which deals with the study of the interrelationship between a magnetic field and atomic and molecular structures. The two most important considerations are magnetic moment (the turning force exerted on an atom, ion, or molecule) and magnetic susceptibility (the extent to which a substance can be magnetized). If a substance turns away from a magnetic force, it is said to be diamagnetic; if it turns toward the force, it is called paramagnetic. Magnetic behaviour studies have been useful in physico-chemical studies, especially in connection with coordination phenomena, spectrographic analysis, and catalytic properties.

The fact that ions are attracted into a curved path when they enter a magnetic field at high velocity makes possible the separat ion of ions which have nearly the same mass; electromagnetic separation of isotopes is utilized in isolating U-235 and is also used in mass spectrometry for analytical purposes. Magnetic fields of high intensity are used to contain, plasmas in fusion research.

magnetomechanical ratio. The ratio of the magnetic moment to the angular momentum, as observed in the gyromagnetic effect. The formula for this is $g'e/2mc$.

magneton. The quantity $eh/4\pi mc$, in which e=the electronic charge, h=Planck's constant, m=the electronic mass, and c = the velocity of light. The numerical value of this quantity also known as the electronic Bohr magneton, is 9.27×10^{-21} erg oersted^{-1}. This quantity is frequently encountered in quantum mechanics.

magnetostriction. Change of body dimensions in magnetic field.

magnons. Quasi-particles ascribed to spin waves introduced in quantum theory of magnetically ordered crystals ; obey Bose-Einstein statistics.

Magnus rule. A metal is deposited from a solution containing metallic salts, at the voltage which is characteristic for that metal.

Majorana effect. A magneto-optic effect that deals with optical anisotropy of colloidal solutions. The effect probably is caused by the orientation of the particles in the magnetic field.

malleability. The property by which a material may be hammered out or rolled into thin sheets without tearing or fracture, or the extent to which a material possesses that property.

malt. The product derived from barley or similar grains as a result of controlled germination followed by heating or drying ; it is the basic material of the brewing industry. Malt contains several enzymes ; diastase, which hydrolyzes the starch to sugars which are later fermented to alcohol ; maltase, which converts maltose to glucose ; and amylase. Malt concentrates rich in these enzymes are used in the food industry. Malt also contains considerable protein and has high nutrient value. Malt extract is called wort.

maltase. An enzyme which hydrolyzes the disaccharide maltose into glucose. It is found in the pancreas, liver, kidney, intestines and blood serum of animals.

Manea test. Vegetable fibres, when dissolved in concentrated sulphuric acid, give with oleic acid a red colour changing to violet on addition of water. Animal fibres do not give this reaction.

manganese. An element.

		Symbol	Mn
		Atomic No.	25
State	Solid	Atomic Wt.	54.938
Group	VIIB	Valence	2,3,4,6,7
		m.p.	1519K

Manganese is a silvers-with metal, and has a cubic (complex) crystal structure, not notably hard (becomes hard upon alloying with carbon), brittle, capable of taking a brilliant polish, but readily oxidized upon heating ; manganese is one of the transition elements of the $3d$ series of the periodic table, falling between chromium and iron. The metal is derived commercially by electrolysis of manganous sulphate. Its multiple valences make manganese a versatile metal for both analytical and industrial procedures ; it can act either as a reducing agent or an oxidizing agent depending on its valence. It is subject to corrosion and is combustible at high temperatures. In the solid state, manganese exists in four allotropic forms designated α, β, γ, and δ. Manganese in either the α or the β modifications at room temperature is both hard and brittle and cannot be plastically deformed to any significant extent.

Its principal uses are in manufacture of manganese salts, as a deoxidizer and purifier in steel manufacture, and as an alloying agent in steel manufacture) and in aluminium and magnesium alloys.

There are eight isotopes of manganese, ^{50}Mn through ^{57}Mn, all radioactive with exception of ^{55}Mn. Half-lives range from a fraction of a second for ^{50}Mn to approximately 140 years for ^{53}Mn.

First ionization potential 7.32 eV; second, 15.7 eV. Oxidation potentials $Mn \rightarrow Mn^{++} + 2e^-$, 1.18 V; $Mn^{2+} + 2H_2O \rightarrow MnO_2 + 4H^+ + 2e^-$, —1.28 V; $Mn^{2+} \rightarrow Mn^{3+} + e^-$, 1.51 V; $Mn^{2+} + 4H_2O \rightarrow MnO_4^- + 8H^+ + 5e^-$, —1.52 V; $MnO_2 + 2H_2O \rightarrow MnO_4^- + 4H^+ + 3e^-$, —0.168 V; $Mn(OH)_2 + OH^- \rightarrow Mn(OH)_3 + e^-$, 0.40 V; $MnO_4^{=} \rightarrow MnO_4^- + e^-$, —0.54V; $MnO_2 + 4OH^- \rightarrow MnO_4^- + 2H_2O + 3e^-$, —0.58 V.

Manganese is an essential trace element in plant nutrition. Its fumes have toxic effect on prolonged inhalation. Chronic manganese poisoning has both psychiatric and neutrological manifestations, the most crippling of which have been related to the extrapyramidal system of the brain.

Manganese group. Elements in seventh sub-group of periodic system with structure of outer electronic sub-shells of atoms : manganese—$3d^5 4s^2$ technetium—$4d^6 5s^1$, rhenium—$5d^5 6s^2$.

mannans. A group of polysaccharides composed chiefly or entirely of D-mannose units. The mannose units linked at the 1,4 positions in the molecule. The simple mannans occur in softwoods (pine, spruce, etc.), as well as in some nuts. A subgroup, called galactomannans, is a combination of galactose and mannose, the two being isomeric sugars ; with slight differences in molecular linkage ; they bear about the same relationship as cellulose and starch. Galactomannans are found in the seeds of such plants as guar, locust, and other rare species.

Mannheim process. A contact process for the manufacture of sulphuric acid, in which the conversion of SO_2 to SO_3 takes place in two stages, the first catalyzed by ferric oxide Fe_2O_3, and the second, by platinized asbestos.

Mannheim process for hydrochloric acid. A method of producing hydrochloric acid gas and sodium hydrogen sulphate from sodium chloride and sulphuric acid which involves :

(*i*) Cooling the HCl-air mixture by scrubbing with a cold, aqueous solution of HCl (concentrated).

(*ii*) Absorbing the cooled HCl gas in a dilute, cold aqueous solution of HCl.

(*iii*) Stripping HCl gas from the strong HCl solution produced by (*ii*).

Mannich reaction. Introduction of aminomethyl group —CH_2NRR' into molecule of compound containing acidic C—H bond (ketone) in place of active hydrogen, due to condensation of that compound with formaldehyde and ammonia (or primary and secondary amine), *e.g.*,

$$C_6H_5COCH_3 + HCHO + (C_2H_5)_2NH.HCl \xrightarrow{-H_2O} C_6H_5COCH_2CH_2N(C_2H_5)_2.HCl$$

Also known as aminomethylation.

manoscopy. The determination of the densities of gases.

marc. Residual vegetable material left after the removal, usually in a press, of the oil or juice of a plant product, such as grapes, oil seeds or kernels, sugar cane, etc.

Marino test reaction. To detect thallic salts in presence of thallous, alkalinize the dilute solution to be tested with potassium hydroxide solution, add saturated α-naphthol solution and a little dimethyl-*o*-phenylenediamine. An indophenol blue colour indicates the presence of thallic salts.

Mariotte's law. Same as Boyle's law.

Markownikoff rule. The addition of Bronsted acids to unsymmetrically substituted double bonds gives almost exclusively that product in which the hydrogen atom from the acid is located at the least substituted carbon atom of the double bond :

$$\overset{X \downarrow}{CH_3CH} = \overset{H \downarrow}{CH_2} \longrightarrow \underset{\text{major product}}{CH_3CHXCH_3}$$

$$(CH_3)_2\overset{X \downarrow}{C} = \overset{H \downarrow}{C}HCH_3 \longrightarrow \underset{\text{major product}}{(CH_3)_2CXCH_2CH_3}$$

Marsh test. A test for the presence of arsenic, performed by treating the solution to be tested with zinc and hydrochloric acid, whereby the arsenic is reduced to its hydride AsH_3. This hydride and the librated hydrogen are passed through a long tube that is heated to decompose the arsine, so that a deposit of metallic arsenic forms in the cool portion of the tube, close to its end. An analogous deposit is obtained for antimony, which is differentiated by the fact that the arsenic deposit is soluble in potassium hypochlorite solution, whereas that of antimony is not. Many modifications of this test are known under names of various investigators.

Martinet dioxindole synthesis. A method of formation of dioxindoles from arylamines and mesoxalic acid esters.

masking. The concealing of a substance by another ; thus a compound is said to mask the properties of a constituent element or ion if the usual, characteristic reactions of the element or radical are not readily obtained.

Masotti field. The electric field that would exist at the position of a molecule in a polarized dielectric if all of the molecules within a sphere of radius R around the molecule in question were removed without disturbing the polarization of the remaining dielectric.

mass. The physical measure of the principal inertial property of a body ; *i.e.*, its resistance to change of motion. At speeds small compared to the speed of light, the mass of a body is independent of its speed. At higher speeds, the mass of a body depends on its speed relative to the observer according to the relation :

$$m = m_0/\sqrt{1-v^2/c^2}$$

where m_0 = mass of the body as found by an observer at rest w.r.t. body ; v = speed of the body relative to the observer who finds its mass m, and c = speed of light.

The term weight is a measure of gravitational attraction and is substantially less on the moon than on the earth.

mass attenuation coefficient. Quotient of linear attenuation coefficient and density of absorbing medium.

mass conservation law. In every chemical reaction or chemical change, the mass (weight) of the substances formed is precisely equal to that of the reacting substances, regardless of any alteration in their form or other properties (provioled no nuclear reaction takes place). This implies the principle of balance in a reaction which means that the products formed contain the same number of atoms of each element as were present in the reacting substances.

mass conservation law in continuous systems. Equation :

$$\frac{\partial \rho}{\partial t} = -\operatorname{div}(\rho v)$$

where t = time, ρ = density, and v = velocity of centre of mass. Also known as conservation equation for mass.

mass defect. The difference in mass between an actual atomic nucleus and the sum of the masses of its constituent protons and neutrons when added as individual units. The mass of a naturally occurring nucleus is found to be very slightly less than that of the sum of its constituents when taken separately; this discrepancy is accounted for by Einstein's equivalence equation $E=mc^2$ which states that mass can be transformed into energy. This refers to the binding energy which holds the nucleus together, a portion of which is released when fission takes place.

Mass defect is given by the relation :

$$\text{Mass Defect} = Zm_{\mathrm{H}} + (A-Z)m_n - M$$

wherein Zm_{H}=the mass of Z hydrogen atoms, Z being the atomic number of the atom ; $(A-Z)m_n$=the mass of $(A-Z)$ neutrons, A being the mass number of the atom ; and M is the determined atomic mass.

massecuite. A term derived from the French, literally meaning a "cooked mass," it is used in sugar technology to denote the thick syrupy mixture to sucrose crystals and molasses resulting from concentration and boiling of the mother liquor.

mass fraction, w_{B}. Ratio of mass of constituent B to general mass of mixture :

$$w_{\mathrm{B}} = \frac{m_{\mathrm{B}}}{\sum_i m_i}$$

where m_{B} = mass of constituent B,

$\sum_i m_i$ = sum of masses of all constituents of mixture.

Massieu function, J. Extensive thermodynamic function $J = -F/T$, where F = Helmholtz free energy and T = thermodynamic temperature.

mass number. The whole number nearest the precise value for the atomic weight of a single atomic species.

It should not be confused with atomic number, which is the number of protons only. For example, hydrogen has a mass number of 1 (one proton, no neutrons), an atomic number of 1, and an atomic weight of 1.008 ; helium, with two protons and two neutrons, has a mass number of 4, an atomic number of 2, and an atomic weight of 4.0026.

mass polymerization. A polymerization reaction carried out with liquid molecules without the addition of any diluent.

mass spectrometry. Analytical and structural research method based on measurement of mass to charge ratio of ions produced from a given sample. A given sample is vaporized and then ionized by electrons, either as the entire molecule or as constituent atoms. The charged particles are accelerated by an electric impulse and then are passed through a magnetic field, which has the effect of changing their path from a straight line to a curve. Since some particles have greater mass than others, the effect is a separation of the particles to an extent dependent on their ratio of mass to charge. Their impact on a photographic plate thus yields a spectrum from which the constituents can be determined. Isotopes and substances present in a mixture in extremely small amounts can be identified in this way. The mass spectrograph is designed especially for mass determinations, as in study of isotopes, whereas the mass spectrometer measures the ion population.

mass stopping power. Average energy lost by charged particle in traversing certain path length and density of medium.

mass-transfer operation. An operation in chemical engineering that involves transfer of material from one phase to another, from one place to another within a single phase.

matrix. In general, an aggregate of ground mass in which a discrete object is embedded. Specifically, the meterial in which a precious or semiprecious stone is embedded; or the earth or rock containing an ore or other mineral ; or the impression left in a rock by a precious or semiprecious stone; a crystal, or a fossil.

In chemical analysis, main component (components) of materials in which trace components are to be determined.

matte. An intermediate, impure product obtained in the process of recovering metals from their ores, which results from smelting operations; or a roughened or fibrous surface which reflects light diffusely such as the surface of uncoated paper.

matter. From the classical macroscopic point of view, it is defined as anything that has mass and occupies space, thus distinguishing it from electromagnetic radiation (light) and thermal activity (heat), which are forms of energy.

Mattox-Kendall method. Preparation of *α*,*β*-unsaturated ketones by elimination of hydrogen bromide from *α*-bromoketones (which are converted first into 2,4-dinitrophenylhydrazones to increase mobility of *α*-bromine atom), *e.g.*,

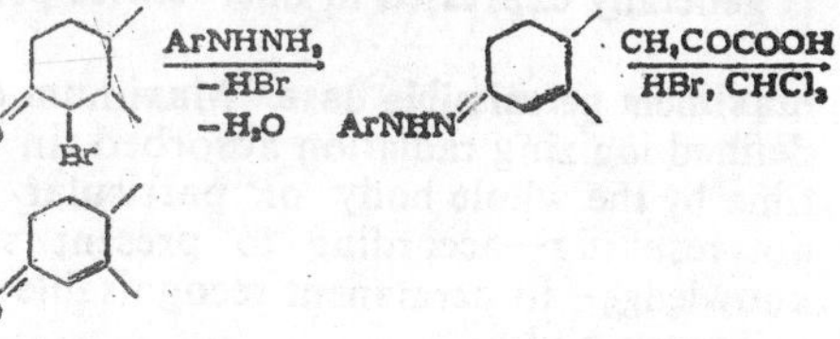

ArNHNH$_2$ / −HBr / −H$_2$O → ArNHN= ... → CH$_3$COCOOH / HBr, CHCl$_3$

This method is mainly used for introduction of double bonds in steroids.

Maumene number. The rise in temperature obtained by mixture of a specified amount of an oil with a specified amount of concentrated sulphuric acid ; the magnitude of the rise indicates the degree of unsaturation and hence the effectiveness of the oil as a drying oil.

maximum boiling point. A two-component or multi-component liquid system in which, for a particular composition, the boiling point is higher than that for any other composition or for the pure component is to have a maximum boiling point at that temperature.

maximum coordination number. Maximum number of coordinate bonds that can be formed by central atom (*cf.* characteristic coordination number).

maximum freezing point. A two-component or multi-component liquid system in which, for a particular composition, the freezing point is higher than that for any other composition or for the pure components is said to have a maximum freezing point at that temperature.

maximum multiplicity rule. An empirical statement that the energy of interaction between the electrons in any one atom is at a minimum when their resultant spin is greatest.

maximum permissible body burden. The maximum amount of a radiactive isotope, (expressed in microcuries) deposited in the human body or in a given tissue, such that the continuous rediation dose rate not exceed the continuous maximum permissible dose rate.

maximum permissible concentration. The maximum concentration of a given radioisotope in air or water such that normal daily intake of air and water will not lead to an accumulated radiation dose in excess of the maximum permissible dose for occupational personnel. It is generally expressed in microcuries per cm^3.

maximum permissible dose. Maximum dose of defined ionizing radiation absorbed in defined time by the whole body or particular organs, not resulting—according to present stage of knowledge—in permanent recognisable damage to human body.

maximum work. Maximum amount of work which can be performed by closed system on surroundings on isothermal transition from state I to state II; equal to loss of Helmholtz free energy of system :

$$\Delta F = F_{\text{I}} - F_{\text{II}}$$

Maxwell-Boltzmann distribution. Equilibrium form of unimolecular partition function :

$$\rho_1 (1) = \lambda \exp \left[- \frac{\epsilon(1)}{kT} \right]$$

where k = Boltzmann constant, T = thermodynamic temperature, λ = absolute activity and ϵ = energy of molecule, ρ_1 = unimolecular partition function and (1) stands for all molecule dynamic variables which characterize its state, Maxwell-Boltzmann distribution is valid for systems of weakly interacting particles and for rarified gases provided quantum effects are negligibly small. Also known as Boltzmann distribution function.

Maxwell's distribution law. Equilibrium distribution of molecular velocities :

$$< N (v_x, v_y, v_z) > =$$

$$<N> \left(\frac{m}{2\pi kT} \right)^{3/2} \exp \left[- \frac{mv^2}{2kT} \right] dv_x \, dv_y \, dv_z$$

where $<N(v_x, v_y, v_z)>$ = average number of molecules with velocity (v_x, v_y, v_z), $<N>$ = average number of molecules in the system, m=molecular mass, k = Boltzmann constant, and T = thermodynamic temperature.

Maxwell's relations. Thermodynamic identities expression dependence of phase entropy S on its volume V and pressure p in terms of easily measurable thermodynamic quantities :

$$\left(\frac{\partial T}{\partial V} \right)_S = - \left(\frac{\partial p}{\partial S} \right)_V$$

$$\left(\frac{\partial S}{\partial V} \right)_T = \left(\frac{\partial p}{\partial T} \right)_V$$

$$\left(\frac{\partial T}{\partial p} \right)_S = \left(\frac{\partial V}{\partial S} \right)_p$$

$$\left(\frac{\partial S}{\partial p} \right)_T = - \left(\frac{\partial V}{\partial T} \right)_p$$

mayer. A unit of heat capacity proposed by Richards. The mayer is the capacity of a body or system which is warmed 1 degree centigrade by 1 joule. The heat capacity of 1 gram of water at 20° is about 4.181 mayers.

Mayer's relation. Formula which for ideal gas determines relation between molar heat capacity at constant pressure Cp and molar heat capacity at constant volume Cv. $Cp - Cv = R$, where R=molar gas constant.

McAfee process. A catalytic cracking process in which the petroleum fraction (which must be free from water) is heated with 5 to 8% by weight of anhydrous aluminium chloride, at a temperature of about 560K., for about two days.

McFadyen-Stevens reduction. A method o converting aromatic esters to aldehydes through their benzenesulphonacylhydrazides ; *e.g.*,

$$RCOOR' + NH_2NH_2 \rightarrow RCONHNH_2 + R'OH$$

$$RCONHNH_2 + C_6H_5SO_2Cl \rightarrow RCONHNHSO_2C_6H_5 + HCl$$

$$RCONHNHSO_2C_6H_5 + Na_2CO_3 \rightarrow RCHO + C_6H_5SO_2Na + N_2 + NaHCO_3$$

mean activity coefficient of ions, $f_\pm$. Quantity defined by formula :

$$f_\pm = \sqrt[\nu]{f_+^{\nu_+} f_-^{\nu_-}}$$

where f_+ and f_- = activity coefficients of ions, ν^+ and ν^- = number of cations and anions respectively which are formed from one molecule of electrolyte ;

$$\nu = \nu^+ + \nu^-$$

mean activity of an electrolyte. The logarithm of the mean activity coefficient of an electrolyte is the arithmetic mean of the logarithms of the individual ionic activity coefficients.

mean free path. A term used to denote the average distance traversed by an atom, molecule, or other particle without collision with another atom or molecule. This distance is much greater in gases than in liquids because of the much lower population of atoms or molecules. It is expressed mathematically as :

$$\lambda = \frac{\bar{c}}{\bar{z}} = \frac{1}{\sqrt{2}\,\pi d^2 n}$$

where $\bar{c}$ = average speed, $\bar{z}$ = mean number of collisions of one molecule during unit time, d = sum of radii of colliding molecules, n = number of molecules in unit volume.

mean ionic concentration, $c_\pm$.

$$c_\pm = \sqrt[\nu]{c_+^{\nu^+} c_-^{\nu^-}}$$

where c_+ and c_- = concentrations of cations and anions respectively, ν^+ and ν^- = number of cations and anions respectively which arise from one molecule of electrolyte ;

$$\nu = \nu^+ + \nu^-$$

mean lifetime. The average period of time that a particle, such as an atom, molecule, nucleus, etc., will remain in a given excited state before undergoing a change.

mean life of radionuclide. Reciprocal of disintegration constant.

mean molal heat capacity, $\bar{C}$. Proportion between amount of heat Q received isochorically or isobarically by one mole of substance over temperature range from T_1 to T_2

$$\bar{C} = \frac{Q}{T_2 - T_1}$$

mechanical mass. The part of the mass of a particle which is supposed to be an intrinsic property of the particle and not due to the interaction of the particle with itself through the medium of some field. The two types of masses are not experimentally distinguishable however.

mechanism of bimolecular electrophilic substitution. *See* S_E2 mechanism.

mechanism of bimolecular elimination. *See* **E_2 mechanism.**

mechanism of bimolecular nucleophilic substitution. *See* S_N2 mechanism.

mechanism of bimolecular nucleophilic substitution with allylic rearrangement. *See* S_N2' mechanism.

mechanism of electrophilic addition to carbon-carbon multiple bonds. The first step in such reactions involves addition of electrophile to carbon-carbon multiple bond with formation of cation. In the second step, trans-addition of nucleophile to cation takes place. Formation of π-complex precedes addition, *e.g.*,

$$\pi\text{-complex } (C{=}C \cdots {:}\overset{\delta\oplus}{Br}{-}\overset{\delta\ominus}{Br}{:}) \xrightarrow{\text{slow}} \text{bromonium cation} + Br^\ominus \xrightarrow{\text{fast}} \text{addition product } (-C(Br)-C(Br)-)$$

mechanism of electrophilic aromatic substitution. The following reaction steps are postulated : first, formation of π-complex due to interaction of ring π-electrons with electrophile X^+ ; secondly, transformation of π-complex into carbonium ion (σ-complex) in which X^+ is bound to one atom of ring (positive charge of carbonium ion is shared over whole system); thirdly, proton elimination from carbonium ion (proton is consumed by nucleophile Y^- present in system) with returning to energetically poor aromatic system. σ-complex formation or proton elimination may be the rate determining step:

$$X^{\oplus} + C_6H_6 \rightleftharpoons [C_6H_6 \cdot X^{\oplus}] \rightleftharpoons [C_6H_6X]^{\oplus} \xrightarrow[-H^{\oplus}]{Y^{\ominus}} C_6H_5X + HY$$

π-complex σ-complex

mechanism of free-radical addition to unsaturated hydrocarbons. This mechanism, typical for addition in the presence of free radical initiators (*e.g.*, light, peroxides), involves the following steps: decomposition of added molecule into free radicals (atoms), addition of free radical (atom) to π-bond and formation of new free radical with unpaired electron on carbon atom, reaction of carbon free radical with added molecule with formation of new addition product and new free radical. The free-radical addition is a typical chain reaction, *e.g.*,

$$Cl_2 \xrightarrow{h\nu} 2Cl^{\cdot}$$

$$Cl^{\cdot} + \rangle C{=}C\langle \rightarrow Cl{-}\overset{|}{\underset{|}{C}}{-}\overset{|}{\underset{|}{C}}^{\cdot}$$

$$Cl{-}\overset{|}{\underset{|}{C}}{-}\overset{|}{\underset{|}{C}}^{\cdot} + Cl_2 \rightarrow Cl{-}\overset{|}{\underset{|}{C}}{-}\overset{|}{\underset{|}{C}}{-}Cl + Cl^{\cdot}$$

mechanism of free-radical substitution. *See* S_R mechanism.

mechanism of internal nucleophilic substitution. *See* $S_{N}1$ mechanism.

mechanism of nucleophilic addition to carbonyl group. Addition to carbonyl group is initiated by nucleophile attack on carbonyl carbon atom, which is electron-deficient due to polarization of carbonyl bond. In the second reaction step, cation adds to ion with negatively charged oxygen atom, *e.g.*,

$$\rangle C{=}O + HCN \xrightarrow[CN^-]{slow} {-}\underset{CN}{\overset{|}{C}}{-}\ddot{O}{:}^- \xrightarrow[H^+]{fast} {-}\underset{CN}{\overset{|}{C}}{-}OH$$

mechanism of nucleophilic addition to ethylenic bond. Addition of nucleophiles to ethylenic bonds conjugated with $-\underset{|}{C}{=}O$, $-C{\equiv}N$ and similar groups. The first reaction step involves addition of anion to terminal carbon atom of the conjugated system. In the second step, addition of cation to atom takes place at position 2- or 4-, *e.g.*,

$$\overset{\delta\oplus}{CH_2}{=}CH{-}C{\equiv}\overset{\delta\ominus}{N} \xrightarrow{RO^{\ominus}} \left[\begin{array}{c} RO{-}CH_2{-}CH{=}C{=}N^{\ominus} \\ \updownarrow \\ RO{-}CH_2{-}\overset{\ominus}{C}H{-}C{\equiv}N \end{array}\right]$$

$$\xrightarrow{ROH} ROCH_2{-}CH_2{-}C{\equiv}N + RO^{\ominus}$$

mechanism of nucleophilic aromatic substitution. This reaction may proceed in two different ways: (*i*) In first, rate-determining step, nucleophile attacks carbon atom linked with leaving group, forming intermediate anion with delocalized charge (Meisenheimer complex). In second step, aromatic system is restored due to elimination of leaving group as anion. (*ii*) Complex mechanism involving elimination with subsequent addition. In first, base-catalized stage, elimination takes place with formation of intermediate dehydrobenzene. The latter reacts readily with nucleophile forming addition product. Nucleophilic aromatic substitution may proceed parallelly by both routes:

1) $$O_2N{-}C_6H_4{-}X \xrightarrow{+Y^{\ominus}} [\text{Meisenheimer complex } (Y, X)]^{\ominus} \xrightarrow{-X^{\ominus}} O_2N{-}C_6H_4{-}Y$$

2) $$C_6H_5Br + {:}\overset{\ominus}{N}H_2 \xrightarrow[-30^{\circ}]{-NH_3} C_6H_4 \text{ (dehydrobenzene)} + {:}NH_3 \rightarrow C_6H_4^{\ominus}{-}\overset{\oplus}{N}H_3 \underset{+H^{\oplus}}{\overset{-H^{\oplus}}{\rightleftharpoons}} C_6H_5NH_2$$

mechanism of unimolecular electrophilic substitution. *See* S_E1 mechanism.

mechanism of unimolecular elimination. *See* E_1 mechanism.

mechanism of unimolecular nucleophilic substitution. *See* S_{N1} mechanism.

median lethal dose, LD_{50}. Dose of ionizing radiation absorbed (by the whole body, human or animal) which after uninterrupted, single irradiation, causes death in 50% of cases after defined period of time. Also, dose after which defined population of living organisms (*e.g.*, of bacteria) suffers 50% death rate after defined period of time.

medicinal chemistry. A branch of chemistry which deals with the effects of drugs and pharmaceuticals on the human body and on various infective organisms and with the systhesis of compounds specifically for certain diseases, such as antimalarials and antihypertensive agents. It is also concerned with such topics as immunology, hormone activity, etc.

Meerwein condensation. Reaction of aromatic diazonium chlorides or bromides with α,β-unsaturated carbonyl compounds, esters and nitriles, in presence of copper salts, resulting in formation of aromatic derivatives at α-position, *e.g.*,

$$[Ar{-}N^{+}{\equiv}N]X^{-} + CH_2{=}CH{-}C{\equiv}N \xrightarrow{Cu^{2+}} Ar{-}CH_2{-}\underset{\displaystyle X}{\underset{|}{CH}}{-}C{\equiv}N + N_2$$

Meerwein-Ponndorf-Verley reaction. A reductive transformation of hydroxy and carbonyl compounds, using metallic alkoxides as catalysts, in which the hydroxy compound becomes a carbonyl compound, and the carbonyl compound becomes an hydroxy compound. This reaction is reversible, *e.g.*,

$$CH_2{=}CHCH_2COCH_3 + (CH_3)_2CHOH \xleftrightarrow{((CH_3)_2CHO)_3Al} CH_2{=}CHCH_2CHOHCH_3 + CH_3COCH_3$$

Meissner effect. The explusion of magnetic flux from the interior of a superconducting metal when it is cooled in a magnetic field to below the critical temperature, near absolute zero, at which the transition to super conductivity takes place.

melamine resin. A thermosetting resin made by a condensation reaction of a melamine derivative, trimethylomelamine,

$$C_3N_3(NHCH_2OH)_3$$

with formaldehyde. Such resins are prepared in the form of moulding powders which can accept colourants and are thus used for production of decorative plastics.

m-electron. An electron characterized by having a principal quantum number of value 3. *See also* M-shell.

melting point. *See* freezing point.

melting point, congruent. *See* congruent melting point.

melting point, incongruent. *See* incongruent melting point.

membrane. An extremely thin, porous layer or film of material, either natural or synthetic ; the thickness is approximately 100 angstrom units, the diameter of the pores ranging from as little as 8 angstroms for natural cellular membranes upto 100 angstroms for manufactured membranes. Membranes which have pores so small that only the molecules of solvents, ions, and a few substances of very low molecular weight can pass through are called semipermeable ; these are characteristic of living cell tissue and are an essential feature of osmosis.

membrane equilibrium. Thermodynamic state of system composed of two phase partitioned by semipermeable membrane and with identical value of chemical potential of any constituent transferred through phase boundary in both phases.

membrane potential. $\Delta\varphi$. Difference of inner potentials of solutions (I) and (II) separated by semipermeable diaphragm ; if diaphragm is permeable for B ions, then

$$\Delta\varphi = \frac{RT}{zF}\ln\frac{a_B^{I}}{a_B^{II}}$$

Also known as Donnan potential.

mendelevium. An element.

	Symbol	Md
State Solid	Atomic No.	101
Group III B	Atomic Wt.	256 (?)
	Valence	2,3

A radioactive metal of the actinide series ; also one of the transuranium elements.

The isotope ^{256}Md was produced by the bombardment of ^{253}Es on gold foil with 48 MeV alpha particles in the 60 in. (152.4-cm) cyclotron at Berkeley. By ion exchange treatment of the dissolved gold foil, only one or two atoms of ^{256}Md were obtained, which decayed ($t_{1/2}$=1.3 hr) by *K*-electron capture to ^{256}Fm, which underwent its characteristic spontaneous fission.

Another isotope, ^{255}Md, is also formed during the bombardment of ^{253}Es by alpha particles. It also decays by electron capture, and has a half-life of 30 minutes.

The element is named for Dmitri Mendeleev, discoverer of the Periodic System. It can be produced only in quantities measured in numbers of atoms. The behaviour of mendelevium in ion-exchange chromatography shows that it exists in the + 3 oxidation state characteristic of the actinide elements. However, it also exhibits +2 and +1 oxidation states.

meniscus. The curved surface of a liquid, particularly noticeable in vessels or tubes of small diameter and due to the surface tension of the liquid. If the liquid wets the containing vessel the meniscus is concave, otherwise it is convex. The meniscus of mercury in glass is convex.

menstruum. A solvent, especially the solvent used in extracting drugs, which is often a complex mixture.

mercaptal. One of a group of sulphur compounds also known as thioacetals, analogous to the acetals, of the general form R'S—CHR—SR", where R' and R" are identical or different alkyl or aryl groups.

mercaptans. Hydrogen sulphide yields two classes of organic compounds: (*a*) hydrosulphides, and (*b*) sulphides. The hydrosulphides are termed mercaptans, a name derived from the Latin phrase mercurium captans, because of their ability to react with mercuric oxide to form crystalline compounds. Mercaptans are also termed thioalcohols and sulphur-alcohols. The more general term thiols is also used. This term not only embraces mercaptans, but also covers thioethers, sulphydrates, and thiophenols. They are liquids of extremely disgusting, garlic odour.

mercaptide. One of a group of metallic derivatives of the mercaptans, *e.g.*, mercury mercaptide, $Hg(C_2H_5S)_2$. They bear the same relation to the mercaptans that the alcoholates do to the alcohols.

mercapto-. The radical HS—.

mercaptol. One of a group of sulphur compounds of the general form.

```
       R'
       |
  SR—C—SR
       |
       R"
```

produced by combination of ketones and mercaptans, in which R' and R" may be identical or different aryl or alkyl groups.

mercerizing. In textile technology, the process of passing cotton fibres through a 20% solution of sodium hydroxide, followed by washing with water. This treatment not only increases the strength of the fibres but develops controlled shrinkage and elasticity. It has been applied to the manufacture of modern stretch fabrics. Mercerizing is the first step in the manufacture of viscose rayon, in which alkali cellulose is formed by reaction of the hydroxyl groups of cellulose fibres with the sodium hydroxide.

Merck's process. A method of making hydrogen peroxide industrially. Sodium peroxide is added to ice-cold 20% sulphuric acid solution. The mother liquor is decanted from the sodium sulphate that crystallises and is distilled in vacuo, a 30% solution of hydrogen peroxide being obtained. Such methods have now been largely replaced by electrolytic and autoxidation processes.

mercuration. The substitution or addition of mercury to an organic compound.

mercuride. A compound of mercury with one or more organic radicals, usually the same radical, as $Hg(C_2H_5)_2$.

mercury. An element

		Symbol	Hg
		Atomic No.	80
		Atomic Wt.	200.59
State	Liquid	Valence	1,2
Group	IIB	Isotopes	7 stable
		m.p.	234.13K
		b.p.	629.58K

Mercury is a noble metal that is soluble only in oxidising solutions, it forms a monatomic vapour and can be compressed to a soft solid state. It is unique among liquids in its very high surface tension (484 dynes/cm) which causes it to fragment into globules rather than to flow ; this property is responsible for the trivial name quicksilver. Solid mercury has a rhombohedral crystal structure.

There are seven stable isotopes of mercury, ^{196}Hg, ^{198}Hg through ^{202}Hg, and ^{204}Hg ; and seven rodioactive isotopes, ^{192}Hg through ^{195}Hg, ^{197}Hg, ^{203}Hg, and ^{205}Hg. With exception of ^{194}Hg ($t_{1/2}$ = approximately 130 days) and ^{203}Hg, ($t_{1/2}$ = approximately 46 days), the half-lives of the radioactive isotopes are short, measured in terms of minutes or hours.

First ionization potential 10.434 eV; second 18.65 eV ; third 34.3 eV. Oxidation potentials $Hg \rightarrow \frac{1}{2}Hg_2^{2+} + e^-$, -0.7986 V ; $Hg \rightarrow Hg^{2+} + 2e^-$, 0.852 V; $Hg_2^{2+} \rightarrow 2Hg^{2+} + 2e^-$, -0.905V. $Hg + 2OH^- \rightarrow HgO + 2H_2O + 2e^-$, -0.098 V ; $2Hg + 2OH^- \rightarrow Hg_2O + H_2O + 2e^-$. -0.123 V.

Elemental mercury is light gray in colour, with a specific gravity 13.6 and high electrical conductivity. It is used in thermometers and barometers, in special lamps, as a component of dental amalgams, as electrodes in electrolytic cells, and in electric switches. It may have toxic effects as a result of long contact with the skin or inhalation of vapour ; while oral intake should be avoided, it is not serious in small amounts. Chronic mercury poisoning presents five main symptoms : numbness, staggering gait, constriction of visual fluid, garbled speech, and tremor. Disposal of mercury in streams and coastal waters is an ecological hazard, due to bacterial conversion of the element into toxic compounds, such as methyl mercury.

mercury cathode. Mercury electrode used in reduction of ions or molecules, as dropping mercury electrode or with large surface for electrolytic separation of certain metals or preparation of certain substances.

merochrome compound. A compound having differently-coloured isomeric forms occuring together, as in a mixed crystal.

meso-. 1. A prefix denoting that the compound lacks optical activity because it contains two asymmetric carbon atoms which rotate plane-polarized light by the same amount in opposite directions, resulting in zero rotation. This is called internal compensation and occurs in, *e.g.*, meso-tartaric acid.

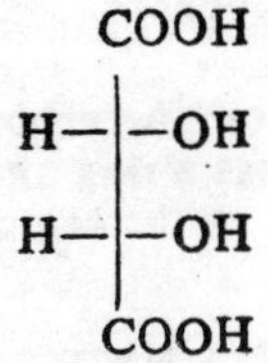

COOH
H—|—OH
H—|—OH
COOH

2. A prefix indicating that certain groups or substituents occupy a middle or central position in the molecule.

mesocolloid. A colloid composed of particles of relatively medium size, *i.e.*, ranging from 0.025 to 0.25 micron.

meso-ionic compounds. 5- or 6-membered heterocyclic compounds whose structure connot be described by simple covalent arrangement of bonds. Such compounds possess electronic sextet covering all atoms of ring and atom linked to it ; *e.g.*, sydnon or nitron :

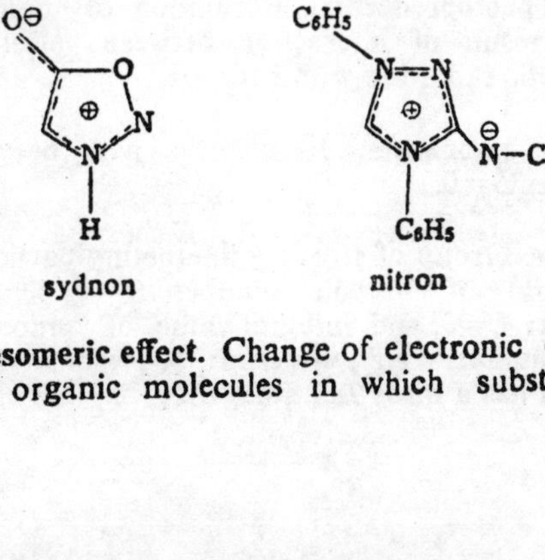

sydnon

nitron

mesomeric effect. Change of electronic density in organic molecules in which substituents containing atoms with free electron pairs (or multiple bonds) are located close to double bonds (especially conjugated double bond systems). Mesomeric effect results from conjugations of π-electrons with free electron pairs of substituent, *e.g.*,

+M effect (electron shift towards the ring)

—M effect (electron shift toward the substituent)

mesomerism. *See* resonance.

mesomethylene carbon. A carbon atom which forms a bridge across a ring and is linked to two methyl groups, as the central carbon atom in camphane.

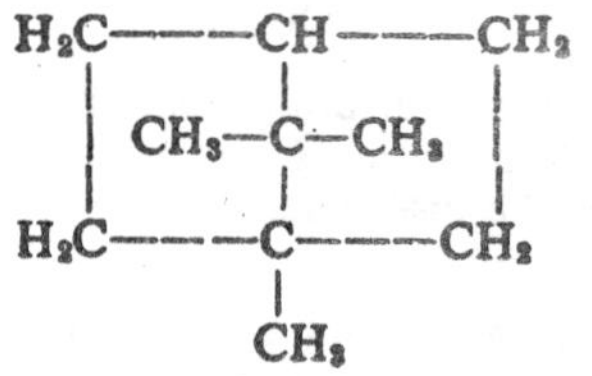

$$\begin{array}{ccccc} H_2C & \text{——} & CH & \text{——} & CH_2 \\ | & & | & & | \\ | & CH_3 & \text{—}C\text{—} & CH_3 & | \\ | & & | & & | \\ H_2C & \text{——} & C & \text{——} & CH_2 \\ & & | & & \\ & & CH_3 & & \end{array}$$

mesomorphic. Having an intemediate form, specifically a form intermediate between the liquid and solid states. The term is applied to the so-called "liquid crystals." This state has considerable order of molecules in liquid and of resulting anisotropy, *e.g.*, optical properties. It occurs in melts of certain organic compounds close to freezing point.

meson photoproduction. Formation of mesons as a result of interaction between electromagnetic radiation with hadrons.

meson resonances. Resonances with baryon number $B=0$.

mesons. Group of strongly interacting particles (hadron) of baryon number $B=0$, lepton number $L=0$, and integral value of quantum spin number ; *e.g.*, π-mesons, K-mesons. π(pi) meson has a mass 285 times that of the electron, and μ-meson has a mass about 215 times that of the electron.

mesothorium I. Radioactive element of the thorium family. Mesothorium I has an atomic number of 88 and mass number 228, and a half-life of 6.7 years. It emits β-rays and is an isotope of radium.

mesothorium II. It has an atomic number of 89 and is isotope of actinium with a half-life of 6.13 hours. Its mass number is 228. It emits β-rays. Mesothorium I yields Mesothorium II by β-ray emission, which, in turn, yields radiothorium by β-ray emission.

messenger. A term often used to describe the function of an active biochemical agent or complex. For example, it is used to characterize the behaviour of hormones, which regulate many essential metabolic functions: it also refers to one type of ribonucleic acid (RNA), which carries essential genetic coding information from DNA molecules to the ribosomes, on the basis of which proteins are built up from various amino acid sequences.

meta-. 1. A prefix used in naming isomers of aromatic compounds and denotes location 3 in a benzene ring. Thus, if substituent atoms or groups replace hydrogen at locations 1 and 3, the compound is a meta-isomer ; often the numerals 1,3- are used to indicate such substitution.

2. The prefix is also used in inorganic nomenclature to indicate a lower state of hydration, *e.g.*, metaphosphoric acid.

metabolism. The chemical and physiochemical changes occurring in a plant or animal in response to intake of nutrients. Plant metabolism involves the assimilation of the major nutrients, *e.g.* nitrogen, potassium, phosphorus trace elements, water, carbon dioxide etc., and their conversion into cellulose, fats, starches, sugars, and proteins within the plant. In animals the entire assimilative process serves to extract the energy values from nutrients provided directly or indirectly by plants in a complex series of steps, from carbohydrate breakdown in the saliva to absorption of glucose and amino acids in the intestines. Digestion of foods is aided by enzymes (pepsin), by hydrochloric acid in the stomach and by bile formed in the liver.

metabolite. An active growth factor in organic systems typified by vitamins, enzymes, proteins, and their various complexes. Substances that are able to inhibit the activity of metabolites because of their chemically similar structure are called antimetabolites or structural antagonists.

metachromatism. Change of the colour of an object or substance with a change in the colour of the light by which it is viewed.

metafiltration. A method of filtration in which the filtering medium is a pile of metallic strips with beveled edges, between which the liquid to be filtered is passed,

metal. An electropositive chemical element. A member of a class of elements characterized by the possession of metallic lustre, ductility, malleability, high electric and thermal conductivity, and chemically, of forming bases which can react with acids.

There is no sharp line of demarcation between metals and non-metals, because many of the latter class possess some metallic properties. Most metals are quite reactive chemically, though a few are not ; they form positive ions and exert electrochemical potential. Physically, a metal atom in the ground state contains a partially filled band with an empty state close to an occupied state.

The atoms of metals are joined by bonds having free electrons, which account for their electrical and thermal conductivity.

Metals fall into several groups : (*i*) alkali metals (Group IA) ; alkaline-earth metals (Group IIA, except beryllium) ; rare earth metals (lanthanide series) ; radioactive metals (polonium, radium, and actinide series) ; and the transition metals (atomic numbers 21-29, 39-47, 72-79). Some authorities include the lanthanide and actinide series in the transition metal group ; the platinum group (atomic numbers 44, 45, 46, 76, 77, 78) are also transition metals.

metal, alkali. *See* alkali metals.

metal, alkaline earths. *See* alkaline earths.

metal-base fuel. A fuel containing a metal of high heat combustion as a principal constituent.

metal carbonyl. Compound formed between metal of zero oxidation number with carbon monoxide; such a compound possesses M—CO bond. Metal carbonyl may be mononuclear $M(CO)_x$ or polynuclear $M_x(CO)_y$.

metal electrode. Electrode (half-cell) constructed from metal dipped into solution containing its ions, M/M^{z+} ; electrode reaction is $M \rightleftharpoons M^{z+} + ze^-$ and potential of electrode,

$$\epsilon = \epsilon^0 + \frac{RT}{zF} \ln a_{M^{z+}}$$

where ϵ^0 = standard electrode potential.

metal glass. A product made by subjecting a molten or alloy to extremely rapid cooling (quenching), thus preventing formation of a crystalline structure. This results in a vitreous material that is predominantly amorphous and has unique behaviour in respect to corrosion resistance, conductivity, and magnetic properties.

metal, heavy. *See* heavy metal.

metal, light. *See* light metal.

metal bond. A strong electrostatic force, existing between atoms in metallic crystals, which binds the crystal together in a close-packed structure ; in this type of bonding, the electrons are distributed among all the available vacancies rather than being paired between specific atoms. Thus, a metallic bond is the attraction between a positively charged metal ion and the unlocalized body of electrons which envelope it. This imparts a number of properties characteristic of metals, such as electrical and thermal conductivity, ductility, hardness, etc. When sufficient energy is supplied, the bonds rupture and the crystal melts.

metallic soap. A compound formed by the reaction of a metal or metal oxide with an organic acid : in other words, a salt of a heavy metal and an organic acid. Metallic soaps are used as driers in the paint industry, and for other industrial purposes.

metallizing. A process for coating objects with thin layers of metal by spraying them with molten metals.

metallocene. Any of a number of organometallic complexes in which a transition metal atom is coordinated with cyclopentadienyl rings (C_5H_5); the metals most often involved are iron (ferrocene) and cobalt (cobaltocene), though the structure can be formed by a number of others. These are sometimes called sandwich structures, since the metal atom lies midway between the two organic rings.

metallography. Study of the properties of metals and alloys as related to their physical structure, involving knowledge of crystal formation and structure, solid solution theory (phase rule), and microscopy at all levels.

metalloid. An obsolete term formerly used to refer to a small group of solid elements which have strong semiconducting properties. These are now preferably called nonmetals or semiconductors.

metallurgy. The science that deals with the processing of metals, from their recovery from ores to their purification, alloying and fabrication into industrial articles. It is generally considered to comprise the following subdivisions : mining and ore separation (extractive metallurgy), alloying, fabrication, and testing (physical metallurgy); and manufacture and fabrication of metal powders (powder metallurgy). Application of the principles of chemical analysis and separation techniques and of electrochemical phenomena are also involved in these subdivisions.

metal-matrix composite. A material consisting of two or more substances, one of which is a metal or metallic alloy, and which exhibits its own distinctive behaviour.

metal, noble. *See* noble metal.

metamagnetic compounds. Antiferromagnetic materials which become ferromagnetic in low external magnetic field strength.

metamerism. A form of structural isomerism in which two or more substances, of the same composition, differ in the position of one or more atoms or radicals or double bonds or triple bonds or other special valences. Frequently the compounds are of different types, but the valency and linkages are the same :

$$\text{(H)(R)C=NOR'} \quad \text{and} \quad \text{(R'O)(R)C=NH}$$

Ketoxime and Imido compound

$$\text{(H}_2\text{N)(RO)C=NH} \quad \text{and} \quad \text{(RHN)(HO)C=NH}$$

Pseudo ureide and Hydroxylimide

metamict state. The amorphous state of substances that have lost their original crystalline structure because of the radioactivity of uranium or thorium.

metasomatism. A process by which the chemical composition of rocks is altered.

metastable electronic state. Excited electronic state of an atom or molecule with radiative dipole transition to lower electronic states forbidden. Also known as metastable state.

metastable equilibrium. A definite equilibrium state which is not the most stable equilibrium under the given conditions. A metastable system will undergo a spontaneous change upon addition of the stable phase, or frequently under the action of vibratory forces.

metastable nucleus. *See* isomeric nucleus.

metastable phase. Phase in state of metastable equilibrium, *e.g.*, supercooled liquid, superheated liquid, supersaturated vapour.

metastable state. 1. A peculiar state of pseudo equilibrium in which the system has acquired, energy beyond that for its most stable state, yet has not been rendered stable.

2. Finite disturbance causes transition of system from metastable state to state of thermodynamic equilibrium.

The term has been used in atomic and nuclear physics for various excited states, but its most general usage today is for an excited state from which all possible quantum transitions to lower states are forbidden transitions by appropriate selection rules.

metastable system. A system capable of undergoing a quantum transition to a state of lower energy, but having a relatively long lifetime in comparison with the most rapid quantum transitions of similar systems.

metastatic electron. An electron that moves from one atom, or from one shall to another in a given atom, or to the nucleus of an atom K-electron capture, whereby the nucleus, usually is an induced radioactive reaction, captures an electron from the K-shell, is an instance of electron metastasis.

metastasis. A fundamental change in the position or orbit of a particle, as in the α-particle emission of certain radioactive nuclei.

metathesis. A chemical reaction in which an element or radical in one compound changes place with another element or radical in another compound, *e.g.*,

$$NaNO_3 + KCl \rightleftharpoons NaCl + KNO_3$$

methanation. A reaction by which methane is formed from the hydrogen and carbon monoxide derived from coal gasification. It requires a catalyst, *e.g.*, nickel, and temperatures in the range of 500K. The reaction is

$$CO + 3H_2 \xrightarrow{Ni} CH_4 + H_2O$$

In one process the reaction is performed in an adiabatic fixed-bed reactor.

methanolysis. Alcoholysis in which the alcohol split out is methyl alcohol.

methylate. 1. To add a methyl group to or substitute methyl in a compound.

2. A metallic compound of methyl alcohol, as sodium methylate $CH_3—ONa$.

methylene. 1. The divalent hydrocarbon group $CH_2—$ in which the carbon atom has its normal valence of 4 ; it is derived from methane by dropping two hydrogen atoms.

methylidyne. The radical $CH\equiv$.

Meyer reaction. A reaction used in the preparation of organic compounds of tin ; alkyl halides react with sodium stannite to give alkyl stannates and sodium halides.

$$NaSnOONa + RX \rightarrow RSnOONa + NaX$$

Meyer-Schuster rearrangement. Rearrangement of tertiary alcohols with alkynyl group at (α-position into α,β-unsaturated ketones in presence of acid catalysts (formic acid, sulphuric acid, acetyl chloride, thionyl-chloride), *e.g.*,

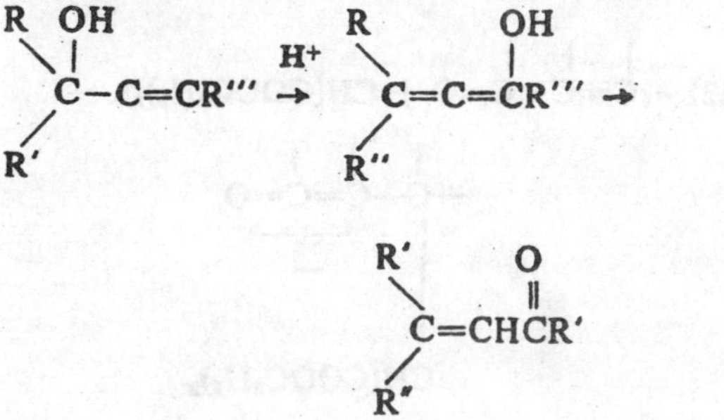

$$(R)(R')C(OH)—C{\equiv}CR''' \xrightarrow{H^+} (R)(R'')C{=}C{=}CR''' \rightarrow (R')(R'')C{=}CHCR'{=}O$$

micelle. Colloidal particle with electrical double layer and solvation sphere. These characteristically occur in such aqueous suspensions as soaps (fatty acids), milk (casein), etc. In soaps, the individual molecules of fatty acids are made up of a positively charged chain of hydrocarbons which is hydrophobic and a negatively charged carboxyl group which is hydrophilic. When many such molecules are present in a solution, they aggregate or unite to form a particle which has properties similar to those of the component molecules. In milk, the casein combines with calcium to form a calcium caseinate complex, or micelle.

Michael addition. Addition of compounds possessing active hydrogen atom to α,β-unsaturated ketones, aldehydes, esters or nitriles catalyzed by bases, *e.g.*,

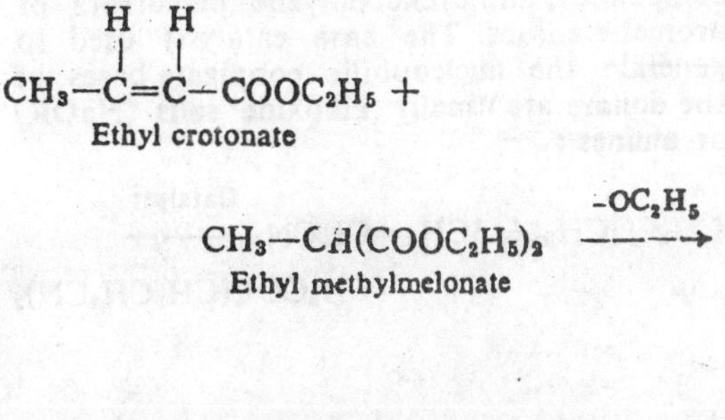

$$CH_3—\overset{H}{C}{=}\overset{H}{C}—COOC_2H_5 +$$

Ethyl crotonate

$$CH_3—CH(COOC_2H_5)_2 \xrightarrow{^-OC_2H_5}$$

Ethyl methylmelonate

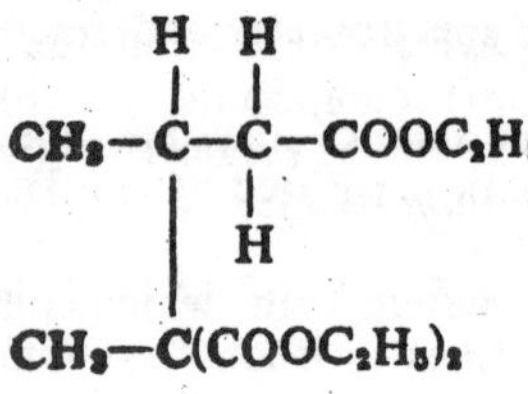

```
     H   H
     |   |
CH3—C———C—COOC2H5
     |   |
     |   H
     |
CH2—C(COOC2H5)2
```

The Michael addition is believed to proceed by the following mechanism (shown for malonic ester):

(1) $CH_2(COOC_2H_5)_2$ + : Base →
$H{:}Base^+ + CH(COOC_2H_5)_2^-$

(2) 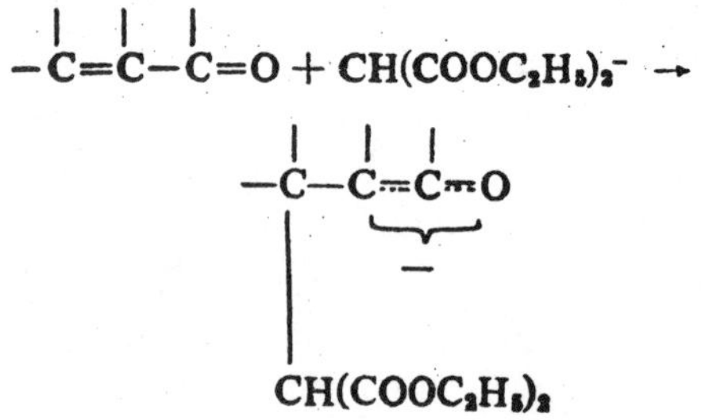 $-\overset{|}{C}=\overset{|}{C}-\overset{|}{C}=O + CH(COOC_2H_5)_2^- \rightarrow$

```
  |   |   |
 —C———C═══C═══O
  |    \____/
  |      —
  |
CH(COOC2H5)2
```

(3) 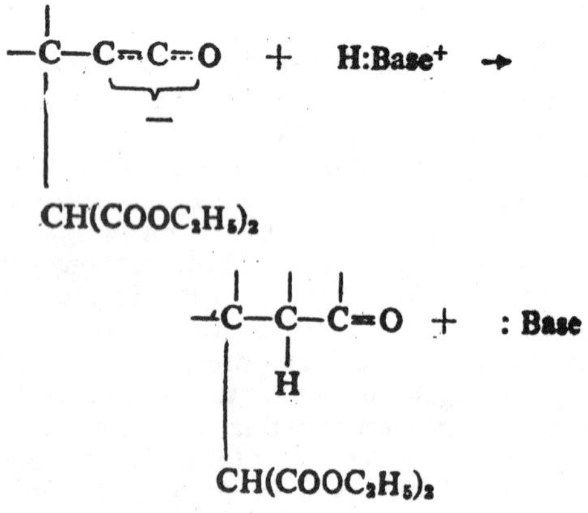
```
  |
 —C———C═══C═══O   +   H:Base+  →
  |    \____/
  |      —
  |
CH(COOC2H5)2
```

```
  |   |   |
 —C———C———C═O  +  : Base
  |   |
  |   H
  |
CH(COOC2H5)2
```

Michael reaction. Carbonyl enolate anions and related intermediates may also serve as nucleophilic donors in a versatile and useful modifications of conjugate addition known as Michael reaction. Possible Michael reaction donors include esters, ketones, nitriles nitro compounds, and cyclic polyene precursors of aromatic anions. The base catalysts used to generate the nucleophilic conjugate bases of the donors are usually alkoxide salts (NaOR) or amines :

$$CH_3COCH_3 + 3CH_2{=}CHCN \xrightarrow{\text{Catalyst}} CH_3COC(CH_2CH_2CN)_3$$

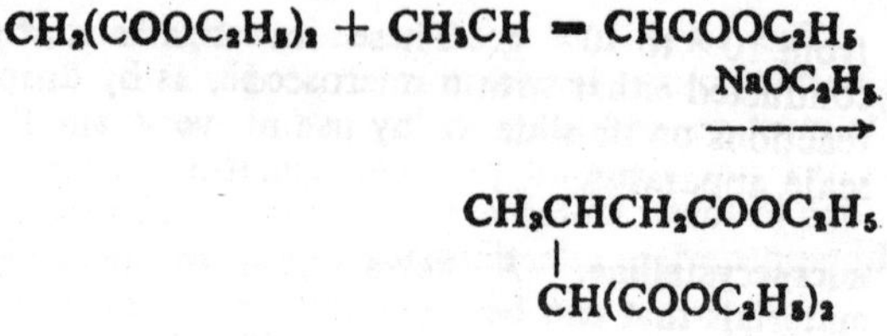

$$CH_2(COOC_2H_5)_2 + CH_3CH = CHCOOC_2H_5 \xrightarrow{NaOC_2H_5}$$

```
CH3CHCH2COOC2H5
   |
CH(COOC2H5)2
```

Michalski reaction. Preparation of oxophosphoranesulphenyl chlorides by treating trialkyl thionophosphoranes with chlorinating agents (Cl_2, SO_2Cl_2), *e.g.*,

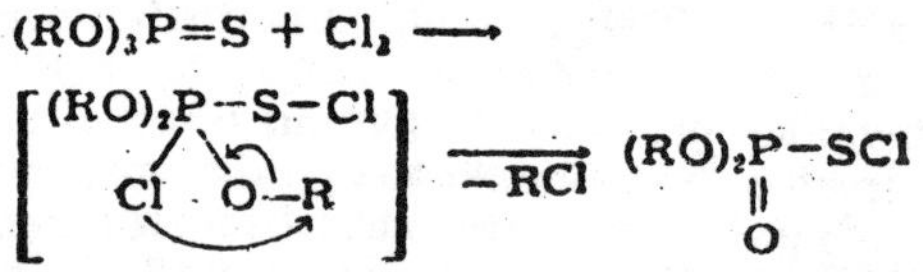

$$(RO)_3P{=}S + Cl_2 \longrightarrow$$

```
[ (RO)2P—S—Cl ]
[   / \        ]   ——————→   (RO)2P—SCl
[  Cl · O—R    ]     —RCl          ‖
                                   O
```

Michalski rearrangement. Preparation of thionophosphoranes (and their analogues) resulting from condensation of oxophosphoranosulphenyl chlorides with di- or trialkyl phosphites, also alkylphosphorane, formed as intermediate, undergoes this reaction :

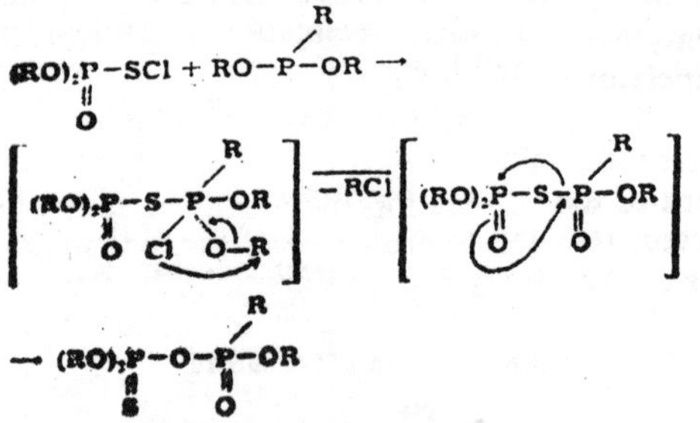

```
                       R
                      /
(RO)2P—SCl + RO—P—OR  →
     ‖
     O

[               R  ]        [               R  ]
[              /   ]  —RCl  [              /   ]
[ (RO)2P—S—P—OR    ]  ————  [ (RO)2P—S—P—OR    ]
[      ‖   / \     ]        [      ‖     ‖     ]
[      O  Cl  O—R  ]        [      O     O     ]

                  R
                 /
→ (RO)2P—O—P—OR
       ‖     ‖
       S     O
```

microanalysis. Analysis of samples weighing from 1/10 milligrams : semimicroanalysis involves samples weighing from 10 to 100 milligrams.

microcanonical assembly. Statistical ensemble given by following probability distribution function $P(Q) = \text{const.}\delta(E(Q)-E_0)$ where δ = Dirac delta-function, $E(Q)$ = energy of system in state Q, E_0 = energy eigenvalue of system ; Microcanonical ensemble is utilized for statistical description of thermodynamic equilibrium in isolated systems. (microcanonical assembly).

micro chemistry. That branch of chemistry devoted to processes of chemical analysis for the investigation of substances of quantities from 10^{-3} to 10^{-2} g. These investigations are conducted either with a microscope, as by drop reactions on its slide, or by use of very small-scale apparatus.

microcrystalline. A term used to describe materials that can be prepared in a form in which the crystals are much smaller than in the natural product. Paraffin-like waxes derived from lubricating oil wastes and residual oil refining are the most important products in commericial use ; they have much higher viscosity and penetration value than normal paraffin wax. They are used in adhesives, paper sizing, carbon paper, cosmetic creams, and many other products. Chlorophyll has a type of structure that is naturally microcrystalline. Some high polymers are now being prepared in this form, including in size from 2.5 to 500 millimicrons.

microgram method. Method of analysis where mass of investigated sample in x.10^{-6}—x.10^{-4}g, or volume *x*.10^{-5}—*x*.10^{-3} cm^3 in the case of gases. ***Also see*** ultramicro method.

micro-heterogeneous catalysis. Multi-phase catalysis due to presence of catalyst in colloidal dispersion.

microspectrophotometry. Method of measurement of absorption by objects with very small surface (ca. 2—20 μm^2) or by very thin objects (*e.g.*, fibres) using microspectometer, *i.e.*, combination of spectrometer and microscope.

micro state. The state of a system specified in the ultimate detail permitted by the Heisenberg uncertainty principle.

State of system in which number of dynamic quantities such as momental particle coordinates, etc., of a given value is maximum ; according to classical statistical mechanics all dynamic variables have precisely defined values at microscopic state; in quantum case not all of them are determined precisely. Also known as microscopic state.

microwave spectroscopy. A type of absorption spectroscopy utilizing the portion of the electromagnetic spectrum lying between the far infrared and radiofrequencies, *i.e.*, wavelengths from 1 to 1000 millimetres. Substances analyzed in this manner must be in the gas phase. The klystron tube is used as a source of microwave radiation. The method is especially suitable for study of internal molecular structure.

microwave spectrum. Spectrum registered in range of frequencies from about 3×10^9 Hz to about 3×10^{12} Hz, associated with transitions between molecular rotational energy levels.

Miescher degradation. The process, which is a modification of the Barbier-Wieland method, accomplishes the removal of three carbons at one time from an aliphatic acid :

$$\mathrm{RR'.CH.CH_2.CH_2CO_2R'} \xrightarrow{\mathrm{C_6H_5MgBr}} \mathrm{RR'.CH.CH_2CH_2C(OH)(C_6H_5)-C_6H_5}$$

$$\xrightarrow{-\mathrm{H_2O}} \mathrm{RR'CHCH_2CH{=}C(C_6H_5)_2}$$

$$\xrightarrow{\text{N-bromo succinimide}} \mathrm{RR'CHCHBrCH{=}C(C_6H_5)_2}$$

$$\xrightarrow[\mathrm{C_6H_5N(CH_3)_2}]{\text{(Dimethylaniline)}} \mathrm{RR'C{=}CHCH{=}C(C_6H_5)_2} \xrightarrow[273\mathrm{K}]{\mathrm{CrO_3}} \mathrm{RCOR'} + \mathrm{CHOCH{=}C(C_6H_5)_2}$$

migration current. Current resulting from electrode process of ions which migrate to electrode surface.

Miller indices. Indices of planes, *h, k, l,* three numbers describing position of any plane of lattice in chosen system of crystallographic axes *a, b, c, e.g.*, plane which intercepts axis *a* at $x = a$ and parallel to *b, c,* has indices (100), a plane parallel to *a,* intercepting axis *b* at $y = b/2$ and axis at $z = c/3$ has indices (023).

Miller reagent for cerium. A 5% solution of sodium arsanilate, of which 5 ml. is added to a mixture of 45 ml. of the solution to be tested and 5 ml. *N* sulphuric acid. A pink to red-brown colour indicates the presence of cerium.

milligram method. Method of analysis where mass of investigated sample is $x.10^{-3}$ g, or volume $x.10^{-2}$—$x.10^{-1}$ cm^3 in the case of gases. Also known as micro method.

mineral. 1. A naturally-occurring inorganic substance which has a characteristic range of chemical composition, usually a definite, crystal form, and which exhibits other specific, physical characteristics such as cleavage, fracture, hardness, luster, colour, specific gravity, and index of refraction.

2. As used by nutritionists, the term refers to such components of food as iron, copper, phosphorus, calcium, iodine, selenium, fluorine. and other trace micronutrients. *See also* geochemistry ; trace element.

3. The term mineral was illogically used by early chemists to describe a variety of substances ; many of these uses are obsolescent, but a few persist, *e.g.*,

mineral acid : many, of the major inorganic acids (sulphuric, nitric, hydrochloric).

mineral black : inorganic black pigments.

mineral blue : varieties of blue pigments.

mineral dust : industrial dust : nuisance dust.

mineral green : copper carbonate.

mineral oil : a liquid petroleum derivative.

mineral pitch : asphalt.

mineral red : iron oxide red.

mineral rubber : blown asphalt.

mineral spirits : a grade of naphtha.

mineral water : natural spring water containing sulphur, iron, etc.

mineral wax : a wax found in the earth (ozocerite), or derived from petroleum.

mineral wool : fibres made by blowing air or steam through molten slag.

4. The term mineral is also extended to include various fossilized organized substances found in nature, such as the bitumens, etc.

mineral dye. An inorganic compound used in dyeing, as ferric hydrate, chromic hydrate, lead chromate, Prussian blue.

mineralization. Complete decomposition and oxidation of analysed organic substance in order to determine its mineral components.

mineral oil. Petroleum, and oils distilled from it ; or, more generally, any oil obtained from inorganic or mineral sources.

mirror nuclei. Pairs of nuclides in which number of neutrons in one nucleus is equal to number of protons in other one (and vice-versa, number of protons in first nucleus equal to number of neutrons in second nucleus).

mirror reflection symmetry. Symmetry of system in which every point has as its counterpart its reflection in the same mirror plane. Also known as reflection plane symmetry.

misch metal. An alloy or mixture of several rare-earth metals, of which cerium constitutes about 50%. It ignites when exposed to heat or friction it is used as a component of numerous alloys, as a reducing agent, and a scavenger (getter) in vacuum devices.

miscibility. The abiltty of two or more substances to mix, and to form a single, homogeneous phase.

miscibility gap. The range of values in a given condition, usually temperature, under which liquids that are otherwise completely miscibile mix only partially, or not at all.

miscible. A term describing the extent to which liquids or gases can be mixed or blended. Substance in the gaseous phase can blend in any proportion : this may or may not be true of liquids. Some, such as ethyl alcohol and water, will blend uniformly in all proportions ; others have limited miscibility, that is, they will blend only until a certain concentration is reached. The term soluble is often used in this sense, but it usually applies to solids.

mixed acid. A blend of nitric and sulphuric acids used in the chemical industries to introduce nitrogen into a compound, for example in the manufacture of nitrocellulose, cotton linters are treated with mixed acid of various strenghts to form lacquers and explosives. The process is called nitration. Standard mixed acid is about two-thirds sulphuric and one-third nitric acid.

mixed-bed. Mixture of cation and anion exchanger in one column. Mixed bed of cation exchanger in hydrogen form and anion exchanger in hydroxyl form is used for deionization of aqueous solutions.

mixed-bed de-ionization. The ion-exchange process carried out with the help of ion-exchange resins in which the cation exchange as well as the anion exchange resins are intermingled in a single bed. The acid that is released by a cation exchange resin is immediately neutralized by neighbouring anion exchange resin, so that H_3O^+ ion concentration never rises enough to cause any mass action reversal of the cation exchange. Regeneration is made possible by having the anion exchange resin considerably lighter than the other resin.

A 4% sodium hydroxide solution is first run in a chamber followed by rinse water. If R^+ represents the giant cation of the anion exchanger and R^- the giant anion of the cation exchanger the reaction for the regeneration of the anion exchanger is :

$$Na^+ + OH^- + [R^+ Cl^-] \rightarrow [R^+ + OH^-] + Na^+ + Cl^-$$

At the same time, Na^+ ions displace most of the Ca^{2+} and Mg^{2+} from the cation exchanger just as they do in the regeneration of a simple softner.

$$2Na^+ + 2Cl^- + [Ca^{2+} + 2R^-] \rightarrow 2[Na^+ + R^-] + Ca^{2+} + 2Cl^-$$

Next the backwash separates the light from the heavy particles. This is called hydraulic classfication. The backwash is slowly turned off and the resin settles down in two separate layers. Next, 10% sulphuric acid is introduced at the top of the lower layer, together with enough water from above to prevent any of the acid from working upward. The reaction is :

$$2H^+ + SO_4^{2-} + 2[Na^+ + R^-] \rightarrow 2[H^+ + R^-] + 2Na^+ + SO_4^{2-}$$

After the excess acid has been rinsed out, the resins are remixed by blowing air through the perforated plate at the bottom of the chamber ; they are then drawn into original operating position.

mixed catalyst. Mixture of catalysts exhibiting different catalytic activity (usually higher) than the one exhibited by each constituent of mixture individually. Also known as compound catalyst.

mixed complex. Complex containing central atom and more than one kind of ligands, *e.g.*, MX_iY_j. Also known as mixed ligand complex.

mixed crystals. A homogeneous solid solution in which the crystal lattice sites are occupied, at random, by the molecules or ions of two different compounds. The property of forming a mixed crystal is typical of isomorphous substances, which must, however, also have similar atomic dimensions.

mixed ligand complex. *See* mixed complex.

mixed polyelectrode potential. *See* mixed potential.

mixed potential. Potential of multiple electrode resultant of potentials of electrode reactions occurring in multiple electrode. Also known as mixed polyelectrode potential.

mixed radiation. Ionizing radiation composed of different particles, or particles and photons.

mixed, salt. A salt of a polybasic acid, in which the hydrogen atoms are replaced by different metallic atoms or positive radicals.

mixture. A mechanical blend of two or more substances in any proportions ; the components may or may not be uniformly dispersed. The substances are not united chemically and can be separated by a number of means, as by filtration, distillation, precipitation, etc. Since they are composed of more than one component, they are heterogeneous in nature. Well-known examples of mixtures are air, milk, alloys, petroleum, blood, gasoline, etc. A mixture in which the components are uniformly dispersed is called a solution.

M-line. One of the lines in the M-series of x-rays that are characteristic of the various elements and are produced by excitation of the electrons of the M-shell.

mobile. A term used to describe the extent to which a liquid moves or flows in response to force. Nonpolar liquids such as hydrocarbon solvents are in general much more mobile than water and somewhat more so than alcohols, because of their lower surface tension. This property is of significance in the handling, transporting, and pouring of such liquids, as well as in fire extinguishment.

mobile phase in chromatography. Gas or liquid flowing through chromatographic column or layer of stationary phase.

modacrylic fibre. Any man-made fibre comprised of a minimum of 35% by weight and a maximum of 85% by weight of acrylonitrile monomer, the balance being made up of various modifying synthetics such as vinyl choride.

moderator. A substance used in nuclear reactors to absorb the energy of the fast neutrons produced by fission, to the point where they will be more likely to induce enough new fissions to maintain a chain reaction. Graphite, berylium, heavy water and ordinary (light) water have been used for this purpose, the last being the most practical. Because the kinetic energy given up by fast neutrons as they collide with the nuclei of the moderating substance appears as heat, the resulting "slow" neutrons are also called "thermal" neutrons.

modification. A form of a substance or system that differs to some extent, usually slight, from another form, which is sometimes the original form ; or the change by which one substance or system is changed to a related one.

Moh's scale. A system in which all solid substances are classified in order of increasing hardness, so that the hardness of any particular substance may be expressed by a number. The numbers were established by assigning the integers from one to ten to arbitrarily chosen substances of increasing hardness, ranging from talc which was given the number one, to diamond which was given the number ten. This was the original Moh scale and is still generally used. In the new Moh scale fifteen substances are used, and diamond has the number fifteen. The hardness of the substances not on the scale is determined by the scratch test, *i.e.*, by comparing its hardness with that of the various substances in the standard scale, utilizing the principle that the harder of the two substances will scratch the softer one, and will not be scratched by it. When a substance is found to have hardness between two of the standard substances in the scale, this fact is expressed by use of decimal notation. Thus, the-mineral having hardness of 6.65 would be harder than feldspar 6, and softer than quartz 7.

The original Moh's scale assigned the integral numbers is as follows : 1 — Talc ; 2 — Gypsum ; 3 — Calcite ; 4 — Fluorite ; 5 — Apatite ; 6 — Orthoclase ; 7 — Quartz ; 8 — Topaz ; 9 — Corundum ; 10 — Diamond.

In the new Moh's scale the numbers above five have been re-assigned as follows : 6 — Orthoclase, Periclase : 7 — Vitreous pure silica ; 8 — Quartz, Stellite ; 9 — Topaz ; 10 — Garnet ; 11 — Tantalum carbide, Fused zirconia ; 12 — Tungsten carbide, Fused alumina ; 13 — Silicon carbide ; 14 — Boron carbide ; 15 — Diamond.

molal. Pertaining to moles, as that term is used masses in chemistry to refer to gram-molecular, which are the molecular weights of substances expressed in grams ; or as of a solution, containing one gram-molecular mass of solute per kilogram of solvent.

molal heat capacity, C. Intensive quantity equal to ratio of elementary heat δQ received isochorically or isobarically by one mole of substance to corresponding temperature change δT caused by this process, *viz* ;

$$C = \frac{\delta Q}{\delta T}$$

Also known as true molal heat capacity.

molal heat capacity at constant pressure, C_p. Intensive quantity defined as :

$$C_p = \left[\frac{\partial H_m}{\partial T}\right]_p$$

where H_m = molal enthalpy, T = thermodynamic temperature and p = pressure.

molal heat capacity at constant volume, C_V. Intensive quantity defined as follows :

$$C_v = \left[\frac{\partial U_m}{\partial T}\right]_v$$

where U_m = molal internal energy, T = thermodynamic temperature, and V = volume.

molality. The number of moles (gram-molecules) of a substance per unit mass of a phase or system, as of solute per kilogram of solvent.

molar. Pertaining to molecules, or to moles per unit volume ; thus a molar solution is one containing one gram-molecular mass of solute per litre of solution.

molar absorptivity, ε. Absorbance of solution of unit molar concentration when path length equals 1 cm. Its numerical value is usually calculated from the Lambert-Beer law applied to measurement results for fairly diluted solutions. Also known as molar absorbancy index.

molar concentration. The number of moles (gram-molecule) of a substance per unit volume of a system. For example, a molar solution contains one mole of solute per litre of solution.

molar conductance. $\Lambda c'$. Conductivity of 1 mole of electrolyte in solution with a given concentration c.

$$\Lambda c' = \frac{1000x}{c}$$

where x = specific conductance of solution with concentration c mol/dm³.

molar mass, M. Mass, in grams, of one mole of given type of particles, *i.e.*, atoms, molecules, ions, free radicals, elementary particles, or atomic groups. Numerically molar mass is equal to corresponding relative atomic or molecular mass—however, in contrast to former, molar mass has dimension.

molar polarization, P_m. Measure of dipole moment induced by electric field of unit strength in 1 mole of substance; scalar quantity defined by :

$$P_m = \frac{1}{3\epsilon_0} N_A [\alpha_1 + \alpha_0] \quad \text{(in SI units)}$$

where N_A = Avogadro constant, α_1 = induced polarizability, α_0 = orientation polarizability, ϵ_0 = permittivity of free space. Also known as molecular polarization.

molar quantities, Z_m. Intensive quantities defined by equation :

$$Z_m = \frac{Z}{\sum_i n_i}$$

where Z = extensive function of state of a given phase and $\sum_i n_i$ denotes sum of number of moles all phase constituents. Also known as proper quantities.

molar refraction, R_m. Constant characteristic for a given substance and defined by

$$R_m = \frac{n^2 - 1}{n^2 + 2} V_m$$

where n = refractive index, V_m = molar volume. Also known as molecular refraction.

molar rotation. Quantity equal to product of specific rotation and 1/100 of molar mass of a given compound.

molar rotation, V_m. Volume of one mole of substance (either single- or multi-component).

molasses. The heavy, viscous liquid remaining after separation of sugar crystals from the mother liquor. In the process of sugar manufacture, this operation is carried out by repeated centrifuging until as much sugar has been recovered as is economically possible. The final molasses (called blackstrap) still contains from 30 to 35% sucrose. Steffen molasses, made from beet sugar, is a source of sodium glutamate. Blackstrap molasses is an important source of ethyl alcohol for industrial use and to some extent for beverage purposes. It can also be used as an animal feed.

mold. 1. A type of fungus ; it has no chlorophyll and thus must derive its nutrients either from dead vegetation or other organic matter, or by acting as a parasite on living organisms. It is smilar to mildew and the so-called rusts or smuts appearing on wheat and other grains. Certain types are cultivated for the manufacture of penicillin, their nutrients being provided in the form of lactose and other sugars, Molds are likely to appear on leather, textiles, and food products in hot, humid climates and can be inhibited by use of benzoic acid (in foods) and formaldehyde (on grain). Metallic naphthenates are used on textiles and similar materials.

2. A metal or plastic case used to impart a specific shape to a product. The term molding is generally used in reference to articles made of rubber or plastics, whereas casting applies to the forming of metals.

mole. Unit of amount of substance ; amount of substance containing number of particles equal to number of atoms in 0.012 kg of pure ^{12}C nuclide. Type of particles should be given, *i.e.*, atoms, molecules, ions, free radicals, elementary particles, atomic groups in molecule etc.

Number of grams of substance equal numerically to its relative molecular mass.

In view of introduction of mole as unit of amount of substance, term molar mass should be used in preference to mole = gram molecule. Also known as gram-mole; gram-molecule; gram-molecular weight.

molecular colloid. Colloidal system, physically homogeneous, in which macromolecules form one component. Also known as macromolecular colloid.

molecular compound. A compound formed by the union of two or more already saturated molecules apparently in defiance of the laws of valence. The class includes double salts, salts with water of crystallization, and metal ammonium derivatives. These salts are usually formed by van der Waal's attraction between the constituent molecules. They do not differ in any characteristic manner from compounds formed in strict accordance with the concept of valence. Also known as addition compounds.

molecular crystals. Crystals whose molecules are bound by van der Waals forces ; they are characterized by low melting points and high compressibility. Also known as van der Waals's crystals.

molecular diagram. Scheme of π-bonds in conjugated systems. Atoms are given their effective charges, and bonds their bond order values and numbers at arrows leaving carbon atoms correspond to free valencies.

molecular distillation. A process by which substances are distilled in high vaccuum at lowest possible temperature and with the least damage to their composition.

molecular equation. An equation expressing a molecular reaction in terms of the formulas of the molecules which react and those which are formed by the reaction, with integral coefficients showing the proportional number of gram molecular masses of each substance. For example :

$$2SO_2 + O_2 \rightleftharpoons 2SO_3$$

is the molecular equation for the combination of sulphur dioxide and oxygen to form sulphur trioxide, in the proportions of two gram-molecular weights of sulphur dioxide and one of oxygen to yield two gram-molecular weights of sulphur trioxide.

molecular field. Hypothetical internal magnetic field, whose strength is proportional to magnetization of substance.

molecular field theory. Phenomenological theory of ferro-, ferri and antiferromagnetic crystals in which exchange interaction leading to magnetic ordering is replaced by interaction of atomic magnetic moments with molecular field.

molecular film. A monomolecular layer, *i.e.*, a, film of a substance, produced on the surface of a liquid, by adsorption, or by other means, that has a thickness of the order of molecular dimensions.

molecular formula. A formula that indicates composition of a substance, which contains two or more molecules. Hydrates, for example, are commonly represented by molecular formulas, as $CuSO_4.5H_2O$ or $Na_2SO_4.7H_2O$. In such formulas the period (.) indicates the interamolecular valence bond or bonds.

molecularity of reaction. The smallest number of elementary entities necessary to create elementary entity (entities) of product (or products) of elementary reaction.

molecular orbital. The wave function of an electron moving in the field of the other electrons and nuclei composing a molecule.

molecular orbital method. Quantum chemistry method based on one-electron approximation. In molecular orbital method each electron is ascribed to some molecular orbital and these are used to construct total molecular wave function. Also known as MO method.

molecular rearrangement. Refers to an irreversible reaction which produces a change in the structural arrangement of the molecule with or without the elimination of simple molecules such as water or a hydrogen halide and which may or may not be unimolecular. Thus Wohler's synthesis of urea to ammonium cyanate is a molecular rearrangement, whereas reactions such as mutarotation, racemization, the Walden inversion, and tautomerism are excluded because they are essentially reversible.

molecular rotational energy levels. Discrete values of molecular rotational energy determined by quantum mechanical conditions. Also known as rotational energy levels of a molecule.

molecular sieve. A term used to describe the function of zeolite materials, which are clay-like in chemical nature (aluminosilicate compounds), and from which all water can be removed without alteration of this molecular structure. As a result of this, the material becomes microporous to such an extent that about half its volume is occupied by very small holes or channels (cages). The material thus readily adsorbs molecules of other substance in much the same manner as activated carbon; however, such molecules must be small enough to enter the pores vacated by the water molecules. Because of the limitation placed by the pores on the size of adsorbed molecules, zeolites act as selective devices which adsorb smaller molecules readily but exclude larger ones. For this reason, they are called molecular sieves. They tend to accept polar molecules as well as unsaturated types. Their more important uses are in water purification by ion exchange and in the cracking of petroleum; they are also active in soil chemistry because of their ion-exchange capability.

molecular spectroscopy. Branch of spectroscopy dealing with investigation of molecular emission and absorption spectra in spectral range from 500 nm to 2000 nm.

molecular spectrum. General term for rotation, vibration-rotation and electronic-vibration-rotation spectra of a given molecule.

molecular vibrational energy levels. Discrete values of molecular vibrational energy determined by quantum mechanical conditions. Also known as vibrational energy levels of a molecule.

molecular weight. The total obtained by adding together the weights of all the atoms present in a molecule. For example, the molecular weight of an oxygen molecule (O_2) is 31.9988; of a molecule of ethyl alcohol (C_2H_5OH), 46.069. In the last case, the arithmetic is: 2(12.011) + 6(1.0079) + 15.999.

An important value in chemistry is the gram-molecular weight (now preferably called the mole); it is the molecular weight expressed in grams; thus, for oxygen it is 31.9988 grams and for ethyl alcohol, 46.069 grams.

molecule. A basic unit of matter which may be comprised of one, two, three, or more elements which are present in the form of atoms (or ions). A molecule of a gas such as hydrogen nitrogen, oxygen, chlorine have 2 atoms (diatomic) while ozone, has 3.

Molecules of compounds are made up of at least two elements, in some cases having only 1 atom of each, as in hydrogen chloride (HCl). In this connection, a molecule may be defined as the smallest amount of a compound that can exist, for if it were further divided, it would cease to be a compound and would become atoms or ions, *i.e.*, HCl would become H^+ and Cl^-. Even the most complex molecules contain only five or six elements, often linked in chains of various combinations; it is the arrangement or sequence of elements in a molecule, rather than their number, that is of critial importance. Molecules of compounds may be gases, liquids or solids. The atoms within a molecule are held together by chemical bonds.

mole fraction. x_B. Ratio of number of moles of constituent B to sum of number of moles of all constituents of mixture

$$x_B = \frac{n_B}{\sum_i n_i}$$

where n_B = number of moles of constituent B, $\sum_i n_i$ = number of moles of all constituents of mixture.

Molisch reagent for albumin. A solution of 200 g. α-naphthol in 1 litre alcohol. It gives a red or violet colour with albumin or peptone on the addition of 5 ml. concentrated sulphuric acid and 2-3 drops of the reagent to 1 ml. of the liquid to be tested.

Molisch test for sugars. To 1 ml. of the solution to be tested, add 2 drops, 15-20% alcoholic α-naphthol solution and 1-2 ml. sulphuric acid. A deep violet precipitate giving a yellow solution in alcohol or ether, a gold-yellow colour in potassium hydroxide solution, and yellowish-brown in ammonia, indicates the presence of sugar.

Mollier diagram. The properties of a vapour, as recorded in vapour tables, may be displayed graphically in a number of ways, among which the most used, and probably the most valuable is the charting upon a plane whose coordinates are entalpy or total heat and entropy. Generally, the total heat is made the ordinate, and entropy the abscissa. This chart of the properties of vapour named the Mollier diagram, and is of considerable use in tracing both theoretical and actual expansions of vapour. A throttled expansion on the Mollier diagram is parallel to the constant heat lines, and adiabatic expansion is parallel to the constant entropy lines. Pressure, quality or superheat, and total temperature are shown on the Mollier diagram as series of lines curved and inclined to the axes. Thus all characteristics of a vapour except volume may be displayed on the the Mollier diagram.

molybdenum. An element.

		Symbol	Mo
		Atomic No.	42
State	Solid	Atomic Wt.	95.95
Group	VIB	Valence	2,3,4,5,6
		Isotopes	7 stable
		m.p.	2883K

Molybdenum, occurs as the sulphide ore molybdenite and has a body-centered cubic crystal structure. Molybdenum is silvery-white, tough malleable, softer than glass, not oxidized by air at ordinary temperatures, but above 600K burns to form white molybdenum oxide.

Seven isotopes occur naturally, ^{92}Mo ^{94}Mo through ^{98}Mo, and ^{100}Mo; and five radioactive isotopes have been identified, ^{90}Mo ^{91}Mo, ^{93}Mo, ^{99}Mo, and ^{101}Mo. With exception of ^{93}Mo, which has a half-life of approximately 10^4 years, the other radioactive isotopes have short half-lives, measured in terms of minutes and hours. The element does not appear on the list of the first 26 most frequently occurring elements in the earth's crust and thus may be considered a scarce element. Molybdenum is listed as the 42nd element in terms of estimated occurrence in the universe, but relatively few deposits are rich enough to warrant recovery costs. Mainly it comes from mines where its recovery is the primary objective of operation. The remainder is recovered as a by-product of certain copper-mining operations. It has the highest melting point of any metal except tungsten and tantalum and has strong thermal and electrical conductivity. It also readily forms coordination or complex compounds. In elemental form its chief uses are in steels, to which it imparts toughness for heavy service, and in heat-resistant alloys. Its compounds have applications in grease lubricants and pigments and as catalysts.

Molybdenum is necessary in trace amounts in plant nutrition and is also valuable in human metabolism. Molybdenum deficiencies are found in plants grown on certain acidic soils, and sometimes the deficiency can be corrected by adding either small quantities of manganese compounds or larger quantities of limestone to the soil. Acute or chronic excessive intake of molybdenum does not produce a defined pathologic lesion in humans, however, in lower animals particularly the ruminants, pastures containing excessive amounts of molybdenum may produce a disease called teart.

monad. An element, atom or radical that has a cheif valence of one, as sodium or fluorine ; cuprous copper or mercurous mercury; methyl or ethyl.

Mond's process. A method of refining nickel after it has been separated from the copper ore with which it is usually associated. Carbon monoxide gas is passed over nickel at a temperature of 316K. The gaseous carbonyl $Ni(CO)_4$ is formed, and this on heating to 443K, decom poses, depositing very pure nickel. The liberated carbon monoxide may be used again.

mono-. A prefix derived from the Greek word for one, appearing in such terms as monoxide, monohydric, monobasic, monomer, and monomoleculor. In common usage, the prefix in such compounds as monochlorobenzene, monoethanolamine, etc., is considered redundant and is usually omitted. The corresponding prefix uni-, with the same meaning, is taken from the Latin ; as a result of semantic convention its use in chemistry is limited to such terms as univalent, uniaxial, and uniform.

monoatomic. (*i*) Containing one atom; a term applied to molecules of certain elements when they are identical with the atoms of that element ; or (*ii*) containing one reactive or replaceable atom; a term applied to certain molecules in regard to certain reactions; or (*iii*) having a valence of one (the term monovalent is preferred for this usage).

monobasic. 1. A term used to describe an acid, either organic or inorganic, whose molecule contains only one hydrogen atom that can be replaced by another element to form a salt ; examples are hydrogen chloride. HCl, and acetic acid, CH_3COOH. Monobasic inorganic acids liberate one hydrogen ion in solution.

2. An inorganic compound containing one atom of a basic element, for example, monobasic sodium phosphate, NaH_2PO_4.

monochromatic. Having one colour, strictly one frequency or wavelength of optical radiation.

monochromatic emissive power. The energy emitted per unit time per unit area per unit wave length for an infinitesimal frequency range near a given frequency in the spectrum of a black body.

monochromator: Device used for selection of monochromatic radition from polychromatic beam of electromagnetic radition.

monodisperse system. *See* isodisperse system.

monogenetic dye. A dyestuff that produces only one colour on the fibre. Cf, dye, polygenetic.

monohydric alcohol. An alcohol whose molecule contains only one hydroxyl group. The paraffinic type, after called simple alcohols, have the generic formula $C_nH_{2n-1}OH$.

monolayer adsorption. *See* unimolecular adsorption.

monomer. A single molecule or a substance consisting of single molecules. The word monomer is used in differentiation of dimer, trimer, etc., words designating polymerized or associated molecules, or substances composed of them, in which each free particle is composed of two, three, etc., molecules. For example, the monomer of natural ruber is isoprene $CH_2{=}C(CH_3)CH{=}CH_2$; when this product is made synthetically, it is called polyisoprene.

monomolecular. Having a thickness of one molecule: usually used to describe a film of fatty acid on water. Fatty acids are long-chain molecules; the carboxyl group at one end, being negatively charged, is attracted by the polar water molecule. Thus, when the acid floats on a water surface, its molecules assume a vertical position, forming a monomolecular layer from 150 to 300 Å thick.

monomolecular reaction. *See* unimolecular reaction.

mononuclear complex. Complex containing one central atom.

monomorphic. Having one form, *i.e.*, one crystal from.

monosaccharide. A class of simple sugars containing a chain of 3-10 carbon atoms in the molecule, known as polyhydroxy aldehydes (aldoses) or ketones (ketoses). They are soluble in water and sparingly solulde in ethanol. The number of monosaccharides know is about 70, of which, about 20 occur in nature. The existence of such a large number of compounds is due to the presence of asymmetric carbon atoms in the molecule. A list of the best known monosaccharides is given below :

Trioses :

$CH_2OH.CHOH.CHO$	Glycerose
$CH_2OH.CO.CH_2OH$	Dihydroxy acetose
Tetroses :	
$CH_2OH.(CHOH)_2.CHO$	Erythrose
$CH_2OH.CHOH.CO.CHO$	Erythrulose
Pentoses :	
$CH_2OH.(CHOH)_3.CHO$	Xylose, arabinose, ribose
$CH_2OH.(CHOH)_2.CO.CH_2OH$	Xylose, ribulose methyl pentoses
$CH_3(CHOH)_4$ CHO	Rhamnose, Fucose
Hexoses :	
$CH_2OH.(CHOH)_4.CHO$	Glucose, Mannose, Galactose
$CH_2OH.(CHOH)_3.CO.CHOH$	Fructose, Sorbose
Heptoses :	
$CH_2OH.(CHOH)_5.CHO$	Glucoheptose, Galamannoheptose
$CH_2OH.(CHOH)_4.CO.CH_2OH$	Sedoheptulose, mannoheptulose

monose. A sugar containing in its molecule one hexose or pentose unit only.

monotropic allotropy. A class of allotropic phenomena in which the transition is irreversible. One allotrope is metastable at all temperatures, *e.g.*, explosive antimony.

monotropy. Property of substance by which it occurs only in one form (commonly only one solid form).

mordant. A term used in dyeing technology to indicate a substance that has the property of fixing or binding dye molecules to textile fibers. Certain mordants act directly on the fibre, making it more susceptible to the dye. Fabrics are them pretreated with the mordant before exposure to the dye. Other mordants function through the formation of a complex with the dye. Mordant and the dye in such case are exposed simultaneously to the fabric. Various metallic salts act in this way, especially those of chromium, aluminium, and tin ; a few organic compounds such as tannic acid are also used.

morphotropism. Similarity of structure, axial ratios, and angles between faces of one or more zones in crystalline substances whose formulae can be derived one from another by substitution.

morphous. A combining term which indicates "form" or "shape," as in isomorphous, dimorphous, etc.

Morse function. Approximate potential energy curve $U(r)$ for diatomic molecule given by

$$U(r) = D\{1 - \exp[-a(r-r_0)]\}^2$$

where D = energy of dissociatiative molecular oscillation energy level, a = constant, r_0 = internuclear distance corresponding to curve minimum.

mosaic crystals. Crystals composed of perfect crystals in blocks 100—1000 nm in size, mutually inclined at very low angles.

mosaic structure. Structure consisting in random deviations (misalignment) of crystal lines from average statistical direction by angles up to 1—2°.

Moseley formula for the energy of *K* x-rays. A relationship of the form :

$$E = 10.25\,(Z - 1)^2$$

where E = the energy of the K x-rays in electron-volts, and Z = the atomic number of the atom emitting the x-rays.

Moseley law. X-ray frequency of given line of atomic spectral series emitted by atom is quadratic function of corresponding atomic number.

Mossbauer effect. Recoilless emission or absorption of gamma radiation originating from certain radionuclide (*e.g.*, ^{191}Ir, ^{57}Fe) incorporated in crystal lattice which takes over the recoil momentum ; it is characterized by exceptionally small width of spectrum lines 10^{-10}—10^{-5} eV). The fundamental physics of this effect involves the transition of a nucleus from an excited state of energy E_e to a ground state of energy E_g with the mission of a gamma ray of energy E_r. If the emitting nucleus is free to recoil, so as to conserve momentum, the emitted gamma ray energy

$$E_r = (E_e - E_g) - E_r$$

where E_r is the recoil energy of the nucleus. The magnitude of E_r, is classically given by the relationship

$$E = E_r^2/2mc^2$$

where m = mass of the recoiling atom. The applications of Mossbauer effect include the measurement of nuclear magnetic and gradrupole moments and of excited-state lifetimes involved in the nuclear decay process ; study of chemical consequences of nuclear decay ; study of the nature of magnetic interactions in iron-containing alloys and of the dependence of the magnetic field in these alloys on various parameters ; study of the effects of high pressure on chemical properties of materials ; investigation of the relationship between chemical composition and structure on the one hand and the superconductive transition on the other ; investigation of the structure of the compounds ; and study of the structure and bonding properties of metal atoms in complex biological molecules.

Mossbauer spectroscopy. Branch of nuclear spectroscopy based on effect of recoilless absorption and emission of γ-rays by atomic nuclei (Mossbauer effect).

most probable velocity of gas molecules, c_{max}. Velocity exhibited by majority of molecules in the given population, corresponding to maximum on Maxwell-Boltzmann curve equal to

$$c_{max} = \sqrt{\frac{2RT}{M}}$$

where R = universal gas constant, T = thermodynamic temperature, M = molar mass.

mother liquor. The residual liquid remaining after crystallization has taken place.

M-radiation. One of a series of x-rays characteristic of each element that is excited when that element, commonly as the metal, is used as an anticathode in an x-ray tube, thus exciting the electrons of the M-shell.

M-shell. The collection of all those electrons in an atom that are characterized by the principal quantum number three. The M-shell consists of one electron in case of sodium and increases by one electron for each element of successively higher atomic number until argon which has 8 electrons in its M shell, is reached. The M-shells of potassium, calcium, scandium, and titanium all contain 8 electrons, the additional electrons of these elements appearing in the beginning N-shell. With vanadium however, there are 10 electrons in the M-shell ; in chromium there are 11 electrons in the M-shell and in manganese there are 13 electrons in the M-shell ; and then the elements of successively higher atomic number increase the number of electrons in the M-shell by one each until zinc is reached. All elements of higher atomic number contain 18 electrons in the M-shell.

mucin. One of the group of glycoproteins that occur in the secretions of the organism.

mucoid. One of a group of glycoproteins which are similiar to the mucins but differ from them in solubility and coagulability.

mu⁻ leption. Elementary particle of mass m= 105.6599 MeV, negative elementary electric charge, baryon number $B = 0$, lepton muonic number $L\mu = 1$, quantum spin number J = 1/2, unstable, of mean lifetime $2.198\ 3 \times 10^{-6}$ s ; μ^--lepton has antiparticle μ^+. Also known as muon.

Mulliken's electronegativity scale. Ordering of atoms according to increasing electronegativity defined as average of atom's ionization potential and its electron affinity.

Mullikan-Scudder test for methanol. The methanol is oxidized to formaldehyde by repeated applications of a hot copper wire, resorcinol is added, and a ring test made with concentrated sulphuric acid. A red colour at the interface indicates formaldehyde. Various modifications of this test have been developed.

multicentre reaction. Reaction proceeding through cyclic transition state, whose formation from substrates and transformation into products is effected by simultaneous electron displacement (with no intervention of ions or radicals).

multicomponent system. System composed of many components which may coexist in one or several phases.

multidentate ligand. Ligand which occupies more than one coordination position around central atom, *e.g.*, oxalic acid, ethylenediaminetetraaceticacid. Also known as polyfuctional ligand.

multilayer adsorption. Adsorption which results in formation of multimolecular layers on surface of adsorbent. Also known as multimolecular adsorption.

multiple bonding. Chemical bond formed by more than one pair of electrons, *i.e.*, double or triple bond, *e.g.*, O=C=O ; N≡N.

multiple coil thermal process. A process for the polymerization of olefinic and paraffinic gaseous hydrocarbons, which operates at a temperature range of 480 to 700 K, and a pressure range of 100 to 200 atmospheres. The sequence of reactions is usually the polymerization of the olefinic hydrocarbons, then the cracking of the paraffins to give olefins, and then the polymerization of the latter. The process produces gasoline, fuel oil, and tar. No catalysts are used in this process.

multiplet. 1. Group of energetic electronic states in atom of close energies, which belong to the same atomic term.

2. Group of spectral lines arising from transitions between energy levels of two atomic multiplet terms.

multiplicity. 1. The number; $2S + 1$, representing the number of ways of vectorially coupling the orbital angular momentum vector L with the spin angular momentum vector S of an atom. This value represents the number of relatively closely spaced energy levels or terms in an atom which result from the coupling process. The value of the multiplicity is added as a left superscript to the term symbol, as ^3P (triplet P), ^4D (quartet D), etc. The multiplicity of molecules is analogous to that of atoms, and is expressed also by the number $2S + 1$.

2. Number of particles formed as a result of high energy particle interaction.

multivalent. Having a valence of three or more.

muon. *See* mu$^-$ lepton.

muonic antineutrino, $\bar{\nu}_\mu$. Antiparticle corresponding to muonic neutrino of muon number $L_{\bar{\mu}} = -1$ and positive (right-handed) helicity, stable.

muonic neutrino, ν_μ. Elementary particle, a lepton, with rest mass probably zero, electrically neutral. of baryon number $B = 0$, quantum spin number $J = 1/2$, muon number $L_\mu = 1$ and negative (left-handed) helicity, stable.

muonium. An exotic atom formed when a positively charged muon and an electron are bound by their mutual electrical attraction. It is a light, unstable isotope of hydrogen, with muon replacing the proton. Muonium has a mass 0.11 times that of an hydrogen atom due to the lighter mass of the muon, and a mean lifetime of 2.2 microseconds.

muon number, L_μ. Number attributed to elementary particles; for μ^--lepton, and muonic netrino, $L_\mu = 1$, for their antiparticles, $L_{\bar{\mu}} = -1$. Other particles and antipaticles have $L_{\bar{\mu}} = 0$. Muon number is conserved in all interactions.

murexide reaction. Murexide is the ammonium salt of purpuric acid and is purple-red or violet in colour. It is produced by oxidation, with nitric acid (followed by treatment with ammonia), of uric acid and related purine compounds.

muriate. An old term for chloride; derived from muriatic acid ; an old term for hydrochloric acid.

Murphree efficiency factor. An expression for the efficiency of an individual plate in a fractionating column. This expression corrects for the departure of the vapour from equilibrium composition. It is of the form :

$$E_m = 100 \frac{(y_n - y_{n-1})}{(y_n^* - y_{n-1})}$$

where E_m = Murphree efficiency factor; y_n = actual composition of the more volatile componet in the vapour leaving plate "n" (mole fraction); y_{n-1} = actual composition of the more volatile component in the vopour leaving plate "$n - 1$" and entering plate "n" (mole fraction); y_n^* = composition in the more volatile component in the vapour in equilibrium (from vapour liquid equilibrium diagram) with the liquid of composition, x_n, on plate "n" (mole fraction).

mutagen. Any agent that causes a modification of deoxyribonucleic acid (DNA) in such a way as to affect the hereditary characteristics transmitted by genes or chromosomes. Among these agenst are ionizing radiation, heat, and some chemical substances (mustards, diethyl sulphate, and nitrous oxide). The mechanism involved in many cases is not clearly understood.

mutamerism. The process or phenomenon of changing of isomeric form, commonly among optical isomers.

mutarotation. Slow change of optical rotation power of solution due to changes of equilibrium between diastereoisomers of solute caused by solvent. Some sugars show a decrease (*i.e.*, glucose, 50%), whereas others (maltose) show an increase, of specific rotation.

myelin. A unique and complex mixture of fatty acids (lipids), proteins, and polysaccharides which forms a laminated sheath around the impulse-transmitting section of nerve cells in the body. It is particularly rich in long-chain fatty acids containing more than 18 carbon atoms; glycerophosphatides are also present.

Mylius salt test. To determine resistance to sea-water erosion of aluminium and other metals, the metals are immersed in a solution of sodium chloride and hydrogen peroxide and the weight loss determined in due course of time.

N

N. Symbol for the element nitrogen (N). Symbol for Avogadro number (N). Symbol for number of molecules (N). Abbreviation for normal (N) or (n) as in a normal solultion; or as in a straight chain aliphatic compound, *i.e.*, *n*-pentane. Symbol for molecular density (n or N). Symbol for molecular density at standard conditions (Loschmidt number) (n_0 or N). Abbrevation for index of refraction (n). Symbol used to designate attachment to a nitrogen atom ; thus N-, when attached to a substituent radical in a chemical name, implies the radical is attached to the nitrogen atom.

n. Symbol for transport number (n). Symbol for rotational frequency (n). Symbol for principal quantum number (n).

nacreous pigment. A pigment containing guanine crystals obtained from fish scales or skin; which produces a pearly lustre. It can be applied as in stimulated pearls, or incorporated in plastics.

Naegeli test reaction for aldehydes and ketones. Aldehydes and ketones, on treatment with hydroxylamine hydrochloride in the presence of sodium carbonate, form oximes having characteristic physical properties.

Naiman reagent for vitamin B_1 (thiamine). Potassium bismuth iodide, which gives an orange-red precipitate with vitamin B_1.

Naiman test reagent for bismuth. A mixture of 1% alcoholic solution of 2-methylbenzothiazole and *N* potassium iodide solution. It gives a deep red precipitate with bismuth even in the presence of antimony.

name reaction. A chemical reaction, usually organic, that is commonly identified by the name of its discoverers, *e.g.*, Diels-Alder, Friedel-Crafts, Ficher-Tropsch, Claisen, Cannizarro, Sandmayar, Wurtz. Many have important industrial applications. For details, *see* each specific name.

Nametkin rearrangement. Rearrangement of retropinacoline type of transient carbocation, formed from halide alcohol or alkene in acidic medium. In case of bicyclic terpenes, this reaction does not change ring system, *e.g.*,

$$\text{camphenilol} \xrightarrow[-H_2O]{+H^{\oplus}} [\;]^{\oplus} \rightarrow [\;]^{\oplus} \xrightarrow{-H^{\oplus}} \text{santen}$$

camphenilol santen

Also known as Nametkin change.

nano-. A prefix meaning one-billionth part; for example, a nanosecond is one-billionth second (often used in expressing the rate of explosion and in advanced computer technology); a nanometre is one-billionth metre, *i.e.*, 1 millimicron or 10 angstrom units.

nanogram method. Method of analysis where mass of investigated sampale is $x.10^{-9}$—$x.10^{-7}$ g, or volume $x.10^{-8}$—$x.10^{-6}$ cm^3 in the case of gases. Also known as submicro method, ultraultramicro method.

napalm. A metallic soap made by reacting an aluminium compound with various mixtures of fatty acids; when added to gasoline, it forms a viscous and highly flammable paste or gel that adheres strongly to objects with which it comes into contact. Its chief use has been for military purposes as an incendiary agent. *See also* soap.

naphtha. Any of several liquid mixtures of hydrocarbons of specific boiling and distillation ranges derived from either petroleum or coal tar. As a group, they are highly volatile and flammable; the grades derived from coal tar are toxic. Naphtha obtained by distillation of petroleum has a confusing number of names, many of which are unscientific or chemically erroneous, *e.g.*, petroleum ether, petroleum spirits, mineral spirits.

narcotic. As a noun, this term refers to various derivatives of opium, a plant alkaloid, among the best known of which are codeine, morphine, and their modifications; it also includes synthetic drugs such as methadone. All these can cause addiction and must be administered under medical supervision. Used as an adjective, the term describes the effects of dizziness and drowsiness induced by vapours of benzene and similar compounds regarded as "narcotic in high concentrations."

nascent. An obsolescent term referring to the unusually active state of an element in the act of splitting off from a parent compound. Oxygen in the atomic state is generated by hydrogen peroxide when in contact with air; certain sulphur-bearing rubber accelerators split off active sulphur atoms on heating, making addition of sulphur unnecessary for vulcanization. The word is derived from the Latin for being born. *i.e.*, generated. It is no longer widely used.

native. Pertaining to an element found in the earth in free state and not combined in a mineral, *e.g.*, gold and sulphur are found uncombined in deposits; they occur as native elements.

natural. Occurring in nature; not artificially prepared.

natural aging. Spontaneous aging at room temperature of a supersaturated metallic solid solution.

natural dye. A dyestuff extracted from animal and vegetable tissues in which they are performed or exist in combination, as indigo, alizarin, logwood, carmine.

natural gas. A combustible gas that occurs in porous rocks and is found with or near accumulations of crude oil. Typical natural gas consists of hydrocarbons having a very low boiling point. Methane makes up approximately 85% of the typical gas. Ethane may be present upto 10%; and propane upto 3%. Butane, pentane, hexane, heptane, and octane may also be present in small amounts. Traces of carbon dioxide, nitrogen, helium, and hydrogen sulphide are also present in the natural gas.

It is also available in liquid form (LNG). In the chemical industries it is an important source of the synthesis gas used in making synthetic organic materials and natural gasoline. Carbon black of the channel or impingement type is manufactured by combustion of natural gas. Natural gas can also be made synthetically (SNG) from petroleum fractions such as naphtha and by gasification of coal.

natural gasoline. A gasoline of low octane number made by extracting and liquefying the C_4 and higher hydrocarbons occurring in natural gas. It is also called casinghead gasoline because the natural gas used as the source is derived from oil wells. It is not suitable for automotive use but is blended with petroleum fractions for use as a source of petrochemicals.

natural glass. An amorphous, vitreous inorganic material that has solidified from magma too quickly to crystallize.

natural line width. Spectral line width as determined by Heisenberg uncertainty principle. Also known as natural breadth of spectral line.

natural product. As customarily used by chemists, this term refer to organic materials originating in or derived from plants and animals; it includes such basic industrials materials as petroleum, cotton, wool, rubber, coal, leather, sugar, and wood, as well as fatty acids, hormones, enzymes, alkaloids, vitamins, etc. Synthetic or man-made products either duplicate the chemical structure of a natural substance or simulate its physical properties. Rubber is a notable example in which both simulation and chemical synthesis have occurred. In spite of the tremendous accomplishments of synthetic organic chemistry, the depletion of the world's supply of some natural products (fuels) is a matter of concern.

natural radiation. Ionizing radiation arising from extraterrestrial sources and from naturally occurring radionuclides contained in earth crust, air and living organisms.

natural radioactivity. Radioactivity of naturally occurring nuclides.

natural radionuclide. Radioactive nuclide occurring naturally.

near infrared. NIR. Electromagnetic radiation range of wavelength between 0.75 μm to 3 μm. Also known as overtone region.

near ultraviolet. Electromagnetic radiation range of wavelength between ca. 200 nm to 400 nm.

Neber reaction. A method of formation of α-amino ketones by reaction of sulphonic esters of ketoximes with potassium ethylate, followed by hydrolysis of the addition product :

$$R'.CH_2.\overset{\displaystyle R'}{\overset{|}{C}}:NOH + C_6H_5SO_2Cl \xrightarrow{-HCl} R'.CH_2.\overset{\displaystyle R'}{\overset{|}{C}}:NOSO_2C_6H_5$$

$$R'.CH_2\overset{\displaystyle R'}{\overset{|}{C}}:NOSO_2C_6H_5 + (H_2O) \xrightarrow{C_2H_5OK} R'.CHNH_2COR' + C_6H_5SO_3H$$

nebulization. Atomization of liquids in air.

Neel point. *See* Neel temperature.

Neel temperature. The transition temperature for an antiferromagnetic material. Maximal values of magnetic susceptibility, specific heat, and thermal expansion coefficient occur at the Neel temperature. Also known as Neel point; antiferromagnetic Curie point.

Nef acetylenic hydroxy compound synthesis. A method of forming acetylenic hydroxy compounds from the action on ketones of sodium derivatives of acetylenic hydrocarbons :

$$R'COR' + NaC \equiv CH \rightarrow R'R'\overset{\displaystyle OH}{\overset{|}{C}}-C\equiv CH + NaOH$$

Nef aldehyde and ketone synthesis. Conversion of sodium (or potassium) salts of primary or secondary nitroparaffins to aldehydes or ketones under action of strong acids :

$$2RCH_2{-}\overset{\overset{O}{\uparrow}}{\underset{\underset{O}{\|}}{N}} \underset{}{\overset{NaOH}{\rightleftharpoons}} 2RCH{=}\overset{\overset{O}{\uparrow}}{\underset{\underset{ONa}{|}}{N}} \overset{H^+}{\rightarrow}$$

$$2RCHO + N_2O + H_2O$$

negative azeotrope. Azeotrope of composition at which there is minimum vopour pressure and correspondingly, maximum boiling temperature.

negative catalysis. The retardation of the velocity of a reaction by a catalyst, *e.g.*, alcohol markedly retards the oxidation of sulphites by free oxygen.

negative catalyst. *See* inhibitor.

negative crystal. A double-refracting crystal in which the difference between the extraordinary ray is negative, *i.e.*, the refractive index of the latter is less than that of the former.

negative valency. Number of electrons moved to atom from atom of positive valency during formation of chemical bond.

negatron. A word sometimes applied to the the normally occurring negatively charged electron when it must be distinguished from a positron. In many parts of the world, the name negaton is used instead of negatron. The word negatron is used in this Encyclopedia wherever distinction is made between positively and negatively charged electrons.

neighbouring-group participation. Adjacent groups to reaction center display inductive, mesomeric and steric effects and sometimes have influence on reaction rate by accelerating or slowing it down (*see* anchimeric assistance effect) or may cause rearrangement in molecules; *e.g.*,

$$(CH_3)_2N{-}CH_2{-}CH(C_2H_5){-}Cl \xrightarrow{-Cl^{\ominus}} (CH_3)_2\overset{\oplus}{N}{-}CH_2{-}CH(C_2H_5) \text{ (cyclic)}$$

$$\xrightarrow{^{\ominus}OH} (CH_3)_2N{-}\underset{\underset{C_2H_5}{|}}{CH}{-}CH_2OH$$

nematicide. A chemical used to destroy plant parasitic nematodes.

nematic phase. One of the forms of the mesomorphic state, the "liquid crystals". The characteristic appearance is that of mobile, thread-like structures, especially visible upon examination of thick specimens with polarized light. This form has a single optical axis, which takes the direction of an applied magnetic field. The liquid appears turbid but does not yield an x-ray diffraction pattern.

Nencki reaction. Acylation of phenols with carboxylic acids (reaction is similar to that of Friedel-Crafts), catalyzed with anhydrous $ZnCl_2$ or $FeCl_3$, *e.g.*,

$$C_6H_4(OH)_2 + RCOOH \xrightarrow{ZnCl_2} C_6H_3(OH)_2COR$$

Nenitzescu acylation reaction. Preparation of acylcycloalkanes from acycloalkenes by treating the latter with acid chlorides in presence of cyclohexane (acting as hydrogen atom donor) and catalytic amount of anhydrous aluminium chloride, *e.g.*,

$$C_6H_{10} + CH_3COCl \xrightarrow{AlCl_3} C_6H_{11}COCH_3 + HCl$$

$$(2C_6H_{12} \rightarrow C_{12}H_{22} + 2H)$$

Reaction also takes place with cycloalkanes often resulting in contraction of ring system, *e.g.*,

$$C_6H_{11}CH_3 + CH_3COCl \xrightarrow{AlCl_3} C_5H_7(CH_3)_2COCH_3 + HCl$$

neo-. A prefix designating a newer compound related in some way to an older one, as neoarsphenamine. Specificaly, indicating a hydrocarbon in which at least one carbon atom is connected directly with four other carbon atoms as neopentane, $(CH_3)_4C$.

neodymium. An element

		Symbol	Nd
		Atomic No.	60
		Atomic Wt.	144.24
State	Solid	Valence	3
Group	IIIB	Isotopes	7 stable
		m.p.	1297K

A rare-earth metal belonging to lanthanide series. It occurs in monazite sands and bastnasite ore. Neodymium also occurs in cerite and other rare minerals.

It readily tarnishes and is attacked by atmsopheric moisture. Elemental neodymium has a close-packed hexagonal crystal structure at 25K. Pure metallic neodymium is a silvery-gray colour, the luster becoming dull upon exposure to moist air at room temperatures.

There are seven natural isotopes, ^{142}Nd, through ^{146}Nd, ^{148}Nd, and ^{150}Nd isotope ^{144}Nd is mildly radioactive ($t_{1/2}=10^{10}-10^{15}$ years), seven artificial isotopes have been produced. Of the light (or cerium-group) rare-earth metal, neodymium is the third most plentiful and ranks 60th in abundance of elements in the earth's crust, exceeding tantalum, mercury, bismuth, and the precious metals, excepting silver. Its scavenging effect makes it useful in refining ferrous alloys. Its salts have found applications in the ceramic industry for coloring glass and for glazes. The glass is particularly useful in goggles used by glass blowers, since it absorbs yellow D-line of sodium present in the flame. The element has also found commercial application in the manufacture of lasers. Some of its compounds have been found to have moderate toxicity for experimental animals.

neon. An element

		Symbol	Ne
		Atomic No.	10
		Atomic Wt.	20.183
Group	Noble Gas	Valence	0
State	Gas	m.p.	24.4K
		b.p.	26.9K

Solid neon has a face-centered cubic crystal structure. At standard conditions, neon is colourless, odorless and does not form stable compounds with other elements under ordinary conditions, though several ions are known.

There are three natural isotopes, ^{20}Ne through ^{22}Ne, and four radioactive isotopes, ^{18}Ne ^{19}Ne, ^{23}Ne, and ^{24}Ne, all with half-lives of less than 5 minutes.

However, the compound-forming capabilities of neon, under any circumstances, appear to be far less than those of argon or krypton. No known hydrates have been identified, even at pressures up to 260 atm. It is a minor component of air (about 0.0001%), from which it can be separated when in liquid form. It produces colours in electric discharge tubes, one of its largest uses being for this purpose: the colour varies with the type of glass, used for the tube and the other gases present (argon or helium). Considerable quantities of neon are used in high-energy physics research. Neon fills spark chambers used to detect the passage of nuclear particles. Neon is also used in fluorescent lights, but in this case the colour produced is due to the phosphors which coat the inner glass lining of the tube. It is also used in lasers and electronic instruments.

nephelauxetic series of ligands. Series of ligands arranged by increasing share of covalent bond in bond between central atom and ligand: $F^- < H_2O < (NH_2)_2CO < NH_3 < NH_2CH_2CH_2NH_2 < C_2O_4^{2-} < NCS^- < Cl^- \backsim CN^- < Br^- < (C_2H_5O)_2PS_2^- \backsim S^{2-} \backsim I^- < (C_2H_5O)_2PSe_2^-$.

nephelometric analysis. The measurement of the concentration, particle size, etc., of suspension by means of its light transmission or dispersion, etc., and the application of the results, especially in chemical analysis. In nephelometry the intensity of the light scattered at right angles to the light beam by a suspension is measured, rather than the decrease in the intensity of directly transmitted light as in turbidimetry. Since a clear solution will scatter no light at right angles to the beam, nephelometry measures the difference between no light and various amounts of scattered light, making it sensitive to the detection of small amounts of turbidity.

neptunium. An element.

		Symbol	Np
		Atomic No.	93
State	Solid	Atomic Wt.	237.0482
Group	IIIB	Valence	3,4,5,6
		m.p.	912K

A artificial radioactive metal of actinide series; also one of the transuranium elements. Neptunium was the first of the transuranium elements to be discovered. Neptunium is produced as a byproduct from nuclear reactors. ^{237}Np is the most stable isotope, with a half-life of 2.20×10^6 year. The only other very long-lived isotope is that of mass number 236, with a half-life of 5×10^3 years. ^{237}Np is the parent of the neptunium ($2n+1$) alpha decay series. Other isotopes include those of mass numbers 229-235 and 238-241; metastable forms of ^{236}Np, ^{240}Np and two of ^{237}Np are known.

The ionic species corresponding to the oxidation states vary with the acidity of the solution; in acid solution of moderate strength the species are Np^{3+}, Np^{4+}, NpO_2^+, and NpO_2^{2+}

as in the case of uranium and plutonium. The potential scheme in 1 *M* HCl is as follows :

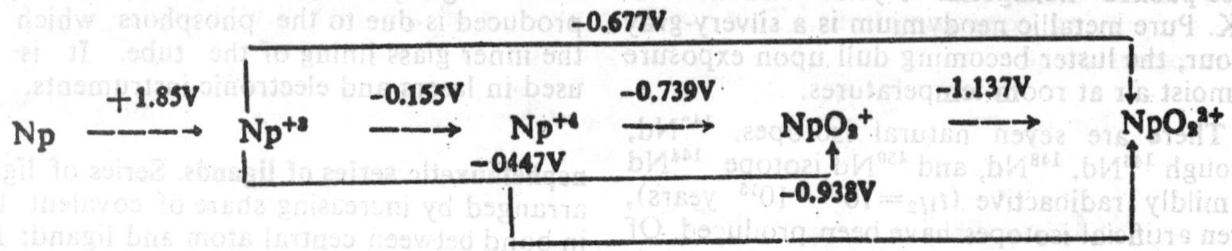

Neptunium ions in aqueous solution possess characteristic colours ; pale purple for Np^{3+}, pale yellow-green for Np^{4+}, green-blue for Np^{5+}, while NpO_2^{2+} varies from colourless to pink or yellow-green depending on the acid present.

The precipitation reactions of Np^{3+} are similar to those of the tripositive rare-earths those of Np^{4+}, to the other tetrapositive actinides and to Ce^{4+}, and those of NpO_2^{2+} to the corresponding ions of uranium and plutonium. All of the simple salts of NpO_2^+ appear to be soluble.

THE NEPTUNIUM SERIES

Element	Symbol	Radiation	Half Life
Plutonium ↓	Pu^{241}	β	~14 yr.
Americium ↓	Am^{241}	α	470 yr.
Neptunium ↓	Np^{237}	α	2.20×10^6 yr.
Protactinium ↓	Pa^{233}	β	27.4 days
Uranium ↓	U^{233}	α	1.63×10^5 yr.
Thorium ↓	Th^{229}	α	7.4×10^3 yr.
Radium ↓	Ra^{225}	β	14.8 days
Actinium ↓	Ac^{225}	α	10.0 days
Francium ↓	Fr^{221}	α	4.9 min.
Astatine ↓	At^{217}	α	2.0×10^{-2} s
Bismuth (96% ↓ Polonium; 4% ↓ Thallium)	Bi^{213}	β and α	47 min.
Polonium ↓	Po^{213}	α	3.2×10^{-6} s
Thallium ↓	Tl^{209}	β	2.2 min.
Lead ↓	Pb^{209}	β	3.3 hr.
Bismuth (End product)	Bi^{209}	Stable	—

Nernst approximation formula. A formula for the equilibrium constant of a gas reaction derived from the Nernst heat theorem by certain simplifying approximations. This formula is expressed as :

$$\log K_p = -\frac{\Delta H}{4.57T} + \Sigma\nu 1.75 \log T + \frac{\beta}{4.57} T + \Sigma\nu I$$

where K_p =the equilibrium constant of the reaction, ΔH = the change in heat content, $\Sigma\nu$=the algebraic sum of the number of moles of the gaseous reactants (or in other words, the change in number of moles of gaseous reactants due to the reaction), T=the absolute temperature, β = a constant, and I = the conventional chemical constant.

Nernst distribution law. In the state of interphase equilibrium the ratio of the activity of a component in two different phases depends only on temperature and pressure.

Nernst heat theorem. For a homogeneous system, the rate of change of the free energy with temperture, as well as the rate of change of heat content with temperature, approaches zero as the temperature approaches absolute zero.

Nernst-Planck theorem. *See* third law of thermodynamics.

nerve gas. One of a group of exceedingly toxic gaseous compounds developed for possible military use. Several types were made in Germany in the 1930s and later in the United States and other countries. Their use in warfare has been prohibited by international agreement. However, many insecticides of the parathion type have been developed and now in use ; though they decompose relatively quickly, they are intensely poisonous and ond extremely dangerous to handle. Chemically, nerve gases are esters of phosphoric acid derivatives; they immobilize the nervous system by preventing the enzyme cholinesterase from deactivating the acetylcholine formed by nerve impulses. They are often referred to as cholinesterase inhibitors.

Nessler reagent. An alkaline, aqueous solution of potassium mercuric iodide, used in the detection and determination of ammonia, various amines, and other substances. Yellow or brown colours or precipitates are obtained. A number of methods are available for the preparation of this reagent.

Nessler reagent for wine. A solution of 7 g. alum and 10 g. sodium acetate in 100 ml. water, used in detecting wine colouring.

Nessler test. A test used to detect the presence of ammonia, certain amines, aldehydes, etc., by colorimetric estimation of the intensity of the reddish-brown colour or precipitate formed with Nessler reagent.

net maximum work. Maximum amount of work which can be performed by closed system on surroundings during isothermal-isobaric transition from state I to state II; net maximum work is equal to loss of Gibbs free energy of system $\Delta G = G_I - G_{II}$. Also known as net useful work ; available net work ; maximum useful work.

network polymer. Polymer having three-dimentional structure, formed by cross-linking of main chains. Also known as space polymer.

neurotoxin. A posion that attacks the nervous system and acts as depressant.

neutral. Derived from the Latin word for neither, this term has two specific meanings in chemistry. An aqueous solution in which the concentration of hydronium ions and hydroxyl ions is exactly equal; such a solution has a *p*H value of 7.0 at room temperature; which is the *p*H of pure water.

neutral atom. An atom in which the positive charge on the nucleus is equal to the total negative charge of the electrons which surround the nucleus. Therefore, the atom does not possess an electric charge.

neutral chelate. Chelate in which positive charge of central ion is compensated for by negative charge of ligand.

neutral compound. A compound that is chemically neutral, *i.e.*, neither acidic nor alkaline.

neutral filter. Filter diminishing radiation intensity to the same extent independently of wavelength (it has this feature only in some wavelength region).

neutral flame. A flame produced by burning fuel in air which is neither oxidising nor reducing.

neutralization. Reaction of acid and base which produces neutral solution, *i.e.*, solution for which activities of both acidic and basic forms of solvent are equal. Usually conducted in an aqueous medium, such as solutions of HCl and NaOH to yield NaCl and H_2O, the reaction may also occur in the absence of water and without forming water, as between a solid and a gas, *e.g.*, CO_2 and CaO to form $CaCO_3$, or between two gases. *e.g.*, NH_3 and HCl to form NH_4Cl. Neutralization does not mean that the *p*H of the final water solution is 7, the neutral *p*H. While true for the reaction of a strong acid and a strong base, such as NaOH and HCl, and of a weak acid and a weak base, such as ammonia and acetic acid, the final *p*H will be above 7 when a strong base and a weak acid react, such as NaOH and acetic acid, and below 7 when a strong acid reacts with a weak base, *e.g.*, NH_3 and H_2SO_4. In each reaction, at least a proton is transferred from the acid to the base.

neutralization indicator. A substance which undergoes a characteristic colour change at the point where an acid has been neutralized by a base used in titrating it, or a base by an acid used in its titration.

neutral point. The point reached in the course of a titration or other chemical operation or process, at which the system contains equal concentrations of hydrogen and hydroxyl ions, each about 1×10^{-7} molar. In practice the neutral point will vary somewhat from this figure, depending upon the method of determining these ionicconcentrations. If indicators are used, their tables of values must be consulted.

neutral salt. A salt which in solution, commonly aqueous solution, does not give an acidic or a basic reaction.

neutral salt effect. The diminution of the ionization of a weak acid or base on the addition of a salt that contains one of the ions of the ionized substance. This is a special case of the common ion effect.

neutrino, ν. General term for two elementary particles : electronic neutrino ν_e, and muonic neutrino ν_μ. Neutrino has zero rest mass and zero electric charge and is classified as lepton.

neutron, *n*. Elementary particle, a hadron, one of isopin doublet state of nucleon, of mass $m = 939.5527$ MeV, electrically neutral, of baryon number $B = 1$, lepton number $L = 0$, quantum spin number $J = 1/2$, strangeness $S = 0$, isospin $I = 1/2$, third component of isospin $I_3 = -1/2$. Neutron is constituent of atomic nuclei. A free neutron is unstable, its mean lifetime is 0.932×10^3 s.

The fact that neutrons have no electric charge enables them, to penetrate the nuclei of atoms in the free state, thus causing fission. Free neutrons are generated by bombarding beryllium with alpha particles (helium nuclei).

Fast neutrons are those emitted by an atomic nucleus during fission; slow or thermal neutrons are those that have been retarded by contact with a moderating substance in a reactor.

neutron absorption analysis. Method of analysis based on measuring of attenuation of neutron flux in layer of material tested. It is applied for determination of elements of high neutron absorption cross-sections.

neutron activation. Activation by neutron irradiation, occurring most often in a (n, γ) nuclear reaction.

neutron activation analysis. Activation method of analysis in which a flux of neutrons is applied for activation.

neutron generator. Accelerator producing neutrons in appropriate nuclear reactions, *e.g.*, $^2H(d, n)^3He$, $^3H(d, n)^4He$.

neutron radiative capture. Nuclear reaction of (n, γ) type, *i.e.*, reaction consisting in absorption of neutron, giving rise to excitation of nucleus, and eventually to return of nucleus to ground state due to emission of γ-quantum.

neutron thermalization. Slowing down of neutrons to reduce their energy to value corresponding to thermal energy of atoms or molecules of medium

Newman formula. Projection formula portraying molecule in a plane, in way convenient for conformation analysis, *e.g.*, conformation of meso-2,3-dibromobutane

$$\overset{1}{CH_3}-\underset{|\atop Br}{\overset{2}{CH}}-\underset{|\atop Br}{\overset{3}{CH}}-\overset{4}{CH_3}$$

Br, H, CH_3, 3, 2, CH_3, H, Br

Formula is viewed from side along the $\overset{2}{C}-\overset{3}{C}$ bond. $\overset{3}{C}$ atom, more distant to observer, is represented as circle ; rest of $\overset{2}{C}-\overset{3}{C}$ atomic bonds from symmetrical system of lines.

Newtonian fluid. A fluid that obeys Newton's law of viscosity, *i.e.*, the viscosity is independent of the rate of shear or the velocity gradient. The tangential force, *F*, between two parallel layers of fluid is given by $F=\eta S.dv/dx$ where S=the area of the fluid layers, dx=the distance between them, and dv=the difference in velocity, η=a constant called the coefficient of viscosity. A large number of liquids obey Newton's law.

Newtonian mechanics. A system of mechanics based on Newton's laws of motion in which mass and energy are considered as separate, conservative, mechanical properties. It provides an accurate means of determining the motions of bodies possessing ordinary velocities.

Newtonian viscosity. Dynamic viscosity independent of change in velocity gradient dv/dx (*see* viscosity coefficient).

Newton's alloy. A fusible alloy that melts at about 365K ; composed of 50% bismuth, 31% lead, and 19% tin. Also known as Newton's metal.

nickel. An element

	Symbol	Ni
	Atomic No.	28
	Atomic Wt.	58.71
State Solid	Valence	2,3
Group VIII	Isotopes	5 stable
	m.p.	1728K

Nickel, is a metallic element of moderate chemical reactivity ; it is particularly resistant to corrosion, one of its major uses being as electroplated portective coatings.

The element ranks 21st among the elements in terms of abundance in the earth's crust, the estimated average content of igneous rocks being about 0.02%. In terms of cosmic abundance; nickel ranks 28th among the elements. Nickel ranks 40th in terms of concentration in seawater.

Finely divided nickel adsorbs 17 times its own volume of hydrogen at standard conditions.

First ionization potential 7.33 eV, second, 18.13 eV. Oxidation potentials $Ni \rightarrow Ni^{2+} + 2e^-$, 0.230 V; $Ni^{2+} + 2H_2O \rightarrow NiO_2 + 4H^+ + 2e^-$, -1.75 V; $Ni + 2OH^- \rightarrow Ni(OH)_2 + 2e^-$, 0.66 V; $Ni(OH)_2 + 2OH^- \rightarrow NiO_2 + 2H_2O + 2e^-$, -0.49 V.

At high temperatures it is attacked by sulphur compounds, and at normal temperatures by moist air containing sulphur dioxide, ammonia, or chlorine. It is highly resistant to alkalies because a film of nickel oxide forms on its surface in the presence of strongly basic compounds, *e.g.*, sodium hydroxide. There are five naturally occurring stable isotopes ^{58}Ni, ^{60}Ni through ^{62}Ni, and ^{64}Ni. Six radioactive isotopes have been identified ^{56}Ni, ^{57}Ni, ^{59}Ni, ^{63}Ni, ^{65}Ni, and ^{66}Ni, ^{59}Ni has a half-life of 8×10^4 years, and ^{63}Ni has a half-life of 80 years. The half-lives of the remaining radioactive isotopes are relatively short, expressed in hours and days. Nickel forms a number of coordination compounds ; the most important of these, nickel carbonyl, $Ni(CO)_4$, is poisonous, and care should be taken to avoid inhalation of its fumes. The chief uses of nickel are as an alloying metal in stainless steel, magnets, and resistance alloys; in cladding and other protective coating; in special types of batteries; and in powder form as a hydrogenation catalyst.

nickel group. Three elements in eighth subgroup of periodic system with structure of outer electronic shells of atoms ; nickel — $3d^84s^2$, palladium — $4d^{10}$, platinum — $5d^96s^1$.

nickel-silver. A group of alloys of copper, nickel, and zinc in varying proportions, containing up to 30% nickel. A typical composition is 60% copper, 20% nickel, 20% zinc. Also known as German silver.

nickel steel. Steel containing up to 9% nickel as a major alloying element.

nicol prism. A polarizing prism prepared by cutting down the end faces of the principal section sf a crystal of calcite (Iceland spar) so that the face angles are reduced to 60°, then slicing the crystal in a plane perpendicular to the ends and the principal section, and cementing it together with Canada balsam, which has an index of refraction less than that of calcite for the ordinary ray, and greater for the extraordinary ray, Thus the ordinary ray may be separated from the extraordinary ray, producing plane polarized light.

Niementowski quinazoline reaction. A method of formation of 4-keto, 3-4-dihydroquinazolines by the action of amides upon anthranilic acids.

$$C_6H_4(NH_2)COOH + R'CO{-}NHR \rightarrow \text{(quinazoline, with } R', N{-}R, C{=}O) + 2H_2O$$

Niementowski quinoline synthesis. Preparation of quinoline and its derivatives by condensation of anthranilic acid with compounds containing $-CH_2-CO-$ group, *e.g.*,

$$C_6H_4(COOH)(NH_2) + R'{-}H_2C{-}CO{-}R \xrightarrow{-2H_2O} \text{(4-hydroxyquinoline with OH, } R', R)$$

Nierenstein reaction. A reaction between an acid chloride (commonly aromatic) and diazomethane which yields the corresponding chloromethylketone:

$$ArCOCl + CH_2N_2 \rightarrow ArCOCH_2Cl + N_2$$

nigre. In soap technology, the brown-to-black liquid remaining after the soap has been separated from the other products of the saponification reaction by the salting-out process. It contains glycerol, sodium chloride, and various impurities.

ninhydrin reaction. Coloured (blue, violet or red) reaction of most α-amino and imino acids, also of amines with ninhydrin in basic medium; applied for detection of proteins.

niobium. An element

	Symbol	Nb
	Atomic No.	41
State Solid	Atomic Wt.	92.906
Group IIIB	Valence	2,3,4,5
	m.p.	2741K
	b.p.	5015K

Elemental niobium has a body-centered cubic crystal structure. The metal has a slightly bluish tinge, is ductile and malleable, and when polished resembles platinum. The metal burns upon being heated in air. There is one natural isotope, ^{93}Nb. Seven radioactive isotopes have been identified, ^{90}Nb through ^{92}Nb and ^{94}Nb through ^{97}Nb, with a wide range of half-lives. The isotopes ^{94}Nb has the longest half-life (2×10^4 years). It is quite stable at room temperature to attack by oxygen and strong acids; it oxidizes readily at high temperatures. Niobium also has gained prominence in research as a superconducting material. At the temperatures of liquid helium, niobium becomes a superconductor and, in the form of a fine wire, has been incorporated in a superconducting cell. The element has both size and cost advantages over electronic materials. The alloy Nb_3Sn becomes superconducting at a somewhat higher temperature. Niobium-titanium and niobium-zirconium alloys also have potential as superconductors.

The principal uses for the element are in alloys. Ferroniobium is a strong carbide-forming material and, when added to 18-8 stainless steel, stabilizes areas that may be heat-affected during welding and thus cause subsequent intergranular corrosion. Niobium steels are used for rotors in gas turbines where temperatures up to 1000K must be withstood. Niobium-base alloys find application in fast reactors.

nitramine. One of many possible compounds derived from nitramide, NO_2NH_2, by replacement of one or both of its hydrogen atoms, commonly by alkyl or aryl radicals.

nitramino. The radicals $NO_2.NH-$.

nitraniline. 1. The compound

$$C_6H_4\begin{cases}NO_2\\NH_2\end{cases}$$

in which the two groups, $-NO_2$ and $-NH_2$ may be at $-o$, $-m$, or $-p$ to each other.

2. One of a class of compounds, representing substitution of both amino- and nitro-groups in benzene and its derivatives.

nitration. Substitution of hydrogen atom in molecule of an organic compound by nitro group $-NO_2$, *e.g.*,

$$C_6H_6 + HNO_3 \xrightarrow{H_2SO_4} C_6H_5NO_2 + H_2O$$

nitridation. In its most common use, nitridation means simply the formation of nitrides, as of certain metals in industry. The term is also used sometimes to indicate the formation of a nitrogen compound by the action of ammonia, analogous to the use of the term oxidation.

nitrification. The formation of nitrates (or nitrites) by oxidation of ammonia and other nitrogen-containing compounds.

nitrifier. A nitrifying agent, *i.e.*, an agent which oxidizes forms of nitrogen at lower valences, as in the form of ammonia and certain organic compounds, to nitrates or nitrites.

nitrifying. Causing oxidation of combined nitrogen or ammonia to nitrates or nitrites, especially microorganisms in the soil.

nitro-aci-nitro tautomerism. Type of prototropic tautomerism connected with reversible rearrangement of primary and secondary nitro compounds in to *aci*-form ;

```
     O            O
  |  ↑        |   ↑
 —C—N    ⇌    C=N
  |  ‖        |   |
  H  O            OH
```

nitro dye. A dyestuff whose chromophore is the nitro group (—NO_2).

nitrogen. An element

		Symbol	N
		Atomic No.	7
		Atomic Wt.	14.0067
State	Gas	Valence	1,2,3,4,5
Group	VA	m.p.	63.14K
		b.p.	77.2K

Nitrogen is a comparatively unreactive element which comprises 78% by volume of air, it is unavailable to plants and man through this source. It is as essential to vital processes as are oxygen or carbon, for it is a constituent of amino acids and proteins, the basis of all animals life. These compounds are synthesized by plants from nitrogen "fixed" in the soil by certain bacteria.

Solid nitrogen has a hexagonal crystal structure. Nitrogen at standard conditions is a colourless, odorless, and tasteless gas. The gas is slightly soluble in water (2.35 parts nitrogen in 100 parts water at 273K), the solubility decreases with increasing temperature (1.55 parts nitrogen in 100 parts water at 293K). Nitrogen is slightly soluble in alcohol and is essentially insoluble in most other known liquids. There are two naturally occurring isotopes, ^{14}N and ^{15}N, with ^{14}N by far the most abundant (99.635%). Four radioactive isotopes have been identified, ^{12}N, ^{13}N, ^{16}N, and ^{17}N, all with extremely short half-lives measured in seconds or minutes.

First ionization potential 14.84 eV ; second, 29.47 eV ; third, 47.17 eV ; fourth, 73.5 eV ; fifth, 97.4 eV. Oxidation potentials $H_2N_2O_2 + 2H_2O \rightarrow 2HNO_2 + 4H^+ + 4e^-$, — 0.80V ; $N_2O_4 + 2H_2O \rightarrow 2NO_3^- + 4H^+ + 2e^-$, —0.81 V ; $HNO_2 + H_2O \rightarrow NO_3^- + 3H^+ + 2e^-$, —0.94 V; $NO + 2H_2O \rightarrow NO_3^- + 4H^+ + 3e^-$, —0.96 V; $NO + H_2O \rightarrow HNO_2 + H^+ + e^-$, —0.99 V; $2NO + 2H_2O \rightarrow N_2O_4 + 4H^+ + 4e^-$, —1.03 V; $2HNO_2 \rightarrow N_2O_4 + 2H^+ + 2e^-$, —1.07 V. $N_2O + 3H_2O \rightarrow 2HNO_2 + 4H^+ + 4e^-$, —1.29 V; $N_2O + H_2O \rightarrow 2NO + 2H^+ + 2e^-$, —1.59 V; $N_2 + H_2O \rightarrow N_2O + 2H^+ + 2e^-$, —1.77 V ; $N_2O_4 + 4OH^- \rightarrow 2NO_3^- + 2H_2O + 2e^-$, 0.85 V; $NO + 2OH^- - NO_2^- + H_2O + e^-$, 0.46 V; $N_2O_2^{2-} + 4OH^- \rightarrow 2NO_2^- + 2H_2O + 4e^-$, 0.18 V; $NO_2^- + 2OH^- \rightarrow NO_3^- + H_2O + 2e^-$, —0.01 V; $N_2O_2^{2-} \rightarrow 2NO + 2e^-$, —0.10 V; $N_2O + 6OH^- \rightarrow 2NO_2^- + 3H_2O + 4e^-$, —0.15 V; $N_2O + 2OH^- \rightarrow 2NO + H_2O + 2e^-$, —0.76V; $2NO_2^- \rightarrow N_2O_4 + 2e^-$, —0.88 V.

Nitrogen is the characteristic element of many chemical groups besides those mentioned: amines, nitriles, alkaloids, azides, and purines. It combines readily with fluorine and is the active element in most explosives, rubber accelerators, fertilizers, and many drugs. Nitrous oxide (N_2O) is an anesthetic, but oxides of nitrogen produced by auto exhausts are toxic air-contaminants, especially nitrogen dioxide, NO_2.

When molecular nitrogen is subjected to the actions of a condensed electrode discharge, or to a high frequency electrodeless discharge, it is partially changed to an activated, unstable condition, from which on standing it returns to its normal state with the emission of a golden-yellow afterglow. In elemental form, nitrogen is used as a protective blanket for highly reactive chemicals, as a blowing agent in foamed plastic, as a scavenging and carrier gas, and in special types of refrigeration. Nitrogen forms dinitrogen complexes with a number of metals of VIII group transition metal family. Such complexes occur in low oxidation state of the metals. It has no active toxicity and is noncombustible.

nitrogen cycle. The general biological series of changes in nature by which the elemental nitrogen of the atmosphere is converted into compounds, used in the nutrition of plants and animals, and ultimately liberated again as free elemental nitrogen. Major events in the natural cycle are the fixation of the atmospheric nitrogen by natural electrical discharges such as lightning, washing of the nitrogen compounds into the soil by rain, then their assimilation for plant use by certain bacteria, followed by their elaboration in the plant into a form available for animal nutrition. The animal produces nitrogenous wastes, and ultimately its body also is decomposed by bacteria ; in both cases the nitrogenous end products return to the soil or the atmosphere to repeat the cycle :

nitrogen fixation. Utilization of the nitrogen of the air by plants to form critically important compounds ; the conversion is performed by certain types of bacteria which live symbiotically on the root hairs of plants, thus enabling them to synthesize nitrogenous compounds (proteins). The term is also applied to various processes for chemically manufacturing ammonia and other nitrogen compounds.

nitrogen group. Elements of fifth main group in periodic system with structure of outer electronic shell of atoms ns^2np^3 : nitrogen, phosphorus, arsenic, antimony, bismuth. Also known as nitrogen family.

nitrogen solution. A mixture of ammonium nitrate and ammonia solution ; used to neutralize super-phosphate in fertilizer manufacture.

nitrol. An organic compound having a nitro group and a nitroso group on the same carbon atom. The typical-formula is :

$$R_2C(-N{=}O)-N(=O)\rightarrow O$$

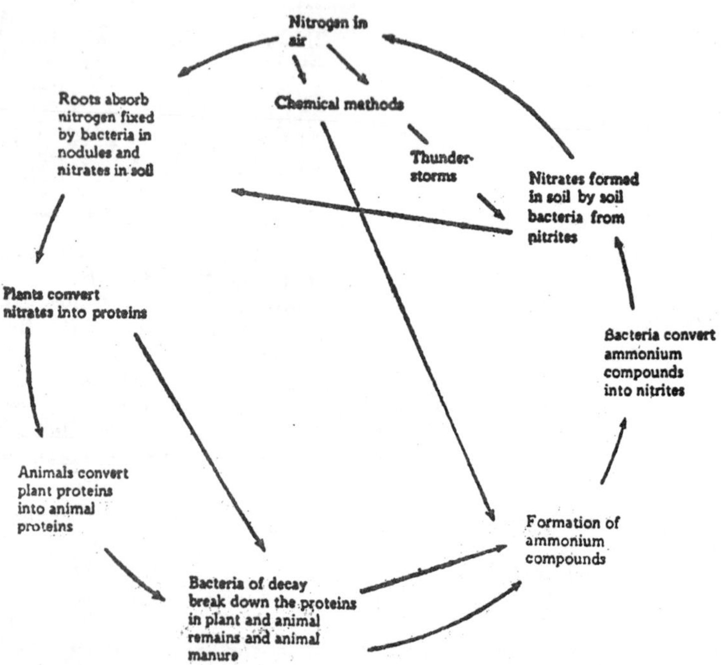

Fig. 28. Nitrogen cycle

nitrosate. One of a series of organic nitrogen compounds, having an oxime group and a nitrate group on adjacent carbon atoms, as isoamylene nitrosate,

$$\begin{array}{l} \quad\;\; CH_3 \quad\;\; O \\ \quad\;\;\; | \qquad\;\;\; \| \\ CH_3-C-O-N\rightarrow O \\ \quad\;\;\; | \\ CH_3-C=N-OH \end{array}$$

nitrosation. Substitution of hydrogen atom in the molecule of an organic compound by nitroso group —NO, resulting in formation of nitroso compounds or their tautomers, oximes; *e.g.*,

$$RCH_2NO_2 \xrightarrow[-H_2O]{HNO_2} \begin{array}{l} RCHNO_2 \\ \;\;| \\ \;\;NO \end{array}$$

$$\begin{array}{c} O \\ \| \\ RCCH_2COOR \end{array} \xrightarrow[-H_2O]{HNO_2} \begin{array}{c} O \\ \| \\ RCCCOOR \\ \| \\ NOH \end{array} \rightleftharpoons \begin{array}{c} OH \\ | \\ RC=CCOOR \\ | \\ NO \end{array}$$

nitrosite. One of a series of organic nitrogen compounds, having an oxime group and a nitrite group on adjacent carbon atoms, as isoamylene nitrosite.

$$\begin{array}{l} \qquad\; CH_3 \\ \qquad\;\; | \\ H_3C-C-O-N=O \\ \qquad\;\; | \\ CH_3-C=N-OH \end{array}$$

nitroso. A prefix indicating the presence of ON- group in an organic compound. It may occur in benzenoid structures, forming compounds that are the basis of dyes (nitrosophenol); it also occurs in fluorocarbon monomers from which socalled nitroso rubbers are made.

nitroso dye. A dyestuff containing the chromophore group —NO.

nitroso-oximino tautomerism. Type of prototropic tautomerism connected with reversible rearrangement of primary and secondary nitroso compounds into oximes (isonitroso compounds).

$$\begin{array}{c} | \\ -C-N=O \\ | \\ H \end{array} \rightleftharpoons \begin{array}{c} | \\ -C=N-OH \end{array}$$

nitrosyl. The univalent radical —N=O in inorganic compounds, *e.g.*, nitrosyl chloride, NOCl.

nitroxyl. The univalent radical $-NO_2$, when it occurs in inorganic compounds, such as nitroxyl chloride, NO_2Cl, or copper nitroxyl, $Cu(NO_2)_2$.

N-line. One of the lines in the N-series of x-rays which are characteristic of the various elements and are produced by excitation of the electrons of the N-shell.

nobelium. An element		Symbol	No
		Atomic No.	102
State	Solid	Atomic Wt.	254(?)
Group	IIIB	Valence	2,3

Nobelium is the thirteenth member of the actinide series. This radioactive element has been isolated by cyclotron experiments, but knowledge of its properties is still fragmentary; ^{254}No has half-life of 55-second; ^{252}No with a 2.3-second half-life; and ^{257}No with a 23-second half-life. Four other isotopes are now recognized, including ^{255}No with a half-life of a few minutes.

In 1973, scientist produced a relatively long-lived isotope of nobelium through the bombardment of ^{248}Cm with ^{18}O ions. A total half-life of 58 ± 5 minutes was computed.

noble. A term used to indicate the relative lack of chemical reactivity of an element.

noble gases. Elements of eighth main group of closed (octetic, except for helium) structure of outer electronic shell of atoms ns^2np^6: helium, neon, argon, krypton, xenon, radon. Of the noble gases, only three (helium, neon, and argon) are actually inert, that is, incapable of forming compounds. Also known as inert gases; rare gases.

noble metal. A term originally applied to gold and silver, and connoting their relative inertness to chemical action, especially to the action of the reagents used by the early chemists and alchemists. Now the term applies generally to the members of the gold and platinum families of elements in the periodic table. Gold is considered more noble than, *e.g.*, silver, because of its comparatively low reactivity. The term should not be confused with "precious" in reference to metals, as it has no economic significance. In the electrode potential series of the elements, an element with the higher potential (Gibbs-Stockholm convention) is referred to as more "noble" than elements of lower potential.

nodule. An aggregate or mixture of manganese and iron (ferromanganese) occurring in huge quantities on the floor of oceans, especially the pacific. The size averages about 4 cm in diameter, varying from small pellets to masses several metres in diameter.

nomenclature, chemical. *See* chemical nomenclature.

nomenclature of naphthalene compounds. The positions in the naphthalene ring are designated as :

8 1 2 3 4 5 6 7

or

α1 β1 β2 α2 α3 β3 β4 α4

Two monosubstitution products are possible according to whether the substituent is adjacent to the central complex or is separated from it by a CH group, *viz.*,

NH_2 $-NH_2$

α-naphthylamine   β-naphthylamine

The disubstitution products are named as follows: 1-2 ortho, 1-3 meta, 1-4 para, 1-5 ana, 1-6 epi, 1-7 kata, 1-8 peri, 2-3 not named, 2-6 amphi, 2-7 pros. Polysubstitution product are designated by numbers. Substituents in the same ring are termed isonuclear ; those in different rings, heteronuclear.

non-bonding electrons. Electrons assumed to occupy molecular orbitals which do not contribute to chemical bonds.

non-bonding orbital. Molecular orbital built of identical atomic orbitals of the same orbital energy ; its energy is equal to that of component atomic orbitals. Appears in Huckel theory of odd alternant hydrocarbons ; also atomic orbital of lone electron pairs.

non-classical ions. Ions with delocalized σ-electrons, introduced to explain certain non-typical rearrangements and reactivity of alicyclic systems ; *e.g.*, non-classical norbornyl cation :

120°

non-destructive activation analysis. Activation method of analysis in which selective measurement of activity of element to be determined is carried out by physical methods without chemical separation of irradiated sample.

nondestructive testing. A type of materials testing made on a finished product rather than on a sample, which involves no damage to the product. Examples are radiography, x-rays, and infrared radiation, which are used to explore large metal structures for flaws, fatigue effects, and similar weaknesses. Same nondestructive tests involve complex high-technology systems, while other which employ the same basic test principle, are easily applied by unskilled operators. Nearly every form of energy is used in nondestructive tests, including all wavelengths of electro-magnetic spectrum, as well as a broad range of frequencies of vibrational mechenical energy. Although there are several methods used for nondestructive testing six are widely applied in industry : visual-optical, liquid-penetrant magnetic-particle, eddy-current, ultrasonic, and radiographic.

non-electrolytes. Substances that do not yield ions in solution and therefore form solution of low or non electrical conductivity.

non-essential amino acid. Amino acid of proteins that can be made by humans and other vertebrates from simpler precursors, and thus not required in the diet.

nonferrous. A term used in metallurgy to refer collectively to all metals other than iron, or to alloys which do not contain iron.

nonheme-iron proteins. Proteins containing iron but no porphyrin groups.

nonhypergolic. Not capable of igniting spontaneously upon contact.

nonideal gas. A gas whose molecules have significant interaction, more than that needed to bring about the equilibrium.

non-isotopic carrier. Carrier for radioactive substance chemically non-identical with substance (usually isomorphic or isodimorphic), *e.g.*, Ba^{2+} ions for Ra^{2+} ions which coprecipitate with precipitates of barium salts.

non-metals. Elements not having the characteristic properties of metals. This term includes two groups of elements ; one group is made up of elements that have little or no similarity to metals, and the other of elements that are somewhat more like metals, especially in their electrical properties. The elements of the latter group are semiconductors. They are still sometimes referred to as metalloids, though this term is obsolescent. The first group is made up of gases (noble gases, oxygen, nitrogen, hydrogen, chlorine, fluorine), a liquid (bromine), and several solids (carbon, phosphorus, sulphur, iodine). The second group includes boron, silicon, arsenic, germanium. selenium, tellurium, antimony, and polonium, all of which are solids having semiconducting properties to some extent, especially germanium and silcon.

nonnutritive sweetener. A synthetic, low-calorie substitute for sugar, for example, the sodium and calcium salts of saccharin (sulphur-bearing derivative of benzoic acid), which are said to have about 300 times the sweetening power of sucrose.

non-osmotic membrane equilibrium. Thermodynamic state of system with electrochemical potential of any kind of ions identical in all phases.

non-stoichiometric compounds. Compounds of composition depending in some degree on mode of preparation. These compounds do not fulfill law of definite proportions. Also known bertholides.

nor. From normal ; a prefix (*a*) indicating the parent from which another compound may be theoretically derived, usually by the removal of one or more carbon atoms (and attached hydrogen), as norcamphane (of which camphane is a trimethyl derivative) ; (*b*) designating a compound of normal structure isomeric with the compound to which it is prefixed, as norleucine.

normal boiling point. Boiling point at pressure of $p = 1.01325 \times 10^{-1}$ MPa (formerly $p = 1$ atm).

normal complex. Complex of ioinic character which dissociates in solution into components, *e.g.*, $[Cd(CN)_4]^{2-}$, $[Co(NH_3)_6]^{3+}$. Also known as ionic complex.

normal compound. An organic compound whose structure is of the straight- or open-chain type, containing no branching or subsidiary groups. This arrangement is characteristic of many hydrocarbons, alcohols, amines, etc. It is usually indicated by a small italic *n*-preceeding the name, as in *n*-butane, *n*-butyl alcohol.

normal concentration. Number of gram-equivalents of substance dissolved in 1 dm^3 of solution. Also known as normality of solution.

normal conditions. *See* standard conditions.

normal electrode potential. *See* standard electrode potential.

normal hydrogen electrode. *See* standard hydrogen electrode.

normalization. A term used by metallurgists to refer to a process of tempering steels and other alloys by heating them to a predetermined temperature and cooling at a controlled rate to relieve internal stresses and improve strength and stability.

normalization of wave function. Procedure to obtain from given wave function Ψ its normalized counterpart $N\Psi$, where N is determined from normalization condition

$\int | N\Psi |^2 d\tau = 1$; $d\tau$=integration volume element and integration is over all spatial and spin variables of system.

normal pressure. The standard pressure to which measurements of volume, especially of gases, and other experimental work which may vary with pressure changes, are usually referred. It is the pressure of a column of mercury 760 millimetres high at sea-level at a latitude of 45°.

normal salt. A salt of a polybasic acid in which all of the replaceable hydrogen atoms have been replaced by other atoms or radicals, or a salt of a polyhydric base in which all the replaceable hydroxyl groups have been replaced by other atoms or radicals.

normal temperature. Average room temperature, to which a value of 293K is assigned.

normal vibrations. Harmonic oscillations in system of material points with all points moving with the same frequency and constant, time-independent phase. Normal vibrations in molecules follow from consideration of molecule as set of material points (atoms).

novolac. A thermoplastic resin of the phenol-formaldehyde type, which can be cross-linked to a thermosetting (cured) state by addition of an amine, usually hexamethylenetetramine. The novolac molecules are made up of chains of several phenol units joined by methylene (CH_2) linkages. When the nitrogen-containing amine is added. a hard, resinous product is formed.

noxious gas. Any gas or vapor having a more or less toxic effect when inhaled. The term is restricted to gases resulting from chemicals or chemical reactions that occur either naturally or as by-products of industrial manufacture or use. It does not include so-called poison gases made specifically for military puposes, nor the asphyxiant gases, which have no positive toxicity. Examples of noxious gases are carbon monoxide, chlorine, and hydrogen sulphide, as well as vapors from carbon tetrachloride and other halogenated hydrocarbons.

N-R transition. *See* Rydberg transiton.

N-shell. The collection of all those electrons in the atom which have the principal quantum number 4. The N-shell is started with the element potassium, atomic number 19, which has one electron in its N-shell, and the N-shell is finally completed (containing 32 electrons) with the element lutecium, atomic number 71. During the progression from potassium to lutecium the difference between elements of consecutive atomic numbers is frequently not in the N-shell, but in an electron increment in the M-shell, or in the O-shell, or the P-shell.

nuclear barrier. The region of high potential energy through which a charged particle must pass on entering or leaving an atomic nucleus. Also known as potential barrier.

nuclear battery. A primary battery in which the energy of radioactive material is converted into electric energy by solar cell or other energy converters.

nuclear breeder. A nuclear reactor in which more fissionable material is formed in each generation than is used up in fission process.

nuclear chemistry. Collective name for a number of particular branches of chemistry, the common feature of which is research and practical utilization of nuclear phenomena.

nuclear energy. Energy of a higher order of magnitude than that of chemical reactions ; the latter is derived from the formation and rupture of bonds (electrons) and amounts to about 5 electron volts per bond, whereas the former is evolved from the nucleus of the atom, yielding, for fission, about 200 million electron volts per nucleus. Nuclear energy is released either by splitting (fission) of an unstable, heavy nucleus (uranium-235 or -233 and plutonium-239) or by union (fusion) of the hydrogen isotopes deuterium and tritium to form helium.

nuclear energy levels. All atomic nuclei have energy levels above their ground state of energy which correspond to the displacement of one or more nucleons within the nucleus. Mathematically, these are eigenvalues of atomic nucleus hamiltonian, *viz.*, energy value defining state of nucleus. Nuclear energy level is often defined as difference between the energy of nucleus in any given state and in lowest (ground) state.

nuclear equation. An equation showing the changes in composition, usually in terms of mass number and charge only, of an atomic nucleus during a nuclear reaction. The equation shows any particles captured, or radiations absorbed by the nucleus, and also the particles or radiations emitted.

nuclear fission. *See* fission.

nuclear forces. Short-range forces occurring among nucleons, in particular binding nucleons into nuclei.

nuclear fuel. Material containing fissionable nuclides in chemical form and geometrical shape ready for use in the particular type of nuclear reactor. Principally, the three fissile isotopes uranium-235, uranium-233, and plutonium-239 are used as nuclear fuel. Of these, uranium-235 is the most important at present as it is the only one which occurs in nature. In addition, the fertile isotopes thorium-237, and uranium-238, which also occur in nature, can be regarded as nuclear fuels because they can be converted to fissile uranium-233 and plutonium-239 respectively.

nuclear fuel cycle. The sequence of processes which nuclear fuel undergoes, from the mine to fuel fabrication plant, nuclear reactor, and finally to reprocessing plant. The cycle also includes the transportation of fuel between each process and the disposal of the radioactive waste produced by each process.

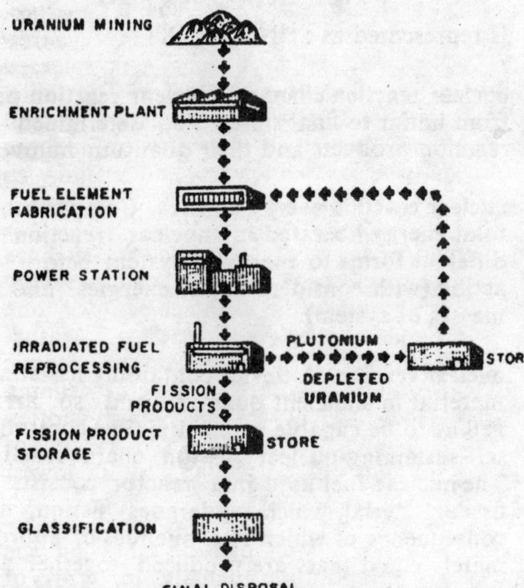

Fig. 29. Nuclear fuel cycle

nuclear fusion. A thermonuclear reaction in which positively charged hydrogen nuclei (protons) unite or fuse to form helium, with evolution of energy. A temperature of several million degrees is necessary to overcome the repulsion of the positive charges. This process occurs in the sun, where it is catalyzed by carbon. Uncontrolled fusion has been achieved in the hydrogen bomb, the initiating temperature being supplied by a fission reaction. Research is now being devoted to developing a controlled and sustained fusion reaction, using the hydrogen isotopes deuterium and tritium. The most efficient experimental reaction is, for each fusion event. $D + T + e \rightarrow {}^4He + n + 17.5$ MeV, where e represents at least 44 million K.

Fusion has two great advantages over fission as an energy source : (*i*) it utilizes water and readily available lithium as its raw material instead of scarce and costly uranium ; (*ii*) it produces no long-lived radioactive fission products, though it does yield high-energy neutrons. Large scale development should not be expected for the indefinite future.

nuclear *g*-factor. Factor in formula for nuclear magnetic moment of paramagnetic nucleus, corresponding to Lande' factor. Also known as nuclear Lande' factor.

nuclear isomerism. A form of isomerism in which two compounds of the same composition differ in the valence linkages by which certain of their atoms are joined in ring structures, or in the relative positions of substituents in a ring.

nuclear isomers. Two (or more) nuclides which have the same mass number and the same atomic number, but have different radioactive properties. They are believed to be composed ultimately of the same number of protons and the same number of neutrons, but to be different in their energy levels. Such isomeric nuclei are found among the naturally radioactive elements as well as among the artificially radioactive elements. Two examples of the latter are a radioactive zinc of mass number 69, which emits a gamma radiation to yield another radioactive zinc of mass number 69; and a radioactive krypton which has a mass number of 83 and is, therefore, a nuclear isotope of ordinary non-radioactive krypton.

nuclear magnetic moment. μ_1. Vector quantity,

defined by $\mu_1 = g_1 I \mu_N$, where g_1 = nuclear g factor, I = spin quantum number, μ_N = nuclear magneton.

nuclear magnetic resonance spectroscopy. Branch of radiospectroscopy which utilizes nuclear paramagnetic resonance for study of physico-chemical properties of materials ; *e.g.*, study of structure of molecules and crystals, study of autodiffusion processes, hindered rotation, etc. It is particularly effective in identifying isomers, elucidating the associative grouping of hydrogen atoms, and establishing important factors of molecular geometry. It can be used in conjunction with other analytical methods, such as infrared and mass spectroscopy, gas chromatography, etc. Its applications extend to inorganic and physical chemistry, biochemistry, and related areas of chemistry. NMR spectroscopy involves the absorption of energy in the range of radiofrequencies by compounds containing certain types of atomic nuclei which have magnetic properties, for example, hydrogen (protons) carbon-13, oxygen-17, fluorine, phosphorus, and nitrogen. The interaction of the magnetic field generated by the rotation of these nuclei with an imposed magnetic field gives rise to NMR spectra when the energy states of the radiation source and the absorbing nucleus are the same (resonance). In this method of analysis, spinning nuclei are examined by measuring the absorption of *rf* radiation that can be induced when a sample is exposed to a strong magnetic field. Hydrogen is the most commonly studied nucleus, the procedure being known as proton-magnetic-resonance (pmr) spectroscopy. By analyzing the shifts in such spectra it is possible to obtain an indication of the internal structure of the molecule. Also known as NMR spectroscopy.

nuclear magneton, μ_N (β_N). Unit of nuclear magnetic moment :

$$1\ \mu_N = \frac{1}{1837}\ \mu_B$$

where μ_B denotes Bohr magneton ; $1\mu_N = 5.050 \times 10^{-27}$ A.m^2.

nuclear potential. Effective potential energy of single nucleon inside atomic nucleus caused by strong nuclear interactions with remaining nucleons.

nuclear purity. Absence in material of elements of such a high degree that it can be used in reactor technique.

nuclear quadrupole moment. Electric quadrupole moment displayed by nuclei with spin $I > 1/2$ due to non-spherical distribution of electric charge.

nuclear quadrupole resonance. Phenomenon associated with quantum transitions between energy levels of electric nuclear quadrupole moments in internal inhomogeneous electric field of molecules and crystals.

nuclear radiation. A term used to denote alpha particles, electrons, neutrons, photons, and other particles which emanate from the atomic nucleus as a result of radioactive decay and nuclear reactions.

nuclear reaction. Any reaction involving a change in the nucleus of an atom, as distinct from a chemical reaction, which only involves the orbital electrons. Such reactions occur in radioactive elements, and in stars as thermonuclear reactions. Nuclear reactions are represented by enclosing within a bracket the symbols for the incoming and outgoing particles or quanta (separated by a comma), the initial and final nuclides being shown outside the bracket. Thus the reaction :

$$^{14}N_7 + {}^4He_2 \rightarrow {}^{17}O_8 + {}^1H_1$$

is represented as : $^{14}N(\alpha,p)^{17}O$.

nuclear reaction channel. Nuclear reaction path from initial to final state, *i.e.*, determined by reaction products and their quantum numbers.

nuclear reaction energy balance. Comparison of total energy liberated in nuclear reaction in different forms to energy of system before reaction (with consideration of energies and list masses of system).

nuclear reactor. A device containing fissionable material in sufficient quantity and so arranged as to be capable of maintainig a controlled, self-sustaining nuclear fission chain reaction. The nuclear fuel used in a reactor consists of fissile material, which undergoes fission, as a consequence of which two nuclides of approximately equal mass are produced together with two or three neutrons and a considerable nmount of energy. These neutron scause further fissions so that chain reaction develops ; in order that the reaction should not get out of control, its progress is regulated by neutron absorbers (*see* control rods), only sufficient free neutrons being allowed to exist in the reactors to maintain the reaction at a constant level. The essential component of a modern nuclear reactor are : (*a*) The core, composed of metals or ceramic-clad rods containing enough fissionable material. (*b*) A source of neutrons to initiate reaction, such as mixture of polonium and beryllium. (*c*) A moderator to reduce the energy of fast neutrons for more efficient fission ; materials such as water, graphite, beryllium are used. (*d*) A coolant to remove generated heat ; water is generally used, which is converted to steam in heat exchangers and used to drive turbines. (*e*) A control system to absorb neutrons rapidly when their concentration becomes too high ; rods of boron or cadmium having high capture cross-sections, are used for this purpose. (*f*) Adequate shielding, remote control equipment, and appropriate instrument, are also required for safety and efficient operation of the nuclear reactor. Also known as atomic pile ; atomic reactor ; fission reactor ; nuclear pile.

nuclear reactor coolant. Liquid or gas removing heat released in core of nuclear reactor. Nuclear reactor coolant may act at the same time as moderator.

nuclear spectroscopy. Branch of nuclear physics dealing with study of absorption and emission of radiation by atomic nuclei.

nuclear spin *J*. Vector equal to geometric sum of total angular momenta of nucleus, expressed in units $h=1.054\ 5919\times10^{-27}$ erg s. Nuclear spin takes values which are multiples of 1/2 in these unit. Nuclear spin describes nucleus and its state. For nuclei in ground state and even number of nucleons, $|J|$ is an integral number of nucleons, $|J|=1/2,\ 3/2,\ 5/2$. Also known as nuclear angular momentum.

nuclear symmetry energy. Difference between binding energy of nucleus with equal number of protons and neutrons and binding energy of nucleus of the same mass number *A* but higher number of neutrons *N* than number of protons *Z*. Nuclear symmetry energy is defined as second derivative of binding energy per nucleon over parameter of excess of neutrons $(N\text{-}Z)/A$ at the same mass number.

nuclear transmutation. The changing of one element into another by suitable nuclear reactions.

nuclear weapon. Weapon in which the explosive power is derived from nuclear fission or a combination of nuclear fusion.

nuclease. An enzyme that catalyses the splitting of nucleic acids to nucleotides, nucleosides, or other components of nucleosides.

nucleation. A term used in crystallography and colloid chemistry to refer to the initiation of crystal formation by microscopic particulates, for example, dust in the air or colloidally dispersed solids in a solution. These act as active centres or nuclei on which water droplets may form or crystal structures may develop. Thus, ice particles induced by quick temperature reduction in moist air can serve as points of formation for raindrops. Various types of crystals prepared or "grown" synthetically under carefully controlled conditions for scientific purposes require a particulate nucleus for initiation.

nucleic acid. An extremely complex compound of high molecular weight which occurs in the nuclei of biological cells ; when associated with a protein, the combined molecule is called a nucleotide. They can be partially hydrolyzed to sugar derivatives (ribosides) of purines and pyrimidines (nucleosides), or to nucleotides (phosphate esters of these compounds). The two major types of nucleic acids are ribonucleic acid, which contains ribose, and deoxyribonucleic acid, containing deoxyribose. Both types are of critical importance in cellular biochemistry, as they establish and execute the genetic mechanisms of the organism. The study of nucleic acids and their stucture and function comprise the science of molecular biology.

nuclein. *See* nucleoprotein.

nucleon, *N*. Elementary particle : proton or neutron (isospin doublet) of baryon number $B=1$, lepton number $L=0$, quantum spin number $J=1/2$, strangeness $S=0$, isospin $I=1/2$ third component of isospin $I_3=1/2$ (for proton) and $I_3=-1/2$ (for neutron).

nucleonics. A term used by nuclear scientists to designate the study of the atomic nucleus and its constituents. It is derived from the word nucleon, that is, a proton, and other particles formed as a result of bombardment of a nucleus with high-energy particles, for example mesons of various types. Nucleonics includes fission, fusion, transmutation, mass defect, binding energy, and the radiation effects that accompany them.

nucleophile. A term and used to designate an agent (ammonia, water, alcohol) that contributes or donates a pair of electrons to a chemical structure (nucleus) to form a covalent bond ; the element or ion that receives the two electrons is called an electrophile.

nucleoprotein. A high molecular weight substance formed by the chemical union of a protein with a nucleic acid in a ratio of about 20 to 1. Such complex molecules are found in cell nuclei of all organisms. They are also called nucleins.

nucleotide. A term applied by biochemists to complex molecules which are usually constituents of nucleic acids ; they are composed of nitrogen-containing bases (purine or pyrimidine) bonded to either ribose or deoxyribose sugars, phosphoric acid being present to form an ester. The purine constituents are adenine and guanine, and the pyrimidines are uracil and cytosine. Some nucleotides are physiologically active complexes called co-enzymes or prosthetic groups. Nucleotides derived from yeast are used as flavor petentiators in the food industy. A well-known nucleotide is adenosine triphosphate (ATP), which is essential to many biochemical processes, including photosynthesis.

nucleus. 1. In physical chemistry, the total number of protons and neutrons, which constitutes virtually the entire mass of an atom. These particles are held together by forces of exceedingly high magnitude known as the binding energy, a portion of which is released by fission.

2. In orgaic chemistry, a fundamental molecular structure which persists with only peripheral changes through many reactions ; examples are the aromatic benzene nucleus ; C_6H_6 and the heterocyclic furan nucleus, C_4H_4O.

3. In crystallograghy, any microscopic particle that serves as a basis for crystal formation.

4. In biochemistry, the central portion of the cell of an organism which contains the essential reproductive chemicals (nucleic acid).

nuclide. Species of atoms characterized by their mass number, atomic number and nuclear state ; each isotope of an element is an individual nuclide ; atoms whose nuclei decay in times too short to be measured are not nuclides.

null electrode. An electrode having a thermodynamic potential of zero ; *i.e.*, an electrode in which there is actually no difference of potential between the metal and the ionic solution. It is believed, however, that no such electrodes have been prepared. Electrodes are known whereby, due to relative motion, it is possible to obtain an electrokinetic potential of zero,but it does not follow that their reversible potential is zero.

null potential. Potential of electrode (half-cell) measused with respect to a given reference electrode, at which electrical charge of metal surface is zero, *e.g.*, for mercury is +0.19 V as compared to normal hydrogen electrode in absence of substance which may be specifically adsorbed on electrode. Also known as zero charge potential.

number average relative molecular mass. Average molecular mass calculated from measurement of effects that depend on number of macromolecules contained in unit volume, *i.e.*, on molar concentration (methods: osmotic, ebullioscopic, cryoscopic, and groups etc.). Also known as number average molecular weight.

number of degrees of freedom. Number of independent random variables minus number of redundancies. When computing variance of series of n independent measurement results, number of degree of freedom is $n-1$ since one of results is related to others by

$$x=(x_1+x_2+\ldots+x_n)/n.$$

number of thermodynamic degrees of freedom. Number of intensive state parameters whose values can be changed independently of each other (in some range) in such a way that number of phases in equilibrium is not changed.

nutrient. Any substance that is essential to the life and growth of plants, or animals, or man either as such or as transformed by chemical or enzymatic reactions. Plant nutrients include numerous mineral elements, as well as nitrogen carbon dioxide, and water. In animals and man the primary nutrients are proteins, carbohydrates, and fats that are obtained from plants, either directly or indirectly, supplemented by vitamins and minerals. Water and oxygen are also considered nutrients, of which three are a total of 43. *See also* food.

nutrient culture. A method of growing flowers and vegetables in the absence of soil by supplying the essential elements in a properly balanced aqueous solution. This technique is especially suitable for localities where good soil is scarce, as in arid areas, small islands, and the like. It is called hydroponics by agriculturalists and is popularly known as soil-less growth.

nutrition. The complex series of synthesis and decomposition reactions that occurs in the growth and maintenance of living organisms. Plants synthesize carbohydrates from carbon dioxide and water by photosynthesis, proteins from nitrogenous compounds, as well as fats, oils, and vitamins. The essential elements required are carbon, hydrogen, nitrogen, phosphorus, potassium, and a number of trace elements. The nutrients of man are supplied by either as such or in the meats resulting from their ingestion by animals all the essential factors being obtained from this source. In man, most of the nutritive processes are of the decomposition type, chiefly hydrolysis and digestion, usually catalyzed by enzymes. Thus, the ultimate products are, to a large extent, carbon dioxide and water, which complete the carbon cycle.

Ny'lander reagent. A solution of Rochelle salt, bismuth subnitrate, and sodium hydroxide in water. This reagent is used for testing glucose in urine. A black colour on boiling indicates the presence of glucose.

nylon. A polyamide resin synthesized by a number of different chemical methods: all types contain the characteristic —$CONH_2$ (amide) grouping.

Nylon has many advantageous properties, among which are strength, resistance to heat and abrasion, colourability, noncombustibility, and nontoxicity. Its lack of toxicity makes it the material of choice for surgical inserts in the body, prosthetic devices, etc.

nylone-6. Nylon made by polycondensation of caprolactum.

nylone-66. Nylon made by the condensation of hexamethylene diamine with sebacic acid.

O

O. Symbol for the element oxygen.

***o*-.** Abbreviation for ortho when this prefix is used to denote the relation of the 1 and 2 positions in benzene, or a compound characterized by it as orthoxylene, orthodichlorobenzene. The abbreviation *o*- is also used for ortho when that prefix is used to designate the ortho-state of an element as *o*-H.

-ocane. A suffix indicating an eight membered ring.

occlusion. A condition of uniform molecular adhesion between a precipitate and a soluble substance, or between a gas and a metal, of such a nature that it is very difficult to separate the occluded substance by washing or other simple mechanical process. Occlusion in precipitates depends upon the distribution of a substance between solvent and solid and is, probably, due to adsorption.

occupation number. Number of particles in given quantum-mechanical state.

-ocin. A suffix indicating an eight-membered ring.

-ocine. A suffix indicating an eight-membered ring.

octahedral complex. Complex of coordination number 6 in which donor atoms of ligands are arranged at vertices of regular or distorted octahedron. Hybridization occuring in this type of complexes is of type d^2sp^3 or sp^3d^2.

octane number. An arbitrary value denoting the antiknock rating of a gasoline ; it is the proportion of the branched-chain hydrocarbon iso-octane that is contained in a test mixture of heptane and iso-octane. The octane number of heptane (a straight-chain hydrocarbon) is rated as zero, while that of iso-octane is 100. Mixing these in various proportions and determining the degree of knocking for each blend establishes value which make up the octane rating scale ; for example, a mixture of 90 parts iso-octane and 10 parts heptane has an octane number of 90. Research octane numbers, (RON) obtained under laboratory conditions, run several points higher than so-called motor octane numbers, (MON) which represent the actual performance of a gasoline in a car engine. Research octane numbers above 100 are possible by using antiknocking agents.

octant rule. Rule permitting forecast of sign and approximate amplitude of Cotton effect in cyclohexanone derivatives.

octose. A carbohydrate which contains a chain of eight carbon atoms.

odd-even nucleus. Atomic nucleus containing odd number of protons and even number of neutrons.

odd molecules. A few, unusual molecules that have an odd number of valence electrons.

odd-odd nucleus. Atomic nucleus containing odd number of protons and odd number of neutrons.

Oddo-Ferrari test reaction for aldehydes. A modified Fischer reagent for aldehydes and ketones whereby ; in acetic acid solution containing fused sodium acetate, aldehydes condense with *sym*-diphenylcarbazide to give carbazoles and aniline.

odor. A response of the olfactory nerves to stimulation by the molecules of an inhaled substance. It is an important and useful property for both identification and warning purposes. The intensity varies greatly at a given concentration, from virtually undetectable to highly penetrating and obnoxious, *e.g.*, sulphur-bearing compounds, of which ethanethiol and hydrogen sulphide are examples. Essential oils in general have a pleasing, sweet odor. The effectiveness of many animal repellents is due to their odor, *e.g.*, sulphur dioxide and citronella oil.

O-electron. An electron having an orbit of such dimensions that the electron constitutes part of the fifth shell of electrons surroundiug the atomic nucleus, counting out from the nucleus the K-shell is the first, the L-, the second, the M-, the third, the N-, the fourth, and the O-shell, the fifth.

Oersted process. A process for making anhydrous aluminium chloride in which a stream of dry chlorine is passed over a strongly heated mixture of aluminium oxide and carbon. Industrially the process is carried on at a temperature of about 1275K.

Ohmic pseudo-polarization. Ohmic drop of voltage in layer of electrolyte between electrode and tip of Luggin capillary during flow of polarizing current through electrolyte.

-oic. A suffix indicating a terminal —COOH group.

oil. A nonspecific term applied to several groups of organic mixtures having quite different chemical composition and properties. Oils are liquids at room temperature, becoming increasingly viscous to semisolid at lower temperatures. The most important groups are ; (*i*) the mineral type (petroleum, shale oil) which are mixtures of hydrocarbons ; (*ii*) the vegetable type (cotton-seed, soybean, etc.) which are mixtures of unsaturated fatty acids, many of which are edible ; (*iii*) the animal type (sperm and fish oils), also containing fatty acids ; and (*iv*) the flower type (essential oils), in which terpenes predominate (though derived from vegetations, they are classified separately from vegetable oils. (The terms oils of mirbane for nitrobenzene and oil of vitriol for sulphuric acid are obsolescent.

oil black. A variety of carbon-black made from oil, usually an aromatic type petroleum oil.

oil, blown. *See* blown oil.

oil, boiled. *See* boiled oil.

oil cake. A mass of oil-seeds (*e.g.*, linseed cottonseed) from which the oil has been expelled in a press (expellers or extracted by a solvent (extractions) : used as cattle feed.

oil colour. A pigment or mixture of pigments which have been ground in oil, and which are used in a mixture with the oil in which they are ground. In use, they require solvents in which the oil is soluble.

oil, drying. *See* drying oil.

oil, essential. *See* essential oil.

oil, fixed. *See* fixed oil.

oil, mineral. *See* mineral oil.

oil sands Porous sandstone structure occurring on the surface and to depths of 750 metres in certain localities : they contain a high proportion of bitument composed chiefly of asphaltenes and maltha, together with substantial percentages of sulphur and heavy metals. Its viscosity is about midway between that of crude oil and soft asphalt. The solid content is reduced to 70% by addition of hot water, after which the oil separates by gravity. As its hydrogen-to carbon ratio is low and its molecular weight is high, it is upgraded by thermal cracking addition of hydrogen, and removal of sulphur. Also known as tar sands.

-ol. A suffix indicating the presence of one or more hydroxyl groups in an organic compound An exception is thiol, a class of compounds similar to alcohol in which the oxygen of the —OH group is replaced by sulphur.

-olane. A suffix indicating a five-membered ring.

-ole. A suffix indicating a five membered ring.

olefine. A member of the olefine series of unsaturated aliphatic hydrocarbons of the general formula C_nH_{2n}, *e.g.*, ethene, C_2H_4. Olefines are named from the corresponding paraffin hydrocarbons by adding the suffix "ylene" to the stem or (Geneva plan), by changing the suffix 'ane" to "ene." For example, the names ethylene and ethene are derived from ethane.

Olefines having only one double bond are called mono-olefines or alkenes, and those with two are diolefines also called alkadienes, or simply dienes. Some olefines have three or more double bonds and are named accordingly (triolefines, etc). The unsaturated linkages are always between adjacent carbons in mono-olefines ; in diolefines they may be between successive carbons (C=C=C) or between alternate pairs of carbons (conjugated) :

C=C—C=C)

olefine complex. Complex of heavy metal (particularly platinum) with hydrocarbons containing double bonds. In this complex coordination bond is formed with participation of π electrons.

oleoresin. A sticky or gummy mixture of essential oils and natural resins occurring in numerous varieties of trees and shrubs, particularly of the evergreen or coniferous type. Turpentine, a well-known example, contains abietic acid, pinene, and dipentene. Most oleoresins have a strong, pleasant aroma; some have value as medicines (cough syrups). *See also* balsam; resin (1); rosin.

oleum. Alternative name for fuming sulphuric acid, *i.e.*, sulphuric acid mixed with sulphur trioxide, used largely as a sulphonating agent. Oleum is the source of the word oil and undoubtedly owes its present meaning to the original name of sulphuric acid (oil of vitriol), derived from the Latin word for grass, because of the refractive appearance of the ferrous sulphate from which it was once made.

oligo-. A prefix derived from the Greek, meaning "several" or "slight", in chemistry, it appears in such terms as oligosaccharides (containing from three to ten monosaccharide units) and oligodynamic (slight bactericidal activity).

oligodynamic. Sterilizing effect of traces of certain metals, *e.g.*, silver in concentration of 0.5 ppm will kill Escherichia coli and staphylococci in 3 hours.

oligomer. Substance composed of molecules containing a few of one or more species of atoms or groups of atoms (called constitutional units or mers) repetitively linked to each sizes that physical properties of oligomer are different from those of both the corresponding monomer and polymer.

oligomeric protein. A protein having two or more polypeptide chains.

oligosaccharide. A sugar composed of two or more monosaccharide units. Those sugars containing upto 6 units, many of which occur in nature, have been isolated as crystalline compounds. Fragments, obtained by controlled hydrolysis of various polysaccharides with acid and consisting of monosaccharides upto 10 units, are also termed oligosaccharides.

The oligosaccharides may be considered as glycosides in which a hydroxyl (OH) group of one monosaccharide is condensed with the reducing group of another, with the loss of (n—1) molecules of water (n=number of monosaccharide residues). The condensation process is shown as :

$$C_6H_{12}O_6 + C_6H_{12}O_6 - H_2O = C_{12}H_{22}O_{11}$$

(Disaccharide)

$$3C_6H_{12}O_6 - 2H_2O = C_{18}H_{32}O_{16}$$

(Trisaccharide)

On the basis of the number of constituent monosaccharide units, the oligosaccharides are classified as disaccharides, trisaccharides, tetrasaccharides, and so on. No sharp distiction can be drawn between the oligosaccharides and polysaccharides; it is chiefly a matter of the latter's possessing higher molecular weights.

The monosaccharide units of an oligosaccharide may be alike, as in maltose, which on hydrolysis gives two molecules of D-glucose, or different, as in sucrose or raffinose.

-olium. A suffix indicating a cation (of -ole base).

omega (ω). The twenty-fourth letter in the Greek alphabet, used to denote the twenty-fourth carbon atom in a straight-chain compound, or a derivative in which the substituent group is attached to the twenty-fourth carbon atom.

Symbol for solid angle. Symbol for angular frequency. Symbol for angular frequency with damping. Symbol for dispersive power.

omega$^-$ hyperon. Elementary particle, a hadron, of mass $m = 1672.5$ MeV, negative elementary electric charge, baryon number $B = 1$, lepton number $L = 0$, quantum spin number $J = 3/2$, strangeness $S = 3$, isopin $I = 0$, third component of isopin $I_3 = 0$, unstable, of mean lifetime 1.3×10^{-10} s. Also known as Ω^--hyperon.

-onane. A suffix indicating a nine-membered ring.

-one. A suffix indicating a ketone.

-onin. A suffix indicating a nine-membered ring.

-onium. Chemical suffix indicating a complex cation, such as hydronium ion, (H_3O^+).

one-component system. System composed of one constituent.

one-electron bond. Chemical bond formed by valence electron present in molecular bonding orbital, *e.g.*, ionized molecule H_2^+ is supposed to have one-electron bond

one electron excitation. Excitation of molecule by raising one of its electrons either from bonding or non-bonding orbital to higher-energetic antibonding orbital.

one particle approximation. Approximation which replaces real interparticle interaction by some self-consistent effective field for each particle. Also known as single particle approximation; single particle model.

Onia-Gegi process. The process for the production of hydrogen-rich gas from methane (natural gas). Methane and steam are passed over a heated nickel catalyst.

Onsager principle. Relations determining symmetry of matrix of phenomenological coefficients of linear phenomenological equations $L_{ik} = L_{ki}$; it follows from Onsager reciprocal relations that each cross effect (*e.g.*, determined by coefficient L_{ik}) has reciprocal cross effect (determined by coefficient L_{ki}).

Onsager theory. Theory of electric polarization in which Lorenz field is replaced by local (Onsager) field.

opacifier. Any substance used to render transparent or translucent substances opaque.

opacity. Imperviousness to radiation, especially to light ; the property of stopping the passage of light rays.

Open-Hearth process. A method of manufacturing steel in a shallow reverberatory furnace (lined with acidic or basic refractories that may combine with impurities in the metal), in which the charge of pig iron, scarp steel, and various fluxes, oxidizing substances, etc., is heated by combustion of gas above the surface of the charge.

open system. System which can exchange energy and mass with surroundings.

Openaur oxidation. Oxidation of primary and secondary alcohols to corresponding aldehydes or ketones, effected by carbonyl compounds in presence of aluminium butanoate, isopropanolate, *e.g.*,

$$RR'CHOH + CH_3COCH_3 \xrightarrow[\text{anisaldehyde}]{[(CH_3)_2CHO]_3Al} RCOR' (CH_3)_2CHOH$$

$$\text{(H}_3\text{C, CH}_3\text{-cyclohexenyl)}-CH_2OH \xrightarrow[\text{anisaldehyde}]{[(CH_3)_2CHO]_3Al} \text{(H}_3\text{C, CH}_3\text{-cyclohexenyl)}-CHO$$

This reaction is reversible. *See also* Meerwein-Ponndorf-Verley reduction.

Oppenheimer-Phillips mechanism. An explanation of the role of deuterons in nuclear bombardment reactions, whereby the deuteron is thought of as behaving as a relatively loose combination of a neutron and a proton, since the binding energy is comparatively small. When the energy of the incident deuteron exceeds this binding energy, the proton portion will break off and be repelled, and the neutron will then enter the target nucleus.

opsonic index. The ratio between the number of bacteria destroyed by the leucocytes in a certain sample of blood to the number destroyed in a normal sample.

optical activity. Property of substance of rotation of plane of polarized light passing through it. Optical activity is caused by chirality of crystals or molecules. All chiral molecules exhibit optical activity in gaseous and liquid states, also in solutions.

optical anisotropy. The behaviour of a medium, or of a single molecule, whose effect on electromagnetic radiation depends on the direction of the propagation of radiation.

optical anomaly. The behaviour of certain organic compounds, such as those whose molecules contain conjugated double bonds, in which the observed values of the molar refraction are not in accord with the values calculated from the known equivalents. When the observed value is higher than the calculated value, the substance is said to exaltation.

optical antipode. *See* enantiomorph.

optical axis. Direction of optical isotropy in crystal. Beam of electromagnetic radiation polarized linearly, which runs in crystal in direction of optical axis has speed independent of orientation of electric vector *E*. Crystals may have one or two optical axes.

optical brightner. A colourless fluorescent organic compound which absorbs ultraviolet light and emits it as visible blue light.

optical density. The negative logarithm of the relative transmittance of a photographic emulsion. $D = -\log_{10} T$, where D = the optical density and T=the relative transmittance.

optical electrons. Electrons occupying atomic valence shell orbitals. They determine character of atomic spectrum.

Term optical electrons is commonly used in the case of alkali metals.

optical exaltation. The phenomenon whereby a compound possesses a refraction different from the value calculated from the various equivalents of the atoms and other structural units of which it is composed. This property is more strictly called optical anomaly, but since in most cases the difference is positive, *i.e.*, the observed value exceeds the calculated one, the term exaltation is used.

optical fiber. An extemely fine-drawn glass fibrè of exceptional purity that will transmit laser light impulses with high fidelity. Such fibres are made from high-purity quartz coated with germanium-doped silica by vapour deposition.

optical frequency. A frequency comparable to that of electromagnetic waves in the optical region, above about 3×10^{11} hertz.

opt cal glass. A type of glass specifically formulated for use in lenses designed to correct astigmatism and other malfunctions of vision, as well as in scientific instruments, cameras, etc. The refractive indices and dispersion properties of such glass can be precisely controlled by proper selection and proportion of ingredients. Optical glass may be of either the crown or flint type, the former containing lime and the latter lead.

optical inversion. The conversion of optically active substances into derivatives of identical structure but of opposite rotation. *l*-Malic acid with phosphorus pentachloride yields *d*-chlorosucccinic acid ; malic acid under the same conditions yields *l*-chlorosuccinic acid. Walden's inversion is the classical instance of optical inversion.

optical interferometer. Instrument for measurement of difference of refractive indices of investigated sample and standard from position of interference lines which appear due to difference of radiation velocities in these two media.

optical isomerism. Type of stereoisomerism caused by chirality of molecules, giving them optical activity. Optical isomers form two main groups : enantiomers (these are mutual mirror images) and diasteroisomers (not mirror images). Diastereoisomers are sub-divided into epimers (including anomers) and meso-isomers, which are optically inactive due to internal compensation of rotation, caused by even number of chiral centres.

optically void liquids. Liquids that do not exhibit the Tyndall effect, *e.g.*, liquids that contain no suspended solids.

optical model. Model representiog atomic nucleus as semitransparent optical medium. Optical model describes deflection of particles by the nucleus as process analogous to dispersion of light.

optical permittivity, ε_{∞}. Electric permittivity at very high ($\nu > 10^{12}$ Hz) frequencies of alternating electric field.

optical purity. Estimate of degree of contamination of enantiomer in terms of another, expressed in percent. When enatiomeric mixture contains 95% of (—) enantiomer and 5% of (+) enantiomer, the former said to be 90% optically pure.

optical rotation. A property of some crystalline substances which enables them to turn the plane of polarized light (vibrations transmitted in one direction only) as is passes through Nicol prisms, the rotation being either to the left (levo) or the right (dextro). Many inorganic materials display this property, *e.g.*, quartz and mercury sulphide. It is also characteristc of organic compounds containing one or more asymmetric carbon atoms (turpentine, tartaric acid) ; most prominent among these are sugars or sugar derivatives, as indicated by the names dextrose and levulose : some acids, including amino acids ; and certain aldehydes and alcohols. The Greek letter alpha is often used as a symbol for optical rotation.

optical spectrum. Most frequently denotes absorption or emission spectrum in visible or ultraviolet region ; sometimes also used in the case of infrared spectra.

Because of its rather imprecise character this term is only rarely used.

optical transition. Radiative transition between two energy states of system accompanied by emission or absorption of light in visible or ultraviolet region.

optical twinning. Simultaneous growth of two crystals which are same excent that mirror image of the other. Also known as chiral twinning.

orbital. A mathematical designation of the wave function or energy level of an electron within a shell. Each shell is composed of several obitals or subshells, the energy state of each being defined by its quantum numbers. No orbital can contain more than two electrons, and these two must have opposite spin

(Pauli exclusion principle). The orbital concept, developed by Heisenberg. Schrodinger, and others, reflects the impact of quantum mechanics on chemistry, espcially as regards bonding and coordination theory. This concept considers the electron as a light wave as well as a particle ; it is described mathematically as a standing wave, the orbital being a function of this wave. The square of the wave function is a real property of the electron, representing the space limits (orbital) within which an electron, is most probably located ; these limits are established by four quantum numbers, which denote its energy level, angular momentum, magnetic moment, and spin. Thus an orbital represents the mathematical probability that an electron will be found at any point in a specific volume of space.

orbital moment (of atom), p_L. Vector quantity, defined by

$$p_L = h\sqrt{L(L+1)}$$

where L = orbital quantum number. Orbital magnetic moment

$$\mu_L = \sqrt{L(L+1)}\ \mu_B$$

corresponds to orbital moment, where μ_B = Bohr magneton.

orbital quantum number, l. Number which defines allowed quantized values of orbital angular momentum of system. For given value of principal quantum number n, l assumes following values 0, 1, ..., $n-1$.

order. The regular arrangement or pattern assumed by atoms or other chemical units in a space lattice ; absence of such an arrangement is known as disorder, or random distribution. The lattices may be of one, two, or three dimensions, depending on the nature of the material (polymer, colloid, crystal, etc.). Maximum order is characteristic of crystals, while liquids are disordered : intermediate structures (proteins) may exhibit reversible change from one state to the other, *e.g.*, from helical form to random coils. Statistical study of such changes is helpful in understanding phase transitions in alloys, colloidal systems, and the structure of macromolecules such as DNA and polypeptides.

order of interference. Value of parameter n=1, 2, 3, ... in formula which gives diffraction maxima for diffraction grating :

$$n\lambda = a(\sin\beta - \sin\alpha)$$

where λ=wavelength of incident light, a=diffraction grating constant, β=incidence angle, and α=diffraction angle.

order of reaction. Sum of exponents over concentrations of reactants in kinetic equation. Also known as overall reaction.

order with respect to a particular substance. Order of reaction equal to exponent with which concentration of this substance appears in kinetic equation.

ore. Any naturally occurring mixture of a metal or metal compound and various silicates, carbonates, etc., found not only in rock strata but also in certain clay or sandy formations. Bauxite is the principal ore of aluminium, and monazite sands are ores from which titanium and rare-earth metals are obtained. Ores have geological names usually ending in *-ite* (taconite, carnotite, ilmenite, bastnasite, hematite). Ore treatment includes separation, beneficiation (dressing), and reduction by any of several methods to extract the metal.

ore dressing. A term used in extractive metallurgy to refer to various nonchemical means of separating metals or their compounds (oxides, sulphides) from the siliceous or calcareous structures in which they occur. Some of the operations performed are beneficiation, elutriation and floatation.

organic. This term basically means "living" as in the biological word organism ; it was thought by early chemists that all organic compounds originated in plants and animals, until the German chemist, Friedrich Wohler (1800-1882), discovered in 1828 that urea could be formed from ammonium cyanate by molecular rearrangement.

organic analysis. Qualitative analysis of an organic compound is the process by which the characterization of its class and structure is determined. Due to the numerous classes of organic compounds and the complexity of their molecular structures, a systematic analytical procedure is often required. A typical procedure entails an initial assignment of compound classification, followed by a complete identification of the molecular structure.

Instrumental methods are also applied for functional group determination and structure identification. Absorption spectroscopy and infrared absorption spectroscopy are among the most important techniques.

In addition to infrared spectroscopy, nuclear magnetic resonance and mass spectrometry are widely used. Other, less common techniques are electron spin resonance, x-ray diffraction, and nuclear quadrupole spectroscopy.

Although the implementation of instrumental methods has greatly simplified qualitative analytical procedures, on individual instrument is capable of complete identification for all samples. A complement of instrumental and wet chemical techniques is required for adequate proof of identification.

organic chemistry. Branch of chemistry dealing with studies of numerous carbon compounds, excluding only a few discussed in inorganic chemistry.

Another view is that organic chemistry deals with the hydrocarbons and their derivatives ; however, it also includes the study of compounds containing nitrogen, oxygen, sulphur, etc, in addition to hydrogen and carbon, *e.g.*, carbohydrates. Developments in modern chemistry have tended to make the division between organic and inorganic less and less definite.

organic compound. One of the great number of compounds consisting of carbon linked in chains or rings ; such compounds usually also contain hydrogen and may contain elements such as oxygen, nitrogen, sulphur, chlorine, etc. Thus organic has come to mean any compound containing the element carbon with several exceptions ; such binary compounds as the carbon oxides, the carbides, and carbon disulphide ; such ternary compounds as the metallic cyanides, metallic carbonyls, phosgene ($COCl_2$), and carbonyl sulphide (COS) ; and the metallic carbonates, such as calcium carbonate and potassium carbonate.

organisol. A dispersion of very finely divided resin particles in organic liquid mixture which cannot dissolve the resin at normal temperatures.

organized ferments. Ferments characterized by connection with living cells, as yeast. Formerly, organized and unorganized ferments were believed to have specific differences. This is known to be untrue, although certain fermentations are not known to take place in the absence of living matter.

organogel. Gel in which organic liquid forms dispersion medium.

organogen. Any one of the four elements, carbon, hydrogen, nitrogen, and oxygen, and by extension, sulphur, phosphorus, and chlorine, characteristic of organic products.

organoleptic. A property which may be perceived by a sense organ, as taste, odor, or colour.

organoleptic analysis. Investigation or identification of substance through the senses *e.g.*, taste and smell. Also known as organoleptic test.

organometallic. A compound containing an organic group bonded to a metal atom. An important and versatile class of organometallics is known as Grignard reagents, in with magnesium appears, together with a halogen atom (CH_3MgI), other examples are metallocenes, tetraethyllead, and triethylaluminum. Names of the many types of organometallic compounds are formed by using the prefix organo- followed by the metal, *e.g.*, organotin, organozinc, organophorus, etc. Many of these are highly toxic, and some are fire and explosion hazards, especially triethylaluminum.

organophilic. A term descriptive of a solid substance which has an affinity for organic solvents, forming viscous solutions or gel-like dispersions. The thick doughs or pastes resulting from dispersion of crude rubber in naphtha or benzene.

organosol. A colloidal solution in which the continuous phase is an organic solvent such as alcohol, benzene, ether, amyl alcohol, pentane, etc.

orientation. From its general meaning of the assumption of a definite position with regard to existing points of reference, this term has acquired a number of specific uses in chemistry. It was applied first to denote the positions assumed by substituents in relation to the configuration of the parent substance and to each other. The term was then applied to the position assumed by a free particle in a field of force or other constraint, as the orientation of fatty-acid molecules in the surface of a polar solvent. The term orientation was also applied to the method of determination of the axial ratios of crystals, by assuming certain axes, and orienting the crystal faces with respect to them.

orientation effect. One of the components of intermolecular force. Orientation effect leads to attractive forces between pair of molecules each one having permanent dipole or higher multipole moment.

orientation in aromatic substitution. Position taken by entering substituent depends on substituents already present in aromatic ring. Electron-donating substituents ($-\bar{N}R_2$, $-\bar{O}H$, $-\bar{O}R$, alkyl) direct entering, substituent to ortho- and para-position; electron-withdrawing group ($-\overset{+}{N}R_3$, $-NO_2$, COOH, $-SO_3H$) direct entering substituent to meta-position.

orientation polarizability, α_o. Dielectric polarization (per molecule) arising in unit local field due to dipole orientation. According to Debye theory it is given by

$$\alpha_o = \frac{\mu^2}{3kT}$$

where : μ =permanent dipole moment, k= Boltzmann constant, T= thermodynamic temperature.

orientation polarization. Dielectric polarization due to orientation of polar molecules or polar groups in molecules with some freedom of internal rotation.

orientation polarization (molar), *Po*. Measure of orientation polarization defined by :

$$P_o = \frac{1}{3\varepsilon_0} N_A\alpha_0 \quad \text{(in SI units)}$$

where N_A=Avogadro constant, α_o=orientation polarizability, ε_0=electric permittivity of free space.

ormulu. An alloy of copper, zinc, and tin in various proportions ; generally containing 50% copper.

-ortho. A prefix that is used for a variety of purposes. Its literal meaning (from the Greek) is "straight" or "regular". It may denote :

(*i*) A particular isomer of the three disubstituted derivatives of benzene, the others being known as "meta" and "para".

(*ii*) The fully hydrated form of an acid *e.g.*, orthophosphoric or orthosilicic acids.

(*iii*) The symmetrical form of the molecule of an element, *e.g.*, ortho-hydrogen ; parahydrogen has a different nuclear spin.

(*iv*) One of the two forms of helium that have different electron spins, the other form being parahelium.

(*v*) One of the seven fundamental systems in crystallography—orthorhombic.

ortho and para hydrogen. Two forms of hydrogen, which constitute about 75%, and 25% respectively, of ordinary hydrogen at room temperature, and which differ somewhat in their physical properties, especially in their specific heats. At very low temperature, as for liquid hydrogen, the para form is present to the extent of 99.7%. The difference between the two forms is explained on the assumption that the two nuclei in the H_2 molecule are spining in anti-parallel directions in the case of para hydrogen and in parallel directions in ortho hydrogen.

orthogonality of wave functions. Two functions φ_1 and φ_2 are orthogonal if

$$\int \varphi_1^+ \varphi_2 \, d\tau = 0,$$

where + denotes complex conjugate, $d\tau$= integration volume element and integration is in region where both functions are defined.

orthokinetic aggregation. Coagulation that occurs due to collision of particles under influence of external force, *e.g.*, gravitational force or centrifugal force in ultra-centrifuge.

orthokinetic flocculation. *See* orthokinetic aggregation.

Orton rearrangement of N-halogenoacylamides. Convertion of N-chloroacylamides into mixture of *o*- and *p*-chloro-N-acylamides, effected by hydrochloric acid, *e.g.*,

Cl—N—COCH$_3$ (benzene ring) $\xrightarrow{HCl}$ NHCOCH$_3$ (ring with o-Cl) + NHCOCH$_3$ (ring with p-Cl)

-osan. A suffix indicating a polysaccharide.

osazone. A diphenylhydrazone. Osazones are often prepared because their crystalline forms and melting points aid in the identification of sugars. The reaction with phenylhydrazine involves the reaction of one molecule of the latter with a carbonyl group to from a phenylhydrazone, followed by oxidation with another molecule of phenylhydrazine of a —CHOH— group that was in the α-position to the carbonyl group, and then the reaction of a third molecule of phenylhdrazine with the carbonyl group formed by the oxidation. A typical osazone is glucosazone,

$$\begin{array}{l} CH_2OH \\ | \\ (CHOH)_3 \\ | \\ C{=}N{-}NH.C_6H_5 \\ | \\ CH{=}N{-}NH.C_6H_5. \end{array}$$

oscillating crystal method. X-ray technique for determination of crystal structure. X-rays are diffracted from crystal oscillating through angle of 5° to 15°. Oscillating crystal method is used in place of rotating crystal method when elementary cell dimensions are relatively large.

oscillations. In general any periodic movements. In molecular spectroscopy periodic movements of molecular fragments (atoms or atomic groups); also oscillations of whole molecule with respect to its equilibrium position.

oscillographic polarograph. Apparatus used for studies of dependence of current on fast linear changes of voltage applied to electrodes; oscillographic polarography is also used with relation $dE/dt = f(E)$, where E = indicator electrode potential and t=time.

oscillometric titration. *See* high frequency titration.

oscillopolarography. Group of electrochemical methods using an oscillograph to observe relationships: $i—E$, $(dE/dt)—E$, or $E—t$, where E=electrode potential, i = electrolysis current, t=time of electrolysis. Also known as cathode-ray polarography.

-ose. A suffix indicating a carbohydrate (specifically, a sugar).

O-shell. The collection of electrons characterized by the quantum number 5. The O-shell starts with element rubidium (atomic number= 37), which has one electron in its O-shell, and the O-shall is finally completed (containing 18 electrons) with the element mercury (atomic number = 80). During the progression from rubidium to mercury, the difference between elements of consecutive atomic number is frequently not in the O-shell, but in an electron increment in the N-shell, or in the P-shell.

osmium. An element.

	Symbol	Os
State Solid	Atomic No.	76
Group VIII	Atomic Wt.	190.2
	Valence	2,3,4,6,8
	Isotopes	7 stable
	m.p.	3321K
	b.p.	5203-5403K

osmium belongs to the platinum group of metals; it is extremely hard and is one of the heaviest elements, with a density about twice that of lead.

The seven stable isotopes of osmium are ^{184}Os, ^{186}Os through ^{190}Os, and ^{192}Os. The six unstable isotopes are ^{182}Os, ^{183}Os, ^{185}Os, ^{193}Os, and ^{194}Os.

Elementary osmium has a closed packed hexagonal crystal structure. Compact osmium is a bluish-white metal and is not attacked by acids.

The chemistry of osmium is very complicated because of the various oxidation states exhibited by it and the tendency of each of these to form numerous complex ions.

When heated to 470K, it forms osmium tetroxide (OsO_4), which has severely toxic properties and is a powerful oxidising agent.

Its ease of formation and volatility make it useful in a purification step for the refining or analysis of osmium. The tetroxide is readily formed by heating the metal in air or distilling an osmium-containing solution from nitric acid.

Osmium forms many complexes with nitrite, oxalate, carbon monoxide, amines, and thio ureas. The latter are important analytically. Osmium forms the interesting aromatic "sandwich" compound, osmocene.

The metal is used chiefly as a component of

hard alloys for specialized applications : the tetroxide as used as an oxidation catalyst and for biological staining.

osmophor. A group or radical that imparts odor to a compound, as a chromophore imparts colour.

osmosis. Diffusion of constituent from solution of higher chemical potential to solution of lower chemical potential, through semi-permeable membrane.

The effect of this is to equalize the concentrations and vapour pressures of the two solutions. The barrier or membrane is called semipermeable if it allows the solvent to diffuse but tends to retain the dissolved substance, which in the case of biological osmosis is sucrose. Considerable pressure is exerted by this phenomenon, which is an essential part of the growth process, as it is the means by which nutrients are furnished to living cells.

osmotic coefficient. *g.* A factor introduced into equation for nonideal solutions to correct for their departure from ideal behavior, as in the equation :

$$\mu = \mu_x^\circ + gRT \ln x_1$$

where μ = chemical potential μ_x° = constant, representing a standard value of the chemical potential, R = gas constant, T = absolute temperature x_1 = the mole fraction of solvent, and g = the osmotic coefficient.

osmotic pressure. Pressure that develops when a pure solvent is separated from a solution by a semipermeable membrane which allows only the solvent molecules to pass through it.

Ostromyslenskii reaction. The direct condensation of alcohols and aldehydes to form diene hydrocarbons. Elevated temperatures and catalysts are required.

$$CH_3CHO + CH_3CH_2OH \xrightarrow[-2H_2O]{\Delta} CH_2{:}CH.CH{:}CH_2$$

Ostwald's dilution law. Formula which describes classical electrolytic dissociation constant Kc

$$K_c = \frac{\Lambda c^2 c}{(\Lambda_0 - \Lambda c)\Lambda c}$$

where Λ_0 and Λ_c = equivalent conductivity of infinitely diluted electrolyte and electrolyte at concentration c respectively; Ostwald's dilution law applies approximately to diluted solutions of weak electrolytes.

Ostwald process. A method for the preparation of nitric acid from ammonia by its oxidation successively to nitric oxide, nitrogen dioxide, and finally nitric acid, using elevated temperatures and platinum gauze as a catalyst.

Ostwald rule. When a substance can exist in more than one form, reactions for its production usually yield the least stable modification, which subsequently undergoes a process of transformation until the most stable form is reached.

Ostwald theory of indicators. Indicators are weak acids or bases, in which the ion differs in colour from the molecule.

Othmer process. A process for the production of pure acetic acid from crude pyroligneous acid ; the crude liquor is distilled, and the vapour is passed through purifying columns, in which the methanol, acetone, tar, and other components are removed by absorption, or solution. The vapours of acetic acid and water than pass to condensers.

Oudeman's law. The molecular rotations of the salts of optically active acids or bases always tend to a definite limiting value as the concentraction of the solution diminishes ; *e.g.*, the soluble salts of α-bromosulphocamphoric acid show identical molecular rotations in hundredth normal solutions.

-ous. A suffix used in naming inorganic compounds to indicate that the multivalent positive element in the compound is in a lower valence state. It is used (a) to designate that the metal in a metallic compound has an oxidation number less than its highest one.

outer-orbital complex. Complex in which, in hybridization of orbitals of central ion, d orbitals have the same principal quantum number as s and p orbitals ; as in octahedral complex nsp^3d^2.

overall instability constant K_n. Equilibrium constant of dissociation reaction of complex

$$MLn \rightleftharpoons M + nL$$

$$K_n = \frac{[M][L]^n}{[ML_n]}$$

where [M], [L] and $[ML_n]$ = equilibrium concentrations of metal, ligand and complex respectively. This constant is equal to product of consecutive instability constants. Also known as cumulative instability constant.

overall stability constant. *See* stability constant.

overlap. Two orbitals φ_1 and φ_2 have non-zero overlap if :

$$\int \varphi_1^{-} \varphi_2 \, d\tau \neq 0$$

where + = complex conjugate and $d\tau$ = volume element of integration region where both functions are defined.

overpotential η. Measure of electrolytic polarization defined by equation $\eta \equiv \epsilon_i - \epsilon$, where ϵ_i= potential of electrode (half-cell) across which there flows electrical current larger than exchange current, ϵ=potential of this electrode at equilibrium. Also known as overvoltage.

oxalene. The radical —N=C(|)—C(|)=N—.

oxazine. One of a number of unsaturated 6-membered, ring compounds, containing one oxygen atom, one nitrogen atom, and four carbon atoms in the ring, and having the formula, C_4H_5ON.

oxidant. Substance that gains electrons from another (oxidized) substance called reducing agent; thus, oxidant is reduced in electron transfer process.

Electronegative elements such as chlorine and other halogens are excellent electron acceptors and thus are strong oxidants. Also known as oxidizing agent ; oxidizer.

oxidase. One of the enzymes which catalyze the oxidation of many substances by free oxygen, *e.g.*, tyrosinase, lactase, uricolase.

oxidation. In its original use, oxidation meant simply combination with oxygen. Its use has, however, been considerably widened to cover a great many processes similar to oxidation, such as chlorination, and other processes of combination with strongly nonmetallic elements, which add electrons readily. In fact the term oxidation in its broadest sense means simply a chemical reaction wherby electrons are removed from one or more of the atoms of a substance. It is, of course, most frequently accompanied by a simultaneous process, in the same reaction, whereby another substance or substances gain the electrons and thus undergo reduction ; therefore, calling the process oxidation, under these circumstances, simply means that it is this part (*i.e.*, loss of electrons) of the particular process that is of greatest interest. Removal of hydrogen atoms (each having one electron) from a hydrogen-containing organic compound (dehydrogenation) is a form of oxidation ; it is effected by a catalytic reaction with air or oxygen, as in the oxidation of alcohols to aldehydes. Free radical chains play an important part in the oxidation of such organic compounds as rubber, drying oils.

oxidation number. For a given element, the number of electrons it can transfer to another element with which it combines. Conversely, it is the number of electrons it is necessary to add to or subtract from a combined atom to restore it to its original uncombined (elemental) state. For example, in the compound magnesium oxide (MgO), the oxidation number of magnesium is +2 and of the oxygen —2 ; since the sum of these is zero, the molecule is electrically neutral. The oxidation number may vary for the same element ; and for different elements it may be positive or negative, depending on the number of valence electrons in the outer shell. Thus, there is a close relation between oxidation number (electrons added or subtracted) and the valence, or combining power, of an element. Some metals have as many as six or seven positive oxidation numbers, and many have two or three. While using the concept of oxidation number, following rules must be observed :

(*i*) The oxidation number of an element is taken to be zero.

(*ii*) The oxidation number of a monoatomic ion is reckoned to be equal to its electric charge, *e.g.*, in $CaCl_2$, Ca^{++} is plus 2, and each Cl^- minus l.

(*iii*) The oxidation number for a covalent compound of known structure is, for each atom, the charge left on that atom when each shared pair of electrons is assigned to the more electronegative of the two atoms which share it, *e.g.*, for H_2O, H is plus 1 and oxygen minus 2.

(*iv*) The sum of oxidation numbers of the atoms making up a molecule of a stable compound is zero. Thus for $K_2Cr_2O_7$ (potassium dichromate) each potassium gives +1, each chromium +6, and each oxygen —2, giving 2 + 12 — 14 = 0.

oxidation-reduction buffer. Solution which contain redox couple in such a concentration that its redox potential changes only slightly after addition of small quantities of oxidant (reductant).

oxidation-reduction catalysis. Catalysis by oxidizing or reducing substances. In this type of catalysis, reaction of catalyst with substrate is connected with transfer of electron.

oxidation reduction cell. A cell in which the electric energy is produced by the interaction of a reducing and an oxidizing substance in separate solutions, each bathing an electrode.

oxidation-reduction equation. A chemical equation expressing a reaction in which there is a transfer of electrons between ions, atoms, or molecules.

oxidation-reduction titration. Volumetric determination of oxidants or reductants present in solution. Also known as redox titration.

oxidative fermentation. Decomposition of hexoses to compounds of simpler structure, occurring under action of bacteria, in which initial degradation of carbohydrate is similar to alcoholic fermentation; final stage leads, however, to products of higher oxidation number.

oxide. A compound of oxygen with another element. Several classes of oxide are recognised :

(*i*) Basic oxide ; an oxide that combines with an acid to form a salt and water only. It is a metallic oxide, and if it is soluble in water (and this is not common) an alkali is formed.

(*ii*) Acidic oxide ; an oxide that combines with a base to form a salt and water only. It is usually a non-metallic oxide and if it is soluble in water (and this is usually the case) an acid is formed.

(*iii*) Amphoteric oxide ; an oxide that possesses both acidic and basic characteristics and can react with both of these.

(*iv*) Neutral oxide ; one that has neither acidic nor basic characteristics.

(*v*) Compound oxide (less appropriately called a "mixed oxide"), is one that behaves chemically as if it were two other oxides combined, *e.g.*, $Fe_3O_4 \equiv Fe_2O_3.FeO$.

(*vi*) Peroxide ; a salt of hydrogen peroxide. Manganese dioxide, lead dioxide, nitrogen "peroxide", are not true peroxides.

(*vii*) Higher oxide : one that contains more oxygen than the normal valency of the element warrants.

Other terms, such as "suboxide" and "sesquioxide", are not well defined and are perhaps best avoided.

From the structural point of view, oxides are conveniently classified as (*i*) ionic, (*ii*) covalent, and (*iii*) intermediate.

oxidizing agent. *See* oxidant.

oxidizing enzyme. An enzyme that catalyzes an organic oxidation, *e.g.*, oxidase, phenolase.

oxime. One of a number of compounds that result from the interaction of aldehydes, ketones, and other carbonyl-containg substances with hydroxylamine, *e.g.*, acetone yields acetoxine

$$(CH_3)_2C{=}O + H_2NOH \rightarrow (CH_3)_2C{=}NOH + H_2O$$

oximido. *See* isonitroso.

oxirane. The radical —C—C— (with both carbons bonded to a bridging O).

oximetry. A technique that employs an an oximeter, a photoelectric photometer, to measure the oxygenated fraction of the hemoglobin.

oxo. The radical O= in organic compounds (both valence bonds joined to some atoms).

oxo complex. Complex in which ligands is (formally) O^{2-} anion.

oxonium compounds. Coordination compounds commonly of certain oxygen-containing organic substances, with mineral acids, of the general type.

$$[R_2O]\ HCl.$$

They bear a strong resemblance to the "oxonium ion," H_3O+, which is a proton, in combination with an H_2O molecule, and is the form in which protons commonly exist in aqueous solution.

oxy. The radical —O— in organic compounds (used as a connective).

oxyazine dye. A dyestuff containing the chromophore, group,

O
R R.
N

oxyazo compounds. Compounds of the type $RN{=}N_6C_4OH$, containing both the azo group —N=N—, and the oxy group (hydroxy group) —OH, both attached to carbon atoms in the same ring. These compounds are commonly produced by the action of diazo compounds upon phenols in alkaline solution. They constitute a class of dyes.

oxygen. An element.

	Symbol	O
	Atomic No.	8
State Gas	Atomic Wt.	15.9994
Group VIA	Valence	2
	Isotopes	3 stable
	Triple point	54.2K
	Boiling point	90.3K

Oxygen about comprises 50% by weight of the earth's crust and oceans and thus is the most abundant terrestrial element, equal to the amount of all the other elements combined. Gaseous oxygen constitutes 21% by volume of the air near the earth's surface, much of which is formed by photosynthesis of plants; water contains 88.8% oxygen by weight. It is vital to all animals and most plants as the supporter of respiration-metabolism processes.

There are three stable isotopes, ^{16}O through ^{18}O. Three radioactive isotopes have been identified, ^{14}O, ^{15}O, and ^{19}O, with short half-lives measured in seconds and minutes.

Though oxygen is the major agency for support or maintenance of combustion of fuels, it is not itself combustible. It is manufactured in large tonnages by fractional distillation of liquefied air for use in the metallurgical industries, in making gas for chemical synthesis and medical applications, and as a rocket fuel (as liquid). In compressed and liquid form, oxygen is stored and shipped in steel cylinders.

First ionization potential 13.614 eV; second, 34.93 *e*V ; third 54.87 *e*V. Oxidation potentials $H_2O_2 \rightarrow O_2 + 2H^+ + 2e^-$, —0.68 V; $3H_2O \rightarrow \frac{1}{2}O_2 + 2H_3O^+$ $(10^{-7}M) + 2e^-$, —0.815 V ; $3H_2O \rightarrow \frac{1}{2}O_2 + 2H^+ + 2e^-$, 1.229 V ; $4H_2O \rightarrow H_2O_2 + 2H_3O^+ + 2e^-$, —1.77 V ; $3H_2O \rightarrow O$ (g) $+ 2H^+ + 2e^-$, — 2.42 V; $HO_2^- + OH^- \rightarrow O_2 + H_2O + 2e^-$, 0.075 V ; $4OH^- \rightarrow O_2 + 2H_2O + 4e^-$, —0.401 V; $3OH^- \rightarrow HO_2^- + H_2O + 2e^-$, —0.87 V; $OH^- \rightarrow OH + e^-$, —1.4 V.

The three known allotropic forms of oxygen are (*i*) the ordinary oxygen in the air, with two atoms per molecuie O_2, (*ii*) ozone O_3 with three atoms per molecule, and (*iii*) the rare, very unstable, nonmagnetic, pale-blue O_4. The latter breaks down readily into two molecules of O_2.

The oxygen molecule is paramagnetic with a moment in accord with two unpaired electrons. In molecular orbital terms, the configuration is written

$$O_2\ [KK(z\sigma)^2\ (y\sigma^*)^2\ (x\sigma)^2\ (w\pi)^4\ (v\pi^*)^2]$$

in which KK designates the completed 1*s* shells of the two atoms, which are non-bonding, the term $(z\sigma)^2$ denotes the O atoms, $(y\sigma^*)^2$ denotes the antibonding effect of the second pair, the $(x\sigma)^2$ term represents the σ-bond formed by one pair of *p*-electrons, $(w\pi)^4$ represents the 2π-bonds formed by the other two pairs of *p*-electrons, while the $(v\pi^*)^2$ term denotes the last pair of *p*-electrons, which go into the next π subshell (two orbitals) with unpaired spins, and are hence antibonding.

Oxygen is a reactive, electronegative element, combining readily with almost all other elements. It forms two covalent bonds and also donates electrons for coordination compounds. Its molecules may be ionized by electric discharge, the ions carrying as many as six positive charges. In animal metabolism, oxygen is transported to the tissues by hemoglobin in the blood.

oxygenase. An enzyme catalyzing a reaction in which oxygen is introduced into an acceptor molecule.

oxygenate. To treat, infuse or combine with oxygen.

oxygen debt. Accumulation of lactic acid in muscles during violent exercise.

oxygen electrode. Electrode (half-cell) consisting of metallic conductor immersed in solution of oxygen and hydroxyl ions, $M, O_2 \mid OH^-$; electrode reactions is

$$4OH^- \rightleftharpoons O_2 + 2H_2O + 4e^-$$

and its potential

$$\epsilon = \epsilon^0 + \frac{RT}{F} \ln \frac{a_{PO_2}^{1/4}}{a_{OH^-}}$$

where ϵ^0= standard electrode potential and a_{PO_2}=volatility of oxygen.

-oyl. A suffix indicating an organic acid radical.

ozocerite. A mixture of hydrocarbons of high molecular weight, probably petrolium residues, occurring in the earth in the vicinity of oil-bearing strata. It is a solid, low-melting material similar to wax (from which the word is derived). When purified, it is known as ceresin wax. It can be used as substitute for more expensive waxes for most of their standard applications.

ozonation. Impregnating or combing with ozone.

ozonide. A compound of ozone with certain unsaturated organic compounds produced by direct addition of ozone of the double bond, *e.g.*,

H H
R—C—O—C—R
O——O

ozonolysis. Degradation (fission) of alkene molecule with formation of carbonyl compounds, effected by ozone and water or any other reducing agent, *e.g.*,

$R^1R^2C{=}CR^3R^4 + O_3 \xrightarrow{CHCl_3}$ [an ozonide] $\xrightarrow{\text{Zn dust or } H_2O_2}$ $R^1R^2C{=}O + O{=}CR^3R^4$

an ozonide

The mechanism of ozonolysis, as suggested by Giegee, is as follows :

ozone
molozonide intermediate
ROH

Ozonolysis can also distinguish cycloalkenes in which both double bonded carbon atoms are part of the same ring from isomers having the double bond outside the ring. In the first case a single ozonolysis product retaining all the carbon atoms of the reactant is formed, and in the second case cleavage at the double bond leads to two smaller fragments. The isomeric pinenes provide a good example of this application :

CH_3 — $\xrightarrow[CHCl_3]{O_3}$ • $\xrightarrow{H_2O_2}$ — CH_3, O, CO_2H

α-pinene — $C_{10}H_{16}O_3$ no loss of carbon

CH_2 — $\xrightarrow[CHCl_3]{O_3}$ • $\xrightarrow{H_2O_2}$ — O + CO_2

β-pinene — $C_9H_{14}O$ loss of one carbon

P

P. Symbol for phosphorus. Abbreviation for pressure. Abbreviation for power. Symbol for electric polarization.

***p*.** Symbol for principal series of spectrum lines. Abbreviation for para, when that prefix is used to designate the relation of the 1 and 4 positions in benzene, or a compound characterized by it, as paraxylene. Symbol for electric moment. Symbol for momentum. Partial potential coefficient. The abbreviation *p* is also used for para when that prefix is used to designate the para-state of an element, as *p*-H.

Paal-Knorr pyrrole synthesis. A method of formation of pyrrole derivatives from 1,4-dicarbonyl compounds and amines (or ammonia.

packing. 1. Any inert material used in absorption, distillation, or rectification columns to baffle the downward flow of countercurrent liquid. It may consist of glass fibre or beads, short pieces of metal tubing, special shapes made of screening or metal, or ceramic forms.

2. A material used in cylinder heads and pipe joints to prevent escape of steam, water, or oil ; it is usually soft enough to conform to the contour of the metals it is intended to seal and thus may be made of a soft metal, plastic, or specially compound rubber (except for oil lines).

packing fraction. An expressson of the fraction by which the atomic weight of an isotope differs from its mass number (defined as the nearest whole number). The actual value of the paking fraction is found by dividing the difference between the isotopic atomic weight and mass number by the mass number, and multiplying by 10,000.

Positive packing fraction values, which are characteristic of unstable elements, occur with mass numbers less than 25 and more than 175 ; negative values occur between mass numbers of 25 and 175. The most unstable element is hydrogen, followed by helium, radium, and uranium. The most stable nuclei occur between mass numbers of 50 and 75. The energy released by the fusion, of hydrogen nuclei to form helium can be predicted from this concept.

paking index. The volume of ion divided by the unit cell in the crystal.

paking radius. One-half of the smallest approach distance of atoms or ions.

paint. A preparation for coating surfaces, for protection. decoration, etc., consisting commonly of finely ground particles of a solid substance or substances, chosen for their stability, colour, and opacity, plus an oil or other substance which dries or oxidizes to form an adherent film ; usually in the presence of ingredients such as solvents, driers, etc. The liquid portion of paint (binder plus solvent) is called the vehicle. Heavy-metal soaps such as cobalt naphthenate are often included to accelerate film formation. Paints containing organic solvents may have a drying oil (linseed or tung) or a synthetic resin (alkyd) as binder, plus pigment. Other colorants such as iron oxide, carbon black, titanium dioxide, or organic pigments may be added for decorative effects. Use of lead compounds is no longer permitted in domestic paints. In emulsion paints, the solvent is water, and the binder an emulsified resin. Acrylic and alkyd resins are widely used in latex emulsion paints for both interior and exterior work. A high-quality binder is essential in exterior paints for weather resistance ; drying is brought about by polymerization induced by atmospheric oxygen after evaporation of solvent.

paint vehicle. The liquid constituent of paint that consists of volatile solvent or thinner and a film-forming material.

paired electrons. Two electrons with different spin functions occupying simultaneously the same atomic or molecular orbital.

pairing energy, *II.* In coordination chemistry, energy necessary for greatest possible pairing of *d*-electrons of central atom.

pair peaks. All the escape peaks generated through annihilation of a positron produced during formation of pairs.

pair production. Formation of particle-antiparticle pair. Process opposite to annihilation, which may occur during collision of particles and lead to formation of baryon-antibaryon or lepton-antilepton pair.

palladium.	An element	Symbol	Pd
		Atomic No.	46
		Atomic Wt.	106.4
State	Solid	Valence	2,3,4
Group	VIII	Isotopes	6 stable
		m.p.	1825K
		b.p.	3412-3414K

A member of the so-called platinum group of melals ; palladium is grayish, comparatively soft, and malleable. Palladium has some similarities with both nickel and silver and to some extent with platinum. Palladium dissolves more readily in acids than any other member of the platinum group of metals. In aqua regia, the melal dissolves quickly. Even the compact metal dissolves slowly in HCl. In finely divided form, it is quite soluble in all acids. When heated in air at red heat, the monoxide, PdO is formed. Palladium is similarly converted to the dihalides under the same conditions when it is exposed to fluorine or chlorine. The metal is not affected by hydrogen sulphide.

Elemental palladium has a face-centered cubic crystal structure. The six stable isotopes of palladium are ^{102}Pd, ^{104}Pd through ^{106}Pd, ^{109}Pd, and ^{110}Pd. The seven unstable isotopes are ^{100}Pd, ^{101}Pd, ^{103}Pd, ^{107}Pd, ^{109}Pd, ^{111}Pd, and ^{112}Pd. In terms of earthly abundance, palladium is one of the scare elements. It is fairly reactive chemically and readily forms metallic complexes. It is widely used (where cost permits) in alloys for special electrical systems. Palladium supported on carbon or alumina is used as a catalyst in a number of chemical processes including hydrogenation in liquid and gas-phase reactions.

Paneth rule. Adsorption of radio-elements is promoted by formation of an insoluble compound with the adsorbing substance, especially when the radio-element is present in a negative radical.

Paneth and Hevesy method. Method of determination of critical potential of deposition or decomposition voltage during electrolysis of extremely diluted solutions based on direct measurement of rate of formation of substance at electrode.

pantachromism. The phenomenon of existing in two or more differently coloured varieties. For example, salts of diphenylvioluric acid exhibit pantochromism.

paper chromatography. A type of chromatography in which the mobile phase is liquid and the stationary phase is a strip of porous paper. A drop of the mixture is placed at one edge of the paper and eluted with the solvent. The components are separated by the rates at which they move across the paper with the solvent. Identification can be done by indicators or by their fluorescence in ultraviolet radiation.

paper electrophoresis. A variation of paper chromatography in which an electric current is applied to the ends of the electrolyte impregnated absorbent paper, thus moving chargeable molecules of the unknown sample toward the respective electrodes.

papite. A poisonous gas consisting of acrolein and stannic chloride.

para-. A prefix used to distinguish between isomers or nearly related compounds. Specifically, (*i*) in organic chemistry the derivatives of cyclic nuclei which contain substituents in the 1-4 position ; (*ii*) some polymers are designated by the prefix para-, as paraldehyde ; (*iii*) in certain acids which have several forms differing in water content, one of the forms may be designated by the prefix para-.

parachor, *P.* Property defined by formula :

$$P=MC^{1/4}=\left(\frac{M}{\rho_l-\rho_v}\right)\sigma^{1/4}=V_m\sigma^{1/4}$$

where M = molar mass, σ = surface tension, ρ_l=density of liquid, ρ_v = density of vapour, Vm = molar volume of liquid, C=characteristic constant independent of temperature for substances not undergoing association. Constant C for associating liquids increases with increase in temperature. Parachor is additive quantity, *i.e.*, it is sum of atomic, bond and ring parachors.

paracyclophanes. Carbocyclic compounds containing two benzene rings linked at para-positions by saturated carbon chains, thus forming ring system of general formula (I), *e.g.*, bi-*p*-xylylene (II) :

$(CH_2)_m$ $(CH_2)_n$ I

H_2C CH_2 H_2C CH_2 II

paraffins. 1. A major group of aliphatic hydrocarbons derived from petroleum ; they may be either straight- or branched-chain ; the term alkane is also applied to this group. Paraffins are saturated hydrocarbons with the generic formula C_nH_{2n+2}; the simplest is methane, CH_4 followed in homologous series by ethane, C_2H_6, propane, C_3H_8, and butane, C_4H_{10}. The structure of *n*-propane, for example, would appears as :

```
  H  H  H
  |  |  |
H—C—C—C—H
  |  |  |
  H  H  H
```

Thus, every paraffin molecule except methane (CH_4) has a CH_3 or methyl group at both ends. In general paraffins are not as reactive as olefins, though substitution of other element or groups readily occurs along the carbon chain : the term is derived from Latin words meaning "very little affinity". The hydrocarbon chain may be extremely long, with correspondingly high molecular weight ; for example, paraffin wax, the distillation end product of aliphatic petroleum, has a chain composed of 36 carbon atoms. Isomeric branched-chain paraffins such as iso-octane are used in gasoline ; the straight-chain types are unsuitable for gasoline but are used in diesel fuels.

2. A white wax of high molecular weight ($C_{36}H_{74}$) derived from aliphatic types of petroleum as a distillation end-product.

parallel band. In vibration spectra band corresponding to vibration with transition dipole moment parallel to molecular symmetry axis.

parallelosterism. A relationship between analogous and isomorphous groups in which similar differences in chemical composition occur with similar differences in molecular volume. Thus the difference in the molar volumes of KCl and KBr is 6.9, between NaCl and NaBr, 6.7, and between AgCl and AgBr, 6.2.

parrallel reactions. System of two or more elementary reactions proceeding simultaneously with one or more common . substrates which changed into different products, *e.g.*,

$$A \rightarrow X,\quad A \rightarrow Y,\quad A \rightarrow Z$$

Also known as simultaneous reactions ; competing reactions.

paramagnetic. Offering less resistance to the passage of magnetic flux than does air, and hence capable of being attracted by a magnet. Paramagnetic substances have, in other words, magnetic permeabilities greater than 1.

They are divided into normal paramagnets, whose magnetic susceptibility satisfies Curie-Weiss law, and metallic paramagnets, whose magnetic susceptibilities slightly increase or decrease with temperature.

paramagnetic element. An element having a magnetic moment greater than unity, which is the value for air.

paramagnetic curie point, θ. Constant, in kelvins, entering Curie-Weiss law positive for ferromagnets and, in general, negative for anti-ferromagnets, provided they satisfy Curie-Weiss law above Curie or Neel temperature, respectively. Also konwn as asymptotic Curie point.

paramagnetic shielding of nucleus. Participation of electrons in magnetic shielding of nucleus leading to chemical shifts of nuclear magnetic resonance in direction of lower static fields or higher frequency alternating magnetic fields. Also known as paramagnetic screening of nucleus.

paramagnetic susceptibility, χ. Positive contribution to magnetic susceptibility of paramagnets. In alternating magnetic field paramagnetic susceptibility becomes complex quantity $\chi=\chi' + i\chi''$, where χ' = real part, χ'' = imaginary part.

paramagnetism. A property exhibited by substances which, when placed in a magnetic field, are magnetized parallel to the field to an extent proportional to the field (except at very) low temperatures or in extremely large magnetic fields. Substance possessing a magnetic permeability slightly greater than unity, *i.e.*, possessing a small positive magnetic susceptibility, are said to be paramagnetic. The atoms of a paramagnetic substance possess a permanent magnetic moment due to unbalanced electron spins or unbalanced orbital motions of the electrons around the nucleus.

paramorph. One of two or more forms of a substance which have the same chemical composition but differ in certain properties.

parasitic ferromagnetism. Weak ferromagnetism of antiferromagnets which diplay small deviations from colinearity of magnetic moments of sublattices.

parasiticide. A substance which kills parisitic organisms.

parent ion. Positive ion formed by detachment of electron in interaction of ionizing radiation with molecule or atom.

parent nuclide. Radioactive nuclide from which another nuclide is formed by decay. Also known as nuclear parent.

parhelium. One group or system of terms in the spectrum of helium that is due to atoms in which the spin of the two electrons are opposing each other. Another group of spectral terms, the orthohelium terms, is given by those helium atoms whose two electrons have parallel spins.

parity, *P*. Quantum number ascribed to particles of integral quantum spin number (photons and mesons), which gives behaviour of wave function for particle undergoing coordinate inversion. If wave function does not change, $P = 1$, but if sign is changed, $P = -1$.

parity conservation law. In strong and electromagnetic interactions, parities of system of initial and final particles in given process are equal. Parity conservation law is not observed in weak interactions.

Parke process. A process for the separation of silver from lead. This process is used extensively in the recovery of silver in the refining of argentiferous lead ores. The process is based on the fact that silver is far more soluble in zinc than in lead, whereas zinc is but very slightly soluble in molten lead. Zinc is added to the silver-containing molten lead, thorough'y mixed, and allowed to stand, whereupon the zinc containing the silver floats to the surface of the molten lead, and is separated. Later the silver is separated from the zinc-silver by distilling off the zinc.

parkerising. A method of protecting iron from corrosion by forming a phosphate film on its surface. The article is immersed in a bath of hot orthophosphoric acid that also contains orthophosphates of the heavy metals. Such coatings are unaffected by expansion or contraction of the metal and form an excellent base for paint.

partial heat of dilution. Enthalpy change of system in process of adding one mole of solvent to such a large bulk of solution of a given concentration that it may be assumed in practice that its concentration remains unaffected. Also known as differential heat of dilution.

partial heat of solution. Enthalpy change of system in process of dissolving one mole of a given substance in such a large bulk of solution of a given concentration that it may be assumed in practice that its concentration remains unaffected. Also known as differential heat of solution.

partially eclipsed conformation, ±ac. Conformation in which the most bulky substituents at two adjacent carbon (or any other element, *e.g.*, silicium or nitrogen) atom are eclipsed by smaller substituents. In Newman's projection formula, bond angles of less remote and more remote substituents equal 0°. This type of conformation is less stable than fully staggered conformation, but more stable than eclipsed :

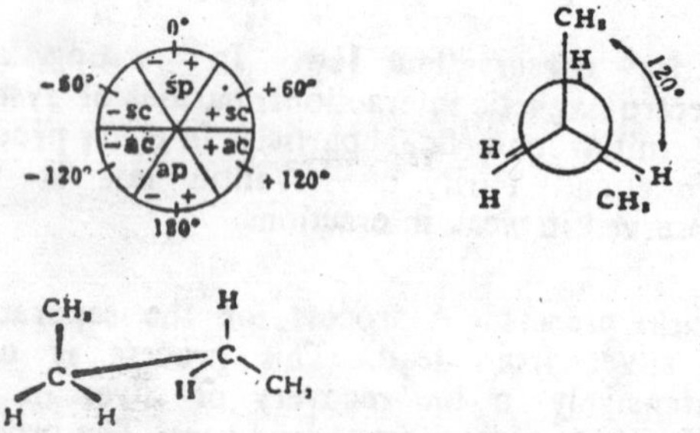

0° −60° sp +60° −sc +sc −ac +ac −120° ap +120° 180°

CH_3 H 120° H H CH_3

CH_3 H C C H H H CH_3

Also known as partly eclipsed conformation ; anti-clinal conformation.

partial miscibility. Ability of mixture to undergo mixing in limited proportion. Also known as limited compatibility.

partial molal volume (of component B), V_B. Intensive quantity, defined by

$$V_B = \left(\frac{\partial V}{\partial n_B}\right)_{T, p, n_c}$$

where n_B = number of moles of component B in a given phase, n_C = number of moles of other components in this phase, V = phase volume, T = thermodynamic temperature, and p = pressure.

partial molar quantities Z_B. Intensive quantities defined by

$$Z_B = \left(\frac{\partial Z}{\partial n_B}\right)_{T, p, n_c}$$

where Z = extensive fuction of state of a given phase, n_B = number of moles of component B in this phase, n_C= number of moles of all remaining components in this phase, T= thermodynamic temperature, p=pressure. Also known as partial molal quantities of component B.

partial pressure, p_B. Intensive thermodynamic function $p_B = x_B p$, where x_B=mole fraction of component B and p=pressure in a given phase.

particle. A term used to refer to individual aggregates of matter having characteristic properties and structure. They include fundamental particles (electrons, protons, and neutrons) ; atoms and ions (atomic weights from 1 to 259) ; molecules (molecular weights from 2 to several thousand) ; macromolecules (weights from about 20,000 to 40 million) ; colloids, carbon black, and up to palpable sizes such as dust, flour, sand, etc. The activity of electrons, protons atoms, and ions is primarily chemical and electrical : from colloidal through optically visible sizes, their behavior becomes increasingly physical. Particle size and shape are critical factors in catalysis, reinforcement, coloration, combustion, etc.

particle energy. Kinetic energy of fast particle (*e.g.*, in beam of ionizing radiation), expressed in electron volts and in SI system in joules.

particle production. Process occurring during collision of high energy particles and leading to formation of other particles.

partition. A term which describes a solvent system in which the solute is divided between two components of the liquid phase, the ratio of their concentrations (partition coefficient) being constant for a given substance. Such a system might be comprised of a solute such as a macromolecular substance (dextran), a low percentage of a polyol (polyethylene glycol), and water. Since the liquids are not miscible, they separate into two layers, the solute being distributed between them in concentrations that vary for different materials, *e.g.*, enzymes, proteins, glucose polymers, etc. Separation or fractionation of the macromolecules can be carried out by several procedures, including partition chromatography.

partition chromatography. Chromatography employing stationary phase, which consists of thin layer of liquid retained on solid support.

partition coefficient. *See* distribution coefficient.

partition function, $Q(T, V, N)$. Function used to express thermodynamic quantities in terms of intermolecular interactions :

$$Q(T, V, N) = \int \exp\left[-\frac{1}{kT}\sum_{i=j} \epsilon(r_{ij})\right] \prod_{i=1}^{N} d^3 x_i$$

where k=Boltzmann constant, T=thermodynamic temperature of N-particle system in equilibrium volume V, d^3x = volume element, r_{ij}=distance beween i-th and j-th particle, and $\epsilon(r)$=inter molecular potential. Also known as configurational partition function ; configurational integral.

Paschen-Back effect. Splitting of energy levels in very strong magnetic fields with mutually independent orientation of angular and spin momenta with respect to magnetic field.

Paschen series. A series of lines in the infrared region of the emission spectrum of atomic hydrogen. The wave numbers of the lines in this series are given by the relationship :

$$\bar{\nu} = R_H\left(\frac{1}{n_1^2} - \frac{1}{n_2^2}\right)$$

where $\bar{\nu}$=the wave number in reciprocal centimeters, R_H = the Rydberg constant, $n_1 = 3$, and n_2 has various integral values.

Passerini reaction. A method of synthesis of aromatic amides of α-acyloxy acids, using aromatic isonitriles, organic acids, and carbonyl compounds :

$$\begin{matrix} R \\ | \\ C{=}O \\ | \\ R' \end{matrix} + Ar{-}N{\equiv}C + R''COOH \rightarrow \begin{matrix} R \\ | \\ R'{-}C{-}C{-}NHAr \\ |\quad\ \| \\ O\quad O \\ | \\ R''C{=}O \end{matrix}$$

$$\xrightarrow{H_2O} \begin{matrix} R \\ | \\ R'{-}C{-}C{-}NH{-}Ar \\ |\quad\ \| \\ HO\quad O \end{matrix} + R''COOH$$

passivity. A term used in chemistry to denote decrease of the reactivity of a metal in an electrochemical system or in a corrosive environment, usually as a result of the formation of an oxide film on its surface. One example of passivity is furnished by immersing iron in nitric acid ; the oxidizing action ends abruptly, and the iron is not further attacked. Another instance is the oxide coating of copper anodes during electrolysis. Passivity is inhibited or destroyed in a reducing environment, or in the presence of halogen ions.

pasteurization. Heat treatment of liquid or semiliquid food products for the purpose of killing or inactivating disease-causing bacteria. It is legally required for milk in most areas, as tuberculosis bacilli from infected cows at one time were a threat to public health. Milk is held at about 340K for half-an hour in the high-temperature short-time method, milk must be heated to 340K, held at that temperature for 15 seconds, and promptly cooled to low temperature (about 275-280 K). The process is also applied to fruit juices. Pasteurization of egg products at 330K for only 3.5 minutes has been mandatory.

Patera process. A metallurgical process for the recovery of silver from its ores by first converting the silver into the insoluble chloride by heating with chlorides, leaching out the soluble chlorides with water, removing the silver by leaching with a hyposulphide from that solution for reduction to the metal.

pathotoxin. A chemical of biological origin, other than an enzyme, that plays an important role in plant disease. Most pathotoxins are produced by plant pathogenic fungi or bacteria but some are produced by higher plants.

pathway. A sequence of reactions, usually of a

biochemical nature, in which more complex substances are converted to simple end products, as in the degradation of the components of foods to carbon dioxide and water. Its course is largely determined by preferential factors involving coenzymes and other catalysis ; for example the TCA, or Krebs cycle.

Pattinson's process. A method of desilverising lead, but this is not so much used nowadays. It takes advantage of the fact that if a very dilute solution of silver in lead is cooled, pure lead crystallises first, leaving the mother liquor richer in silver. A continuous repetition of the prcoess may bring the silver content up to 2%, after which it may be cupelled. The laborious application of this principle, using rows of now little used.

Pauli exclusion principle. In system of identical fermions each quantum mechanical state can be occupied at most by single fermion, *i.e.*, it is impossible for two electrons in the same atom to have the same value for all four quantum numbers ; two electrons occupy the same orbital only if they have opposite spin, or direction of rotation, *i.e.*, $+\frac{1}{2}$ and $-\frac{1}{2}$. This principle explains the arragement of elements in the Periodic Table and accounts for the maximum number of electrons that can occur in the seven shells, *i.e.*, 2 in the first, 8 in the second 18 in the third, and 32 in the fourth Also known as exclusion principle.

Pauling's electronegativity scale. Ordering of atoms according to increasing electronegativity computed from Pauling's definition.

Pavy solution. A test reagent for glucose, prepared either by adding an aqueous solution of sodium and ammonium hydroxides to Fehling solution ; or by mixing an aqueous solution of cupric sulphate with an aqueous solution of Rochelle salt, ammonium hydroxide, and potassium hydroxide ; or (in a two-solution form), by preparing separate solutions of cupric sulphate, and of Rochelle salt, potassium hydroxide, and ammonium hydroxide.

Payne process. A process for the impregnation of wood with iron and calcium salts by treating it with solutions of ferrous sulphate and calcium chloride, commonly to render it resistant to attack by minute animals or fire.

P-branch. In rotation-oscillation band, set of transitions corresponding to change of rotational quantum by —1.

peak resolution. Quantity describing degree of separation of two chromatographic peaks.

pearlite. A macroconstituent of iron or steel consisting of alternate layers of ferrite and cementite.

peat. The semicarbonized remains of plants formed in bogs and marshes. It occurs in surface layers from 3 to 10 feet thinck. It has a water content of up to 80%, which is reduced to about 35% by drying. The dried product must be protected from autoignition when stored. Peat is easily converted to hydrocarbons and is a good source of gaseous fuel; it can be burned directly after through drying. Sources in the U.S. are chiefly in the north central states and Alaska. Besides gas, substantial amounts of oil, ammonia, and sulphur are obtainable as by-products.

Pechmann condensation. The formation of coumarin derivatives by condensation of phenols with *β*-keto esters or similar compounds, *e.g.*,

$$C_6H_5OH + CH_2(COOC_2H_5)(COCH_3) \rightarrow C_6H_4(OH)\text{-}C(OH)(CH_3)\text{-}CH_2\text{-}COOC_2H_5 \xrightarrow[-C_2H_5OH]{-H_2O} \text{4-methylcoumarin } (CH_3)$$

Pechmann coumarin synthesis. *See* Pechmann condensation.

Pechmann pyrazole synthesis. Direct union of acetylenes and dioxomethane to give pyrazoles.

pectic acids. A term applied to pectic substances mostly composed of colloidal polygalacturonic acids and essentially free from methyl ester groups. The salts of pectic acids are either normal or acid pectates.

pectic substances. A group designation for those complex, colloidal carbohydrate derivatives which occur in, or are prepared from, plants and contain a large proportion of anhydrogalacturonic acid units that are through to exist in a chain-like combination. The carboxyl groups of polygalacturonic acids may be partly esterified by methyl groups and partly or completely neutralized by one or more bases.

pectin. A group of polysaccharides occurring in cell walls and intercellular layers of all land plants. They are extractable with hot water, dilute acids and are capable of forming gels with sugar and acid under suitable conditions.

pectinic acids. A term used for colloidal polygalacturonic acids containing more than a negligible proportion of methyl ester groups. Pectinic acids, under suitable conditions, are capable of forming gels with sugar and acid, or, if suitably low in methoxyl content, with certain metallic ions. The salts of pectinic acids are either normal or acid pectinates.

pectise. To gelate or gelatinize.

Pedersen process. A process for producing alumina, in which bauxite, lime, iron ore, and coke are smelted to yield by-product iron and a low-silica calcium aluminate slag, which is leached with a dilute sodium carbonate solution and the resulting sodium aluminate solution is carbonated with carbon dioxide to precipitate aluminum hydroxide (yielding alumina on dehydration) and to regenerate the sodium carbonate solution. The process has been modified by using, as raw materials, clay and limestone, which, on sintering, yield calcium aluminate and dicalcium silicate, and then recovering alumina from the sinter by a method similar to Pedersen's.

Pedretti tests for hair dye intermediates. Many of the intermediates used in hair dyes give characteristic colours with (*i*) dilute sodium nitrite solution followed by hydrochloric acid, and (*ii*), potassium hypochlorite solution followed by hydrochloric acid.

P-electron. An electron having an orbit of such dimensions that the electron constitutes part of the sixth shell of electrons surrounding the atomic nucleus, counting out from the nucleus (*i.e.*, the K-shell is the first; the L-, the second; the M-, the third; the N-, the fourth; the O-, the fifth; and the P-shell, the sixth).

Pelouze synthesis. A method for the formation of nitriles from alkyl sulphates and potassium cyanide.

$$RSO_4K + KCN \rightarrow RCN + K_2SO_4$$

penetration. 1. In general, the process of entering, saturating or piercing.

2. The passage of particles or radiation through solids.

3. The consistency of a material in terms of the depth it is entered by a standard needle under standard conditions.

penetration complex. Complex of generally covalent character which does not decompose in solution, *e.g.*, $[Fe(CN)_6]^{4-}$, $[Co(NH_3)_6]^{3+}$.

penfield scale. A series of integral numbers used to designate materials, chiefly minerals, according to their fusibility—the higher numbers corresponding to higher fusing points. The substance whose fusing point (melting points) constitute the integral values on the scale are: (*i*) stibnite, (*ii*) chalcopyrite, (*iii*) almandite, (*iv*) actinolite, (*v*) orthoclase, (*vi*) bronzite (*vii*) infusible.

pentolite. An highly explosive mixture of pentaerythritol tetranitrate and trinitrotoluene in equal quantities.

pentosan. One of a group of carbohydrates which, on hydrolysis, yield pentoses, as cherry gum while yields *l*-arabinose. They are classed as polysaccharides.

pepsin. A digestive enzyme produced in the stomach that converts proteins into peptone in it acts only in an acidic medium.

peptidase. An enzyme that attacks peptide linkages and splits off amino acids.

peptization. The stabilization of colloidal solutions (called sols) by means of a so-called electric layer of adsorbed ions, derived either from a small amount of added electrolyte (peptizing agent) or from water (hydroxyl ions). This results in a liquefying or softening action; the term peptization was applied to it by analogy with the digestive action of pepsin on proteins. It is considered to be a form of aggregation.

peptone. A secondary protein derivative that is

water-soluble, not coagulated by heat, and not precipitated on saturation of its solutions with ammonium sulphate.

peptonization. Conversion into peptones.

per-. Complete, thorough, extreme ; the prefix specifically denoting : (*i*) a compound containing an element in the highest (or a high) state of oxidation, as perchloric acid, manganese peroxide (better, dioxide (*ii*) presence of —O—O group, as barium peroxide, perbenzoic acid, peracid (better peroxy acid) ; (*iii*) exhaustive substitution or addition, as perchloroethylene, C_2Cl_4 : perhydronaphthalene, $C_{10}H_{18}$. In naming halogenated organic compounds or groups, the terms "perbromo," "perchloro," "perfluoro," and "periodo" denote substitution of all hydrogen atoms attached to carbon atoms except those whose substitution would affect the nature of the functional groups present. "Per" may refer to the whole word or to part of the word to which it is attached, but not to more than one word. Parentheses are used where necessary to avoid ambiguity as to whether "per" refers to part of a name or to a whole name. Examples : $C_6F_{11}CF_3$, perfluoro (methylcyclohexane) ; C_3F_7CHO, perfluorobutyraldehyde: $C_2H_5CO_2C_4Cl_9$, perchlorobutyl propionate : $CBr_3CBr_2CH{=}NOH$, perbromopropionaldoxime ;

$$(CCl_3)_2CCl(CCl_2)_3CCl_3,$$

perchloro(2-methylhexane) ; $C_6H_5C_5Cl_{11}$, (perchloropentyl)benzene.

An inorganic compound comprised of three elements, in which the central element is in its maximum oxidation state ; for example, in potassium permanganate ($KMnO_4$) the oxidation states of the three elements are +1 for potassium, +7 for manganese, and —2 for oxygen. Some acids fall into this group, *i.e.*, perchloric, permanganic, and periodic ; these should not be confused with the oxygen acids.

per-acids. 1. Oxy-acids in which $[O{-}O]^{2-}$ or $[O{-}OH]^-$ groups have replaced oxide in oxyanions (compound containing the superoxide ion $[O_2]^-$ are formally not per-acids but the distinction is often difficult to make). The O—O group may be bonded end on [M—O—O] or symmetrically [M ← O].

                                                    |
                                                    O

Prepared by the use of H_2O_2 or by electrolytic oxidation. It may be noted that permanganates, perchlorates and periodates are not are of much importance. Of the organic peracids, perbenzoic is quite stable and converts olefines to epoxide, which on hydrolysis yield *trans*-glycols. Perethanioic and permethanoic acids give glycol monoesters with olefines.

percarbonates. Carbonates with varying amounts of H_2O_2 of crystallization are stable as solids and $2Na_2CO_3{\cdot}3H_2O_2$ is used in laundering and for cleaning dentures.

percolation. A process for the continuous extraction of soluble matter from its admixture with insoluble material by a suitable solvent conducted in such a way that the solvent travels through the mass to be extracted, from one surface of which the partially saturated solution is removed while fresh solvent is admitted at the opposite surface.

percrystallization. The crystallization of a dissolved substance from a solution, during or after dialysis.

perfect. This term is used in chemistry in several senses. (*i*) In reference to gases, it describes a theoretically ideal gas, which behaves in accordance with Boyle's law ; in reality there is no such gas. *See* ideal.

(*ii*) In reference to elasticity it describes a substance which recovers completely after application of stress, for exmple, glass ; it also is used to denote atomic and molecular collisions in which there is no gain or loss of energy as a result of impact.

(*iii*) As applied to crystals, it means that all lattice locations ore occupied by the atoms or ions required by the nature of the molecule, and by no others.

perfect crystal. *See* perfect.

perfect gas. *See* perfect ; ideal gas.

perfect gaseous mixture. Mixture in which chemical potential of each component is equal to chemical potential of this component in state of pure ideal gas at the some temperature and pressure as mixture. Also known as multicomponent ideal gas.

perfect gas laws. Empirical laws established for so-called stable gases by Boyle and Mariotte, Gay-Lussac, Charles, Avogadro, Dalton, and Amagat ; set of these laws describes properties of perfect gases.

perfume. Any of a wide range of liquids having an intense, pleasant smell and derived by steam distillation or extraction with solvents from essential oils occurring in flowers, or sometimes from other parts of the plant. The selection and blending of these is an ancient art.

perhalo. In naming halogenated organic compounds or groups, the term perhalo denotes substitution of all hydrogen atoms attached to carbon atoms except those whose substitution would affect the nature of the functional groups present. "Per" may refer to the whole word or to part of the word to which it is attached, but not to more than one word. Parenthese are used where necessary to avoid ambiguity as to whether "per" refers to part of a name or to a whole name. ; for example, C_3F_7CHO, perfluorobutyraldehyde ; C_6H_6, perfluorobenzene ; C_6H_5COOH, perfluorobenzoicacid.

peri-. (Greek, around, about) A perfix indicating (*i*) the relation between positions 1 and 8 of naphthalene ; (*ii*) in polycyclic ring systems, fusion of a ring to two or more adjoining rings, as peri-dinitronaphthalene.

pericyclic reaction. A reaction which appears to proceed by a simultaneous or concerted making and breaking of two or more covalent bonds, often to stereospecific products. Many of such reactions take place under milder conditions. Reactions of this kind usually have transition status involving a cyclic interchange of bonds around a ring of atoms, *e.g.*,

sunlight →

pericyclo. A term proposed by Bredig for a valence bond extending partly around a ring, as in the case of the position (or linkage) *a—b* in R-hexane derivatives, *viz.*,

a | | b
HC—CH——CH
C(CH₃)₂
H₂C—C——CH₂
CH₃

perikinetic aggregation. Coagulation that occurs due to collision of particles caused only by Brownian movement. Also known as perikinetic flocculation.

period. In periodic system, horizontal series of elements showing regular changes in properties; ordinal number of period corresponds to particular value of main quantum number ; in conventional periodic system period begins with an alkali metal and ends with a noble gas.

periodic. A term which has the same spelling two quite different meanings and pronunciation (*i*) When divided pe-ri-od-ic, it describes a quality, condition, or action that repeats itself at regular intervals, for example, the periodic nature of the chemical elements, or periodic temperature increase. (*ii*) When divided per-i-o-dic, it refers to an iodine compound in which the iodine is in its highest oxidation state, *i.e.*, +7. *See also* Periodic classification ; per-.

Periodic law. One of the most important generalizations in the history of chemistry. Essentially it states that the arrangement of electrons in the atoms of the chemical elements and the properties determined by this arrangement (bonding, reactivity, etc.) are closely related to the atomic number, and that the arrangement changes in a regularly repeated (periodic) sequence as the atomic number increases from one element to the next. This law is the basis of the Periodic Table.

periodic classification. A systematic classification of the chemical elements based on the Periodic Law ; it was originally worked out by the Russian chemist, Dmitri Mendeleev in 1869 by listing the then-known elements in the order of increasing atomic weight. It was later modified by the English physicist, Henry G.J. Moseley, and others, who showed that the periodicity actually depends on the atomic number. Thus, the location of an element in the periodic table is an indication of its electronic structure and chemical properties ; elements having a similar electronic pattern occur on a regularly repeating (periodic) basis. There are seven horizontal divisions, called periods, containing, respectively, 2, 8, 8, 18, 18, 32, and 19 , elements, (Elements 93-106 are synthetic radioactive elements of the transuranic series.) Each period begins with an element having one outermost electron and ends with one having eight outermost electrons (except helium). The vertical divisions of the table comprise nine major groups I through VII are divided into two subgroups designated A and B. Thus, Group IA is a vertical series of univalent, reactive elements, while those in the last (noble) group are inert, or nearly so, the first three having zero valence. Many variations of the table have been proposed and used ; in that now widely approved the groups are as follows :

IA IIA IIIB IVB VB VIB VIIB VIII IB IIB IIIA IVA VA VIA VIIA Noble gases. Also known as periodic system.

periodicity. The recurrence of an event, phenomenon, or characteristic feature at regular intervals of time, distance, or other variable, specifically the variation of the physical or chemical properties of an element in relation to its atomic number, as shown by its position in the periodic system.

peritectic point. Incongruent melting point identical with discontinuity on liquidus curve.

peritectic process. Process of melting of polyconstituent phase in which both liquid phase and another solid phase are formed ; new phases are of different chemical composition.

Perkin, Jr. reaction. A reaction between the sodium compound of either acetoacetic ester or malonic ester and a dibromide (as ethylene dibromide) which results in the formation of a cyclic compound, *e.g.*,

$$\begin{matrix} CH_2Br \\ | \\ | \\ CH_2Br \end{matrix} + \begin{matrix} COOEt \\ | \\ Na_2C \\ | \\ COOEt \end{matrix} \rightarrow \begin{matrix} CH_2 \\ | \\ CH_2 \end{matrix} \!\!>\! C \!<\! \begin{matrix} COOEt \\ \\ COOEt \end{matrix} + 2NaBr.$$

Perkin reaction. A condensation reaction between sodium salts of carboxylic acids and aldehydes, usually in the presence of acid anhydrides, resulting in the formation of an unsaturated carboxylic acid, for example ;

$$C_6H_5CHO + (CH_3CO)_2O \xrightarrow{CH_3COOK} C_6H_6CH{=}CHCOOH + CH_3COOH$$

Perkin rearrangement. A reaction of 3-halocoumarins with alkali to yield benzofuran-2 carboxylic acids.

Perkin synthesis of alicyclic compounds. A method of formation of alicyclic compounds from dihalogenated compounds and compounds containing active methylene groups :

$$\begin{matrix} CHBr.R' \\ | \\ CH_2 \\ | \\ CHBr.R'' \end{matrix} + CH_2(COOC_2H_5)_2 + 2NaOC_2H_5 \rightarrow CH_2 \begin{matrix} CHR' \\ \\ CHR'' \end{matrix} C(COOC_2H_5)_2 + 2NaBr + 2C_2H_5OH.$$

Perkov reaction. Preparation of O,O-dialkyl-O-vinylphosphoranes by treating α-haloaldehydes, α-haloketones or α-haloesters with trialkyl phosphites, *e.g.*,

$$(CH_3O)P + ClCH_2CHO \rightarrow (CH_3O)\overset{+}{P}{-}\underset{\underset{O}{|}}{CH}{-}\dot{C}H_2{-}Cl$$

$$\rightarrow (CH_3O)_2\overset{\delta\oplus}{P} \cdots \overset{\delta\ominus}{O} \cdots CH \; (O{-}CH_3,\; CH_2{-}Cl) \xrightarrow{-CH_3Cl}$$

$$(CH_3O)_2\underset{\underset{O}{\|}}{P}{-}O{-}CH{=}CH_2$$

permafil. A mixture in which the liquid completely undergoes polymerization and hardens without any evaporation.

permanent dipole. Electric dipole existing independently of presence of external electric field.

permanent gases. An historic classfication that included those gases which are very difficult to liquefy and which were thought to be non-liquefiable. The distinction has vanished since all the gases have been liquefied beacase of the advance in low temperature techniques.

permanent hardness. The presence in water of certain chiefly sulphates or carbonates of calcium or magnesium, which can not be removed by boiling, and require chemical treatment of the water (or its passage through ion-exchange media) to prevent scale formation in boilers. the precipitation of soap, and other undesired effects.

permeability. 1. The capacity of a membrane or other material to allow another substance to penetrate or pass through it ; or specifically, the quantity of a specified gas or other substance which passes through under specified conditions.

2. Magnetic permeability is the value of the total magnetic induction in a unit field.

permease. Any of a group of enzymes which mediate the phenomenon of active transport.

permendur. A magnetic alloy composed of equal parts of iron and cobalt and has an extremely high permeability when saturated.

permenorm alloy. An alloy containing equal amounts of nickel and iron ; used as magnetic core material and in magnetic amplifiers.

permittivity, ε. Ratio of dielectric shift and electric field strength in dielectric or ratio of capacity of condenser filled with given dielectric to that of empty one. Also known as electric permittivity.

permittivity of free space, ε_0. In SI units ε_0= 8.855.10^{-12} F/m (previously in CGS electrostatic units $\varepsilon_0=1$).

permutation. A term used in some cases and by writers as equivalent to transmutation and by others for chemical substitution.

peroxidase. One of a class of enzymes that activate hydrogen peroxide, and probably other peroxides, and catalyze oxidation reactions that do not proceed with appreciable velocity in their absence.

peroxide. The anion O_2^{2-} or HO_2^-, or a compound containing one of these anions.

peroxy-. A prefix denoting presence of the peroxide group, —O—O— as peroxymonosulphuric acid, $HOSO_2OOH$ (now considered preferable to per- in this sense).

perpendicular band. In vibration spectra band corresponding to rotation-vibration transition with transition dipole moment perpendicular to molecular symmetry axis.

perpetuum mobile of the first kind. Heat engine could perform cyclic process and could do work during this process without accepting any energy ; such an engine cannot exist according to the first law of thermodynamics.

perpetuum mobile of the second kind. Heat engine which could perform cyclic process with energy accepted in form of heat from bath of constant (positive) thermodynamic temperature and returned quantitatively in form of work ; such an engine cannot exist according to the second law of thermodynamics.

Perrin determination of the Avogadro number. A method of determination of the Avogadro number, based upon the distribution of colloidal particles, subject to the Brownian movement, of known mass and density, at two different levels in a suspension in equilibrium with gravity. From a series of experiments made with mastic and gamboge suspensions, over a wide range of particle sizes, values of Avogadro's number lying consistently between 6.5 × 10^{23} and 7.3 × 10^{23} were obtained.

Perrin rule. A generalization derived from certain results on electroosmosis, to the effect that ions of charge opposite to that of the diaphragm have by far the greatest effect upon endosmosis, and that the higher their valence (if it is of opposite sign) the greater the reduction of electro-osmotic flow.

Persoz reagent. A mixture of zinc chloride and zinc oxide in water ; used to detect the presence of silk with wool (only silk dissolves in it).

perspective formula. Formula portraying three-dimentional model of molecule as simplified perspective drawing with all interatomic bonds and distances, *e.g.*, formula of chair or boat forms of cyclic compounds, or sawhorse formula of open-chain compounds.

persulphide. A sulphide which contains a larger proportion of sulphur than is necessary to satisfy the highest ; as FeS_2.

pervaporation. Evaporation through a semi-permeable membrane.

pervious. Permitting the passage of radiations or substances commonly liquids, or gases. The negative term, impervious, is more frequently used.

pesticide. A broad term that includes all chemical agents used to kill animal and vegetable life which interferes with agricultural productivity; thus, insecticides, herbicides, herpicides, fungicides, and rodenticides are special types of pesticides, regardless of their mode of action. Fumigants, used in orchards and on stored grain, which are toxic to bacteria as well as to animals, also may be considered pesticides. All pesticides are poisonous in varying degress when ingested directly, and care should be used in their handling and application. The most hazardous are those in the parathion groups ; next in order are chlorinated hydrocarbons. The chief risks from pesticide intake are exposure during application and accidental ingestion, rather than from intake of residues on agricultural products.

Peterson reagent. Two solutions used in testing for tartrates and citrates. They are : (*i*) an aqueous solution of 0.116 *g.* sodium salicylate made up to 1 litre ; and (*ii*) a solution of 1 ml. 10% ferric chloride solution in 50 ml. water, alkalized with ammonium hydroxide until the precipitate just redissolves, then 1 drop acetic acid is added, and the volume made up to 100 ml. with water. On testing with these solutions, citrates and tartrates give a violet colour or; in small concentrations, an opalescence.

Petrenko-Kritshenko piperidone synthesis. A method of formation of piperidones by condensation of esters of acetone dicarboxylic acid with aldehydes and primary amines, *e.g.*,

$$ROOC{-}CH_2{-}\overset{\overset{O}{\|}}{C}{-}CH_2{-}COOR + R'{-}CHO + R'CHO + R''NH_2 \xrightarrow{-2H_2O}$$

(4-piperidone ring: C=O at top, flanked by ring carbons bearing ROOC and COOR, then carbons bearing R' and R', ring N bearing R'')

petrochemical. A chemical intermediate obtained directly from petroleum or natural gas by cracking or pyrolysis, or an end-product derived by subsequent chemical processing. The term is so general that its usefulness has been questioned by some authorities. The primary petrochemicals are methane, ethane, propane, ethylene, acetylene, benzene, hydrogen, etc., from which hundreds of chemicals are produced by a variety of reactions. For example, ethylene, obtained largely by heat treatment of hydrocarbon gases, is further reacted to yield such chemicals as ethylene dichloride, ethyl alcohol, ethyl chloride, and polyethylene some of these are end-products, but others are intermediates for acrylonitrile, ethylene glycol, vinyl chloride, and many other synthetic organics.The same is true of the other primary petrochemicals. The vast number of derivatives are used as solvents, plasticizers, elastomers, fibers, pharmaceuticals, explosives, dyes, fertilizers, etc. Petroleum-derived materials that are used directly as energy sources (gasoline, fuel oil) are not usually considered to be petrochemicals.

Petroff medium. A culture medium for micro-organisms prepared by the extraction of beef with glycerol-water solution followed by the addition of eggs beaten in a strong alcohol-water solution, the addition of crystal violet indicator, and coagulation by heating.

petrolatum. A purified mixture of hydrocarbons consisting of a semi-solid whitish or yellowish mass. Also known as vaseline; petroleum jelly.

petroleum. This term literally means "rock oil." Petroleum is thought to have originated from decomposition of animal life which inhabited the ocean floor in early geologic periods. It is a complex mixture of all types of hydrocarbons the paraffins predominating in some areas, and aromatics and cycloparaffins in others. It occurs in numerous locations in the world, usually in rock strata, but sometimes close to the surface. The leading producing areas in the U.S. are California and Texas. Deposits have been brought on stream in Alaska and the North Sea, and extensive resources have been found in Mexico ; elsewhere it is found in northern Canada, the Mid-east Persian Gulf area, and the Baku peninsula in the Caspian Sea. It is not only the primary source of automotive fuels but of thousands of organic chemicals used in medicines, plastics, dyes, solvents, lubricants, etc. The molecules of some of its components contain up to 50 carbon atoms.

petroleum gas. Any of a number of flammable gases obtained by refining of petroleum and used both for organic synthesis and in liquefied form as fuels. Most important are the saturated compounds butane, isobutane, and propane and the unsaturated butylenes and propylene. Methane is obtained not only from petroleum, but also from other sources such as coal and natural gas.

Pettenkofer's method. For the estimation of atmospheric carbon dioxide. A large known volume of air is shaken with a measured volume of standard baryta-water and then the excess of baryta titrated against standard acid with phenolphthalein as indicator.

pewter. An alloy of approximately 4 parts of tin to 1 part of lead, with small amounts of antimony.

Pfitzinger reaction. A method of formation of quinoline carboxylic acids by condensation of isatins with α-methylenecarbonyl compunds :

$$\text{C}_6\text{H}_4(\text{NH}_2)\text{CO-COOH} + \text{CH}_2\text{-R}'\text{-CO-R} \rightarrow \text{quinoline-COOH (R, R')} + 2\text{H}_2\text{O}$$

Pfund series. A series of lines in the infrared region of the emission spectrum of atomic hydrogen. The wave numbers of the lines in this series are given by the relationship :

$$\bar{\nu} = R_H\left(\frac{1}{n_1^2} - \frac{1}{n_2^2}\right)$$

where $\bar{\nu}$ = wave number in reciprocal centimeters, R_H=Rydberg constant, n_1=5, and n_2 has various integral values.

pH. A scale indicating the acidity or alkalinity of aqueous solutions ; it was developed in 1909 by S P.L. Sorensen, a Danish biochemist. *p*H is conventionally defined as the negative logarithm of hydrogen-ion activity, $p\text{H} \equiv -\log a_{\text{H}_3\text{O}^+}$, used for convenience, since individual-ion activities cannot be measured, as a scale based on standard buffer solutions and EMF's measured with electrodes reversible with respect to hydrogen ions :

$$p\text{H}(x) = p\text{H}(s) + \frac{(E_x - E_s)F}{2.303\,RT}$$

*p*H (*s*) and *p*H(*x*) being the *p*H's of the standard buffer and the test solution and E_s and E_x their respective EMF's.

*p*H value is a number from 1 to 14, which represents a logarithmic scale indicating the concentration of hydrogen ions. These number are actually exponents expressing the molar concentration ; water molecules dissociate into H^+ and OH^- and recombine at such a rate that there is at any instant a concentration of these ions of 1/10.000.000 mole per liter, *i.e.*, $1/10^7$ or 10^{-7}. This is the neutrality point of pure water (*p*H 7), at which the concentrations of H^+ and OH^- ions are equal. When an acid added to the water, numbers from 1 to 7 are used to indicate the acidity of the solution, *i.e.*, the predominance of hydrogen ions ; if alkalies are added to the water, numbers from 7 to 14 indicate the alkalinity, *i.e.*, the predominance of hydroxyl ions in the solution. A *p*H of 1.0 is represented by 0.1N hydrochloric acid, and a *p*H of 14 is that of 0.1N sodium hydroxide. Since the ionic concentration increases logarithmically, the values on the *p*H scale differ by a factor of 10; a *p*H of 5 is ten times as acidic as a *p*H of 6.

pharmaceutical chemistry. A branch of applied chemistry that deals with the composition and preparation of medicinal materials.

pharmacology. The entire body of scientific knowledge dealing with drugs, their source, composition, identification, and physiological action.

pharmacophore. A structural arrangement of atoms that is considered to impart pharmacological activity to a chemical substance.

phase. 1. Part of system separated from the rest by distinct boundaries and differing from the rest discontinuously as concerns thermodynamic properties. Thus a gas, a homogeneous liquid, or a homogeneous solid is a single phase, while, for example, a system of two insoluble or partly-soluble liquids which form separate layers has two phases, and a system of two solids in equilibrium with their solution has three phases.

2. In colloid chemistry, this term is used to designate the portions of a solution or dispersion, namely, the disperse phase and the continuous phase (sometimes called internal and external, respectively). For example, in an oil-in-water emulsion, the oil droplets are the dispersed phase and water the continuou sphase; in a water-in-oil emulsion, the reverse is the case.

3. The term phase is used to express one of two behaviour exhibited by the same entity.

phase cell. Volume in phase space which represents microscopic states of system, indistinguishable by macroscopic methods.

phase diagram. Plot showing zones of existence of particular phase and conditions of change of one phase into another in the given system, as function of qualitative and quantitative composition and of state variables.

phase equilibrium. Thermodynamic state of multiphase system with the same value of chemical potential of each component in all coexisting phases.

phase point. In statistical mechanics point in phase space. Phase point represents microscopic state of system and is determined by values of all its coordinates and momenta.

phase rule. A mathematical expression which shows the conditions of equilibrium in a system as a relationship between the number of phases, the number of components, and the degrees of freedom possible under the given conditions. If C represents the number of components, P, the number of phases, and F, the degrees of freedom, then $C+2-P=F$

phase space. In statistical mechanics $2f$-dimensional space; each point of this space represents some microscopic state of system with f degrees of freedom.

phase transition. Thermodynamic process of vanishing (gradually or suddenly) of one phase and simultaneous appearance of another. Also known as phase change.

phasine. One of a group of nitrogenous substances found in seeds, barks, and probably other plant tissues, which agglutinate red blood corpuscles, although most of the phasines are nontoxic. They are found in beans (Phaseolus vulgaris), whence the name phasine. They act like strong bases and can be recovered from the agglutinate with dilute HCl. Phasines are digested and detoxicated in the intestinal tract; they lose their agglutinating power on heating.

phasotropy. A pnenomenon shown by certain diazoamino compounds, amidines, and formazyl derivatives in which isomerism occurs by the "shift" of a hydrogen atom and a double bond between nitrogen atoms, *viz.*,

Also **known as virtual** tautomerism.

pheno-, phen-. The prefix meaning relation to phenyl or benzene, as phenacyl; specifically, denoting the presence of two benzene rings in a complex, as phenazine, phenothiazine.

phenolate. A phenol in which a hydroxyl hydrogen atom is replaced by a positive radical, commonly a metal.

phenol extraction process. A process for the refining of lubricating oil, involving extraction with phenol.

phenolic. General name for a class or group of chemicals derived from benzene by substitution of one or more hydroxyl groups, and in some cases methyl groups as well, for hydrogen atoms on the benzene ring. Phenolic compounds are widely used as starting points for synthetic resins, disinfectants, herbicides, pharmaceutical products, and chemical synthesis. In addition, there are a number of special uses for each type.

phenomenological coefficients, L_{ik}. Quantities

$$L_{ik} = \left(\frac{\partial J_i}{\partial X_k}\right)_0$$

where J_i = thermodynamic flux and X_k=thermodynamic force; "0" subscript denotes derivative calculated at equilibrium.

phenomenological equations. Equations expressing thermodynamic fluxes J_i in terms of thermodynamic force X_i or vice versa; they give dependence of thermodynamic forces on fluxes in system; in linear thermodynamics of irreversible process phenomenological equations have linear form, most frequently expressed by:

$$J_i = \sum_k L_{ik} X_k$$

where L_{ik} = phenomenological coefficients.

phenonium ion. Ion formed in reactions of nucleophilic substitution of compounds containing aromatic ring in position adjacent to substituted group. Such an ion is formed due to interaction of π-electrons (of ring) with electrophilic reaction centre. Nucleophile attack in the second stage of reaction may take place at 1- or 2-position:

$$-\overset{2}{C}-\overset{1}{C}(OTs)- \xrightarrow{-OTs^{\ominus}} \text{phenonium ion} \xrightarrow{AcO^{\ominus}} -C-C(OAc)- \text{ or } -C(OAc)-C-$$

phenonium ion

where Ts = tosyl ($-SO_2C_6H_4CH_3$), Ac = acyl ($-COR$)

phenoxy. The radical C_6H_5O-

phenyl. The unsaturated aromatic group C_6H_5-, representing a benzene molecule with one open valence where any of numerous atoms, groups, or side chains may be attached. For example, in phenol (C_6H_5OH), the hydrogen originally present in benzene is replaced by a hydroxyl group.

phenylene. The radical $-C_6H_4-$ (*o*, *m*, or *p*), as in phenylenediamine, $C_6H_4(NH_2)_2$, where two amino groups replace the hydrogens.

pheromone. Any substance produced by an organism that serves to induce a behavioral or developmental response in an individual of the same species. Pheromones include sex attractants, alarm substances, trail substances, trail markers, and aggregation-inducing compounds. Animals and plants produce other substances as well, which some behaviorists call allomones and kairomones, that transmit information to individuals of different species.

Now that the chemical structure of many pheromones has been determined and the compounds synthesized, a number of them have been used in integrated control programs. For example sex and food attractants of certain moths and beetles that destroy stored food products have been used for the early detection of infestations in granaries, mills, and warehouses, and to prevent the increase of pest populations by mass trapping. The use of these pheromone traps minimizes the need for treatment with insecticides. Sex pheromones have been used to disrupt sexual communication among moths and to prevent mating. In this method the sex pheromones are evaporated from many sources to confuse the males and prevent their locating conspecific females. The technique has shown promise in control of the plum fruit moth, codling moth, larch bud moth, and grape moth.

The odorous secretions of mammals have been of interest to perfume makers for ages, but little is known about their role in animal communication, and the chemical structure of the compounds is largely unknown. Studies indicate that mammals do not give an automatic, standardized response to their odor signals in the way that insects react to their pheromones, and the term semiochemicals (chemical or odor signals) has been suggested for mammalian scents.

In mammals, only the male pheromone of the domestic pig has been applied to practical purpose. The saliva and sweat glands of the sexually aroused boar contain two steroids which induce the mating stance in estrous sows. The compounds have been used to facilitate the artificial insemination of pigs.

phi. (ϕ, ϕ or φ). The twenty-first letter in the Greek alphabet, used to denote the twenty-first carbon atom in a straight-chain compound, or a derivative in which the substituent group is attached to that carbon atom (ϕ-). Symbol for angle (ϕ). Symbol for angle of incidence (ϕ). Symbol for angle of refraction (ϕ'). Symbol for critical angle (ϕ^c). Symbol for function (of) (ϕ). Abbreviation for phenyl (ϕ). Symbol for fluidity (ϕ). Symbol for electron affinity or net work function per unit charge (ϕ). Symbol for gross electron affinity or gross work function per unit charge (ϕ_g). Symbol for magnetic flux or radiant flux (ϕ). Symbol for velocity potential (ϕ).

***p*H metry.** Group of methods based on *p*H measurements.

phonon. Quantum of harmonic vibrations *viz.*, the imaginary boson, which describes various types of quantized vibrations, *e.g.*, crystalline lattice vibrations or vibrations on surface of atomic nucleus.

phosphatide. Any of a number of complex lipids which contain phosphorus in the molecule ; they occur in all living cells and have significant metabolic functions, many of which are not fully elucidated. The alternative name for such compounds is phospholipid. In addition to phosphorus in the form of phosphoric acid, they are comprised of polyhydric alcohols, fatty acids, and a basic group containing nitrogen, all of which can be obtained by hydrolysis. Lecithin and sphingomyelin are among the better-known phosphatides.

phospholipid. *See* phosphatide.

phosphor. 1. A substance which emits radiation in the ultraviolet, visible, or infrared wavelengths during or following excitation by an external energy source ; it may be either fluorescent or phosphorescent depending on whether or not it emits light after the exciting source has been removed. Inorganic phosphors such as metallic tungstates, zinc sulphide, etc. are produced in quantity for use in fluorescent lights, colour television, scintillation counters, etc. ; hundreds of such materials have been prepared for these and similar purposes. For satisfactory results they require the presence of trace quantities of such metals as silver, copper, or manganese, which are called activators. Organic phosphors have also been used for display colour effects and textile brighteners. Riboflavin and chlorophyll are examples of natural organic phosphors.

2. The term phosphor is used adjectively, as in phosphor bronze; to indicate the presence of a low percentage of phosphorus as a deoxidizing additive.

phosphorescence. Type of photoluminescence which consists in emission of light accompanying spin-forbidden radiative transition between two electronic states of different multiplicity, *e.g.*, from triplet to singlet state. This phenomenon occurs naturally in many minerals and metallic compounds, in some types of organic compounds, and in some living organism (marine fauna and insects such as the firefly). Phosphorescence is distinguished from fluorescence in two ways ; (*i*) there is a longer time period between excitation and the emission of light, ranging from one-thousandth of a second to several hours, whereas fluorescence occurs almost instantaneously ; (*ii*) and phosphorescence may continue for some hours after the exciting source has been removed, the length of emanation depending on the substance, whereas fluorescence ceases when the source is cut off. Thus, phosphorescent materials glow in darkness, but fluorescent materials do not.

phosphoric. 1. Containing pentavalent phosphorus.

2. Related to phosphoric acid (ortho), H_3PO_4, phosphoric acid (meta), HPO_3, or phosphoric acid (pyro), $H_4P_2O_7$.

phosphoro. The radical —P=P—, in organic compounds.

phosphoroso. The radical OP—, in organic compounds.

phosphorus. An element.

	Symbol	P
State Solid	Atomic No.	15
Group VA	Atomic Wt.	30.9738
	Valence	3,5

Phosphorus is a nonmetallic element having several allotropic forms, designated by their colour—two white forms differing in their crystal structure, a red-violet, and a black allotrope, the last two being either amorphous or crystalline. The white allotropes are pyrophoric, but the black does not ignite easily. Phosphorus also resembles carbon in its tendency to form covalent bonds, though it does not bond to itself as readily as carbon. Research in phosphorus chemistry indicates that there may be as many compounds based on phosphorus as on carbon.

First ionization potential 11.0 eV ; second, 19.81 eV ; third, 30.04 eV ; fourth, 51.1 eV ; fifth, 64.698 eV. Oxidation potentials $H_3PO_2 + H_2O \rightarrow H_3PO_3 + 2H^+ + 2e^-$, 0.59 V ; $P + 3H_2O \rightarrow H_3PO_3 + 3H^+ + 3e^-$, 0.49 V; $P + 2H_2O \rightarrow H_3PO_2 + H^+ + e^-$, 0.29 V; $H_3PO_3 + H_2O \rightarrow H_3PO_4 + 2H^+ + 2e^-$, 0.20 V; $PH_3(g) \rightarrow P + 3H^+ + 3e^-$, 0.04 V; $P + 2OH^- \rightarrow H_2PO_2^- + e^-$, 1.82 V; $P + 5OH^- \rightarrow HPO_3^{2-} + 2H_2O + 3e^-$, 1.71 V; $H_2PO_2^- + 3OH^- \rightarrow HPO_3^{2-} + 2H_2O + 2e^-$, 1.65 V; $HPO_3^{2-} + 3OH^- \rightarrow PO_4^{3-} + 2H_2O + 2e^-$, 1.05 V; $PH_3(g) + 3OH^- \rightarrow P + 3H_2O + 3e^-$, 0.87 V.

Phosphorus is an essential nutrient for plants and animals and has complex metabolic function (as adenosine triphosphate) in addition to its hardening effect on bones and teeth (as hydroxyapatite). In elemental form it is highly toxic, and some of its organic compounds (nerve gases and insecticides of the parathion type) are lethally poisonous.

Like carbon, phosphorus is covalently bound to its neighboring atoms in all of its compounds, except perhaps for some metallic phosphides. Indeed, the chemistry of carbon and that of phosphorus are somewhat similar as might be expected from the diagonal retationship of these elements in the periodic table.

Probably the major difference between carbon and phosphorus is that the former element is quite closely restricted to the use of *s*- and *p*-orbitals, because of the relatively high energy of *d*-orbitals in the case of second period elements; whereas, phosphorus, being a third period element, can utilize *d*-orbitals in bonding.

The known coordination numbers exhibited by phosphorus within the molecule and the ions containing this element are 1, 3, 4, 5, and 6 which, to at least a first approximation, exhibit the symmetry of p, p^3, sp^3, sp^3d and sp^3d^2 hybridization, respectively. A very large number (several thousand in each case) of triply- and quadruply-connected phosphorus compounds are known ; but there are only a few compounds of higher coordination number in which *d*-orbitals are involved in the σ-bond base structure.

The chief uses of elemental phosphorus are in the manufacture of numerous compounds (phosphoric acid, combinations with halogens, sulphur, etc., and organophosphorus compound). as a semiconductor and catalyst, in pyrotechnic devices, and in deoxidizing metals.

Phosphorus-containing fertilizers, such as single superphosphate, wet-process orthophosphoric acid, triple superphosphate, ammonium phosphate and nitrophosphates do not require elemental phosphorus (or the resulting pure P_2O_5) in their preparation, but are manufactured by directly reacting phosphate rock with requisite chemicals, such as H_2SO_4 or HNO_3.

phosphoryl. The radical $\equiv P=O$, as in phosphoryl chloride $POCl_3$.

phosphorylation. Introduction of phosphoryl group —PO into chemical compound molecule, usually by displacing hydrogen atom.

It is important in cellular metabolism, vitamin activity, and enzyme formation. It is used to produce a modification cellulose for cation exchange in chromatographic separations.

photoactivation analysis. Activation method of analysis in which a beam of γ-quanta is used for activation. Also known as γ-ray activation analysis, photonuclear activation analysis

photocatalysis. The catalysis of a chemical reaction achieved by irradiation with light, usually in the optical or the ultraviolet region of the spectrum.

photocatalyst. A substance which promotes a reaction that is catalyzed by light. The most universal reaction of this type is the photosynthesis of carbohydrates in green plants from carbon dioxide and water. It is accelerated by light in the presence of chlorophyll, the photocatalyst of the reaction.

photocathode. A cathode that emits electrons when it is illuminated, *i.e.*, as a result of the photoelectric effect.

photochemical. Related to the effects of radiation, commonly in the region of visible or ultraviolet light, upon a chemical reaction.

photochemical equilibrium. A position of equilibrium reached in a reversible chemical change in which one or both of the reaction are sensitive to light and with presence of the effective radiation postulated as one of the conditions under which the equilibrium is reached.

photochemical quantum yield. Ratio between number of molecules which undergo a given photochemical reaction and total number of photons previously absorbed.

photochemical reaction. A reaction brought about or markedly accelerated by exposure to electromagnetic radiations in the spectrum of visible light, the ultraviolet, and (rarely) the near infrared. This type of reactions are initiated by absorption of photons with appropriate energy by at least one component of reacting system composed of atoms or molecules.

Such reactions include most, if not all, the major types—oxidation, reduction, decomposition, hydrolysis, synthesis, etc. The photosynthesis of carbohydrates from carbon dioxide and water in the presence of chlorophyll is a photochemical reaction of the most universal significance.

photochemistry. A subdivision of chemistry dealing with the study of the chemical changes induced by various wavelengths of radiation, often brought about through the agency of molecular fragments known as free radicals. Absorption of radiant energy is involved, and the effects of this are permanent rather than temporary, as in spectroscopy, where no chemical changes occur.

photochromic. Derived from two words meaning "light" and "colour" this term denotes a material to which has been added a low percentage of a light-sensitive chemical, the effect of which is to cause the material to darken in the presence of strong light and to resume its original transparency when the light intensity is decreased. This effect is brought about in optical glass by addition of silver bromide, which reduces the light transmission by about 50%. Certain classes of organic dyes exhibit photochromic behaviour, changing from colourless to coloured by absorption of ultraviolet radiation, which causes a reversible chemical change in the dye molecule.

photoconductivity. In general, the increase in electrical conductivity of a substance when illuminated, commonly by visible or ultraviolet light. Specifically, the effect is most marked in some crystals which show a substantial change in conductivity when illuminated. Photoconduction arises from the absorption of light causing electrons to be promoted from the valence band of the solid into the conduction band.

photoconductor. Semiconductor exhibiting increase of electrical conductivity under illumination.

photodisintegration. The break up of an atomic nucleus into two or more fragments as a result of bombardment by gamma radiation.

photodissociation. *See* photolysis.

photoelectric effect. Emission of electrons from metal surface due to its bombardment by stream of photons. Also known as external photoelectric effect, normal photoelectric effect.

photoelectron. Orbital electron of electromagnetic radiation, *i.e.*, through the external photoelectric effect.

photofission. Division of atomic nucleus into two heavy fragments induced by absorption of γ-quantum of sufficienly high energy.

photoionization. Ionization initiated by absorption of photons of equal or greater energy than that of ionization energy.

If the frequency of the ratiation is ν, each photon will have an energy $h\nu$ where h is Planck's constant. Photons with energies in excess of the ionization potential of the atoms struck will cause ionization to occur.

photoisomerization. The conversion of one isomer into another as a result of the action of light, *e.g.*, antinitro-benzaldoxime changes, when exposed to light, into the more stable *syn* form, and anthracene dimerize to dianthracene.

photolysis Fission (dissociation) of molecule induced by photon absorption, *e.g.*,

$$HI + h\nu \rightarrow H\cdot + I\cdot$$

Photolysis can be regarded as the opposite of photosynthesis. Also known as photodissociation; photochemical dissociation. *See also* flash photolysis.

photolytic. Pertaining to a reaction in which a

substance is decomposed or split by radiant energy.

photomeson. A meson produced by the interaction between a photon and an atomic nucleus.

photometric. Relating to measurements or methods of intensity of light.

photometric analysis. Chemical analysis by means of absorption or emission of radiation, primarily in the near ultraviolet, visible, and infrared portions of the electromagnetic spectrum. It includes such techniques as spectrophotometry, spectrochemical analysis, colourimetry, and fluorescence measurements.

photometry. Group of measurement techniques for determination of radiation intensity in visible, ultraviolet and infrared region.

photon. The ultimate unit (quantum) of electromagnetic energy which comprises the entire spectrum of radiation, from cosmic and gamma rays to the longest radiofrequencies. An objective description of a photon is a discontinuous "packet of energy" behaving as a wave ; an accurate understanding can be gained only from the mathematics involved in quantum mechanics. Photons are usually considered as elementary particles with rest mass equal to zero and spin quantum number $J=1$.

An electron gives off one or more photons in coming from a higher to lower energy level. Molecules are capable of absorbing the energy of photons, as occurs with chlorophyll, and thus chemical reactions can be activated by this means.

photonuclear reaction. Nuclear reaction caused by absorption of γ-quantum by nucleus. Also known as photodisintegration.

photooxidation. Photochemical reaction of oxidation which consists either in transfer of electron from excited molecule or addition of molecular oxygen to it or, alternatively, in its dehydrogenation.

photophoresis. Production of unidirectional motion in a collection of very small particles suspended in a gas or falling in a vacuum by a strong light-beam.

photopolymer. A polymer of plastic that undergoes a change on exposure to light. The effect of light may be to cause further polymerization on crosslinking, or may cause degradation.

photopolymerization. Photochemical reaction of polymerization initiated by free radicals or excited molecules very often in triplet state. Also known as photosensitized polymerization.

photoreduction. Photochemical reduction reaction of electronically excited molecules, *e.g.*, photoreduciton of benzophenone to benzopinacone.

photosensitization. The initiation of a chemical reaction by irradiation of an intermediary substance. The intermediary absorbs the radiation and initiates the process by collisions with the reactants, thereby transferring part or all of its excess energy to the reactants.

photosensitized reaction. Reaction initiated by radiative energy absorbed by certain atoms or molecules which, however, do not react themselves but transfer their excessive excitation energy to appropriate coexistent substrates of reaction.

photosensitizer. Molecule or the atom which is capable by itself to absorb the radiative energy of light and to transfer it to coexistent substances which than undergo photochemical reactions.

photosynthesis. The chemical synthesis of carbohydrates (sugars, starches, and cellulose) performed in the cells of plants, the necessary energy being supplied by sunlight. Plant cells absorb water from the soil and carbon dioxide from the air, the reaction being catalyzed by the green pigment chlorophyll. The basic reaction is : $6CO_2+6H_2O+\text{energy} \rightarrow C_6H_{12}O_6+6O_2$. This is of the utmost importance, not only for the food substances formed but for the oxygen evolved. Virtually all the oxygen of the air results from photosynthesis, well over half of it being produced by algae and other aquatic plants. Thus, plant life is the primary means of converting radiant energy to chemical energy. The ability of plants to synthesize organic compounds from inorganic constituents is unique, and no life would be possible without it. In the absence of light, oxygen is absorbed and carbon dioxide evolved, with no sugar formation. Combustion can be regarded as the reverse of photosynthesis, yielding carbon dioxide and water, with release of the original energy input.

phototrophism. A type of nutrition in which the source of energy for synthesis of organic compounds is light. Most phototrophic organisms are autotrophic ; these include the green plants, blue-green algae, and some photosynthetic bacteria.

phototropism. A directional growth movement of part of a plant in response to light. The phenomenon is clearly shown by growth of shoots and coleoptiles towards light. A reversible change in the structure of a solid exposed to light or other radiant energy, accompanied by a change in colour. *See also* photochromic.

phycocolloid. Any of several colloidal macromolecular substance occurring in seaweeds ; they are chemically classified as polysaccharides, or polymeric forms of certain sugars. They are strongly hydrophilic, forming gelatinous pastes by absorption of water. The most important phycocolloids are obtained from algae (agar) and Irish moss (carrageenan).

physical adsorption. Increase in concentration of any adsorbed substance (adsorbate) at interfacial surface of adsorbent caused by attractive intermolecular forces. Also known as physisorption ; van der Waals adsorption.

physical chemistry. The branch of chemistry dealing with studies on interdependence between physical properties and chemical structure of substances or system as well as on physical phenomena accompanying chemical transformations.

Physical chemistry includes those areas of chemistry which involve an understanding of the physical principles of mass, motion, electricity, radiation, heat and related phenomena ; they include nuclear chemistry, spectroscopy, electrochemistry, atomic structure, chemical kinetics, and colloid chemistry.

physical photometry. The brach of photometry; radiation intensity is determined by measurement of changes of some physical quantity, *e.g.*, photoelectric or thermoelectric current, caused by radiation.

physiological saline. An isotonic solution of salts in distilled water used for preserving cells. Such solutions contain no food for the cells and their survival in them is therefore restricted.

phyt-, phyto-. A prefix relating to plants, as phytosterol, phytase.

phytochemistry. That branch of chemistry which deals with the nutrition and metabolism of plants and with the chemical products obtained from them. It thus includes the utilization of mineral nutrients, carbon dioxide, and water, and their transformation into carbohydrates, proteins, oils vitamins, alkaloids, etc., as well as plant growth regulators, osmosis, soil *p*H, and other factors affecting growth.

pi (Π or π). The sixteenth letter in the Greek alphabet, used to denote the sixteenth carbon atom in a straight-chain compound, or a derivative in which a substituent group is attached to that carbon atom (π-).

pi bond. Chemical bond formed by valence electrons present in molecular π-bonding orbital, antisymmetric with respect to nodal plane passing through bond axis, *e.g.*, bond between carbon atoms in ethylene.

π molecular orbitals

picean ring. A four-membered ring which exists in certain terpenes, *viz.*,

```
       CH₂
      /   \
—HC         CH—
      \   /
        C
        ‖
```

pickling. 1. In metal technology this term refers to descaling and cleaning of metallic surfaces with a strong acid such as sulphuric or hydrochloric acid.

2. Preservation of certain food products by the use of various spices, sodium chloride solution, vinegar (acetic acid), or sodium benzoate in low concentrations. Salt solution is also used in the preliminary treatment of skins for the tanning process in leather technology.

pick-up reaction. Nuclear reaction in which incident particle removes nucleon from surface shell of target nucleus, and proceeds together with picked up nucleon in slightly changed direction.

picogram method. Method of analysis where mass of investigated sample is $x.10^{-12}$ — $x.10^{-10}$ *g.*, or volume $x.10^{-9}$ cm^3 in the case of gases.

pi-complex. Labile complex formed of π-electrons of unsaturated molecule and cation, or electron-deficient atom of polarized molecule *e.g.*,

$$C_6H_6 \rightarrow NO_2^{\oplus} \qquad >C{=}C< \;\downarrow\; H^{\delta\oplus}\!-\!Cl^{\delta\ominus}$$

Pictet-Gams isoquinoline synthesis. A method of formation of isoquinolines from acylated aminoethylphenyl alcohols or their ethers.

$$C_6H_5\text{-}CH(OH)\text{-}CH_2\text{-}NH\text{-}C(=O)\text{-}R \xrightarrow[-2H_2O]{P_2O_5} \text{isoquinoline (1-R)}$$

Pictet-Hubret reaction. A method of formation of phenanthridine derivatives by dehydration of acyl-orthoxenylamines. The Pictet-Hubert method involves heating at 520-570K, with zinc chloride ; while the Morgan-Walls method involves treatment with $POCl_3$ in nitrobenzene.

Pictet-Spengler isoquinoline synthesis. A method of formation of tetrahydroisoquinoline derivatives from β-aromatic ethylamines and aldehydes (and other carbonyl compounds).

$$(RO)(R''O)C_6H_2\text{-}CH_2CH_2NH_2 + R'CHO \xrightarrow{-H_2O} \text{tetrahydroisoquinoline (RO, R''O, NH, R')}$$

Pidgeon process. A process for the production of metallic magnesium from magnesium oxide by reduction with ferrosilicon, and volatilization of the magnesium.

pi-electrons. Electrons assumed to occupy π-molecular orbitals. Also known as π-electrons.

Pier process. The utilization of bituminous coal instead of coke in generators during the manufacture of fuel and illuminating gases. The generator and fuel are arranged in such a manner as to insure the use of all the bituminous coal present.

piezoelectric effect. The generation of opposite electric charges in certain dielectric crystals as a result of the application of mechanical stress conversely, the property of expansion along one axis and contraction along another when subjected to an electric field.

pig iron. A crude form of iron having high carbon content obtained from iron ores by the blast furnace process.

pigment. Any substance, either inorganic or organic, which has positive tinctorial power. Synthetic organic pigments are usually called dyes, though there is no entirely satisfactory line of demarcation between a dye and an organic pigment. A distinction that is more conventional than scientific is that dyes are applied almost exclusively to fibers and fabrics, whereas organic pigments are used for other materials, such as paints, plastics, and ceramics. Inorganic pigments are often insoluble powders, *e.g.*, oxides of metals such as iron, chromium, and cobalt, either made by chemical reaction or occurring naturally as earthy mixtures (ocher). These are less brilliant than dyes but are more stable to heat and light. Natural organic pigments are produced by both plants and animals.

Piloty alloxazine synthesis. A method of condensation of violuric acids and *m*-aromatic diamines to form alloxazine, isoalloxazine, or their derivatives :

Piloty-Robinson pyrrole synthesis. Ring closure to form pyrroles from azines of enolizable ketones :

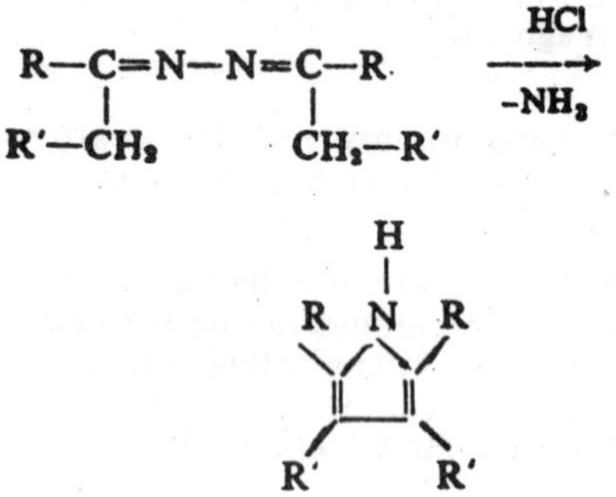

$$\underset{R'-CH_2}{R-C}=N-N=\underset{CH_2-R'}{C-R} \xrightarrow[-NH_3]{HCl}$$

(pyrrole ring: N–H at top, R on both α-carbons, R′ on both β-carbons)

pi-meson. Elementary particle, a hadron, of baryon number $B=0$, lepton number $L=0$, quantum spin number $J=0$, strangeness $S=0$, isospin $I=1$, parity $P=-1$, unstable, π-meson occurs in three states of charge (isospin triplet): with positive elementary electric charge (π^+-meson ; mass $m=139.576$ MeV, third component of isospin $I_3=1$, mean lifetime 2.6024×10^{-8} s); electrically neutral (π^0-meson ; $m=134.972$ MeV, $I_3=0$, mean lifetime 0.84×10^{-16}s); and of negative elementary electric charge (π^--meson ; $I_3=-1$, mass and mean lifetime as π^+-meson).

pinacol rearrangement. *See* Pinacolone rearrangement.

pinacolone rearrangement. Acid-catalyzed rearrangement of α-glycols (most often di-ternary) to ketones, involving elimination of water molecule and anionic migration (with rearrangement-1,2) of alkyl or aryl group, or of hydride anion from diol molecule, *e.g.*,

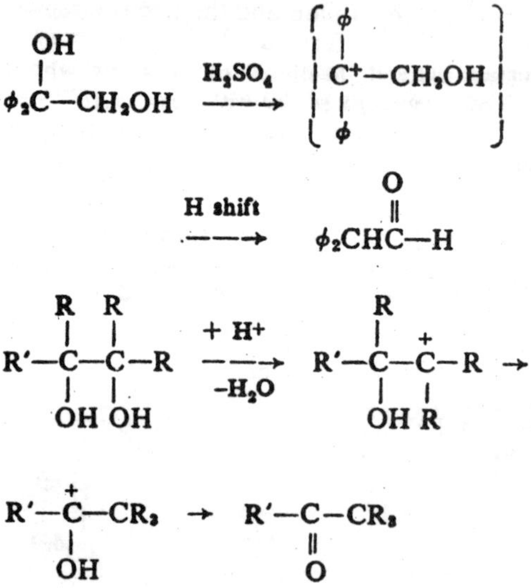

$$\phi_2\overset{OH}{\overset{|}{C}}-CH_2OH \xrightarrow{H_2SO_4} \left[\phi-\overset{+}{C}(\phi)-CH_2OH\right] \xrightarrow{\text{H shift}} \phi_2CH\overset{O}{\overset{\|}{C}}-H$$

$$R'-\underset{OH}{\overset{R}{C}}-\underset{OH}{\overset{R}{C}}-R \xrightarrow[-H_2O]{+H^+} R'-\underset{OH}{\overset{R}{C}}-\underset{R}{\overset{+}{C}}-R \rightarrow$$

$$R'-\underset{OH}{\overset{+}{C}}-CR_3 \rightarrow R'-\underset{O}{\underset{\|}{C}}-CR_3$$

Also known as pinacol rearrangement.

Pinner amidine synthesis. A method of formation of amidines from nitriles by treatment first with HCl and alcohol (to form the imidoester) and than with amines.

$$R'CN+HCl+R''OH \rightarrow R'\overset{NH.HCl}{\overset{\|}{C}}OR''$$

$$R'\overset{NH.HCl}{\overset{\|}{C}}OR''+R'''R''''NH \longrightarrow R'\overset{NH.HCl}{\overset{\|}{C}}NR'''R''''$$

Pinner method. A method of production orthoesters by the action of alcohols on imidoesters, which may be made by condensing an alcohol and a nitrile with HCl.

$$ROH+R'CN+HCl \rightarrow R'\overset{OR}{\overset{|}{C}}=NH.HCl$$

$$\xrightarrow{2R''OH} R'\underset{OR''}{\overset{OR}{C}}-OR''+NH_4Cl$$

pion. *See* pi-meson.

pionium. An exotic atom which is similar in structure to the hydrogen atom but with the proton replaced by a pion and the electron replaced by muon. It is formed during the decay of a certain heavier particle called the neutral kaon. Also known as pi-mu atom.

pi-orbital. Molecular orbital antisymmetric with respect to nodal plane which contains bond axis.

Piria reaction. Sulphonation and reduction of an aromatic nitro-compound by treatment with sulphite and a mineral acid, such as hydrochloric acid. For example, nitrobenzene gives sulphanilic acid, nitrotoluene gives the corresponding toluidinesulphonic acid, and α-nitronaphthalene gives naphthionic acid.

NO_2 $\xrightarrow[HCl]{Na_2SO_3}$ NH_2 / SO_3H

pitch. A carbonaceous residue obtained by distillation of such substances as coal tar, pine tar, rosin, petroleum, and fatty acids. Some types occur naturally, *e.g.*, glance pitch. Most types are of dark brown to black colour and are characterized by extreme thickness, especially when warm. They are used as sealants, in roofing compounds, and in road paving.

pitzer strain. Strain resulting from total (or partial) overwhelming of rotational barrier hindering free rotation about single bond in different conformational system.

***p*K.** Negative logarithm of equilibrium constant of reaction.

Planck's constant. The quantity 6.61×10^{-34} joule-second ; first introduced into physical theory by Max Planck in 1901, is a basic ingredient of the formalism of quantum mechanics. Planck's constant commonly is denoted by the letter h ; the notation $\hbar = h/2\pi$ also is standard.

Planck's distribution law. A relation for the intensity of radiation emitted by a black body with a narrow band of frequencies, as a function of frequency, and of the body's temperature. Also known as Planck's radiation formula Planck's law.

Planck's law of radiation. The energy of electromagnetic radiation (including light) is composed of discrete quanta, the magnitude of which is given by the product of Planck's constant h and the frequency of the radiation f.

Planck's function, *Y*. Extensive thermodynamic function $Y = -G/T$, where G = isothermal-isobaric thermodynamic potential (free enthalpy) and T=thermodynamic temperature.

Planck's method for calculation of diffusion potential. Method based on assumption that boundary layer between two electrolyte solutions may be considered as porous layer in contact with both electrolytes with concentrations constant with time.

Planck's oscillator. In old quantum theory, harmonic oscillator or total energy $E_n = nh\nu$, where n=principal quantum number, h= Planck's constant, ν=frequency of oscillations. Also known as classical harmonic oscillator.

plane of polarization. Plane containing the electric vector and the direction of propagation of electromagnetic wave.

plane of symmetry. An imaginary plane by which body is divided into two parts, each of which is the exact mirror image of the other.

plant fermentation. A type of plant metabolism in which carbohydrates are partially degraded without consuming molecular oxygen.

plant hormone. One of a group of substances which is formed in plants, and which initiates, controls, or retards various metabolic processes within the plant, acting in the nanner of, if not as, a positive or negative catalyst. Plant hormones include auxin *a* and *b*, traumatic acid, ethylene, and many other substances. In recent years, there has been a great expansion in the use of these substances, as, for instance, 2,4-dichlorophenoxyacetic acid, its sodium salt and its esters, for the control of weeds.

plasma. 1. Quasi-neutral highly ionized gas (*i.e.*, population of positive ions and electrons) of such density, that every charge is surrounded by charges of opposite sign (*i.e.*, screening takes place); thus electric field induced by and charge in plasma is shielded by neighbouring charges of opposite sign.

Two kinds of plasma are recognized by physicists, namely, a particle plasma and a reactor plasma. A particle plasma is a neutral mixture of positively and negatively charged particles interacting with an electromagnetic field, which dominates their motion. Temperatures of 10000 to 15,000K can be reached. Such plasma, formed by sudden energy releases, can be utilized as an energy source, as in magnetohydrodynamics. Reactor plasmas, on the other hand, are composed of positively charged ions of hydrogen isotopes (deuterium, tritium); the electric charge is the controlling factor. These are used in nuclear fusion devices called tokamaks, where temperatures of 74 million K have been attained. These plasmas also respond to electromagnetic forces, which are used to confine them.

2. In medicine, this term refers to human blood from which the red and white corpuscles have been removed; it is used primarily to replace fluids lost from the body as a result of burns or excessive bleeding. It is often supplemented by so-called volume expanders such as dextran or polyvinylpyrrolidone.

plasma chromatography. A trace analysis technique in which trace molecules in a gas are detected by subjecting them to an ion-molecule relation and measuring the ion-molecules produced. It is capable of detecting and identifying a substance present in concentrations far below the ppm range.

plasma spectroscopy. Branch of physics covering investigation of components of radiation emitted by ionized plasma in order to determine its composition, concentration of charged particles, temperature strength of electric and magnetic field.

plasma substitute. A product prepared from chemical substances for use in solution for intravenous injection in shock or other conditions for which injections of widely-used substances in formulating plasma substitutes is polyvinyl pyrrolidone.

plasmin. A proteolytic enzyme in plasma which can digest many proteins through the process of hydrolysis.

plasminogen. The inert precursor, or zymogen, of plasmin. Also known as profibrinolysin.

plasmolysis. Abstraction of water from cells by bathing them in hypertonic solutions of salts, *e.g.*, employing osmotic pressure to concentrate the cell sap. It is evident that, if the osmotic pressure of the cell is known, plasmolysis offers a means of approximately determining the osmotic pressure of "unknown" solutions.

plasticizer. A nonvolatile substance added to an organic mixture or material to keep it soft and to avoid the cracking, checking and other undesirable effects of brittleness. Plasticizers are widely used in the plastics, lacquer, and synthetic fabric industries. Though hundreds of plasticizers have been developed, those most widely used are ethylene glycol derivatives, tricresyl phosphate, dibutyl phthalate, blown castor oil, etc. Camphor was the first plasticizer.

plastics. Collective term for high polymers (resins) to which various modifying materials have been added, so that the product can be manufactured in whatever degree of quality, hardness, colour, and shape is desired. Synthetic resins are the basis of most plastics, but some are also made from modified cellulose, proteins, rubber, etc. The basic material plus added ingredients can by formed by calendering, extrusion, injection molding, foaming, etc. The more important types are derived ultimately from petroleum. Plastics can be broadly classified into two groups: (*i*) thermoplastic (those that soften when heated) and (*ii*) thermosetting (those that retain their hardness when heated). During the last 50 years, manufacture of plastics has become a dramatically successful industry both in the entire world. Not only are plastics used for innumerable utiltarian products, but they have expanded into many fields in which they have been successful substitutes for many natural materials: silk, cotton, animal glues, drying oils, metals, wood, rubber, and leather.

plastic state. State of solid crystalline or amorphous substance in which its properties resemble liquid of high viscosity and low rigidity. It occurs *e.g.*, in metals beyond range of elastic strain (deformation), or in polymers above flow temperature.

plastisol. A term used in plastics technology to denote a mixture of vinyl polymer (usually polyvinyl chloride) and from 30 to 50% of a plasticizer ; this results in a thick, rubbery mass which is used as the basis for thermoplastic moulded products. Various plasticizers are used, among them acetyl tributyl citrate. *See also* plasticizer.

platinic. Containing or relating to quadrivalent platinum.

platinize. To coat, plate. or combine with platinum.

platinoid. An alloy of 60% copper, 24% zinc, 14% nickel, and about 2% tungsten.

platinous. Containing or relating to bivalent platinum.

platinum. An element

		Symbol	Pt
		Atomic No.	78
		Atomic Wt.	195,09
State	Solid	Valence	2,3,4
Group	VIII	Isotopes	5 stable
		m.p.	2044K
		b.p.	4073K

The most important of a closely related group of six metals (ruthenium, rhodium, palladium, osmium, iridium, and platinum) placed in Group VIII of the Periodic Table, all of which are considered to be rare metals.

Platinum is a grayish-white, ductile metal, which is resistant to oxidation and tarnish ; it tends to take up large percentages of hydrogen. It is one of the heaviest elements, with a density, 21.45 g/cc, almost twice that of lead. It is quite reactive chemiçally, especially in powder form (platinum black), and is one of the most effective catalysts known for the reactions involved in making high-octane motor fuels (platinum sponge) by the reforming process. Platinum can be made into a spongy form by thermally decomposing ammonium chloroplatinate or by reducing it from an aqueous solution. In this form it exhibits a high absorptive power for gases, especially oxygen, carbon monoxide, and hydrogen. The high catalytic activity of platinum is related directly to this property. It has many applications in the electrical and medical fields and is also used in spinneret nozzles, special laboratory vessels, etc., usually in the form of alloys with other members of the group. The extremely high cost of platinum restricts its use to specialized applications.

platinum electrode. Electrode constructed from platinum wire, foil or gauze used as indicator electrode in potentiometric or voltammetric measurements and in electrogravimetry for electrodeposition of electrolyzed substance.

REPRESENTATIVE PROPERTIES OF PLATINUM GROUP METALS

Property	Iridium	Osmium	Palladium	Platinum	Rhodium	Ruthenium
Atomic volume, cm^3 g-atom	8.54	8.34	8.88	9.09	8.27	8.29
Atomic radius	1.355	1.350	1.373	1.335	1.342	1.336
Crystalline form	fcc	hcp	fcc	fcc	fcc	hcp
Lattice parameters, A, *a*	3.8389	2.7341	3.8902	3.9310	3.804	2.7041
b	—	4.3197	—		—	4.2814
Thermal conductivity at 293K, (cal)(cm)(s)(cm^3)(K)	0.14	—	0.168	0.166	0.21	—
Electrical resistivity at 273K micro-ohm-cm	5.3	9.5	10.8	10.6	4.5	7.2
Thermal expansivity, $K \times 10^6$ at 293K	6.6	6.6	12.4	9.0	8.3	9.6
Hardness, Mohs scale	6.5	7.0	4.8	4.3	—	6.5
Specific heat, cal/g-atom at 293K	0.031	0.031	—0.0584	0.031	0.059	0.057
Heat of fusion kcal/mole	6.3	7.0	4.0	4.7	5.2	6.1
Heat of vaporization, kcal/mole	134.7	150	90	122	118.4	135.7

platinum metals. Elements forming two triads in eighth sub-group of periodic system (in periods V and VI): ruthenium, rhodium, palladium and osmium, iridium, platinum. Because of their unique properties and in spite of their high initial cost, the platinum metals find many applications in industry. Since used platinum metals retain a large portion of their initial value, many scrap materials are a major source of recoverable platinum metals. Practically every application of platinum generates scrap in some form which is eventually returned to the platinum refiner for recycling. Although there are ample mine reserves, they soon would be depleted without constant scrap recycling.

platosammine. An ammonium compound of platinum of the general formula, $Pt(NH_3)_2X_2$, in which X represents an univalent acid radical.

Plattner process. A metallurgical process for the recovery of gold as the trichloride by chlorination with gaseous chlorine and leaching.

plumbite. The anion PbO_2^{2-}, or a compound containing it.

plumbous. Containing or pertaining to bivalent lead.

plumbum. The Latin name of lead.

plutonium. An element.

	Symbol	Pu
State Solid	Atomic No.	94
Group IIIB	Atomic Wt.	239.11
	Valence	3,4,5,6
	m.p.	914K

A highly radioactive and fissionable element of the transuranium series.

The ionic species corresponding to the four oxidation states of plutonium vary with the acidity of the solution. In moderately strong (one-molar) acid the species are Pu^{3+}, Pu^{4+}, PuO_2^{+}, and PuO_2^{2+}. The ions are hydrated but it is not possible at present to assign a definite hydration to each ion. The potential scheme of these ions in one molar perchloric acid is the following:

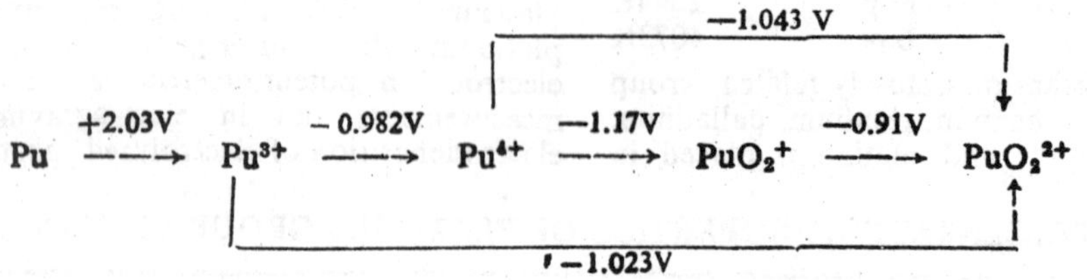

$$Pu \xrightarrow{+2.03V} Pu^{3+} \xrightarrow{-0.982V} Pu^{4+} \xrightarrow{-1.17V} PuO_2^{+} \xrightarrow{-0.91V} PuO_2^{2+}$$

$$Pu^{4+} \xrightarrow{-1.043\ V} PuO_2^{2+} \qquad Pu^{3+} \xrightarrow{-1.023V} PuO_2^{2+}$$

The potentials are in volts relative to the hydrogen-hydrogen ion couple as zero.

The values given for the potential scheme in one-molar acid may be altered extensively by a change in hydrogen ion concentration (pH) or as a result of the addition of substances capable of forming complex ion with the plutonium species.

It exists in six allotropic crystalline forms. It is a much more efficient fissioning agent than uranium-235, which it has largely replaced as a nuclear reactor fuel. It is now made in a reactor from natural uranium by neutron bombardment of the 238 isotope to form plutonium 239.

Plutonium-239 emits an α-particle from its nucleus in normal radioactive disintegration, for which it has a half life period of 24,131 years. However, by the action of slow neutrons, the

pleochromatism. A phenomenon observed in the trasmission of polarized light by bi-axial crystals, whereby a polarized ray is observed at right angles to the axial ray, and is of a colour complementary to it.

pleomorphism. The property of crystallizing in two or more forms. The term includes dimorphism and trimorphism.

Plews process. A method of recovery of antimony by volatilizing its oxide from sulphide ores by heating in a roasting furnace.

plumbate. An anion containing tetravalent lead and oxygen, or a compound containing such an anion.

plumbic. Containing or pertaining to quadrivalent lead.

nucleus of the plutonium atom disintegrates in an entirely different way to form a number of products consisting of elements having mass numbers on the order of one half that of plutonium. This process is attended by an over-all loss of mass which appears as energy. Its commercial use is chiefly in electric power reactors is extremely dangerous to handle, and operations must be done by remote control and with adequate shielding.

Plutonium has also been produced in other ways, *e.g.*, in the form of plutonium-238, by bombardment of uranium-238, with deuterons, forming neptunium-238 and 2 neutrons, and followed by the beta disintegration of the neptunium-238 to yield.

Care must be taken in the handling of plutonium to avoid unintentional formation of a critical mass. Plutonium in liquid solutions is more apt to become critical than solid plutonium. The shape of the mass also determines criticality. Plutonium's chemical properties also increase handling difficulty. Metallic plutonium is pyrophoric, particularly in finely divided form. Because of the high rate of emission of alpha particles, and the physiological fact that the element is specifically absorbed by bone marrow, plutonium, like all of the transuranium elements, is a radiological poison and must be handled with special equipment and precautions. Plutonium operations are normally handled in an essentially closed system, such as a glovebox. In addition, shielding is required when certain isotopes, including plutonium-240 and plutonium-241, are present in appreciable quantity.

pneumatic. Related to, or pertaining to, air or derivatively to other gases. Thus, a pneumatic trough is a small tank, containing a shelf with small holes. It is used to collect gases in the laboratory, by pouring water into it to a level above the shelf, on which are placed inverted gas collecting bottles filled with water, which is displaced from them by gas from tubes passing under the shelf and into the bottles through the holes in the shelf.

pnicogens. A collective term sometimes used (but not recommended) for the elements nitrogen, phosporus, arsenic, antimony, and bismuth. Pnictides contain M^{3-} species.

Poggendorf cell. A voltaic cell, used as a standard in measurement of electrical potential. It consists of a mercury-zinc anode and carbon cathode in a dilute sulphuric acid solution of potassium dichromate.

Poggendorff's compensation method. Method based on compensation of EMF of cell by oppositely directed known potential difference.

***p*OH.** Negative logarithm of hydroxyl ion activity $pOH \equiv -\log a_{OH^-}$.

point defects. Irregularities in structure of crystal lattice with dimensions, of order of space occupied by one atom. Also known as point imperfections.

point group. Set of symmetry operations (rotation around axis, reflection across plane or combination of planes), not including translation, which when carried out on periodic arrangement to points in space, brings that system of points to self-coincidence.

point imperfections. *See* point defects.

poise. The unit of viscosity in the centimeter-gram-second system, equal to one dyne per square centimetre per second.

Poiseuille's equation. A relationship for determining the viscosity of a fluid by the use of a capillary tube. The form of this relationship is :

$$\eta = \frac{\pi p r^4 t}{8 V l}$$

in which η=the coefficient of viscosity, p=the pressure difference across the tube, r=its radius, t=the time required to deliver volume V, and l=the length of the tube.

poison. 1. A term used by organic chemists to denote a substance which contaminates a catalyst to the point where its activity is greatly reduced or destroyed altogether, such poisons are often present as impurities in the reactants. Arsenic and sulphur have this effect when adsorbed on the catalyst, for example, on platinum in the oxidation of sulphur dioxide to sulpher trioxide.

2. In medicinal chemistry, a poison is a substance which exerts a detrimental effect on the life of an organism, often in minute dosage ; the adverse effect may range from severe illness to death. Poisons are chemically active principles, often affecting the central nervous

system ; among the most severe are arsenic, various cyanides, alkaloids, phosphoric acid ester, carbon monoxide, and mercury compounds. Inorganic substances which cause death by asphyxia (water, carbon dioxide, etc). are not considered as poisons. *See also* toxicity.

Poisson's equation. Equation of adiabatic of perfect gas, whose heat capacity is temperature-independent, pV^x=constant, where p=pressure, V=volume, and $x=Cp/Cv$, Cp=heat capacity at constant pressure and Cv at constant volume.

polar adsorption. Adsorption of electrically unequal amounts of ions, so that the adsorbed film has an over-all electrical charge. Also adsorption chiefly attributable to attraction between polar groups of adsorbent and adsorbate.

polar bond. *See* ionic bond.

polar compound. In general, a compound that exhibits polarity, or local differences in electrical properties, and has a dipole moment associated with one more of its interatomic valence bond. Polar compounds have relatively high dielectric constants, associate readily in most cases, and include the substances that exhibit tautomerism. In the most general use of the term, polar compounds include all electrolytes, most inorganic substances, and many organic ones. Specifically, the term polar compound is frequently applied to the extreme type of polarity which arises in the presence of an electrovalent bond or in wave-mechanical terms, to cases in which one ionic term dominates in the orbital function of the molecule. Such compounds are exemplified by the inorganie acids, bases, and salts which possess, to a greater or lesser degree, the power to conduct electricity, associate, form double molecules and complex ions, etc.

polar group. Arrangement of atoms in molecule, having permanent dipole moment, *e.g.*,

$$C{-}H,\ C{-}Cl,\ C{=}O,\ C{-}NH_2,\ C{-}C{\equiv}N$$

polarimetry. Method of analysis used for identification (specific rotation measurement) or quantitative determination of optically active substances based on measurement of angle of rotation of polarization plane of polarized light.

polarity. A partial separation of positive and negative charges exhibited by substances. This separation may persist in the natural state (as in dipolar molecules) or may be induced or maintained by the action of an external field.

polarizability, molecular. The constant of proportionality between the electrical moment of the dipole induced in a molecule and the field intensity, as in the relationship :

$$m=\alpha F$$

in which m = the electrical moment of the induced dipole, α = the molecular polarizability, and F = the field intensity.

polarization. 1. The process of confining the vibrations of the magnetic (or electric field) vector of light to one plane.

2. The process to bring about a partial separation of electrical charges of opposite sign in a body by the superposition of an external field.

3. The formation of localized regions near the electrodes of electric cell during electrolysis of products which modify (usually adversely) the further flow of current through cell.

polarization potential. The total counterelectromotive force of an electrolytic (voltaic) cell, which increases as the process of polarization within the cell proceeds, in the course of many electrolytic process.

polarized bond. Chemical bond with non-zero dipole moment.

polarized covalent bond. Intermediate bond between the covalent and ionic bonds, characterized by various probabilities of finding electrons near linked atoms. This bond occurs always between different atoms and is often identified (when strongly polarized) with ionic bond.

polarized light. Light without properties of cylindrical symmetry in direction of propagation.

Polarized light, circular. Polarized light composed of vibrations of circular, rather than the common linear, motion in the plane normal to the direction of transmission.

Polarized light, elliptical. Polarized light composed of vibrations of elliptical, rather than the common linear, motion in the plane normal to the direction of transmission.

polar molecule. Molecule with permanent dipole moment.

polarogram. Curve representing dependence of current on potential, recorded during polarography experiment.

polarograph. Apparatus for automatic recording of current changes with slowly linearly changing voltage (0.1 – 1.0 V/min) applied to electrodes.

polarographic maxima. In polarography, characteristic increase of current above value predicted by Ilkovic equation.

polarographic wave. Sharply rising part of polarographic curve.

polarography. The methods of measurement of potential difference-current relationships in solutions by means of a polarized microelectrode ; and the interpretation of data or records so obtained in terms of the nature and behaviour of many substances and systems. In electrolytic cell having one electrode large in area, and the other electrode very small, the polarization of the latter approaches a maximum, and variations in the electromotive force of the cell are due almost entirely to changes in the potential of this electrode. Consequently, this microelectrode can function as an indicator electrode to measure changes in potential while current is flowing.

Many types of microlectrodes have been used sucessfully in polarographic work. The solid micraoelectrodes have been used extensively, both in stirred solutions, and by rotating the solid microelectrode in a stationary solution. Another important type is the dropping-mercury electrode, consisting of a slowly-growing drop of mercury issuing in small uniform drops from a glass capillary of small size (approximately 0.05 mm. in diameter).

polaron. The object that results when an electron in the conduction band of a crystalline insulator or semiconductor polarizes or otherwise deforms the lattice in its vicinity. The polaron comprises the electron plus its surrounding lattice deformation. Polarons can also be formed holes in the valence bond.

Polenske number. A quantity which expresses the relative water-insoluble volatile fatty acid content of fats, soaps, and similar substances. The actual value of this quantity is the number of cubic centimeters of tenth-normal alkali required to neutralize an alcohol solution of the water-insoluble volatile fatty acids obtained by saponifying a 5 g. sample.

poling. A technique used in refining of copper in which green-wood poles are dipped into molten metal to generate the reducing gases that react with the oxides in the liquid metal.

polish. Any compound or mixture applied to the surface of a material to give a brilliant decorative finish or to remove minor imperfections. Glass is mechanically treated with rouge (red iron oxide) and for special purposes with heat (flame-polishing) ; metals and ceramic products leather, wood, and many other materials are finished with a variety of mixtures containing waxes, solvent, and colourant,

2. The outer coating or husk of cereal grains, which often contains valuable vitamins and is usually removed in processing, for example, rice polish,

Pollacci test for iodic acid. Red phosphorus reduces iodic acid, liberating free iodine.

Pollard test. Gold is detected in solution by acidifying 10 ml. of the solution with hydrochloric acid and adding 1 ml. of a solution of 0.1g. *o*-toluedine in 100 ml. 1 : 10 hydrochloric acid. A yellow colour appears if gold is present.

pollution. Destruction or impairment of the purity of environment, *i.e.*, introduction into any environment of substances that are not normally present therein and that are ojectionable.

polonium. An element.

	Symbol	Po
State Solid	Atomic No.	84
Group VIA	Atomic wt.	210
	Valence	2,4,6
	m.p.	527K
	b.p.	1233K

It is a silvery crystalline metal, which resembles lead and bismuth in physical properties more than it does tellurium, the element above it in the Periodic Table. Polonium is a radioactive element ; the isotope 210 is the form produced commercially : it emits alpha particles. It is produced by irradiation of bismuth with neutrons, with subsequent chemical treatment and concentration.

It is used as a neutron source in nuclear reactors and as an alpha particle generator. Polonium-plated metal rods and strips have been used as static dissipators in textile coating equipment and in various element. The alpha particles from the polonium ionize the air. causing it to conduct and draw off accumulations of static electrical charges.

Investigations as a potential power source have been carried out . Like other radioactive elements, polonium is a hazardous toxic agent and should be handled with proper protective equipment.

Three isotopes of polonium occur in the uranium ($4n+2$) radioactive series : ^{218}Po (radium A), $t_{1/2}$ 3.05 min ; ^{214}Po (radium C′), $t_{1/2}$ 1.6 × 10^{-4} s ; and ^{210}Po (radium F) $t_{1/2}$ 138.4 days, and the most stable isotope of polonium. It is used as a source of α-radiation. The thorium ($4n$) series has two isotopes, ^{216}Po (thorium A), $t_{1/2}$ 0.16 s, and ^{212}Po (thorium C′) $t_{1/2}$ 3×10^{-7} s. The actinium ($4n+3$) series also has two isotopes, ^{215}Po (actinium A), $t_{1/2}$ 1.83 ×10^{-3} s, and ^{211}Po (actinium C′) $t_{1/2}$ 0.52 s, which occurs in a 0.3% branched chain disintegration of ^{211}Bi (actinium C). Several other isotopes of polonium have been prepared, one of which occurs in the neptunium ($4n+1$) series as ^{213}Po, $t_{1/2}$ 4.2×10^{-6} s.

Poluetkov test for gallium. 1. Gallium forms a light red lake with an alcoholic solution of alizarin, in the presence of ammonium chloride and ammonium hydroxide.

2. One ml. of the neutral or weakly-acid solution tested is treated whith 3 ml. 0.5% manganese chloride solution in 6-7 N potassium ferrocyanide solution containing a little potassium bromate. A red-brown precipitate or turbidity indicates the presence of gallium.

Poluetkov test for rhenium. One drop of the solution tested is mixed with 1 drop of a solution of 10 g. stanous chloride in 20 ml. hydrochloric acid. A black colour or precipitate on addition of sodium tellurate indicates the presence of rhenium.

poly-. A prefix widely used in chemistry with the general meaning of " many" or "several') (or more than one).

polyacid. Product of condensation of certain number of simple molecules of oxy-acid, having more than one mole of acid anhydride per one mole of water.

polyaddition. Generally—addition polymerization. Particular meaning—polymerization by repeated addition process of monomers not containing carbon-carbon double bonds (*e.g.*, reaction of epoxy monomers, isocyanates or lactams).

polyallomer resins. These are black copolymers prepared by polymerizing monomers in the presence of anionic coordination catalysts. The polymer chains in polyallomers are composed of homopolymerized segments of each of the monomers employed. The structure of a typical polyallomer can be represented as :

$$(PPPPPPPP.\,.\,.\,.\,.)_x\ (EEEE.\,.\,.\,.)_y$$

where P represents a propylene molecule and E an ethylene molecule. The number and length of the individual segments can be varied within wide limits depending on the process conditions, monomer concentrations, and catalyst systems employed. The copolymers exhibit the crystallinity normally associated only with the stereoregular homopolymers of these monomers.

Polyallomers can be synthesized in slurries by contacting the parent monomers with anionic coordination catalysts of the Ziegler-Natta type at temperatures of 340-350K. Polyallomers are also synthesized in solution at 400-500K by contacing the parent monomers with hydrogen-reduced alpha-titanium trichloride and a lithium-containing cocatalyst. In both the slurry and solution process the polyallomers are formed by alternate polymerization of the monomers employed. In the synthesis of polyallomers from monomers which differ widely in polymerization rates it is sometimes desirable to alternately polymerize a single monomer and then a mixture of monomers to obtain the most desirable properties.

polyamide. A class of high-polymer substances characterized by a —$CONH_2$ grouping ; it includes such naturally occurring materials as the proteins, casein, found in milk, and zein in corn.

polyatomic. Containing more than two atoms or, derivatively, containing more than two of a particular kind of atom, indicated by the term modified by the word polyatomic.

polycarbonate. A type of polyester resin resulting from the catalytic condensation reaction of bisphenol A with a carbonyl-containing compound such as diphenyl carbonate or phosgene (carbonyl chloride). The product is a linear polymer of carbonic acid ester represented by the structure

$$[-OC_6H_5-C(CH_3)_2-C_6H_5-O-C\cdots O]_n.$$

Reaction techniques are by emulsion polymerization at room temperature, by direct reaction under vacuum with heat and catalyst (transesterification), or by polymerization in solution with an organic base as solvent, *e.g.*, ethanolamine.

polychromic. Having two or more colours. Also known as polychromatic.

polycrystalline aggregate. Solid substance composed of large number of small, irregularly shaped and differently oriented crystal.

polycyclic. Having two or more rings, as a compound having a structure containing two or more rings of atoms.

polydisperse system. A colloidal system that consists of particles of sedimentation constant has different values for a polydisperse system.

polydispersity. Dispersion of mass of particles in suspensions and colloids.

polyelectrode. Electrode (half-cell) at which simultaneously two or more electrode reactions determining potential occur. Also known as multiple electrode.

polyelectrolyte. An ionically active, electrically conducting high polymer, either natural or synthetic, used for water conditioning, colloidal clay dispersion, inhibition of calcium carbonate deposition, etc. Polyelectrolytes may exhibit either applications depend to some extent on the individual substance. Examples of natural polyelectrolytes are gum arabic, carrageenan, and proteins ; sodium polyphosphate is one of a number of synthetic types ; ion-exchange resins function in the same manner.

polyene. A compound which contains more than two double bonds.

polyester. Any of a broad class of synthetic resins made by a condensation reaction between a dihydric alcohol such as ethylene glycol and a dicarboxylic acid, *e.g.*, phthalic or maleic. Some types, such as alkyd resins, require the presence of a drying oil. Polyester resins are unsaturated, cross-linked polymers which are made thermosetting by use of a peroxide-type catalyst.

polyethylene. One of the most versatile and widely used types of plastics ; it is also called polythene. It is an addition polymer synthesized by free radical-activated polymerization of ethylene $(C_2H_4)_n$, where the molecular weight may be as low as from 2000 to 4000 ; in so-called linear polyethylene, it is much greater, the macromolecule containing as many as 10,000 hydrocarbon units arranged in long coiled chains, *i.e.*, amorphous or thermoplastic polyethylene, which may be either high or low density. Polyethylene can be cross-linked, either with a peroxide or by radiation, in which case it becomes thermosetting, with high strength and electrical resistance. A crystalline modification can be made by synthesis with stereospecific catalysts of the Ziegler type.

polyform process. A method of petroleum cracking in which thermal cracking and naphtha reforming take place in the same reaction zone specifically by preheating a mixture of naphtha and C_3 and C_4 hydrocarbons and passing them together through the heating coil.

polygenetic dye. A dyestuff which yields different colours on the fibre according to the mordant used, *e.g.*, alizarin.

polyhydrate. A compound containing more than two associated molecules of water.

polyhydric. Containing more than two hydroxyl groups.

polymer. Substance composed of molecules containing many of one or more species of atoms or groups of atoms (called constitutional units or mers) repetitively linked to each other.

A polymer molecule may be formed naturally or made synthetically either by (*i*) the chemical union of five or more molecules of a monomer (addition polymer) or (*ii*) a series of condensation reactions between two or more chemicals, *e.g.*, phenol and formaldehyde (condensation polymer). If only a few monomer units combine, the products are low polymers; when only two, three, or four molecules are present, the combination are called dimers, trimers, and tetramers respectively.

polymeric composite. Any of the combinations or compositions that comprise two or more materials as separate phases, at least one of which is a polymer. By combining a polymer with another material, such as glass, carbon, or another polymer, it is often possible to obtain unique combinations or levels of properties.

polymerization. In general, a reaction in which a complex molecule of relatively high molecular weight is produced from a number of simpler molecules. The reaction may proceed by mere addition of molecules of a single molecular species; it may include more than one species; or it may involve condensation, *i.e.*, elimination of water, ammonia, or other simple substance, or their elements.

Polymerization may be carried out catalytically at temperatures and pressures ranging from normal to high. Synthetic resins, elastomeric dispersion (latexes), and certain types of gasoline and lubricants are made in this way. It may be noticed that initiating agents such as peroxides, free radicals, or short-wave radiation; are essential factors in the polymerization mechanism. Condensation polymerization involves a multistep catalytic reaction of two chemical compounds, *e.g.*, phenol and formaldehyde in addition polymerization, identical molecules (monomers) of olefinic substance such as styrene combine to form polystyrene. When molecules of two or more such substances are used the result is a copolymer (styrene-butadiene). In many cases the reactions can be controlled by use of selective catalysts to give "tailor made" molecular structures called stereospecific polymers. Polymerization techniques are quite varied, including gas phase, solution. batch or block, emulsion, and oxidative coupling. Some substances, notably acrylic acid, polymerize spontaneously at room temperature; inhibitors must be incorporated in handling and storage to prevent this reaction.

Polymerization occurs naturally in plants, forming, cellulose from sugars and starches, proteins and polypeptides from amino acids, and terpenes from hydrocarbons. The drying of certain vegetable oils is another instance of natural polymerization.

polymerization, bulk. *See* bulk polymerization.

polymerization, co-. *See* coplymerization.

polymerization, condensation. *See* condensation polymerization.

polymerization, emulsion. *See* emulsion polymerization.

polymerization isomerism. Occurrence of complex compounds of the same empirical formula but different molecular masses, it may result from coordination polymerization, *e.g.*, $[Co(NH_3)_3(NO_2)_3]$ and $[Co(NH_3)_6][Co(NO_2)_6]$; or nuclear polymerization, *e.g.*,

$$\left[(H_3N)_3Co \begin{matrix} OH \\ -OH- \\ OH \end{matrix} Co(NH_3)_3\right] X_3$$

and

$$\left[Co\left\{\begin{matrix} OH \\ OH \end{matrix}\right\rangle Co(NH_3)_4\right\}_3\right] X_6$$

polymerization, mass. *See* mass polymerization.

polymolecularity. Dispersion of molecular mass of polymer. Also known as polydispersity of molecular weight.

polymorph. A substance that exhibits two or more crystalline forms.

polymorphism. A phenomenon in which a substance exhibits different forms. Dimorphic substances appear in two crystal forms, whereas trimorphic exist in three, as sulphur, carbon, tin, silver iodide, and calcium carbonate. Polymorphism is restricted to the solid state. Polymorphs yield identical solutions and vapours (if vapourizable). The relation between them has been termed "physical isomerism" and the polymorphs have been termed "physical isomers."

polynuclear complex. Complex composed of two or more central atoms with ligands forming coordination spheres linked by atoms or bridge groups. Also known as bridged complex.

polynuclear hydrocarbon. One of a class of hydrocarbons posscsing more than one ring.

The aromatic polynuclear hydrocarbons may be divided into two groups. In the first, the rings are fused, which means atleast two carbon atoms are shared between adjacent rings, *e.g.*, naphthalene. In second group of polynuclear hydrocarbons the aromatic rings are joined either directly, or through a chain of one or more carbon atoms.

polyol. Contracted form of polyhydric alcohol *i.e.*, one that contains three or more hydroxyl groups.

polyolefin. A general term referring to any high polymer made by addition polymerization of unsaturated, straight-chain hydrocarbons by catalytic reactions at high temperature. They are thermoplastic resins ; some are useful in their linear form, but cross-linking is generally required. Polyethylene is a typical example.

polypeptide. A compound composed of two or more amino acids and similar in many properties to the natural peptones. The amino acids are joined by peptide groups $-NH-\overset{\overset{O}{\parallel}}{\underset{|}{C}}$ formed by the reaction between an $-NH_2$ group and a $-\overset{\overset{O}{\parallel}}{\underset{\underset{OH}{|}}{C}}$ group, whereby there is elimination of a molecule of water, and formation of a valence bond. They may be termed di-, tri-, tetra-, etc., peptide according to the number of amino acids present in the molecule. The molecular weight may range as high as 40 million (for bushy stunt virus). Both acidic and basic groups are present, and the products are thus amphoteric. Polypeptides are proteins in all essential respects.

polyploidy. Having more than twice the normal haploid number of chromosomes in a cell. Artificial polyploidy can be induced (*e.g.*, by colchicine), and is used to produce fertile hybrids with desired characteristics.

polysaccharide. One of a class of carbohydrates characterized by amorphous, complex structure and lack of sweet taste, as cellulose, amylose, galactose, mannose, starch, dextrin, inulin. On hydrolysis they yield, after a series of reactions, several molecules of monosaccharide. Among the subgroups are phycocolloids found in seaweeds, water-soluble gums produced by certain species of tropical trees, and mucilages (guar gum).

polytropic process. A process which occurs with an interchange of both heat and work between the system and its surroundings. Quasistatic process with constant heat capacity $C=\frac{\delta Q}{\delta T}$. In ideal gas of constant C_v polytropic process is described by equation

$$pV^n = \text{const.}$$

where δQ=elementary heat of quasistatic process, T=thermodynamic temperature and $n=(C_p-C)/(C_v-C)$; C_p=heat capacity at constant pressure and C_v=heat capacity at constant volume.

polyunsaturate. This term is usually applied to a type of unsaturated fatty acid found in vegetable fats and oils which has two or more double bonds, *e.g.*, linoleic and linolenic acids. Foods containing these are considered less likely to cause cholesterol deposition than those containing saturated fatty acids (animal-derived).

polywater. A reported form of water differing in properties (such as density, viscosity) from normal water. These properties are due to the presence of colloidal particles derived from impurities rather than to any differences in the molecular structure of the water itself. Also known as anomalous water.

Pomeranz-Fritsch reaction. A method of formation of isoquinolines by condensing aryl aldehydes and amino acetals, followed by ring closure in the presence of acid., *e.g.*,

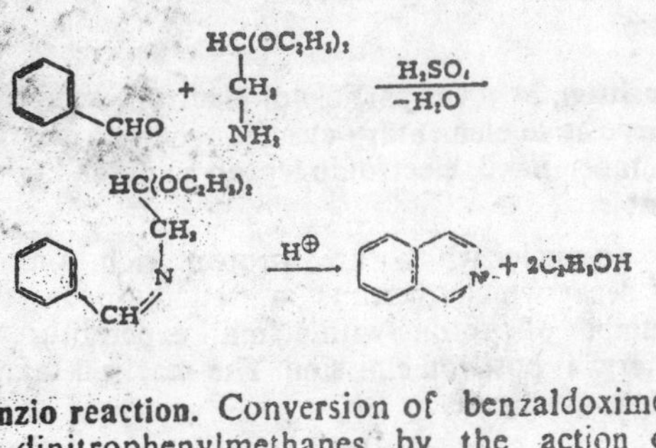

$$C_6H_5CHO + \underset{NH_2}{\underset{|}{CH_2}}\text{-}HC(OC_2H_5)_2 \xrightarrow[-H_2O]{H_2SO_4} C_6H_5CH{=}N\text{-}CH_2\text{-}HC(OC_2H_5)_2 \xrightarrow{H^{\oplus}} \text{isoquinoline} + 2C_2H_5OH$$

Ponzio reaction. Conversion of benzaldoximes to dinitrophenylmethanes by the action of nitrogen dioxide in ethereal solution :

$CH{=}NOH$ $\xrightarrow{N_2O_4}$ $CH(NO_2)_2$

NO_2 NO_2

poromeric. A term used to describe a material usually organic in nature, which has a great number of extremely small pores per unit area. This is characteristic of human and animal skins, which transmit moisture from the body; it is also true of leather and some types of synthetic resins used as leather substitutes. These are particularly suitable for shoes, as the pores are so formed as to allow the passage of air and vapour from the inside outward.

porphyrin. Any of a number of natural nitrogenous organic compounds characterized by four heterocyclic pyrrole groups, which have high pigmenting power. There are two central hydrogen atoms which can be replaced by metal atoms, forming coordination compounds. The porphyrin molecule has both strong pigmenting properties and catalytic activity. Two of the most important porphyrin derivatives are chlorophyll, where magnesium replaces the central hydrogens, and hemin, in which iron is the central metal atom.

position isomerism. Type of structural isomerism caused by different location of substituents on identical carbon skeleton (straight-chained or cyclic) of isomeric compounds, *e.g.*, propan-1-ol and propan-2-[illegible] o-xylene and *m*-xylene.

positive azeotrope. Azeo[illegible] composition at which there is maximum [illegible]ar pressure and correspondingly, minimum boiling temperature.

positron, e^+. Antiparticle of electron, a lepton, of positive elementary electric charge, baryon number $B=0$, electronic lepton number $L_e=1$, stable.

In nuclei which are proton rich, a mode of decay which permits a reduction in the number of protons with a small expenditure of energy is positron emission. The reaction taking place during decay is

$$p^+ \rightarrow n^0 + e^+ + \mu$$

where p^+ represents the proton; n^0, the neutron; e^+, the positron; and μ a massless, chargeless entity called a neutrino. *See also* neutrino. The positron and neutrino are emitted from the nucleus while the neutron remains bound within the nucleus. Although none of the naturally occuring radioactive nuclides are positron emitters, many artificial radioisotopes which decay by positron emission have been produced. The first observed case of positron decay of nuclei was also the first observed case of artificial radioactivity. An example of such a nuclear decay is

$$_{11}Na^{22} \rightarrow {}_{10}Ne^{22} + e^+ + \mu \text{ (half-life} \backsim 2.6 \text{ years).}$$

This decay provides a particle, usable source of positrons for experimental purposes.

The life span of positrons is very short; positron-electron pairs appear momentarily upon the absorption of γ rays or cosmic rays; positrons are also commonly emitted in many nuclear reactions.

positronium. Unstable system consisting of electron and positron, analogous to hydrogen atom (proton is replaced by positron); it is formed, *e.g.*, during the slowing down of positrons in matter. Positronium is of particular interest because it is the two-body system to which quantum electrodynamics is applicable, and its study has served as an important confirmation of the theory of quantum electrodynamics.

Its set of energy levels is similar to that of the hydrogen atom (electron and proton). However, because of the different reduced mass, the frequencies associated with the spectral lines are less than half of those of the corresponding hydrogen lines. The mean life of positronium is at most about 10^{-7} seconds, its existence being terminated by negatron-positron annihilation.

potash. A generic and commercial name for naturally occurring potassium salts; derived from "pot ashes".

potassium. An element.

	Symbol	K
State Solid	Atomic No.	19
Group IA	Atomic Wt.	39.098
	Valence	1
	Isotopes	2 stable
	m.p.	
	b.p.	

Potassium is a very abundant element, ranking

seventh among all the elements in the earth's crust, 2.59% of which is potassium in combined form. In sea water, potassium is present upto 380 ppm. Potassium, is one of the reactive of the alkali-metal group.

There are three naturally occurring isotopes, ^{39}K through ^{41}K, of which ^{40}K is radioactive ($t_{1/2}=1.3\times10^9$ years). In ordinary potassium this isotope represents only 0.0119% of the content. There are four other known isotopes, all radioactive, ^{38}K and ^{42}K through ^{44}K, all with relatively short half-lives-measured in minutes and hours. Elemental potassium has a body-centered cubic crystal structure. Potassium is a silvery-white metal, can be readily moulded, and cut by a knife, oxidizes instantly on exposure to air. and reacts violently with water, yielding potassium hydroxide and hydrogen gas, which burns spontaneously in air with a violet flame due to volatilized potassium. In these respects, potassium behaves much like sodium. The element is preserved under kerosene.

Its salts, chiefly KCl, occur in many natural deposits. It readily combines with halogens and other elements, and its principal use is in the form of these compounds, as fertilizers and explosives. It is a vital element in plant nutrition and occurs and metabolic functions in animal organism. In combination with sodium (NaK), it is used as a heat-transfer agent.

potassium-argon dating. A method of dating geological specimens based on the decay of the radioisotope potassium-40 to argon-40. The half-life of potassium-40 is about 1.3×10^9 years and an estimate of the ratio of the two isotopes in a specimen give an indication of its age.

potency. In its original mathematical sense, this term connoted the power of a term, *i.e.*, the number of times a number was multiplied by itself. It is used in the therapeutics to denote the power of a drug in the sense of its therapeutical activity.

potential. Ratio of potential energy of system in potential field to same scalar quantity characteristic for system and denoting its interaction with field.

potential barrier. Spatial region with local maximum of potential energy. Repulsive forces tend to remove particle from this region.

potential, contact. *See* contact potential.

potential, critical. *See* critical potential.

potential, diffusion. *See* diffusion potential.

potential, discharge. *See* discharge potential.

potential, electrode. *See* electrode potential.

potential energy curve, $U(r)$. Curve representing functional dependence of potential energy U of pair of particles on their relative distance r, *e.g.*, potential energy curve for diatomic molecule.

potential energy surface (in chemical kinetics). Population of all points of coordinates r_1, r_2, $E(r_1, r_2)$ where r_1 = distance between centres of atoms X and Y, r_2 = distance between centres of atoms Y and Z, $E(r_1, r_2)$ =potential energy depending on r_1 and r_2, in reacting systems $XY+Z \rightarrow X+YZ$.

potential field. Field derived as negative gradient of some scalar function (potential, potential energy).

potential, liquid junction. *See* diffusion potential.

potential-time curve. Dependence of potential of indicator electrode on time of chronopotentiometric analysis.

potential well. Potential given by $U(x) = 0$ for $0\leq x\leq a$, $U(x) = U_0$ for either $x<0$ or $x>a$:

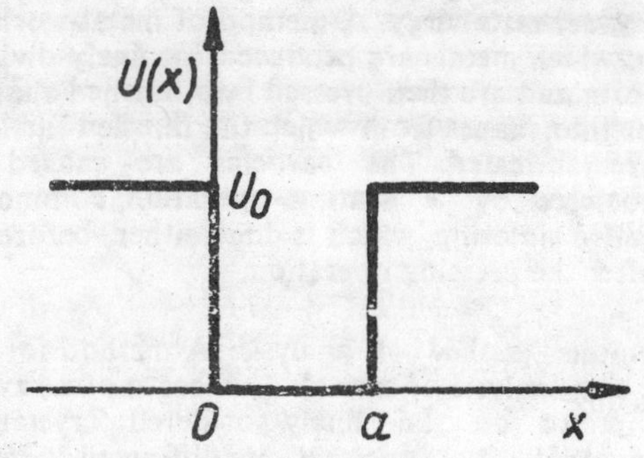

also known as a potential box.

potentiator. A term used in the food and flavor industries to characterize a substance that intensifies the taste of a food product to a far greater extent than an enhancer. The most important of these are certain enzyme-like nucleotides such as riboflavin 5'- phosphate; the effective concentration is measured in parts per billion, whereas that of enhancers such as monosodium glutamate is in parts per thousand. The effect is thought to be due to synergism. Potentiators do not impart any taste of their own, but intensify the taste response to substances already present in the food.

potentiometric titration. A method of titrating a solution by determining, after each addition of standard solution, the potential of a suitably-chosen electrode in equilibrium with that solution. If the system is properly arranged, a marked change in potential will be found at the end point of the titration. The method frequently uses a potentiometer to determine the changing values of the electrode potential.

potentiostatic methods. Methods of study of kinetics of electrode reactions consisting in recording and analysis of current changes during electrolysis carried out at constant potential of electrode.

pour point. A term used to denote the lowest temperature at which a lube oil will flow by gravity from a specified container under standard conditions. Since this point is largely dependent on the wax content of the oil, agents called pour-point depressant are added to reduce the melting point of the wax. Acrylic acid esters and alkylated naphthalenes have been used for this purpose.

powder metallurgy. A method of metal-working in which metals are produced in finely-divided form and are then pressed into finished shapes, or into shapes from which the finished articles are fabricated. The particles are caused to coalesce by a heating operation, commonly called sintering, which is done either before or after the pressing operation.

powder method of analysis. A method for the x-ray analysis of crystals. A beam of x-rays is directed on the finely-powdered crystalline material, by which it is diffracted. Many minute crystals in the powder are oriented in the correct diffraction for the Bragg equation to be applied to the determination. The diffracted x-rays are allowed to impinge on a film strip which surrounds the powder; characteristic ring patterns are then obtained. The x-ray photograph made in the process is characteristic of each crystalline material, and so can be used in identification.

power factor, sin δ. Sine of loss factor.

Pozzi-Escot test for nickel in presence of cobalt. A neutral or weakly-acid solution of cobalt and nickel chlorides, on addition of excess saturated ammonium molybdate solution, gives a greenish-white precipitate of the nickel, the cobalt remaining in solution.

Pozzi-Escot test for tungsten or molybdenum. To the neutral solution tested, add 1 drop saturated mercurous nitrate solution, 1-1.5 ml. concentrated hydrochloric acid, and excess potassium iodide. Shake until any precipitate dissolves. A transitory blue colour indicates the presence of tungsten or molybdenum.

Prager-Jacobson classification. The system of classification of organic compounds used in the Beilstein Handbuch der Organischen Chemie.

Prandtl number. A dimensionless number used in the study of forced and free convection; equal to the dynamic viscosity times the specific heat at constant pressure divided by the thermal conductivity. The lower the number, the higher is the convection capacity of the substance.

praseo-. A prefix from the Greek praseos, which denotes a green colour.

praseodymium. An element.

	Symbol	Pr
State Solid	Atomic No.	59
Group IIIB	Atomic Wt.	140.91
	Valence	3,4
	m.p.	935K

Praseodymium is a member of rare-earth group of elements, and is a rather soft crystalline solid; obtained from monazite sands. The metallic form is similar to iron in colour, and many of its compounds have a pronounced greenish shade. It has limited use in ceramics and glass manufacture and as a catalyst and phosphor. It has a number of specialized applications in metallurgy.

pre-arc period in emission spectral analysis. Time interval between arc initiation and spectrum recording for analytical purposes.

Prebula-McCollum reaction for vitamin B_1 (thiamine). Vitamin B_1, when treated with a diazotized solution of *p*-aminoacetanilide or methyl-*p*-aminophenylketone, gives a purple-red stable colour, insoluble in water and soluble in xylene.

precipitate. Solid particles formed as a product of a chemical reaction which can be separated from the reaction medium by gravity settling (including cyclone separators, which intensify the force of gravity), centrifuging, coagulation, and filtration. A precipitate also forms when the solubility limit of a substance is reached by cooling (crystallization) or by removal of the solvent from the reaction system (evaporation).

precipitation titration. Titration with solution of substance of known concentration which forms poorly soluble compound with analysed substance.

precipitin. The visible result of the chemical interaction of antigen and antibody. Not all antibodies will result in precipitation, yet they may participate in agglutination reactions or add on to particulate antigens, and evidence for their occurrence together with precipitating antibody can be obtained for most sera.

precision spectrophotometry. Spectrophotometric method of determination of concentration based on measurements with respect to one or two standard solutions of known concentration, used to fix 100 per cent and/or 0 per cent point of transmittance scale.

precritical state. State of substance under conditions close to critical state, characterized by considerable fluctuations of physical properties.

precursor. A term used in biochemistry to denote an organic compound occurring naturally in plants or animals which is comparatively inactive until subjected to an external stimulus; when this occurs, the compound assumes an active form which has a definite function, *e.g.*, vitamin, often as a result of enzymatic activity. Examples are the conversion of prothrombin to thrombin in the blood brought about by release of blood from the circulatory system, which induces clotting; and the activation of ergosterol to calciferol (vitamin D) by ultraviolet light. In these cases, prothrombin and ergosterol are precursors (inactive forms). the term literally means "running before."

predissociation. Blurring of vibrational energetic levels of molecule due to radiationless transitions between two electronic states, the first of which is stationary excited state of molecule, whereas the second corresponds configuration of nuclei.

pre-exponential factor, *A*. Coefficient occurring in Arrhenius equation, specific for given reaction.

Pre-exponential factor is interpreted in different ways in theory of absolute reaction rate (*see* entropy factor) and collision theory (*see* steric factor). Also known as frequency factor.

preferential. Selectivity of action, either chemical or physicochemical, exhibited by a substance in contact with two other substances ; it may be due either to chemical affinity or to surface phenomena. An example of a preferential chemical combination is that of hemoglobin for carbon monoxide, with which it unites 200 times as readily as with oxygen when exposed to a mixture of the two ; such phenomena as adsorption, corrosion, and the wetting of one material by another are subject to this selectivity.

Prelog's rule. Rule permitting to forecast of configuration of asymmetric synthesis product formed in excess from dicarbonyl compounds. Accordinig to rule, substituents at chiral (L>M>S) acquire conformation in which S is coplanar with two anti-parallely oriented carbonyl groups. Nucleophile Y^- will preferentially attack carbonyl group from the less covered side, *i.e.*, from M substituent :

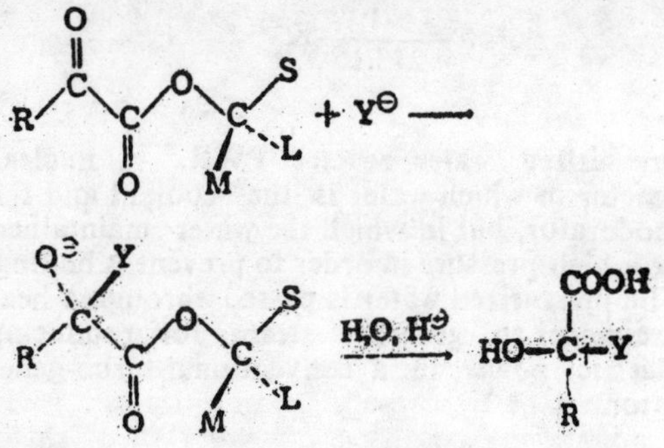

R—C(=O)—C(=O)—O—C(S)(L)(M) + $Y^{\ominus}$ ⟶

R—C($O^{\ominus}$)(Y)—C(=O)—O—C(S)(L)(M) $\xrightarrow{H_2O,\ H^{\oplus}}$ HO—C(COOH)(Y)(R)

prepolymer. A liquid, partially polymerized mixture of a polyhydric alcohol and an isocyanate prepared for on-the-spot formation of urethane foams. The mixture is supplied to the user together with a second mixture containing the blowing agent, catalyst, and alcohol; the foam is formed when the two mixtures are blended. The term also applies to other thermosetting resins, such as diallyl phthalate.

prepreg. A shortened form of the term preimpregnated, used by plastics engineers to refer to a material used as the basis for a composite, such as glass fiber or a textile, which has been coated or impregnated with a thermosetting resin prior to assembly and curing.

preservative. Any substance that prolongs the useful life of an organic material, usually in low concentrations. Though generally applied to food additives such as benzoic acid, acetic acid, and ascorbic acid, which have antimicrobial and antioxidant value, the term applies equally well to antioxidants used in petroleum products, rubber, and similar materials. It also includes the various alcohol and aldehydes used in preventing deterioration of biological specimens, *e.g.*, formaldehyde, though in this case a high concentration is necessary, either by injection or immersion.

pressure coefficient (of gas), β. Relative change of pressure p of gas, caused by change of thermodynamic temperature T by 1 K at constant volume V

$$\beta = \frac{1}{p}\left(\frac{\partial p}{\partial T}\right)_V \quad [\mathrm{K}^{-1}]$$

Pressure coefficient of ideal gas is

$$\beta = \frac{1}{273.15}\,\mathrm{K}^{-1}$$

pressurized water reactor PWR. A nuclear reactor in which water is the coolant and the moderator, but in which the water maintained at a high pressure in order to prevent it boiling. The pressurized water is passed through a heat exchanger to generate steam for producing electric power in a conventional turbo-generator.

Prevost reaction. The production of α-glycol benzoates from olefins by the action of iodo-silver benzoate, which can be obtained by direct action of iodine upon silver benzoate.

$$>C{=}C< \xrightarrow[-AgI]{I_2 + CH_3COOAg} -\underset{|}{\overset{I}{\overset{|}{C}}}-\underset{OOCCH_3}{\underset{|}{C}}- \xrightarrow[-AgI]{Ag^{\oplus}}$$

$$\left[\begin{array}{c} -C-C- \\ | \quad | \\ O \quad O \\ \diagdown \diagup \\ C^{\oplus} \\ | \\ CH_3 \end{array}\right] \xrightarrow{CH_3COO^{\ominus}} -\underset{|}{\overset{CH_3COO}{\overset{|}{C}}}-\underset{OOCCH_3}{\underset{|}{\overset{|}{C}}}-$$

Prileschajew reaction. The action of organic peroxides upon alkenes to yield epoxides:

$$>C{=}C< + C_6H_5COOOH \rightarrow -\overset{|}{C}-\overset{|}{C}- + C_6H_5COOH$$
$$\quad\ \diagdown_{O}\diagup$$

primary alcohol. A monohydric alcohol in which one of the hydrogen atoms attached to the methanol carbon is replaced by an alkyl group; if the carbon chain is not branched, the alcohol is called normal. Examples are ethyl alcohol (CH_3CH_2OH) and normal butyl alcohol, $CH_3(CH_2)_2CH_2OH$. The term is also applied to amines and numerous other compounds in an analogous manner.

primary cell. A system in which electrical energy is obtained as the result of a chemical reaction or reactions. Although the reactions are usually reversible, the primary cell is not arranged to operate reversibly, cells so constructed being called secondary cells. Primary cells consist commonly of an electrode of a metal or other substance in contact with a solution containing its ions, and the solution being electrolytically connected, in a manner that will avoid mixing, with another solution in contact with another electrode. To complete the circuit, electrical contact is made between the electrodes, commonly through an external circuit which consumes the electrical energy produced by the cell.

primary interfering reaction. In activation analysis, nuclear interfering reaction caused by stream of bombarding primary particles. Also known as primary interference.

primary ionization. Ionization produced directly by interaction of charged particle with atoms of matter through which it is passing.

primary photochemical process. Photochemical reaction which takes place in electronically excited state immediately after absorption of photon by a given atom or molecule, *e.g.*, photolysis, photoisomerization.

primary reaction. Initiating reaction in system of coupled reactions which determines path of secondary reaction, *i.e.*, of induced reaction.

primary salt effect. Influence of non-reacting electrolytes present in solution on change in rate of proceeding ionic reaction. Primary salt effect is expressed by difference of activity coefficients of substrates and activated complex.

primary standard (in volumetric analysis). Substance of high purity samples of which are used to standardize solution or to prepare solutions of known concentrations.

primary standard substance (in thermochemistry). High-purity substance recommended by IUPAC for calibration of calorimetric systems, *e.g.*, pure benzoic acid is recommended as standard for determination of combustion heats of solids, whereas hydrogen is used for volatile liquids and gases.

primary valency. According to Werner's theory valency characteristic for dissociating compounds (with ionic bonds) and corresponding to atom's oxidation number in given compound.

primitive cell. Unit cell in which identical points are on corners of parallelepiped only. Also known as primitive unit cell.

primitive unit cell. *See* primitive cell.

primer. 1. A substance or material used to start an action, or used as the first stage in an operation. Thus, detonators for explosives are called primers.

2. The term is also used to denote a coat of a finishing material that is applied to an uncoated surface before painting.

principal axis. 1. The longest axis of a crystal.

2. The optical axis of a crystal.

principal polarizabilities. Molecular polarizability values along three mutually perpendicular axes chosen in such a way that the first polarizability value is maximum and the third one minimum for given molecule. Polarizability is arithmetic mean of three principal components.

principal quantum number, *n*. Positive integer which determines energy levels of atom or ion. In the theory of quantum mechanics the principal quantum number is used mostly to identify the electronic orbital of the electron.

principal series. A series of lines in the spectra of many atoms which have one, two, or three electrons in their outer shells, either in their neutral state or as a result of ionization. (Excluded are the atoms which have only one electron in all, such as hydrogen, singly-ionized helium, doubly-ionized lithium, etc.). The principal series differs from the other series for such elements in having a somewhat distinctive physical appearance, and in having a characteristic formula,

$$\bar{\nu}_p = L - \frac{R}{(m+c)^2}$$

where ν_p is the wave number of a line in the principal series, L and c are constants for the principal series, m is a variable integer, whose values give the various lines in the principal series, and R is the Rydberg constant.

principle of corresponding states. For real gases there is some identical equation of state formulated in terms of reduced temperature, reduced pressure and reduced volume.

principle of detailed balancing. Fundamental principle of statistical mechanics according to which in state of thermodynamic equilibrium the same (average) number of particles passes in time unit from state I to state II and from state II to state I. In particular each elementary chemical reaction proceeds with the same velocity in both directions.

principle of increase of entropy. Spontaneous adiabatic transition is always accompanied by system entropy increase.

principle of least structural changes. In chemical reaction formation of new bond (at atom of reactive centre) is accompanied by cleavage of bond, taking place at the same atom. Rearrangement reactions proceed against this principle.

principle of superposition. If quantum mechanical system is allowed to have states ψ_1, ψ_2, ψ_3, ..., then in state given by

$$\psi = \sum_i c_i \psi_i$$

probability that measurement of some quantity will give value characteristic for state ψ_j is equal c_j^2. Also known as superposition principle.

Prins reaction. A method of formation of glycol and dioxane (1,3 position) and their derivatives from olefins, formaldehyde, and organic acid in the presence of mineral acid :

$$2CH_3CH{=}CH_2 + HCHO + 2CH_3COOH \xrightarrow{H^+}$$

$CH_3CHCH_2CH_2$ (with CH_3COO and $OOCCH_3$ attached) + H_3C-substituted 1,3-dioxane ring (O, O)

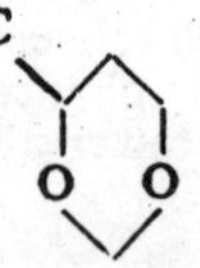

priority rule. Rule on which R-S and E-Z systems and names of conformation systems are based. Atoms and groups of atoms attached to chiral centre (R-S system) or to double bond system (E-*Z* system), are arranged in sequence of decreasing atomic number. If two or more of these atoms have the same atomic number, selection is made by comparing atomic numbers of second group of atoms attached to first atoms. If ambiguity still persists, the third, fourth, etc., sets (working onwards from asymmetric carbon atom) are compared until selection is made.) Substituents are given in order of decreasing priority : I, Br, Cl, SR, SH, F, OH, NO_2, NH_2, CCl_3, COCl, CHO, CH_2OH, C_6H_5, CH_3, D, H. Also known as sequence rule.

pro-. A prefix denoting an antecedent substance, as proenzyme, provitamin.

process. As used in chemical engineering. This term indicates an industrial production method in which a chemical or physicochemical change occurs, as distinguished from an operation, in which there is no chemical change. Among the chemical reactions involved in processes are oxidation, reduction, ionization polymerization, hydrogenation, halogenation, hydrolysis, and saponification.

prochirality. Formation of chirality centre in molecule, resulting from substitution of one of the identical ligands linked with given moiety of molecule (named prochirality centre) by another ligand.

producer gas. A manufactured mixture of gases made by incomplete combustion of coal or by contact of steam with hot coke ; carbon monoxide and hydrogen comprise about 40% of the gas, most of the remainder being nitrogen. It is used chiefly as a low-cost fuel, usually on-site.

product formula. A list of the ingredients and their amounts or percentage required in an industrial product. Such formulas (or recipes) are mixtures. not compounds ; they are generally used in such industries as adhesives, food paint, rubber, and plastics. Selection of ingredients to provide optimum specific properties for a given end use or for specification requirements is made by experienced technologists.

proenzyme. A cell substance or constituent from which enzymes are derived.

proferment. A cell substance or constituent from which ferments are derived.

progesterone. A steroid hormone produced in the body of the female during pregnancy ; formula $C_{21}H_{30}O_2$. It is extracted from an ovrian ductless gland of pregnant animals and can also be synthesized. It is also able to inhibit ovulation when injected but has little effect when take orally.

projection formula. Formula portraying three-dimentional model of molecule as perpendicular projection on a plane.

proliferation. A term used in biochemistry to denote production within a plant or animal of specific types of cells or chemical compounds ; it implies the idea of abundant multiplication, as occurs in the budding of plants, bacterial growth, and formation of diseased tissue cells.

promethium. An element.

	Symbol	Pm
State Solid	Atomic No.	61
Group IIIB	Atomic Wt.	147(?)
	Valence	3
	m.p.	1315K
	b.p.	3273K

A radioactive rare-earth metal; its longest-lived isotope (145) has a half-life of 18 years. The element has been isolated only in trace quantities.

Elemental promethium has a double hexagonal close-packed crystal structure at 300K. Pure metallic promethium is a silvery-white coloured, soft, and can be cast or machined. The naturally occurring isotope, ^{147}Pm, is radiactive ($t_{1/2}$=2.52 years). Consequently, the element must be handled within a shielded area. Eighthen artificially-produced isotopes, ranging from ^{140}Pm to ^{146}Pm and from ^{148}Pm to ^{158}Pm have been identified, all with very short half-lives. Many of the properties of promethium remain classified, or are known only by proprietary sources. It is produced artificially in nuclear reactors, since it is one of the products that results from the fission of uranium, thorium, and plutonium.

Beads containing ^{147}Pm mixed with a phosphor provide a long-lived, reliable green light and were used by astronauts to assist in docking and other maneuvers in outer space. Commercial applications of ^{147}Pm as a power source include betavoltaic cells for surgical implant with heart pumps and pacemakers. Promethium forms only a few compounds, which are of chiefly theoretical interest.

promoter. A substance of little or no catalytic activity which increases the catalytic activity of a catalyst; the total catalytic activity of promoter and catalyst is greater than would be expected from their individual activities.

prompt critical. Capable of sustaining a nuclear fission chain reaction on the prompt neutrons along, without contribution from delayed neutrons.

prompt gamma. In activation analysis, γ-quanta emitted by atoms from target material instantaneously after radiative neutron capture reaction, *i.e.*, (n,γ) reaction. Also known as prompt gamma radiations.

prompt neutrons. Fission neutrons emitted in time shorter than 10^{-13} s. Prompt neutrons constitute about 99% of all neutrons emitted in fission reactions.

proof. An arbitrary term used to designate the volume content of ethyl alcohol in a spiritous liquor or an industrial alcohol. It is twice the percentage of ethyl alcohol present at room temperature; thus, 100-proof alcohol contains 50% of ethyl alcohol and 86-proof alcohol contains 43%, both on a volume basis.

propanolysis. Alcoholysis in which the alcohol split is propyl alcohol.

propellant. 1. A term used in aerosol technology to denote a gas used to drive or push various materials through an orifice in the form of a spray or foam. A simple example is a perfume atomizer where air expelled by pressure on a bulb disperses the liquid into droplets as it leaves the nozzle. Propellants of this type are gases such as carbon dioxide, air, nitrous oxide, butane, and propane. They are used to disperse paints, whipped cream, insecticides, and numerous household cleansers and purifiers.

2. In combustion technology, the term refers to rocket fuels of various types, among which are liquid hydrogen peroxide, hydrazine, boron hydride, etc., and solids such as plasticized nitrocellulose, ammonium nitrate, etc.

property. Any of a number of physical and chemical characteristics that establish the identity of an element or compound. Important among these are the following:

colour
odour
state (gas, liquid, solid)
taste
boiling point
freezing point (liquids)
melting point (solids)
atomic weight (elements)
molecular weight (compounds)
refractive index
toxicity
specific gravity (density)
reaction with standard reagents
energy absorption and emission (infrared, ultraviolet, etc.)
solubility (in water and organic solvents)
combustibility

property, additive. A property of a system that is equal to the sum of the values of that property for the constituents of the system.

property, colligative. A property that depends for the most part on the number of molecules involved and not on their nature.

property, constitutive. A property that depends for the most part on the arrangement of the molecule and, to a lesser degree, on their number and nature.

property, extensive. A property of a system that varies in its value with the quantity of material contained in the system.

property, intensive. A property of system that is independent of the quantity of material contained in the system.

prophylactic. A substance or agent that aids in or contributes to prevention of infection or of a disease.

pros position. In general, any nearby position; or specifically, the 2,3 position in the naphthalene ring and similar condensed rings.

prostaglandins. A group of fatty acid derived molecules containing 20 carbon atoms. They have been detected in practically every part and organ in the human body with especially high concentrations in seminal fluid. They are active biologically causing smooth muscle preparations to contract at concentrations of 10^{-9} g/ml and having definite effects on human blood pressure at doses as 0.1 microgram per kilogram of body weight they are thought to have critical functions in both male and female reproductive processes. Active research is continuing on their possible medical and pharmaceutical applications, as well as on their sources; their presence in unusually high concentrations in sea organisms living in coral beds has been discovered.

prosthetic group. That portion of a protein molecule which is not protein in nature, *e.g.*, nucleic acids in the nucleoproteins, or carbohydrate groups in the glycoproteins.

An active chemical group or metabolite which promotes essential chemical reactions and transformations within the body, for example, oxidation-reduction, decarboxylation, phosphorylation, etc. The term actually means "replacement of a missing part (of the body)," and is used in this sense in medicine. In biochemistry, the meaning is more sophisticated; prosthetic groups function by "fitting in" to active sites afforded by the configurations of molecular complexes. A mechanical analogy would be the teeth on a gear, where each tooth, makes an active but temporary connection with a mating gear by locking into an aperture. Some types prosthetic groups are composed of metal ions bound to porphyrin structures, their effect being produced, at least in part, by chelation, *e.g.*, chlorophyll. Other types are coenzymes, which are organic groups associated with enzymes but easily separated from them. Vitamins of the B complex function by prosthetic mechanisms.

prot-, proto-. (Greek, first) A prefix specifically designating: (*i*) first in an organic series as protoxide (now little used); (*ii*) parent or immediate antecedent, as protoactinium, protochlorophyll.

protactinium. An element.

	Symbol	Pa
State Solid	Atomic No.	91
Group IIIB	Atomic Wt.	231.0359
	Valence	4,5
	m.p.	>1800K

Protactinium is, formally, the third member of the actinide series of elements and the first in which a 5*f* electron appears, but its chemical behaviour in aqueous solution resembles that of tantalum and niobium more closely than that of other actinides.

A radioactive element whose longest-lived isotope is 231, with a half-life of about 32500 years; it occurs naturally in trace quantities in uranium ores and is about as abundant as radium. Isotopes of mass numbers 216, 217, and 222-238 are known, all of them radioactive. The 233 isotope is made artificially by decay a thorium isotope.

Protactinium-231 yields actinium-227 by alpha-particle emission and has a half-life of 3.43×10^4 years. Its other isotopes include two isomers of mass number 234: uranium X_2, with a half-life of 1.17 minutes, and uranium Z, with a half-life of 6.7 hours, the former being an excited state which undergoes deexcitation to give the latter. Other nuclear species have mass numbers 225-230, 232, 233, 235, and 237.

protamine. Any of a class of simple proteins of relatively low molecular mass found in association with the chromosomal DNA of vertebrate male germ cells. They contain a single polypeptide chain comprising about 67% arginine. Protamines are supposed to protect and support the chromosomes.

protecting group. Grouping of atoms attached temporarily to functional group to protect the latter from entering into unwanted reaction.

protection of functional group. Conversion of one of the several functional groups present in molecule of organic compound into another (protective) group, which can easily be removed to restore the primary functional group. This protective group is to be left unchanged in course of reactions carried out with other fuctional groups present in molecule.

protease. A group of enzymes capable of breaking up proteins into amino acids, or building up amino acids into proteins, and of substituting one amino acid by another in protein molecules. Occurring in all living tissues ; they conduct the processes of protein metabolism in the living organism. Also known as proteinase.

protective action. The effect of a substance which stabilizes a system of colloidal particles against coagulation by electrolytes or other means.

protective coating. A general term including all types of surface coatings applied primarily to prevent or inhibit deterioration due to oxidation, corrosion, bacterial attack, and the like.

protective colloid. A hydrophilic high polymer whose particles (molecules) are of colloidal size, such as a protein or gum ; it may be either naturally present in such systems as milk and rubber latex, or intentionally added to mixtures to prevent coagulation of coalescence of the particles of fat or other dispersed material. Protective colloids are also called stabilizing, suspending, or thickening agents ; they also act as emulsifiers. Examples are (*a*) a thin coating of protein on hydrocarbon particles of latex which keeps them from cohering as a result of the impact due to their Brownian motion ; (*b*) gelation, sodium alginate, or gum arabic which are added to ice cream, confectionery, and other food products to obtain a smooth, creamy mixture. They are readily adsorbed by the suspended particles and reinforce the protective effect of proteins that may be naturally present. *See also* gelatin ; gum ; emulsion.

protective effect (in radiation chemistry). Influence of minor additions of chemical compounds affecting yield of radiolysis of main constituent of system or diminution of biological consequences of irradiation.

proteidin. A generic term for a class of bacteriolytic enzymes "combined" with blood albumins which have immunizing and curative properties.

proteinate. A protein compound, commonly formed by reaction with a metallic hydroxide or other base.

protein error. Indication error of acid-base indicators due to presence of proteins in solution.

protein. (pro-te-in). Any of a large class of natural polymers, often having a molecular mass of a million or more ; such macromolecules are made up of amino acid units linked together with amide groups to form a chain-like polypeptide structure of colloidal dimensions. The chains are sometimes crosslinked with disulphides, as in wood. As proteins contains both acidic (COOH) and basic (NH_2) groups, they react in either way and are thus amphoteric. Simple proteins may have only a few amino acid units, but in more complex types there may be several thousand. The sequence in which the amino acids occur in protein molecules is controlled by the nucleoproteins DNA and RNA and is of vital significance in genetic mechanisms. A nucleoprotein is a combination of a protein with a nucleic acid.

Proteins are synthesized by plants from nitrogen fixed by bacteria and from the carbohydrate products of photosynthesis. Though animals can elaborate special types of proteins, they depend on ingestion of plant forms for most of their protein requirements. Proteins are major components of such biologically active complexes as hormones, enzymes, genes, bacteria, and viruses. They are hydrolyzed to their constituent amino acids by proteolytic enzymes of various types.

They are classified in several ways ; the system adopted by the American Society of Biological Chemists is as follows :

I. Simple proteins. On hydrolysis these yield amino acids or their derivatives alone.

A. Albumins. Soluble water and dilute saline solutions, coagulable by heat. Egg albumin, serum albumin.

B. Globulins. Insoluble in water, soluble in dilute saline solutions, coagulable by heat. Edestsn, serum globulin.

C. Glutelins. Insoluble in water or dilute salt solution, soluble in very dilute acid or alkalies, coagulable by heat. Glutenin.

D. Prolamines. Insoluble in water, soluble in 80% alcohol. Gladin, hordein zein.

E. Albuminoids. Insoluble in dilute acid, alkali, water, or salt solutions. Elastin, keratin, collagen. (Also called scleroproteins.)

F. Histones. Soluble in water and dilute acids, precipitated by ammonia, strongly basic, not coagulable by heat. Histone.

G. Protamines. Soluble in ammonia, not coagulable by heat, strongly basic, yielding large amounts of diamino acids on hydrolysis. Sturnin, salmin, clupein.

II. Conjugated proteins, called protcides. Compounds of simple prosthetic with prosthetic groups.

A. Hemoglobins (Chromoproteide.) The prosthetic group is coloured. Hemoglobin, hemocyanin, phycoerythrin.

B. Glycoproteides. (Glucroteides). The prosthetic group contains a carbohydrate residue. mucin, ichthuliun.

C. Phosphoproteins. Proteins of cytoplasm. The prosthetic group contains phosphoric acid but neither nucleic acid nor a phospholipin. Casein, vitellin.

D. Nucleoproteides. The prosthetic group is nucleic acid. Nuclein, nucleohistone.

E. Lecithoproteides. The prosthetic group is lecithin or a phospholipin. Lecithoproteides are soluble in ether.

F. Lipoproteides. (Mathews.) The prosthetic group is a higher fatty acid.

III. Derived proteins. Decomposition products of the natural proteins and synthetic products.

A. Primary protein derivatives.

a. Derived proteins, the first products of the action of acids, enzymes, or water. Insoluble in water. (Proteins.)

b. Metaproteins, produced by further action of acids or alkalies. Insoluble in neutral solution, soluble in weak acids and alkalies. Acid albumin.

c. Coagulated proteins, produced by the action of heat or alcohol, insoluble.

B. Secondary protein derivatives.

a. Proteoses. Hydrolytic decomposition products of proteins, soluble in water, not coagulable by heat, precipitated by saturating their solutions with ammonium sulphate.

b. Peptones. Hydrolytic decomposition products of proteins, not coagulable by heat, soluble in water, not precipitated by saturation with ammonium sulphate.

c. Peptides. Compounds of amino acids of known composition. The synthetic polypeptides are included in this class.

The system of classification proposed by the English Society of Physiologists is :

I. Simple proteins.

1. Protamines.
2. Histones.
3. Globulins.
4. Albumins.
5. Glutelins.
6. Glaidins (prolamines).
7. Scleroproteins.
8. Phosphoproteins.

II. Conjugated proteins.

1. Chromoproteins.
2. Nucleoproteins.
3. Glucoproteins.

III. Hydrolyzed proteins.

1. Metaproteins.
2. Albumoses or proteoses.
3. Peptones.
4. Polypeptides.

proteolysis. Catalytic (*e.g.*, enzymatic) hydrolysis of protein resulting in formation of peptones, polypeptides or amino acids.

proteolytic. A term used in biochemistry to describe enzymes which have the ability to decompose proteins to their component amino acids, usually by a hydrolytic reaction. This occurs, for example, in the digestion of foods which is catalyzed by the enzyme pepsin, present in gastric juice. Other enzymes of this type are trypsin and pepsin.

protium. The name sometimes given to the lighter isotope of hydrogen, which consists of a single proton and electron, has an atomic number of 1 and a mass number of 1, and constitutes about 99.98°/ₒ of ordinary hydrogen.

protogenic solvent. Solvent, which gives proton to dissolved substance, *e.g.*, glacial acetic acid, liquid hydrogen fluoride anhydrous sulphuric acid (*see* Bronsted's theory of acids and bases). Also known as proton donor solvent, acidic solvent.

protolysis. Exchange of protons between two pairs of acids and conjugate bases ; second acid-base pair is usually the solvent.

$$HA + B \rightleftharpoons A + HB$$

HA and A as well as HB and B represent these conjugated pairs (*see* Bronsted's theory of acids bases). Also known as protolytic reaction.

proteolytic enzyme. An enzyme such as pepsin and papain, that catalyzes the hydrolysis of proteins. Also known as protease, proteoclastic enzyme.

protolytic reaction. *See* protolysis.

proton, *p*. Elementary particle, a hadron, one of isospin doublet state of necleon, stable, of mass m=932.2592 MeV, positive elementary electric charge, baryon number $B=1$, lepton number $L=0$, quantum spin number $J=1/2$, strangeness $S = 0$, isospin $I = 1/2$, third component of isospin $I_3=1/2$. It is assumed that parity of proton is $P=+1$. Proton is constituent of all atomic nuclei.

The proton is the nucleus of a hydrogen atom, *i.e.*, it is a hydrogen atom without its electron, and is one of the basic "building-blocks" of the nuclei of all atoms.

protonated double bond. One of the conceptions of boron-boron bond in B_2H_6 molecule, proposed by Pitzer ; two bridge-forming protons are closely located to B—B bond axis :

```
 H       H
 |   H   |
H—B:   :B—H
     H
```

protone. One of a class of substances intermediate between the amino acids and the protamines, prepared from the latter by mild hydrolysis. The protones bear to :

$$HOOC—CH_2—CH=CH—COOH \rightleftharpoons HOOC—CH=CH—CH_2—COOH$$

the protamines a relation similar to that which the peptones bear to the proteins.

protopectin. A term applied to the water-insoluble parent pectic substance which occurs in plants and which upon restricted hydrolysis, yields pectin or pectinic acids.

protophile. A substance which accepts (*i.e.*, forms combinations with) protons (hydrogen ions) readily.

protoplasm. A complex mixture of components of plant and animal cells. The more diffused portion lying between the nucleus and the cell wall or membrane is called cytoplasm. The exact compositions of protoplasm is uncertain though amino acids, phosphorus, and ribose sugars are known to occur in nucleotide.

proton-proton chain. Series of thermonuclear reactions leading to synthesis of helium from hydrogen :

$$^1H(p,\beta^+\nu)\ ^2H(p,\gamma)\ ^3He \begin{cases} ^3He,\ 2p)\ ^4He \\ (\alpha,\gamma)\ ^7Be \begin{cases} (\beta^-,\nu^-)\ ^7Li(p,\alpha)\ ^4He \\ (p,\gamma)\ ^8B(\beta,\gamma)\ ^8Be(\alpha)\ ^4He \end{cases} \end{cases}$$

According to Salpeter, proton-proton chain is source of energy of stars.

protophilic solvent. Solvent with affinity for proton, *e.g.*, liquid ammonia, amines water ether dioxane (*see* Bronsted's theory of acids bases). Also known as proton acceptor solvent; basic solvent.

prototropy. In general, the shifting of a proton or hydrogen atom in a compound to yield an isomeric substance. Thus, in β-dicarbonyl compounds, a prototropic change to the enol-form accounts for many of the reactions of these substances :

$$-\overset{O}{\overset{\|}{C}}-\overset{H}{\overset{|}{C}}-\overset{O}{\overset{\|}{C}}- \rightleftharpoons -\overset{OH}{\overset{|}{C}}=C-\overset{O}{\overset{\|}{C}}-$$

especially those reactions in which the enol-form yields protons. Cf. ionotropy. Another example of this type of prototropic change is that of phenylnitromethane :

$$C_6H_5-CH_2-NO_2 \rightleftharpoons C_6H_5-CH=N(O)OH$$

A somewhat different type of situation is that three-carbon prototropic system :

$$-CH=CH-CH_2- \rightleftharpoons -CH_2-CH=CH-$$

The mobility of the H in this system explains many types of chemical behaviour, as for example, the fact that glutaconic acid, unlike maleic acid, does not exhibit cis- and trans-isomerism.

provitamin. The inactive form of a vitamin, known as a precursor, which is converted to an active form by catalytic mechanisms in the liver (carotene), or by ultraviolet irradiation (ergosterol), forming vitamin A and vitamin D_2 (calciferol), respectively. *See also* precursor.

proximate analysis. The separation into and determination of the classes of components of a mixture. In this process no attempt is made to determine the elementary composition of the various components. Commonly the moisture ash, alcohol extract, petroleum ether extract, water extract, hydrochloric acid extract, resin, starches, reducing sugars, protein, fat, free acids, esters, etc. are reported.

prussate. A term used for various negative radicals derived from the cyanide group, as well as for the cyanide group itself.

Pschorr reaction. A method of formation of phenanthrene derivatives by ring closure of diazotized α-aryl-*o*-cinnamic acids, which may be prepared from *o*-nitrobenzaldehydes (or other aromatic nitrocarbonyl compounds) and aryl acetic acids followed by reduction of the nitro group :

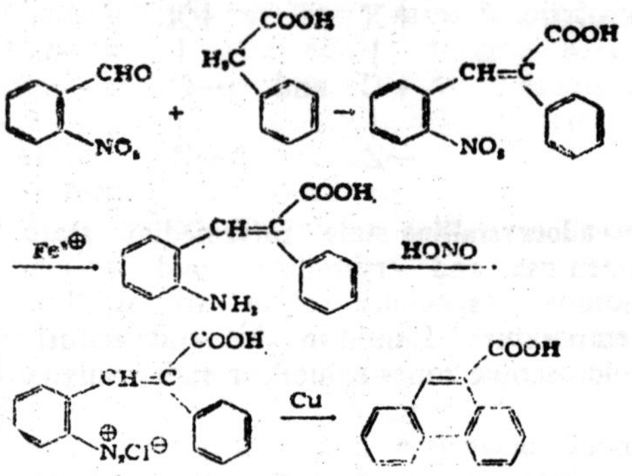

CHO, NO_2 + H_2C, COOH → CH=C, COOH, NO_2 —Fe^{2+}→ CH=C, COOH, NH_2 —HONO→ CH=C, COOH, $N_2Cl^{\ominus}$ —Cu→ COOH

pseudo-acid. A substance that exhibits ionic isomerism (*see* isomerism, ionic), wherein one of the forms exhibits acidic properties. For example various compounds containing the group—NO_2 and which are neutral may become acid by the tautomeric change of the —NO_2 group to =NO.OH and exhibit the characteristic properties of acids.

pseudo-alum. One of a series of double sulphates consisting of a double salt of a sulphate of a trivalent metal of the aluminum group and a sulphate of one of certain bivalent metals (manganese, ferrous iron, copper, zinc, and magnesium). Thus, a representative pseudo-alum is :

$$Al_2(SO_4)_3.MnSO_4.24H_2O.$$

The pseudo-alums receive their name from their resemblance to the alums.

pseudo-asymmetry. Asymmetry caused by a nonasymmetric carbon atom becoming asymmetric due to a change in the configuration of asymmetric groups with which it is associated. Thus in an asymmetric compounds of the type :

$$(H)-\underset{Z}{\underset{|}{\overset{X}{\overset{|}{C}}}}-(OH)$$

where X and Z are asymmetric groups and C is inactive, as long as X and Z are of the same rotation C remains inactive ; but let X and Z assume opposite rotations and C becomes asymmetric and, although it does not affect the optical rotation of the compound, it does produce two different inactive substances, *viz.*,

```
+X          +X
 |           |
+C   and    —C.
 |           |
—Z          —Z
```

pseudocrystalline state. Intermediate state between gas and crystalline solid, specific for liquids, especially close to solidification temperature. Liquid in this state consists of microscopic zones exhibiting short-range order.

pseudohalogens. Compounds with molecules containing at least two electronegative atoms. Such compounds display considerable similarity to fluorine derivatives in their properties and chemical reactions. *e.g.*, $(CN)_2$, $(SCN)_2$, IN_3, $(SCSN_3)_2$, ClO_2.

pseudomeric isomerism. A form of isomerism in which two or more substances of the same composition differ in the valence of certain atoms and in their chemical nature. The classic examples are the cyanates KOCN and the isocyanates KCNO ; as well as the cyanides and the isocyanides KCN and KNC.

pseudomorphism. A phenomenon in which a substance exhibits an abnormal crystalline form. Substances which show this are termed pseudomorphous.

pseudo-salt. A compound that has some of the normal characteristics of a salt, but lacks certain others, notably the ionic lattice in the solid state and the property of ionizing completely in solution. The absence of these properties is due to the fact that the bonds between the metallic and nonmetallic radicals are covalent or semi-covalent instead of polar. Because these salts do not ionize completely, they are also called weak salts.

pseudo-symmetry. 1. The condition of certain inactive indivisible types of asymmetric compounds which contain two structurally similar asymmetric carbon atoms and are without a plane of symmetry, yet whose reflected image is identical with them, as a compound of the type :

```
a     ⋮     b
|  X——⋮——Y  |
c             c
|  Y——⋮——X  |
b     ⋮     a
```

in which the *a-c-b* groups are assumed to be at right angles to the plane of the ring. One half of the compound must be rotated through an angle of 180° to make the configuration symmetrical. This type is not a meso-type.

2. In crystals, twins or fourlings which show forms that apparently belong to crystal systems of higher symmetry than the system of the single individual. These are termed pseudo-symmetric or mimetic. Also known as compound symmetry, indirect symmetry.

pseudo-unimolecular reaction. First-order reaction of molecularity higher than one.

p-shell. The collections of electrons characterized by the principal quantum number six. The P-shell is started with the element cesium (atomic number=55), which has one electron in its P-shell, and the P-shell is not completed, as far as is known, even with the transuranic element mendelevium. Elements in the progression from cesium upward differ in an increment of electrons in the N-shell, or the O-shell, or the Q-shell, as well as in the P-shell.

ptomaine. Any of a number of extremely poisonous substances derived from decomposition products of proteins formed in animal bodies after death. These toxins are a serious risk in improperly refrigerated meats, especially fish and chicken. A typical ptomaine is cadaverine. $NH_2(CH_2)_5NH_2$. Ptomaine poisoning is a loose term for any type of food poisoning, whether or not it is due ptomaines.

puckering. Corrugations in metals parts resulting from pressing or drawing.

puddling. An almost obsolete method of preparing nearly pure wrought iron from cast iron that contains a high percentage of carbon. The cast iron is heated with haematite, Fe_2O_3, the oxygen in which oxidizes the carbon, silicon, phosphorus, and manganese to their corresponding oxides.

pulping. A term used primarily in industry to refer to any of a number of methods of preparing woody fibres for the paper-making operation. The chief purposes of pulping are the separation and removal of lignin from cellulosic compounds of the wood, and softening of the fibers. These are accomplished in the following ways : (*i*) chemical pulping, which involves digestion or cooking of softwood pulp in either an acidic (sulphite pulp) or a basic medium (sulphate or kraft pulp); (*ii*) semichemical pulping, designed chiefly for hardwoods, in which chemical and physical methods are combined ; and (*iii*) mechanical or groundwood pulping, mainly for newsprint, in which the pulp is formed by abrading the wood with a rotating stone.

pulse irradiation. Irradiation with ionizing radiation in pulses of microsecond, nanosecond or as short as pico-second duration.

pulse polarography. Variation of polarography where current or charge is measured during application to indicator electrode of short pulses potential of amplitude linearly increasing with time. In another modification short pulses of low-amplitude potential are superimposed on potential linearly increasing with time.

pulse radiolysis. Radiolysis with a large dose of ionizing radiation over period of micro- or nanoseconds.

purdie methylation. The use of methyl iodide and silver oxide as methylating agents for carbohydrates ; this method requires a preliminary treatment to protect the reducing groups from oxidation, as by changing them into glycosides.

purgative. A drug that causes violent bowel evacuation.

push-pull mechanism. Trimolecule mechanism of nucleophilic substitution describing reaction as result of simultaneous pushing of carbon atom engaged in substitution by nucleophile Y, and pulling of substituent X by solvent (or electrophile), *e.g.*,

$$Y{:}+ \;-\overset{|}{\underset{|}{C}}-X + ROH \rightarrow$$

$$\left[Y\cdots{:}\overset{|}{\underset{\wedge}{C}}\cdots X\cdots H-OR \right] \rightarrow$$

activated complex

$$\rightarrow \; Y-\overset{|}{\underset{|}{C}}- + X^- \;\; HOR$$

putrefaction. A form of decomposition of organic material, especially proteins, brought about by microorganisms and characterized by complexity of process and by the offensive odour of the products.

pyran. One of a group of cyclic compounds, which are the parent substances of a number of important compouds. The pyrans all have the formula C_5H_6O, and consist of six-membered rings, containing five carbons and one oxygen atom.

pyrazolone. One of a group of cyclic compounds which are the parent substances of a number of compounds, especially drugs. The pyrazolones have the formula $C_3H_6N_2O$, and consist of five-membered rings, containing two nitrogen atoms and three carbon atoms, one of which has a doubly-bonded (carbonyl) oxygen atom.

pyro-, pyr-. A prefix indicating formation by heat, as pyrocinchonic acid, pyrene : specifically, designating an acid derived from two molecules of an "ortho" acid by loss of 1 H_2O, as pyrophosphoric acid,

$$H_4P_2O_7(2H_3PO_4-H_2O).$$

pyroacid. An acid containing less water than the orthoacid of the same elemental name. Thus, pyrophosphoric acid has the formula $H_4P_2O_7$, whereas orthophosphoric acid is H_3PO_4.

pyroelectric effect. Appearance of macroscopic dipole moment due to temperature changes.

pyrognes. Substances produced by living bacteria (not yeasts or moulds) that cause a rise in body temperature on injection. Thus any material that has been infected may, despite subsequent sterilization contain pyrogents and be unsuitable for injection. Pyrogens are not destroyed by heat ; sometimes water supplies can be pyrogenic.

pyrolysis. A chemical change brought about by heat along ; in the case of inorganic materials (limestone or metal ores) it is synonymous with calcination. It is distinguished from combustion by the fact that oxidation does not occur. It is usually applied to the conversion of organic compounds not only into smaller and simpler compounds but also into substance of higher molecular weight than the original compound. Thus, its meaning is not limited to "thermal decomposition." The temperatures involved may be as high as 1370K, as in the formation of carbon and hydrogen from methane : usually they range from 430 to 820K in which hydrocarbon gases are thermally cracked to olefins (ethane to ethylene, propane to propylene, etc.), with evolution of hydrogen. One type of artificial graphite is made by pyrolysis; it is also applied to conversion of organic wastes to fuel gases.

pyrometallurgy. Processes employing chemical reactions at elevated temperatures for the extraction of metals from ores and concentrates.

pyronine dye. A dyestuff having the chromophore group,

pyrophoric. 1. Igniting on contact with air.

2. Producing sparks when ground or abraded. Typical of such substances are phosphorus and lithium hydride. A number of substances such as sodium, potassium, butyllithium, etc. are spontaneously flammable in contact with humid air, as they react exothermally with water. Pyrophoric materials must be protected from air and moisture by storage in an atmosphere of inert gas or under kerosine. Some alloys (misch metal) are called pyrophoric because they will ignite as a result of friction.

pyrosol. Colloidal system stable only at higher temperatures, *e.g.*, gold in fused borax.

pyrotechnics. The compounding, manufacture, and engineering of fireworks, signal flares, etc. It involves the use of potassium nitrate, chlorate, dichromate, phosphorus, magnesium, and numerous other flammable and explosive compounds which emit coloured light when deflagrated.

Q

Q. Symbol for quantity of electricity. Symbol for quantity of heat.

q. Symbol for volumetric rate of flow. Symbol for rate of heat transfer.

Q-branch. In rotation-oscillation band, set of transitions which do not involve any change of rotational quantum number.

Q-electron. An electron having an orbit of such dimensions that the electron constitutes part of the seventh shell (or Q-shell) of electrons surrounding the atomic nucleus, counting out from the nucleus (*i.e.*, the K-shell is the first ; the L-, the second ; the M-, the third ; the N-, the fourth ; the O-, the fifth ; the P-, the sixth ; and the Q-, the seventh).

Q-factor. A measure of the ability of a system with periodic behaviour to store energy equal to 2π times the average energy stored in the system divided by the energy dissipated per cycle ; *i.e.*, $\Delta E/E = 2\pi/\theta$. Also known as quality factor ; storage factor.

Q-shell. The seventh layer of electrons in motion about the nucleus of an atom ; the first, or innermost layer being the K-shell ; the second, the L-shell ; the third, the M-shell ; the fourth, the N-shell ; the fifth, the O-shell ; and the sixth, the P-shell. The Q-shell is started, it is believed, with the element francium (atomic number =87) and the elements of higher atomic number have electrons in Q-shells.

quad. An energy unit that has come into use in recent years in predicting future energy requirements on a national basis. One quad equals 10^{15} Btu, which is the energy equivalent of 10^{12} cubic feet of natural gas, or 182 million barrels of oil, or 42 million tons of coal, or 293 billion kw-hr of electricity.

quadrature. The condition in which the phase angle between two alternating quantities is 90°, corresponding to one-quarter of an electrical cycle. The electric and magnetic fields of electromagnetic radiation are in space quadrature, which means that they are at right angles in space.

quadribasic. 1. Capable of neutralizing four molecules of monacid base, as pyrophosphoric acid.

2. Having four hydrogen atoms replaceable by bases.

quadrimolecular. Involving, or pertaining to four molecules. There are quadrimolecular reactions if the term is used in the sense of a reaction involving four molecules; but it is unlikely that there are quadrimolecular reactions in the sense of fourth-order reactions, *i.e.*, reactions having a rate that depends upon four concentration terms.

quadrivalent. The accepted meaning of this term is having four valencies. The term has also been used to mean having a valence of four, but the latter meaning is now more commonly expressed by the term tetravalent.

quadruple point. The temperature at which four phase.s are in equilibrium. An example is the case in which an anhydrous salt, a hydrate of the salt, its saturated solution, and its water vapour are in equilibrium in a salt-water system.

quadrupole. System of two mulually compensating electric (electric quadrupole) or magnetic (magnetic quadrupole) moments. The following quadrupoles may be distinguished according to relative position of dipoles : (*a*) regulate, (*b*) axial, (*c*) general.

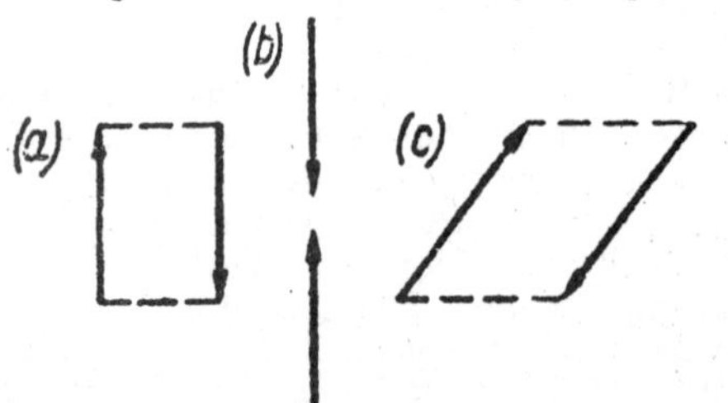

quadrupole moment, *Q*. Quantity which determines electric field of quadrupole. Symmetric second-rank tensor, traceless. In Cartesian coordinate system quadrupole moment of any charge distribution is given by :

$$Q_{xx}=\sum_i q_i\, x_i^2,\quad Q_{xy}=Q_{yx}=\sum_i q_i\, x_i\, y_i$$

$$Q_{xz}=Q_{zx}=\sum_i q_i\, x_i\, z_i,\quad Q_{yy}=\sum_i q_i\, y_i^2$$

$$Q_{yz}=Q_{zy}=\sum_i q_i\, y_i\, z_i\quad Q_{zz}=\sum_i q_i\, z_i^2$$

where q_i= i-th charge value, x_i, y_i, z_i = its coordinates.

quadrupole relaxation. Relaxation in nuclear magnetic resonance determined by interaction between quadrupole nuclear moments and surrounding inhomogeneous electric field.

qualitative chemical analysis. The branch of chemistry concerned with indentifying the elements and compounds present in a sample of matter. Inorganic qualitative analysis traditionally used classical "wet" methods to detect elements or groups of chemically similar elements, but instrumental methods have largely superseded the test-tube methods. Methods for the detection of organic compounds or classes of compounds have become increasingly available and important in organic, forensic, and clinical chemistry.

quality. A term used in chemistry to express the relative excellence, or, more commonly, the degree of purity.

quality control. A system of inspection, analysis, and action applied to a manufacturing operation so that, by inspecting a small portion of the product currently produced, an estimate of the overall quality of the product can be made to determine what, if any, changes must be made in the operation in order to achieve or maintain the required level of quality.

The term is usually applied in the context of manufacturing operations.

quality factor, k. Factor from which hypothetical radiation dose producing any given effect may be calculated on multiplication by absorbed dose from the particular radiation.

Term is used in radiobiology only; it is used seldom in radiation chemistry, since it is not precise enough.

quantitative chemical analysis. That branch of analytical chemistry which deals with the determination of the relative proportions of constituents in a compound or of components in a mixture.

In an ultimate analysis, the amount of a single element or compound is determined. In a proximate analysis, certain constituents are determined as a group of indefinite relative composition, for example, the determination of ash in a sample of coal. Conventional methods volumetric and gravimetric determination are still used for routine work, but instrumental methods are required for precise evaluation. The introduction of such techniques as gas chromatography and mass spectrometry has made continuous analyses possible. Methods of analysis may be direct or indirect. In a direct gravimetric method, the desired constituent is converted to a compound of definite, known composition and this compound is weighed. In a direct volumetric method, the desired constituent is determined by measuring the volume of reagent of known concentration required to react completely with the constituent.

In an indirect gravimetric method, a mixture of substances which includes the desired constituent is weighed and then wholly, or in part, converted to some other substance, or mixture of substances, of known composition and weighed. The amount of desired constituent can then be calculated.

quantization. A term applied to the transition from a description of a system of particles or fields in the classical approximation where canonically conjugate variables commute to a description where these variables are treated as noncommuting operators. In classical physics the possible numerical values of each observable, meaning the possible results of exact measurement of the observable, generally form a continuous set. For example, the x coordinate of the position of a particle may have any value between $-\infty$ and $+\infty$. In quantum mechanics the possible numerical values of an observables, the possible results of exact measurement form a discrete set ; for other observables, the possible numerical values are partly discrete, partly continuous ; for example, the total energy of an electron in the field of a proton may have any positive value between 0 and $+\infty$, but may have only a discrete set of negative values, namely, —13.6, —13.6/4, —13.6/9, —13.6/16 eV, ... Such observables are said to be quantized ; often there are simple quantization rules determining the quantum numbers which specify the allowable discrete values. Spectroscopy, especially the study of atomic spectra, probably provides the most detailed quantitative confirmation of quantization.

quantized vortices. A type of flow pattern exhibited by superfluids, such as liquid ^4He below 2.17K. The term vortex designates the familiar whirlpool pattern where the fluid moves circularly around a central line and the velocity diminishes inversely proportionally to the distance from the center. The strength of a vortex is determined by the circulation, which is the line integral of the velocity around any path enclosing the central line.

Quantized vortex lines are usually produced by rotating a vessel containing superfluid helium. At very low rotation speeds, no vortices exist : the superfluid remains at rest while the vessel rotates. At a certain speed the first vortex appears and corresponds to the first excited rotational state of the system. If the container continues to accelerate, additional quantized vortices will appear. At any given speed the vortices form a regular array which rotates with the vessel.

quantum. A unit quantity of energy which is bound during absorption of radiation or set free during emission of radiation. It is symbolized by ε and is expressed by the formula, $\varepsilon = h\nu$, where ν is the frequency number of the radiation (the quotient of the velocity of light divided by the wave length of the radiation), and h is the Planck constant.

quantum chemistry. Branch of theoretical chemistry which deals with study of chemical systems by using quantum-mechanical methods. More specifically, it is concerned with the electronic structure of molecules.

quantum chromodynamics. A theory of the strong ("nuclear") interactions among quarks, which are regarded as fundamental constituents of matter. Quantum chromodynamics (QCD) seeks to explain why quarks combine in certain configurations to form the observed patterns of subnuclear (or "elementary") particles, such as the proton and pi meson. According to this picture, the strong interactions among quarks are mediated by a set of force particles known as gluons. Strong interactions among gluons may lead to new structures that correspond to as yet undiscovered particles. The long-studied nuclear force which binds protons and neutrons together in atomic nuclei is regarded as a collective effect to the elementary interactions among constituents of the composite protons and neutrons.

Quantum chromodynamics has not yet been subjected to rigorous experimental tests. Several qualitative predictions of quantum chromodynamics do seem to have been borne out.

quantum efficiency. In a photochemical reaction (*see* reaction, photochemical), the ratio of the number of molecules transformed to the number of quanta of radiation absorbed.

quantum electrodynamics. The study of the properties of electromagnetic radiation and its interaction with electrically charged matter; in particular, with atoms and their constituent electrons. The fundamental equations governing quantum electrodynamics actually are believed to encompass all of atomic physics, chemistry, properties of bulk matter, and classical electromagnetic theory. Almost all of the phenomena readily perceived by the senses are believed to be ultimately understandable in terms of the laws of quantum electrodynamics.

quantum electronics. A loosely defined term concerned with the interaction of radiation and matter, particularly those interactions involving quantum energy levels and resonance phenomena, and especially those involving lasers and masers. Quantum electronics encompasses useful devices such as lasers and masers and their practical applications; related phenomena and techniques, such as nonlinear optics and light modulation and detection; and related scientific problems and applications, such as quantum noise processes, laser spectroscopy, picosecond spectroscopy, and laser-induced optical breakdown.

quantum energy. Photon energy usually given in electronvolts: in SI units expressed in joules.

quantum field theory. Quantum theory of physical systems possessing an infinite number of degrees of freedom, such as the electromagnetic field, gravitational field or wave fields in a medium. Its major applications lie in the attempted description of fundamental particles and their associated wave fields under circumstances in which both the effects of quantum mechanics and of special relativity are important. Quantum field theory is also used in nonrelativistic quantum theory for systems of many particles such as electrons in a metal, or for sound waves in liquids and solids.

quantum mechanical operators. In quantum mechanics, operators replacing dynamic variables of classical mechanics; constructed according to quantum mechanics postulates.

quantum mechanical. Four postulates which establish following assumptions:

(*i*) for each quantum mechanical state of system there is wave function depending on either generalized coordinates, or generalized momenta of particles;

(*ii*) superposition principle if valid;

(*iii*) each dynamic variable is represented by quantum mechanical operator with given rule for calculation of average values;

(*iv*) time evolution of system is given by solution of time-dependent Schrodinger equation. Also known as postulates of quantum mechanics.

quantum mechanical state. State of system with wave function.

quantum mechanics. The modern theory of matter, of electromagnetic radiation, and of the interaction between matter and radiation; also, the mechanics of phenomena to which this theory may be applied. It deals with the description and molecular properties based on the dualistic relation between matter and wave radiation. It is characterized by the fact that many of the variables investigated by use of this theory can assume only discrete values. Quantum or wave mechanics developed around the turn of the century from the theories of electromagnetism advanced by Maxwell, Planck, and Einstein, ultimately proved that matter is essentially a form of energy and can be transformed into it, as occurs in nuclear fission and fusion.

In chemistry, this concept was applied to electrons by Schrodinger, Heisenberg, De-Broglie, and others ; electron is an electromagnetic wave function rather than a solid particle and that its energy state is defined by four quantum numbers. This discovery gave rise to the orbital concept, which has provided a better understanding of the electronic structure of the elements, chemical bonding, photochemical reactions, catalysis, resonance and other chemical phenomena.

The formalism of quantum mechanics is not the same in all domains of applicability. In approximate order of increasing conceptual difficulty, mathematical complexity, and likelihood of future fundamental revision, these domains are the following : (*i*) Nonrelativistic quantum mechanics, applicable to systems in which particles are neither created nor destroyed, and in which the particles are moving slowly compared to the velocity of light. Here a particle is defined as a material entity having mass, whose internal structure either does not change or is irrelevant to the description of the system. (*ii*) Relativistic quantum mechanics, applicable in practice to a single relativistic particle (one whose speed equals or nearly equals *c*) ; here the particle may have zero rest mass, in which event, its speed must equal *c*. (*iii*) Quantum field theory, applicable to systems in which particle creation and destruction can occur, the particle may have zero or nonzero rest mass.

quantum notation. One of various systems of symbols for indicating the quantum numbers (energy levels) of electrons, and sometimes the electronic transitions, accompanying the emission of various radiation frequencies.

quantum numbers. The set of quantities, usually discrete with integer or half-integer values, which are needed to characterize a physical system of one or more atomic or subatomic particles. Specification of the set of quantum numbers serves to define such a system or, in other words, to label the possible states the system have. In general, quantum numbers are obtained from conserved quantities determinable by performing symmetry transformations consisting of arbitrary variations of the system which leave the system unchanged. For example, since the behaviour of a set of particles should be independent of the location of the origin in space and time (that is, the symmetry operation is translation in space time), it follows that momentum and energy are rigorously conserved.

In general, each physical system must be studied individually to find the symmetry transformations, and thus the conserved quantities and possible quantum numbers. The quantum numbers themselves, that is, the actual state labels, are usually the eigenvalues of the physical operators corresponding to the concerved quantities for the system in question.

quantum number, azimuthal. *See* azimuthal quantum number.

quantum number, inner. *See* inner quantum number.

quantum number, magnetic. *See* magnetic quantum number.

quantum number, principal. *See* principal quantum number.

quantum number, spin. *See* spin quantum number.

quantum solids. A class of solids whose atoms or molecules undergo large zero point motion even in the quantum ground state (at temperature $T=0$ K as a result of their small mass and the weak attractive part of their interaction potential. The most striking examples are the isotopes of helium, ^3He and ^4He, which have a root-mean-square displacement from their lattice sites of approximately 25°/₀. Further examples are the molecular hydrogens, H_2, D_2, and HD, as well as some heavier molecular solids.

quantum state. The condition of a physical system as described by a wave function, the function may be simultaneously an eigenfunction of one or more quantum-mechanical operator, the eigenvalues are than the quantum numbers that lebel the state.

quantum statistics. A method of statistical analysis of the behavior of the fundamental particles of matter, and their higher aggregates, such as atoms and molecules, from the standpoint of quantum mechanics. One of its basic postulates is that similar particles are not distinguishable. Two widely known systems of quantum statistics are the Bose-Einstein statistics and the Fermi-Dirac statistics.

quantum theory. A theory concerning the behavior of atoms and molecules, characterized by the limitation that most of the variables discussed in the theory can assume only a restricted number of discrete values.

quantum yield. 1. Ratio between number of photons emitted in luminescent process (*see* luminescence) and total number of photons absorbed.

2. For a photochemical reaction, the number of moles of a reactant disappearing, or the number of moles of a product formed, per einstein of light of the stated wavelength absorbed.

quarkonium. It was suggested that the bound system of an extremely massive quark with its antiquark would be so small that the strong force would be extremely feeble. In this case, the binding between quark and antiquark is mediated by the exchange of a single massless gluon, and the spectrum of bound states resembles that of an exotic atom composed of an electron and an antielectron (positron) bound electromagnetically in a Coulomb potential generated by the exchange of a massless photon. Since the electron-positron atom is known as positronium, the heavy quark antiquark atom has been called quarkonium. Two families of heavy quark-antiquark bound states, the Ψ/J system composed of charmed quarks and the Y system made up of b quarks, have been discovered. Both have level schemes characteristic of atomic spectra, which have been analyzed by using tools of nonrelativistic quantum mechanics developed for ordinary atoms.

quarks. Hypothetical particles of electric charge equal to 1/3, —1/3 or —2/3 of elementary charge. Quarks are considered to be the basic constituent particles, of which "elementary" particles are now believed to be composed. Theoretical models built on the quark concept have been very successful in understanding and predicting many phenomena in particle physics. However, the experimental observation of free quarks remains ambiguous.

The properties of quarks, to the extent that they are now understood, are present in the table.

Properties of quarks

	u	*d*	*c*	*s*	*t**	*b*
Mass (GeV/c^2)†	0.39	0.39	1.55	0.51	(>15)	4.72
Electric charge	+2/3	—1/3	+2/3	—1/3	(+2/3)	—1/3
Baryon number	1/3	1/3	1/3	1/3	(1/3)	1/3
Spin (in units of $\hbar$)	1/2	1/2	1/2	1/2	(1/2)	1/2
Isotopic spin	+1/2	—1/2	0	0	(0)	0
Strangeness	0	0	0	—1	(0)	0
Charm	0	0	+1	0	(0)	0

*The *t* quark has not yet been found. Listed are its predicted properties.

†Masses are uncertain. Values listed here are half the mass of the lowest-lying quark-antiquark vector meson.

Physicists now believe that the proton and neutron are not fundamental constituents of matter but they are made of quarks, very much as the nuclei of ^3H and ^3He are made of protons and neutrons and as the molecules O_2 and CO are made of oxygen and carbon atoms.

quartation. A method of assay of silver or gold ores, or other materials containing one of these precious metals. In order to effect this separation accurately, which is done by differential solution in nitric acid, the amount of gold present should be about one-quarter of the total gold and silver, and the ratio is adjusted by estimating the original concentrations and adding the calculated amount (usually of silver) before separating. Then the process is repeated by adjusting the amount of silver added to the results of the first analysis, and a closer approximation to the correct result is obtained. If necessary, the process of successive analysis is repeated until a sufficiently consistent result is obtained.

quartz. A hard crystalline form of silica (SiO_2) which occurs freely in natural rock formations; it is usually white to grayish but may have a pink colouration due to traces of dispersed iron. Quartz crystals are also produced artificially for special purposes. When melted it is called fused silica, a form of silica used in power tubes, lamps, and electronic devices.

quasi racemates. Equimolecular compounds formed of two optically active compounds of similar structure and opposite configurations existing in solid state only, *e.g.*, (+)-chlorosuccinic and (—)-bromosuccinic acids from quasi-racemates in solid state.

quasistatic process. Thermodynamic process with thermodynamic equilibrium (at any instant) inside system and without any dissipative processes within this system. According to second law of thermodynamics each quasistatic process is reversible and each reversible process is quasistatic. Also known as quasistatic change.

quaternary. A term having the general meaning of the fourth, or of the fourth order. It is used most commonly in chemistry to indicate certain compounds in which four hydrogen atoms are substituted, as a quaternary ammonium or a quaternary phosphonium compound ; or to indicate a compound composed of four different atoms or radicals.

quaternary ammonium compound. A versatile group of ionizing compounds derived from reactions between amines and alkyl-or aryl-containing materials. They comprise a nitrogen atom to which four organic groups (R) are attached (the cation) and a negatively charged group or atom (the anion) ; thus, the molecule would appear as :

$$\left[\begin{array}{c} R \\ | \\ R—N—R \\ | \\ R \end{array}\right]^{+} Z^{-}$$

quaternary structure. The three-dimensional structure of an oligomeric protein ; particularly the manner in which the sub-unit chains fit together.

queen's metal. An alloy of tin containing antimony, zinc, lead, and/or copper.

quench. The cool suddenly, commonly by immersion in a liquid ; a process applied in metallurgy to obtain (1) alloys and other metallic systems which retain certain of the characteristics of forms stable at higher temperatures, which would otherwise undergo complete transition on slow cooling, or (2) to obtain a metal structure of characteristic grain-size. The brittleness resulting from the sudden cooling is frequently modified by subsequent partial reheating.

quench aging. Aging of metal induced by rapid cooling from solution heat-treatment temperatures.

quench annealing. Annealing an austenitic ferrous alloy by heating followed by quenching solution temperature.

quench bath. A liquid medium, such as oil, fused salt, or water, into which a material is plunged for heat-treatment purposes

quenching of luminescence. Drop in quantum yield of luminescence of substance A caused either by admixture of substance B, due to intermolecular transfer of energy from A to B or to their chemical reaction, or by increase in temperature (due to increased rates is non-radiative transitions).

quinhydrone electrode. An electrode of quinhydrone, which accepts protons (hydrogen ions) to yield hydroquinone, and donates protons to yield *p*-benzoquinone, and has, therefore, a definite relation between its potential and the *p*H of the solution. Its values have been recorded at definite temperatures, and it is used as a standard electrode in *p*H measurement. Quinhydrone electrode (half-cell) is constructed from platinum (or gold) dipped into quinhydrone solution ; electrode reaction is :

$$C_6H_4(OH)_2 + 2H_2O \rightleftharpoons C_6H_4O_2 + 2H_3O^+ + 2e^-$$

and potential of electrode :

$$\epsilon = \epsilon^0 + \frac{RT}{2F} \ln \frac{a_{quinone} a^2_{H_3O^+}}{a_{quinhydrone}}$$

where ϵ^0=standard electrode potential.

quinocarbonium salt. One of a group of salts of nonnitrogenous organic compounds with mineral acids in which the acid is combined with carbon (carbonium valence). A rearrangement of the molecule occurs with production of quinoid structure and development of colour. They have the general structure :

in which A is commonly an acid radical, and the remaining quinoid oxygen, shown above, is usually replaced by substituents.

quinoid form. The atomic grouping :

$$=C\langle \begin{matrix} C=C \\ C=C \end{matrix} \rangle C=$$

characteristic of quinones and believed to be the chromophore in certain coloured benzene derivatives. Cf. benzenoid. Since the preparation of *o*-quinone derivatives it has been necessary to distinguish the above grouping as the "*p*-quinoid" to avoid confusion. The unqualified term "quinoid," however, always refers to the above group.

quinole. One of a class of substance allied to *p*-benzoquinone, having the general type-formula :

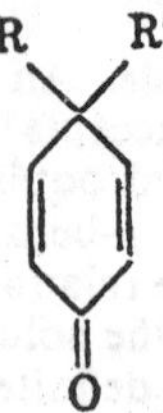

in which R an alkyl group, and R′ a hydroxy or halogenated alkyl group.

quintuple point. The temperature at which five phases are in equilibrium. For a ternary system, the Phase Rule shows that five coexistent phases will be invariant. The system silver perchlorate/water/benzene shows six quintuple points.

Q-unit. A unit of energy used in measuring the heat energy of fuels reserves ; equal to 10^{18} British thermal units, or approximately 1.055×10^{21} joules.

Q-value. The net amount of energy released or absorbed in a nuclear reaction ; usually expressed in million electron-volts, MeV, per individual reaction. Also known as nuclear energy change; nuclear heat of reaction; disintegration energy.

R

R. 1. The universal gas constant, *R*, equal to $p_o v_o/273$. If p_o is one atmosphere and v_o is the volume of one mole, expressed in liters, the numerical value of *R* is $22.4/273=0.08057$ liter-atmosphere per degree per mole. Also, $R=8.31441$ joule per mole kelvin.

2. Symbol used in generalized formulas of organic compounds to represent a hydrocarbon (alkyl or aryl) group, *e.g.*, CH_3, C_2H_5, C_6H_5, etc.

3. The letter R with a superior dot (R·) is used to indicate a free radical, that dot indicating its free valence.

R_∞. Symbol for Rydberg constant, its numerical value is 1.097373177×10^7 m^{-1}.

Ry· Symbol for Rydberg energy ;

$$Ry = R_\infty \cdot h \cdot c = 1.3605804 \text{ eV}$$
$$= 2.1799072 \times 10^{-18} \text{J}$$

rabbit. Device used for transfer of short-lived radioisotopes by means of pneumatic-tube conveyor.

racemate. *See* racematic compound.

racemate. *See* racemic modification.

racemation. *See* racemization.

racemic compound. One form of racemic modification in solid state mixture consisting of two opposite enantiomers, paired up in unit cell of crystal, which thus contains equal numbers of (+) and (—) molecules. Melting point of racemic compound is generally higher than those of enantiomers ; other physical properties are also different. Also known as *dl*-compound, recemate.

racemic mixture. One form of racemic modification in solid state—gross mixture of enantiomer crystals ; racemic mixture forms in crystallization from solution of racemic modification, each enantiomer crystallizes separately. Melting point of racemic mixture is lower than those of enantiomers and eutectic is formed. Solubility of racemic mixture is higher than those of enantiomers. Also known as conglomerate.

racemic modification. Equimolecular, optically inactive mixture of enantiomeric molecules, existing in gaseous and liquid states, also in solution. In solid state, racemic modification exists in one of three kinds of crystals (depending on its chemical character and crystallization conditions—temperature and solvent) ; racemic mixture, racemic compound or *dl* racemic mixture. Also known as dextro-laevo modification, racemate.

racemization. The rendering inactive of an optically active substance by converting it into the racemic form. Heating is the usual method of effecting the conversion. Some substances racemize spontaneously at ordinary temperatures (autoracemization) ; others are not completely racemized but sometimes only a single asymmetric group is affected (partial racemization). Also known as racemation.

racemized proteins. Proteins that have been treated with concentrated alkali thereby diminishing their optical activity.

rad. Obsolete unit of absorbed dose of ionizing radiation carresponding to 100 ergs of absorbed energy per 1 g of medium. In SI system 1 rad =0.01 Gy (*see* gray).

Abbreviation from radiation absorbed dose.

radial chromatography. Technique of paper chromatography in which sample is transferred onto centre (or close to it) of filter disk and chromatogram is developed in direction from centre towards edges.

radial distribution function $g(r)$. Probability density of finding particle at point r and another particle at position $r=0$.

radiant. A term denoting motion on a radius or, more particularly, along a very great number of radii, as the emission of energy from a point source, which travels along the various radii of a sphere of constantly-increasing radius, so that the radiation-pattern at any instant occupies, in a perfectly homogeneous medium, the position of the surface of a sphere. From this original meaning, the term has been extended in its application to connote either particles of matter or electromagnetic energy emerging from a more or less sharply defined region, or the substance or entity which emits such particles or radiations.

radiant energy. A form of energy propagated in defined wave lengths at a velocity of 299,790 kilometers per second. Radiation energy is electromagnetic in nature. It is readily transformed into other forms of energy, especially chemical energy (photochemical processes). The main source of radiant energy is the sun.

radiant flux density. Product of density of particles or photons (number of particles or photons per unit volume) and their mean velocity, its dimension being $m^{-2}s^{-1}$. Also known as flux density.

radiation. The terms radiant energy and light are essentially synonymous with radiation. Radiation is electromagnetic energy composed of waves of massless units (photons or quanta) emitted as a result of nuclear transformations in astral bodies and moving through space at constant speed (186,000 miles per second). The wavelengths range from a fraction of an angstrom unit (gamma radiatian) to several miles for radio and electric waves. The classic mathematical evaluation of radiation is that formulated by Planck in 1903, $E=h\nu$, where ν is frequency and h is a universal constant. The total range of wavelengths comprises the electromagnetic spectrum, which includes the following subdivisions, from short to long ; cosmic, gamma, x-rays, ultraviolet, infrared, microwave and radiofrequencies. Less specifically, the term is also applied to particulate emanations of unstable or split atomic nuclei. These include high-energy electrons (beta), protons or helium nuclei (alpha), and (in the case of fission) neutrons. Gamma radiation is also emitted in the decay of uranium and radium. The many types of spectroscopy utilize radiation of various wavelengths ; it is also used in medicine (radioactive isotopes), in industrial measuring devices, and in communications equipments.

radiation catalysis. Catalysis caused by influence of ionizing radiation or by modification of catalyst by ionizing radiation.

radiation chemistry. Branch of chemistry dealing with chemical effects resulting from absorption of ionizing radiation.

radiation damage. Undesirable permanent changes in a material caused by absorption of ionizing radiation.

radiation dose. General description of extent of influence of ionizing radiation on object of consideration ; an unprecise definition.

radiation equilibrium. In radiation chemistry, state in which concentration of at least one of the components of irradiated system is constant with time. In radiation equilibrium, reaction rates of formation and disappearance of a chemical individual (or individuals) are equal.

radiation induced activation. Process of incidental induction of radioactivity in material irradiated with ionizing radiation which produces chemical or biological effects.

radiation induced mutation. Abrupt change of properties of plant or animal organisms, inherited by progeny and caused by absorption of energy of ionizing radiation in certain stages of development or reproduction of living organism.

radiation induced reactions. Chemical reactions initiated by ionizing radiation.

radiationless transition. Transition between energy states of system without emission of photon. Also known as non-radiative transition.

radiation protection. All provisions to protect personnel against action of ionizing radiation and personnel and laboratories against radioactive contamination ; and for decontamination.

radiation quality. Value or values characterizing ionizing radiation in terms of its penetrability.

radiation source. Device or substance capable of emitting ionizing radiation. Sources most often used are : isotopic sources, nuclear reactors, accelerators and X-ray tubes.

radiation yield, *Gx*. Number of indexed chemical changes (*x*) due to irradiation, per 100 eV absorbed energy of ionizing radiation.

radiative collision. A collision between charged particles in which part of the kinetic energy is converted into electromagnetic radiation.

radiative life-time. Life-time of electronically excited state given by reciprocal of rate constant of luminescence originating from this excited state.

radiative transition. Transition between higher and lower energy state of system accompanied by photon emission.

radical. This term strictly denotes any ionized group of atoms characteristic of dissociated inorganic compounds, which behaves as a single unit. Among the more common radicals are the nitrite $(NO_2)^-$, the sulphate $(SO_4)^{2-}$, hydroxyl $(OH)^-$, the ammonium $(NH_4)^+$, and the carbonate $(CO_3)^{2-}$. It is also (but less correctly) used in the organic field to designate alkyl, aryl, and other groups which are not charged. A specialized meaning includes the active molecular fragments known as free radicals (indicated by R') which initiate reactions by a chain mechanism.

radical products of radiolysis. Radiolysis products containing unpaired electron, *e.g.*, e^-aq, HO in case of water.

radio-. A prefix which denotes a relationship with the phenomena of radiant energy or of radioactivity.

radioactinium. Isotope of thorium. Atomic number 90. Mass number 227. Radioactinium emits α-particles (half-life period 18.8 days) to give radium 223.

radioactive. Emitting radiation or particles of sub-atomic size.

radioactive constant. The proportionality constant which expresses the relationship between the rate of decay of the activity of a radioactive element, and its activity at any time. It is defined by the expression :

$$\lambda I = -\frac{dI}{dt}$$

where λ radioactive constant of an element, $I=$ its instantaneous activity, and $-dI/dt=$its rate of decay.

radioactive dating. Determination of age of minerals, materials or objects from their content of radioactive nuclides or daughter products.

radioactive decay. Spontaneous transformation of unstable nucleus into another nucleus with emission of corpuscular or electromagnetic radiation. Also known as radiactive disintegration.

radioactive displacement law. The statement of the changes in mass number and take place during various nuclear transformations, is summarized in the table shown below :

posited on the earth's surface following the explosion of nuclear weapons.

radioactive indicator. A radioactive substance which is used, because of the convenience and ease of its detection, to investigate chemical and biochemical processes, commonly those of a nonradioactive atomic species of the same atomic number, and hence the same chemical properties.

radioactive isotope. An unstable form of an element (also called a radioisotope) whose major isotopes are stable. For example, the 14 isotope of carbon is naturally radioactive, though carbon is a stable element, as less than 1°/。 of its atomic weight is represented by the unstable isotope. Similarly, bismuth has five radioactive isotopes, and potassium, platinum, and lead have one or more. Carbon-14 is used as a tracer and in chemical dating. The nuclei of many stable elements are made artificially radioactive by neutron irradiation in a nuclear reactor ; these are used for curative purposes in medicine and for specialized industrial used such as detection of leaks and various types of measuring devices. *See also* radioactivity.

Radiation			*Changes in nucleus*	
Type	*Mass No.*	*Change*	*Mass No.*	*Atomic No.*
α	4	+2	decreases by 4	decreases by 2
β⁻	0	−1	no change	increases by 1
β⁺	0	+1	no change	decreases by 1
Electron capture			no change	.decreases by 1
γ	0	0	no change	no change

radioactive equilibrium. In a system containing two or more radioactive elements, in which each element (except the first) is formed by radioactive disintegration of the element preceding it in the series present, radioactive equilibrium is reached when the rate of formation of any element from its parent is equal to its own rate of disintegration. This statement does not apply to the terminal element of the series present which is nonradioactive.

radioactive fall-out. Radioactive material de-

radioactive kryptonate. Solid into which radioactive krypton ^{85}Kr in the loosely bonded form has been introduced.

radioactive purity. Amount of radioactive nuclides of desired type, expressed as percentage of all radioactive nuclides present in substance.

radioactive series. Series of genetically connected radioactive nuclides each of which is formed by radioactive decay of its predecessor. Each series starts with a long-lived radioactive nuclide and ends with a stable nuclide. Also known as radioactive families.

radioactive source. Sources of ionizing radiation produced by radioactive nuclide.

radioactive substance. Substance containing natural or artificial radioactive nuclides.

radioactive tracer. Radioactive nuclide which is introduced into a system in order to examine it.

radioactive tracer method. Method for tracing course of chemical and physical processes by means of compounds labelled with radioactive tracer. Absence of isotopic effects is essential for applicability of this method.

radioactive wastes. Materials or objects containing radioactive substances, further use of which is impossible or unprofitable.

radioactivity. Spontaneous nuclear transformation of nuclide into another nuclide, accompanied by emission of nuclear radiation, either corpuscular or electromagnetic. It may be natural, as with radium, artificial (caused by bombardment of a stable nucleus with neutrons or deuterons), or induced, as in radioactive carbon. The emanations are in the form of alpha, beta, and gamma rays. The natural radioactive elements are uranium, radium, radon, and thorium (the principal members of the uranium decay series), the ultimate end-products being stable isotopes of lead, and helium. A number of elements, *e.g.*, sodium, iodine, etc., can be made radioactive by bombardment with neutrons, deuterons, or other heavy particles.

radiocarbon. Isotope of carbon. Atomic number 6. Mass number 14. Also known as natural radiocarbon.

radiocarbon dating. A method of determining quite accurately the age of a carbon-bearing material derived from living plants or animals within the last 70,000 years. It is based on the ratio of carbon-14 in the material to that in a modern reference sample by measuring the radioactivity of the carbon-14 in the material. Since the half-life of carbon 14 is 5730 ± 30 years, and the living precursor utilized CO_2 from the atmosphere or some other part of the earth's dynamic carbon reservoir, a process that ceased when the original plant or animal died, the amount of carbon-14 now present gives directly the age of the material. The carbon-14 in the reservoir is constantly being replaced by the sequence :

$$N^{14} \rightarrow C^{14} + O_2 \rightarrow C^{14}O_2.$$

This has maintained the ratio of carbon isotopes constant during the ages, but burning of fossil fuels since the Industrial Revolution has lowered somewhat the quantity of carbon-14 in the atmosphere during the last few centuries, an effect that does not affect measurements on older objects. The sample to be tested must be carefully prepared to prevent contamination by younger carbon.

The radiocarbon technique was discovered by Willard F. Libby (1908-1980. Nobel Prize 1960) and has been applied with great success in the field of archeology, geology, geochemistry, and geophysics. Its accuracy has been checked and verified by use of tree-ring counts (dendrochronology) and with the known ages of objects from ancient cultures, such as Egyptian and Chinese. The former shows that, for the 2400-6000 B.P. (before present) age of bristlecone pine tree-rings, 5200C^{14} years equal 6,000 calendar years.

radiochemical analysis. Detection or determination of components of substance examined based on detecting and measuring radiation emitted by radioactive nuclides. Also known as radiochemical analytical methods, analytical radiochemistry.

radiochemical yield. Percentage recovery of an element after chemical separation.

radiochemistry. A subdivision of chemistry which deals with the study of radioactive substances. It includes the nuclear transformations involved, transmutation of one element into another, and the nature and properties of the radiation emitted. It also deals with the use of this radiation in chemical tracer analysis, for geological and archeological (chemical dating), and for initiation of cross-lining (polymerization).

radiochromatography. Chromatography of substance labelled with radioactive tracers, whose radioactivity is used subsequently for qualitative and/or quantitative evaluation of chromatograms.

radiocobalt. Isotope of cobalt. Atomic number 27. Mass number 60. Also known as cobalt-60.

radiocolloids. Colloids composed of particles of radioactive substance with colloidal dispersion or pseudoradiocolloids which are products of adsorption of rodioactive substance on foreign colloidal particles.

radioelement. Chemical element having no stable natural isotopes. Also known as radioactive element.

radiography. Use of ionizing radiation for studying internal structure of solid ; a photographic emulsion being most often used as the detector of radiation.

radioimmunoassay. Sensitive quantitative determination of trace amounts of hormone (or some other biomolecule) by its capacity to displace the radioactive form of combination with its specific antibody.

radioiron. Isotope of iron. Atomic number 26. Mass number 59. Also known as iron-59.

radioluminescence. Any kind of luminescence caused by absorption of ionizing radiation. Also known as radiation induced luminescence.

radiolucent. Almost transparent to radiation, especially *x*-ray and radio waves.

radiolysis. Chemical decomposition of materials by ionizing radiation.

radiometric analysis. 1. Analytical techniques in which use is made of various nuclear phenomena and interaction between ionizing radiation and matter, and also methods of radiotracers for determination of non-radioactive elements.

2. Method for determination of a radioactive component of a mixture based on measurement of its radioactivity.

radiometric titration. Titration in which titrant or substance titrated is labelled with radioactive tracer and end point is determined by radiometric measurement.

radiometry. Methods for measuring radiation and determining activity of radioactive preparations.

radiomimetic substances. Chemicals which cause biological effects similar to those caused by ionizing radiations.

radionuclide. Unstable nuclide under going spontaneous radioactive transformation with emission of particle or photon.

radio opaque. Not appreciably penetrable by *x*-rays or other forms of radiation.

radiophosphorus. Isotope of phosphorus. Atomic number 15. Mass number 32. Also known as phosphorus-32.

radioresistance. Property of material responsible for specially low yields of radiolysis.

radiosensitivity. Qualitative character and quantitative extent of changes caused by absorption of ionized radiation in pure chemical compounds, synthetic materials and living organisms.

radiosensitizer. Chemical compound added to irradiated system for purpose of enhancing a particular chemical effect. Also known as radiation sensitizer.

radiosodium. Isotope of sodium. Atomic number 11. Mass number 24. Also known as sodium-24.

radiospectroscopy. Branch of spectroscopy comprising nuclear magnetic, electron spin and nuclear quadrupole resonance phenomena and others in which one observes stimulated quantum transitions between energy levels produced according to given conditions (*e.g.*, in magnetic field) and corresponding to absorption or emission of electromagnetic radiation in radiofrequency region.

radiospectrum. The entire range of frequencies in the radio range to about 300,000 megahertz. Also known as radio-frequency spectrum.

radiostrontium. Isotope of strontium. Atomic number 38. Mass number 90. Also known as strontium-90.

radiosulphur. Isotope of sulphur. Atomic number 16. Mass number 35. Also known as sulphur-35.

radiothermoluminescence. Thermoluminescence of solid substance irradiated previously with ionizing radiation.

radiothorium. Isotope of thorium. Atomic number 90. Mass number 228 ; produced naturally by β-decay of actinium 228 (mesothorium II). Radiothorium emits α-particles (half-period 1.90 years) to give radium 224.

radiotoxicity. Toxicity connected with radiation of radioactive nuclide present in organism.

radium. An element.

	Symbol	Ra
State Solid	Atomic No.	88
Group IIA	Atomic Wt.	226.0254
	Valence	2
	m.p.	973K
	b.p.	1413K

A strongly radioactive element, occurring in extremely small percentages in uranium ores (pitchblende and carnote). Radium is formed by radioactive transformation of uranium, about 3 million parts of uranium being accompanied in nature by one part radium. Radium spontaneously generates radon gas at approximately the rate of 100 mm^3 per day per gram of radium, at standard conditions.

Radium is a highly dangerous substance and must be kept in heavy lead containers to block off its ionizing radiation. Its major use is in cancer therapy in the form of salts.

The radium isotope of mass number 226 occurs in the uranium $(2n + 2)$ alpha-decay series. Its half-life is 1,620 years, and it yields radon-222 by α-disintegration. Other naturally occurring isotopes of radium are ^{228}Ra in the thorium series, half-life 6.7 years, producing actinium-228 by β-decay which yields by β-decay thorium-228, which in turn yields ^{224}Ra half-life 3.64 days, giving radon-220 by α-decay. Another naturally occurring isotope of radium is found in the actinium series : it is ^{223}Ra, half-life 11.7 days, giving radon-219 by α-decay. In the neptunium series there is ^{225}Ra, half-life 14.8 days, undergoing β-decay to actinium-225. Other isotopes of radium include those of mass numbers 219, 221, 225, 227, 229, and 230. Chemical properties of radium are similar to those of barium.

radium-D. Isotope of lead. Atomic number 82. Mass number 210.

radium emanation. Isotope of radon. Atomic number 86. Mass number 222.

radium-G. Isotope of lead. Atomic number 82. Mass number 206. Also known as radium lead.

radius of ionic atmosphere, $1/x$. Concept from Debye-Huckel theory of strong electrolytes :

$$x^2 = \frac{8\alpha e_0^2 N_A}{1000\epsilon_r kT}$$

Introduction of numerical values of constants gives :

$$1/x = 1.988 \times 10^{-10} \sqrt{\frac{\epsilon_r T}{J}} \text{ [cm]}$$

where e_0=charge of electron, n_A=Avogadro's constant, ϵ_r=relative permittivity, k=Boltzman constant and J=ionic strength.

radon. An element.

	Symbol	Rn
State Gas	Atomic No.	86
Group Noble Gas	Atomic Wt.	222(?)
	m.p.	202K
	b.p.	211.2K

Radon is the heaviest of all gases with a density of almost 10 grams per litre (air=1.3g/l). Isotope ^{222}Rn is formed by the alpha disintegration of ^{226}Ra. Actinon, its isotope of mass number 229, is produced by alpha disintegration of ^{223}Ra (AcX) and is a member of the actinium series. Similarly, thoron, its isotope of mass number 220, is a member of the thorium series. Since the name "radon" may be considered to be specific for the isotope of mass number 222 (from the radium series), the term "emanation" is sometimes used for element number 86 in general. Other isotopes of radon include those of mass numbers 209-118 and 221.

Radon has limited use in cancer therapy and in research in chemical kinetics. Like radium, it is hazardous to handle and should be used with adequate protective shielding.

Radziszewski amide synthesis. Synthesis of amides by treating nitrile with hydrogen peroxide in basic medium.

Radziszewski imidazole synthesis. Preparation of imidazole derivatives by heating **mixture of** 1,2-diketone, ammonia and aldehyde **in etha**nolic solution, *e.g.*,

$$\begin{matrix} R-C=O \\ | \\ R'-C=O \end{matrix} + 2NH_3 + R''CHO \rightarrow$$

$$\begin{matrix} R-C & — & N \\ \| & & \| \\ R'-C & & C-R'' \\ & \diagdown N \diagup & \\ & | & \\ & H & \end{matrix}$$

raffinate. 1. A refined petroleum product, produced by fractionation of a crude charge.

2. Any refined product obtained by fractional distillation.

Raies ultimes. Analytical lines of a given element which disappear last when concentration of this element in analytical gap is reduced to zero.

Raikow test for methanol. The method is converted nitromethane, which, on treatment with sodium nitroprusside in ammoniacal solution, gives a deep-blue colour, changing to green yellow, and red-yellow.

Raman effect. A phenomenon observed in scattering of light when it passes through a transparent medium. When monochromatic light passes through a transparent medium, some of the light is scattered. If the spectrum of this scattered light is examined, it is found to contain, apart from light of the original wavelength, weaker lines differing from this by constant amounts. Such lines are called Raman lines, and they are due to the loss or gain of energy experienced by the photons of light as a result of interaction with the vibrating molecules of the medium through which they pass.

Raman frequency. Wave number of rotational or vibrational transition recorded from Raman spectrum as difference of Rayleigh and Raman line positions.

Raman line. Spectral line of scattered electromagnetic radiation with frequency either decreased (Stokes line) or increased (anti-Stokes line with respect to frequency of excitation line (Rayleigh line). Frequency of Raman line corresponds to rotations or oscillation transitions in target molecules.

Raman spectrometry. Method of analysis utilizing Raman spectra for identification and qualitative and quantitative analysis, and for determination of primary components in multicomponent mixtures.

Raman spectrum. A spectrum obtained by illuminating a substance with radiation of a single frequency, and obtaining from the radiations scattered at right angles a spectrum of those frequencies differing from the incident radiation.

Ramsay-Young rule. An empirically-derived relationship between two sets of temperature at which two chemically-similar liquids have the same vapour pressures of the form :

$$T_1/T_2 + T_1'/T_2' \; P'$$

in which two similar liquids have the same vapour pressure P, and T_1' and T_2' are temperature at which the substances have the same vapour pressure P'. This relationship is useful in comparing vapour pressures at different temperatures, and boiling points at different pressures, of similar compounds.

Raney nickel. Nickel produced in a particularly finely-divided state for use as catalyst by the Raney Catalyst Co. (Davidson Chemical Corp.) in the U.S.A. An alloy of aluminium and nickel is treated with caustic soda solution, dissolving the aluminium and leaving the nickel in this special form—particularly useful for hydrogenation.

Rankine temperature scale. A temperature scale which corresponds tc the Kelvin scale, but is based on the absolute zero of the Fahrenheit system, so that 0° Rankine = —159.69°F.

Raoults law. Partial pressures at constant temperature of vapours of constituents of perfect solution are proportional to concentrations of these constituents in liquid phase, expressed in mole fractions :

$$p_B = p_B^* x_B$$

where p_B=partial pressure of constituent B in gas over solution, p_B^* = vapour pressure of pure constituent B, x_B=mole fraction of constituent B in liquid phase.

rapid coagulation. Coagulation of colloidal particles completely discharge when their electrokinetic potential £ is equal to zero. **Rate of coagulation is independent of both electrokinetic concentration and particular features of ions causing coagulation.**

rare. A term applied to several groups of elements to indicate that they occur in very low concentration or in exceedingly small amounts, (*i*) the rare gases, *i,e.*, the noble gases in the zero group of the Periodic Table, (*ii*) the rare metals, which include the alkaline-earth series as well as many others such as cadmium, beryllium, cobalt, the platinum metals, and uranium.

rare earth elements. Sometimes referred to as the "fraternal fifteen," beacause of similarities in physical and chemical properties, the rare earth elements actually are not so rare. The term rare arises from the fact that these elements were discovered in scare materials. The term earth stems from the fact that the elements were first isolated from their ores in the chemical form of oxides and that the old chemical terminology for oxide is earth.

rare gases. *See* noble gases.

rare metal. *See* rare.

Raschig process for making hydrazine. This is the usual method for making hydrazine ($NH_2.NH_2$), by the action of large excess of ammonia on sodium hypochlorite. The reaction is best carried out at about 170K. and 40 atmospheres pressure. A little glue or gelatin catalyses the reaction. The name Raschig's process is also used for a method of preparing phenol from benzene. (*See* Section Three).

Raschig process for making phenol. The catalytic conversion of benzene phenol, which takes place in two stages, as follows :

$$2C_6H_6 + 2HCl + O_2 \rightarrow 2C_6H_5Cl + 2H_2O$$

$$C_6H_5Cl + H_2O \rightarrow C_6H_5OH + HCl$$

The hydrochloric acid is distilled off the water fraction obtained from the second stage, and is returned to the first stage. The first stage takes place, with the catalysts in use (*c*, 1948) at about 230K, and the second stage at about 425K. Although the percentage conversion in both reactions is only about 10%, giving the process the disadvantage of low operating capacity it has a relatively high yield, because only a very small amount of by-products is obtained.

Rast molecular weight method. A micro method for the determination of molecular weights. The method consists of dissolving a small weighed amount of the substance in molten camphor and determining the depression of the freezing point of the camphor attributable to the substance. By conducting the test in a capillary tube attached to a thermometer, close temperature readings are obtained.

rate-determining step. Slowest step determining overall rate of process.

Raybin test reaction for vitamin B_1 (thiamine). About 0.001 g. of vitamin B_1 is dissolved in several ml. of a borax solution of *p*H 9.6, and a drop added of an alcoholic solution of 2,6-dibromoquinonechloroimide. An orange colour, soluble in chloroform and other organic solvents, forms at once.

Rayleigh equation. An expression for the separation by distillation of one component of a liquid system. It is of the form :

$$\frac{dN}{N} = \frac{dx}{(y-x)}$$

where N is the total number of moles of liquid, dN is an infinitesimal amount distilled off, x is the composition of the original liquid with respect to one component, and y is the composition (determined as a function of x) of the distillate dN.

This expression has been integrated for a number of cases, *i.e.*, for certain binary mixtures, dilute solutions, and others.

Rayleigh line. Scattered electromagnetic radiation spectral line of the same frequency as that of incident radiation.

Rayleigh scattering. Scattering of light on molecules without frequency change in scattered light.

rayon. A semisynthetic fibre made by chemical treatment of wood pulp ; it is also called regenerated cellulose. It can be made by either the cuprammonium (copper and ammonia) or the viscose process. the latter being the more common. The chemically modified cellulose in liquid form is then extruded through a fine orifice (spinneret) into a hardening bath which causes fomation of a smooth, fairly strong fiber. Various modifications with proteins such as casein have been introduced to increase strength and durability. The fibers can be spun to extreme fineness (denier), making them especially suitable for hosiery and other garments. Its applications in recent years have been restricted by the appearance of many synthetic fibers of superior properties.

Cellophane is also regenerated cellulose made by the viscose process and extruded through slits of various widths to form film suitable for packaging. It was the first widely used transparent packaging film, but its use has decreased since the development of synthetic high-polymer films.

R band. Band in electronic spectra of organic molecules containing heteroatoms; R band corresponds to n-π^* electronic transitions and is of much lower intensity than K band.

R-branch. In rotation-oscillation band, set of transitions corresponding to change of rotational quantum number by +1.

reactant. One of the chemical substances that take part in a chemical reaction. (*See* reaction).

reaction. 1. Any chemical change, regardless of rate, amount of product formed, or whether it occurs naturally (as in plant and animal metabolism) or is purposely induced in a laboratory or in large-scale production. Chemical reactions involved only the electrons of an atom, and the energy absorbed or emitted is small compared with that of nuclear reactions.

Natural reactions usually occur below 310K, but the rate of many induced reactions is greatly increased by high temperatures and by use of catalysts: the concentration of reactants and the particle size of the solids involved are also important factors in the efficiency of reactions. Among the more important types are decomposition, replacement, condensation, neutralization, oxidation-reduction, rearrangement, saponification, and polymerization.

2. Disintegration of the nucleus of an atom either by natural radioactivity or by fission due to bombardment with high-energy particles. A thermonuclear reaction involves the fusion or union of hydrogen nuclei to form helium, with evolution of energy, *See also* change, chemical; chain reaction; fission; fusion.

reaction coordinate. Coordinate (*e.g.*, distance between atoms or time) denoting path of potential energy changes in system of particles of elementary reaction during transition from substrates over activated complex to products.

reaction isotherm. Relation between chemical affinity A and thermodynamic chemical equilibrium constant Ka and activities α_B of reagents before reaching chemical equilibrium

$$A = RT \ln \frac{Ka}{\prod_B \alpha_B^{\nu_B}}$$

where R = molar gas constant, T = thermodynamic temperature, ν_B = stoichiometric coefficient of reactant B. $\prod_B$ = product of all reactants.

reaction kinetics. Although the ultimate state of a chemical system is specified by thermodynamics, the time required to reach that equilibrium state is highly variable. As a consequence, determining the rate of chemical reactions has proved to be important for practical reasons. For example, diamonds are thermodynamically unstable with respect to graphite, but the rate of transformation of diamonds to graphite is negligible. Rate studies have also yielded fundamental information about the details of the nuclear rearrangements which constitute the chemical reaction.

Traditional chemical kinetic investigations of the reaction between species A and B to form C and D, reaction (1), sought a rate of the form given in Eq. (2), where $d[C]/dt$ is the rate of

$$A + B \rightarrow C + D \quad (1)$$

$$d[C]/dt = kf([A], [B], [C], [D]) \quad (2)$$

appearance of product C, f is some function of concentrations of A, B, C, and D which are themselves functions of time, and k is the rate constant.

With few exceptions, the rate law for an elementary reaction $A+B \rightarrow C+D$ is given by $d[C]/dt = k[A][B]$. The order (sum of the exponents of the concentrations) is two, which is expected if the reaction is bimolecular (requires only species A to collide with species B). The rate constant k for such a reaction depends very strongly on temperature.

In some instances, particularly for decomposition reactions $AB \rightarrow A+B$, the elementary reaction step is first-order, Eq. 3,

$$d[A]/dt = d[B]/dt = k[AB] \quad (3)$$

which means that the reaction is unimolecular. The species AB does not spontaneously dissociate it must first be given some critical amount of energy usually through collisions, to form an excited species AB*. It is the species AB* which decompose unimolecularly.

reaction mechanism. Description of subsequent changes which substrate undergoes to yield reaction product.

reaction of fractional order. Reaction with kinetic equation characterized by fractional sum of exponents in which concentrations of reactants occur. Examples of reactions of fractional order are some chain reactions and catalyzed reactions.

reaction polarization. Type of concentration polarization consisting in slow achievement of equilibrium of chemical reactions preceding or following electrode process proper, in comparison to rate of electrode reaction. Reaction polarization is expressed by reaction overvoltage. Also known as chemical polarization.

reaction product. Substance formed as result of chemical reaction. In stoichiometric equation corresponding symbol (formula) appears on its right.

reaction rate. Diminution of mass of substrate referred to unit time and volume. In homogeneous system, v is equal to loss of substrate concentration in unit time and is expressed as derivative of concentration c of substrate with respect to time t, $v = -dc/dt$. Also known as chemical reaction rate.

raaction-rate constant. Coefficient, constant at defined temperature and pressure, specified for given reaction, occurring in kinetic equation for reaction $v = kc^n$, where v=reaction rate, c=substrate concentration, n=order of reaction. Also known as rate constant.

reactive intermediate. A short-lived molecule, atom, or ion formed during the course of a chemical reaction.

reactivity indices. Numbers describing quantitatively reactivity of given position in molecule for different reaction types.

reactor. A device for maintaining a controlled nuclear reaction, chiefly for electric power production, but also for the manufacture of radioisotopes and military equipment. The essential components of a power reactor are (*i*) a fissionable element, or fuel, such as uranium-235 or plutonium ; (*ii*) a neutron source to initiate the reaction ; (*iii*) a moderator to retard fast neutrons for more efficient fission ; (*iv*) a coolant (water or liquid sodium) ; (*v*) control rods made of cadmium, which absorb neutrons and thus maintain any desired level of output. Electric power production is now possible with a minimum evolution of waste heat. The term fuel element, used by reactor technologists, refers to the "package" of nuclear fuel in a ceramic or metal coating, rather than to the fissionable material itself, the word element being used in its electrical rather than its chemical sense.

reagent. In the original use of the term, a substance used to react with another substance or mixture of substances in order to dissolve, them, to oxidize or to reduce them etc., in order that they might be analyzed or utilized. The present meaning of the term is more closely limited to those substances that produce reactions of use in analysis, including all phases of analysis from solution of the sample to detection and determination of specific substances.

reagent's purity. Purity determined as content of impurities in reagent (in weight per cent).

real gas. Gas which does not satisfy equation of state for ideal gas. Particles of real gas interact with each other. Also known as imperfect gas ; non-ideal gas.

real solution. Solution with properties differing from those of ideal mixture. Also known as non-ideal solution.

rearrangement. Process proceeding against principle of least structural changes, involving modification of systems of arrangements of atoms (or groups of atoms) and covalent bonds in molecule, thus causing structural isomerization of the latter. In this type of chemical reaction the atoms of a single compound recombine usually under the influence of a catalyst, to form a new compound having the same molecular weight but different properties. Thus, ammonium cyanate in solution will rearrange to form urea, in which the four hydrogen atoms are equally distributed between the two nitrogen atom :

$$NH_4OCN \rightarrow (NH_2)_2CO$$

rearrangement-1,2. Rearrangement of organic molecule involving migration of atom or group of atoms from given atom to adjacent one, *e.g.*,

$$X\text{—}A\text{—}B \rightarrow A\text{—}B\text{—}X$$

rearrangement, carbonium-ion-induced. Carbonium-ion intermediates in which the positively charged centre is adjacent to a highly branched (substituted) carbon atom may rearrange by a shift of one of the neighboring substituents :

$$R\text{—}\underset{R}{\overset{R}{C}}\text{—}\underset{R}{\overset{+}{C}}\text{—}R' \xrightarrow{\text{R shift}} R\text{—}\underset{R}{\overset{+}{C}}\text{—}\underset{R'}{\overset{R}{C}}\text{—}R'$$

Such carbonium-ion rearrangement are most often observed when they result in an improvement in ion stability or in a relief of ring strain or nonbonded repulsions :

$$R_3CCH_2Cl \xrightarrow{H_2O}$$

$$\left\{ R_3C\text{—}\overset{+}{C}H_2 \xrightarrow{\text{R shift}} R\text{—}\underset{R}{\overset{+}{C}}\text{—}CH_2R \right\} \rightarrow$$

$$R\text{—}\underset{R}{\overset{OH}{C}}\text{—}CH_2R \quad + \quad \underset{R}{\overset{R}{C}}=\underset{H}{\overset{R}{C}}$$

Such rearrangements do not usually involve more than one functional group in the commonly used sense of the term.

Reaumur. A rarely used scale for measuring temperature invented by Rene Reaumur (1683-1757). French physicist. As on the centigrade scale, the freezing point of water is 0°, but the boiling point is 80°. Thus, each, °R is 1.25K, so that 10°R equals 12.5K, 40°R equals 50K, and so on. *See also* centigrade.

recalescence. The phenomenon of growing hot again, The term is commonly met in connection with the slow cooling of red-hot iron. At about 1175K, there is sudden change from α- to β-iron and the red-hot iron is seen to glow brightly. The phenomenon of recalescene when observed during the cooling of alloys usually betrays a change of allotropic form or the nature of the solid solution.

recalescent point. A temperature at which a change in the allotropic form, or solid solution occurs during the cooling of alloys, especially steel.

recarbonize. To add carbon to a substance or system from which carbon has been removed. In various metallurgical processes, metals are purified by treatment which reduces the carbon content, as by oxidation, to a value below that desired in the finished product. According, the value is adjusted by the addition of carbon, a carbide, or other carbonaceous substance.

reciprocity law. Amount of products obtained in any photochemical reaction is directly proportional to product of intensity of incident light and time of its action. Also known as Bunsen-Roscoe law.

reclaiming. Any of various processes for recovering the values from scrap or used materials so that they can be incorporated in the manufacturing of new products. Waste paper is shredded and deinked by solvents and adsorptive agents ; glass and metals are fregmented, and added to fresh batches in limited proportions ; scrap rubber is devulcanized" by heat and solvents or by destructive distillation. The percentage of such reclaimed materials that can be added to new products is restricted, as in many cases their quality has been permanently impaired ; often so many impurities and degradation products are present that reclaiming is not economically practicable. The feasibility of reclaiming agricultural wastes for fuels, fodder, and industrial products has been researched ; such wastes include corn cobs, bagesse and others, as well as manures.

recombinant DNA. Genetic materials transferred from the genes of one species to those of another by uniting a portion of the DNA of one organism with extranuclear section of DNA from another organism. The technique has made possible the synthesis not only of certain complex molecules (proteins) but also of entirely new life forms (bacteria). It is being utilized in basic genetic research sponsored by the Institutes of Health in various countries. Experimental work has already produced a number of important results: (*i*) the production of human insulin from the bacterium E. coli by implantation of synthesized genetic material ; (*ii*) creation of artifical interferon, used in cancer therapy ; (*iii*) a synthetic bacterium that consumes oil spills more efficiently than natural type. Many more achievements of this nature are likely, and the potential for the chemical, agricultural, food and pharmaceutical industries is enormous. Also known as gene-splicing.

recombination coefficient. A quantity entering into calculations of the decrease in concentration of ionized pairs by recombinations of ions. In its simplest application, it is shown in the expression,

$$\beta N_1 N_2 = -\frac{dN_1}{dt} = -\frac{dN_2}{dt}$$

where N_1 and N_2 are the numbers of positive and negative ion per cubic centimeter, $-\frac{dN_1}{dt}$ and $-\frac{dN_2}{dt}$ are their respectives of disappearance, and β is the recombination coefficient.

recombination energy. The energy released when two oppositely charged portions of an atom or molecule rejoin to form a neutral atom or molecule.

recombination radiation. The radiation emitted in semiconductors when electrons in conduction band recombine with holes in the valence band.

reconstitution. In food technology, replacement at the time of use of the water removed from a dehydrated food product, thus restoring the food to its original edible condition.

recrystallization. Repeated crystallization, a process used to purify substances.

rectification. 1. The interaction of a partial condensate with the vapour rising through a fractionating column, resulting in further enrichment of the vapour in the low boiling component. This specific use of the term rectification is commonly extended to cover the entire process of distillation, as used in the purification of liquids.

2. The adjustment of alcoholic content, of alcoholic beverages, etc., to obtain a product of predetermined strength.

rectifying column. A fractionating column in which the direct interchange of heat, and consequent evaporation and condensation, takes place.

recycling. 1. Return of a portion of a reaction product to the beginning of a processing sequence. Separation and recirculating of unreacted components increases the efficiency of conversion and also permits reuse of processing aids that remain unchanged. Recycling is standard procedure in distillation (reflux), the cracking of petroleum, and synthesis of ammonia and other chemicals.

2. In popular use, the term refers to reclamation of waste paper, glass, etc., a limited proportion of which can be incorporated in new product manufacture. *See also* reclaiming.

redox. A shortened expression for "reduction-oxidation" or "oxidation-reduction."

redox electrode. Electrode (half-cell) usually constructed from noble metal dipped into solution which contains ions or compounds of different oxidation states, *e.g.*, Pt | Fe^{3+}, Fe^{2+} or Pt | quinone, hydroquinone ; electrode reaction is :

$$\text{Red} \rightleftharpoons \text{Ox} + ze^-$$

where Red and Ox=reduced and oxidized form respectively ; electrode potential is :

$$\varepsilon = \varepsilon^0 + \frac{RT}{zF} \ln \frac{a_{\text{Ox}}}{a_{\text{Red}}}$$

where ε^0=standard electrode potential.

Redox indicator. A substance that undergoes a characteristic colour change at a definite state of oxidation of a solution or, rather, at a definite value of the oxidizing potential.

reduced equation of state. Thermal equation of state of real gas expressed by reduced parameters ; reduced pressure p_r, reduced volume V_r and reduced thermodynamic temperature T_r, *e.g.*, reduced van der Waals equation has the form :

$$\left(P_r + \frac{3}{V_r}\right)(3V_r - 1) = 8T_r$$

reduced mass, μ. Quantity used in description of relative motion of two particles of mass m_1 and m_2, with respect to their centre of mass :

$$\mu = \frac{m_1 m_2}{m_1 + m_2}$$

reduced parameters. Dimensionless quantities defined as ratios of parameters of state and corresponding critical parameters of the given substance $Xr=X/Xc$, where X=reduced parameter of state, Xc=corresponding critical parameter of discussed substance. Also known as reduced variables.

reduced pressure, p_r. Dimensionless quantity :

$$p_r = \frac{p}{p_c}$$

where p=pressure and p_c=critical pressure.

reduced temperature, Ta. Dimensionless magnitude $T_r=T/Tc$, where T=thermodynamic temperature, T_c=critical temperature of a given substance.

reduced viscosity, ηred. Ratio of specific viscosity to concentration of solution :

$$\eta_{red} = \frac{\eta_{sp}}{c} = \frac{\eta - \eta_0}{\eta_0 \, c}$$

where η=viscosity coefficient of solution, η_0= viscosity coefficient of solvent, ηsp=specific viscosity, c=concentration of solution. Also known as Staudinger function.

reduced volume, V_r. Dimensionless quantity $V_r=V_m/V_c$, where V_m=molar volume and Vc=critical volume.

reducing agent. Substance giving up its electrons to another (reduced) substance called oxidizing agent which gains electrons ; thus, reducer of electron transfer. Also known as reductant.

reducing enzyme. An enzyme that reduces certain organic or inorganic substance, *e.g.*, catalase.

reducing flame. A flame in which substances undergo reduction reactions, as the reduction of a metallic oxide to the free metal. The term is applied commonly to the luminous inner portion of the flame of gas burners, blowpipes, etc., which, because of its content of carbon monoxide and other reducing substances, has a marked reducing action.

reducing sugar. Any mono- or disaccharide, such as glucose or fructose, which reduces silver or copper salts in alkaline solution, beacause of the presence of free aldehyde or ketone groups.

reduction. 1. Addition of hydrogen to or subtraction of oxygen from a substance. The term originally referred to a reaction in which oxygen is removed from a compound and transferred to an element called a reducing agent, for example, $ZnO+C \rightarrow Zn+CO$. Though reduction can be regarded simply as the removal of oxygen, it also has a broader meaning ; the acceptance of one or more electrons (or their equivalent) from another substance. For example ; it may be accomplished by transfer of chlorine atoms, as in the Kroll magnesium reduction process, where the metal chloride is reduced to elemental metal while the magnesium is oxidized by combination with chlorine ; $2Mg+XCl_4 \rightarrow X+2MgCl_2$ where X is a metal. Oxygen is not essential to the reaction. Reduction can also be effected by addition of hydrogen to a molecule.

2. Lowering the valence of an element in combination, as reducing ferric chloride to ferrous chloride.

3. Both the preceding processes, and the complete reactions of which they are a part, involve an interchange of electrons between atoms, whereupon the atom gaining the electron or electrons is reduced, and the atom losing the electron or electons is oxidized.

4. Comminution of larger solid units to smaller ones by crushing, grinding, or similar disintegrating methods, as expressed by the term size reduction.

5. In metallurgy, separation of a metal ore into its wanted and unwanted components by any of several methods. *e.g.*, roasting, flotation elutriation, etc.

reduction ratio. A term, used specifically in connection with milling and grinding processes, to indicate the ratio of particle sizes before and after crushing or grinding. The particle chosen from a given mass of material may be the average or mean of the aggregation of particles, or more commonly, the largest.

reductometry. Determination of oxidants in solution by means of titration with standardized solution of raductants. Also known as reductometric titration.

Reed reaction Direct treatment of paraffin or alicyclic hydrocarbons with chlorine and sulphur dioxide to produce their sulphonyl chlorides.

$$RH + SO_2 + Cl_2 \rightarrow RSO_2Cl + HCl$$

The reaction is catalyzed by light.

reference. In optical absorption technique, precisely defined object used as reference for absorption measurements of a given object in order to eliminate certain factors like reflection, scattering, etc. Also known as reference material.

reference band. Spectral band of auxiliary sample of known frequency, superimposed on investigated spectrum in order to obtain reference point on frequency scale.

reference electrode. Electrode with respect to which potentials of other electrodes are measured as EMF of cell constructed with that electrode. Usually it is electrode of second kind with stable and reproducible potential with respect to normal hydrogen electrode, whose potential is assumed equal to zero.

reference solution. Solution with respect to which relative measurements of studied solution are conducted.

reference source. Radiation source of parameters (*e.g.*, activity, purity) determined with sufficient accuracy to apply source as standard. Also known as radioactive standard.

refining. 1. In the petroleum industry, this term refers to chemical reactions performed on the various fractions from petroleum by distillation; these include cracking, reforming, polymerization, dehydrogenation, etc., usually with catalysts, for production of gasoline and other derivatives.

2. In food industry, refining involves a sequence of operations employed to remove impurities and to concentrate the desirable portion of a food product to improve its suitability for consumption. Typical is the refining of sugar by such operations as filtration, adsorption on charcoal, centrifuging, crystallization, etc. Flours and other cereals are refined by grinding and sifting. Purification of vegetable oils by adsorption on clays or carbon and the rectification of spiritous liquors are other instances of food product refining. Chemical reactions are not involved in these methods.

3. In metallurgy, the term also implies removal of impurities by various separation techniques, important among which are electrolysis used for aluminum, copper, and the precious metals) and a specialized operation called zone refining.

4. In the rubber reclaim industry, refining involves passing the reclamate repeatedly between close-set metal rollers at high speed, and afterward through a straining device, to remove particles of dirt, metal, and other foreign matter.

reflection spectroscopy. Method of optical analysis used for investigation of solids. Quality of a given product (*e.g.*, whiteness of sugar or paper) or concentration of a given component is evaluated from measurement of diffusionally reflected radiation at some wavelength or in some spectral range.

reflux. Literally means "flowing back". For reflux condensing, the condenser is placed upright on the neck of the vessel in which the liquid is boiled. Vapour condenses and the liquid runs back into the vessel and their is no loss in weight. The arrangement is very useful for slow organic reactions which may have to be maintained at boiling-point for some hours, Without the refluxing arrangement, the liquid would soon boil away.

Reformatsky reaction. The condensation reaction between an α-haloester and a carbonyl compound (such as an aldehyde, ketone, or ester) in the presence of zinc. This reaction is used in organic synthesis as a means of preparing β-hydroxy esters and the corresponding unsaturated acids and esters, as well as a means of adding two carbon atoms to the carbon chain, *e.g.*,

$$C_2H_5OOC{-}CH_2Br + Zn \rightarrow C_2H_5COOC{-}CH_2{-}ZnBr$$

$$[C_2H_5OOC{-}CH_2{-}ZnBr] + O{=}C(R')(R'') \rightarrow C_2H_5OOC{-}CH_2{-}C(OH)(R')(R')$$

reforming process. A cracking process for transforming hydrocarbon mixtures of low octane number into fuels having high octane numbers. The process involves, to a greater or lesser degree, all three of the reactions; dehydrogenation decomposition, and aromatization. The process is commonly carried out at temperatures of 750-1070K in the presence of catalysts such as platinum and molybdenum. The reactions most commonly involved are dehydrogenation and isomerization. When platinum is the catalyst, it is necessary to add hydrogen to the catalyst by contamination with carbon. This type of reforming is called hydroforming.

refractometry. Analytical methods based on the measurement of refractive index. Used for identification purposes, purity control and for quantitative analysis of mostly two-component mixtures of components with substantially different refractive indices.

refractory. Resistant to the action of heat, especially in the sense of having a high melting point, or any substance which possesses this property. Refractories are used extensively in the construction of furnaces and other apparatus which operates at high temperatures.

refrigerant. Any substance or mixture used in the production of reduced temperatures. Refrigerants range from the various substances which are used as working media in refrigeration apparatus to substances or mixtures which are used without apparatus to produce reduced temperatures, such as ice, brines, ammonia, solid carbon dioxide, sulphur dioxide, and ethyl chloride. The first three are still in wide use in food packing and storage plants.

regeneration. 1. Returning a raw material or natural product to its original state or condition after it has been chemically modified for processing purposes. Examples are regeneration of cellulose to rayon after it has been solubilized with sodium hydroxide and carbon disulphide to permit extrusion into fiber, and regeneration of collagen by neutralization with acid after purification in alkaline solution for use in sausage casings. Regeneration should not be confused with reclaiming, which only partially restores the original properties of a material.

2. Renewing or reactivating a catalyst, molecular sieve, or ion-exchange medium (zeolite) by any of several methods. Catalysts fouled with coke or other deposits are regenerated by treatment with hot reactive gases such as oxygen, hydrogen, steam, etc. Zeolites are regenerated by replacing the sodium ions exchanged during the removal of calcium compounds from water by treatment with a solution of sodium chloride.

regioselective reaction. Formation of one of possible isomers in predominant amount with respect to other isomeric products, *e.g.*,

$$CH_3{-}CH_2{-}\underset{Br}{\overset{CH_3}{C}}{-}CH_3 \xrightarrow[-HBr]{t\text{-}BuO^-} \underset{72\%}{CH_3{-}CH_2{-}\overset{CH_3}{C}{=}CH_2} + \underset{23\%}{CH_3{-}CH{=}\overset{CH_3}{C}{-}CH_3}$$

Electrophilic, nucleophilic and free-radical aromatic substitutions can be *o*-, *m*- or *p*-regioselective.

regiospecific reaction. Formation of one of possible isomers, due to absence of rearrangements in system, *e.g.*,

$$(CH_3)_3C{-}CH{=}CH{-}CH_3 + IN_3 \rightarrow (CH_3)_3C{-}CH{-}\underset{I}{\overset{N_3}{CH}}{-}CH_3$$

regular polymer. Polymer is regular when its macromolecules can be split into constitutional units of one species and in one sequential arrangement only.

regular solution. Solution with enthalpy of mixing H^M (*see* functions of mixing) different from zero, *i.e.*, having value other than in ideal solution, but with entropy of mixing S^M equal to entropy of mixing of ideal solution :

$$S^M = -R \sum_i x_i \ln x$$

where R = universal gas constant, x_i = molar fraction of constituent of solution, $\sum_i$ = summation of all constituents of solution.

regulatory enzyme. An enzyme having a regulatory function through its capacity to undergo a change in catalytic activity by non-covalent binding of a specific modulating metabolite.

Reichert numbers. Various methods of expressing the volatile water-soluble organic acids in a fat, which are usually determined by first saponifying the fat, distilling, and then titrating the liberated fatty acids. The specific Reichert numbers, which are designated usually by the name of Reichert and some other investigator, as the Reichert-Meissl or Reichert-Wollny numbers, are the volume in cubic centimeters of a standard alkali solution of specified concentration, (commonly 0.1 N NaOH) required to titrate the volatile water-soluble fatty acids from a specified amount of fat (5 grams).

Reichstein reagents. 1. 3,5-Dinitrobenzoylchloride, which forms crystalline esters of characteristic melting point with alcohols. These esters give deep-red to orange colours with α-naphthylamine.

2. Anthraquinone-β-carboxylic acid chloride gives characteristic compounds with primary and secondary alcohols. The reaction also takes place with many phenols, enolic compounds, mercaptans, amines, etc.

Reimer-Tiemann reaction. The preparation of oxy-aldehydes by the interaction of a phenol, chloroform, and aqueous alkalies. The aldehyde group enters the ortho and para positions with respect to the hydroxyl group. Oxyacids are similarly produced from carbon tetrachloride :

$$CHCl_3 \xrightarrow[-HCl]{HO^-} :CCl_2$$

$$C_6H_5O^{\ominus} + :CCl_2 \longrightarrow \left[\text{dienone}(=O)\text{–}C(H)\text{–}\overset{\ominus}{C}Cl_2 \right] \longrightarrow$$

$$o\text{-}(CHCl_2)C_6H_4O^{\ominus} \xrightarrow{2H_2O} o\text{-}(CHO)C_6H_4OH$$

reinecke. A hydrated salt resulting from combination of two ammonium compounds, one containing a thiocyanate group (SCN) and the other a diammonochromate group, $Cr(NH_3)_2$. The product is a water- and alcohol-soluble red powder used as a reagent in organic analysis (amines and other organic bases). The formula is $NH_4[Cr(NH_3)_2(SCN)_4] \cdot H_2O$.

reinforced plastic. A composite structure composed of a thermoplastic or a thermosetting resin and a fibrous filler material ; the components are pressed together to give an extremely strong product with high impact resistance. Glass fiber is usually used as the reinforcing material, for both lightness and strength. Such composites are called fibre glass-reinforced plastics (FRP); they have many structural uses, especially for bullet-proof fuselages, building panels, automobile and boat bodies, switchboards, and filament winding. Their corrosion-resistant properties make them preferable to steel and other metals on an economic basis, for such uses as oil-well drilling equipment, chemical piping, tanks, and similar equipment. Numerous resins are used, epoxy being one of the most important.

reinforcing agent. A term used in rubber and plastics technology to denote any material that increases the toughness, abrasion resistance, or impact strength of the base material when added to it in substantial quantities. Finely divided powders such as carbon black and zinc oxide greatly enhance these properties in rubber and other elastomers. The impact strength of plastics can be increased by incorporation of asbestos or glass fibres and by fabric insertions.

Reinsch test. A qualitative test for arsenic. The element is reduced, and deposited from a hydrochloric acid solution on a small piece of burnished copper as a characteristic black stain.

rennin. An enzyme used in commercial practice for coagulation of milk to obtain the grade of casein used in making buttons and other small plastic items, and also as a food additive. It is one of the digestive enzymes secreted in the stomach and is produced commercially by extraction from the organs of young animals. In commercial terminology it is also called rennet.

Reissert reaction. A method of synthesis of the

"Reissert Compounds," which are 1-acyl-2-cyano-1,2 dihydroquinoline derivatives, by the direct action upon quinoline of acid chlorides and alkali cyanides, *e.g.*,

$$RCOCl + KCN + \text{quinoline} \longrightarrow \text{1-acyl-2-cyano-1,2-dihydroquinoline (N–COR, CN)}$$

(Reissert compound)

$$\xrightarrow[\text{hydrolysis}]{H^{\oplus}} RCHO + \text{quinaldic acid (COOH)} + NH_4$$

"Reissert compound" thus obtained yields upon acid hydrolysis aldehyde and quinaldic acid.

relative atomic mass *Ar*. Ratio of mean atomic mass of given element and 1/12 of mass of ^{12}C nuclide ; mean atomic mass is calculated as average of natural abundance of nuclides ; *e.g.*, $Ar(Cl) = 35.453$.

Concept of relative atomic mass can be extended to any mixture of nuclides. However, natural mixture is assumed if not stated otherwise. Also known as atomic weight.

relative configuration. Determination of configuration around chiral centre, related to conventionally adopted model ; for instance, in the case of hydroxyaldehydes—to one of the enantiomers of glyceraldehyde. It has been arbitrarily adopted that dextro-rotary glyceraldehyde enantiomer possesses configuration shown in projection formula, in which hydroxyl group is located on right side of carbon chain ; this configuration is denoted as D ; configuration of laevo-rotary glyceraldehyde enantiomer is denoted as L.

D-(+)-glyceraldehyde: CHO (C=O, H) at top; H on left, OH on right; CH_2OH at bottom.

L-(—)-glyceraldehyde: CHO (C=O, H) at top; HO on left, H on right; CH_2OH at bottom.

relative electrode potential. EMF of cell constructed from normal hydrogen electrode and particular given electrode.

The term relative electrode potential is traditional : more appropriate term is EMF of reference cell.

relative molecular mass M_r. Ratio of mean mass of molecule, as given by its formula and natural abundance of nuclides, to 1/12 of mass of ^{12}C nuclide ; *e.g.*, M_r (KCl) = 74.555.

Concept of relative molecular mass can be extended to any mixture of nuclides. However, natural mixture is assumed if not stated otherwise.

relative reaction rate. Ratio of rate of one selected chemical reaction from among several reactions proceeding in identical conditions to rate of reaction chosen from that group as reference reaction. Generally, reaction-rate constants of reactions of the same order are compared, at the same temperature.

relative viscosity η_{rel}. Ratio of viscosity coefficient of pure solvent $\eta_{rel} = \eta/\eta_0$, where η = viscosity coefficient of solution, η_0 = viscosity coefficient of solvent. Also known as viscosity ratio.

relativistic mass. The mass of a body that is travelling at a speed comparable to the velocity of light. The relativistic mass, *m*, of a body travelling at a velocity, *v*, is given by :

$$m = m_0 \sqrt{1 - v^2/c^2}$$

where m_0 = the rest mass and c = the velocity of light.

relativistic particle. A particle that has speed comparable to the velocity of light ; *i.e.*, a particle with a relativistic mass substantially in excess of its rest mass.

relativistic velocity. A velocity, approaching the velocity of light, at which the effect of the theory of relativity is significant.

relaxation methods. Considerable use has been made of perturbation techniques to measure rates and determine mechanisms of rapid chemical reactions. These methods provide measurements of chemical reaction rates by displacing equilibria. In situations where the reaction of interest occurs in a system at equilibrium, perturbation techniques called relaxation methods have been found most effective for determining reaction rate constants.

A chemical system at equilibrium is one in

which the rate of a forward reaction is exactly balanced by the rate of the corresponding back reaction. Examples are chemical reactions occurring in liquid solutions, such as the familiar equilibrium in pure water, shown in reaction :

$$H_2O \underset{k_b}{\overset{k_f}{\rightleftharpoons}} H^+(aq) + OH^-(aq) \quad (1)$$

The essence of any of the relaxation methods is the perturbation of a chemical equilibrium (by a small change in temperature, pressure, electric-field intensity, or solvent composition) in so sudden a fashion that the chemical system in seeking to reachieve equilibrium, is forced by the comparative slowness of the chemical reactions to lag behind the perturbation.

The temperature jump (T-jump) relaxation method has proved to be very versatile. The choice of the particular means of effecting the temperature perturbation is dictated only by the requirement that the temperature rise somewhat more rapidly than the time constant of the chemical reaction to be explored, so that a tedious deconvolution can be avoided.

In a situation, such as reaction (1), in which electrically neutral reactant species dissociate into oppositely charged ions, an especially sensitive tool for measuring rate constants of forward and backward reactions is the electric-field jump (E-jump) technique with conductometric detection. In a strong electric field (of the order of 4×10^6 V m^{-1}), a weak acid in solution is caused to dissociate to a greater degree than it would be in the absence of the electric field. With a sensitive, high-voltage, Wheatstone bridge, the exponential increase with time in the concentration of ions following a precipitous increase in electronic-field strength is readily detected. The measured relaxation time (τ) is clearly that corresponding to the high-electric-field environment, but since the rate constants for these reactions differ little in and out of the electric field, no serious problem is posed.

Two other relaxation methods widely used than the E-jump technique are pressure jump (P-jump) and ultrasonic absorption. Each relies its effectiveness on a volume change, $\triangle V^0$, occurring in an aqueous sample equilibrium undergoing kinetic investigation. As electrically neutral, weak electrolyte species dissociate into ions in aqueous solution, there is an increase in the number of solvent molecules drawn into a highly ordered solvation sheath. The higher the charge density of the ion, the more water molecule dipoles are bound and the greater the change in V^0 as reactants become products. Unlike the T-jump and E-jump relaxation methods, which usually employ step function perturbations, the ultrasonic absorption techniques are continuous-wave experiments in which the sample chemical equilibrium absorbs a measusable amount of the sound wave's energy when the frequency of the sound wave (f) and the relaxation time of the chemical equilibrium bear the relation to one another given by Eq. (2). *See* ultrasonics.

$$\tau^{-1} = 2\pi f \quad (2)$$

The typical pressure-jump (P-jump) experiment is one in which a liquid sample under about 200 atmospheres (20 megapascals) pressure is suddenly brought to atmospheric pressure by the bursting of a metal membrane in the sample cell autoclave. Relaxation times measured spectrophotometrically or conductometrically are thus accessible if $\pi > 100$ microseconds. This technique has proven particularly useful in the elucidation of micellar systems of great interest for catalysis and for petroleum recovery from apparently depleted oil fields.

The continuous- and stopped-flow techniques antedate somewhat the relaxation techniques described above, and have the sometimes important advantage of permitting kinetic measurements in chemical systems far from equilibrium. The stopped-flow experiment is one in which two different liquids in separate syringes are mixed rapidly in a tangential jet mixing chamber and then the rapid flow of mixed reactants is almost immediately brought to a halt in a spectrophotometric, conductometric, or calorimetric observation chamber.

relaxation time. In relaxation phenomena, the time interval which is required for a predetermined portion of the system to respond to a sudden change in external conditions, forces, or effects :

$$\Delta f_t = \Delta f_{t=0}\, e^{-\frac{t}{\tau}}$$

where relaxation time is period in which initial change $\Delta f_{t=0}$ of investigated value f from value in steady state diminishes e times :

$$\Delta f_{t=\tau} = \frac{\Delta f_{t=0}}{e},$$

where t=time, e=base of natural logarithms.

rem. Obsolete unit of relative biological efficiency equal to absorbed dose of any ionizing radiation causing the same biological effect as 1 rad of X-ray radiation with specific ionization of 100 ions pairs in water layer of 1 nm thickness.

Abbreviation from rontgen equivalent man.

remanence. The residual magnetization of a ferromagnetic substance subjected to a hysteresis cycle when the magnetizing field is reduced to zero.

Remy test. Ruthenium is detected by mixing the material tested with 1 ml. hydrochloric acid, and passing in chlorine. An intense blue colour indicates the presence of ruthenium.

Renner effect. Inseparability of nuclear and electronic motions in degenerate electronic states of linear polyatomic molecules.

Renz test reaction. Thallium salts, when in alcoholic solution, give a violet colour or precipitate with α-naphthylamine. With β-naphthylamine a double compound with a silvery luster is obtained.

rep. Obsolete unit of absorbed dose of ionizing radiation of any kind (in SI system substituted by unit gray); dose of 1 rep is equal to 93 erg/g, *i.e.*, to dose absorbed by approximately 1 g of substance from exposure dose of 1 rontgen of hard gamma or X-ray radiation.

Abbreviation from rontgen equivalent physical.

repeatability. A measure of deviation of test results from their mean value, all determinations being carried out by one operator without change of apparatus in those cases where the manner of handling apparatus can alter results.

repellent. 1. In materials technology, any substance that is not penetrated or wetted by water, *i.e.*, hydrophobic. Chief among these are hydrocarbon solvents, oils, fat, waxes, rubber, and such finely divided materials as carbon black, magnesium carbonate, etc.

2. In agricultural chemistry, a substance which is so repugnant to an animal or insect as to prevent its approach. Repellents are not necessarily toxic but are offensive to the subject either because of smell or taste. They are quite specific in their action, no single type being generally effective. They are used on a wide range of living beings, including mosquitoes, rabbits, deer, birds, and sharks.

replication. Making a reverse image of a surface by means of an impression on or in a receptive material. This technique is used in electron microscopy to obtain plastic replicas of observed objects. In biochemistry, the term refers to the reproduction of the deoxyribonucleic acid molecule, which is composed of two interlocking chains of nucleotide substances, forming a double helix. It reproduces itself by forming two identical daughter molecules, each of which receives one of the two chains of the original molecule, the other chain in each case being synthesized from nucleic acids by the action of enzymes (DNA polymerases). In the over-simplified drawing, the solid lines represent the strands contributed by the original molecule, and the broken lines are the synthesized strands. *See also* deoxyribonucleic acid ; genetic code.

parent DNA daughter

Reppe reactions. Syntheses applying acetylene under pressure and elevated temperatures for vinylation, ethynylation, carbonylation and cyclic polymerization.

Reppmann test. Arsenic is detected by placing 1 drop of the solution tested on filter, moistening with hydrochloric acid and a 0.5% solution of N-ethyl-8-hydroxytetrahydroquinoline hydrochloride. Then 1 drop ferric chloride solution is added and the paper is warmed. A red-brown colour indicates the presence of arsenic.

reprecipitation. Repetitive precipitation of analysed component using the same or in succession different precipitating reagents to obtain better separation from impurities.

reprocessing. Treatment of spent nuclear reactor fuel to recover the unconsumed uranium-235 and plutonium ; the method comprises a series of complex chemical separations involving solvent extraction, ion-exchange, and precipitation (Purex process). The reclaimed material is sent to fabrication plants for ultimate reuse. Serious radiation hazards are present in reprocessing, which requires shielding and remotecontrol handling.

residual current. In electroanalysis, usually small electrolysis current at potentials not exceeding decomposition potential. Residual current is due to charging current and reduction or oxidation of impurities.

residual magnetization. Magnetization of previously saturated ferro- or ferrimagnet which remains when external magnetic field is removed.

resin. 1. A group of natural products of vegetable origin, commonly the solid exudation-products of plants, frequently formed by polymerization of esssential oil constituents. Chemically, they are largely mixtures of oxygen derivatives of cyclic hydrocarbons, resin acids, and phenolic derivatives. Resins are characterized by lack of crystalline structure, low melting point, strong, pleasant odour, insolubility in water, solubility in alkalies, alcohol, and most organic solvents. They are hard and brittle when cold, and soft and tacky when warm. On fusion with alkalies resins yield phenols (resorcinol, phloroglucinol, etc.) and on distillation with zinc dust they yield benzene, naphthalene, and similar hydrocarbons.

2. Any synthetic high polymer usually resulting from an addition or a condensation reaction *e.g.*, polystyrene, phenolformaldehyde. Such substances were originally called resins probably because some early types, such as coumarone-indene, physically resembled natural resins. Thus, the term synthetic resin, though still widely used, is strictly inappropriate, since the substances are polymeric compounds rather than mixtures of simple substances. Characteristic properties of such polymers are insolubility in water, resistance to attack by chemicals, high electrical resistivity, and a smooth hard finish.

resinoid. A term used by materials engineers to denote a liquid, semisolid thermosetting resin or plastic, especially those used for bonding agents in such composites as abrasive wheels plywood, etc. It also includes semipolymerized (heat-bodied) linseed oil and A-stage phenolformaldehyde resins (also called resols).

resolution. A term used in a number of specific cases in science to denote the process of separating closely-related forms or entities. The term is most frequently used in optics to denote the smallest extension which a magnifying instrument is able to separate or the smallest change in wave length which a spectrometer can differentiate. In this last sence, it is defined as the ratio of the average wave length (wave number or frequency) of two spectral lines, which can just be detected as a doublet, to the difference in their wave lengths (wave numbers or frequencies). The term resolution is also applied to such varied processes as the separation of a racemic mixture into its optically-active components or as the breaking up of a vectorial quantity into component.

resonance. 1. Mathematical concept based on quantum mechanical considerations (*i.e.*, the wave functions of electrons), which expresses the true nature of certain compounds which cannot be accurately represented by any one valence-bond. Valence electrons in such molecules are able to acquire slightly different energy levels. These levels can be described by various non-existing resonance structures. The real electronic structure of molecule lies somewhere in-between resonance structure and is called resonance hybrid, *e.g.*,

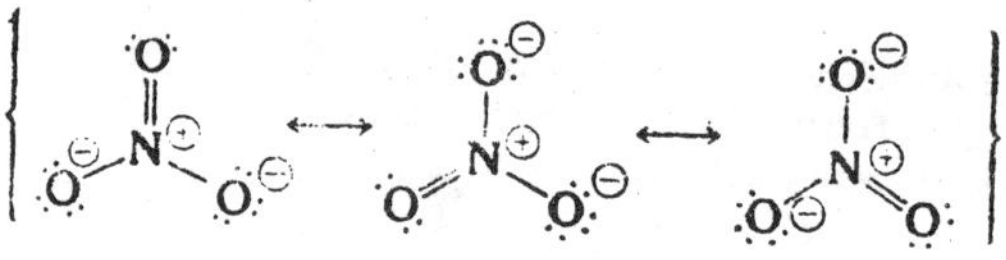

The term mesomerism is used synonymously with resonance.

2. In spectroscopy, resonance refers to a condition in which a source of radiant energy is in the same energy state as the atom or molecule that absorbs the radiation, as in nuclear magnetic resonance. Thus, the radiation emitted has the same wavelength as the exciting source.

resonance capture. Capture of neutron of resonance energy.

resonance effect. In coordination chemistry, increase in stability constant of chelate complex occurring number of possible resonance structures.

resonance fluorescence. The emission by an excited atom of a radiation of the same frequency as the exciting radiation. Also called resonance radiation.

resonance neutron activation. Activation by resonance neutrons, the energy of which causes the resonance induction of the particular kind of atomic nuclei.

resonance neutron detector. Neutron detector in which intensity of neutron flux of different energies is determined by measuring activity of a metal foil (*e.g.*, cobalt, manganese, copper) activated by neutrons of specified energy.

resonance peak. Peak in curve relating cross-section of a nuclear reaction to energy of bombarding particle (excitation function) it corresponds to resonance absorption.

resonances. Systems of hadrons in resonance state decaying in 10^{-23}—10^{-22} s, characterized by discrete quantum numbers.

resorption. The absorption, or less commonly, the adsorption by a body or system of material previously released from absorption or adsorption by that same body or system.

respiratory quotient. The ratio of the volume of oxygen inhaled by an organism to the volume of carbon dioxide exhaled. This ratio is generally less than 1, due to the volume of expired carbon dioxide being less than the volume of inspired oxygen.

rest mass. The mass of a body when at rest relative to the observer. The mass of a body varies with its velocity.

restricted rotation. Lack of free rotation, about single bond in molecule, resulting from considerable difference in potential energies at defined temperature of conformers (unstable one with high energy and stable with low energy). Rotational barrier of restricted rotation is ca. 75—85 kJ/mol. Also known as restricted internal rotation, hindered rotation.

retarder. A benzenoid compound such as salicylic or benzoic acid added to rubber and plastic mixes during processing in low concentrations to prevent cross-linking action (curing) from taking place at the temperatures prevailing during extrusion and other manufacturing steps. They are also used in sponge rubber formulations to withhold vulcanization until the material has had a chance to form a foam. Retarders are special types of inhibitors.

retention. In radiochemistry, ratio of activity which cannot be separated from irradiated target to total primary activity of target ; frequently expressed as a percentage.

retention of configuration. Retention of configuration at chiral centre in chemical reaction, when cleavage of previous and formation of new bonds with chiral atom take place.

retention volume. Volume of gas or liquid needed for elution of given compound from chromatographic column (measured upto moment when its concentration in effluent reaches maximum. Also known as total retention volume.

Retger liquid. Methylene iodide (sp. gr. 3.3) which is miscible with benzene and suitable for specific gravity determinations and separations of minerals and other solids.

retonation. The repetition of a detonation ; an explosion-wave which travels again from the origin of explosion through the substances that have already exploded.

retrograde condensation. Partial liquefaction of two component mixtures of gases during their isothermal expansion. Retrograde condensation occurs in neighbourhood of critical state in the case of two component systems in which liquid phase may exist in a certain range of temperatures above critical temperature due to condition $(\partial^2 H_m/\partial x^2_i)=0$ (where H_m =molar enthalpy at critical state, x_i=mole fraction of constituent in phase).

retrovirus. RNA virus containing a reverse transcriptase, *i.e.*, an RNA-directed DNA polymerase.

Reverdin rearrangement. The migration of iodine that occurs during the nitration of iodophenolic ethers.

$$\text{OR-}C_6H_4\text{-I (para)} + HNO_3 \rightarrow \text{OR-}C_6H_3(\text{I})\text{-}NO_2 + H_2O$$

reverse isotope dilution. Isotope dilution in which substance labelled with isotopic tracer is determined by addtion of the substance with natural isotopic composition.

reversible cell. A storage battery, or any electric cell in which the chemical reaction by which the cell produces its electromotive force and current is reversible by application to the cell terminals (emergent part of the electrodes) of an e.m.f. opposite in sign to that of cell and great enough in magnitude to force a current to flow through the cell in the opposite direction to that prevailing when the cell is producing current. The result of the process is to restore the electrodes and electrolyte to their original chemical condition.

reversible coagulation. Coagulation in which product (usually gel) can be reconverted into sol state, *e.g.*, coagulation of lyophilic colloids by action of electrolytes.

reversible colloid. A colloidal system such as a gel or suspension that can be changed back to it's original liquid form by heating, addition of water, or other method. For example, evaporated egg white can be restored (reconstituted) by addition of water, pastes of starch or soap are also reversible.

reversible cycle. Simultaneously cyclic and reversible thermodynamic process. Also known as reversible cyclic process.

reversible electrode. An electrode used in a reversible electrochemical reaction. There are three types of reversible electrodes used in reversible cells. The first type consists of a metal which is in contact with a solution containing its ions. The second type consists of a metal and one of its insoluble salts in contact with a solution containing a soluble salt with the same anion. This type of electrode is reversible with respect to the anions. The third type of electrode is a metal which is resistant to acids and bases, in contact with a solution which contains ions in two valence states. Oxidation or reduction is the reversible reaction which occurs at this type of electrode.

reversible process. Thermodynamic process with entropy source vanishing in system as well as at boundary between system and surroundings. Also known as reversible change.

reversible reaction. A chemical reaction which can proceed first to the right and then to the left when the conditions are changed ; in other words the product of the first reaction can decompose to the original components as a result of different conditions of temperature or pressure, *e.g.*, $H_2O+CO_2 \rightleftharpoons H_2CO_3$; $NH_4Cl \rightleftharpoons NH_3 + HCl$, in which the ammonium chloride decomposes on heating to ammonia and hydrogen chloride, which recombine on cooling.

Reynold's number. A dimensionless quantity applied to a liquid flowing through a cylindrical tube, given by $(R_e)=udl/\eta$, where u=velocity of flow, d=density of the liquid, l=the diameter of the tube, and η=the coefficient of viscosity of the liquid. At low velocities, the flow of the liquid is streamline. At a certain value of (R_e), corresponding to critical velocity u_c, the flow becomes turbulent.

rH. The oxidation-reduction potential, expressed as the logarithm of the reciprocal of the hydrogen pressure (in atmospheres) :

$$rH = \log\left(\frac{1}{p_{H_2}}\right),$$

where the partial pressure of the hydrogen is given in atmospheres.

rhamnogalactoside. One of a group of glycosides which, on hydrolysis, yield rhamnose and galactose, as robinin and xanthorhamnin.

rhamnoglucoside. One of a group of glycosides which yield rhamnose and glucose on hydrolysis, as hesperidin, rutin, sophorin.

rhamnomannoside. One of a group of glycosides which yield rhamnose and mannose on hydrolysis, as strophanthin.

rhamnoside. One of a group of glycosides which yield rhamnose upon hydrolysis, as quercitin, baptisin, frangulin, etc.

rhe. The absolute unit by which fluidity is measured or expressed. It is the reciprocal centipoise, which is in turn, one-hundredth of the poise, the c.g.s. unit of viscosity. One poise is equal to one dyne second per square centimeter.

rheid. A substance below its melting points. which deforms by viscous flow during applied stress at an order of magnitude at least three times that of elastic deformation under similar circumstances.

rhenium. An element.

	Symbol	Re
State Solid	Atomic Wt.	186.2
	Atomic No.	75
Group VIIB	Valence	1,2,3,4,5,6,7
	m.p.	3450K
	b.p.	5893K

Rhenium is a silver-gray metal ; its density 21.02 (g/cc) is almost twice that of lead, and it has a very high melting point, which places it in the category of refractory metals. It is quite stable but forms compounds with all the halogens and oxidizes strongly on heating. It is resistant to hydrochloric acid but is attacked by nitric and sulphuric acids. It forms a number of complexes with oxidation state in the range +1 to +7. It is moulded by powder metallurgy techniques, is a component of thermocouple alloys, and has numerous applications in electronic devices. It can also be electroplated. Its high cost limits its use to speciality items.

rheology. The study concerned with processes involving flow of matter, or more generally, of time-dependent deformation processes. Rheological studies concern mainly mechanical properties (viscosity, plasticity and disappearing of stresses).

rheopexy. Reverse process to thixotropy, isothermal reversible conversion of some sols into gels under influence of very slow flowing or mixing.

rheostan. An alloy of 52% copper, 25% nickel, 18% zinc, and 5% iron ; used for electrical resistance wire.

Rh factor. An active substance occurring in the red blood cells of most humans and also of the Rhesus monkey, from which it was named. Humans whose blood contains this factor are said to be Rh-positive, and those who lack it Rh-negative. The transmission of this blood characteristic is hereditary. If Rh-positive blood is introduced into the blood of an Rh-negative individual, as by transfusion or during pregnancy.

rhigioline. A name used for the first fraction from the distillation of crude petroleum. It consists mainly of butane and pentane and boils at 290°-300°K. It is used as a solvent, and as a local anaesthetic.

rho (P, ρ or *ο*). The seventeenth letter, in the Greek alphabet, use to denote the sixteenth carbon atom in a straight-chain compound, or a derivative in which the substituent group is attached to that carbon atom.

Symbol for density.

rhod-. A prefix derived from the Greek, rhodon, rose (red), as rhodamine.

Rhodes reagent. A solution of 200 g. mercuric iodide and 160 g. potassium iodide in 1 litre water, to which is then added 10 litres 3 N sodium hydroxide solution. It is used in detecting oxycellulose in artificial silk. Characteristic dark stains are obtained under the test conditions.

rhodium. An element.

	Symbol	Rh
State Solid	Atomic No.	45
Group VIII	Atomic Wt.	102.9055
	Valence	3,4
	m.p.	2276—2280K
	b.p.	4000K

Rhodium is one of the members of the so-called platinum group which comprises six of the nine transition metals in Group VIII. It has about the same density as palladium, *i.e.*, it is only about half as heavy as other metals in this group. Elemental rhodium has a face-centered cubic crystal structure. The one stable isotope is ^{103}Rh. The seven unstable isotopes are ^{99}Rh through ^{101}Rh and ^{104}Rh through ^{107}Rh. In terms of earthly abundance, rhodium is one of the scarce elements. No notable presence of rhodium in seawater has been detected.

It has very high melting point, and good electrical conductivity, which makes it suitable for high-temperature alloys, electrical devices, furnace windings, and other refractory uses. It can also b eelectro plated and vacuum deposited for coatings for specialized purposes. It has only one stable form.

rhodopsin. A visual pigment present in light-sensitive colour receptors located in the retina of the eyes. It is also called visual purple. It is composed of the aldehyde of vitamin A (carotene) and the protein opsin. A reversible colour change similar to bleaching occurs when the pigment absorbs light ; this reduces the sensitivity of the eye until the rhodopsin is restored, largely by the action of opsin.

rhombohedral lattice. A crystal lattice in which the three axes of a unit cell are of equal length and three angles between them are the same and are not right angles.

rH scale. A scale of hydrogen pressures that gives a measure of the strength of a reducing agent. The *rH* value is defined as $\log_{10} 1/[H]$, where [H]=the hydrogen pressure that would produce the same electrode potential as that of a given redox reaction at the same *pH* value.

ribonuclease. A nuclease that catalyzes the hydrolysis of certain internucleotide linkages of ribonucleic acid.

ribonucleic acid (RNA). A nucleotide molecule, similar in composition to deoxyribonucleic acid, which performs a number of important functions in programming the genetic code in cells. There are several types, the most important being messenger RNA, ribosomal RNA, and transfer RNA, the latter including 20 or more variations which correspond to the amino acids of which proteins are composed. RNA molecules impart the amino acid coding information received from DNA to nucleoproteins called ribosomes, the code designating not only the amino acids required for the particular protein under construction, but also (and equally important) the sequence in which they are to be assembled in the chain, the location of disulphide cross-links, etc.

ribosomal RNA (rRNA). A class of RNA molecules serving as components of ribosomes.

ribosome. A macromolecular assembly of rRNAs and proteins, about 20 nm in diameter, which serves as the site of protein synthesis.

Richter cinnoline synthesis. A method of formation of cinnoline derivatives from *o*-amino aromatic propiolic acids, by diazotization and ring closure :

C≡C—COOH
—NH_2
+ HNO_2 + H

↓

→ C≡C—COOH
—N_2Cl
+ $2H_2O$

↓

OH
COOH
N
N
→ + HCl.

Riehm quinoline synthesis. A method of formation of quinoline derivatives by condensation of aniline hydrochloride (or other aromatic amine hydrochlorides) with ketones :

Riley oxidation. Selenium dioxide oxidation of active methyl or methylene group to carbonyl group, *e.g.*,

$$CH_3CH_2CHO + SeO_2 \rightarrow CH_3COCHO + H_2O + Se$$

ring. A cyclic molecular arrangement whose structure is represented by polygons having four to eight sides (cyclooctatetraene). The principal element (the atom at each vertex of the polygon) is usually carbon, as in the hexagonal benzene ring (homocyclic). If an element other than carbon appears in the ring, the compound is called heterocyclic, for example, the pentagonal furane ring. Alicyclic hydrocarbons such as cyclohexane have a ring structure which may have varied configurations, such as boats, chairs, birdcages, etc. Not all rings are completely closed, especially in sterols. Fused rings are those arranged in a pattern of two, three, or more, each pair having one side in common, as in anthracene and phenanthrene.

ring-chain tautomerism. A special type of prototropic tautomerism, caused by reversible rearrangement of the ring compounds into the open-chain compounds, *e.g.*,

$$\underset{\mathrm{OH}}{\mathrm{CH_2}}-\mathrm{CH_2}-\mathrm{CH_2}-\underset{\mathrm{H}}{\mathrm{C}}=\mathrm{O} \rightleftharpoons$$

$$\mathrm{CH_2-CH_2-CH_2-C}\langle^{\mathrm{H}}_{\mathrm{OH}} \quad (\text{ring closed through } \mathrm{O})$$

ring closure. The formation of cyclic compounds from open-chain compounds. Numerous methods are used, most of them based on the elimination of simple groups or atoms from a bifunctional open-chain system, *i.e.*, an intramolecular coupling ; *e.g.*,

$$\begin{matrix}\mathrm{CH_2-CH_2Br}\\ |\\ \mathrm{CH_2}\\ |\\ \mathrm{CH_2-CH_2Br}\end{matrix} + \mathrm{Zn} \rightarrow \begin{matrix}\mathrm{CH_2-CH_2}\\ \mathrm{CH_2}\\ \mathrm{CH_2-CH_2}\end{matrix} + \mathrm{ZnBr_2}$$

Also known as cyclization.

ring contraction. The conversion of a cyclic system into one containing one carbone atom less in the ring, *e.g.*, the conversion of a six-membered ring into five-membered ring, the sixth carbon atom usually appearing as a substituent on the new ring. *See also* Wagner rearrangement.

ring expansion. The conversion of a substituted cyclic compound into a new compound containing a larger ring, *e.g.*,

$$\begin{matrix}\mathrm{CH_2-CH_2}\\ |\\ \mathrm{CH_2-CH_2}\end{matrix}\rangle \mathrm{CO} + \mathrm{CH_2N_2} \rightarrow$$

$$\begin{matrix}\mathrm{CH_2-CH_2}\\ \mathrm{H_2C} \qquad \mathrm{CO}\\ \mathrm{CH_2-CH_2}\end{matrix} + \mathrm{N_2}$$

ring opening. Reaction involving fission of ring with formation of open-chain compound, *e.g.*,

$$\text{cyclohexanone} \xrightarrow{[\mathrm{O}]} \begin{matrix}\mathrm{CH_2}\\ \mathrm{CH_2\ COOH}\\ |\\ \mathrm{CH_2\ COOH}\\ \mathrm{CH_2}\end{matrix}$$

Rinmann's green. The green mass obtained by fusing a zinc compound with a trace of cobalt salt. It contains zinc cobaltate, possibly represented $ZnCo_2O_4$; used as a test for zinc.

ripening agent. A chemical substance (commonly ethylene) used to accelerate the internal changes in various fruits and vegetables so as to hasten ripening ; one of the accelerated change and probably the most important is the destruction of chlorophyll with the subsequent production of the ripe aspect of the fruit of vegetable.

Ritter reaction. Preparation of N-substituted carboxylic acid amides involving addition of nitriles to alkenes in presence of concentrated sulphuric acid, followed by hydrolysis, *e.g.*,

$$\mathrm{CH_3-C\equiv N} + \begin{matrix}\mathrm{CH_2}\\ \|\\ \mathrm{C-CH_3}\\ |\\ \mathrm{CH_3}\end{matrix} \ (+\mathrm{H_2O}) \xrightarrow{\mathrm{H^+}}$$

$$\mathrm{CH_3}\underset{\mathrm{O}}{\underset{\|}{\mathrm{C}}}-\mathrm{NH}-\overset{\mathrm{CH_3}}{\underset{\mathrm{CH_3}}{\mathrm{C}}}-\mathrm{CH_3}$$

Ritz combination principle. The Ritz combination principle states that the wave number of any spectral line for a given atom can be calculated by means of the formula :

$$\bar{\nu} = R\left(\frac{1}{x^2} - \frac{1}{y^2}\right)$$

in which $\bar{\nu}$ = the wave number, R = a constant, x = constant for a given series, and y = varies from term to term in the series.

RNA polymerase. An enzyme that catalyzes the formation of RNA from ribonueleoside 5′-triphosphates, using a strand of DNA or RNA as a template.

roast. A term used in metallurgy to denote high-temperature treatment of sulphide-bearing ores in air or oxygen preparatory to chemical separation of the metal values. The roasting process oxidizes the ores. The non-metal is commonly driven off as its oxide.

Roentgen ray. The familiar X-rays, a type of radiation produced whenever cathode rays (streams of high-speed electrons) impinge on any solid substance such as the walls of a gas-discharge tube or upon obstacles placed within their path. X-rays penetrate many substances through which the cathode rays do not pass, are not deflected by a magnet, excite phosphorescence in many substances and ionize gases. They occupy a range of the electromagnetic spectrum from about 20 to 0.04 Angstrom units.

Roentgen, *R*. The amount of radiation which, on passage through dry air under standard conditions, produces an electrostatic unit of ions, of either plus or minus charge, per cubic centimetre. In SI system, 1 R=0.258 mC/kg.

Roesler process. A metallurgical process for the separation of copper and silver from gold, by taking advantage of their greater reactivity with sulphur, so that copper and silver sulphides are formed by heating with sulphur, under conditions that leave the gold unaffected.

Rohrbach solution. A high-density solution of mercuric chloride and barium chloride in water, used in the classification of minerals by their specific gravity.

rolled gold. Same as gold-filled except that the proportion of gold alloy to total weight of the article may be less than 1/20 ; fineness of the gold alloy may not be less than 10 carat.

root mean square velocity. Velocity of gaseous molecules square of which is equal to mean of squares of velocities of all molecules in particular population, equal to :

$$\sqrt{\overline{c^2}} = \sqrt{\frac{3RT}{M}}$$

where R = universal gas constant, T = thermodynamic temperature, M = molar mass.

Rosenheim-Drummond test for vitamin-A. One ml. arsenic trichloride is added to one drop of the oil to be tested, which is then dissolved in petroleum benzene and shaken. If vitamin A is present, the oil dissolves with a blue colour, changing to purple, then becoming yellowish. The test can be used for the colorimetric determination of the vitamin.

Rosenmund arsonic acid reaction. A reaction for the preparation of aromatic arsonic acids by the interaction of sodium or potassium arsenite with aryl halides :

$$ArX + K_3AsO_3 \rightarrow Ar.AsO(OK)_2 + KX$$

Rosenmund reduction reaction. A method for synthesizing aromatic and aliphatic aldehydes by the hydrogenation of a carboxylic acid chloride in the presence of palladium sulphate as catalyst :

$$RCOCl + H_2 \rightarrow RCHO + HCl$$

Rosenmund-von Braun synthesis. A method of formation of aryl nitriles from aryl bromides and cuprous cyanide.

$$RBr + CuCN \xrightarrow{750K} RCN + CuBr$$

Rosenstein process. A process for the reduction of chlorine to hydrochloric acid by carbon monoxide (from water gas). The complete equation is believed to be :

$$Cl_2 + CO + H_2O \rightarrow 2HCl + CO_2$$

rotated ring disc-electrode. Rotating disc electrode with disc surrounded by layer of insulator and ring electrode around disc ; in electrochemical experiments both electrodes are placed exactly on the same surface and are polarized independently from two circuits.

rotating crystal method. X-ray technique for determination of crystal structure. X-rays are diffracted by crystal rotating 360°.

rotating-crystal photograph. X-ray image obtained by rotating crystal method ; population of spots placed on parallel lines (strata) formed on cylindrical photographic film surrounds crystal which rotates slowly around chosen crystallographic axis. Wavelength of applied radiation (monochromatic beam) and angle of inclination of beam against rotation axis are defined.

rotating platinum electrode. Electrode constructed from platinum wire ratated in examined solution at constant rate ; this electrode is used for estimation of current-potential relationship at positive potential of indicator electrode and also in amperometric titrations.

rotating sector method. Method of experimental investigation of photolysis or radiolysis ; light or beam of ionizing radiation is supplied to system in intermittent way due to revolution of disc with cut-off window (sector).

rotational barrier. Energy necessary to overcome restriction of rotation about single or double bond. In the case of single bond, rotational barrier is ca. 8—40 kJ/mol in conformers and 80—150 kJ/mol in atropisomers. rotational barrier of ethylenic bond (change of configuration from *cis*- to *trans*-) is approximately 160—250 kJ/mol.

rotational energy of molecules. That fraction the total energy of a molecule which is associated with the rotation of the molecule about an internal axis.

rotational partition function, $r(T)$. Function defined by :

$$r(T)=\sum_{J=0}^{\infty}(2J+1)\exp\left[-J(J+1)\frac{\theta_r}{T}\right]$$

where T=thermodynamic temperature, θ_r= characteristic rotational temperature and J= rotational quantum number. Rotational partition determines influence of rotation of nuclei in diatomic molecule on thermodynamic properties of corresponding gas. For $T>>\theta_r$ rotational partition function simplifies to :

$$r(T)=\frac{T}{\theta_r}$$

rotational quantum number J. In quantum mechanics, number which determines energy of rigid rotator ; J assumes non-negative integral values.

rotational spectra. Spectra in the far infrared portion of the spectrum that are caused by rotational transitions within a molecule.

rotation-vibration band. In vibration spectra band corresponding to simultaneous transition between rotational and vibrational molecular energy levels ; if difference of vibrational quantum numbers is constant then rotational quantum numbers change.

rotatory reflection. A method for securing superposition in crystals of 2-, 4-, or 6-fold axes, consisting of rotation around an axis followed by reflection in a plane normal to the axis of rotation.

Roth solution. Sulphuric acid saturated with nitrogen trioxide, used in testing fatty oils. This is the "Claidin" test for olive oil, and is based upon the time required for solidification after addition of the reagent.

row lines. Lines formed by the diffraction spots on a rotation photograph of a crystal as obtained by rotation of crystal in a beam of X-rays, and photographing the diffraction pattern.

R-S nomenclature. Cahn-Ingold-Prelog unambiguous system for specification of absolute configuration. If molecule contains chirality centre, four atoms attached to that centre are arranged in sequence of decreasing atomic numbers *e.g.*, $a>b>c>d$. Three-dimensional model of molecule is viewed from side remote to group of the lowest priority and sequence (decreasing priority) of other three groups is recorded as clockwise or anti-clockwise. When it is clockwise symbol R (rectus is used to denote configuration. When it is anti-clockwise, symbol S (sinister) is employed :

d—C(a)(b)(c) ← viewing direction → (a)(b)(c)C—d

R configuration S configuration

Also known as R-S system.

rubber. A natural elastomeric polymer of isoprene ; it is an unsaturated hydrocarbon, *cis*-1,4-polyisoprene :

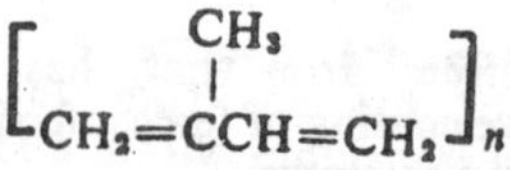

$$\left[CH_2{=}\overset{\overset{\displaystyle CH_3}{|}}{C}CH{=}CH_2 \right]_n$$

In its original state, rubber is nearly useless for anything but adhesive purposes; it is highly temperature-sensitive (thermoplastic) and has little strength until vulcanized with sulphur, aided by organic accelerators. This has the effect of cross-linking the hydrocarbon chains into a thermosetting structure possessing a unique elastic modulus (recovery after deformation), though there is some permanent loss of strength and resilience on repeated extension. When reinforced with carbon black (30 to 40%) it has remarkable abrasion resistance. Though subject to oxidation and to degradation by fatty acids petroleum products, considerable protection from these can be provided by antioxidants. The term has been extended to include any synthethic elastomeric substance that has the essential properties of natural rubber.

rubefacient. A drug or other substance that produces a reddening of the skin, due to congestion with blood of superficial capillaries.

rubidium. An element.

		Symbol	Rb
		Atomic No.	37
State	Solid	Atomic Wt.	85.467
Group IA		Valence	1
		m.p.	312K

Rubidium is a member of the alkali group and hence extremely reactive, especially with air and water, it should be stored in an inert atmosphere or under kerosine. It has only one stable form. It is classed as a flammable material.

Small quantities of rubidium are found in certain foods, including coffee, tea, tobacco, and several other plants. There is evidence indicating that trace quantities of the element are required by living organisms.

The main uses of rubidium are in photocathodes and photo-electric cells. However, rubidium cells are inferior to cesium cells in their sensitive and range. Although very small quantities are involved, rubidium gas cells now perform as secondary time standards, on the order of quartz crystal oscillators, inasmuch as they must be referenced to more accurate systems. Potential uses of rubidium include uses as a fuel for ion propulsion engines and as a heat-transfer medium.

Rubidium alloys easily with potassium, sodium, silver and gold, and forms amalgams with mercury. Rubidium and potassium are completely miscible in the solid state. Cesium and rubidium form an uninterrupted series of solid solutions. These alloys, in various combinations, are used mainly as getters for removing the last traces of air in high-vacuum devices and systems.

rubidium-strontium dating. A method of dating rocks, used for specimens over 10^9 years old. It is based on the decay of rubidium-87 (half-life 5×10^{11} years) to yield strontium-87. An estimate of the sample's age is given by the ratio of the two isotopes.

Rubin number. Amount of protective colloid, expressed in mg per 100 g of solution of Congo red at final concentration of 0.01% which prevents colour change during 10 minutes on addition of 160 m moles of KCl. Also known as Congo-Rubin number.

Rubner test for dextrose and lactose. Add lead acetate and ammonium hydroxide to the dilute solution tested until a permanent precipitate is formed, and boil for 20-25 seconds. A red colour indicates dextrose. Lactose gives a pale red colour after 2-3 minutes boiling.

Ruff-Fenton degradation. A method of shortening the carbon chain of a sugar by oxidizing the aldonic acid or its calcium salt with hydrogen peroxide in the presence of ferric salts, *e.g.*,

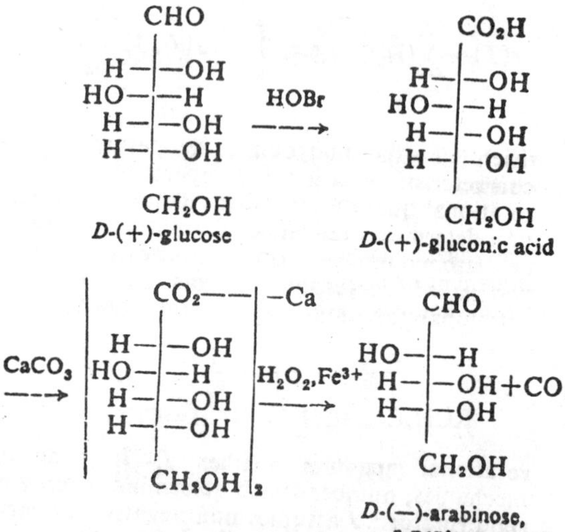

$$\begin{array}{c} CHO \\ H-\!\!|\!\!-OH \\ HO-\!\!|\!\!-H \\ H-\!\!|\!\!-OH \\ H-\!\!|\!\!-OH \\ CH_2OH \end{array} \xrightarrow{HOBr} \begin{array}{c} CO_2H \\ H-\!\!|\!\!-OH \\ HO-\!\!|\!\!-H \\ H-\!\!|\!\!-OH \\ H-\!\!|\!\!-OH \\ CH_2OH \end{array}$$

D-(+)-glucose *D*-(+)-gluconic acid

$$\xrightarrow{CaCO_3} \left| \begin{array}{c} CO_2\!-\!\!-\!|-Ca \\ H-\!\!|\!\!-OH \\ HO-\!\!|\!\!-H \\ H-\!\!|\!\!-OH \\ H-\!\!|\!\!-OH \\ CH_2OH \end{array} \right|_2 \xrightarrow{H_2O_2, Fe^{3+}} \begin{array}{c} CHO \\ HO-\!\!|\!\!-H \\ H-\!\!|\!\!-OH + CO_2 \\ H-\!\!|\!\!-OH \\ CH_2OH \end{array}$$

D-(—)-arabinose, a pentose

rule of Dulong and Petit. *See* Dulong and Petit law.

rule of maximum multiplicity. An empirical statement that the energy of interaction between the electrons in any one atom is at a minimum when their resultant spin is greatest.

rule of six. An empirical rule stating that in addition reactions to an unsaturated group (*e.g.*, carbonyl) considerable steric hindrance will be exerted by atoms in the sixth position (giving the numbers 1 and 2 to the unsaturated group) :

```
           6
           H
           |
    C—C—C—C—C=O
    6  |5  4  3  2  1
       |
       H
       6
```

The more atoms are in the sixth position, the slower will reaction go in which the double has to be attacked ; *e.g.*, the esterification of :

$$\overset{6}{H_3}\overset{5}{C}-\overset{4}{CH_2}-\overset{3}{CH_2}-\overset{2}{C}(OH)=\overset{1}{O}$$

which has three hydrogen atoms in the sixth position, is some 3000 times faster then that of :

$$(\overset{6}{H_3}\overset{5}{C}-\overset{4}{CH_2})_3-\overset{3}{C}-\overset{2}{C}(OH)=\overset{1}{O}$$

which has nine hydrogen atoms in the sixth position.

Rupe rearrangement. The acid-catalysed rearrangement of acetylenic alcohols to α, β-unsaturated ketones ; *e.g,*

$$RCH_2C(OH)(CH_3)C\equiv CH \rightarrow RCH=C(CH_3)COCH_3$$

Russell-Saunders coupling. *See* L-S coupling.

Russia iron. Iron that has been given a protective coating of ferrosoferric oxide (Fe_3O_4) by heating in steam.

ruthenium. An element.

		Symbol	Ru
		Atomic No.	44
		Atomic Wt.	101.07
State	Solid	Valence	3,4,5,6,8
Group	VIII	m.p.	2583K
		b.p.	4173-4200K

Ruthenium is a hard metal, and is a member of the platinum group ; it is present in low concentrations in platinum ores. Elemental ruthenium has a close-packed hexagonal crystal structure. The seven stable isotopes are ^{96}Ru, ^{98}Ru through ^{102}Ru, and ^{104}Ru. The five unstable isotopes are ^{95}Ru, ^{97}Ru, ^{103}Ru, and ^{106}Ru. In terms of earthly abundance, ruthenium is one of the scarce elements. No notable presence of ruthenium has been detected in seawater. It is used in the alloys in combination with platinum as a means of increasing its hardness ; it also has some application as a catalyst in the petroleum industry, in special alloys for electrical devices and as electrodeposited coatings. It is active in chemical combination and forms a number of coordination compounds.

Rutherford, *Rd.* Obsolete unit of activity, quantity of radioactive material which undergoes 10^6 disintegrations per second ; in SI system 1Rd=MBq, *see* becquerel.

Rutherford solution. A mixture of 25 ml 10% hydrogen peroxide with 60 ml. glacial acetic acid, used in etching lead and it alloys.

Ruzicka large ring synthesis. A method of formation of large-ring alicyclic hydrocarbons, in the form of their ketones, by ring closure on heating of the salts of the proper dicarboxylic acids. Ruzicka used salts of metals of the third and fourth groups of the periodic system.

```
      CH2COO                CH2
     /      \              /   \
(CH2)n       Th   →   (CH2)n    CO
     \      /              \   /
      CH2COO                CH2
```

R_f value. In paper and thin-layer chromatography, ratio of distance migrated by given substance to that migrated by solvent (both measured from place of application of sample). R_f value characterizes substance in given conditions of obtaining chromatogram.

R_M value. In paper and thin-layer chromatography, quantity linearly dependent upon free energy of transfer of substance from one phase to another ($R_M = \lg 1/R_f - 1$). R_M value is additive quantity for separate component parts of chemical compound in given chromatographic system.

Rydberg, Ry. Energy unit used in atomic and molecular spectroscopy equal to product of Rydberg constant *h*, and velocity of light in vacuum *c*

$$1 \text{ Ry} = Rhc = 2.17972 + 0.00017).10^{-18} \text{ J}$$

Rydberg constant, R_H. Constant with dimension of wavenumber, used in atomic and molecular spectroscopy:

$$R_H = \frac{\mu_0^2 m_e e^4 c^3}{8h^3}$$

$$= (1.0973731 \pm 0.0000003)10^{-7}\text{m}^{-1}$$

where μ_0=magnetic permittivity in vacuum, m_e=electronic rest mass, e=electronic charge, c=velocity of light in vacuum, h=Planck's constant.

Rydberg constant is used in various fundamental formulas which express the wave number of spectral lines in terms of differences of two numerical terms. Thus, for the lines in the various spectra of atomic hydrogen, this general relationship becomes :

$$\frac{1}{\lambda} = R_H\left(\frac{1}{n_1^2} - \frac{1}{n_2^2}\right)$$

in which λ = the wave length of a given line, R_H = the Rydberg constant for hydrogen, 109,677.8 cm^{-1}, n_1=the series term (its value is 1 in the Lyman series of spectral lines, 2 in the Balmer series, 3 in the Paschen series, 4 in the Brackett series, and 5 in the Pfund series). The term n_2 has various integral values for the lines within a given series.

The relationship applies to other atomic species, such as singly-ionised helium, sodium and potassium atoms, and others which have only one electron in the outer shell.

Rydberg transition. High-energy electronic transition from molecular ground state to excited state whose wave function is approximate described by atomic orbital of one-electron atom. Also known as N-R transition.

Rymsza test for picric acid. On heating picric acid, potassium cyanide and sodium hydroxide solution, or on evaporating picric acid solution and adding potassium cyanide and ammonium hydroxide, a blood-red colour is produced.

S

S. Symbol for the element sulphur. Symbol for total spin quantum number. Symbol for entropy.

s. Abbreviation for symmetrical. Abbreviation for secondary (*s* or *sec*). Symbol for "spin" number. Symbol for scattering coefficient (turbidity).

Sabanin-Laskowsky test. A test for citric acid performed by heating a little citric acid with ammonia in a sealed glass tube or small flask for several hours at 400 K. The mixture becomes blue or green upon standing exposed to the air.

Sabatier-Senderens reaction. The catalytic hydrogenation of unsaturated organic compounds by action of hydrogen in the vapour phase. The usual catalyst is finely-divided nickel.

Sabatier-Senderens test. A test for distinguishing between primary, secondary, and tertiary alcohols ; the vapour of the alcohol are passed over finely divided copper heated to 575K. Primary alcohols are decomposed into aldehydes and hydrogen ; secondary into ketones and hydrogen, and tertiary into unsaturated hydrocarbons and water.

Sabetay reagent. A solution of 30 g. antimony chloride in 70 g. chloroform used for detecting unsaturation in organic substances. Many unsaturated compounds, chiefly those having double bonds, give characteristic colour reactions.

Saccharify. To convert into or impregnate with sugar or a sugar, especially to starches into maltose, as in the malting grains.

Sachse-Mohr theory. Theory, according to which six-membered rings of cyclohexane type and more-membered ones can be strainless, on assumption that cycles are not planar but buckled. Also known as theory of strainless rings.

Sachse reaction. A reaction of methane at high temperature to produce ethni ;

$$2CH_4 \rightarrow C_2H_2 + 3H_2$$

The reaction occrs at about 177SK, the high temperature being obtained by burring part of methane in air

Sachse solution. An aqueous solution of mercuric iodide, potassium iodide, and potassium hydroxide in the ratio of 2 : 3 : 10; used for detecting and estimating glucose, which reduces it on boiling.

Sackur-Tetrode equation. An equation giving the translational entropy of an ideal gas. With certain simplifying approximations, it becomes :

$$S_{tr} = R\left[\ln \frac{(2\pi mkT)^{1/2}}{h^3N} V + \frac{5}{2}\right]$$

in which S_{tr}=translational entropy of one mole of gas, R=gas constant, m=molecular mass, k= Boltzmann constant, T=absolute temperature, h=Planck's constant, N=Avogadro number, and V=molecular volume.

sacrificial. A term used by electrochemists to denote a type of galvanic corrosion in which a coating, most commonly zinc, is attacked in preference to the underlying metal, that is, the coating is "sacrificed" in order to preserve the base metal.

Sah-Chang-Lei test reagent. The compound, *p*-bromophenylisothiocyanate, use as a test reagent for aromatic amines. It condenses with aromatic amines to form substituted thioureas which have characteristic melting points.

Sah-Lei reagents. *p*-Tolylhydrazine and *p*-chlorophenylhydrazine, which are used to produce compounds of definite melting points with aldehydes and ketones.

Saint Clair-Blue process. Molten zinc is used to treat a crude aluminiumsilicon alloy, in order to dissolve the aluminium. The molten aluminium-zinc is filtered through crushed basalt and the zinc removed by distillation.

Saint Pfau-Plattner azulene synthesis. A method of formation of azulenes, starting from indanes and using diazoacetic ester.

$+ N_2CHCOOC_2H_5 \xrightarrow{-N_2}$

$CHCOOC_2H_5$

H

$\downarrow +HO$

$+ 2H_2 + CO_2$

H

$\xleftarrow{Pd}$ CHCOOH

H

sal. A prefix that indicates a salt, as in sal ammoniac.

salify. To convert into a salt as to salify a base. Substances which can react to form salts are termed saliliable, and the process is known as salilication.

saline. Of pertaining to, or containing, a salt Of the nature of a salt; salty, as saline substances, saline springs, etc.

salinity. The degree of salt in sea water. In the open sea salt makes up about 30,000 mg/litre of the fluid. But near seacoasts this value slackens somewhat because of dilution from rain.

salt. One of the products resulting from a reaction between an acid and a base, in which the hydrogen atom of the acid replaces the metal atom or NH_4 group of the base, the other reaction product being water. Salts may be either inorganic or organic, depending on the nature of the reactants. An example of an inorganic salt-forming reaction is $2NaOH + H_2SO_4 \rightarrow Na_2SO_4 + 2H_2O$; an organic salt, *e.g.*, of acetic acid, is formed by the reaction $2CH_3COOH + CuO \rightarrow Cu(C_2H_3O_2)_2 + H_2O$. In the former case a sulphate results, and in the latter case, an acetate; thus, salts of most acids ending in -ic have the suffix -ate. However, salts of such acids as hydrochloric have the suffix -ide, and those of acids ending in -ous have the suffix -ite, *e.g.*, sodium chloride from hydrochloric acid and sodium sulphite from sulphurous acid, respectively.

salt, acid. *See* acid salt.

salt, amphoteric. *See* amphoteric.

salt bridge. Usually U-shaped glass tubing filled with solution of electrolyte (mostly saturated KCl); its role is to connect electrolytically two solutions and to decrease diffusion potential. Also known as electrolytic bridge.

salt, complex. *See* complex salt.

salt, double. *See* double salt.

salt effect. 1. The tendency of ions of a strong electrolyte to increase the degree of ionization of a solution of a weak electrolyte, provided that ions of the strong electrolyte are not the same as those formed by the weak electrolyte.

2. In regard to the kinetics of ionic reactions, and especially their catalysis, there are two types of salt effect, primary and secondary. The primary salt effect is the influence of concentration of the electrolyte on activity coefficients of reaction. The secondary salt effect refers to the change in the concentration of the reacting ions brought about by the addition of electrolytes, and derives from the definition (1).

salt error. Indication error of acid-base indicators due to high concentration of ions in solution.

salting out. An operation used chiefly in the soap industry involving the incorporation of common salt in the product at the end of the mixing cycle to cause aggregation of the desired ingredients and thus the seperation of these ingredients from unwanted reaction products.

salt, inner complex. *See* inner complex salt.

salt, internal. *See* internal salt.

salt, mixed. *See* mixed salt.

salt, neutral. *See* neutral salt.

salt, normal. *See* normal salt.

salvage. Any material that has been used in a product, or the actual product itself, if it has been used, lends itself to reuse or sale. If it is saleable it is salvage and if it is not saleable, it is refuse.

samarium. An element.

		Symbol	Sm
		Atomic No.	62
State	Solid	Atomic Wt.	150.4
Group	IIIB	Valence	2,3
	(Lan-	Isotopes	7 stable
	thanide	m.p.	1345K
	Series)	b.p.	2051K

Samarium is a member of the rare-earth series of metals. It is very hard and steel-like in appearance. Elemental samarium has a rhombohedral crystal structure (300 K). Pure metalic samarium is a silvery-gray colour, retaining a luster in dry air but is only moderately stable in moist air with formation of an adherent oxide. When pure, the metal is soft and malleable, but must be worked and fabricated under an inert gas atmosphere. There are seven natural isotopes of samarium, ^{144}Sm, ^{147}Sm, through ^{150}Sm. ^{152}Sm, and ^{154}Sm. Elevan artificial isotopes have been identified. The natural ^{147}Sm isotope is weakly radioactive ($t_{1/2}=2.5 \times 10^{11}$ years). The samarium isotope mixture is the second highest (after gadolinium) of all elements in terms of its thermal-neutron-absorption cross section (5800 barns at 0.025

eV.) The cross section of ^{149}Sm is about 40,000 barns, but no chain reaction exists because of separation by low-cross-section isotopes.

Samarium has been alloyed with gadolinium and aluminium to produce nuclear reactor hardware that will absorb neutrons for short periods. The use of samarium in intermetallics, cermets, and other chemical forms for use in nuclear applications hold promise. Current and possible applications include electric motors, line printers, frictionless bearing, jewelry, and hospital surgical uses.

It is a reducing agent for many metallic oxides, carbon monoxide, and carbon tetrachloride. It is combustible at about 425K.

Sanchez test for differentiating ammonium salts, amines, and amides. An aqueous solution of an ammnium salt containing potassium iodide, added to a hypochlorite solution, darkens the solution and then nitrogen iodide, NI_3 precipitates. If an amide is used instead of ammonium salt, the liquid merely turns yellow from free iodine dissolved by potassium iodide. If an amine is used, a yellow, red, or brown precipitate of varying composition is formed.

Sanchez test for primary cyclic amines. All compounds containing an amino group attached directly to the benzene ring, regardless of the other substituted groups, when treated with a saturated aqueous solution of furfural slightly acidified with acetic acid, produce immediately or after adding hydrochloric acid, a red orange or purple colour. Arsenic or antimony in the compound do not interfere; but if the amino group is on the carbon of the side chain, no colour is produced.

Sandmeyer diazo reaction. Preparation of haloaromatic (or cyanoaromatic) derivative from diazonium salt by catalytic action of cuprous halide or cyanide, *e.g.*,

$$C_6H_5NH_2 \xrightarrow[HCl]{NaNO_2} C_6H_5N_2Cl \xrightarrow[320K]{CuCN + KCN} C_6H_5CN + N_2$$

Sandmeyer isatin synthesis. Methods of formation of isatin derivatives by ring closure of thioamides or isonitrosodiphenylamidines. The starting materials of this synthesis are aniline (or other arylamine and carbon disulphide, or aniline and chloral hydrate.

sandwich compound. Complex compound in which metal atom is between two planar (or nearly planar) organic ring molecules. Bond in such compound is result of coordination of π elections of organic molecule by central atom, *e.g.*, in ferrocene :

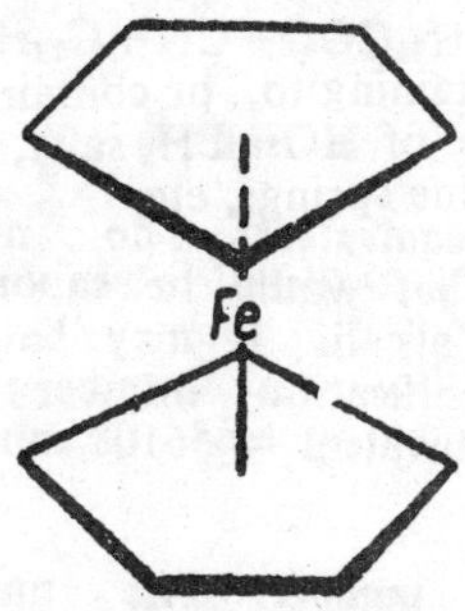

sapiphores. Atomic groups which bear to taste the same relation that an harmonic chord does to hearing. Substances which contain these groups are generally sweet.

saponification. A special case of hydrolysis in which an ester is converted into an alcohol and a salt of the appropriate acid by reaction with an alkali. The esters may be of mono- or polybasic acids and mono- or polyhydric alcohols, the physical conditions under which the reaction occurs being suitably varied to secure an adequate rate. The alkali most commonly used is sodium hydroxide, because of cost and water solubility, but other appropriate alkaline materials are also suitable.

The saponification of stearin (glycerol tristearate) is commonly shown as :

$$\begin{array}{l} C_{17}H_{35}COO-CH_2 \\ \qquad\qquad\quad | \\ C_{17}H_{35}COO-CH + 3NaOH \rightarrow \\ \qquad\qquad\quad | \\ C_{17}H_{35}COO-CH_2 \end{array}$$

$$3C_{17}H_{35}COONa + \begin{array}{l} HO-CH_2 \\ \qquad | \\ HO-CH \\ \qquad | \\ HO-CH_2 \end{array}$$

Actually, the saponification appears to progress stepwise, the first hydrolytic reaction taking place as follows :

$C_{17}H_{35}COO-CH_2$
$C_{17}H_{35}COO-CH+NaOH \rightarrow$
$C_{17}H_{35}COO-CH_2$

$C_{17}H_{35}COO-CH_2$
$C_{17}H_{35}COO-CH+C_{17}H_{35}COONa$
$HO-CH_2$

saponification equivalent. The number of grams of a fat that would be saponified by 1 liter of normal alkali. It may be calculated from the saponification number: Saponification equivalent = 56108/saponification number.

saponification number. The number of milligrams of potassium hydroxide consumed in the complete saponification of 1 gram of a fat or wax. A constant of a fat or wax. Also known as Koettstorfer number.

saponin. One of a class of glycosidal substances of high molecular weight characterized by (*i*) solubility in water and slight solubility in cold alcohol; (*ii*) a persistent foaming of their aqueous solutions; (*iii*) giving a greenish colouration with ferric chloride in the presence of alcoholic sulphuric acid; (*iv*) production of strong irritation of mucous membranes; (*v*) producing hemolysis in the blood stream. They occur naturally in plants, *e.g.*, Quillaja saponaria.

Sargent curves. Graphs obtained by plotting for various β-particle-emitting radio-elements, the logarithms of their radioactive decay constant against the corresponding values of the logarithm of their maximum β-particle energies. For the naturally radioactive elements, most of the points fall on two roughly-parallel straight lines called, as stated above,, Sargent curves; calculations using the artificial radioelements indicate the existence of other Sargent curves.

Sargent rule. An inverse proportionality between the half-period of a natural radioactive element and the fifth power of its maximum energy of β-radiation. It holds for many elements and can be extended to others by use of another proportionality constant.

sattellite DNA. Highly repeated nontranslated segments of DNA in eukaryotic chromosomes.

saturated compound. A compound containing carbon atoms, each of whose valences forms a single bond with another atom, which may be carbon or some other element.

saturated solution. Solution remaining in equilibrium with another phase (solid, liquid or gaseous) which contains dissolved constituent. A solution that contains the highest possible concentration of a solute at a given temperature without becoming unstable.

saturated vapour. Vapour in equilibrium with condensed phase.

saturation activity. Radioactivity induced in a given material under specified conditions of irradiation, reached after an infinitely long time of activation.

saturation factor. Given by the equation:

$$1 - e^{-\lambda t}$$

where λ=disintegration constant of radioactive isotope formed during activation, and t=time of activation. Saturation factor defines ratio of activity induced in time t, to activity induced in the same conditions after an infinite time of irradiation (*i.e.*, until saturation activity is reached). Also known as growth factor.

Savelle test. A test for fusel oil in alcohol made by boiling together equal amounts of the sample and sulphuric acid. If a brown colour develops, fusel oil is present.

sawhorse formula. Perspective formula portraying conformations of open-chain compounds, *e.g.*,

CH_3 H
H H
CH_3 CH_3

Saytzeff rule. The rule which helps in predicting the structure of the elements of water, or hydrogen halide, from a secondary or tertiary alkyl alcohol, or halide resulting in formation of alkene with the highest number alkyl substituents at double bond (when formation of two isomeric alkenes is possible):

$$CH_3CH_2\underset{|}{\overset{Br}{C}}HCH_3 \xrightarrow{OH^-} \begin{cases} CH_3CH{=}CHCH_3 & \text{main product} \\ CH_3CH_2CH{=}CH_2 & \text{byproduct} \end{cases}$$

scale. 1. A deposited layer or incrustation of calcium carbonate or calcium sulphate on the lining of boilers or in water pipes, resulting from prolonged contact with hard water.

2. A series of marking at regular intervals which are used for measurement or computation.

3. Any standard set of values or gradations for measuring a property of condition, such as temperature, viscosity, *p*H hardness, etc.

4. An extremely accurate type of weighting device used in analytical laboratories, commonly called a balance.

5. A type of paraffin wax which retains several percent of liquid distillate; scale wax has a lower melting point, 325K, than fully pressed and refined wax and is type commonly used for packaging, candles, etc.

scandium. An element.

	Symbol	Sc
	Atomic No.	21
State solid	Atomic Wt.	44.9559
Group IIIB	Valence	3
	m.p.	1813K
	b.p.	3105K

Scandium is classed as a rare metal and is obtained in very small quantities from the ores of other metals. The alpha form is close-packed hexagonal. The face centered cubic allotrope, although generally accepted, has not received full recognition. Scandium is a relatively soft metal with a silvery luster. The metal oxidizes, rapidly in air. Scandium combines readily with water oxygen acids, halogens, and chalcogenides. The isotope ^{45}Sc occurs in nature and is not radioactive. Nine radioactive isotopes have been indentified, ^{40}Sc through ^{44}Sc and ^{46}Sc through ^{49}Sc, all with relatively short half-lives, ranging from a fraction of a second up to 84 days.

To date, the applications for scandium and its compounds have been very limited, mainly because of its high reactivity and high cost. In exotic light sources, scandium iodide enhances luminosity. Minor inclusions of scandium are made in substituted yttrium garnets for electronic applications. At one time, it was believed that scandium might serve as a substitute for aluminium, particularly for aircraft applications.

scandium group. Element in third sub-group of periodic system with structure of outer electronic shells of atoms $(n\text{-}1)d^1ns^2$: scandium, yttrium, lanthanum, actinium.

scattering of particles. Interaction of particles (also of atomic nuclei) with other particles or systems (atomic nuclei, atoms etc.) leading in general to change of direction of their movement and to change of their internal state.

scattering of radiation. In quantum electrodynamics general concept describing all possible forms of interaction between radiation and matter. In spectroscopy radiation scattering usually denotes effects arising when radiation propagates through optically inhomogeneous media ; if frequency of radiation does not change upon scattering, scattering is said to be elastic ; in the case of inelastic scattering either frequency change (Raman effect) or complete disappearance of scattered radiation (absorption) is observed.

scavenger. 1. Any metal or alloy which has the ability to remove traces of gaseous impurities from molten metals by combination or adsorption ; these are used in the manufacture of steel to eliminate oxygen, nitrogen etc., during the melting process. They are also used in vacuum devices to pick up stray gaseous molecules , in this application they are called getters.

2. Gases such as ammonia and nitrous oxide, as well as radioactive carbon and iodine, have been used in research on free radicals and other active entities induced by radiation ; by reacting a particular manner with the latter, they act as indicators.

3. In radiochemistry, substance used to remove unwanted radioactive impurities by their co-precipitation or adsorption. The scavenger is usually a precipitate with a well developed surface.

4. Chemical compound reacting at high rate constant with specified free radicals.

Schaer reagent. A saturated alcoholic or aqueous solution of chloral hydrate; used as an extraction medium for investigation of alkaloids, resins, etc.

Schaudinn fluid. A mixture of 20 ml, of a saturated aqueous solution of mercuric chloride, with 10 ml. alcohol; used as a fixative.

Scheller reaction. A modification of Bart reaction in which aromatic acids are prepared from diazonium compounds in methanol or acetic acid solution with arsenic trichloride in the presence of Cu_2Cl_2;

$$(ArN_2)^+ [HSO_4]^- + AsCl_3 \rightarrow ArAsCl_3(OSO_3A) \xrightarrow{H_2O} ArAsO_3H_2$$

Schemjakin-Belokon micro-reactions. Micro-reactions for vanadates and molybdates. (*i*) With an alkaline solution of a vanadate, a saturated alcoholic solution of 1-nitroso-β-naphthol gives a dark green precipitate. with a solution acidified with hydrochloric acid, a brownish-red precipitate, and with a neutral solution, there, is no precipitation. (*ii*) With an acidified solution of 1-nitroso-β-naphthol in acetic acid or alcohol, it form a red precipitate. If the test is made by "spotting" the reagent and the solution to be tested on paper, four rings, (inner) orange, lilac, yellow, and blue, may appear.

Schemjakin test reactions. Tests for rare earths as follows : (*i*) Cerium forms a dark or chocolate precipitate with a solution of morphine hydrochloride in aqueous ammonia. (*ii*) Ceric ions form a stable pink colour with a brucine solution in acetic acid. (*iii*) Ceric ions form a dark brown precipitate in alkaline medium with a brucine solution. Cerous, lanthanum, and thorium ions from gelatinous precipitates.

Schenk-Burmeister test. A test for benzaldehyde or cinnamic acid. With phenol and sulphuric acid, traces of benzaldehyde produce a quince-yellow colour. To test for cinnamic acid the acid is first converted into benzaldehyde by alkaline permanganate solution.

Schewket test reaction for di- and tri-phenols. This test is performed by adding a few drops of 1% iodine-potassium iodide solution to 1 ml. of the phenol solution, diluting with water and adding a few drops of 5% solidium hydroxide solution. Pyrocatechol (a diphenol) produces a green colour which changes to brown when warmed, and back to green when shaken with a few drops of hydrogen peroxide. The return to green differentiates it from hydroquinone and resorcinol. Pyrogallol (a tri-phenol) produces a transistory blue-violet or red-violet colour. Phloroglucinol produced a light brown colour.

Schiemann reaction. Preparation of fluoroaromatic derivatives by pyrolytic decomposition of diazonium fluoroborates, *e.g.*,

$$ArNH_2 + HNO_2 + [BF_4]^+ \xrightarrow{\Delta} [ArN_2]^+[BF_4]^+ \xrightarrow{\Delta} ArF + N_2 + BF_3$$

Schiff bases. Compounds formed by the condensation of an amine and an aldehyde, with loss of water, and the formation of a double bond between the carbon atom of the amine. Commonly, aromatic amines and aliphatic aldehydes are used in preparing Schiff bases, but there are also well-known cases in which both the reacting molecules are aromatic, as in the case of the benzylidene anilines :

$$C_6H_5CHO + C_6H_5NH_2 \rightarrow C_6H_5CH{=}NC_6H_5 + H_2O$$

Schiff test for carbohydrates. Mix equal parts of glacial acetic acid and xylidine in a little alcohol and saturate strips of paper with this mixture. Heat the sample with hydrochloric acid or sulphuric acid and expose the strips to the vapours. A red colour indicates the presence of carbohydrates.

Schiff test for cholesterol. 1. With cholesterol, concentrated sulphuric acid and iodine produce a green colour.

2. Cholesterol produces a red colour when boiled with hydrochloric acid and ferric chloride.

3. On evaporating cholesterol with nitric acid, the residue obtained is coloured red by ammonia.

4. A solution of cholesterol in concentrated sulphuric acid is coloured red by ammonia.

Schiff test for chromate. With a 1 : 100 solution of chromic acid or chromates weakly acidified with sulphuric acid produces an intense colour.

Schiff reagents for aldehydes. Various dyes which have been decolourized by sulphurous acid ; the addition of these reagents to the solution containing aldehydes causes the colour of the dye to reappear. Fuchsin, rosaniline, and magenta are among the dyes used for this purpose.

Schiff test solution for allantoin or urea. A solution of furfural in hydrochloric acid, used to test for urea or allantoin with which it gives a yellow colour, changing to violet.

Schiff test solution for hydrogen peroxide. A titanium sulphate solution prepared by boiling titanium oxide with concentrated sulphuric acid, precipitating with ammonium hydroxide, and redissolving the precipitate in dilute sulphuric acid ; it is used in testing for hydrogen peroxide, which gives a yellow colour with it.

Schirm reagent. A reagent for determining zinc, manganese, cobalt ; nickel, copper, and cadmium. This reagent is prepared by dissolving 17 g. trimethylphenyl ammonium carbonate and 3 g. triethyl phenylammonium iodide in 80 g. water.

Schlittler-Muller reaction. A method of formation of isoquinolines by condensing benzylamines with glyoxal semiacetal, followed by ring closure in the presence of acid.

$$C_6H_4(NH_2)CHR + HC(OR)_2CHO \rightarrow C_6H_4(CHR{-}N{=}CH{-}HC(OR)_2) + H_2O \xrightarrow{HCl} \text{isoquinoline (R)} + 2ROH$$

See also Pomeranz-Fritsch reaction.

Schlosing test. A test for potassium made with perchloric acid and fairly strong solutions of potassium salts. A crystalline precipitate is formed.

Schlossberger test. A test for differentiating silk, wool, and cotton fibres made by adding the sample to a freshly precipitated solution of nickelous hydroxide in concentrated ammonia. Silk fibres are dissolved but not of wool or cotton.

Schlotterbeck reaction. A reaction between diazoparaffins and aldehydes which results in the replacement of the aldehyde hydrogen atom by an alkyl group :

$$RCHO + N_2CHR' \rightarrow RCOCH_2R' + N_2$$

This reaction is most successful with the diazo derivatives of the lower paraffins, especially diazomethane.

Schmidlin ketene synthesis. Direct formation of ketene by decomposition of acetone vapour :

$$CH_3COCH_3 \xrightarrow{800K} CH_2{=}C{=}O + CH_4$$

Schmidlin-Massini test reaction. A test for permonophosphoric acid, made by adding a dilute manganese sulphate solution to the acid. A pale-violet colour is produced slowly in the cold solution and rapidly when heated, if permonophosphoric acid is present.

Schmidt-Hinderer test for metals. A test for zinc, cadmium, and copper, made by adding the samples to be tested to an aqueous solution of 2,7-diaminofluorene. White precipitates form with zinc and cadmium, and a blue precipitate and a blue-green solution with copper.

Schmidt-Lumpp reagent. A reagent for nitrate which is made by dissolving 0.1 g. di-(9,10-monohydroxyphenanthryl) amine in one litre concentrated sulphuric acid. The blue reagent is changed to blue-red and to wine-red by nitric acid, nitrates or their solutions in concentrated sulphuric acid.

Schmidt reaction. Conversion of carbonyl compounds by hydrazoic acid in sulphuric (or polyphosphoric) acid medium ; amines are formed for carboxylic acids, nitriles from aldehydes and acid amides from ketones, *e.g.*,

$$RCOOH + HN_3 \xrightarrow{H_2SO_4} RNH_2 + CO_2 + N_2$$

A plausible mechanism for such transformation is shown below :

In the presence of excess hydrazoic acid the Schmidt reaction sometimes leads to substantial and substituted tetrazoles :

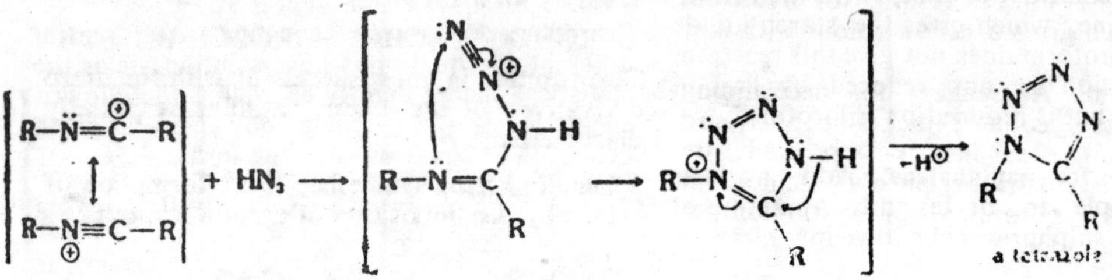

$$\left[\begin{matrix} R-\ddot{N}=\overset{\oplus}{C}-R \\ \updownarrow \\ R-\underset{\oplus}{N}\equiv C-R \end{matrix}\right] + HN_3 \longrightarrow [\ldots] \longrightarrow \ldots \xrightarrow{-H^{\oplus}} \text{a tetrazole}$$

Schoenherr process. One of the processes used for the production of nitrates directly from the air by the combination of oxygen and nitrogen under the action of an electric arc.

Schmidt's rule. Double bond strengthens adjacent single bond, simultaneously weakening next single bond ; *e.g.*, free-radical fission of alkenes takes place most readily in allylic position.

Schmidt test reactions for gelatin. 1. Add ammonium molybdate solution to the sample. A white flocculent precipitate indicates the presence of gelatin. The precipitate dissolves partially on warming and reappears on cooling.

2. Acidify Nessler reagent with sulphuric acid and filter. This reagent produces a white precipitate, which dissolves in alkalies, if gelat in is present in the sample.

Schmiedel process. A variation of the chamber process for the manufacture of sulphuric acid, in which nitrosylsulphuric acid is sprayed into the sulphur dioxide.

Schmiedel test. A test for methanol which is based on the oxidation of methanol in alkaline solution with 30% hydrogen peroxide. The resulting formic acid is detected or determined by its reducing action on mercuric chloride.

Schmiz test. A test for ammonia or alkali performed by mixing 1 ml. cupric sulphate solution with 1 ml. of 3% hydrogen peroxide and floating 0.5 ml. of the sample to be tested on the mixture, If ammonia or alkali is present, a brown-black precipitate forms ; with weaker concentrations of ammonia or alkali (such as 0.001% or less), a yellow colour appears.

Schneider aceto-carmine solution. A saturated solution of carmine in 45% acetic acid, used as a stain.

Schoenflies' symbols. Symbols for representation of symmetry elements of point group.

Scholl reaction. A method of ring closure of polynuclear ketones by heating with aluminium chloride :

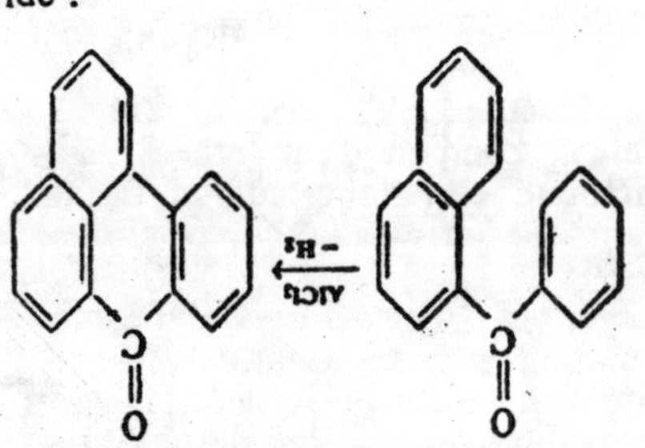

$$\xrightarrow[AlCl_3]{-H_2}$$

The method can be utilized for the preparation of condensed heterocyclic ring systems.

Scholler saccharification process. Hydrolysis of wood to form sugars by heating at 440-450 K. and high pressure with ½% aqueous sulphuric acid.

Schonbein test for nitrite in the presence of nitrate. Acidify with phosphoric acid a very dilute solution of the sample to be tested and add potassium iodide-starch paste. A blue colour indicates the presence of nitrate. Several modifications of this test have been developed.

Schonbein test for nitrite in nitric acid. Add some of the nitric acid to be tested to the brown solution of potassium ferricyanide and ferric nitrate. Prussian blue forms if nitrite is present. This test must be made at room temperature.

Schonvogel test. A test for differentiating animal and vegetable oils which is made by shaking the sample with a saturated aqueous solution of borax. An emulsion is produced by vegetable oils ; whereas animal oils, including butter and olive oil. produce no emulsion, but sharply separated layers.

Schoorl test for differentiating chloroform and carbon tetrachloride. Heat 1 drop of the liquid carefully in a loosely stoppered test tube. Carbon tetrachloride oxidizes with the formation of chlorine, which gives the starch-iodide test, but chloroform does not give this reaction. Fehling solution is not reduced by carbon tetrachloride but is reduced by chloroform.

Schoorl test for naphthalene. Add a little of the sample to be tested to a mixture of concentrated sulphuric acid and yellow mercuric oxide and boil for several minutes. Then add a little resorcinol to the reaction product and heat. When cold, add this material to water and make alkaline with sodium hydroxide solution. If napthalene is present, a green fluorescence will appear, due to the oxidation of the naphthalene to phthalic anhydride.

Schorigin reaction. A reaction involving a sodium-alkyl compound or other Grignard-type compound containing sodium in place of magnesium. *See also* Wanklyn reaction.

Schossberger test. A test for sulphide made by supersaturating a dilute solution of sodium molybdate with hydrochloric acid. This solution is coloured blue by hydrogen sulphide or by metal sulphides.

Schotten-Baumann acylation reaction. Acylation of hydroxylic and amine groups with acid chlorides in presence of dilute alkaline solutions, *e.g.*,

$$C_6H_5OH + C_6H_5COCl + NaOH \rightarrow C_6H_5COOC_6H_5 + NaCl + H_2O$$

$$C_4H_9NH_2 + CH_3COCl + NaOH \rightarrow CH_3CONHC_4H_9 + NaCl + H_2O$$

Schottky defects. Defects of crystal lattice consisting in transfer of certain number of atoms or ions from nodes inside crystal to its surface. Therefore some nodes in lattice remain unoccupied, *see* vacancy (atomic, ionic).

Schreinemakers residue method. A method of determining the true composition of a solid multi-component phase in equilibrium with the mother-liquid, from the analysis of the wet solid which separates. The liquid is also analyzed, and a line is extended through the two points plotted from these data. Then the process is repeated for another solution and the wet solid which has separated from it, and another line is drawn. The point of intersection of these two lines gives the true composition of the dry solid.

Schrodinger wave equation. A partial differential equation whose solution yields the statistical charge density as well as the allowed energy levels of a particle moving in a given fields. The equation is of the form :

$$\nabla^2\Psi + 8\pi^2 m(E-U)\Psi/h^2 = 0$$

in which ∇^2=the Laplace operator, m = the mass of the particle, h=the Planck constant, E=the total energy of the particle, and U=its potential energy.

Schulze-Hardy rule. Coagulation power of electrolyte increases considerably with increasing valency of ions of sign opposite to that of colloidal particles (counter-ions).

Schutz and Borrissow law. The amount of material digested by an enzyme is propotional to the square root of the amount of enzyme.

$$x = tK\sqrt{C_f}$$

Where t=the time, C_f = concentration of the enzyme, and x=the amount digested,

This rule holds only under very limited conditions, as in the determination of pepsin by Mott's method. This rule does not apply at all when the enzyme concentration is either very low or very high in proportion to the concentration of substrate.

Schwarz test for lime in magnesite. After calcination, the sample is placed on a watch glass or microscope slide and treated with a few drops of 0.33 N ammonium citrate, followed by a little thymolphthalein solution. If calcium is present, the material will be dyed blue.

Schweissinger test for pyridine. Add 10 drops of a saturated alcoholic solution of mercuric chloride to 10 ml. of the alcoholic liquid to be tested. If pyridine is present, a crystalline precipitate will appear.

Schweizer test for xanthine. A test for xanthine made by heating a trace of xanthine with a few crystals of potassium chlorate and a few drops of hydrochloric acid, then evaporating to dryness on a watch glass, The alloxan formed gradually passes into its red modification, on prolonged heating of the residue on the water bath. If 1-2 drops of potassium hydroxide are added to the carmine-red residue, an intense ultramarine-blue colour forms immediately.

scintillation counter. Counter in which light flashes produced in a scintillator by ionizing radiation are transformed in electrical pulses by means of a photomultiplier.

scintillator. Phosphor which emits a light flash under the influence of absorbed particle or photon.

scleroprotein. One of a group of proteins which form the skeletal structure of animal (*see* proteins).

Scoville test. A test for differentiating benzoic and cinnamic acids in which some manganese sulphate is added, if the solution to be tested forms a yellow colour with ferric chloride. A white crystalline precipitate develops within an hour if cinnamic acid is present. If this precipitate does not appear, the colour developed by ferric chloride can be ascribed to the presence of benzoic acid.

screen analysis. The classification of material by size, accomplished by shaking it on screens of successively smaller sizes, and collecting separately the portions that fail to pass through the various screens.

screening constant: 1. A quantity occurring in the relationship between the frequency of a line in a particular x-ray series, and the atomic number of the element emitting the rays of the form :

$$\sqrt{\nu} = a(Z - \sigma)$$

where, ν = the frequency of the line, a = a constant, Z = the atomic number of the element, and σ=the screening constant, that is the same for all the lines in a given series.

2. In theory of NMR chemical shifts dimensionless quantity which defines effective magnetic field at a given nucleus,

$$H_{ef} = H_{extern}(1-\sigma)$$

Also known as shielding constant.

screening effect. Since the orbital electrons surrounding an atomic nucleus are arranged in shells, it is logical that the attractive force of the nucleus for an electron in an outer shell is weakened by the presence of electrons in inner shells, whose negative charges act partly to "screen" the positive nucleous from the outer electrons, and thus to decrease the effective charge of the nucleus. It is assumed that this screening effect bears a definite relationship to the electrical charges involved, and is an inverse function of the distance of the screening electrons from the nucleus.

screw axis. Coupling of *n*-fold rotation axis with translation in direction parallel to axis by fraction of period indicated by axis symbol ; *e.g.*, 3_2 denotes three-fold screw axis ; this action consists in combination of revolution by angle of 120° with shift by 2/3 of period in direction parallel to axis.

screw dislocations. Rows of atoms around which vertical lattice planes change into screw surfaces.

scrub. A term used by chemical engineers to designate an operation by which impurities are removed from gases and vapours by contact with a countercurrent liquid. It is usually performed in a column or tower through which the gaseous mixture rises through the downflowing liquid. Solid and liquid impurities are removed in this way, and unwanted gases can also be separated. The method is used for elimination of dust particles from air, purification of blast-furnace gases, and numerous other industrial purposes.

Seaboard purification process. A process for the purification of manufactured fuel gas, which consists of scrubbing with an aqueous solution of 2-3% sodium carbonate to absorb the hydrogen sulphide ; the scrubbing solution is regenerated by spraying it in a tower against a current of air. A modification of the process uses for the scrubbing a sodium phenolate solution, which is regenerated by boiling.

sealant. A soft, tacky organic material which will flow into, or be easily inserted in cracks, holes, and other small orifices where it will subsequently harden or polymerize to afford a tight, waterproof joint. Most sealants in use today are synthetic self-curing high polymers (organic cements) typified silicone resins, urethanes, acrylics, and polyethylene. A few are of natural origin, especially linseed oil (putty) and asphalt, the latter used chiefly in highway construction.

sec-. Abbreviation of secondary, as *sec*-butyl.

secondary. 1. A monohydric alcohol in which two of the hydrogen atoms attached to the methanol carbon are replaced by alkyl group, *e.g.*, $CH_3CH_2CHOHCH_3$ (*sec*-butyl alcohol). The term is also applied to amines and other compounds in an analogous manner. In such cases it is conventionally abbreviated *sec*-.

2. When referring to metals or other mineral products, this term denotes recovery from scrap or other waste products ; when applied to petroleum, it indicates exploitation by means of pressurized water and other special methods of wells that can no longer be pumped. *See also* primary ; tertiary.

secondary cell. An electroytic cell which the interacting substances may be restored to their original chemical form by sending a direct current of electricity through the cell in reverse direction to that of the discharge. Secondary cells are commonly used to store and furnish electricity.

secondary electrons. Electrons formed in interaction between primary particle or photon and electrons of medium.

secondary ionization. Ionization of atoms of matter caused by their collision with fast electrons (δ-rays) produced during primary ionization.

secondary photochemical reaction. Reaction which may proceed readily without absorption of any radiative energy because of presence of very active products (*e.g.*. electronically excited molecules, ions or free radicals) formed during primary photochemical process.

secondary reaction. *See* induced reaction.

secondary salt effect. Influence of electrolytes present in solution on rate constant of proceeding reaction catalyzed by acid or base. Secondary salt effect is expressed as change of equilibrium state of ionization of acid or base.

secondary standard. 1. In volumetric analysis substance for which content of active comparison with primary standard ; it is used in standardization of solutions.

2. Substance used for calibration of calorimetric systems after its previous comparison with any primary standard substance.

secondary structure. The residue-by-residue conformations of the backbone of a polypeptide chain.

secondary valency. According to Werner's theory, valency characteristic for compounds unable to dissociate ; corresponds to coordination bond.

second coordination sphere. Surroundings of complex ion composed, among others, of ions beyond first coordination sphere neutralizing charge of complex. Also known as outer coordination sphere.

second law of thermodynamics. For each *c*-component phase there is a function of state *S*, called entropy of this phase :

$$S^{\alpha} = S^{\alpha}(U^{\alpha}, V^{\alpha}, n_1^{\alpha}, n_2^{\alpha}, \ldots, n_c^{\alpha})$$

(where U=internal energy, V=volume. n, n_2. . , n_c=numbers of moles of phase components, and α numbers system phases) such that (*i*) Gibbs equation is satisfied, (*ii*) entropy of system is extensive quantity $S = \sum_{\alpha} S^{\alpha}$, and (*iii*) principle of entropy increase is satisfied for all possible adiabatic transi ions between local equilibrium states of system.

second-order asymmetric transformation. Process of privileged crystallization of one of the epimers taking part in first-order asymmetric transformation. Constant lack of equilibrium in solution of epimers is caused by precipitation of less soluble epimer. This effect enables almost quantitative conversion of one epimer into another to take place.

second-order phase transition. Process accompanied by sudden change of second order derivatives of Gibbs free energy with respect to pressure and temperature, *i.e.* compressibility and molal heat capacity.

second order reaction. Reaction in which kinetic equation is marked by sum of powers of concentrations of reactants being equal to two.

second virial coefficient. Coefficient *B* in virial equation of state. *B* has the same dimension as molar volume, depends on temperature and is characteristic of a given gas.

secular determinant. An equation in the form of a determinant whose solution yields the eigenvalues which the quantized system under consideration can assume.

secular equilibrium. Stationary state between radioactive parent nuclide and its daughter for the case when half-life of parent nuclide is very long compared with that of daughter. For this equilibrium, the relation is :

$$N_1\lambda_1 = N_2\lambda_2 = \ldots = N_i\lambda_i$$

where N_i=number of nuclei of i-th member of radioactive series ; λ_i=disintegration constant of this member.

sedimentation. A separation operation in which particles dispersed in a liquid medium are allowed to fall to the bottom of a container, by gravity. It differs from precipitation in respect to the time required; precipitation is rapid, whereas sedimentation may take hours or even days if the particles approach colloidal dimensions. Sedimentation is applied as a large-scale water purification method, in blood analyses, and in metallurgical operations.

sedimentation analysis. Method of mechanical analysis based on difference of rate of sedimentation of particles of investigated substance dispersed in a given medium in order to determine concentration of particles of different size.

sedimentation balance. Balance allowing study rate of gravitational sedimentation of suspensions, *e.g.*, Figurowski balance.

sedimentation constant. A quantity obtained in investigating the behaviour of colloidal particles under the action of forces, chiefly centrifugal forces. This quantity for a given particle and medium is defined by the expression :

$$S = \frac{2r^2 (p - p')}{9\eta}$$

in which S = the sedimentation constant r=the radius of the particle, p and p' are the reciprocals of the partial specific volumes of particle and medium, respectively, and η=the viscosity of the medium.

sedimentation equilibrium. Equilibrium state between sedimentation and diffusion of particles of dispersed phase, *i.e.*, equilibrium state in outer field of forces (gravitational field, centrifugal field) leading to formation of concentration gradient.

sedimentation potential. *See* Dorn effect.

sedimentation rate, *U*. Rate of sedimentation of particles due to gravitational or centrifugal forces which, in case of spherical particles of radius r, can be expressed as :

$$U = \frac{2}{g}\frac{(\gamma - \gamma_0)a}{\eta} r^2$$

whare γ and γ_0=densities of dispersed phase and dispersion medium respectively, η=viscosity coefficient of sol $a=g$=constant of gravitation (sedimentation due to gravitation), or $a=\omega^2x$ (where ω=angular velocity of rotation of centrifuge x=distance of particle from axis of rotation for sedimentation due to rotation).

Seeliger reagent. A solution of 1.0 g. potassium iodide, 0.2 g. iodine, and 60 g. calcium nitrate (crystalline), in 50 ml. water, used in testing for lignin in paper. It colours cellulose light blue to dark blue, linen and half linen wine red, and wood pulp and strongly-lignified fibres yellow-brown.

segregation. Differentiation of composition of alloy which occurs, *e.g.*, during solidification in its various parts.

selection rules. Rules which govern possibility of radiative transitions between quantum mechnical states of system.

selective adsorption. Adsorption from multicomponent mixture which selectively increases concentration of one of components on surface of adsorbent ; it is due to different adsorptive powers of components for definite adsorbent.

selective reduction. Preferential reduction of one (or more) functional groups from among other groups, which could be reduced, present in molecule of organic compound.

selectivity of ion exchanger. Ability of ion exchanger to prefer some ions in comparison with others.

selectivity coefficient, $k_{A,B}$. Product of concentrations of ion exchange reaction (raised to appropriate powers) divided by analogous product of substrate concentrations. Also known as equilibrium quotient.

selenium. An element.

		Symbol	Se
		Atomic No.	34
State	Solid	Atomic Wt.	78.96
Group	VIA	Valence	2,4,6
		Isotopes	6 stable
		m.p.	490K
		b.b.	958K

A semiconducting element, classed as a non-metal ; it is mostly recovered as a byproduct of copper ore refining.

Selenium has a large number of allotropes, some of which have not been fully investigated. On heating selenium above its melting point and cooling it, a red vitreous mass is formed, probably a mixture of allotropes. A red amorphous allotope is precipitated by sulphur dioxide from selenious acid solution. On heating above 423K, the red vitreous form changes to a gray hexagonal form, the stable form of selenium at ordinary temperatures, with metallic properties, one of which is photoconductivity. By evaporation of a carbon bisulphide solution of the red vitreous form below 345K, a red α-monoclinic form is obtained ; evaporation above 345K gives β-monoclinic selenium. Black hexagonal selenium, believed to have a ring structure, is produced, by heating amorphous selenium to near its melting point. Unlike sulphur, liquid selenium apparently has only one form.

Its electrical properties make it particularly suitable for use in rectifiers ; its electrical conductivity is increased on exposure to light by the effect of photons, which proliferate electrons and energy deficits (holes) within the atoms. Selenium is thus used in photocells, solar batteries, and similar devices. It has specialized applications in rubber vulcanization and catalysis and as a colorant in glass and ceramic products.

There are six natural occuring isotopes ^{74}Se, ^{76}Se, through ^{7}S^{8}e, ^{80}Se, and ^{82}Se, and seven known radioactive isotopes ^{72}Se, ^{73}Se, ^{75}Se, ^{79}Se, ^{81}Se. ^{83}Se, and ^{84}Se. With exception of ^{79}Se, which has a half-life of something less than 6×10^{4} years the half-lives of the other isotopes are comparatively short, measured in minutes, hours, or days. In terms of abundance, selenium ranks 34th among the elements occurring in the earth's crust.

Selenium itself is not poisonous, but many of its compounds are (*e.g.*, hydrogen selenide); toxic effects on cattle grazing in locations where selenium is present in the soil have been reported from time to time.

selenium dioxide oxidation. The controlled oxidation of various organic compounds by selenium dioxide (SeO_2). The method is used for the oxidation of (*i*) active methylene groups attached to the corresponding carbonyl compounds ; (*ii*) unsaturatad compounds to alcohols without attaching the double or triple bond ; (*iii*) oxidation of methyl or methylene groups attached to aromatic rings to the corresponding aldehyde or ketone ; *e.g* ,

$$RCH_2CH{=}CHR' \xrightarrow{SeO_2} RCHOHCH{=}CHR'$$

$$C_6H_5COCH_3 \xrightarrow{SeO_2} C_6H_5COCHO$$

$$C_6H_5CH_2C_6H_5 \xrightarrow{SeO_2} C_6H_5COC_6H_5$$

self-absorption. The reduction in radiant power at the center of emission lines, resulting, from selective absorption of radiation emitted by the hot central core into the cooler outer vapour of the source envelope.

self-consistant field. Effective potential field acting on particles in single-approximation for many-particle systems ; it follows from averaging inter-particle interaction.

self-diffusion. Spontaneous displacement of chemical components in their own medium caused by thermal movement of particles, *e.g* , self-diffusion of lead ions in crystals of a lead salt. It is usually observed and measured by isotopic tracers.

self-diffusion coefficient. Proportionality coefficient *D* in Fick's laws applied to self diffusion. The true self-diffusion should be distinguished from that of an isotopic tracer because of isotopic effects.

self-irradiation. Partial (in case of γ-emitters) or practically complete (in case of soft radiation from β- and α-emitters) absorption energy of ionizing radiation by the medium in which a radioactive nuclide is present.

self-reversal (in emission spectral analysis). Limiting case of self-absorption when radiation corresponding to spectral line centre is completely absorbed.

self-scattering. Scattering of radiation by meterial that emits it.

semi-. A prefix which means (*i*) "half", and (*ii*) "imperfectly."

semicarbazido. The radical $H_2NCONHNH—$.

semicarbazone. A compound formed by reaction between semicarbazide and many carbonyl compounds, especially aldehydes and ketones. The general form of the reaction :

$$R—\overset{O}{\overset{\|}{C}}—R' + NH_2—NH—\overset{O}{\overset{\|}{C}}—NH_2 \rightarrow$$

$$RR'C=N—NH—\overset{O}{\overset{\|}{C}}—NH_2 + H_2O$$

semiconductor. An element or compound whose electrical properties are midway between a conductor and an insulator. Semiconduction was first discovered in the element germanium and subsequently in the nonmetals selenium and silicon and in the compounds silicon carbide, lead sulphide, and a few others. It is caused by two factors ; (*i*) free electron ejected from low-energy covalent bonds at the site of the lattice defect, leaving an energy deficit called a hole (positively charged) ; and (*ii*) electrons supplied by atoms of impurity elements. Electrons from both sources pass through the crystal from one energy deficit location to another, so that the deficit itself can be regarded as a flow of positive electricity. If enough electrons are present to satisfy the energy deficit by saturating the covalent bond, the electrons become the conducting medium, and the semiconductor is said to be *n*-type ; but if too few electrons are available, the conductivity is by the positively chariged holes, which move through the crystal as the electrons shift location from one bond to another. In this case the semiconductor is *p*-type.

Semiconductors are characterized by specific conductance of 10^{-9} to $10^{-2}\,\Omega^{-1}\,cm^{-1}$ (at room temperature), increasing with temperature, according to relation (valid in defined temperature ranges) :

$$\sigma = \sigma_0 \exp\left(-\frac{E}{kT}\right)$$

where σ=specific conductance at temperature T, E=activation energy, k=Boltzmann constant, and σ_0=empirical constant.

Semidine rearrangement. A special case of the benzidine rearrangement which occurs when one of the benzene nuclei in the hydrazobenzene is substituted in the para-position, so that the rearrangement to the *p,p'*-diamino-biphenyl compound is partly blacked. In this case, a para-aminodiphenylamine is formed (in the presence of strong acid). Some of the product may also be the orthoaminodiphenylamine derivative, *e.g.*,

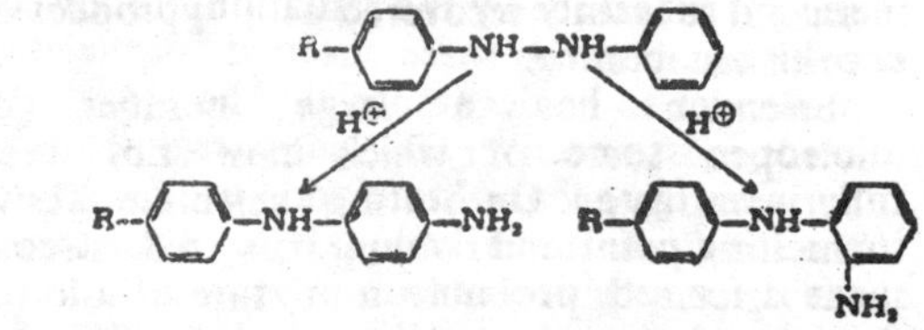

R—C_6H_4—NH—NH—C_6H_5

$H^{\oplus}$ ↙ ↘ $H^{\oplus}$

R—C_6H_4—NH—C_6H_4—NH_2 R—C_6H_4—NH—C_6H_4(NH_2)

semimicro-analysis. Analysis of sample with mass of 0.01—0.1 g and for gases of volume 1—10 cm^3.

semipermeable membrane. A membrane or septum through which a solvent but not certain dissolved or colloidal substances may pass through; used in osmotic pressure determinations. Many natural membranes are semipermeable, *e.g.*, cell walls ; other membranes may be made artificially, *e.g.*, by precipitating copper ferrocyanide in the interstices of a porous cup, the cup serving as a frame to give the membrane stability. Also known as semipermeable diaphragm.

semisynthetic. A substance or material made by chemical modification of an existing natural material, as opposed to a true synthetic resulting from reactions between chemicals. Examples are the many products derived from the natural polymer cellulose (rayon, paper, nitrocellulose, carboxymethyl cellulose, etc.) ; glass (a mixture of sand, soda, lime, etc.) ; and soap (from natural fats and oils). Though most semisynthetics are made by reaction with one or more chamicals, the base materials occur as such in nature.

sensitivity of determination or analytical method. Lowest value of concentration (or content) of constituent determined by a given method, which allows two values to be treated as different at assumed level of probability.

sensitization. The process of rendering susceptible to the action of some force or state, as radiant energy, acidity, etc. In colloid chemistry, effect of certain substances added in very small quantities to sol on its sensitivity to action of electrolytes.

sensitized chemiluminescence. Emission of light by atoms or molecules excited by energy transferred from other molecules previously excited in chemical reaction.

sensitized decompositions. A chemical decomposition that is brought about by the presence of a second substance which absorbs an exciting radiation. The essential mechanism of the reaction is the excitation of particles of the second subsatnce by the radiation, followed by collisions between these excited particles and molecules to be decomposed. The process proceeds most effectively if the energy difference between the ground state and excited state of the sensitizer is nearly equal to the energy of the decomposition reaction.

sensitized fluorescence. Fluorescence of molecules or atoms excited by other molecules or atoms which have previously absorbed photon.

separation. The division of a mixture into its component substances by either chemical or physical methods. Chemical methods include precipitation, reduction, acid-base reactions, recrystallization, etc. ; physical methods are fractionation, solvent extraction, chromatography, adsorption, sedimentation, flotation, dehaydration and drying, filtration, centrifugation, and magnetic techniques. All these methods, have several variations ; for example fractionation is performed by distillation, freezing techniques (helium), and gel filteration ; chromatographic separations include gas-phase, liquid-phase, thinlayer, paper, etc.

separation energy. Energy necessary to detach a particle from system in which it is bound, *e.g.*, energy needed for separation of electron from atom, or of nucleon from atomic nucleus.

separation factor. A relationship used to express the efficiency of any operation or process for the separation of isotopes; it is the ratio of the isotopic forms in the initial phase divided by their corresponding ratio in the final phase.

sequence. In vibrational structure of electronic spectrum, group of oscillation bands with the same value of difference of vibrational quantum numbers.

sequestering agent. A type of chelating or coordination compound (also called a metal-ion deactivator) which immobilizes (sequesters) the ions of such metals as copper, iron, calcium etc., by binding them into complexes that are both stable and soluble. As a result, the ions are prevented from acting as oxidation catalysts and from forming insoluble precipitates, *e.g.*, boiler scale. Ethylenediaminetetraacetic acid (EDTA) is particularly effective.

Sequestering agents are used in a broad range of industrial products such as antioxidants, preservatives, and purifying agents, for example, to retard formation of precipitates (gumming) in gasoline and fuel oil, to decontaminate materials subjected to radioactivity, to inhibit catalytic breakdown of hydrogen peroxide, and for many similar applications where ion deactivation is required.

Serini reaction. Preparation of ketones from seconday acetate from secondary-tertiary 1,2-glycol with zinc dust. In chemistry of steroids this reaction is applied for removal of residual acetic acid from 17-hydroxy-20-acetoxy-derivatives :

CH_3
$CH_3CO-O-CH$ $\xrightarrow[\text{toluene}]{\text{Zn}}$ $C=O$
OH 17 $\quad$ CH_3 H 17

serum. 1. The liquid portion of a suspension such as milk after removal of all the solid particles, including those in the colloidal size range. Milk from which the fat particles and casein micelles have been separated is a serum called whey ; it contains chiefly water in which sugars, minerales, and vitamins are present in true solution, *i.e.*, in molecular form. Another example is the serum obtained from rebber latex by precipation of the rubber hydrocarbon micelles.

2. Blood from which corpuscles, platelets, and some protiens have been separated by centrifugation, especially after it has been treated with an antigen for cure of a disease by inoculation.

sesqui. A prefix which indcates a proportion of two to three, as a sesquioxide in which the atomic proportions of metal and oxygen are as two or three, *e.g.*, Fe_2O_3. The term is also used to indicate "half."

sesquioxide. An oxide in which the ratio of metal to oxygen is as two to three' as in ferric oxide, chromic oxide, etc.

sesquiterpene. A terpene of the formula

$C_{15}H_{24}$, as distinguished from the ordinary terpenes which have the formula, $C_{10}H_{16}$.

sewage treatment. *See* activated sludge; aerobic; biodegradability; BOD.

sharp series. A series of lines in the spectra of many atoms which have one, two, or three electrons in their outer shells, either in their neutral state or as a result of ionization. (Excluded are the atoms which have only one electron in all, such as hydrogen, singly-ionized helium, doubly-ionized lithium, etc.). The sharp series differs from the other series for such elements in having a somewhat distinctive physical appearance, and being representable by the characteristic formula,

$$\bar{\nu}s = L - \frac{R}{(m + c)^2}$$

where $\bar{\nu}s$=the wave number of a line in the sharp series, *L* and *c* are constants for the sharp series, *m*=a variable integer, whose values give the various lines in the sharp series and *R*=the Rydberg constant.

Sharples process. One of a number of methods for the dewaxing of petroleum fractions by solvent extraction, centrifuging, and refrigeration.

Sheinkman test. A test for carbonate in the presence of sulphite made by heating the sample in a flask with water, adding sulphuric acid, and passing the gases evolved successively through a permanganate solution and through clear lime water. The presence of carbonates is indicated if turbidity appears in the lime water.

shell. A term applied by physical chemists to the various energy levels of groups of orbitals occupied by electrons as they resolve around atomic nuclei. There are seven possible shells, designated as K, L, M, N, etc.; the number varies with the element from 1 in the lightest (hydrogen and helium) to 7 in the heaviest (uranium). Each shell can contains only a certain number of electrons, for example, 2 for K, 8 for L, 18 for M, and 32 for N; the shells may or may not be valence electrons, which are directly involved in chemical bonding. *See also* orbital; electron; Pauli exclusion principle.

shell model. Model of atomic nucleus based on concept of similarity between structure of energetic levels in nucleus to structure of electron shells in atom. Energy levels of nucleus are arranged in groups. Levels within a particular group do not differ greatly in energy and belong to one shell.

sherardizing. A process for covering the surface of ferrous materials with a protective coating of zinc. The articles are treated with zinc dust in a closed vessel at a temperature of about 1100K.

shift of spectral line. A small displacement in the position of a spectral line that is caused by a corresponding change in frequency which is due, in turn, to one or more of a variety of causes, such as the Doppler effect, etc.

1, 2-shifts. Rearrangement reactions in which a group migrates from the atom to which it was originally bound to am adjacent atom, *i.e.*,

```
C'—C"    →    C'—C"
|                 |
R                 R
```

Reactions of this type are for example, neopentyl, pinacol, Lossen, Curtius, and Demjanov rearrangements. In most cases the actual isolated rearrangement product is one obtained after one or more additional steps after the 1, 2-shift.

shielding. Protection of personnel by placing adequate thickness of appropriate materials around nuclear reactors, and sources of high-energy *x*-rays and radioactive emanations. Lead is most frequently used for *x*- and gamma-ray protection because of its high density. Boron and cadmium are most effective as neutron absorbers. Hydrogen rich materials as hydraulic cements, polythylene, paraffin, and water also afford protection, but only in rather large amounts.

shielding constant. *See* screening constant.

shielding effect. In S_N1 reaction, effect of protecting reaction centre by leaving group; due to this nucleophile can attack electrophilic centre opposite side.

shielding of nuclear charge. Apparent decrease of nuclear charge interacting with outer electrons due to screening of nucleus by the other electrons.

shielding of nucleus. *See* screening effect.

side chain. System of chain-like linked atoms branching from main chain of atoms or from cyclic arrangement of atoms, *e.g.*,

$CH_3-(CH_2)_3-CH_2-CH(CH_2-CH_3)-CH_2-CH_2-CH_3$

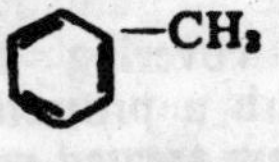

(cyclohexane ring)$-CH_3$

side reaction. When two or more reactions occurring simultaneously to the same reactant or reactants giving rise to different products. the predominating reaction is termed the main or principal reaction, the other, the secondary reaction. The term side reaction is often used in the sense of the secondary reaction.

Sidgwick-Powell theory. Theory which assumes that electrostatic repulsion forces, acting between electron pairs (bonding or non-bonding of valence shells of atoms, are of decisive character with respect to spatial structure of the molecule.

Siemens-Halske process. An electrolytic process for the metallurgical extraction of copper from its sulphide ores, in which the metal is dissolved in sulphuric acid and ferrous sulphate and the solution electrolyzed.

Siemens-Martin process. An open-hearth process used for producing steel. It operates at high temperatures, and its charge usually consists of pig iron, scrap steel, and other materials, with iron oxide added to the slag to oxidize impurities.

sigma bond. Chemical bond formed by valence electrons present in molecular σ-bonding orbital, symmetric with respect to bond axis, *e.g.*, C—H bonds in methane. Also designated as σ-bond.

sigma complex. Product of addition of cation to one of two carbon atoms of double bond system, requiring π-electron pair trom that system to form σ-bond. The σ-complex is formed from the π-complex, *e.g.*,

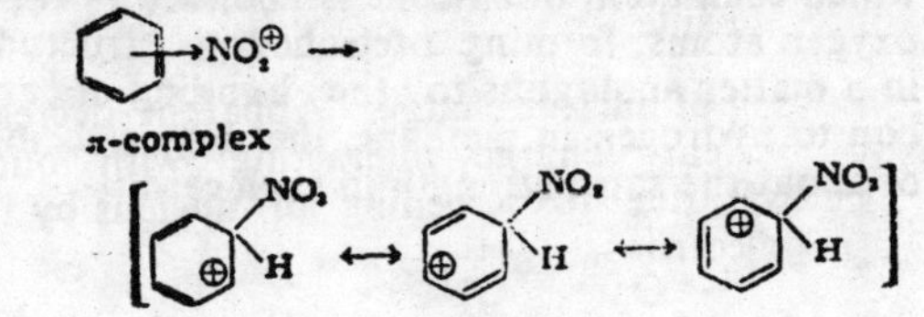

(benzene) $\rightarrow NO_2^{\oplus} \longrightarrow$

π-complex

[(⊕)(H)(NO_2) ⟷ (⊕)(H)(NO_2) ⟷ (⊕)(H)(NO_2)]

σ-complex

sigma electrons. Electrons assumed to occupy σ-molecular orbitals. Also designated as σ-electrons.

sigma hyperon. Elementary particle, a hadron, of baryon number $B=1$, lepton numper $L=0$, spin quantum number $J=1/2$, strangeness $S=-1$, isospin $I=1$, unstable. Σ-hyperon occurs in three states of charge (isospin triplet) ; of positive elementary electric charge (Σ^+-hyperon; mass $m=1189.42$ MeV, third component of isospin $I_3=1$, mean life-time 0.800×10^{-10} s), electrically neutron ; $m=1192.51$ MeV, $I_3=0$, mean life-time less than 1.0×10^{-11}s) and of negtive electric charge (Σ^--hyperon ; $m=1197.37$ MeV, $I_3=-1$, of mean lifetime 1.489×10^{-10} s). Also designated as Σ-hyperon.

sigma orbital. Molecular orbital symmetric with respect to rotation about bond axis. Also designated as σ-orbital.

sigmatropic reaction. Molecular rearrangement in which a σ-bond, flanked to be one or more α-electron systems, shifts to a new position. Such rearrangements are classified by two numbers set in brackets, which refer to the relative distance (in atoms) each end of the migrating σ-bond has moved. The Cope rearrangement is an important example of a [3, 3] sigmatropic reaction :

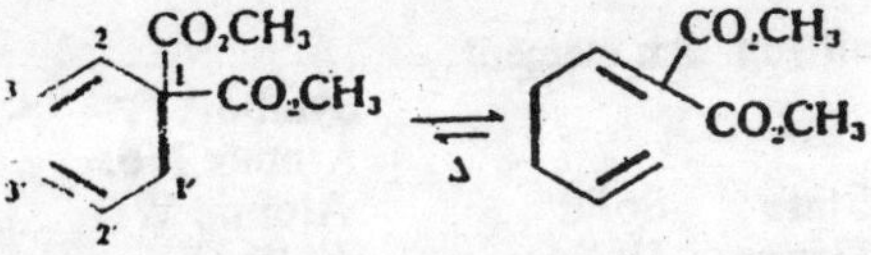

(1,5-diene with positions 1, 2, 3, 1′, 2′, 3′; CO_2CH_3, CO_2CH_3 at C-1) $\underset{\Delta}{\rightleftharpoons}$ (cyclic diene with CO_2CH_3, CO_2CH_3)

silanes. The compound SiH_4 is called silane ; compounds having the general formula $H_3Si(SiH_2)_nSiH_3$ are called disilane, trisilane, etc., according to the number of silicon atoms present. (In disilane, n in the above formula has a value of 0, in trisilane n has value of 1, etc.)

silazanes. Compounds having the general formula $H_3Si(NHSiH_2)_nNHSiH_3$ are called disilazane, etc., according to the number of silicon atoms present. They have the generic name silazanes. (In disilazane, n in the above formula has a value of 0; in trisilazane, a value of 1, etc.

silicane. This is used by different authorities to mean three entirely different compounds and types of compounds. It many denote (*i*) monosilane, SiH_4, which is discussed under silane ; (*ii*) all compounds of silicon and hydrogen, (*iii*) a compounds of the general formula SiR_4 in which R_4 may denote four identical hydrocarbon radicals or any combination of hydrocarbon radicals.

silicate. Any of a broad range of mineral compounds comprised of from one to six silica groups (SiO_2), arranged in either rings or chains. These include many of the more familiar gemstones (zircon, garnet, beryl, emerald), as well as asbestos (magnesium silicate), mica, and various types of clay (aluminium), A well-known synthetic silicate is (sodium silicate), a water-soluble glass commonly called water glass. Silicates are used in the manufacture of water-softening agents (zeolites).

siliceous. Containing silicon dioxide or one of its compounds.

silicic. 1. Containing or pertaining to silicon.

2. Containing silicic acid (ortho) H_4SiO_4 ; or silicic acid (meta) H_2SiO_3 ; or silicic acids of a higher degree of hydration (disilicic acids, trisilicic acids, etc.).

silicide. A binary compound of silicon.

silico-. A combining term indicating content to silica or silicon.

silicon. An element.

		Symbol	Si
		Atomic No.	14
State	Solid	Atomic Wt.	28.086
Group	IVA	Valence	4
		Isotopes	3 stable
		m.p.	1680-1692K
		b.p.	2628K

Silicon, is the most abundant solid element ; it rarely occurs in elemental form, virtually all of it existing as compounds (silicon dioxide, silicates, etc.

Elemental silicon has a face-centered cubic crystal structure (diamond structure). The existence of a hexagonal form of silicon with a wurtzite-type structure and with lattice parameters of $a = 3.80$ Å and $c = 6.28$ Å was established in 1963. Silicon is a nonmetal, like carbon, to which it is chemically similar ; it has the same valence and is next below carbon in the Periodic Table.

There are three naturally occurring isotopes ^{28}Si, through ^{30}Si, and three radioactive isotopes have been identified ^{27}Si, ^{31}Si, and ^{32}Si,. The latter isotope has a half-life of approximately 700 years, while the half lives of the other two are short, measured in terms of seconds and hours. Silicon forms single bonds with itself and with carbon, oxygen , hydrogen, and halogens, but it does not form double or triple bonds nor chains of more than six silicon atoms. This similarity to carbon accounts for its ability to form silanes (with hydrogen), siloxanes (with oxygen), and the industrially important silicon compounds (with oxygen and organic groups). Silicone is one of the few element that have pronounced semiconducting properties. The production of raw steel requires about 1.6-1.7 kilograms of silicon per metric ton of steel. The silicon is used in the form of ferrosilicon, which contains about 20% silicon. It is estimated that about 3 million metric tons of ferrosilicon are consumed annually in steel-making. It is also used as a semiconductor, *e.g.*, in solar cells and solid state devices. Though normally crystalline, silicon can be prepared in amorphous form, which has been found especially effective in solar cells.

silicone. A linear polymeric structure derived from siloxanes by substitution of an organic group for the oxygen atoms above and below the silicon atom; chlorine or other halogen may also be included in the compound :

$$-\underset{R}{\overset{R}{\underset{|}{\overset{|}{Si}}}}-\left[O-\underset{R}{\overset{R}{\underset{|}{\overset{|}{Si}}}}-\right]_n-O-\underset{R}{\overset{R}{\underset{|}{\overset{|}{Si}}}}-O-$$

$R{=}CH_3$

Silicone polymers may be liquids or resinous products ; the liquids (sometimes called silicone oils) are used for water-repellency, heat-transfer, and dielectric liquids and foam-inhibiting agents ; the resins form excellent adhesive bonding agents, antivibration pads, and electric insulating materials. They have unique elastomeric properties. especially when cross-linked with organic peroxides to given so-called silicone rubber.

siloxane. A compound of silicon and oxygen in which each atom of silicone is bonded to four oxygen atoms, forming a tetrahedral structure in a matter analogous to the bonding of carbon to hydrogen in methane, the bonds being of about the same strength in each case ;

$$-O-\underset{\underset{|}{O}}{\overset{\overset{|}{O}}{Si}}-O-\underset{\underset{|}{O}}{\overset{\overset{|}{O}}{Si}}-O-$$

This structure is found in the dioxide and in silicates generally, where the SiO_4 groups occur in chains or rings.

silthianes. Compounds having the general $H_3Si(SSiH_2)_nSSiH_3$ which are called disilthiane, trisilthiane, etc., according to the number of silicon atoms present. They have the generic name silthianes. (In disilthiane, n in the above formula has a value of 0, in trisilthiane, a value of 1, etc.)

silver. An element.

	Symbol	Ag
State Solid	Atomic Wt.	107.868
Group IB	Atomic No.	47
	Valence	1
	Isotopes	2 stable
	m.p.	1235K
	b.p.	2435K

Elemental silver has a face-centered cubic crystal structure. Silver is a white metal, softer than copper and harder than gold. When molten, silver is luminescent and occludes oxygen, but the oxygen is released upon solidification. As a conductor of heat and electricity, silver is superior to all other metals. It is extremely sensitive to contamination by sulphur and its compounds (tarnish). It has antiseptic properties which are utilized in medicine and dentistry, and it plays an essential part in the formation of photographic images. Other applications are in special batteries, alloys and linings for chemical equipment. First ionization potential is 7.574 eV, second, 21.4 eV; third, 35.9 eV. Oxidation potentials: $Ag \rightarrow Ag^+ + e^-$, $E^0 = -0.799$ V; $Ag^+ \rightarrow Ag^{2+} + e^-$, -1.98 V; $2Ag + 2OH^- \rightarrow Ag_2O + H_2O + 2e^-$, -0.344 V; $Ag_2O + 2OH^- \rightarrow 2AgO + H_2O + 2e^-$, -0.57 V; $2AgO + 2OH^- \rightarrow Ag_2O_3 + H_2O + 2e^-$, -0.74V. Silver forms compounds with the halogen elements, oxygen, and nitrogen. The light-sensitive halides are used in photography; the iodide is effective in atmospheric nucleation for rain-making. There are two stable, naturally occurring isotopes, ^{107}Ag and ^{109}Ag. In addition, there are reported to be 25 less-stable isotopes, ranging in half-life from 5 seconds to 253 days.

silvicide. This term refers to nonselective herbicides which kill or defoliate woody plants, bushes and small trees. Ammonium sulphamate has been used effectively for this purpose. Defoliants such as picloram may also be classed as silvicides if the trees die as a result.

similar chiral centres. Chiral centres identical with respect to chemical structure but different in configuration, *e.g.*, each molecule of the three tartaric acids, (+), (−) and meso, has two equivalent chiral centres. Also known as identical chiral centres.

Simon-Chavaune test reactions. 1. A test for ethyl glyoxalate made by heating the sample with ammonia. A black substance, soluble in water and insoluble in alcohol, is produced if glyoxalates are present; it dissolves in alkali hydroxides and carbonates with a deep red colour.

2. Ethylglyoxalate condenses with phenylhydrazine, hydroxylamine, or semi carbazide.

Simonini reaction. Formation of ester from two molecules of silver salt of carboxylic acid and one molecule of iodine, *e.g.*,

$$2RCOOAg + I_2 \rightarrow RCOOR + CO_2 + 2AgI$$

Simonis reaction. Preparation of chromone and coumarine from phenols and β-ketoesters in presence of phosphorus pentoxide, *e.g.*,

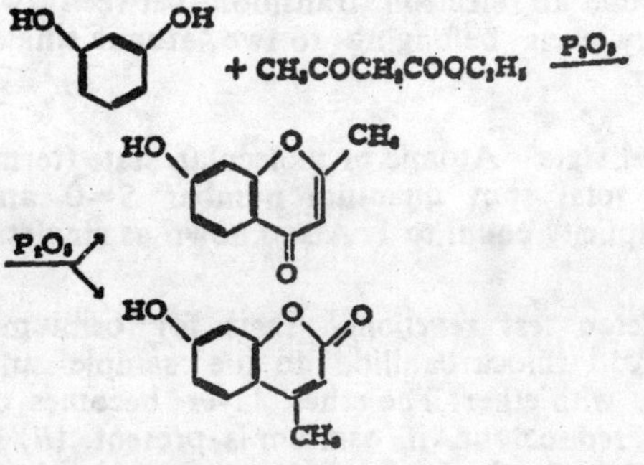

$$+ CH_3COCH_2COOC_2H_5 \xrightarrow{P_2O_5}$$

Simon reaction for phenylhydrazine. Add a few drops of an aqueous solution of trimethylamine and of dilute sodium nitroprusside solution to a solution of phenylhydrazine and heat. The mixture becomes blue, and this colour is darkened by potassium hydroxide and changed to sky-blue by acetic acid. The permanence of this colour distinguishes it from the aldehyde reaction.

Simon test for aldehydes. Add to the liquid to be tested, a few drops of aqueous trimethylamine solution and some very dilute sodium nitroprusside solution. A blue colour is given by aldehydes.

Simon test for amines. A test for the differentiation of primary amines by the use of acetaldehyde and sodium nitroprusside. Primary amines give a red colour, and other amines give a blue one.

simple electrode. Electrode (half-cell) at which only one electrode reaction occurs.

single escape peak. Peak in gamma radiation spectrum generated due to formation of electron-positron pair, annihilation of positron formed and escape of one annihilation photon from detector.

single-sweep voltammetry. Electrochemical method which consists in determination of current-potential relationship during electrolysis of non-stirred solution or molten salt ; voltage linearly increasing with time is applied to microelectrode with constant surface and to large reference electrode. Also known as voltammetry with continuously changing potential; stationary electrode voltammetry.

singlet line. In atomic spectroscopy spectral line due to electron transition between two energy levels belonging to two atomic singlet terms.

singlet state. Atomic or molecular state (term) with total spin quantum number $S=0$ and multiplicity equal to 1. Also known as singlet.

Singleton test reactions. Tests for osmium : (*i*) Add thiocarbanilide to the sample and shake with ether. The ether layer becomes of deep red colour if osmium is present. (*ii*) If osmium is in the form of osmate, a red colour is given with thiourea solution.

sinter. Heating of metal powders, clays and similar earths to a temperature well below the melting point ; this treatment results in softening and agglomeration of the particles to form a microporous product which can be pressed or molded to desired shape. The temperatures and pressures used are critical for any given material, since the size and distribution of "voids" can be closely controlled. Sintering is the major operation of powder metallurgy.

Sivadjian test reaction for amines. With primary amines, chloranil produces a red colour with secondary amines, a violet colour : and with tertiary amines, emerald-green colour.

sizing. An adherent coating of a soft, tacky nature applied to textile fibres, paper and various other products to give a smooth finish to decrease water absorption, and (for paper) to furnish a glossy surface suitable for halftone reproduction. Materials often used are solution containing starch, rosin, natural gums, casein, etc. Special types of sizing materials called slashing compounds are used in weaving cotton and rayon fibres.

Skey test reaction for cobalt. Add some citric or tartaric acid to the solution and followed by the addition of an excess of ammonia and some potassium ferricyanide. A dark red colour indicates the presence of cobalt.

Skraup reaction. The preparation of quinoline and its derivatives from an aromatic amine (aniline and its derivatives), glycerol sulphuric acid, and an oxidizer (nitrobenzene or arsenic oxide), The glycerol probably yields acrolein, which condenses with the aniline, and the acrolein, aniline thus produced condenses to quinoline :

$$CH_2OHCHOHCH_2OH \xrightarrow{\Delta,\ H_2SO_4} CH_2{=}CH{-}CHO$$

$$C_6H_5NH_2 + CH_2{=}CH{-}CHO \rightarrow C_6H_5NH{-}CH_2CH_2CHO \xrightarrow{-H_2O} \text{dihydroquinoline} \xrightarrow{C_6H_5NO_2} \text{quinoline}$$

Skraup test. A test for thalline solutions, which are coloured green by oxidizers such as ferric chloride, chlorine, or chromic acid.

slack. 1. Descriptive of a soft paraffin wax resulting from incomplete pressing of the settings from the petroleum distillate. Though it has some applications in this form, it is actually an intermediate product between the liquid distillate and the scale wax made by expressing more of the oil.

2. Specifically, to react calcium oxide (lime)

with water to form calcium hydroxide (slacked or hydrated lime); the reaction is

$$CaO + HO_2 \rightarrow Ca(OH)_2 + \text{heat}.$$

slag. The material which separates from the molten metal during the smelting of ores; it consists largely of the nonreduced portion of the ore, in combination with any flux that may have been used in the smelting. Slag usually floats on the molten metal and solidifies on cooling.

Slater's orbital. Atomic orbital of the form:

$$\Psi = Nr^{n^*-1} e^{-Z^* r/n^* a_0} Y_{lm}(\theta, \varphi)$$

where n^*=effective quantum number, Z^*= effective nuclear charge, r = distance from nucleus, θ and φ = angular coordinates of electron, a_0=Bohr radius, N=normalization constant, Y_{lm}=hydrogen-like angular part of orbital.

slime. A solution of a solid in a liquid, or more commonly a suspension, which because of the presence of gelatinous substances, colloids, or even very fine mineral particles, often feels slippery to the touch. Mineral slimes are produced by the very fine grinding rocks often necessary in the flotation process.

slip. A rather thin aqueous dispersion of clays (aluminium silicates) used for coating ceramic ware; a fluxing agent is often added to facilitate melting when the assembly is fired. A glassy finish called a glaze is thus obtained.

slow coagulation. Coagulation of colloidal particles partially discharged when their electrokinetic potential ζ is between critical potential value and zero This coagulation increases with increasing concentration of electrolyte used and depends on particular features of its ions.

slow neutrons. Neutrons having kinetic energies from zero up to about 1000 eV.

sludge. A solid residue, usually containing liquid which is often the end-product or waste-product of various process.

slurry. A dilute suspension of particulate solids in water, for example, the aqueous dispersions of clay, fibre particles, or metal powders. Slurry explosives are suspensions of ammonium nitrate in water, also containing low percentages of aluminium powder or active explosives.

SE1 mechanism. Substitution reaction involving formation of carbanion as a result of ionization of organic molecule with subsequent reaction of carbanion with electrophile Y^+, *e.g.*,

$$-\overset{|}{\underset{|}{C}}:X \rightarrow -\overset{|}{\underset{|}{C}}:^- + X^+$$

$$-\overset{|}{\underset{|}{C}}:^- + Y^+ \rightarrow -\overset{|}{\underset{|}{C}}Y$$

SE2 mechanism. Substitution reaction involving attack of electrophile Y^+ on carbon atom from which exchanged group separates off simultaneously as cation X^+, *e.g.*,

$$Y^\ominus + -\overset{|}{\underset{|}{C}}-X \rightarrow \left[\overset{\delta\ominus}{Y}\cdots\overset{\diagdown\,\diagup}{\underset{|}{C}}\cdots\overset{\delta\ominus}{X}\right] \rightarrow Y-\overset{|}{\underset{|}{C}}- + X^\ominus$$

activated complex

Also known as mechanism of bimolecular electrophilic substitution.

SN1 mechanism. Substitution involving carbonium ion formation (due to dissociation of RX molecule) as rate-determining step with subsequent reaction of carbonium ion with nucleophile Y^+, *e.g.*,

$$-\overset{|}{\underset{|}{C}}-X \underset{}{\overset{\text{slow}}{\rightleftharpoons}} \overset{\diagdown\,\diagup}{\underset{|}{C}}\oplus + X{:}^\ominus$$

$$\overset{\diagdown\,\diagup}{\underset{|}{C}}\oplus + Y^\ominus \xrightarrow{\text{fast}} -\overset{|}{\underset{|}{C}}-Y$$

The stereochemistry of SN1 reaction with suitable example is shown below:

I

II

carbonium-ion intermediate

fast | $Y:^{\ominus}$

The reaction rate varies with (*i*) R according to carbonium ion stability (3°>2°>1°), (*ii*) the solvent, since ions are stabilized by solvation, the reaction rate is unaffected by changes in Y^-; as long as the solvent remains unchanged. During the course of reaction molecular rearrangements may occur. Also known as mechanism of unimolecular nucleophilic substitution.

SN2 mechanism. Substitution involving indirect formation of active complex (the rate-determining step), containing group X^+ and attacking group Y^-, both partly bound to carbon atom on which substitution occurs, *e.g.*,

$$\bar{Y} + -\overset{|}{\underset{|}{C}}-X \rightarrow \left[\overset{-\delta}{Y}\cdots C \cdots \overset{-\delta}{X}\right] \rightarrow Y-\overset{|}{C}- + X^-$$

activated complex

The reaction rate varies (*i*) with R according (1°>2°>>3°); (*ii*) increase with the nucleophilicity of Y^-; ($SH^- > I^- > CN^- > OR^- > Br^- > Cl^- > F^-$); (*iii*) varies with X (F<<Cl<Br<I); (*iv*) and is not greatly affected by changes in the solvent. Stereoisomeric halides react stereospecifically with inversion of configuration. Also known as mechanism of bimolecular nucleophilic substitution.

SN2′ mechanism. Mechanism of nucleophilic substitution connected with rearrangement observed with allylic derivatives. Nucleophile attacks allylic atom (not carbon atom originally substituted by leaving group). Migration of double bond takes place simultaneously with substitution, *e.g.*,

$$R_3N: + CH_2{=}CH{-}CHCH_3(Cl) \rightarrow R_3\overset{\oplus}{N}CH_2{-}CH{=}CHCH_3 + Cl^{\ominus}$$

SNi mechanism. Mechanism involving intramolecular nucleophile attack on carbon atom at which substitution occurs. Nucleophile attacks from direction of leaving group. Thus, reaction proceeds with total retention of configuration, *e.g.*,

$$-\overset{|}{C}-O-\underset{\underset{O}{\|}}{S}-Cl \rightarrow \; \rightarrow -\overset{|}{C}-Cl + SO_2$$

Also known as mechanism of internal nucleophilic substitution.

SNi′ mechanism. Mechanism of internal nucleophilic substitution with rearrangement observed in case of allylic derivatives. Reaction involves intramolecular nucleophile attack on allylic carbon atom with subsequent migration of double bond, *e.g.*,

$$R{-}CH{=}CH{-}CH_2{-}OH \xrightarrow[-HCl]{SO_2Cl_2}$$

$$\rightarrow R{-}\underset{\underset{Cl}{|}}{C}H{-}CH{=}CH_2 + SO_2$$

SR mechanism. Mechanism of radical substitution involving homolytic fission of bonds. Initiated reaction proceeds in chain process, *e.g.*,

$$Cl_2 \xrightarrow{light} 2Cl\cdot$$

$$Cl\cdot + CH_4 \rightarrow CH_3\cdot + HCl$$

$$CH_3\cdot + Cl_2 \rightarrow CH_3Cl + Cl\cdot \text{ etc}$$

Also known as mechanism of free-radical substitution.

smectic phase. One of the forms of the mesomorphic state, or the "liquid crystals." In the smectic phase, flow does not occur normally substance often forms drops which show a series of fine lines especially on examination with polarized light. The liquid motion is more of a "gliding" that a flowing action, and x-ray diffraction patterns are obtained in one direction only.

smelt. A term used by metallurgists to denote the separation of a metal from its ore by heating at high temperature in a confined vessel; the liquefied metal falls to the bottom of the container, the lighter ore components remaining on the surface as slag. A reduction reaction is involved.

Smiles rearrangement. A rearrangement of diaryl sulphones, sulphides, ethers, and similar compounds containing, in a position ortho to the groups named above, a hydroxy, amino, or similar group. The rearragement results in the breaking of the bond between the sulphone, sulphide, etc., group and one of the aryl groups and the formation of a new bond linking the aryl groups through the hydroxy, amino, or similar group.

$$H_2C{-}CH_2 \text{ (HO, SO–}C_6H_4{-}NO_2) \xrightarrow{OH^-} H_2C{-}CH_2 \text{ (HOS, O–}C_6H_4{-}NO_2)$$

smoke. An aerosol composed of colloidal particles of combustion products dispersed in air combined with the gases resulting from combustion. Specialized types of smoke include the fumes from heated metal sulfaces and so-called military or chemical smoke, which is evolved by reaction of appropriate compounds, *e.g.*, titanium tetrachloride.

soap. A compound of one of the higher fatty acids or a mixture of such compounds. The true soaps are salts of the alkali metals and are soluble in water but the term has been extended to include the salt of other metals, some of which are insoluble in water combinations of fatty acids and certain organic bases, such as ethanolamine; mixtures of the foregoing substances with alkaline silicates, glycerol, and other additives.

soap, metallic. *See* metallic soap.

Soddy-Fajans displacement laws. Rules which define changes in mass number *A* and atomic number *Z* of nuclei produced in radioactive transformations with respect to *A* and *Z* values of the parent nuclides: (*i*) in α-decay, *A* decreases by 4, *Z* decreases by 2; (*ii*) in β-decay, *A* does not change, *Z* increases by 1; (*iii*) in β-decay, *A* does not change, *Z* decreases by 1.

Soderberg cell. A cell for the production of aluminum by electrolysis of alumina dissolved in a bath of molten salts. This cell uses a large electrode, cylindrical in form, which originates as a carbonaceous mixture in a hopper above the cell, and becomes hard and conductive by heating as it moves down into the cell.

sodium. An element.

	Symbol	Na
State Solid	atomic No.	11
Group AI	Atomic Wt.	22.98977
	Valence	+1
	m.p.	370.8K
	b.p.	1156K

Sodium, the sixth most abundant element in the earth's crust and the most common alkali metal (Group IA) within average of 2.9%

sodium in igneous rocks. In terms of content in seawater, the element ranks fourth with an estimated 10.8 million metric tons per cubic kilometre of seawater is a soft electropositive metal, its compounds are more numerous than those of any other metal. It occurs in many natural compounds in the form of chloride, borate, carbonate, sulphate and others. The metal is made on a large scale by the electrolysis of molten sodium chloride mixed with calcium chloride or potassium fluoride. It reacts vigorously with water with formation of hydrogen and sodium hydroxide and the strong evolution of heat, and should be kept out of contact with water, as well as with air and oxygen. It readily forms compounds with the halogens, oxygen, and many other nonmetals, and alloys with a large number of metals, especially lead and mercury. Sodium ion is essential to man and other animals whose chief intake of it is in the form of sodium chloride. Sodium is dangerous to handle, as it is corrosive to the skin, and also flammable when exposed to heat.

Among the attractions of molten sodium metal as a heat transfer medium (*i*) low density compared with other metals and combinations of salts, contributing to low cost per unit volume and also to relative ease of pumping. (*ii*) relatively low vapour pressure even at temperatures as high as 800K. (*iii*) greater heat capacity than most common metals in liquid form, the thermal conductivity being 5-10 times greater than the conductivities of lead or mercury and 50 times greater than the most organic heat-transfer media ; and (*iv*) viscosity of molten sodium is quite low. Despite these qualifications, however, the use of sodium as a heat-transfer medium enjoyed mixed reception over the years, partially attributable to a lack of marketing thrust on its behalf.

softener. This term is widely used in chemical technology in its common meaning to denote a material or agent which is added to a product or process to increase the pliability or plasticity of any substance. A special usage is in the treatment of water in which the term "water softener" is applied to a substance used to remove undesirable salts.

softening temperature. A more or less definite physical constant of a substance that does not have a definite melting point, defined as the temperature at which viscous flow changes to plastic flow.

soft radiation. Ionizing radiation of low energy and poor penetrating power, *e.g.*, β-radiation and x-rays of energy up to several hundred keV.

sogasoid. A dispersed system of a solid in a gas.

sol. A term used by physical chemists to denote a liquid colloidal dispersion of solid particles, for example, gold, in water the dispersion is stabilized by electric charges, either all negative or all positive, the particles being kept from colliding or flocculating by mutual electrical repulsion. The "sol" state is opposed to the "gel" state, in which the dispersion is a thick, semisolid mass. The word is a shortened form of solution, not of solid.

solation. In colloidal nomenclature, the process of change from a gel to a sol. The gel is said to solate.

solder. An alloy which applied in fused form to join two metallic surfaces.

solid. A state of aggregation in which the substance possesses both definite volume and definite shape. Solids possess elasticity both of shape and bulk, *i.e.*, they resist any force that tends to alter their volume or form. Solids are characterized by very stable surfaces of distinct outline on all sides.

The crystals of solid elements and compounds are three-dimensional structures (cubes, rhomboids, tetrahedrons, etc.) held together by chemical bonds of one kind or another in a geometrical pattern called a lattice. Much has been learned about the shape and internal arrangement of crystals by x-ray diffraction.

solid solution. Solution characterized by miscibility of constituents in solid phase. Also known as mixed crystals.

solidus. Plot of temperature at which the last of liquid phase solidifies, with respect to composition. Also known as solidus curve.

soliquid. A dispersed system of a solid in a liquid.

solubility. A property of a substance by virtue of which it forms mixtures with other substances which are chemically and physically homogeneous throughout. The degree of solubility (often spoken of as "solubility") is the concentration of a solute in a saturated solution at any given temperature. The degree of solubility of most substances increases with rise in temperature, but there are cases (notably the organic salts of calcium) where a substance is more soluble in cold than in hot solvents.

solubility diagram. Plot of solubility of substance in solvent, as function of temperature (two component systems) and also as function of presence of other substances (multicomponent systems).

solubility product, K_s. Ionic product of weakly soluble electrolyte. Equilibrium constant for equilibrium between weakly soluble electrolyte and its saturated solution (ions) is written as :

$$K_s = a_+^{\nu+} \cdot a_-^{\nu-}$$

where a_+ and a_- =concentration activities of cation and anion, respectively, ν_+ and ν_- =number of cations and anions resulting from one molecule of electrolyte. Value for solubility product depends on temperature ; in formula for solubility product for very weakly soluble electrolytes activities can be subsituted by conentrations. Also known as activity solubility product.

solute. The dissolved substance in a solution.

solutide. A true solution.

solution. A uniform molecular or ionic mixture of one (or more) substance(s) (solute) in another (solvent). This is called a true solution in contrast to a colloidal solution, in which the dispersed material in the form of extremely small particles (1 micron or less) ; these systems are more properly called dispersions. The molecules of ions of a solution are the solute, and the substance in which they are dissolved is the solvent. Polar compounds, for example, metal hydroxides and halides, form ions in water solutions, but nonpolar compounds such as sugar remain in molecular form. Concentrations of solutions are indicated by such standard definitions as molarity, normality, and molality.

The most familiar type of solution is that of a solid in a liquid. Glass is an undercooled solution of metallic oxides in molten silica, which is technically liquid but physically rigid. There are many instances of solutions of liquids in liquids (alcohol-water). There are also solutions of solids in solids (alloys.). Polymerization is often carried out in a solution in which the monomer is the solute.

solution pressure. 1. The force impelling molecules or atoms to cross a phase boundary and enter into solution.

2. A term introduced by Nernst to denote the property possessed by metals, hydrogen, and certain non-metals, whereby they tend to pass into solution as ions. However, it has not been found possible to device a method for the measurement of the absolute potential between an electrode and a solution of its ions.

solvate. Addition compound formed in solution as result of solvation.

solvated electron, $e^-_{solv.}$ Electron attached to one or several molecules in liquids.

solvation. A term used to denote the tendency of finely divided solid surfaces to absorb a diffuse layer or film of a solvent in which they are dispersed as a result of electrostatic forces between the surface of the particle and the solvent molecules. The process utilizes the stabilizing interaction of solute molecules with solvent molecules, particularly important for ions in solution. When the solvent is water, the process is termed hydration.

solvation number of ion. Number of solvent molecules in first solvation sphere.

solvation shell. Zone around ion or molecule formed by solvent molecules, as result of solvation.

solvatochromism. Solvent induced shift of absorption bands in electronic spectra.

Solvay process. A process involving synthesis, of sodium bicarbonate ($NaHCO_3$) and sodium carbonate (soda ash) (Na_2CO_3) from sodium chloride, ammonia and carbon dioxide obtained from calcium carbonate ($CaCO_3$) derived from limestone. Essentially the reactions involve formation of ammonium bicarbonate (NH_4HCO_3) from ammonia, water and carbon dioxide ; this reacts with sodium chloride to yield sodium bicarbonate and ammonium chloride. The sodium bicarbonate breaks down to sodium carbonate (soda ash) on heating. Ammonia is regenerated by reacting the ammonium chloride previously formed with calcium hydroxide, calcium chloride being the by-product. Also known as ammonia-soda process.

solvent. Derived from the Latin, meaning "set free" or "losen," this term designates a liquid which can reduce certain solids to molecular or ionic form by relaxing the intermolecular forces that unite them. This is the exact meaning of dissolve, which comes from the same root as solvent and solution. By far the most common inorganic solvent is water (often erroneously called the universal solvent). It dissolves such solids as sugar, starch, and many ion-forming metal salts, as well as numerous liquids and gases (sulphuric acid, alcohol, formaldehyde, hydrogen chloride). Hydrocarbon liquids such as benzene dissolve organic materials such as fats, waxes, resins, resins, and oils. In all cases the system is a uniform mixture of the solvent and the dissolved substance (the solute) in either molecular or ionic form.

solvolysis. Metathesis between solvate and solvent, the latter acting as a nucleophile, *e.g.*,

$$C_2H_5OH + (CH_3)_3CBr \rightarrow C_2H_5{-}O{-}C(CH_3)_3 + HBr$$

Sommelet aldehyde synthesis. Preparation of aldehydes by hydrolysis of adduct of hexamethylenetetramine and organic halides (usually arylic), *e.g.*,

$$ArCH_2X \xrightarrow{C_6H_{12}N_4} [ArCH_2{-}C_6H_{12}N_4]^+X^- \xrightarrow{H_2O} ArCHO$$

Sommelet rearrangement. The acid-catalyzed rearrangement of benzyltrimethylammonium hydroxide to *o*-benzylbenzyldimethylamine:

$$(C_6H_5)_2CHN(CH_3)_3OH \xrightarrow{H_2SO_4} C_6H_5.CH_2.C_6H_4.CH_2.N(CH_3)_2 + H_2O$$

Sonn-Muller aldehyde synthesis. A method of conversion of amides to aldehydes, involving dehydration to imidochlorides, followed by reduction to imines and hydrolysis to the aldehydes:

$$RCONH_2 \xrightarrow{SOCl_2} RCCl{=}NH \xrightarrow{SnCl_2+HCl} RCH{=}NH.HCl \xrightarrow{H_2O} RCHO + NH_4Cl$$

sonochemistry. Branch of chemistry dealing with applications of ultrasonic or acoustic waves for initiation or catalysis of certain chemical reactions. Also known as phonochemistry.

sorbent. Substance able to take up another substance in process of sorption.

sorption. General term employed for description of ability of taking up given substance (sorptive) from liquid bulk by another condenced phase. This term is also used by chemists in cases when it is not clear whether adsorption or absorption is involved, or when both are occurring simultaneously.

space formula. A structural formula, or more commonly a group of structural formulas grouped to show differences between stereoisomers, or compounds identical in composition but differing in spatial arrangement. A simple space formula is that showing the two stereoisomers of lactic acid:

```
 H  OH   O          H  H    O
 |  |   /           |  |   /
H—C—C—C           H—C—C—C
 |  |   \           |  |   \
 H  H    OH         H  OH   OH
```

space group. Group of symmetry elements transforming space lattice into itself (self-coincidence). Except elements of symmetry characteristic for elementary cell, every space group contains elements of translation symmetry, and may also contain screw axis of symmetry and mirror translation planes. There are 230 three-dimensional Fedorov and Schoenflies space groups.

space lattice. In general, an arrangement of particles in space; specifically the arrangement in a crystal of the constituent atoms or radicals which is determined from the diffraction patterns obtained by x-ray photography and other methods

space quantization. Limitation of allowed direction of spin, orbital or total magnetic moment of atom or molecule in magnetic or electric field to discrete, small number of orientations defined by corresponding magnetic quantum number.

spallation. Smashing of atomic nucleus into several fragments by high energy particle. This type of nuclear reaction result from bombardment of atoms with high energy projectiles, such as 200 meV protons and 400 meV alpha particles, whereby nuclei having atomic numbers 10 to 20 lower than the bombarded nucleus are obtained. The difference is largely in the form of ejected protons and alpha particles. Spallations differ from ordinary nuclear reactions in that the latter rarely yield, at first instance, atoms differing in atomic number by more than 2, from the bombarded nucleus. Spallations differ from nuclear fission process in that the reaction is not self sustaining and that the changes in nuclear mass in spallation are not large as usually encountered in fission.

spalling. The splitting-off portions of solid as a result of internal thermal or mechanical stresses.

spar. 1. A term used by mineralogists to designate a type of crystalline material such as Iceland spar or feldspar, usually containing calcium carbonate or aluminium silicate; fluorspar is calcium fluoride.

2. A weather-resistant varnish originally used for coating wooden decks of ships, which may be the reason for its name. It contains a drying oil, rosin or phenolic resin, and solvent. Some early type also contained sulphur.

spark line (ion line). A spectral line produced by radiation from ions.

spark spectrum. Emission spectrum of element obtained by electric spark excitation; it contains chiefly emission lines of singly ionized atoms, but also spectral lines of multiply ionized and neutral atoms.

specific. 1. Related to a particular class or entity.

2. A drug that has a direct action, or a specially action, toward the treatment or cure of a particular disease.

specific acid-base catalysis. Acid-base catalysis due to only acid or base coupled with solvent.

specific activity. Activity of a radioactive material with reference to unit mass or unit volume (for solutions). Also known as specific radioactivity.

specific coagulation time. Time in which initial number of colloidal particles in unit volume decreases due to coagulation to half its initial value.

specific conductance, x. The electrical conductance of a centimeter cube of a substance or a solution. It is measured in mhos (reciprocal ohms). For solutions, the specific conductance varies with the concentration, *e.g.*,

$$R = \rho \frac{l}{S} \qquad x = \frac{1}{\rho}$$

where R=resistance of conductor, l and S its length and cross-section area respectively, ρ= specific resistance.

specific ion exchanger. Ion exchanger that, due to presence of special functional groups, shows distinct preference for one or several ions. Also known as chelating resin.

specific ionization. Number of ion pairs formed per unit distance along track of ionizing particle passing through matter.

specific polarization, p. A quantity defined by the formula:

$$p = \frac{\varepsilon_r - 1}{\varepsilon_r + 2} \frac{1}{\rho}$$

where; ε_r=relative permittivity of medium, and ρ=its density.

specific reagent. Reagent reacting under specified conditions only with one ion or compound.

specific rotation. Rotation of polarization plane of monochromatic light by liquid layer of thickness 10 cm and containing 1 g of a given substance in 1 cm^3; measured in degrees.

specific surface. The surface, or area, of a substance or entity per unit volume; obtained by dividing the area by the volume, and expressed in reciprocal units of length.

specific viscosity, η_{sp}. Ratio of difference between viscosity coefficients of solution and pure solvent to viscosity coefficent of pure solvent ;

$$\eta_{sp} = \frac{\eta - \eta_0}{\eta_0} = \eta_{rel} - 1$$

where η=viscosity coefficent of solution, η_0= viscosity coefficient of pure solvent, η_{rel}=relative viscosity of solution. Also known as viscosity ratio excess.

specific volume. The volume of a substance or entity per unit mass, obtained by dividing the volume by the mass ; and expressed in units of length to the third power and reciprocal units of mass.

spectral distribution curve. The curve showing the radiant power emitted by a source as a function of wave length or frequency.

spectral ghosts. False spectral lines arising from imperfection of diffraction monochromator.

spectral line. Slit image in focal plane of spectrograph or spectrometer created by electromagetic radiation.

spectral pure reagent. Reagent provided with certificate indicating spectral lines of impurities detectable under specified conditions of excitation. Also known as spectral pure reagent; specpure reagent.

spectral series. In atomic spectroscopy group of lines corresponding to some fixed value of principal quantum number of either initial or final energetic level. Also known as series of spectral line.

spectral term. In hydrogen atom spectroscopy, ratio of Rydberg constant and square of principal quantum number of a given electronic state. Generally, in atomic spectroscopy, energy of a given electronic energy level in kaysers (cm^{-1}). Also known as spectroscopic term.

spectroanalysis. Qualitative and quantitative determination of sample's chemical composition by measurement of its spectra. Also known as spectrum analysis; spectroscopic analysis.

spectrochemical analysis. Spectroscopic determination of sample's qualitative and quantitative chemical composition.

spectrochemical buffer. In emission spectral analysis substance added to sample in order to minimize influence of other elements of sample on spectrum of a given element.

spectrochemical carrier. Substance added to spectral sample in order to facilitate its transition to gaseous state.

spectrochemical series. Series of ligands arranged by value of energy splitting (Δ or 10 *Dq*) in octahedral complexes formed by these ligands : $I^- < Br^- < Cl^- < F^- < H_2O << NH_3 < H_2N(CH_2)_2NH_2 < CN^-$.

spectrofluorimetry. Measurement of intensity of split fluorescence spectrum. This term is frequently applied in context of fluorimetric analysis utilizing spectrofluorimeter. Also known as spectrofluorometry.

spectrogram. A record produced by a spectrograph, *i.e.*, a record of a spectroscopic process commonly one obtained by photographic methods.

spectrographic analysis. Spectroanalysis based on measurement of sample emission spectrum record on photogrophic plate.

spectrometric analysis. Emission spectral analysis using photoelectric detectors for direct measurement of intensity of spectral lines.

spectrophotometric titration. Titration method with end point determined by spectrophotometer from point of inflection on curve representing dependence of absorption coefficient on amount of added reagent. Also known as photometric titration.

spectrophotometry. Branch of science dealing with investigation of dependence between intensity of electromagnetic radiation interacting with matter (emission, absorption, reflection scattering) and radiation wavelength ; this term usually refers to ultraviolet, visible and infrared region.

spectropolarimetry. Analytical method based on measurement of dispersion of optical rotation ; used for determination of optically active compounds, structural research and for identification of some optically active groups.

spectroscopy. A branch of analytical chemistry that deals with the determination of the structure of atoms and the chemical composition of molecules by measuring the radiant energy they absorb or emit in any of the wavelengths of the electromagnetic spectrum (gamma and x-radiation, ultraviolet, infrared, visible, microwave, and radiofrequency). When atoms or molecules are excited by energy input from an arc, spark, or flame, they respond in a characteristic manner; their identity and composition are signaled by the wavelengths of incident light they absorb or emit, the emission spectra being in the form of lines (atoms) of distinctive colour, such as the yellow sodium D-line, or bands (molecules). The intensity of these varies with the amount of an element present and thus affords a basis for quantitative analysis of the sample.

spectrum. 1. The resolution pattern of a group of radiations into its component parts over a surface or region in which radiation of any given wave length is physically separate from radiations of neighbouring wavelengths.

2. The resolution pattern of a group of masses over a region according to increasing mass, in which particles of a given mass are physically isolated from those of neighbouring masses.

3. A mathematical concept denoting the types of solutions which are associated with a given partial differential equation.

Sperry process. An electrolytic method for the production of white lead, litharge, lead borate, copper carbonate, lead chromate, and similar compounds. As used for white lead, the apparatus consists of a concrete tank containing lead anodes and insoluble iron cathodes. The cathodes are suspended in porous fabric envelopes which separate the electrolytes. The catholyte is an aqueous solution of 1-3% sodium acetate, 7-14% sodium carbonate, and 5% sodium hydroxide. The anolyte is an aqueous solution of 3-5% sodium acetate, and very little of the other salts. The complex ionic interaction results in the precipitation of the lead ions dissolved from the anode as a complex compound in the proportions of basic lead carbonate, which are those of white lead.

spin. Intrinsic particle angular momentum; vector quantity of no classical counterpart. Term spin is also used to denote spin quantum number. Also known as spin angular momentum.

spin decoupling. Elimination of coupling between two nuclear spins I_1 and I_2 which had formed multiplet structure of nuclear magnetic resonance line during observation of resonance signal of nuclei of spin I_1. Achieved by irradiating sample with alternating magnetic field of frequency corresponding to resonance frequncy of nuclei of spin I_2; technique used for analysing complex NMR spectra.

spin echo. Additional signal observed in pulse techniques of paramagnetic resonance when high frequency electromognetic field has been switched off.

spinel. Any of a group of hard, glassy minerals of various colours of quite wide geographical occurrence. Chemically, spinels are compounds or double oxides of such metals as iron, magnesium, aluminium, chromium, etc., common types being magnesium aluminate ($MgAl_2O_4$) and magnetite ($FeFe_2O_4$). Some types can be made synthetically. They have useful crystallographic properties and are closely related to ferrites.

spin-free complex. *See* high-spin complex.

spin-lattice relaxation. Relaxation in nuclear magnetic resonance arising from energy exchange between spin system and crystal lattice. Also known as longitudinal relaxation.

spin moment, *p*. Vector quantity defined by $p_S = h\sqrt{S(S-1)}$, where S=spin quantum number.

Spin magnetic moment $\mu_S = \sqrt{S(S-1)}\mu_B$ corresponds to spin moment, where μ_B=Bohr magneton.

spin orbital. One-electron wave function in atom or molecules given as product of electron.

spin-orbital coupling. Interaction between spin of electron (or total spin of electrons) with angular momentum of electron (or total angular momentum of electrons) giving total angular momentum of system.

spin quantum number. An integral term in the expression for the contribution to the total angular momentum of the electron that is due to the rotation of the electron on its own axis. This contribution is quantized, having two values $\frac{1}{2}$ and $-\frac{1}{2}$, in terms of $h/2\pi$ units of angular momentum (h=Planck's constant). The spin quantum number gives a numerical basis for the occurrence of many multiplet lines in ordinary spectra.

spin-spin coupling. Isotropic interaction of nuclear spins through molecular bonding electrons producing multiplet structure of NMR lines. Also known as spin-spin interaction.

spin-spin coupling constant, *J*. Constant expressed in Hz, which determines isotropic indirect spin-spin interaction between nuclear spins leading to formation of multiplet structure of NMR lines.

spin temperature, T_s. Concept introduced in consideration of the population of Zeeman levels in spin-lattice relaxaion. For two levels with $M=+1/2$ and $M=-1/2$ spin temperature is defined by ratio of their populations :

$$\frac{n_{+1/2}}{n_{-1/2}} = \exp\,(2\mu H/kT_s)$$

where μ=magnetic moment, H=magnetic field strength, k=Boltzmann constant, M=projection of spin onto direction of external magnetic field.

spin waves. Concept utilized in quantum mechanical theory of magnetism in order to describe propagation of spin-excited states in magnetically ordered crystals (*e.g.*, in ferromagnets).

spirit. In chemistry a term applied to ethyl alcohol, or to solutions in ethyl alcohol of volatile substances, or (less commonly) to any distillate.

spiro atom. Atom shared by two ring systems, *e.g.*, carbon atom in spirobicyclobutane or nitrogen atom in 1,1′-spirobipiperidinium bromide :

[Structures: spirobicyclobutane $C(CH_2)_4$ rings; 1,1′-spirobipiperidinium bromide $N^{\oplus}$ with CH_2 groups, $Br^{\ominus}$]

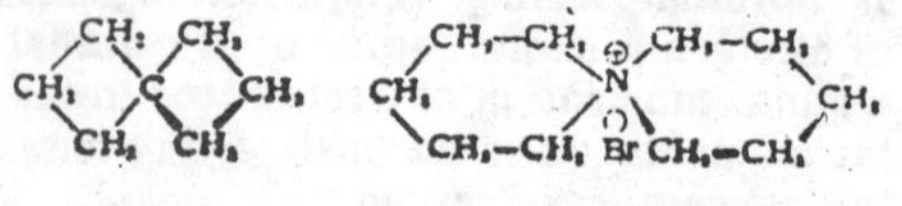

spiro-compound. An organic compound in which two ring structures have one carbon atom in common. *See also* spiro atom.

sponge. 1. Any material, natural or synthetic, which has or can be made to have a cellular structure, that is dispersions of gas globules within the solid. They are thus solid foams, exemplified by cake, bread and cellular plastics as well as by natural sponges.

2. A metal converted to a porous particulate form by reduction of its oxide for use as a catalyst or adsorbent ; iron and nickel are prepared in this way. Also, the initial porous form of metal obtained by the reduction of a metal compound, *e.g.*, the oxide or chloride, with such agents as carbon, hydrogen, magnesium, etc., usually at temperatures below the melting point of the metal.

spontaneous. Occurring by virtue of inherent properties or energy as distinguished from processes carried out by deliberate application of external force, as spontaneous evaporation, combustion, oxidation, etc.

spontaneous fission. Radioactive decay of the heaviest nuclei, consisting their spontaneous decay to two (rarely three or four) fragments which are nuclei of elements appearing in centre of periodic system.

spot test analysis. Technique in trace analysis ; it is based on reaction carried out with one drop of solution on surface of sample, on porcelain plate or paper. Appearance of appropriate colour, precipitate or gas bubbles indicates presence of suspected component.

Sometimes the test is made by "spotting" the drops so that their peripheries just meet.

spreading coefficient. A thermodynamic expression for the work done in the spreading of one liquid on another. It is the difference between the work of adhesion between the two liquids and the work of cohesion of the liquid spreading which may be expressed by the equation :

$$K_s = \gamma_B - \gamma_A - \gamma_{AB}$$

where K_s=the spreading coefficient, γ_B = the surface tension of the stationary liquid, γ_A = the surface tension of the spreading liquid, and γ_{AB} = the interfacial tension between the liquids.

spur. Group of ionic and free radical products of radiolysis located close to one another in zone of primary ionization of high energy particle or photon. Spur region diffuses with time and eventually becomes indistinguishable with bulk of liquid.

sputter. A method of producing systems containing very small particles of metals, as, *e.g.*, metals sols, by passing an electrical arc between two metallic electrodes placed the surface of a liquid or, sometimes, in a gas.

square planar complex. Complex of coordination number 4 in which donor atoms of ligands are distributed at corners of square (hybridization of dsp^2 type).

square-wave polarography. Method based on recording and analysis of square-wave alternating current which flows in polarographic circuit when voltage linearly increasing with time applied to electrodes is modulated with square-wave voltage of frequency 200—250 Hz and amplitude 5—50 mV.

stability constant, βn. Equilibrium constant of formation reaction of complex $M+nL \rightleftharpoons ML$. Under conditions guaranteeing constancy of activation coefficients :

$$\beta_n = \frac{[ML_n]}{[M][L]^n}$$

where $[MLn]$, $[M]$ and $[L]$ = equilibrium concentrations of complex, metal and ligand respectively.

stabilizer. Any substance added to another substance or mixture to prevent or retard a chemical or physicochemical change, at least for a considerable time. As this function can occur in many different ways, the term is a very general one, which includes antioxidants, inhibitors, emulsifiers protective colloids, etc.

The antioxidants stabilize the product in which they are contained by rendering it more resistant to oxidation, because they act as negative catalysts for reactions of the other components with oxygen, or because the stabilizers undergo preferential oxidation. Another use of the term "stabilizer" is to denote a substance used to render in emulsion more permanent, or more resistant to changes in temperature, *pH*, or other conditions.

stable complex. Complex which under specified conditions, practically does not dissociate in solution, and is characterized by large value of stability constant (generally $>10^8$).

stable nuclide. Nuclide not undergoing spontaneous measurable radioactive decay.

stable state. State of system in which all conditions of diffusion, mechanical and thermal stability are fulfilled.

Staddon test. A test for arsenic and antimony made by dissolving 0.5—2 g. of the sample to be tested in about 5 ml. water and adding 0.5—2 g. sodium hydrosulphite and warming the solution. If arsenic and antimony are precipitated, varying in colour from light to dark brown, forms in proportion to the amount present.

Staedel-Bugheimer pyrazine synthesis. A method of formation of pyrazines by condensation of α-halogenated ketones with ammonia.

Stahl reaction for orientation of hydroxyl group. Aromatic compounds having a hydroxyl group in the ortho position (*e.g.*, pyrocatechol) reduce molybdic acid or ammonium molybdate solution. However, the isomers with the group in the meta or para position (*e.g.*, hydroquinone and resorcinol) exert no reducing effect.

Stahl test for pyrogallol. Traces of pyrogallol give a blue colour with a mixture of ferric chloride and potassium ferricyanide solutions.

standard cell. Galvanic cell used as standard in measurements of EMF of cells ; currently exclusively Weston normal cell.

standard conditions. Temperature 273.16 K and and pressure 1.01325×10^{-1} MPa (formerly $p=1$ atm).

For a solid element, the allotropic form in which it most commonly occurs and at ordinary temperature, and at one atmosphere pressure. Also known as normal conditions.

standard curve method. Method of colorimetric analysis based on determination of concentration dependence of absorption of standard solutions. Unknown concentration of investigated substance is then determined by absorption measurement.

standard electrode potential. Potential of electrode (half-cell) with activity of components which take part in electrode potential equal to unity. Standard potentials are expressed usually with respect to potential of normal hydrogen electrode or saturated calomel electrode. Also known as normal electrode potential.

standard electromotive force. Electromotive force cell in which all substances participating in reactions occurred in cell are in standard state. Also known as normal electromotive force.

standard enthaply of reaction. Extensive quantity, measure of heat effect in isothermal-isobaric chemical reaction,

$$\Delta \overset{\circ}{H}_{T,p} = \sum_{B} \nu_B H^\circ_B$$

where ν_B=stoichiometric coefficient of reagent B (positive for products and negative for substrates), H°_B =molar enthaply of reagent B in standard state (of temperature and pressure indentical for all reactants), $\sum_B$ denotes summ-aiton over all reactants Also known as standard heat of reaction.

standard heat of reaction. *See* standard enthaply of reaction.

standard entropy. The total entropy of a substance in a state defined as standard. Thus the standard states of a solid or a liquid are regarded as those of the pure solid or the pure liquid, respectively, and at a stated temperature. The standard state of a gas is at 1 atmosphere pressure (1.01325×10^{-1} MPa), specified temperature, and its standard entropy is the change of entropy accompanying its expansion to zero pressure, or its compression from zero pressure to 1 atmosphere. The standard entropy of an ion is defined in a solution of unit activity, by assuming that the standard entropy of the hydrogen ion is zero.

standard free energy change. The value of the free energy change of a reaction existing when all the substances taking part in it are in their standard states of unit activity.

standard hydrogen electrode. Hydrgoen electrode taken as having a zero potential at all temperatures and one atmosphere pressure of hydrogen, *i.e.* in SI system $p_{H_2}=0.1325 \times 10^5$Pa, in solution of unit hydrogen activity, $a_{H_3O^+}=1$. Also known as normal hydrogen electrode.

standardization. The process of determining the precise assay of a complex substance, or the composition of a solution, which may then be used with the factor so determined, or adjusted to the desired value.

standard sample. Substance with strictly defined chemical composition given in producer's certificate, determined by large number of analyses carried out in various laboratories. Standard sample is used in comparative analyses, estimation of analytical methods etc.

standard solution. A solution of definite or known described properties such as *p*H, colour, electrical conductivity, or concentration for which the concentration (or other desired property) factor has been determined by analysis or method of preparation.

standard state (of component in a given phase). Arbitrarily chosen thermodynamic state with respect to which thermodynamic quantities of component in a given phase are determined. In simplest case standard state can be chosen as state of pure component or state of component in indefinitely diluted solution.

standard states of unit activity. Reference states for calculating thermodynamic activity such that : (i) in solutions diluted with respect to component B, activity of this component a_B tends to concentration value c_B, when this concentration tends to zero :

$$\lim_{c_B \to 0} \frac{a_B}{c_B} = 1$$

(*ii*) activity of pure substances under pressure of one atmosphere is equal to unity.

standard temperature. In general, a standard temperature established by some unvarying process, such as melting or boiling point or pressure or volume of a substance under fully-defined conditions. In common use, the term is applied to the temperature of a mixture of pure ice and water when the pressure on the water surfane is one atmosphere. This is the temperature of 0°C on the centigrade scale, or 273.16K on the absolute scale.

standard volume. The volume of one mole of a substance, in the form of a gas at a temperature of 273.16K., and a pressure of 1.01325×10^{-1} MPa.

stannane. One of various compounds of tin with hydrogen or with organic radicals, in which the metal usually has a valence of four.

Stark effect. Splitting of atomic or molecular

energy levels or splitting of spectral lines due to external electric field.

Stark-Einstein equation. The equation which is based on the law of Stark-Einstein, gives the amount of energy absorbed in a photochemical reaction. It is of the form :

$$E = Nh\nu$$

in which E=the amount of energy absorbed by one mole reactant, N = the Avogadro number, h=the Planck constant, and ν=the frequency of the radiation. Since N and h are constants, E is a function only of the frequency. This quantity E for a given wave length is frequently referred to as one einstein of radiation.

Stark-Einstein law of photochemical equivalence. Each molecule engaged in primary photochemical process absorbs only one quantum of radiation initiating this reaction.

Stark test. A test for antipyrine performed by mixing sulphuric acid and a little dillute potassium nitrate solution and adding the solution to be tested. A characteristic green colour is produced if antipyrine is present.

state. In its fundamental connotation, this term refers to the condition of a substance, as its state of aggregation, which may be solid, liquid, or gaseous—massive or dispersed. As extended to particle, the state may denote its condition of oxidation, as the state of oxidation, of an atom, or its energy level, as the orbit of an electron about the atomic nucleus, or in fact, the energy level of any other particle possessing rotational or vibrational energy.

state of aggregation. Physical state in which matter exists at defined conditions of pressure and temperature. Differences between particular states of aggregation are determined by interactions between particles and their mutual distances. Also known as physical state.

state quantities. *See* thermodynamic quantities.

state variable. Quantity used to characterize state of thermodynamic system. Also known as thermodynamic parameter ; coordinate of thermodynamic system; macroscopic parameter; state parameter.

Stathis test. A test for mercury performed by adding 0.5 ml. of 1% potassium iodide, 1 ml. of 20% potassium hydroxide, and 5 ml. of 0.01% gold chloride solution to 1 ml. of the solution to be tested. A violet colour is formed immediately, if mercury is present.

static reactivity indices. Reactivity indices following from consideration of electronic structure of molecule in preliminary stage of chemical reaction. At this stage changes in molecular electronic structure due to approach of reagent are rather small (polarization of electronic cloud). One of these indices is given by π-electron density.

stationary phase in chromatography. Adsorbent ion exchanger or liquid on solid support that is able to retain components being separated, and through which flows stream of mobile phase.

stationary state. State in which all properties have time-independent values. Also known as steady state.

statistical ensemble. Virtual set of statistically independent physical systems satisfying following conditions ; (*i*) particles of systems are all of the same type and interact through the same interaction potential, (*ii*) distribution of probability of microstates of these systems is given. In statistical mechanics it is convenient to consider given system as randomly chosen from some appropriate statistical ensemble. Also known as statistical assembly ; representation ensemble ; Gibbs assemble.

statistical mechanics. Branch of theoretical physics which deals with description and interpretation of microscopic properties of matter by using known particle properties (*i.e.*, properties of atoms, molecules, ion, etc.) and interactions between them.

statistical operator. Operator which in statistical quantum mechanics determines probability of result of measurement of any quantity. Statistical operator allows determination of all macroscopic properties of given system. Also known as density matrix ; density operator.

statistical thermodynamics. Branch of statistical mechanics dealing with dependence of thermodynamic functions on structure and mutual interactions of particles composiong macroscopic systems.

steam distillation. A simultaneous distillation of a substance immiscible with water and of water at a temperature such that the combined vapour pressure of the substance and of the water is equal to the external (usually atmospheric) pressure. Volatilization of high boiling substances or of substances which would decompose at their normal boiling points is readily effected in this manner.

steel. Basically, an alloy of iron and carbon made from molten pig iron from which all but a controlled percentage of residual carbon has been removed by oxidation Steels containing from 0.03 to 0.3% carbon are called low-carbon while those having from 0.75 to 1.7% are known as high-carbon. The presence of some carbon is essential, for it has a significant effect on the physical properties of steel, such as hardness strength, machinability, etc. Modern research has led to the employment of less highly carbonized or mild steels in a variety of forms, either as castings, or as forgings, or rolled sections, thus displacing cast and wrought iron. Steels are often alloyed with other metals to increase toughness corrosion resistance, and heat resistance. Stainless steels (noncorrosive) contain chromium and nickel (a well-known type having 18% chromium and 8% nickel) ; tool steels designed for high-speed metal-cutting are alloyed with molybdenum, tungsten, vanadium, etc., often in combination.

Stefan-Boltzman constant. *See* Stefan-Boltzman equation.

Stefan-Boltzmann equation. An equation expressing the law of Stefan and Boltzman which state that the total energy radiated by a black body is proportional to its absolute temperature raised to the fourth power :

$$E = \sigma(T^4 - T_0^4)$$

in which E=the total energy radiated, T=the absolute temperature of the source, T_0 = the absolute temperature of the surroundings, and σ=the Stefan-Boltzmann constant, which is equal to 5.67032×10^{-8} W/(m^2 . K^4).

Stefanelli test. A test for alcohol in either made by shaking the sample with a little aniline violet. If alcohol is present, the ether becomes coloured, but if no alcohol is present it remains colourless.

Steffens process. A series of operations used to recover the sugar from beet molasses. The molasses is treated with lime which reacts with sucrose to form saccharates of calcium. These are then extracted and treated with carbon dioxide which releases the sucrose and precipitates calcium carbonate. The sucrose is then purified.

Steiger test. A test for flouride in which small amounts of fluoride can be detected and estimated by the bleaching action of fluorine on the yellow colour produced by oxidizing a titanium solution with hydrogen peroxide.

Stein test for free alkali in soaps. An alkali soap solution forms a yellow-red precipitate with an aqueous solution of mercuric chloride. A white precipitate is formed with neutral soap solutions.

Stein test for iodine in nitric acid or nitrates. Acidify the acid or the nitrite with nitric acid and digest with tin sticks until red vapours are no longer produced. Then shake the liquid with carbon disulphide. If iodine is present the carbon disulphide becomes red.

Steinle-Kahlenberg test reaction. A test for cholesterol. A chloroform solution of antimony pentachloride with a dilute solution of cholesterol forms a muddy brown precipitate. In more chloroform, the precipitate dissolves and forms a clear, purple liquid which rapidly changes to cobalt-blue on exposure to light.

stem correction. A correction to be made in the reading of a thermometer which has part of its stem containing a portion of the thermometric-fluid column outside the region at the temperature being measured, so that amount of the thermometric fluid is not at the correct temperature.

step filter. Quartz, occasionally glass plate which enables intensity of passing radiation to be weakened in controlled way, different for distinct weakener steps. Also known as step weakener.

Stephen reaction. Preparation of aldehydes from nitriles by action of anhydrous stannous chloride in diethyl ether saturated with hydrogen chloride, *e.g.*,

$$RCN + HCl \rightarrow RC(Cl){=}NH \xrightarrow{SnCl_2}$$

$$RCH{=}NH.HCl \xrightarrow[-NH_4Cl]{H_2O} RCHO$$

step weakener. *See* step filter.

stepwise dissociation constant. *See* consecutive instability constant.

stepwise elution. Elution of mixture with aid of several successively introduced eluents, each of which selectively elutes single substances (ions) or their groups.

stepwise formation constant. *See* consecutive stability constant.

ster-, stereo-. A term derived form the Greek, meaning "three-dimensional" which appears in a number of chemical words both as a prefix and as a basic term. Stereochemistry and stereospecific refer to the special configurations of molecular structures; compounds classed as sterols and steroids are so named because of their three-dimensional structure. The same applies to steric hindrance."

sterobase unit. Smallest set of one, two or more successive configurational base units, that prescribes repetition in polymer macromolecule.

stereochemical effect (in coordination chemistry). Influence of size and spatial structure of ligand on stability of complex. In chelate complexes this effect is manifested by influence of substituents in chelating agent on formation and stability of these complexes (*cf.* steric hindrance in chelate complexes.

stereochemistry. The aspect of chemistry which is concerned with the three-dimensional structure of organic compounds and the spatial relationships of their constituent atoms or groups. The major subdivisions of this study are in the fields of high-polymer chemistry (stereoregular or stereospecific polymers); isomerism, both optical and geometric; and conformational analysis.

stereoisomer Isomers having same constitution but differing in the spatial arrangement of their atoms. Such pairs of compounds may be either (cis-trans) isomers or optical (D, L) isomers. Among the former are a number of metal coordination complexes, especially of cobalt, where the metal acts as a ligand. In the case of asymmetric (mirror image) compounds, the enantiomorphs formed are stereoisomers. The four-carbon sugars, for example, have two pairs of enantiomorphs (D and L configurations); in such instances, the two D and the two L forms which are not enantiomorphs are called diastereoisomers. Stereoisomers occur widely in natural products, particularly among the carotenoids some of which have over 100; for example, beta-carotene has 20.

stereoisomerism. Type of isomerism caused by different configuration of molecules (stereoisomers) which are not structural isomers.

stereometric formula. Chemical formula portrayings spatial arrangements of atoms in molecule thus enabling differentiation between steroisomers, *e.g.*,

$$\begin{array}{c} CHO \\ \vdots \\ H\blacktriangleright C \blacktriangleleft OH \\ \vdots \\ CH_2OH \end{array} \qquad \begin{array}{c} CHO \\ \vdots \\ HO\blacktriangleright C \blacktriangleleft H \\ \vdots \\ CH_2OH \end{array}$$

D-(+)-glyceric aldehyde **L-(−)-glyceric aldehyde**

Also known as stereoisomeric formula, stereoformula.

stereoregular polymer. Regular polymer composed of macromolecules have regular repetition of identical stereobase units at all stereoisomeric sites of main chain.

stereoselective polymerization. Polymerization in which polymer macromolecule is formed from mixture of stereoisomeric monomer molecules by preferential incorporation of one species into growing polymer chain.

stereoselective reaction. Formation of one of possible stereoisomer in predominant amount; such isomer possesses defined configuration, *e.g.*,

$$(\pm)C_6H_5-\underset{\displaystyle Cl}{\underset{|}{CH}}-CH_2-C_6H_5 \xrightarrow[-HCl]{OH^-}$$

$$\underset{70\%}{\begin{array}{ccc} C_6H_5 & & H \\ & C=C & \\ H & & C_6H_5 \end{array}} \quad + \quad \underset{30\%}{\begin{array}{ccc} C_6H_5 & & C_6H_5 \\ & C=C & \\ H & & H \end{array}}$$

stereospecific reaction. Formation of product of strictly defined steric structure from substrate of known configuration, *e.g.*, trans-but-2-ene on treatment with bromine forms only meso-2,3-dibromobutane.

steric effect. Effect exerted by steric system of atoms in molecule on its physical properties and chemical reactivity (or conformation).

Term has wide application, *see* shielding effect, hindering effect, transannular effect, internal strain.

steric factor. A corrections factor applied, in cases of many "slow" reactions, to correct the values calculated for the reaction rates by the collision theory. It is believed that the reason for the discrepancy, or, in other words, the physical meaning of the steric factor, may be the large number of degrees of freedom in which energy transformations must occur, in certain reactions, to form the activated complex. Also known as probability factor.

steric hindrance. 1. Specific interaction between atoms or groups of atoms in molecule, influencing reactivity of a site in compound, for instance, by interfering in coupling in acquiring given conformation or by decreasing reaction rate.

2. In coordination chemistry, chelating agent group which decreases stability of complex by steric hindrance, *e.g.*, derivatives of 8-hydroxyquinoline (in position 2) form less stable chelate complexes than parent reagent alone (cf. steric effect in coordination chemistry).

sterile. Free from living microorganisms.

sterilize. To render free from living microorganisms.

Sterkin-Helfgat solution. A mixture of 25 ml, of a 0.12% aqueous solution of sodium arsenate, 25 ml, of a 2% aqueous solution of ammonium molybdate, and 25 ml. of 2% hydrochloric acid, used as a test reagent for quinine. A permanent opalescence is formed with acidified quinine solutions.

Stern's theory of double layer. Theory which unites basic ideas of theories of structure of double layer of Helmholtz and Gouy and Chapman at electrode-electrolyte interface; it assumes existence on solution side next to metal surface of compact layer (Helmholtz) and further away of diffuse layer (Gouy and Chapman).

Stern-Volmer reactions. Exchange of atoms between two molecules, at least one of which is in excited state.

steroid. Any of a considerable number of organic compounds having a polycyclic 17-carbon phenanthrene nucleus. Steroids include the monohydric alcohols called **sterols,** of which cholesterol is a well-known example, hormones such as progesterone, testosterone bile acids (cholic acid and its derivatives), and provitamins ergosterol) :

[Structures: testosterone (OH, CH_3, H labels; O at C-3) and progesterone (CH_3, C=O, H labels; O at C-3)]

Steudel reaction for nucleic acid. Doubly refractive crystals, consisting of the purine bases, are obtained if nucleic acid is treated on a slide with concentrated nitric acid. Concentrated hydrochloric acid acts similarly.

Stevens α-methoxyketone synthesis. A method of formation of α-methoxyketones by treatment of α-bromoketones with sodium methylate to form epoxy ethers, which are rearranged by catalysts to give the α-methoxyketones :

$$R'COCBrR_2 + NaOCH_3 \rightarrow$$

$$R'-\underset{OCH_3}{\overset{O}{C}}-CR_2 + NaBr \quad \text{(epoxide)}$$

$$\downarrow \text{Catalyst}$$

$$R'-\underset{OCH_3}{\overset{R}{C}}-\overset{O}{\overset{\|}{C}}-R$$

Stevens rearrangement. Migration of benzyl group, for instance, in phenacylbenzyldimethylammonium bromide, caused by heating it with dilute solution of sodium hydroxide or by action of sodium amalgam on aqueous bromide solution :

$$C_6H_5COCH_2-\overset{\overset{CH_3}{|}}{\underset{\underset{CH_3}{|}}{N^+}}-CH_2-C_6H_5 \; Br^- \xrightarrow[-HBr]{OH} C_6H_5COCH(CH_2-C_6H_5)-N(CH_3)_2$$

stibarseno. The radical $-Sb{:}As-$.

stibic. Containing or pertaining to pentavalent antimony.

stibinic. The radical $>Sb({:}O)OH$, (attached to 2 radicals).

stibinico. The radical $HOOSb=$.

stibino. The radical H_2Sb-.

stibinous. The radical $>Sb(OH)$, (attached to two radicals).

stibious. Containing or pertaining to trivalent antimony.

stibium. Latin name for antimony.

stibo. The radical O_2Sb-.

stibonic. The radical $-Sb({:}O)(OH)_2$.

stibonium radical. The radical $-SbH_4$.

stibono. The radical $(HO)_2OSb-$.

stibonous. the radical $-Sb(OH)_2$.

stiboso. The radical $O{:}Sb-$.

stibyl. *See* stibino.

stibylene. The radical $HSb=$.

Stieglitz rearrangement. The course of this rearrangement of triphenylmethyl hydroxylamines and related compounds is such that there is possible the existence of intermediate univalent nitrogen compounds :

$$(C_6H_5)_3CN(OH)(H) \xrightarrow[\text{or Base}]{\text{Acid}} [(C_6H_5)_3C-N=] \rightarrow (C_6H_5)_2C=NC_6H_5$$

Instead of hydroxylamines, haloamines, dihaloamines, or other compounds can also be used.

Stobbe condensation. Condensation of aldehydes and ketones with succinic acid esters in presence of sodium ethanolate ; products are monoesters of alkylidenosuccinic acids, which upon hydrolysis yield alkylidenosuccinic acids, *e.g.*,

$$(CH_3)_2C=O + CH_2(COOC_2H_5)-CH_2-COOC_2H_5 \xrightarrow[H^+]{C_2H_5ONa} (CH_3)_2C=C(COOH)-CH_2-COOC_2H_5$$

$$\xrightarrow{\text{hydrolysis}} (CH_3)_2C=C(COOH)-CH_2-COOH$$

Stoeltzner test. A characteristic test reaction for vitamin D. If an oil, such as olive oil, containing about 1% of vitamin D, is treated with phosphorus pentoxide a reddish-brown colour develops which gradually becomes darker until it is almost black. Codliver oil also gives this reaction.

stoichiometric coefficient. Number in front of symbol (formula) of reactant in chemical equation. Stoichiometric coefficient determines number of moles of reactant taking part in a given reaction.

stoichiometric compounds. Chemical compounds fulfilling law of definite proportions. Also known as daltonides.

stoichiometry. Study of the mathematics of the material and energy balances (equilibrium) of chemical reactions. It is based on the laws of conservation of mass and energy and on the combining weights of elements. In a given case, it concerns the molecular amounts of the reacting substances and their products at a specific temperature and pressure, which is normally 1 atmosphere and 273.16K, as well as the heat absorbed or evolved (energy balance). Such analysis of a reaction shows that the total material and energy input is equal to the total output, that is, the mass-energy relationship is constant.

stoke(s). The CGS unit of kinematic viscosity ; fluid has a kinematic viscosity of unity when its dynamic viscosity is one poise and its density is one g. per cm^3 ; equal to 10^{-4} metre sequared per second.

stokes law. Wave length of luminescent light is longer than that of corresponding radiation.

stokes line. Raman line with frequency decreased with respect to that of excitation line.

stokes reagent. A reducing agent consisting of a solution of 3 g. ferrous sulphate and 2 g. tartaric acid in 100 ml. water.

Stolle synthesis. A method of formation of indole derivatives from aromatic amines or diamines by the action of oxalyl chloride (or α-haloacid chlorides).

stopping power. Measure of effect of a substance upon kinetic energy of charged particle passing through it. It is equal to energy loss of the particle per unit length.

storage cell. A cell in which the original active materials can be regenerated by forcing a current through in the opposite direction to that in which it flows during discharge. *See also* lead storage cell.

Stormer test reaction. A test for thymol. When a little thymol, dissolved in concentrated potassium hydroxide solution, is heated with a few drops of chloroform, a violet colour forms immediately. On shaking, the colour becomes violet-red.

STP. Conventional abbreviation for standard temperature and pressure. The standard temperature is 273.16K and the pressure is 1 atmosphere (760 mm of mercury).

strain. Any structural factor (such as angle distortion, bond eclipsing, or crowding) that raises the potential energy of a molecule constrained in due unfavorable configuration. The chemical reactivity of strained molecules is usually greater than that of similar unstrained molecules.

strain theory. A theory according to which five or six-membered carbon rings are the most stable. Rings comprising a larger or smaller number of carbon atoms may be formed, but are not as stable, since the structure of such a ring is strained.

strangeness, *S*. Additive quantum number attributed to hadrons and photons. Sum of strangeness is preserved in strong and electromagnetic interactions, but changes in weak interactions. Strangeness has integral values.

strange particles. Group of unstable particles of non-zero strangeness *S* (*K*-mesons, Λ-, Σ-, Ξ-, Ω-hyprons and a series of resonances).

streak. A term used in mineralogy to denote the more or less characteristic line produced by rubbing a mineral across a surface. Examination of the streak for colour and other characteristic qualities frequently gives valuable clues to the nature of the mineral. For best results, the testing surface should be clean and absorbent, such as that provided by unglazed porcelain.

streaming mercury electrode. Electrode consisting of jet of mercury flowing from capillary under pressure. In practice its surface is constant in time.

streaming potential. A difference of electrical potential between a porous diaphragm, or other permeable solid, and a liquid which is passing through it.

Strecker amino acid degradation. The reaction of α-amino acids with various oxidising agents such as O_3, H_2O_2, $K_2S_2O_8$ etc. to give aldehydes or ketones containing one less carbon atom, and carbon dioxide. Under certain conditions, the evolution of carbon dioxde can be determined quantitatively, and used to determine the α-amino acid content.

$$\underset{\displaystyle \mathrm{NH_2}}{\mathrm{RCHCOOH}} \rightarrow \mathrm{RCHO}$$

$$\mathrm{R'{-}\overset{\displaystyle R}{\underset{\displaystyle NH_2}{C}}{-}COOH} \rightarrow \mathrm{\overset{\displaystyle R}{\underset{\displaystyle R'}{C}}{=}O}$$

Strecker amino acid synthesis. A method of synthesizing α-amino acids from aldehydes (or ketones) by treatment with a cyanide and ammonia (or an amine), followed by hydrolysis. The course of the reaction is believed to be as follows :

$$\mathrm{RCHO + HCN + NH_3 \rightarrow RCH(NH_2)CN \xrightarrow{3H_2O} RCH(NH_2)COOH + NH_4OH}$$

The use of an alkali cyanide and ammonium chloride (instead of hydrogen cyanide and ammonia) is the Zelinsky-Stadnikoff synthesis.

Strecker synthesis. A method of formation of alkyl sulphonates from alkyl halides and alkali sulphites :

$$RBr + Na_2SO_3 \rightarrow RSO_3Na + NaBr$$

stretching vibrations. Normal vibrations in molecules which approximately correspond solely to change of bond lengths. Also known as valence vibration.

stripping. Nuclear reaction of direct interaction, consisting in addition of one or several nucleons of incident particle to target nucleus. Remaining part of incident particle continues its route with slight deflection.

stripping analysis. Method of determination of low concentrations of metal ions based on preliminary electro-deposition of determined metals on hanging mercury drop electrode from intensely stirred solution during controlled time. Resulting amalgam is oxidized (usually in stationary electrode voltammetry conditions) and concentration of ions in solution, from which amalgam was formed is determined from observed current value.

Strohmeyer test. A test for xanthine performed by adding mercuric chloride solution to the sample to be tested. A distinct turbidity is produced if xanthine is present.

strong electrolyte. Electrolyte with degree of dissociation approximately equal to one, regardless of concentration (complete dissociation).

strong interaction. Interaction of particles resulting in processes which take place in time range of 10^{-24} — 10^{-21}s (rapid processes). Strong interaction fullfils the greatest number of conservation laws.

strong ligand field. Crystal ligand field causing splitting of energy levels (terms) of central ion, large compared with distances between energy levels (atoms) of free ion. In complex of such field, number of unpaired electrons may be decreased compared with free ion (cf. crystal field splitting energy, low-spin complex.)

strontium. An element.

		Symbol	Sr
		Atomic No.	38
State	Solid	Atomic Wt.	87.62
Group	IIA	Valence	2
		Isotopes	4 stable
		m.p.	1043K
		b.p.	1657K

Strontium is a comparatively soft metal of the alkaline-earth group, similar in many respects to calcium.

Below 488K, elemental strontium has a face-centered cubic crystal structure ; between 488 and 878K, a hexagonal close-packed crystal structure ; and above 605K, a body-centered cubic crystal structure. It is quite reactive and quickly forms an oxide coating when exposed to dry air. It has strong reducing properties, decomposing water to evolve hydrogen ; it must be protected from moist air by storage under naphtha. In powder form it catches fire spontaneously at room temperature. It has no important commercial uses ; though the bright red colour of its flame is utilized in pyrotechnic devices. There are four stable isotopes, ^{84}Sr and ^{86}Sr through ^{88}Sr, and seven known radioactive isotopes ^{82}Sr, ^{83}Sr, ^{85}Sr, and ^{89}Sr through ^{92}Sr, all with relatively short half-lives measurable in hours or days, except ^{90}Sr ($t_{1/2}=26$ years). The latter isotope represents a hazard from nuclear blasting activities because of its long half-life, tendency to contaminate food products, such as milk, and retention in the body. In terms of abundance, strontium is 21st among the elements, occurring in the rocks of the earth's crust. In terms of content in seawater, the element ranks 11th, with an estimated 38,000 tons of strontium per cubic mile (8208 metric tons in a cubic kilometer) of seawater.

Stroup test. A test for differentiating caffeine and theobromine made by triturating a sample in a porcelain dish and adding 1 drop of a 5 : 100 solution of potassium dichromate in sulphuric acid. Caffeine gives a light blue-green colour ; theobromine gives a dark purple colour which gradually changes to purple-green, olive-green, then to blue-green.

structural formula. A formula which shows all the valence bonds and the atoms that they join within the molecule, *e.g.*, structure of water, ammonia, and methane are H—Ö—H,

$$H-\ddot{N}-H \text{ (with H below N)}, \quad \text{and} \quad H-C-H \text{ (with H above and below C)}$$

respectively.

structural chemistry. That branch of chemistry which deals with the grouping and linkages of atoms within the molecule.

structural isomerism. A form of isomerism in which two or more substances possess the same elementary composition, but differ in their structures, commonly their plane-structures, by having the same substituent attached to defferent atoms in a chain, the same atoms in a chain, the same atoms or groups in different positions on a ring, double or triple bonds in different positions, or a difference in the chain arrangement of the atoms.

structural viscosity. Excess of viscosity coefficient of sol over Newtonian viscosity, *i.e.*, difference between viscosity coefficients of sol in the case of small and very great velocity gradients. Change in viscosity coefficient with changing velocity gradient is most frequently caused by formation of internal structures.

Stuffer rules. 1. Gamma disulphones are split by alkali into a sulphinate and an alcohol. Other disulphones do not undergo this reaction :

$$RSO_2CH_2CH_2SOR + NaOH \rightarrow RSO_2CH_2CH_2OH + RSO_2Na$$

All sulphones in which sulphone groups are attached to adjacent carbon atoms can be saponified, Ethylenediethyl sulphone is an example of such a compound :

$$\begin{array}{l} CH_2-SO_2-C_2H_5 \\ | \\ CH_2-SO_2-C_2H_5 \end{array}$$

sub-. Under, below. Denoting (*i*) a low, or the lowest, proportion, as subiodide, suboxide ; (*ii*) any of certain "basic salts," as aluminium subacetate.

subatomic. Pertaining to processes or reactions in which atoms undergo disintegration, as in natural or artificial radioactivity ; or to particles or radiations yielded by such reactions, such as electrons, positrons, protons, neutrons, helium nuclei, and nuclear fragments of larger size.

subexcitation electrons. Final generations of secondary electrons having energies lower than minimum energy of electron excitations in a given system.

sub-group. Part of group of periodic system composed of transition element. Also known as odd series; B family.

sublimate. The condensed vapour from the process of sublimation, analogous to the distillate from distillation.

sublimation. The direct transition, under suitable conditions between the vapour and the solid state of a substance. If solid iodine is placed in a tube and slightly warmed, it vapourizes and the vapour re-forms into crystals on the cooler parts of the tube. Many craystalline substances, both metallic and non-metallic, may be similarly sublimated in a vacuum ; fairly large crystals of selenium have been thus prepared. The most familiar sublimates are frost and snow. As in the case of other changes of state, sublimation is accompanied by the absorption or evolution of heat, the quantity of which per unit mass is called the heat of sublimation of the substance. At pressures near the triple point the heat of sublimation is approximately equal to the sum of the heats of fusion and vaporization. In physical and chemical literature, it is customary to regard as sublimation only the transition from solid to vapour, not from vapour to solid ; but meterologists do not make this distinction.

Sublimation plays a major role in the freeze drying of foods.

sublimation temperature. Temperature at which substance is converted from solid into gaseous state without attaining the liquid state.

submicron. In Zsigmondy's nomenclature, submicrons are particles between 5×10^{-9} and 10^{-7} metres in diameter,

subsesqui-. A prefix indicating combination in the proportion of two to three, particularly where the acidic radical is in the proportion of two. In "sesqui" compounds the acidic radical is in the proportion of three to two of base.

subsidiary reaction. A special type of simultaneous reaction in which a transformation of one of the reaction products concomitantly with, and dependently on, the main reaction which, in turn, is dependent upon this subsidiary reaction, *e.g.*, if the reaction :

$$HBrO_3 + 6HI \rightarrow HBr + 3H_2O + 3I_2$$

is written in its ionic form,

$$6H^+ + BrO_3^- + 6I^- \rightarrow Br^- + 3H_2O + 3I_2$$

it may be dissected into two processes,

$$6H^+ + BrO_3^- + 6e^- \rightarrow Br^- + 3H_2O$$

and

$$6I^- \rightarrow 3I_2 + 6e^-,$$

in which the second of the two ionic reactiens is the subsidiary one, since it furnishes the six electrons necessary to neutralize the hydrogen atoms in the main reaction. Although this breakdown of the reaction explains, in certain cases, some of the kinetic factors, there is far from complete evidence that it represents the actual mechanism.

substance. Any unit of matter at or above the atomic level that is of identical composition throughout (homogeneous) and that cannot be separated by mechanical means. Thus, all chemical elements and compounds are substances, whereas solutions, dispersions, alloys, and composite materials are mixture. For example, carbon, water and alcohol are substances ; milk and petroleum are mixtures.

substantive dye. A dyestuff which yields colours directly to the fibre without the use of a mordant.

substituent. Any chemical entity that takes the place of another during the course of a replacement reaction (also called a substitution reaction), for example, where the hydrogen of an acid is replaced by a metal. The substituents may be atoms, ions, groups, or radicals.

substitution. Replacement of atom (or group of atoms) in molecule by another atom (or group of atoms). The following types of substitution are distinguished in organic chemistry ; nucleophilic S_N, electrophilic S_E and free radical S_R, depending on mechanism of particular reaction.

substitutional solid solution. Solid solution in which atoms or ions of dissolved substance substitute atoms or ions in matrix substance ; crystallographic conditions are defined by Grimm's law.

substoichiometric isotope dilution. Isotope dilution in which for separation of the constituent to be determined a substoichiometric quantity of reagent is used.

substoichiometric separation. Separation of component in sample by means of reagent added in a quantity smaller than the stoichiometric one.

substrate. 1. A term used by biochemists to denote any organic compound that ts acted upon by an enzyme, *e.g.*, a protein, carbohydrate, fat, or sugar. The name of the enzyme itself is usually formed by adding the suffix ase to the name of the activated substance ; for example, protease, lipase, etc., though there are some exceptions.

2. The term is also loosely used in the pigment and coatings fields to refer to the material being electroplated, painted, etc.

subtractional solid solution. Solid solution with excess of one of constituents, due to fact that some nodes in lattice are left unoccupied by second constituent.

Suchier reagent. A mixture of equal volumes of a 20% alcoholic solution of diphenylamine and 20% alcoholic solution of *p*-dimethyl-*p*-aminobenzaldehyde, which is used to impregnate paper for testing for phosgene. A brown colour is obtained if phosgene is present.

sucroclastic enzyme. An enzyme that catalyzes the splitting of a sugar into simpler sugar molecules. Also known as glycolytic enzyme.

sucrose. A disaccharide sugar whose molecule is formed of two glucose units ; it contains two alcohol groups ($-CH_2OH$) and six additional hydroxyl groups, the formula being $C_{12}H_{22}O_{11}$. It has a strong positive optical rotation.

sugar. The simplest of the broad carbohydrate, series of compounds formed from carbon dioxide and water by the photosynthetic activity of (*i*) The simple sugars are called monosaccharides, as they contain but one characteristic molecular unit having six carbon atoms (hexose sugars). (*ii*) More complex types (oligosaccharides) have from two to ten such units. (*iii*) There are also high-polymer sugars called polysaccharides which occur in natural gums, pectins, seaweeds, as weel as in starch and cellulose. Glucose (dextrose) is a typical monosaccharide :

```
     CH=O
      |
   H—C—OH
      |
  HO—C—H
      |
   H—C—OH
      |
   H—C—OH
      |
     CH₂OH
```

a simple sugar
(monosaccharide)

it is found in corn and grapes, and sucrose (table sugar) is a disaccharide obtained from beets and sugarcane. These compounds are characterized by optical activity, that is, their molecules rotate plane-polarized light either to the right (dextrose) or to the left (levulose). Invert sugars are slightly levorotatory mixture of dextrose and levulose cbtained by hydrolysis of sucrose. Ethyl alcohol is readily formed from sugars in fermentation reactions catalyzed by enzymes. Sugar also occurs in milk (lactose) and in blood (glucose).

Suida test reaction. A test for aspartic acid. Basic dyes, such as crystal violet, Nile blue, and safranine precipitate the hydrochloride of acid from an aqueous solution.

Suitsu-Okuma test reaction. A test for magnesium made by alkalinizing the solution to be tested with sodium hydroxide and adding a few drops of a 0.5% solution of *o*-dihydroxyazo-*p*-nitrobenzene (Magneson) in 1% sodium hydroxide solution. A sky-blue lake forms if magnesium is present.

sulphamic acid. An organic sulphur acid of the general formula :

```
R  O
|  ||
N—S—OH
|  ||
R′ O
```

sulphamide. A sulphone-containing derivative of one of the secondary amines, *e.g.*, tetramethylsulphamide,

$$(CH_3)_2N—SO_2—N(CH_3)_2$$

sulphamine. A compound of the general formula $R—S(=O)_2—NH_2$, where R is an organic group.

sulphamino. The radical $HO_3SHN—$.

sulphamyl. The radical $H_2NO_2S—$.

sulphanilamido. The radical

$$p\text{-}H_2NC_6H_4SO_2NH—$$

(from sulphanilamide).

sulphate process. A procedure for obtaining strong wood pulp by treating wood with a solution of sulphide, containing some sulphate and carbonate. The cooking liquid used is alkalized with sodium hydroxide and the pulp is intentionally undercooled to make it stronger. The woods used in the process are long-fibered pine woods. The pulp made by the sulphate process is called kraft pulp.

sulphazide. A sulphone derivative of a hydrazo compound of the general formula R.NH.NH.SO_2.R′, *e.g.*, phenylbenzenesulphazide, $C_6H_5NH.OH.SO_2.C_6H_5$.

sulphenic. The radical —SOH.

sulphimide radical. A sulphate radical, in which one of the hydroxy groups of sulphuric acid has been replaced by an imino group :

```
   O
   ||
 —S—NH—
   ||
   O
```

sulpho. The radical $HO_3S—$ in organic compounds.

sulphonate. A derivative of sulphuric acid ; or a compound containing a sulphonic acid group, commonly an ester of general formula :

$$R{-}\overset{\overset{\displaystyle O}{\|}}{\underset{\underset{\displaystyle O}{\|}}{S}}{-}OH$$

or the action of conducting a sulphonation reaction.

sulphonation. Substitution of hydrogen atom in organic compound molecule by sulphonic group $-SO_3H$, effected by sulphuric acid or sulphur trioxide, *e.g.*,

$$C_6H_6 + HO{-}SO_2H \xrightarrow{SO_3} C_6H_5{-}SO_3H + H_2O$$

The resulting compounds are called sulphonic acids (*e.g.*, benzene-sulphonic acid) and are formed by reaction with sulphuric acid. Since the inclusion of this group provides water-solubility, compounds containing it in combination with amines and various benzene derivatives are widely used as dyes and dye intermediates.

sulphone. An organic sulphur derivative of the type $R-SO_2-R'$.

sulphonic. The radical $-S(=O)_2OH$.

sulphonic acid. A member of an important class of organic acids characterized by the presence of the group :

$$R{-}\overset{\overset{\displaystyle O}{\|}}{S}{=}O \atop \quad | \atop \quad OH$$

the "sulphonic acid" group. Sulphonic acids are formed by digesting certain hydrocarbons or other compounds with either concentrated or fuming sulphuric acid, and they react as acids. They are usually very soluble in water and alcohol and only slight soluble in ether and nonoxygenated solvents.

sulphonyl. The radical $-SO_2-$ in organic compounds.

sulphoxide. A sulphur analogue of a ketone, *e.g.*, dimethyl sulphoxide $(CH_3)_2S=O$.

sulphoylate. The anion SO_2^{2-}, or a compound containing it.

sulphur. An element.

		Symbol	S
		Atomic No.	16
		Atomic Wt.	32.06
State	Solid	Valence	2,4 6
Group	VIA	Isotopes	4 stable
		m.p.	385.9K (rhom.)
			392K (mono)
			393K (ampor.)

Sulphur is a yellow solid which occurs in elemental form. Its low melting point permits extraction in liquid form by pumping superheated water into the limestone deposit (*see* Frasch process). It is also extracted from certain iron ores (pyrites) and from gypsum, as well as from smelting wastes and petroleum fractions, *e.g.*, fuel oil.

Both rhombic and monoclinic forms contain S_8 molecules, when melted, produce the same liquid, which is also compose of S_8 molecules. As the temperature of the liquid is raised S_8 rings are broken into chain by the thermal collisions.

The stable isotopes of sulphur are ^{32}S, ^{33}S, ^{34}S and ^{36}S. There are three known radioactive isotopes ^{31}S, ^{35}S, and ^{37}S, with ^{35}S having the longest half-life ($t_{1/2}$=87 1 days). *See* Radioactivity. Electronic configuration is $1s^22s^22p^63s^23p^4$. Ionic radius, S^{2-}, 1.855 Å, S^{6+}, 0.29 Å (Pauling). Covalent radius, 1.07 Å. In terms of abundance, sulphur ranks fourteenth among the element occurring in the earth's crust, with an estimated 520 grams per metric ton. In seawater, the element ranks fifth, with an estimated 894 gram per metric ton.

First ionizatton potential 10.357 eV ; second, 23 3 eV ; third, 34.9 eV ; fourth, 47 08 eV fifth, 63.0 eV, sixth 87.67 eV Oxidation potentials $H_2S(aq) \rightarrow S + 2H^+ + 2e^-$, -0.141 V ; $H_2SO_3 + H_2O \rightarrow SO_4^{2-} + 4H^+ + 2e^-$, -0.20 V ; $S + 3H_2O \rightarrow H_2SO_3 + 4H^+ + 4e^-$, -0.45 V ; $SO_3^{2-} + 2OH^- \rightarrow SO_4^{2-} + H_2O + 2e^-$, 0.90 V; $S^{2-} \rightarrow S + 2e^-$, 0.508 V ; $HS^- + OH^- \rightarrow S + 2e^-$, 0.478 V.

The liquid abruptly increases in viscosity at 433K and acquires unique viscoelastic properties.

Sulphur has chemical properties similar to those of oxygen ; it reacts strongly with alkali and alkaline-earth metals, as well as with bromine and chlorine.

Sulphur has a large number of allotropes.

The ordinary form, α-sulphur, is rhombic having a crystal unit cell composed of sixteen S_8 molecules. At 368.5K it undergoes transition to β-sulphur, which is monoclinc and also has a molecular weight (in solution in carbon disulphide) corresponding to S_8. Four other monoclinic forms have been identified microscopic ; γ-sulphur, prepared by heating α-sulphur to 423K, cooling to 363K, and inducing crystallization by friction, ρ-sulphur, S_6, prepared by extracting an acidulated sodium thioslphate solution with toluene, as well as ν-sulphur, and δ-sulphur. There is also a tetrahedral form, θ-sulphur, crystallyized from a carbon disulphide solution of rhombic sulphur treated with balsam. The first liquid form to appear is λ-sulphur, a pale yellow liquid, obtained on heating sulphur to 393K. Above 433K, this form changes to a viscous, dark brown liquid consisting mainly of μ-sulphur. A third liquid allotrope, π-sulphur is considered to exisit a molten sulphur, in equilibrium with the other forms, having its greatest concentration at about 453K. Sulphur vapour has been show to contain S_8, S_6, S_4, and S_2 molecules. Several other allotropes of sulphur have been produced including two paramagnetic forms, purple and green in colour, by low temperature processing. Its major uses are in the manufacture of useful chemicals, *e.g.*, sulphuric acid, vulcanization of rubber, processing of paper pulp, certain dayes animal repllents, and insecticides. Sulphur is a constituent of most proteins. It may be safely ingested and is an ingredient of curative tonics: it also occurs in certain spring waters.

sulphur group. Elements of sixth main group of periodic system, except for oxygen (sulphur, selenium, tellurium, polonium).

Term previously used to denote present oxygen family.

sulphuric. 1. Containing hexavalent sulphur.

2. Related to sulphuric acid, H_2SO_4 or $(HO)_2SO_2$.

3. Related to a number of acids of the type formula $H_xS_yO_z$, such as persulphuric acid, metasulphuric acid, etc., which are listed under the corresponding adjectives.

sulpurization. Introduction of sulphur into the molecule of a chemical compound.

sum peak. Peak and gamma radiation spectrum formed as a result of simultaneous photoelectric absorption of two γ-photons of different energies.

super-. Above, over. Denoting a high, or the highest, proportion ; as superoxide (peroxide) (now little used).

superalloy. A term used by mettallurgists to designate a group of refractory alloys which resist heat-deterioration up to 1650K. The basic component metals are iron, cobalt, and nickel, together with small proportions of molybdenum, chromium, or tungsten.

superconductivity. Disappearence of electric resistance below certain temperature (usually in range 15—0.4K). At the same time material becomes perfectly diamagnetic. Recently, materials showing superconductivity upto 200K have been developed.

Superconductivity does not occur in alkali metals, noble metals, ferro- and antiferromagnetic metals. It is well-known in elements having 3, 5 or 7 valence electrons per atom, and is associated with high room-temperature resistivitry. A system for transmitting electric current underground by means of superconducting cables has been developed. Superconduction is being used in advanced computer research ; it is expected to make an improvement in response time comparable to that obtained when vacuum tubes were replaced by semiconductors.

suporconductivity model. Model of atomic nucleus which takes into account residual interaction between nucleons. This interaction causes association of protons and neutrons into pairs of zero-spin and gives rise to effects similar to the superconductivity which occurs in conductor due to strong correlation of electron pairs. Also known as superfluid model; pairing correlations model.

supercooling. The cooling of a liquid below its freezing point without the separation of the solid phase. This is a condition of metastable equilibrium, as is shown by solidification of the supercooled liquid upon the addition of the solid phase, or the application of certain stresses, or simply upon prolonged standing.

superexchange. In magnetochemistry, mechanism of strong indirect exchange interactions between paramagnetic ions through diamagnetic ion positioned between them (*e.g.*, oxide ion). Exhibited by magnetically ordered crystals (ferro-, antiferro- and ferrimagnetic).

superexcited molecule. Molecule with about 10 eV excess energy, sufficient usually for scission to free radicals and for reactions with zero activation energy.

superfludity. Property of helium II to flow through narrow capillary tubes without friction.

superheated liquid. Fluid in metastable state, heated at constant pressure to temperature higher than boiling temperature or subjected isothermally to pressure lower than pressure of saturated vapour. Disturbance of this metastable state causes violent change of liquid into gaseous phase.

superheated vapour. Vapour of pressure which is lower than pressure of saturated vapour at the same temperature.

superlattice. A type of arrangement of atoms in a multicomponent solid system, in which the atoms of an element occupy certain regular positions in the atomic lattice of another element, even though no compound between the two elements of that composition can be separated or otherwise identified.

supernatant liquor. The liquid standing above a precipitate or sediment.

superoxide. The anion O_2^- or a compound containing it.

superparamagnetism. Quasi-paramagnetism displayed by highly disintegrated ferromagnets (particle volume of 10^{-18} cm^3 or lower).

superphosphate. A mixture of compounds obtained as a result of a long established process for the production of chemical fertilizers is the treatment of phosphate rock with concentrated sulphuric acid. The product of this reaction, as practiced in industry, is a mixture of calcium sulphates and calcium phosphates containing more or less of the acid salts, which is called superphosphate. Derivatively this term is also applied to an acid phosphate.

superposition principle. *See* principle of superposition.

supersaturated solution. Solution in which concentration of dissolved constituent is higher than concentration of saturated solution in the same conditions. Supersaturated solution is metastable system.

supersaturated vapour. Vapour in unstable state, isobarically cooled below boiling point, or compressed isothermally to pressure larger than pressure of saturated vapour ; supersaturation disappears in presence of condensation seeds and vapour transforms into saturated state.

supersaturation. A condition in which a solute is present in a solution beyond its limit of solubility.

supplied entropy. Part of entropy increase which (*i*) is due to exchange of heat and mass with surroundings, and (*ii*) changes sign if direction of exchange is reversed. Also known as exchanged entropy.

supporting electrode. In spark and arc spectroscopy electrode prepared of material different from that of sample ; sample is then placed on/in this electrode.

supporting electrolyte. In polarography or other electrochemical techniques, electrolyte introduced to examined solution in large concentration in order to increase its conductivity ; ions of supporting electrolyte should not react with electrode over large potential range.

suppressor mutation. A mutation that totally or partially restores a function lost by a primary mutation ; located at a site in the gene different from the site of primary mutation.

surface. As used in physical chemistry, this term refers to a type of interface, or area of contact, that exists between two different phase of matter. Examples are the surfaces between (*i*) finely divided solid particles and air (solid-gas) ; (*ii*) liquids and air (liquid-gas or gas-liquid) ; (*iii*) insoluble particles and a liquid (solid-liquid). Such surfaces are sites of physicochemical activity between the phases, which is responsible for such phenomena as adsorption, evaporation, surface tension, reactivity, and catalysis,

surface-active agent. This term and its condensed synonym surfactant conventionally refer to substances that reduce the interfacial or surface tension of liquids ; it could logically be applied to catalysts also, since their action depends directly on surface activity. The terms detergent, wetting agent, and emulsifier are also used, with only a slight difference in meaning. Detergents aid in cleaning by lowering the surface tension of water, thus enabling the water to form emulsions with fatty and oily materials ; acids, long-chain alcohols and various synthetic products (dodecylbenzene) have this property, and hence they are called emulsifiers. Reduction of surface tension is also the function of wetting agents, permitting water to cover particles of dry powders and other finely divided materials more effectively than would otherwise be possible. *See also* emulsion ; detergent ; wet ; surface tension.

surface-active film. Thin layer of insoluble (or very slightly soluble) substance at surface of liquid which changes its surface tension.

surface activity. Ability of some solutes to accumulate on (or near) solvent surface, thus lowering its surface tension.

surface area. The total area of exposed surface of a solid material, usually in the form of a powder, including all irregularities, pores, etc. Since activity is greatest at the surface, that is the interface between the particle and its environment, the larger the surface area of a given substance, the more reactive it becomes. Thus reduction to small particles is a means of increasing the efficiency of both chemical and physical reactions ; for example, twigs and wood fragments ignite more easily than large slabs, and potatoes cook faster when cut into small pieces. The coloring effect of pigments is increased by size reduction. Carbon black is notable among solid for its huge surface area the activity of its surface accounts for its outstanding ability to increase the strength and abrasion resistance of rubber. The ability of activated carbon to adsorb molecules of gases is due to this factor. Surface area is measured most accurately by nitrogen adsorption techniques. *See also* particle.

surface compounds theory. Theory of heterogeneous catalysis, explaining mechanism of catalysis by formation of intermediate, unstable compounds of substrates with atoms or ions present in surface layers of catalyst.

surface diffusion. Diffusion occurring in two-dimensional layer of adsorbate along surface of adsorbent.

surface film. A film of an insoluble substance, on the surface of a liquid, and consisting of a monolayer of closely packed molecules, at or near the point at which further compression of the film causes the formation of additional layers. Also known as condensed surface film.

surface phenomena. Group of all physicochemical phenomena observed at interfaces between different phases.

surface potential, x. Difference of electrical potentials between point inside phase and point separated 10^{-6} m from phase surface. Also known as surface electric potential difference.

surface tension, σ. Free surface energy required to develop defined unit of free surface area. It is expressed as the work required to increase the surface area by one unit and is usually expressed as newton per metre (N/m). Values for surface tension are usually measured at a liquid-gas interface, commonly air, and vary with the composition of the liquid and the solutes in it. Mercury has the highest surface tension of any liquid at ordinary temperatures. Polar liquids, of which water is typical, have pronounced surface tension, which limits thier ability to "wet" solids and to blend with dissimilar liquids. This accounts for the formation of water droplets and the ability of a water surface to sustain the weight of a razor blade.

suspended transformation. The cessation of action before true equilibrium has been reached, or the failure of a system to readjust itself immediately when conditions are changed. Metastable equilibrium, supercooling, etc., are examples.

suspension. Disperse system in which particles of solid dispersed phase have dimensions greater than 500 nm.

suspensoid. Historical term denoting an irreversible lyophobic sol. Do not confuse with suspension, *i.e.*, mechanical suspension.

Sutherland constant. A constant in an equation for the variation of the viscosity of a gas with temperature, of the form :

$$\eta = \eta_0 \frac{\sqrt{T}}{1 + C/T}$$

where η = the viscosity, η_0 = a constant for the particular gas, T=the absolute temperature, and C=Sutherland constant.

Sutherland equation. A relationship between the mean free path of a molecule and the molecular diameter. This relationship is expressed in the following equation :

$$d \propto \frac{1}{n\, l\sqrt{1+C/T}}$$

where d = the molecular diameter, n = the number of molecules per unit volume, l = the mean free path, T = the absolute temperature and C=Sutherland constant.

Svanberg-Struve test reaction. A test for phosphate, performed by adding strong nitric acid solutions of ammonium molybdate to phosphoric acid or its salts. A yellow precipitate of ammonium phosphomolybdate forms. This is soluble in ammonia and other alkalies and form more rapidly on warming. Several modifications of this reactions have been developed.

Svedberg. A unit of measure of the rate at which a particle sediments in a centrifugal field.

Swain equation. An equation correlating the rate coefficients of nucleophilic reactions on saturated carbon atoms assuming simultaneous nucleophilic and electrophilic attacks :

$$\log (k/k_0) = sn + s'e$$

where k=rate coefficient of the reaction, n= nucleophilicity of the reagent, e=electrophilicity of the simultaneously attacking agent, s and s' =sensitivity of the reaction to nucleophilic and electrophilic attack respectively, and k_0= rate coefficient of reference reaction which is chosen so that for it both n and e equal zero.

Swarts reaction. A method of particl replacement by fluorine of other halogens in polyhalo compounds by the action of certain metallic fluorides.

$$Cl_2C{=}CCl.CHCl_2 + SbF_3 \xrightarrow[\text{(Trace)}]{SbCl_5} ClCH{=}CClCF_3 + SbCl_3$$

swelling. Process of binding liquid or gas by gel or solid accompanied by increase in volume (shape of material that swells does not change in principle.

symbiosis. A condition in which the simultaneous presence of two organic species in the same environment favours the development of both species, as the symbiosis of leguminous plants and nitrifying bacteria. The microorganisms which are found in symbiosis are termed symbions.

symmetric top molecule. Molecule, all principal momenta of inertia of which are finite and two of them are different, *e.g.*, CH_3Cl.

symmetry. 1. Invariance of physical systems or interactions with respect to a certain transformation (leads usually to cooresponding conservation law).

2. Attribute of physical object (*e.g.*, geometrical structure) consisting in equivalency *i.e.*, indistinguishability of its properties in defined directions. These direction are called equiponderant with respect to symmetry of considered property.

It is described in terms of three parameters called elements of symmetry, namely ; (*i*) The centre of symmetry, around which the constituent atoms are located in an ordered arrangement ; there is only one such centre in a molecule, which may or may not be an atom. (*ii*) Planes of symmetry, which represent division of a molecule into mirrorimage segments. (*iii*) Axes of symmetry, represented by lines passing through the center of symmetry ; if the molecule is rotated it will have the same position in space more than once in a complete 360° turn *e.g.*, the benzene molecule, with six axes of symmetry, requires a 60° rotation to return to its identical position. *See also* stereochemistry ; asymmetry.

symmetry class. Population of objects (both physical like crystals and abstracts. *e.g.*, vectors functions etc.) undergoing identical transformation into self-coincidence with respect to all symmetry elements belonging to the same point group.

Symbol of this point group is used to denote symmetry class, sometimes leading to confusion of class of objects with group of optrations which may be performed on these objects.

symmetry element. Operator which transforms defined mathematical or physical objects into repetition of itself. Basic symmetry elements are : centre of symmetry, rotation axis and symmetry plane.

symmetry number (of molecule). Number of identical molecular configurations obtained by rotation of molecule wite identical nuclei.

symmetry operations. Displacement of geometric objects bringing them to self-coincidence. Principal symmetry operations for finite objects are : revolution around *n* fold axis by $360/n^{\circ}$ angle where *n* is a natural number, reflection at point ; for infinite objects (space lattices) ; translations and their combinations with revolutions where number of axes is limited ; $n=$ 2, 3, 4 and 6.

syn-anti isomerism. Obsolete term formerly denoting cis-trans isomerism in compounds containing C=N or —N=N— groups, *e.g.*,

```
 ϕ                 ϕ   OH
 |   ..            |   |
 C = C             C = N
 |   |             |   ..
 H   OH            H
```

syn-benzaldehyde   anti-benzaldehyde

synartetic acceleration. The acceleration of the reaction rate in Wagner-Meerwein rearrangements in which the migration of, *e.g.*, an alkyl group R occurs synchronously with the ionization of a C—X bond ;

```
   R              R
   |             / \
 —C—C—X   →   —C — C...X   →
   |            |    |

                   R
                +  |
              —C—C— + X⁻
               |  |
```

Here the migration of R assists and accelerates the rate of ionization of the C—X group.

syndiotactic. A type of stereospecific polymer whose molecules are comprised of atoms (hydrogen) and organic groups (R) arranged in a specific and predetermined sequence above and below a chain of carbon atoms. The molecule of a syndiotactic polymer might have the arrangement RHHHRHHH above the carbon chain and HHRHHHRH below it, as indicated :

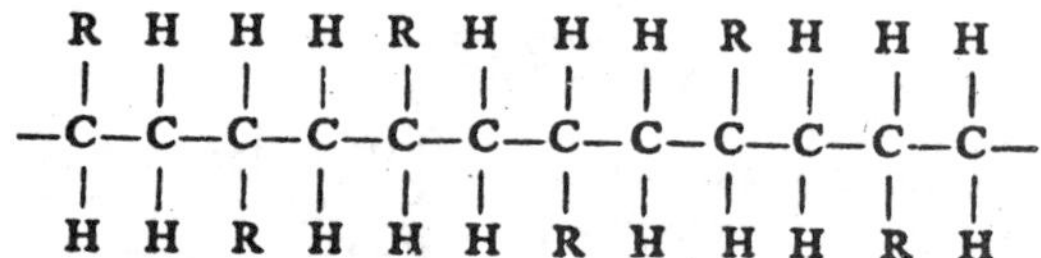

Such polymers can be obtained by use of Ziegler and Natta catalysts.

syneresis. Separation of water or other suspending liquid from a uniformly dispersed colloidal gel, with resulting contraction of the gel. This action is probably caused by a decrease in the capacity of the protein portion of the gel to bind water, induced by change in *p*H, temperature, surface tension, etc. Examples of syneresis are the formation of whey in cheese-making and the watery exudation from injured tissue. The separated aqueous liquid is actually a solution.

synergism. A phenomenon often encountered in chemistry in which one or more properties of a mixture are affected to a far greater extent than would be indicated by adding the values for the components taken individually. For example, the toxicity to house flies of a mixture of pyrethrum and kerosine is increased by a factor of 10 by the presence of a low percentage of sesame oil, though the latter alone has no effect.

synergistic coagulation. Coagulation of sol by mixture of electrolytes, when presence of one coagulant makes sol sensitivity to action of another coagulant ; hence sumconcentration of electrolytes required for coagulation is considerably lower than would seem necessary from additive action.

synfuel. Any fuel, either liquid or gaseous, made by chemical treatment of coal, naphtha, shale oil, or agricultural wastes.

synthesis. The combination of elements or compounds to produce compounds of one kind, *e.g.*, $H_2+Cl_2 \rightarrow 2HCl$ is a synthesis or synthetic reaction. In organic chemistry the term synthesis was originally applied to the process of preparing a compound from its elements or from other compounds which can be synthesized from their elements, nothing being used that is a product of a living organism.

synthesis gas. A blend of hydrogen and carbon monoxide in varying proportions obtained from coke, natural gas, or other carbonaceous materials, usually by reaction with steam in the presence of air. It contains a law percentage of nitrogen. It is used for a number of important synthesis operations, including production of ammonia, methanol, and a wide ranged of organic compounds.

synthetic chemistry. That branch of chemistry which is concerned with the the preparation or production of relatively complex substances from simpler ones.

synthetic natural gas. Any manufactured fuel gas of approximately the same composition and heating value as gas obtained directly from oil fields. It contains about 85% methane and 15% ethane. It is derived from such carbon-rich material as coal ; naphtha, and agricultural wastes.

system. 1. A specified region, or portion of of matter, containing a definite amount of a substance or substances, arranged in one or more phases.

2. A plan of arrangement of terms or entities especially those composing a larger aggregate.

Szebelledy-Jonas test. A test for molybdate performed by adding tincture of cochineal to the acid solution. A fire-red fluorescence indicates the presence of molybdate.

Szebelledy-Tanay test. A test for zinc performed by mixing on a spot plate, 6 drops of freshly prepared 2% potassium ferricyanide solution with 2 drops of N sulphuric acid and 12 drops of 1% phenetidine hydrochloride solution. To another cavity on the spot plate, transfer 0.1 ml. of the mixture and add carefully about 0.01 precipitate or colour is formed at the zone of contact if zinc is present.

Szent-Gyorgyi test. A test for ascorbic acid, performed by mixing a slightly alkaline 1% solution of ascorbic acid with some ferrous sulphate solution. It is allow to stand while exposed to the air. A dark violet colour develops rapidly if ascorbic acid is present.

Szilard-Chalmers effect. Rupture of chemical bond between recoiling atom and molecule in which it was incorporated due to nuclear transformation or reaction.

Szyszkowski's equation. Equation giving dependence of surface tension σ of aqueous solution of surface-active substance (surfactant) on its concentiation *c*, *viz.*,

$$\sigma_0 - \sigma = a \log (1+bc)$$

where σ_0=surface tension of water, *a*, *b*=constants characteristic of a given surfactant ; equation is true for solutions of substance which do not form micelles.

T

T. Symbol for tritium, *i.e.*, H^3. Abbreviation for absolute temperature. Symbol for transport number.

tacticity. A term used denote various arrangements or sequences of atoms in the molecules of high polymers. Those in which the sequence of substituent atoms on both sides of the carbon chain is random are called atactic and the polymers are amorphous. Advances in the art of controlled catalysis have made it possible to synthesize crystalline polymeric structures in which the arrangement of substituents is predetermined ; these are called stereospecific polymers, which may be isotactic or syndiotactic.

tactic polymer. Regular polymer in whose macromolecules, there is an ordered structure with respect to configurations around at least one main-chain site of stereoisomerism per constitutional base unit.

Tafel reaction for anilides. The substance to be tested is dissolved in concentrated sulphuric acid and some potassium dichromate is added to it. Acetanilide produces a red-violet colour ; benzanilide, violet ; and propionanilide, blood-red.

Tafel rearrangement. A rearrangement of substituted acetoacetic esters during electrolytic reduction to hydrocarbons in alcoholic sulphuric acid solution at a lead cathode. Some unrearranged hydrocarbon is also formed, *e.g.*,

$$\underset{\text{R.CO.CH.COOR}}{\overset{CH_2.CH_2.CH_3}{|}} \;\Big\rangle\; \begin{cases} R.CH_2.CH_2.CH_2.CH_2.CH_2.CH_3 \\ \underset{R.CH_2.CH.CH_3}{\overset{CH_2.CH_2.CH_3}{|}} \end{cases}$$

Taft equation. An equation correlating the rate coefficients in various esterification and hydrolysis reactions :

$$\log (k/k_0) = fA$$

where, k_0 = rate coefficient of a standard reaction, k = rate coefficient of a similar reaction under identical conditions, f = a constant depending on the nature of the reaction, and A=constant depending on the nature of the substituents.

tagged atom. *See* tracer element.

Tagliavini test. A test for tartaric acid in which the solution of free acid is heated with minimum (Pb_3O_4) and filtered, a little potassium thiocyanate is added to the filtrate and boiled. There is an evolution of hydrogen sulphide. The appearance of a black colour (due to lead sulphide) shows the presence of tartaric acid in the solution tested.

tailing. In chromatography asymmetric spreading of rear edge of chromatographic band during development.

Tamm test. A test for copper made by adding sodium bisulphide solution and potassium thiocyanate solution to a cupric salt solution. A white precipitate of cuprous thiocyanate is produced.

Tananaev-Dolgov tests for gold, palladium, and platinum. 1. *Gold :* A drop of the solution to be tested is placed on a strip of filter paper and a drop of a solution of benzidine in acetic acid is added. A blue or green colour indicates the presence of gold.

2. *Palladium :* A filter paper is moistened with a drop of saturated thallium nitrate solution and gold chloride solution added, followed by the solution to be tested. The spot darknes if palladium is present.

3 *Platinum :* A drop of thallium nitrate is placed on a filter paper, followed wi'h a drop of the solution to be tested, and another drop of thallium nitrate. Any free acid is neturalized with a drop of dilute ammonia applied to the center of the spot. Then stannous chloride is added. An orange or yellow colour indicates the presence of platinum.

Tananaev-Panchenko tests for titanium and uranium. A drop of titanium sulphate solution is placed on a filter paper and a drop of chromotropic acid added to the same spot. An intense brown colour is obtained. Addition of stannous chloride weakens the colour slightly by preventing interference by ferric iron or uranyl ions. To test for uranyl ions, the brown colour formed with potassium ferrocyanide is a suitable test.

Tananaev test for tin. A drop of the solution to be tested is placed on a strip of filter paper which has been moistened with mercuric chloride solution and dried. A drop of aniline is added. A dark strin indicates the presence of tin must be reduced with magnesium in acid solution before the test is made.

Tananaev test for mercury. A drop of stannous chloride solution is placed on a strip of filter paper and a drop of the solution to be tested and a drop of aniline added. Mercury produces a dark stain.

Tantar-Petroff test for thallium. A test for thallium in slightly acid solution, for which sodium cobaltinitrite serves as a very sensitive reagent. A red, crystalline precipitate is formed which is insoluble in hot water or in cold dilute acid. The precipitate dissolves with evolution of oxides of nitrogen, on boiling with acids. The thallium and cobalt pass into solution.

tankage. A by-product of the meatpacking industry made by boiling slaughterhouse scrap. It contains substantial percentages of ammonia and phosphates extracted from the bones, as well as fats and proteins ; used as fertilizer components.

tannin. One of a group of naturally occurring carbon compounds characterized by the following properties ; the are amorphous and astringent ; they precipitate gelatin from solution, convert hide into leather, precipitate many alkaloids and glycosides from solution, form insoluble compounds with lead and copper, react with ferric salts to produce deep blue or green colours. In alkaline solution they absorb oxygen, and produce a deep red colour with ammonia and aqueous potassium ferricyanide. The chemistry of the tannins is not fully understood, but some of them appear to be glycosides.

tanning. Conversion of the soft, perishable proteins of the skin or hide to a durable but flexible material (leather) by treatment with chemical compounds ; also called curing. There are two major types of tanning ; (*i*) vegetable tanning, in which the active agent is tannic acid derived from the bark of certain rare trees (quebracho and wattle), which functions as a cross-linking agent for the skin proteins ; (*ii*) chrome tanning, in which salts of various metals act as complexing agents, *e.g.*, chromium, aluminium, and zirconium ; hydrogen bonding is also inolved in the conversion.

Tanret reagent for albumin. A solution which gives a white precipitate with albumin and some alkaloids. It is prepared by mixing a solution of 3.3 g. pottasium iodide in 25 ml. water of 1.35 of mercuric chloride in 25 ml. water, adding 20 ml. of glacial acetic acid, and the volume of the solution reaches 60 ml.

Tanret reagent for alkaloids. A reagent which precipitates alkaloids from acidified solution. It is an aqueous solution of 13.55 g. mercuric chloride and 50 g. potassium iodide, made up to one liter.

tantalum. An element.

		Symbol	Ta
		Atomic No.	73
State	Solid	Atomic Wt.	180.948
Group	VB	Valence	V
		m.p.	3269K
		b.p.	5700K

A metal, which forms compounds with most other elements; its most common oxidation state is 5, though it has lower oxidation states which are unstable, *i.e.*, 3 and 2. Elemental tantalum has a body-centered cubic crystal structure. Because of its high m.p., it is considered a refractory metal.

There is one naturally occurring stable isotope. ^{181}Ta. Isotope ^{180}Ta also occurs naturally (isotopic abundance of 0.012%), with a half-life of something greater than 10^7 years. At least nine other radioctive isotopes have been identified, ^{176}Ta through ^{179}Ta, and ^{182}Ta through ^{186}Ta. With exception of ^{179}Ta ($t_{1/2}$=abont 600 days), the remaining half-lives are expressed in minutes, hours, or days. Isotope ^{182}Ta has been used as a source of gamma rays.

It forms complexes with both organic and inorganic substances. It is not readily attacked by chemicals and forms an oxide film on its surface which increases its electrical resistivity.

Tantalum is used widely, although in small quantities, in the electronics industry for electrolytic capacitors, emitters, and getters. The corrosion resistance of tantalum has been compared with that of glass.

target. Substance or subject exposed to action of nuclear radiation or bombarded with accelerated ions or elemantary particles. During these processes specific nuclear reactions occur in the target.

tarnish. A gray-to-black film of sulphide formed on surfaces of silver and gold when exposed over a period of time to sulphur or its compounds. Most tarnishing is due to sulphur dioxide in the air or to sulphur compounds in eggs or other food products in contact with silverware. It does no permanent damage and can be effectively removed with prepared cleaners. A transparent water-insoluble film is sometimes applied to reduce susceptibility to tarnish.

tartar. The hard crust that forms on the side of a cask of completely fermented wine. It consists of impure acid, potassium tartrate. The term is also used for the deposit that forms on teeth, but this is mainly calcium phosphate.

Tarugi-Lenci reaction for amino and imino groups. Treat about 0.5 g. of the substance to be tested with an excess of phenol crystals and add, drop by drop, a solution of sodium hypochlorite (containing about 3% active chlorine and of an alkalinity equivalent to 4% of sodium hydroxide). Amino acids, amino aldehydes, and in general, all substances containing the groups $-NH_2$ or $=NH$ given an intense blue colour.

Tassinari-Piazza test. A test for nitrate made by heating the substance to be tested with potassium hydroxide solution and zinc dust. If nitrate is present, ammonia is evolved. Several modification of the test have been developed.

tast polarography. Variation of polarogaphy consisting in recording of current at end of drop life; due to this influence of capacity current is eliminated to some extent and limiting currents are larger than those recorded in classical polarography.

Tattersall reaction for morphine. Add a little concentrated sulphuric acid and some sodium arsenate to a little morphine. The mixture becomes dirty violet and then sea-green.

Tauber benzidine reagent. A solution of 4 g. benzidine in 100 g. glacial acetic acid. It is used in testing for pentoses, by boiling 0.5 ml. of the unknown solution with 1 drop of the reagent. A red colour on cooling indicates the presence of pentoses.

Tauber reagent for vitamin C. A reagent prepared by dissolving 1 ml. ferric sulphate in 80 ml. water and 18 ml. phosphoric acid (85%), and oxidizing with 1% potassium permanganate solution. In conducting the test 5 g. of sample are ground with 15 ml. 8% acetic acid, then filtered, and the filtrate is spot tested on filter paper with the reagent. A blue colour indicates the presence of vitamin C (ascorbic acid).

Tauber reagents for monose sugars. There are two Tauber reagents for monose sugars. One is an aqueous solution of lactic acid and cupric acetate; and the other is prepared by dissolving molybdenum trioxide in an aqueous sodium carbonate solution, and then adding phosphoric acid (85%). A blue colour, obtained under test conditions, shows the presence of monose sugars.

Tauber test reaction for vitamin B_1 (thiamine). A test for vitamin B_1 made by placing about 2-4 mg. of the vitamin and about 5 mg. *p*-dimethylaminobenzaldehyde in a small crucible, adding 0.1 ml. glacial acetic acid, evaporating, then cooling and adding 1 drop glacial acetic acid. A deep brick-red colour is produced immediately. Amino acids and proteins interfere.

tautomeric equilibrium. Thermodynamic equilibrium of mutual conversion of tautomeric forms, *e.g.*, for keto-enolic tautomerism, this equilibrium is expressed by equation :

$$K_T = \frac{[EH]}{[KH]} = \frac{K_{KH}}{K_{EH}}$$

where K_T = tautomeric equilibrium constant, [EH] and [KH] = concentrations of enol and ketone forms, K_{KH} and K_{EH} = acid constants of either form in mixture is expressed in percent.

tautomerism. Type of structural isomerism caused by existence of thermodynamic equilibrium between isomers (tautomers) whose molecules differ by arrangement of atoms and electron density distribution. The change from one form to the other is generally rapid and reversible, so that if one form is removed from the mixture by a chemical reaction, this is formed newly from the second form until whole of the material is consumed in the reaction. There are many types of tautomeric systems. A partial list of the (three-atom) prototropic (proton-shifting) tautomeric systems is shown :

Some Triad Prototropic Tautomeric Systems

Name Commonly Used	*Tautomeric System*
Three carbon	[H]C—C=C ⇌ C=C—C[H]
Keto-enol	[H]C—C=O ⇌ C=C—O[H]
Nitro-acinitro	[H]C—N=O ⇌ C=N—O[H]
Azo-hydrazone	[H]C—N=N ⇌ C=N—N[H]
Amidine	[H]N—C=N ⇌ N=C—N[H]
Nitroso-oximino	[H]C—N=O ⇌ C=N—O[H]
Nitrosoamino-diazohydrate	[H]N—N=O ⇌ N=N—O[H]
Amide-iminol	[H]N—C=O ⇌ N=C—O[H]
Imino-enamine	[H]C—C=N ⇌ C=C—N[H]
Carboxyl group	[H]O—C=O ⇌ O=C—O[H]
Methylene-azomethine	[H]C—N=C ⇌ C=N—C[H]
Diazoamino	[H]N—N=N ⇌ N=N—N[H]

The simplest approach to the mechanism of tautomerism is that of cationotropy, where the process may be considered to consist of (*i*) the separation of a positive ion, such as a proton (*ii*) the redistribution of the negative charge by electromeric rearrangement in the residual anion, and (*iii*), the re-coordination of the positive ion at the new site of the negative charge.

tau value. Number characterizing proton chemical shift in NMR spectra : $\tau = 10 - \delta$, where δ=chemical shift in ppm, measured with respect to tetramethylane standard.

tawing. A tanning process in which mineral agents, as alum or chromium salts, are employed to convert the hide into leather.

technetium. An element.

		Symbol	Tc
		Atomic No.	43
State	Solid	Atomic Wt.	98.9062
Group	VIIB	Valence	2,4,5,6,7
		m.p.	2443K
		b.p.	5149K

This radioactive element, was artificially formed in 1937 from molybdenum by deuteron bombardment. Three of its isotopes have half-lives of over 100,000 years, but the others are quite short ; the most stable isotope is ^{99}Tc (half-life 2.12×10^5 years), it is used in diagnostic. The element has superconducting properties. Its radioactice nature (gamma) makes it dangerous to handle without adequate protection. The properties technetium are intermediate between manganese and rhenium, the resemblance to the latter being perhaps greater than to the former. The metal has been shown to have the same structure as rhenium and the adjacent elements osmium and ruthenium. Superconductivity has been observed in technetium metal and in alloys based on technetium with additions of palladium, osmium, rhodium, tin, vanadium, carbon, or tungsten.

Tellera test. A test for petrolatum in lanolin in which 1 g. of the lanolin is dissolved in 15 ml, ether with the aid of heat ; allowed to cool, the precipitate stearin filtered off and 5 ml. absolute alcohol added to the filtrate. A flocculent precipitate indicates the presence of petrolatum.

telluric. 1. Containing or pertaining to hexavalent tellurium.

2. Related to telluric acid, H_2TeO_4.

telluride. A binary compound of tellurium, usually one in which that element is bivalent.

tellurinic. The radical —Te(:O)OH.

tellurium. An element.

		Symbol	Te
		Atomic No.	52
		Atomic Wt.	127.60
State	Solid	Valence	2,4,6
Group	VIA	Isotopes	8 stable
		m.p.	723K
		b.p.	1663±K

Tellurium is silvery white soft solid, classed as a nonmetal and recovered as a by-product of copper ore refining ; it is similar in many respects to sulphur and especially, to selenium, which is regarded as its sister element. It has semiconducting properties and forms compounds with many other elements, especially halogens, hydrogen, and oxygen.

Elemental tellurium has a hexagonal crystal structure with trigonal symmetry. There are several natural occurring isotopes ^{120}Te, ^{122}Te, through ^{126}Te, ^{128}Te, and ^{130}Te. Nine radioactive isotopes have been identified ^{118}Te, ^{119}Te, ^{123}Te, ^{127}Te, ^{129}Te, and ^{131}Te through ^{133}Te. With exception of ^{123}Te which has a half-life greater than 10^{13} years, all of the other isotopes have lives measurable in terms of minutes, hours, or days.

First ionization potential, 9.01eV ; second 18.6 eV; third, 30.5 eV ; fourth, 37.7 eV ; fifth, 59.95 eV.

Oxidation potentials :

$H_2Te\,(aq) \rightarrow Te + 2H^+ + 2e^-$; 0.69V

$Te + 2H_2O \rightarrow TeO_2(s) + 4H^+ + 4e^-$; —0.529V

$TeO_2(s) + 4H_2O \rightarrow H_6TeO_6(s) + 2H^+ + 2e^-$; —1.02V

Te^{2-} — $Te + 2e^-$; 0.92V

$Te + 6OH^- \rightarrow TeO_3^{2-}$; $+ 3H_2O + 4e^-$; 0.02V

$Te \rightarrow Te^{4+} + 4e^-$; —0.564V

Its major uses are as an alloying agent in steels, copper, etc., as a rubber accelerator, and particularly as a semiconductor. It is also used in electric power generation for specified purposes (cooling, relay signals, and the like). Tellurium and its compounds are toxic. Acceptable concentration limit for an 8-hour daily exposure to dust and fumes in air is 0.1 mg of tellurium per cubic meter air.

telomer. Product of telomerization, oligomer composed of molecules containing terminal groups incapable (under conditions of synthesis) to react with added monomer to give larger molecules of identical chemical composition.

telomerization. A polymerization reaction between two substances in which one substance breaks up, commonly into two parts which constitute the terminal groups of the new polymer molecule, while the other substances furnish the unsaturated groups or structural elements which form the links that constitute the interior of the polymer chain.

temperature, *t*. Intensive function of state which has following property : if system in thermodynamic equilibrium is composed of two diathermally partitioned parts A and B then their temperatures are equal, $t_A = t_B$. Also known as empirical temperature.

temperature, absolute. *See* absolute temperature.

temperature coefficient of reaction rate. Ratio of reaction rate constant at two temperatures ; in particular, quotient *n*, of rate constant *k* at temperature *t* divided by *k* measured at temperature 10 degrees lower :

$$n = \frac{k_t}{k_{t-10^\circ}}$$

for many reactions $2<n<3$.

temperature, critical. *See* critical temperature.

temperature, inversion. *See* inversion temperature.

temperature, kindling. *See* kindling temperature.

temperature of inversion. The temperature at which a substance undergoes a change in optical rotatory power due to a change in chemical structure ; or, in general, the temperature at which a substance undergoes a change to an isomeric form.

temperature, transition. *See* transition temperature.

tempering. In general, the process of rendering a material more suitable for its purpose. The tempering of metals is a process of heating or reheating, followed by cooling, at predetermined rates and temperatures to obtain a desired degree of clays or plastics is a process of mixing, to obtain a more uniform product. The tempering of sugar solutions is a treetment with lime for clarification.

temporary hardness. The presence in water of certain salts, such as bicarbonates of calcium or magnesium, which can be removed by boiling, and which, if not removed, cause scale formation in boilers, the precipitation of soap, and other undesired effects.

tensammetry. Alternating-current polarography applied to study of adsorption and desorption phenomena of various substances on dropping mercury electrode.

Tentelew process. A contact process for the manufacturing of sulphuric acid, in which the burner gases containing the sulphur dioxide are purified by dry filtration and scrubbing with water.

terbium. An element.

		Symbol	Tb
		Atomic No.	65
State	Solid	Atomic Wt.	158.9254
Group	IIIB	Valence	3,4
		m.p.	1633K
		b.p.	3503K

Terbium, is a rare-earth metal occurring in low concentration in monazite stands. Elemental terbium has a classed-packed hexagonal crystal structure at 298K. Pure metallic terbium is silver-gray colour, but oxidises readily in moist air. It is the most reactive of the heavy rare-earth metals and must be handled and worked in a vacuum or inert atmosphere.

The metal is extracted by chemical purification techniques, *i.e.*, by reducing the fluoride. It is extremely reactive when exposed to air or oxygen and must be kept in an inert atmosphere. To date, the uses of terbium are quite limited. The element currently is undergoing extensive studies to determine its future in photoconductive, semiconductor, or thermoelectric applications.

Ter Meulen method. The determination of oxygen in an organic compound by pyrolysis and hydrogenation of the substance at high temperatures in the presence of a nickel-catalyst. Under these conditions, all oxygen present in the compound is converted into water, which is absorbed and weighed, making the calculation of the percentage of oxygen in the given compound possible.

termolecular reaction. Elementary reaction of molecularity equal to three. Also known as trimolecular reaction.

ternary. A uniformly dispersed mixture (solution or alloy) having three components ; also, a chemical compound having three constituent elements or groups.

terpenes. The class of organic compounds characterized by the presence of the repeating carbon skeleton of isoprene :

$$CH_2{=}\underset{|}{\overset{CH_3}{C}}{-}CH{=}CH_2$$

These compounds are widely distributed in natural. The name terpene used properly refers to the hydrocarbons which are exact multiples of the skeletal isoprene unit. However the name "terpene", sometimes used loosely include not only hydrocarbons but also other functional types of naturally occurring organic compounds which contain the reoccurring isoprene skeletal. In the strictest sense, the name terpenoid or isoprenoid should be used instead of the more loosely applied usage of terpene.

Terpenoids are divided into subclasses as follows :

Subclass name	No. of carbon atoms	No. of isoprene skeletal units
Hemiterpenoids	C_5	1
Monoterpenoids	C_{10}	2
Sesquiterpenoids	C_{15}	3
Diterpenoids	C_{20}	4
Sesterterpenoids	C_{25}	5
Triterpenoids	C_{30}	6
Tetraterpenoids	C_{40}	8
Polyterpenoids	$(C_5)^n$	*n*

terpenoids. *See* terpenes.

tertiary. A term meaning literally "of the third order," which has two important meanings in chemestry. It is applied to compounds of tribasic acids, such as phosphoric or arsenic acids, to denote the replacement of all three acidic hydrogen atoms by metals or radicals.

In reference to alcohols this term denotes the presence of three alkyl groups attached to amines, it denotes the attachment of three alkyl groups to the nitrogen atom. It is customarily abbreviated *tert*.

test solution. A solution used in the determination of the properties or composition of a substance or sample. A great variety of test solutions are used in qualitative and quantitative analysis and other chemical laboratory work. Many of them are known by the names of the investigators who first suggested them, and a great many of these solutions are defined in this book under the name of various investigators.

tetra-. A prefix indicating the presence of four atoms of an element or four groups in a compound, *e.g.*, silicon tetrachloride ($SiCl_4$), tetraethyllead, $Pb(C_2H_5)_4$.

tetragonal hybrid. One of four equivalent hybridized atomic orbitals formed from one *s* and three *p* orbitals. Angle between two sp^3 hybrids is 109°27′ ; used for instance to explain structure of methane molecule. Also know as sp^3 hybrid.

tetrahedral complex. Complex of coordination number 4, in which donor atoms of ligands are distributed at vertices of regular or distorted tetrahedron. In this complex hybridization sp^3, is involved.

tetramer. A macromolecule comprised of four monomer units.

tetramine. A compound that contains four amino groups ($-NH_2$). These compounds are also called tetramino or tetramido compounds, as tetraminobenzene, $C_6H_2(NH_2)_4$.

tetrammine. A coordination compound in which four molecules of ammonia (NH_3) are coordinated around a metal ion. Each ammonia molecule donates a pair of electrons to form a coordinate bond with the metal ion, *e.g.*,

$$[Cu(NH_3)_4]^{2+}$$

tetragonal lattice. A crystal lattice in which the axes of a unit cell are perpendicular, and two of them are equal in length to each other, but the third axis different in length.

tetragonal system. A crystal system divided into seven symmetry classes, as shown in the following table :

	Symbol	Centre	Planes of symmetry	Axes of rotation symmetry	Axes of rotary inversion	Examples
1	4/mmm	C	3	4 ii, 1 iv	—	Zircon, Cassiterite, Rutile
2	42m	—	2	2 ii	1 iv	Chalcopyrite, Melilite
3	4mm	—	4	1 iv		Rare
4	422	—	—	4 ii, 1 iv	—	Phosgenite ($PbCl_2.PbCO_3$
5	4/m	C	1	1 iv	—	Wulfenite ($PbMoO_4$) Scheelite ($CaWO_4$)
6	4	—	—	—	1 iv	Rare
7	4	—	—	1 iv	—	—

thallium. An element.

		Symbol	Tl
		Atomic No.	81
		Atomic Wt.	204.37
State	Solid	Valence	1,3
Groups	IIIA	Isotopes	2 stable
		m.p.	576.5K
		b.p.	1730K

Thallium is a relatively metal of low melting point, occurring at an average concentration of about 1 gram per ton in the earth's crust ; its highest concentrations are in potassium-containing minerals. Elemental thallium has a hexagonal close-packed crystal structure normally, but also exhibits a face-centered cubic crystal structure. Thallium compounds can be recovered from by-products of zinc smelting, and the metals obtained by various separation techniques. The metal oxidizes in air to from a protective oxide coating.

Thallium occurs naturally as ^{203}Tl and ^{205}Tl. Eleven radioactive isotopes have been identified, ^{198}Tl through ^{202}Tl, ^{204}Tl, and ^{206}Tl though ^{201}Tl. With the exception of ^{204}Tl, which has a half-life of 4.07 years, the other isotopes have relatively short half-lives expresed in minutes, hours, and days. Thallium is not considered an abundant, estimates of occurrence in the earth's curst ranging from 0.3 to 3.0 ppm. In a allist of 65 chemical elements found in seawater, thallium does not appear.

Electron configuration is $1s^2 2s^2 2p^6 3s^2 p^6 3d^{10} 4s^2 4p^6 4d^{10} 4f^{14} 5d^2 5p^6 5d^{10} 6s^2 6p^1$. First ionization potential, 6.106 eV ; second, 20.32 eV ; third, 29.7 eV. Oxidation potentials : $Tl \rightarrow Tl^+ + e^-$, 0.336V ; $Tl^+ \rightarrow Tl^{3+} + 2e^-$, —1.25 V ; $Tl + OH^- \rightarrow TlOH + e^-$, 0.3445 V ; $TlOH + 2OH^- \rightarrow Tl(OH)_3 + 2e^-$, 0.05 V. Its uses in metallic form are chiefly in alloys with bismuth, cadmium, mercury, etc. Thallium and thallium compounds are toxic and skin contact must be avoided. Impervious gloves and aprons should be worn and excellent ventilation and masks should be provided where dusts and fumes may be present.

Its compounds have been used in rodenticides and various insecticides ; it also has limited application in photoelectric devices.

Thaw-Melt method. A method of obtaining accurate thermal data needed in the study of equilibria between solid and liquid phase of systems containing two or more components. The finely-divided solid of known composition is headed slowly in a glass tube and is pressed from time to time to expel the first drops of liquid as soon as they are formed, giving the "thaw point" or the temperature at which fusion commences (the point on the solidus curve). Then slow heating is continued until the solid melts completely, giving the "melt point," or the temperature at which the solid phase disappears (the point on the liquids curve).

Thenard blue. A blue fusion-product, consisting chiefly of cobalt aluminate, obtained by heating aluminium salts which have been moistened with cobalt nitrate. This reaction is used as a test for aluminium.

theoretical chemistry. Branch of physical dealing with applications of theory for description of various physico-chemical phenomena.

theoretical plate. A term used in chemical engineering to describe a contacting device that yields the same separation of the components of a liquid mixture in a fractionating column as does one simple distillation.

theoretical plate number, *n.* In chromatography parameter characterizing column performance ;

$$n = 16\left(\frac{\text{retention volume}}{\text{peak width}}\right)^2$$

where peak width is denoted by base of triangle with sides tangent to inflection points of peak.

therm. A unit of heat equivalent to 1,000 large calories used in expressing the calorific value of feeds.

thermal. Of or pertaining to heat, as thermal capacity, thermal conductivity.

thermal analysis. Method based on investigation of temperature changes of investigated system in time of its heating or cooling in order to determine its chemical composition and/or phase change of substance.

thermal column. Block of graphite, several metres thick, leading from nuclear reactor core through reflector and shield, used for thermalization of neutrons.

thermal conductance. The ability to conduct heat in an unequally heated system from a region of high to one of lower temperature. The coefficient of thermal conductivity is the time rate of heat conduction per unit area unit temperature gradient.

thermal conductivity. cell. Device that records composition of gas leaving chromatographic column by measuring its thermal conductivity. Also known as katharometer.

thermal de Broglie wavelength. Parameter

$$\lambda = \sqrt{\frac{h^2}{2\pi mkT}}$$

(m=particle mass, k=Boltzmann constant, and h=Planck's constant) which represents order of magnitude of de Broglie wavelength for typical in thermodynamic system at temperature T ; if $\lambda << \sqrt[3]{v}$, where v denotes average volume per particle, quantum effects are negligible ; they become important for λ comparable to or greater than $\sqrt[3]{v}$.

thermal equation of state. Equation with gives dependence of phase pressure p on its temperature T, volume V and number of moles of its constituents n_1 n_2, ..., nc

$$p=p(T, V, n_1, n_2, ..., n^c)$$

thermal equilibrium. Thermodynamic state of system with the same temperature in all coexisting phases.

thermal excitation. The acquisition of excess energy by atoms or molecules by collision processes with other particles.

thermal neutrons. Neutrons in thermal equilibrium with substance in which they exist. In normal conditions energy of thermal neutrons is 0.01—0.1 eV ; most probable speed of thermal neutrons at 293K is 2200 m/s.

thermal spike. Local heating of liquid or solid medium, confined to a molecular scale, due to the stopping of ion or neutral heavy particle of high kinetic energy.

thermionic effect. The emission of electrons by a heated cathode, *i.e.*, by a heated substance maintained at a negative electrical potential. The term thermionic effect is also applied to the ionization of a gas in contact with a heated cathode.

thermionic work function. The energy required

to release an electron from the metal in the photoelectric effect. It is equal to the difference between the energy of the photon of incident radiation and the kinetic energy of the emitted electron.

thermite. A strongly exothermic mixture of finely divided aluminium and iron oxide which, when ignited, reacts to produce molten iron and aluminum oxide by the reaction

$$2Al+Fe_2O_3 \rightarrow 2Fe + Al_2O_3 + 44.2\ kJ$$

The temperatures attained reach about 3500K. When used for welding massive iron parts, the mixture is placed in a magnesia crucible above the site of the joint to be made, is ignited, and the molten iron flows into the space to make the weld. Thermite is also used in incendiary military bombs.

thermochemical equation. Stoichiometric representation of chemical reaction or physical process which takes into account both amounts and nature of all reactants or constituents, their aggregation state, value of heat effect as well as temperature and pressure, *i.e.*, condition of the transformation.

thermochemistry. The branch of chemistry that embraces the determination and study of the heat absorbed or evolved in the formation and dissociation of compounds in chemical reactions and in changes of phase (liquid to vapour, solid to liquid, etc.).

thermochromism. Reversible change of colour of a chemical compound with temperature; usually high-temperature form absorbs at longer wavelength than the low-temperature one. Bianthron is typical thermochromic compound.

thermodiffusion potential. Difference of inner potentials resulting from temperature gradient in phase.

thermodynamic calorie, cal_{th}. The obsolete unit of energy; in SI system 1 cal_{th}=4.1840 J.

thermodynamic equation of state. Any equation derived by consideration of reversible energy changes, which gives a relationship between pressure, volume, and temperature for a state of matter.

thermodynamic equilibrium. Thermodynamic state in which entropy source and all thermodynamic forces vanish; in thermodynamic equilibrium no irreversible process is possible. Also known as complete internal equilibrium.

thermodynamic equilibrium constant, K_a. Ratio of product of equilibrium activities of product and product of equilibrium activities of substrates. Activity of each reactant is raised to power equal to corresponding stoichiometric coefficient. Thermodynamic equilibrium constant depends on temperature and pressure.

thermodynamic fluxes. Quantities characterizing velocities of individual irreversible processes; they vanish at thermodynamic equilibrium. Also known as fluxes; thermodynamic fluxes; generalized fluxes.

thermodynamic forces. Gradients of intensive quantities characterizing distance from thermodynamic equilibrium. Also known as affinities.

thermodynamic functions. Extensive functions of state parameters such that all thermodynamic properties can be expressed in terms of them and their derivatives with respect to state parameters, which are arguments of these functions. Also known as characteristic functions.

thermodynamic limit. Limit for which volume of system approaches infinity, $V \rightarrow \infty$; particle number density remains constant, $\frac{\langle N \rangle}{V}$ =constant. Average values in assembly composed of finite volume systems become extensive or intensive as characteristic for thermodynamic quantities only in thermodynamic limit. Also known as infinity volume limit

thermodynamic potential. An extensive property of a system, defined as the difference between the heat content and the product of the entropy and temperature. The thermodynamic potential is also called the free energy or Gibbs function.

thermodynamic process. Transition of system from one thermodynamic state to another (which can also be identical with initial one) accompanied macroscopically by chemical reaction, mass transport, or energy transfer within system and surroundings. Also known as thermodynamic change; thermodynamic transition.

thermodynamic properties. *See* thermodynamic quantities.

thermodynamic quantities. Quantities which depend only one state of system. Change of state depends solely on initial and final state of system and does not depend on way in which state is changed. Also known as state quantities ; thermodynamic properties; functions of state; macroscopic variables.

thermodynamics of irreversible processes. Phenomenological theory of dissipative processes in macroscopic systems in thermodynamic non-equilibrium states. Also known as irreversible thermodynamics ; non-equilibrium thermodynamics.

thermodynamic system. System composed of large number of particles (most frequently molecules), which behaves according to laws of macroscopic thermodynamics. Also known macroscopic system.

thermodynamic temperature, *T*. Intensive thermodynamic quantity :

$$T=\left(\frac{\partial U}{\partial S}\right)_V$$

where U=internal energy, S=entropy, and V=phase volume. Thermodynamic temperature is equivalent to temperature determined by gas thermometer. *See also* absolute temperature.

thermodynamic transition. *See* thermodynamic process.

thermodynamics. The study which of relationships between heat and other forms of energy and the laws which govern their interconversion. Thermodynamics treats systems whose states are determined by thermal parameters, such as temperature, in addition to mechanical and electromagnetic parameters. By system we mean a geometric section of the universe whose boundaries may be fixed or varied, and which may contain matter or energy or both. The state of a system is a reproducible condition, defined by assigning fixed numerical values to the measurable attributes of the system.

thermodynamics, first law of. *See* first law of thermodynamics.

thermodynamics, second law of. *See* second law of thermodynamics.

thermodynamics, third law of. *See* third law of thermodynamics.

thermodynamic work function. The difference between the intrinsic energy of a system, and the product of the entropy and the temperature it is called the work function because in an isothermal system it is equal to the maximum work done on the system.

thermoelectromotive force. Electromotive force produced by differences in temperature between two dissimilar metals. Specifically, the total electromotive force that arise from a temperature difference at the junction of two dissimilar metals, as in a thermocouple.

thermofor catalytic cracking process. A continuous, catalytic cracking process for petroleum, consisting of a moving bed in which one chamber serves as reactor and another to regenerate the catalyst.

thermogravimetry. Method of thermal analysis involving the use of thermobalance to determine change of mass of investigated substance in relationship to temperature or time.

thermolabile. Destroyed or greatly altered by moderate heating. Coagulable proteins, microorganisms, bacterial toxins, and certain isomers are thermolabile.

thermoluminescence. Emission of radiation by increasing temperature of system excited at lower temperature. It arises when the electrons and holes, trapped in a solid as a result of exposure to ionizing radiation, unite and emit photons of light. The process is made use of in thermoluminescent dating, which assumes that the number of electrons and holes trapped in a sample of pottery is related to the length of time that has elapsed since the pottery was fired. By comparing the luminescence produced by heating a piece of pottery of unknown age with the luminescence produced by heating similar materials of known age, a fairly accurate estimate of the age of an object can be made.

thermomagnetic analysis. Method of analysis and determination of phase components of materials containing ferromagnet (*e.g.*, catalysts) and method of investigation of appearance of ferromegnetic phases during recrystallization of metal alloys ; it utilizes measurements of magnetization as function of temperature.

thermometric titration. Titration for which end point is determined on basis of changes of temperature of analysed solution (liquid or gas) resulting from heat of reaction.

thermonuclear reaction. *See* nuclear fusion.

thermoplastic. Any substance that is solid or semisolid at room temperature but that softens or melts without decomposition at higher temperatures, regaining its original physical characteristics on cooling. Such materials can be moulded or shaped and will retain their shape until their softening point is reached, for example, waxes, butter and hard fats. In the plastics industry, the term is applied to high-polymer resins or plastics which can be moulded either at room temperature or under low heat but which will soften under high heat Thermoplastic materials are generally linear polymer in which no bonds exist between the chains, *e.g.*, polyethylene, polystyrene, acrylic polymers etc. Such materials (with a few exceptions) are soluble in common solvents. Thermoplastic materials can be made thermosetting by cross-linking agents or exposure to high-energy radiation ; among these are polyethylene and rubber.

thermoset. Any substance which requires exposure to high temperature to yield a useful article that will be permanently hard, infusible and relatively insoluble. Compared with thermoplastic polymers, the thermosetting ones are generally more stable, harder, and also more brittle. When heated at high temperatures, they decompose without melting. Thermosetting polymers have a three-dimensional, cross-linked structure, such as glyptal resins and bakelite.

thiazine dye. A sulphur-containing dyestuff having the chromophore group,

```
     S
   /   \
  R     R
   \   /
     N
```

thiazole. One of two isomeric compounds having the formula C_3H_3NS, and having a ring structure consisting of three carbon atoms, one nitrogen atom, and one sulphur atom.

Thiele reaction. An acetylation of quinones with acetic anhydride that forms the triacetoxy compounds. Sulphuric acid or boron fluoride catalyze the reaction.

Thiele's theory of conjugation. A pre-electronic theory stating that conjugated double bonds interact with each other. By using the concepts of residual affinity (or partial valency), Thiele tried to explain the reactions of compounds like butadiene or benzene. The theory has now only historical interest.

thin. In spite of its apparent simplicity, this term has several meanings in material technology. (*i*) In electronic metallurgy, a thin film is a vapour-deposited coating having a thickness of only a single atom; such monatomic films, *e.g.*, thorium, on tungsten, are used in electronic devices such as cathodes. (*ii*) A coating or film of a fatty acid on water which is one molecule thick (about 200 angstroms) is called a monolecular film. (*iii*) In thin-layer chromatography, the term applies to a specially prepared mixture of adsorbents spread on glass slides to a thickness of about 10^{-2} mm. (*iv*) The term is also used in the sense of liquid of low viscosity as in paint thin-boiling starch.

thin-layer chromatography. A technique for the analysis of liquid mixtures using chromatography. The stationary phase is a thin layer of an absorbing solid (e.g. alumina) prepared by spreading a slurry glass) and drying it in an oven. A spot of the mixture to be analysed is placed near one edge and the plate is stood upright in a solvent. The solvent rises through the layer by capillary action carrying the components up the plate at different rates (depending on the extent to which they are absorbed by the solid). After a given time, the plate is dried and the location of sports noted. It is possible to identify constituents of the mixture by the distance moved in a given time. The technique needs careful control of the thickness of the layer and of the temperature.

thin layer-electrochemistry. Electrolysis of thin layer (1—100μm) of electrolyte solutions carried out under various conditions (chronoamperometry, chronopotentiometry, stationary electrode voltammetry).

thinner. A low-viscosity liquid such as hydrocarbon (naphtha, benzene, etc,) and tarpentine, which are added to oil-base paints to adjust their viscosity to a suitable point for application.

thio-. A prefix denoting the divalent sulphur atom especially but not necessary, when it replaces oxygen.

thioacid. An organic acid in which one or more of the oxygen atoms have been replaced by divalent sulphur atoms. If the hydroxyl oxygen has been replaced by sulphur as R—COSH, the compound is a thiolic acid. If the carbonyl oxygen has been replaced (as, R—CSOH), the compound is a thionic acid. When both have been replaced (as, R—CSSH), a dithionic or thionthiolic acid results.

thiocyanation. The replacement of a hydrogen atom contained in a reactive aromatic compound (generally a phenol or aniline) by the thiccyano group (—SCN) using thiocyanogen $(SCN)_2$, as the substituting agent.

$$H_2N-C_6H_4 + (SCN)_2 \rightarrow H_2N-C_6H_4-SCN$$

Some polynuclear aromatic hydrocarbons containing highly reactive sites (*e.g.*, anthracene) also undergo this reaction.

thiocyanogen value. The quantity of a thiocyanate solution calculated as thiocyanogen $(SCN)_2$, required in a given titration, or equivalent to the iodine (which is titrated with thiocyanate solution) that is absorbed by unit mass of an organic compound or product.

thiodiazine. One of two isomeric compounds having the formula $C_3H_4N_2S$, and having a ring structure consisting of three carbon atoms, two nitrogen atoms, and one sulphur atom.

thiodiazole. One of four isomeric compounds having the formula $C_2H_2N_2S$, and having a structure consisting of two carbon atoms, two nitrogen atoms, and one sulphur atoms.

thiols. Organic compounds that contain the group—SH (called the thiol group, mercapto group, or sulphydryl group). Thiols are analogues of alcohols in which the oxygen atom is replaced ay a sulphur atom. They are named according to the parent hydrocarbon ; *e.g.*, ethane thiol (C_2H_5SH). A characteristic property is their strong unpleasant odour. For example the odour of garlic is produced by ethane thiol. Unlike alcohols they are acidic, reacting with alkalis and certain metals to form saltlike compounds. The older name, mercaptan, comes from their ability to react with ('seize') mercury. Also known as mercaptans ; thio alcohols.

thiono. The radical=CS. The use of the term thiono commonly of the oxygen in a carbonyl group by sulphur.

thiozonide. A member of a class of sulphur compounds to the ozonides and formed from thiozone.

third law of thermodynamics. Only finite amount of energy can be taken out of equilibrium system in form of heat and during this process thermodynamic temperature tends to zero and entropy to some value S_0, which (*i*) is equal to zero for one-component phases, (*ii*) in case of disordered multicomponent phases is positive and depends only on number of components. Also known as Nernst-Planck theorem.

third-order reaction. Reaction with kinetic equation characterized by sum of powers, in which concentration terms of reactants occur being equal to three.

thixotropy. A term literally means a change of form caused by slight pressure. It is applied to certain types of solid dispersions such as clay-water pastes, sand saturated with water, concentrated points, and colloidal gel structure. Application of slight pressure causes such mixtures to liquefy while the pressure maintained, after which they resume their original form.

Thompson-Beamish-Scott tests for osmium. 1. Add a drop of hydrochloric acid to the solution to be tested, followed by a drop of concentrated pyrogallol solution. A distinct blue colour indicates the presence of osmium.

2. Add a drop of a saturated aqueous solution of ephederine hydrochloride to a solution of sodium osmate, and alkalinize with sodium hydroxide. An orange colour is obtained.

Thoms reagent for copper. This reagent, which is potassium iodide solution, is used by itself or with starch solution. A cupric sulphate solution turns yellow when this reagent is added. A distinct violet colour forms on adding a few drops of starch solution.

thorium. An element.

		Symbol	Th
		Atomic No.	90
State	Solid	Atomic Wt.	232.0381
Group	IIIB	Valence	4
		m.p.	2013-33K
		b.p.	5023-73K

Thorium is a relatively heavy, radioactive metal, occurring in monazite sands, and is associated with the rare-earth elements of the lanthanide series. It is quite soft and can be easily machined. First ionization potential. 5.7 eV ; second, 16.2 eV ; third, 29.4 eV. Oxidation potentials : $Th \rightarrow Th^{4+} + 4e^-$, 1.90 V ; $Th + 4OH^- - ThO_2 + 2H_2O + 4e^-$, 2.48 V.

The isotopes of thorium include mass numbers 223-234. Isotone ^{232}Th has a half-life of 1.39×10^{10} years. It emits an alpha particle and forms meso-thorium 1 (radium 228), which is also radioactive, having a half-life of 6.7 years, emitting a beta particle. Since ^{232}Th captures slow neutrons to form by a series of nuclear reactions, ^{233}U, which is fissionable, thorium can be used as a fuel for nuclear reactors of the breeder type. Thorium occurs in earth minerals, an average content estimated at about 12 ppm. Findings of the Apolo-11 space flight indicated that thorium concentrations in some lunar rocks are about the same as the concentrations in terrestrial basalts.

Thorium occurs in greater volume in the earth's crust than does uranium and is thus important for future supply of nuclear fuel. It has limited use in alloys with magnesium, in photoelectric cells, x-ray tubes, etc. Cathodes of thoriated tungsten are used in electronic devices. Thorium is toxic when taken internally

thorium-D, ThD. Isotope of lead. Atomic number 82. Mass number 208.

thorium series. Naturally occurring series with first and last members thorium, ^{231}Th, and lead, ^{208}Pb, respectively. The mass number of each member of this series is $A=4n$, where $n=$ natural number.

thoron, Tn. Isotope of radon. Atomic number 86. Mass number 220. Also known as thorium emanation.

Thorpe reaction. In general, the reaction between active methylene groups and nitrile groups ; sometimes denoting specifically the reaction between a compound containing a nitrile group, and a compound in which the methylene group is activated by a nearby nitrile group. The reaction is catalyzed by bases.

$$2\,NC{-}CH_2{-}COOR \rightarrow ROOC{-}CH(CN){-}C(=NH){-}CH_2COOR$$

This method may be applied to the preparation of cyclic compounds by the base-catalysed intramolecular condensation of dinitriles :

$$CH_2CH_2CN{-}CH_2CH(CN)COOEt \xrightarrow[\text{(ii) hydrolysis, (iii) decarboxylation}]{\text{(i) condensation}} \text{cyclopentanone } (CH_2{-}CH_2{-}C{=}O{-}CH_2{-}CH_2 \text{ ring})$$

three carbon tautomerism. Type of prototropic tautomerism connected with reversible rearrangement of α, β-ethylenic compounds into corresponding β,γ-derivative, *e.g.*,

$$C_6H_{10}{=}CHCOOH \rightleftharpoons C_6H_9{-}CH_2COOH$$

Three-carbon tautomerism is a special case of triad tautomerism :

$$X{=}Y{-}Z{-}H \rightleftharpoons HX{-}Y{=}Z.$$

The atoms X, Y and Z may be carbon, oxygen, or nitrogen.

three-centre bond. Conception of bond present in molecule with electron deficiency, postulated by Longuet-Higgins, *e.g.*, B—B bond in B_2H_6. According to it, B—B bond is formed by electrons present in three-centred molecular

THE THORIUM SERIES

Radioelement	Corresponding Element	Symbol	Radiation	Half Life
Thorium ↓	Thorium	^{232}Th	α	1.39×10^{10} yr.
Mesothorium I ↓	Radium	^{228}Ra	β	6.7 yr.
Mesothorium II ↓	Actinium	^{228}Ac	β	6.13 hr.
Radiothorium ↓	Thorium	^{228}Th	α	1.90 yr.
Thorium X ↓	Radium	^{224}Ra	α	3.64 days
Th Emanation ↓	Radon	^{220}Rn	α	54.5 s.
Thorium A (~100% ↓ Thorium B; 0.014% ↓ Astatine-216)	Polonium	^{216}Po	β and α	0.158 s.
Thorium B ↓	Lead	^{212}Pb	β	10.6 hr.
Astatine-216 ↓	Astatine	^{216}At	α	3×10^{-4} s.
Thorium C (66.3% ↓ Thorium C′; 33.7% ↓ Thorium C″)	Bismuth	^{212}Bi	β and α	60.5 min
Thorium C′ ↓	Polonium	^{212}Po	α	3×10^{-7} s.
Thorium C″ ↓	Thallium	^{208}Tl	β	3.1 min.
Thorium D (End Product)	Lead	^{208}Pb	Stable	—

orbitals overlapping atom and two boron atoms :

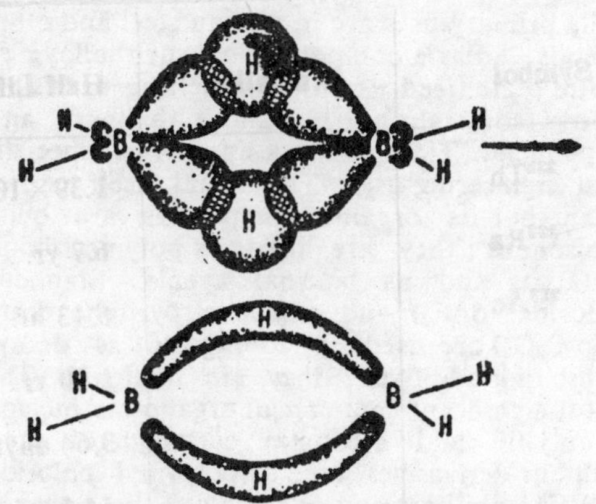

threo form. Diastereoisomer having two adjacent non-equivalent chiral centres of specific configuration: two identical or similar atoms (or groups of atoms) as are situated on opposite sides of Fischer projection formula, *e.g.*,

$$\begin{array}{c} CH_3 \\ Br-\!\!\!-\!\!\!-H \\ H-\!\!\!-\!\!\!-OH \\ CH_3 \end{array}$$

threshold energy. The smallest energy that a particle or quantum must have to cause, for instance, ionization of a molecule, displacement of an atom in crystal lattice, nuclear activation by ionizing radiation or nuclear reaction.

throwing. 1. In textile technology, this term refers to an auxiliary called a throwing oil ; it is applied to rayon and other fibers as a lubricant in making yarn from filaments, which involves a twisting or "throwing" action. The oil is later removed by scouring.

2. In electroplating, the term throwing power denotes the ability of an electrolytic solution (electroplating bath) to deposit a uniform coating of metal on all parts of the object being plated, including any recessed or intricate surfaces that may be present on hollow or irregular pieces. Throwing power is related to the temperature of operation and the current density of the bath.

Thrun test reaction. A test for magnesium made by adding curcumin to the solutions to be tested. A yellow to orange lake is formed if magnesium is present.

thulium. An element.

		Atomic No	69
		Symbol	Tm
State	Solid	Atomic Wt.	168.9342
Group	IIIB	Valence	3
		m.p.	1818K
		b.p.	2183K

Thulium is a minor element of the rare-earth group, occurring in association with yttrium in a number of ores such as xenotime and euxenite found in monazite sands. Elemental thulium has a closed-packed hexagonal structure at 298K. The pure element is grey, with no evidence of tarnishing upto a temperature of 473K. It is stable in air and reacts slowly with halogen elements at room temperature ; it also forms compounds with oxygen, carbon, nitrogen, and hydrogen at high temperatures. It has few important uses ; small pellets can be used as a portable source of diagnostic x-rays, and there is also a possibility of application in magnetic ceramic materials (ferrites). Significant scientific and industrial applications for thulium and its compounds remain to be developed. In particular the photoelectric, semiconductor, and thermoelectric properties of thulium and its compounds, mainly behaviour in the near-infrared region of spectrum, are being investigated.

Tiemann reaction. A rearrangement of amidoximes by treatment with benzenesulphonyl chloride and water or phosphorus pentachloride to yield asymmetric urea.

$$\underset{\displaystyle RC{=}NOH}{\overset{\displaystyle NH_2}{|}} \xrightarrow[H_2O]{C_6H_5SO_2Cl} RNHCONH_2$$

The practical applications of this method are very limited.

Tiffenau reaction. A rearrangement reaction whereby cyclic amino alcohols contained from reduction of cyanohydrins) having their amino and hydroxy groups attached to adjacent carbon atoms are converted to carbonyl compound by nitrous acids. As in the reaction shown, changes in the ring often accompany the reaction, *e.g.*,

$$\text{C=N, OH cyclopentane} \xrightarrow[CH_3COOH]{H_2/Pt} \text{CH}_2\text{NH}_2\text{, OH} \xrightarrow[CH_3COOH]{NaNO_2} \text{cyclohexanone} + N_2 + 2H_2O$$

Tillmans-Hirsch test reactions for ascorbic acid. 1. Ascorbic acid reduces 2,6-dichlorophenolindop henol to a leuko-dye.

2. With naturally acid lemon juice, a 10% phosphomolybdic acid solution can be used as a reagent. The ascorbic acid produces a blue colour, which is not characteristic in alkaline solution.

time-dependent Schrodinger equation. Equation which determines time evolution of quantum mechanical system ;

$$H\varphi = ih\frac{\partial\varphi}{\partial t}$$

where H = hamiltonian of system, φ = wave function, which depends on spatial and spin coordinates and time, $i=\sqrt{-1}$, h=Planck's constant divided by 2π.

time-independent Schrodinger equation. Equation which determines stationary states of quantum mechanical systems ; $H\varphi=E\varphi$, where H = hamiltonian of system, φ and E = wave function and corresponding stationary state energy respectively.

time-resolved spectroscopy. Technique of spectrophotometric measurements with recording of absorption spectra in time intervals of 5 μs to 0.01 s. Most frequently used for study of kinetics of fast processes.

tin. An element.

		Symbol	Sn
State	Solid	Atomic No.	50
Group	IVB	Atomic Wt.	118.69
		Valence	2,4
		m.p.	505K
		b.p.	2543K

Tin is obtained by roasting or smelting the ore cassiterite. It is relatively soft and has a comparatively low melting point. Tin has the largest number of naturally occurring isotopes ^{112}Sn, ^{114}Sn through ^{120}Sn, ^{122}Sn, and ^{124}Sn. Five radioactive isotopes have been identified ^{111}Sn ^{113}Sn, ^{121}Sn, ^{123}Sn, and ^{125}Sn.

Its primary uses are in plating steel and other metals and as a component of such alloys as terne plate (lead + tin), low-melting or fusible alloys (solders), bearing alloys (babbitt), and type metal. Tin also has a number of specialized engineering uses. The metal itself is not toxic, but its organic compounds are quite poisonous ; they are used as polymerization catalysts and as biocidal agents. Stannous fluoride (SnF_2) and stannous pyrophosphate ($Sn_2P_2O_7$) are used in toothpaste as decay-inhibiting additives ; they are nontoxic. The most significant commercial organotins include dibutyltin and dioctyltin carboxylates and sulphur derivatives, used as polyvinyl chloride (PVC) stabilizers and as catalysts in polymer systems ; *bis*(tributyltin)oxide, triphenyltin fluoride, and tributyltin fluoride, used as antifoulants for marine paints, fungicides, bactericides, sanitizing agents, and wood preservatives ; tricyclohexyltin hydroxide as an insecticide ; triphenyltin hydroxide and triphenyltin acetate as agricutural fungicides ; and dibutyltin dilaurate as a poultry anthelmintic.

tincture. An alcoholic liquid containing a soluble extract of a drug, as Tincture Nux Vomica, or a dissolved compound or element such as Tincture Ferric Chloride or Tincture Iodine. Tinctures are more dilute than fluid extracts and differ from spirits in not being wholly volatile. Most tinctures used in medicine contain a concentration of the drug obtained by extracting thoroughly 10 grams of the drug with 100 cubic centimetres of ethyl alcohol.

tin pest. If metallic tin is kept at a temperature around zero for some length of time there will be a partial transition from the normal white tin to the allotropic grey tin, giving the metal a spotted appearance. Although the transition temperature from one allotrope to the other is about 13°C. little change takes place unless the metal is kept at a temperature well below this for some time. Also known as tin plague.

tin plague. *See* tin pest.

Tishchenko preparation of esters. Preparation of esters by intermolecular condensation of aldehydes in presence of alcoholates of aluminium, magnesium or sodium, *e.g.*,

$$2RCH_2CHO \xrightarrow{Al(OC_2H_5)_3} \left[\begin{array}{l} RCH_2CH{-}O{-}Al(OC_2H_5)_3 \\ \quad\;\; | \quad\;\; + \\ \quad\; O{-}\overset{+}{C}HCH_2R \end{array}\right] \rightarrow RCH_2COOCH_2CH_2R$$

titanium. An element.

		Symbol	Sn
		Atomic No.	22
State	Solid	Atomic Wt.	47.90
Group	IVB	Valence	2,3,4
		Isotopes	5 stable
		m.p.	1924K
		b.p.	3553K

Titanium is derived chiefly from the ores ilmenite and rutile, though it occurs in low concentrations in most of the rocky structures in the earth's crust and was originally discovered in beach sand. Elemental titanium has a hexagonal close-packed crystal structure below 1158K ; above this temperature, it has a body-centered cubic crystal structure.

It is produced commercially by reduction of titanium tetrachloride with magnesium (Kroll process) or sodium, or by electrolytic means. It is flammable in power form, and the bulk metal will catch fire at about 1473K (2200°F). There are five natural isotopes, ^{46}Ti through ^{50}Ti, and three radioactive isotopes have been identified, ^{44}Ti, ^{45}Ti, and ^{51}Ti, the latter two having relatively short half-lives measured in minutes and hours. The isotope ^{44}Ti has a half-life of approximately 10^3 years, Titanium is relatively abundant, ranking 8th in the list of chemical elements occurring in the earth's crust. Titanium ranks 35th among the elements in terms of content in seawater, with an estimated 1080 kilograms per cubic kilometer of seawater.

First ionization potential, 6.83 eV ; second 13.60 eV ; third, 27.6 eV ; fourth, 44.66 eV. Oxidation potential : $Ti + 2H_2O \rightarrow TiO_2 + 4H^+ + 4e^-$, 0.95 V ; $Ti \rightarrow Ti^2 + 2e^-$, 1.75 V : $Ti^{2+} \rightarrow Ti^{3+} + e^-$, 0.37 V.

Its outstanding property is its lightness, which, combined with sufficient strength, makes it of uniqne value as a structural metal in airplanes and acrospace vehicles. It is also useful in manufacture of chemical plant and desalination equipment because of its high resistance to chlorine. Its most important compound is titanium dioxide. TiO_2, used principally as white pigment in paints, rubber, plastic and paper. The major uses for titanium are in various alloys, although unalloyed titanium also finds some applications. Titanium alloys are classified as alpha, alpha-beta, or beta, determined by the phases present in the alloy at room temperature. The alpha alloys usually result when the main elements present are the alpha stabilizers, *e.g.*, oxygen, nitrogen, hydrogen, and carbon. Alpha-beta alloys and beta alloys contain increasing amounts of beta stabilizers, mainly vanadium, molybdenum, iron, chromium, manganese, tantalum, and niopium (columbium).

titanium group. Elements in fourth sub-group of periodic system with structure of outer electronic shells of atoms $(n-1)d^2ns^2$: titanium, zirconium, hafnium (thorium). Also known as titanium family.

titer. With one exception, the various meanings of this term all relate directly to the process of titration. Thus titer means (*i*) the normality of a solution ; (*ii*) the number of grams of an element, ion, or compound per unit volume of solution ; (*iii*) the number of cubic centimeters per liter by which a normal solution differs from a true solution. The meaning of titer that relates only indirectly to the process of titration is its use in oil and fat analysis, where it means the melting point of the fatty acids obtained by saponification. Also spelled titre.

titrant. Solution with precisely known titre used in volumetric analysis.

titration A method of volumetric analysis in which a volume of one reagent is added to a known volume of another reagent slowly from a burette until an end point is reached (*see* indicator). The volume added before the end point is reached is noted. If one of the solutions has a known concentration, that of the other can be calculated.

titre. *See* titer.

titrimetric factor. A number used to multiply the volume result of a given titrimetric analysis in order to obtain the amount of the substance to be determined ; often termed the volumetric factor.

Toisson fluid. A reagent used in diluting blood for microscopic examination, especially for counting erythrocytes. It is prepared by dissolving 2 g. sodium chloride, 0.05 g. methyl violet

5B, 16 g. sodium sulphate, and 60 ml. glycerol in 320 ml. water.

tokamak. A transliterated Russian word for an assembly for producing nuclear fusion (thermonuclear) reactions experimentally. It consists essentially of a doughnut-shaped evacuated chamber called a torus, 0.45 m in cross section, through which plasma circulates. Surrounding the torus is an electromagnetic field powerful enough to confine the energized plasma sufficiently to achieve the required density of 10^{14} particles perceper second and a temperature of 44 million degrees C. The vacuum chamber and the magnetic field simulate conditions on the sun ; namely, absence of air and immense gravitational force. Larger and more powerful tokamaks up to about 1 metre in cross-section are under development, in which temperatures up to 100 million degrees C may be achieved.

Tollens reagent for aldehydes. A solution of 10 g. silver nitrate in 60 ml. concentrated ammonium hydroxide and 40 ml. water ; a small quantity of this solution is mixed immediately before using with an equal quantity of a 10% aqueous solution of sodium hydroxide It is used as a test reagent for aldehydes, being mixed with the sample in a test tube. The formation of a silver mirror in the test tube indicates the presence of aldehydes.

Tollens test for galactose. A test based on the oxidation of the suger by nitric acid (sp. gr. 1.15), to mucic acid melting at 484-485K.

Tollens test for glycuronic acid. A granule of the substance to be tested is boiled with 5 ml, water, 1 ml. of 1% alcoholic naphthoresorcinol solution, and 6 ml. hydrochloric acid for 1 about minute, then cooled and shaken with ether. The ether become red to blue-red in the presence of glycuronic acid.

Tommila test for bismuth. Treat the solution to be tested with fairly concentrated hydrochloric acid dilute, and add a large excess of potassium thiocyanate either as a concentrated solution or as the solid salt. A distinct yellow colour is given by bismuth. The colour is easily extracted by ethyl acetate and amyl alcohol.

Tonegutti test. A test for differentiating coal tar and wood tar by use of alcohol, chloroform or benzene. Wood tar is completely soluble in these substances, but coal tar is incompletely soluble. A greenish fluorescence is given by the coal tar constituents which do dissolve.

toner. Any of a group of organic pigments that are free from the inorganic components or substrates which characterize lakes. Among them are various phthalocyanine, diazo, and triphenylmethane pigments.

topotactic. A reaction in which the product has an ordered geometric relation to the reactant.

tosylation. The introduction of the tosyl (*p*-toluenesulphonyl) group into an organic compound.

$$ROH + CH_3.C_6H_4.SO_2Cl \rightarrow CH_3.C_6H_4.SO_2R + HCl$$

tor. A unit of pressure ; 1 tor = 1 mm Hg pressure.

total angular momentum. Vector quantity defined as sum of orbital and spin angular momentum of system.

total heat of solution. Enthalpy change of system in process of dissolving one mole of a given substance in such an amount of pure solvent as finally to reach saturation point.

total ion exchange capacity. Number of equivalents of ionogenic groups per unit of dry mass (mass capacity), or bed volume (volume capacity) of exchanger. Also known as ion exchange capacity.

toxalbumin. A toxic substance of protein nature similar to the bacterial toxins, but not produced by microorganisms. Representative toxalbumins are the toxins of rattlesnake and cobra venom, and the plant toxalbumins ricin, abrin, and robin.

toxic dose. The minimum dose that gives characteristic symptoms of poisoning.

toxicity. The extent to which a substance adversely affects the life process or any of its subcritical aspects as a result of chemical reactions involving tissue or metabolic functions. Many diseases are caused by the toxic product of infectious organisms ; other toxic agents act directly on the central nervous system, on the blood, or on the muscular and digestive systems. In all such cases one or more chemical reactions are involved. Toxicity standards are usually based on results of animal experiments the results of which are presented as LD_{50} ratings (lethal dose 50%), which means that half of the exposed animals die from a given dosage of the substance tested. Toxicity is affected by fineness of subdivision, solubility, and chemical state ; many metals that are relatively harmless in elemental form are severely toxic as compounds, for example mercury and beryllium. *See also* poison.

The following list includes chemical individuals and groups that are generally regarded as having toxic properties. There is considerable variation in the degree of roxicity among these and the listing is by no means exhaustive.

Individuals	*Groups*
aniline	aldehydes
arsenic and its compounds	alkaloids
asbestos (carcinogen)	allyl compounds
barium and soluble compounds	barbiturates
berylium and soluble compounds	chlorinated hydrocarbons
benzidine (carcinogen)	corrosive materials
cadmium and compounds	cyanides
benzpyren (carcinogen)	organic phosphate esters
carbon monoxide	radioactive elements
chlorin	
chromium (hexavalent compounds)	
coal-tar pitch (carcinagen)	
cresol	
fluorine and compounds	
hydrogen peroxide	
hydrogen sulphide	
hydrogen selenide	
lead compounds	
mercury (soluble compounds)	
methyl alcohol	
nickel carbonyl	
osmium tetroxide	
oxalic acid	
ozone	
phenol	
pyrene	
pyridine	
phosphine	
selenium compounds	
stibin	
sulphur dioxide	
sulphur trioxide	
thallium (soluble compounds)	
tin (organic compounds)	
vinyl chloride monomer (carcinogen)	

toxicology. The science that deal with the study of the nature, action and relations of poisonous substances and the methods for detecting and treating poisoning.

toxin. 1. Any poisonous substance.

2. A plant poison of unknown composition.

3. A bacterial toxin, *i.e.* a poisonous substance produced by microorganisms.

4. A toxalbumin or venin.

toxophore groups. The portion of a bacterial toxin which has the specific poisonous properties shown by the toxin.

trace analysis. Identification or determination of trace components of sample.

trace elements. This term refers to five elements necessary for plane nutrition which are present in the soil in minute concentrations (less than 1000 parts per million). These are generally considered to be boron, copper, manganese, molybdenum, and zinc. Additional elements required in trace concentrations in animal and human nutrition are fluorine, iodine, and selenium. Element present in the soil in higher concentrations are not regarded as trace elements. The term micronutrient is synonymous with trace element. Trace elements should not be confused with tracer elements.

tracer element. A radioactive isotope, either natural or artificial introduced into a system to determine its behaviour in and reactivity with the other constituents present. This is made possible by the emission of radiation from the tracer which is detected by a sensing device, so that the movement of the isotope can be followed continuously. This method is used in studies of biochemical reactions (carbon-14) as well as in medical research ; for example, radioactive iodine is used in treatment of the thyroid gland, which concentrates this element. The terms labelled or tagged are frequently used to designate these elements or the compounds in which they occur.

tracer technique. The use of isotopes for the study of chemical (including biological) reactions. Isotopes incorporated into one of the components taking part in a reaction make it possible to study the fate of this component, to follow its pathway in a system, and to deduce the mechanism of a reaction. Radioactive isotopes of carbon, halogens, or tritium are the easiest to use for such studies as their presence can be ascertained by relatively simple instruments (radiation counters) The use of non-radioactive isotopes (deuterium ^{18}O, ^{15}N, etc.) involves a more complicated technique (mass-spectrometric analysis).

tranquilizer. More properly called a psychotropic drug, a tranquilizer is a pharmaceutical compound used in treating psychic problems of emotionally unstable persones. Contrary to the meaning of the term in popular usage, some of these agents act as stimulants rather than relaxant, though their therapeutic effect is equally beneficial. The so-called major tranquilizers are derivatives of butyrophenone and phenothiazine (chloropromazine); their clinical action is quite different from that of the minor group, which includes benzodizepine and glycerol derivatives such as meprobamate. There are three classifications of psychotropic drugs based on their functional effect, namely, antipsychotics, antidepressants, and antianxiety agents. Such drugs should not be taken without the advice of a physician.

trans. *See* trans form.

transalkylation. A catalytic reaction of the disproportionation type by which benzene and xylene are formed from toluene by hydrogenation without production of methane, that is, by hydrodealkylation.

transaminases. Enzymes catalysing the transfer of amino groups, and found in all organisms. Many transfer $-NH_2$ group to and from glutamine and asparagine. Glutamic acid is thus of considerable importance in the formation of amino acids from keto-acids and ammonia.

transamination. Reaction between amino acid and α-ketoacid, involving migration of amino group, *e.g.*,

$$H_2N-\underset{}{\overset{R}{\overset{|}{C}}}H-COOH + O=\overset{R'}{\overset{|}{C}}-COOH \rightleftharpoons O=\overset{R}{\overset{|}{C}}-COOH + H_2N-\overset{R'}{\overset{|}{C}}H-COOH$$

transannular effect. Mutual influence exerted by atoms (or groups of atoms) located in remote points of medium-sized ring, for instance, at 1,5- or 1,6-position of 8–12 membered ring. This effect is accompanied by specific physical constants and very often by specific chemical reactions (*see* transannular migration).

transannular migration. Type of rearrangement characteristic for multi-membered alicyclic compounds, (8—12 carbon atoms) involving hydrogen atom (or group of atoms) migration to carbon atom sterically close, but situated further in the ring (3 to 4 carbon atoms away), *e.g.*,

trans effect. Effect of weakening of bond of each group in trans position with respect to coordinating ligand (cf. trans effect series).

trans effect series. Ligands arranged by increasing trans effect, *e.g.*, $H_2O < OH^- < NH_3 <$ pyridine $< Cl^- < Br^- < NCS^- \sim I^- \sim \sim NO_2^- \sim SO_3H^- \sim PR_3 \sim R_2S \sim SC(NH_2)_2 < NO < CO \sim C_2H_4 \sim CN^-$. Also known as order of increasing trans effect.

transesterification. Reaction of ester with alcohol (alcoholysis), ester with acid (acidolysis) or between two different esters, leading to exchange of alkoxyl or acyl group of ester, *e.g.*,

$$CH_3COOC_2H_5 + C_4H_9OH \overset{H^+}{\rightleftharpoons} CH_3COOC_4H_9 + C_2H_5OH$$

$$CH_2{=}CHCOOCH_3 + HCOOH \overset{H^+}{\rightleftharpoons} CH_2{=}CHCOOH + HCOOCH_3$$

$$C_6H_5COOC_2H_5 + CH_3COOC_4H_9 \overset{H^+}{\rightleftharpoons} C_6H_5COOC_4H_9 + CH_3COOC_2H_5$$

transference number. The fraction of the total current carried by each of the ionic species of an electrolyte. Thus, in the simple case of an electrolyte having two ions, such as sodium chloride solution, the transport number of the sodium ion is the ratio of the current it carries to the total current carried by both ions, while the transferenee number of chloride ion is the ratio of the current it carries to the total current carried by both ions. Also known as transport number.

trans form. Diastereoisomer in which identical or similar groups are situated on opposite sides of plane passing through double bond or through ring surface, *e.g.*, trans-2-butene :

```
CH3       H
   \     /
    C=C
   /     \
  H       CH3
```

Also known as trans isomers.

transformation. A term having the general meaning of a change in structure or arrangement. It is applied most commonly to certain rearrangements of organic structures, such as the Beckmann rearrangement (they are defined in this book under their specific names), and to changes among and within atoms, especially within atomic nuclei.

transformation series. This term is commonly used in reference to radioactive elements to denote a series of elements which are produced by successive radioactive disintegrations from the parent element to their successors. *See* element, radioactive, for details of the various series.

transient equilibrium. Stationary state between radioactive parent nuclide and its daughter for the case when parent nuclide's half-life is up to a hundred times more than that of daughter. Also known as transient radioactive equilibrium.

trans isomer. 1. *See* trans form.

2. In coordination chemistry, isomer in which two similar ligands are in opposite positions, *i.e.*, in square complexes $[Ma_2b_2]$ ligand occupy opposite vertices of square, and in octahedral complexes $[Ma_2b_2]$ opposite corners of octahedron.

transition cell. 1. In electrochemistry, a voltaic cell containing an electrolyte which undergoes a chemical transition that is accompanied by a corresponding electromotive force, and that usually occurs at a definite temperature.

2. In biology, a living cell with characteristics between two other types of cells, into which it may changed, under suitable conditions.

transition elements. Elements the atoms of which have partly-filled outermost electronic d sub-shell. Structure of outer electronic shells of atoms of these elements can, in general, be represented by $(n-1)d^{1-9}ns^2$, although there exist elements in which number of electrons in ns sub-shell is smaller than 2. Four series of transition elements are distinguished which correspond to filling of 3*d*, 4*d*, 5*d*, and 6*d* sub-shells. Specifically, they are as follows :

Period 4	*Period 5*
scandium	yttrium
titanium	zirconium
vanadium	niobium
chromium	molybdenum
manganese	technetium
iron	ruthenium
cobalt	rhodium
nickel	palladium
copper	silver

Period 6	*Period 7*
lanthanum	actinium
lanthanide series	actinide series
hafnium	
tantalum	
tungsten	
rhenium	
osmium	
iridium	
platinum	
gold	

The transition elements or metals are so named because they represent a gradual shift from the strongly electropositive elements of Groups IA and IIA to the electronegative elements of Groups VIA and VIIA. They are also more versatile in their chemical bonding properties than are other elements, using the two outer shell orbitals instead of only those of the outermost shell.

transition moment. Matrix element of dipole moment operator between wave functions of two energetic states of the system. Direction of transition moment determines polarization of radiative transition. Squared absolute value of transition moment is proportional to dipole transition probability.

transition point. 1. The temperature at which one crystalline form of a substance changes to another form.

2. The temperature at which a substance changes phase.

3. The temperature at which a substance becomes superconducting.

4. The temperature at which some other change, such as a change of magnetic properties, takes place. Also known as transition temperature.

transition polarization. Type of electrolytic polarization consisting in transfer of electrons or ions across interphase, slow in comparison with other steps of electrode reaction. Transition polarization is expressed by transition overvoltage.

transition probability. Number which expressed fractions of system of quantum mechanical statistical ensemble undergoes transition from one stationary state φ_1 to other stationary state φ_2 in unit time interval due to some perturbation.

transition state. The association of atoms of highest energy formed during a chemical reaction. The transition state can be regarded as a short-lived intermediate that breaks down to give the products. For example, in a S_N2 substitution reaction, one atom or group approaches the molecule as the other leaves. The transition state is an intermediate state in which both attacking and leaving groups are partly bound to the molecule, *e.g.*,

$$B + RA \rightarrow B—R—A \rightarrow BR + A.$$

In the theory of reaction rates, the reactants assumed to be in equilibrium with this activated complex, which decomposes to the products.

transition time. In chronopotentiometry, time which elapses from beginning of electrolysis to moment at which concentration of electrolyzed substance at electrode surface drops to zero.

translation. Operation consisting in parallel shift by a given displacement of all points belonging to defined geometrical structure. Translation is described explicitly by direction sense of vector, and length of section through which operation was conducted.

translational energy. Kinetic energy of translation of molecule.

tronslation partition function, f_{tr}. Function defined by $f_{tr}=V/\lambda^3$, where V=volume of gas and λ=thermal de Broglie wavelength. Translational partition function determines influence of translational degrees of freedom of molecule on thermodynamic properties of corresponding ideal gas.

translational symmetry. Symmetry of system in which surroundings of two points of this system are congruent with respect to the same translation.

transmethylation. Migration of methyl group $—CH_3$, from one molecule to another, stimulated by chemical or biochemical catalyst.

transmission. The ratio of the radiant power transmitted by a sample to the radiant power incident on the sample, both being measured at the same spectral position and with the same slit width The beam is understood to be parallel radiation and incident at right angles to plane parallel surfaces of the sample. Also known as transmittance ; transmittancy.

transmission coefficient. Fraction of activated complexes which decay into products. Transmission coefficient is almost invariably equal to one and differs from one only in reactions accompanied by changes in electronic energy.

transmutation. Conversion of one element into another by introducing one more subatomic particle (generally proton into its nucleus by nuclear bombardment, *e.g.*, one of the protons and the two neutrons of the helium enter the nitrogen nucleus (atomic number 7), thus increasing its atomic number by 1 and its atomic weight by 3, so that it becomes the 17 isotope of oxygen (atomic number 8). The additional proton is emitted as a hydrogen nucleus The reaction is represented as $_2^4He + _7^{14}N \rightarrow _8^{17}O + _1^1H$.

transmutation equation. An equation for the change of one atom into another, which differs from it in nuclear charge, mass, or stability. Such changes occur in natural radioactive processes, but the general need for a systematic notation for expressing them came only with the investigation of artificial radioactive and the great number of changes discovered.

Two representative transmutation equations are :

$$_{13}^{27}Al + _0n^1 \rightarrow _{12}^{27}Mg + _1H^1$$

which shows the transmutation of aluminium atoms of mass number 27, and of atomic number 13, by bombardment with neutrons, to magnesium atoms of mass number 27, and of atomic number 12, with the emission of a proton, and :

$$_4^9Be + \gamma \rightarrow _4^8Be + _0^1n$$

which shows the transmutation of beryllium atoms of mass number 9, under gamma rays bombardment, to beryllium atoms of mass number 8, with the emission of a neutron.

The two reactions above may also be expressed in condensed form as :

$$^{27}Al\ (n\ ;\ p)\ ^{27}Mg$$

and $$^{9}Be\ (\gamma\ ;\ n)\ ^{8}Be$$

transport coefficients. Proportionality constants between flux (*e.g.*, of heat, electric charge, particles) and corresponding force responsible for it (*e.g.*, temperature gradient, electrostatic potential gradient, concentration gradient).

transuranic. A term used by chemists to denote the series of synthetic or artificially created elements which lie beyond uranium in the Periodic Table, beginning with neptunium (atomic number 93) and extending to the most recently discovered element 106. These are : neptunium, plutonium, americium, curium, berkelium, californium, einsteinium, fermium mendelevium, nobelium, lawrencium, 104, 105, 106.

trap. Localized energetic state in solids or liquids able to catch electrons (electron trap), to give up electrons (hole-trap), to participate in both processes with equal probability (recombination centre), or to catch specified free radicals (radical trap). Also known as trapping state.

Trapani reagent. A solution of 2.5 g. mercuric cyanide and 5 g. potassium hydroxide in 100 ml. water. It is used as a test reagent for bilirubin, giving a red colour that is discharged by acetic acid.

trapped electron, e^-_{tr}. Electron, knocked out in absorption of high energy radiation, and after being slowed down to appropriate energy, caught in specific electron trap.

trapping of radicals. Stabilization of radicals for period of time as long as needed, in medium preventing their diffusion and recombination.

Traube purine synthesis. A method of formation of purines by the action of formic acid or chlorocarbonic ester on 5,6-diaminopyridimines, which may be prepared from urea and α-nitrile esters :

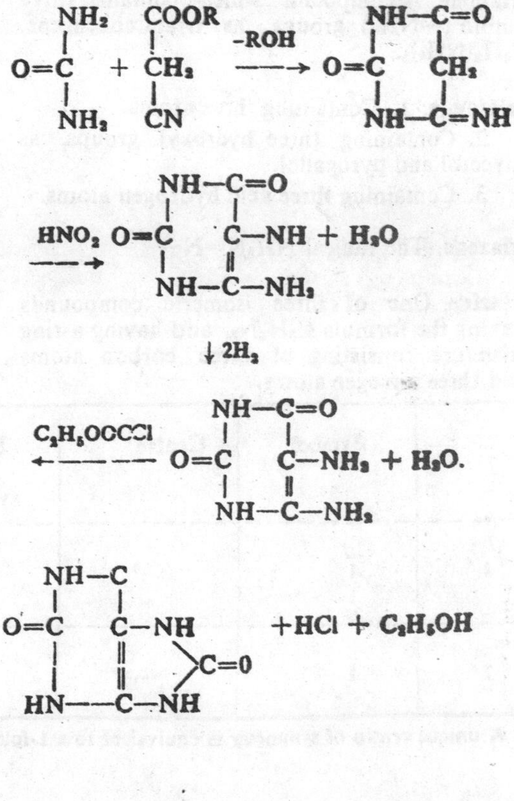

```
  NH2       COOR                   NH—C=O
  |         |         -ROH         |   |
O=C     +   CH2      ——→    O=C    CH2
  |         |                      |   |
  NH2       CN                     NH—C=NH

                   NH—C=O
                   |   |
HNO2          O=C   C—NH + H2O
——→                |   ||
                   NH—C—NH2

                     ↓ 2H2

                   NH—C=O
C2H5OCCl           |   |
←————         O=C   C—NH2 + H2O.
                   |   ||
                   NH—C—NH2

  NH—C
  |   |
O=C   C—NH                +HCl + C2H5OH
  |   ||   \
  |   ||    >C=0
  |   ||   /
  HN———C—NH
```

Traube's rule. A relationship between the effects upon the surface tension of water produced by the addition of organic substances in various homologous series. In dilute aqueous solutions of surface-aqueous substance (surfactants) whose hydrophobic groups are long aliphatic carbon chains, surface activity increases with increase in length of chains.

Traube test for hydrogen peroxide. A test for hydrogen peroxide made by adding a little sulphuric acid and zinc iodide-starch solution to 8 ml. of the solution to be tested, then adding no more than 4 drops of cupric sulphate solution and a little of 0.5% ferrous sulphate solution. A blue colour indicates the presence of hydrogen peroxide.

triacid. A base capable of neutralizing three equivalents of monobasic acid.

triad. A class of tautomeric compounds in which the shifting hydrogen atom is supposed to travel from one polyvalent atom past a second to a third in a chain of three such atoms.

triamine. A compound which contains three amino ($—NH_2$) groups, as triaminobenzene, $C_6H_3(NH_2)_3$.

triatomic. 1. Containing three atoms.

2. Containing three hydroxyl groups, as glycerol and pyrogallol.

3. Containing three acid hydrogen atoms.

triazeno. The radical $NH_2N{=}N—$

triazine. One of three isomeric compounds having the formula $C_3H_3N_3$, and having a ring structure consisting of three corbon atoms and three nitrogen atoms.

triazinyl. The radical $C_3H_2N_3—$ (from traizine).

triazole. One of six isomeric compounds having the formula $C_2H_3N_3$, and having a ring structure consisting of two carbon atoms and three nitrogen atoms. Two of these compounds are named isotriazoles.

triazolyl. The $C_2H_2N_3—$ (from triazole).

tribasic. 1. An acid, either inorganic or organic, whose molecule contains three hydrogen atoms that can be replaced by basic elements to form salts.

2. An inorganic compound whose molecule contains three atoms of a basic univalent elements, *e.g.*, tribasic sodium phosphate (Na_3PO_4)

triboluminescence. Luminescence caused by friction; for example, some crystalline substances emit light when they are crushed as a result of static electric charges generated by the friction.

trichroism. The property of exhibiting three different colours when viewed in as many different directions.

triclinic crystal. A crystal whose unit cell has axes which are not at right angles, and are unequal. Also known as an anorthetic crystal.

triclinic system. A crystal system of one-fold symmetry, with three unequal axes intersecting obliquely. It has been divided into two classes.

This system includes all those crystals that are referred to three axes—of which one is at right angle to any other and having unequal parameters. Elements of triclinic system will thus include the three parameters and three interaxial angles :

	Symbol	Centre	Planes of symmetry	Axes of rotations symmetry	Axes of rotary inversion symmetry
1	$\bar{1}$	(C)*	—	—	1
2	1	—	—	—	—

* A unique centre of symmetry is equivalent to a 1-fold inversion axes of symmetry.

tricyclic. 1. A ring composed of three atoms. 2. A molecule containing three rings of atoms.

triglyceride. An easter of glycerol (propane-1,2,3-triol) in which all three hydroxyl groups are esterified with a fatty acid. Triglycerides are the major constituent of fats and oils and provide a concentrated food energy store in living organisms as well as cooking fats and oils, margarines, soaps, etc. Their physical and chemical properties depend on the nature of their constituent fatty acids. In simple triglycerides all three fatty acids are identical; in mixed triglycerides two or three different fatty acids are present. Also known as triacylglycerol.

trigonal hybrid. One of three equivalent hybridized atomic orbitals formed from one *s* and two *p* atomic orbitals. Angle between two sp^2 hybrids is 120°; used for instance to explain structure of ethylene molecule. Also known as sp^2 hybrid.

trigonal system. A crystal system divided into five classes (the modern practice of considering this system separately rather than with the hexagonal system is followed here). Trigonal crystals are usually referred to the same set of axes as for the hexagonal system. However, an alternative set of axes consisting of three non-orthogonal axes, equally inclined to the three-fold axis of symmetry (or the three-fold inversion axis) and making equal angles with each other, is available. They are, in fact, parallel to three edgedirections of a rhombohedron, and when using them the characteristic feature is not the axial ratio but the axial angle.

Trillat-Turchet test. A test for ammonia in water performed by adding 3 drops of a 10% potassium iodide solution to 20-30 ml. of the water and then adding 2-3 drops of concentrated sodium hypochlorite solution. If ammonia is present a dark colour develops.

trimer. Oligomer whose molecule is composed of three units of the same monomer.

trimolecular reaction. *See* termolecular reaction.

	International symbol	Centre	Planes of symmetry	Axes of rotation symmetry	Axes of rotary inversion	Examples
1	$\bar{3}$m	C	3	3 ii	1 iii	Calcite and related carbonates; Corundum; haematite
2	3m	—	3	—1 iii	—	Tourmaline
3	32	—	—	3 ii, iii	—	Quartz; Cinnabar
4	$\bar{3}$	C	—	—	1 iii	Dolamite; Willemite (Zn_2SiO_4) Dioptase ($CuSiO_3.H_2O$) Phenacite (Be_2SiO_4)
5	3	—	—	—1 iii	—	—

trimorphism. The property of crystallizing in three forms.

trinitride. *See* azide.

triese. A monosaccharide which contains carbon atoms, as glyceric aldehyde,

$$CH_2OH—CHOH—CHO$$

trioxazole. One of the isomeric compounds having the formula CHO_3N, and having a ring structure consisting of one carbon atom, one nitrogen atom, and three oxygen atoms.

triphenylmethane dye. A dyestuff derived from $(C_6H_5)_3CH$, having the chromophore group,

```
      C=C
     /   \
  =C       C=
     \   /
      C=C
```

e.g., crystal violet, *p*-rosaniline and methyl green.

triple bond. Chemical bond formed by three pairs of valence electrons; one is present in molecular bonding σ-orbital and two others occupy molecular bonding π-orbitals with nodal planes perpendicular to one another, *e.g.*, C≡C bond in acetylene. Its presence indicates a highly unsaturated and reactive compound. Triple bonds are more stable to high temperature than single and double bonds and are strong electron receptors. They are active in many type of reactions, *e.g.*, Diels-Alder, vinylation, and polymerization with Ziegler catalysts.

triple ions. The aggregation of these ions, two of similar and one of opposite charges, *i.e.* + — + or — + —. In solvents of low dielectric constant, there is a tendeney for ion pairs to attach to themselves another ion, especially at high sat concentrations. Triple ions contribute towards the conductivity of the solution as they have a net positive or negative charge. Also known as ion triplets.

triple point. The temperature and pressure at which the vapour, liquid. and solid phases of a substance are in equilibrium. For water the triple point occurs at 273.16 K and 611.2 Pa. This value forms the basis of the definition of the kelvin and the thermodynamic temperature scale.

triplet. In atomic spectroscopy group of spectral lines arising due to transition between energy levels corresponding to two atomic triplet terms.

triplet state. Atomic or molecular state (term) with total spin quantum number $S = 1$ and three possibilities of projection of spin angular-momentum onto direction of the external magnetic field, corresponding to three values of magnetic spin quantum number $M_s = \pm 1$ and 0; triplet multiplicity is equal to 3.

triplet-triplet annihilation. Transition of two colliding molecules from their triplet state to corresponding ground and excited singlet state due to their intermolecular energy exchange. Molecule raised to singlet state subsequently displays delayed fluorescence.

tris-. A prefix indicating that a certain chemical grouping occurs three times in a molecule, for example, tris(hydroxymethyl)aminomethane $(CH_2OH)_3CNH_2$. *See also* bis-.

tritium. *T.* The radioactive isotope of hydrogen (H^3); its nucleus contains two neutrons and one proton, giving an atomic weight of 3.017. It is made by impingement of slow neutrons on lithium nuclei and has a half-life of about 12 years. It is used to induce thermonuclear (fusion) reactions, as well as in biochemical tracer work and specialized research.

triton. A hydrogen nucleus of mass number 3, the term being derived from tritium, the hydrogen isotope of mass number 3.

trituration. The process of grinding substance together, usually with a little liquid, thus promoting reaction by intimate contact. The form of mercuric sulphide known as vermilion for example, is usually prepared by triturating mercury and sulphur with a little potassium hydroxide solution.

tritylation. The introduction of trityl (triphenylmethyl) group, $(C_6H_5)_3C—$, into an organic compound, *e.g.*, by the reaction of hydroxyl group with trityle chloride. Also known as triphenylmethylation.

trivalent. Having a valence of three, as exemplified by the elements aluminum, chromium, and nitrogen.

trivial name. A name applied by early chemists to a number of simple organic compounds, usually based on their sources or properties, *e.g.*, acetone and acetic acid (from Latin acetum, vinegar); urea (from urine); glucose and glycerol from Greek glyc- (sweet).

Trotarelli test. A test for ptomaines which is based on the colour reactions obtained with palladium nitrate and sodium nitroprusside.

Trouton's rule. Molai latent heat of vaporization of liquid (at normal boiling point under atmospheric pressure) divided by this boiling temperature on absolute scale is nearly the same for a great number of substances and approximately equal to 21 cal $mole^{-1}$ K^{-1}.

Truchot reagent. A solution of 0.2 g. diphenylamine in 100 ml. concentrated sulphuric acid. It is used in the identification of nitrocellulose silk, which dissolves in it with the formation of a blue solution.

true activation energy. Apparent activation energy of reaction in multiphase system E^x increased by value of adsorption heat of substrate λ_A and diminished by value of adsorption heat of product λ_B:

$$E = E^x + \lambda_A - \lambda_B$$

true half-width. Spectral line width as given by features of emitting or adsorbing species, free of instrument factors; it is usually given as true half-width $\Delta\nu^t_{1/2}$. Also known as true width.

true solution. Limiting case of dispersed system in which particles of dispersed phase have dimensions smaller than 1 nm, therefore of order of simple molecules.

trypsin. An enzyme that digests proteins. It is secreted in an inactive form (trypsinogen) by the pancrease into the duodenum. There, trypsinogen is acted on by an enzyme (enterokinase) produced in the duodenum to yield trypsin. The active enzyme plays an important role in the digestion of proteins in the anterior portion of the small intestine.

Tsalapatani reaction for quinine. Add a 20% trichloroacetic acid solution to an aqueous solution of quinine hydrochloride. This forms a white precipitate which, when dried and heated to 370-380K. for 5-10 minutes, evolves chloroform and becomes red.

Tschirch test for shellac and its substitutes. The shellac is dissolved in alcohol, to settle, filtered and then ether added to the filterate. A yellow solution is obtained which, when shaken with dilute sodium carbonate, causes the yellow colouring matter to pass into the soda solution and impart a redviolet colour. Subsequently, the aqueous solution is acidified, and it again becomes yellow. When shaken, the colouring matter dissolves inthe ether which is a yellow colour. No colouring matter obtained with shellac substitutes.

Tschugaev reagent and test for nickel. The reagent is α-dimethylglyoxime. The liquid to be tested is made strongly ammonical, shaken, and the powdered reagent added, then the mixture is heated to boiling. A scarlet precipitate forms in the presence of nickel. Several modifications of this test have been developed.

Tschugaev test for differentiation borneol and isoborneol. Nitrous gases are evolved on treating borneol at ordinary temperatures with concentrated nitric acid but isoborneol, when similarly treated remains unchanged. If the reaction mixture is diluted with water, borneol produces crystals and isoborneol a thick oil.

Tseou-Chow test. A reaction for differentiating acetals from ethers conducted by adding 4 drops of the solution to be tested to 5 ml. of 10% alcoholic resorcinol solution and then pouring 1 ml. of 20% sulphuric acid down the side of the inclined tube. Acetals form a precipitate, usually red in colour, at the junction of the two layers and show a further change of colour on the addition of 6 N sodium hydroxide or ammonia. Ethers do not show this test.

tungsten. An element.

		Symbol	W
		Atomic No.	74
State	Solid	Atomic Wt.	183.85
Group	VIB	Valence	2,4,5,6
		Isotopes	5 stable
		m.p.	3683K
		b.p.	5933K

Tungsten does not occur as such in nature but is obtained in the form of the compound tungstic oxide, WO_3, by reduction of the ores wolframite and scheelite.

Two forms of metallic tungsten are known α-tungsten, which has a body-centered cubic crystal structure, and β-tungsten which has a face-centered cubic crystal structure. The metal exhibits the phenomenon of passivity so that it is quite resistant to chemical action even though it has a strong reducing action when a fresh surface is exposed, or in potentiometric titrations. Tungsten has four naturally occurring isotopes, ^{180}W, and ^{182}W through ^{184}W. The isotope ^{180}W is radioactive with a half-life approximately 3×10^{14} years. Six other radioactive isotopes have been identified, ^{176}W through ^{178}W, ^{185}W, W^{187} and ^{188}W. All have half-lives considerably less than 4 months.

The major properties of tungsten which make it an essential natural resource are its extremely high melting point and its strong electrical conductivity. It is one of the heaviest metals, with a specific gravity of 19.3. Approximately one half of the tungsten produced is in the form of sintered tungsten carbides. These compounds are used for cutting tools and wear-resistant parts. About 15% of production in consumed for making wire used in lamps and also for various shapes used in aerospace and defense products. Another 15% of production is used far high-temperature alloys and powder metallurgy. Approximately 10% goes into high-speed tools. The remaining production goes into a wide variety of applications.

Tunmann test reaction for nicotine. A test for nicotine made by permitting a solution of *p*-dimethylaminobenzaldehyde in fuming hydrochloric acid to come in contact with a drop of nicotine on a slide. A violet colour is formed.

tunnel effect An effect in which electrons are able to tunnel through a narrow potential barrier that would constitute a forbidden region if the electrons were treated as classical particles. That there is a finite probability of an electron tunnelling from one classically allowed region to another arises as a consequence of *quantum mechanics. The effect is made use of in the tunnel diode.

turbidimetry. Analytical method based on light transmittance measurements related to changes of solution opacity due to isolation of determined component in form of deposit of emulsion.

twin crystal. A crystal made up of two parts which are orientated differently but in a regular fashion related to the crystallography of each portion. Two kinds of twin may be recognised :

(*a*) Interpenetration or contact twins. These involve the idea of two simple crystals interpenetrating in such a way that one individual appears to have been rotated 180° about a twin axis relative to the other.

(*b*) Rotation twins. These are conventionally derived by assuming the following operation. A simple unturned crystal is divided along a plane, *i.e.*, the twin plane, which may or may not have a plane of symmetry, but which is invariably paralled to a possible crystal face. At right angles to the twin plane is the twin axis (which cannot be an evenfold axis of symmetry) about which one-half of the crystal is rotated through 180° relative to the other half. The two halves of the crystal are then united along a composition plane, which may or may not be the same as the twin plane. A characteristic feature of twin crystals is the occurrance of re-entrant angles.

twin gliding. Crystal gliding that results in the formation of crystal twins.

twin law. A statement relating two or more individuals of a twin to one another in terms of their crystallography.

twinning. The formation of twin crystals by growth, translation, or gliding.

twinning axis. The crystal axis about which one individual of a twin crystal may be rotated; usually 180° to bring it into coincidence with the other individual. It cannot be coincident with the axes of the two-fold, four-fold, six-fold symmetry.

twinning displacement. Displacement in a crystal due to twin gliding.

twinning plane. The common plane across which individual components of a crystal twin are symmetrically arranged or reflected. It is parallel to a crystal face but not to a plane of symmetry of a single crystal. It is usually identical with the composition plane.

Twitchell process. An industrial process for the production of glycerine and fatty acids by the acid hydrolysis of fats or oils.

two-dimensional chromatography. Chromatographic technique used in paper or thin-layer chromatography in which development is carried out successively in two perpendicular directions.

two-quantum transition. Simultaneous absorption of two photons by atom or molecule.

Tyndall effect. The reflection or scattering of light by colloidal particles suspended in a gas or liquid. As the light beam passes through the suspension, the particles (which are too small to be seen in an optical microscope) indicate their presence by reflecting the light at various angles, depending on their position relative to the incident beam. As a result, a visible path or cone of light appears. A similar effect car be seen by passing an intense light beam through a darkened room.

Tyrer process. The direct sulphonation of benzene with sulphuric acid to produce benzenesulphonic acid. The process is carried out at 450-460 K, so that the water produced in the reaction is removed simultaneously.

U

U. Symbol for the element uranium.

Udranszky test reaction for cholesterol. A test for cholesterol made by adding 5 drop of 0.5% aqueous furfural solution to 5 ml. of the alcoholic solution to be tested, mixing, and then floating the mixture on 5 ml. of concentrated sulphuric acid. An intense red colour, gradually changing to blue, is given by cholesterol.

Uffelmann reaction for acid. A solution of 0.3 g. phenol and 1 drop of a saturated aqueous solution of ferric chloride in 50 ml. water. This reagent is used in testing for lactic acid in gastric juice. A colour change from blue to yellow indicates the presence of lactic acid.

Uhlenhut test. A test for copper made by adding a solution of 0.5 g. 1,2-diaminoanthraquinone-3-sulphionic acid in 500 ml. water and 40 ml. of 35% sodium hydroxide to a solution to be tested. If copper is present, an intense blue colour is produced.

Ullmann reaction. Condensation of two aryl groups in reaction of haloarenes in presence of powdered copper, at 370—470 K, resulting in formation of biaryls, *e.g.*,

$$2C_6H_5I + Cu \xrightarrow{\Delta} C_6H_5{-}C_6H_5 + CuI_2$$

This reaction is also utilized for the synthesis of aryl ethers and derivatives of phenylanthranilic acid, *e.g.*,

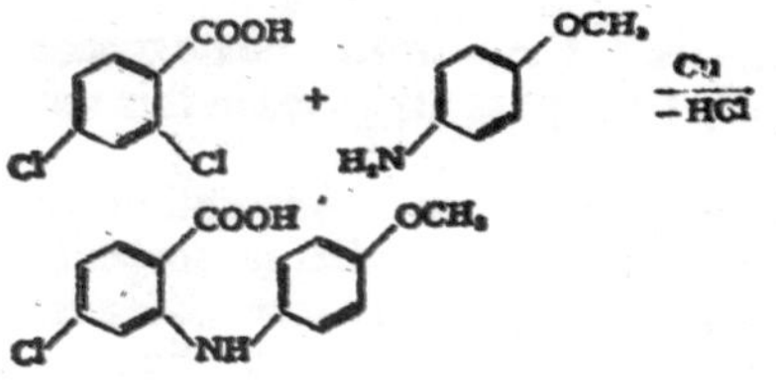

Ultee cyanhydrin method. A method of forming cyanhydrins of ketones or aldehydes by treatment with anhydrous hydrogen cyanide containing a trace of alkali cyanide at 273K.

ultimate analysis. A quantitative elementary analysis. This term is used commonly by the organic chemist to denote an analysis for the determination of the quantities of the elements in a chemical substance, in contrast with a proximate analysis.

ultracentrifuge. A centrifuge of high speed which provides convection-free conditions and which is used for quantitative measurement of sedimentation velocity or sedimentation equilibrium or for the separation of particles (solute) in liquid solution.

ultrafiltration. Filtration though membranes whose pores are small enough to retain colloidal particles. Ultrafilters differ from ordinary filters only in the fineness of the pores through which the liquid must pass. By using a series of filters of graduated fineness it is possible to prepare a series of sols in which the size of the disperse phase particles progressively decreases.

ultramicroscopy. A method for extending the range of vision of the ordinary microscope in which a powerful beam of light is focussed into a liquid under examination in such a way that the direction of the light is at right angles to the line of vision in the instrument. The ultramicroscopic particles, *i.e.*, those smaller than 0.25μm in diameter, are then surrounded by visible diffraction rings and may thus be perceived. Particles as small as 1 nm in diameter have been observed in this way.

ultramicrospectrophotometry. Spectroscopic technique used for absorption measurements for microgramme samples by utilization of so-called microvessels made of capillary tubes which enable spectrophotometric studies to be conducted on 20—30 nm^3 of liquids.

ultraphotic rays. Rays beyond the visible region of the spectrum. This term is used as a general expression for ultraviolet and infrared rays.

ultrasonic. The science of effects of sound vibrations beyond the limit of audible frequencies. Used for dust, smoke and mist precipitation ; preparation of colloidal dispersions ; cleaning of metal parts, precision machinery, fabrics, etc ; fraction welding ; formation of catalysts ; degassing and solidification of molten metals ; extracting flavor oils in brewing : electroplating ; drilling hard material ; fluxless soldering ; nondestuctive testing. Also used for investigating the physical properties, determination of molecular weights of liquid polymers, degree of association of water, and for inducing chemical reaction. Biological effects are also under study.

ultraviolet radiation. Electromagnetic radiation range of wavelength between 1nm to about 400 nm. Most UV radiation for practical use is produced by various types of mercury-vapour lamps. Ordinary glass absorbs UV radiation and therefore lenses and prisms for use in the UV are made from quartz.

ultraviolet absorber. An organic compound which absorbs the ultraviolet radiation present in sun light; it is added to products which tend to deteriorate from prolonged exposure to light for example, various plastics and rubber. Various derivatives of benzene, and acrylonitrile are used. Though not usually classed as a U.V. absorber in the chemical additive sense, glass does not transmit ultraviolet radiation.

ultraviolet spectrum. Spectrum in ultraviolet wavelength region with bands corresponding to transitions between different electronic state of atoms or molecules. Also known as UV spectrum.

uncertainty principle. In classical physics the observables characterizing a given system are assumed to be simultaneously measurable (in principle) with arbitrarily small error. For instance, it is thought possible to observe the initial position and velocity of a particle and therewith, using Newton's laws, to predict exactly its future path in any assigned force field. According to the uncertainty principle, accurate measurement of an observable quantity necessarily produces uncertainties in one's knowledge of the values of other observables. In particular, for a single particle relation (1) holds Δx :

$$\Delta x \Delta p_x > h/2\pi \quad (1)$$

represents the uncertainty (error) in the location of the x coordinate of the particle at any instant, and Δp_x is the simultaneous uncertainty in the x component of the particle momentum. Relation (1) asserts that under the best circumstances, the product $\Delta x \Delta p_x$ of the uncertainties cannot be less than about 10^{-34} joule second.

The uncertainty relation (2) is derived and interpreted :

$$\Delta t \Delta E \vee \hbar \quad (2)$$

somewhat differently than relation (1) ; it asserts that for any system, an energy measurement with error ΔE must be performed in a time not less than $\Delta t \gtrsim h/\Delta E$. If system endures for only Δt sec, any measurement of its energy must be uncertain by at least

$$\Delta E \gtrsim h \Delta t.$$

uncompensated heat, Q_n. Quantity defined as :

$$Q_n = TdS - \delta Q$$

where δQ= elementary heat, S=entropy of system, T=thermodynamic temperature. In irreversible processes Q_n is never equal to zero and always positive.

unidentate ligand Ligand which occupies only one coordination position around central atom. Also known as monofunctional ligand.

uniaxial. Characteristic of or by a single axis, as an object which has only one axis, or a flow of energy that travels only along one axis of a crystal or other medium.

uniaxial crystal. A doubly refracting crystal which has but one optic axis and which shows characteristic interference figures, as Iceland spar, quartz, and tourmaline.

unified model. Model of atomic nucleus as system consisting of a core, described by collective model and one or several external (valency) nucleons. Unified model is combination of collective and shell models.

uniform dispersion. A mixture of two or more substances (gas-in-gas, solid-in-solid, liquid-in-liquid, or solid-in-liquid) in which the proportion of components is exactly the same in all parts of the mixture. For example, air at sea level is a uniform mixture of oxygen, nitrogen, carbon dioxide, etc. ; a properly blended point is a uniform dispersion of its solid and liquid components. The word homogeneous is frequently (but inexactly) used in this sense.

unimolecular adsorption. Adsorption on surface of solid or liquid bodies (adsorbents) with formation of unimolecular layer of adsorbate. Also known as monolayer adsorption.

unimolecular reaction A chemical reactions or step involving only one molecule. An example is the decomposition of dinitrogen tetroxide :

$$N_2O_4 \rightleftharpoons 2NO_2$$

Molecules colliding with other molecules acquire sufficient activation energy to react, and the activated complex only involves the atoms of a single molecule.

unit. A specified measure of a physical quantity, such as length, mass, time, etc. specified multiples of which are used to express magnitudes of that physical quantity. For scientific purposes previous systems of units have now been replaced by SI units.

unit cell. The smallest parallelepiped which exhibits all characteristic geometric features of space lattice (besides transtation symmetry) and enables reconstruction of it by simple repetition of cell in directions of its three edges.

unit operation. A term used in chemical engineering to designate an action performed on a material or mixture of materials for a particular purpose which does not involve a chemical change (though it often does involve a physical change); examples are filtration (separation without physical change), distillation (separation with physical change), and heat exchange (energy transfer with or without physical change). Unit operations are distinguished from unit process, which involve chemical change, *e.g.*, hydrolysis, polymerization, etc.

unit process. Certain chemical reactions, commonly organic reactions, which are so widely used that their general characteristics have been studied by chemists and chemical engineers. Among these important general reactions are halogenation, hydrolysis, esterification, nitration, amination, diazotization, coupling, oxidation, hydrogenation, Friedel-Crafts reaction, alkylation, polymerization, pyrolysis, cracking, isomerization, and cyclization. All these processes and a large number of others are described in this book together with many less commonly-used reactions, under the term reaction, followed by the specific name, or under the name of the discoveror investtgator to whom the reaction is attributed.

unitary thermal process. A process for the polymerizatian of cracked or paraffin hydrocarbon gases made up of propane and propene, butanes and butenes etc., in order to polymerize them to produce such liquid products as gasoline and gas oil. This process is conducted at temperatures of 775-800 K., and at high pressure and no catalysts are used.

united atom. Atom obtained by artificial process of uniting nuclei of diatomic molecule.

univalent. In its most common use, this term indicates an element or radical having only one valence, as, *e.g.*, sodium. However the term is also used to indicated an element or radical having a valence of 1, although the term monovalent is preferable for this meaning.

univariant system. According to the phase rule a system which has but one degree of freedom, *e.g.*, the system liquid water ⇌ water vapour.

universal constants. Physical constants whose numerical values (according to present status of knowledge) do not depend on such parameters as pressure, volume, temperature and properties of substance or systems which are used for their measurement but on system of units; examples of universal constants are : velocity of light in vacuum, absolute zero point temperature, gas constant, Avogadro constant, gravitational constant, charge and rest mass of electron, etc. Also known as absolute constant fundamental constants.

universal indicator. Mixture of several *p*H indicators which changes continuously over large *p*H range ; it is used for approximate determination of *p*H. Also known as multiple range indicator.

Unna-Golodetz test. A test for many proteins, based on their reducing power, whereby sulphur suspended in water is converted into hydrogen sulphide which is detectable by its odour and exposure to lead acetate paper.

unorganized ferment. An enzyme unconnected with living cells and capable of acting in sterile media.

unpaired electrons. Electrons on singly occupied atomic or molecular orbitals ; they are responsible for instance for paramagnetism of atoms and molecules.

unsaturated bond. Multiple bond characterized by its special reactivity, *e.g.*, double bond in alkenes or triple bond in alkynes. Also known as unsaturated linkage.

unsaturated compound. A substance that contains one or more elements of which the total valence is either not satisfied or is satisfied by union with another atom on the same element. $C \leftrightarrows O$ is an example of the first class ; $H_2C{=}CH_2$, an example of the second. Unsaturated compounds usually add hydrogen, halogens, ozone, halogen acids, and other compounds, directly producing saturated compounds, *viz.*,

$$C \leftrightarrows O + Cl_2 \rightarrow COCl_2$$

$$HC{\equiv}CH + 2HCl \rightarrow Cl_2CH{-}CH_3$$

unsaturated solution. A solution that can dissolve more solute under the given conditions of temperature and pressure, before reaching equilibrium with the solid phase.

unsaturated weston cell. Weston cell with cadmium sulphate solution saturated at 277K (unsaturated at room temperature) ; it has very low temperature coefficient of EMF.

unstable. A substance or system which assumes an entirely new condition or arrangement when disturbed from its initial state. Thus, unstable systems readily revert to a condition of greater entropy.

unstable complex. Complex which readily undergoes dissociation in solution, *i.e.*, is characterized by small value of stability constant. Also known as thermodynamically unstable complex.

unsymmetrical. Asymmetrical, or not symmetrical.

1. Of a crystal, having no plane of symmetry.

2. Of a tetravalent atom, having four dissimilar atoms or groups bonded to it. (*See* isomerism, optical.)

3. Of a derivative of a benzene having three substituents which do not occupy the 1, 2, 3, (*i.e.*, symmetrical) position.

ur-acid. A hydrolytic product of a cyclic ureide, as oxaluric acid,

```
NH—CO—COOH
|
C—NH₂
||
O
```

The energy yield per atom of 235 is about 200 million electron volts, plus two to three neutrons, which is turn initiate new fissions. Plutonium is made from uranium by neutron absorption. Uranium has four oxidation states (III), (IV), and (V), and (VI), and the ions in aqueons solution are usually represented as U^{3+}, U^{4+}, UO_2^+, and UO_2^{2+}. The oxidation-reduction scheme, on the hydrogen scale (in which the potential for $\frac{1}{2}H_2 \rightarrow H^+$ is taken as zero) is indicated as follows :

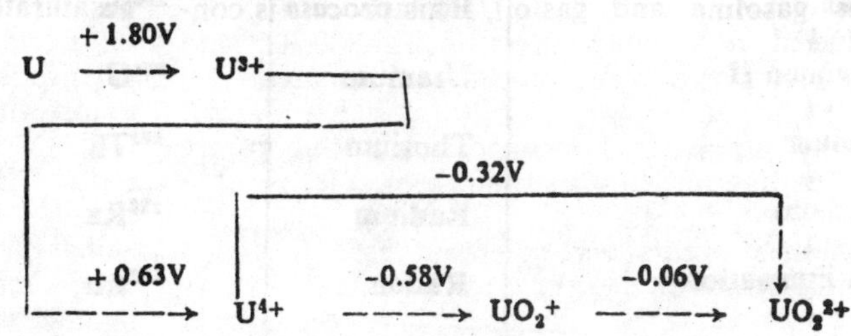

Oxidation-Reduction Potentials of Uranium Ions (in 1-molar hydrochloric acid)

uranium. An element.

		Symbol	U
		Atomic No.	92
		Atomic Wt.	238.03
State	Solid	Valence	3,4,6
Group	IIIB	Isotopes	3
		m.p.	1405K
		b.p.	4091K

A heavy and strongly radioactive metal, member of actinide series, extracted from the ores pitchblende and carnotite. The total uranium content of the earth's crust to a depth of 25 km is estimated to be 10^{17} kg ; the oceans may contain 10^{13} kg of uranium.

Uranium metal is found in three allotropic forms : (*a*) alpha phase, stable below 941K, orthorhombic, (*b*) beta phase, existing between 941-1047K, tetragonal and (*c*) gamma phase above 1047K, body-centred cubic crystal structure. The gamma phase behaves most nearly like that of a true metal. The alpha phase has several nonmetallic feature in its crystallography The beta phase is brittle.

The element uranium found in nature consists of the three isotopes of mass numbers 238, 235, 234 with relalive abundence 99.28, 0.71, and 0.006% respectively. The isotope 235 can be split by neutron bombardment to yield nuclear energy. The artificial isotope U-233, derived from thorium, is also fissionable, The third natural isotope, U-234, has little importance.

The UO_2^+ ion is unstable in solution and undergoes disproportionation to U^{4+} and UO_2^{2+}. A few solid compounds of this oxidation state are known, as for example, UF_5 and UCl_5,

The ion U^{3+} forms intense red solutions in H_2O and is oxidized by water at an appreciable rate, The rate of oxidation appears to increase with increasing ionic strength, although concentrated solutions are said to be stabilized by strong acids such as hydrochloric. Solutions of uranium (IV) are green, and uranium (VI) solutions, yellow.

uranium-lead dating. A group of methods of dating certain rocks that depends on the decay of the radioisotopes uranium-238 to lead-206 (half-life 4.5×10^9 years) or the decay of uranium-235 to lead-207 (half life 7.1×10^8 years). One form of uranium-lead dating depends on measuring the ratio of the amount of helium trapped in the rock to the amount of uranium present (since the decay $^{238}U \rightarrow {}^{206}Pb$ release eight alpha-particles). Another method of calculating the age of the rocks is to measnre the ratio of radiogenic lead (^{206}Pb, ^{207}Pb, and ^{208}Pb) present to nonradiogenic lead (^{204}Pb). The methods give reliable results for ages of the order 10^7 to 10^9 years.

THE URANIUM SERIES

Radiolement	Corresponding Element	Symbol	Radiation	Half Life
Uranium I ↓	Uranium	^{238}U	α	4.5×10^{9} yr.
Uranium X_1 ↓	Thorium	^{234}Th	β	24.1 days
Uranium X_2 ↓	Protactinium	^{234}Pa	β	1.2 min.
Uranium II ↓	Uranium	^{234}U	α	2.50×10^{5} yr.
Ionium ↓	Thorium	^{230}Th	α	8.0×10^{4} yr.
Radium ↓	Radium	^{226}Ra	α	1.62×10^{3} yr.
Ra Emanation ↓	Radon	^{222}Rn	α	3.82 days
Radium A (99.96% → Radium B; 0.04% → Astatine-218)	Polonium	^{218}Po	α and β	3.05 min.
Radium B	Lead	^{214}Pb	β	26.8 min.
Astatine-218	Astatine	^{218}At	α	1.3 s.
↓ Radium C (99.96% → Radium C′; 0.04% → Radium C″)	Bismuth	^{214}Bi	β and α	19.7 min
Radium C′	Polonium	^{214}Po	α	1.64×10^{-4} s.
Radium C″	Thallium	^{210}Tl	β	1.3 min.
↓ Radium D ↓	Lead	^{210}Pb	β	22 yr.
Radium E (~100% → Radium F; ~10^{-5}% → Thallium-206)	Bismuth	^{210}Bi	β and α	5.0 days
Radium F	Polonium	^{210}Po	α	138.3 days
Thallium-206	Thallium	^{206}Tl	β	4.23 min.
↓ Radium G (End Product)	Lead	^{206}Pb	Stable	—

uranium series. Naturally occurring series with first and last members uranium ^{238}U, and lead, ^{206}Pb, respectively. The mass number of erch member of this series is $A=4n+2$, where $n=$ natural number.

uranoids. Elements of actinide family starting with uranium (uranium, neptunium, plutonium, americium, curium, californium, einsteinium, fermium, mendelevium, nobelium lawrencium). Also known as uranides.

urea cycle. The series of biochemical reactions that converts ammonia to urea during the excertion of metabolic nitrogen. Urea formation occurs in animals and, to a lesser extent, in some other animals. The liver converts ammonia to the much less toxic urea, which is excreted in solution in urine. Also known as ornithine cycle.

urease. An enzyme obtained from the soyabean. It is used for the quantitative estimation of urea, which it hydrolyses, giving off ammonia gas. With urine its use is specific, as it does not affect other nitrogen compounds present—only the urea.

Urech cyanhydrin method. A method of forming cyanhydrins of ketones by treatment of a mixture in equivalent proportions of the ketone and an alkali cyanide, with acetic or sulphuric acid.

Urech hydantoin synthesis. A method of formation of hydantoins by addition of α-amino acids to potassium cyanate, followed by ring closure :

$$RCH(NH_2)COOH + KOCN \rightarrow \left[\begin{array}{l} R-CH-COOK \\ \quad\;\; | \\ \quad\; NH \\ \quad\;\; | \\ O=C-NH_2 \end{array}\right] \xrightarrow[\Delta]{HCl}$$

$$\text{(hydantoin ring: R, O; HN, NH; C=O)} + KCl + H_2O.$$

ureide. In general a derivative of urea, either by substituting for one or more of its hydrogen atom, as for one of its NH_2-groups, or for its carbonyl oxygen atom, as far more than one of the these. The term is.

urethane. An ester of carbamic acid of the general form :

$$\begin{array}{c} H_2NC-OR \\ \| \\ O \end{array}$$

urethane resins. Synthetic resins containing the repeating group —NH—CO—O—. There are numerous types made by copolymerizing isocyanate esters with polyhydric alcohols. They have a variety of uses in plastics, paints, and solid foams. Also known as polyurethanes.

uricolytic enzyme. An enzyme that catalyzes the metabolizing of uric acid to urea.

Usanovich-Ebert-Konopik's theory of acids and bases. The most general contemporary theory of acids and bases ; acids are species having tendecy to lose protons or arbitrary cations or to add on electrons or arbitrary anions, bases are species having tendency to add on protons or arbitrary cations or to lose electrons or arbitrary anions.

Utz test for formaldehyde in milk. Equal volumes of milk and concentrated hydrochloric acid are heated with a few granules of vanillin. A pale-violet colour is produced if the milk is free from formaldehyde ; if formaldehyde is present, a yellow colour is obtained.

Utz test for mineral acids in vinegar. To 10 ml. of the vinegar, add about 4g. of cane sugar and invert in the usual manner. Shake about 3 times with ether ; and after filtering the ether solution, evaporate it. Dry the residue on the steam bath and add a few drops of 1 : 100 resorcinol-hydrochloric acid. A rose to red colour is given if mineral acids are present.

U.V. Abbreviation for ultraviolet light.

V

V. Symbol for the element vanadium. Abbreviation for volume

vacancy. 1. A term used in crystallography to describe a defect in a crystal due to the absence of an atom or ion in the lattice structure. Such defects are common in crystals; they cause energy imbalances within the crystal which often result in marked changes in their electrical and optical properties. *See also* hole; semiconductor.

2. It also refers to the absence of one or more electrons in the valence shell of an atom.

vaccine. This term was applied originally to the preparation obtained by Jenner from lymph exuded from lesions developed by cows suffering from cow pox and which represented the poineer work on immunization for smallpox. The term vaccine has been extended to cover any bacterial suspension used to confer immunity against a disease.

vaccum distillation. A method of distillation conducted under pressure so as to lower the boiling point of a volatile substance, usually resorted to in order to avoid the decomposition or other alteration of the substance which might occur at high temperature, or to reduce a very high boiling point to a temperature that is more reasonably accessible in the laboratory.

Vageler equation. An expression relating the degree of exchange and the concentration in an ion exchange system, of the form:

$$X = \frac{S \cdot a}{a + c}$$

where X=amount exchanged, a=electrolyte added, and S and c are constants.

Valdiguie' test reaction. A test for aminopyrine made by adding several drops of Schiff reagent to an aqueous or alcoholic solution to be tested. A red colouration is produced if aminopyrine is present.

valence. A whole number indicating for any element its ability to combine with another element. In inorganic compounds, characterized by ionic bond, this is equivalent to the positive oxidation number, as it represents the number of electrons that the electropositive atom transfers its partner in a compound, that is, the number of electrons in its out or valence shell. Negative or polar valences characterize electronegative atoms, which tend to acquire electrons and are thus usually oxidizing agents (oxygen, chlorine, and other halogens). Since a molecule is always electrically neutral, the algebraic sum of the valences of its constituent atoms must equal zero. Many metals have several positive valences. Chlorine (a nonmetal) is exceptional, as under various conditions it can have valences of -1, $+1$, $+3$, $+4$, $+5$, and $+7$. In organic compounds, the valence represents the number of electrons shared between the atoms of compound as covalent bonds, exeept in the case of organic nitrogen compounds in which one electron is transferred in addition to those shared. Also known as valence number; valency.

valence-band (in band theory of solids). Energy band originating from overlap of highest completely filled electronic levels of all atoms or ions forming crystal lattice.

valence-bond method. Quantum chemistry method used to compute approximate wave functions of many-electron systems in form of linear combinations of known functions corresponding to same preselected electron distributions (*viz.*, so-called resonance structures). Also known as VB method.

valence-bond theory. Theory which assumes that formation of complex compound is accompanied by transfer of electrons of ligands into hybridized orbitals of central ion. Characteristic features of this theory is preservation, in general, of individuality of atoms within complex and action of exchange forces between ligand and central ion, which corresponds to complete covalence of bonds. Considering assumed hybridization, theory makes possible easy explanation of directed valence bonds and stereochemistry of complexes.

valence electrons. Electrons of outer electronic shell in atom. They play decisive role in formation of chemical bonds. Also known as valency electrons.

valence number. *See* valence

valence shell. Outer electron shell of atom, occupied in its ground state

valency. *See* valence.

valency electrons. *See* valence electrons.

Valenta reagent for differentiating aliphatic and aromatic hydrocarbons. This reagent is dimethyl sulphate, which dissolves aromatic hydrocarbons in the cold, but not aliphatic hydrocarbons.

Valenta reagent for fats. This reagent is glacial acetic acid, which produces clear solution with fats and fatty oils at various temperatures.

Valser solution. A 10% aqueous solution of potassium iodide which is saturated with mercuric iodide and used as a test reagent for alkaloids. A white precipitate is given by most alkaloids.

Vamvakas test. A test for gelatin (in starch syrup). On boiling a 10% gelatin solution with Nessler solution an immediate, lustrous, lead-gray precipitate is formed. The precipitate is duller in colour with more dilute solutions.

vanadium. An element.

		Symbol	V
		Atomic No.	23
		Atomic Wt.	50.9414
State	Solid	Valence	2,3,4,5
Group	VB	Isotopes	2 stable
		m.p.	2163K
		b.p.	3653K

One of the softer metals, vanadium, has unusual resistance to corrosion and has no toxic properties in elemental form. It occurs only in the form of ores, among which are carnotite and phosphate rock, from which it is extracted as V_2O_5 ; the metal is obtained by the reduction of the oxide with calcium. It is an important transition metal and complexing agent. Its principal use as a metal is as an alloying ingredient (ferrovanadium) for corrosion-resistant steels, especially for those exposed to saline atmospheres and seawater ; its resistance to liquid sodium has led to its use in nuclear reactors. Its most important compound is vanadium pentoxide (V_2O_5), which is the chief catalyst used for the manufacture of sulphuric acid by the contact process ; it also has other catalytic applications. Most of the vanadium compounds are considered to be toxic.

vanadium group. Elements in fifth sub-group of periodic system with structure of outer electronic shells of atoms $(n-1)d^3ns^2$; vanadium, niobium, tantalum, (protactinium). Also known as vanadium family.

van Deen test. A test for blood made by adding several drops of tincture of guaiac resin and red (ozonized) turpentine oil to the sample to be tested. A blue colour indicates the presence of blood.

van der Waals bond. This type of linkage considerably weaker than ordinary chemical linkage, is caused by van der Waals forces. It occurs *e.g.*, between atoms of noble gases and between molecules in molecular crystals. Also known as molecular bond.

van Der Waals equation of state. Empirical (thermal) equation of state for real gas :

$$\left(p+\frac{a}{V_m^2}\right)(V_m-b)=RT$$

where p = pressure, Vm = molar gas volume, T = thermodynamic temperature, R = universal gas constant, a, b = constants characteristic for the given gas ; value of a/V_m^2 represents correction for force of mutual attraction of molecules, constant b is correction for molecules' own molar volume.

van der Waals forces. Extremely weak forces of interaction between unexcited atoms or molecules of gases ; they account for the fact that gases do not behave strictly in accordance with theory, *i.e.*, their behaviour varies slightly from that described by the ideal or perfect gas laws. They are weaker than hydrogen bonds and are not involved in chemical bonding. Van der Waals forces include interaction of temporary fluctuating multipole moments (dispersion effect), interaction of permanent multipoles with induced multipoles (induction effect), and interactian of permanent multipoles (orientation effect).

van der Waals isotherm. p-V isotherm described by van der Waals equation.

van der Waals radius. One half of distance between two identical atoms when repulsive and attractive forces are completely balanced. Sum of van der Waals radii of two atoms is called van der Waals distance.

van Ekenstein-Blanksma test reaction. A test for furfural performed by adding albumin and concentrated hydrochloric acid to the solution to be tested. A dirty red to brown colour indicates the presence of furfural.

Vanino test. A test for colloidal metal solutions in which barium sulphate precipitates and decolorizes colloidal solutions of gold, silver, etc. Dissolved substances, like aniline dyes, are not disturbed.

van Itallie test reaction for antipyrine. Heat the solution to be tested with nitric acid. A cherry-red colour is given by antipyrine.

van Itallie test reaction for thymol. Add 1 drop potassium hydroxide solution to a solution containing thymol and enough iodine-potassium iodide solution to colour the liquid yellowish. A red colour is given on gentle warming.

van Slyke method. A method for determination of primary amines, and hence compounds which yield primary amines on hydrolysis, such as proteins, by reaction with nitrous acid warming. The evolved nitrogen is measured. the reaction is :

$$RNH_2+HNO_2 \rightarrow N_2+ROH+H_2O$$

van't Hoff complex. In homogeneous catalysis, rate of decay of substrate—catalyst complex into starting compounds is considerably lower than rate of decay into reaction products.

van't Hoff factor. A factor which expresses the ratio of the observed osmotic pressure of a solution to the value calculated upon the basis of the osmotic pressure to the product of the temperature and the constant, divided by the volume.

van't Hoff isobar. Equation which determines influence of isobaric temperature change on thermodynamic constant of chemical equilibrium

$$\left(\frac{\partial \ln K_a}{\partial T}\right)_p = \frac{\Delta H}{RT^2}$$

where K_a=thermodynamic chemical equilibrium constant, T=thermodynamic temperature, p=pressure, ΔH=standard enthalpy of chemical reaction, and R=molar gas constant. Also known as **van't Hoff equation**; **van't Hoff relation**.

van't Hoff isochore. Equation which determines influence of isochoric temperature changes on thermodynamic constant of chemical equilibrium

$$\left(\frac{\partial \ln K_a}{\partial T}\right)_v = \frac{\Delta U}{RT^2}$$

where K_a=thermodynamic chemical equilibrium constant, T=thermodynamic temperature, V=volume, ΔU=standard internal energy of chemical reaction, and R=molar gas constant. Also known as **reaction isochore**.

van't Hoff law. A dissolved substance has the same osmotic pressure as the gas pressure it would exert in the form of an ideal gas occupying the same volume as that of the solution. The formula describing dependence of osmotic pressure π of infinitely diluted solution of non-electrolyte on thermodynamic temperature T and molar concentration of solution c, is

$$\pi = cRT$$

where R=molar gas constant.

van't Hoff rule. Increase of temperature by 10 degrees (kelvins) doubles (roughly) rate of reaction.

van't Hoff rule of optical superposition. The molar rotation of compound containing several chiral centres is the sum of rotations of particular chiral centres in molecule. Rule does not hold when chiral centres are located in direct neighbourhood.

van Urk test differentiating chloramine-T from hypochlorites. 1. With a resorcinol solution, hypochlorites give a purple-red colour immediately while chloramine-T gives a green and then a yellow colour which becomes red on heating.

2. Hypochlorite gives a blue-green colour with β-naphthol on boiling while chloramine-T gives a yellow colour.

3. With reduced indigo solution, hypochlorite bleaches out the blue colour while chloramine-T does not.

van Zijp test for cholesterol. A test for cholesterol made by exposing, for 1—4 hours, a thin layer of cholesterol (such as the evaporation residue from a solution in chloroform) to the vapours of concentrated hydroiodic acid containing iodine. Blue or bluished-black crystals are obtained. This reaction is not given by ergosterol and phytosterols.

vapour. A term applied to a gas that is at a temperature below its critical temperature, which can, therefore, be condenced by pressure alone.

vapour density. The density of a gas referred to the density of hydrogen or air as unity. If the density of hydrogen is taken as 2, the vapour density is approximately the molecular weight ; if it is taken as one, the vapour density equals half the molecular weight.

vapour pressure. A value characteristic of all liquids and some solids. It is the pressure exerted by the vapour when evaporation and condensation exactly balance each other in a closed system, that is when as many molecules are entering the liquid as are leaving it. This is called the equilibrium state between a liquid and its vapour. It is function of the substance and of its temperature. This pressure rises with temperature because of the increase in molecular kinetics caused by the added energy. When the pressure of the vapour reaches that of the atmosphere, the liquid boils.

vapour tension. The tendency of a liquid to enter the vapour state, balanced by, and numerically equal to the vapour pressure.

varnish. A solution of a resin or a drying oil in a volatile solvent or in a drying oil. Which solidifies on evaporation of solvent due to polymerization of the oil or resin base. Varnishes are classified as spirit, turpentine, and linseed oil varnishes, according to the solvent used.

vaseline. A mixture of paraffins obtained from the residues of the distillation of crude petroleum. It consists chiefly of hydrocarbons $C_{22}H_{46}$ and $C_{33}H_{68}$ and melts between 310 and 320K.

Vassallo test reaction. A test for tin and bismuth made by heating 50 g. hematoxylone wood with 100 g. alcohol for 3 hours under a reflux condenser and filtering. Strips of filter papar are then dipped into the extract and dried. Under certain conditions, tin and bismuth salt solutions produce a violet colour.

vat dye. A term used in dyeing technology to refer to a group of organic dyes derived from indigo or anthraquinone ; the essential process involved in making such dyes is reduction of the insoluble compound to a soluble form to enable it to penetrate the fibre, after which it is oxidized back in the original insoluble state. The reducing agent is sodium hydrosulphite. Indanthrene blue is a well-known dye of this type. Vat dyes are notably stable to water and are used for textiles requiring a high degree of light-fastness and colour permanence. The term vat was presumably adopted from the equipment used in their manufacture.

vector. 1. An animal or insect that harbors infectious bacteria or viruses and thus trasmits a disease.

2. A quantity that has both magnitude and direction.

vegetable alkali. An alkaloid ; the term is also applied at times to potash or potassium carbonate.

vegetable oil. An oil (or when solid, a fat) obtained from a wide variety of vegetable and some fruits and characterized by relatively high percentages of unsaturated fatty acids, though low percentages of saturated acids are often present. These oils are classified as drying, semidrying, or nondrying, based on their tendency to undergo oxygen-catayzed polymerization on exposure to air which depends on their content of unsaturated components. The fatty acids occur in the form of esters called glycerides, usually as mixtures of several types. Some of the fatty acids commonly occurring in vegetable oils are : saturated—palmitic, myristic, stearic, lauric, and arachidic ; unsaturated —oleic, linoleic, linolenic, eleostearic.

vehicle. A term used to refer to those components of a paint that are in the form of liquids, solutions or (in the case of emulsion paints) water suspensions. Thus, the vehicle is composed of the binder (drying oil or synthetic resin) plus the solvent or thinner, in which the dry ingredients (pigments, extenders, and driers) are dispersed. It is so-called because the liquid acts as a carrier for the solids.

Velardi test. A test aldehydes, performed by heating a few drops of the oil with some alcoholic potassium hydroxide and a trace of benzenesulphhydroxamic acid. The solution is then cooled, diluted with water and a little ether added. It is then neutralized with hydrochloric acid and a little ferric chloride solution added. A red to yellow colour is produced if aldehyde is present.

Venable test reaction. A test for ferric iron made by adding the sample to be tested to a cobalt nitrate solution which has been coloured blue by adding concentrated hydrochloric acid. Traces of ferric salts will turn the solution green.

Ventre test reaction. A method for detecting sugar, the reagents for which are (*a*) a mixture of equal parts alcohol and nitrobenzene ; (*b*) a saturated aqueous solution of ammonium molybdate. Ten ml. of the solution to be tested are boiled for 3 minutes with 5 drops of solution (*a*), 20 drops of solution (*b*), and 12 drops of concentrated sulphuric acid. If sugar is present, a blue colour develops, the intensity of which is proportional to the sugar content.

Verhassel test reactions. Reactions for α- and β-naphthols. (*i*) Chlorinated lime solution added to an aqueous solution of α-naphthol gives a violet colour, added to β-naphthol a green-yellow colour. (*ii*) Potassium ferrocyanide added to an aqueous solution of α-naphthol gives a violet colour, added to β-naphthol a light yellow colour. (*iii*) Potassium ferricyanide added to an aqueous solution of α-naphthol gives a brown colour, added to β-naphthol a green-yellow colour. (*iv*) Ferric chloride added to an alcoholic solution of α-naphthol gives a violet precipitate, added to β-naphthol a greenish precipitate.

Vesterberg dehydrogenation. The dehydrogenation of a compound by heating it with sulphur at high temperatures. It is often used for the dehydrogenation of alicyclic hydrocarbons to the corresponding aromatic derivatives.

vibrational characteristic temperature (of a molecule), θ_v. Parameter expressed in units of temperature :

$$\theta_v = \frac{h\nu}{k}$$

where h=Planck constant, k=Boltzmann constant, and ν=classical nuclear vibration frequency in molecule. Vibrational characteristic temperature enters expression for molecular vibrational partition function.

vibrational energy of molecules. Diatomic molecules may possess vibrational energy, produced by relative oscillation of the two constituent atoms. Polyatomic molecules exhibit vibrational energy by oscillations in the directions of the valence bonds and by oscillations perpendicular to that direction ; a molecule of n atoms usually has $3n - 6$ modes of vibration, increasing to $3n - 5$ modes in the case of a linear molecule.

vibrational partition function, $\nu(T)$. Function defined by :

$$\nu(T) = \left[2 \sin h \frac{\theta_v}{2T} \right]^{-1}$$

where T=thermodynamic temperature, and θ_v=characteristic vibration temperature ; vibrational partition function determines influence of vibrations of nuclei in diatomic molecule on thermodynamic properties of corresponding gas.

vibrational quantum number, n. In quantum mechanics number which determines energy E_n of harmonic oscillator according to $E_n = h\nu(n + 1/2)$; where h=Planck constant, ν= vibration frequency ; n assumes non-negative integral values.

vibration band. In IR spectroscopy band corresponding to vibrational transition. There is also simultaneous change of rotational energy.

vibration-rotational spectrum. Spectrum corresponding to transitions between two vibrational levels of the same electronic state with simultaneous change of rotational energy. Such are useful in calculating force constants, and other molecular constants.

vibration spectrum. Spectrum in infrared region arising from transition between vibration energy levels of the same electronic state. Also known as oscillation spectrum.

vibrations. *See* oscillations.

vibronic level. Vibrational-electronic molecular energy level.

vic-. Abbreviation of vicinal, as vic-triazine.

vicinal. A term derived from the Latin word for near or neighbouring ; in chemical terminology, it refers to locations on a carbon backbone or cyclic structure which are immediately next to each other, Vicinal locations on the molecule shown are occupied by the hydrogen atoms and the hydroxyl groups :

```
 H  H
 |  |
—C—C—
 |  |
HO  OH
```

Victor Meyer synthesis. A method of formation of aliphatic nitro derivatives (and nitrites) by action of metallic nitries on aliphatic halides,

$$RCl + M{-}NO_2 \rightarrow RNO_2 \text{ (or RONO)} + MCl$$

Vignon test. A test for free phosphorus in phosphorus sulphide made by passing hydrogen over the phosphorus sulphide. If white free phosphorus is present, the hydrogen becomes phosphorescent and burns with a green flame.

Villiers Fayolle reagent for free chlorine. A mixture of 20 ml. of a saturated aqueous solution of *o*-toluidine, 100 ml. of a saturated aqueous solution of aniline, and 30 ml. acetic acid, used in detecting free chlorine. A blue colour is obtained if free chlorine is present.

Vincent test reaction for α- and β-naphthol. A reaction of α-naphthol and β-naphthol with iodic acid. α-Naphthol gives a yellowish, flocculent precipitate which soon becomes violet. β-Naphthol gives a precipitate which gradually becomes red. and after a short time the solution turns reddish and the precipitate red-brown.

vinyl. The unsaturated organic group $H_2C{=}CH$ occurring in a large number of reactive compounds which polymerize readily and are thus of great importance in high-polymer chemistry.

vinylation. Introduction of vinyl group $—CH{=}CH_2$ into molecule of organic compound, usually by addition of compound with active hydrogen atoms to acetylene or its derivative, *e.g.*,

$$HC{\equiv}CH + CH_3OH \xrightarrow{KOH} H_2C{=}CH{-}OCH_3$$

vinylene. The radical $—CH{=}CH—$.

vinylidene. The radical $H_2C{=}C{=}$.

vinylogs. Compounds which differ from each other by a $—CH{=}CH—$ unit ; *e.g*, cinnamic aldehyde, $C_6H_5CH{=}CHCHO$ is a vinylog of benzaldehyde, C_6H_5CHO.

vinylogy rule. Influence of functional group on certain other group of atoms in molecule may spread beyond α-position, especially if the latter group is separated from the former by one or more conjugated double bonds, *e.g.*, aldehyde group activates methyl group in crotonaldehyde (vinylogue of acetaldehyde) similary to acetaldehyde.

virial. Statistical average :

$$\sum_{\nu} x_\nu \cdot \frac{\partial U}{\partial x_\nu}$$

where ν enumerates gas molecules, $x=$ position vector of centre of mass of molecule, and $U=$ potential energy of intermolecular interactions. Virial determines influence of intermolecular interactions on gas pressure.

virial coefficients. Coefficients *B*, *C*, ... in virial equation of state (respectively called : second, third etc, virial coefficient) ; values characteristic for the given gas and depending on temperature.

virial equation of state. Thermal equation of state of real gas in the form of power series with respect to molar volume *Vm* or pressure *p*

$$pV_m = RT\left(1 + \frac{B}{V_m} + \frac{C}{V_m^2} + \cdots\right)$$

or

$$pV_m = RT(1 + B'p + C'p^2 + \ldots)$$

where T = thermodynamic temperature, R = universal gas constant, B, C ... or B', C' ... = virial coefficients.

virus. A colloidal complex composed of one or more nucleic acid linked to a protein ; most are too small to be retained by the finest filter media and hence are called filterable viruses. Viruses are not true organisms, as are bacteria; they do not absorb nutrients and thus are unable to grow. They do reproduce within cellular tissue and initiate a large number of infectious diseases in man, among which are smallpox, influenza, and poliomyelitis ; such animal diseases as rabies, Newcastle disease, and hoof-and-mouth disease are due to viruses. In plants, bushy stunt and tobacco mosaic viruses are well-known ; the latter is a nucleoprotein which is about 95% protein and 5% ribonucleic acid. Viruses behave like parasites and have a number of different shapes (fibrous, spherical, etc.), which can be observed clearly in an electron microscope. They are on the borderline between animate and inanimate.

viscoelasticity. Rheological properties of such amorphous plastic polymers which, with respect to violent and brief forces, behave like an plastic body, and with respect to long-acting forces behave like a viscous liquid displaying increasing deformation with time. This phenomenon is caused by rates of relaxation much faster than in typical solids, but slower than in typical liquids. Also known as viscoelastic behaviour; viscoelastic properties.

viscose process. A method for the manufacture of rayon. Purified sulphite pulp and cotton linters are used as raw material. Sheets of this material are dipped in sodium hydroxide, then shredded. The shredded material is treated with carbon disulphide, then dissolved in sodium hydroxide solution. This solution is forced through spinnerettes and comes in contact with a coagulating bath which hardens each jet into a filament. The fibres are then washed, desulphurized, and bleached.

viscometry. Branch of physical chemistry concerned with the study of viscosity of different systems.

viscocity. A measure of the resistance to flow that a fluid offers when it is subjected to shear stress. For a Newtonian fluid, the force, F, needed to maintain a velocity gradient. dv/dx, between adjacent planes of a fluid of area A is given by : $F = \eta A(dv/dx)$, where η is a constant, called the coefficient of viscosity. In SI units it has the unit pascal second (in the c.g.s. system it was measured in *poise). Non-Newtonian fluids, such as clays, do not conform to this simple model. Viscosity is affected by temperature, especially for liquids comprised of large, complicated molecules such as asphalt or heavy oils. The more complex the molecular organization, the greater is the viscosity of a liquid. Pragmatic tests of viscosity involve either dropping a small metal sphere through a container of the liquid being measured and noting its times of fall placing the test liquid in a glass tube provided with a small outlet and observing the rate of escape (Saybolt method).

viscosity coefficient. η. The force per unit area necessary to sustain unit difference of velocity between parallel layers of fluid unit distance apart. Measure of viscosity, coefficient determined by formula :

$$\eta = \frac{F}{A\frac{dv}{dx}} \quad \text{...(1)}$$

where F = tangent force necessary to displace liquid layer of surface area A with velocity dv with respect to second layer at distance dx. Unit of viscosity in SI system is pascal-second.

Also,

$$\eta = \frac{2gr^2(\rho - \rho_l)}{9u} \quad \text{...(2)}$$

where g = gravitational constant, r = the radius of the sphere, ρ = its density, ρ_l = the density of the liquid, and u = the maximum velocity of fall of the sphere in the liquid.

Expression (2) is obtained from the limiting, or maximum velocity of fall of a small sphere under free gravitational fall.

The expression for the coefficient of viscosity of a liquid flowing through a narrow tube. It has the form :

$$\eta = \frac{\pi pr^4 t}{8vl} \quad \text{...(3)}$$

where η = the coefficient of viscosity, p = the pressure on the liquid, r = the radius of the tube, t = the time in which a volume v flows through the tube, and l = the length of the tube.

A relationship between the viscosity of a solution having a given concentration of solute and the viscosity of the pure solvent, has the form :

$$\text{Specific viscosity} = \frac{\eta - \eta_0}{\eta_0} \quad \ldots(2)$$

where η = the viscosity of the solution, and η_0 = the viscosity of the pure solvent.

visible region. Electromagnetic radiation range of wavelength between ca. 400 nm and ca. 750 nm to which human eye is sensitive.

visible spectrum. Spectrum in visible wavelength region with lines or bands corresponding to transitions between different electronic energy levels of atoms or molecules.

visual titration. Titration in which end point is determined visually (on basis of colour changes appearnce or disappearance of fluorescence etc.)

vitagen. One of a group of substances essential not only for transformation of enery or regulation of the metabolism of structural units but also in that they supply energy and/or structural building units. The last two properties, *i.e.*, the function of supplying energy and structural units, are not possessed by vitamins, which are thus differentiated from vitagens. Examples of vitagen are the essential amino acids, carbohydrates, fatty acids, sulphur-containing compounds, and transferable methyl compounds.

Vitali test for ethyl alcohol. The solution to be tested is treated with carbon disulphide, ammonium molybdate, potassium hydroxide, and excess dilute sulphuric acid. A red colour is produced, due to the formation of molybdenum xanthogenate, if ethyl alcohol is present.

Vitali test reaction for bromide. An adaptation of Cresti's test for copper. made by adding a little sulphuric a very dilute solution of hydrobromic acid or of a bromide and evaporating As the mixture becomes concentrated, it becomes violet-brown and turbid; however, the turbidity disappears on dilution.

Vitali test reaction for chlorate. An intense blue colour is produced by chlorate with aniline sulphate and concentrated sulphuric acid.

Vitali test reaction for formaldehyde. A modification of the Fischer test made by adding a not too concentrated solution of phenylhdrazine to the solution to be tested. A whitish. milky turbidity indicates the presence of formaldehyde.

Vitali test reaction for iodoform. When iododorm is fused with a little potassium hydroxide and thymol, a violete mass forms which dissolves in alcohol. Upon addition, the violet colour is changed to scarlet.

vitamin. A class of biochemically active organic compounds which profoundly affect many metabolic functions, either alone or in conjunction with enzymes or coenzymes ; their chemical behaviour is essentially catalytic, for example, ascorbic acid (vitamin C) catalyzes cellular oxidation-reduction reactions, and calciferol (vitamin D_2) facilitates deposition of calcium in bony structures. Vitamins include various types of compounds, among which are hydrocarbons, amino complexes, sterols, and acids. All are ultimately derived from plant products, though two (A and D) are present in the body in the form of provitamins and are either elaborated in the liver or activated ultraviolet radiation. Most important from a nutritional standpoint are the B complex and vitamins A, D and C.

vitazyme. A compound term indicating a substance possessing certain characteristics or properties of both a vitamin which has a vitamin as a posthetic group.

vitreous state. Amorphous state characterized by rigid arrangement of molecules, occupying defined, unchangeable positions. Deformation caused by external force is elastic and is described by Hook's law. Also known as glassy state.

vitriol. A name applied to sulphuric acid, also known as oil of vitriol. Certain sulphates which crystallize in the rhombic system with seven molecules of water (or form isomorphous crystals with those that do, as $CuSO_4$) are termed vitriols. Thus ferrous sulphate (green vitriol), zinc sulphate (white vitriol), copper sulphate (blue vitriol), magnesium sulphate, manganous sulphate, cobalt sulphate and nickel sulphate, all crystallized with water constitute the vitriols.

Vogel test for alcohol in chloroform. Add a little

dry potassium hydroxide to the chloroform, then pour off the chloroform. Some of the potassium hydroxide is dissolved if alcohol is present and, on adding a little pyrogallol, a yellow to brown colour develops in the chloroform.

Voigt reaction. The addition of amines to benzonis to form aminodesoxybenzenes :

$$R'-\overset{\overset{O}{\|}}{C}-\overset{\overset{OH}{|}}{CH}-R' + R''NH_2 \xrightarrow{P_2O_5} R'-\overset{\overset{NHR''}{|}}{CH}-\overset{\overset{O}{\|}}{C}R' + H_2O$$

volatile alkali. Ammonia ; ammonium hydroxide.

volatility. Literally meaning "to fly away," this term refers to the ease with which a liquid or solid passes into its vapour phase (evaporates or sublimes). The rate increases with temperature. Ethyl alcohol and hydrocarbon liquids are more volatile than water ; solid carbon dioxide (dry ice) sublimes at 222K and is thus more volatile than ice or snow.

volatility coefficient, f_p. Measure of deviation of real gas properties from those of ideal gas, defined by ratio of volatility of a given gas a_p to pressure p of ideal in the same conditions,

$$f_p = a_p / p$$

Volcy-Boucher test reaction for α- and β-naphthol. A reaction for α-and β-naphthol made by dissolving 0.5 g. of the naphthol in a very small quantity of alcohol and adding 2 ml. of 10% cupric sulphate solution and 4 ml. freshly prepared 10% potassium cyanide solution. A violet precipitate is given by α-naphthol and a yellow precipitate by β-naphthol.

Volhard-Erdmann thiophene synthesis. A reaction of sodium succinate (or related compounds) with phosphorus sulphides, yielding thiophene (or related compounds).

$$\underset{NaOOC}{\overset{RCH}{|}}-\underset{COONa}{\overset{CHR'}{|}} \xrightarrow{P_2S_3} \begin{matrix} RCH-CR' \\ \| \quad\quad \| \\ HC \quad\quad CH \\ \diagdown \;\; \diagup \\ S \end{matrix}$$

Volland test. A test for cod liver oil made by adding concentrated sulphuric acid. True cod liver oil is colour first violet, then brown-red, and finally black.

voltammetry. Electrochemical method consisting in recording and analysis of dependence of electric current on potential of working electrode.

volume. The space occupied by any body. It is definite for any specific temperature and pressure. The metric units of volume are the cubic centimeter and the litre. The volume of one gram molecule of a gas at standard temperature and pressure is about 22.4 litres.

volume fraction, ϕ_B. Ratio of volume of dissolved substance B and volume of solution :

$$\phi_B = \frac{n_B \; V_B}{\sum_i n_i V_i}$$

where n_B=number of moles of dissolved substance B, V_B=molar volume of dissolved substance B, $\sum_i n_i V_i$ = sum of volume of all constituents in solution.

volume of activation, ΔV^*. Difference of volume of initial and transition state experimentally determined by measurement of pressure dependence of rate constant of a given process (chemical reaction, diffussion, viscosity) and using formula :

$$\left(\frac{\partial \ln k}{\partial p}\right)_T = \frac{\Delta V^*}{RT}$$

where k=rate constant of a given process, p= pressure, R=molar gas constant and T=thermodynamic temperature.

volumetric analysis. *See* titrimetric analysis.

Von Auwers-Skita rule. Cis-isomers of disubstituted cycloalkane derivatives (mainly C_5 and C_6) usually have higher boiling points, higher densities and higher refractive indices than trans-isomers.

Von Bitto test for monohydric alcohols. A solution of 0.5 g. methyl violet in 1 litre water is the reagent used. One ml. of an alkali polysulphide solution and 1-2 ml. of the reagent are shaken with the liquid to be tested. If the liquid becomes cherry-red to violet-red and remains clear, a monohydric alcohol is present.

Von Bitto test reactions for aldehydes and ketones. 1. Add 1 ml. freshly prepared 0.3-0.5% aqueous sodium nitroprusside solution to the aldehyde or ketone solution and make alkaline with sodium hydroxide solution A red-yellow to violet-red colour forms which is characteristic of the aldehyde or ketone in question.

2. In the liquid aldehyde or ketone or its alcohol solution, dissolve a few crystals of *m*-dinitrobenzene. On addition of a few drops sodium hydroxide solution, a blue colour developes which is changed to violet-red by acetic acid.

Von Bitto test reaction for creatinine. Creatinine gives a violet-red colour with *m*-dinitrobenzene and sodium hydroxide solution, in the presence of acetone. On the addition of metaphosphoric acid the colour changes to cherry-red.

Von Braun cyanogen bromide reaction. Breaking of C—N bond in tertiary amines with cyanogen bromide, *e.g.*,

$$R_3N + BrCN \rightarrow [R_3\overset{+}{N}\text{—}C{\equiv}N]^{+}Br^{-} \xrightarrow{\Delta} R_2N\text{—}C{\equiv}N + RBr$$

Von Braun reaction. Decomposition of acyclated aliphatic amine derivatives to alkyl halides and nitriles, effected by heating with PBr_5 or PCl_5, *e.g.*,

$$RNH\overset{O}{\overset{\|}{C}}C_6H_5 + PBr_5 \xrightarrow{\Delta} RBr + HBr + C_6H_5C{\equiv}N + POBr_3$$

Von Braun reaction causes also decyclization of secondary derivatives of aromatic amines, *e.g.*,

$$\text{Pyridine} + PBr_3 \xrightarrow{\Delta} C_6H_5C{=}O$$

$$C_6H_5C{\equiv}N + BrCH_2(CH_2)_3CH_2Br + POBr$$

Von Braun reaction for carbonyl compounds. The compound diphenylmethanedimethydrazine, made by reduction with zinc dust, dilute acetic acid, and alcohol, of dinitrosodimetyldiaminodiphenylmethane. It forms condensation products with aldehydes and ketones, useful in their identification.

Von Hevesy Logstrup test reaction. To detect zirconium or hafnium, prepare their acetylacetonates by reaction of acetylacetone and sodium carbonate with zirconium oxynitrate or hafnium oxychloride. A carbon disulphide solution of the acetylacetonates becomes red on standing.

Von Kobell scale. A series of integral numbers used to designate materials, chiefly minerals, according to their fusibility—the higher numbers corresponding to higher fusing points. The substances whose fusing points (melting points) constitute the integral values in this scale are : (*i*) stibite ; (*ii*) natrolite ; (*iii*) garnet; lime alumina variety ; (*iv*) hornblende ; (*v*) orthoclase ; (*vi*) bronzite ; (*vii*) (infusible).

Von Neumann's equation. Conservation equation for statistical operator.

$$\frac{\partial\rho}{\partial t} - \frac{i}{h}(H\rho - \rho H) = 0$$

where ρ=statistical operator, H=Hamiltonian of system, t=time, $i=\sqrt{-1}$ and h=Planck constant divided by 2π. In quantum statistical mechanics von Neumann's equation determines times evolution of isolated system. Also known as Liouville-von Neumann equation; quantum mechanical Liouville equation.

Von Richter reaction. The action upon aromatic nitro compounds of potassium cyanide in alcoholic solution, whereby the nitro group is eliminated, and a carboxyl group is joined to the ring in a position ortho to that occupied by the nitro group.

Von Weimarn equation. An expression for the rate of formation of particles of colloidal size from smaller particles such as ions and molecules. It has the form :

$$V_i = k\,\frac{P_1}{P_2},$$

in which Vi=the initial rate of "condensation" or coalescence, k=a constant, P_1=the condensation pressure, and P_2=the condensation resistance.

Vorlander test for differentiating allyl and propenylphenol ethers. Propenylphenol ether produces a red to brown colour within a few minutes with hydrobromic acid dissolve in glacial acetic acid, but allylphenol ether does not give the reaction until several hours have passed.

Vorlander test for hydrochloric acid in chloroform. Add about 0.01 mg. powdered *p*-dimethylaminoazobenzene to 10 ml. of the chloroform. A violet-red colour shows the presence of hydrochloric acid.

Vortmann test reaction for phenol. A dark red precipitate forms on heating phenol with iodine and sodium hydroxide to 325-35K.

Votocek test for ketoses. Mix 2 ml. of glacial acetic acid, a small quantity of carbazole and 1 drop of fuming hydrochloric acid in an evaporating dish, add a drop of the sugar to be tested and place on the water bath for 10 minutes. A cherry-red colour shows the presence of ketoses.

Votocek test for sulphite in the presence of thiosulphate. A solution of 0.075 g. fuchsin in 300 ml. water is mixed with a solution of 0.025 g. malachite green in 100 ml. water. A few drops of this solution are added to 2-3 ml. of the liquid to be tested. Sulphites effect immediate decolourization but thiosulphates or thionates do not.

Vreven test for differentiating creosote and guaiacol. One drop of the liquid to be tested is shaken with 3 drops of ether, 2 drops of concentrated nitric acid, and 2 drops hydrochloric acid. The ether is allowed to evaporate spontaneously. Creosote forms oily drops, whereas guaiacol forms acicular crystsls.

Vreven test reaction for fats. Fats and oils treated with cane sugar and sulphuric acid, produced a yellow to brown colour which changes to rose in 10 minutes, and then to a persistent lilac colour.

vulcanite. A hard insulating substance made by heating natural rubber with a larger quantity of sulphur than that needed merely to "vulcanize" it. In the ordinary vulcanizing process the employment of a small amount of sulphur takes away the stickiness and improves the elastic qualities and toughness of the rubber. Vulcanites is also known as "ebonite".

vulcanization. Cross-linking of rubber hydrocarbon and similar elastomers with sulphur, usually with the aid of heat ; the time required is notably reduced by use of organic accelerators. Vulcanization without heat, and even without sulphur (with peroxides), is possible under special conditions. This process transforms rubber from a soft, hydrocarbon-soluble material that is unstable to temperature changes to a strong, resilient, water-resistant, insoluble product having manifold used over a wide range of temperatures. High-energy radiation may be used to induce vulcanization. With highly accelerated mixtures, from 2 to 3% sulphur is required, and the time for the process may by as short as minutes.

Vulkollan process. A method of producing synthetic elastomers by reaction of ethylene glycol and adipic acid to yield a polyester, which on subsequent treatment with (*i*) a diisocyanate, and (*ii*) water or ethylene glycol, yields the desired elastomer.

Vulpius test for tartaric acid in citric acid. Add 1 ml. of the 1:2 aqueous citric acid solution to 2 ml. of a solution of 1 g. potassium acetate in 20 g. of 90% alcohol. If the citric acid is pure, at first a precipitate forms and the solution becomes clear. A crystalline. precipitate of potassium bitartrate forms immediately, if tartaric acid is present to the extent of 2% : the precipitate forms after vigorous shaking with 1% tartaric acid.

W

W. Symbol for the element tungsten. Symbol for work (external work).

Wachsmith test. A test for nitrogen bases made by adding 0.5 ml. of 15% cupric sulphate solution and 1-2 drops of 1% potassium cyanide solution to 10 ml. of a very dilute solution of the substance to be tested. A colour is produced immediately if nitrogen bases are present. If the solution is too concentrated, a turbidity may form and an excess of potassium cyanide is undesirable. The colours given are: animopyrine, violet; epinephrine, red; apomorphine, a red colours which passes through rose to brown to grey and finally to green; morphine and codeine, yellow-green.

Wackenroder reaction. The reaction between sulphur dioxide and hydrogen sulphide, in the presence of water, which results in the formation of various polythionic acid (H_2S^xOx), as, *e.g.*,

$$3SO_2 + H_2S \rightarrow H_2S_4O_6$$

Wacker process A process for the manufacture of ethanal by the air oxidation of ethene. A mixture of air and ethene is bubbled through a solution containing palladium(II) chloride and copper(II) chloride. The Pd^{2+} ions form a complex with the ethene in which the ion is bound to the pi electrons in the C=C bond. This decreases the electron density in the bond, making it susceptible to nucleophilic attack by water molecules. The complex formed breaks down to ethanal and palladium metal. The Cu^{2+} ions oxidize the palladium back to Pd^{2+}, being reduced to Cu^{+} ions in the process. The air present oxidizes Cu^{+} back to Cu^{2+}. Thus the copper(II) and palladium(II) ions effectively act as catalysts in the process, which is now the main source of ethanal and, by further oxidation, ethanoic acid. It can also be applied to other alkenes.

Wacker reagent for alcohols, aldehydes, or carbohydrates. A solution of *p*-phenylhydrazinesulfonic acid. This reagent must be well shaken. It gives a red colour with aldehydes, alcohols, or carbohydrates in the presence of air and an excess of sodium hydroxide solution. Other hydrazine compounds may be used in this test.

Waegner reagent. A reagent for absorption of carbon monoxide (a modification of the Winkler reagent) which is made by dissolving 5 g. cuprous chloride in 25 ml. of water and 10 g. concentrated hydrochloric acid, heating to boiling, and, after removing the flame but while swirling, adding sodium hypophosphite in small portions until the mixture has become colourless. It is cooled rapidly, concentrated ammonia in excess is added, and then ammonia (sp. gr. 0.96) is added to the desired volume.

Wagenaar test for distinguishing citric, oxalic and tartaric acids. Add 0.3 g. aminopyrine and 0.03 g. resorcinol to a mixture of a few drops of ferric chloride solution and 20 drops of water. Then add 0.05 g. of the acid to be tested and 3 ml. of concentrated sulphuric acid and warm over a small flame. Citric acid gives a yellowish-brown colour; oxalic acid a dark green, changing to pale green on standing; and tartaric acid gives a deep red colour; changing to raspberry-red on standing.

Waggoner solution. A solution of 50 ml. 85-90% C.P. formic acid in 35 ml. distilled water. It is mixed with an aqueous solution of sodium citrate, and the mixture is used to decalcify bones.

Wagner-Jauregg reaction. A method of synthesis of aromatic ring systems by the addition of maleic anhydride to substituted arylethylenes. The initial products of the addition are *bis*-adducts which are decarboxylated to yield the aromatic ring systems.

Wagner-Meerwein rearrangement. Acid-catalyzed conversion of pinacoline alcohol (and its analogues) into alkenes, involving anionic migration (in 1,2-rearrangement) from alkyl or aryl group and elimination of water molecule, *e.g.*,

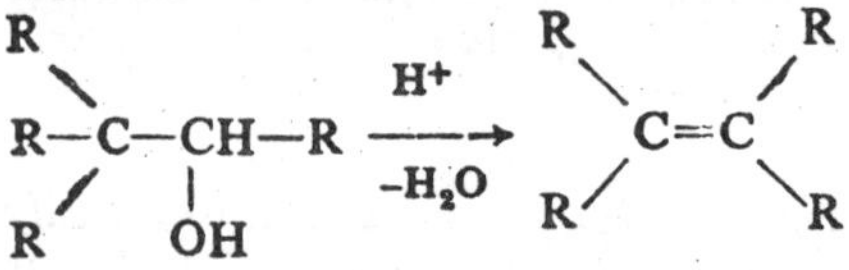

$$R_3C-CH(OH)-R \xrightarrow[-H_2O]{H^+} R_2C=CR_2$$

In case of bicyclic terpenes, this reaction results in expansion or diminishing of rings, *e.g.*,

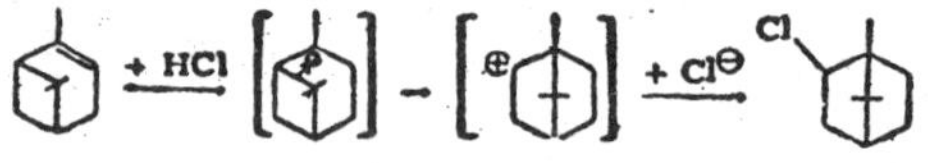

$$\xrightarrow{+HCl} [\;] - [\oplus] \xrightarrow{+Cl^\ominus} Cl$$

Wait test reaction. A test for vitamins A, C, and D made by adding a 1% solution of phosphomolybdic acid in acetic acid to the sample to be tested. Vitamins A and C give a blue colour. Substances containing both vitamins A and D yield first a green colour and then a blue colour.

Walden inversion. Inversion of configuration of molecule taking place in SN2 reaction at atom forming chirality centre. Attacking substituent approaches from opposite side to group leaving molecule, *e.g.*,

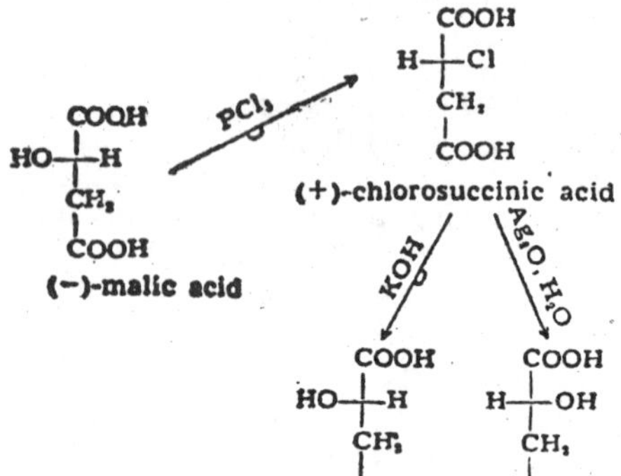

(−)-malic acid (COOH, HO—C—H, CH_2, COOH) $\xrightarrow{PCl_5}$ (+)-chlorosuccinic acid (COOH, H—C—Cl, CH_2, COOH)

(+)-chlorosuccinic acid $\xrightarrow{KOH}$ (−) (COOH, HO—C—H, CH_2, COOH)

(+)-chlorosuccinic acid $\xrightarrow{Ag_2O, H_2O}$ (+) (COOH, H—C—OH, CH_2, COOH)

The concept of rearward attack mechanism gives experimental evidence that in most metathetical reactions the entering group attaches itself to the back face of the atom from that occupied by the displaced group, although the process is not readily detectable except in optically active substances.

Walden's rule. Independently of nature of solvent, $\Lambda_0\eta_0$ = const., where Λ_0 = limiting equivalent conductance of electrolyte in a given solvent, η_0 = viscosity of solvent; empirical rule holds for small ions.

Wallach degradation reaction. The conversion of cyclohexanones to cyclopentanones through a series of reactions including bromination, rearrangement and oxidative decarboxylation :

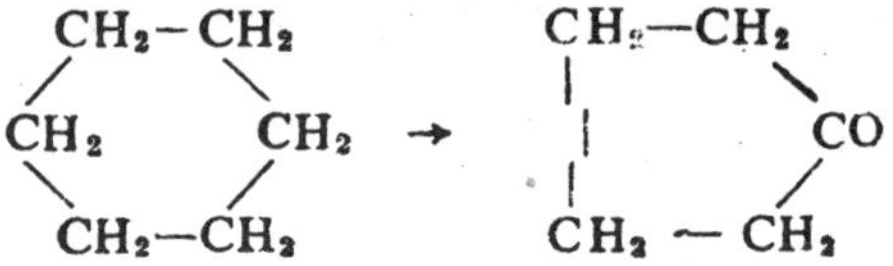

$$\text{cyclo-}(CH_2)_6 \rightarrow (CH_2)_4CO$$

Wallach rearrangement. The acid-catalysed conversion of azoxybenzenes into *p*-hydroxyazobenzene.

$$C_6H_5-N(=O)=N-C_6H_5 \xrightarrow{H_2SO_4} C_6H_5-N=N-C_6H_4-OH(p)$$

Some *o*-hydroxybenzene is also formed as by product.

Wanklyn reaction. The synthesis of salt of monobasic acids from sodium alkyls and carbon dioxide,

$$RNa + CO_2 \rightarrow RCONNa.$$

Ware test for phenol, cresol, naphthol, and thymol. 50 mg. of the substance to be tested are triturated with 10 ml. concentrated hydrochloric acid and 0.5 g. of a mixture of 1 part sodium nitrate and 2 parts anhydrous sodium sulphate. The mixture is let stand for 5 minutes and the colour noted, and then 1 ml. of it is added to excess of 10% ammonia. Characteristic colours are given.

water gas. A gaseous mixture derived by reacting steam with not coke or natural gas in the presence of air ; it contains chiefly carbon monoxide and hydrogen admixed with nitrogen and carbon dioxide. The basic reaction is $C + H_2O \rightarrow CO + H_2$. It has a higher calorific value than producer gas and is also called blue gas. It is used in some processes for ammonia synthesis. It can be carburetted by passing it through hydrocarbon vapours to increase combustibility for fuel purposes. Its composition is 49.51% CO, 49.93% H, 0.35% H_2O, 0.21%

CO_2. In practice the product contains much more carbon dioxide, nitrogen, water, etc.

water glass. A water soluble silicate of sodium (the simplest glass known) made by melting together sand and soda ash. In solid form it hard and brittle, but when heated with steam, it becomes a colourless liquid with a wide range of viscosities according to water content. Silica gel is formed when the material is neutralized by addition of acid. The major uses of water glass are as a dispersing agent for clay suspensions, as a fire retardant coating for paper and fiberboard, as a binder for foundry cores, and as a detergent builder. A similar is made from potassium silicate.

water of crystallization. A form in which water molecules are present in chemical compounds, whereby the H_2O molecule retains its structural identity. Commonly, such H_2O molecules are tetrahedrally or octahedrally coordinated around the cations in the crystal lattice.

water softening. Removel of salts from water especially those that cause hardness, by heating, chemical precipitation, base exchange, or other processes.

wave function. When the system is known to be in the eigenstate corresponding to $A=\alpha$, the eigenfunction $u(x,\beta)$ is the wave function ; that is, it is the function whose projection on an eigenfunction $v(x,\beta)$ of any observable B gives the probability of measuring $B=\beta$. The wave function $\Psi(x)$ may be known exactly ; in other words, the state of the system may be known as exactly as possible (within the limitations of uncertainty and complementarity), even though $\Psi(x)$ is not the eigenfunction of a known operator. This circumstance arises because the wave function obeys Schrodinger's wave equation. Knowing the value of $\Psi(x)$ at time $t=0$, the wave equation completely determines $\Psi(x)$ at all future times. In general, however, if $\Psi(x,0) = u(x,\alpha)$, that is, if ($\Psi(x,t)$ is an eigenfunction A at $t=0$, then $\Psi(x,t)$ will not be an eigenfunction of A at later times $t > 0$.

A system described by a wave function is said to be in a pure state. Not all systems are described by wave functions, however. For example, a beam of hydrogen atoms streaming out of a small hole in a hydrogen discharge tube can be regarded as a statistical ensemble or mixture of pure states oriented with equal probability in all directions.

wave mechanics. *See*. quantum mechanics.

wave number. The number of waves per unit length in vacuum, the reciprocal of λ_{vac}. The usual unit of wave number is the reciprocal centimeter, cm^{-1}.

Term frequency ($\bar{\nu}$) is often misused for wavenumber (ν). They are related by equation : $\bar{\nu}=\nu/c$ where ν=frequency, c=speed of light.

wave particle duality. It is natural to identify such fundamental constituents of matter as protons and electrons with the mass points or particles of classical mechanics. According to quantum mechanics, however, these particles, in fact all material systems, necessarily have wavelike properties. Conversely, the propagation of light, which, by Maxwell's electromagnetic theory, is understood to be a wave phenomenon, is associated in quantum mechanics with massless energetic and momentum-transporting particles called photons. The quantum mechanical synthesis of wave and particle concepts is embodied in the de Broglie relations, given by Eqs. 1 and 2

$$\lambda=h/p \quad (1)$$

$$\nu=E/h \quad (2)$$

These give the wavelength λ and wave frequecy f associated with a free particle (moving freely under no forces) whose momentum is p and energy is E ; the same relations give the photon momentum p and energy E associated with an electromagnetic wave in free space (that is, in a vacuum) whose wavelength is λ and frequency is ν.

The wave properties of matter have been demonstrated conclusively for beams of electrons, atoms (hydrogen, H, and helium, He), and molecules (H_2). When incident upon crystals, these beams are reflected into certain directions forming diffraction patterns. Diffraction patterns are difficult to explain on a particle picture ; they are readily understood on a wave picture, in which wavelets scattered from regularly spaced atoms in the crystal lattice interfere constructively along certain directions only.

The particle properties of light waves are observed in the photoelectric effect and the compton effect.

wave packet. Wave function different from zero only in very limited part of space.

wave vector. Vector perpendicular to head of

wave, of absolute value $k=2\pi/\lambda$, where $\lambda=$ wavelength (*e.g.*, of elastic wave in crystal).

wax. A thermoplastic solid of high molecular weight which may be a hydrocarbon derived from distillation of an aliphatic petroleum (paraffin wax) or an ester of unsatusated fatty acids and alcohols which are endproducts of plant and animal metabolism. Of the latter, beeswax, spermacetic, and wool wax (lanolin) from animals and candelilla, carnauba, and bayberry from plants are in most common use. There is also a group of mineral or earth waxes, chief among which is ozocertite or its purified form, cresin. Certain waxes which has a structure of extremely small crystals are called microcrpstalline waxes ; examples are paraffin derived from petroleum wastes and also the chlorophyll of plants.

Waxes are physically plastic but are sensitive to temperature. As their chemical structure is not polymeric or resinous, they are not plastics in the accepted sense of the word.

weak electrolyte. Electrolyte with degree of dissociation changing from value close to one for very diluted solutions to zero for very concentrated ones (partial dissociation).

weak interaction. Interaction of particles resulting in process which takes place in time range of 10^{-10}—10^{-6} s (slow processes). Weak interaction satisfies only a few laws of conservation.

wave ligand field. Crystal ligand field causing splitting of energy levels (terms) of central ion, small compared with distances between energy levels (terms) of free ion. In complex of such field, number of unpaired electrons remains the same as in free ion (*cf*, crystal field splitting energy, spin-free complex).

Weber-Koch test. A test for propyl, butyl, isobutyl, and isoamyl alcohols, made by gently heating 1 ml. of the alcohol with 2-8 drops of Beckmann chromic acid mixture. The corresponding aldehyde is formed. After any precipitate has settled, the clear, centrifuged solution is treated with sodium hydroxide and a little *o*-nitrobenzaldehyde. Characteristic colours are given by the various alcohols.

Weber-Tollens test reaction. A test for formaldehyde or hexamethylenetetramine that gives, on treatment with hydrochloric acid and phloroglucinol, a whitish flocculent precipitate, which becomes yellowish-red on standing.

Weerman degradation. Preparation of aldehydes inpoverished by one carbon atom by action of aqueous solution of sodium hypochlorite on appropriate α-hydroxyacid amides. This reaction is utilized for shortening carbon chain in aldoses :

$$\begin{array}{l} CHO \\ | \\ CHOH \\ | \\ CHOH \\ | \end{array} \xrightarrow[3.\ +NH_3]{1.\ \text{oxydation}\quad 2.\ \text{lactonization}} \begin{array}{l} CONH_2 \\ | \\ CHOH \\ | \\ CHOH \\ | \end{array} \xrightarrow[NaOH]{NaOCl}$$

$$\left[\begin{array}{l} N{=}C{=}O \\ CHO{-}H \\ | \\ CHOH \\ | \end{array}\right] \xrightarrow{NaOH} \begin{array}{l} NaNCO \\ CHO \\ | \\ CHOH \\ | \end{array}$$

Weil test reaction. A reaction for cobalt and nickel obtained by treating the solution to be tested with potassium chromate. Cabalt solutions give a brownish-red precipitate of basic cobaltous chromate, whereas nickel solutions react only slowly in the cold but, on boiling, a chocolatebrow precipitate of the basic chromate forms.

Weinland-Dottinger test reaction. A reaction for cobalt in which ammonia is added to an aqueous solution containing catechol and a suitable cobalt salt in the necessary proportions. A red precipitate is obtained.

Weizmann process. The bacterial fermentation of starch to yield a mixture of butanol, acetone, and ethanol.

Weizsacker's mass formula. Semiempirical formula for mass or atomic nucleus binding energy as function of its mass number *A* and atomic number Z, based on liquid-drop model of nucleus.

Weldon process. A method for manufacturing chlorine from hydrochloric acid by the action of manganese dioxide, which is reduced in the process to manganous chloride. The latter is in turn reconverted to manganese dioxide, for re-use in the process, by treatment with lime, and oxidation.

Welter rule. A method for approximating the heat of combustion of carbon compounds which contain hydrogen and oxygen. The rule is to subtract the oxygen with as much hydrogen as is necessary to form water with it, then the heats of combustion of the residual carbon and hydrogen gives an approximate value of the heat of combustion of the whole compound. This rule gives results about 10% low.

Werner theory. Theory of structure of complex compounds which assume coordination of ligands around central atom. Assumed presence of principal and auxilliary valences is characteristic for this theory. It explains the formation of coordination compounds by postulating that, even when the combining power of certain atoms is exhausted (as judged by the valence number), such atoms still posses, in some instances, the ability of constructing complex molecules by the formation of definite atomic linkages. This action was attributed to the fact that atoms have in addition to their principal valences, the ability to form other bonds which are termed auxiliary valences.

Weston normal cell. Cell represented by scheme:

Hg, $HgSO_4(s)$ | $CdSO_4 \cdot \frac{8}{3}H_2O$ (sat. solution) | Cd(Hg) (12.5%). EMF of this cell at 293K is 1.01830 V and is standard of international volt. Also known as Weston standard cell, Weston cadmium cell.

wet. When used as a verb, this term refers to the ability of a liquid to spread readily and uniformly over the surface of another liquid or of solid, especially when the solid is in powder form. A liquid of very high surface tension and electrical conductivity, such as mercury, has virtually no wetting capacity; water, with moderately high surface tension and low conductivity, has reasonably good wetting ability but requires a surfactant (also called a wetting or dispersing agent) for maximum effect. Petroleum solvents and fatty acids, which have low surface tension and conductivity, have excellent wetting ability; for example, a hydrocarbon liquid will quickly spread on a water surface, forming a thin, continuous film. The chemical nature of the substance being wet is also a factor; hydrophobic solids repel water and hydrophilic solids attract it.

wetting. Establishment of certain definite wetting angle θ in gas-liquid-solid three-phase system; when $\theta > 90°$ liquid is said in practice not to wet solid, whereas complete (idea) wetting implies contact angle of 0°.

wetting agent. A substance that causes a liquid to spread more readily upon a solid surface, owing its action chiefly to its effect in reducing the surface tension. Specific wetting agents have been developed in many industries. Wetting ability is of critical importance in dyeing, cleaning, painting, and any operation involving suspensions of dry powders. A notable case is the wetting action exerted by stearic acid on carbon black-rubber mixtures. The wetting phenomenon is closely related to emulsification.

Wheeler-Tollens test. A test for pentoses made by heating a 20% hydrochloric acid solution and phloroglucinol with xylose, arabinose, or any substance that splits off a pentose. A cherry-red colour is produced which shows an absorption spectrum between 5200 and 5900 Å.

whiskers. Fibrous single crystals of metals such as aluminium, cobalt, tungsten, and others made synthetically by crystal-growing techniques. They may be up to 0.05 m in length by 10 microns in diameter. They are notable for their fantastically high strength and excellent heat resistance and are used in composites for aeraspace construction (ablative agents) and other engineering applications involving high-temperature exposure.

white arsenic. Trivial name of arsenic trioxide (As_2O_3).

white gold. This term, which has on occasion been used to describe platinum, normally refers to an alloy of gold with nickel or tellurium that in appearance closely resembles platinum.

white spirit. When crude petroleum, is first distilled under atmospheric pressure, the fraction boiling between 420 and 470 K, is often separated for use as a solvent. The paraffins present usually contain a little sulphur and, if the spirit is intended for the paint industry ("turpentin"), this must be removed.

white tin. The common form of tin, *i.e.*, the allotrope stable between the temperatures 286° and about 433 K.

Widman Stoermer synthesis. A method of formation of cinnoline derivatives by diazotization and cyclization of *o*-aminoaryl ethylenes.

$$\text{o-}(NH_2)C_6H_4\text{-}C(R){=}CH_2 + HNO_2 \xrightarrow{HCl} \text{o-}(N_2Cl)C_6H_4\text{-}CR{=}CH_2 \xrightarrow{-HCl} \text{cinnoline (R)}$$

Wiedemann-Franz law. Ratio of thermal conductivity λ and electric conductivity σ is constant at a defined temperature *T* for all metals and is described by formula :

$$\frac{\lambda}{\sigma} = -LT$$

where $L = 2.45 \times 10^{-8}\ V^2/K^2$ is Lorentz number.

Wien effect. The increase in conductance of an electrolyte at high potential gradients.

Wien equation. A relationship between the intensity of radiation of any wave length yielded by a perfect radiator (black body) at a given temperature, of the form :

$$I = a\lambda^{-5} e^{C/\lambda T}$$

in which I=the intensity of radiation at wave length λ, T=the absolute temperature, a and C are constants, and e=the logarithmic base (natural).

Willgerodt reaction. A reaction of a substituted ketone, commonly a substituted alkyl ketone, with a solution of ammonium polysulphide to form an aliphatic acid amide, containing the aryl group. The effect of the reaction is to reduce the carbonyl group and oxidize a terminal, methyl group. In the Kindler variation, a dry amine and sulphur, in equimolecular proportions, replace the ammonium polysulphide, giving a thioamide :

$$C_6H_5.CO.CH_3 \xrightarrow[H_2O]{(NH_4)_2S_x} C_6H_5.CH_2.CO.NH_2$$

$$C_6H_5.CO.CH_3 + R'R''NH + S \rightarrow C_6H_5.CH_2.CS.NR'R'' + H_2O$$

Williamson ether synthesis. Preparation of ethers by treating alcoholates with alkyl halides *e.g.*,

$$R\overset{-}{O}\overset{+}{Na} + R'CH_2X \rightarrow RO{-}CH_2R' + NaX$$

Since alkoxide ions can also function as strong bases, elimination products often accompany the ethers formed by the synthesis. When unsymmetrical ethers are being prepared by this method it is therefore best to choose that combination of reagents which will give the most favourable SN_2 reaction.

$$C_6H_{11}O^{\ominus}Na^{\oplus} + CH_3CH_2Br \longrightarrow C_6H_{11}\text{-}O\text{-}CH_2CH_3 + NaBr$$

ethyl cyclohexyl ether

Since the ratio of substitution to elimination products is usually higher for primary halides than for secondary and tertiary halides, so in Williamson synthesis should employ primary halides whenever possible.

Windaus test reaction for cholesterol. Reactions for cholesterol : (*i*) To cholesterol dissolved in as little ether as possible, add a solution of bromine in glacial acetic acid until a distinct yellow-brown colour results. A crystalline precipitate of cholesterol dibromide, melting at 396-97 K is produced immediately.

(*ii*) Cholesterol in alcoholic solution is precipitated almost quantitatively, as the double compound, by addition of an alcoholic solution of digitonin.

Windisch test for lactic acid. A test for detecting slight quantities of lactic acid is made by distilling the material with potassium dichromate and sulphuric acid and receiving the distillate in Nessler's reagent. A colour, due to the aldehyde formed, is produced in the presence of lactic acid.

Winkler reagent for absorbing carbon monoxide. A solution of 200 g. cuprous chloride and 225g. ammonium chloride in 1 litre water, to which ammonium hydroxide is then added until the solution is clear. This reagent is used to absorb carbon monoxide.

Winkler reagent for nitric oxide gas. A concentrated aqueous solution of ferrous chloride or sulphate which, with nitric oxide, produces a brown to black colour.

Winkler reagent for absorbing oxygen. 50 g. pyrogallol are dissolved in 1 litre potassium hydroxide solution to form a reagent which absorbs oxygen from gas mixtures and is so used in gas analysis.

Winkler test for dissolved oxygen in water, A manganese chloride solution, and a sodium hydroxide solution containing potassium iodide are added to the sample to be tested. The precipitate of manganous oxide is oxidized by any oxygen present to mangano manganite. On dissolving the precipitate by addition of acid, iodine is liberated which can be determined with 0.02 N thiosulphate.

Winstein-Grunwald equation. An equation correlating the rates of nucleophilic unimolecular solvolysis in solvents of varying ionizing abilities ;

$$\log (k/ko) = mY$$

where, k = rate coefficient of a solvolysis in a solvent which has the ionizing ability, m = constant which is characteristic of the compound undergoing solvolysis.

Wittig reaction. Preparation of alkenes from aldehydes and ketones and phosphoric acid yields (alkylidenetriphenylphosphates). Extensive study of this reaction has produced evidence of one or more intermediates, such as the betaine and oxaphosphetane as shown below :

$$\overset{\delta\ominus}{RCH}=\overset{\delta\oplus}{P}\phi_3 + R'_2C=O \longrightarrow \left[\begin{array}{c}\phi_3P^{\oplus}\;\ddot{O}^{\ominus}\\ |\quad\;\; | \\ R-C-C-R' \\ |\quad\;\; | \\ H\quad R'\end{array}\right] \longrightarrow$$

a betaine

$$\left[\begin{array}{c}\phi_3P-\ddot{O}\\ |\quad\;\; | \\ R-C-C-R' \\ |\quad\;\; | \\ H\quad R'\end{array}\right] \longrightarrow \phi_3P=O + \begin{array}{c}R \qquad R' \\ C=C \\ H \qquad R'\end{array}$$

an oxaphosphetane

Witt test reactions for *p*-diamines. 1. An intense blue colour is produced by diamines with an alkaline phenol solution containing calcium hypochlorite.

2. A blue or green colour, changing to red on boiling with water, is produced by diamines with an alcoholic solution of aniline and ferric chloride.

Wohl-Zemplen degradation of sugars. Shortening of carbon chain in aldoses ; acetylation of aldose oxime with acetic anhydride in presence of sodium acetate leads to formation of acetylated nitrile of aldonic acid. The latter on treatment with sodium methylate releases hydrogen cyanide, forming aldose having one carbon atom less :

$$\begin{array}{c}CHO\\ |\\ CHOH\\ |\\ CHOH\\ |\end{array} \xrightarrow{NH_2OH} \begin{array}{c}CH=NOH\\ |\\ CHOH\\ |\\ CHOH\\ |\end{array} \xrightarrow[CH_3COONa]{(CH_3CO)_2O}$$

$$\begin{array}{c} C{=}N \\ | \\ CHOCOCH_3 \\ | \\ CHOH \\ | \end{array} \xrightarrow[CHCl_3]{CH_3ONa} \begin{array}{c} HC{=}N \\ \\ CHO \\ | \\ CHOH \\ | \end{array}$$

Wohl-Ziegler reaction. A method of halogenation by the use of *N* haloamides, used especially in such special cases the substitution of a halogen atom in an unsaturated compound without affecting the unsaturated linkage,

$$RCH{=}CH{-}CH_3 + \text{(N-bromosuccinimide, N–Br)} \longrightarrow$$

$$RCH{=}CH{-}CH_2Br + \text{(succinimide, NH)}$$

Wohler-Metz test reactions. Ruthenium solutions, heated a short time with thiourea and concentrated hydrochloric acid, give a blue colour. A more sensitive reaction can be made by substituting thiocarbanilide for thiourea. A blue green colour forms which can be shaken out with ether. Osmium solutions in concentrated hydrochloric acid, heated for 2 minutes with thiocarbanilide, give a red colouration which can be shaken out with ether to increase the sensitiveness. When metals of the iron and platinum groups are treated with trithiocarbonate in hydrochloric acid salution and shaken out with ether, characteristic colour are obtained. Osmium gives an olive green colour.

Wohler synthesis. The pioneer organic synthesis (really a rearrangement) in which urea was obtained by heating ammonium cyanate :

$$NH_4OCN \xrightarrow{\text{Heat}} \begin{array}{c} H_2N \\ | \\ C{=}O \\ | \\ H_2N \end{array}$$

Wolff-Kishner reduction. Reduction of carbonyl compound to hydrocarbon involving hydrazone formation and heating the latter to 425—450K in presence of strong bases *e.g.*,

$$\begin{array}{c} R \\ \diagdown \\ C{=}O \\ \diagup \\ R' \end{array} \xrightarrow[\Delta]{N_2H_4} \left[\begin{array}{c} R \diagdown C{=}\ddot{N} \\ R' \diagup \quad \diagdown \ddot{N}H_2 \\ \Big\Updownarrow OH^{\ominus} \\ R \diagdown \; H \\ C \\ R' \diagup \; \diagdown N{=}\ddot{N}H \end{array} \right] \xrightarrow{-N_2} \begin{array}{c} R \diagdown \; \diagup H \\ C \\ R' \diagup \; \diagdown H \end{array}$$

Wolff reaction for benzidine and tolidine. A very small quantity of the substance is dissolved in glacial acetic acid, diluted with water and lead peroxide added. A blue colour, disappearing on heating, is produced in the presence of benzidine or toluidine.

Wolff reaction for thiocyanate. An excess of an alcoholic ammonium thiocyanate solution added to a very dilute neutral or nearly neutral alcoholic cobaltous salt solution produces a blue colour which shows a characteristic absorption spectrum.

Wolff rearrangement. A rearrangement of diazoketones, on reaction with alcohols or amines or water, to form esters or amides or acids, and free nitrogen, in the presence of a metallic catalyst, *e.g.*,

$$RCOCHN_2 \xrightarrow{Ag_2O} [HCH{=}C{=}O] \xrightarrow{H_2O} RCH_2COOH$$

Wolffenstein-Boters reaction. A method of production of certain nitrophenols from aromatic compounds (chiefly hydrocarbons) by simultaneous oxidation and nitration. A well-known application of this reaction is in the formation of picric acid by heating benzene with nitric acid in the presence of a mercury salt.

Woodward *cis*-hydroxylation. The treatment of an olefin by a mixture of iodine and silver acetate. Subsequent treatment with silver acetate in aqueous acetic acid and finally hydrolysis results in a product in which the original olefinic group is converted to a *cis*-glycol :

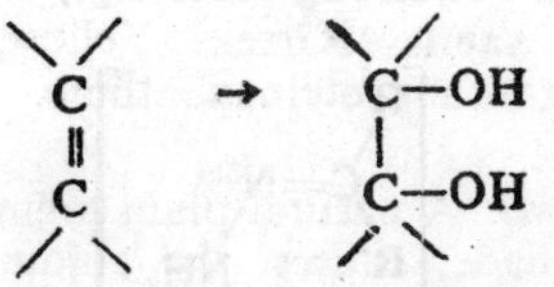

$$>C=C< \rightarrow >C(OH)-C(OH)<$$

Woodward-Fieser rules. A set of empirical rules for calculating λmax from the molecular structure of the compound. There is generally good agreement between the calculated and observed values. but notable exceptions are five-membered ring α, β-unsaturated ketones. λmax about 10 nm longer then the observed value.

Woodward-Hoffmann rules. Orbital symmetry rules relating to ring formation and ring opening.

work function. A quantity that determines the extent to which thermionic or photoelectric emission will occur according to the Richardson equation or Einstein's photoelectric equation. It is sometimes expressed as a potential difference (symbol ϕ) in volts and sometimes as the work to be done by the exciting electron (symbol W) in electron volts or joules. The former has been called the work function potential and the latter the work function energy.

work hardening. An increase in the hardness of metals as a result of working them cold. It causes a permanent distoration of the crystal structure and is particularly apparent with ions, copper, aluminium, etc., whereas with lead and zinc it does not occur as these metals are capable of recrystallizing at room temperature.

wort. In the brewing of beer, sprouted barley is baked to arrest development. This product is known as "malt" and contains the enzyme diastase. The cereal to be used is mashed with water and malt at temperature of 325 K. The resulting mixture, containing the sugar maltose is known "wort".

Wurster salts. Salts obtained by the oxidation of *p*-phenylenediamine derivatives. They contain one nitrogen atom in the state of a free-radical ion, and are strongly coloured owing to the quinonoid structures contributing to their reasonance :

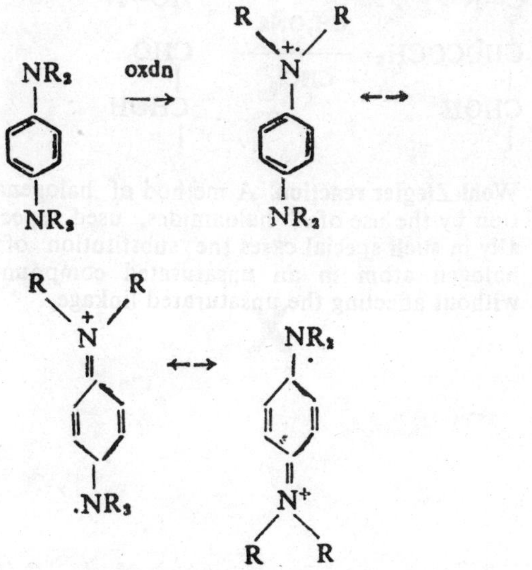

NR₂–C₆H₄–NR₂ —oxdn→ [R₂N⁺· –C₆H₄–NR₂ ←→ R₂N⁺=C₆H₄=NR₂· ←→ ·NR₂–C₆H₄=N⁺R₂]

Wurtz-Fittig reaction. The synthesis of mixed alkyl-aryl hydrocarbons by treatment of halogen-substituted alkyl and aryl compounds with metallic sodium. Thus bromobenzene and methyl bromide yield toluene :

$$C_6H_5Br + CH_3Br + 2Na \rightarrow C_6H_5CH_3 + 2NaBr$$

The yield is reduced by the reaction of two molecules of the bromobenzene to form biphenyl, and the reaction of two molecules of the methyl bromide to form ethane.

Wurtz reaction. Preparation of alkanes by action of sodium on alkyl halides

$$2RX + 2Na \rightarrow R{-}R + 2NaX$$

$$RX + R'X + 2Na \rightarrow R{-}R + R{-}R' + R'{-}R' + NaX$$

X

X. Symbol for a radical (X). Symbol for mole fraction in liquid (x).

xanthate. A salt of an alkyl dithiocarbonic acid in which the acidic portion of the molecule is represented by OCSSH, the alkyl substituent usually being an ethyl group and the metal, one of the alkali series (sodium or potassium). Xanthates of this type are used in metal separation operations. The most familiar variation is cellulose xanthate, used in the viscose rayon process ; it is obtained by reacting alpha-cellulose with carbon disulphide and sodium hydroxide. Xanthates have a characteristic orange-yellow colour, from which the name is derived.

xanthine dase. One of a number of proximate principles of plants, formerly classed alkaloids, and some products of the animal economy derived from xanthine. Representative xanthine compounds are caffeine, theobromine, theophylline, heteroxanthine, paraxanthine. Xathine is 2,6-dihydroxypurin, having the formula :

```
        N=C—OH
        |   |
  OH—C   C—N—H
     ‖   ‖    \
     ‖   ‖     C—H
     ‖   ‖    /
     X—C—N
```

or the di-keto form of this structure.

xantho-, xanth. (Greek) Yellow, as xanthocobaltic xanthoprotein, xanthine.

xanthophyll. A natural plant pigment of bright yellow shade, causes the colour of autumn foliage as well as of many flowers ; is also formed in certain animals and is present especially in egg yolk. Chemically, it belongs to the carotenoid group of compounds ; it is an oxygenated derivative (alcohol) of the hydrocarbon pigment carotene, with two hydroxyl groups. $C_{40}H_{45}(OH)_2$. Xanthophyll is thus entirely different from chlorophyll (a porphyrin), in spite of the similarity in names and its presence in leaves and green vegetation.

xantho-protein reaction. Colourd (yellow) reaction of amino acids containing aromatic nucleic acid ; applied for detection of protein.

xenon. An element.

		Symbol	Xe
		Atomic No.	54
State	Gas	Atomic Wt.	131.3
Group	Noble Gas	Valence	2,4,6,8
		Isotopes	9 stable
		m.p.	161K
		b.p.	166K

Xenon is a heavy, unreactive stable gas occurring in air in precentages. Until recent years, it was thought to be unable to form compounds but it is now known to combine with fluorine oxygen, caesium, and alkali metals to form the correponding fluorides, oxides, and salts, as well as number of metallic complexes. All its compounds are toxic, though the gas itself is not. It is obtained from the oxygen portion of liquid air by specialized vapourization and adsorption techniques. It has been used as an anesthetic and also in flash lamps and light bulbs. Some of its compounds have limited application as oxidizing agents in laboratory analysis.

xerogel. Dry gel formed from lyogel after separation of dispersion medium with simultaneous decrease in volume,

XI hyperon. Elementary particle, a hadron, of baryon number $B=1$, lepton $L=0$, quantum spin number $J=1/2$, strangeness $S=-2$, isospin $I=1/2$, unstable, Ξ-hyperon occurs in two states of charge (isospin doublet) : electrically neutral (Ξ^0-hyperon ; mass $m=1314.7$ MeV, third component of isospin $I_3=1/2$, mean lifetime 3.03×10^{-10} s) and of negative elementary electric charge (Ξ^--hyperon ; $m=1321.31$

MeV, $I_3 = -1/2$, mean lifetime 1.660×10^{-10} s). also known as Ξ-hyperon; cascade particle.

X-ray. Electromagnetic radiation of shorter wavelength than ultraviolet radiation and longer wavelength than gamma radiation. The range of wavelengths is 10^{-11} m to 10^{-9} m. Atoms of all the elements emit a characteristic X-ray spectrum when they are bombarded by electrons. The X-ray photons are emitted when the incident electrons knock an inner orbital electron out of an atom. When this happens an outer electron falls into the inner shell to replace it, losing potential energy (ΔE) in doing so. The wavelength λ of the emitted photon will then be given by

$$\lambda = ch/\Delta E$$

where, c = speed of light, and h = Planck's constant.

x-ray background radiation. X-ray continuous radiation produced by rapid hindrance of movement of charged particles (*e.g.*, electrons) in Coulomb field of atomic nuclei. Also known as white radiation.

x-ray crystallography. The use of X-ray diffraction to determine the structure of crystals or molecules. The technique involves directing a beam of X-rays at a crystalline sample and recording the diffracted X-rays on a photographic plate. The diffraction pattern consists of a pattern of spots on the plate, and the crystal structure can be worked out from the positions and intensities of the diffraction sports. X-rays are diffracted by the electrons in the molecules and if molecular crystals of a compound are used, the electron density distribution in the molecule can be determined.

X-ray diffraction. The diffraction of X-rays by a crystal. The wavelengths of X-rays are comparable in size to the distances between atoms in most crystals, and the repeated pattern of the crystal lattice acts like a diffraction grating for X-ray. Thus, a crystal of suitable type can be used to disperse X-rays in a spectrometer. X-ray diffraction is also the basis of X-ray crystallography.

X-ray diffraction analysis. Qualitative and quantitative determination of composition of crystalline substances by X-ray diffraction measurement.

X-escape peak. Peak in gamma radiation or X-Spectrum caused by escape of X-rays emitted by an atom of the detector material after photoelectron emission.

X-ray fluorescence. X-radiation emitted when atoms are ionized by incident X-ray photons which eject electrons from their shells (mainly *K* and *L*). Also known as secondary radiation. The wavelengths of the fluorescent X-rays can be measured by an X-ray spectrometer as a means of chemical analysis. X-ray fluorescence is used in such techniques as electron-probe microanalysis.

X-ray fluorescence analysis. Spectroanalysis based on investigation of X-ray fluorescence spectra, *i.e.*, analysis of secondary x-ray radiation spectrum excited by primary one.

X-ray hardness. The penetrating power of x-ray which is an inverse function of the wave length.

X-ray spectrochemical analysis. Spectoanalysis based investigation of X-ray spectrum.

xylo-, xyl (greek, xyion, wood). Relating to wood, xylene, or xylose, as xyloidin, xyloquinone xylonic.

Y. Symbol for the element yttrium. Symbol for mole fraction.

Yb. Symbol for the element ytterbium.

yeast. A biochemically active material composed of fungus-like, single-celled organisms which are high in protein. It is able to convert carbohydrates into water and carbon dioxide in the presence of air, and into alcohol and carbon dioxide in the absence of air (fermentation). It is an important source of vitamines. Its activity is largely due to the enzyme zymase. Common commercial types used in the food industries are bakers, yeast and brewers yeast. Yeasts are grouped as top yeasts which are carried to the surface of the vat by the carbon dioxide they produce, and bottom yeasts, which remain on the bottom of the vat and act at lower temperature than the top yeasts. Compressed yeasts are made by callecting the yeast plants by filteration, mixing with 25% of starch and pressing Wild yeasts are yeast plants about which little is known and which are often deterimental in their actions. Forulae are also industrially important yeasts, but they are not saccharomyces ; and they do not have spores.

yellow antimony. An allotrope of antimony prepared, and only stable, at very low temperatures.

yellow arsenic. An unstable allotrope of arsenic obtained by the rapid cooling of arsenic vapour, The name is also somtimes used for the natural sulphide—or pigment (As_2S_3).

yellow phosphorus. A common allotrope of phosphorus that is usually known as "white phosphorus". White phosphorus turns yellow on exposure to air.
water under which the sticks are kept).

yield (of reaction). Ratio of amount of product obtained in chemical reaction and theoretical amount of product following from stoichiometry for the same amount of substrates ; expressed as percentage.

ylid. Neutral mesomeric molecule in which the carbanion is linked directly to the electropositive heteroatom :

$$\overset{+}{Z}-\overset{-/}{C} \leftrightarrow Z=\overset{/}{C}$$

ytterbium. An element.

		Symbol	Yb
		Atomic No.	70
State	Solid	Atomic Wt.	173.04
GrouP	IIIB	Valence	2,3
	(Lan-	Isotopes	7 stable
	thandide	m.p.	1092K
	Series)	b.p.	1569K

A rare-earth metal, obtained from several ores (monazite, gadolinite) It is subject to attack by acids and is soluble in ammonia. It forms compounds with oxygen, the halogens, and with carbon and other nonmetals. Its most important use is as a doping agent for garnet crystals in lasers. It has limited use in catalysts composed of mixtures of rare earths. It is not toxic and has several radioactive isotopes, one of which is used in radiography of metal parts and in medical diagnostic work.

yttrium. An element.

		Symbol	Y
		Atomic No.	39
State	Solid	Atomic Wt.	88.9059
Group	IIB	Valence	3
		m.p.	1795K
		b.p.	3611K

Though it is not one of the rare-earth metals' yttrium, is very similar to them and is always associated with them in such ores as monazite and gadolinite. It forms compounds with oxygen and the halogen elements, and with carbon. The major use of the metal is as an additive or alloying ingredient with a number of other metals ; additions of small percentages increase resistance to oxidation at high temperatures and have other beneficial effects upon the alloy systems to which it is added. Yttrium oxide is used with europium in phosphors for the red colour in TV tubes, in yttrium-iron garnets for microwave filters, and in nuclear technology. Yttrium has only one stable form and is non-toxic. It is classed as a rare-metal.

yttrium earths. Oxides of yttrium and lanthanoids from europium (Z=63) to lutetium (Z=71).

Yvon reagents for α-water β-naphthol. 1. Two ml. nitric acid, 2 ml, alcohol, and 10 drops nitrate solution.

2. Two ml. alcohol, 3 drops concentrated

potassium nitrate solution, and 10 drops sulphuric acid. On adding the reagents to 10 ml. of the aqueous naphthol solution, colour reactions are obtained.

Yvon reagent for water in alcohol. Calcium carbide ; when added to alcohol containing traces of water, acetylene is evolved.

Yvon test for alcohol in chloroform. Add a solution of 1 g. potassium permanganate and 10 g. potassium hydroxide in 250 ml. water to the solution to be tested and shake. If the violet colour changes to green, the presence of alcohol in indicated.

Z

Z. Symbol for gram-equivalent weight. Symbol for atomic number.

Zaffre. The mass obtained when native cobalt arsenide ($CoAs_2$) is roasted in air. It contains a mixture of cobalt oxides and arsenate, from this smalt can be obtained.

Zaffuto test reaction. A test for molybdenum made by acidifying the solution with nitric acid, adding ammonium nitrate and 1 ml. of alcohol and shaking ; then some crystals of sodium hydrosulphite ($Na_2S_2O_4$) are added. The solution turns brown, then greenish-blue and, when shaken and heated at 325-335 K., dark blue, if molybdenum is present.

Zamparo test for the differentiation of the naphthols. 1. Sulphuric acid in alcohol containing hydrogen peroxide.

2. Formaldehyde and hydrochloric acid are used to differentiate the two naphthols by colour reactions.

Zeeman effect. Splitting of atomic or molecular energy levels or splitting of spectral lines due to external magnetic field.

When a source of light is placed in an intense magnetic field, its spectral lines are broken up into two or more components, and these components are polarized. In the simplest case, when viewed in a direction perpendicular to the field, three lines appear, the cental one being plane polarized at right angles to the field and having the same wave length as the original line, the other two components being plane polarized parallel to the field, and being, respectively, of shorter and longer wave length than the original line, the difference in wave length being the same in both cases. In this simplest case, when viewed in a direction parallel to the magnetic field, two components are seen, having the same wave lengths as the outside components previously mentioned, but being circularly polarized in opposite directions.

However, most spectral lines show a much more complex resolution than the simplest case. Instead of three components in a transverse magnetic field, there are observed a larger number, some having the same state of polarization as the central component mentioned above, and others similar to the outer components, the number of each class varying with the spectral type of the line. Since it was observed in the simplest case that the change in frequency of each out component could be calculated by the relationship :

$$\Delta\nu_n = \frac{eH}{4m_0} = 1.400 \times 10^6 H$$

Where H is the magnetic field intensity, the designation of normal Zeeman effect was applied to cases for which this relationship held, while the more complex types of resolution were called the anomalous Zeeman effect.

Zeeman levels. Sublevels arising from splitting of energetic level of atom, ion, molecule or paramagnetic nucleus in magnetic field.

zein. The characteristic protein corn, from which it is extracted on a commercial. Its molecule contains the amide group —$CONH_2$. It has good nutritional value and thus is used in coatings for capsules and for dielectric and special food preparations. It also has some application in paper coatings and in the textile field, both as a sizing agent and as a fibre for blending with wood.

Zeisel method. A method of determination of methoxy groups in organic compounds by means of hydriodic acid, whereby the methyl group is replaced by hydrogen, leaving a hydroxy group in place of the methoxy group and forming methyl iodide, which can be determined in various ways.

Zeisel reaction. The demethylation of an organic compound by treatment with hydriodic acid, which leaves a hydroxy group in place of the methoxy group, and forms methyl iodide, which may readily be determined quantitatively as in the study of the amount of methoxy groups present.

Zelensky-Stadnikoff aminonitrile synthesis. Preparation of α-aminonitriles by the reaction of an aldehyde or a ketone with an alkali cyanide and ammonium chloride.

$$\begin{matrix} R' \\ \diagdown \\ C{=}O \\ \diagup \\ R \end{matrix} \xrightarrow{KCN + NH_4Cl} \begin{matrix} R' & & NH_2 \\ & \diagdown \diagup & \\ & C & \\ & \diagup \diagdown & \\ R & & CN \end{matrix}$$

The reaction is a variation of Strecker synthesis.

Zenger test. A test for arsenic made by distilling the unknown substance with hydrochloric acid or with sodium chloride and sulphuric acid. The arsenic in the distillate is then precipitated as the trisulphide, removed by filtration, after which it is redissolved, oxidized with nitric acid and precipitated with magnesia mixture.

Zenker fluid. An aqueous solution of sodium sulphate, potassium dichromate, glacial acetic acid, and mercuric chloride, used as a fixative.

zeolite. Clay-like structures (alumino silicates) which have ion exchange properties and exhibit the behaviour of molecular sieves. They are crystalline compounds of tetrahedrons of silicon in which aluminium atoms have replaced some of the silicon. The crystalline complex forms channels and cages of varying size which are capable of exerting an ionic selectivity or "sievin" effect when placed in salt solutions. Thus, zeolite ion-exchange units are extensively used in water conditioning to remove calcium and magnesium ions by replacing them with sodium ions. These units can be regenerated by treatment with sodium chloride solutions. Modified zeolites are now widely used in the petroleum refining industry as cracking catalysts and in water softening.

zeotropic system. System with no external vapour pressure or extreme of boiling point.

zeotropy. Property of systems characterized by non-existence of either external vapour pressure or extreme of boiling point.

Zerewitinoff determination. A method of analysis of organic compounds containing active hydrogen atoms, as in hydroxy, carboxy, or amino groups, by reaction with methyl magnesium halide to yield methane quantitatively.

$$ROH + CH_3MgX \rightarrow CH_4 + ROMgX$$

zero charge potential. *See* null potential.

zero group. The gases comprising the righthand column of the Periodic Table (or in older variations, the left-hand column). It is variously designated as the "inert gas," "rare gas," or "noble gas" group. The first three elements of this group do not enter into chemical combination. The zero group was so named at a time when all its members were thought to have zero valence ; but it was later found that last three members (krypton, xenon, and radon) have limited compound-forming ability. The most reasonable name for this group is the noble gas group.

zero order reaction. Reaction with kinetic equation characterized by sum of exponents in which concentrations of reactants occur being equal to zero ; *i.e.*, reaction of rate which does not change with change of concentration of reactants.

zero-point energy. The energy possessed by a molecule at its lowest energy level, *i.e.*, at a temperature of absolute zero. According to quantum mechanics this energy is finite, and it has been calculated for many molecules.

zero point entropy. According to third law of thermodynamics, the entropy of a system in equilibrium at the absolute zero must be zero. Such systems, as for instance a glass which can have finite entropy at absolute zero, are not in thermodynamic equilibrium.

zero point field. In quantum electrodynamics, the electromagnetic field is quantized and, like any other quantum mechanical system, has a zero point energy, of one-half quantum per state of the field. The field associated with these zero point energies is known as the zero point field.

zero point fluctuations. Fluctuations in the zero point field.

zero point vibrations. *See* lattice vibrations.

zeroth law of thermodynamics. If two systems are in thermal equilibrium with a third, then are in mutual thermal equilibrium. It is assumed that partitions between these systems are all diathermal.

zeta potential. Difference of electrical potentials between sliding surface and interior of liquid phase moving in respect to solid phase. Also known as electrokinetic potential.

Ziegler bromination. The direct substitutions of a hydrogen atom in the allylic position of an unsaturated compound by N-bromosuccinimide.

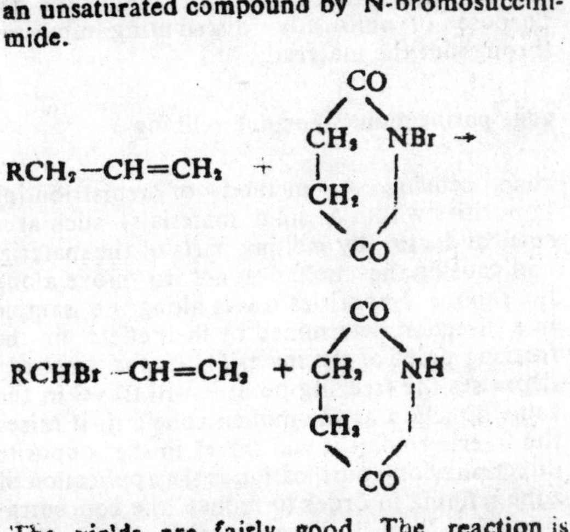

$$RCH_2-CH=CH_2 + \begin{matrix} & CO & \\ CH_2 & & NBr \\ | & & | \\ CH_2 & & \\ & CO & \end{matrix} \rightarrow$$

$$RCHBr-CH=CH_2 + \begin{matrix} & CO & \\ CH_2 & & NH \\ | & & | \\ CH_2 & & \\ & CO & \end{matrix}$$

The yields are fairly good. The reaction is carried out without a catalyst in boiling CCl_4 as solvent. Lewis acids ($AlCl_3$) promote nuclear brominations of aromatic compounds by the same brominating agents.

Ziegler catalyst. A type of organometallic catalyst. There are many variations in compositiion, but in general these catalysts are made up of an alkyl (the metal being in Groups I, II, or III of the Periodic Table of a transition metal (Groups IV to VIII). An example would be triethyluminum, $(C_2H_5)_3Al$, plus titanium dichloride ($TiCl_2$) dispersed in a hydrocarbon solvent. These catalysts are of the stereospecific type, permitting close control of the chemical structure of the polymers formed.

Ziegler method. A method of obtaining cyclic ketones from dinitriles by cyclization with metal amides, followed by hydrolysis and decarboxylation.

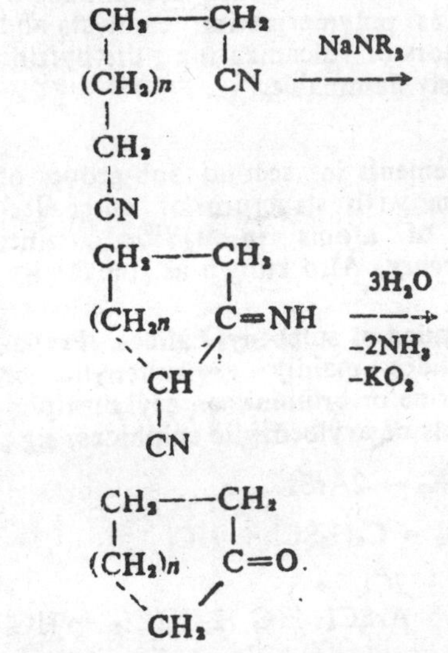

$$\begin{matrix} CH_2 & - & CH_2 \\ | & & | \\ (CH_2)_n & & CN \\ | & & \\ CH_2 & & \\ | & & \\ CN & & \end{matrix} \xrightarrow{NaNR_2}$$

$$\begin{matrix} CH_2 & - & CH_2 \\ | & & | \\ (CH_2)_n & & C=NH \\ & CH & \\ & | & \\ & CN & \end{matrix} \xrightarrow[-2NH_3,\ -KO_2]{3H_2O}$$

$$\begin{matrix} CH_2 & - & CH_2 \\ | & & | \\ (CH_2)_n & & C=O. \\ & CH_2 & \end{matrix}$$

Zirvogal process. A metallurgical process for the recovery of silver from sulphide ores, involving oxidation by roasting in air, solution of the silver sulphate in water, and displacement of the metallic silver from solution by treatment with metallic copper.

zinc. An element.

		Symbol	Zn
		Atomic No.	30
State	Solid	Atomic Wt.	65 3 8
Group	IIB	Valence	2
		Isotopes	5 stable
		m.p.	692.5K
		b.p.	1180K

Zinc, is widely distributed in the earth's crust, usually as a sulphide ore ; large deposits are in British Columbia, Ontario, Quebec, Utah, Colorado, and Australia. The metal is obtained by pyrometallurgical and electrochemical techniques. The most notable chemical property of zinc is its pronounced electropositive nature ; it is third among the common metals in this respect, exceeded only by aluminium and magnesium. For this reason it is particularly effective as a protective coating for steel (galvanized coatings), in which the phenomenon called sacrificial protection occurs. Other important applications are in alloys with copper (brass) and with aluminium (die castings). Neither the metal nor its inorganic compounds are toxic. The most important of the latter are zinc oxide and zinc sulphide used in paint pigment (lithopone), and zinc chloride used in dry cell batteries, textile printing, and as a fireproofing agent for timber and growing trees. Organic compounds of zinc are used as polymerization catalysts and ultra-accelerators of vulcanization ; diethylzinc is spontaneously flammable.

zinc group. Elements in second sub-group of periodic system with structure of outer electronic shell of atoms $(n-1)d^{10}ns^2$, zinc, cadmium, mercury. Also known as zinc family.

Zincke preparation of sulphenyl halides. Preparation of halides, mainly arylsulfenylic, by action of chlorine or bromine on aryl disulphides, thiophenols or arylbenzylic sulphides, *e.g.*,

$$ArS{-}SAr + X_2 \rightarrow 2ArSX$$

$$C_6H_5SH + Cl_2 \rightarrow C_6H_5SCl + HCl$$

$$ArSCH_2C_6H_5 + 2Cl_2 \rightarrow ArSCl + C_6H_5CHCl_2 + HCl$$

Zinke nitration reaction. A method of preparing certain halogen-substituted nitrophenols by replacement of some bromine or iodine or substituents by nitro groups by treatment with nitrous acid.

zirconium. An element

State	Solid	Symbol	Zr
Group	IVA	Atomic No.	40
		Atomic Wt.	91.22
		Valence	4
		Isotopes	5 stable
		m.p.	2126K
		b.p.	4649K

Zirconium, is a strong metal with good mechanical properties. It is found in nature as zircon, zirconium silicate, in beach sands and the beds of streams and lakes, chiefly in Australia and Florida, and is always associated in nature with hafnium. After separation of the hafnium by solvent extraction of the tetrachlorides of the two elements, it is reduced to metal by magnesium (Kroll process). It has a density of 6.5 g/cc and while chemically reactive has excellent resistance to corrosion by most acids and alkalis. It has very low neutron absorption capability and thus an important application is in cladding uranium fuel element in nuclear reactors, usually in the form of a series of alloys trademarked "Zircaloy." It is also used in the manufacture of corrosion-resistant equipment for the chemical industries. In the form of sponge, powder, or scrap, it will ignite spontaneously at room temperature. Its compounds have many miscellaneous applications in ceremics, catalysts, and special alloys, the sulphate is used in tanning white leather. Neither the metal nor its compounds are toxic.

zone axis. The axis through the centre of a crystal which is parallel to the edge of a zone.

zonal crystals. Crystals characterized by their stratified (zonal) structure which is due to change in growth of crystals.

zone law. Every face of crystal belongs to at least two interesting zones.

zone leveling. The passage of one or more molten zones along a semiconductor body for the purpose of uniformly distributing impurities throughout the material.

zone purification. *See* zone refining.

zone refining. A method of redistributing impurities within a solid materials, such as a semiconductor, by melting parts of the material and causing the molten zones to move along the sample. Impurities travel along the sample in a direction determined by their effect on the freezing point of the material. If the impurity depresses the freezing point it will travel in the same direction as the molten zone ; if it raises the freezing point it will travel in the opposite direction. Zone purification is the application of zone refining in order to reduce the concentration of an impurity in a material.

In zone refining the sample of the material is moved slowly past a heater so that the molten zone effectively moves along the length of the bar. Melting is achieved by induction heating, electron bombardment, or the heating effect of a current through a resistance coil. Zone purification carried out using a large number of heaters can reduce the impurity concentration to such an extent that the impurity is of order of 99.999999%.

Zulkowsky reagent. The reagent prepared by heating 60 g. starch with 1litre glycerol until the mixture is soluble in water. It is used as a reagent for iodine, which gives a deep blue colour with it.

zwitterion. An ion that has a positive and negative charge on the same group of atoms. Zwitterions can be formed from compounds that contain both acid groups and basic groups in their molecules. For example, aminoethanoic acid the (amino-acid glycine) has the formula $H_2N.CH_2.COOH$. However, under neutral conditions, it exists in the different form of the zwitterion $^{+}H_3N.CH_2.COO^{-}$, which can be regarded as having been produced by an internal neutralization reaction (transfer of a proton from the carboxyl group to the amino group). Aminoethanoic acid, as a consequence, has some properties characteristic of ionic compounds; *e.g.*, a high melting point and solubility in water. In acid solutions, the positive ion $^{+}H_3NCH_2COOH$ is formed. In basic solutions, the negative ion $H_2NCH_2COO^{-}$ predominates. The name comes from the Germah zwei, two.

zymo-, zym-. Relating to a ferment or fermentation as zymophosphate, zymase.

zymase. A major enzyme occurring in yeast which catalyzes the fermentation of sucrose to alcohol and carbon dioxide.

zymogen. A progenitor of an enzyme in the organisum ; a substance from which an enzyme is supposed to be formed, as pepsin from pepsinogen, trypsin from trypsinogen or thrombin from prothrombin.

Zymolytic reaction. Any chemical reaction brought about by the catalytic effect of an enzyme. This is usually a hydrolysis, for which the term "zymohydrolytic reaction" is also used.